CONDITIONED TASTE AVERSION

Behavioral and Neural Processes

CONDITIONED TASTE AVERSION

Behavioral and Neural Processes

Edited by

Steve Reilly
Todd R. Schachtman

UNIVERSITY PRESS

2009

Oxford University Press, Inc., publishes works that further
Oxford University's objective of excellence
in research, scholarship, and education.

Oxford New York
Auckland Cape Town Dar es Salaam Hong Kong Karachi
Kuala Lumpur Madrid Melbourne Mexico City Nairobi
New Delhi Shanghai Taipei Toronto

With offices in
Argentina Austria Brazil Chile Czech Republic France Greece
Guatemala Hungary Italy Japan Poland Portugal Singapore
South Korea Switzerland Thailand Turkey Ukraine Vietnam

Published by Oxford University Press, Inc.
198 Madison Avenue, New York, New York 10016
www.oup.com

Library of Congress Cataloging-in-Publication Data
Conditioned taste aversion : behavioral and neural processes /
edited by Steve Reilly and Todd R. Schachtman.
p. ; cm.
Includes bibliographical references and index.
ISBN 978-0-19-532658-1 (cloth)
1. Taste.   2. Aversive stimuli. I. Reilly, Steve. II. Schachtman,
Todd R. [DNLM: 1. Taste—physiology.   2. Behavior—physiology.
3. Conditioning (Psychology)—physiology   4. Neuronal Plasticity—physiology.
WI 210 C745 2008]
BF261.C66 2008
152.1'67—dc22
2008012840

9 8 7 6 5 4 3 2 1

Printed in the United States of America
on acid-free paper

For Elaine and Becky

Contents

Part III. Neural Analysis and Physiological Mechanisms

Part IV. Clinical Application of Research and Target Populations

Foreword

THE EVOLUTION AND MATURATION OF CTA RESEARCH

They sell a T-shirt in Texas that says, "I wasn't born in Texas but I came as fast as I could." That characterizes my relation to conditioned taste aversion (CTA). I did not begin my career studying taste aversion learning, but I got into the area as soon as I could, publishing my first paper on the topic in 1972 (Domjan, 1972). The issue that brought me into the field was the suggestion that CTA was an adaptive specialization of learning that did not follow conventional rules (Rozin & Kalat, 1971; Seligman, 1970). This was a radical idea at the time, and much research in the next 10 years focused on whether CTA was or was not consistent with general process learning theory (Domjan, 1983). Although I later moved from CTA to study sexual conditioning, I continued to be deeply interested in adaptive specializations of learning and how such specializations could be incorporated into a general theory of learning (Domjan, 2005, 2008). The present book illustrates that numerous other investigators also have been captivated by research questions raised by CTA. What is perhaps most remarkable about the current book is that CTA research has extended in so many different directions.

In their elegant account of the history of CTA research, Freeman and Riley note in their chapter that CTA originated in two seemingly unrelated applied problems, pest control to limit infestations of rats and mice and concerns about radiation safety. Had the research remained focused on those questions, most of us would not have paid much attention to it. However, one of the early investigators of CTA, John Garcia, was steeped in traditional learning theory and recognized that CTA had two unusual properties. The taste aversions could be acquired despite delays of several hours between the taste and subsequent poison or radiation-induced illness (Garcia, Ervin, & Koelling, 1966), and the aversion learning was specific to taste cues or reflected a selective association (Garcia & Koelling, 1966).

The phenomena of long-delay learning and cue–consequence specificity attracted a great deal of attention starting in late 1960s, during what was a turbulent time for traditional learning theory. Kamin's blocking effect (1969) and the relative validity effect demonstrated by Wagner and his colleagues (Wagner, Logan, Haberlandt, & Price, 1968) challenged the long-held assumption that temporal contiguity is sufficient for associative learning. Long-delay CTA indicated that temporal contiguity is not even necessary. Adding fuel to the debate, Bolles (1970) argued that much of what occurs in avoidance learning is not reinforced by the avoidance contingency, and Breland and Breland (1961) showed that positive reinforcement fails to strengthen behavior in numerous situations where the requirement of response–reinforcer contiguity is well satisfied. To further the insult to general process learning theory, Brown and Jenkins (1968) showed that the pigeon's key peck response is an outstanding example of Pavlovian rather than instrumental conditioning.

John Garcia's long-delay CTA and cue–consequence specificity held center stage among the various challenges to traditional learning theory and captivated the attention of wide range of scientists. Some, like myself, focused on the implications of CTA for learning theory. Others regarded CTA, along with taste neophobia and conditioned food preferences, as mechanisms determining food choice. Still others focused on comparative, developmental, and pharmacological aspects of CTA. All of these themes were represented at the Baylor Symposium that culminated in the first comprehensive book devoted to CTA (Barker, Best, & Domjan, 1977). The book included 22 chapters. Three chapters dealt exclusively with the mechanisms of long-delay learning, and four chapters were devoted to nongustatory aspects of food aversion learning, reflecting the interest in selective associations.

The Baylor Symposium volume, edited by enthusiastic scientists who were active in the field and in frequent contact with many of the participants, had a profound impact and remains available 30 years later on Amazon.com. It was soon followed by another edited volume, *Food Aversion Learning* (Milgram, Krames, & Alloway, 1977), which included seven chapters. Four of those chapters focused on learning issues and were written by contributors who also participated in the Baylor Symposium. The three remaining chapters dealt with CTA and drug abuse, the use of toxicosis conditioning to suppress aggression, and the neurobiology of CTA. These chapters illustrated the beginnings of the expansion of CTA into new areas of inquiry.

The increase in the range of topics studied with CTA techniques continued with the next major volume devoted to CTA, which consisted of papers presented at a symposium at the New York Academy of Sciences (Braveman & Bronstein, 1985). That volume included 28 chapters. Issues related to learning theory remained well represented (five

chapters). But, focus on neurobiological issues was now evident in 6 chapters, and 11 other chapters were devoted to use of CTA in pharmacology, toxicology, aversion therapy, cancer treatment, and psychoneuroimmunology.

The current book illustrates that CTA has become a well-established behavioral method that is useful in studying a wide range of behavioral, pharmacological, and neurobiological issues. Interestingly, none of the chapters in the current book is concerned with adaptive specializations in learning or deals exclusively with the two phenomena that fueled initial interest in CTA: long-delay learning and selective associations. As is appropriate, the field has moved on. Only three of the contributors to the present book (Sam Revusky, James C. Smith, and Anthony L. Riley) participated in the 1976 Baylor Symposium. The present book reports on new advances in a few of the areas that were entertained at the Baylor Symposium, such as the unitary nature of CTA, the deleterious effects of preexposure to the conditioned and unconditioned stimulus, and chemical aversion treatment of alcoholism. However, most of the chapters in the present book describe lines of research that people did not even speculate about 30 years ago. Furthermore, many of the research techniques that are represented in the current book (behavioral, genetic, and neurobiological) were unavailable when CTA first became popular.

In Part I of the book, Freeman and Riley provide a beautiful account of the history of CTA research in their chapter and describe the early theoretical debates that CTA stimulated in psychology and learning theory. Part II, devoted to "Behavioral Processes," is the largest section of the book including 12 chapters. The section begins as Lubow provides a detailed account of the deleterious effects of preexposure to the conditioned stimulus (CS) on CTA (latent inhibition) in his chapter and also discusses the role of contextual cues in retrieval of the memories of preexposure and conditioning. In his chapter, Hall provides a detailed analysis of the deleterious effects of preexposure to the unconditioned stimulus (US) on CTA, concluding that most of the effect is due to blocking by drug administration cues. However, US habituation also may be involved.

Part II then gets right into some of the thorniest behavioral issues in the field with two chapters that deal with the paradox that aversions are learned to tastes paired with drugs of abuse even if those drugs are reinforcing and self-administered. In their chapter, Grigson, Twining, Freet, Wheeler, and Geddes review numerous studies that support the "reward comparison hypothesis" that solves the paradox by treating the problem as a case of anticipatory contrast. According to this hypothesis, the flavor loses value because of the anticipated reinforcing drug that usually follows. In her chapter, Parker takes a different approach, emphasizing that not all CTAs are created equal. More specifically, taste aversions conditioned with drugs of abuse do not result in disgust reactions, unlike taste aversions conditioned with lithium chloride. Comparing CTA in rats (which cannot vomit) and shrews (which can vomit), Parker argues that nausea rather than emesis is critical for a bona fide CTA. The paradox of CTA induced by drugs of abuse that are self-administered is analyzed further in the chapter by Riley, Davis, and Roma, who employ a behavioral genetic approach comparing inbred lines of rats (Fischer and Lewis) that differ in CTA and drug self-administration behavior.

Memory mechanisms are the focus of the chapter by Meehan and Riccio, who provide a wide-ranging review of retention interval, context shift, and retrograde amnesia manipulations in CTA. Memory and retrieval mechanisms in CTA are discussed further in the chapter by Schachtman, Ramsey, and Pineño who focus on how CTA can be altered by various postconditioning manipulations in single-cue learning and cue–competition situations. These include extinction, reminder, US reinstatement, renewal, and reacquisition. Boakes and Nakajima describe effects using running and swimming as USs in CTA and show that such USs can result in many of the learning effects found with other USs. Moreover, wheel running, like drug consumption, may induce many processes concomitantly such as appetive effects as well as aversive effects.

In their chapter, Batsell and Paschall tackle complex problems of compound conditioning in which the presence of a competing cue can facilitate or interfere with the conditioning of a target stimulus. They describe how perceptual and associative mechanisms may lead to one or the other of these outcomes. Issues related to the representation of taste stimuli are also the subject of the chapter by Holland and Wheeler, who describe how CTA may result from associatively activating a taste representation before illness. Such associatively mediated CTA may contribute to unusual

eating habits and eating disorders. How tastes are represented also plays an important role in instrumental behavior reinforced by ingested substances. The chapter by Balleine describes the role of taste representation and CTA in studies of the associative and motivational bases of instrumental behavior. Misanin, Anderson, and Hinderliter describe the rich literature on CTA in rats across the life span in their chapter, from prenatal ages to senescence. Comparing CTA across such a broad developmental range is challenging methodologically, but there is intriguing evidence that older subjects are more capable of long-delay learning and such learning may be facilitated by slowing the subject's metabolic rate.

Part III on "Neural Analysis and Physiological Mechanisms" includes six chapters. By coincidence, this is the same number of chapters that appeared in the 1985 New York Academy of Sciences volume dealing with physiological mechanisms of CTA. However, the coverage in the present book is both broader and deeper. The chapter by Reilly provides a thoughtful and detailed review of lesion studies of CTA. This and other chapters in this part are mindful that disruptions of CTA can occur because of disruptions in taste perception, US salience, acquisition, retention, and retrieval of the CTA. Thus, physiological manipulations that disrupt CTA could do so for a variety of reasons that have to be sorted out. The chapter by Bernstein, Wilkins, and Barot reviews the literature on early gene expression (cFos) in mapping the circuitry of CTA. The familiarity of the taste and the method of its exposure (ingestion vs. oral infusion) are critical in this line of work, which has identified the central nucleus of the amygdala as critical for CTA. The discussion of cFos expression in studies of CTA continues in the chapter by Barki-Harrington, Belelovsky, Doron, and Rosenblum, who also discuss other molecular techniques, with special emphasis on glutamate and its receptors during memory formation and consolidation and mRNA translation regulation.

The last three chapters in Part III take contrasting approaches to the neurobiology of CTA. Chambers and Hintiryan review studies of the role of hormones (testosterone, estradiol, and adrenocorticotropin hormone [ACTH]) in CTA in their chapter. They report that the primary effect of these hormones is to prolong extinction, probably by inducing an aversive state. Cunningham, Gremel, and Groblewski provide a detailed review of the use of a variety of genetic techniques to study CTA in their chapter. These techniques include inbred strains, gene–behavior correlations, selective breeding, knockout and transgenic mice, and gene transcription, expression, and protein translation studies. Houpt and Smith describe how CTA was used originally to study the aversive effects of exposure to irradiation (in pioneering work by Smith) in their chapter and also discuss how that approach is being used now to examine the biological effects of exposure to high-strength (3–14 Tesla) magnetic fields. They report that the threshold for CTA is 3–4 Tesla and magnet sensitivity is mediated by the vestibular system.

The last section of the book (Part IV: "Clinical Application of Research and Target Populations") consists of four chapters. The chapter by Revusky reviews the use of CTA in the treatment of alcoholism. As Revusky points out, even though this application dates back to the 1930s, therapists still have a lot to learn from the animal literature to design effective treatment protocols. The chapter by Pacheco-López, Engler, Niemi, and Schedlowski brings us up to date on an important line of research started by Ader and Cohen (1975) on taste–immune associative learning. As they point out, anticipatory immune responses can be of considerable benefit, since even minor cuts and scratches can mobilize the immune system. In their chapter, Baley, Dye, and Hill describe studies of CTA induced by pregnancy in women. Nausea and vomiting is a common occurrence in pregnant women and may be related to their peculiar food preferences and aversions. Scalera and Bavieri study CTA induced by the side effects of chemotherapy in human patients, who may develop both food aversions and anticipatory nausea, in their chapter. The use of overshadowing "scapegoat" cues to disrupt such learning has met with some success.

The present book is important because it documents the many ways in which CTA has been used to advance our understanding of learning, behavior, and its neurobiology and neurocircuitry. This book demonstrates that CTA research has become much more sophisticated, both at the level of behavioral analysis and at molecular, genetic, and systems levels of analysis. This book is an outstanding example of the power of modern neuroscience in providing an integrated description of how learning is organized by neurobiological and hormonal systems to generate adaptive behavior. But, science advances not just by the accumulation

of new findings. It also advances by the nurturing of an interactive community of scholars. The last roll call of the CTA community was more than 20 years ago (Braveman & Bronstein, 1985). The present book is a roll call of the current CTA community and shows that the community is well and thriving. It has numerous new participants and many new exciting ideas and areas of research.

Michael Domjan

Department of Psychology
The University of Texas at Austin

References

Ader. R., & Cohen, N. (1975). Behaviorally conditioned immunosuppression. *Psychosomatic Medicine, 37*, 333–340.

Barker, L. M., Best, M. R., & Domjan, M. (Eds.) (1977). *Learning mechanisms in food selection*, Waco, TX: Baylor University Press.

Bolles, R. C. (1970). Species-specific defense reactions and avoidance learning. *Psychological Review, 77*, 32–48.

Braveman, N. S., & Bronstein, P. (Eds.). (1985). *Experimental assessments and clinical applications of conditioned food aversions. Annals of the New York Academy of Sciences*, Vol. 443. New York.

Breland, K., & Breland, M. (1961). The misbehavior of organisms. *American Psychologist, 16*, 681–684.

Brown, P. L., & Jenkins, H. M. (1968). Autoshaping the pigeon's key peck. *Journal of the Experimental Analysis of Behavior, 11*, 1–8.

Domjan, M. (1972). CS preexposure in taste-aversion learning: Effects of deprivation and preexposure duration. *Learning and Motivation, 3*, 389–402.

Domjan, M. (1983). Biological constraints on instrumental and classical conditioning: Implications for general process theory. In G. H. Bower (Ed.), *The psychology of learning and motivation*, Vol. 17 (pp. 215–277). New York: Academic Press.

Domjan, M. (2005). Pavlovian conditioning: A functional perspective. *Annual Review of Psychology, 56*, 179–206.

Domjan, M. (2008). Adaptive specializations and generality of the laws of classical and instrumental conditioning. In R. Menzel (Ed.), *Learning theory and behavior. Vol. [1] of Learning and memory: A comprehensive reference*, 4 vols. (J.Byrne Ed.) (pp. 327–340). Oxford: Elsevier.

Garcia, J., Ervin, F. R., & Koelling, R. A. (1966). Learning with prolonged delay of reinforcement. *Psychonomic Science, 5*, 121–122.

Garcia, J., & Koelling, R. A. (1966). Relation of cue to consequence in avoidance learning. *Psychonomic Science,* 4, 123–124.

Kamin, L. J. (1969). Predictability, surprise, attention, and conditioning. In B. A. Campbell & R. M. Church (Eds.), *Punishment and aversive behavior* (pp. 279–296). New York: Appleton-Century-Crofts.

Milgram, N. W., Krames, L., & Alloway, T. M. (Eds.), (1977). *Food aversion learning.* New York and London: Plenum Press.

Rozin, P., & Kalat, J. W. (1971). Specific hungers and poison avoidance as adaptive specializations of learning. *Psychological Review,* 78. 459–486.

Seligman, M. E. P. (1970). On the generality of the laws of learning. *Psychological Review,* 77, 406–418.

Wagner, A. R., Logan, F. A., Haberlandt, K., & Price, T. (1968). Stimulus selection in animal discrimination learning. *Journal of Experimental Psychology,* 76, 171–180.

Contributors

MATTHEW J. ANDERSON
Department of Psychology
Saint Joseph's University
Philadelphia, PA
United States

BERNARD W. BALLEINE
Department of Psychology
University of California
Los Angeles, CA
United States

LIZA BARKI-HARRINGTON
Department for Neurobiology
   and Ethology
University of Haifa
Israel

SABIHA K. BAROT
Program in Neurobiology
   and Behavior
University of Washington
Seattle, WA
United States

W. ROBERT BATSELL, JR.
Department of Psychology
Kalamazoo College
Kalamazoo, MI
United States

MARIO BAVIERI
Department of Oncology
   and Haematology
Section of Respiratory Diseases
University of Modena
   and Reggio Emilia
Italy

TRACY M. BAYLEY
Clinical Psychology Unit
Department of Psychology
University of Sheffield
United Kingdom

KATYA BELELOVSKY
Department for Neurobiology
   and Ethology
University of Haifa
Israel

ILENE L. BERNSTEIN
Department of Psychology
University of Washington
Seattle, WA
United States

ROBERT A. BOAKES
School of Psychology
University of Sydney
Australia

KATHLEEN C. CHAMBERS
Department of Psychology
University of Southern California
Los Angeles, CA
United States

CHRISTOPHER L. CUNNINGHAM
Department of Behavioral Neuroscience
    and Portland Alcohol Research Center
Oregon Health and Science University
Portland, OR
United States

CATHERINE M. DAVIS
Psychopharmacology Laboratory
Department of Psychology
American University
Washington, DC
United States

GUY DORON
Department for Neurobiology and Ethology
University of Haifa
Israel

LOUISE DYE
Institute of Psychological Sciences
University of Leeds
United Kingdom

HARALD ENGLER
Institute for Behavioral Sciences
ETH Zurich
Switzerland

KEVIN B. FREEMAN
Division of Neurobiology and Behavior Research
Department of Psychiatry
    and Human Behavior
University of Mississippi Medical Center
Jackson, MS
United States

CHRISTOPHER S. FREET
Department of Neural and Behavioral Sciences
Pennsylvania State University College
    of Medicine
Hershey, PA
United States

RASTAFA I. GEDDES
Department of Neural and Behavioral Sciences
Pennsylvania State College of Medicine
Hershey, PA
United States

CHRISTINA M. GREMEL
Department of Behavioral Neuroscience
    and Portland Alcohol Research Center
Oregon Health and Science University
Portland, OR
United States

PATRICIA S. GRIGSON
Department of Neural and Behavioral Sciences
Pennsylvania State College of Medicine
Hershey, PA
United States

PETER A. GROBLEWSKI
Department of Behavioral Neuroscience
    and Portland Alcohol Research Center
Oregon Health and Science University
Portland, OR
United States

GEOFFREY HALL
Department of Psychology
University of York
United Kingdom

ANDREW J. HILL
Academic Unit of Psychiatry
    and Behavioural Sciences
Institute of Health Sciences
Leeds School of Medicine
United Kingdom

CHARLES F. HINDERLITER
Department of Psychology
University of Pittsburgh at Johnstown
Johnstown, PA
United States

HOURI HINTIRYAN
Department of Psychology
University of Southern California
Los Angeles, CA
United States

PETER C. HOLLAND
Department of Psychological and Brain Sciences
Johns Hopkins University
Baltimore, MD
United States

THOMAS A. HOUPT
Department of Biological Science
Florida State University
Tallahassee, FL
United States

CHERYL L. LIMEBEER
Department of Psychology
University of Guelph
Canada

R. E. LUBOW
Department of Psychology
Tel Aviv University
Israel

SUSANNE M. MEEHAN
Department of Psychology
University of Akron – Wayne College
Orrville, OH
United States

JAMES R. MISANIN
Department of Psychology
Susquehanna University
Selinsgrove, PA
United States

SADAHIKO NAKAJIMA
Department of Integrated
   Psychological Science
Kwansei Gakuin University
Japan

MAJ-BRITT NIEMI
Institute for Behavioral Sciences
ETH Zurich
Switzerland

GUSTAVO PACHECO-LÓPEZ
Institute for Behavioral
   Sciences
ETH Zurich
Switzerland

LINDA A. PARKER
Department of Psychology
University of Guelph
Canada

GAYLA Y. PASCHALL
Department of Psychology
Southern Methodist University
Dallas, TX
United States

OSKAR PINEÑO
Department of Psychology
Hofstra University
Hempstead, NY
United States

ASHLEY RAMSEY
Department of Psychological Sciences
University of Missouri
Columbia, MO
United States

SHADNA A. RANA
Department of Psychology
University of Waterloo
Canada

STEVE REILLY
Department of Psychology
University of Illinois at Chicago
Chicago, IL
United States

SAM REVUSKY (RETIRED)
Department of Psychology
Memorial University of Newfoundland,
   St. John's
Canada

DAVID C. RICCIO
Department of Psychology
Kent State University
Kent, OH
United States

ANTHONY L. RILEY
Psychopharmacology Laboratory
Department of Psychology
American University
Washington, DC
United States

PETER G. ROMA
Psychopharmacology Laboratory
Department of Psychology
American University
Washington, DC
United States

KOBI ROSENBLUM
Department for Neurobiology
   and Ethology
University of Haifa
Israel

GIUSEPPE SCALERA
Department of Biomedical Sciences
Section of Physiology
University of Modena
   and Reggio Emilia
Italy

TODD R. SCHACHTMAN
Department of Psychological Sciences
University of Missouri
Columbia, MO
United States

MANFRED SCHEDLOWSKI
Division of Medical Psychology
   and Behavioral Immunobiology
University of Duisburg-Essen
Germany

JAMES C. SMITH
Department of Psychology
Florida State University
Tallahassee, FL
United States

ROBERT C. TWINING
Department of Neural and Behavioral Sciences
Pennsylvania State College of Medicine
Baltimore, MD
United States

DANIEL S. WHEELER
Department of Psychological
   and Brain Sciences
Johns Hopkins University
Baltimore, MD
United States

ROBERT A. WHEELER
Department of Psychology
University of North Carolina
Chapel Hill, NC
United States

EMILY E. WILKINS
Department of Psychology
University of Washington
Seattle, WA
United States

PART I

INTRODUCTION AND HISTORICAL SIGNIFICANCE

1

Introduction

STEVE REILLY AND TODD R. SCHACHTMAN

In this brief introduction, we describe the ways that we have benefited from putting together this edited book, point out a few of the findings involving conditioned taste aversion (CTA) that we found intriguing, and express our appreciation to the contributors. Our initial sense of satisfaction in putting together this book stemmed, of course, from the great need for it. In the past 20 years, there has also been a substantial amount of research exploring the neural substrates of CTA including its neuroanatomy and pharmacology and also the molecular and cellular basis of plasticity. There has also been much work examining the phases of information processing that are involved in certain manipulations of conditioned responding using CTA. CTA has also continued to be an important procedure in the field of animal learning. This critically important phenomenon and methodology persists in having a substantial impact on theory and on clinical concerns. CTA is used to explore the neural mechanisms of learning and the selective processes involved in the pathology of emotional and consummatory disorders. For instance, Cameron et al. (2001) noted that symptoms resulting from the anticipation of chemotherapy (subjects that had already received many pairings of the cues with chemotherapy) can affect a person's quality of life and these anticipatory symptoms may be due to classical conditioning (see Morrow & Dobkin, 1988, as cited by Cameron et al.).

Given the importance of these topics, it is surprising that there has not been, to our knowledge, an edited book on this topic in over 20 years. The three previous edited books in the area (Barker, Best, & Domjan, 1977; Braveman & Bronstein, 1985; Milgram, Krames, & Alloway, 1977) had a notable impact on the research conducted on this topic. Putting this book together and reading the contents of this book caused us to reflect on certain findings in the field and a few of these findings that struck us as particularly notable will be mentioned briefly later. We will focus our reactions to the behavioral analysis of CTA—the results of which benefit neuroscience work as well as other research areas (such as clinical interventions as well as attribution theory in social psychology to name two examples).

METHOD OF ASSESSING CTA

One issue that stands out as important to the demonstration of CTA is the method of assessment. There are numerous ways to assess taste aversions: these include single-bottle tests, two-bottle tests, and the taste reactivity tests involving ingestive and aversive orofacial responses. Some of these behavioral tests have proven to be more sensitive to experimental manipulations. For instance, Thiele, Kiefer, and Bailey (1996) found that a one-bottle test as well as aversive "taste reactivity responses" were more sensitive than "ingestive responses" when saccharin was used as the test conditioned stimulus (CS). One study showing how unusual tests can sometimes yield fruitful results is Ader and Peck (1977); they used an interesting assessment procedure (as cited in Misanin, Anderson, & Hinderliter, Chapter 14). Although young rats showed no evidence of CTA after a 6-day retention interval using either a one- or two-bottle test, the conditioned rats did show evidence of CTA when they were placed in a competitive situation with nonconditioned rats for access to the drinking tube during testing. The aforementioned methods share at least one feature in common: all require the subject to make consummatory contact with the CS at the time of the test. Such test methods ensure that the acquired aversive qualities of the CS can provide feedback and contribute to the level of manifest performance at the time of test. Whether explicitly acknowledged or implicitly accepted, this aspect is considered an important attribute of consummatory intake tests. There are, however, situations when it is diagnostically important to assess knowledge about an aversive ingestible stimulus in the absence of consummatory contact with that stimulus. Using instrumental methodologies, postacquisition devaluation of the instrumental outcome through CTA has revealed important new aspects of the associative structure of instrumental conditioning by analyzing performance in extinction. The analysis assesses the incentive value of the outcome in the absence of consummatory contact which, by itself, may bias or distort the test performance (see, e.g., Adams & Dickinson, 1981; Colwill & Rescorla, 1986; see also Balleine, Chapter 13).

Some work using CTA has focused on qualitatively distinct forms of learning or attributes of the stimuli. For instance, Berridge has provided the frequently cited distinction between wanting versus liking—two qualitative features of palatable flavors or drugs of abuse. Balleine (Chapter 13) has distinguished between a taste cue's ability to activate an aversive system or a disgust system. It is interesting that the field of animal learning has been moving toward what might be called an "attribute approach" to learning or a learning approach in which more than one system of processing can be engaged. Such approaches are not new as many systems have been previously put into place, such as Garcia's theory from the 1980s (Garcia, Lasiter, Bermudez-Rattoni, & Deems,

1985) and Konorski's (1967) preparatory and consummatory distinction (see also Craig, 1918; Delamater & LoLordo, 1991) to name a few. Regarding this attribute approach to "what is learned," it reminds us of work by Harry Fowler in the 1970s on the signaling versus affective properties of CSs (Ghiselli & Fowler, 1976; see also Dickinson & Pearce, 1977). The following text regarding Baeyens theorizing also discusses distinct processing systems.

OCCASION-SETTING

Baeyens and colleagues (Baeyens et al., 1996, 1998; see De Houwer et al., 2001 for a review) used an evaluative conditioning procedure with human participants and were not able to find any evidence that flavors could set the occasion for other flavors as predictors of an aversive Tween unconditioned stimulus (US). In reviewing their findings, De Houwer et al. (2001) distinguished between expectancy learning (which concerns traditional Pavlovian learning effects) and referential learning. In expectancy learning, a cue signals the presence or absence of an outcome (the US) and an expectancy regarding this outcome is produced. In referential learning (which underlies evaluative conditioning), the "CS merely makes one (consciously or unconsciously) think of the US without activating an expectancy that the US is actually going to occur" (p. 864)—as applied to human evaluative conditioning work. This distinction may have some merit and deserves exploration in future work.

RETRIEVAL AND COGNITIVE PROCESSES IN CTA

It is interesting to us that several chapters address or mention retrieval processes (e.g., Batsell & Paschall, Chapter 10; Hall, Chapter 4; Holland & Wheeler, Chapter 11; Meehan & Riccio, Chapter 7; Misanin et al., Chapter 14; Reilly, Chapter 15; Schachtman, Ramsey, & Pineño, Chapter 8). The field of animal learning and conditioning has progressed greatly in considering nonacquisition determinants of conditioned performance. Given that the acquisition of taste aversion is often viewed as a more primordial process, it is interesting that such learning may involve processes of a more cognitive nature such as retrieval and the learning about events which—at the time of testing—are not currently present (Holland & Wheeler, Chapter 11; see Dickinson & Burke, 1996; Van Hamme & Wasserman, 1994, for theorizing regarding this issue). On the other hand, it is interesting that some researchers continue to describe CTA as a noncognitive process; for instance, Stewart-Williams and Podd (2004, p. 333) have recently cited an early report by Seligman and Hager (1972) in suggesting that CTAs do not involve expectancies.

IMPLICIT PROCESSING OF TASTE AVERSIONS IN HUMANS

Despite the potential involvement of these more cognitive processes, it is interesting that taste aversions do appear to have an implicit nature to them such that conscious, explicit knowledge cannot readily override CTA learning. For instance, Rozin and Fallon (1987, p. 31, citing Logue et al., 1981) point out that "People often report, without prompting, that a food aversion they developed from getting sick after eating a food occurred even though they know the food did not cause the illness." This finding reminds us of the fact that humans are subject to biases and heuristics that can produce less than perfect performance and, yet, giving subjects training on such processes (teaching people about such biases to try to keep them from being influenced by them) does not always override the original bias (see, e.g., Arkes, 1981 for a discussion).

BLOCKING

It is perplexing that blocking is so difficult to attain using a CTA preparation whereas there are hundreds of demonstrations using other procedures, such as fear conditioning. It is easy to assume that the reason is that within-compound associations are quickly formed during compound conditioning phases with flavors that reduce the probability of obtaining a blocking effect (e.g., see Nicholas, Dickinson, & Mackintosh, 1983 for a demonstration using fear conditioning); but—given the extreme paucity of published findings obtaining blocking (Gallo & Candido, 1995; Reilly, Bornovalova, Dengler, & Trifunovic, 2003; see also Schachtman et al., 1992; Gustavson et al., 1992)—perhaps other factors contribute as

well, but the identity of such factors remains elusive. The rarity of blocking effects in CTA stands in marked contrast to other effects such as latent inhibition and the US preexposure effect and extinction-related phenomena (Batsell & Paschall, Chapter 10; Hall, Chapter 4; Lubow, Chapter 3; Meehan & Riccio, Chapter 7; Rosas & Bouton, 1996, 1997; St. Andre & Reilly, 2007; Schachtman et al., Chapter 8).

POTENTIAL ROLE OF NAUSEA AND CUE-INDUCED NAUSEA ON FEAR CONDITIONING

It is interesting to consider the role of nausea and the induction of nausea by associated cues on other kinds of learning. Rachman (1977, p. 385) mentioned that fears are more likely to be conditioned when an organism is in a compromised state such as being emotionally upset or physically ill (dizzy, weak), and he mentioned nausea as one circumstance in which fear conditioning may be more likely to occur in humans. An exploration of such interactions may prove valuable.

CTA AS A MODEL OF ANXIETY

There has been an enormous amount of research on fear conditioning in the past two decades. Some researchers have described CTA as a model of anxiety much like that of fear conditioning procedures that use footshock as the US or consequence. That is, the CTA avoidance response and its presumed emotional correlates have resulted in CTA being purported as a model of anxiety (Guitton & Dudai, 2004; Mickley et al., 2005, 2007; see also Fendt et al., in press) and the defensive reaction to a conditioned flavor has implications for the development of fears, phobias, and posttraumatic stress responses (Mickley et al., 2005, 2007). Years ago, Rachman wrote (1977, p. 378) that "if we also agree to an equation between the acquisition of a taste aversion and the acquisition of a fear, this recent literature [on CTA] may yet provide the best evidence for a conditioning theory of fear acquisition." Rachman goes on to say that "The idea that taste aversions and fear are related, receives some indirect support from the findings such as the elevated incidence of food aversions among neurotic subjects." Rachman then describes a study by Wallen (1945) which found exactly that.

PACEMAKER EFFECT AND LONG INTERSTIMULUS INTERVALS IN CTA

We found Misanin et al.'s pacemaker effect intriguing (see Misanin et al., Chapter 14). That is, the faster metabolic rate for younger rats may influence the temporal pacemaker such that intervals of time are perceived as longer relative to older adults. Longer delays between the taste and illness during CTA treatment are able to be bridged for older rats because the delays (based on slower pacemaker counts) are, indeed, calculated as shorter.

APPRECIATION

This book is expected to have the somewhat unique quality of serving the interests of many researchers, educators, and clinicians: neuroscientists, learning and conditioning researchers, psychopharmacologists, those interested in dietary and ingestive behaviors, clinical psychopathologists, and those in the medical field. We especially wish to thank the authors of the individual chapters. Nearly all senior authors read and commented on at least one of the other chapters in addition to putting together their own chapters. This "crossfostering" by various authors allowed for more cross-referencing as well as provided "reviews" in addition to those provided by the editors. We want to make a special note of appreciation to four of the individuals who have been a critical part of the CTA literature and history almost since the time of its inception: Drs. Mike Domjan, Sam Revusky, Tony Riley, and Jim Smith. Mike Domjan digested all of the chapters in order to produce the Foreword for this book. Sam Revusky wrote about the underappreciated role of CTA as a treatment for alcoholism, a contribution that ranks among the most interesting and thought-provoking of his career. Jim Smith's chapter (with Tom Houpt) on magnetism-induced taste aversions is as timely and as important today as his prior work on radiation-induced CTAs. Tony Riley, a source of encouragement and support throughout this project, wrote two chapters for the book, a historical perspective (with Kevin Freeman) and a provocative contribution concerning animal models of addiction (with Catherine Davis and Peter Roma). This book is much more strongly rooted in the history of the field with the contributions of these individuals in this volume; they each have our gratitude and thanks. Unbeknown to us, while writing (with Dr. Mario Bavieri) the chapter on conditioned taste aversion and chemotherapy Giuseppe Scalera was himself receiving that treatment. Giuseppe, friend, collaborator, and colleague, lost his battle with cancer in the summer of 2008—we will miss him. Finally, we would like to thank Oxford University Press and our editor, Catharine Carlin, for providing the opportunity and support to make this book possible.

References

Adams, C. D., & Dickinson, A. (1981). Actions and habits: Variations in associative representations during instrumental learning. In N. E. Spear & R. R. Miller (Eds.), *Information processing in animals: Memory mechanisms* (pp. 143–155). Hillsdale, NJ: Erlbaum.

Ader, R., & Peck, J. H. (1977). Early learning and retention of a conditioned taste aversion. *Developmental Psychobiology, 10*, 213–218.

Arkes, H. R. (1981). Impediments to accurate clinical judgment and possible ways to minimize their impact. *Journal of Consulting and Clinical Psychology, 49*, 323–330.

Baeyens, F., Crombez, G., De Houwer, J., & Eelen, P. (1996). No evidence for modulation of evaluative flavor–flavor associations in humans. *Learning and Motivation, 27*, 200–241.

Baeyens, F., Hendriekx, H., Crombez, G., & Hermans, D. (1998). Neither extended nor simultaneous feature positive training result in modulation of evaluative flavor conditioning in humans. *Appetitive, 31*, 185–204.

Barker, L. M., Best, M. R., & Domjan, M. (Eds.). (1977). *Learning mechanisms in food selection*. Waco, TX: Baylor University Press.

Braveman N. S., & Bronstein P. (Eds.) (1985). *Experimental assessments and clinical applications of conditioned food aversions*. Annals of the New York Academy of Sciences, 443, New York: New York Academy of Sciences.

Cameron, C. L., Cella, D., Herndon, J. E., Kornblith, A. B., Zuckerman, E., Henderson, E., et al. (2001). Persistent symptoms among survivors of Hodgkin's disease: An explanatory model based on classical conditioning. *Health Psychology, 20*, 71–75.

Colwill, R. M., & Rescorla, R. A. (1986). Associative structures in instrumental learning. In G. H. Bower (Ed.), *The psychology of learning and motivation* (Vol. 20, pp. 55–104). New York: Academic Press.

Craig, W. (1918). Appetites and aversions as constituents of instinct. *Biological Bulletin, 34*, 91–107.

De Houwer, J., Thomas, S., & Baeyens, F. (2001). Associative learning of likes and dislikes: A review of 25 years of research on human evaluative conditioning. *Psychological Bulletin, 127*, 853–869.

Delamater, A. R., & LoLordo, V. M. (1991). Event revaluation procedures and associative structures in Pavlovian conditioning. In L. Drachowski & C. F. Flaherty (Eds.), *Current topics in animal learning: Brain, emotion, and cognition* (pp. 55–94). Hillsdale, NJ: Erlbaum.

Dickinson, A., & Burke, J. (1996). Within-compound associations mediate the retrospective revaluation of causality judgements. *Quarterly Journal of Experimental Psychology, 49B*, 60–80.

Dickinson, A., Nicholas, D. J., & Mackintosh, N. J. (1983). A re-examination of one-trial blocking in conditioned suppression. *Quarterly Journal of Experimental Psychology, 35B*, 67–79.

Fendt, M., Schmid, S., Thakker, D., Jacobson, L. H., Yamamoto, R., Mitsukawa, K., et al. (in press). mGluR7 facilitates extinction of aversive memories and controls amygdala plasticity. *Molecular Psychiatry*. Advance online-publication, August 21, 2007; doi:10.1038/sj.mp.4002073

Gallo, M., & Candido, A. (1995). Dorsal hippocampal lesions impair blocking but not *Behavioral Neuroscience, 109*, 413–425.

Garcia, J., Lasiter, P. S., Bermudez-Rattoni, F., & Deems, D. A. (1985). A general theory of aversion learning. In N. S. Braveman & P. Bronstein (Eds.), *Experimental assessments and clinical application of conditioned food aversions, 443* (pp. 8–22). New York: New York Academy of Sciences.

Ghiselli, W. B., & Fowler, H. (1976). Signaling and affective functions of conditioned aversive stimuli in an appetitive choice discrimination: US intensity effects. *Learning and Motivation, 7*, 1–16.

Guitton, M. J., & Dudai, Y. (2004). Anxiety-like state associates with taste to produce conditioned taste aversion. *Biological Psychiatry, 56*, 901–904.

Gustavson, K. K., Hart, J. A., Calton, J. L., & Schachtman, T. R. (1992). Effects of extinction and US reinstatement of a blocking CS–US association. *Bulletin of the Psychonomic Society, 30*, 247–250.

Konorski, J. (1967). *Integrative activity of the brain.* Chicago, IL: University of Chicago Press.

Logue, A. W., Ophir, I., & Strauss, K. E., (1981). The acquisition of taste aversions in humans. *Behavioral Research and Therapy, 19*, 319–333.

Mickley, G. A., Hoxha, Z., Bacik, S., Kenmuir, C. L., Wellman, J. A., Biada, J. M., & DiSorbo, A. (2007) Spontaneous recovery of a conditioned taste aversion differentially alters extinction-induced changes in c-Fos protein expression in rat amygdala and neocortex. *Brain Research, 1152*, 139–157.

Mickley, G. A., Kenmuir, C. L., Yocum, A. M., Wellman, J. A., & Biada, J. M. (2005). A role for prefrontal cortex in the extinction of conditioned taste aversion. *Brain Research, 1051*, 176–182.

Milgram, N. W., Krames, L., & Alloway, T. M. (Eds.) (1977). *Food aversion learning.* New York: Plenum Press.

Morrow, G. R., & Dobkin, P. L. (1988). (in Cameron) Anticipatory nausea and vomiting in cancer patients undergoing chemotherapy treatment: Prevalence, etiology, and behavioral interventions. *Clinical Psychology Review, 8*, 517–556.

Pelchat, M. L., Grill, H. J., Rozin, P., & Jacobs, J. (1983) Quality of acquired responses to tastes by *Rattus norvegicus* depends on type of associated discomfort. *Journal of Comparative Psychology, 97*, 140–153.

Rachman, S. (1977). The conditioning theory of fear-acquisition: A critical examination. *Behaviour Research and Therapy, 15*, 375–387.

Reilly, S., Bornovalova, M., Dengler, C., & Trifunovic, R. (2003). Effects of excitotoxic lesions of the gustatory thalamus on latent inhibition and blocking of conditioned taste aversion in rats. *Brain Research Bulletin, 62*, 117–128.

Rosas, J. M., & Bouton, M. E. (1996). Spontaneous recovery after extinction of a conditioned taste aversion. *Animal Learning and Behavior, 24*, 341–348.

Rosas, J. M., & Bouton, M. E., (1997). Renewal of a conditioned taste aversion upon return to the conditioning context after extinction in another one. *Learning and Motivation, 28*, 216–229.

Rozin, P., & Fallon, A. E. (1987). A perspective on disgust. *Psychological Review, 94*, 23–41.

St. Andre, J., & Reilly, S. (2007). Effects of central and basolateral amygdala lesions on conditioned taste aversion and latent inhibition. *Behavioral Neuroscience, 121*, 90–99.

Schachtman, T. R., Gustavson, K. K., Chelonis, J. J., & Bourne, M. J. (1992). Effects of US reinstatement on the potential of an extinguished CS to attenuate manifest learning about another CS. *Learning and Motivation, 23*, 250–268.

Seligman, M. E. P., & Hager, J. L. (1972). *Biological boundaries of learning.* Englewood Cliffs, NJ: Prentice-Hall.

Stewart-Williams, S., & Podd, J. (2004). The placebo effect: Dissolving the expectancy versus conditioning debate. *Psychological Bulletin, 130*, 324–340.

Thiele, T. E., Kiefer, S. W., & Bailey, S. A. (1996). Taste reactivity and consumption measures in the assessment of overshadowing: Modulation of aversive, but not ingestive activity. *Psychonomic Bulletin and Review, 3*, 199–203.

Van Hamme, L. J., & Wasserman, E. A. (1994). Cue competition in causality judgments: The role of nonpresentation of compound stimulus elements. *Learning and Motivation, 25*, 127–151.

Wallen, R. (1945). Food aversions of normal and neurotic males. *Journal of Abnormal and Social Psychology, 40*, 77–81.

2

The Origins of Conditioned Taste Aversion Learning: A Historical Analysis

KEVIN B. FREEMAN AND ANTHONY L. RILEY

In describing the history of any phenomenon, one difficulty is determining the extent of the analysis. That is, given that history covers considerable ground (i.e., from then to now), the point where one is talking of the past versus the present is somewhat blurred. In the present chapter, we have traced what we see as the beginnings of the phenomenon of conditioned taste aversion (CTA) learning. In so doing, our focus is on its origins and the immediate impact of and reaction to the introduction of the phenomenon to the field. From these beginnings, research on aversion learning has been extensive and has taken many routes, from attempts to reinforce its apparent adaptive nature to empirical demonstrations of the conditions under which such learning occurred to its use as a clinical tool (see Riley & Freeman, 2004). These latter issues bring us to the immediate present which is the focus of the remainder of the current book. Although some of the history we are describing is certainly familiar to some (especially those who were part of its development), it is likely new to many. Seeing CTAs in the context of its origins may give some insight into how it came about, what it meant to those investigating this rather unique form of learning, and how it set the stage for the voluminous efforts that followed.

The origins of CTA learning as an empirically demonstrated phenomenon began with the conclusion of the Second World War, rising from the investigation of problems related to military applications. The first of these was a familiar issue: the need to manage rodent pestilence in foxholes and on beachheads. The second, however, was a new artifact of the atomic age: the need to study and understand the effects of radiation on biological systems. Each of these issues generated an extensive body of research in a relatively short time that spanned a wide range of topics and methodologies with the first empirical reports of CTA learning appearing almost simultaneously within each of these areas.[1]

BAIT-SHYNESS

In 1939, when war with Germany seemed inevitable, academic researchers in England were informed that they would be withheld from military service in order to conduct applied research relevant to war needs. However, this was an open-ended declaration because the British government often did little to provide direction in the development of programs for the various academic institutions. To that end, Charles Elton of the Bureau of Animal Population (BAP) proposed that his institute shift its focus from basic research on the ecology of wildlife populations to applied research on rodent control methodology (Elton, 1954). Thus began a rigorous program of field and laboratory investigation with the explicit aim of improving technologies for rodent elimination (Elton, 1954). The proposed agenda was diverse, including the assessment of numerous poisons (Chitty, 1954; Freeman et al., 1954), the base types in which the poisons could be mixed (e.g., bread mash or kibble; Leslie, Ranson, & Freeman, 1954; Thompson, 1954), the containers in which baits (defined as poisoned bases) were placed (Elton & Ranson, 1954), the eating behavior and stomach contents of poisoned rats in the wild (Rzóska, 1954b and 1954c), and census surveys of rat and mouse populations (Elton & Laurie, 1954).

The need for improvements implied a deficit in the current methodology, and one of the issues most pressing was the general effectiveness of poisons in field conditions. During initial field trials, the BAP used a method wherein novel baits (i.e., a poison mixed with some food base) were offered, that is, the animals had no prior experience with either the food base itself or the added poison. Thus, the bait presented to the rat was functionally a novel stimulus. Success under these conditions was minimal, as rats tended to sample amounts of the bait below what was necessary for lethal toxicosis. This might have been expected, as it was well known at that time that rats exhibited a neophobic response toward novel foods (Barnett & Spencer, 1949). To circumvent the fact that rats sampled too little of the novel baits for the poison to be effective, it was common practice when trying to poison rodents to use a method called prebaiting, wherein bases (not to be mistaken with baits) were placed in areas of pestilence so that rodents could sample the novel food, habituate to it, and eventually reach a reliably high level of consumption. Once a regular pattern of base consumption was established, the bait could be presented with some assurance that the rodent would consume a lethal amount of poison (Barnett & Spencer, 1949).

For unspecified reasons, the prebaiting method was not used in the initial field trials conducted by the BAP. This was a fortuitous decision for the discovery of CTA, however, as it led the investigators to consider what factors were causing rats to avoid baits under field conditions. One interesting interpretation was that "rats might be getting conditioned against the baits by taking sublethal doses of poison and afterwards associating some ingredient of the bait with their unpleasant experience" (Elton, 1954, p. 12). This assumption led to a series of investigations on this phenomenon, termed "bait-shyness" by the BAP.

In 1954, Julian Rzóska, one of the BAP researchers, published a paper entitled "Bait shyness, a study in rat behavior," which summarized research that he and his colleagues conducted on this issue during the Second World War (Rzóska, 1954a). The general aim of this research was to identify empirically the various factors contributing to the avoidance of poisoned baits. To that end, Rzóska and colleagues fed food-restricted laboratory rats a bait comprised of bread-paste and poison (arsenic, barium carbonate, or red squill). Although the laboratory rats initially accepted the bait (a curious absence of neophobia),[2] over successive presentations they either reduced their consumption or refused the bait outright. Thinking that the rats were somehow detecting the presence of the poisoned substance in the base, Rzóska offered the same base laced with a different poison. However, this modified bait was refused in a similar manner. Initially, Rzóska interpreted this as a "cross prejudice" wherein rats avoided "one poison on the basis of harmful experience with another" (Rzóska, 1954a, p. 129). However, this conclusion would prove to be inaccurate. In a following study, rats that had eaten a poisoned bait were offered, after 7 days, a new base laced with the familiar poison. Remarkably, they readily consumed this new bait, thus marginalizing the role of the poison cue itself in the expression of bait-shyness. The obvious factor was now the base itself. To test this, rats that had previously experienced a poisoned bait were then offered, on a subsequent occasion, the familiar base *without* any poison. The base itself was rejected in a manner similar to the avoidance seen with familiar poisoned baits. This was a clear indication that cues from the base (one might venture to say taste) rather than the poison itself were generating the avoidance behavior. In summarizing these findings, Rzóska (1954a, p. 130) stated that the laboratory rats in his experiments generally followed four rules after an initial experience with a poisoned bait:

1. An identical poison bait was refused on successive occasions.
2. A new poison in a base harmfully experienced was rejected.
3. An experienced poison in a new base was accepted.
4. A new poison in a new base was accepted.

Rzóska observed that "the poison makes the animal ill or uncomfortable, but mostly it appeared to be recognized through the medium of the base and not for itself" (Rzóska, 1954a, p. 130). Then, offering a seminal interpretation, he posited that "an 'association' was formed between the particular base and the illness felt when it was consumed with a poison" (Rzóska, 1954a, p. 130). Thus, food aversion (bait-shyness) was interpreted from these empirical findings as an associative learning phenomenon, that is, the animal appeared to learn an association between a nonpoison stimulus (taste) and the effects of poisoning (malaise, toxicity, etc.).

In addition to characterizing food aversion as an associative phenomenon, Rzóska (1954b) noted that the magnitude of the avoidance behavior was directly related to the dose of poison used in the bait. Furthermore, in testing the retention of the learned bait-shyness, he noted that rats avoided the poison-associated base as long as 374 days after being poisoned. This early work demonstrated for the first time that the expression of CTAs was dose-dependent and that the association could be retained for great lengths of time. The fact that bait-shyness was a function of the dose of the poison further supported the notion that it was a learning phenomenon, as stimulus intensity was known to be a mediating factor in the development of conditioning (Schwartz & Reisberg, 1991).

Rzóska did not pursue the characterization of "bait-shyness" as a learning phenomenon beyond its application to rodent control. Summarizing the narrow scope of the BAP's research focus, one researcher noted:

Rat control is a technology and its study therefore differs from a scientific investigation in having limited and practical aims. The success of any such study is determined by the extent to which these aims are met and not by any contributions which may be made towards science.

Chitty, 1954, p. 160[3]

However, it should also be noted that the BAP was primarily staffed by biologists. Understandably, their interest in animal behavior was not focused on traditional learning theory and the conditions under which learning was generally reported to occur. As such, it is not surprising that the importance of "bait-shyness" as a unique form of learning was not distilled from the research. However, this factor would not escape the attention of a student in psychology studying radiation in California.

THE STIMULUS PROPERTIES OF RADIATION

During the Second World War, the development of atomic weaponry ushered in a new age largely defined by the presence of this novel technology. In addition to its potential combat use, research on atomic energy offered the possibility of a bountiful energy source and an alternative to petroleum-based fuels. However, the generation of atomic energy produced radioactive by-products that were as harmful as they were poorly understood. The U.S. government placed a high premium on research into the effects of radiation (and their associated mechanisms) on living systems. One of the facilities conducting such research was the Radiological Defense Laboratory at Hunters Point in San Francisco, California.

In 1951, John Garcia, a graduate student in Psychology at the University of California at Berkeley, left before completing his Ph.D. and joined the team of Donald J. Kimeldorf and Edward L. Hunt at Hunters Point. According to Garcia, "the mission of the laboratory seemed simple enough: Determine the effects of ionizing radiation on biological systems and develop methods of protection against its hazards" (Garcia, 1980, p. 38). The research conducted in this laboratory examined the effects of radiation on a broad range of physiological and behavioral processes such as survivability in the cold (Kimeldorf & Newsom, 1952), sensitivity to low oxygen tension in a low pressure environment (Kimeldorf & Newsom, 1953), exercise performance (Kimeldorf, Jones, & Castanera, 1953), and alterations in body growth (Kimeldorf & Baum, 1954). However, in the midst of these numerous preparations, Garcia noticed a peculiar pattern in the rats' food and water consumption under conditions of irradiation which led to his work on aversion learning.

In one of the preparations Garcia used, rats were irradiated in a standard testing apparatus. This apparatus typically was a concrete encasement in which food and water were generally available ad libitum. Interestingly, water in this testing chamber was always offered in plastic bottles, while glass bottles were used in the rats' home cages. Garcia noticed that water consumption, along with food intake, decreased over successive treatments in the radiation testing chamber. However, no such effect was evident for either water or food in the home cages (J. Garcia, 2006, personal communication).

Naturally, Garcia considered the two things that varied between the testing chamber and the home cages: the type of water container and the presence or absence of radiation. He hypothesized that the plastic bottle lent a distinctive flavor to the water offered in the testing chamber and that this modified taste served as a discriminable cue that was somehow being associated with radiation-induced sickness. It was this association, he hypothesized, that led to the avoidance of the water consumed from the plastic bottles. As a preliminary assessment, he gave rats that had previously avoided water in the testing chamber the same plastic bottles of water when they were returned to their home cages (in lieu of the usual glass bottles). Remarkably, they avoided the water just as they did in the testing chamber, demonstrating that the previously noted suppression of consumption was a function of the plastic water bottle and independent of the location of its presentation. Thus, it seemed that a plastic bottle filled with water offered some kind of avoidance cue, a possibility that Garcia's colleague Robert A. Koelling, who hated the taste of coffee in a plastic cup, found quite believable (J. Garcia, 2006, personal communication).

To explain these findings, Garcia suggested that "the progressive change in consummatory behavior during repetitive exposure [to radiation] may be, in part, a conditioned response in which the avoidance of water and food is strengthened by learning through repeated coupling with the radiation situation" (Garcia, Kimeldorf, & Koelling, 1955, p. 157). This hypothesis was tested and the results reported in a seminal paper published in the journal *Science* entitled "Conditioned aversion to saccharin resulting from exposure to gamma radiation" (Garcia et al., 1955). In this study, Garcia and his colleagues, Kimeldorf and Koelling, paired a distinctive flavor with radiation exposure, after which they tested for an aversion to the flavor in the absence of radiation. Specifically, rats were initially given a choice between saccharin-flavored water and plain water to quantify the preference for the sweetened solution. Prior to any treatment, this preference was approximately 86% (i.e., the average fluid intake was 86% saccharin solution and 14% water), thus, demonstrating a clear baseline preference for saccharin over unflavored water.

Following this assessment, rats were placed in the radiation chamber for 6 h, during which time they had access to the saccharin solution. While in the chamber, the rats were administered radiation at one of two doses (30 or 57 roentgens [r]). Control subjects were treated similarly except that they received sham irradiation (with access to saccharin and placed in the chamber with the radiation source off). Then, beginning on the third day post-treatment, all animals were given access to water and saccharin on a continuous basis for the next 2 months, during which time the consumption of each solution was measured daily for each animal. Radiation was not administered during this assessment (i.e., the test was done under an extinction condition). The results of this study are summarized in Figure 2.1[4] which depicts saccharin preference over the 63 days of extinction. Rats that had saccharin paired with radiation during training showed a clear dose-dependent reduction in saccharin preference (relative to their initial preference). Although the preference for saccharin gradually increased over extinction, Garcia et al. (1955) noted that *the conditioned aversion to the discriminate fluid* was still present 30 days after irradiation (p. 158, italics added). Sham-treated subjects (data not shown) maintained their high level of saccharin consumption following "conditioning" and throughout "extinction," indicating that any change in saccharin preference seen in the radiated groups was not a function of mere exposure or habituation to saccharin.

Garcia et al. (1955) went on to argue in this paper that "the use of saccharin solution in the present study has made it possible to demonstrate the effectiveness of ionizing radiation to act as an unconditioned stimulus in animal behavior" (p. 158). Thus, CTA learning was introduced as a form of classical conditioning wherein radiation, when paired with a distinct flavor cue, could come to suppress the subsequent consumption of that flavor (as a result of the previously acquired association). In Pavlovian terms, taste, functioning as a conditioned stimulus (CS), was being associated with radiation administration, an unconditioned stimulus (US). In speculating on the nature of the radiation stimulus, Garcia introduced the concept of nausea:

The processes through which radiation is capable of operating as an unconditioned stimulus are unknown. Since consummatory behavior

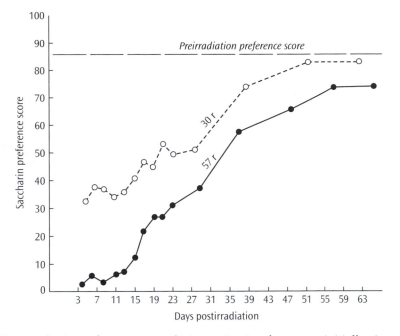

Figure 2.1. Median saccharin preference scores during extinction for groups initially given access to saccharin and exposed concurrently to gamma radiation (at 30 and 50 r). Preference for saccharin was significantly reduced and remained below preirradiation baselines for over a month. From "Conditioned aversion to saccharin resulting from exposure to gamma radiation," by J. Garcia et al., 1955, *Science*, *122*, 157–158. Copyright 1955 by The American Association for the Advancement of Science. Reprinted with permission.

is partially a reflection of gastric function, it is plausible to suspect gastrointestinal disturbances as the physiological events that motivate the animal in the learning situation. Gastrointestinal functions are known to be disturbed during radiation and are responsive to the same magnitude of radiation dose [used in the current study].

Garcia et al., 1955, p. 158

If CTA learning was indeed a form of conditioning (i.e., an association between the taste and the illness-inducing effects of radiation), then it stood to reason that it should fit into established conditioning models. To test this, Garcia and Kimeldorf (1957) conducted a temporal analysis study to "test how well these effects of irradiation fit the paradigm of conditioning with respect to temporal sequences of paired presentation of the stimuli" (p. 180). To that end, Garcia and Kimeldorf varied the order of presentation of saccharin and radiation using trace, simultaneous, and backwards conditioning arrangements, that is, where the CS was

followed by the US, where the CS was concurrent with the US, and where the US was followed by the CS, respectively (see Figure 2.2a). Backwards conditioning proved to be the only ineffective configuration (see Figure 2.2b), thus demonstrating that CTA learning was amenable to the same ordinal manipulations of stimulus arrangement generally accepted to impact the acquisition of Pavlovian learning (Pavlov, 1927).[5] Because conditioning with taste and radiation apparently occurred under the same temporal parameters supporting other forms of Pavlovian learning (Schwartz & Reisberg, 1991), it seemed relatively clear that taste aversions induced by radiation constituted a true conditioning process. However, this interpretation was complicated by a widely held belief that radiation possessed no stimulus properties and was therefore "imperceptible to the senses" (Garcia, 1980, p. 38). Furthermore, histological studies examining the effects of radiation on the mammalian nervous system had not yielded consistent results (Furchgott, 1963). Therefore, when Garcia reported that radiation could be used as a US in a procedure

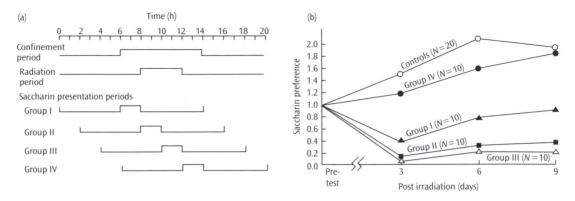

Figure 2.2. (a) Schematic for the experimental design of Garcia and Kimeldorf (1957). Time is measured in hours. Confinement period is time spent in the radiation apparatus. Radiation period is time spent during irradiation. Presentation periods are time in which saccharin was available. (b) Mean saccharin preference following irradiation for Groups I–IV (depicted in a) and for nonirradiated controls. From "Temporal relationship within the conditioning of a saccharine aversion through radiation exposure," by J. Garcia and D. J. Kimeldorf, 1957, *Journal of Comparative and Physiological Psychology, 50,* 180–183. Copyright 1957 by The American Psychological Association. Reprinted with permission.

of Pavlovian learning, there was some reluctance to accept this as a demonstration of radiation's stimulus effects, and, by extension, conditioning. In response to Garcia's findings, one prominent radiobiologist noted that "we have been radiating animals for years and no one has ever observed an avoidance response" (Garcia, 1980, p. 39).

Garcia, however, believed that most of this reluctance was based on presumption, as the notion of radio-insensitivity seemed to be supported mostly by a lack of disputing evidence (Garcia, 1980; Garcia & Buchwald, 1963; Garcia, Buchwald, Hull, & Koelling, 1964). To address this issue, Garcia and Buchwald (1963) demonstrated that low-dose, flash presentations (approximately 2 s) of radiation, when directed at the head, could serve as a CS in a shock-avoidance procedure, that is, acute radiation was an effective stimulus for the prediction of shock. This did much to resolve the uncertainty over whether or not radiation administration could induce a stimulus effect, and thus strengthened the case (at the very least by marginalizing one point of criticism) that radiation-induced taste aversions were, in fact, the result of an association (i.e., between taste and the effects of radiation). However, the mechanism by which radiation was capable of conditioning avoidance behavior was still unknown.

In an effort to better characterize the nature of radiation as a US in aversion learning (specifically, to delineate an anatomical location of the radiation-induced effects), Garcia and Kimeldorf (1960) carried out an experiment in which the administration of radiation was varied across different parts of the rat's body. Specifically, different groups of rats were allowed to drink a saccharin solution and were then exposed to radiation (administered locally to the head, thorax, abdomen, or pelvis). A final group was given saccharin access and exposed to whole-body radiation similar to the procedure used in the previous CTA experiments (Garcia et al., 1955; Garcia & Kimeldorf, 1957). Although whole-body radiation produced the strongest aversion, direct application of radiation to the abdomen was much more effective at producing aversions than the other localized applications, despite the constancy of dose. This led Garcia and Kimeldorf (1960) to conclude that "sensations triggered by gastric dysfunction may represent the stimuli through which radiation acts to condition behavior in animals" (p. 726), further extending Garcia's previously-stated hypothesis that visceral nausea was mediating CTA learning with radiation (see Garcia et al., 1955). In discussing these findings, Garcia and Kimeldorf (1960) made an interesting prediction: "Taste cues may be dependent on the relatively close relationship of consummatory behavior and gastric function so that sensations triggered by gastric dysfunction are *readily associated by the animal*" (italics added, pp. 725–726). This would, indeed, turn out to be the case, as was later demonstrated in his seminal selective association work (Garcia & Koelling, 1966; see following text for a full discussion of this issue).

Although it appeared that the aversive effects were concentrated in the gastrointestinal area, there still remained the problem that aversions were found when other areas of the body were irradiated (Garcia & Kimeldorf, 1960). Within the same laboratory at Hunters Point, Hunt and colleagues speculated that radiation administration could be releasing a toxin-like substance into the blood, which could then be transported anywhere in the body to interact with systems that mediated radiation's aversive effects (Hunt, Carroll, & Kimeldorf, 1965). To test this, rat pairs were made to share blood supplies through a skin-vascular anastomosis, that is, their vascular systems were functionally integrated. Following this, one of the rats in the parabiont pair was irradiated, after which the other rat, shielded from the radiation, was offered a saccharin solution.[6] A control group of parabiont rats was given the same treatment, but the rats were merely tied together to simulate the proximal pairing without the sharing of a blood supply. A third group was anastomized, but in this case the nonirradiated partner received water instead of saccharin. Anastomized rats that drank saccharin following their partners' irradiation showed marked aversions to saccharin on a subsequent test. However, neither the tethered controls nor the anastomized water controls showed an aversion to saccharin (see Figure 2.3).

Hunt et al. (1965) concluded that "our results show that a noxious effect of irradiation can be mediated by a systemic humoral factor" (p. 1748). This was further validated in a study in which transplanted serum from irradiated donors was used to condition taste aversions in nonirradiated rats (Garcia, Ervin, & Koelling, 1967). Thus, it seemed that radiation, in addition to its gastrointestinal perturbation, induced its aversive effects through the release of some by-product into the circulatory environment.

A UNIQUE FORM OF LEARNING?

Up until the mid-1960s, Garcia's empirical demonstrations of taste aversion learning centered around the characterization of radiation's stimulus (cueing and aversive) effects. However, as his research progressed, he and his colleagues began to interpret

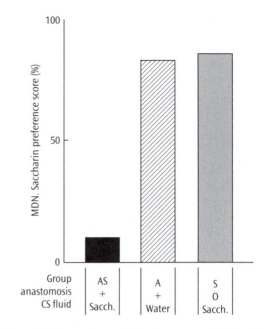

Figure 2.3. Aversive conditioning to saccharin fluid obtained in shielded parabiont rats that experienced the taste of saccharin after the partner was exposed to 360 r of X-rays. AS—experimental group; A—control group (anastomized but drank water); S—control group (tied together, not anastomized); MDN—Median. From "Humoral mediation of radiation-induced motivation in parabiont rats," by E. L. Hunt et al., 1965, Science, 150, 1747–1748. Copyright 1965 by The American Association for the Advancement of Science. Reprinted with permission.

their data in a way that gave increasing emphasis to taste aversions as a specialized type of learning. In the initial 1955 report (Garcia et al., 1955), Garcia and his colleagues noted that the evidence for aversion conditioning with radiation was limited to a single behavior, that is, taste discrimination. However, they posited that aversions "may be symptomatic of broader behavioral disturbances instigated during radiation exposure. If this is true, then it should be possible to detect avoidance behavior with stimuli other than taste" (p. 158). Following up on this, he and his colleagues demonstrated that rats would avoid distinct environmental cues that had been previously paired with radiation (Garcia, Kimeldorf, & Hunt, 1957). However, this contextual conditioning lacked the robustness of that when taste was used as the CS. Specifically, aversions to contextual cues required repeated conditioning trials, whereas taste aversion conditioning could be acquired after a single taste-radiation pairing (Garcia et al., 1955). Furthermore, taste aversions induced by radiation were more stable over time than similarly conditioned contextual aversions (Garcia et al., 1964). Speculating on these differences, Garcia et al. (1964) said the following:

> It seems plausible to assume that evolutionary pressures have produced organisms designed to learn quickly the relationships between these internal states and information received via the chemical senses (taste and smell) which sample the substances which are soon incorporated into the internal environment.
>
> p. 110

This introduced the notion (at least in the context of taste aversions) that adaptive specializations within the organism could be governing learning processes in a way that favored the development of certain associations beneficial to the animal's survival. Garcia and Koelling tested this inference and reported their findings in another seminal

paper entitled "Relation of cue to consequence in avoidance learning" (Garcia & Koelling, 1966). In this study, rats were offered a compound CS that included a distinctive taste and an audiovisual cue activated by the rats' licking of the drinking spout ("bright noisy" water). These animals were then divided into separate groups based on whether they were given exposure to radiation or foot shock. Specifically, one group of rats had the compound taste/audiovisual cue paired with radiation, while the second group had the same compound stimulus paired with foot shock. On a subsequent test, subjects were given access to either saccharin *or* bright noisy water (plain water and the lick-induced activation of the audiovisual cue). Rats that were initially conditioned with radiation avoided consumption of saccharin but continued to lick the plain water that resulted in the presentation of the audiovisual cue. Conversely, rats conditioned with foot shock reduced the licking of the plain water that triggered the presentation of the audiovisual cue, but readily consumed saccharin (see Figure 2.4). These differential patterns of consumption (or suppression) apparently reflected a selective association between gustatory cues and

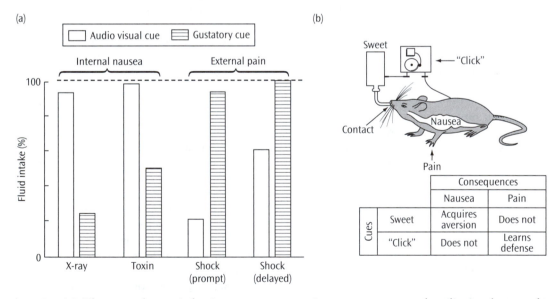

Figure 2.4. (a) The secondary reinforcing property accruing to gustatory and audiovisual cues after conditional pairing with either internal nausea or peripheral pain (shock). The y-axis represents percentage of saccharin intake relative to total fluid intake. From "Gustatory–visceral and telereceptor–cutaneous conditioning—adaptation in internal and external milieus," by J. Garcia and F. R. Ervin, 1965, *Communications in Behavioral Biology, 1*, 389–415. Copyright 1968 by Elsevier. Reprinted with permission. (b) The effects of pairing a gustatory cue or an auditory cue with pain or nausea. From *Perspectives in ethology* (p. 24), by J. Garcia et al., 1972, New York: Plenum. Copyright 1972 by Springer. Reprinted with permission.

nausea and between audiovisual cues and foot shock. Similar data were subsequently reported by Garcia and his colleagues demonstrating that rats readily associated the taste of distinctively flavored food pellets with illness, but not the size of the pellets, whereas food pellets of a particular size (but not of a particular taste) could be readily conditioned by foot shock (Garcia, McGowan, Ervin, & Koelling, 1968).

In discussing the 1966 findings, Garcia and Koelling said "it seems that given reinforcers are not equally effective for all classes of discriminable stimuli. The cues…appear to be related to the consequences of the subsequent reinforcer" (p. 124). The title of the Garcia and Koelling paper "Relation of cue to consequence in avoidance learning" defined the concept of the importance of the relationship between stimuli in associative learning, a concept incongruent with popular learning theory which considered reinforcement to be generally applicable to all discriminable stimuli, regardless of the qualitative nature of the stimuli involved (Kimble, 1961). Garcia and Koelling posited that these selective associations were a form of adaptive specialization, honed through natural selection, which increased an organism's chance at forming associations between stimuli that were contingently related and biologically relevant. This was reflected in the conclusion to the paper demonstrating these specific and selective associations: "Natural selection may have favored mechanisms which associate gustatory and olfactory cues with internal discomfort since the chemical receptors sample the materials soon to be incorporated in the internal environment" (Garcia & Koelling, 1966, p. 124).

In addition to selective associations, research conducted in CTA learning during this period offered another caveat to general learning theory. At the time of CTA's appearance in the literature, there was a widely accepted view that associative conditioning required close stimulus–reinforcer contiguity, measured in milliseconds to seconds, for learning to occur (Kimble, 1961). However, in a paper published in 1963, McLaurin and Scarborough noted that in a standard CTA procedure in which rats are "presented with saccharin solution for 20 minutes or more, imbibing of the fluid by the subjects would not be continuous throughout the duration of the CS period. Thus, varying subject interstimulus intervals…would be expected to exist" (p. 317). Given that some of these animals might have gone a minute or more between drinking and being irradiated, there was

an obvious problem when considering the tenet of traditional learning theory that close interstimulus contiguity was required for learning to occur. Therefore, to more systematically assess the effects of varying the delay between the taste and illness, McLaurin and Scarborough conducted a trace conditioning experiment wherein the interstimulus interval between the saccharin CS and the radiation US was varied such that one group of animals was exposed to radiation immediately following saccharin access, while an additional two groups were exposed 25 or 50 min, respectively, following saccharin removal. A final group received sham irradiation 25 min following saccharin access. When the animals were subsequently tested for saccharin preference, *all* irradiated groups showed robust and equivalent aversions, that is, the magnitude of the aversion was not affected by the imposed delays in the CS–US interval (McLaurin & Scarborough, 1963). Although there were no differences in aversions induced by the immediate versus delayed radiation, the fact that aversions were evident in the 25 and 50 min delay conditions presented a clear problem for the contiguity principle in associative learning, wherein extensions of the CS–US interval, even as long as 1 s, proved detrimental to the development of associations in other learning preparations (Kimble, 1961; Warner, 1932). Interestingly, in light of this apparent violation, McLaurin and Scarborough (1963) interpreted their data *not* as evidence of long-delay learning, but rather as a nonassociative phenomenon of unknown origin:

It is concluded under the conditions of this study that factors other than the association of stimuli are contributing to the intensity and duration of the saccharin avoidance response. The avoidance response may be due in part to generalized avoidance behavior of the organism after irradiation manifested toward unfamiliar stimuli in a familiar environment…Until the specific mechanisms involved in the saccharin avoidance behavior under irradiation which produces such intense avoidance over extended interstimulus intervals can be ascertained, *there is a question as to the appropriateness of the term "conditioning" as applied to this phenomenon.*

p. 323 (italics added)

Three years later, Garcia, Ervin, and Koelling published similar data showing that conditioning could occur with extended CS–US intervals

(Garcia, Ervin, & Koelling, 1966; see Figure 2.5). As with the McLaurin and Scarborough (1963) paper, Garcia and his colleagues varied the interval between the CS (saccharin) and US (apomorphine, a drug shown to produce gastrointestinal disturbances) and assessed the effects of these extended CS–US intervals on taste aversion learning. Specifically, they gave different groups of rats access to saccharin followed at different times by an injection of vehicle or apomorphine (from 0.5 to 3 h), and like the earlier report, aversions to saccharin were conditioned at delays of 45–70 min (but not when the drug was delayed longer). Although the data were similar to those reported by McLaurin and Scarborough (1963), the interpretation was very different, one consistent with that given to the findings of selective associations noted before. In discussing their findings, Garcia et al. (1966) noted the following:

> These data indicate anew that the mammalian learning mechanisms do not operate randomly, associating stimuli and reinforcers only as a function of recency, frequency, and intensity. The omnivorous rat displays a bias, probably established by natural selection, to associate gustatory and olfactory cues with internal malaise even when these stimuli are separated by long time periods.
>
> p. 122

Clearly, Garcia and his colleagues were adding a new layer to their previously stated position that CTA learning was an adaptive specialization. In addition to an organism's inherent ability to selectively associate gustatory cues with nausea (and audiovisual cues with external pain such as shock), there was evidence that this associative mechanism was further refined and safeguarded by a system that enabled the association to form over extended delays. This made logical sense in an ecological context. Given that toxicity was likely to follow consumption of a toxin after some delay (a natural function of digestion) and that numerous types of stimuli were sure to be encountered during that interval, being able to make selective associations after relatively long taste-illness intervals was arguably essential to an organism's survival.

INTERPRETING THE PHENOMENON

By 1966, CTA learning had gone from being an observed artifact within the context of other research (rodent control and radiation assessments) to an independently investigated and empirically validated phenomenon. With the introduction of selective associations and long-delay learning, CTA presented a challenge to general-process learning theory, which favored the position that all discriminable stimuli were equally susceptible

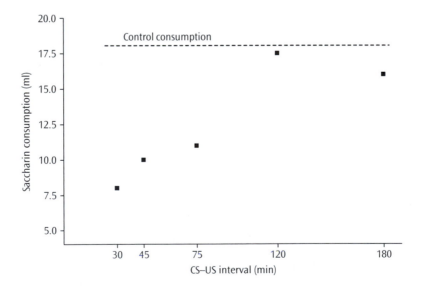

Figure 2.5. Mean intake of saccharin-flavored water on the first extinction day following saccharin-apomorphine pairings at CS–US intervals of 30, 45, 75, 120, and 180 min. Dashed line represents saccharin consumption of vehicle-treated animals. Data redrawn from Garcia et al. (1966).

to reinforcement and that close stimulus–reinforcer contiguity was required for learning to occur (Kimble, 1961; Pavlov, 1927; Thorndike, 1911). This apparent challenge attracted numerous researchers to the investigation and interpretive discussion of CTA learning. In the resulting discourse, two major themes were prevalent: (1) the exceptional nature of CTA learning and the implications of its incongruence with contemporary learning theory, that is, the fact that it could occur in a single trial, could develop under conditions of long delay between the CS and US, and could show evidence of selective CS–US associations and (2) the ecological utility of the phenomenon, including its physiological underpinnings and the selective pressures that honed its development. In almost every case, some aspect of the latter was used to explain the former.

Three seminal reviews written between 1968 and 1971 took on the ambitious task of offering empirically-based explanations of the exceptional nature of CTA learning. The first of these, entitled "Gustatory–visceral and telereceptor-cutaneous conditioning—adaptation in internal and external milieus" (Garcia & Ervin, 1968), argued that the demonstration of selective associations and long-delay learning in CTA necessitated two "amendments to the Law of Effect" (see Thorndike, 1911): (1) "Not all of the stimuli which impinge upon the organism, and are followed by an effective reinforcer, acquire secondary reinforcing properties," and (2) "Immediate reinforcement is not a general requirement for all learning" (p. 390). According to the authors, these exceptions arose from adaptive specializations in physiology that enabled the animal to make associations important for survival more readily than other associations. This specialized apparatus also prevented concurrent, but irrelevant, stimuli (e.g., visual cues during the interstimulus interval) from impinging on or interfering with the development of the taste-illness association. Stressing the need to consider biological factors in this apparent constraint on learning, Garcia and Ervin (1968) noted:

We now argue that the effectiveness of learning also depends upon specific sensory channels used to stimulate the organism and their particular relation to the afferent consequences of reinforcement. The fact that an animal can make some cue-consequence connections much more readily than others can only be understood in terms of the biological structure of that organism.

p. 403

Garcia and Ervin (1968) later noted:

The fact that these new acquisitions [i.e., associations] are formed in one or two trials indicates that a central associative mechanism connects the gustatory and visceral systems. However, the animal cannot readily associate sights and sounds with the effects of food, indicating that these exteroceptive afferents are probably not directly connected to this particular central integrative system.

p. 405

Thus, a system was proposed in which the sources of aversive impingements on the internal and external "milieu" could be delineated from one another via specializations in the animal's physiology, with the purpose of generating behavior that avoided further insult. Reviewing evidence for the existence of such an apparatus, Garcia and Ervin described some findings within the nervous systems of various organisms in which sensory channels carrying gustatory and visceral stimuli were integrated subcortically, thus providing a direct center for the fast organization of gustatory–visceral associations. Because tele- and cutaneous-receptor afferents did not share this integrative apparatus with the gustatory system, the authors argued that audiovisual cues could not be as readily associated with malaise as could taste cues. The implication was that an animal's predisposition to learn certain associations more robustly than others stemmed, at least in part, from the organization of sensory and integrative neurocircuitry (systems shaped presumably by evolution). In speculating on the selective advantage of long-delay learning in CTA, Garcia and Ervin (1968) noted: "Since the ultimate effects of ingested materials are often delayed, effective gustatory–visceral associations would necessarily need to span long[er] temporal intervals than would telereceptor-cutaneous connections" (p. 409). This highlighted the obvious ecological advantage of long-delay learning in CTA and further stressed the role of adaptive specialization in its development.

In 1970, a second comprehensive review, entitled "Learned associations over long delays" by Sam Revusky and John Garcia, addressed long-delay taste aversion learning and its reception into the field of learning (Revusky & Garcia, 1970). The apparent aim of this review was not only to cite supporting evidence and logic for the phenomenon's existence but also to defend it against a rising tide of criticism (see discussion of this later). In addressing the delays supported in taste aversion learning, Revusky and Garcia (1970) noted at the outset of the review "all we know about the delay-of-reinforcement (or punishment) gradient is that there is such a gradient for each experimental situation, but that the shape of the gradient can vary" (p. 19). This implied that the weakening of stimulus–reinforcer associations seen with delay of reinforcement was applicable to all learning, CTA included (which it was; see Garcia et al., 1966), and irregardless of its quantitative uniqueness (i.e., the fact that relatively long interstimulus intervals could support taste aversion conditioning), the qualitative patterns seen with delayed reinforcement in other preparations should also occur in CTA.

For Revusky and Garcia, the theoretical explanation of long-delay taste aversion learning was in terms of processes operative for all learning. Thus, they noted that long-delay associations also occurred in a variety of other preparations, for example, see Capaldi and Spivey (1964) and Tinklepaugh (1932). Building on the selective association findings of Garcia et al. (1966), Revusky and Garcia (1970) used the concept of stimulus relevance (a term initially coined by Dietz & Capretta, 1967), defined as "the principle that the associative strength of a cue with some consequence depends, in part, on the nature of the consequence" (p. 21). Furthermore, they added that in the case of CTA, "a flavor has high associative strength relative to a physiological consequence, while an exteroceptive stimulus has low associative strength" (p. 21). This had bearing on the validity of long-delay taste aversion learning as an associative process because it provided a means by which a gustatory cue and subsequent malaise, together sharing stimulus relevance, were able to be associated despite having a protracted interstimulus interval over which a barrage of extraneous stimuli were sure to impinge on the organism. As such, the associative apparatus was constructed in such a way that these extraneous stimuli could not easily be associated with malaise, and, therefore, were not likely to overshadow (or interfere with) the previous, but more

relevant, taste stimulus. Thus, in the absence of this interference, the only remaining threat to the taste-stimulus association was the natural process of memory decay.

According to Revusky and Garcia (1970), if stimulus relevance was governing the process of selective association, it should have been possible to overshadow the saccharin taste cue with another novel stimulus of equal relevance, that is, a new distinct taste. The logic here was that the intervening stimulus would itself become associated with subsequent illness and, therefore, detract from the associability of the more temporally separated saccharin cue. However, if the animal had prior nonreinforced experience with this intervening stimulus, the interference should be much weaker due to latent inhibition, that is, the animal's previous experience with the intervening taste stimulus in the absence of reinforcement should retard its associability with the subsequent malaise, thus diminishing its ability to overshadow the novel saccharin stimulus (see Revusky & Bedarf, 1967; see also Lubow, Chapter 3). This effect was demonstrated in data reported in the Revusky and Garcia review. Specifically, rats were allowed to drink 4 ml of saccharin and were injected 100 min later with LiCl. However, some of the animals were given a novel flavor to consume during the interstimulus interval (either coffee or vinegar), while the others were presented with a familiar flavor (again, coffee or vinegar). Presentation of the familiar flavor during the interval had no effect on the acquisition of an aversion to saccharin. However, when animals consumed a novel flavor during the interval, the aversion to saccharin was attenuated. Thus, interference appeared to be a function of the associative strength of the intervening stimuli which in turn supported the authors' notion that "it is the occurrence of interfering associations involving intervening stimuli that usually prevents association over long delays" (Revusky & Garcia, 1970, p. 35).

This made sense in an ecological context because animals experiencing an ingestion-associated illness were likely to have consumed more than one candidate food in recency. Logically, it would most likely be something novel in the diet, as the familiar food had proven to be safe in the past. This theoretical mechanism, subsequently coined concurrent interference, accounted for long-delay learning through the process of selective association, and, in so doing, provided the animal with a tool for food selection that enabled it to discern between harmful and safe foods.

In 1971, Paul Rozin and Jim Kalat published an important review entitled "Specific hungers and poison avoidance as adaptive specializations of learning." While the Garcia and Ervin (1968) and Revusky and Garcia (1970) reviews focused on specialized processes that allowed for the perceived "exceptional learning" seen in CTA (i.e., selective associations and long-delay learning), Rozin and Kalat (1971) sought to remove this emphasis on CTA's uniqueness by arguing that what was perceived as "special" in the phenomenon was actually representative of a process of adaptive specialization that shaped many, if not all, forms of learning. The authors introduced this idea in the following:

Learning and memory, being the result of natural selection, should be expected to be best developed in situations and species where other solutions to the problems at hand are less adaptive. Furthermore, when learning or memory capacities are brought to bear on a particular type of problem or situation, it stands to reason that these capacities should be shaped by or adapted to the situation. We propose to treat learning and memory as any other biological characteristic, subject to natural selection and therefore adapted to handle specific types of problems.

Rozin & Kalat, 1971, p. 459

In supporting this argument, the authors reviewed work (theirs and others) on specific hungers, a phenomenon in which animals deficient in a nutrient exhibited preferences for diets enriched by that nutrient (Richter, 1943). The issue of interest for Rozin and Kalat (1971) was the mechanism by which animals selectively chose diets that contained a nutrient in which they were deficient. Early evidence suggested that some specific hungers were derived from a learning process (Scott & Verney, 1947). Specifically, rats were allowed to eat a distinctly flavored enriched diet (i.e., one containing a needed nutrient) versus an unflavored one deficient in the nutrient. Over time, they developed a preference for the flavored, enriched food. When subsequently offered the deficient diet (but with the distinct flavor), the rats then showed a preference for the flavored deficient diet, suggesting that they

had learned something about the flavor relative to the dietary deficiency. Beyond establishing that learning was involved in food selection with specific hungers, however, there remained the question as to whether this represented an acquired preference for the enriched diet or an acquired aversion to the old deficient diet. If the latter were the case, then what appeared to be a preference for the enriched diet might have been nothing more than the consumption of an alternative to the deficient food. This "aversion" interpretation was demonstrated by showing that rats maintained on a nutrient-deficient diet would continue to avoid that diet, even after they were allowed to recover from the deficiency via consumption of an enriched diet made available at a separate time (Rozin, 1967). Furthermore, the deficient diet was still rejected when the rats were in a food-deprived (but nutrient-replete) state, that is, they rejected the food in spite of hunger. Commenting on this, Rozin and Kalat (1971) noted that "preference of hunger (eating nothing) to ingestion in hungry rats and the similarity in the rat's behavior toward deficient and highly unpalatable (quinine adulterated) diets suggests strongly that we are dealing with an aversion to the familiar food" (Rozin & Kalat, 1971, p. 463). Then, making a comparison between specific hungers and poison avoidance, the authors noted:

We can consider the deficient diet as a CS and the nausea or other ill effects produced by its ingestion as a UCS. Presumably, the classically conditioned "ill effects" lead to avoidance of the familiar [deficient] food...To the extent that specific aversions play a key role in the specific hungers, there is an obvious parallel between specific hungers and poisoning. Both involve learned aversions; [a] vitamin deficient diet is a slowly acting poison.

Rozin & Kalat, 1971, p. 463

This broadened the functional scope of aversion learning, because it not only enabled the animal to avoid the consumption of toxic substances, but it also maximized its chances of eating beneficial foods by leading it away from less nutritious alternatives. Furthermore, in each case, the qualities of long-delay learning and selective association [termed "belongingness" in Rozin & Kalat (1971)] were apparent (Garcia et al., 1966;

Garcia & Koelling, 1966; Rozin, 1967; Rozin & Kalat, 1971). The importance of this was reflected in the following:

> Both principles, belongingness and long-delay learning, seem highly adapted to the properties of the feeding system. Tastes are, in fact, causally linked to gastrointestinal events, and there is a long inherent delay between the taste and its consequences. We suggest that specific learning mechanisms have evolved in response to specific problems.
>
> Rozin & Kalat, 1971, p. 470

This placed CTA learning within an adaptive framework, suitably developed to meet the challenges of food selection. The implication was that any quality of learning considered "peculiar" in CTA (e.g., long-delay learning) was best understood when viewed as a refinement in the learning process, shaped by selective pressure, to tackle a specific problem. In the case of long-delay learning, the challenge was in bridging the stimulus gap between the tasting of a food and the effects of its consumption, which would not occur until "many minutes or hours after ingestion" (Rozin & Kalat, 1971). Thus, in the particular case of the feeding system, some means of making associations between stimuli that were separated by relatively long intervals was required. However, there was no reason to expect this feature in all cases of learning. Rozin and Kalat (1971) expressed this notion in the following: "The long-delay learning found in feeding is probably not characteristic of other 'prepared' associations, and in our view, it should not be, since in most cases close temporal contiguity is the best predictor [of reinforcement]" (p. 481). As such, parametric differences (e.g., long-delay learning or lack thereof) across learning preparations should be expected because these processes were differentially shaped by evolution to meet distinct environmental challenges. Interestingly, one could argue that this brought a degree of generality back to learning, a point the authors noted in the closing of their review:

> Given the constraints on adaptations produced by basic properties of the nervous system, the cost of evolving specializations, and the fact that most species face a common set of problems, we doubt that a separate learning

mechanism would exist for every situation, or that there would be separate laws for each species. It may be possible to formulate laws of some degree of generality, taking ecological factors into account.
>
> Rozin & Kalat, 1971, p. 481

Their position that such adaptations were widespread and that many types of learning may be constrained or shaped by the animal's biological history was quite different from those who saw taste aversion learning as unique or special. The authors noted this in the final section of their review "Adaptive specializations of learning: generality and relation to other positions." In discussing taste aversion learning (and other examples of biologically relevant learning, e.g., imprinting), they concluded:

> Feeding and imprinting can be considered as two exceptions to an otherwise correct 'general process' view of learning. Or they can be considered as examples of a basic adaptational principle pervading much or all of learning. We prefer the latter alternative...We differ from all the other authors in the sense that they see belongingness, in one form or another, as *the* unique phenomenon to be explained, whereas we see it as an example of the general adaptational principle; animals may not only learn some things more easily than others, but they may also learn some things in a different way than others.
>
> Rozin & Kalat, 1971, pp. 479 and 481

Rozin and Kalat's (1971) argument fit well within the context of concurrent research looking at biological constraints on other forms of learning. In addition to poison avoidance and specific hungers, constraints on learning were being characterized in species-specific defense reactions (Bolles, 1972), autoshaping (Brown & Jenkins, 1972), the misbehavior of organisms (Breland & Breland, 1972), and differential cue conditioning with auditory and visual stimuli (Shettleworth, 1972a). Furthermore, these positions were in accordance with current ethological thinking which emphasized the role of evolution in the shaping of behavior (Alcock, 1979; Eibl-Eibesfeldt, 1970; Tinbergen, 1951).

REACTIONS TO THE INTERPRETATIONS

The three major reviews published between 1968 and 1971 (Garcia & Ervin, 1968; Revusky & Garcia, 1970; Rozin & Kalat, 1971) addressed the apparent uniqueness of CTA learning, that is, selective associations and long-delay learning. Although each review approached this topic from its own individual perspective, the net effect was to bring to the literature an integrated hypothesis that could account for its physiological underpinnings (Garcia & Ervin, 1968), the mechanisms of its learning specializations (Revusky & Garcia, 1970), and the basis for its development as an instrument in food selection (Rozin & Kalat, 1971). And, although the emphasis varied with respect to the status of CTA as a unique form of learning (Garcia & Ervin, 1968; Revusky & Garcia, 1970) or as a particularly salient example of an adaptive specialization seen with other learning phenomena (Rozin & Kalat, 1971), there was unanimous consent that (1) CTA was indeed learning, (2) what were observed as selective associations and long-delay learning were indeed just that, and (3) quantitatively speaking, the features of these parameters set CTA apart from most other learning preparations.

Although such implications resonated with others working on related behavioral constraints (see Hinde & Stevenson-Hinde, 1973; Lehrman, Hinde, & Shaw, 1972; Seligman, 1970; Seligman & Hager, 1972), there were reactions to these findings and their interpretation. While some reactions denied the findings (see Seligman & Hager, 1972),[7] others raised interesting issues and alternative interpretations. As early as 1975, Bitterman questioned the premise of both selective associations and long-delay learning. In relation to the work on selective association in which taste cues (flavored food pellets) appeared selectively associable with the effects of radiation, whereas a visual cue (the size of the food pellet) was effectively paired with shock (see Garcia et al., 1968), Bitterman (1975) noted:

> The results for irradiation may be attributed to the fact that gustatory stimuli persisted in the interval between irradiation and illness whereas visual stimuli, of course, did not. The results for shock may be attributed to the fact that the visual stimuli antedated shock by a short interval favorable for conditioning, whereas the gustatory stimuli were at best simultaneous with shock and may even have followed it (since the animals were shocked immediately upon taking the food).

p. 708

In relation to long-delay learning, Bitterman (1975) noted that the extended CS–US interval could be illusory because of "the possibility that smell and taste receptors are stimulated again at the time of illness by food returned to the mouth from the stomach" (p. 708). Naturally, this would have provided the close temporal contiguity necessary for learning to occur under the framework of traditional learning theory (however, see Rozin & Kalat, 1971, for commentary on this issue). Thus, according to Bitterman, research on aversion learning had not provided sufficient evidence to necessitate a reformulation of traditional learning theory. Further, Bitterman argued that the lack in CTA experiments of pseudoconditioning controls precluded a means for ruling out unconditioned suppressive effects related to the administration of the aversive US, effects that might impact the relative salience of cues in specific conditioning situations that favored specific associations (independent of any biologically specialized learning thought to underlie CTA).

Concerns about CTA went beyond these procedural challenges. Others raised questions about the very uniqueness of aversion learning and, in so doing, whether it had implications for general-process learning theory (Logue, 1979; Spiker, 1977; Wallace, 1976). As noted by Logue (1979) in a review of CTA and its implications for general laws of learning, "the traditional laws of learning used for comparison were not clearly specified" (p. 277). That is, selective associations and long-delay learning in CTA may provide no clear violation of traditional learning theory because the parameters being violated (see Garcia & Ervin, 1968) were never explicitly defined in the first place. According to this view, all forms of learning, despite the apparent *quantitative* dissimilarities, could be generalized into a common theoretical framework if there were *qualitative* trends that pervaded the full range of processes. Logue (1979) supported this assertion by highlighting work outside of CTA in which most of the features considered unique to CTA, most notably one-trial learning (Bolles, 1970), selective associations (Shettleworth, 1972b), and long-delay learning (Lett, 1977), were observed in other preparations. In light of these accompanying "exceptions," it was concluded that "the characteristics of taste aversion learning that are said to be unique appear frequently to be better described as characteristics of prepared or feeding behavior" (Logue, 1979, p. 289). This point was interesting in that by questioning the uniqueness of aversion learning it raised the general importance of evolution and environmental context for all learning. This view actually fit well with the position expressed earlier by Rozin and Kalat (1971), who emphasized the likelihood that all forms of learning, despite showing some parametric differences, were most likely derived from a single baseline learning process. Accordingly, parametric variations across learning preparations could be accepted without necessitating a reformulation of basic learning theory, and considerations of adaptive specialization could be integrated into a broader approach to the study of learning.

Although the position that learning in general may have had an evolutionary underpinning that shaped it to the specific environmental and ecological context in which the animal lived seemed reasonable and intuitively sound, the adaptive interpretation as a means of explaining the exceptional nature of CTA (or for that fact any "unique" learning) was considered by many to be ad hoc. As such, many in the field of learning expressed concern that the special nature of CTA learning was being explained as a product of evolution in a manner that did little to generate subsequent functional analysis (Bitterman, 1975; Domjan & Galef, 1983; Goudie, 1980; Mackintosh, 1975). This concern was reflected in the following:

> The similarities between [flavor aversion learning (FAL)] and other forms of conditioning are probably more significant than the differences. It would certainly seem premature to appeal to somewhat dubious concepts such as "preparedness" to explain the FAL phenomenon. Such concepts have post hoc value only. They generate few, if any, empirically testable hypotheses and are therefore of little use in the analysis of learning mechanisms.
>
> Goudie, 1980, p. 594

In a review specifically addressing this issue, Domjan and Galef (1983) argued that the consideration of preparedness (the concept that organisms were predisposed to associate certain stimulus events more readily than others) and biological constraints had failed to generate any novel and progressive research in the field of associative learning. And although Rozin and Kalat (1971) suggested a means to make predictions based on the particular environmental challenges that a given organism might encounter, Domjan and Galef (1983) noted that "this approach to the discovery of new instances of specialized learning is rather informal and has been rarely used since it was proposed" (p. 154). As a remedy, it was suggested by the authors that more comparative analyses be conducted, particularly between the "behaviors of taxonomically related species subjected to different pressures," (e.g., white vs. wild rats; Domjan & Galef, 1983, p. 157). To that end, predictions could be made about behavior patterns based on variant selective pressures, and then verified through correlational analyses. In this way, biological constraints on learning could be studied in a systematic and empirical way, thus marginalizing the abovementioned criticisms of the adaptive interpretations applied to CTA learning.

FROM SPECIALIZATION TO ANALYSIS AND APPLICATION

As might be expected, these critical responses evoked reactions in which answers to challenges were presented, new procedural variations were assessed (to control for stated prior deficiencies), and the uniqueness of aversion learning as an adaptive specialization was defended (for discussions, see Garcia, Hankins, & Rusiniak, 1976; Revusky, 1977, Appendix 1). What is most interesting about the period in which taste aversions were being interpreted, questioned, and reframed, however, was that the interest in CTA as an empirical phenomenon remained quite high. In the period from 1968 to 1983 (see Figure 2.6) when the seminal reviews of aversion learning were being published and its implications were being questioned and challenged, there were a total of 1055 published papers on CTA learning (roughly 66 per year).

While some of these papers were attempts to reinforce (or challenge) its uniqueness as a

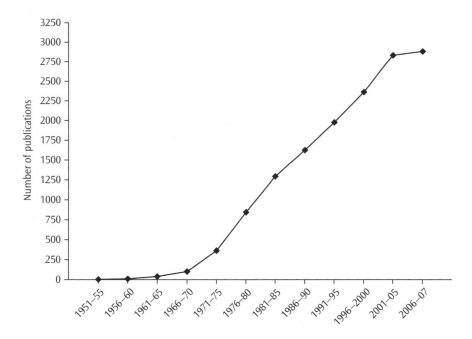

Figure 2.6. The cumulative publication record of all CTA literature, both empirical and review, starting with the original paper (Rzóska, 1954a) and up to the present. Time is expressed in 5-year blocks. [See www.CTAlearning.com]

specialized form of learning (especially in the years immediately after the publication of the 1966 papers by Garcia and coworkers and the reviews that followed), others had what appeared to be quite a different focus. Specifically, these latter papers (which were, in fact, the vast majority of the published work on aversion learning) explored the characterization of aversion learning, the conditions under which it could be demonstrated and the effects of various manipulations on its acquisition and display. It was this second focus that generated a burgeoning growth of research.

In this context, the phenomenon of taste aversion conditioning became like any other behavioral phenomenon, that is, something of interest and something to investigate. During this period, aversions were conditioned to a wide range of tastes (Brackbill, Rosenbush, & Brookshire, 1971), and issues such as salience (Kalat & Rozin, 1970), novelty (Kalat, 1974), and the amount (Bond & Di Guisto, 1975) and duration (Barker, 1976) of the taste stimulus were being manipulated. While taste was still the major sensory modality being investigated, conditioning was being examined

using cues such as odor (Pain & Booth, 1968), texture (Domjan & Hanlon, 1982), temperature (Nachman, 1970), and intravascular stimulation (Bradley & Mistretta, 1971), and the interaction of taste with these other modalities (in terms of potentiated aversions; Rusiniak, Hankins, Garcia, & Brett, 1979) was being highlighted. Along with variations in the stimuli that might serve as conditioned stimuli, the range of compounds that could condition aversions was growing and aversion conditioning was evident not only with radiation and classical toxins but also with drugs of abuse (to the considerable surprise to many; see Berger, 1972; Cappell & LeBlanc, 1977; Gamzu, 1977). Concurrent with these demonstrations, there was an interest, as well, in factors affecting the ability of an agent to condition an aversion, for example, its route of administration (Brown, Amit, Smith, & Rockman, 1978; Nachman & Ashe, 1973), distribution (Domjan, Foster, & Gillan, 1979), and novelty, with drug history receiving major research effort (Braveman, 1975; Brookshire & Brackbill, 1976; Riley, Jacobs, & LoLordo, 1976). At this time, not only did drugs prove to be effective in inducing aversions, but so did their absence in nutrient-deficient (Rozin, 1967; see earlier text) or drug-dependent animals. In relation to drug dependency, animals made dependent on morphine displayed aversions to tastes associated with withdrawal (Parker, Failor, & Weidman, 1973; Parker & Radow, 1974; see also Vitiello & Woods, 1977 for similar conditioning with caffeine). The temporal parameters of conditioning were still being investigated (Buresova & Bures, 1974; Deutsch, 1978), along with the role of contingency in taste aversion learning (Monroe & Barker, 1979). Related to this focus on the conditioning nature of CTA were papers addressing latent inhibition (Batson & Best, 1982; Tarpy & McIntosh, 1977), sensory preconditioning (Revusky, 1980), higher-order conditioning (Archer & Sjoden, 1982), within-stimulus associations (Lavin, 1976), and general information processing (Gillan & Domjan, 1977). The role of neophobia (and, thus, the role of learning itself) in the acquisition and display of taste aversions also was examined during this period (Braveman & Jarvis, 1978; Mitchell, Winter, & Moffitt, 1980; Riley, 1978), raising issues about the relative contribution of associative and nonassociative factors in conditioned avoidance. Memory issues were being investigated along several fronts, including the extension of the CS–US interval (Etscorn & Stephens, 1973), the longevity of conditioning (in adults and weanling rats; Campbell & Alberts, 1979; Howard, Marsh, & Cole, 1977), the nature of its memory function (Biederman, Milgram, Heighington, & Stockman, 1974), as well as the effects of amnesic agents on developing and established learning (Nachman, 1979; Shaw & Webster, 1979). Various papers reported that aversions could be conditioned in males and females (albeit with different rates of acquisition and extinction; Chambers, 1976; Chambers, Sengstake, Yoder, & Thornton, 1981), that different patterns of learning (and memory) of aversions were seen in animals of different ages (Guanowsky & Misanin, 1983; Ingram & Peacock, 1980), and that aversions could be demonstrated in a range of different strains and species (although the relative ease of conditioning with different conditioned stimuli varied in these comparisons; see Gustavson, 1977). Also at this time, aversions were reported to be blocked by a variety of pharmacological agents (Kral & St. Omer, 1972; LeBlanc & Cappell 1975), allowing for the initial attempts to isolate and identify the biochemical and neurophysiological substrates of

such conditioning. These assessments were reinforced by both the lesioning (Best & Orr, 1973; Elkins, 1980; see Gaston, 1978) and stimulation (Brozek, Siegfried, Klimenko, & Bures, 1979; Buresova & Bures, 1979) of a number of brain areas, giving some insight into the peripheral and central components, as well as the cortical and subcortical substrates, of aversion learning.

Although some of the aforementioned work may have been discussed in terms of its biological importance, it was the phenomenon of taste aversion learning itself that appeared to have generated the interest. It is important to note that these more analytical assessments did not occur after any specific resolution of the debate about the importance of its nature as a "constraint on learning" (see the section titled Reactions to the Interpretations). This work was concurrent with the debates and challenges. These concurrent approaches to taste aversion learning were nicely illustrated in the first major compilation of work on taste aversion learning that appeared in 1977. Organized by Bud Barker, Mike Best, and Mike Domjan, a host of investigators in food aversion learning met in Waco, Texas in 1976 to discuss the field and its direction. In the collection of chapters that appeared in the book *Learning Mechanisms in Food Selection* (edited by Barker, Best, & Domjan, 1977), there was a clear blend of efforts devoted toward understanding CTA in the context of learning theory (see chapters by Best et al.; Braveman; Capretta; Garcia and Hankins; Gustavson; Revusky; Rozin; Testa and Ternes; Wilcoxin; Zahorik), but there was an equally important presence of work examining its foundation as a behavioral phenomenon (see chapters by Barker et al.; Best and Barker; Braveman; Domjan; Galef; Gamzu; Hawkins; Hogan; Kalat; Nachman et al.; Solomon). A similar blend of theoretical and practical interests was evident in a companion compendium, *Food Aversion Learning* edited by Milgram, Krames, and Alloway in 1977.

For the past 25 years, work in the area of food aversions has not abated (since the major empirical demonstration and theoretical challenges between 1975 and 1983; see Figure 2.6), although there has been a clear shift away from demonstrations of aversions as being a specialized form of learning to more work assessing the nature of the phenomenon itself (Klosterhalfen & Klosterhalfen, 1985; Riley & Freeman, 2004). With this focus, the number of publications in the field has increased dramatically (to roughly 75 papers each year) as new drugs have been examined, new procedures employed, and new physiological and pharmacological assessments tried (Reilly & Bornovalova, 2005; Riley & Simpson, 2001; Scalera, 2002). Although much of the work since the initial introduction of aversion learning has been in this vein, reports before and since this introduction have noted the use of CTA in applied settings. These initial forays into applications were concerned primarily with alcoholism and its treatment (covert desensitization and chemical aversion therapy; Boland, Mellor, & Revusky, 1978; Elkins, 1975; Jackson & Smith, 1978; Revusky, 1973; Voegtlin, Lemere, & Broz, 1940). Work at this time was also being reported on the use of the aversion design in a variety of other clinical settings, for example, in the examination of conditioned immunosuppression (and the implications of conditioning for the autoimmune disease Lupus and its treatment; Ader & Cohen, 1982), as a potential explanation of dietary changes associated with chemotherapy (and how such an understanding may allow procedural modifications to abate the effects of aversion learning in this setting; Bernstein, 1978; Bernstein, Vitiello, & Sigmundi, 1980), in the control of wildlife predation (Gustavson, Garcia, Hankins, & Rusiniak, 1974), in the elucidation of mechanisms underlying normal feeding control (Geary & Smith, 1982), and in understanding the nature of addiction and how a drug's aversive effects might factor into its abuse liability and overall acceptability (Baker & Cannon, 1982; Cappell & LeBlanc, 1977; Goudie, Dickens, & Thornton, 1978; Stolerman & D'Mello, 1981). By 1985, when the proceedings of a conference on food aversion learning that was held at the New York Academy of Sciences were published (see *Experimental Assessments and Clinical Applications of Food Aversion Learning*, edited by Norm Braveman and Paul Bronstein), a full 40% of the book was devoted to the application of aversion learning as a behavioral tool (with chapters on its use as an animal model of drug addiction, a model for the assessment of drug interactions [with a focus on drug treatment], a model of drug toxicity, a model to understand human dietary preferences, a procedure to discriminate satiety from toxicity, a tool to control wildlife predation, a model to treat alcoholism, and a procedure to model the progression and treatment of cancer; see Braveman & Bronstein, 1985).

Today, aversion learning is still being analyzed and characterized, as new parameters are being assessed, for example, the types of drugs that can induce aversions, the specific brain loci and pathways mediating such learning, and the demonstration of sex differences and their hormonal basis (see Riley & Freeman, 2004). Its use as a tool continues with its application to a broader range of topics, for example, in the molecular biology of learning and memory (Hatakeyama et al., 2006), in the assessment of the stimulus and subjective properties of drugs (Stevenson et al., 2002), in the modeling of the genetics of drug vulnerability (Broadbent, Muccino, & Cunningham, 2002; Phillips et al., 2005). This blend of analysis and application that directed research until the present is quite evident in the contents of the present book with the majority of chapters describing the effects of varying parameters on aversion learning (and its biological, physiological, neurochemical, and anatomical mediation) as well as its use as a preclinical and clinical tool. It is interesting that a phenomenon with origins primarily in rat poisoning and the effects of radiation has its empirical strength as a biologically important behavior and its clinical potential as a behaviorally important tool. At this point in time, few papers on aversion learning are still devoted exclusively to its discussion as a unique form of learning. The interest and direction of the field has changed, both appropriately and naturally.

CONCLUSIONS

We began the chapter by offering some restriction on what would be covered in a historical sketch of the field, that is, where it began, what it meant, and what reactions were generated to the basic findings. With its roots in poison control and radiation (ala Rzóska and Garcia, respectively), CTAs have, in fact, evolved considerably. From attempts to rid rats from foxholes and to explain an unusual effect on water intake concurrent with radiation exposure, aversions have become a freestanding major field of research (now with clear utility as a research and clinical tool). After over 50 years, it is obvious that many questions remain about what is learned, whether the learning is the same across all aversion preparations, how taste aversion learning is mediated (both chemically and anatomically), what this rather unique form of learning means (as a biological phenomenon in the context of other forms of learning), and how aversion learning as a tool can be used and applied. We close our chapter on the origins of aversion learning, thus, peering a bit into the future. We anticipate that such questions will continue to drive research on aversion learning and that the next historical sketch will have a considerable amount to summarize.

6. Although this appeared to be a backward conditioning design (previously reported to be ineffective; see above), it should be noted that the subsequent effects of radiation that constituted the aversive US may have occurred after drinking.

7. From Seligman and Hager (1972): "This article [Garcia & Koelling, 1966] did not receive a congenial reception in some quarters. One investigator, who had worked for years on delay of reinforcement, remarked publicly, 'those findings are no more likely than birdshit in a cuckoo clock'."

Notes

1. The history we are describing here is not the only history of the phenomenon of acquired aversions. As early as 1939, Windecker reported the conditioned avoidance of the caterpillar of the cinnabar moth by young birds (for this and related examples in aposematism and Batesian and Mullerian mimicry, see Edmunds, 1974; Wickler, 1968). Further, in the late 1930s and throughout the 1940s, chemical aversion therapy was regularly used by Voegtlin and his colleagues in the treatment of alcoholism (for a review, see Revusky, Chapter 21). The account presented in the present chapter is primarily a review of the specific historical lineage associated with the seminal work of Garcia and his colleagues at the Radiological Defense Laboratory at Hunters Point in San Francisco, California. It was the investigations of this researcher (along with a host of others) that eventuated in a direct challenge to learning theory, resulting in a reformulation of the ways in which learning was viewed and examined.

2. Differences in neophobic reactions to novel foods have been reported to occur between wild rats and domestic laboratory stock (Mitchell, 1978).

3. The wartime work of the BAP is summarized in a three-volume set, *Control of Rats and Mice* (1954) edited by Dennis Chitty. Interestingly, most of the chapters were written by 1947, and the editing was complete by 1949. However, various issues withheld its publication until 1954. Any researcher of CTA with a minor in anthropology will certainly enjoy mining the allusions to phenomena that are well characterized in the CTA literature today.

4. In the interest of maintaining a historical perspective, figures, where possible, were scanned from the original publication. In some cases, minor graphic enhancement was required to improve clarity.

5. It should be noted that what appears to be simultaneous conditioning in this preparation may actually be trace conditioning due to the delayed effects of radiation.

References

Ader, R., & Cohen, N. (1982). Behaviorally conditioned immunosuppression and murine systemic lupus erythematosus. *Science, 215,* 1534–1536.

Alcock, J. (1979). *Animal behavior: An evolutionary approach.* Sunderland, MA: Sinauer.

Archer, T., & Sjoden, P. (1982). Higher-order conditioning and sensory preconditioning of a taste aversion with an exteroceptive CS. *Quarterly Journal of Experimental Psychology, 34B,* 1–17.

Baker, T. B., & Cannon, D. S. (1982). Alcohol and taste-mediated conditioning. *Addictive Behaviors, 7,* 211–230.

Barker, L. M. (1976). CS duration, amount, and concentration effects in conditioning taste aversions. *Learning and Motivation, 7,* 265–273.

Barker, L. M., Best, M. R., & Domjan, M. (Eds.). (1977). *Learning mechanisms in food selection.* Waco, TX: Baylor University Press.

Barnett, S. A., & Spencer, M. M. (1949). Sodium fluoroacetate (1080) as a rat poison. *Journal of Hygiene, 47,* 426–430.

Batson, J. D., & Best, M. R. (1982). Lithium-mediated disruptions of latent inhibition: Overshadowing by the unconditioned stimulus in flavor conditioning. *Bulletin of the Psychonomic Society, 18,* 328–330.

Berger, B. D. (1972). Conditioning of food aversions by injections of psychoactive drugs. *Journal of Comparative and Physiological Psychology, 81,* 21–26.

Bernstein, I. L. (1978). Learned taste aversions in children receiving chemotherapy. *Science, 200,* 1302–1303.

Bernstein, I. L., Vitiello, M. V., & Sigmundi, R. A. (1980). Effects of tumor growth on taste-aversion learning produced by antitumor drugs in the rat. *Physiological Psychology, 8,* 51–55.

Best, P. J., & Orr, J. (1973). Effects of hippocampal lesions on passive avoidance and taste aversion conditioning. *Physiology and Behavior, 10,* 193–196.

Biederman, G. B., Milgram, N. W., Heighington, G. A., & Stockman, S. M. (1974). Memory of conditioned food aversion follows a U-shape function in rats. *Quarterly Journal of Experimental Psychology, 26*, 610–615.

Bitterman, M. E. (1975). The comparative analysis of learning. *Science, 188*, 699–709.

Boland, F. J., Mellor, C. S., & Revusky, S. (1978). Chemical aversion treatment of alcoholism: Lithium the aversive agent. *Behavior Research & Therapy, 16*, 401–409.

Bolles, R. C. (1970). Species-specific defense reactions and avoidance learning. *Psychological Review, 77*, 32–48.

Bolles, R. C. (1972). Species-specific defense reactions and avoidance learning. In M. E. P. Seligman & J. L. Hager (Eds.). *Biological boundaries of learning* (pp. 189–211). New York: Appleton-Century-Crofts.

Bond, N., & DiGuisto, E. (1975). Amount of solution drunk is a factor in the establishment of taste aversion. *Animal Learning & Behavior, 3*, 81–84.

Brackbill, R. M., Rosenbush, S. N., & Brookshire, K. H. (1971). Acquisition and retention of conditioned taste aversions as a function of the taste quality of the CS. *Learning and Motivation, 2*, 341–350.

Bradley, R. M., & Mistretta, C. M. (1971). Intravascular taste in rats as demonstrated by conditioned aversion to sodium saccharin. *Journal of Comparative and Physiological Psychology, 75*, 186–189.

Braveman, N. S. (1975). Formation of taste aversions in rats following prior exposure to sickness. *Learning and Motivation, 6*, 512–534.

Braveman, N. S., & Bronstein, P. (Eds.). (1985). *Experimental assessments and clinical applications of conditioned food aversions, Volume 443*. New York: The New York Academy of Sciences.

Braveman, N. S., & Jarvis, P. S. (1978). Independence of neophobia and taste aversion formation: Implications for learned safety. *Animal Learning & Behavior, 6*, 406–412.

Breland, K., & Breland, M. (1972). The misbehavior of organisms. In M. E. P. Seligman & J. L. Hager (Eds.), *Biological boundaries of learning* (pp. 181–186). New York: Appleton-Century-Crofts.

Broadbent, J., Muccino, K. J., & Cunningham, C. L. (2002). Ethanol-induced conditioned taste aversion in 15 inbred mouse strains. *Behavioral Neuroscience, 116*, 138–148.

Brookshire, K. H., & Brackbill, R. M. (1976). Formation and retention of conditioned taste aversions and UCS habituation. *Bulletin of the Psychonomic Society, 7*, 125–128.

Brown, Z. W., Amit, Z., Smith, B., & Rockman, G. E. (1978). Differential effects on conditioned taste aversion learning with peripherally and centrally administered acetaldehyde. *Neuropharmacology, 17*, 931–935.

Brown P. L., & Jenkins, H. M. (1972). Autoshaping of the pigeon's key-peck. In M. E. P. Seligman & J. L. Hager (Eds.), *Biological boundaries of learning* (pp. 146–156). New York: Appleton-Century-Crofts.

Brozek, G., Siegfried B., Klimenko, V. M., & Bures, J. (1979). Lick triggered intracranial stimulation interferes with retrieval of conditioned taste aversion. *Physiology & Behavior, 23*, 624–631.

Buresova, O., & Bures, J. (1974). Functional decortication in the CS–US interval decreases efficiency of taste aversion learning. *Behavioral Biology, 12*, 357–364.

Buresova, O., & Bures, J. (1979). The anterograde effect of ECS on the acquisition, retrieval, and extinction of conditioned taste aversion. *Physiology & Behavior, 22*, 641–645.

Campbell, B. A., & Alberts, J. R. (1979). Ontogeny of long-term memory for learned taste aversions. *Behavioral and Neural Biology, 25*, 139–156.

Capaldi, E. J., & Spivey, J. E. (1964). Intertrial reinforcement and after effects at 24-hour intervals. *Psychonomic Science, 1*, 181–182.

Cappell, H., & LeBlanc, A. E. (1977). Gustatory avoidance conditioning by drugs of abuse: Relationships to general issues in research on drug dependence. In N. W. Milgram, L. Krames, & T. M. Alloway (Eds.), *Food aversion learning* (pp. 133–167). New York: Plenum Publishing.

Chambers, K. C. (1976). Hormonal influences on sexual dimorphism in rate of extinction of a conditioned taste aversion in rats. *Journal of Comparative and Physiological Psychology, 90*, 851–856.

Chambers, K. C., Sengstake, C. B., Yoder, R. L., & Thornton, J. E. (1981). Sexually dimorphic acquisition of a conditioned taste aversion in rats: Effects of gonadectomy, testosterone replacement and water deprivation. *Physiology & Behavior, 27*, 83–88.

Chitty, D. (1954). The study of the brown rat and its control by poison. In D. Chitty (Ed.), *Control of rats and mice: Vol. 1* (pp. 160–299). Oxford, England: Clarendon Press.

Deutsch, R. (1978). Effects of CS amount on conditioned taste aversion at different CS–US intervals. *Animal Learning & Behavior, 20*, 482–492.

Dietz, M. N., & Capretta, P. J. (1967). *Modification of sugar and sugar-saccharin preference in rats as a function of electric shock to the mouth.* Proceedings of the 75th Annual Convention of the American Psychological Association, Washington, D.C., 161–162.

Domjan, M., Foster, K., & Gillan, D. J. (1979). Effects of distribution of the drug unconditioned stimulus on taste-aversion learning. *Physiology & Behavior, 23*, 931–938.

Domjan, M., & Galef, B. G. (1983). Biological constraints on instrumental and classical conditioning. *Animal Learning & Behavior, 11*, 151–161.

Domjan, M., & Hanlon, M. J. (1982). Poison-avoidance to food-related tactile stimuli: Avoidance of texture cues by rats. *Animal Learning & Behavior, 10*, 293–300.

Edmunds, M. (1974). *Defence in animals.* Essex, England: Long Group Limited.

Eibl-Eibesfeldt, I. (1970). *Ethology: The biology of behavior.* Austin, TX: Holt, Rinehart & Winston.

Elkins, R. L. (1975). Aversion therapy for alcoholism: Chemical, electrical, or verbal imaginary. *International Journal of the Addictions, 10*, 157–209.

Elkins, R. L. (1980). Attenuation of x-ray-induced taste aversions by olfactory-bulb or amygdaloid lesions. *Physiology & Behavior, 24*, 515–521.

Elton, C. (1954). Research on rodent control by the bureau of animal population, September 1939 to July 1947. In D. Chitty (Ed.), *Control of rats and mice: Vol. 1* (pp. 1–23). Oxford, England: Clarendon Press.

Elton, C., & Laurie, E. M. O. (1954). A sample census of rats and house mice in English corn-ricks in January to July 1943–7. In D. Chitty (Ed.), *Control of rats and mice: Vol. 2* (pp. 449–468). Oxford, England: Clarendon Press.

Elton, C., & Ranson, R. M. (1954). Containers for baiting. In D. Chitty (Ed.), *Control of rats and mice: Vol. 1* (pp. 147–159). Oxford, England: Clarendon Press.

Etscorn, F., & Stephens, R. (1973). Establishment of conditioned taste aversions with a 24-hour CS–US interval. *Physiological Psychology, 1*, 251–253.

Freeman, R. B., Elton, C., Leslie, P. H., Ranson, R. M., Rzóska, J., & Thompson, V. (1954). Properties of the poisons used in rodent control. In D. Chitty (Ed.), *Control of rats and mice: Vol. 1* (pp. 25–136). Oxford, England: Clarendon Press.

Furchgott, E. (1963). Behavioral effects of ionizing radiations. 1955–61. *Psychological Bulletin, 60*, 157–199.

Gamzu, E. (1977). The multifaceted nature of taste-aversion-inducing agents: Is there a single common factor? In L. M. Barker, M. R. Best, & M. Domjan (Eds.), *Learning mechanisms in food selection* (pp. 477–510). Waco, TX: Baylor University Press.

Garcia, J. (1980). John Garcia [A biographical sketch]. *American Psychologist, 35*, 38–40.

Garcia, J., & Buchwald, N. A. (1963). Perception of ionizing radiation: A study of behavioral and electrical responses to very low doses of x-ray. *Boletín del Instituto de Estudios Médicos y Biológicos, 21*, 391–405.

Garcia, J., Buchwald, N. A., Hull, C. D., & Koelling, R. A. (1964). Adaptive responses to ionizing radiation. *Boletín del Instituto de Estudios Médicos y Biológicos, 22*, 101–113.

Garcia, J., & Ervin, F. R. (1968). Gustatory-visceral and telereceptor–cutaneous conditioning: Adaptation in internal and external milieus. *Communications in Behavioral Biology, Part A, 1*, 389–415.

Garcia, J., Ervin, F. R., & Koelling, R. A. (1966). Learning with prolonged delay of reinforcement. *Psychonomic Science, 5*, 121–122.

Garcia, J., Ervin, F. R., & Koelling, R. A. (1967). Toxicity of serum from irradiated donors. *Nature, 213*, 682–683.

Garcia, J., Hankins, W. G., & Rusiniak, K. W. (1976). Flavor aversion studies. *Science, 192*, 265–267.

Garcia, J., & Kimeldorf, J. K. (1957). Temporal relationship within the conditioning of a saccharine aversion through radiation exposure. *Journal of Comparative and Physiological Psychology, 50*, 180–183.

Garcia, J., & Kimeldorf, D. J. (1960). Some factors which influence radiation conditioned behavior of rats. *Radiation Research, 12*, 719–727.

Garcia, J., Kimeldorf, D. J., & Hunt, E. L. (1957). Spatial avoidance in the rat as a result of exposure to ionizing radiation. *British Journal of Radiology, 30*, 318–321.

Garcia, J., Kimeldorf, D. J., & Koelling, R. A. (1955). Conditioned aversion to saccharin resulting from exposure to gamma radiation. *Science, 122*, 157–158.

Garcia, J., & Koelling, R. A. (1966). Relation of cue to consequence in avoidance learning. *Psychonomic Science, 4*, 123–124.

Garcia, J., McGowan, B. K., Ervin, F. R., & Koelling, R. A. (1968). Cues: Their relative effectiveness as a function of the reinforcer. *Science, 160*, 794–795.

Gaston, K. E. (1978). Brain mechanisms of conditioned taste aversion learning: A review of the literature. *Physiological Psychology, 6*, 340–353.

Geary, N., & Smith, G. P. (1982). Pancreatic glucagons and postprandial satiety in the rat. *Physiology & Behavior, 28*, 313–322.

Gillan, D. J., & Domjan, M. (1977). Taste-aversion conditioning with expected versus unexpected drug treatment. *Journal of Experimental Psychology: Animal Behavior Processes, 3,* 297–309.

Goudie, A. J. (1980). Conditioned food aversion: An adaptive specialisation of learning? *IRCS Journal of Medical Science, 8,* 591–594.

Goudie, A. J., Dickens, D. W., & Thornton, E. W. (1978). Cocaine-induced conditioned taste aversions in rats. *Pharmacology, Biochemistry & Behavior, 8,* 757–761.

Guanowsky, V., & Misanin, J. R. (1983). Retention of conditioned taste aversions in weanling, adult, and old-age rats. *Behavioral and Neural Biology, 37,* 173–178.

Gustavson, C. R. (1977). Comparative and field aspects of conditioned taste aversions. In L. M. Barker, M. R. Best, & M. Domjan (Eds.), *Learning mechanisms in food selection* (pp. 23–44). Waco, TX: Baylor University Press.

Gustavson, C. R., Garcia, J., Hankins, W. G., & Rusiniak, K. W. (1974). Coyote predation control by aversive conditioning. *Science, 184,* 581–583.

Hatakeyama, D., Sadamoto, H., Watanabe, T., Wagatsuma, A., Kobayashi, S., Fujito, Y., et al. (2006). Requirement of new protein synthesis of a transcription factor for memory consolidation: Paradoxical changes in mRNA and protein levels of C/EBP. *Journal of Molecular Biology, 256,* 569–577.

Hinde, R., & Stevenson-Hinde, J. (Eds.). (1973). *Constraints on learning.* New York: Academic Press.

Howard, W. E., Marsh, R. E., & Cole, R. E. (1977). Duration of associative memory to toxic bait in deer mice. *Journal of Wildlife Management, 41,* 484–486.

Hunt, E. L., Carroll, H. W., & Kimeldorf, D. J. (1965). Humoral mediation of radiation-induced motivation in parabiont rats. *Science, 150,* 1747–1748.

Ingram, D. K., & Peacock, L. J. (1980). Conditioned taste aversion as a function of age in mature male rats. *Experimental Aging Research, 6,* 113–123.

Jackson, T. R., & Smith, J. W. (1978). A comparison of two aversion treatment methods for alcoholism. *Journal of Studies on Alcohol, 39,* 187–191.

Kalat, J. W. (1974). Taste salience depends on novelty, not concentrations in taste aversion learning in the rat. *Journal of Comparative and Physiological Psychology, 86,* 47–50.

Kalat, J. W., & Rozin, P. (1970). "Salience": A factor which can override temporal contiguity in taste-aversion learning. *Journal of Comparative and Physiological Psychology, 71,* 192–197.

Kimble, G. A. (1961). *Hilgard and Marquis' conditioning and learning.* New York: Appleton-Century-Crofts.

Kimeldorf, D. J., & Baum, S. J. (1954). Alterations in organ and body growth of rats following daily exhaustive exercise, x-irradiation and post-irradiation exercise. *Growth, 18,* 79–96.

Kimeldorf, D. J., Jones, D. C., & Castanera, T. J. (1953). Effect of x-irradiation upon the performance of daily exhaustive exercise by the rat. *American Journal of Physiology, 174,* 331–335.

Kimeldorf, D. J., & Newsom, B. D. (1952). Survival of irradiated rats during prolonged exposure to environmental cold. *American Journal of Physiology, 171,* 349–353.

Kimeldorf, D. J., & Newsom, B. D. (1953). The sensitivity of irradiated rats to conditions of low oxygen tension at reduced barometric pressures. *Journal of Aviation Medicine, 24,* 57–62.

Klosterhalfen, W., & Klosterhalfen, S. (1985). Conditioned taste aversion and traditional learning. *Psychological Research, 47,* 71–94.

Kral, P. A., & St. Omer, V. V. (1972). Beta-adrenergic receptor involvement in the mediation of learned taste aversions. *Psychopharmacologia, 26,* 79–83.

Lavin, M. J. (1976). The establishment of flavor–flavor associations using a sensory preconditioning training procedure. *Learning and Motivation, 7,* 173–183.

Leblanc, A. E., & Cappell, H. (1975). Antagonism of morphine-induced aversive conditioning by naloxone. *Pharmacology, Biochemistry & Behavior, 3,* 185–188.

Lehrman, D. S., Hinde, R. A., & Shaw, E. (Eds.). (1972). *Advances in the study of behavior.* New York: Academic Press.

Leslie, P. H., Ranson, R. M., & Freeman, R. B. (1954). The amount of wheat consumed by the brown rat. In D. Chitty (Ed.), *Control of rats and mice: Vol. 2* (pp. 335–350). Oxford, England: Clarendon Press.

Lett, B. T. (1977). Long delay learning in the T-maze: Effect of reward given in the home cage. *Bulletin of the Psychonomic Society, 10,* 211–214.

Logue, A. W. (1979). Taste aversion and the generality of the laws of learning. *Psychological Bulletin, 86,* 276–296.

Mackintosh, N. J. (1975). A theory of attention: Variations in the associability of stimuli with reinforcement. *Psychological Review, 82,* 276–298.

McLaurin, W. A., & Scarborough, B. B. (1963). Extension of the interstimulus interval in saccharin avoidance conditioning. *Radiation Research, 20,* 317–323.

Milgram, N. W., Krames, L., & Alloway, T. M. (Eds.). (1977). *Food aversion learning.* New York: Plenum Press.

Mitchell, D. (1978). The psychological vs. the ethological rat: Two views of the poison avoidance behavior of the rat compared. *Animal Learning & Behavior, 6,* 121–124.

Mitchell, D., Winter, W., & Moffitt, T. (1980). Cross-modality contrast: Exteroceptive context habituation enhances taste neophobia and conditioned taste aversions. *Animal Learning & Behavior, 8,* 524–528.

Monroe, B., & Barker, L. M. (1979). A contingency analysis of taste aversion conditioning. *Animal Learning & Behavior, 7,* 141–143.

Nachman, M. (1970). Learned taste and temperature aversions due to lithium chloride sickness after temporal delays. *Journal of Comparative and Physiological Psychology, 56,* 343–349.

Nachman, M. (1979). Limited effects of electroconvulsive shock on memory of taste stimulation. *Journal of Comparative and Physiological Psychology, 73,* 31–37.

Nachman, M., & Ashe, J. H. (1973). Learned taste aversions in rats as a function of dosage, concentration, and route of administration of LiCl. *Physiology and Behavior, 10,* 73–78.

Pain, J. F., & Booth, D. A. (1968). Toxiphobia for odors. *Psychonomic Science, 10,* 363–364.

Parker, L. A., Failor, A., & Weidman, K. (1973). Conditioned preferences in the rat with an unnatural need state: Morphine withdrawal. *Journal of Comparative and Physiological Psychology, 82,* 294–300.

Parker, L. A., & Radow, B. L. (1974). Morphine-like physical dependence: A pharmacologic method for drug assessment using the rat. *Pharmacology, Biochemistry & Behavior, 2,* 613–618.

Pavlov, I. P. (1927). *Conditioned reflexes.* New York: Oxford University Press.

Phillips, T. J., Broadbent, J., Burkhart-Kasch, S., Henderson, C., Wenger, C. D., McMullin, C., et al. (2005). Genetic correlational analyses of ethanol reward and aversion phenotypes in short-term selected mouse lines bred for ethanol drinking or ethanol-induced conditioned taste aversion. *Behavioral Neuroscience, 119,* 892–910.

Reilly, S., & Bornovalova, M. A. (2005). Conditioned taste aversion and amygdala lesions in the rat: A critical review. *Neuroscience and Biobehavioral Reviews, 29,* 1067–1088.

Revusky, S. (1973). Some laboratory paradigms for chemical aversion treatment for

alcoholism. *Journal of Behavioral Therapy & Experimental Psychiatry, 4,* 15–17.

Revusky, S. (1977). Learning as a general process with an emphasis on data from feeding experiments. In N. W. Milgram, L. Krames, L., & T. M. Alloway (Eds.), *Food aversion learning* (pp. 1–71). New York: Plenum Press.

Revusky, S. (1980). A sensory preconditioning effect after a single flavor–flavor pairing. *Bulletin of the Psychonomic Society, 15,* 83–86.

Revusky, S. H., & Bedarf, E. W. (1967). Association of illness with prior ingestion of novel foods. *Science, 155,* 219–220.

Revusky, S., & Garcia, J. (1970). Learned associations over long delays. In G. Bower & J. Spence (Eds.), *Psychology of learning and motivation: Advances in research and theory: Vol. 4* (pp. 1–84). New York: Academic Press.

Richter, C. P. (1943). Total self-regulatory functions in animals and human beings. *Harvey Lectures Series, 38,* 63–103.

Riley, A. L. (1978). In response to and in defense of Mitchell and Revusky: An analysis of nonassociative effects. *Animal Learning & Behavior, 6,* 472–473.

Riley, A. L., & Freeman, K. B. (2004). Conditioned flavor aversions: Assessment of drug-induced suppression of food intake. In J. N. Crawley, C. Gerfen, R. McKay, M. Rogawski, D. R. Sibley, & P. Skolnick (Eds.), *Current protocols in neuroscience* (pp. 8.6E.1–8.6R.12). New York: Wiley.

Riley, A. L., Jacobs, W. J., & LoLordo, V. M. (1976). Drug exposure and the acquisition and retention of a conditioned taste aversion. *Journal of Comparative and Physiological Psychology, 90,* 799–807.

Riley, A. L., & Simpson, G. R. (2001). The attenuating effects of drug preexposure on taste aversion conditioning: Generality, experimental parameters, underlying mechanisms and implications for drug use and abuse. In R. R. Mowrer & S. B. Klein, (Eds.), *Contemporary learning theory* (2nd ed., pp. 505–559). Hillsdale, NJ: Lawrence Erlbaum Associates.

Rozin, P. (1967). Specific aversions as a component of specific hungers. *Journal of Comparative and Physiological Psychology, 64,* 237–242.

Rozin, P., & Kalat, J. W. (1971). Specific hungers and poison avoidance as adaptive specializations of learning. *Psychological Review, 78,* 459–486.

Rusiniak, K. W., Hankins, W. G., Garcia, J., & Brett, L. P. (1979). Flavor–illness aversions: Potentiation of odor by taste in rats. *Behavioral and Neural Biology, 25,* 1–17.

Rzóska, J. (1954a). Bait shyness, a study in rat behavior. *British Journal of Animal Behavior,* 1, 128–135.

Rzóska, J. (1954b). Stomach analysis of brown rats poisoned in the field. In D. Chitty (Ed.), *Control of rats and mice: Vol. 2* (pp. 395–413). Oxford, England: Clarendon Press.

Rzóska, J. (1954c). The behavior of white rats towards poison baits. In D. Chitty (Ed.), *Control of rats and mice: Vol. 2* (pp. 374–394). Oxford, England: Clarendon Press.

Scalera, G. (2002). Effects of conditioned food aversions on nutritional behavior in humans. *Nutritional Neuroscience, 5,* 159–188.

Schwartz, B., & Reisberg, D. (1991). *Learning and memory.* New York: Norton & Company.

Scott, E. M., & Verney, E. L. (1947). Self selection of diet. VI. The nature of appetites for B vitamins. *Journal of Nutrition, 34,* 471–480.

Seligman, M. E. P. (1970). On the generality of the laws of learning. *Psychological Review, 77,* 406–418.

Seligman, M. E. P., & Hager, J. L. (Eds.). (1972). *Biological boundaries of learning.* New York: Appleton-Century-Crofts.

Shaw, N., & Webster, D. M. (1979). Disruption of taste aversion learning by pentylenetetrazol. *Psychopharmacology, 66,* 195–198.

Shettleworth, S. J. (1972a). Conditioning of domestic chicks to visual and auditory stimuli: Control of drinking by visual stimuli and control of conditioned fear by sound. In M. E. P. Seligman & J. L. Hager (Eds.), *Biological boundaries of learning* (pp. 228–236). New York: Appleton-Century-Crofts.

Shettleworth, S. J. (1972b). Stimulus relevance in the control of drinking and conditioned fear responses in domestic chicks (*Gallus gallus*). *Journal of Comparative and Physiological Psychology, 80,* 175–198.

Spiker, V. A. (1977). Taste aversion: A procedural analysis and an alternative paradigmatic classification. *Psychological Record, 27,* 753–769.

Stevenson, G. W., Canadas, F., Gomez-Serrano, M., Ullrich, T., Zhang, X., Rice, K. C., et al.

(2002). Delta opioid discrimination learning in the rat: Assessment with the selective delta agonist SNC80. *Pharmacology, Biochemistry and Behavior, 71,* 283–292.

Stolerman, I. P., & D'Mello, G. D. (1981). Oral self-administration and the relevance of conditioned taste aversions. In T. Thompson, P. B. Dews, & W. A. McKim (Eds.), *Advances in behavioral pharmacology* (pp. 169–214). Hillsdale, NJ: Lawrence Erlbaum.

Tarpy, R. M., & McIntosh, S. M. (1977). Generalized latent inhibition in taste-aversion learning. *Bulletin of the Psychonomic Society, 10,* 379–381.

Thompson, H. V. (1954). The consumption of plain and poisoned cereal baits by the brown rat. In D. Chitty (Ed.), *Control of rats and mice: Vol. 2* (pp. 352–373). Oxford, England: Clarendon Press.

Thorndike, E. L. (1911). *Animal intelligence.* New York: Macmillan.

Tinbergen, N. (1951). *The study of instinct.* New York: Oxford University Press.

Tinklepaugh, O. L. (1932). Multiple delayed reactions with chimpanzeees and monkeys. *Journal of Comparative and Physiological Psychology, 13,* 207–243.

Vitiello, M. V., & Woods, S. C. (1977). Evidence for withdrawal from caffeine by rats. *Pharmacology, Biochemistry & Behavior, 6,* 553–555.

Voegtlin, W. L., Lemere, F., & Broz, W. R. (1940). Conditioned reflex therapy of alcoholic addiction. III. An evaluation of present results in light of previous experiences with this method. *Quarterly Journal of Studies on Alcohol, 1,* 501–505.

Wallace, P. (1976). Animal behavior: The puzzle of flavor aversion. *Science, 193,* 989–991.

Warner, L. H. (1932). The association span of the white rat. *Journal of Genetic Psychology, 41,* 57–90.

Wickler, W. (1968). *Mimictry in plants and animals.* London: World University Library.

PART II

BEHAVIORAL PROCESSES

3

Conditioned Taste Aversion and Latent Inhibition: A Review

R. E. LUBOW

Although laboratory studies of conditioned taste aversion (CTA) go back to the pioneering work of Garcia, Kimmeldorf, and Koelling (1955), the first demonstrations of latent inhibition (LI) with a CTA preparation did not appear until the 1960s. By the early 1970s, there were at least nine studies that had demonstrated that prior exposure to a to-be conditioned flavor interfered with CTA (Lubow, 1973). That conditioned aversion to a familiar stimulus appears to be weaker than to the same stimulus when it is novel is, of course, identical to the results from scores of LI experiments that have used a variety of learning paradigms.

In a CTA–LI review conducted almost 20 years ago, the robustness of the basic effect was simply confirmed, and it was noted that CTA, like avoidance conditioning and conditioned suppression, had become a prominent procedure for studying LI (Lubow, 1989, pp. 20–23, 59–61). As such, LI research has had an impact on general learning theory (e.g., McLaren & Mackintosh, 2000; Schmajuk, 2005), on theoretical models of schizophrenia, both behavioral (e.g., Escobar, Oberling, & Miller, 2002; Lubow, 2005) and neurophysiological (e.g., Bethus, Muscat, & Goodall, 2006; Weiner, 2003), as well as on applications such as the screening of antipsychotic drugs, particularly for schizophrenia (e.g., Russig, Kovacevic, Murphy, & Feldon, 2003).

Given the extensive use of the CTA–LI protocol, this chapter will begin with some cautionary comments. This will be followed by a brief update on the earlier summary and conclusions regarding basic parameters. The next sections will present several new stimulus preexposure–CTA research topics, including LI effects from preexposure and/or conditioning to compound flavors, the role of flavor preexposure in affecting subsequent generalization/discrimination (perceptual learning effects as opposed to LI effects), and the effects of retention interval duration and retention interval context on LI. After summarizing the empirical findings, a general framework for understanding stimulus preexposure effects will be presented.

SOME CAUTIONS

Although it is desirable to be able to extend LI findings beyond CTA, or at least to know what is restricted to it, there are paradigm-specific and other, more general, considerations that may interfere with obtaining this goal. In addition to the usually noted idiosyncratic characteristics of CTA, such as its capacity to withstand very long CS–US intervals, there are a number of special problems, particularly from the use of three-stage procedures.

The Three-Stage Procedure

The early *non*-CTA–LI experiments used two-stage procedures, stimulus preexposure and a combined acquisition/test, with LI being defined as poorer evidence of learning in stage-2 by the stimulus preexposed (PE) group compared to the non-preexposed (NPE) group. The prototypical three-stage CTA–LI experiment also has PE and NPE groups that are differentiated by their treatment in the preexposure stage. In the second stage, both groups have access to the PE flavor that is then followed by the US. In the test stage, the groups are presented with the CS-flavor. LI is exhibited when the PE group consumes more of the previously conditioned flavor than the NPE group. As illustrated in Figure 3.1, this apparently simple LI effect can be accounted for, *en large*, in three different ways. Stage-3 performance may reflect either the strength

of the stage-2 association (A-theories; e.g., Lubow, Weiner, & Schnur, 1981; Mackintosh, 1975; Pearce & Hall, 1980) or a competition between associations learned in stage-1 and stage-2 (R-theories; e.g., Bouton, 1993; Miller, Kasprow, & Schachtman, 1986) or by some combination of the two (A/R theories; e.g., Lubow & Gewirtz, 1995; McLaren & Mackintosh, 2000).

There is no simple way of differentiating among these three possibilities. On the one hand, if there are multiple CS–US pairings, a measure of conditioning strength can be obtained in stage-2. If there is no difference between the PE and NPE groups in stage-2, but the LI effect appears in stage-3, this would appear to support the R-theories. Fortunately, one need not be concerned about using the absence of differences in stage-2 to support a theoretical position, since LI, indeed, has been obtained in many two-stage preparations (e.g., avoidance conditioning). On the other hand, by themselves, these latter data do not support the A-theories. First, LI can be assessed only *after* at least one CS–US pairing. Consequently, R-theories may rightfully claim that any difference that appears on the second trial already reflects a competition between the associations acquired during preexposure and the association acquired on trial-one of the conditioning stage. Second, the presence of two-stage LI does not preclude the possibility that an LI effect observed in stage-3 is composed of an associative deficit component from stage-2 *plus* a retrieval component from stage-3 (A/R theories).

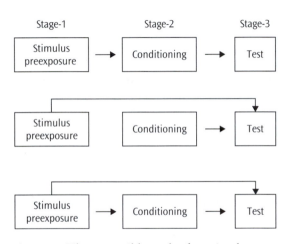

Figure 3.1. Three possible paths for stimulus pre-exposure effects in three-stage preparations (stimulus preexposure, conditioning, and test). The arrows represent the flow of information from one stage to another stage. Route A (top) describes the attentional/associative deficit model, whereby the test-stage results represent the effects of pre-exposure on conditioning. Route R (middle) describes the retrieval/competition model, whereby the test-stage results represent independent inputs from the preexposure and conditioning stages, the final output of which is resolved by a competition process. Route A/R (bottom) represents a combination of the A- and R-paths. As described in the text, a retrieval model might claim that the acquisition of a CS–0 association in stage-1 can affect stage-2 performance by interfering with the within-trial retrieval of prior stage-2 CS–US associative strengths. However, such a position would appear to be indistinguishable from that of A-theories, at least in terms of testable predictions.

Does the LI Effect Reflect a Process in the PE Group or the NPE Group?

In any LI experiment, whether two- or three-stage, the nominal PE–NPE variable is confounded with the type of transition from preexposure to conditioning stages. For the PE group, the first stage-2 conditioning trial is marked by the appearance of a *familiar* conditioning-stage CS in a *familiar* context, the same one that was present in preexposure. On the other hand, for the NPE group, when the CS is presented for the first time in the conditioning stage, it appears as a *novel* stimulus in a *familiar* context. As such, the NPE stimulus may be more salient than the PE stimulus, thus providing it with an advantage in acquiring new associations (e.g., Lubow, Alek, & Rifkin, 1976) or performing any attention-related task, as, for example, visual search (Johnston & Hawley, 1994; Lubow & Kaplan, 1997). Thus, the LI effect, which results in poorer test performance by the PE as compared to the NPE group, traditionally attributed to a process uniquely occurring in the PE group, may have two sources, one from each of the two groups.

Effects due to Reduction of Neophobia in PE as Compared to NPE Groups

Preexposure trials with the flavored solution can result in the habituation of neophobia. As a consequence, the PE group would drink more of the familiar test flavor than the NPE group, for whom the test flavor is novel. Thus, greater consumption of the target flavor in the test by the PE than the NPE group, nominally described as an LI effect, may have a component from the habituation of neophobia (for other neophobia-induced misattributions in CTA research, see Reilly & Bornovalova, 2005). Furthermore, habituation of neophobia may result in the PE group drinking more of the CS than the NPE group in the conditioning stage. Since conditioning strength is affected by the volume and/or duration of flavor consumed (e.g., Bennett, Tremain, & Mackintosh, 1996; Deutsch, 1978; Kalat, 1976), this can adversely influence the size of the LI effect in the test stage. This latter problem can be overcome, at least to some extent, by equating the amounts consumed by the PE and NPE groups. Alternatively, one can record consumption in the conditioning stage. If there is no significant difference between the PE and NPE groups, then this also would ensure that the LI effect in the test stage was not contaminated. However, the presence of such differences would require other precautionary tactics, either using additional groups that would allow one to partial out the effects of neophobia habituation, or analyzing the test-stage results using the amount consumed in the conditioning stage as a covariate.

The Atypical Context Conditions of Most CTA Experiments

In principle, experimental procedures can be conducted in a variety of locations. However, in practice, these places are largely determined by the experimental paradigm. Thus, with CTA, where the basic equipment consists of one or two bottles,

it is customary to do everything in the home cage. Most other paradigms (e.g., conditioned suppression, conditioned avoidance) require a specially instrumented enclosure for delivering stimuli and measuring responses. Thus, the experimental stages need to be conducted in some context *other than* that of the home cage; if there are lengthy intervals between stages, then these are spent in the home cage. Although these differences in apparatus-driven procedures have been largely disregarded (but see, Killcross, Kiernan, Dwyer, & Westbrook, 1998), recent CTA–LI studies indicate that the relationship between the retention interval context and the other contexts of the experiment does influence the direction of retention interval duration effects, producing either attenuated or potentiated LI (see following sections, also see Lubow & De la Casa, 2005a; Meehan & Riccio, Chapter 7).

The Confounding of Context Change and Context Familiarity

Relatedly, because of the frequent use of the home cage in CTA experiments, procedures used to assess the effects of context change on LI often end up by having the context of the *un*changed condition more familiar than the context of the changed condition. Familiarity of the same and different contexts should be equated in a counterbalanced design that alternates the consumption of the PE target flavor in one context and the consumption of water in the second context (e.g., Hall & Channell, 1986, Experiment 3).

Analytic versus Synthetic Processing of Flavor Compounds

Explaining the results from experiments that use compound flavors must take into consideration the nature of perceptual processing of those stimuli. In this regard, it is important to know whether a tastant that is composed of two different flavors is processed synthetically, such that it is perceived as a unitary whole, or analytically as a set of discrete qualities that retain their original identities. On the one hand, an element (X) may be responded to differently from the compound in which it is embedded (XY) because the perceived intensity of X is changed, either reduced by simple dilution or masked by Y, or even increased by dint of contrast effects (e.g., adding salt to melon). On the other hand, XY may be perceived as *qualitatively* different from A. The problem is made even more complex because flavors have taste and odor components, which also may interact in different ways (Prescott, Johnstone, & Francis, 2004; Small & Prescott, 2005). The synthetic/analytic distinction affects the interpretation of data from CTA experiments that use compound stimuli, particularly as they relate to theories that make distinctions between elemental (e.g., Harris, 2006; McLaren & Mackintosh, 2000) and configural (e.g., Pearce, 2002; Wagner & Brandon, 2001) representations of the stimuli that enter into associations.

Ceiling/Floor Effects

Using CTA, it is sometimes difficult to assess the effects of variables that are thought to modulate LI. On the one hand, a single pairing of the flavor and the typical LiCl produces strong conditioning, such that on the first few test-stage trials the NPE group may consume little or none of the CS-flavor (floor effect). On the other hand, the same preparation is very sensitive to the effects of flavor preexposure, such that on the first and all subsequent test-stage trials the PE group may consume the maximum possible amount of the CS-flavor (ceiling effect). Although one can find US concentrations and CS preexposure values that will not produce floor or ceiling effects, this issue is often ignored, and the true effects of a particular variable on LI may be obscured.

The Special Status of Flavored-Solution Preexposure

In general, LI–CTA effects are in accord with what would be expected from other classical conditioning procedures. However, in the vast majority of LI–CTA studies, flavor preexposure occurs while the animal is thirsty. This is very different from the stimulus preexposure conditions in other LI-paradigms, where the stimulus is presented passively and not associated with any drive reduction (e.g., a tone in conditioned suppression). Thus, in LI–CTA, but not in other LI protocols, the preexposed stimulus may acquire secondary reinforcing properties, thereby accounting for more test-stage consumption of the PE flavored solution than the novel flavored solution, but by a process that is different from any of the ones proposed for LI effects generated with non-CTA procedures.

As an argument against this interpretation, Domjan (1972) found *weaker* aversion conditioning to a PE saccharin solution compared to a novel saccharin solution when preexposure was accomplished while the subjects were relatively satiated for water (Experiment 1), and no difference in the magnitude of the LI effect when the amount of flavor preexposure was equated across groups with different deprivation levels (Experiment 2). Although both cases argue against secondary reinforcement as an explanation for the *basic* CTA–LI effect, the ingestion of the PE flavored solution by the thirsty rat may still contribute to the observed size of the LI effect. Indeed, there are many demonstrations of conditioned taste *preferences* that result from pairing a flavor with a substance that reduces some induced-deprivation state (e.g., for sodium depleted rats, pairing salt and almond flavor, Westbrook et al., 1995; for a review, see Capaldi, 1991).

Relatedly, since flavor exposure is accompanied by thirst reduction in stage-1 and by thirst reduction *plus* illness in stage-2, CTA–LI may be considered as an instance of counterconditioning (e.g., Wheeler, Stout, & Miller, 2004). Such an account is not relevant to non-CTA protocols since the PE stimulus is presented independently of the response that will subsequently become the dependent variable in the test stage.

Alternatively, consuming a flavored solution while thirsty can be viewed as an example of a masked presentation of the to-be CS, such that attention allocated to the thirst-reducing liquid qualities of the solution is at the expense of the flavor qualities. Masking tasks during preexposure have been shown to play an important role in generating LI in humans (Lubow & Gewirtz, 1995).

AN UPDATE OF BASIC LI–CTA EMPIRICAL FINDINGS

Types of Stimuli

CTA–LI can be obtained with a wide range of PE and conditioned stimuli not only with flavors that are affectively negative, such as vinegar and salt, or affectively positive, such as sucrose and milk, but also with odors, and food-related objects (e.g., food container qualities). However, there are a few exceptions. Barot and Bernstein (2005, Experiment 2) failed to find an LI effect for Polycose, a highly palatable polysaccharide, even though the same procedures produced LI to a saline solution (Experiment 4). The fact that novel and PE Polycose were treated similarly by the rat was interpreted as indicating that both were regarded as familiar. This conclusion was reached because novel Polycose failed to elicit the normal neural correlates for taste novelty, elevated c-Fos-like immunoreactivity in the central amygdala and insular cortex (Koh & Bernstein, 2005; Koh, Wilkins, & Bernstein, 2003).

Methods of Stimulus Delivery

The conventional procedure for presenting the PE to-be CS, as well as the CS when it is paired with the US, allows the thirsty subject access to a bottle containing the flavored solution. However, other modes of flavor preexposure, such as infusion, have been used (e.g., Rudy, Rosenberg, & Sandell, 1977). More recently, there have been some attempts to examine effects of shifting modes of presentation from the preexposure to conditioning stages, a topic that also relates to context-change effects (see subsequent text).

Fouquet, Oberling, and Sandner (2001, Experiment 4) preexposed rats to the target flavor, either actively (A; licking) or passively (P; intraoral infusion), following which one A-group was conditioned in the P-mode and one in the A-mode. The PE P-group was conditioned in the A-mode. When the three groups were tested (all in the A-mode), the A–A and A–P groups consumed more of the target flavor than the P–A group. However, since there was no NPE group, it is difficult to assess LI per se. Furthermore, it is not clear whether the differences in test-stage consumption of the target flavor by the P–A group compared to the A–P and A–A groups were due to the method of flavor presentation in *preexposure*, or to the fact that only the P–A group had a change of presentation-mode from preexposure to test (local context change).

In a second study, Yamamoto, Fresquet, and Sandner (2002, Experiment 2b) compared two different active modes of CS delivery, standard tube-licking and nose-poke-elicited oral infusion, in a 2 × 2 design (two delivery modes in preexposure × two delivery modes in conditioning). The group that was preexposed to the flavor by self-activated oral perfusion, but conditioned to the flavor when it was presented under standard conditions, showed significantly less test-stage consumption of the target flavor than the other three groups. As in

the previous study, the relevance of these findings to LI is unclear since all groups were tested with the standard tube-licking procedure and there was no NPE group.

An earlier CTA study by Domjan (1972) did use PE *and* NPE groups. A significant LI effect was obtained when the flavored liquid was delivered by oral infusion in the preexposure and conditioning stages and by normal bottle-mode presentations in the test stage. Although the experiment did not directly compare liquid deliveries by infusion and bottle, a comparison of data across Experiments 1, 2, and 3 suggests that the LI effect was independent of the presentation mode.

In summary, LI does not appear to be affected by the mode of delivery of the PE flavor. However, the studies cited earlier do not provide a definitive answer regarding the role of changing the delivery modes across experimental stages. Nevertheless, on the basis of the context specificity of LI (see following text), and, in particular, the effects from changes in *local* context, either across sensory modalities (e.g., Archer, Mohammed, & Jarbe, 1986) or within modalities (as in reduced LI from element and compound switching between preexposure and conditioning/test; see following text), it would be reasonable to assume that such changes would attenuate LI.

Amounts of Stimulus Preexposure

In general, CTA–LI increases as a function of the amount of preconditioning exposure to the flavor (number of preexposures × duration of preexposure; see, Lubow, 1989, Table 9, p. 60). This relationship was confirmed by De la Casa and Lubow (1995), who varied the number and duration of flavor preexposures (Experiment 1). In a second experiment, the number and duration of the flavor preexposure sessions was held constant while manipulating the level of liquid deprivation. As would be expected, the consumption of the flavored solution during the preexposure session increased with an increase in deprivation level. This, in turn, led to more LI in the postconditioning test. DiBattista, Hollis-Walker, and Hague (2003), using Golden Hamsters, also found that LI increased with the amount of flavor preexposure. However, very small quantities (1 ml) of the PE flavor can *enhance* CTA, at least with a complex flavor (Bennett et al., 1996; also, see following text). Relatedly, Hoffman and Spear (1989), using infant rats in an odor–shock conditioning procedure, also found enhanced conditioning when the number of odor preexposures was small but found LI when it was large. On the other hand, De la Casa and Lubow (2002, Experiment 1) reported significantly more LI with two as compared to four flavor preexposure trials (5 min each) when the conditioning–test interval was 21 days but not when it was 1 day. In summary, it appears that LI can be produced with few flavor preexposures, but if the amount of the flavor solution is severely limited, then the preexposure may generate an enhanced CTA effect rather than LI.

Intensity of the Preexposed Stimulus

CTA–LI increases as a function of concentration of the PE flavor (Rodriguez & Alonso, 2002; Gilley & Franchina, 1985). Irrespective of flavor preexposure, CTA is also a function of CS intensity (Barker, 1976; Dragoin, 1971), as well as salience (Kalat, 1974).[1]

Stimulus Specificity of CTA–LI

An early review of six experiments that investigated the generalization of CTA–LI (Lubow, 1989, p. 59) concluded that LI was relatively stimulus specific, at least when comparing the PE flavor to one that was qualitatively different from it. As might be expected, a small change on a single stimulus dimension from preexposure to test produces sizeable generalization of CTA–LI, while larger changes result in significant attenuations of CTA–LI. The same effects have been reported with infant rats (Chotro & Alonso, 1999). As will be seen later, stimulus specificity of LI, as reflected in generalization decrements, has been used to explain a variety of effects when preexposure and conditioning are conducted with the various combinations of a flavor element and a compound that includes that element (see also Meehan & Riccio, Chapter 7).

Numbers of Conditioning and Test Trials

In most LI experiments with multiple conditioning trials, as the number of CS–US trials increases, the PE and NPE groups approach asymptotic levels of conditioning. As a consequence, the observed CTA–LI effect is larger at the beginning than at the

end of the conditioning sessions. The same is true for CTA–LI (e.g., Rodriguez & Alonso, 2002).

On the other hand, the effects of number of test-stage trials, which are presented after the conditioning stage and conducted in the absence of the US (extinction), are more complex. If conditioning was strong, then the consumption of the target solution, at least initially, would recover faster for the PE group than the NPE group. This would be reflected as an increase in LI with repeated test trials (e.g., De la Casa & Lubow, 2002; three trials). However, with an extended number of test trials both groups would eventually reach similar asymptotic levels, culminating in the disappearance of the LI effect. Interestingly, an extended number of extinction trials (nine vs. three) by itself may also produce a CTA–LI effect, as indicated by retarded reacquisition of target flavor aversion (Brooks, Bowker, Anderson & Palmatier, 2003).

Retention Interval Durations

The retention of LI can be influenced by several temporal parameters, including the time intervals between (1) stage-1 preexposure and stage-2 conditioning; (2) stage-1 preexposure and stage-3 test; and (3) stage-2 conditioning and stage-3 test. Experiments designed to assess the effects of any one of these intervals will necessarily involve manipulating other intervals as well. Although the ensuing confoundings have not always been controlled for, the general picture that emerges is reasonably clear (see also Meehan & Riccio, Chapter 7).

Preexposure–Conditioning Interval
Various experiments have compared a 1- or 2-day delay to those of anywhere from 10 to 100 days (usually about 20 days). Typically, CTA–LI decreases as a function of the duration of the interval between preexposure and conditioning stages (Ackil, Carman, Bakner, & Riccio, 1992; Aguado, Symonds, & Hall, 1994, Experiment 3; DiBattista et al., 2003; Elkins & Hobbs, 1979; Ishii, Yamada, Hishamura, & Haga, 2002, Experiments 1 and 2; Kraemer & Roberts, 1984, Experiment 4; McIntosh & Tarpy, 1977; but see, Kalat & Rozin, 1973).

Notably, the retention intervals in the studies mentioned were spent in the *same* context as that of the preexposure and conditioning stages. Since recent studies had shown that the context of the retention interval between acquisition and test stages modulates CTA–LI (see subsequent text), De la Casa and Lubow (2002, Experiment 3) conducted an experiment in which the preexposure–conditioning interval (1 or 21 days) was spent in a *different* context than that of the other stages. Under such circumstances, LI was *not* attenuated by a longer retention interval. Although the design did not include a same-context condition, a comparison to studies that did use the same-context condition suggests that the interval context may modulate the effects of time between the preexposure and conditioning stages on CTA–LI.

Preexposure–Test Interval

Ishii et al. (2002) observed attenuated LI with a 21-day delay (Experiment 1) and a 12-day delay (Experiment 2) between flavor preexposure and test, both as compared to a 3-day delay.

Conditioning–Test Interval

It has been generally accepted that an increase in the time between conditioning and test attenuates the LI effect, a finding that has been used to support retrieval/competition accounts of LI (see p. 38), as opposed to the older associative deficit accounts (i.e., that CS preexposure results in a weak CS–US association). Such results have been obtained mostly in CTA–LI experiments that have compared a 1- or 2-day delay with longer delays, typically 21 days (Aguado, de Brugada, & Hall, 2001, Experiment 2; Aguado et al., 1994, Experiment 1; Bakner, Strohen, Nordeen, & Riccio, 1991, Experiments 1 and 2; Ishii, Yamada, Hishimura, & Haga, 2002, Experiments 1 and 2; Kraemer & Spear, 1992, with saccharin but not maple).

As with the earlier CTA–LI studies that manipulated the preexposure–conditioning interval, subjects in these experiments also spent the retention interval in the same context as that of the preexposure, conditioning, and test stages. However, recent studies have found that when the retention interval context is *different* from the context of the other stages, an increase in retention interval duration *potentiates* LI (De la Casa, Diaz, & Lubow, 2003; De la Casa & Lubow, 2000, 2002, 2005; Lubow & De la Casa, 2002, 2005b; for a review, see Lubow & De la Casa, 2005a). In these studies, thirsty rats were either preexposed or not to the to-be conditioned flavor (saccharin), following which the PE stimulus was paired with the

US. After either a 1- or 21-day retention interval, spent in either the same or a different context from that of the other experimental stages, saccharin consumption was assessed in the same context as that of preexposure and conditioning. In the short retention interval condition, and irrespective of the retention interval context, the usual LI effect was obtained. With a long retention interval, the retention interval context determined the direction of the LI effect relative to the short interval. When the retention interval context was the same as that of the other contexts, LI was attenuated. When the retention interval context was different from that of the other contexts, there was a super-LI effect.

Context Change Effects

There is abundant evidence from a variety of research paradigms that LI is context specific, namely that LI is more robust when the context in which the preexposure stage is conducted is the same as the contexts of the conditioning and/or test stages than when those contexts are different from each other. However, an early review of the literature (Lubow, 1989, pp. 74–81) suggested that CTA–LI might be a special case. At that time, the preponderance of data indicated that CTA–LI was attenuated by interstage changes of *local* context (stimuli whose presence is contingent on the ingestion of the flavored liquid, such as a spout that makes a sound when it is licked (e.g., Archer et al., 1986)) but not of *global* context (stimuli that are continuously present, even in the absence of the target stimulus, such as drug state, time of testing, or, more typically, testing apparatus (e.g., Best & Meachum, 1986, but see Hall & Channell, 1986)). The deleterious effect of local context changes on CTA–LI can also be seen in recent studies in which there is a switch from a compound flavor to an element of that compound (or vise versa) from preexposure to conditioning (see following text).

In a study that varied global *and* local contexts, Alvarez and Lopez (1995, Experiment 3) preexposed rats to either an element of a flavor compound, or to the compound, or to water (NPE), all in global context A. After preexposure, animals were conditioned to the compound in the vivarium and spent the rest of the day in their home cages. On the next day, all animals were presented with the flavor compound in context A and in context B. Element and compound preexposures both produced LI effects.

However, LI was larger in the same global context condition than in the different global context condition, but only for the compound-PE group. This suggests that context is a particularly powerful mediator of LI effects when the PE stimulus is relatively complex.

More recently, Moron et al. (2002) failed to find disrupted LI for global context changes between preexposure and conditioning stages. This was true for apparatus/place (Experiment 1; also see Chamizo, 1996) and time (Experiment 2), even though these manipulations did affect the expression of CTA itself, as well as the renewal of CTA after extinction. In a modification of Moron et al.'s Experiment 2, Manrique et al. (2004) used 5 days, instead of 2 days, of apparatus habituation prior to initiating the flavor preexposure sessions. Under these conditions, LI was significantly less when the

preexposure and conditioning stages occurred at different as compared to the same times of day.

Table 3.1 summarizes the literature on the effects of global context changes on CTA–LI. As can be seen, there is, at best, only weak evidence for the context specificity of CTA–LI. As such, these data complement Garcia's (1989) claim that CTA should be relatively independent of context because CTA reflects a special relationship between food-related stimuli and digestive system activity. Nevertheless, there are many examples of context manipulations that *do* modulate other CTA-related behaviors. Not only is CTA–LI diminished by changes in *local* context, but changes of *global* context from conditioning to test stages reduce CTA itself, that is, a specific aversion acquired in one context transfers poorly to a different context (e.g., Boakes, Westbrook, Elliot, & Swinbourne,

Table 3.1 Latent Inhibition Decrements (Yes or No) as a Function of Changes in Global Contexts in Preexposure (PE), Conditioning (Cond), and Test Stages with CTA Procedures.

Experiments	PE	Cond.	Test	Results
Alvarez and Lopez (1995,	A	H	A	Yes/no[a]
Experiment 3)	A	H	B	
Best and Meachum (1986)	A	A	A	
	H	A	A	No
Chamizo (1996)				
Experiment 1	A	A	A	
	A	B	A	No[b]
Experiment 2	A	A	A	
	A	B	A	No
Hall and Channell (1986)				
Experiment 2	H	H	H	
	H	A	A	No
Experiment 3[c]	A	A	A	
	A	B	B	Yes
Kurz and Levitsky (1982)	A	A	A	
	A	B	B	No
Manrique et al. (2004) (time)	A	A	A	
	A	B	A	Yes
Moron et al. (2002)				
Experiment 1 (place)	A	A	A	
	A	B	A	No
Experiment 2 (time)	A	A	A	
	A	B	A	No

Note: Letters indicate contexts; the same letters signify the same contexts; H indicates that the context is the home cage.
[a]LI attenuated with context change for compound but not for elemental stimuli.
[b]$p = 0.055$.
[c]The only experiment in the table that equated familiarity of the A and B contexts.

1997; Bonardi, Honey, & Hall, 1990, Experiment 2; Ishii, Iguchi, & Sawa, 2006; Murphy & Skinner, 2005, Experiments 1 and 2). Furthermore, Hall and Symonds (2006) recently presented evidence suggesting that not only can one condition an aversion to a specific context by pairing it with a typical CTA US, but that prior exposure of that context can induce an LI effect for that context as well. In addition,

1. preexposure of the acquisition context prior to CS–US pairing facilitates CTA (Mitchell, Winter, & Moffitt, 1980; also see Hinderliter & Misanin, 1993);
2. postconditioning exposure to the conditioning context (a context extinction procedure) weakens CTA, at least when exposures are accompanied by the consumption of water (Murphy & Skinner, 2005, Experiment 2);
3. a return to the conditioning context after extinction, as opposed to a return to a different context, elevates conditioned performance (the renewal effect; e.g., Chelonis, Calton, Hart, & Schachtman, 1999; Rosas & Bouton, 1997);
4. pairing the US with context prior to pairing the flavor with the US in that same context reduces CTA (context blocking, e.g., Batsell, 1997; see also Hall, Chapter 4);
5. on a similar note, the debilitating effect of US-presentations prior to flavor–US pairing on CTA is reduced when the preexposure context is familiar (e.g., Cole, VanTilburg, Burch-Vernon, & Riccio, 1996);
6. finally, as noted in the section on conditioning–test interval, the context of a long retention interval dramatically affects CTA–LI (also see following text, as well as Meehan & Riccio, Chapter 3, and for a review, Lubow & De la Casa, 2005a).

Considering the extensive literatures that document the global context specificity of LI in *non*-CTA preparations and the context-related CTA effects described earlier, it is puzzling that reports of debilitating effects of global context change on CTA–LI remain scant. There are several possible reasons for this situation:

1. Unlike in other preparations, the home cage often plays a role in CTA–LI procedures.
2. Relatedly, many of the studies of global context effects with CTA–LI confound context novelty/familiarity with the different-/same-context manipulation. Indeed, when Hall and Channell (1986, Experiment 3) equated the familiarity of the same and different contexts, they found some evidence for a context-specific LI effect. Interestingly, with these same flavor preexposure manipulations, rats exhibit no difference in the amounts of the PE flavor consumed when tested in the same context or a different context from that of preexposure, that is, habituation of neophobia is not context specific (Honey, Pye, Lightbrown, Rey, & Hall, 1992).
3. Alternatively, the relatively weak global context effects in CTA–LI as compared to other LI preparations may stem from the fact that global context effects are stronger for conditions in which the target stimulus is not accompanied by reinforcement, as in the preexposure stages of non-CTA–LI procedures or extinction (e.g., Bouton, Nelson, & Rosas, 1999). As opposed to this, preexposures to flavored solutions in CTA–LI experiments are presented to water-deprived rats, thus reinforcing the drinking response and perhaps making the flavor a secondary reinforcer.

Clearly, there is a need to determine why CTA–LI is, at best, only weakly global context specific. Furthermore, the sources of any putative global context effect, as well as of the better established local context effects, must be identified. Whether they are consequences of the relationship between the preexposure and conditioning contexts or between the preexposure and test contexts, or both, has important implications for theories of learning in general, and for LI specifically.

PREEXPOSURE AND CONDITIONING OF FLAVOR ELEMENTS AND COMPOUNDS

During the preexposure stage, the to-be target flavor (X) may be accompanied by a second flavor (Y) that either overlaps X, creating a simultaneous compound (XY), or immediately follows X, creating a serial compound (X–Y). In addition, Y may appear at any point in time during the preexposure stage but not contingent on the presentation of X (X, Y). In the conditioning stage, either X, Y, or

XY can be paired with the US. In the test stage, consumption of one or more of the X, Y, or XY solutions can be assessed. Within the large number of designs that can be generated from various combinations of these variables, one can identify several clusters of CTA–LI experiments, as well as related ones in which particular stimulus preexposure conditions produce *enhanced* learning.

Preexposing One Group to X, Another to XY, and Conditioning to XY

In one set of studies, some groups are preexposed to X and/or Y individually, and another group is preexposed to the XY compound. Both groups are then conditioned with the compound, and LI to the compound is assessed in the test stage. In one of the earliest of these studies, Holland and Forbes (1980) reported that preexposure to the flavor elements produced more LI to the compound than preexposure to the compound itself. However, Baker, Haskins, and Hall (1990) found the opposite pattern of results, namely greater LI in the group preexposed and conditioned to the compound than to the groups preexposed to the elements and conditioned to the compound. In an effort to reconcile these contradictory findings, Lopez and Aguado (1992) reduced the number of preexposures to elements and compound and manipulated the interval between preexposure and conditioning. They reported no difference in the size of the LI effect for elements and compound with a 48-h interval, but they reported the same results as Baker et al. with a 4-h interval. Alvarez and Lopez (1993) replicated the results obtained by Baker et al. with both time intervals (also see, Alvarez & Lopez, 1995).

On the whole, it appears that preexposing elements of a to-be conditioned compound produces less LI than preexposing the compound itself, a result that has also been reported with preparations other than CTA (e.g., Ishii, 1999). There are several explanations for these findings, the foremost of which is that of generalization decrement (e.g., Honey & Hall, 1989; Kaye, Swietalski, & Mackintosh, 1988), according to which the magnitude of LI is a positive function of the perceived similarity between the PE stimulus and the CS. Relatedly, since LI is context specific, the results can be accounted for by a change of local context from preexposure to conditioning (e.g., Archer et al., 1986).

Preexposing One Group to X, Another to XY, and Conditioning to X

As opposed to the designs mentioned, some studies have preexposed groups to either the X or Y element or to the XY compound, but conditioned to X and tested with X. These experiments, designed to assess the influence of distractors on the processing of the PE to-be CS, generally find that adding an irrelevant element (Y) to the to-be relevant element (X), either simultaneously or serially, increases the effectiveness of the subsequent conditioning episode to X (i.e., decreases LI). In one such study, normal LI was reduced when the preexposed to-be CS was *immediately* followed by an irrelevant flavor (Best, Gemberling, & Johnson, 1979; but see Honey & Hall, 1988, Experiment 1; Westbrook, Provost, & Homewood, 1982; for a discussion of differences among these studies, see Lubow, 1989, pp. 86–87). The LI-attenuating effect can be reduced by either prior familiarization with the irrelevant stimulus or by increasing the temporal interval (3 h) between the presentations of the two stimuli (Best et al., 1979).

Ishii, Haga, and Hishimura (1999) combined the conditions described in the previous section with those of the present one. Groups were preexposed either to water or to the to-be target element or to the compound of the to-be target and distractor. Half of each group was conditioned to the target element and half to the compound. There were two counterbalanced test trials, one with the compound CS and one with the element CS. Consumption of the CS in test (either element or compound) indicated that LI was attenuated by *any change* from preexposure to acquisition, whether from element to compound or compound to element. Consequently, these results cannot be interpreted purely in terms of distractor effects, namely that the additional irrelevant stimulus interferes with the processing of the target stimulus *during the preexposure phase*. However, the data are compatible with the generalization decrement hypothesis, as well as with related explanations, such as that of local context change. One also can appeal to association-based accounts. For example, Y may *overshadow* X. As such, during the preexposure stage, associative strength, whether of an X-no consequence or X-context association, or some combination of them, would accumulate more slowly to X in the XY compound than to X alone.

Independent Preexposures of X and Y

The effects of nominally distracting stimuli on LI can also be studied by presenting Y independently of the to-be CS (i.e., neither as a simultaneous nor serial compound). Kaye et al. (1988) showed that adding a distractor stimulus 5 min after preexposure to the target flavor disrupted LI, as did presenting the distractor 5 min after the conditioning trial. Relatedly, Killcross (2001) found that postconditioning exposure to a compound flavor composed of the PE element and a novel Y element also reduced LI.

Kaye et al. (1988) argued that their results reflected a target stimulus generalization decrement rather than an effect of distraction. However, there are several reasons for questioning the generalization decrement account.

1. Although the 5-min separation between X and Y creates problems for a distraction explanation, that interval also would seem to be sufficiently long to prevent the configural processing that is required by the generalization decrement hypothesis.
2. Although the distractors had the same effects when applied after the preexposure stage and after the conditioning stage, the similarity of effects does not necessarily require a common process.
3. Furthermore, other studies have found that when Y is neither part of a simultaneous nor a serial compound, it does not significantly reduce CTA–LI (Kasprow & Schachtman, 1993; Westbrook et al., 1982). However, in these studies, Y was presented *prior* to the conditioning stage.

In summary, it may be conceptually difficult to separate Y-effects into those that arise from distractor- or from generalization decrement processes. In either case, LI may be a function of the location of Y, at least in the three-stage CTA–LI procedure.

STIMULUS PREEXPOSURE AFFECTS GENERALIZATION/DISCRIMINATION (PERCEPTUAL LEARNING)

Given that LI is stimulus specific, it should come as no surprise that preexposure of a flavor also will improve its discriminability from other flavors,

a perceptual learning effect (Gibson, 1969; Hall, 1991). This simply follows from the fact that stimulus specificity, by definition, requires encoding of the sensory/perceptual properties of that stimulus. Indeed, although preexposure to a single flavor induces an LI effect, it also diminishes the generalization of CTA to a novel test-stage flavor (e.g., Best & Batson, 1977; Domjan, 1975). Relatedly, preexposure to one flavor, and conditioning to a second flavor, also reduces the amount of postconditioning generalization between them (Burch-Vernon & Riccio, 1997; Honey & Hall, 1989).

Likewise, if two flavors are individually preexposed, the generalization of CTA between them can be reduced (e.g., Alonso & Hall, 1999; Bennett, Wills, Wells, & Mackintosh, 1994; Blair & Hall, 2003a, 2003b; Honey & Hall, 1989; Mackintosh, Kaye, & Bennett, 1991; Symonds & Hall, 1995, 1997; Bennett et al., 1996). Similar results have been reported for infant rats (Chotro & Alonso, 1999, 2001, 2003). Relatedly, preexposure to a flavor compound (XY) followed by conditioning to XZ decreases the generalization of CTA to XY (e.g., Bennett et al., 1994). In summary, evidence for enhanced discriminability as a result of flavor preexposure is unequivocal, and it only remains to identify the variables that modulate the effect, and, of course, to provide a theoretical framework.

Similarity of the Two Preexposed Flavors

Increasing the similarity between two PE flavors, as by using two compounds with a common element, reduces the generalization between them (e.g., Mackintosh et al., 1991; Symonds & Hall, 1995). Although Chotro and Alonso (1999, Experiment 3A) at first failed to obtain preexposure-induced reduced generalization with infant rats, they achieved that effect by combining increases in the concentration of the common element in the two compounds with a larger number of preexposures (Experiment 4).

Alternating Flavor Preexposure Trials

Preexposing the two flavors on alternate trials, as opposed to preexposing each flavor individually in separate blocks of trials, increases their discriminability (e.g., Bennett & Mackintosh, 1999; Blair & Hall 2003a, 2003b; Blair, Wilkinson, & Hall, 2004;

Mondragon & Hall, 2002; Rodriguez & Alonso, 2004, Symonds & Hall, 1995, Experiments 2 and 3; Sanjuan, Alonso, & Nelson, 2004, Experiment 1, but see Experiments 2 and 3). Human participants, tested with procedures that are analogous to those of the animal CTA studies, also exhibit a greater reduction in generalization when two compound flavors are preexposed on an intermixed as compared to a blocked schedule (Dwyer, Hodder, & Honey, 2004; Mundy, Dwyer, & Honey, 2006).

These findings suggest that discrimination between stimuli is enhanced by procedures that support stimulus comparisons. However, Alonso and Hall (1999) found that when the two PE flavors were presented side by side, a procedure that should promote comparison, generalization was increased. Relatedly, Bennett and Mackintosh (1999) reported that the alternation procedure maintained discriminability when the trial intervals were as little a few minutes or as much as several hours, but not when the interval was reduced to zero. Although these findings undermine the stimulus-comparison hypothesis, they are congruent with the position that perceptual learning may be the result of the establishment of mutually inhibitory links between the distinctive features of the two flavors (McLaren, Kaye, & Mackintosh, 1989; McLaren & Mackintosh, 2000). This view requires that each of the two PE stimuli has a unique element with respect to the other stimulus. Using a preexposure procedure that was designed to preclude the formation of mutually inhibitory associations by excluding the common element from one of them (AX and X; where X is not a unique element since it is also a part of the AX compound), Rodriguez and Alonso (2004) presented the two flavors either on alternating or blocked trials. Conditioning was conducted with X, and generalization of the conditioned aversion was tested with AX. The alternating condition still produced less generalization between the two flavors than the blocked condition, thereby not supporting the mutual inhibitory links explanation.

Hall and colleagues also have presented evidence that the perceptual learning effect is independent of mutual inhibitory links (Artigas, Sansa, Blair, Hall, & Prados, 2006; Blair & Hall, 2003a, 2003b; Hall, Blair, & Artigas, 2006). They have shown that the perceptual learning effect that stems from the alternation of two PE flavors, AX and BX, as compared to CX in a separate block

of trials, occurs because the alternation preserves the salience of the unique elements of the compounds. They offered an explanation for salience maintenance based on the associative activation of stimulus representations. Presentations of BX trials during the preexposure session produce a within-compound excitatory association that is maintained by the intervening AX trials because the representation of B is associatively activated by the X component. Thus, unlike in the McLaren account, it is not the unique feature (A) that is important for generating the effect, but rather the common feature (X).

Preexposing AX and BX and Conditioning to A: Does B Become an Inhibitor? (Espinet Effect)

Clearly, intermixed preexposures to AX and BX flavor compounds increase the discriminability between them. However, following such preexposures, if the animal is then given A-US conditioning trials, B will develop into a conditioned inhibitor for that US (e.g., Bennett, Scahill, Griffiths, & Mackintosh, 1999; Espinet, Iraola, Bennett, & Mackintosh, 1995). McLaren and Mackintosh (2000) again invoke inhibitory associations between A and B during the preexposure stage to account for this effect.

THE RETENTION INTERVAL DURATION × RETENTION INTERVAL CONTEXT INTERACTION

As described earlier, many CTA–LI experiments have investigated the effects of retention interval duration. More recently, there also has been an interest in the interaction between retention interval duration and the context in which that interval is spent (same or different from that of the other stages). In a series of experiments by De la Casa and Lubow (De la Casa et al., 2003; De la Casa & Lubow, 2000, 2002, 2005; Lubow & De la Casa, 2002, 2005b; for a review, see Lubow & De la Casa, 2005a), thirsty rats were either preexposed or not preexposed to a flavored solution (saccharin), following which it was paired with the injection of a US (LiCl). After either a short or long retention interval (typically 1 and 21 days) that was spent in either the same context as that of the other experimental stages or a different context, saccharin consumption was assessed in the same-context as that of preexposure and conditioning. The short retention interval condition, irrespective of its context, provided the standard LI effect, less CTA in the PE than the NPE group. On the other hand, LI in the long retention interval condition was significantly affected by the context in which the interval was spent. When the retention interval context was the same as that of the contexts of the other experimental stages, LI was attenuated, a finding that appears in a number of other reports with similar retention interval context conditions (e.g., Aguado et al., 2001; Bakner et al., 1991; Ishii et al., 2002; Kraemer & Spear, 1992). However, when the retention interval context was different from that of the other contexts, there was a *super-LI* effect.

The traditional account of LI-loss in the long-interval, same context condition acknowledges that the PE group acquires a CS–no consequence association (CS–0) association in stage-1 that, in turn, becomes associated with the context in which the preexposure occurred. These associations cannot be acquired by the NPE group. In stage-2, conditioning, both groups acquire a CS–US association that is relatively *context independent*. When the context of the conditioning–test retention interval is the *same* as that of the preexposure stage, the PE group's CS–context association undergoes extinction, which becomes stronger with increasing time in that context. As a result, in the test stage, which has the same context as the other stages, the CS–US association dominates the CS–0 association, and LI is weaker after a long as compared to a short retention interval. This, then, can explain the time-induced LI attenuations that have been reported when all stages of the experiment, *including the retention interval*, are conducted in the same context.

Alternatively, Lubow and De la Casa (2005a) have proposed a context differentiation hypothesis, which not only can account for the attenuated LI in the long-interval, same-context condition but also can explain the source of the super-LI effect in the long-interval, different-context condition. The context differentiation hypothesis proposes that the *perceived similarity* of the context in which the CS–0 and CS–US associations were acquired to the test context is, of course, a function of their physical similarity. However, the perceived similarity is also a function of the physical similarity of the *retention interval* context to the other contexts

and of the *duration* of that interval. Specifically, spending extended periods of time in the *same* context (preexposure, conditioning, retention interval, and test stages) increases the differentiation amongst those contexts. Conversely, if the interval context is *different* from that of the other contexts, then, with an increase in retention interval duration, the perceived similarity of those contexts is increased. Thus, if one accepts that CTA–LI is attenuated when there are different preexposure and test contexts (e.g., Hall & Channell, 1986; but see section on the effects of context change), then the conditions that produce context differentiation should reduce LI. On the other hand, given the context specificity of LI, increasing the perceived similarity between preexposure and test contexts should enhance the LI effect, perhaps by strengthening the ability of the test-stage context to serve as a retrieval cue for the CS–0 association.

Admittedly, the context differentiation hypothesis is an after-the-fact explanation. Nevertheless, it concisely accounts for a disparate set of data and it is testable. Furthermore, there is presently no alternative account of the super-LI effect.

IMPLICATIONS FOR THEORIES OF LI

The wide-ranging flavor preexposure effects are not likely to be encompassed by either A- or R-theories individually. This conclusion follows directly from two cardinal facts. (1) CTA strength is strongly affected by a variety of different stimulus *preexposure* conditions. For example, CTA may be potentiated by using only a very few preexposures, but increasingly large LI effects can be generated after additional preexposures (e.g., Bennett et al., 1996; also see *amount of stimulus preexposure*, p. 41). (2) *Identical* stimulus preexposure conditions can lead to *different* outcomes, each of which depends on the subsequent post-preexposure conditions. Thus, post-preexposure changes of local context (and perhaps global context) result in less LI than the absence of such changes. LI also is affected by such post-preexposure variables as retention interval context and duration (see the relevant sections).

The modulation of CTA–LI by pre- *and* post-conditioning variables suggests that the observed test-stage effects are the products of multiple interacting systems (partially illustrated at the bottom of Figure 3.1). The following sections outline a proposal by which the A- and R-theories that characterize the older accounts of LI can be viewed within a more unified framework, a position anticipated in other writings (e.g., Lubow, 1989; Lubow & De la Casa, 2005a; Lubow & Gewirtz, 1995; McLaren & Mackintosh, 2000; Schmajuk, 2005).[2] As applied to LI, it is proposed that the A-factor, operating during the preexposure stage, but expressed in later stages, is composed of two processes, one that encodes stimulus *properties* (attributes, features, or elements) and one that encodes the *relationships* or associations among stimuli.

Processing during the Preexposure Stage

Stimulus Property Encoding

The encoding of stimulus properties during the preexposure stage is reflected in the stimulus specificity of LI. This point is reinforced by the fact that changes in *local* context from preexposure to test disrupt LI, a finding that represents a stimulus generalization decrement. Similarly, the global context specificity of LI, amply demonstrated at least in non-CTA preparations, provides evidence for the encoding of the context stimuli during the preexposure stage.

Since the acquisition of *any* association requires some degree of *prior* stimulus property encoding, it follows that property encoding must be initiated *before* the encoding of any of the several stimulus relationship associations that are presumed to be the basis of the LI effect (see following text). As a consequence of this priority, with very few stimulus preexposures, the subsequent association of that stimulus with a US should be *facilitated* rather than retarded, as compared to a NPE group (because the PE group has already encoded the stimulus properties and not yet encoded the CS–0 association) or to a PE group that has received a relatively large number of stimulus preexposures. Indeed, as noted, CTA is enhanced by few preexposures to the target flavor, and CTA–LI is obtained only with more extensive preexposures. The benefits from the prior encoding of stimulus attributes would be most prominent in tests that involve a difficult discrimination between the PE and novel stimulus.

Stimulus property encoding also has perceptual consequences that, in part, can be independent of the preparation for the acquisition of associations,

as, for example in the novel pop-out effect (e.g., Johnston & Hawley, 1994, see pp. 38–39). Similarly, perceptual learning effects, as illustrated by increased discriminability between two PE stimuli or between a PE and novel stimulus, have been accounted for by a stage-1 stimulus encoding process. Thus, preexposure of two stimuli would provide the organism with more contact with their common elements than with their unique elements. As a result, the salience of the common elements would be reduced more than that of the unique elements, thereby increasing the discriminability of the two stimuli (McLaren, Kaye, & Mackintosh, 1989; McLaren & Mackintosh, 2000).

Stimulus Relationship Encoding

All theories of LI depend on the acquisition of one or more associations during the stimulus preexposure stage (e.g., Lubow et al., 1982; Mackintosh, 1975; Pearce & Hall, 1980; Wagner, 1976). The encoding of the relationship between stimuli, involving a contingency-governed process, generates associative links between the PE stimuli and other events that occur in their presence. For the PE group, these associations may include (1) CS–0, when the to-be CS is not followed by any event of significance (not entirely true for CTA, see earlier sections); (2) Context–CS, when the to-be CS is presented in a particular context; (3) Context–[CS–0], a higher-order conditional association whereby the context may become an occasion setter for the expression of a CS–0 association. On the other hand, since the typical NPE group is merely preexposed to the context, it can only acquire a Context–0 association. A viable theory of LI should specify the role of each of these associations, both in regard to their acquisition in stage-1 preexposure and to their retrieval in stage-3 test.

Processing during the Test Stage

It is evident that the same two encoding processes described for stage-1 (preexposure) would also be operative in stage-2 (conditioning), but they would have a different impact on the PE and NPE groups. However, since acquisition data are usually not collected in stage-2, it will suffice to assume that, by the end of stage-2, the PE group will have learned that the target flavor, previously not followed by a consequence (CS–0, but see p. 40) is now also followed by a negative consequence CS–US. In the stage-3 test, the response to the CS flavor may be the result of a *competition* between these two retrieved associations, a rivalry that is absent in the NPE group. This difference between the PE and NPE groups provides the basis for the LI effect as described by R-theories.

R-theories of LI have been supported by CTA experiments that varied the time between acquisition and test, and which found that LI, present in the short retention interval condition, was absent in the long retention interval condition. Such results suggest that the stage-2 CS–US associations acquired by the short-delay PE and NPE groups had the same underlying strengths, but that the test-stage difference between the PE and NPE groups were due to the retrieval/competition processes (e.g., Bakner et al., 1991; Kraemer & Ossenkopp, 1986; Kraemer, Randall, & Carbary, 1991; Kraemer & Roberts, 1984; Kraemer & Spear, 1992). However, as already noted, in all of these studies the retention interval context was the same as that of the other experimental contexts. More recent experiments have reported an *increase* in LI when the long delay was spent in a *different* context than that of the other stages (De la Casa et al., 2003; De la Casa & Lubow, 2000, 2002, 2005; Lubow & De la Casa, 2002, 2005b; for a review, see Lubow & De la Casa, 2005a). Although these newer data also require the engagement of a retrieval/competition process, neither current R- nor A- theories can accommodate the *differential* context-dependent retention interval effects.

Similarly, neither A- nor R-theories address order-dependent CTA effects. CS–0 followed by CS–US (LI procedure) and CS–US followed by CS–0 (extinction procedure) do not produce the same response strength to the CS in a stage-3 test. Lubow and De la Casa (2002) failed to observe symmetry of LI and extinction effects, even with controls for differences in time between the first two stages and the test. Ishii et al. (1999) also found that presentation order affected LI. Thus, a distractor (Y) added to a flavor to create an XY compound reduced LI to the conditioned X. However, when X was preexposed alone and conditioning was conducted with the XY compound, there was no comparable loss of LI. Explanations of retention interval context effects and order effects would seem to require special provisions, even to an integrated A/R-theory, as for example the context differentiation hypothesis (Lubow & De la Casa, 2005a) for the former, and a primacy principle for the latter (e.g., De la Casa & Lubow, 2002; Wheeler, Stout, & Miller, 2004).

SUMMARY AND CONCLUSIONS

CTA–LI is an exceedingly robust phenomenon that can be generated by exposure to almost any flavor prior to conditioning with that flavor. Simple CTA–LI is largely stimulus specific, and it increases as a function of the amounts and intensity/salience of the PE flavor. However, the LI effect is reduced with an increase in the number of conditioning trials. CTA–LI effects appear to be independent of the mode of preexposure as long as that mode is consistent across experimental stages. Relatedly, a change of local context from preexposure to conditioning and/or test stages diminishes LI. It is not yet clear whether such a context-specific effect can be obtained with similar changes in global context. Nevertheless, the global context of the conditioning-to-test retention *interval* does affect CTA–LI. CTA–LI is less when the retention interval is long, compared to short, but only when that interval is spent in the same context as that of the other experimental stages. If the long retention interval is spent in a different context from that of the other stages, then a super-LI effect is produced.

In general, preexposure to a flavor element and conditioning to a compound containing that element, or vise versa, reduces LI as compared to when the PE and conditioned flavors are identical. Such effects are similar to those obtained by changes in local context, and probably reflect a simple generalization decrement of the normally stimulus-specific LI. As opposed to LI effects, flavor preexposures also can induce a perceptual learning effect, namely an increase in the discriminability between two PE flavors or between a PE and novel flavor. Relatedly, a small number of flavor preexposures enhances CTA to that flavor, reflecting the operation of an encoding process, which, on the one hand, underlies the stimulus-specificity of CTA–LI, and, on the other hand, contributes to the perceptual learning effects. In short, flavor familiarity impedes the formation of new associations with that stimulus, but at the same time increases its discriminability from other stimuli.

Finally, it appears that a comprehensive explanation of the wide array of stimulus preexposure effects would have to begin with an amalgamation of A- and R-theories, with special provisions to account for the interaction of retention interval duration and retention interval context. Together with our rodent subjects, we would happily drink to such an achievement!

Notes

1. For rats familiarized with a particular concentration of a flavored solution, a less concentrated flavor was more readily associated with the US than the original higher concentration. This suggests that CTA intensity effects are a special case of novelty or, in other words, of stimulus salience.

2. The A–R duality is not unique to theories of LI; it mirrors the long-standing oppositional tensions in the learning and cognition literature, as reflected in such controversies as learning versus performance (for a brief review, see Miller & Escobar, 2001), encoding versus retrieval (e.g., Tulving & Thomson, 1973), and the source of amnesic effects in animals (Gold & King, 1974; Miller & Springer, 1973), as well as others.

References

Ackil, J. K., Carman, H. M., Bakner, L., & Riccio, D. C. (1992). Reinstatement of latent inhibition following a reminder treatment in a conditioned taste aversion paradigm. *Behavioral and Neural Biology, 58,* 232–235.

Aguado, L., de Brugada, I., & Hall, G. (2001). Tests for inhibition after extinction of a conditioned stimulus in the flavour aversion procedure. *Quarterly Journal of Experimental Psychology, 54B,* 201–217.

Aguado, L., Symonds, M., & Hall, G. (1994). Interval between preexposure and test determines the magnitude of latent inhibition: Implications for an interference account. *Animal Learning & Behavior, 22,* 188–194.

Alonso, G., & Hall, G. (1999). Stimulus comparison and stimulus association processes in the perceptual learning effect. *Behavioural Processes, 48,* 11–23.

Alvarez, R., & Lopez, M. (1993). Latent inhibition to a compound following exposure to the elements or the compound. *Bulletin of the Psychonomic Society, 31,* 569–570.

Alvarez, R., & Lopez, M. (1995). Effects of elements or compound preexposure on conditioned taste aversion as a function of retention interval. *Animal Learning & Behavior, 23,* 391–399.

Archer, T., Mohammed, A. K., & Jarbe, T. U. C. (1986). Context-dependent latent inhibition in taste aversion learning. *Scandinavian Journal of Psychology, 27,* 277–284.

Artigas, A. A., Sansa, J., Blair, C. A. J., Hall, G., & Prados, J. (2006). Enhanced discrimination between flavor stimuli: Roles of salience modulation and inhibition. *Journal of Experimental Psychology: Animal Behavior Processes, 32,* 173–177.

Baker, A. G., Haskins, C. E., & Hall, G. (1990). Stimulus generalization decrement in latent inhibition to a compound following exposure to the elements of the compound. *Animal Learning & Behavior, 18,* 162–170.

Bakner, L., Strohen, K., Nordeen, M., & Riccio, D. C. (1991). Post-conditioning recovery from latent inhibition effect in conditioned taste aversion. *Physiology and Behavior, 50,* 1269–1272.

Barker, L. M. (1976). CS duration, amount, and concentration effects in conditioning taste aversions. *Learning and Motivation, 7,* 265–273.

Barot, S. K., & Bernstein, I. L. (2005). Polycose taste pre-exposure fails to influence behavioral and neural indices of taste novelty. *Behavioral Neuroscience, 119,* 1640–1647.

Batsell, W. R. (1997). Retention of context blocking in taste aversion learning. *Physiology & Behavior, 61,* 437–446.

Bennett, C. H., & Mackintosh, N. J. (1999). Comparison and contrast as mechanism of perceptual learning? *Quarterly Journal of Experimental Psychology, 52B,* 253–272.

Bennett, C. H., Scahill, V. L., Griffiths, D. P., & Mackintosh, N. J. (1999). The role of inhibitory associations in perceptual learning. *Animal Learning & Behavior, 27,* 333–345.

Bennett, C. H., Tremain, M., & Mackintosh, N. J. (1996). Facilitation and retardation of flavor conditioning following prior exposure to the CS. *Quarterly Journal of Experimental Psychology, 49,* 220–230.

Bennett, C. H., Wills, S., Wells, J. O., & Mackintosh, N. (1994). Reduced generalization following preexposure: Latent inhibition of common elements or a difference in familiarity? *Journal Experimental Psychology: Animal Behavior Processes, 20,* 232–239.

Best, M. R., & Batson, J. D. (1977). Enhancing the expression of flavor neophobia: Some effects of the ingestion-illness contingency. *Journal Experimental Psychology: Animal Behavior Processes, 3,* 132–143.

Best, M. R., Gemberling, G. A., & Johnson, P. E. (1979). Disrupting the conditioned stimulus preexposure effect in flavor aversion learning: Effects of interoceptive distractor manipulations. *Journal of Experimental Psychology: Animal Behavior Processes, 5,* 321–334.

Best, M. R., & Meachum, C. L. (1986). The effects of stimulus preexposure on taste-mediated environmental conditioning: Potentiation and overshadowing. *Animal Learning & Behavior, 14,* 1–5.

Bethus, I., Muscat, R., & Goodall, G. (2006). Dopamine manipulations limited to preexposure are sufficient to modulate latent inhibition. *Behavioral Neuroscience, 120,* 554–562.

Blair, C. A. J., & Hall, G. (2003a). Perceptual learning in flavor aversion: Evidence for learned changes in stimulus effectiveness. *Journal of Experimental Psychology: Animal Behavior Processes, 29,* 39–48.

Blair, C. A. J., & Hall, G. (2003b). Changes in stimulus salience as a result of stimulus preexposure: Evidence from aversive and appetitive testing procedures. *Learning & Behavior, 31,* 185–191.

Blair, C. A. J., Wilkinson, A., & Hall, G. (2004). Assessments of changes in the effective salience of stimulus elements as a result of stimulus preexposure. *Journal of Experimental Psychology: Animal Behavior Processes, 30,* 317–324.

Boakes, R. A., Westbrook, R. F., Elliot, M., & Swinbourne, A. L. (1997). Context dependency of conditioned aversion to water and sweet tastes. *Journal of Experimental Psychology: Animal Behavior Processes, 23,* 56–67.

Bonardi, C., Honey, R. C., & Hall, G. (1990). Context specificity of conditioning in flavor-aversion learning- extinction and blocking tests. *Animal Learning & Behavior, 18,* 229–237.

Bouton, M. E. (1993). Context, time, and memory retrieval in the interference paradigms of Pavlovian conditioning. *Psychological Bulletin, 114,* 80–99.

Bouton, M. E., Nelson, J. B., & Rosas, J. M. (1999). Stimulus generalization, context change, and forgetting. *Psychological Bulletin, 125,* 171–186.

Brooks, D. C., Bowker, J. L., Anderson, J. E., & Palmatier, M. I. (2003). Impact of brief or extended extinction of a taste aversion on inhibitory associations: Evidence from summation, retardation, and preference tests. *Learning & Behavior, 31,* 69–84.

Burch-Vernon, A., & Riccio, D. C. (1997). The effects of CS-preexposure in conditioned taste aversion: Enhanced flavor discrimination. *Learning and Motivation, 28,* 170–187.

Capaldi, E. D. (1991). Hunger and the learning of flavor preferences. In R. C. Bolles (Ed.), *The hedonics of taste* (pp. 127–142). Hillsdale, NJ: Lawrence Erlbaum.

Chamizo, V. D. (1996). Absence of contextual specificity of latent inhibition in taste aversion learning. *Psicológica, 17,* 307–321.

Chelonis, J. J., Calton, J. L., Hart, J. A., & Schachtman, T. R. (1999). The renewal effect in conditioned taste aversion. *Learning and Motivation, 30,* 1–14.

Chotro, M. G., & Alonso, G. (1999). Effects of stimulus preexposure on the generalization of conditioned taste aversion in infant rats. *Developmental Psychobiology, 35,* 304–317.

Chotro, M. G., & Alonso, G. (2001). Some parameters of stimulus preexposure that affect conditioning and generalization of taste aversions in infant rats. *International Journal of Comparative Psychology, 14,* 43–63.

Chotro, M. G., & Alonso, G. (2003). Stimulus preexposure reduces generalization of conditioned taste aversions between alcohol and non-alcohol flavors in infant rats. *Behavioral Neuroscience, 117,* 113–122.

Cole, K. C., VanTilburg, D., Burch-Vernon, H., & Riccio, D. C. (1996). The importance of context in the US preexposure effect in CTA: Novel versus latently inhibited contextual stimuli. *Learning and Motivation, 27,* 362–374.

De la Casa, L. G., Diaz, E., & Lubow, R. E. (2003). Effects of post-treatment retention interval and context on neophobia and conditioned taste aversion. *Behavioural Processes, 63,* 159–170.

De la Casa, G., & Lubow, R. E. (1995). Latent inhibition in conditioned taste aversion: The roles of stimulus frequency and duration, and amount of fluid ingested during preexposure. *Neurobiology of Learning and Memory, 64,* 125–132.

De la Casa, L. G., & Lubow, R. E. (2000). Super-latent inhibition with delayed conditioned taste aversion testing. *Animal Learning & Behavior, 28,* 389–399.

De la Casa, G., & Lubow, R. E. (2002). An empirical analysis of the super-latent inhibition effect. *Animal Learning & Behavior, 30,* 112–120.

De la Casa, L. G., & Lubow, R. E. (2005). Delay-induced super-latent inhibition as a function of order of exposure to two flavours prior to compound conditioning. *Quarterly Journal of Psychology, 58B,* 1–18.

Deutsch, R. (1978). Effects of CS amount on conditioned taste aversion at different CS–UCS intervals. *Animal Learning & Behavior, 6,* 258–260.

DiBattista, D., Hollis-Walker, L., & Hague, L. (2003). The CS-preexposure effect in conditioned taste-aversion learning in golden hamsters. *Journal of General Psychology, 130,* 446–461.

Domjan, M. (1972). CS preexposure in taste aversion learning: effects of deprivation and preexposure duration. *Learning and Motivation, 3,* 389–402.

Domjan, M. (1975). Poison-induced neophobia in rats- role of stimulus generalization of conditioned taste aversions. *Animal Learning & Behavior, 3,* 205–211.

Dragoin, W. B. (1971). Conditioning and extinction of taste aversions with variations in intensity of CS and US in two strains of rats. *Psychonomic Science, 22,* 303–305.

Dwyer, D. M., Hodder, K. I., & Honey, R. C. (2004). Perceptual learning in humans: The roles of preexposure schedule, feedback, and discrimination assay. *Quarterly Journal of Experimental Psychology, 57B,* 245–259.

Elkins, R. L., & Hobbs, S. H. (1979). Forgetting, preconditioning familiarization and taste aversion learning: An animal experiment with implications for alcoholism. *Behaviour, Research and Therapy, 17,* 567–573.

Escobar, M., Oberling, P., & Miller, R. R. (2002). Associative deficit accounts of disrupted latent inhibition and blocking in schizophrenia. *Neuroscience and Biobehavioral Reviews, 26,* 203–216.

Espinet, A., Iraola, J. A., Bennett, C. H., & Mackintosh, N. J. (1995). Inhibitory associations between neutral stimuli in flavor aversion conditioning. *Animal Learning and Behavior, 23,* 361–368.

Fouquet, N., Oberling, P., & Sandner, G. (2001). Differential effect of free intake versus oral perfusion of sucrose in conditioned taste aversion in rats. *Physiology & Behavior, 74,* 465–474.

Garcia, J. (1989). Food for Tolman: Cognition and cathexis in concert. In T. Archer & L. G. Nilsson (Eds.), *Aversion, avoidance and anxiety* (pp. 45–85). Hillsdale, NJ: Lawrence Erlbaum.

Garcia, J., Kimmeldorf, D. J., & Koelling, R. A. (1955). Conditioned aversion to saccharin resulting from exposure to gamma radiation. *Science, 122,* 157–158.

Gibson, E.J. (1969). *Principles of perceptual learning and development.* New York: Appleton-Century-Crofts.

Gilley, D. W., & Franchina, J. (1985). Effects of preexposure flavor concentration on conditioned aversion and neophobia. *Behavioral and Neural Biology, 44,* 503–508.

Gold, P. D., & King, R. A. (1974). Retrograde amnesia: Storage failure versus retrieval failure. *Psychological Review, 81,* 465–469.

Hall, G. (1991). *Perceptual and associative learning.* Oxford: Clarendon Press.

Hall, G., Blair, C. A. J., & Artigas, A. A. (2006). Associative activation of stimulus representations restores lost salience: Implications for perceptual learning. *Journal of Experimental Psychology: Animal Behavior Processes, 32,* 145–155.

Hall, G., & Channell, S. (1986). Context specificity of latent inhibition in taste aversion learning. *Quarterly Journal of Experimental Psychology, 38B,* 121–139.

Hall, G., & Symonds, M. (2006). Overshadowing and latent inhibition of context aversion conditioning in the rat. *Autonomic Neuroscience: Basic and Clinical, 129,* 42–49.

Harris, J. A. (2006). Elemental representations of stimuli in associative learning. *Psychological Review, 113,* 584–605.

Hinderliter, C. F., & Misanin, J. R. (1993). Context familiarity and delayed conditioned taste-aversion in young-adult and old-age rats. *Perceptual and Motor Skills, 77,* 1403–1406.

Hoffmann, H., & Spear, N. E. (1989). Facilitation and impairment of conditioning in the preweanling rat after prior exposure to the conditioned stimulus. *Animal Learning & Behavior, 17,* 63–69.

Holland, P. C., & Forbes, D. T. (1980). Effects of compound or element preexposure on compound flavor aversion conditioning. *Animal Learning & Behavior, 8,* 199–203.

Honey, R. C., & Hall, J. (1988). Overshadowing and blocking procedures in latent inhibition. *Quarterly Journal of Experimental Psychology, 40B,* 163–186.

Honey, R. C., & Hall, G. (1989). Enhanced discriminability and reduced associability following flavor preexposure. *Learning and Motivation, 20,* 262–277.

Honey, R. C., Pye, C., Lightbrown, Y., Rey, V., & Hall, G. (1992). Contextual factors in neophobia: The role of absolute and relative novelty. *Quarterly Journal of Experimental Psychology, 45B,* 265–284.

Ishii, K. (1999). Attenuation of latent inhibition after compound conditioning. *Japanese Psychological Research, 41,* 101–111.

Ishii, K., Haga, Y., & Hishimura, Y. (1999). Distractor effect on the latent inhibition of conditioned flavor aversion in rats. *Japanese Psychological Research, 41,* 229–238.

Ishii, K., Iguchi, Y., & Sawa, K. (2006). Context dependency of conditioned aversions to familiar and novel fluids. *Learning and Motivation, 37,* 113–130.

Ishii, K., Yamada, Y., Hishimura, Y., & Haga, Y. (2002). The effects of preexposure–test and conditioning–test intervals on the magnitude of latent inhibition. *Japanese Psychological Research, 44*, 51–56.

Johnston, W. A., & Hawley, K. J. (1994). Perceptual inhibition of expected inputs: The key that opens closed minds. *Psychonomic Bulletin and Review, 1*, 56–72.

Kalat, J. W. (1974). Taste salience depends on novelty, not concentration in taste-aversion learning in the rat. *Journal of comparative and Physiological Psychology, 86*, 47–50.

Kalat, J. W. (1976). Should taste aversion learning experiments control duration or volume of drinking on the training day? *Animal Learning & Behavior, 4*, 96–98.

Kalat, J. W., & Rozin, P. (1973). "Learned safety" as a mechanism in long-delay taste aversion learning in rats. *Journal of Comparative and Physiological Psychology, 83*, 198–207.

Kasprow, W. J., & Schachtman, T. R. (1993). Differential effects of distractor stimuli and the interval between flavor exposures on neophobia and latent inhibition. *Psychological Record, 43*, 25–38.

Kaye, H., Swietalski, N., & Mackintosh, N. J. (1988). Distractor effects on latent inhibition are a consequence of generalization decrement. *Quarterly Journal of Experimental Psychology, 40B*, 151–161.

Killcross, A. S. (2001). Loss of latent inhibition in conditioned taste aversion following exposure to a novel flavour before test. *Quarterly Journal of Experimental Psychology, 54B*, 271–288.

Killcross, A. S., Kiernan, M. J., Dwyer, D., & Westbrook, R. F. (1998). Loss of latent inhibition of contextual conditioning following non-reinforced context exposure in rats. *Quarterly Journal of Experimental Psychology, 51B*, 75–90.

Koh, M. T., & Bernstein, I. L. (2005). Mapping conditioned taste aversion associations using C-Fos reveals a dynamic role for the insular cortex. *Behavioral Neuroscience, 119*, 388–398.

Koh, M. T., Wilkins, E. E., & Bernstein, I. L. (2003). Novel tastes elevate C-Fos expression in the central amygdala and insular cortex. *Behavioral Neuroscience, 117*, 1416–1422.

Kraemer, P. J., & Ossenkopp, K. P. (1986). The effects of flavor preexposure and test interval on conditioned taste aversions in rats. *Bulletin of the Psychonomic Society, 24*, 219–221.

Kraemer, P. J., Randall, C. K., & Carbary, T. J. (1991). Release from latent inhibition with delayed testing. *Animal Learning & Behavior, 19*, 139–145.

Kraemer, P. J., & Roberts, W. A. (1984). The influence of flavor preexposure and test interval on conditioned taste aversion in the rat. *Learning and Motivation, 15*, 259–278.

Kraemer, P. J., & Spear, N. E. (1992). The effect of nonreinforced stimulus exposure on the strength of a conditioned taste aversion as a function of retention interval: Do latent inhibition and extinction involve a shared process? *Animal Learning & Behavior, 20*, 1–7.

Kurz, E. M., & Levitsky, D. A. (1982). Novelty of contextual cues in taste aversion learning. *Animal Learning & Behavior, 10*, 229–232.

Lopez, M., & Aguado, L. (1992). Effects of element or compound preexposure on taste-aversion learning with simultaneous and serial compounds. *Bulletin of the Psychonomic Society, 30*, 279–282.

Lubow, R. E. (1973). Latent inhibition. *Psychological Bulletin, 79*, 398–407.

Lubow, R. E. (1989). *Latent inhibition and conditioned attention theory.* New York: Cambridge University Press.

Lubow, R. E. (2005). The construct validity of the animal-latent inhibition model of selective attention deficits in schizophrenia. *Schizophrenia Bulletin, 31*, 139–153.

Lubow, R. E., Alek, M., & Rifkin, B. (1976). The context effect: The relationship between stimulus preexposure and environmental preexposure determines subsequent learning. *Journal of Experimental Psychology: Animal Behavior Processes, 2*, 38–47.

Lubow, R. E., & De la Casa, G. (2002). Super-latent inhibition and spontaneous recovery: Differential effects of pre- and post-conditioning CS-alone presentations after long delays in different contexts. *Animal Learning & Behavior, 30*, 376–386.

Lubow, R. E., & De la Casa, L. G. (2005a). There is a time and a place for everything: Bi-directional modulations of latent inhibition by time-induced context differentiation. *Psychonomic Bulletin & Review, 12*, 806–821.

Lubow, R. E., & De la Casa, G. (2005b). Time-induced super-latent inhibition is dependent on the distinctiveness of the retention-interval context from the other experimental contexts. *Learning and Motivation, 36*, 322–330.

Lubow, R. E., & Gewirtz, J. C. (1995). Latent inhibition in humans: Data, theory, and implications for schizophrenia. *Psychological Bulletin, 117*, 87–103.

Lubow, R. E., & Kaplan, O. (1997). Visual search as a function of type of prior experience with target and distractor. *Journal of Experimental Psychology: Human Perception and Performance, 23*, 14–24.

Lubow, R. E., Weiner, I., & Schnur, P. (1981). Conditioned attention theory. In G. Bower

(Ed.), *The psychology of learning motivation,* Vol. 15. New York: Academic Press.

Mackintosh, N. J. (1975). A theory of attention: Variations in the associability of stimuli with reinforcement. *Psychological Review, 82,* 276–298.

Mackintosh, N. J., Kaye, H., & Bennett, C. H. (1991). Perceptual learning in flavour avoidance conditioning. *Quarterly Journal of Experimental Psychology, 43B,* 297–322.

Manrique, T., Molero, A., Ballesteros, M. A., Moron, I., Gallo, M., & Fenton, A. A. (2004). Time of day-dependent latent inhibition of conditioned taste aversion in rats. *Neurobiology of Learning and Memory, 82,* 77–80.

McIntosh, J. M., & Tarpy, R. M. (1977). Retention of latent inhibition in a taste aversion paradigm. *Bulletin of the Psychonomic Society, 9,* 411–412.

McLaren, I. P. L., Kaye, H., & Mackintosh, N. J. (1989). An associative theory of the representation of stimuli: Applications to perceptual learning and latent inhibition. In R. G. M. Morris (Ed.), *Parallel distributed processing: Implications for psychology and neurobiology.* (pp. 102–130). New York: Oxford University Press.

McLaren, I. P. L., & Mackintosh, N. J. (2000). An elemental model of associative learning: I. Latent inhibition and perceptual learning. *Animal Learning & Behavior, 28,* 211–246.

Miller, R. R., & Escobar, M. (2001). Contrasting acquisition-focused and performance-focused models of acquired behavior. *Current Directions in Psychological Science, 10,* 141–145.

Miller, R. R., Kasprow, W. J., & Schachtman, T. R. (1986). Retrieval variability: Sources and consequences. *American Journal of Psychology, 99,* 145–218.

Miller, R. R., & Springer, A. D. (1973). Amnesia, consolidation, and retrieval. *Psychological Review, 80,* 69–79.

Mitchell, D., Winter, W., & Moffitt, T. (1980). Cross-modality contrast: Exteroceptive context habituation enhances taste neophobia and conditioned taste aversions. *Animal Learning & Behavior, 8,* 524–528.

Mondragon, E., & Hall, G. (2002). Analysis of the perceptual learning effect in flavour aversion learning: Evidence for stimulus differentiation. *Quarterly Journal of Experimental Psychology, 55B,* 153–169.

Moron, I., Manrique, T., Molero, A., Ballesteros, M. A., Gallo, M., & Fenton, A. (2002). The contextual modulation of conditioned taste aversions by the physical environment and time of day is similar. *Learning & Memory, 9,* 218–233.

Mundy, M. E., Dwyer, D. M., & Honey, R. C. (2006). Inhibitory associations contribute to perceptual learning in humans. *Journal of Experimental Psychology: Animal Behavior Processes, 32,* 178–184.

Murphy, M., & Skinner, D. M. (2005). Contextual control of fluid consumption: The effects of context extinction. *Learning and Motivation, 36,* 297–311.

Pearce, J. M. (2002). Evaluation and development of a connectionist theory of configural learning. *Animal Learning & Behavior, 30,* 73–95.

Pearce, J. M., & Hall, G. (1980). A model for Pavlovian conditioning: Variations in the effectiveness of conditioned but not unconditioned stimuli. *Psychological Review, 87,* 332–352.

Prescott, J., Johnstone, V., & Francis, J. (2004). Odor–taste interactions: Effects of attentional strategies during exposure. *Chemical Senses, 29,* 331–340.

Reilly, S., & Bornovalova, M. A. (2005). Conditioned taste aversion and amygdala lesions in the rat: A critical review. *Neuroscience and Biobehavioral Reviews, 29,* 1067–1088.

Rodriguez, G., & Alonso, G. (2002). Latent inhibition as a function of CS intensity in taste aversion learning. *Behavioural Processes, 60,* 61–67.

Rodriguez, G., & Alonso, G. (2004). Perceptual learning in flavor-aversion learning: Alternating and blocked exposure to a compound of flavors and to an element of that compound. *Learning and Motivation 35,* 208–220.

Rosas, J. M., & Bouton, M. E. (1997). Renewal of a conditioned taste aversion upon return to the conditioning context after extinction in another one. *Learning and Motivation, 28,* 216–229.

Rudy, J. W., Rosenberg, L., & Sandell, J. H. (1977). Disruption of a taste familiarity effect by novel exteroceptive stimulation. *Journal of Experimental Psychology: Animal Behavior Processes, 3,* 26–36.

Russig, H., Kovacevic, A., Murphy, C. A., & Feldon, J. (2003). Haloperidol and clozapine antagonize amphetamine-induced disruption of latent inhibition of conditioned taste aversion. *Psychopharmacology, 170,* 263–270.

Sanjuan, M. C., Alonso, G., & Nelson, J. B. (2004). Blocked and test-stimulus exposure effects in perceptual learning re-examined. *Behavioural Processes, 66,* 23–33.

Schmajuk, N. A. (2005). Brain–behaviour relationships in latent inhibition: A computational model. *Neuroscience and Biobehavioral Reviews, 29,* 1001–1020.

Small, D. M., & Prescott, J. (2005). Odor/taste integration and the perception of flavor. *Experimental Brain Research, 166,* 345–357.

Symonds, M., & Hall, G. (1995). Perceptual learning in flavor aversion conditioning: Roles of stimulus comparison and latent inhibition of common stimulus elements. *Learning and Motivation, 26,* 203–219.

Symonds, M., & Hall, G. (1997). Stimulus pre-exposure, comparison, and changes in the associability of common stimulus features. *Quarterly Journal of Experimental Psychology, 50B,* 317–331.

Tulving, E., & Thomson, D. M. (1973). Encoding specificity and retrieval processes in episodic memory. *Psychological Review, 80,* 352–373.

Wagner, A. R. (1976). Priming in STM: An information processing mechanism for self-generated or retrieval-generated depression in performance. In T. Tighe & R. N. Leaton (Eds.), *Habituation: perspectives from child development, animal behavior, and neurophysiology* (pp. 95–128). Hillsdale, NJ: Lawrence Erlbaum.

Wagner, A. R., & Brandon, S. E. (2001). A componential theory of Pavlovian conditioning. In R. R. Mowrer & S. B. Klein (Eds.), *Handbook of contemporary learning theories.* (pp. 23–64). Hillsdale, NJ: Lawrence Erlbaum.

Weiner, I. (2003). The "two-headed" latent inhibition model of schizophrenia: modeling positive and negative symptoms and their treatment. *Psychopharmacology, 169,* 257–297.

Westbrook, R. F., Duffield, T. Q., Good, A. J., Halligan, S., Seth, A. K., & Swinbourne, A. L. (1995). The extinction of within-event learning is contextually controlled and subject to renewal. *Quarterly Journal of Experimental Psychology, 48B,* 357–375.

Westbrook, R. F., Provost, S. C., & Homewood, J. (1982). Short-term flavor memory in the rat. *Quarterly Journal of Experimental Psychology, 34B,* 235–256.

Wheeler, D. S., Stout, S. C., & Miller, R. R. (2004). Interaction of retention interval with CS-preexposure and extinction treatments: Symmetry with respect to primacy. *Learning & Behavior, 32,* 335–347.

Yamamoto, J., Fresquet, N., & Sandner, G. (2002). Conditioned taste aversion using four different means to deliver sucrose to rats. *Physiology & Behavior, 75,* 387–396.

4

Preexposure to the Unconditioned Stimulus in Nausea-Based Aversion Learning

GEOFFREY HALL

Learned flavor aversion is a familiar and widespread phenomenon. Every year I conduct an informal poll of my undergraduate students, asking how many have, at some time, developed an aversion to a particular food (or drink). They respond readily (they apparently have the concept of an acquired aversion prior to any formal teaching on the topic), and each year about 50% of the class report an aversion—usually to a specific alcoholic drink, and often with a vivid report of the specific episode of overindulgence and its immediate consequence.

Evidently flavor–nausea associations are readily established. From one point of view this is not surprising. The flavor that acts as the conditioned stimulus (CS) in the conditioning trials that my students inflict on themselves is usually quite novel—that is, the student in question is usually trying brandy (or whisky or champagne) for the first time. Novel flavors are highly associable; it is well established that prior exposure to a given flavor will dramatically reduce the ease with which it forms a conditioned aversion (the well-known phenomenon of *latent inhibition*, e.g., Lubow, 1989). Nausea (the putative unconditioned stimulus, US), on the other hand, is a state that my students will undoubtedly have experienced a number of times before. Nonetheless, it is still clearly able to operate as a powerful reinforcer. Is it perhaps immune from the effects of preexposure that CSs are susceptible to? Introspection suggests that, as years

go by, later episodes (however produced) seem no less unpleasant than earlier ones. Indeed, there is some evidence to suggest that they might become more so—patients undergoing chemotherapy for cancer sometimes report that the nausea induced by a given drug infusion grows increasingly worse over the course of treatment (Stockhorst et al., 1998).

However this may be (and we will return to this last observation later), there is clear experimental evidence from the study of flavor aversion learning in the rat that the effectiveness of nausea as a reinforcer can be diminished by prior exposure. Figure 4.1 shows the results of one such experiment (Aguado, De Brugada, & Hall, 1997, Experiment 1). It shows the amount of a saccharin solution consumed by two groups of rats on a test trial given 2 days after a conditioning trial on which consumption of saccharin had been followed by an intraperitoneal injection of lithium chloride (LiCl). (LiCl acts on the area postrema of the hindbrain, a structure associated with distress in the upper gastrointestinal tract, Tsukamoto & Adachi, 1994.) Control subjects showed a marked aversion to saccharin, drinking very little on test. Preexposed subjects differed from controls in that they had been given three previous injections of LiCl, the last of these 2 days before the conditioning trial. These subjects showed much less of an aversion to saccharin. This effect, the retardation of conditioning produced by prior exposure to the US, has been labeled (unimaginatively) as the *US-preexposure effect* (there is no equivalent to the term latent inhibition, used for the CS-preexposure effect). The effect is robust and widespread, being found with almost all the procedures and drugs capable of establishing flavor aversion (as is fully documented in the review by Riley & Simpson, 2001). My analysis of the nature of the effect will, however, concentrate on the effect as it is shown by rats that are given LiCl as the US, a procedure for which a substantial body of, theoretically relevant, experimental work is now available.

In an early review of the US-preexposure effect, Randich and LoLordo (1979) identified two general classes of explanation for the effect—nonassociative and associative—and examples of each of these remain the central concern for this chapter. In the first category, Randich and LoLordo concentrated on *habituation*, suggesting that the effectiveness of a US as a reinforcer might decline simply as a consequence of repeated presentations of that US. The categorization of this proposed

explanation as being necessarily nonassociative was rendered inappropriate by the development of accounts of habituation that relied on associative mechanisms (e.g., Wagner, 1981), but the process involved may still be distinguished from that postulated by the most widely considered associative explanation. This account, often called *context blocking* (although blocking by context would be a better term), takes as its starting point the observation that presenting a US without an explicit CS (as in the US-preexposure procedure) does not preclude the occurrence of conditioning. Each presentation of the US occurs in the presence of a distinctive set of cues, including those associated with handling and the injection procedure, and those that characterize the place in which the illness is experienced. These contextual cues could come to function as CSs, and since they will be present during the formal conditioning stage of the procedure, when a flavor CS is presented prior to the US, they could therefore act to *block* (Kamin, 1969) conditioning of the flavor, with the result that acquisition of an aversion is attenuated.

In what follows I will assess recent experimental evidence that bears on each of these proposals. It should be noted that these interpretations are not mutually exclusive; both could be operating and contribute to most instances of the US-preexposure effect. Equally, of course, there could be examples of the effect that are not explained by either.

Group	Pre	Cond	Test
Pre	3 Li	Sac → Li	Sac
Control	3 Sal	Sac → Li	Sac

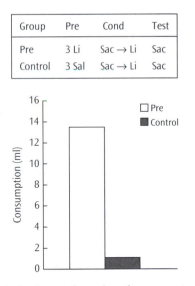

Figure 4.1. Design and results of an experiment by Aguado et al. (1997, Experiment 1). Group Pre (preexposed) had experienced three daily intraperitoneal injections of lithium chloride (Li) followed by a conditioning (Cond) trial in which consumption of a saccharin (Sac) solution was followed by an injection. The control group received injections of isotonic saline (Sal) in the preexposure phase. On the test, which followed conditioning after 2 days, consumption of saccharin was measured.

HABITUATION: AN INITIAL CONSIDERATION

At the level of behavioral observation, habituation refers to the waning in the magnitude or probability of an unconditioned response (UR) as a result of repeated presentations of the US. (When the stimulus in question is the administration of a given dose of a drug, the phenomenon may also be referred to as the development of *tolerance*; Riley & Simpson, 2001.) If the suggestion that the US-preexposure effect is a consequence of US habituation is to be anything more than a redescription of the observed results, it seems necessary to show that the learning process that is responsible for the loss of the UR is also responsible for the reduced ability of nausea to act as a reinforcer. A first step, then, would be to show that the UR evoked by an injection of lithium is attenuated by a preexposure procedure of the sort that generates

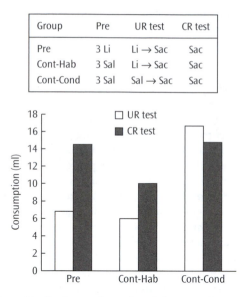

Group	Pre	UR test	CR test
Pre	3 Li	Li → Sac	Sac
Cont-Hab	3 Sal	Li → Sac	Sac
Cont-Cond	3 Sal	Sal → Sac	Sac

Figure 4.2. Design and results of the experiment by De Brugada et al. (2003a). Group Pre (preexposed) received three intraperitoneal injections of lithium chloride (Li); control groups (Cont) received saline injections. On the UR test, all groups drank saccharin (Sac) after an injection of Li or of Sal. The CR test assessed consumption of saccharin.

a US-preexposure effect. The available results are not encouraging.

An injection of LiCl produces a range of observable reactions. For the sort of dose used in flavor aversion conditioning, it produces a lowering of body temperature and a reduction in activity level. Batson (1983) examined these URs in rats that were given a series of eight injections of LiCl, but found no sign of habituation in them. Nonetheless, rats given this preexposure showed poor conditioning when LiCl was used as the US for conditioning. A similar dissociation was obtained in a study by De Brugada, González, and Cándido (2003a), the results of which are illustrated in Figure 4.2. An immediate effect of an injection of LiCl is that rats will refuse to consume an otherwise palatable substance (Domjan, 1977; Symonds & Hall, 2002). This was the UR measured by De Brugada et al. (the UR test in Figure 4.2). As the figure shows, control rats (the Cont-Cond group) drank a saccharin solution readily, but rats given an injection of LiCl just before the saccharin was offered showed a suppression of consumption. This was true both for rats that experienced LiCl

for the first time (group Cont-Hab) and for rats that had had three previous injections (group Pre); that is, there was no indication of habituation. But preexposure did produce an attenuation of conditioning. The procedure that was used for testing the UR means that animals in the Pre and Cont-Hab groups drank some saccharin while under the effects of the LiCl injection, allowing the possibility that an association might be formed between the taste and nausea. The aversion that was conditioned on the UR test trial was assessed in a subsequent test on which saccharin was made available, and given a day later when the immediate effects of the injection had worn off (the CR test of Figure 4.2). On this test the Cont-Hab group showed a marked aversion to saccharin, whereas the Pre group drank the saccharin as readily as animals (group Cont-Cond) that had received no injection of LiCl.

This preliminary survey of the implications of the habituation hypothesis yields a clear outcome. The effects of an injection of LiCl appear not to habituate, within the parameters investigated, and yet the US-preexposure effect is still obtained. Some other process must be responsible for the effect seen in these conditions. We turn, therefore, to a consideration of the context-blocking hypothesis.

CONTEXT AVERSION CONDITIONING

A first requirement, if the context-blocking hypothesis is to be supported, is that it should be possible to demonstrate that injections of LiCl are capable of establishing a context as a CS for nausea. And this is precisely what has been denied by some. Thus, for example, Garcia and his colleagues (e.g., Garcia, 1989; Garcia, Brett, & Rusiniak, 1989), have asserted that nausea activates a special "gut-defense" system that specifically allows learning about tastes but which will not normally support learning about exteroceptive cues (such as contextual cues). The only exception allowed was to accommodate the phenomenon of *potentiation*—the discovery that the presence of a taste might foster learning about other cues. It was thus allowed that exteroceptive cues might be capable of acquiring aversive properties if they were presented in conjunction with taste cues. (According to the analysis offered by Garcia et al., the presence of the taste cues opens a "gate" that allows the exteroceptive cues to sneak into a learning system to which otherwise they would be denied access.)

Potentiation and the Consumption Test

The experimental evidence lends support to this suggestion. Several studies (e.g., Best, Brown, & Sowell, 1984; Boakes, Westbrook, & Barnes, 1992; Mitchell & Heyes, 1996) have shown that context conditioning occurs more readily when rats are permitted to drink a solution with a novel flavor during the conditioning phase. And although this effect is most apparent when the flavor is novel, simply giving access to unflavored water can generate the same outcome. Symonds et al. (1998, Experiment 1) conducted trials on two groups of rats in two different contexts (distinctive cages, different from each other, and both different from the home cage). Exposure to context A was followed by an injection of LiCl, exposure to context B was not. Contextual conditioning was assessed by means of a consumption test in which the rats were offered a sucrose solution in each of the contexts—we know that the state induced by an injection of LiCl suppresses consumption; if contextual cues, by way of conditioning, acquire the power to evoke some properties of this state then they too might be capable of suppressing consumption.[1] The two groups differed only in that one was allowed to drink (water) during the context conditioning trials whereas the other was not. The results (Figure 4.3) show that the rats that drank water during training showed a suppression of consumption when tested in context A, consistent with the notion that this context had acquired aversive properties. Rats that were not allowed to drink during conditioning did not show this effect.

This result immediately raises doubts about the context-blocking hypothesis. There is no reason to think that the US-preexposure effect will be found only when the rats are allowed to drink during preexposure trials, and yet this appears to be necessary for context conditioning to occur. Worse, although this pattern of results has been taken as demonstrating potentiation of context conditioning, an alternative interpretation is available that denies that context conditioning has occurred at all. The problem is that allowing the animal to ingest something prior to the injection allows the possibility that what is ingested will acquire aversive properties. This can occur even when what is

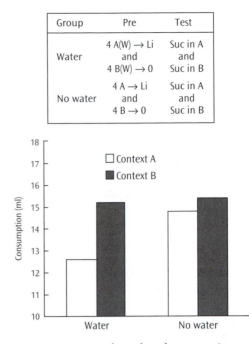

Group	Pre	Test
Water	4 A(W) → Li and 4 B(W) → 0	Suc in A and Suc in B
No water	4 A → Li and 4 B → 0	Suc in A and Suc in B

Figure 4.3. Design and results of an experiment by Symonds et al. (1998, Experiment 1). During preexposure (Pre), all subjects experienced context A followed by an injection of lithium chloride (Li); no injection followed exposure to context B. The water group (W) was permitted to drink during this phase. On the test, consumption of a sucrose (Suc) solution was assessed in both contexts.

consumed is just plain water (Boakes, Westbrook, Elliott, & Swinbourne, 1997). Suppression of consumption of a different substance on the test might thus be a consequence of direct generalization from one flavored substance to another, rather than an indication that the contextual cues have acquired associative strength. It is true that suppressed consumption is seen only when the test is given in the trained context and not when it is given elsewhere (Mitchell & Heyes, 1996), but this observation does not require us to assume that the context has acquired aversive properties. It is known that flavor aversions can become context dependent so that they will be fully expressed only in the presence of the context used in training (Bonardi, Honey, & Hall, 1990). This phenomenon appears to be an instance of *occasion setting*, in which the context fosters the retrieval of associative information (Boakes et al., 1997; Puente, Cannon, Best, & Carrell, 1988). The context specificity demonstrated by Mitchell and Heyes (1996) could thus have occurred because their context acted as an occasion setter allowing a generalized aversion to the test fluid to show itself.

Other Procedures

To show that a context has indeed come to function as a Pavlovian CS requires a different procedure. I will describe two that have been used with some success. The first uses a different test procedure, the second a modified training procedure.

One strategy is to use a measure other than the suppression of consumption, and this has been arranged by making use of *blocking* as a test. It is well established that when one element of a compound stimulus has been pretrained as a signal for a given US, its presence in the compound will block conditioning to the other. Thus it should be possible to assess the aversive properties of a context previously paired with nausea in terms of its ability to block the acquisition of an aversion to a novel flavor, when this flavor and the contextual cues are conditioned as a compound. With this procedure, evidence for a context aversion would be provided by a failure of conditioning to the novel flavor (i.e., by a high level of consumption). Direct generalization from any flavor aversion formed during training could not generate such a result.

This strategy has been used a number of times (e.g., Best et al., 1984; Symonds et al., 1998; Symonds & Hall, 1997; Westbrook & Brookes, 1988; Willner, 1978). The design and results of one of these experiments (Symonds & Hall, 1997, Experiment 2) are shown in Figure 4.4. The initial training procedure, given to two groups of rats, was identical to that used for the water group of Figure 4.3, with one context (A) being paired with LiCl and another (B) not. In the next phase (compound conditioning), the rats were allowed to drink a sucrose solution in the home cage, and were then exposed to context A (the blocking group) or context B (the control group) prior to a further injection of LiCl. The aversion to sucrose was assessed in a final test given in the home cage. As the figure shows, the control group showed a strong aversion and drank rather little. Subjects in the blocking group drank rather more, an outcome consistent with the notion that the pretrained context (context A) had been able to block the acquisition of the aversion to sucrose.

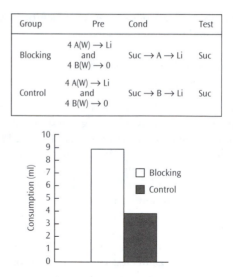

Group	Pre	Cond	Test
Blocking	4 A(W) → Li and 4 B(W) → 0	Suc → A → Li	Suc
Control	4 A(W) → Li and 4 B(W) → 0	Suc → B → Li	Suc

Figure 4.4. Design and results of an experiment by Symonds and Hall (1997, Experiment 2). During preexposure (Pre), all subjects experienced context A followed by an injection of lithium chloride (Li); no injection followed exposure to context B. In the conditioning (Cond) phase, consumption of sucrose (Suc) was followed by exposure to context A (the blocking group) or to context B (the control group) and an injection of Li. Consumption of sucrose in the home cage was measured in the test phase.

The blocking test appears to be a rather sensitive procedure for detecting context conditioning. In a study otherwise identical to that just described, Symonds et al. (1998) gave no access to water for any of the rats during the context conditioning phase. Recall that in these conditions the suppression-of-consumption test revealed no evidence of context conditioning (Figure 4.3). But Symonds et al. were able to detect clear evidence of context conditioning using the blocking test. A possible interpretation of this finding is that pairing a context with nausea *can* produce conditioning, even in the absence of a flavor, but the effect is small and difficult to detect. This brings us to the second strategy, which is simply to find a way of enhancing conditioning in these situations, to make it evident on the consumption test. This was achieved by Rodriguez, Lopez, Symonds, and Hall (2000) who introduced the technique of injecting the rat with LiCl shortly before it was put into the training context. Previous work had routinely used the procedure of exposing the rat to the context prior to the injection (in line with many other conditioning procedures in which the CS precedes the US). It turns out, however, that giving the injection first, so that the rat experiences the illness in the presence of the contextual cues, produces a context that is very effective at suppressing consumption of an otherwise palatable substance. This effect is seen in rats that are not permitted to eat or drink in the context, and thus cannot be the consequence of a generalized flavor aversion.

Nature of the CR

It remains to establish the nature of the CR established by this context conditioning procedure. One reason for using the suppression-of-consumption test was that it matches the UR; if the suppressed consumption produced directly by an injection of LiCl indicates a state of nausea, it seems reasonable to assume that suppression in the presence of conditioned contextual cues reflects conditioned nausea. Parker (2003) has argued, however, that an injection of LiCl not only induces nausea, it also produces a novel change in physiological state that signals danger to the rat. Both these effects might support conditioning. A taste associated with LiCl does indeed appear to acquire nausea-inducing properties. These can be made evident by the *taste reactivity* test in which a small amount of the conditioned substance is introduced into the rat's oral cavity by way of a cannula. The rat will show a characteristic open-mouthed gaping response (the sort of response that precedes vomiting in species capable of antiperistalsis). But this conditioned aversion need not be responsible for the suppression of intake seen in a standard consumption test for flavor aversion. The taste avoidance shown on such a test, Parker suggests, is supported by an association (akin to fear conditioning) between the taste and the dangerous change of physiological state. A possible implication of this analysis is that the learning produced by context conditioning procedures might be based on this second form of learning—that the context comes to signal potential danger, but does not actually evoke a state of conditioned nausea. A rat might be expected to be reluctant to consume an otherwise palatable substance when it is presented in a fear-evoking context (thus generating the suppression seen in the consumption test).

To investigate this possibility, Limebeer, Hall, and Parker (2006) conducted a study of context conditioning that made use of the taste reactivity

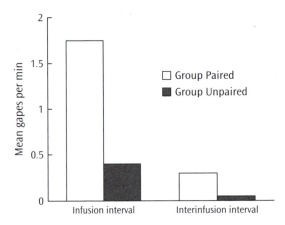

Figure 4.5. Design and test results of an experiment by Limebeer et al. (2006, Experiment 1). The paired group had received pairings of a distinctive context and injections of LiCl; the unpaired group had experienced context and injections on separate occasions. The results show the number of gaping responses made by each group in the context, both during intraoral infusions of saccharin and in the interval between infusions.

test. One group of rats (the paired group) received exposure to a distinctive context while suffering the effects of an injection of LiCl; control subjects (unpaired) experienced the context and the injection on separate occasions. The context was a box specially adapted for recording the rat's orofacial reactions. After conditioning, the rats were put back in the box and a saccharin solution was infused through an intraoral cannula. Subjects in the unpaired group accepted this readily, but, as Figure 4.5 shows, those in the paired group showed the gaping response, taken to be characteristic of nausea. Although their frequency is low, gaping responses do sometimes occur even in the absence of an infusion, and, as Figure 4.5 also shows, they did so more often in the paired than in the unpaired group. Parker's (2003) avoidance learning mechanism may well contribute to the suppression of consumption seen in the presence of conditioned contextual cues, but these new results indicate that conditioned nausea is at work too.

Potentiation Reconsidered

Finally, in this section of the chapter, we need to reconsider the notion of potentiation. We have established that context aversion conditioning can be demonstrated when the subjects do not eat or drink during the conditioning phase. Where does this leave the many demonstrations of potentiation? One possibility is that the effect is not all or none—that context conditioning can be obtained when ingestion is not permitted but is enhanced when it is. A second, more intriguing, is that the potentiation effect, at least with regard to context conditioning, is artifactual. The most substantial body of evidence for the effect comes from experiments that make use of a consumption test, and it is most reliably obtained when solutions with a distinctive novel flavor are used both in conditioning and on test (most commonly saccharin or sucrose has been used in training, and saline as the test flavor; see Symonds & Hall, 1999, for a review). This immediately suggests the possibility that the effect is a consequence, not of potentiation of learning about the context but of the direct generalization to the test flavor of an aversion established to the flavor present during conditioning.

This problem can be overcome by using the blocking test rather than the consumption test. Figure 4.6 shows the design of an experiment (Symonds & Hall, 1999, Experiment 2) that does this. Two groups of thirsty rats received conditioning trials in which two distinctive context were associated with injections of LiCl. In one of these contexts (A) the rats were allowed to drink water flavored with the distinctive sour taste of an acid (H: HCl). They then received a compound trial in which consumption of sucrose in the home cage was followed by exposure to one of the contexts (A for the experimental group, B for the control group) and then by an injection of LiCl. When tested with sucrose in the home cage both groups showed an aversion to sucrose that extinguished over successive test trials, but the aversion was more profound in the experimental group. We may deduce, therefore, that the context was *less* effective at blocking conditioning to sucrose in this group—that the context had gained less strength in this group than in the control group. Far from potentiating conditioning to the context, the presence of a novel flavor during the first phase of training detracted from it. From one point of view, this result should not be surprising—*overshadowing* (the attenuation of conditioning to a target cue by the concurrent presence of another competing cue) is routinely found in standard conditioning preparations and is predicted by standard theories of conditioning (e.g., Pearce & Hall,

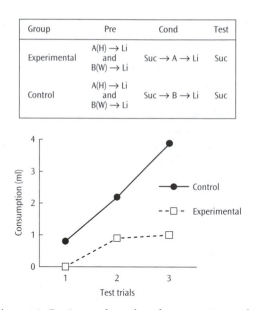

Figure 4.6. Design and results of an experiment by Symonds and Hall (1999, Experiment 2). During preexposure (Pre), all subjects experienced both context A and context B along with an injection of lithium chloride (Li). The sour taste of acid (H) was available in context A, plain water (W) in context B. In the conditioning (Cond) phase, consumption of a sucrose (Suc) was followed by exposure to context A (the experimental group) or to context B (the control group) and an injection of Li. Consumption of sucrose in the home cage was measured in the test phase.

1980; Rescorla & Wagner, 1972). Symonds and Hall (1999) concluded that the potentiation effect in context aversion conditioning is likely to be an artifact of the use of the consumption test and that context aversions seem to be acquired in the same way and according to the same rules as other CS–US associations.

BLOCKING BY CONTEXT

The Role of Cage Cues

What we have now established, after a good deal of effort, is that the procedure of giving a series of injections of LiCl in order to produce a US-preexposure effect is likely to result in establishing the context as a CS for nausea. The way seems clear, therefore, for an explanation of the effect in terms of blocking by context. Indeed, one of the procedures already discussed can be seen as supplying evidence that directly supports the explanation. In the study presented in Figure 4.4, preexposure to injections of LiCl resulted in retarded acquisition of an aversion to sucrose, but only when the context used for preexposure was present on the conditioning trials.

In the absence of a control condition that was given no preexposure to LiCl, this experiment does not include a demonstration of the basic US-preexposure effect itself, but other experiments have addressed this issue fully. The critical prediction of the context-blocking account is that the US-preexposure effect should be found only when conditioning is given in the presence of the contextual cues that were present during US preexposure. A change in context between preexposure and conditioning should abolish or (allowing for the possibility of generalization between contexts) attenuate the effect. This prediction has gained ample support from studies by Willner (1978), Batson and Best (1979), Domjan and Best (1980), and Dacanay and Riley (1982). All these experiments included a condition in which the initial exposure to LiCl was given in a novel context. Some rats then received flavor aversion conditioning in this same context prior to a test given in the home cage; for other subjects, both conditioning and the test occurred in the home cage. Both groups showed some retardation of conditioning (with respect to control subjects given no preexposure to the US), but the effect was less profound in those that experienced the change of context prior to conditioning.

A further prediction of the context-blocking account is that manipulations that limit or reduce the strength of the context–US association should attenuate the US-preexposure effect. Evidence is available on three such manipulations: overshadowing, extinction, and latent inhibition. The first of these has already been discussed. The results presented in Figure 4.6 can be taken as showing that the US-preexposure effect was less profound (i.e., the aversion to sucrose was stronger) in the experimental group than in the control group. The experimental group received its preexposure to the US after consuming a salient flavor, an arrangement that might be expected to overshadow acquisition by the context and thus limit the ability of the context to block in the next stage of the experiment.

The effect of extinction has been investigated by Batson and Best (1979, Experiment 4). They obtained a strong US-preexposure effect when preexposure and conditioning trials occurred in a distinctive black box, but the effect was attenuated when eight trials of exposure to the box were interpolated between the two stages. Batson and Best suggested that these trials allowed extinction of the association between the context and nausea and thus reduced the ability of the context to block subsequent acquisition. Further results consistent with this interpretation come from experiments investigating the effects of inserting a delay (a retention interval) between the phase of exposure to the US and the conditioning and test phases. This procedure has been found to reduce the size of the US-preexposure effect (Aguado et al., 1997; Cannon, Berman, Baker, & Atkinson, 1975). Since, in these experiments, all the procedures were carried out in the rats' home cages, this means that the rats spent the retention interval in the place in which preexposure to the US was given. As Aguado et al. pointed out, this would give ample opportunity for extinction of the context–US association, with the result that blocking by context, and hence the US-preexposure effect, would be less likely to occur (but see Miller, Jagielo, & Spear, 1993, for an alternative analysis).

Evidence on latent inhibition comes from a study by Cole, VanTilburg, Burch-Vernon, and Riccio (1996). They simply compared a condition in which all phases of the procedure (preexposure, conditioning, and the test) were given in the home cage, with a condition in which the procedures occurred in a novel context, different from the home cage. The US-preexposure effect was significantly weaker in the latter case. This outcome, Cole et al. suggested, was a consequence of the fact that the home cage, being very familiar, would have suffered extensive latent inhibition. Context conditioning during the US-preexposure phase would therefore be retarded, and the possibility of context blocking would be reduced. In fact, comparison with a non-preexposed control yielded no indication of any US-preexposure effect in animals trained in the home-cage condition.

Qualifications

This last observation may look like strong evidence in favor of the possibility that context blocking is the entire explanation of the US-preexposure effect, but in fact, closer examination reveals the need to refine this notion. Although Cole et al. (1996) found no US-preexposure effect in rats trained and tested in the home cage, many others have done so (the results presented in Figure 4.1 are just one example). This is not, in itself, evidence against the adequacy of the context-blocking explanation—it is quite likely that, in some circumstances, the latent inhibition suffered by the home cage would not be complete and would not be enough to totally preclude context conditioning and thus context blocking. There are, however, two arguments, one based on empirical evidence and one theoretical, that give grounds for doubting that context blocking, as we have understood it so far, is responsible for the effect in this case.

The empirical evidence comes from the experiment by De Brugada, González, and Cándido (2003b) depicted in Figure 4.7. The two bars on the left of the figure show the US-preexposure effect (a lesser aversion in the preexposed group than in the control group) for rats that remained in the home cage throughout all phases of the experiment. The two bars on the right are the results for rats given similar treatment except that they were switched to a novel context for conditioning and testing. For these subjects, the role of context blocking should be attenuated or even abolished. But although the aversion was somewhat stronger for these subjects, this was true for both the preexposed and the control groups and there was no statistically reliable evidence for any diminution in the size of the US-preexposure effect. De Brugada et al. concluded that contextual cues may play an important role in the US-preexposure effect when these cues are novel during preexposure, but that they have a negligible role when the context is familiar (i.e., when the cues have undergone latent inhibition). In these circumstances some other factors must be responsible for the effect.

The second argument arises from the fact that when the entire experimental procedure is carried out with the rats in the home cage, the magnitude of the CR is necessarily tested in the same context as that used for preexposure, and thus in the presence of the putative blocking cues. In the standard blocking procedure (e.g., Kamin, 1969) the failure of the blocked cue to control a strong CR is evident only when that cue is tested on its own—the compound of blocked and blocking cue evokes a strong CR. It is not easy then for the

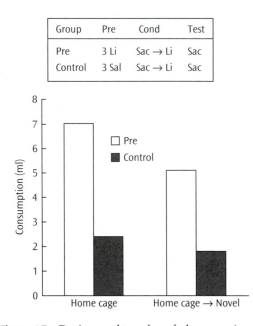

Group	Pre	Cond	Test
Pre	3 Li	Sac → Li	Sac
Control	3 Sal	Sac → Li	Sac

Figure 4.7. Design and results of the experiment by De Brugada et al. (2003b, Experiment 1). The Pre (preexposed) groups received three intraperitoneal injections of lithium chloride (Li); the control groups (Cont) received saline injections. Conditioning (Cond) consisted of consumption of saccharin (Sac) followed by an injection of LiCl (Li). Saccharin consumption was measured on the test. For one pair of groups all these procedures occurred in the home cage. For a second pair (Home cage → Novel), Pre occurred in the home cage, Cond and Test in a novel context.

context-blocking account to predict a weak CR to the flavor CS when the test is given in the presence of the pretrained contextual cues. To maintain this explanation it is necessary to assume that the associative strength gained by contextual cues is capable of restricting the acquisition of strength by the flavor CS during the conditioning phase of the procedure, but not of summating with such strength as the CS may have acquired when it comes to the test. There is reason to doubt the general validity of this assumption—that conditioned taste aversions tend to be stronger when tested in the training context rather than in some other context may be determined by several factors (see, e.g., Boakes et al., 1997), but in at least some cases, the effect seems to depend on a summation of the Pavlovian properties of the context and the substance being ingested (Loy, Alvarez, Rey, & Lopez, 1993).

Injection-Related Cues

These observations lead to the following conclusions. First that the acquisition of strength by distinctive contextual cues (such as those supplied by a novel cage) will allow them to block conditioning to a flavor CS and that the effects of this blocking (a weak CR) will be evident when the flavor is presented in a different context (e.g., back in the home cage). Second that this analysis cannot apply to the US-preexposure effect as it is shown by rats trained and tested in the home cage, at least, if by context we mean just the set of environmental cues that define a particular place. But, as was noted some time ago (e.g., Rudy, Iwens, & Best, 1977), administration of an intraperitoneal injection involves a range of handling and other cues that might well be regarded as constituting a part of the context in which the effects of the injection are experienced.

However we categorize them, such cues are prime candidates when it comes to blocking of flavor aversion learning. Although the environmental context of a US-preexposure experiment may have suffered latent inhibition, the injection-related cues will be novel and will be perfectly correlated with the occurrence of nausea. They can thus be expected to acquire associative strength readily during US preexposure. Because they are present on the conditioning trials they will be able to block acquisition by the flavor CS, and because they are absent on the test trial the full effect of the blocking should be evident.

Empirical support for this interpretation of the US-preexposure effect comes from studies in which the associative strength of the injection-related cues has been manipulated. Willner (1978) included a condition in which saline injections were intermixed with LiCl injections during preexposure, a procedure that reduces the reliability of the injection as a signal for nausea, and might thus be expected to limit the acquisition of associative strength by injection-related cues. The magnitude of the US-preexposure effect was reduced in this condition. Similarly, De Brugada and Aguado (2000; see also De Brugada et al., 2003b) demonstrated an attenuation of the effect in rats given a series of saline injections between the US-preexposure phase and the conditioning phase.

Such injections can be expected to bring about extinction of the association between injection-related cues and the US, and thus reduce the ability of these cues to produce blocking. But perhaps the most striking evidence on the role of injection-related cues comes from a series of studies by De Brugada, Hall, and Symonds (2004) in which use was made of a technique that allows LiCl-based conditioning to occur, but does not involve an intraperitoneal injection (or indeed, any handling of the rats at all).

Thirsty rats will readily drink a solution of LiCl—at least, once. Thereafter they will refuse it (and other salty solutions such as NaCl). Loy and Hall (2002) investigated this effect, and demonstrated it to be a consequence of associative learning in which the salty taste of LiCl becomes associated with the nausea induced by its consumption. (The size of the aversion produced in this way proved to be exactly comparable to that produced by intraperitonal injection of the same quantity of LiCl.) Orally consumed LiCl is evidently an effective reinforcer; Loy and Hall went on to show that drinking LiCl can establish an aversion to another taste (such as sucrose) that was consumed at the same time. This phenomenon makes it possible to investigate the effects of preexposure to injections on LiCl on the ability of orally consumed LiCl to support flavor aversion learning and thus to investigate the US-preexposure effect in circumstances in which blocking by injection-related cues cannot play a part.

The design of such an experiment (De Brugada et al., 2004, Experiment 1b) is shown at the top of Figure 4.8. The group labeled LI-LO (LI: lithium by injection; LO: oral consumption of lithium) received US preexposure consisting of three injections of LiCl prior to a conditioning trial on which they drank flavor A followed immediately by oral consumption of a solution of LiCL. The control group SI-LO (SI: saline by injection; LO: oral consumption of lithium) experienced the same conditioning procedure but received saline injections in the preexposure phase. Three injections of LiCl will produce a robust US-preexposure effect when orthodox conditioning procedures are used; the question of interest was whether the effect would be obtained when no injection-related cues were present in the conditioning phase. A further control group SI-SO (SI: saline injections in preexposure; SO: oral consumption of saline on the conditioning trial) that drank a saline solution

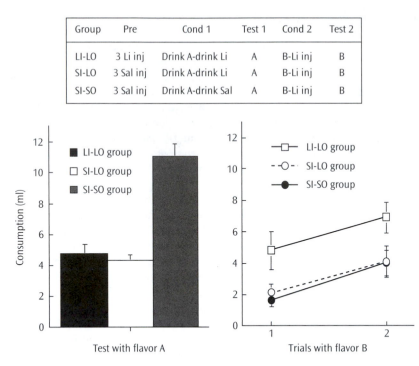

Group	Pre	Cond 1	Test 1	Cond 2	Test 2
LI-LO	3 Li inj	Drink A-drink Li	A	B-Li inj	B
SI-LO	3 Sal inj	Drink A-drink Li	A	B-Li inj	B
SI-SO	3 Sal inj	Drink A-drink Sal	A	B-Li inj	B

Figure 4.8. Design and test results of the experiment by De Brugada et al. (2004, Experiment 1b). Test 1, with flavor A, was given after rats in the LI-LO and SI-LO groups had experienced A prior to drinking LiCl (Li) (Cond 1). Test 2, with flavor B, was given after all rats had experienced B followed by an injection of LiCl (Cond 2). A and B were solutions of saccharin and vinegar, counterbalanced. Rats in the LI-LO group had received three LiCl injections (inj) during preexposure (Pre). Abbreviations in group labels: L = lithium; S = saline; I = injected; O = oral administration.

rather than LiCl after drinking flavor A in conditioning was included to confirm that oral consumption of lithium could indeed serve as an effective US in this procedure.

The results of a test trial with flavor A are presented in the lower left panel of Figure 4.8. The control group that did not experience lithium on the conditioning trial (group SI-SO) drank A readily, whereas the SI-LO control group showed a marked aversion, thus demonstrating the effectiveness of this conditioning procedure. The important result, however, is that for the LI-LO group. These subjects showed no less of an aversion than group SI-LO; that is, prior experience of injections of LiCl produced no US-preexposure effect when the US during conditioning was administered orally rather than by injection. The critical role of injection-related cues was confirmed by a further test. After the subjects had received the test with flavor A they all (see Figure 4.8) experienced a standard flavor aversion conditioning trial

in which consumption of a new flavor (B) was followed by an injection of LiCl. The results of the subsequent tests of consumption of B are shown in the lower right panel of Figure 4.8. On these tests, both control groups showed a strong aversion, whereas that shown by the LI-LO group was markedly less. In this case, then, the US-preexposure effect was obtained. The conclusion prompted by this pattern of results seems clear—prior exposure to (injections of) LiCl retards subsequent flavor aversion learning only when the US is delivered by injection; the US-preexposure effect seen in this situation is entirely a consequence of blocking by injection-related cues.

Conclusions

The general conclusions justified by the results discussed so far can be stated briefly. First, the effects produced by administration of LiCl to the rat will support conditioning not just to flavors, but to a range of exteroceptive cues. These include the physical context (the cage) in which the effects are experienced and also the cues that arise from the procedure of giving an intraperitoneal injection. The associative strength acquired by these cue will block subsequent flavor aversion conditioning resulting in the US-preexposure effect. When the physical context is novel during preexposure (and the test for aversion learning is given elsewhere) contextual (cage) cues contribute to the blocking effect. When the context is familiar, injection-related cues appear to have the dominant role. In no case does habituation (or the development of tolerance) appear to be involved—injections of LiCl that produce the US-preexposure effect do not result in a reduced UR (Figure 4.2) and do not produce any US-preexposure effect when conditioning is achieved by oral administration of LiCl (Figure 4.8).

HABITUATION RECONSIDERED

In spite of what has just been said, there are features of the results discussed in the previous section that might make us want to think again about the role of habituation. Specifically, the fact that contextual (including injection-related) cues can come to function as CSs for nausea complicates interpretation of the habituation test of De Brugada et al. (2003a), presented in Figure 4.2. This study used postinjection suppression of consumption as its measure, and it demonstrated that the size of this response was not influenced by experience of prior injections of LiCl. The conclusion that no habituation had occurred rests, however, on the assumption that this response is a simple UR, something that we now have reason to doubt. Since contextual cues can acquire associative strength, preexposure trials are conditioning trials, and the response shown on the test trial will be combination of the UR evoked by the injection on that trial and the CR elicited by contextual cues.

Symonds and Hall (2002) have investigated this matter directly. They demonstrated that the immediate effects of an injection of LiCl were enhanced when these were experienced in a context that had previously been paired with nausea. They concluded that the suppression of consumption seen in these circumstances reflected a summation of the UR with the CR

to the context. What follows is that the development a CR over a series on injections might act to obscure any loss of the UR produced by habituation—that the performance of the Pre group in the experiment by De Brugada et al. (2003a) might indicate not the absence of habituation, but the development of a CR that compensates for the habituation effect. (Indeed, it is quite possible that in some circumstances the development of the CR may more than just compensate, and the summation of CR and UR will make the net effect of a later injection more powerful than that of an earlier one. Symonds and Hall, 2002, offered this as an explanation for the increase in the severity of posttreatment nausea reported by some chemotherapy patients; see also Stockhorst et al., 1998.)

In order to assess the role of habituation it is necessary to have a test procedure that avoids these complications—a test that reflects just the UR and is not contaminated by the CR. The lithium-drinking procedure of De Brugada et al. (2004) can provide what is needed. Here, since the preexposure procedure is carried out in the home cage, the only contextual cues that are of importance are the injection-related cues. These will acquire strength, but this will not be relevant if the LiCl on test is administered orally. The response evoked by such a dose of LiCl may be taken, therefore, to be a pure UR. How is it influenced, if at all, by prior experience of LiCl?

This issue has been addressed in an experiment by De Brugada, González, Gil, and Hall (2005). The critical features of their experimental design are shown in Figure 4.9. In this study the experimental group (the E group in the table) received six injections of LiCl in the preexposure phase (earlier work, see De Brugada et al., 2004, having indicated that habituation effects might be difficult to obtain with fewer preexposure trials). Control subjects were injected with saline during this phase. On the UR test the E group and one of the control groups (C-1) drank a LiCl solution and then were given immediate access to a novel flavor (A). The other control group (C-2) was given A after drinking saline. It was expected that suppression of consumption of A would be seen in rats that had just drunk LiCl; the question of interest was whether the degree of suppression would be influenced by preexposure to LiCl. The results, amounts of flavor A consumed by the three groups, are displayed on the left of the lower left panel of Figure 4.9. They

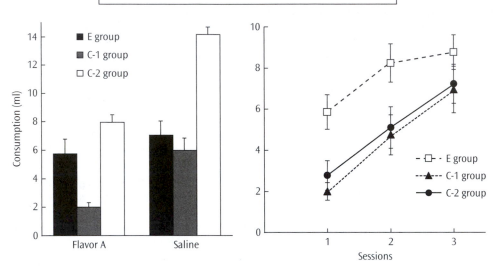

Group	Preexposure	UR Test	Test Sal	Cond	CR Test
E	6 Li inj	Drink Li -- A	Sal	B-Li inj	B
C-1	6 Sal inj	Drink Li -- A	Sal	B-Li inj	B
C-2	6 Sal inj	Drink Sal -- A	Sal	B-Li inj	B

Figure 4.9. Design and test results of the experiment by De Brugada et al. (2005, Experiment 2). The lower left panel shows scores for the UR test (consumption of flavor A) given after consumption of LiCl (Li) in groups E and C-1, and for a test with saline (Sal) given 1 day later. Subjects in group C-2 drank saline rather than LiCl on the UR test. Rats in group E had received preexposure consisting of six injections (inj) of LiCl. The lower right panel shows consumption of flavor B (the CR test) given after conditioning (Cond) in which, for all subjects, drinking B was followed by an injection of LiCl.

show that prior consumption of LiCl resulted in a suppression of consumption of A; the C-1 group drank much less of A than did the C-2 group. But this effect was much attenuated in rats given preexposure to LiCl—the E group drank more than the C-1 group—in other words, habituation was obtained.

The results of the first phase of this experiment establish, for the first time, that habituation to LiCl can occur. It remains to determine what role such habituation might play in the US-preexposure effect. This was the purpose of the subsequent stages of the experiment. The first of these consisted of a test in which the rats were given access to a saline solution. It may be recalled that Loy and Hall (2002) have shown that drinking LiCl establishes a conditioned aversion to salty tastes. This means that the trial labeled UR Test in the table, not only served to

test the UR to flavor A but also constituted a conditioning trial for the groups that drank LiCl (groups E and C-1). And indeed, these groups showed an aversion to saline in the subsequent test (see lower left panel of the figure), whereas the C-2 group drank it readily. But the result of central interest for our present concern is that there was no difference between the E group and the C-1 group in the degree of aversion they showed. The preexposure given to the E group appears to produce habituation to the effects of LiCl (the UR test), but it does not result in retarded conditioning (i.e., does not produce a US-preexposure effect).

The final phase of the experiment confirmed that a US-preexposure effect can be obtained in this training preparation, provided the blocking mechanism is permitted to operate. As Figure 4.9 shows, all the rats were given standard flavor aversion conditioning in which consumption of a new flavor (B) was followed by an injection of LiCl. The results of three test trials with B are shown in the lower right panel of the figure. Now the two control groups both show strong aversions, whereas that shown by the E group was much less. This outcome confirms the earlier finding of De Brugada et al. (2004)—preexposure to injections of LiCl will produce the US-preexposure effect, but only when injection-related cues are present in the conditioning phase.

Previous studies (such as those by De Brugada et al., 2003a, 2004) have shown that the US-preexposure effect can be obtained in the absence of any sign of habituation. The experiment just described allows us to take the argument a step further. Clearly, when habituation does not occur it cannot be responsible for the US-preexposure effect. In this experiment, however, we have been successful in obtaining evidence of habituation, allowing us to ask whether habituation contributes to the US-preexposure effect in this case. And the answer appears to be no—when blocking by contextual (injection-related) cues is eliminated, the aversion acquired by preexposed subjects is as great as that shown by controls.

SUMMARY AND CONCLUSIONS

I began this chapter by noting that the UR of nausea appears not to habituate, but that preexposure to a nausea-inducing treatment (a series of injections of LiCl for the rats), nonetheless, reliably reduces the effectiveness of nausea to serve as a US in flavor aversion conditioning. An explanation for both these facts can be provided by the application of standard principles of associative learning. Preexposure to LiCl injections is itself a conditioning procedure that allows contextual cues (those that characterize the place in which the injection is given plus those associated with the injection procedure itself) to become established as CSs for nausea. This has two relevant consequences.

First, it means that our standard tests for habituation, which assess the UR evoked by an injection of LiCl, will be "contaminated" by the fact that the injection procedure will also evoke a CR that can summate with the UR. When this effect is controlled for, a habituation effect (albeit not very powerful, and requiring extensive preexposure)

can be obtained. Second, it provides, in itself, an explanation for the US-preexposure effect—the associative strength acquired by contextual cues will be able to block acquisition during flavor conditioning and thus retard the acquisition of an aversion.

What follows is that both of the possibilities mentioned earlier as explanations for the US-preexposure effect (i.e., habituation of the reinforcing power of the US and blocking by context) remain viable. The experimental evidence that has been discussed has amply confirmed the reality of the blocking-by-context effect. The role of habituation, however, is less secure. Not only do we obtain the US-preexposure effect when there is no sign of habituation but also as the last experiment discussed has shown, the effect can fail to occur even in the presence of habituation. This last effect is particularly intriguing theoretically and demands further study. At the very least, it requires us to acknowledge that the event described simply as "the US" in these experiments is rather more complex than this label implies. Standard associative theory (e.g., Wagner, 1981) has assumed that the application of a US activates a single representational node, and that the level of activity in this node determines both the magnitude of the UR and the reinforcing power of the US. The present results may indicate the need to distinguish two nodes, one susceptible to habituation by repeated US presentation and responsible for the UR, and one responsible for conditioned suppression of consumption and susceptible to associative modulation (and thus blocking effects).

It remains to be seen whether these conclusions, derived as they are from a single specific instance of the US-preexposure effect, will have general applicability. A clear and reliable effect has been repeatedly demonstrated with electric shock as the US for rats trained in the conditioned suppression (conditioned emotional response) paradigm. Blocking by context (i.e., by cage cues—there is no equivalent of injection-related cues when the US is a shock) may well play a role here, but the evidence is far from compelling. And the observation that the perceived intensity of a shock (and the UR it evokes) declines substantially and rapidly with repeated applications increases the plausibility of an explanation in terms of habituation. It will be an irony if the US-preexposure effect observed in this procedure (much used in the development of modern associative theory) turns out to be nonassociative in nature, whereas that obtained in nausea-based learning (said by some to be a unique form) turns out to be explicable in terms of standard associative principles.

Note

1. We will examine the validity of this assumption later in the chapter.

References

Aguado, L., De Brugada, I., & Hall, G. (1997). Effects of a retention interval on the US-preexposure phenomenon in flavor aversion learning. *Learning and Motivation, 28,* 311–332.

Batson, J. D. (1983). Effects of repeated lithium injections on temperature, activity, and flavor conditioning in rats. *Animal Learning & Behavior, 11,* 199–204.

Batson, J. D., & Best, P. J. (1979). Drug-preexposure effects in flavor-aversion learning: Associative interference by conditioned environmental stimuli. *Journal of Experimental Psychology: Animal Behavior Processes, 5,* 273–283.

Best, M. R., Brown, E. R., & Sowell, M. K. (1984). Taste-mediated potentiation of noningestional stimuli in rats. *Learning and Motivation, 15,* 244–258.

Boakes, R. A., Westbrook, R. F., & Barnes, B. W. (1992). Potentiation by a taste of toxicosis-based context conditioning. *Quarterly Journal of Experimental Psychology, 45B,* 303–325.

Boakes, R. A., Westbrook, R. F., Elliott, M., & Swinbourne, A. L. (1997). Context dependency of conditioned aversions to water and sweet tastes. *Journal of Experimental Psychology: Animal Behavior Processes, 23,* 55–67.

Bonardi, C., Honey, R. C., & Hall, G. (1990). Context specificity of conditioning in flavor-aversion learning: Extinction and blocking tests. *Animal Learning & Behavior, 18,* 229–237.

Cannon, D. S., Berman, R. F., Baker, T. B., & Atkinson, C. A. (1975). Effect of preconditioning unconditioned stimulus experience on learned taste aversions. *Journal of Experimental Psychology: Animal Behavior Processes, 1,* 270–284.

Cole, K. C., VanTilburg, D., Burch-Vernon, A., & Riccio, D. C. (1996). The importance of context in the US preexposure effect in CTA: Novel versus latently inhibited contextual stimuli. *Learning and Motivation, 27,* 362–374.

Dacanay, R. J., & Riley, A. L. (1982). The UCS preexposure effect in taste aversion learning: Tolerance and blocking are drug specific. *Animal Learning & Behavior, 10,* 91–96.

De Brugada, I., & Aguado, L. (2000). El efecto de preexposición al EI en la aversión gustativa condicionada: Papel relativo del contexto y de las claves de inyección [The effect of preexposure to the US in flavor-aversion conditioning: The role of context and injection cues]. *Psicológica, 21,* 23–37.

De Brugada, I., González, F., & Cándido, A. (2003a). Repeated administration of LiCl produces an unconditioned stimulus preexposure effect in backward excitatory CTA but not habituation of the unconditioned increment in neophobia. *Behavioural Processes, 60,* 227–223.

De Brugada, I., González, F., & Cándido, A. (2003b). The role of injection cues in the associative control of the US pre-exposure effect in flavour aversion learning. *Quarterly Journal of Experimental Psychology, 56B,* 241–252.

De Brugada, I., González, F., Gil, M., & Hall, G. (2005). The role of habituation of the response to LiCl in the US-preexposure effect. *Learning & Behavior, 33,* 363–370.

De Brugada, I., Hall, G., & Symonds, M. (2004). The US-preexposure effect in lithium-induced flavor-aversion conditioning is a consequence of blocking by injection cues. *Journal of Experimental Psychology: Animal Behavior Processes, 30,* 58–66.

Domjan, M. (1977). Selective suppression of drinking during a limited period following aversive drug treatment in rats. *Journal of Experimental Psychology: Animal Behavior Processes, 3,* 66–76.

Domjan, M., & Best, M. R. (1980). Interference with ingestional learning produced by preexposure to the unconditioned stimulus. *Learning and Motivation, 11,* 522–537.

Garcia, J. (1989). Food for Tolman: Cognition and cathexis in concert. In T. Archer & L.-G. Nilsson (Eds.), *Aversion, avoidance, and anxiety* (pp. 45–85). Hillsdale, NJ: Lawrence Erlbaum.

Garcia, J., Brett, L. P., & Rusiniak, K. W. (1989). Limits of Darwinian conditioning. In S. B. Klein & R. R. Mowrer (Eds.), *Contemporary learning theories: Instrumental conditioning and the impact of biological constraints on learning* (pp. 181–203). Hillsdale, NJ: Lawrence Erlbaum.

Kamin, L. J. (1969). Predictability, surprise, attention, and conditioning. In B. A. Campbell & R. M. Church (Eds.), *Punishment and aversive behavior* (pp. 279–296). New York, NY: Appleton-Century-Crofts.

Limebeer, C. L., Hall, G., & Parker, L. A. (2006). Exposure to a lithium-paired context elicits gaping in rats: A model of anticipatory nausea. *Physiology & Behavior, 88*, 398–403.

Loy, I., Alvarez, R., Rey, V., & Lopez, M. (1993). Context–US associations rather than occasion-setting in taste aversion learning. *Learning and Motivation, 24*, 55–72.

Loy, I., & Hall, G. (2002). Taste aversion after ingestion of lithium chloride: An associative analysis. *Quarterly Journal of Experimental Psychology, 55B*, 365–380.

Lubow, R. E. (1989). *Latent inhibition and conditioned attention theory.* New York, NY: Cambridge University Press.

Miller, J. S., Jagielo, J. A., & Spear, N. E. (1993). The influence of retention interval on the US preexposure effect: Changes in contextual blocking over time. *Learning and Motivation, 24*, 376–394.

Mitchell, C., & Heyes, C. (1996). Simultaneous overshadowing and potentiation of taste and contextual cues by a second taste in toxicosis conditioning. *Learning and Motivation, 27*, 58–72.

Parker, L. A. (2003). Taste avoidance and taste aversion: Evidence for two different processes. *Learning & Behavior, 31*, 165–172.

Pearce, J. M., & Hall, G. (1980). A model for Pavlovian learning: Variations in the effectiveness of conditioned but not of unconditioned stimuli. *Psychological Review, 87*, 532–552.

Puente, G. P., Cannon, D. S., Best, M. R., & Carrell, L. E. (1988). Occasion setting of fluid ingestion by contextual cues. *Learning and Motivation, 27*, 58–72.

Randich, A., & LoLordo, V. M. (1979). Associative and nonassociative theories of the UCS preexposure phenomenon: Implications for Pavlovian conditioning. *Psychological Bulletin, 86*, 523–548.

Rescorla, R. A., & Wagner, A. R. (1972). A theory of Pavlovian conditioning: Variations in the effectiveness of reinforcement and nonreinforcement. In A. H. Black & W. F. Prokasy (Eds.), *Classical conditioning II: Current research and theory* (pp. 64–99). New York, NY: Appleton-Century-Crofts.

Riley, A. L., & Simpson, G. R. (2001). The attenuating effects of drug preexposure on taste aversion conditioning: Generality, experimental parameters, underlying mechanisms, and implications for drug use and abuse. In R. R. Mowrer & S. B. Klein (Eds.), *Handbook of contemporary learning theories* (pp. 505–559). Mahwah, NJ: Lawrence Erlbaum.

Rodriguez, M., Lopez, M., Symonds, M., & Hall, G. (2000). Lithium-induced context aversion in rats as a model of anticipatory nausea in humans. *Physiology & Behavior, 71*, 571–579.

Rudy, J. W., Iwens, J., & Best, P. J. (1977). Pairing novel exteroceptive cues and illness reduces-illness induced taste aversions. *Journal of Experimental Psychology: Animal Behavior Processes, 3*, 14–25.

Stockhorst, U., Wiener, J. A., Klosterhalfen, S., Klosterhalfen, W., Aul, C., & Steingrüber, H.-J. (1998). Effects of overshadowing on conditioned nausea in cancer patients: An experimental study. *Physiology & Behavior, 64*, 743–753.

Symonds, M., & Hall, G. (1997). Contextual conditioning with lithium-induced nausea as the US: Evidence from a blocking procedure. *Learning and Motivation, 28*, 200–215.

Symonds, M., & Hall, G. (1999). Overshadowing not potentiation of illness-based contextual conditioning by a novel taste. *Animal Learning & Behavior, 27*, 379–390.

Symonds, M., & Hall, G. (2002). Postinjection suppression of drinking is modified by the presence of conditioned contextual cues: Implications for both anticipatory and post-treatment nausea in humans. *Animal Learning & Behavior, 30*, 355–362.

Symonds, M., Hall, G., Lopez, M., Loy, I., Ramos, A., & Rodriguez, M. (1998). Is fluid consumption necessary for the formation of context-illness associations? An evaluation using consumption and blocking tests. *Learning and Motivation, 29*, 168–183.

Tsukamoto, G., & Adachi, A. (1994). Neural responses of rat area postrema to stimuli producing nausea. *Journal of the Autonomic Nervous System, 49*, 55–60.

Wagner, A. R. (1981). SOP: A model of automatic memory processing in animal behavior. In N. E. Spear & R. R. Miller (Eds.), *Information processing in animals: Memory mechanisms* (pp. 5–47). Hillsdale, NJ: Lawrence Erlbaum.

Westbrook, R. F., & Brookes, N. (1988). Potentiation and blocking of conditioned flavour and context aversions. *Quarterly Journal of Experimental Psychology, 40B*, 3–30.

Willner, J. A. (1978). Blocking of a taste aversion by prior pairings of exteroceptive stimuli with illness. *Learning and Motivation, 9*, 125–140.

5

Drug-Induced Suppression of Conditioned Stimulus Intake: Reward, Aversion, and Addiction

PATRICIA S. GRIGSON, ROBERT C. TWINING, CHRISTOPHER S. FREET, ROBERT A. WHEELER, AND RASTAFA I. GEDDES

According to figures provided by the National Institute on Drug Abuse http://www.nida.nih.gov/Infofacts/index.html, in 2004, 34.2 million Americans used cocaine at least once, 7.8 million Americans used crack at least once, 2.4 million Americans used heroin (87% under the age of 26), and there were 450,000 current users of ecstasy. There were 14.6 million users of marijuana in 2004 and 70.3 million Americans smoking cigarettes. These large numbers are even more problematic because many become addicted and addiction is not resolved following even long periods of abstinence. In fact, addiction is a disease of chronic relapse (Leshner & Koob, 1999), costing society hundreds of billions of dollars each year as the addict repeatedly cycles from addiction to abstinence, withdrawal, drug-seeking, and relapse.

Along with society, the addict and his or her family are also adversely affected as addiction is associated with an apparent devaluation of, and inattention to, natural rewards. According to *DSM-IV*, substance abuse and dependence involve a failure to fulfill major obligations at work, school, or home, the giving up of important social, occupational, or recreational activities, and continued drug use despite recurrent physical, legal, social, or psychological problems. These findings are substantiated by published data showing that the human addict weighs less, is more often absent from work, fails to respond appropriately to monetary rewards, and more often has his or her children removed from the home due to neglect (Goldstein et al., 2006; Jones, Casswell, & Zhang, 1995; Nair et al., 1997; Santolaria-Fernandez et al., 1995).

Addiction, then, is a two-part problem involving both chronic relapse and the devaluation of natural rewards. There are several critical animal models for the study of craving and relapse (Grimm, Hope, Wise, & Shaham, 2001; Neisewander et al., 2000; See, 2002; Weiss et al., 2000). There are, however, no recognized animal models for the systematic study of drug-induced devaluation of natural rewards. The data outlined below demonstrate that the long-standing model of drug-induced conditioned taste aversion (CTA) likely has been misinterpreted and actually serves as the first animal model for the study of drug-induced devaluation of natural rewards (Grigson, 1997). In addition, the natural reward cue also signals the availability of the drug and, as such, the paradigm serves as a model for the study of cue-induced craving as well. Finally, the central nervous system (CNS) effects of these agents are not benign and are, therefore, likely offset by a myriad of conditioned compensatory (preparatory) responses. Thus, while evidence indicates that drugs of abuse do not support the development of a classic CTA, our data suggest that these drugs can support the development of a conditioned compensatory state, such as cue-induced craving/withdrawal that is, itself, aversive

(McDonald, Parker, & Siegel, 1997) and predicts drug-seeking and drug-taking behavior (Wheeler et al., 2008; Grigson & Twining, 2002). This outcome is best accounted for by the reinforcing/addictive properties of the drug.

CTA AND DRUGS OF ABUSE: THE PARADOX

A CTA occurs when rats avoid intake of a gustatory conditioned stimulus (CS) after it has been paired with an aversive, illness-inducing agent such as lithium chloride (LiCl) or X-radiation (Garcia, Kimmeldorf, & Koelling, 1955; Nachman & Ashe, 1973; Smith, Morris, & Hendricks, 1964). These CTAs are pervasive and they occur with all gustatory CSs tested, so long as the tastant is salient and, preferably, novel (Kalat, 1974; Kalat & Rozen, 1970). Not long after CTAs were discovered with emetic agents serving as the unconditioned stimulus (US), Le Magnen (Le Magnen, 1969) reported that rats also avoid intake of a similar gustatory CS when paired with a drug of abuse. Since this time, drug-induced suppression of CS intake has been found with a range of abused substances including morphine (Cappell, LeBlanc, & Endrenyi, 1973; Miller, Kelly, Neisewander, McCoy, & Bardo, 1990; Sherman, Pickman, Rice, Liebeskind, & Holman, 1980), cocaine (Glowa, Shaw, & Riley, 1994), amphetamine (Cappell & LeBlanc, 1971), ethanol, flurazepam, chlordiazepoxide (Cappell et al., 1973; Lester, Nachman, & Le Magnen, 1970; Vogel & Nathan, 1975), nicotine (Castane, Soria, Ledent, Maldonado, & Valverde, 2006), and amobarbital and phenobarbital (Vogel & Nathan, 1975). Indeed, the only drug found not to support the reduction in CS intake was heroin (Switzman, Hunt, & Amit, 1981) and our data now show that heroin is no exception (Grigson, Twining, & Carelli, 2000). Rats, then, avoid intake of a taste cue following pairings with all drugs of abuse tested, across a range of doses (Parker, 1991), and when administered intraperitoneally (IP), subcutaneously (SC), intravenously (IV), or, in some cases, even when administered directly into the nucleus accumbens (NAc; Bechara & van der Kooy, 1985; Cappell & LeBlanc, 1971; Mucha & Herz, 1986; Shoaib & Stolerman, 1995; Wise, Yokel, & DeWit, 1976).

This phenomenon, which is both robust and pervasive, was interpreted as a CTA as early as 1970 (Lester et al., 1970). Thus, here began the paradox—the paradox whereby highly rewarding drugs of abuse, drugs that rats and man readily self-administer (van Ree, 1979), also were shown to have aversive properties in the CTA paradigm. Indeed, quintessential evidence of this paradox was provided when several laboratories showed that avoidance of the taste cue (CTA, if you will) was, in the same experiment, accompanied by increased speed in a runway for the drug (White, Sklar, & Amit, 1977), more time spent in the drug-paired compartment in a conditioned place preference task (Reicher & Holman, 1977), and avid self-administration of the drug (Wise et al., 1976). Since this time, additional evidence has been provided for the aversive properties of addictive agents (Bechara & van der Kooy, 1985; Blanchard & Blanchard, 1999; Ettenberg & Geist, 1991), and the conditioned aversion has been attributed to a range of factors including stimulus novelty, drug shyness, fear (see Parker, Chapter 6), and even positive conditioned suppression (Goudie, 1979; Hunt & Amit, 1987; Parker, 2003; Stolerman & D'Mello, 1981).

Conditioned Suppression of CS Intake: Anticipatory Contrast

About a decade after drugs of abuse were found to support CTA learning, Flaherty reported that rats avoid intake of a saccharin CS when paired, in once daily sessions, with a highly preferred 32% sucrose solution (Flaherty & Checke, 1982). This phenomenon was referred to as an *anticipatory* contrast effect because reduced intake of the saccharin cue was thought to be due to anticipation of the availability of the preferred sucrose reward in the very near future. Indeed, in a subsequent study, Flaherty and Rowan (1985) showed that the reduction in intake of the taste cue depended on the value of the anticipated 32% sucrose reward, not on the memory of the 32% sucrose solution received 24 h earlier. Anticipatory contrast effects, then, depend on the development of a Pavlovian associative relationship between the saccharin CS and the sucrose US (Flaherty & Grigson, 1988). The lesser reward CS is avoided in anticipation of the imminent availability of the preferred reward US (Flaherty, 1996; Flaherty & Grigson, 1988). This effect can occur whether the rats are food deprived or free feeding (Flaherty, Grigson, Checke, & Hnat, 1991) and regardless of whether the preferred reward does or does not have caloric value (Flaherty & Rowan, 1986).

Reward Comparison:
A Solution to the Paradox?

Given this information, we reinterpreted published data showing that rats avoid intake of a taste cue when paired with a drug of abuse. Specifically, we hypothesized that, if one were to view drugs of abuse as rewarding, then the resultant reduction in CS intake is simply another form of anticipatory contrast (Grigson, 1997). Thus, we proposed that rats avoid intake of a drug-associated taste cue because the value of the taste cue pales in comparison to the powerful drug reward anticipated in the very near future.

Drugs of Abuse: Evidence
against a CTA Account

Despite the conditioned reduction in CS intake (i.e., the operational definition of a CTA), other data suggest that these drugs are rewarding and that the resultant reduction in CS intake is not like that mediated by LiCl. Specifically, drugs of abuse are readily self-administered by humans and other animals (for review, see van Ree, 1979) and, unlike LiCl, they sustain the development of conditioned place preferences (Bardo, Miller, & Neisewander, 1984; Blander, Hunt, Blair, & Amit, 1984; Katz & Gormezano, 1979; Reilly, Grigson, & Norgren, 1993). Further, while LiCl suppresses both instrumental and consummatory responding (White et al., 1977), drugs of abuse, as discussed, simultaneously augment instrumental performance and suppress conditioned consummatory behavior. Thus, rats bar press to self-administer apomorphine while reducing intake of a saccharin solution that predicts its availability (Wise et al., 1976); they increase running speed in a runway for morphine, but simultaneously decrease intake of an associated food cue (White et al., 1977); and they increase the amount of time spent in an amphetamine-associated environment, but decrease intake of the gustatory CS that predicts the drug's administration (Reicher & Holman, 1977). Finally, Parker (1984, 1988, 1991, 1993, 1995) used the taste reactivity test of Grill and Norgren (1978) to assess the palatability of gustatory CSs and dissociated LiCl-induced CTAs from the suppressive effects of abused substances. LiCl-induced CTAs were associated with a decrease in ingestive responses, such as tongue protrusions, paw licking, and mouth movements,

and with an increase in active rejection responses, such as gapes, chin rubs, and paw treading. The suppressive effects of drugs of abuse, in contrast, were accompanied only by a decrease in ingestive responses following the intraoral (IO) delivery of the CS, with no clear increase in active rejection responses (Parker, 1984, 1988, 1993; Parker & Carvell, 1986). These findings led Parker (1988) to conclude that "positively reinforcing drugs may produce a different type of CTA than do drugs which are not positively reinforcing."

DRUGS OF ABUSE: EVIDENCE
IN SUPPORT OF THE REWARD
COMPARISON HYPOTHESIS

The reward comparison hypothesis states that rats avoid intake of a taste cue when paired with a drug of abuse because the value of the taste cue pales in anticipation of the highly rewarding properties of the drug. We reasoned that if this hypothesis was correct, then drug-induced suppression of CS intake should be sensitive to factors that affect anticipatory contrast. LiCl-induced CTAs, on the other hand, should be relatively impervious to these factors/manipulations.

Nature and Intensity of the CS

The suppressive effects of sucrose and drugs of abuse, but not LiCl, are affected by the nature of the gustatory CS. In the anticipatory contrast paradigm, rats avoid intake of a sweet-tasting saccharin CS when it predicts access to a preferred sucrose reward, but they will not avoid (in fact they prefer) a more neutral water cue when it predicts access to the same sucrose reward (Flaherty, Turovsky, & Krauss, 1994). Likewise, rats avoid intake of the same sweet-tasting saccharin cue when it predicts access to morphine or cocaine, but they fail to avoid intake of a similarly associated, but more neutral, salt CS (Grigson, 1997). When paired with LiCl-induced illness, on the other hand, rats avoid intake of both the palatable saccharin and the more neutral salt cue (Grigson, 1997). This saccharin/salt dissociation between abused substances and LiCl has been replicated in mice (Risinger & Boyce, 2002) and was shown in rats previously (Bevins, Delzer, & Bardo, 1996), even when using a very potent 2% NaCl solution as the CS. In this case, however, indirect evidence for suppression to the salt CS was obtained when examined using a second-order saccharin cue. Suppression, however, may have developed because of the intrinsic value of the second-order saccharin cue.

Later, Sorge et al. (2002) challenged our hypothesis that drug-induced suppression of CS intake depended on the rewarding value of the taste cue by demonstrating that rats failed to avoid intake of a salt CS following salt–morphine pairings even when the salt solution was made highly palatable by the induction of a furosemide-induced sodium appetite. Indeed, if anything, both the intake data and the taste reactivity data showed that the induction of the sodium appetite led to the development of a conditioned *preference* for the morphine-associated salt cue, not to a conditioned reduction in CS intake as would have been predicted by the reward comparison hypothesis. The same sodium appetite did not alter the taste reactivity behavior toward the LiCl-paired salt solution, which continued to elicit aversive orofacial responses (e.g., gapes).

These data, while taken as strong evidence against the reward comparison hypothesis are, upon closer analysis, actually consistent with the anticipatory contrast literature. That is, while anticipatory contrast effects generally increase in magnitude with an increase in the concentration (i.e., value) of the gustatory CS from neutral to palatable (Flaherty et al., 1994), the anticipatory contrast effect actually reverses to a conditioned increase in CS intake when the value of the CS approaches that of the US. This pattern of behavior has been shown with both saccharin and sucrose concentration pairs (Flaherty & Rowan, 1986; Flaherty et al., 1991). By this analysis, rats would have demonstrated an increase, rather than a decrease, in responding for the morphine-associated salt CS following the induction of the sodium appetite because the salt CS gained enough reinforcement value to now approach that of the drug US. Support for this interpretation is provided by the fact that Sorge et al. used an extremely high dose of furosemide (100 mg/kg). The minimal dose of furosemide found effective to induce a robust sodium appetite is approximately 5 mg/kg (Lundy, Jr., Blair, Horvath, & Norgren, 2003). The highest dose used in the Lundy et al. study was 25 mg/kg, which is standard. In contrast, Sorge et al. used a dose that was 4 times greater than the highest dose used by Lundy et al. and 20 times greater than the minimum dose employed. The rats in the Sorge et al. study, then, would have been

extremely sodium deficient, making salt a highly rewarding stimulus—one that likely approached the otherwise powerful drug of abuse.

Finally, while anticipatory contrast effects vary as a function of the relative value of the CS and the US (Flaherty et al., 1991, 1994), recent unpublished data from our laboratory show that the CS actually need not be rewarding at all. It can, in fact, be aversive. Thus, we have found that fluid deprived rats also will greatly avoid intake of a fairly unpalatable malic acid CS when paired with either morphine or cocaine. Although interesting, this finding posed a bit of an interpretative problem for the reward comparison hypothesis. Thus, it was essential that we test whether rats might also avoid intake of an aversive malic acid CS when paired with a putatively rewarding 1.0-M sucrose solution. The results of this study showed that they did (unpublished data). In sum, rats will avoid intake of a taste cue when paired with a drug of abuse and the degree of suppression of CS intake depends upon the nature of the CS. Specifically, this general finding appears to depend upon the relative value of the CS and the drug US, with suppression augmented with an aversive CS, reduced with a neutral CS, augmented again as the CS gains in value, but finally reduced (or even reversed) as the value of the CS approaches that of the US. LiCl-induced CTAs, on the other hand, are marked with all CSs tested and differ little as a function of concentration of the CS (Ellins & Kennedy, 1995). If the rat can detect the CS, it will reject the CS if the CS has been paired with LiCl-induced malaise. This is not true of drugs of abuse.

Deprivation State of the Rat and Caloric Value of the CS

Later papers showed that the suppressive effects of sucrose and drugs of abuse, but to a lesser extent LiCl, are affected by deprivation state (Flaherty et al., 1991; Gomez & Grigson, 1999; Grigson, Lyuboslavsky, Tanase, & Wheeler, 1999). In anticipatory contrast, rats will avoid intake of a saccharin cue following saccharin–sucrose pairings whether tested in a nondeprived or a food-deprived state. The effects are, however, slightly smaller when tested in food-deprived rats, as food deprivation drives intake of even the noncaloric saccharin cue. This mild disruptive effect of food deprivation in contrast, however, becomes glaring when a low concentration of sucrose, rather than saccharin, serves as the taste cue. In this case, hungry rats will suppress intake of the sucrose cue only if access to the weak sucrose cue is *immediately* followed by access to the strong sucrose reward. If, on the other hand, the rats have to wait 5 min for access to the preferred sucrose US, then food-deprived rats will not forego access to a lesser, but still caloric, sucrose cue. A similar pattern was obtained with morphine, but not LiCl, in water-deprived rats. That is, water-deprived rats failed to suppress intake of a range of sucrose CSs when paired with a standard 15 mg/kg dose of morphine, but they suppressed intake of the same sucrose CSs when paired with LiCl (Grigson et al., 1999). Like water deprivation, food deprivation also served to reduce the magnitude of the suppressive effects of morphine, cocaine, and sucrose on intake of a saccharin CS. The suppressive effects of a matched dose of LiCl, on the other hand, were much more intransigent (Gomez & Grigson, 1999). Thus, as with the suppressive effects of a sucrose US, the suppressive effects of drugs of abuse are greatest when examined in a nondeprived state (Grigson, 2000; Grigson, Wheeler, Wheeler, & Ballard, 2001) and when using a noncaloric solution as the gustatory CS because deprivation of either food or water drives intake and, thereby, offsets the suppression of CS intake. In this light, it is interesting to note that fluid-deprived shrews, insectivores with very high metabolic rates, also fail to exhibit suppression of CS intake (in fact, they demonstrate what appears to be a conditioned preference) following pairings of saccharin or sucrose with amphetamine or morphine (Parker, Corrick, Limebeer, & Kwiatkowska, 2002; Parker, 2006).

Selectively Bred Strains

The suppressive effects of a rewarding sucrose US and cocaine, but not LiCl, are greater in drug-sensitive Lewis rats than in the less-sensitive Fischer 344 inbred strain. Lewis rats show a greater conditioned preference for a location that has been paired with morphine or cocaine than do Fischer 344 rats (Guitart, Beitner-Johnson, Marby, Kosten, & Nestler, 1992; Kosten, Miserendino, Chi, & Nestler, 1994), but see (Davis, Roma, Dominguez, & Riley, 2007). Compared to Fischer rats, Lewis rats also more readily self-administer cocaine, ethanol, and opiates (Ambrosio, Goldberg, & Elmer, 1995; George & Goldberg, 1989; Kosten et al., 1997; Suzuki, George, & Meisch, 1988). Once

having established stable self-administration, however, both strains of rat administer the drug at the same rate (Kosten et al., 1997). Together, these findings suggest that Lewis rats are more sensitive than Fischer rats to the rewarding properties of these drugs. This observation supports a specific prediction regarding the means by which drugs of abuse suppress intake of a gustatory CS. That is, if the suppressive effects of drugs of abuse are mediated by aversive properties (i.e., CTAs), then the degree of suppression by cocaine, for example, should not differ between the two strains of rats. If, on the other hand, rewarding drug properties mediate the suppression of CS intake, then the magnitude of cocaine-induced suppression should be greater in the drug-preferring Lewis rats. This is, in fact, what we found (see Figure 5.1, Grigson & Freet, 2000). The suppressive effects of cocaine and a rewarding sucrose US, but not LiCl, were greater in Lewis (Figure 5.1b) than Fischer rats (Figure 5.1a).

This finding is consistent with an earlier report on cocaine (Glowa et al., 1994), but opposite to the pattern reported for nicotine (Pescatore, Glowa, & Riley, 2005) or morphine. Regarding morphine, Lancellotti, Bayer, Glowa, Houghtling, and Riley (2001) found that morphine-induced suppression of CS intake was actually greater in Fischer than in Lewis rats. Recent data, however, may provide an explanation. Specifically, Wheeler et al. (2002) used the kappa agonist, spiradoline, and showed that Fischer rats are more sensitive to the aversive kappa-receptor-mediated properties of opiates than Lewis rats. The two strains, however, do not differ in their response to the suppressive effects of the μ agonist, DAMGO, when administered directly into the lateral ventricles (Liu & Grigson, 2005). Thus, Fischer rats may be exhibiting a CTA to the morphine US, as mediated by an increased sensitivity to kappa agonist activity, while Lewis rats are exhibiting a reward comparison effect. The reward comparison effect, in this particular case, is smaller in magnitude. Evidence in further support of this conclusion is provided in the following section.

Chronic Drug Treatment

A history of chronic morphine treatment exaggerates the suppressive effects of a rewarding sucrose US and cocaine, but not those induced by a matched dose of LiCl. The increase in drug sensitivity in Lewis rats is thought to be associated

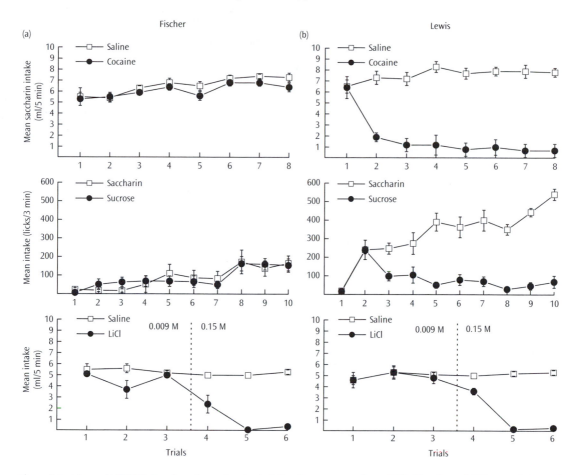

Figure 5.1. Mean (±SEM) intake of saccharin (ml/5 min, top panels or licks/3 min, middle panels) or of saline or LiCl (ml/5 min, bottom panels) for (a) Fischer or (b) Lewis rats following repeated pairings with saline or 10 mg/kg cocaine (top panels), saccharin or 1.0-M sucrose (middle panels), or with saline or LiCl-induced malaise (bottom panels). From "Drugs of abuse and reward comparison: A brief review," by Grigson, 2000, *Appetite, 35,* 89–91. Copyright 2000 Academic Press.

with a number of innate neurochemical characteristics in the dopaminergic pathway projecting from the ventral tegmental area (VTA) to the NAc. These include decreased tyrosine hydroxylase in the axon terminals of VTA neurons in the NAc, decreased neurofilament protein in the VTA, increased glial fibrillary acidic protein, suppressed G_i proteins, and enhanced adenylate cyclase and cyclic AMP-dependent protein kinase in the NAc (Beitner-Johnson, Guitart, & Nestler, 1991, 1992b, 1993; Guitart et al., 1992, 1993). These same neurochemical characteristics can be induced in Sprague-Dawley rats following chronic treatment with morphine (Beitner-Johnson, Guitart, & Nestler, 1992a; Beitner-Johnson & Nestler, 1993). Thus, we hypothesized that the exaggerated

cocaine- and sucrose-induced suppression seen in Lewis rats would be mimicked in Sprague-Dawley rats after chronic morphine treatment. The hypothesis proved correct (see Figure 5.2). Chronic treatment with morphine exaggerated the suppressive effects of an otherwise ineffective dose of cocaine and of a rewarding sucrose US in Sprague-Dawley rats. The suppressive effects of the aversive LiCl US, on the other hand, were not altered (Grigson et al., 2001).

NEUROCIRCUITRY

Recently, we have begun to use lesions, microdialysis, and electrophysiology to investigate the

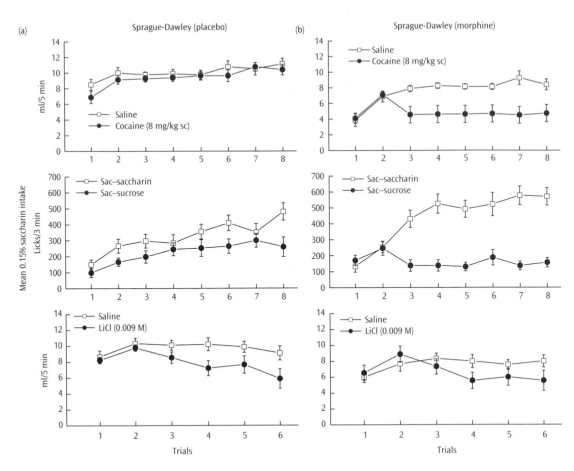

Figure 5.2. Mean (±SEM) intake of saccharin (ml/5 min, top and bottom panels or licks/3 min, middle panels) following repeated pairings with saline or a low 10 mg/kg dose of cocaine (top panels), 3-min access to saccharin or 1.0-M sucrose (middle panels), or an IP injection of saline or LiCl (0.009 M) in rats with a history of chronic treatment with (a) placebo or (b) morphine pellets. Redrawn from "Chronic morphine treatment exaggerates the suppressive effects of sucrose and cocaine, but not lithium chloride, on saccharin intake in Sprague-Dawley rats," by Grigson et al., 2000, *Behavioral Neuroscience, 115,* 403–416. Copyright 2000 American Psychological Association, Inc.

circuitry mediating drug-induced suppression of CS intake. Current evidence implicates the gustatory thalamus, the gustatory cortex, and dopaminergic transmission from the VTA to the NAc.

Neurocircuitry: Thalamus and Cortex

Lesions of the gustatory thalamus (THLX) also serve to dissociate the phenomena in Sprague-Dawley rats (Grigson, Lyuboslavsky, & Tanase, 2000; Reilly & Pritchard, 1996; Schroy et al., 2005). Bilateral electrolytic or ibotenic acid lesions of the gustatory thalamus have no impact on the development of a LiCl-induced CTA (Flynn, 1991; Reilly & Pritchard, 1996; Scalera, Grigson, &

Norgren, 1997). The same lesion does, however, fully disrupt avoidance of the same taste cue in the anticipatory contrast paradigm when predicting subsequent access to the preferred sucrose reward (Reilly, Bornovalova, & Trifunovic, 2004; Schroy et al., 2005). Given this dichotomy, we hypothesized that bilateral lesions of the gustatory thalamus also would serve to disrupt the suppressive effect of a drug of abuse on CS intake. This prediction was confirmed despite multiple pairings of a gustatory CS with a 15 mg/kg dose of morphine (Grigson, 2000; see Figure 5.3). The gustatory thalamus, then, appears to play a critical role in the comparison of a palatable taste cue with the memory of the preferred sucrose US or the drug US anticipated in the near future. A similar dissociation has been

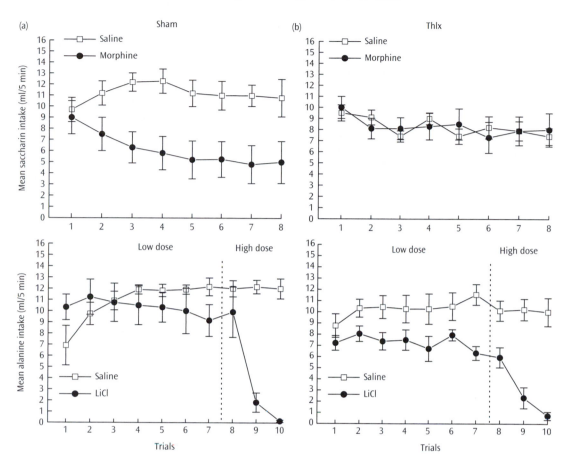

Figure 5.3. Mean (±SEM) intake (ml/5 min) of 0.15% saccharin (top panels) or 0.3-M alanine (bottom panels) following pairings with saline or 15 mg/kg morphine (top panels) or with saline or 0.009-M then high 0.15-M LiCl (bottom panels) in (a) Sham lesioned rats or (b) rats with electrophysiologically guided bilateral lesions of the gustatory thalamus (Thlx). From "Bilateral lesions of the gustatory thalamus disrupt morphine- but not LiCl-induced intake suppression in rats: evidence against the conditioned taste aversion hypothesis," by Grigson et al., 2000, *Brain Research, 858,* 327–337. Copyright 2000 by Elsevier Science B.V.

obtained between morphine and LiCl in rats with lesions of the gustatory cortex (Mackey, Keller, & van der Kooy, 1986) and between cocaine and LiCl (Geddes, Han, Baldwin, Norgren & Grigson, in press). Taken together, these data suggest that drug-induced suppression of CS intake may be mediated by the thalamus, the cortex, or by communication between the two structures (i.e., the thalamocortical loop). Support for a mediating role for the thalamocortical loop is provided by the recent finding that morphine-induced, but not LiCl-induced, suppression of CS intake is prevented by unilateral asymmetric lesions of the gustatory thalamus (e.g., left) and the gustatory cortex (e.g., right; Geddes et al., unpublished

data). Thus, despite repeated taste–morphine or taste–LiCl pairings, the suppressive effects of morphine-, but not LiCl, were disrupted by disconnection of the taste thalamus from the taste cortex.

This picture, while consistent with the reward comparison hypothesis, grows more complex when using cocaine as the US. As described earlier, bilateral lesions of the gustatory thalamus disrupt the suppressive effects of morphine. This is so when using either a lower (15 mg/kg IP) or a higher (30 mg/kg IP) dose of morphine as the US. The same lesion also disrupts the suppressive effects of a standard 10 mg/kg dose of cocaine when administered SC, but the disruptive effect of the lesion is overridden when the taste cue is paired with a higher 20 or 40 mg/kg dose of the drug (Twining et al., unpublished data). A similar pattern occurs following bilateral lesions of the gustatory cortex (Geddes et al., in press). Taken together, these data demonstrate that suppression of CS intake can be mediated by multiple means that differ, potentially, as a function of drug, dose, route of administration, sex, strain, experience, and history, for example. In this light, studies are underway to determine whether the suppression of CS intake as mediated by a low versus a high dose of cocaine represents a quantitative or a qualitative shift. Has the drug simply become so rewarding/addictive at 20 mg/kg that other structures are recruited outside of the thalamocortical loop? Or, alternatively, has the phenomenon switched from one that is mediated by reward to one that is mediated by aversion? This issue will be revisited in the following section.

Neurocircuitry: VTA, NAc, and Dopamine

It is nearly impossible to consider substances of abuse without making mention of the dopaminergic projection from the VTA to the NAc. The role of dopamine in reward is nothing, if not complex. In general, evidence shows that accumbens dopamine tracks stimuli that are of import, regardless of valance, and the response to these stimuli in the accumbens is altered by experience. Accumbens dopamine is elevated following the presentation two novel, neutral stimuli (Young, Ahier, Upton, Joseph, & Gray, 1998), following the presentation of aversive stimuli (Young, 2004), and following the presentation of rewarding stimuli such as sweets (Hajnal, Smith, & Norgren, 2004) or drugs of abuse (DiChiara, Acquas, Tanda, & Cadoni, 1993). Recent electrophysiological data also show that neuronal activity in the NAc tracks both rewarding (sucrose) and aversive (quinine) taste stimuli (Roitman, Wheeler, & Carelli, 2005).

In addition to tracking significant stimuli, accumbens dopamine also tracks cues that have come to predict the availability/presentation of those stimuli. Dopamine is elevated in the Nac following the presentation of conditioned cues that have been associated with stimuli that are aversive (Young, 2004) or rewarding (Datla, et al., 2002; Kiyatkin & Stein, 1996; Mark, Smith, Rada, & Hoebel 1994; Young, 2004), and similar conditioned changes in the neural activity of accumbens cells have been reported (Carelli & Deadwyler,

1997; Roitman et al., 2005). Accumbens dopamine levels can also be suppressed. Specifically, accumbens dopamine levels were reduced to approximately 60% of baseline following presentation of a LiCl-paired saccharin cue (Mark, Blander, & Hoebel, 1991). In addition to classical conditioning (i.e., CTA), accumbens dopamine levels can also be reduced by contrast (i.e., by an unexpected loss of reward). Genn, Ahn, and Phillips (2004) reported that the dopamine response elicited by a palatable 4% sucrose solution was fully blunted in the successive negative contrast paradigm when rats were unexpectedly downshifted from a highly preferred 32% sucrose solution to the less concentrated 4% sucrose solution.

This finding suggests that a similar blunting of accumbens dopamine should occur when the saccharin cue is devalued following saccharin–morphine pairings. To test this hypothesis, cannulae were placed in the NAc of nondeprived Sprague-Dawley rats (Grigson & Hajnal, 2007). The rats were given 20 min access to 0.15% saccharin followed immediately by an ip injection of saline (saline controls, $n = 7$) or 15 mg/kg morphine (conditioning group, $n = 10$). Explicitly unpaired controls ($n = 7$) were injected with morphine approximately 24 h after access to the saccharin cue. Forty-eight hours after the conditioning trial, all rats were presented with the saccharin cue and intake and accumbens dopamine were measured. The results showed that the saline treated and the explicitly unpaired controls did not differ from one another. Relative to these combined controls, rats in the saccharin–morphine group greatly suppressed intake of the saccharin cue at test following a single saccharin–morphine pairing (see Figure 5.4a; Grigson & Hajnal, 2007). Consistent with the findings of Genn et al. (2004), the conditioned reduction in CS intake was associated with a full blunting of the dopamine peak to the saccharin cue at test (Figure 5.4b). Importantly, reduced levels of accumbens dopamine were not due merely to reduced CS intake, because performance on these two indices was not correlated. Instead, the reduction in dopamine appears to reflect the reduced perceived palatability of the saccharin cue as a result of a single pairing with the preferred morphine reward. The reduction in accumbens dopamine also may be due to the onset of cue-induced withdrawal, as a single exposure to morphine is sufficient to elicit the onset of withdrawal (Parker, Corrick, Limebeer, & Kwiatkowska, 2002). This possibility will be discussed later. Finally, while

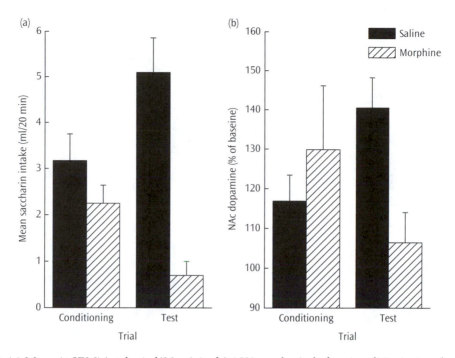

Figure 5.4. (a) Mean (±SEM) intake (ml/20 min) of 0.15% saccharin before (conditioning) and after (test) a single pairing with an IP injection of saline (solid bars) or a 15 mg/kg dose of morphine sulfate (hatched bars). (b) Mean dopamine (% of baseline) in nucleus accumbens (NAc) before (conditioning) and after (test) a single pairing with an IP injection of saline (solid bars) or a 15 mg/kg dose of morphine sulfate (hatched bars). Redrawn from "Once is too much: Conditioned changes in dopamine following a single saccharin-morphine pairing," by Grigson & Hajnal, 2007, *Behavioral Neuroscience, 121,* 1234–1242.

some consideration must be given to the possibility that the phenomenon reflects a classic CTA, all of the foregoing evidence suggests that reward comparison mediates the reduction in intake of the saccharin cue when paired with this drug, at this dose, in this strain of rat. We conclude, then, that accumbens dopamine tracks both absolute and relative properties of reward (Taha & Fields, 2005; Wheeler, 2005) and that levels of this important neurotransmitter can be conditioned and reduced following a single pairing of the saccharin cue with morphine (Grigson & Hajnal, 2007).

Although it is the case that the accumbens tracks both innate and learned absolute and relative properties of reward, it must be noted that the VTA–NAc pathway need not be intact for the avoidance of a saccharin cue when paired with a rewarding sucrose solution (Leszczuk & Flaherty, 2000) or when paired with either morphine or cocaine (Twining, 2005). Leszczuk and Flaherty showed that bilateral lesions of the NAc failed to disrupt the anticipatory contrast effect that occurred following saccharin–sucrose pairings. Likewise, Twining et al. (2005) showed that bilateral 6-OHDA lesions of the VTA,

resulting in at least an 80% reduction in accumbens dopamine as verified by HPLC, also failed to prevent either morphine- or cocaine-induced suppression of CS intake. These same lesions, however, fully prevented the morphine- and chlordiazepoxide-induced appetite stimulating effects which were, otherwise, robust. This finding is a bit surprising, given the wealth of evidence outlined earlier for the role of dopamine in reward. It makes it quite clear, however, that, at least with respect to the comparison of disparate rewards over time, dopamine tracks, but does not mediate, the experience of reward or reward comparison (i.e., contrast).

SELF-ADMINISTRATION: EXPANSION OF THE MODEL

The data suggest that the phenomenon at hand has more to do with substance abuse and addiction than with classic CTA learning. If this is so, then suppression of CS intake should have some impact on, or some relationship to, responding to the drug of abuse. Of course, we already know that avoidance

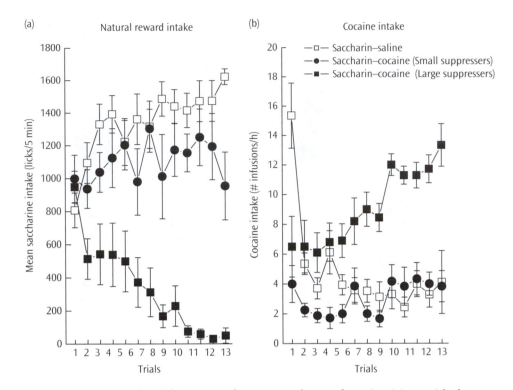

Figure 5.5. (a) Mean (±SEM) intake (licks/5 min) of 0.15% saccharin after 13 pairings with the opportunity to self-administer either saline or cocaine (0.33 mg/infusion) for 1 h, using a fixed-ratio 10-lick contingency on an empty spout. The rats in the cocaine group are divided into small suppressers ($n = 8$) and large suppressers ($n = 10$). (b) Mean (±SEM) number of infusions per hour of either saline or cocaine (0.33 mg/infusion) after 13 saccharin–cocaine pairings in rats classified as the small or the large suppressers. Redrawn from "Cocaine-induced suppression of saccharin intake: A model of drug-induced devaluation of natural rewards," by Grigson & Twining, 2002, *Behavioral Neuroscience, 29(3)*, 239–246.

of the taste cue is accompanied by an increase in operant responding for the drug that mediates the reduction in CS intake (Reicher & Holman, 1977; White et al., 1977; Wise et al., 1976). In a more recent analysis, we directly addressed this issue by using catheterized rats to better model the anticipatory contrast paradigm whereby the rats could consume not only the saccharin CS but also the cocaine US (via a 10-lick contingency on an empty spout). As with passive administration (Gomez, 2000), the rats suppressed intake of the saccharin CS following daily pairings with self-administered cocaine (0.33 mg/infusion for 1 h). Individual differences were evident whereby some rats (referred to as large suppressers) were more likely than others (referred to as the small suppressers) to avoid intake of the saccharin cue following daily saccharin–cocaine pairings (see Figure 5.5a; Grigson & Twining, 2002). Importantly, these individual differences in intake of the CS also translated into individual differences in "intake"

of the drug US. Specifically, greater avoidance of the taste cue, as seen in Figure 5.5a, was correlated with greater cocaine self-administration (see Figure 5.5b) and with greater drug-seeking following a period of 1–6 months of abstinence (data not shown, Grigson & Twining, 2002).

SELF-ADMINISTRATION AND AVERSIVE TASTE REACTIVITY

These data show that avoidance of the taste cue and the propensity to self-administer drug go hand in hand. This finding is in keeping with the hypothesis that the reduction in intake of the gustatory CS is due to the rewarding properties of the drug. We believe this is the case and, as such, that this paradigm is the first animal model for the systematic study of drug-induced devaluation of natural rewards. What remains unclear, however, is whether the taste cue is simply perceived as less rewarding as a result of its predictive relationship with the powerful drug of abuse or whether, in fact, the taste cue can actually become aversive. In an effort to address this question, Wheeler et al. (2008) used a within subjects design where the IO delivery of one flavored saccharin solution (200 μl every minute over a 30-min period) predicted the opportunity to self-administer cocaine for 2 h, while the IO delivery of another flavored saccharin solution, on a different day, predicted the opportunity to self-administer saline for 2 h. Taste reactivity behavior was measured using an EMG electrode placed into the anterior digastric muscle (a requisite jaw opener) and videotape. Single unit activity was also recorded in real time using a fine microwire array in the NAc. The results showed that avoidance of the cocaine-associated taste cue was accompanied by (actually correlated with) aversive taste reactivity (i.e., gapes). The magnitude of this unexpected rejection response predicted faster load up behavior and was correlated with faster acquisition of steady-state responding for cocaine. Finally, this shift in the affective response to the saccharin cue from reward to aversion was tracked by a similar shift in the coded response of single cells in the NAc from primarily inhibitions (as seen with the IO delivery of putatively rewarding gustatory stimuli) to primarily excitations (as seen with the IO delivery of putatively aversive gustatory stimuli Roitman et al., 2005).

So, it is clear, rats emit gapes (aversive taste reactivity) when a cocaine-associated CS is infused directly into the oral cavity. The question is why. Why was aversive taste reactivity obtained here when Parker found no evidence of aversive taste reactivity following the IO delivery of a gustatory cue that had been paired with a range of drugs of abuse across a range of doses (Parker, 1984, 1988, 1991, 1993, 1995, 2003; Parker & Carvell, 1986)? There are three primary differences between the protocol used here and that used by Parker. First, the drug was actively (i.e., self-), rather than passively, administered. Second, the CS was a Kool-Aid adulterated saccharin solution rather than 0.5 M sucrose, as is more often used by Parker. Third, the saccharin CS was delivered into the oral cavity (200 μl in 3.5 s) at 1 min intervals over an entire 30-min session rather than at a rate of 1 ml/min over just a 2-min test session. It is likely that not one, but all of these factors had an impact on the data. Thus, while it is easy to imagine that route of administration (i.e., self-administration) contributed to the finding of gapes in this study, the

nature of the CS and the time frame over which the CS was delivered also are highly suspect. As discussed, palatable taste cues (like sucrose) elicit less drug-induced suppression of CS intake (Gomez, 1999; Grigson et al., 1999) and, as such, also may be less likely to support aversive taste reactivity. Further, while it is generally concluded that Parker did not find aversive taste reactivity following the IO delivery of CSs paired with a range of drugs of abuse across a range of doses, close analysis of the data reveals a low level of aversive taste reactivity behavior in the 2-min tests (Parker, 1991, 1995). Data for aversive taste reactivity behaviors may have become evident, even with passive drug delivery, had the CS been presented over a longer period of access at test. In support, humans, like rats, it appears, emit aversive facial responses when cues indicate that they must wait for access to drug (Sayette et al., 2003). The response to cues that predict the availability of drug, then, is not necessarily the same as the response to cues that predict that one must wait for the availability of drug. In the Wheeler et al. report, the rats had to wait 30 min for access to the drug.

CONCLUSIONS

Together, we believe, these parametric factors (route of administration, nature of the gustatory CS, length of the CS access period, and dose of the drug) have allowed for the assessment of aversive taste reactivity to the drug-associated CS. Is this evidence that the drug is aversive or, more specifically, that aversive drug properties are responsible for the conditioned reduction in CS intake? Not necessarily. The weight of the evidence shows that these drugs are primarily rewarding and avoidance of the drug-associated taste cue is more akin to avoidance of a sucrose-associated taste cue than to the avoidance induced by an aversive LiCl US (see Table 5.1).

When taken in total, the data show that the reduction in intake of a taste cue following pairings with a drug of abuse is mediated, in large part, by reward comparison (i.e., by drug-induced devaluation of the natural reward). In this paradigm, however, the taste cue is not only devalued by the drug, it also becomes, by its associative relationship, a highly reliable predictor of the administration of the rewarding/addictive substance. In so doing, the taste cue can support the establishment of a preparatory, conditioned compensatory response

Table 5.1 The impact of a range of manipulations on the development of a sucrose-induced anticipatory contrast effect (ACE) on the suppressive effects of drugs of abuse (DOA) such as morphine and cocaine (m/c), and on the establishment of a LiCl-induced conditioned taste aversion (CTA).

	Nature of the CS	Food Deprivation	Intensity of the CS	Calories and Deprivation	Selected Strains	History of Chronic Drug Treatment	Lesions of the Gustatory Thalamus
ACE Sucrose	+	+	+	+	+	+	+
DOA M/C	+	+	+	+	+	+	+
CTA LiCl	–	–	–	–	–	–	–
	Grigson, 1997; Bevins et al., 1996; Flaherty et al., 1994	Gomez & Grigson, 1999; Flaherty et al., 1991	Grigson, 1997; Flaherty et al., 1994	Grigson et al., 1999; Flaherty et al., 1991	Grigson & Freet, 2000; Glowa et al., 1994	Grigson et al., 2001	Grigson et al, 2000; Reilly & Pritchard, 1996; Scalera et al., 1997; Flynn et al., 1991; Schroy et al., 2005

Notes: (+) indicates that a phenomenon is affected by the manipulation.

(–) indicates that a phenomenon is not affected by the manipulation.

(Siegel & Ramos, 2002). Parker and her colleagues (Rana & Parker, 2007) have data showing that an amphetamine-associated taste cue elicits fear. This may well be the case. We propose, however, that fear and likely anxiety, for example, are only components of a larger phenomenon, that is, a conditioned compensatory response involving cue-induced craving and withdrawal. Lower doses of drug, we believe, support the development of cue-induced craving and, thereby, elicit seeking, but not necessarily aversive taste reactivity (i.e., gapes). The suppressive effects of these doses, like the suppressive effects of sucrose, are prevented by bilateral lesions of the gustatory thalamus and cortex.

As discussed, the lesions of the taste thalamus or cortex, in rats, fail to suppress intake of the taste cue when paired with higher doses of cocaine and/or extended training. This suggests the involvement of another mechanism that is dependent upon recruitment of additional circuitry. Evidence indicates that cue-induced withdrawal is this other mechanism.

1. Koob's group has provided ample evidence that conditioned withdrawal is associated with anhedonia in rats (Kenny, et al., 2006) and, of course, in our studies the rats suppress intake of the taste cue as though it is not rewarding.

2. Drug-associated taste cues elicit a conditioned elevation of circulating corticosterone (Gomez, Leo, & Grigson, 2000) and corticosterone levels are known to be elevated during naloxone-precipitated withdrawal (Nunez, et al., 2007).

3. Presentation of the taste cue is associated with a blunted accumbens dopamine response (Grigson & Hajnal, 2007). Accumbens dopamine levels also are blunted to baseline following the onset of naltrexone-induced withdrawal (Shaham & Stewart, 1995).

4. When intraorally delivered, rats exhibit aversive taste reactivity behaviors to a taste cue that was previously paired with the opportunity to self-administer cocaine (Wheeler et al., 2008). McDonald et al. (1997) have shown that gapes also are elicited by the IO infusion of a taste cue that has been paired with naloxone-induced withdrawal.

5. Finally, as might be expected if the taste cue were eliciting conditioned withdrawal, greater avoidance of the taste cue is associated with greater cocaine self-administration and greater cocaine-seeking following a period of extended abstinence (Grigson & Twining, 2002). It also is correlated with greater aversive taste reactivity which, in

turn, predicts faster load up behavior—a most effective correction for the onset of cue-induced withdrawal (Wheeler et al., 2008).

Future studies will examine conditions (e.g., nature of the CS, length of CS access, drug, dose, number of trials, drug history, strain, and individual differences) that support the development of suppression of CS intake by drug-induced devaluation (reward comparison), by cue-induced craving, and by the onset of cue-induced withdrawal and the associated underlying circuitry. According to Parker (2006), animals that can vomit will do so when exposed to naloxone-precipitated withdrawal. Thus, other studies will examine whether the gapes found following the IO delivery of the cocaine-associated saccharin cue are mediated by the nausea associated with withdrawal. Finally, we will examine the degree to which the onset and magnitude of the conditioned withdrawal response (as indexed by the measures described earlier) predict the eventual development of "addiction-like" behaviors as outlined by Deroche-Gamonet, et al. (2004).

In sum, it is now clear that a classic CTA interpretation does little to account for the data. The reward comparison hypothesis, on the other hand, explains a great deal of the data, as evidence suggests that the taste cue is devalued in anticipation of the availability of the highly rewarding drug of abuse. Unlike a highly preferred sweet US, however, the drug US exerts a profound impact on the CNS. This, in turn, necessitates the development of a conditioned compensatory response to offset the impact of the impending and potent drug of abuse. As with humans (O'Brien, et al., 1992), it appears that drug-associated cues elicit a conditioned compensatory response that may be experienced as craving and withdrawal in the rat. This, in turn, initiates a correction via drug-seeking and drug-taking behavior.

References

Ambrosio, E., Goldberg, S. R., & Elmer, G. I. (1995). Behavior genetic investigation of the relationship between spontaneous locomotor activity and the acquisition of morphine self-administration behavior. *Behavioural Pharmacology, 6*(3), 229–237.

Bardo, M. T., Miller, J. S., & Neisewander, J. L. (1984). Conditioned place preference with morphine: The effect of extinction training on the reinforcing CR. *Pharmacology, Biochemistry, and Behavior, 21*(4), 545–549.

Bechara, A., & van der Kooy, D. (1985). Opposite motivational effects of endogenous opioids in brain and periphery. *Nature, 314*(6011), 533–534.

Beitner-Johnson, D., Guitart, X., & Nestler, E. J. (1991). Dopaminergic brain reward regions of Lewis and Fischer rats display different levels of tyrosine hydroxylase and other morphine- and cocaine-regulated phosphoproteins. *Brain Research, 561*(1), 147–150.

Beitner-Johnson, D., Guitart, X., & Nestler, E. J. (1992a). Common intracellular actions of chronic morphine and cocaine in dopaminergic brain reward regions. *Annals of the New York Academy of Sciences, 654*, 70–87.

Beitner-Johnson, D., Guitart, X., & Nestler, E. J. (1992b). Neurofilament proteins and the mesolimbic dopamine system: Common regulation by chronic morphine and chronic cocaine in the rat ventral tegmental area. *Journal of Neuroscience, 12*(6), 2165–2176.

Beitner-Johnson, D., Guitart, X., & Nestler, E. J. (1993). Glial fibrillary acidic protein and the mesolimbic dopamine system: Regulation by chronic morphine and Lewis–Fischer strain differences in the rat ventral tegmental area. *Journal of Neurochemistry, 61*(5), 1766–1773.

Beitner-Johnson, D., & Nestler, E. J. (1993). Chronic morphine impairs axoplasmic transport in the rat mesolimbic dopamine system. *Neuroreport, 5*(1), 57–60.

Bevins, R. A., Delzer, T. A., & Bardo, M. T. (1996). Second order conditioning detects unexpressed morphine-induced salt aversion. *Animal Learning & Behavior, 24*, 221–229.

Blander, A., Hunt, T., Blair, R., & Amit, Z. (1984). Conditioned place preference: An evaluation of morphine's positive reinforcing properties. *Psychopharmacology (Berl), 84*(1), 124–127.

Blanchard, D. C., & Blanchard, R. J. (1999). Cocaine potentiates defensive behaviors related to fear and anxiety. *Neuroscience and Biobehavioral Reviews, 23*(7), 981–991.

Cappell, H., & LeBlanc, A. E. (1971). Conditioned aversion to saccharin by single administrations of mescaline and D-amphetamine. *Psychopharmacologia, 22*(4), 352–356.

Cappell, H., LeBlanc, A. E., & Endrenyi, L. (1973). Aversive conditioning by psychoactive drugs: Effects of morphine, alcohol and chlordiazepoxide. *Psychopharmacologia, 29*(3), 239–246.

Carelli, R. M., & Deadwyler, S. A. (1997). Cellular mechanisms underlying reinforcement-related processing in the nucleus accumbens: Electrophysiological studies in behaving animals. *Pharmacology, Biochemistry, and Behavior, 57*(3), 495–504.

Castane, A., Soria, G., Ledent, C., Maldonado, R., & Valverde, O. (2006). Attenuation of nicotine-induced rewarding effects in A2A knockout mice. *Neuropharmacology, 51*(3), 631–640.

Cosgrove, K. P., Hunter, R. G., & Carroll, M. E. (2002). Wheel-running attenuates intravenous cocaine self-administration in rats: Sex differences. *Pharmacology, Biochemistry, and Behavior, 73*(3), 663–671.

Datla, K. P., Ahier, R. G., Young, A. M., Gray, J. A., & Joseph, M. H. (2002). Conditioned appetitive stimulus increases extracellular dopamine in the nucleus accumbens of the rat. *European Journal of Neuroscience, 16*(10), 1987–1993.

Davis, C. M., Roma, P. G., Dominguez, J. M., & Riley, A. L. (2007). Morphine-induced place conditioning in Fischer and Lewis rats: acquisition and dose-response in a fully biased procedure. *Pharmacology, Biochemistry, and Behavior, 86*(3), 516–523.

Deroche-Gamonet, V., Belin, D., & Piazza, P. V. (2004). Evidence for addiction-like behavior in the rat. *Science, 305*(5686), 1014–1017.

DiChiara, G., Acquas, E., Tanda, G., & Cadoni, C. (1993). Drugs of abuse: Biochemical surrogates of specific aspects of natural rewards? *Biochemical Society Symposia, 59*, 65–81.

Ellins, S., & Kennedy, D. K. (1995). Differential effects of saccharin concentrations on taste aversion conditioning and taste potentiation of an auditory food cue in rats. *Behaviorology, 3*, 121–133.

Ettenberg, A., & Geist, T. D. (1991). Animal model for investigating the anxiogenic effects of self-administered cocaine. *Psychopharmacology (Berl), 103*(4), 455–461.

Flaherty, C. F. (1996). *Incentive relativity.* New York: Cambridge University Press.

Flaherty, C. F., & Checke, S. (1982). Anticipation of incentive gain. *Animal Learning & Behavior, 10*, 177–182.

Flaherty, C. F., & Grigson, P. S. (1988). From contrast to reinforcement: Role of response contingency in anticipatory contrast. *Journal of Experimental Psychology: Animal Behavior Processes, 14*(2), 165–176.

Flaherty, C. F., Grigson, P. S., Checke, S., & Hnat, K. C. (1991). Deprivation state and temporal horizons in anticipatory contrast. *Journal of Experimental Psychology: Animal Behavior Processes, 17*, 503–518.

Flaherty, C. F., & Rowan, G. A. (1985). Anticipatory contrast: Within-subjects analysis. *Animal Learning & Behavior, 13*, 2–5.

Flaherty, C. F., & Rowan, G. A. (1986). Successive, simultaneous, and anticipatory contrast in the consumption of saccharin solutions. *Journal of Experimental Psychology: Animal Behavior Processes, 12*(4), 381–393.

Flaherty, C. F., Turovsky, J., & Krauss, K. L. (1994). Relative hedonic value modulates anticipatory contrast. *Physiology & Behavior, 55*(6), 1047–1054.

Garcia, J., Kimmeldorf, K. J., & Koelling, R. A. (1955). Conditioned aversions to saccharin resulting from exposure to gamma radiation. *Science, 122*, 157–158.

Geddes, R. I., Han, L., Baldwin, A. E., Norgren, R., & Grigson, P.S. (in press). Gustatory insular cortex lesions disrupt drug-, but not LiCl-, induced suppression of CS intake. *Behavioral Neuroscience.*

Genn, R. F., Ahn, S., & Phillips, A. G. (2004). Attenuated dopamine efflux in the rat nucleus accumbens during successive negative contrast. *Behavioral Neuroscience, 118*(4), 869–873.

George, F. R., & Goldberg, S. R. (1989). Genetic approaches to the analysis of addiction processes. *Trends in Pharmacological Sciences, 10*(2), 78–83.

Glowa, J. R., Shaw, A. E., & Riley, A. L. (1994). Cocaine-induced conditioned taste aversions: Comparisons between effects in LEW/N and F344/N rat strains. *Psychopharmacology (Berl), 114*(2), 229–232.

Goldstein, R. Z., Cottone, L. A., Jia, Z., Maloney, T., Volkow, N. D., & Squires, N. K. (2006). The effect of graded monetary reward on cognitive event-related potentials and behavior in young healthy adults. *International Journal of Psychophysiology, 62*(2), 272–279.

Gomez, F., Leo, N. A., & Grigson, P. S. (2000). Morphine-induced suppression of saccharin intake is correlated with elevated corticosterone levels. *Brain Research, 863*(1–2), 52–58.

Gomez, F., & Grigson, P. S. (1999). The suppressive effects of LiCl, sucrose, and drugs of abuse are modulated by sucrose concentration in food-deprived rats. *Physiology & Behavior, 67*(3), 351–357.

Goudie, A. J. (1979). Aversive stimulus properties of drugs. *Neuropharmacology, 18*, 971–979.

Grigson, P. S. (1997). Conditioned taste aversions and drugs of abuse: A reinterpretation. *Behavioral Neuroscience, 111*(1), 129–136.

Grigson, P. S., & Freet, C. S. (2000). The suppressive effects of sucrose and cocaine, but not lithium chloride, are greater in Lewis than in Fischer rats: Evidence for the reward comparison hypothesis. *Behavioral Neuroscience, 114*(2), 353–363.

Grigson, P.S., & Hajnal, A. (2007). Once is too much: Conditioned changes in dopamine following a single saccharin-morphine pairing. *Behavioral Neuroscience, 121*, 1234–1242.

Grigson, P. S., Lyuboslavsky, P., & Tanase, D. (2000). Bilateral lesions of the gustatory thalamus disrupt morphine- but not LiCl-induced intake suppression in rats: Evidence against the conditioned taste aversion hypothesis. *Brain Research, 858*(2), 327–337.

Grigson, P. S., Lyuboslavsky, P. N., Tanase, D., & Wheeler, R. A. (1999). Water-deprivation prevents morphine-, but not LiCl-induced, suppression of sucrose intake. *Physiology & Behavior, 67*(2), 277–286.

Grigson, P. S., & Twining, R. C. (2002). Cocaine-induced suppression of saccharin intake: A model of drug-induced devaluation of natural rewards. *Behavioral Neuroscience, 116*(2), 321–333.

Grigson, P. S., Twining, R. C., & Carelli, R. M. (2000). Heroin-induced suppression of saccharin intake in water-deprived and water-replete rats. *Pharmacology, Biochemistry, and Behavior, 66*(3), 603–608.

Grigson, P. S., Wheeler, R. A., Wheeler, D. S., & Ballard, S. M. (2001). Chronic morphine treatment exaggerates the suppressive effects of sucrose and cocaine, but not lithium chloride, on saccharin intake in Sprague-Dawley rats. *Behavioral Neuroscience, 115*(2), 403–416.

Grill, H. J., & Norgren, R. (1978). The taste reactivity test. I. Mimetic responses to gustatory stimuli in neurologically normal rats. *Brain Research, 143*(2), 263–279.

Grimm, J. W., Hope, B. T., Wise, R. A., & Shaham, Y. (2001). Neuroadaptation: Incubation of cocaine craving after withdrawal. *Nature, 412*(6843), 141–142.

Guitart, X., Beitner-Johnson, D., Marby, D. W., Kosten, T. A., & Nestler, E. J. (1992). Fischer and Lewis rat strains differ in basal levels of neurofilament proteins and their regulation by chronic morphine in the mesolimbic dopamine system. *Synapse, 12*(3), 242–253.

Guitart, X., Kogan, J. H., Berhow, M., Terwilliger, R. Z., Aghajanian, G. K., & Nestler, E. J. (1993). Lewis and Fischer rat strains display differences in biochemical, electrophysiological and behavioral parameters: Studies in the nucleus accumbens and locus coeruleus of drug naive and morphine-treated animals. *Brain Research, 611*(1), 7–17.

Hajnal, A., Smith, G. P., & Norgren, R. (2004). Oral sucrose stimulation increases accumbens dopamine in the rat. *American Journal of Physiology—Regulatory, Integrative and Comparative Physiology, 286*(1), R31–37.

Hunt, T., & Amit, Z. (1987). Conditioned taste aversion induced by self-administered drugs: Paradox revisited. *Neuroscience and Biobehavioral Reviews, 11*(1), 107–130.

Jones, S., Casswell, S., & Zhang, J. F. (1995). The economic costs of alcohol-related absenteeism and reduced productivity among the working population of New Zealand. *Addiction, 90*(11), 1455–1461.

Kalat, J. W. (1974). Taste salience depends upon novelty, not concentration, in taste-aversion learning in the rat. *Journal of Comparative and Physiological Psychology, 86*, 47–50.

Kalat, J. W., & Rozen, P. (1970). "Salience": A factor which can override temporal contiguity in taste-aversion learning. *Journal of Comparative and Physiological Psychology, 71*, 192–197.

Katz, R. J., & Gormezano, G. (1979). A rapid and inexpensive technique for assessing the reinforcing effects of opiate drugs. *Pharmacology, Biochemistry, and Behavior, 11*(2), 231–233.

Kenny, P. J., Chen, S. A., Kitamura, O., Markou, A., & Koob, G. F. (2006). Conditioned withdrawal drives heroin consumption and decreases reward sensitivity. *Journal of Neurosciences, 26*(22), 5894–5900.

Kiyatkin, E. A., & Stein, E. A. (1996). Conditioned changes in nucleus accumbens dopamine signal established by intravenous cocaine in rats. *Neuroscience Letters, 211*(2), 73–76.

Kosten, T. A., Miserendino, M. J., Chi, S., & Nestler, E. J. (1994). Fischer and Lewis rat strains show differential cocaine effects in conditioned place preference and behavioral sensitization but not in locomotor activity or conditioned taste aversion. *Journal of Pharmacology and Experimental Therapeutics, 269*(1), 137–144.

Kosten, T. A., Miserendino, M. J., Haile, C. N., DeCaprio, J. L., Jatlow, P. I., & Nestler, E. J. (1997). Acquisition and maintenance of intravenous cocaine self-administration in Lewis and Fischer inbred rat strains. *Brain Research, 778*(2), 418–429.

Lancellotti, D., Bayer, B. M., Glowa, J. R., Houghtling, R. A., & Riley, A. L. (2001). Morphine-induced conditioned taste aversions in the LEW/N and F344/N rat strains. *Pharmacology, Biochemistry, and Behavior, 68*(3), 603–610.

Le Magnen, J. (1969). Peripheral and systemic actions of food in the caloric regulation of intake. *Annals of the New York Academy of Sciences, 157*(2), 1126–1157.

Leshner, A. I., & Koob, G. F. (1999). Drugs of abuse and the brain. *Proceedings of the Association of American Physicians, 111*(2), 99–108.

Lester, D., Nachman, M., & Le Magnen, J. (1970). Aversive conditioning by ethanol in the rat. *Quarterly Journal of Studies on Alcohol, 31*(3), 578–586.

Leszczuk, M. H., & Flaherty, C. F. (2000). Lesions of nucleus accumbens reduce instrumental but not consummatory negative contrast in rats. *Behavioural Brain Research, 116*(1), 61–79.

Liu, C., & Grigson, P. S. (2005). Mu opioid receptor agonist DAMGO-induced suppression of saccharin intake in Lewis and Fischer rats. *Brain Research, 1064*(1–2), 155–160.

Lundy, R. F., Jr., Blair, M., Horvath, N., & Norgren, R. (2003). Furosemide, sodium appetite, and ingestive behavior. *Physiology & Behavior, 78*(3), 449–458.

Mackey, W. B., Keller, J., & van der Kooy, D. (1986). Visceral cortex lesions block conditioned taste aversions induced by morphine. *Pharmacology, Biochemistry, and Behavior, 24*(1), 71–78.

Mark, G. P., Blander, D. S., & Hoebel, B. G. (1991). A conditioned stimulus decreases extracellular dopamine in the nucleas accumbens after the development of a learned taste aversion. *Brain Research, 551,* 308–310.

Mark, G. P., Smith, S. E., Rada, P. V., & Hoebel, B. G. (1994). An appetitively conditioned taste elicits a preferential increase in mesolimbic dopamine release. *Pharacology Biochemistry and Behavior, 48,* 651–660.

McDonald, R. V., Parker, L. A., & Siegel, S. (1997). Conditioned sucrose aversions produced by naloxone-precipitated withdrawal from acutely administered morphine. *Pharmacology, Biochemistry, and Behavior, 58*(4), 1003–1008.

Miller, J. S., Kelly, K. S., Neisewander, J. L., McCoy, D. F., & Bardo, M. T. (1990). Conditioning of morphine-induced taste aversion and analgesia. *Psychopharmacology (Berl), 101*(4), 472–480.

Mucha, R. F., & Herz, A. (1986). Preference conditioning produced by opioid active and inactive isomers of levorphanol and morphine in rat. *Life Science, 38*(3), 241–249.

Nachman, M., & Ashe, J. H. (1973). Learned taste aversions in rats as a function of dosage, concentration, and route of administration of LiCl. *Physiology & Behavior, 10*(1), 73–78.

Nair, P., Black, M. M., Schuler, M., Keane, V., Snow, L., Rigney, B. A., et al. (1997). Risk factors for disruption in primary caregiving among infants of substance abusing women. *Child Abuse & Neglect, 21*(11), 1039–1051.

Neisewander, J. L., Baker, D. A., Fuchs, R. A., Tran-Nguyen, L. T., Palmer, A., & Marshall, J. F. (2000). Fos protein expression and cocaine-seeking behavior in rats after exposure to a cocaine self-administration environment. *The Journal of Neuroscience, 20*(2), 798–805.

Nunez, C., Foldes, A., Laorden, M. L., Milanes, M. V., & Kovacs, K. J. (2007). Activation of stress-related hypothalamic neuropeptide gene expression during morphine withdrawal. *Journal of Neurochemistry, 101*(4), 1060–1071.

O'Brien, C. P., Childress, A. R., McLelan, A. T., & Erhrman, R. (1992). Classical conditioning in drug-dependent humans. *Annals of the New York Academy of Sciences, 564,* 400–415.

Parker, L. A. (1984). Behavioral conditioned responses across multiple conditioning/testing trials elicited by lithium- and amphetamine-paired flavors. *Behavioral and Neural Biology, 41*(2), 190–199.

Parker, L. A. (1988). Defensive burying of flavors paired with lithium but not amphetamine. *Psychopharmacology (Berl), 96*(2), 250–252.

Parker, L. A. (1991). Taste reactivity responses elicited by reinforcing drugs: A dose-response analysis. *Behavioral Neuroscience, 105*(6), 955–964.

Parker, L. A. (1993). Taste reactivity responses elicited by cocaine-, phencyclidine-, and methamphetamine-paired sucrose solutions. *Behavioral Neuroscience, 107*(1), 118–129.

Parker, L. A. (1995). Rewarding drugs produce taste avoidance, but not taste aversion. *Neuroscience and Biobehavioral Reviews, 19*(1), 143–157.

Parker, L. A. (2003). Taste avoidance and taste aversion: Evidence for two different processes. *Learning & Behavior, 31*(2), 165–172.

Parker, L. A. (2006). The role of nausea in taste avoidance learning in rats and shrews. *Autonomic Neuroscience, 125*(1–2), 34–41.

Parker, L. A., & Carvell, T. (1986). Orofacial and somatic responses elicited by lithium-, nicotine- and amphetamine-paired sucrose solution. *Pharmacology, Biochemistry, and Behavior, 24*(4), 883–887.

Parker, L. A., Corrick, M. L., Limebeer, C. L., & Kwiatkowska, M. (2002). Amphetamine and morphine produce a conditioned taste and place preference in the house musk shrew (Suncus murinus). *Journal of Experimental Psychology. Animal Behavior Processes, 28*(1), 75–82.

Pescatore, K. A., Glowa, J. R., & Riley, A. L. (2005). Strain differences in the acquisition of nicotine-induced conditioned taste aversion. *Pharmacology, Biochemistry, and Behavior, 82*(4), 751–757.

Rana, S. A., & Parker, L. A. (2007). Effect of prior exposure to a lithium- and an amphetamine-paired flavor on the acoustic startle response in rats. *Journal of Experimental Psychology. Animal Behavior Processes, 33*(2), 172–184.

Reicher, M. A., & Holman, E. W. (1977). Location preference and flavor aversion reinforced by amphetamine in rats. *Animal Learning & Behavior, 5,* 343–346.

Reilly, S., Bornovalova, M., & Trifunovic, R. (2004). Excitotoxic lesions of the gustatory thalamus spare simultaneous contrast effects but eliminate anticipatory negative contrast: evidence against a memory deficit. *Behavioral Neuroscience, 118*(2), 365–376.

Reilly, S., Grigson, P. S., & Norgren, R. (1993). Parabrachial nucleus lesions and conditioned taste aversion: Evidence supporting an associative deficit. *Behavioral Neuroscience, 107*(6), 1005–1017.

Reilly, S., & Pritchard, T. C. (1996). Gustatory thalamus lesions in the rat: II. Aversive and appetitive taste conditioning. *Behavioral Neuroscience, 110*(4), 746–759.

Risinger, F. O., & Boyce, J. M. (2002). Conditioned tastant and the acquisition of conditioned taste avoidance to drugs of abuse in DBA/2J mice. *Psychopharmacology, 160,* 225–232.

Roitman, M. F., Wheeler, R. A., & Carelli, R. M. (2005). Nucleus accumbens neurons are innately tuned for rewarding and aversive taste stimuli, encode their predictors, and are linked to motor output. *Neuron, 45*(4), 587–597.

Santolaria-Fernandez, F. J., Gomez-Sirvent, J. L., Gonzalez-Reimers, C. E., Batista-Lopez, J. N., Jorge-Hernandez, J. A., Rodriguez-Moreno, F., et al. (1995). Nutritional assessment of drug addicts. *Drug and Alcohol Dependence, 38*(1), 11–18.

Sayette, M. A., Wertz, J. M., Martin, C. S., Cohn, J. F., Perrott, M. A., & Hobel, J. (2003). Effects of smoking opportunity on cue-elicited urge: A facial coding analysis. *Experimental and Clinical Psychopharmacology, 11*(3), 218–227.

Scalera, G., Grigson, P. S., & Norgren, R. (1997). Gustatory functions, sodium appetite, and conditioned taste aversion survive excitotoxic lesions of the thalamic taste area. *Behavioral Neuroscience, 111*(3), 633–645.

Schroy, P. L., Wheeler, R. A., Davidson, C., Scalera, G., Twining, R. C., & Grigson, P. S. (2005). Role of gustatory thalamus in anticipation and comparison of rewards over time in rats. *American Journal of Physiology— Regulatory, Integrative and Comparative Physiology, 288*(4), R966–980.

Shaham, Y., & Stewart, J. (1995). Stress reinstates heroin-seeking in drug-free animals: an effect mimicking heroin, not withdrawal. *Psychopharmacology (Berl), 119*(3), 334–341.

Sherman, J. E., Pickman, C., Rice, A., Liebeskind, J. C., & Holman, E. W. (1980). Rewarding and aversive effects of morphine: Temporal and pharmacological properties. *Pharmacology, Biochemistry, and Behavior, 13*(4), 501–505.

Shoaib, M., & Stolerman, I. P. (1995). Conditioned taste aversions in rats after intracerebral administration of nicotine. *Behavioural Pharmacology, 6*(4), 375–385.

Siegel, S., & Ramos, B. M. (2002). Applying laboratory research: drug anticipation and the treatment of drug addiction. *Experimental and Clinical Psychopharmacology, 10*(3), 162–183.

Smith, J. C., Morris, D. D., & Hendricks, J. (1964). Conditioned aversion to saccharin solution with high dose rates of X-rays as the unconditioned stimulus. *Journal of Radiation Research, 22*, 507–510.

Sorge, R.E., Fudge, M.A., & Parker, L.A. (2002). Effect of sodium deprivation on morphine- and lithium-induced conditioned salt avoidance and taste reactivity. *Psychopharmacology, 160*, 84–91.

Stolerman, I. P., & D'Mello, G. D. (1981). Oral self-administration and the relevance of conditioned taste aversions. In T. Thompson, P. Dews, & W. A. McKim (Eds.), *Advances in behavioral pharmacology* (pp. 169–214). New York: Academic Press.

Suzuki, T., George, F. R., & Meisch, R. A. (1988). Differential establishment and maintenance of oral ethanol reinforced behavior in Lewis and Fischer 344 inbred rat strains. *Journal of Pharmacology and Experimental Therapeutics, 245*(1), 164–170.

Switzman, L., Hunt, T., & Amit, Z. (1981). Heroin and morphine: Aversive and analgesic effects in rats. *Pharmacology, Biochemistry, and Behavior, 15*(5), 755–759.

Taha, S. A., & Fields, H. L. (2005). Encoding of palatability and appetitive behaviors by distinct neuronal populations in the nucleus accumbens. *Journal of Neurochemistry, 25*(5), 1193–1202.

Twining, R. C., Hajnal, A., Han, L., Bruno, K., Hess, E. J., & Grigson, P. S. (2005). Lesions of the ventral tegmental area disrupt drug-induced appetite stimulating effects but spare reward comparison. *International Journal of Comparative Psychology, 18*, 372–396.

Van Ree, J. M. (1979). Reinforcing stimulus properties of drugs. *Neuropharmacology, 18*(12), 963–969.

Vogel, J. R., & Nathan, B. A. (1975). Learned taste aversions induced by hypnotic drugs. *Pharmacology, Biochemistry, and Behavior, 3*(2), 189–194.

Weiss, F., Maldonado-Vlaar, C. S., Parsons, L. H., Kerr, T. M., Smith, D. L., & Ben-Shahar, O. (2000). Control of cocaine-seeking behavior by drug-associated stimuli in rats: Effects on recovery of extinguished operant-responding and extracellular dopamine levels in amygdala and nucleus accumbens. *Proceedings of the National Academy of Sciences of the United States of America, 97*(8), 4321–4326.

Wheeler, R. A., Liu, C., Sanchez, K.W., Sublette, N., Leuenberger, E., & Grigson, P. S. (2002). Fischer 344 rats are more sensitive to the aversive kappa-mediated effects of opioids than Lewis rats. *Appetite, 39*, 106.

Wheeler, R. A., Twining, R. C., Jones, J. L., Slater, J. M., Grigson, P. S., & Carelli, R. M. (2008). Cue-induced negative affect: A behavioral and neural mechanism of cocaine seeking. *Neuron, 57*(5), 774–785.

White, N., Sklar, L., & Amit, Z. (1977). The reinforcing action of morphine and its paradoxical side effect. *Psychopharmacology (Berl), 52*(1), 63–66.

Wise, R. A., Yokel, R. A., & DeWit, H. (1976). Both positive reinforcement and conditioned aversion from amphetamine and from apomorphine in rats. *Science, 191*(4233), 1273–1275.

Young, A. M. (2004). Increased extracellular dopamine in nucleus accumbens in response to unconditioned and conditioned aversive stimuli: Studies using 1 min microdialysis in rats. *Journal of Neuroscience Methods, 138*(1–2), 57–63.

Young, A. M., Ahier, R. G., Upton, R. L., Joseph, M. H., & Gray, J. A. (1998). Increased extracellular dopamine in the nucleus accumbens of the rat during associative learning of neutral stimuli. *Neuroscience, 83*(4), 1175–1183.

6

Conditioned Disgust, but Not Conditioned Taste Avoidance, May Reflect Conditioned Nausea in Rats

LINDA A. PARKER, CHERYL L. LIMEBEER, AND SHADNA A. RANA

Garcia and colleagues (e.g., Garcia, Hankins, & Rusiniak, 1974) pioneered the study of conditioned taste aversion learning; in fact, taste aversion learning is often called the Garcia effect. These early investigations were specifically directed toward understanding the nature of associations formed between flavors and toxic compounds with known emetic properties. According to Garcia (1989), a conditioned taste aversion resulted when a novel flavored food or fluid was paired with nausea produced by activation of the emetic system of the gut and the brainstem. Typically, rats served as subjects in these experiments. Although rats are incapable of vomiting, they were observed to display conditioned disgust reactions (i.e., gaping, chin rubbing) when exposed to a taste previously paired with drug-induced nausea. Garcia and colleagues (1974) argued that conditioned disgust resulted in subsequent avoidance of the taste and that these disgust reactions were established by the association between the taste and activation of the emetic neural circuitry.

The current chapter reviews evidence showing that these conditioned disgust reactions, but not taste avoidance, in rats are exclusively produced by agents capable of producing vomiting in other species. In rats, conditioned disgust reactions may serve as an effective measure of conditioned nausea, but nausea is not necessary for the establishment of conditioned taste avoidance. In the absence of nausea, some other mechanism, such as conditioned fear, may motivate conditioned taste avoidance in rats.

CONDITIONED DISGUST AS A TASTE AVERSION

Garcia's descriptions of conditioned disgust reactions were later experimentally verified by Grill and Norgren (1978a) who developed a systematic test for assessing palatability using rodent models. The taste reactivity (TR) test has since become a standard measure of not only disgust reactions but also hedonic reactions that rats display when tasting a highly palatable sweet solution (e.g., Berridge, 2000). These initial hedonic reactions are replaced with disgust reactions following a sucrose–toxin pairing. Grill and Norgren (1978b) showed that the expression of *conditioned* disgust reactions relies on forebrain circuitry, although brainstem circuitry mediates the display of *unconditioned* disgust reactions to unpalatable flavors.

The typical measure of a flavor–illness association is the amount consumed from a bottle containing the flavored solution—a measure of conditioned taste avoidance. This consumption measure requires that the rat approach the bottle in order to sample the flavored solution. Therefore, measuring taste avoidance involves both appetitive and consummatory responses (Konorski, 1967).

The TR test is an alternative measure of a flavor–illness association. In the TR test, the experimenter controls exposure to the conditioned stimulus (CS) flavored solution and the rat reacts with only the consummatory phase of responding. When intraorally infused with a flavored solution previously paired with nausea, rats display conditioned disgust reactions—a direct measure of taste aversion. These disgust reactions are similar in form to those elicited by bitter quinine solution.

The TR test has revealed that rats display conditioned disgust reactions to flavored solutions that have been paired with low to high doses of lithium chloride (LiCl; Berridge, Grill, & Norgren, 1981; Grill & Norgren, 1978a; Parker, 1982), cyclophosphamide (Parker, 1998; Limebeer & Parker, 1999), high doses of nicotine (Parker, 1993) and apomorphine (Parker & Brosseau, 1990), naloxone-precipitated morphine withdrawal (McDonald, Parker, & Siegel, 1997), and full body rotation (Cordick, Parker, & Ossenkopp, 1999; Ossenkopp et al., 2003). Each of these agents produces vomiting in species that are capable of vomiting (see Parker, Limebeer, & Kwiatkowska, 2005).

MEASURES OF CONDITIONED DISGUST

The measures of conditioned disgust reactions vary among laboratories. Grill and Norgren (1978a) originally defined the following responses as disgust reactions: gaping (large openings of the mouth and jaw), chin rubbing (bringing the chin in direct contact with the floor and projecting the body forward), paw treading (forward and backward movement of the forepaws in synchronous alternation), forelimb flailing (shaking of the forelimbs back and forth), head shaking (rapid lateral vibration of the head and neck), and locomotor activity. The response of passive dripping first described as a mildly aversive/neutral response (Berridge et al., 1981) has since been described by some investigators to reflect aversion (e.g., Schafe, Thiele, & Bernstein, 1998; Thiele, Kiefer, & Badia-Elder, 1996). Therefore, a reader must critically evaluate the means of measuring aversion when comparing results from different laboratories.

In order to clarify the relationships among disgust reactions, we (Parker, 1995) evaluated the taste reactions that co-occurred (using factor analysis) during exposure to a drug-paired flavor, using a pooled large data set (a total of 299 male Sprague-Dawley rats) across six experiments that used a similar procedure, but with different unconditioned stimulus (US) drugs. We found that the responses of gaping, chin rubbing, and paw treading were highly correlated with one another and were negatively correlated with tongue protrusions and mouth movements (which correlated positively with each other). Three factors emerged:

1. Hedonic/ingestion with primary positive loadings of tongue protrusions and mouth movements and negative loadings of gaping, chin rubbing, and passive dripping.
2. Disgust reactions with primary positive loadings of gaping, chin rubbing, and paw treading and negative loadings of mouth movements and tongue protrusions.
3. Motoric responding with primary positive loadings of forelimb flails, head shakes, and locomotion, with no contribution from gaping, chin rubbing, or paw treading.

Therefore, we define disgust reactions as the combination of gaping, chin rubbing, and paw treading. The most sensitive and predominant conditioned disgust reaction is that of gaping (Breslin, Spector, & Grill, 1992; Parker, 2003). In fact, Travers and Norgren (1986) suggest that the muscular movements involved in the gaping response mimic those seen in species capable of vomiting. As seen in Figure 6.1 (see also Color Figure 6.1 in the color insert), the orofacial topography of a rat gape is very similar to the retch that precedes an emetic response in the insectivore shrew, *Suncus murinus*, which vomits when injected with emetic agents such as LiCl (Parker & Kemp, 2001; Parker, Kwiatkowska, Burton, & Mechoulam, 2004). The gaping response in the rat may represent an incipient vomiting response in this animal that does not display the full vomiting response.

TASTE AVOIDANCE PRODUCED BY REWARDING DOSES OF DRUGS

Taste avoidance is not only produced by nauseating doses of drugs, but it is also produced by drugs that animals choose to self-administer or that establish a preference for a distinctive location (e.g., Berger, 1972; Reicher & Holman, 1977; Wise, Yokel, & DeWit, 1976). In fact, when a taste

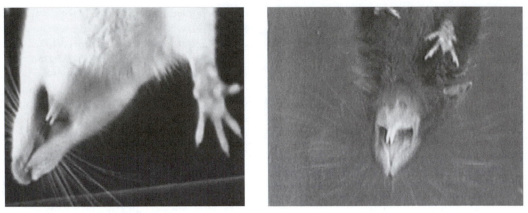

Rat gape   Shrew prevomiting oral response

Figure 6.1. Conditioned gaping in rats reflects nausea "incipient vomiting response." The orofacial characteristics of the rat gape are very similar to those of the shrew retch. Unlike the rat, the shrew vomits in response to emetic stimulation. (See also Color Figure 6.1 in the color insert section.)

is presented prior to a drug self-administration session, the strength of subsequent avoidance of the taste is a direct function of intake of the drug during the self-administration session (Grigson & Twining, 2002; Wise, et al., 1976). This paradoxical phenomenon was initially interpreted as another instance of taste aversion learning. Because Garcia et al. (1974) had developed a model to account for taste aversion produced by emetic agents, it was reasonable for early investigators to assume that rewarding doses of drugs also produce taste avoidance because they produce a side effect of nausea that becomes selectively associated with a flavor (Reicher & Holman, 1977).

If the taste avoidance produced by a rewarding dose of a drug is mediated by conditioned nausea, then the avoidance of the taste should be accompanied by conditioned disgust reactions (e.g., Garcia, 1989; Garcia et al., 1974; Grill & Norgren, 1978a); however, considerable evidence indicates that it is not (e.g., Parker, 1982; Parker, 1995; Parker, 2003). Unlike emetic agents, rewarding doses of drugs do not produce conditioned disgust reactions in rats. This phenomenon has been demonstrated with rewarding doses of amphetamine (Parker, 1982, 1988, 1991; Parker & Carvell, 1986; Zalaquett & Parker, 1989), cocaine (Mayer & Parker, 1993; Parker, 1993), methamphetamine (Parker, 1993), methylphenidate (Parker, 1995), LSD (Parker, 1996), morphine (Parker, 1988, 1991), phencyclidine (Parker, 1993), and low doses of nicotine (Parker & Carvel, 1986).

Each of these agents produced conditioned taste avoidance, but not conditioned disgust reactions at doses that are self-administered and/or produce a conditioned place preference. Rewarding drugs do, however, produce suppressed ingestive responding and enhanced passive dripping (e.g., Parker, 1995). The failure of rewarding agents to produce conditioned disgust reactions is not simply the result of the relative weakness of the acquired taste–drug association. When doses of amphetamine and LiCl were adjusted to produce weaker taste avoidance with LiCl (12 mg/kg) than with amphetamine (3 mg/kg), only the LiCl-paired flavor elicited conditioned disgust reactions (Zalaquett & Parker, 1989). Therefore, although the avoidance test suggests that both amphetamine and LiCl produce a similar aversive effect, the taste reactivity test shows that the avoidance produced by these two drugs is not motivated by the same process.

Table 6.1 (adapted from Parker, 2003) summarizes the results from numerous experiments in our laboratory and other laboratories that have compared the capacity of doses of drugs to produce a place preference or avoidance and to produce conditioned disgust. The upper left quadrant shows that none of the doses of drugs that have been tested have the capacity to produce both a place preference and conditioned disgust reactions. On the other hand, as seen in the upper right quadrant, many drugs produce both place avoidance and conditioned disgust—these drugs also produce vomiting in species capable of vomiting at the

Table 6.1 Place Conditioning and Disgust Reactions.

	Place Preference	Place Avoidance
Disgust reactions and taste avoidance	None	Alcohol (novel; 1–2 g/kg, IP) Amphetamine[a] (10 mg/kg, IP) Apomorphine[a] (15 mg/kg, IP) Chlordiazepoxide (5–20 mg/kg, IP) Cyclophosphamide (10–40 mg/kg, IP) Fenfluramine (2.5–10 mg/kg, IP) Lithium chloride (12–127 mg/kg, IP) Naloxone-precipitated morphine withdrawal Nicotine[a] (1.2–2 mg/kg, SC) $\triangle$-9-THC[a] (1.5–2.5 mg/kg, IP)
No disgust reactions and taste avoidance	Alcohol (familiar; 1–2 g/kg, IP) Amphetamine[a] (1–5 mg/kg, IP) Apomorphine[a] (1–7.5 mg/kg, IP) Cocaine (5–20 mg/kg, SC) LSD (0.025–0.2 mg/kg, IP) Methylphenidate (5–30 mg/kg, IP) Morphine (2–80 mg/kg, IP) Nicotine (0.2–0.8 mg/kg, SC, 1 mg/kg, IP) Phencyclidine[a] (0.5 mg/kg, IP) Pentobarbital[b] (1–20 mg/kg, IP) $\triangle$-9-THC[a,b] (0.25–1.0 mg/kg)	Footshock Naltrexone (1–10 mg/kg, IP) Pentobarbital[b] (1–20 mg/kg, IP) Phencylidine[a] (2–20 mg/kg, IP)

[a] Biphasic drug effects across dose range.
[b] Conflicting reports.

indicated doses. Doses of drugs producing a place preference do not produce disgust reactions (lower left quadrant). Finally there are drugs that are aversive for some reason other than nausea that do not produce conditioned disgust reactions (lower right quadrant); for instance naltrexone may produce an effect that is more similar to pain than to nausea (Lett, 1985).

Nausea appears to be crucial for the establishment of conditioned disgust reactions, but not taste avoidance (Grant, 1987; Ionescu & Buresova, 1977; Nachman & Hartley, 1975). In fact, many investigators (Berger, 1972; Goudie, Stolerman, Demellweek, & D'Mello 1982; Grill, 1985; Hunt & Amit, 1987) have suggested that the nomenclature commonly used to describe suppression of consumption of an illness-paired flavor, that is "conditioned taste aversion learning" is inaccurate. A conditioned taste aversion is better assessed by the presence or absence of conditioned disgust reactions in the TR test (Grill, 1985). Additional evidence for this distinction was reported by Pelchat, Grill, Rozin, and Jacobs (1983) who videotaped rats while they licked from

a tube containing sucrose solution that had been previously paired with a low dose of LiCl (in a single trial) or paired with shock (multiple trials). The groups were equated for the strength of taste avoidance as their sucrose intake was equivalent in the subsequent test, but both groups drank less sucrose than saline control groups. On the other hand, the videotapes revealed that the orofacial reactions displayed while consuming the LiCl-paired and the shock-paired sucrose differed dramatically. Rats displayed conditioned disgust reactions only during consumption of the LiCl-paired sucrose. Pelchat et al. (1983) concluded that the LiCl- and shock-paired sucrose solution was avoided for different reasons—LiCl-paired sucrose became distasteful, but shock-paired sucrose became a danger signal. Clearly, the potential of a drug to produce taste avoidance need not relate to its potential to produce illness (Grant, 1987).

The failure of some toxins to produce at best only a weak avoidance of a taste (Ionesco & Buresova, 1977; Nachman & Hartley, 1975) may also be explained by their potential to produce pain (like shock) rather than nausea (Lett, 1985). Strychnine or cyanide (which immediately produce anoxia and convulsions) and gallamine (which produces muscular paralysis interfering with respiration) produce only weak taste avoidance, even at near lethal doses. Ionesco and Buresova (1977) suggested that poisons must produce gastrointestinal distress to produce strong taste avoidance; however, clearly a number of agents (such as amphetamine, morphine, and cocaine) produce taste avoidance in the absence of gastrointestinal distress (e.g., Reicher & Holman, 1977). Lett (1985) reported that when paired with a chamber cue, gallamine produced a stronger place aversion than did LiCl; however, when paired with a taste cue, LiCl produced the stronger association. Gallamine produced paralysis of the peripheral musculature shortly after its administration, which may produce a painful event more like electric shock than a slower onset change in internal homeostasis that is evident with LiCl, morphine, or amphetamine. As demonstrated by Lett (1985) some drug-induced effects may become more readily associated with exteroceptive cues than with interoceptive food-related cues. Garcia (e.g., Garcia & Koelling, 1966) and others (Revusky & Garcia, 1970; Pelchat et al., 1983) have consistently demonstrated that electric shock is less effectively associated with flavor cues than with exteroceptive cues. The possibility that drugs that do not readily produce taste avoidance produce a painlike effect is consistent with the biological model originally proposed by Garcia and his associates (Garcia & Ervin, 1968; Garcia et al., 1974), which explained why taste stimuli are more easily associated with nausea whereas audiovisual or tactile stimuli are more easily associated with pain.

As described in this section, treatments that are sought after by rats (in other paradigms) also produce taste avoidance, but they do not produce conditioned disgust. Furthermore, painful shock produces avoidance, but not conditioned disgust. Therefore, conditioned disgust is a better measure of the potential of an agent to produce nausea than is taste avoidance.

EFFECT OF ANTINAUSEA TREATMENTS ON CONDITIONED DISGUST AND TASTE AVOIDANCE

Another approach to understanding the role that nausea plays in the establishment of taste avoidance in rats is to evaluate the potential of

antinausea treatments to interfere with avoidance of a flavor paired with an emetic treatment. Early work suggested that antinausea agents interfered with the expression of previously established taste avoidance produced by LiCl (Coil, Hankins, Jenden, & Garcia, 1978); however, more recent findings suggest that similar antinausea treatments (Goudie et al., 1982; Parker & McLeod, 1991; Rabin, & Hunt, 1983) and different antinausea treatments (Gadusek & Kalat, 1975; Levy, Carroll, Smith, & Hofer, 1974; Limebeer & Parker, 2000, 2003; Parker et al., 2003; Parker, Mechoulam, & Schlievert, 2002) failed to interfere with the expression of LiCl-induced taste avoidance. Furthermore, there is considerable evidence that antinausea treatments either do not interfere with the establishment of conditioned taste avoidance learning (Limebeer & Parker, 2000; Parker, Mechoulam, et. al., 2002; Rabin & Hunt, 1983; Rudd, Ngan, & Wai, 1998) or at least only interfere with the establishment of very weak LiCl-induced taste avoidance (Gorzolka, Hanson, Harrington, Killam, & Campbell-Meiklejohn, 2003; Wegener, Smith, & Rosenberg, 1997). Two prominent antinausea treatments include drugs that reduce serotonin availability and drugs that elevate the activity of the endocannabinoid system (see Parker et al., 2005). These treatments interfere with the establishment and/or the expression of conditioned disgust reactions, but not conditioned taste avoidance (for review, see Parker, 2003).

Serotonergic Agents

Serotonin (5-hydroxytryptamine, 5-HT) released from the gastrointestinal enterochromaffin cells is implicated in the emetic response during cisplatin chemotherapy treatment (Andrews, Rapeport, & Sanger, 1988). Peripheral actions of 5-HT on $5-HT_3$ receptors located on vagal afferents appear to trigger nausea and vomiting. It is at this site that $5-HT_3$ receptor antagonists, such as ondansetron, exert their antiemetic effects and relieve the deleterious side effects that often accompany cancer chemotherapy. Similar mechanisms are believed to operate in the rat despite this animal's inability to vomit (Hillsley & Grundy, 1998; Higgins, Kilpatrick, Bunce, Jones, & Tyers (1989) also reported that central injections of $5-HT_3$ receptor antagonists into the area postrema inhibit cisplatin-induced vomiting in ferrets, suggesting that central mechanisms may also be involved in 5-HT-induced emesis.

Serotonin agonists would, therefore, be expected to produce conditioned disgust reactions in rats by producing nausea. Indeed, when paired with a flavored solution, fenfluramine (3 mg/kg, intraperitoneal [IP]), a drug that nonspecifically facilitates the release of serotonin both peripherally and centrally (Blundell, 1984), produced conditioned disgust reactions in rats (Parker, 1988). Furthermore, we have recently found (Parker & Limebeer, 2006) that the antidepressant 5-HT reuptake inhibitor, fluoxetine, also produces dose-dependent (>20 mg/kg, IP) conditioned disgust reactions when paired with saccharin solution. Because fluoxetine has been reported to produce the side effects of nausea and gastrointestinal distress in some patients (Brambilla, Cipriani, Hotopf, & Barbui, 2005), the conditioned disgust reaction model may serve as a tool for detecting the side effects of nausea produced by newly developed pharmaceutical compounds.

The most typical emetic treatment used in the study of flavor–drug associations is LiCl. Indeed, LiCl produces vomiting in species capable of vomiting, such as the *S. murinus* (Parker, Corrick, Limebeer, & Kwiatkowska, 2002; Smith, Friedman, & Andrews, 2001). LiCl-induced nausea and vomiting may also be at least partially mediated by serotonin release. In animal brain tissue, LiCl inhibits the release of norepinepherine and dopamine, but not serotonin (Baldessarini & Vogt, 1988). In fact, LiCl has been reported to enhance the release of serotonin especially in the limbic system (Manji et al., 1999; Treiser et al., 1981; Wang, & Friedman, 1989). Using microdialysis to monitor extracellular levels of serotonin, West, Mark, and Hoebel (1991) reported that 5-HT was elevated in the lateral hypothalamus, but not the hippocampus, following an intraoral infusion of saccharin that had previously been paired with LiCl.

If conditioned disgust reactions are only produced by nauseating treatments in rats, then pretreatment with drugs that attenuate toxin-induced vomiting in emetic species (e.g., Matsuki et al., 1988) might also attenuate conditioned disgust reactions in rats. Two such drugs are the $5-HT_3$ antagonist, ondansetron, and the $5-HT_{1A}$ autoreceptor agonist, 8-OH-DPAT that reduce toxin-induced vomiting in animal models (e.g., Parker et al., 2005, for review). Studies from our laboratory have demonstrated that ondansetron and 8-OH-DPAT interfere with both the establishment and the expression of LiCl-induced conditioned disgust reactions, but not conditioned taste avoidance (Limebeer & Parker, 2000, 2003; see also Rudd et al., 1998). Limebeer and Parker (2000) showed that pretreatment with ondansetron (0.01 or 0.1 mg/kg) interfered with the establishment of LiCl-induced conditioned disgust reactions as well as with the expression of previously established disgust reactions. The effect could not be explained as a state-dependent learning decrement, because in a separate experiment, rats were injected with ondansetron prior to conditioning and testing and still showed no conditioned rejection reactions. On the other hand, pretreatment with ondansetron did not interfere with either the establishment or the expression of LiCl-induced taste avoidance whether assessed in a one-bottle or a two-bottle test. In fact, when disgust reactions were measured during a consumption test, ondansetron selectively attenuated disgust reactions, with only a slight modification of consumption. Limebeer and Parker (2003) also found that 8-OH-DPAT, a drug that reduces serotonin availability by acting as a presynaptic $5-HT_{1A}$ autoreceptor agonist, produces a very similar pattern of interference with the establishment and expression of LiCl-induced conditioned disgust reactions without modifying taste avoidance. These results suggest that conditioned disgust reactions, but not conditioned taste avoidance, reflect nausea in rats that can be attenuated by a reduction in serotonin availability. The effect of serotonin antagonism is specific to conditioned disgust reactions, because ondansetron pretreatment did not interfere with unconditional disgust reactions elicited by bitter quinine solution.

Another way to reduce serotonin availability is to lesion the raphe nuclei with the selective serotonin neurotoxin, 5,7-dihyroxytryptamine (5,7-DHT). Limebeer, Parker, and Fletcher (2004 evaluated the potential of 5,7-DHT lesions of the dorsal raphe and the median raphe to interfere with LiCl-induced conditioned disgust reactions in rats. The neurotoxin, 5,7-DHT, is taken up by the 5-HT containing neurons and results in degeneration of axons and terminals containing 5-HT. To inhibit uptake of 5,7-DHT by noradrenergic neurons, rats can be injected with desipramine prior to the intracranial delivery of the 5,7,-DHT (Baumgarten et al., 1978). The central 5-HT system consists of two distinct subdivisions associated with the midsagittal seam (raphe) of the brainstem: a rostral division that projects to the forebrain, and a caudal division that projects to the spinal cord (Tork, 1990). The rostral division consists of the dorsal raphe and the median raphe, which both project axons to multiple areas in the forebrain. Grill and Norgren (1978b) demonstrated that an intact forebrain is necessary for the establishment and/or expression of LiCl-induced conditioned disgust reactions. Furthermore, kainic acid lesions of the midline brainstem region, including the rostral raphe nuclei, attenuated vomiting in cats (Miller, Nonaka, Jakus, & Yates, 1996).

Limebeer et al. (2004) found that these 5,7-DHT lesions of the dorsal and median raphe nuclei prevented the establishment of LiCl-induced conditioned disgust reactions; however, the lesions did not prevent the establishment of conditioned taste avoidance. This latter finding is consistent with that of Kostowski and colleagues who report that neither intracerebroventricular (Bienkowski, Iwinska, Piasecki, & Kostowski, 1997) nor dorsal raphe (Piasecki, Bienkowski, Dudek, Koras, & Kostowski, 2001) administration of 5,7-DHT affected saccharin–ethanol (>1 g/kg) conditioned taste avoidance. Such high doses of ethanol, like LiCl, produce conditioned disgust reactions in rats, suggesting that they produce nausea (Parker, 1998). Furthermore, LiCl-induced conditioned taste avoidance has been reported to be unaffected by electrolytic median raphe lesions (Asin, Wirtshafter, & Kent, 1980) and intracerebroventricular administration of 5,7-DHT (De Olivera Mora et al., 1999).

To summarize, the emetic effects of compounds can be reduced by treatments that reduce serotonin availability. These treatments selectively attenuate toxin-induced conditioned disgust reactions, but do not attenuate toxin-induced conditioned taste avoidance. These findings suggest that in the absence of nausea even taste avoidance produced by LiCl may be mediated by some process other than nausea.

Cannabinoid Agents

The marijuana plant has been used for several centuries for a number of therapeutic results, including relief of nausea and vomiting (see Parker et al., 2005); however, it was only recently that Gaoni and Mechoulam (1964) isolated the major psychotropic component, Δ^9-tetrahydrocannabinol (Δ^9-THC). Twenty-five years later, the specific brain receptors for this compound, Cannabinoid$_1$ (CB$_1$) and Cannabinoid$_2$ (CB$_2$), were identified (Devane, Dysarz, Johnson, Melvin, & Howlett, 1988) and cloned (Matsuda, Lolait, Brownstein, Young, & Bonner, 1990). Therefore, it was only natural to start the search for an endogenous ligand for the cannabinoid receptor, which was discovered 2 years later (Devane et al., 1992). This ligand was the ethanol amide of arachidonic acid and was called anandamide. A second type of endocannabinoid was discovered in 1995 (Mechoulam et al., 1995), which was also a derivative of arachidonic acid, but its ester, 2-arachidonoyl glycerol (2-AG). Both anandamide and 2-AG are rapidly inactivated after their formation and release by the enzyme fatty acid amide hydrolase (FAAH; Deutsch & Chin, 1993).

The antiemetic effects of cannabinoids appear to be mediated by action at the CB$_1$ receptor. CB$_1$ receptors are found in the gastrointestinal tract and its enteric nervous system (Pertwee, 2001) as well as within the emetic system of the brain (Van Sickle et al., 2001; Van Sickle, Oland, Mackie, Davison, & Sharkey, 2003) in the dorsal vagal complex (DVC), consisting of the area postrema (AP), nucleus tractus solitarius (NTS), and the dorsal motor nucleus of the vagus (DMNX) in the brainstem of rats, ferrets, and the least shrew (Simoneau et al., 2001; Van Sickle et al., 2001). Cannabinoid agonists act mainly via peripheral CB$_1$ receptors to decrease intestinal motility (Pertwee, 2001), but they appear to act centrally to attenuate emesis (Pertwee, 2001; Van Sickle et al., 2001). The DVC is involved in the nausea or vomiting reactions induced by either vagal gastrointestinal activation or by several humoral cytotoxic agents—it is considered the starting point of a final common pathway for the induction of emesis in vomiting species. When emesis is pharmacologically induced, Δ^9-THC reduces the emetic reaction by activation of CB$_1$ receptors in the NTS, and this antiemetic effect can be reversed by the action of CB$_1$ receptor antagonists/inverse agonists, SR-141716 (Darmani & Johnson, 2004) and AM251 (Van Sickle et al., 2001) at the same site. c-Fos expression induced by cisplatin in the DMNX, specific subnuclei of the nucleus tractus solitarius and area postrema, is significantly reduced by Δ^9-THC (Van Sickle et al., 2001, 2003). In addition, endogenous cannabinoid ligands, such as anandamide, as well as synthetic cannabinoids, such as WIN 55,212–2, act on these receptors (Simoneau et al., 2001). The natural endo-cannabinoids most likely play a role in the control of nausea and vomiting, because the CB_1 antagonist/inverse agonist SR-141617 produces vomiting on its own (Darmani, 2001). Darmani et al. (2005) recently reported that cisplatin increases endogenous brain 2-AG and concomitantly decreases intestinal 2-AG and anandamide levels in the least shrew.

Recent evidence suggests that the cannabinoid system interacts with the serotonergic system in the control of emesis. The DVC not only contains CB_1 receptors but is also densely populated with $5\text{-}HT_3$ receptors (Himmi, Dallaporta, Perrin, & Orsini, 1996; Himmi, Perrin, El Ouazzani, & Orsini, 1998), potentially a site of antiemetic effects of $5\text{-}HT_3$ antagonists. Anandamide has also been reported to interact with serotonin (Kimura, Ohta, Watanabe, Yoshimura, & Yamamoto, 1998). Cannabinoid receptors are co-expressed with serotonin $5\text{-}HT_3$ receptors in some neurons in the central nervous system (CNS; Hermann, Marsicano, & Lutz, 2002), and inhibitory functional interactions have been reported between cannabinoid CB_1 and $5\text{-}HT_3$ receptors (Barann et al., 2002; Fan, 1995). In addition, cannabinoids reduced the ability of $5\text{-}HT_3$ agonists to produce emesis in the least shrew (Darmani & Johnson, 2004), and this effect was prevented by pretreatment with the selective cannabinoid CB_1 receptor antagonist/inverse agonist, SR-141716. Cannabinoids may act at CB_1 presynaptic receptors to inhibit release of newly synthesized serotonin (Darmani & Johnson, 2004; Howlett et al., 2002; Schlicker & Kathman, 2001). Using the house musk shrew model of emesis, Kwiatkowska, Parker, Burton, & Mechoulam (2004) found that ondansetron and Δ^9-THC both suppressed vomiting and retching with increasing efficacy as the dose increased; however, the minimally effective dose of ondansetron (0.2 mg/kg, IP) was considerably lower than the minimally effective dose of Δ^9-THC (2.5 mg/kg, IP). A combined pretreatment of doses of the two drugs that were ineffective alone (0.02 mg/kg ondansetron and 1.25 mg/kg Δ^9-THC) completely suppressed cisplatin-induced vomiting and retching. These results suggest that a combination of lower doses of ondansetron and Δ^9-THC may be an effective alternative treatment of the acute phase of chemotherapy-induced vomiting, and the combination may have fewer side effects than higher doses of either agent alone.

The marijuana plant contains over 60 cannabinoids, but the two principal components are the psychoactive compound, Δ^9-THC, and the non-psychoactive compound, cannabidiol (CBD). CBD, unlike Δ^9-THC, does not bind to known cannabinoid receptors (Mechoulam et al., 2002). In shrews, low doses of CBD (5–10 mg/kg, IP) inhibit cisplatin-induced (Kwiatkowska et al., 2004) and LiCl-induced (Parker et al., 2004) emesis. The mechanism by which CBD suppresses emesis is presently unknown.

Cannabinoids not only produce antiemetic effects in species capable of vomiting, but they also interfere with the establishment of conditioned disgust reactions produced by nauseating treatments in rats. Limebeer and Parker (1999) demonstrated that a low dose (0.5 mg/kg, IP) of Δ^9-THC interfered with the establishment of cyclophosphamide-induced conditioned disgust reactions and with the expression of previously established conditioned disgust reactions in rats. Cyclophosphamide is an agent used in chemotherapy treatment in humans that produces the side effect of nausea and vomiting. In collaboration with Raphael Mechoulam, we have found that Δ^9-THC and the potent synthetic cannabinoid agonist, HU-210, interfere with LiCl-induced conditioned disgust reactions in rats, and the CB_1 receptor antagonist/inverse agonist, SR-141716, blocks this effect (Parker et al., 2003; Parker & Mechoulam, 2003). Most interestingly, SR-141716 actually potentiated LiCl-induced conditioned disgust, suggesting that natural cannabinoids set an endogenous tone in the regulation of nausea.

Although low doses of the CB_1 antagonists/inverse agonists SR-141716 (Parker et al., 2003) and AM251 (McLaughlin et al., 2005) did not produce conditioned disgust reactions on their own, higher doses of AM251 (>8 mg/kg, IP) produced conditioned disgust reflective of nausea. This finding suggests that the appetite suppressant effect of the newly marketed CB_1 antagonist/inverse agonist, rimonabant, may be partially mediated by the side effect of nausea which is the most commonly reported side effect in human randomized control trials (Pi-Sunyer et al., 2006). Most recently, we evaluated the effect of the silent CB_1 antagonist, AM4113, that does not have inverse agonist properties and found that it did not produce conditioned disgust at doses that produced equivalent feeding suppression as evident with AM251 (Sink et al., 2008). AM251-induced conditioned disgust may thus be mediated by its inverse agonist properties.

More compelling evidence that the endocannabinoid system may serve as a regulator of nausea is our recent finding that prolonging the duration of action of anandamide by pretreatment with URB 597, a drug that inhibits the enzyme FAAH, also disrupts the establishment of LiCl-induced conditioned disgust reactions in rats (Cross-Mellor, Ossenkopp, Piomelli, & Parker, 2007). Rats pretreated with URB 597 (0.3 mg/kg, IP) 2 h prior to a saccharin–LiCl pairing displayed suppressed conditioned disgust reactions in a subsequent drug-free test. Rats given the combination of URB 597 (0.3 mg/kg, IP) and anandamide (5 mg/kg, IP) displayed even greater suppression of conditioned disgust reactions.

Even the nonpsychoactive cannabinoid compound found in marijuana, CBD, reduces LiCl-induced conditioned disgust in rats. CBD (5 mg/kg, IP) and a more potent synthetic analog, cannabidiol-DMH (5 mg/kg, IP), both interfered with LiCl-induced conditioned disgust reaction in rats without interfering with conditioned taste avoidance (Parker & Mechoulam, 2003; Parker, Mechoulam et al., 2002).

Conclusion

Treatments that reduce serotonin availability or that activate the endocannabinoid system both interfered with the establishment and/or expression of conditioned disgust reactions produced by emetic treatments in rats. The establishment of toxin-induced conditioned disgust is prevented by pretreatment with antinausea treatments, presumably by interfering with toxin-induced nausea during conditioning. Furthermore, the expression of previously established toxin-induced conditioned disgust reactions during testing can also be prevented by pretreatment with these antinausea treatments. On the other hand, these antiemetic treatments neither modify the establishment nor the expression of conditioned taste avoidance. That is, drugs that should reduce LiCl-induced nausea do not interfere with LiCl-induced taste avoidance.

Evidence from human self-report studies also suggests that nausea plays a special role in the establishment of conditioned disgust, but not necessarily conditioned taste avoidance. Hedonic ratings of dislike are also more predictive of nausea than are consumption patterns in humans reexperiencing an illness-paired flavor (Pelchat & Rozin, 1982; Schwarz, Jacobsen, & Bjovberg, 1996). Human chemotherapy patients were allowed to consume a novel flavored solution prior to their chemotherapy session during which they rated the severity of nausea that they experienced. When they were subsequently presented with the chemotherapy-paired solution, their hedonic ratings of liking of the flavor (reflective of a change in its incentive properties) were more predictive of self-reported ratings of nausea during the session than was the amount of the solution consumed. Furthermore, in humans, nausea seems to be a better predictor of the development of conditioned disgust than are other nongastrointestinal aversive experiences. Pelchat and Rozin (1982) describe a scenario in which shrimp produces food poisoning in one person and produces hives in another person. Although both people avoid eating shrimp in the future, only the poisoned person comes to dislike the taste of shrimp. That is, the people avoid the shrimp for different reasons. They suggest that food avoidance can be based on distaste or perceived danger.

In the Absence of Nausea, What Motivates Conditioned Taste Avoidance in Rats: Role of Conditioned Fear?

Nausea does not appear to be necessary for the establishment of conditioned taste avoidance in the rat (Grant, 1987; Hunt & Amit, 1987; Limebeer & Parker, 2000; Nachman & Hartley, 1975). As reviewed before, the findings that rats learn to avoid a flavor paired with LiCl even if the nausea is prevented by pretreatment with an antiemetic drug (e.g., Limebeer & Parker, 2000) and that rats learn to avoid a flavor paired with a drug that has rewarding (rather than emetic) properties (e.g., Parker, 1995) demonstrate that rats learn to avoid a drug-paired (be it an emetic or a rewarding drug) flavor even in the absence of nausea. Some other effect of these drug treatments must serve the role of the US that produces avoidance of the flavor.

On the basis of considerable evidence that drug preexposure reduces the likelihood that the same drug or even a different drug would produce taste avoidance, Gamzu (1977) suggested that (since a rat cannot vomit) any novel change in its affective homeostatic state following the ingestion of a food may signal danger. A taste paired with this change in state may therefore come to conditionally signal danger (e.g., Pelchat et al., 1983) resulting in subsequent avoidance of that taste. That is, conditioned taste avoidance produced in the absence of nausea may be mediated by conditioned fear rather than conditioned nausea. The gradual change in affective homeostasis is not necessarily fear inducing on its own when it does not follow consumption of new foods, because rats learn to self-administer and to develop a preference for a cue paired with a rewarding drug. Furthermore, drugs are not equally effective USs in producing taste avoidance (Ionesco & Buresova, 1977; Nachman & Hartley, 1975). Some drugs (e.g., gallamine) may produce a painlike effect, such as shock, that is less likely to become associated with interoceptive, food-related cues (Lett, 1985) than is LiCl.

If avoidance of a taste is mediated by conditioned fear, then exposure to the taste might be expected to potentiate a rat's reaction in a behavioral test of fear. A simple measure of conditioned fear is conditioned suppression of licking during exposure to a tone previously paired with shock (Leaf & Leaf, 1966). Using a similar conditioned suppression paradigm, Parker (1980) reported that preexposure to a LiCl-paired flavor, but not a saline-paired flavor, elicited conditioned suppression of licking of both a novel flavored solution and unflavored water. The strength of the suppression increased as the dose of the LiCl (US) increased. These findings parallel those of traditional conditioned suppression elicited by a shock-paired cue, which has been interpreted as a measure of conditioned fear (e.g., Kamin Brimer & Black, 1963).

Do flavors paired with rewarding drugs elicit conditioned fear in rats? We have begun to use typical measures of conditioned fear to examine this question. Rana and Parker (2007) evaluated whether rats may learn to fear a novel flavor paired with amphetamine and/or LiCl using a modified fear-potentiated acoustic startle response (ASR). The ASR is enhanced when elicited in the presence of a cue (tone or light) previously paired with shock, a measure of conditioned fear/arousal (Brown, Kalish, & Farber, 1951; Davis, Falls, Campeau, & Kim, 1993). On the other hand, treatments that produce sickness, including naloxone-precipitated withdrawal from chronic morphine exposure (Mansbach, Gold, & Harris, 1992) and the proinflammatory cytokine IL-1β (Beck & Servatius, 2003), have been reported to produce an attenuated ASR. Therefore, if the drug-paired flavor elicits conditioned fear/arousal, then it would be expected to potentiate the amplitude of an ASR.

On the other hand, if the drug-paired flavor elicits conditioned sickness, then it would be expected to attenuate the amplitude of an ASR.

In order to closely approximate the fear-potentiated ASR procedure using a shock-paired cue, Rana and Parker (2007) presented either a LiCl-paired flavor or an amphetamine-paired flavor intraorally during the startle session a few seconds prior to presentation of white noise bursts, which elicited a startle response. It was found that intraoral exposure to amphetamine-paired saccharin elicited a potentiated startle response as is seen with a shock-paired cue. On the other hand, an intraoral infusion of LiCl-paired saccharin solution elicited a blunted startle reaction as is seen when rats are made ill prior to the test (Beck & Servatius, 2003; Mansbach et al., 1992). However, when the nausea produced by LiCl was prevented prior to conditioning by pretreatment with ondansetron, the rats reacted to LiCl-paired saccharin in the same manner that they responded to the amphetamine-paired saccharin; that is they displayed a potentiated startle reaction. Ondansetron pretreatment, however, did not interfere with the avoidance of the saccharin solution displayed in a subsequent test, in support of previous findings (Limebeer & Parker, 2000; Rudd et al., 1998). That is, when the nausea was prevented by pretreatment with ondansetron, the remaining change in the rat's internal milieu produced by LiCl was sufficient to produce taste avoidance and conditioned fear to the taste. The results of this study suggested that the conditioned response elicited by intraoral exposure to a LiCl-paired flavor is one of conditioned nausea (evident as the blunted ASR). This conditioned nausea is also reflected by the presence of disgust reactions when assessed by the TR test (Grill & Norgren, 1978a). However, if the LiCl-induced nausea is overcome by pretreatment with ondansetron during conditioning, then the remaining affective changes produced by LiCl become associated with the taste. In the absence of nausea, the rats treat the taste as a danger signal and display a potentiated ASR (and conditioned avoidance) as they do following exposure to amphetamine-paired saccharin or a shock-paired cue.

Taste Avoidance/Preference Learning in the *S. murinus*

Further evidence that taste avoidance in the non-emetic rat may be at least partially mediated by conditioned fear in the absence of nausea is provided by comparative experiments the *S. murinus* (house musk shrew). The *Suncus* is an insectivore that, unlike rats, vomits in response to gastrointestinal and blood-borne toxins (Uneo, Matsuki, & Saito, 1988). Since the *Suncus* is capable of vomiting, it may not need to be as careful as the nonemetic rat in its selection of food. Like the nonemetic rat, however, the *Suncus* has been reported to avoid a taste paired with the emetic drug, LiCl (Smith et al., 2001). In fact, even doses of LiCl that do not provoke vomiting in this species are capable of establishing taste avoidance, suggesting that nausea is the effective US.

Although emetic drugs have been shown to produce taste avoidance in diverse species (Gustavson, Garcia, Hankins, & Rusiniak, 1974), there has been little comparative investigation of taste avoidance produced by rewarding drugs (although, see Rabin & Hunt, 1992). Rats consistently avoid consumption of a flavor paired with amphetamine or morphine at the same doses that produce a preference for a place (see Parker, 1995). Unlike the nonemetic rat, we have found that the *Suncus* develops a *preference* for rather than an avoidance of a novel sucrose or saccharin flavor that has been paired with moderate to high doses of amphetamine or morphine (Parker, Corrick, et al., 2002). In addition, when evaluated in a conditioned place preference paradigm, the same doses of amphetamine and morphine that produced a taste preference also produced a place preference in this species.

An explanation of the difference between rats and shrews in flavor conditioning produced by rewarding drugs may be linked to their different capabilities for emesis. The central emetic circuitry of the shrew is very similar to that of the rat (Ito & Seki, 1998). As noted before, early investigators speculated that drug-induced novelty is responsible for taste avoidance produced by rewarding drugs in rats, a species that is not capable of regurgitating ingested materials (Amit & Baum, 1970; Gamzu, 1977; Hunt & Amit, 1987). It would be advantageous for the nonemetic rat to monitor any change in internal state that follows ingestion of a distinctive novel food and avoid consuming that food in the future. Certainly, the rat has adapted to its lack of vomiting reflex by displaying the behavior of neophobia, an extreme wariness of new foods (Rzoska, 1953). It is thus easily conceivable that even a novel change in physiological state that is rewarding in nature may be sufficient to produce taste avoidance in this species. But, different pressures would be exerted on a species capable of vomiting.

Do Antiemetic Drugs Prevent Lithium-Induced Taste Avoidance in Shrews, Unlike Rats?

Like the nonemetic rat, the *Suncus* avoids consumption of a taste that is paired with LiCl (Smith et al., 2001). As reviewed before, attenuation of nausea during conditioning by pretreatment with an antiemetic drug does not attenuate subsequent avoidance of a LiCl-paired taste in rats (Limebeer & Parker, 1999, 2000, 2003), indicating that the nausea component of the affective state produced by LiCl may not be necessary for subsequent avoidance of the taste in the wary nonemetic rat. On the other hand, nausea may be necessary for the avoidance of a taste in a less wary animal capable of vomiting, the *Suncus*, an animal that does not display neophobia to a novel saccharin or sucrose solution (Parker, Corrick, et al., 2002). This hypothesis is supported by reports that the *Suncus* selectively avoids flavors paired with emetic drugs (LiCl; Smith et al., 2001), but actually prefers flavors paired with rewarding drugs (amphetamine and morphine; Parker, Corrick, et al., 2002). Therefore, it might be expected that pre-treatment with an antiemetic drug would prevent the establishment of LiCl-induced taste avoidance in the *Suncus*, unlike the nonemetic rat.

In a series of experiments, Kwiatkowska and Parker (2005) evaluated the potential of the antiemetic agents, ondansetron and Δ^9-THC, to interfere with LiCl-induced taste avoidance in the *Suncus*. At a dose (1.5 mg/kg) that did not modify saccharin (Experiment 1) or sucrose (Experiment 2) intake, ondansetron prevented the establishment of LiCl-induced taste avoidance (and prevented vomiting) in the shrew. A low dose of Δ^9-THC (1 mg/kg), that did not modify sucrose intake during conditioning, also prevented the establishment of LiCl-induced taste avoidance (and prevented vomiting) in the shrew. Higher doses of Δ^9-THC (2.5–10 mg/kg) were also effective, but they also suppressed sucrose consumption during conditioning. These results suggest that nausea is a necessary component of the US for the establishment of conditioned taste avoidance in the emetic shrew, unlike the nonemetic rat.

In the nonemetic rat, even when LiCl-induced nausea (expressed as conditioned disgust reactions) is prevented by pretreatment with an antiemetic drug, LiCl-induced taste avoidance is not attenuated. On the other hand, the establishment of conditioned taste avoidance in the shrew can be prevented by a reduction of the nausea/emesis produced by LiCl (Kwiatkowska & Parker, 2005). These results confirm our previous reports that taste avoidance in the shrew appears to be mediated by nausea/emesis (Smith et al., 2001), but taste avoidance in the rat may be mediated by conditioned fear, at least in the absence of nausea (Parker, 2003).

Anticipatory Contrast: A Reward Comparison Hypothesis

A very interesting recent theory to explain why rewarding drugs produce taste avoidance has been posited by Patricia S. Grigson and her group (Grigson, 1997). Grigson argues that the mechanism responsible for taste avoidance produced by rewarding drugs is similar to the mechanism responsible for saccharin avoidance produced by the subsequent opportunity to consume sucrose; that is, anticipatory contrast effects. When saccharin consumption repeatedly precedes sucrose consumption, rats eventually suppress their intake of saccharin (Flaherty & Checke, 1982)—an effect that looks like taste avoidance produced by a drug. The anticipatory contrast account for this phenomenon suggests that the rats suppress their consumption of a good flavor in anticipation of subsequently receiving an even better tasting flavor. When applied to taste avoidance produced by a rewarding drug, the anticipatory contrast theory suggests that rats suppress their intake of the flavored solution in anticipation of receiving an even better reward—an injection of morphine or cocaine, for example.

The strength of the anticipatory contrast effect produced by sucrose is determined by the relative rewarding properties of both the CS and the US; that is, reward comparison. According to this hypothesis, the reward comparison can be manipulated by varying the palatability of the CS. For instance, Flaherty, Turovsky, and Krauss (1994) reported that the magnitude of sucrose-induced suppression of saccharin consumption is increased as the palatability of the CS increased—that is, contrast effects were greater when the palatability of the CS more closely approximated the palatability of the

US. Therefore, if suppressed consumption of a flavored solution previously paired with a rewarding drug is another instance of an anticipatory contrast effect, then the strength of suppressed consumption should also vary (at least within limits) as a function of the palatability of the CS flavor. Grigson (1997) used two CS flavors that varied in palatability; rats preferred 0.15% saccharin to 0.58% NaCl in a two-bottle preference test. In different groups, each solution was paired with morphine (15 mg/kg, IP), cocaine (10 mg/kg, subcuatneous [SC]), LiCl (84.6 mg/kg, IP), or saline. In a subsequent 5-min single-bottle test, LiCl suppressed the intake of both saccharin and NaCl, but morphine and cocaine only suppressed the intake of the more palatable saccharin solution. Grigson argues that if the rats avoid the taste because of some aversive effects of all drugs, then rats treated with morphine and cocaine should behave as the rats treated with lithium, but they did not. The pattern of findings is better explained by a reward comparison mechanism; "that is, like the reward comparison effects that occur when saccharin predicts the future availability of a preferred concentration of sucrose, the suppressive effects of morphine also varied as a function of the relative value of the predictive CS" (Grigson, 1997, p. 134).

Grigson and her colleagues have provided additional evidence for the hypothesis that rats avoid intake of a flavor cue paired with a drug of abuse because they are anticipating the rewarding, rather than the aversive effects of the drug. Lesions of the gustatory thalamus prevent the suppressive effects of both rewarding sucrose solution and morphine, but not LiCl (Grigson, Lyuboslavsky, & Tanase, 2000; Reilly & Trifunovic, 1999; Scalera, Grigson, & Norgren, 1997; Schroy et al., 2005). Additionally, the suppressive effects of a rewarding sucrose solution and cocaine, but not LiCl, are exaggerated in reward-preferring Lewis rats and in Sprague-Dawley rats after chronic morphine treatment (Glowa, Shaw, & Riley, 1994; Grigson, 2000; Grigson & Freet, 2000; Grigson, Wheeler, Wheeler, & Ballard, 2001). The suppressive effects of morphine, but not LiCl, are prevented when using a highly palatable sucrose CS and water-deprived rats (Grigson, Lyuboslavsky, Tanase, & Wheeler, 1999) or food-deprived rats (Gomez & Grigson, 1999). Finally, when given the opportunity to self-administer cocaine by making the operant response of licking saccharin in a tube, the rats that self-administer the most (suggesting that they find cocaine highly rewarding) also show greater suppression of subsequent saccharin intake (Grigson & Twining, 2002).

Although considerable evidence supports the reward comparison explanation of suppressed consumption produced by a drug of abuse, other evidence does not fit as well within this framework. Such an account may not be able to explain species difference in the capacity of rewarding drugs to produce taste avoidance. That is, why do shrews prefer a taste paired with amphetamine or morphine that also produces a place preference (Parker, Corrick, et al., 2002)? Perhaps shrews, unlike rats, do not show anticipatory contrast effects when sucrose serves as the US; however, this is currently unknown. Furthermore, the reward comparison hypothesis argues that when a taste is paired with morphine, intake of the solution is expected to decrease as the palatability of the CS taste increases. However, morphine is less effective in producing conditioned suppression of salt consumption when salt is made more palatable by prior sodium deprivation (Sorge, Fudge, & Parker, 2002). In fact, when the palatability of salt was enhanced by sodium depletion, morphine also produced a mild conditioned salt preference in both a two-bottle preference test and enhanced ingestion reactions in the taste reactivity test, but morphine produced conditioned saccharin avoidance. Further research is needed to better understand these inconsistencies.

Clearly, the potential of a drug to produce both seeking behaviors and taste avoidance presents an interesting puzzle that is better understood in light of recent research. Whether the mechanism can be explained as an instance of conditioned fear or anticipatory contrast may motivate future researchers to structure interesting experiments toward solving this puzzle.

Taste Avoidance and Conditioned Disgust Methodology Differences

Flavor–drug associations are generally established by presenting thirsty rats with a bottle containing a novel flavored solution and injecting them with an illness-inducing drug on completion of the specified drinking period. The strength of the learning is generally assessed a number of days later by giving the rats the opportunity to consume the illness-paired flavor from a bottle for a specified time. If the rat has learned the flavor–illness association,

it will drink less than a rat that was injected with saline during the conditioning trial instead of the toxin. This procedure requires the rat to display both appetitive and consummatory responses (Craig, 1918) during both the conditioning and testing procedure. Since both responses are present during conditioning, it is conceivable that the rat learns the Pavlovian contingency between the taste CS and the illness US and/or that the rat learns the instrumental contingency between approaching the bottle (instrumental response) and illness (reinforcer) in the presence of the saccharin taste (discriminative stimulus). During testing, the subsequent suppressed consumption of the illness-paired flavor, therefore, may include the learned instrumental response (suppressed approach) and the Pavlovian conditioned response (conditioned disgust).

In the laboratory, another way of establishing a flavor–drug association is to intraorally infuse the flavored solution via a permanently implanted cannula for a specified time immediately prior to injecting an illness-producing drug or saline. The strength of the association is typically then measured by the orofacial reactions that the rats display when reexposed to the flavored solution in the TR test (Grill & Norgren, 1978a). If the rat learned the flavor–illness association, it will display conditioned disgust reactions (e.g., gaping) during the intraoral infusion test. Neither the acquisition nor expression of a flavor–illness association by this method includes the appetitive phase of responding. Without the instrumental response requirement, the intraoral method of conditioning contains only the Pavlovian contingency. When subsequently tested, the rat displays conditioned disgust reactions.

It is also possible to condition using one method (bottle or intraoral) and test using the other method. The bottle conditioned rats tested by intraoral infusion have the opportunity to learn the instrumental and the Pavlovian contingency, but the test only evaluates the Pavlovian response. Rats conditioned by intraoral infusion that are tested by bottle, have the opportunity to learn only the Pavlovian contingency, but the test also includes the instrumental approach response. It is not surprising, then, that when rats are tested by a bottle, they display a stronger avoidance response if they had been conditioned by bottle than if they had been conditioned by intraoral infusion (Limebeer & Parker, 2006). This is not simply a function of bottle conditioning producing a stronger association (Domjan & Wilson, 1972; Fouquet, Oberling, & Sandner, 2001; Revusky, Parker, Coombes, & Coombes, 1976; Wolgin & Wade, 1990; Yamamoto, Fresquet, & Sandner, 2002), because rats conditioned by intraoral infusion also show stronger conditioned disgust reactions in the intraoral test than rats conditioned by bottle (Limebeer & Parker, 2006).

Schafe et al. (1998) suggested that the intraoral conditioning method may produce a different neural and/or cognitive representation than the bottle conditioning method. They provide evidence that the amygdala is critical for intraoral established conditioning, but not for bottle established conditioning. These results are consistent with the theory that multiple memory systems are involved in the acquisition and expression of complex behaviors (e.g., McDonald & White, 1993). These results are very promising for providing a better understanding of the nature of the representation of a taste–drug association. However, it is crucial to keep in mind that weaker conditioning would be more vulnerable to disruption by lesion than stronger conditioning. Since, conditioning and testing using the same procedures (either bottle or intraoral) produces greater evidence of a saccharin–LiCl association than when they are not consistent (Limebeer & Parker, 2006), it is important to ensure that the differential effects of lesions on the bottle versus intraoral conditioning memory traces is not simply a difference in the strength of that trace produced by different training and testing methods.

Avoidance and Disgust: Multiple Memory Systems?

Garcia and colleagues (1974) argued that taste–illness memories are stored in different memory systems than buzzer-shock memories: "The way in which food-effects are stored in memory may be fundamentally different from the way in which memories of specific time–space strategies devised by external contingencies are understood" (Garcia et al., 1974, p. 829). McGowan, Hankins, and Garcia (1972) found that hippocampal lesions disrupted conditioning to a buzzer that was followed by shock, but facilitated conditioning to a taste that was followed by LiCl. Recently, Stone, Grimes, and Katz (2005) also reported that taste avoidance learning is enhanced by temporary inactivation of the hippocampus.

The distinction between conditioned disgust and conditioned avoidance suggests that even food–illness associations may have multiple memory representations. The neural representation of a flavor–illness association has been mostly assessed using a standard taste avoidance procedure. There has been relatively little investigation of the neural mechanisms involved in the establishment and/or the expression of conditioned disgust reactions. Grill and Norgren (1978b) showed that forebrain mechanisms are necessary for rats to acquire conditioned disgust for a LiCl-paired taste. Since the decerebrate rats were unable to drink, they were not tested in a taste avoidance procedure. More recently, Kiefer and Orr (1992) showed that rats lacking a gustatory cortex learned to avoid drinking sucrose and salt that was paired with LiCl (albeit at a slower rate than controls), but they failed to display aversive reactivity to the tastes. This was not a function of their inability to make aversive responses or to detect aversive tastes, because they showed normal reactivity to quinine solution. Therefore, rats lacking a gustatory cortex learned to avoid the taste, but not because it was conditionally disgusting. On the other hand, lesions of the area postrema (Eckel & Ossenkopp, 1996) and the parabrachial nucleus of the pons (Flynn, Grill, Schulkin, & Norgren, 1991), but not the nucleus of the solitary tract (Flynn et al., 1991) prevented both LiCl-induced taste avoidance and conditioned disgust. Finally, as reported before, Limebeer et al. (2004) found that 5,7-DHT lesions of the dorsal and median raphe nuclei (depleting forebrain 5-HT) prevented the establishment of LiCl-induced conditioned disgust but not taste avoidance.

The role of the amygdala in the establishment of conditioned taste avoidance learning has been the subject of much controversy (Reilly & Bornovalova, 2005, for review), but its involvement in conditioned disgust has only recently been evaluated. Schafe et al. (1998) reported that neurotoxin-induced amygdala lesions interfered with taste aversion only when the taste was delivered intraorally during conditioning, but not when delivered by bottle. However, the measures reported included consumption and latency to continuously passive drip (a neutral/mildly aversive reactions according to Berridge et al., 1981 and Parker, 1995), not conditioned disgust reactions. Using more discrete electrolytic lesions, Galaverna et al. (1993) reported that lesions of the central nucleus of the amygdala effected neither LiCl-induced taste avoidance (as has been consistently reported in the literature, see Reiley & Bornovalova, 2005, for review) nor conditioned disgust reactions. Rana and Parker (2008) have recently replicated the finding of Galaverna et al. (1993) using neurotoxin-induced (ibotenic acid) lesions.

Rana and Parker (2008) also evaluated the role of the basolateral amygdala (BLA) in conditioned disgust reactions. Neurotoxin-induced lesions of the BLA attenuated the strength of LiCl-induced saccharin avoidance, but did not affect the strength of LiCl-induced conditioned disgust reactions among rats that had been conditioned intraorally. Since conditioned taste avoidance may be at least partially motivated by conditioned fear, but conditioned disgust may be motivated by conditioned sickness, it is conceivable that the BLA lesions reduced the capacity of LiCl-paired saccharin to signal danger but not illness. This interpretation is consistent with the large body of literature demonstrating that the BLA is necessary for the establishment of conditioned fear (e.g., Killcross, Robbins, & Everitt, 1997; Melia, Falls, & Davis, 1992; Selden, Everitt, Jarrard, & Robbins, 1991). Alternatively, the BLA may be necessary for response requirements of avoidance, but not conditioned disgust. Since BLA lesions have been reported to interfere with shock motivated instrumental avoidance, but not Pavlovian conditioned suppression responses (Killcross et al., 1997), it is also possible that the BLA lesion may have interfered with instrumental avoidance of the spout of the bottle, while sparing Pavlovian conditioned disgust reactions (Rana & Parker, 2008). Recent fMRI data with humans demonstrated that the BLA is also not involved in disgust sensitivity to pictures of disgusting foods (Calder et al., 2007); however, the anterior insula was implicated in coding this emotion. This finding is consistent with the rat disgust literature (Kieffer & Orr, 1992; Rana & Parker, 2008).

Conclusion

The rat has been the subject of most investigations (over 2600 papers, see Riley & Freeman, 2004) of conditioned taste avoidance learning. Because this species does not vomit in response to a toxin challenge, it is likely to have developed an extremely keen ability to recognize foods likely to produce toxic effects. In fact, the rat avoids food previously paired with almost any drug state (hedonic or aversive); that is, it avoids any food that predicts a novel change in its affective homeostatic state and nausea is not a necessary component of that state. When nausea is explicitly prevented by pretreatment with an antiemetic drug, rats still learn to avoid a taste paired with LiCl. On the other hand, the emetic shrew need not be as wary as the rat. Although the emetic drug, LiCl, produces conditioned taste avoidance in the shrew, the rewarding drugs, amphetamine and morphine, produce a conditioned taste preference in the *Suncus*. It appears that nausea is necessary for the establishment of conditioned taste avoidance in this emetic species, because unlike the rat, antiemetic drug pretreatment blocks taste avoidance produced by LiCl. We hypothesize that the ability of a species to vomit plays a crucial role in the associative processes that govern food selection across species.

Although there has been considerable investigation of the neural mechanisms responsible for taste avoidance in the rat, clearly conditioned disgust and taste avoidance have been behaviorally dissociated in the studies reported earlier. There is also emerging evidence that different neural mechanisms may be involved in the establishment and/or expression of taste avoidance and conditioned disgust in the rat. Future research aimed at better understanding the neural mechanisms responsible for conditioned disgust in the rat may give us a better understanding of the central mechanisms involved in nausea. Although much is known about the neural system responsible for emesis, little is known about the distinct neural system for nausea (Andrews & Horn, 2006). The rat may serve as a better model than the shrew for these investigations, because nausea can be evaluated in the absence of emesis.

Acknowledgments This research was supported by a grant (OGP-92057) from the Natural Sciences and Engineering Research Council of Canada to Linda Parker.

References

Amit, Z., & Baum, M. (1970). Comment on the increased resistance to extinction of an avoidance response induced by certain drugs. *Psychological Reports, 27*, 310.

Andrews, P. L., & Horn, C. C. (2006). Signals for nausea and emesis: Implications for models of upper gastrointestinal diseases. *Autonomic Neuroscience: Basic and Clinical, 125*, 100–115.

Andrews, P. L., Rappaport, W. G., & Sanger, G. J. (1988). Neuropharmacology of emesis induced by anti-cancer therapy. *Trends in Pharmacology Sciences, 9*, 334–341.

Asin, K. E., Wirtshafter, D., & Kent, E. W. (1980). The effects of electrolytic median raphe lesions on two measures of latent inhibition. *Behavioral and Neural Biology, 28*, 408–417.

Baldessarini, R. J., & Vogt, M. (1988). Release of 3H-dopamine and analogous monoamines from rat striatal tissue. *Cellular and Molecular Neurobiology, 8*, 205–216.

Barann, M., Molderings, G., Bruss, M., Bonisch, H., Urban, B. W., & Gothert, M. (2002). Direct inhibition by cannabinoids of human 5-HT3A receptors: Probably involvement of an allosteric modulatory site. *British Journal of Pharmacology, 137*, 589–596.

Baumgarten, H. G., Klemm, H. P., Lachenmayer, L., Bjorklund, A., Lovenberg, W., & Schlossberger, H. G. (1978). Mode and mechanism of action of neurotoxic indoleamines: A review and a progress report. *Annals of the New York Academy of Sciences, 305*, 3–24.

Beck, K. D., & Servatius R. J. (2003). Stress and cytokine effects on learning: What does sex have to do with it? *Integrative Physiological and Behavioral Science, 38*, 179–188.

Berger, B. (1972). Conditioning of food aversions by injections of psychoactive drugs. *Journal Comparative and Physiological Psychology, 81*, 21–26.

Berridge, K. C. (2000). Measuring hedonic impact in animals and infants: Microstructure of affective taste reactivity patterns. *Neuroscience and Biobehavioral Reviews, 24*, 173–198.

Berridge, K. C., Grill, H. J., & Norgen, R. (1981). Relation of consummatory responses and preabsorptive insulin release to palatability and learned taste aversions. *Journal of Comparative and Physiological Psychology, 95*, 363–382.

Bienkowski, P., Iwinska, K., Piasecki, J., & Kostowski, W. (1997). 5,7-Dihydroxytryptamine lesion does not affect ethanol-induced conditioned taste and place aversion in rats. *Alcohol, 14*, 439–443.

Blundell, J. E. (1984). Serotonin manipulations and the structure of feeding behaviour. *Appetite, 7*(Suppl), 39–56.

Brambilla, P., Cipriani, A., Hotopf, M., & Barbui, C. (2005). Side-effect profile of fluoxetine in comparison with other SSRIs, tricyclic and newer antidepressants: A meta-analysis of clinical trial data. *Pharmacopsychiatry, 38*, 69–77.

Breslin, P. A., Spector, A. C., & Grill, H. J. (1992). A quantitative comparison of taste reactivity behaviors to sucrose before and after lithium chloride pairings: A unidimensional account of palatability. *Behavioral Neuroscience, 106*, 820–836.

Brown, J. S., Kalish, H. I., & Farber, I. E. (1951). Conditioned fear as revealed by magnitude of startle response to an auditory stimulus. *Journal of Experimental Psychology, 41*, 317–328.

Calder, A. J., Beaver, J. D., Davis, M. H., van Ditzhuijzen, J., Keane, J., & Lawrence, A. D. (2007). Disgust sensitivity predicts the insula and pallidal response to pictures of disgusting foods. *European Journal of Neuroscience, 25*, 3422–3428.

Coil, J. D., Hankins, W. G., Jenden, D. J., & Garcia, J. (1978). The attenuation of a specific cue-to-consequence association by antiemetic agents. *Psychopharmacology, 56*, 21–25.

Cordick, N., Parker, L. A., & Ossenkopp, K. P. (1999). Rotation-induced conditioned rejection in the taste reactivity test. *NeuroReport, 10*, 1157–1159.

Craig, W. (1918). Appetites and aversions as constituents of instinct. *Biological Bulletin, 34*, 91–107.

Cross-Mellor, S. K., Ossenkopp, K. P., Piomelli, D., & Parker, L. A. (2007). Effects of the FAAH inhibitor, URB 597, and anandamice on lithium-induced taste reactivity responses: A measure of nausea in rats. *Psychopharmacology, 190*, 135–143.

Darmani, N. A. (2001). Delta-9-tetrahydrocannabinol and synthetic cannabinoids prevent emesis produced by the cannabinoid CB_1 receptor antagonist/inverse agonist SR 141716A. *Neuropsychopharmacology, 24*, 198–203.

Darmani, N. A., McClanahan, B. A., Trinh, C., Petrosino, S., Valent, M., & DiMarzo, V. (2005). Cisplatin increases brain 2-arachidonoylglycerol (2-AG) and concomitantly reduces intestinal 2-AG and anandamide levels in the least shrew. *Neuropharmacology, 49*, 502–513.

Darmani, N. S., & Johnson, C. J. (2004). Central and peripheral mechanisms contribute to the antiemetic actions of delta-9-tetrahydrocannabinol against 5-hydroxytryptophan-induced emesis. *European Journal of Pharmacology, 488*, 201–212.

Davis, M., Falls, W. A., Campeau, S., & Kim, M. (1993). Fear-potentiated startle: A neural and pharmacological analysis. *Behavioral Brain Research, 58*, 175–198.

De Olivera Mora, P., Fouquet, N., Oberling, P., Gobaille, S., Graeff, F. G., & Sandner, G. (1999). A neurotoxic lesion of serotonergic neurons using 5,7-dihydroxytryptamine does not disrupt latent inhibition in paradigms sensitive to low doses of amphetamine. *Brain Research 100*, 167–175.

Deutsch, D. G., & Chin, S. (1993). Enzymatic synthesis and degradation of anandamide, a cannabinoid receptor agonist. *Biochemical Pharmacology, 46,* 791–796.

Devane, W. A., Dysarz, F. A., Johnson, M. R., Melvin, L. S., & Howlett, A. C. (1988). Determination and characterization of a cannabinoid receptor. *Molecular Pharmacology, 34,* 605–613.

Devane, W. A., Hanus, L., Breuer, A., Pertwee, R. G., Stevenson, L. A., Griffin, G., et al. (1992). Isolation and structure of a brain constituent that binds to the cannabinoid receptor. *Science, 258,* 1946–1949.

Domjan, M., & Wilson, N. E. (1972). Contribution of ingestive behaviours to taste-aversion learning in the rat. *Journal of Comparative and Physiological Psychology, 80,* 403–412.

Eckel, L. A., & Ossenkopp, K. P. (1996). Area postrema mediates the formation of rapid, conditioned palatability shifts in lithium-treated rats. *Behavioural Neuroscience, 110,* 202–212.

Fan, P. (1995). Cannabinoid agonists inhibit the activation of $5-HT_3$ receptors in rat nodose ganglion neurons. *Journal of Neurophysiology, 73,* 907–910.

Flaherty, C. F., & Checke, S. (1982). Anticipation of incentive gain. *Animal Learning & Behavior, 10,* 177–182.

Flaherty, C. F., Turovsky, J., & Krauss, K. L. (1994). Relative hedonic value modulates anticipatory contrast. *Physiology & Behavior, 55,* 1047–1054.

Flynn, F. W., Grill, J. H., Schulkin, J., & Norgren, R. (1991). Central gustatory lesions: II Effects on sodium appetitie, taste aversion learning, and feeding behaviors. *Behavioral Neuroscience 105,* 944–954.

Fouquet, N., Oberling, P., & Sandner, G. (2001). Differential effect of free intake versus oral perfusion of sucrose in conditioned taste aversion in rats. *Physiology & Behavior 74,* 465–474.

Gadusek, F. J., & Kalat, J. W. (1975). Effects of scopolamine on retention of taste-aversion learning in rats. *Physiological Psychology, 3,* 130–132.

Galaverna, O. I. G., Seeley, R. J., Berridge, K. C., Grill, H. J., Epstein, A. N., & Schulkin, J. (1993). Lesions of the central nucleus of the amygdale I: Effects on taste reactivity, taste aversion learning and sodium appetite. *Behavioral Brain Research 59,* 11–17.

Gamzu, E. (1977). The multifaceted nature of taste aversion inducing agents: Is there a single common factor? In L. Barker, M. Domjan, & M. Best (Eds.), *Learning mechanisms of food selection* (pp. 447–511). Waco, TX: Baylor University Press.

Gaoni, Y., & Mechoulam, R. (1964). Isolation, structure and partial synthesis of an active constituent of hashish. *Journal of the American Chemical Society, 86,* 1646–1647.

Garcia, J. (1989). Food for Tolman: Cognition and cathexis in concert. In T. Archer & L.-G. Nilsson (Eds.), *Aversion, avoidance and anxiety* (pp. 45–85). Hillsdale, NJ: Lawrence Erlbaum Associates, Inc.

Garcia, J., & Ervin, F. R. (1968). Gustatory-visceral and telereceptor–cutaneous conditioning: Adaptation in internal and external milieus. *Communications in Behavioral Biology, 1,* 389–415.

Garcia, J., Hankins, W. G., & Rusiniak, K. W. (1974). Behavioral regulation of the milieu interne in man and rat. *Science, 185,* 824–831.

Garcia, J., & Koelling, R. A. (1966). Relation of cue to consequence in avoidance learning. *Psychonomic Science, 4,* 123–124.

Glowa, J. R., Shaw, A. E., & Riley, A. L. (1994). Cocaine-induced conditioned taste aversions: Comparison between effects in LEW and F344/N rat strains. *Psychopharmacology, 114,* 229–232.

Gomez, F., & Grigson, P. S. (1999). The suppressive effects of LiCl, sucrose, and drugs of abuse are modulated by sucrose concentration in food-deprived rats. *Physiology & Behavior, 67,* 351–357.

Gorzalka, B., Hanson, L., Harrington, J., Killam, S., & Campbell-Meiklejohn, D. (2003). Conditioned taste aversion: Modulation by 5-HT receptor activity and corticosterone. *European Journal of Pharamcology, 47,* 129–134.

Goudie, A. J., Stolerman, I. P., Demellweek, C., & D'Mello, G. D. (1982). Does conditioned nausea mediate drug-induced conditioned taste aversion? *Psychopharmacology, 78,* 277–282.

Grant, V. L. (1987). Do conditioned taste aversions result from activation of emetic mechanisms? *Psychopharmacology, 93,* 405–415.

Grigson, P. S. (1997). Conditioned taste aversions and drugs of abuse: A reinterpretation. *Behavioral Neuroscience, 111,* 129–136.

Grigson, P. S. (2000). Drugs of abuse and reward comparison: A brief review. *Appetite, 35,* 89–91.

Grigson, P. S., & Freet, C. S. (2000). The suppressive effects of sucrose and cocaine, but not LiCl, are greater in Lewis than Fischer rats: Evidence for the reward comparison hypoghesis. *Behavioral Neuroscience, 114,* 353–363.

Grigson, P. S., Lyuboslavsky, P., & Tanase, D. (2000). Bilateral lesions of the gustatory thalamus disrupt morphine- but not LiCl-induced intake suppression in rats: Evidence against the conditioned taste aversion hypothesis. *Brain Research, 858,* 327–337.

Grigson, P. S., Lyuboslavsky, P. N., Tanase, D., & Wheeeler, R. (1999). Water-deprivation prevents morphine-, but not LiCl-induced, suppression of sucrose intake. *Physiology and Behavior, 76,* 277–289.

Grigson, P. S., & Twining, R. (2002). Cocaine-induced suppression of saccharin intake: A model of drug-induced devaluation of natural rewards. *Behavioral Neuroscience, 116,* 321–333.

Grigson, P. S., Wheeler, R. A., Wheeler, D. S., & Ballard, S. M. (2001). Chronic morphine treatment exaggerates the suppressive effects of sucrose and cocaine, but not lithium chloride, on saccharin intake in Sprague-Dawley rats. *Behavioral Neuroscience, 115,* 403–416.

Grill, H. C. (1985). Introduction: Physiological mechanisms in conditioned taste aversions. In N. Braveman & P. Bronstein (Eds.), *Experimental assessments and clinical applications of conditioned food aversion.* New York: New York Academy of Sciences; *Annals of the New York Academy of Sciences, 443,* 67–88.

Grill, H. C., & Norgren, R. (1978a). The taste reactivity test. I: Mimetic responses to gustatory stimuli in neurologically normal rats. *Brain Research, 143,* 263–279.

Grill, H. C., & Norgren, R. (1978b). Chronically decerebrate rats demonstrate satiation but not bait shyness. *Science, 201,* 267–269.

Gustavson, C. R., Garcia, J., Hankins, W. G., & Rusiniak (1974). Coyote predation control by aversive conditioning. *Science, 184,* 581–583.

Hermann, H., Marsicano, G., & Lutz, B. (2002) Coexpression of the cannabinoid receptor type 1 with dopamine and serotonin receptors in distinct neuronal subpopulations of the adult mouse forebrain. *Neuroscience, 109,* 451–460.

Higgins, G. A., Kilpatrick, G. J., Bunce, K. T., Jones, B. J., & Tyers, M. B. (1989). 5-HT$_3$ receptor antagonists injected into the area postrema inhibit cisplatin-induced emesis in the ferret. *British Journal of Pharmacology, 97,* 247–255.

Hillsley, K., & Grundy, D. (1998). Serotonin and cholecystokinin activate different populations of rat mesenteric vagal afferents. *Neuroscience Letters, 255,* 63–66.

Himmi, T., Dallaporta, M., Perrin, J., & Orsini, J. C. (1996). Neuronal responses to delta9-tetrahyrocannabinol in the solitary tract nucleus. *European Journal of Pharmacology, 312,* 273–279.

Himmi, T., Perrin, J., El Ouazzani, T., & Orsini, J. C. (1998). Neuronal responses to cannabinoid receptor ligands in the solitary tract nucleus. *European Journal of Pharmacology, 359,* 49–54.

Howlett, A. C., Barth, F., Bonner, T. I., Cabral, P., Casellaa, G., Devane, W. A., et al. (2002). International Union of Pharmacology. XXVII. Classification of cannabinoid receptors. *Pharmacological Reviews, 54,* 161–202.

Hunt, T., & Amit, Z. (1987). Conditioned taste aversion by self-administered drugs: Paradox revisited. *Neuroscience and Biobehavioral Reviews, 11,* 107–130.

Ionesco, E., & Buresova, O. (1977). Failure to elicit CTA by severe poisoning. *Pharmacology, Biochemistry, and Behaviour, 6,* 251–254.

Ito, H., & Seki, M. (1998). Ascending projections from the area postrema and nucleus of the solitary tract of *Suncus murinus*: Anterograde tracing study using *Phaseolus vulgaris* leucoagglutinin. *Okajimas Folia Anatomy Japan, 75,* 9–31.

Kamin, L. J., Brimer, C. J., & Black, A. H. (1963). Condiitioned suppression as a monitor of fear of the CS in the course of avoidance training *Journal of Comparative and Physiological Psychology, 56,* 497–501.

Kiefer, S. W., & Orr, M. S. (1992). Taste avoidance, but not aversion, learning in rats lacking gustatory cortex. *Behavioral Neuroscience, 106,* 140–146.

Killcross, S., Robbins, T. W., & Everitt, B. J. (1997). Different types of fear-conditioned behaviour mediated by separate nuclei within amygdala. *Nature, 388,* 377–380.

Kimura, T., Ohta, T., Watanabe, K., Yoshimura, H., & Yamamoto, I. (1998). Anandamide, an endogenous cannabinoid receptor ligand, also interacts with 5-hydroxytryptamine (5HT) receptor. *Biological & Pharmaceutical Bulletin, 21,* 224–226.

Konorski, J. (1967). *Integrative activity of the brain: An interdisciplinary approach.* Chicago, IL: University of Chicago Press.

Kwiatkowska, M., & Parker, L. A. (2005). Ondansetron and Δ-9-tetrahydrocannabinol interfere with the establishment of lithium-induced conditioned taste avoidance in the house musk shrew (*Suncus murinus*). *Behavioral Neuroscience, 119,* 974–982.

Kwiatkowska, M., Parker, L. A., Burton, P., & Mechoulam, R. (2004). A comparative analysis of the potential of cannabinoids and ondansetron to suppress cisplatin-induced emesis in the *Suncus murinus* (house musk shrew). *Psychopharmacology, 174,* 254–259.

Leaf, R. C., & Leaf, S. R. (1966). Recovery time as a measure of degree of conditioned suppression. *Psychological Reports, 18,* 265–266.

Lett, B. T. (1985). The painlike effect of gallamine and naloxone differs from sickness induced by lithium chloride. *Behavioral Neuroscience,* 99, 145–150.

Levy, C. J., Carroll, M. F., Smith, J. C., & Hofer, K. G. (1974). Antihistamines block radiation-induced taste aversions. *Science, 186,* 1044–1045.

Limebeer, C. L., & Parker, L. A. (1999). Delta-9-tetrahydrocannabinol interferes with the establishment and the expression of conditioned rejection reactions produced by cyclophosphamide: A rat model of nausea. *NeuroReport, 10,* 3769–3772.

Limebeer, C. L., & Parker, L. A. (2000). Ondansetron interferes with lithium-induced conditioned rejection reactions, but not lithium-induced taste avoidance. *Journal of Experimental Psychology: Animal Behavior Process, 26,* 371–384.

Limebeer, C. L., & Parker, L. A. (2003). The 5-HT$_{1A}$ agonist 8-OH-DPAT dose-dependently interferes with the establishment and expression of lithium-induced conditioned rejection reactions in rats. *Psychopharmacology, 166,* 120–126.

Limebeer, C. L., & Parker, L. A. (2006). Effect of conditioning method and testing method on strength of lithium-induced taste aversion learning. *Behavioral Neuroscience, 120,* 963–969.

Limebeer, C. L., Parker, L. A., & Fletcher, P. J. (2004). 5,7-Dihydroxytryptamine lesions of the dorsal and median raphe nuclei interfere with lithium-induced conditioned gaping, but not conditioned taste avoidance, in rats. *Behavioral Neuroscience, 118,* 1391–1399.

Manji, H. K., Bebchuck, J. M., Morre, G. J., Glitz, D., Hasanat, K. A. & Chen, G. (1999). Modulation of CNS signal transduction pathways and gene expression by mood-stabilizing agents: Therapeutic implications. *Journal of Clinical Psychiatry, 60,* 27–39.

Mansbach, R. S., Gold, L. H., & Harris, L. S. (1992). The acoustic startle response as a measure of behavioral dependence in rats. *Psychopharmacology, 108,* 40–46.

Matsuda, L. A., Lolait, S. J., Brownstein, M. J., Young, A. C., & Bonner, T. I. (1990). Structure of a cannabinoid receptor and functional expression of the cloned cDNA. *Nature, 346,* 561–565.

Matsuki, N., Ueno, S., Kaji, T., Ishihara, A., Wang, C. H., & Saito, H. (1988). Emesis induced by cancer chemotherapeutic agents in the *Suncus murinus*: A new experimental model. *Japanese Journal of Pharmacology, 48,* 303–306.

Mayer, L. A., & Parker, L. A. (1993). Rewarding and aversive properties of IP versus SC cocaine: Assessment by place and taste conditioning. *Psychopharmacology, 112,* 189–194.

McDonald, R. J., & White, N. (1993). A triple dissociation of memory systems: Hippocampus, amygdala, and dorsal striatum. *Behavioral Neuroscience, 107,* 3–22.

McDonald, R. V., Parker, L. A., & Siegel, S. (1997). Conditioned sucrose aversions produced by naloxone-precipitated withdrawal from acutely administered morphine. *Pharmacology, Biochemistry, and Behaviour, 58,* 1003–1007.

McGowan, B. K., Hankins, W. G., & Garcia, J. (1972). Limbic lesions and control of the internal and external environment. *Behavioral Biology, 7,* 841–852.

McLaughlin, P. J., Winston, K. M., Limebeer, C. L., Parker, L. A., Makriyannis, A., & Salamone, J. D. (2005). The cannabinoid antagonist AM 251 produces food avoidance and behaviors associated with nausea but does not impair feeding efficiency in rats. *Psychopharmacology, 180,* 286–293.

Mechoulam, R., Ben-Shabat, S., Hanus, L., Ligumsky, M., Kaminski, N. E., Schatz, A., et al. (1995). Identification of an endogenous 2-monoglyceride, present in canine gut, that binds to cannabinoid receptors. *Biochemical Pharmacology, 50,* 83–90.

Mechoulam, R., Parker, L. A., & Gallily, R. (2002). Cannabidiol: An overview of some pharmacological aspects. *Journal of Clinical Pharmacology, 42,* 11S–19S.

Melia, K. R., Falls, W. A., & Davis, M. (1992). Involvement of pertussis toxin sensitive G-proteins in conditioned fear-potentiated startle: Possible involvement of the amygdala. *Brain Research, 584,* 141–148.

Miller, A. D., Nonaka, S., Jakus, J., & Yates, B. J. (1996). Modulation of vomiting by the medullary midline. *Brain Research, 737,* 51–58.

Nachman, M., & Hartley, P. L. (1975). The role of illness in inducing taste aversions in rats: A comparison of several rodenticides. *Journal of Comparative and Physiological Psychology, 81,* 1010–1018.

Ossenkopp, K. P., Parker, L. A., Limebeer, C. L., Buron, P., Fudge, M. L., & Cross-Mellor, S. K. (2003). Vestibular lesions selectively abolish rotation-induced, but not lithium-induced, conditioned taste aversions (oral rejection responses) in rats. *Behavioral Neuroscience, 117,* 105–112.

Parker, L. A. (1980). Conditioned suppression of drinking: A measure of the CR elicited by a lithium-conditioned flavor. *Learning and Motivation, 11,* 538–559.

Parker, L. A. (1982). Nonconsummatory and consummatory behavioral CRs elicited by lithium- and amphetamine-paired flavors. *Learning and Motivation, 13,* 281–303.

Parker, L. A. (1984). Behavioral conditioned responses across multiple conditioning/testing trials elicited by lithium- and amphetamine-paired flavors. *Behavioral and Neural Biology, 41,* 190–199.

Parker, L. A. (1988). Positively reinforcing drugs may produce a different kind of CTA than drugs which are not positively reinforcing. *Learning and Motivation, 19*, 207–220.

Parker, L. A. (1991). Taste reactivity responses elicited by reinforcing drugs: A dose–response analysis. *Behavioral Neuroscience, 105*, 955–964.

Parker, L. A. (1993). Taste reactivity responses elicited by cocaine-, phencyclidine-, and methamphetamine-paired sucrose solutions. *Behavioral Neuroscience 107*, 118–129.

Parker, L. A. (1995). Rewarding drugs produce taste avoidance, but not taste aversion. *Neuroscience and Biobehavioral Reviews, 19*, 143–151.

Parker, L. A. (1996). LSD produces a place preference and taste avoidance, but does not produce taste aversion. *Behavioral Neuroscience, 109*, 503–508.

Parker, L. A. (1998). Emetic drugs produce conditioned rejection reactions in the taste reactivity test. *Journal of Psychophysiology, 12*, 3–13.

Parker, L. A. (2003). Taste avoidance and taste aversion: Evidence for two different processes. *Learning & Behavior, 31*, 165–172.

Parker, L. A., & Brosseau, L. (1990). Apomorphine-induced flavor–drug associations: A dose–response analysis by the taste reactivity test and the conditioned taste avoidance test. *Pharmacology, Biochemistry, and Behaviour, 35*, 583–587.

Parker, L. A., & Carvell, T. (1986). Orofacial and somatic responses elicited by lithium-, nicotine- and amphetamine-paired sucrose solution. *Pharmacology, Biochemistry, and Behaviour, 24*, 883–887.

Parker, L. A., Corrick, M. L., Limebeer, C. L., & Kwiatkowska, M. (2002b). Amphetamine and morphine produce a conditioned taste and place preference in the house musk shrew (*Suncus murinus*). *Journal of Experiment Psychology: Animal Behavior Processes, 28*, 75–82.

Parker, L. A., & Kemp, S. W. (2001). Tetrahydrocannabinol (THC) interferes with conditioned retching in *Suncus murinus*: An animal model of anticipatory nausea and vomiting (ANV). *NeuroReport, 12*, 749–751.

Parker, L. A., Kwaitkowska, M., Burton, P., & Mechoulam, R. (2004). Effect of cannabinoids on lithium-induced vomiting in the *Suncus murinus* (house musk shrew). *Psychopharmacology, 171*, 156–161.

Parker, L. A., Kwiatkowska, M., & Mechoulam, R. (2006). Delta-9-tetrahydrocannabinol and cannabidiol, but not ondansetron, interfere with conditioned retching reactions elicited by a lithium-paired context in *Suncus murinus*: An animal model of anticipatory nausea and vomiting. *Physiology & Behavior 87*, 61–71.

Parker, L. A., Limebeer, C. L., & Kwiatkowska, M. (2005). Cannabinoids: Effects on vomiting and nausea in animal models. In R. Mechoulam (Ed.), *Cannabinoids as therapeutics* (pp. 183–200). Basel, Switzerland: Birkhauser Verlag.

Parker, L. A., & McLeod, K. B. (1991). Chin rub CRs may reflect conditioned sickness elicited by a lithium-paired sucrose solution. *Pharmacology, Biochemistry, and Behaviour, 40*, 983–986.

Parker, L. A., & Mechoulam, R. (2003). Cannabinoid agonists and an antagonist modulate lithium-induced conditioned gaping in rats. *Integrative Physiological and Behaviorioal Science, 38*, 134–146.

Parker, L. A., Mechoulam, R., & Schlievert, C. (2002a). Cannabidiol, a non-psychoactive component of cannabis, and its synthetic dimethylheptyl homolog suppress nausea in an experimental model with rats. *NeuroReport, 13*, 567–570.

Parker, L. A., Mechoulam, R., Schlievert, C., Abbott, L. A., Fudge, M. L., & Burton, P. (2003). Cannabinoid agonists attenuate and a cannabinoid antagonist potentiates lithium-induced conditioned rejection reactions in a rat model of nausea. *Psychopharmacology, 166*, 156–162.

Pelchat, M. L., & Rozin, P. (1982). The special role of nausea in the acquisition of food dislikes in humans. *Appetite, 3*, 343–351.

Pelchat, M. L., Grill, H. J., Rozin, P., & Jacobs, J. (1983). Quality of acquired responses to tastes by *Rattus norvegicus* depends on type of associated discomfort. *Journal of Comparative Psychology, 97*, 140–153.

Pertwee, R. G. (2001). Cannabinoids and the gastrointestinal tract. *Gut, 48*, 859–867.

Piasecki, J., Bienkowski, P., Dudek, K., Koros, E., & Kostowski, W. (2001). Ethanol-induced conditioned taste aversion in the rat: Effects of 5,7-dihydroxytryptamine lesion of the dorsal raphe nucleus. *Alcohol, 24*, 9–14.

Pi-Sunyer, F. X., Aronne, L. J., Heshmati, H. M., Devin, J., Rosenstock, J., & RIO-North America Study Group (2006). Effect of rimonabant, a cannabinoid-1 receptor blocker, on weight and cardiometabolic risk factors in overweight or obese patients. *Journal of American Medical Association, 295*, 761–775.

Rabin, B. M., & Hunt, W. A. (1983). Effects of anti-emetics on the acquisition and recall of radiation and lithium chloride induced conditioned taste aversions. *Pharmacology, Biochemistry, and Behavior, 18*, 629–636.

Rabin, B. M., & Hunt, W. A. (1992). Relationship between vomiting and taste aversion learning in the ferret: Studies with ionizing radiation, lithium chloride, and amphetamine. *Behavioral and Neural Biology, 58*, 83–93.

Rana, S. A., & Parker, L. A. (2007). Effect of exposure to a lithium-paired or an amphetamine-paired flavor on the acoustic startle response in rats. *Journal of Experimental Psychology: Animal Behavior Processes, 33*, 172–184.

Rana S. A., & Parker L. A. (2008). Differential effects of neurotoxin-induced lesions of the basolateral amygdala and central nucleus of the amygdala on lithium-induced conditioned disgust reactions and conditioned taste avoidance. *Behavioural Brain Research*, 189, 284–292.

Reicher, M. A., & Holman, E. W. (1977). Location preference and flavor aversion reinforced by amphetamine in rats. *Animal Learning & Behavior, 5*, 343–346.

Reilly, S., & Bornovalova, M. A. (2005). Conditioned taste aversions and amygdala lesions in the rat: A critical review. *Neuroscience and Biobehavioral Reviews, 29*, 1067–1088.

Reilly, S., & Trifunovic, R. (1999). Gustatory thalamus lesions eliminate successive negative contrast in rats, *Behavioral Neuroscience, 113*, 1242–1248.

Revusky, S., & Garcia J. (1970) Learned associations over long delays. In G. H. Bower (Ed.) *The psychology of learning and motivation: Advances in research and theory, IV* (pp. 1–83). New York: Academic Press.

Revusky, S., Parker, L. A., Coombes, J., & Coombes, S. (1976). Rat data which suggest alcoholic beverages should be swallowed during chemical aversion therapy, not just tasted. *Behaviour Research and Therapy, 14*, 189–194.

Riley, A. L., & Freeman, K. B. (2004). Conditioned taste aversion: A database. *Pharmacology, Biochemistry, and Behaviour, 77*, 655–666.

Rodriguez, M., Lopez, M., Symonds, M., & Hall, G. (2000). Lithium-induced context aversion in rats as a model of anticipatory nausea in humans. *Physiology & Behavior, 71*, 571–579.

Rudd, J. A., Ngan, M. P., & Wai, M. K. (1998). 5-HT$_3$ receptors are not involved in conditioned taste aversions induced by 5-hydroxytryptamine, ipecacuanha or cisplatin. *European Journal of Pharmacology, 352*, 143–149.

Rzoska, J. (1953). Bait shyness, a study in rat behaviour. *British Journal of Animal Behavior, 1*, 128–135.

Scalera, G., Grigson, P. S., & Norgren, R. (1997). Gustatory functions, sodium appetite, and conditioned taste aversion survive excitotoxic lesions of the thalamic taste area. *Behavioral Neuroscience, 111*, 633–645.

Schafe, G. E., Thiele, T. E., & Bernstein, I. L. (1998). Conditioning method dramatically alters the role of amygdala in taste aversion learning. *Learning & Memory, 5*, 481–492.

Schlicker, E., & Kathman, M. (2001). Modulation of transmitter release via presynaptic cannabinoid receptors. *Trends in Pharmacological Sciences, 22*, 565–571.

Schroy, P. L., Wheeler, R. A., Davidson, C., Scalera, G., Twining, R. C., & Grigson, P. S. (2005). Role of gustatory thalamus in anticipation and comparison of rewards over time in rats. *American Journal of Physiology: Regulatory, Integrative and Comparative Physiology, 288*, 966–980.

Schwarz, M. D., Jacobsen, P. B., & Bjovberg, D. H. (1996). Role of nausea in the development of aversions to a beverage paired with chemotherapy treatment in cancer patients. *Physiology & Behavior, 59*, 659–663.

Selden, N. R. W., Everitt, B. J., Jarrard, L. D., & Robbins, T. W. (1991). Complementary roles for the amygdala and hippocampus in aversive conditioning to explicit and contextual cues. *Neuroscience, 42*, 335–350.

Simoneau, I. I., Hamza, M. S., Mata, H. P., Siegel, E. M., Vanderah, T. W., Porreca, F., et al. (2001) The cannabinoid agonist WIN55, 212-2 suppresses opioid-induced emesis in ferrets. *Anesthesiology, 94*, 882–887.

Sink, K. S., McLaughlin, P. J., Brown, C., Fan, P., Vemuri, V., Keran, V., et al. (2008). The novel cannabinoid CB1 receptor neutral antagonist, AM4113, suppresses food intake and food-reinforced behaviour but does not induce signs of nausea in rats. *Neuropsychopharmacology, 33*, 945–955.

Smith, J. E., Friedman, M. I., & Andrews, P. L. R. (2001). Conditioned food aversion in *Suncus murinus* (house musk shrew) a new model for the study of nausea in a species with an emetic reflex. *Physiology & Behavior, 73*, 593–598.

Sorge, R. E., Fudge, M. A., & Parker, L. A. (2002). Effect of sodium deprivation on morphine- and lithium-induced conditioned salt avoidance and taste reactivity. *Psychopharmacology, 160*, 84–91.

Stone, M. E., Grimes, B. S., & Katz, D. B. (2005). Hippocampal inactivation enhances taste learning. *Learning & Memory, 12*, 579–586.

Thiele, T. E., Kiefer, S. W., Badia-Elder, N. E. (1996). Delayed generalization testing produces enhanced alcohol aversions in rats. *Alcohol, 13*, 201–207.

Tork, I. (1990). Anatomy of the serotonergic system. *Annals of the New York Academy of Sciences, 600,* 9–34.

Travers, J. B., & Norgren, R. (1986). Electromyographic analysis of the ingestion and rejection of sapid stimuli in the rat. *Behavioral Neuroscience, 100,* 544–555.

Treiser, S. L., Cascio, C. S., O'Donohue, T. L., Thao, N. B., Jacobowitz, D. M., & Kellar, K. J., et al. (1981). Lithium increases serotonin release and decreases serotonin receptors in the hippocampus. *Science, 213,* 1529–1531.

Uneo, S., Matsuki, N., & Saito, H. (1988). *Suncus murinus* as a new experimental model for motion sickness. *Life Science, 43,* 413–420.

Van Sickle, M. D., Oland, L. D., Ho, W., Hillard, C. J., Mackie, K., Davison, J. J., et al. (2001). Cannabinoids inhibit emesis through CB1 receptors in the brainstem of the ferret. *Gastroenterology, 121,* 767–774.

Van Sickle, M. D., Oland, L. D., Mackie, K., Davison, J. S., & Sharkey, K. A. (2003). Δ^9-Tetrahydrocannabinol selectively acts on CB_1 receptors in specific regions of dorsal vagal complex to inhibit emesis in ferrets. *American Journal of Physiology: Gastrointestinal and Liver Physiology, 285,* G566–G576.

Wang, H. Y., & Friedman, E. (1989). Lithium inhibition of protein kinsase C activation-induced serotonin release. *Psychopharmacology, 99,* 213–218.

Wegener, G., Smith, D. F., & Rosenberg, R. (1997). 5-HT1A receptors in lithium-induced conditioned taste aversion. *Psychopharmacology, 133,* 51–54.

West, H. L., Mark, G. P., & Hoebel, B. G. (1991). Effects of conditioned taste aversion on extracellular serotonin in the lateral hypothalamus and hippocampus of freely moving rats. *Brain Research, 556,* 95–100.

Wise, R., Yokel, P., & DeWit, H. (1976). Both positive reinforcement and conditioned aversion from amphetamine and from apomorphine in rats. *Science, 191,* 1273–1274.

Wolgin, D. L., & Wade, J. V. (1990). Effect of lithium chloride-induced aversion on appetitive and consummatory behavior. *Behavioral Neuroscience, 104,* 438–440.

Yamamoto, J., Fresquet, N., & Sandner, G. (2002). Conditioned taste aversion using four different means to deliver sucrose to rats. *Physiology & Behavior, 74,* 387–396.

Zalaquett, C., & Parker, L. A. (1989). Further evidence that CTAs produced lithium and amphetamine are qualitatively different. *Learning and Motivation, 20,* 413–427.

7

Memory Phenomena and Conditioned Taste Aversion

SUSANNE M. MEEHAN AND DAVID C. RICCIO

Unlike many other learning paradigms, conditioned taste aversion (CTA) can often be acquired in a single trial and hence learning need not be measured online. Rather, it is often assessed after the conditioning is completed. Following a pairing of a taste with induced illness, a period of time, typically 24 or 48 h, is interpolated to permit recovery from the malaise at the time of testing. So, in a sense, almost all CTA studies involve a retention interval, albeit a relatively brief one.

Given CTA's well-deserved reputation as a phenomenon that is resistant to forgetting, one might wonder why a chapter on memory and CTA is needed. Our view would be that if we broaden the scope to include the variety of phenomena associated with CTA, then there are a number of findings that prove relevant for discussion.

We should note that over the past 25 years or so, much of the research on memory in nonhuman animals has shifted from an emphasis on storage failure to a focus on retrieval impairments (e.g., Spear, 1978; Spear & Riccio, 1994). An important guiding principle has been the importance of a match between the cues (such as context) present at the time of learning and those present at the time of testing or retrieval (Tulving & Thomson, 1973). One implication of the retrieval position is that many cases of memory loss might be attenuated or reversed by reinstating critical cues. With a few important exceptions, however, the CTA studies of memory have not focused on issues of retrieval, a point that will be noted where appropriate.

RETENTION OF THE CONDITIONED RESPONSE

Age-Related Differences

As indicated above, it is well established that there is relatively little forgetting of taste–illness associations over long (up to 90-day) postconditioning retention intervals in mature animals (e.g., Biederman, Milgram, Heighington, Stockman, & O'Neill, 1974; Dragoin, Hughes, Devine, & Bentley, 1973) and the magnitude of retention is dependent upon the strength of the initial conditioning (Elkins, 1984). In one study comparing young adult and 2-year-old rats on several forms of aversively motivated learning, CTA was found to be well retained by both age groups over long intervals (e.g., 6 and 12 weeks). In contrast, after 3 weeks the aged rats showed poorer inhibitory (passive) avoidance than the younger group (Martinez & Rigter, 1983).

But are there other age-related differences that point to a unique persistence of memory for CTA? The substantial evidence of relatively rapid forgetting in immature nonhuman and human animals, or "infantile amnesia" as it is termed, raises the question of whether the durability of CTA might prove to be an exception to this general rule. One could argue that CTA, unlike many other learning tasks, is particularly biologically relevant and thus may have different ontogenetic characteristics. To examine this possibility, Campbell and Alberts (1979) carried out a series of experiments with rats of different ages and found that while preweanling 18-day-old rats exhibited a weaker flavor aversion than adults, neither age exhibited significant forgetting over a 56-day retention interval. Interestingly, and consistent with other work, the pups did show more rapid forgetting of a conditioned emotional response (CER; lick suppression arranged like the taste aversion) than did adults, suggesting that CTA may be a qualitatively different form of learning. However, additional data in that study revealed that younger animals (10–12 days of age) did experience a marked decline in retention for the aversion over a 5- to 10-day interval (Campbell & Alberts, 1979). Comparable age-related effects were observed by Schweitzer and Green (1982). In contrast, Steinert, Infurna, and Spear (1980) observed greater forgetting in 18-day-old animals relative to adults over a 60-day retention interval following a single sucrose–LiCl pairing.

Other studies of retention for taste aversion in weanling animals provide discrepant results with respect to long-term retention for a conditioned taste aversion. Klein, Mikulka, Domato, and Halstead (1977) found that retention of a sucrose–LiCl aversion was equivalent for 23-day-old weanling and adult rats tested 28 days after conditioning. Robust aversions have also been observed following a 21-day interval in weanling rats exposed to a single pairing of chocolate milk and LiCl (Kraemer, Lariviere, & Spear, 1988). However, while weanling rats trained with a saccharin–LiCl exposure showed aversions comparable to adults at 1-day retention interval, marked retention loss was observed in the pups following a 28-day interval (Guanowsky, Misanin, & Riccio, 1983). Taken together, the findings suggest that retention of CTA, while relatively robust even in immature rats, does show improvement with development. It may be that subtle changes in parametric manipulations might contribute to altered patterns of long-term retention for CTA in younger organisms.

STIMULUS GENERALIZATION AND RETENTION INTERVAL

It is well recognized that as the retention interval increases, subjects show increased generalized responding to stimuli other than the nominal conditioned stimulus (CS; e.g., Perkins & Weyant, 1958). This flattening of the stimulus generalization gradient has been interpreted as evidence for

the forgetting of specific CS attributes over time (e.g., Riccio & Ebner, 1981; Riccio, Richardson, & Ebner, 1984). Such time-dependent generalization has been exhibited within the CTA paradigm (Richardson, Williams, & Riccio, 1984). Rats were trained with a 10% (w/v) sucrose solution presented in conjunction with LiCl injection and tested 2, 7, or 21 days later with 2.5%, 10%, or 32% sucrose. At the short retention interval, subjects showed marked discriminative responding, that is, suppressed consumption of the 10% training concentration only. Following the extended retention intervals, generalized aversive responding was expressed to the 2.5% and 32% concentrations. These results clearly indicate that while the response memory is retained over a long period of time, memory for the specific aspects of CS declines during the same retention interval.

In a related study using alcohol as the taste CS, Thiele, Kiefer, and Badia-Elder (1996) paired a 4% concentration with LiCl and then tested rats either 2 or 21 days later for aversion to the training stimulus or to generalized stimuli (1% and 7% concentrations). In addition to a strong aversion to the CS, the rats showed greater aversion to the nonpaired cues (i.e., the other concentrations) after the long interval. To reduce a floor effect, a second experiment reduced the strength of the unconditioned stimulus (US). Again, the aversion to the generalized cues increased over the delay, consistent with the Richardson et al. (1984) findings. However, since CTA to the target stimulus also increased in the second experiment, the authors suggested that aversions to alcohol became stronger over time, rather than suggesting that the attributes of the cues were no longer discriminable, although the two views do not seem mutually exclusive.

Using a different approach to examine the forgetting of attributes in a CTA paradigm, Metzger (1997) took advantage of the phenomenon of latent inhibition (LI; i.e., attenuated responding to the CS at testing following CS preexposure prior to conditioning). To remove the possible influence of differences in preferences for different sucrose concentrations on consumption at testing, rats were preexposed to a generalized solution but tested on one target CS. Control rats exposed to 10% sucrose solution prior to conditioning to the 10% CS either 1 or 8 days later showed the expected attenuation of CTA, that is, the LI effect. However, when rats drank 20% sucrose 1 day before conditioning to the 10% target solution there was no evidence of LI, indicating that the two concentrations were highly discriminable. In contrast, the same preexposure produced generalized LI when conditioning to the target was delayed for an 8-day retention interval, suggesting that the attributes of the two stimuli were no longer distinguished, that is, a loss of memory for characteristics of the cues.

CONTEXT CHANGE AND RETENTION INTERVAL

Many studies have found that performance is disrupted when the context at testing does not coincide with the context present at the time of conditioning (e.g., Spear & Riccio, 1994). This "context shift effect" has attracted considerable attention as well as some dispute over its theoretical role in long-term memory loss (Bouton, Nelson, & Rosas, 1999; Riccio, Richardson, & Ebner, 1999). However, there is general agreement based on empirical evidence that the disruptive effect of context change is related to removal of retrieval cues rather than distraction by the test context.

In this vein, a number of different studies employing several procedural variations have also found that the expression of CTA is context dependent. Specifically, a change in context between training and testing has been shown to attenuate performance of a conditioned response following a short retention interval. Studies using either single- or multiple-trial conditioning procedures have shown that extinction proceeds more rapidly when the context is altered between training and extinction phases (Archer & Sjoden, 1980; Archer, Sjoden, Nilsson, & Carter, 1979, 1980; Bonardi, Honey, & Hall, 1990; Sjoden & Archer, 1981). However, it should be noted that some studies have failed to observe an effect of contextual shift following a single-trial conditioning episode (e.g., Bonardi et al., 1990; Rosas & Bouton, 1997).

Investigations employing discriminative CTA training vary the conditioning regimen such that, over the course of several cycles, animals are exposed to a flavor–illness pairing in one context but receive access to the flavor solution in the absence of illness in an alternative context. Studies employing this method have found that whereas strong CTA is observed in the conditioning context, aversions are attenuated when testing occurs in the alternative context (Boakes, Westbrook, Elliot, & Swinbourne, 1997; Loy, Alvarez, Rey, & Lopez-Ramirez, 1993; Loy & Lopez, 1999). These studies provide clear evidence for the role of contextual control in the mediation of expression for CTA (but see Rosas & Bouton, 1997), but it may be viewed as conceptually distinct from the effects of a context shift observed when testing occurs in a novel context in the absence of any explicit discriminative training between drug and no-drug contexts.

RETENTION INTERVAL EFFECT

Another phenomenon related to the retention for flavor aversion has been labeled the "retention interval effect" (RIE). Initially observed by Biederman et al. (1974), this effect is characterized by a decline in the conditioned aversion that is expressed following a short retention interval (1–2 days) compared with briefer (90-min post-LiCl recovery) or longer intervals (see also Batsell & Best, 1992a, 1992b, 1993, 1994; Batsell & Pritchett, 1995). The RIE has been interpreted as reflecting the potentiation of the conditioned aversion over long retention intervals (e.g., De le Casa, Diaz, & Lubow, 2003). However, Batsell and Best (1994) and Batsell and George (1996) have argued that RIE is the result of a temporary retrieval deficit at the intermediate interval produced by the effects of the novel or surprising US *at the time of conditioning*. Thus, the phenomenon appears akin to the nonmonotonic pattern of deficits seen in avoidance, that is, the Kamin effect, which has been convincingly interpreted as a retrieval impairment in other aversively motivated conditioning paradigms (e.g., Klein & Spear, 1970; Spear, Klein, & Riley, 1971). While the RIE is not a ubiquitous phenomenon in CTA (see, e.g., Kraemer et al., 1988; Miller et al., 1990; Steinert et al., 1980), it does reinforce the notion that patterns of retention can be nonmonotonic and raises an important methodological consideration for studies examining memory for CTAs.

MEMORY FOR AN EXTINGUISHED CONDITIONED RESPONSE

Extinction, a reduction in the magnitude of the conditioned response (CR) to the CS as the result of repeated presentation of the CS alone following conditioning (Pavlov, 1927), has been reliably observed for CTA in a number of laboratories (e.g., Archer & Sjoden, 1980; Archer, Sjoden, Nilsson, & Carter,

1979, 1980; Rosas & Bouton, 1997; Schachtman, Brown, & Miller, 1985). From the standpoint of memory retrieval, the process of extinction establishes a CS–no US representation that interferes with the expression of the taste–illness memory at the time of retrieval (Kasprow, Schachtman, & Miller, 1985). This view is substantiated by data indicating that presentation of a US reminder in the absence of the CS can reinstate the aversion following extinction. Schachtman et al. conditioned animals with a single saccharin–LiCl pairing. Subjects received extinction with the CS alone for 3 days. On the following day, animals were given a single administration of the LiCl US in a novel context. In subsequent testing 48 h later, subjects showed strong saccharin aversions indicating that the reinstatement procedure induced recovery from extinction.

Additional work by Bouton (see Bouton, 1993) has indicated that context also plays a role in mediating the expression of extinction. Specifically, when a CS–US association is conditioned in one context but extinguished in another, subjects show a resurgence of conditioned responding when they are returned to the original training context. This "renewal effect" has been observed with CTA. Following 3 days of preexposure to two different contexts (A & B), animals were conditioned with a flavor–illness pairing in Context A. Over the following 4 days, half of the animals were extinguished with the flavor in Context A and were exposed to water in Context B. The remaining subjects were extinguished in Context B and were given access to water in Context A. All subjects were then tested for their aversion to the flavor in Context A. A renewal effect was demonstrated by the return of a moderate aversion to the flavor in animals extinguished in Context B but tested in Context A (Rosas & Bouton, 1997). Similarly, Chelonis, Calton, Hart, and Schachtman (1999) extinguished a flavor aversion in either the training context, a single alternative context, or multiple alternative contexts. All subjects were then tested for sucrose aversions in the original training context. Extinction in a single alternative context produced a renewal effect in that animals showed greater aversion to sucrose compared to rats extinguished in the original training context. However, extinction in multiple training contexts did reduce the magnitude of the renewal effect.

Spontaneous recovery (a return of responding to the CS) occurs if a long retention interval is imposed between extinction and a subsequent representation of the CS (Pavlov, 1927). The first clear demonstration of spontaneous recovery in CTA was reported by Rosas and Bouton (1996). The aversive response to a single-trial saccharin–LiCl aversion was extinguished over three sessions and spontaneous recovery of the taste aversion was observed following an 18-day postextinction interval (Rosas & Bouton, 1996). Spontaneous recovery over long postextinction intervals is attributed to the forgetting of the extinction experience over time, which in turn allows for the expression of the stronger CS–US association when the CS is presented again (e.g., Bouton, 1991, 1993). Support for this perspective is supplied by evidence indicating that a specific reminder associated with extinction can obviate spontaneous recovery. In a replication of Rosas and Bouton, Brooks, Palmatier, Garcia, and Johnson (1999) exposed rats to an auditory cue (buzzer) during extinction sessions. Presentation of this buzzer during testing 18-days later attenuated the degree of spontaneous recovery, presumably by reminding animals of the extinction episode.

Bouton (e.g., Bouton et al., 1999) has noted that both a change in context (renewal effect) and the passage of time (spontaneous recovery) can alleviate the CR deficits observed with extinction and has suggested that "physical contexts are naturally imbedded in a superordinate context provided by the passage of time" (Rosas & Bouton, 1998, p. 80). On the basis of this notion, context change and retention interval should act in an additive fashion. This idea was examined in a CTA study examining extinction effects as a function of context change and retention interval. Following preexposure to two distinctive contexts (A & B), animals were conditioned with a saccharin–LiCl pairing. Animals were extinguished in either the training context (A) or the alternative context (B) and tested in Context A either 1 day or 24 days following extinction. Animals tested in the alternative context after a 24-day retention interval displayed greater CS aversions than animals subjected to spontaneous recovery (extinguished in context A and tested after 24 days) or renewal (extinguished in context B and tested after 1 day) procedures (Rosas & Bouton, 1998).

CTA AND RETROGRADE AMNESIA

Are there manipulations introduced after the taste–illness pairing that can impair memory for

CTA? From the perspective of memory processes, this question, basically similar to that in research on retrograde amnesia (RA), has the methodological advantage that the subjects are undisturbed at the time of conditioning. Unlike anterograde amnesia, in which treatments precede acquisition, retrograde interventions avoid potential alterations in sensory or motivational properties of the CS or US, or changes in the associative processes themselves. By varying the training to treatment interval, investigators can determine if memory loss in CTA follows a temporal gradient, as is found in many other studies of RA. A further relevant consideration is the use of a reversible agent to help determine whether any deficits are produced at the time of storage ("consolidation") or at retrieval (testing). In this connection, the difficulty with interpreting deficits from postacquisition lesions is that the damage may have impaired storage, or retrieval, or both. (For a discussion of these and other issues see Bures, Bermudez-Rattoni, & Yamamoto, 1998.)

The robust nature of CTA might suggest that it is quite impervious to manipulations (such as seizure activity produced by electroconvulsive shock [ECS] or other agents or administration of protein synthesis inhibitors) that are typically used to produce RA in other tasks. In line with this prediction, some early studies failed to find convincing evidence of memory loss for a conditioned taste aversion when the agent was not applied between the CS and US. However, it now seems clear that CTA, like many other learning phenomena, is subject to RA. In one early study, Ahlers and Best (1972) obtained substantial loss of taste aversion when they administered Metrazol (pentylenetetrazol) 2 h after pairing saccharin (CS) with apomorphine (US), although a possible temporal gradient was not explored.

A series of studies by Shaw using ECS have further documented induced memory impairment for CTA. The window of susceptibility to ECS after the CS–US pairing was relatively limited, with only marginal memory loss when ECS was delayed for more than 10 min after the LiCl injection (Shaw, 1986). Furthermore, the intensity of the US was important, as RA was prevented if a stronger dose of LiCl was employed (Shaw, 1993).

An unusually prolonged temporal gradient has been reported by Ivanova and Bures (1990), who used intracerebral injection of tetrodotoxin (TTX), an agent that interferes with neuronal activity by blocking voltage-dependent sodium channels. On administering TTX 1, 2, or 4 days after conditioning, the investigators obtained impaired memory for CTA at testing. Importantly, the agent had no effect after an 8-day interval, thus ruling out interference from the drug during retrieval or general impairments of test performance.

To determine whether protein synthesis is important in memory processing in very young rats, Gruest, Richer, and Hars (2004) administered anisomycin (ANI), a protein synthesis inhibitor, to 3-day-old rat pups after CTA conditioning. Odorized milk delivered via a surrogate nipple served as the CS and was followed by an injection of LiCl as the US. Anisomycin injected systemically either immediately or 15 min following training produced substantial RA, but no such outcome was obtained when ANI was administered 6 or 24 h after conditioning. Their finding extends the generality of memory impairment of CTA to a very early stage of ontogeny. Interestingly, Rosenblum, Meiri, and Dudai (1993) did not find memory loss in young adult rats when they injected ANI into gustatory cortex immediately following pairing of saccharin and LiCl, although performance was significantly impaired when the drug was applied either before exposure to the CS or both before the CS and after the US.

Electrical stimulation of selected areas of the brain provides a form of reversible lesion that can be useful in identifying neuranatomical substrates of memory. We do not attempt to review that literature here, but instead we focus on a study by Phillips and LePiane (1980) that examined disruption of the memory for CTA induced by stimulation of the amygdala. In one of their conditions, stimulation delivered immediately following the US (LiCl injection) produced impaired memory of the aversive CR. However, noting that few studies considered the possible role of brain stimulation as a cue, they included a group that received stimulation at testing as well as conditioning. Clear evidence of a state-dependent-like outcome was observed, with the group receiving stimulation both at training and at testing showing strong CTA, that is, intact memory. Whether the memory impairment obtained in the single stimulation condition is viewed as a generalization decrement, that is, impaired performance due to changing from a compound to a single stimulus or a mismatch of brain "states," the finding suggests that in some cases the RA is not due to disruption of storage of information. The degree to which this view can be extended to other sources of memory loss in CTA is not clear; however, the authors' interpretation is echoed in some concepts of RA for shock-induced inhibitory avoidance (e.g., Hinderliter, Webster, & Riccio, 1975; Riccio & Richardson, 1984).

In CTA, as in other learning paradigms, the temporally restricted period of vulnerability would seem to imply that a manipulation such as ECS applied long after conditioning would have little consequence for memory. That this prediction might not be supported is suggested by some early findings demonstrating RA for old memory in fear conditioning tasks (Mactutus, Riccio, & Ferek, 1979; Misanin, Miller, & Lewis, 1968; Przybyslawski & Sara, 1997). The critical feature in these experiments was that the old information had to be reactivated, typically by a brief reexposure to the CS alone (see also Richardson, Riccio, & Mowrey, 1982).

This phenomenon has recently received renewed attention in the neuroscience community, in large part due to a *Nature* paper by Nader (Nader, Schafe, & LeDoux, 2000) and subsequent commentaries (e.g., Miller & Matzel, 2000; Millin, Moody, & Riccio, 2001; Nadel & Land, 2000; Sara, 2000). Although conveniently labeled "reconsolidation," that term seems unfortunate as it conveys a particular theoretical interpretation that is subject to many of the same criticisms that are applied to the concept of "consolidation" (Millin et al., 2001). Nevertheless, the phenomenon itself is of considerable interest and importance.

The bulk of the research on the issue has used traditional fear conditioning as the target task, but a series of studies from Dudai's lab have used CTA to investigate the characteristics of "reconsolidation." As the reactivation treatment nominally involves an extinction exposure to the CS, and extinction is now widely seen as another form of learning (a putative CS–no US association), an important question then arises: Why does the amnesic agent not block the last learning (extinction) and leave the original conditioning intact? Eisenberg, Kobilo, Berman, and Dudai (2003) showed that in the CTA paradigm the answer depends on the strength of the initial conditioning. With a modest level of learning, ANI injected into the insular cortex following cueing (retrieval) impairs memory for extinction, such that the taste aversion persists relative to controls. However, with a stronger CTA established by multiple training trials, the same treatment impairs retention of the original memory, that is, RA occurs for the old reactivated memory.

A lively issue of debate in the "reconsolidation" research domain focuses on whether the initial storage processes ("consolidation") and the processes reactivated at retrieval are identical, or even similar (for reviews see, e.g., Dudai, 2006; Riccio, Millin, & Bogart, 2006). Evidence that these phenomena reflect separate processes in CTA comes from studies using a double dissociation strategy. In research on new memory, Bahar, Samuel, Hazvi, and Dudai (2003) found that inhibition of protein synthesis with anisomycin in the central amygdala (CeA) impaired memory for CTA, while a similar treatment in the basolateral amygdala (BLA) had no effect on CTA. Conversely, anisomycin slowed extinction when injected into the BLA but did not affect extinction when injected in the CeA.

Subsequently, Bahar, Dorfman, and Dudai (2004) extended this approach to the issue of reconsolidation. After establishing a strong CTA with multiple training trials, Bahar et al. (2004) reactivated memory by testing the rats with a choice between saccharin (CS) and water, followed immediately by microinfusion of ANI into either the CeA or the BLA. In contrast with newly established memory, neither condition had any effect on the reactivated information, implying that different amygdalar circuits underlie these memory processes.

Finally, in their study of RA for CTA in rat pups, Gruest et al. (2004) also provided evidence that reactivation renders their memory susceptible to disruption. Two days after training, pups were cued by inserting the artificial nipple with aromatized milk for a few minutes, followed by systemic injection of ANI. At testing the pups showed RA that again followed a time-dependent pattern, with memory loss occurring with delays of 0, 15, or 30 min between reactivation and administration of ANI, but no impairment when the delays were extended to 6 or 24 h.

DELAY CONDITIONING—RETENTION OF THE NOMINAL CS

A hallmark characteristic of the CTA paradigm is its ability to withstand long delays between exposure of the nominal flavor CS and the onset of internal malaise resulting from US administration (see Garcia, Hankins, & Rusiniak, 1974; Riley & Tuck, 1985). One explanation for this delay gradient is that the presentation of a flavor stimulus elicits a neural trace of the CS that persists over time (e.g., Rozin & Kalat, 1971). More recent work on the neurobiology of CTA (Bermudez-Rattoni & Yamamoto, 1998) has postulated that this memory trace, or gustatory short-term memory (GSTM), consists of a subcortical buffer system that is activated by taste signals from the gustatory cortex. Presentation of a taste stimulus results in activation of a circuit priming the specific CS input into the GSTM. Once established, the activity in this priming circuit persists even in the presence of cortical blockade (Buresova & Bures, 1973). Circuit activity escalates to a maximum level between 10 and 60 min following CS exposure and then declines gradually over an 8–12 h period. This putative neural model defines the parameters under which associations may occur between the GSTM circuit and neural signals evoked by a US resulting in the encoding of an aversion in gustatory long-term memory (GTLM). According to the model, the strength of aversive conditioning should be maximal during the build up of GSTM circuit activity and should exhibit progressive decline as the integrity of the GSTM signal diminishes. In addition, according to this model, the absence of an illness-inducing US during the period of waxing and waning of GSTM activity should result in the encoding of a CS–no US association in GTLM, producing responses observed as attenuated neophobia or learned safety (Bermudez-Rattoni, & Yamamoto, 1998).

One restriction on the model concerns the nature of the outcome predicted by the flavor CS. Although highly effective in entering into an association with malaise over long intervals, the representation of the CS has much shorter viability in other paradigms. For example, in a CTA study that utilized a sensory preconditioning task, the two flavors (S1 and S2) failed to show evidence of becoming associated with each other when the interstimulus interval was around 30 s (Lavin, 1976). A very similar conclusion was reached in an experiment on conditioned flavor preference that investigated sensory preconditioning intervals (Lyn & Capaldi, 1994). Despite this restriction, the GSTM model proposed by Bermudez-Rattoni and Yamamoto (1998) provides a valuable heuristic to aid in the examination of variables that effect delay conditioning and the retention of the CS in the CTA paradigm.

AGE-RELATED DIFFERENCES IN DELAY CONDITIONING

Ontogenetic studies reveal age-related changes in the functional capacity of animals to condition a CTA over long delay intervals, and hence suggest age-related differences in the STM for gustatory stimuli. While adult rats appear to be able to tolerate CS–US delays of about 1.5 h before marked reductions in the response to the flavor–illness association is observed (Misanin, Greider, & Hinderliter, 1988; Westbrook & Homewood, 1982), preweanling and weanling rats under these conditions show disruptions in CTA when the CS–US interval is extended beyond the point of contiguous presentation (Misanin et al., 1988; Steinert, Infurna, Jardula, & Spear, 1979). These data, suggesting greater forgetting of the gustatory taste stimulus over the delay interval, are commensurate with numerous results indicating more rapid forgetting of response memory in young organisms compared to adults (e.g., Campbell & Spear, 1972; Spear, 1978).

Although this developmental pattern in learning and memory has been attributed to the functional immaturity of the nervous systems of altricial animals (Nadel & Zola-Morgan, 1984), more recent work has suggested a role for experiential factors in mediating long delay CTA deficits in young animals. Specifically, weanling rats given an odor or different taste contiguously paired with LiCl 24 h prior to delayed (1.5 h) conditioning with saccharin and LiCl showed robust aversions to saccharin relative to controls (Kraemer, Miller, Jagielo, & Spear, 1992). Interestingly, the attenuation of CTA following longer CS–US duration in adult rats can also be eliminated by contiguous presentations of a different taste + illness prior to delay conditioning (Westbrook & Homewood, 1982). Relatedly, Kraemer, Kraemer, Smoller, and Spear (1989) found that exposure to LiCl, signaled by a novel odor, facilitated subsequent CTA to saccharin. Taken together, these results suggest that young organisms may not necessarily lack the requisite neurological maturity to maintain the representation of the gustatory CS, rather prior experience with taste (or odor) + illness associations may be necessary to allow an association when a long interval is imposed between the new CS and the malaise.

In contrast to the effects observed in younger animals, aged rats appear to tolerate CS/US delays better than young-adult rats. Misanin et al. (1988) observed that aged rats were able to demonstrate strong conditioned aversions to a gustatory CS with delay intervals up to 3 h, whereas young-adult animals show evidence of CTA only at delays of up to 1.5 h. This effect does not appear to be due to age-related differences in perceived US intensity (Misanin & Hinderliter, 1994), relative CS novelty (Hinderliter & Misanin, 1993), or the formation of context–illness associations (Misanin & Hinderliter, 1995). Moreover, increasing the US intensity led to enhanced CTA over longer-delay intervals in aged rats, yet comparable results were absent in young-adults (Misanin, Goodhart, Anderson, & Hinderliter, 2002). According to these authors, the results suggest that the increasing US intensity might have a facilitative effect in the older rats as the CS memory trace begins to fade over the interval, whereas the lack of effect in young adults may point to a more rapid loss of a viable STM trace over time. Hence, in the context of the model proposed by Bermudez-Rattoni and Yamamoto (1998) the waning of the GSTM might become more protracted as the animal ages and biological activity slows. Indeed, the amnestic effects produced by interpolated anesthesia and hypothermia have been postulated to result from a functional slowing of a "biological pacemaker" thus retarding metabolic processes associated with declining functional integrity of the memory trace (or GSTM; Misanin, Anderson, et al., 2002; Misanin, Goodhart, et al., 2002; Misanin, Wilson, Schwarz, Tuschak, & Hinderliter, 1998).

FORGETTING OF CS ATTRIBUTES IN DELAY CONDITIONING

Clearly, the preponderance of the literature on CS–US delay has focused on factors influencing the relative strength of the CTA that is established to the nominal CS. Little attention has been paid to how the nature of the CS representation may alter as conditioning parameters change from a contiguous CS–US presentation (waxing GSTM) to a long delay between CS and US (waning GSTM)

presentation. To examine this issue, and as part of a more general interest in forgetting of features or attributes of stimuli, Land, Harrod, and Riccio (1998) exposed rats to a milk CS and administered LiCl either contiguously or following a 2-h delay. Forty-eight hours later, animals were tested with both the training CS and a new flavor (chocolate milk). Animals trained with an immediate delay discriminated between flavors, displaying a greater aversion to the milk CS relative to the novel chocolate milk. However, animals that experienced a 2-h CS–US delay showed relatively low but similar levels of consumption of both fluids. This lack of differential CTA to the two flavors suggests that the specific attributes of the CS were forgotten over the delay interval. Thus the temporal modulation of GSTM activity may not only impact the relative strength of the CTA response but also alter what is learned about the attributes of the target CS as a function of interstimulus delay.

EFFECTS OF ELECTROCONVULSIVE SHOCK DURING DELAY CONDITIONING

Evidence suggests that stressful events interpolated within the CS–US delay period can retard the subsequent development of CTA (e.g., Bourne, Calton, Gustavson, & Schachtman, 1992; Revusky & Reilly, 1989). ECS is well established as an agent that produces RA for responses that recently preceded it (e.g., Lewis, Miller, & Misanin, 1967). Accordingly, one might expect to find that administering ECS following exposure to the target flavor would disrupt the CS representation. Specifically, Kral (1970, 1971a, 1971b) found that administration of ECS between taste exposure and illness induction attenuated the observed CTA in rats. Nachman (1970) also found a weak temporal gradient for ECS administered during the CS–US delay. Relatedly, Kasprow, Schachtman, and Miller (1985) administered ECS 5-, 10-, or 20-min postingestion. Since the US was administered 30-min postingestion in all groups and the greatest CTA disruption was observed in animals with the shortest CS–ECS interval, these data suggest that the ECS has a retrograde effect on the memory for the ingested fluid rather than an anterograde disruption of memory for the illness experience. Shaw (1993, 1988) suggested that the neural trace representing the gustatory cue may be weakened by this ECS. Essentially, the administration of ECS might serve to diminish the integrity of the GSTM (i.e., disrupt consolidation of the taste memory) with a functional outcome similar to that seen with the waning of the GSTM signal over long delay. Since a number of studies have shown that RA for responses can be attenuated by pretest reminder treatments (e.g., Miller & Springer, 1972, 1973), it would be of interest to know if recovery could also be induced for the memory of the CS since such data would address the notion of consolidation disruption produced by the putative weakening of the gustatory neural trace by ECS. As the consolidation model implies a failure of storage, the memory impairment should be permanent. However, to our knowledge there has been no investigation as to the efficacy of reminder treatments on the recovery of CTA following ECS exposure during CS–US delay.

EFFECTS OF ANESTHESIA AND HYPOTHERMIA IN DELAY CONDITIONING

Certain interstimulus events have been shown to enhance the strength of the taste aversion response conditioned over long delays. Employing halothane or equithesin anesthesia during the CS–US interval, Rozin and Ree (1972) found that CTA could be conditioned despite an interstimulus delay of up to 9 h. Similarly, Buresova and Bures (1977) reported the presence of a CTA formed after a 5-h CS–US interval spent under the influence of allobarbital anesthesia. More recently, introduction of Ketaset–Rompun (KR) anesthesia during long interstimulus delay has been shown to enhance the establishment of CTA relative to unanesthetized controls (Misanin, Christianson, Anderson, Giovanni, & Hinderliter, 2004). Although KR itself may serve as an effective malaise-inducing US for conditioning a CTA (Metzger, Flint, & Riccio, 1997), data from Misanin et al. (2004) suggest that the potentiation of CTA over the delay was not the result of increased illness produced by exposure to summative aversive effects of KR and LiCl following CS presentation. This suggests that the actions of anesthetics may prolong the waxing or forestall the waning of the gustatory CS signal in GSTM.

A series of experiments from the Misanin lab have shown that hypothermia produces effects similar to those of anesthetic administration when deep body cooling is interpolated during CS–US delay. Misanin et al. (1998) found that deep body cooling after CS consumption resulted in the establishment of a CTA in animals whose exposure to the US was delayed by 3 h. According to the authors, these results could not be attributed to a lingering systemic CS or a cold-induced increase in US intensity. Moreover, delaying the hypothermic treatment 45, 90, or 170 min into the 3-h CS–US interval resulted in graded performance disruptions that were similar to those observed for animals receiving the LiCl (US) 45, 90, or 170 min after CS exposure. Further studies (Misanin, Anderson, et al., 2002) manipulated the magnitude of post-CS hypothermia (0°C, 4.5°C, 7°C, or 10°C) as well as the CS–US delay interval (90, 135, 180, or 225 min). Normothermic control animals failed to develop CTA with the 90-min delay; however, animals whose temperatures were lowered by 4.5°C, 7°C, or 10°C were able to display flavor aversions despite 135-, 180-, and 225-min CS–US delays, respectively. Taken together, these results suggest that hypothermia may also act to modulate the waxing and waning of the GSTM circuit. Finally, it should be noted that hypothermia has been shown to function as an amnestic agent for response memory (e.g., Hamm, 1981; Riccio, Hodges, & Randall, 1968). However, Misanin has suggested that in order to obtain amnesia the rats must be returned to normal body temperature relatively rapidly, whereas in the delay interval studies described here the hypothermia was maintained for a prolonged period of time (Misanin & Hoover, 1971).

STIMULUS PREEXPOSURE STUDIES—INTERFERENCE EFFECTS

Presenting subjects with either the CS or the US prior to training produces a disruption in the production of the CR at test. Both CS and US preexposure effects have been well documented in a variety of Pavlovian conditioning paradigms (see Lubow, 1973 and Randich & LoLordo, 1979, respectively), and CTA is no exception (Best, 1975; Kalat & Rozin, 1973; Revusky & Bedarf, 1967; Riley & Simpson, 2001; Siegel, 1974). One account of the impact of stimulus preexposure attributes the deleterious effects to a disruption of acquisition of the CS–US association during training (e.g., Mackintosh, 1975; Pearce & Hall,

1980; Rescorla & Wagner, 1972). An alternative view contends that memory for the stimulus preexposure competes or interferes with expression of the training memory at the time of testing (e.g., Bouton, 1991, 1993; Kasprow, Schachtman, & Miller, 1987; Miller & Matzel, 1988). Owing to the nature of this chapter we will consequently limit our discussion to data that address this latter theoretical perspective.

US PREEXPOSURE EFFECT

Attenuation with Long Preexposure to Conditioning Retention Interval

The US preexposure effect (also termed context blocking) is defined as an attenuation of conditioned responding observed when the US is presented alone prior to CS–US pairings (see Radich & Lolordo, 1979). In CTA, pretraining administration of the illness-inducing agent retards the flavor avoidance observed at test. Presumably, the pairing of the US with contextual cues present during US exposure elicits a context–US association. Increasing the intensity of the US or the number of preexposures strengthens this association and often produces weaker CTA (see Riley & Simpson, 2001). Extending the duration of the retention interval between US preexposure and conditioning has been shown to modify this effect. Aguado, De Bruga, and Hall (1997) exposed rats to the US (0.3 M, 10 ml/kg LiCl) once a day for 3 days. A strong attenuation of CTA was found when conditioning occurred 2 days later, but the effect was eliminated following a 15-day preexposure to conditioning interval. Similar results were obtained by Cannon, Berman, Baker, and Atkinson (1975). These findings suggest that the preexposure experience was forgotten over the long delay interval.

Attenuation of US Preexposure with Long Conditioning to Test Retention Interval

Increasing the duration of the retention interval between conditioning and testing may also serve to decrease the magnitude of the US preexposure effect. Preexposure to LiCl has been found to attenuate aversion to the taste component of an odor–taste compound after a 2-day retention interval. However, when testing was conducted after a 15-day interval strong CTA was observed (Miller,

Jagielo, & Spear, 1993). On the other hand, Cole, Bakner, Vernon, and Riccio (1993) examined the effects of LiCl preexposure using a single element taste and found no differences in performance between animals tested following short or long retention intervals (see also Aguado et al., 1997).

Batsell (1997) noted that Cole et al. (1993) preexposed animals with 1-M LiCl but trained them with a 0.25-M dose. This type of regimen, that is, high exposure dose and low training dose, has been shown to produce a strong US-preexposure effect (Klein, Mikulka, & Lucci, 1986). Cole et al. also preexposed animals in a novel context and context–US associations may be formed more readily if preexposure occurs in an unfamiliar location (Klein et al., 1987). Thus, Batsell suggested that the strength of the retention interval effect would depend on the initial strength of the context–US association, that is, weaker associations would be forgotten more readily resulting in the loss of a US preexposure effect at longer conditioning to test intervals. Batsell manipulated the number of US preexposures as well as the familiarity of the preexposure location in an attempt to produce both weak and strong context–US associations during the preexposure phase. Animals received either 0, 2, or 4 administrations of 0.15-M LiCl in a novel context prior to conditioning and were tested after either 3 or 14 days. Relative to controls, animals that received two US presentations in the unfamiliar context showed a marked attenuation of CTA when tested after 3 days (i.e., a US preexposure effect was observed). Following a 14-day retention interval, animals suppressed consumption of the CS fluid, indicating a loss of the US preexposure effect over time. Rats exposed to four presentations of the US (that presumably established a stronger context–US association) failed to show a similar effect; a US preexposure effect was observed at both intervals.

Consistent with the view that context–US associations are less readily established in a familiar context, Batsell found that employing a familiar preexposure context yielded a different pattern of results. Animals given two preexposure trials failed to show an attenuation of CTA at either interval. Subjects that received four preexposure trials showed a US preexposure effect at the 3-day interval but this effect was eliminated following a 14-day retention interval. These results suggest that weaker context–US associations, like weak CS–US associations, are more susceptible to forgetting over the course of a long retention interval.

Effect of Context Change on US Preexposure

Like proactive and retroactive interference, context shifts are considered to be an important source of forgetting. Presumably, under naturalistic conditions, the learning context changes more as the retention interval increases and this shift removes a source of retrieval cues (Spear & Riccio, 1994). In support of this view, a number of laboratory studies have found that introducing a change in context shortly after learning has a disruptive effect on test performance (e.g., Millin & Riccio, 2004; for review see Riccio et al., 1984). Consistent with this evidence, context change between US preexposure and training also weakens or eliminates the attenuated CTA observed at testing. The effect is observed when exposure to the US occurs in one context and subsequent training is conducted in an alternative context as compared with training in the original preexposed context (e.g., Batson & Best, 1979; Dacanay & Riley, 1982; Domjan & Best, 1980). Similar results have also been obtained with discriminative preexposure studies in which one context is paired with the US administration and the alternative context is paired with vehicle exposure prior to training (Prados & Sansa, 2002; Symonds & Hall, 1997; Westbrook & Brookes, 1988). These effects are taken as evidence that a context–US association is formed during preexposure and the removal of these retrieval cues results in the attenuation of the context preexposure effect on the subsequent CTA.

LATENT INHIBITION

Attenuation of LI with Long Preexposure to Conditioning Retention Interval

Preexposure to taste stimuli prior to taste–illness pairings produce an attenuation of the CTA response at testing, that is, latent inhibition (LI). The degree of CS preexposure appears to modulate this effect with greater preexposure associated with more substantial retardation of CTA (e.g., Franchina, Domato, Patsiokas, & Griesemer, 1980). However, this pattern of responding has been shown to vary as the duration of the retention interval between preexposure and conditioning increases. Elkins and Hobbs (1979) observed

that extending the retention interval (20 or 100 days) between taste preexposure and conditioning resulted in the prevention of LI and the establishment of a CTA in preexposed subjects. Kraemer and Roberts (1984, Experiment IV) obtained similar results following a 21-day retention interval, although the preexposed stimulus was a generalized flavor (apple juice) as opposed to the actual CS (saccharin). More recently, Ackil, Carmen, Bakner, and Riccio (1992) examined retention interval effects on LI employing the nominal CS as the preexposed stimulus. Rats were preexposed to a 10% sucrose solution in the home cage and were trained with a sucrose–LiCl pairing either 1 day or 10 days later. Subjects that received sucrose preexposure 1 day prior to training showed LI in that their aversions to the CS were attenuated. In contrast, animals subjected to the 10-day preexposure to training interval displayed strong aversions to the target CS that were comparable to nonpreexposed controls. Moreover, this study found that rats exposed to a preconditioning reminder (brief access to 10% sucrose in a novel location) 24 h prior to conditioning on day 10 showed the return of the LI effect at testing. Importantly, this reminder procedure was ineffective in subjects trained in the absence of preexposure, indicating that the reminder exposure itself was too brief to produce LI. Hence, these data suggest that forgetting of the nonreinforced CS over the course of the preexposure to conditioning retention interval impedes the expression of LI at test.

In a related study, Alvarez and Lopez (1995) preexposed animals to a compound flavor or its elements either 1 or 21 days prior to conditioning on the compound. Unlike the aforementioned studies, LI remained strong for animals receiving a 21-day interval between preexposure and conditioning. As generalization decrement would suggest, at the short retention interval subjects exposed to the elements showed less LI than animals exposed to the compound. However, at the long interval, the two groups exhibited equivalent attenuation of CTA. These results suggest that while memory for the preexposure experience was retained over the 21-day interval, the memory for the specific stimulus attributes of the elements declined, thus increasing the generalization between the elemental preexposure experience and the compound presented at training (Riccio, Ackil, & Burch-Vernon, 1992).

A phenomenon likely related to LI is the CS– effect in discrimination learning. Exposure to the CS− prior to training can facilitate the acquisition of a subsequent discrimination (e.g., Kucharski, Richter & Spear, 1985). One interpretation of the effect is that the preexposure reduces the tendency for the CS− to acquire associative strength through generalization from the target CS+. An important study by Domjan (1975) provided an early demonstration of value of preexposure in reducing generalization in CTA. Rats preexposed to nontarget flavors prior to pairing of the CS with illness showed an aversion more restricted to the target flavor than controls.

The nature of CTA, in which subjects tend to refrain from consuming a range of flavors after being poisoned, can make it difficult to establish a discrimination through nonreinforced exposure to a CS−. Put differently, since sampling the flavor is under the control of the subjects, how does one get them to taste other substances to learn that they are safe? On the basis of Domjan's study, one strategy would be to expose the subjects to the safe (CS−) cue prior to conditioning, an approach successfully employed by Honey and Hall (1989).

A study by Burch-Vernon and Riccio (1997) extended these findings in several ways. Of relevance here were two experiments designed to explore the possibility that the flattening of generalization gradients over time (i.e., the forgetting of specific stimulus attributes at longer retention intervals) would reduce the CS− effect as the CS− became less distinguishable from the target flavor. No evidence of a weakening of the preexposure effect was seen when subjects were tested 1 or 14 days after conditioning was completed. However, when the interval between preexposure and conditioning was varied (1, 10, or 21 days) there was a modest reduction in the CS− effect, that is, the discrimination was moderately attenuated.

Effect of ECS in the Preexposure to Conditioning Retention Interval

Application of an amnestic agent during the preexposure to training interval also appears to disrupt the emergence of LI at testing (Misanin, Kniss, Yoder, & Yazujian, 1984). Animals were given 15-min access to saccharin solution followed by ECS exposure. The following day, saccharin exposure was paired with LiCl. Testing after a 1-day interval indicated that animals receiving ECS failed to show an LI effect relative to non-ECS treated controls. This effect followed a temporal gradient

with maximal efficacy achieved when ECS was administered immediately after flavor exposure. This observation mirrors that obtained by employing ECS during CS–US delay (e.g., Kasprow et al., 1985; Kral, 1971b) and suggests that ECS may have disrupted memory for the nonreinforced CS presentation (Riccio & Richardson, 1984). As is the case for ECS delay interval effects, there is no current evidence as to whether or not reminder procedures might effectively lead the reappearance of LI in this situation.

Attenuation of LI with Long Conditioning to Test Retention Interval

CTA studies manipulating the duration of the postconditioning retention interval also have noted persistent aversions in the LI paradigm at long intervals. The increase in CTA over time appears paradoxical if preexposure impaired acquisition. To address this issue, a competing memories interpretation was suggested by Kraemer and Roberts (1984), who first observed the phenomenon. They proposed that the LI observed at the shorter interval is the result of conflicting representations (specifically, memory for the preexposure experience and memory for the conditioning episode) that compete for expression at the time of test. As testing is delayed, memory for the nonreinforced CS declines more rapidly than the conditioning memory, resulting in a reduction in interference and an expression of the training memory (see Riccio et al., 1992; Riccio, Rabinowitz, & Axelrod, 1994).

An unusual feature of the Kraemer and Roberts study was that the condition producing the increase in CTA with a long retention interval involved preexposure to a flavor different from the CS. Subsequent research attempted to replicate the "Kraemer effect" using the same flavor in preexposure and conditioning. In one such study, Bakner, Strohen, Nordeen, and Riccio (1991) preexposed rats to a sucrose solution followed by sucrose–LiCl pairing. An LI effect was obtained when testing occurred after a 2-day retention interval. In contrast, animals tested after 11 or 21 days showed marked attenuations of LI, and the data suggested that strength of the conditioned aversion increased as a function of the duration of the training to test interval. Similar results have been obtained in other laboratories (e.g., Aguado, Symonds, & Hall, 1994; Batsell & Best, 1992).

Pursuing the conflicting memories interpretation, Alvarez and Lopez (1995) argued that similar effects should be obtained whether the long interval was interpolated between preexposure and training or between training and testing. In one experiment, rats were preexposed either to a compound flavor or the separate elements 1 or 21 days prior to conditioning with the compound; in a second experiment, the interval was following conditioning. The outcomes were similar in both cases in that LI was observed in the compound preexposure group after the long as well as the short interval. Although not replicating the recovery of CTA, another interesting finding was obtained. Exposure to the elements failed to produce LI at the 1-day interval independent of where the delay was introduced. However, in both cases, LI was observed in element preexposed animals after the 21-day intervals. As mentioned earlier, these results suggest that the specific stimulus features of the elemental preexposure experience were forgotten over time.

Effects of Context Change on LI

There is some suggestion that alterations in contextual stimuli can effectively mediate the presence or absence of LI observed at testing. Archer, Mohammed, and Jarbe (1986) preexposed animals to saccharin using either quiet or noisy bottles. During a taste–illness pairing and testing, subjects consumed saccharin from the noisy bottles. An attenuation of LI was observed in animals shifted from the quiet to noisy conditions.

Using a different contextual manipulation, Hall and Channell (1986) exposed animals to two distinctive contexts prior to training. In one context, animals received the CS flavor while tap water was available in the alternate context. Subjects were subsequently conditioned and tested in either the same context as CS preexposure or in the alternative context. Results showed that changing the context between preexposure and testing attenuated the LI effect. Similar results were reported by Alvarez and Lopez (1995). In this latter study animals were preexposed to a compound CS (or its elements) in one context and tap water in another. Animals were given flavor–illness pairings in the home cage followed by testing in the two contexts. Subjects exposed and trained with the compound showed a reduction in LI when tested in a context different from that of preexposure. These results

suggest that, at test, altered contextual cues fail to promote the retrieval of the preexposure episode. In the absence of this interfering memory, a strong CTA is observed.

Relevance of Retention Interval Context

Recent studies by Lubow and colleagues (see Lubow & De la Casa, 2005) have articulated a potential interaction between context and retention interval that accounts for some of the disparity in results obtained when LI is observed after long retention intervals. Specifically, while some researchers find a loss or attenuation of LI after long postconditioning intervals, others find an enhanced LI effect (super LI). The relevant variable that appears to differentiate these findings is the context in which the animal spends the retention interval. This is a particularly critical observation for the CTA paradigm since frequently preexposure, training, retention interval, and testing all occur in the home cage. Hence the same contextual elements are maintained throughout the study. A systematic review of the LI data (Lubow & De la Casa, 2005) revealed that subjects who spent the retention interval in the same context that was present during preexposure and testing showed either a loss or a reduction of LI after a long interval (e.g., Aguado et al., 1994; Bakner et al., 1991; Kraemer & Roberts, 1984). Conversely, animals that spent the retention interval in a different context showed a super LI effect (e.g., De la Casa & Lubow, 1995, 2000; Lubow & De la Casa, 2002). This effect is attributed to the differential actions of extinction and forgetting that occur during the retention interval. Assuming that preexposure and training occur in the same context, then the preexposed animal enters the retention interval with a CS–no US preexposure association that is context dependent and a CS–US association that is relatively context independent. When the retention interval context is the same, the context-dependent preexposure association is extinguished over the long interval and the subsequently more dominant CS–US association is readily accessible at the time of test. The result is an observed attenuation of LI. If, however, the retention interval context is different, then extinction of the preexposure memory does not occur. Moreover, the precise stimulus characteristics of the preexposure context are forgotten over time and the ability of the test context to serve as a generalized retrieval cue for the pre-exposure memory is enhanced resulting in super LI at the time of test (for a detailed account see Lubow & De la Casa, 2005).

SUMMARY

In this chapter we have presented a representative sample of studies to indicate how a number of diverse phenomena are associated with CTA and memory. In some cases the focus is on the retention of the aversion itself or aspects of the aversion, as in developmental studies of memory for CTA or in memory for the attributes of the stimuli that predicted malaise. In other cases, we discussed the memory for variables that influence the acquisition of CTA, as in various delay conditioning manipulations and in the effects of preexposure to the CS or the US. The nature of the long delay conditioning, protracted retention, and the variety of interference phenomena inherent in the CTA paradigm provide multiple points of access for examining more general issues of retention, forgetting, retrieval, and reconsolidation.

Acknowledgment Preparation of this chapter was supported in part by University of Akron Faculty Improvement Leave to S.M.M. and NIMH Grant 37535 to D.C.R.

References

Ackil, J. K., Carman, H. M., Bakner, L., & Riccio, D. C. (1992). Reinstatement of latent inhibition following a reminder treatment in a conditioned taste aversion paradigm. *Behavioral & Neural Biology, 58*(3), 232–235.

Aguado, L., De Brugada, I., & Hall, G. (1997). Effects of a retention interval on the US-preexposure phenomenon in flavor aversion learning. *Learning and Motivation, 28*(3), 311–322.

Aguado, L., Symonds, M., & Hall, G. (1994). Interval between preexposure and test determines the magnitude of latent inhibition: Implications for an interference account. *Animal Learning & Behavior, 22*(2), 188–194.

Ahlers, R. H., & Best, P. J. (1972). Retrograde amnesia for discriminated taste aversions: A memory deficit. *Journal of Comparative and Physiological Psychology, 79*(3), 371–376.

Alvarez, R., & Lopez, M. (1995). Effects of elements or compound preexposure on conditioned taste aversion as a function of retention interval. *Animal Learning & Behavior, 23*(4), 391–399.

Archer, T., Mohammed, A. K., & Jarbe, T. U. (1986). Context-dependent latent inhibition in taste aversion learning. *Scandinavian Journal of Psychology, 27*(3), 277–284.

Archer, T., & Sjoden, P. (1980). Context-dependent taste-aversion learning with a familiar conditioning context. *Physiological Psychology, 8*(1), 40–46.

Archer, T., Sjoden, P., Nilsson, L., & Carter, N. (1979). Role of exteroceptive background context in taste-aversion conditioning and extinction. *Animal Learning & Behavior, 7*(1), 17–22.

Archer, T., Sjoden, P., Nilsson, L., & Carter, N. (1980). Exteroceptive context in taste-aversion conditioning and extinction: Odour, cage, and bottle stimuli. *Quarterly Journal of Experimental Psychology, 32*(2), 197–214.

Bahar, A., Dorfman, N., & Dudai, Y. (2004). Amygdalar circuits required for either consolidation or extinction of taste aversion memory are not required for reconsolidation. *European Journal of Neuroscience, 19*(4), 1115–1118.

Bahar, A., Samuel, A., Hazvi, S., & Dudai, Y. (2003). The amygdalar circuit that acquires taste aversion memory differs from the circuit that extinguishes it. *European Journal of Neuroscience, 17*(7), 1527–1530.

Bakner, L., Strohen, K., Nordeen, M., & Riccio, D. C. (1991). Postconditioning recovery from the latent inhibition effect in conditioned taste aversion. *Physiology & Behavior, 50*(6), 1269–1272.

Batsell, W. R. (1997). Retention of context blocking in taste-aversion learning. *Physiology & Behavior, 61*(3), 437–446.

Batsell, W. R., & Best, R. (1992a). Variations in the retention of taste aversions: Evidence for retrieval competition. *Animal Learning & Behavior, 20*(2), 146–159.

Batsell, W. R., & Best, R. (1992b). Investigation of replacement fluids and retention-interval effects in taste-aversion learning. *Bulletin of the Psychonomic Society, 30*(5), 414–416.

Batsell, W. R., & Best, R. (1993). One bottle too many? Method of testing determines the detection of overshadowing and retention of taste aversions. *Animal Learning & Behavior, 21*(2), 154–158.

Batsell, W. R., & Best, R. (1994). The role of US novelty in retention interval effects in single-element taste-aversion learning. *Animal Learning & Behavior, 22*(3), 332–340.

Batsell, W. R., & George, W. (1996). Unconditioned stimulus intensity and retention interval effects. *Physiology & Behavior, 60*(6), 1463–1467.

Batsell, W. R., & Pritchett, P. (1995). Retention of rotationally induced taste aversions. *Physiology & Behavior, 58*(4), 815–818.

Batson, J. D., & Best, J. (1979). Drug-preexposure effects in flavor-aversion learning: Associative interference by conditioned environmental stimuli. *Journal of Experimental Psychology: Animal Behavior Processes, 5*(3), 273–283.

Bermudez-Rattoni, F., & Yamamoto, T. (1998). Neuroanatomy of CTA: Lesion studies. In J. Bures, F. Bermudez-Rattoni, & T. Yamamoto (Eds.), *Conditioned taste aversion: Memory of a special kind* (pp. 28–44). New York: Oxford University Press.

Best, M. R. (1975). Conditioned and latent inhibition in taste-aversion learning: Clarifying the role of learned safety. *Journal of Experimental Psychology: Animal Behavior Processes, 1*(2), 97–113.

Biederman, G. B., Milgram, N. W., Heighington, G. A., Stockman, S. M., & O'Neill, W. (1974). Memory of conditioned food aversion follows a U-shape function in rats. *Quarterly Journal of Experimental Psychology, 26*, 610–615.

Boakes, R. A., Westbrook, R. F., Elliott, M., & Swinbourne, A. L. (1997). Context dependency of conditioned aversions to water and sweet tastes. *Journal of Experimental Psychology: Animal Behavior Processes, 23*(1), 56–67.

Bonardi, C., Honey, R. C., & Hall, G. (1990). Context specificity of conditioning in flavor-aversion learning: Extinction and blocking tests. *Animal Learning & Behavior, 18*(3), 229–237.

Bourne, M. J., Calton, J. L., Gustavson, K. K., & Schachtman, T. R. (1992). Effects of acute swim stress on LiCl-induced conditioned taste aversions. *Physiology & Behavior, 51*(6), 1227–1234.

Bouton, M. E. (1991). Context and retrieval in extinction and in other examples of interference in simple associative learning. In L. W. Dachowski & C. F. Flaherty (Eds.), *Current topics in animal learning: Brain, emotion, and cognition* (pp. 25–52). Hillsdale, NJ: Lawrence Erlbaum.

Bouton, M. E. (1993). Context, time, and memory retrieval in the interference paradigms of Pavlovian learning. *Psychological Bulletin, 114*(1), 80–99.

Bouton, M. E., Nelson, J. B., & Rosas, J. M. (1999). Stimulus generalization, context change, and forgetting. *Psychological Bulletin, 125*(2), 171–186.

Brooks, D. C., Palmatier, M. I., Garcia, E. O., & Johnson, J. L. (1999). An extinction cue reduces spontaneous recovery of a conditioned taste aversion. *Animal Learning & Behavior, 27*(1), 77–88.

Burch-Vernon, A. S., & Riccio, C. (1997). The effects of CS-super(–) preexposure in conditioned taste aversion: Enhanced flavor discrimination. *Learning and Motivation, 28*(2), 170–187.

Bures, J., Bermudez-Rattoni, F., & Yamamoto, T. (1998). *Conditioned taste aversion: Memory of a special kind*. New York: Oxford University Press.

Buresova, O., & Bures, J. (1973). Cortical and subcortical components of the conditioned saccharin aversion. *Physiology & Behavior, 11*(4), 435–439.

Buresova, O., & Bures, J. (1977). The effect of anesthesia on acquisition and extinction of conditioned taste aversion. *Behavioral & Neural Biology, 20*(1), 41–50.

Campbell, B. A., & Alberts, R. (1979). Ontogeny of long-term memory for learned taste aversions. *Behavioral & Neural Biology, 25*(2), 139–156.

Campbell, B. A., & Spear, E. (1972). Ontogeny of memory. *Psychological Review, 79*(3), 215–236.

Cannon, D. S., Berman, R. F., Baker, T. B., & Atkinson, C. A. (1975). Effect of preconditioning unconditioned stimulus experience on learned taste aversions. *Journal of Experimental Psychology: Animal Behavior Processes, 1*(3), 270–284.

Chelonis, J. J., Calton, J. L., Hart, J. A., & Schachtman, T. R. (1999). Attenuation of the renewal effect by extinction in multiple contexts. *Learning and Motivation, 30*(1), 1–14.

Cole, K. C., Bakner, L., Vernon, A., & Riccio, D. C. (1993). The effect of US preexposure on conditioned taste aversion: Lack of postconditioning recovery of the aversion. *Behavioral & Neural Biology, 60*(3), 271–273.

Dacanay, R. J., & Riley, L. (1982). The UCS preexposure effect in taste aversion learning: Tolerance and blocking are drug specific. *Animal Learning & Behavior, 10*(1), 91–96.

De la Casa, L. G., Diaz, E., & Lubow, R. E. (2003). Effects of post-treatment retention interval and context on neophobia and conditioned taste aversion. *Behavioural Processes, 63*(3), 159–170.

De la Casa, L. G., & Lubow, E. (1995). Latent inhibition in conditioned taste aversion: The roles of stimulus frequency and duration and the amount of fluid ingested during preexposure. *Neurobiology of Learning and Memory, 64*(2), 125–132.

De la Casa, L. G., & Lubow, E. (2000). Super-latent inhibition with delayed conditioned taste aversion testing. *Animal Learning & Behavior, 28*(4), 389–399.

Domjan, M. (1975). Poison-induced neophobia in rats: Role of stimulus generalization of conditioned taste aversions. *Animal Learning & Behavior, 3*(3), 205–211.

Domjan, M., & Best, R. (1980). Interference with ingestional aversion learning produced by preexposure to the unconditioned stimulus: Associative and nonassociative aspects. *Learning and Motivation, 11*(4), 522–537.

Dragoin, W., Hughes, G., Devine, M., & Bentley, J. (1973). Long-term retention of conditioned taste aversions: Effects of gustatory interference. *Psychological Reports, 33*(2), 511–514.

Dudai, Y. (2006). Reconsolidation: The advantage of being refocused. *Current Opinion in Neurobiology, 16*(2), 174–178.

Eisenberg, M., Kobilo, T., Berman, D. E., & Dudai, Y. (2003). Stability of retrieved memory: Inverse correlation with trace dominance. *Science, 301*(5636), 1102–1104.

Elkins, R. L. (1984). Taste-aversion retention: An animal experiment with implications for consummatory-aversion alcoholism treatments. *Behaviour Research and Therapy, 22*(2), 179–186.

Elkins, R. L., & Hobbs, H. (1979). Forgetting, preconditioning CS familiarization and taste aversion learning: An animal experiment with implications for alcoholism treatment. *Behaviour Research and Therapy, 17*(6), 567–573.

Franchina, J. J., Domato, G. C., Patsiokas, A. T., & Griesemer, H. A. (1980). Effects of number of pre-exposures on sucrose taste aversion in weanling rats. *Developmental Psychobiology, 13*(1), 25–31.

Garcia, J., Hankins, W. G., & Rusiniak, K. W. (1974). Behavioral regulation of the milieu interne in man and rat. *Science, 185*(4154), 824–831.

Gruest, N., Richer, P., & Hars, B. (2004). Emergence of long-term memory for conditioned aversion in the rat fetus. *Developmental Psychobiology, 44*(3), 189–198.

Guanowsky, V., Misanin, R., & Riccio, D. C. (1983). Retention of conditioned taste aversion in weanling, adult, and old-age rats. *Behavioral & Neural Biology, 37*(1), 173–178.

Hall, G., & Channell, S. (1986). Context specificity of latent inhibition in taste aversion learning. *Quarterly Journal of Experimental Psychology B: Comparative and Physiological Psychology, 38*(2), 121–139.

Hamm, R. J. (1981). Hypothermia-induced retrograde amnesia in mature and aged rats. *Developmental Psychobiology, 14*(4), 357–364.

Hinderliter, C. F., & Misanin, R. (1993). Context familiarity and delayed conditioned taste aversion in young-adult and old-age rats. *Perceptual and Motor Skills, 77*(3, Pt. 2), 1403–1406.

Hinderliter, C. F., Webster, T., & Riccio, D. C. (1975). Amnesia induced by hypothermia as a function of treatment-test interval and recooling. *Animal Learning & Behavior, 3,* 257–263.

Honey, R. C., & Hall, G. (1989). Attenuation of latent inhibition after compound preexposure: Associative and perceptual explanations. *Quarterly Journal of Experimental Psychology B: Comparative and Physiological Psychology, 41*(4-B), 355–368.

Ivanova, S. F., & Bures, J. (1990). Conditioned taste aversion is disrupted by prolonged retrograde effects of intracerebral injection of tetrodotoxin in rats. *Behavioral Neuroscience, 104*(6), 948–954.

Kalat, J. W., & Rozin, P. (1973). "Learned safety" as a mechanism in long-delay taste-aversion learning in rats. *Journal of Comparative and Physiological Psychology, 83*(2), 198–207.

Kasprow, W. J., Schachtman, T. R., & Miller, R. R. (1985). A retrograde gradient for disruption of a conditioned aversion to drinking cold water by ECS administered during the CS–UCS interval. *Physiology & Behavior, 34*(6), 879–882.

Kasprow, W. J., Schachtman, T. R., & Miller, R. R. (1987). The comparator hypothesis of conditioned response generation: Manifest conditioned excitation and inhibition as a function of relative excitatory strengths of CS and conditioning context at the time of testing. *Journal of Experimental Psychology: Animal Behavior Processes, 13,* 395–406.

Klein, S. B., Becker, T., Boyle, D., Krug, D. E., Underhill, G., & Mowrer, R. R. (1987). The influence of context and UCS intensity on the UCS preexposure effect in a flavor aversion paradigm. *Learning and Motivation, 18*(4), 356–370.

Klein, S. B., Mikulka, P. J., Domato, G. C., & Hallstead, C. (1977). Retention of internal experiences in juvenile and adult rats. *Physiological Psychology, 5*(1), 63–66.

Klein, S. B., Mikulka, P. J., & Lucci, K. (1986). Influence of lithium chloride intensity on unconditioned stimulus-alone interference in a flavor aversion paradigm. *Learning and Motivation, 17*(1), 76–90.

Klein, S. B., & Spear, E. (1970). Forgetting by the rat after intermediate intervals ("Kamin effect") as retrieval failure. *Journal of Comparative and Physiological Psychology, 71*(1), 165–170.

Kraemer, P. J., Kraemer, E. G., Smoller, D. E., & Spear, N. E. (1989). Enhancement of flavor aversion conditioning in weanling but not adult rats by prior conditioning to an odor. *Psychobiology, 17*(1), 34–42.

Kraemer, P. J., Lariviere, N. A., & Spear, N. E. (1988). Increase in retention of a taste aversion by weanling rats after a long interval. *Animal Learning & Behavior, 16*(2), 191–194.

Kraemer, P. J., Miller, J. S., Jagielo, J. A., & Spear, N. E. (1992). Facilitation of long-delay conditioned taste aversion in weanling rats. *Psychobiology, 20*(3), 223–228.

Kraemer, P. J., & Roberts, A. (1984). The influence of flavor preexposure and test interval on conditioned taste aversions in the rat. *Learning and Motivation, 15*(3), 259–278.

Kral, P. A. (1970). Interpolation of electroconvulsive shock during CS–US interval as an impediment to the conditioning of taste aversion. *Psychonomic Science, 19*(1), 36–37.

Kral, P. A. (1971a). Electroconvulsive shock during taste-illness interval: Evidence for induced disassociation. *Physiology & Behavior, 7*(5), 667–670.

Kral, P. A. (1971b). ECS between tasting and illness: Effects of current parameters on a taste aversion. *Physiology & Behavior, 7*(5), 779–782.

Kucharski, D., Richter, N. G., & Spear, N. E. (1985). Conditioned aversion is promoted by memory of CS–. *Animal Learning & Behavior, 13*(2), 143–151.

Land, C., Harrod, S. B., & Riccio, D. C. (1998). The interval between the CS and the UCS as a determinant of generalization performance. *Psychonomic Bulletin & Review, 5*(4), 690–693.

Lavin, M. J. (1976). The establishment of flavor–flavor associations using a sensory preconditioning training procedure. *Learning and Motivation, 7*(2), 173–183.

Lewis, D. J., Miller, R. R., & Misanin, J. R. (1967). ECS-induced retrograde amnesia for one trial active avoidance. *Psychonomic Science, 8*(11), 485–486.

Loy, I., Alvarez, R., Rey, V., & Lopez-Ramirez, M. (1993). Context-US associations rather than occasion setting in taste aversion learning. *Learning and Motivation, 24*(1), 55–72.

Loy, I., & Lopez, M. (1999). Conditional control of toxicosis-based conditioning by context. *Behavioural Processes, 46*(2), 173–179.

Lubow, R. E. (1973). Latent inhibition. *Psychological Bulletin, 79*(6), 398–407.

Lubow, R. E., & De la Casa, G. (2002). Superlatent inhibition and spontaneous recovery: Differential effects of pre- and postconditioning CS-alone presentations after long delays in different contexts. *Animal Learning & Behavior, 30*(4), 376–386.

Lubow, R. E., & De la Casa, G. (2005). There is a time and a place for everything: Bidirectional modulations of latent inhibition by time-induced context differentiation. *Psychonomic Bulletin & Review, 12*(5), 806–821.

Lyn, S. A., & Capaldi, D. (1994). Robust conditioned flavor preferences with a sensory preconditioning procedure. *Psychonomic Bulletin & Review, 1*(4), 491–493.

Mackintosh, N. J. (1975). A theory of attention: Variations in the associability of stimuli with reinforcement. *Psychological Review, 82*(4), 276–298.

Mactutus, C. F., Riccio, D. C., & Ferek, J. M. (1979). Retrograde amnesia for old (reactivated) memory: Some anomalous characeristics. *Science, 204*(4399), 1319–1320.

Martinez, J. L., & Rigter, H. (1983). Assessment of retention capacities in old rats. *Behavioral & Neural Biology, 39*(2), 181–191.

Metzger, M. M. (1997). *An investigation of the forgetting of stimulus attributes in the conditioned taste aversion paradigm: Conditioned stimulus, unconditioned stimulus, and context.* Unpublished doctoral dissertation, Kent State University, Kent.

Metzger, M. M., Flint, R. W., & Riccio, D. C. (1997). Ketaset–Rompun anesthesia induces a conditioned taste aversion in rats. *Psychological Record, 47*(3), 473–482.

Miller, J. S., Jagielo, J. A., & Spear, N. E. (1990). Changes in the retrievability of associations to elements of the compound CS determine the expression of overshadowing. *Animal Learning & Behavior, 18*(2), 157–161.

Miller, J. S., Jagielo, J. A., & Spear, N. E. (1993). The influence of retention interval on the US preexposure effect: Changes in contextual blocking over time. *Learning and Motivation, 24*(4), 376–394.

Miller, R. R., & Matzel, L. D. (1988). The comparator hypothesis: A response rule for the expression of associations. In G. H. Bower (Ed.), *The psychology of learning and motivation* (pp. 51–92). San Diego, CA: Academic Press.

Miller, R. R., & Matzel, L. D. (2000). Memory involves far more than "consolidation." *Nature Reviews Neuroscience, 3*, 214–216.

Miller, R. R., & Springer, D. (1972). Induced recovery of memory in rats following electroconvulsive shock. *Physiology & Behavior, 8*(4), 645–651.

Miller, R. R., & Springer, D. (1973). Amnesia, consolidation, and retrieval. *Psychological Review, 80*(1), 69–79.

Millin, P. M., Moody, E. W., & Riccio, D. C. (2001). Interpretation of retrograde amnesia: Old problems redux. *Nature Reviews Neuroscience, 2*, 68–70.

Millin, P. M., & Riccio, C. (2004). Is the context shift effect a case of retrieval failure? The effects of retrieval enhancing treatments on forgetting under altered stimulus conditions in rats. *Journal of Experimental Psychology: Animal Behavior Processes, 30*(4), 325–334.

Misanin, J. R., Anderson, M. J., Christianson, J. P., Collins, M. M., Goodhart, M. G., Rushanan, S. G. et al. (2002). Low body temperature, time dilation and long-trace conditioned flavor aversion in rats. *Neurobiology of Learning and Memory, 78*(1), 167–177.

Misanin, J. R., Christianson, J. P., Anderson, M. J., Giovanni, L. M., & Hinderliter, C. F. (2004). Ketaset-Rompun extends the effective interstimulus interval in long-trace taste-aversion conditioning in rats. *Behavioural Processes, 65*(2), 111–121.

Misanin, J. R., Goodhart, M. G., Anderson, M. J., & Hinderliter, C. F. (2002). The interaction of age and unconditioned stimulus intensity on long-trace conditioned flavor aversion in rats. *Developmental Psychobiology, 40*(2), 131–137.

Misanin, J. R., Greider, D. L., & Hinderliter, C. F. (1988). Age differences in the outcome of long-delay taste-aversion conditioning in rats. *Bulletin of the Psychonomic Society, 26*(3), 258–260.

Misanin, J. R., & Hinderliter, F. (1994). Efficacy of lithium chloride in the taste-aversion conditioning of young-adult and old-age rats. *Psychological Reports, 75*(1, Pt. 1), 267–271.

Misanin, J. R., & Hinderliter, F. (1995). Lack of age differences in context–illness associations in the long-delay taste-aversion conditioning of rats. *Perceptual and Motor Skills, 80*(2), 595–598.

Misanin, J. R., & Hoover, M. (1971). Recovery rate as a determinant of the amnesic-like effect of hypothermia. *Physiology & Behavior, 6*(6), 689–693.

Misanin, J. R., Kniss, D. A., Yoder, S. D., & Yazujian, D. L. (1984). The effect of electroconvulsive shock on the attenuation of taste-aversion conditioning produced by flavor preexposure. *Behavioral & Neural Biology, 41*(1), 30–40.

Misanin, J. R., Miller, R. R., & Lewis, D. J. (1968). Retrograde amnesia produced by electroconvulsive shock after reactivation of a consolidated memory trace. *Science, 160*(3827), 554–555.

Misanin, J. R., Wilson, H. A., Schwarz, P. R., Tuschak, J. B., & Hinderliter, C. F. (1998). Low body temperature affects associative processes in long-trace conditioned flavor aversion. *Physiology & Behavior, 65*(3), 581–590.

Nachman, M. (1970). Limited effects of electroconvulsive shock on memory of taste stimulation. *Journal of Comparative and Physiological Psychology, 73*(1), 31–37.

Nadel, L., & Land, C. (2000). Memory traces revisited. *Nature Reviews Neuroscience, 1*, 209–212.

Nadel, L., & Zola-Morgan, S. (1984). Infantile amnesia: A neurobiological perspective. In M. Moscovitch (Ed.), *Infant memory* (pp. 145–172). New York: Plenum.

Nader, K., Schafe, G. E., & LeDoux, J. E. (2000). Fear memories require protein synthesis in the amygdala for reconsolidation after retrieval. *Nature, 406*, 722–726.

Pavlov, I. P. (1927). *Conditioned reflexes*. Oxford: Oxford University Press.

Pearce, J. M., & Hall, G. (1980). A model for Pavlovian learning: Variations in the effectiveness of conditioned but not of unconditioned stimuli. *Psychological Review, 87*(6), 532–552.

Perkins, C. C., Jr., & Weyant, R. G. (1958). The interval between training and test trials as determiner of the slope of generalization gradients. *Journal of Comparative Physiological Psychology, 51*, 596–600.

Phillips, A. G., & LePiane, G. (1980). Disruption of conditioned taste aversion in the rat by stimulation of amygdala: A conditioning effect, not amnesia. *Journal of Comparative and Physiological Psychology, 94*(4), 664–674.

Prados, J., & Sansa, J. (2002). Differential acquisition of aversion by two distinctive contexts paired with lithium-induced illness. *Learning and Motivation, 33*(2), 253–268.

Przybyslawski, J., & Sara, J. (1997). Reconsolidation of memory after its reactivation. *Behavioural Brain Research, 84*(1–2), 241–246.

Randich, A., & LoLordo, M. (1979). Associative and nonassociative theories of the UCS preexposure phenomenon: Implications for Pavlovian conditioning. *Psychological Bulletin, 86*(3), 523–548.

Rescorla, R. A., & Wagner, A. R. (1972). A theory of Pavlovian conditioning: Variations in the effectiveness of reinforcement and nonreinforcement. In A. H. Black & W. F. Prokasy (Eds.), *Classical conditioning II* (pp. 64–99). New York: Appleton-Century-Crofts.

Revusky, S., & Bedarf, E. W. (1967). Association of illness with prior ingestion of novel foods. *Science, 155*, 219–220.

Revusky, S., & Reilly, S. (1989). Attenuation of conditioned taste aversions by external stressors. *Pharmacology, Biochemistry and Behavior, 33*(1), 219–226.

Riccio, D. C., Ackil, J. K., & Burch-Vernon, A. (1992). Forgetting of stimulus attributes: Methodological implications for assessing associative phenomena. *Psychological Bulletin, 112*(3), 433–445.

Riccio, D. C., & Ebner, D. L. (1981). Post-acquisition modifications of memory. In N. E. Spear & R. R. Miller (Eds.), *Information processing in animals: Memory mechanisms* (pp. 291–317). Hillsdale, NJ: Erlbaum.

Riccio, D. C., Hodges, L. A., & Randall, P. K. (1968). Retrograde amnesia produced by hypothermia in rats. *Journal of Comparative and Physiological Psychology, 66*(3, Pt.1), 618–622.

Riccio, D. C., Millin, P. M., & Bogart, A. R. (2006). Reconsolidation: A brief history, a retrieval view, and some recent issues. *Learning and Memory, 13*(5), 536–544.

Riccio, D. C., Rabinowitz, V. C., & Axelrod, S. (1994). Memory: When less is more. *American Psychologist, 49*(11), 917–926.

Riccio, D. C., & Richardson, R. (1984). The status of memory following experimentally induced amnesias: Gone, but not forgotten. *Physiological Psychology, 12*(2), 59–72.

Riccio, D. C., Richardson, R., & Ebner, D. L. (1984). Memory retrieval deficits based upon altered contextual cues: A paradox. *Psychological Bulletin, 96*(1), 152–165.

Riccio, D. C., Richardson, R., & Ebner, D. L. (1999). The contextual change paradox is still unresolved: Comment on Bouton, Nelson, & Rosas. *Psychological Bulletin, 125*(2), 187–189.

Richardson, R., Riccio, D. C., & Mowrey, H. (1982). Retrograde amnesia for previously acquired Pavlovian conditioning: UCS exposure as a reactivation treatment. *Physiological Psychology, 10*(4), 384–390.

Richardson, R., Williams, C., & Riccio, D. C. (1984). Stimulus generalization of conditioned taste aversion in rats. *Behavioral & Neural Biology, 41*(1), 41–53.

Riley, A. L., & Simpson, G. R. (2001). The attenuating effects of drug preexposure on taste aversion conditioning: generality, experimental parameters, underlying mechanisms, and implications for drug use and abuse. In R. R. Mowrer & S. B. Klein (Eds.), *Handbook of contemporary learning theories* (pp. 505–559). Mahwah, NJ: Lawrence Erlbaum.

Riley, A. L., & Tuck, L. (1985). Conditioned food aversions: A bibliography. *Annals of the New York Academy of Sciences, 443*, 381–437.

Rosas, J. M., & Bouton, E. (1996). Spontaneous recovery after extinction of a conditioned taste aversion. *Animal Learning & Behavior, 24*(3), 341–348.

Rosas, J. M., & Bouton, E. (1997). Renewal of a conditioned taste aversion upon return to the conditioning context after extinction in another one. *Learning and Motivation, 28*(2), 216–229.

Rosas, J. M., & Bouton, E. (1998). Context change and retention interval can have additive, rather than interactive, effects after taste aversion extinction. *Psychonomic Bulletin & Review, 5*(1), 79–83.

Rosenblum, K., Meiri, N., & Dudai, Y. (1993). Taste memory: The role of protein synthesis in gustatory cortex. *Behavioral & Neural Biology, 59*(1), 49–56.

Rozin, P., & Kalat, W. (1971). Specific hungers and poison avoidance as adaptive specializations of learning. *Psychological Review, 78*(6), 459–486.

Rozin, P., & Ree, P. (1972). Long extension of effective CS–US interval by anesthesia between CS and US. *Journal of Comparative and Physiological Psychology, 80*(1), 43–48.

Sara, S. J. (2000). Retrieval and reconsolidation: Toward a neurobiology of remembering. *Learning and Memory, 7*, 73–84.

Schachtman, T. R., Brown, A. M., & Miller, R. R. (1985). Reinstatement-induced recovery of a taste–LiCl association following extinction. *Animal Learning & Behavior, 13*(3), 223–227.

Schweitzer, L., & Green, L. (1982). Acquisition and extended retention of a conditioned taste aversion in preweanling rats. *Journal of Comparative and Physiological Psychology, 96*(5), 791–806.

Shaw, N. (1986). Disruption of conditioned taste aversion: The effect of ECS after the taste–illness interval. *Physiology & Behavior, 38*(3), 431–434.

Shaw, N. A. (1988). Disruption of conditioned taste aversion: Evidence that ECS weakens the gustatory engram. *Behavioral & Neural Biology, 49*(3), 302–309.

Shaw, N. A. (1993). Impairment of the gustatory engram by generalised seizure activity without associated loss of conditioned taste aversion. *Physiology & Behavior, 53*(5), 839–843.

Siegel, S. (1974). Flavor preexposure and "learned safety." *Journal of Comparative and Physiological Psychology, 87*(6), 1073–1082.

Sjoden, P., & Archer, T. (1981). Associative and nonassociative effects of exteroceptive context in taste-aversion conditioning with rats. *Behavioral & Neural Biology, 33*(1), 74–92.

Spear, N. E. (1978). *The processing of memories: Forgetting and retention.* Hillsdale, NJ: Erlbaum.

Spear, N. E., Klein, S. B., & Riley, E. P. (1971). The Kamin effect as "state-dependent learning": Memory-retrieval failure in the rat. *Journal of Comparative and Physiological Psychology, 74*(3), 416–425.

Spear, N. E., & Riccio, D. C. (1994). *Memory: Phenomena and principles.* Boston, MA: Allyn and Bacon.

Steinert, P. A., Infurna, R. N., Jardula, M. F., & Spear, N. E. (1979). Effects of CS concentration on long-delay taste aversion learning in preweanling and adult rats. *Behavioral & Neural Biology, 27*(4), 487–502.

Steinert, P. A., Infurna, R. N., & Spear, N. E. (1980). Long-term retention of a conditioned taste aversion in preweanling and adult rats. *Animal Learning & Behavior, 8*(3), 375–381.

Symonds, M., & Hall, G. (1997). Contextual conditioning with lithium-induced nausea as the US: Evidence from a blocking procedure. *Learning and Motivation, 28*(2), 200–215.

Thiele, T. E., Kiefer, S. W., & Badia-Elder, N. E. (1996). Delayed generalization testing produces enhanced alcohol aversions in rats. *Alcohol, 13*(2), 201–207.

Tulving, E., & Thomson, M. (1973). Encoding specificity and retrieval processes in episodic memory. *Psychological Review, 80*(5), 352–373.

Westbrook, R. F., & Brookes, N. (1988). Potentiation and blocking of conditioned flavour and context aversions. *Quarterly Journal of Experimental Psychology B: Comparative and Physiological Psychology, 40*(1, Sect. B), 3–30.

Westbrook, R. F., & Homewood, J. (1982). The effects of a flavour–toxicosis pairing upon long-delay, flavour aversion learning. *Quarterly Journal of Experimental Psychology B: Comparative and Physiological Psychology, 34*(2), 59–75.

8

Postconditioning Event Manipulations on Processing of the Target Conditioned Stimulus in Conditioned Taste Aversion

TODD R. SCHACHTMAN, ASHLEY RAMSEY, AND OSKAR PINEÑO

POSTCONDITIONING EVENT MANIPULATIONS

Several major innovations occurred in the field of animal learning in the 1960s and early 1970s. First, there was the discovery of conditioned taste aversion (CTA) and its distinguishing properties (Garcia, Ervin, & Koelling, 1966; Garcia & Koelling, 1966). Second, prior to the 1970s a vast majority of the research on classical conditioning focused almost exclusively on the processes supporting or limiting the *acquisition* of associations following simple CS–US pairings (CS: conditioned stimulus; US: unconditioned stimulus). The influence of other forms of information processing (e.g., retrieval, rehearsal, and interference) was previously ignored for the most part in the literature. Such processes began to receive more attention in the 1970s. Third, the importance of the interactions between the target CS with other cues (e.g., contextual cues and other CSs) was given more focus.

There are a few reasons why researchers may have strayed from focusing on nonacquisition-based influences on conditioned performance prior to the 1970s. On one hand, theories and models at the time did not address these forms of information processing. Also, the experimental techniques (such as the use of postconditioning treatments) were not available (or acknowledged) to examine such processes in animals. However, research in the past few decades has provided many insights into the varied forms of processing that can occur during conditioning as well as ways to examine the contents of learning (i.e., what information is acquired and stored in memory).

Many of the experimental techniques that are currently used to assess the information processing that underlies conditioned performance involve treatments that occur after the initial conditioning experience and prior to the test for the conditioned response (CR) elicited by the target CS. In classical conditioning, initial training might involve pairing one or more CSs with the US. Later, the CS of interest (i.e., the "target CS") is presented to test for the degree of the CR it elicits. Treatments occurring between training and testing have been very valuable in isolating the various processes presumably involved in the learning that occurred as well as the associative content of the memory. Much of the research in this chapter will be concerned with such processes and these associative structures. One such treatment involves changing the conditions at the time of testing relative to what was experienced during the conditioning phase. The use of a change of context to influence conditioned performance and to reveal the nature of the processing deficit is not new: similarity between the training and test contexts in modulating information retrieval in humans has been long acknowledged in research on human memory.

Tulving's notion of encoding specificity (Tulving & Thompson, 1973) described how a match in the circumstances (i.e., context) during training and testing would facilitate retrieval of the target information at test (for a recent review, see Smith & Vela, 2001). Changing the context between training and testing along with other manipulations that occur after an initial conditioning phase and prior to testing can influence the retrievability and/or expression of the target CS–US association in classical conditioning. Moreover, numerous studies with animals have shown that conditioned performance is usually worse if the contextual cues (cues of the apparatus used for the experiment) are changed between conditioning and testing (e.g., Archer, Sjödén, & Nilsson, 1985; Riccio, Urda, & Thomas, 1966). Similarly, experiments on state-dependent learning (Deutsch & Roll, 1973; Overton, 1985) have shown that training under one drug-induced state (e.g., drugged) and testing with another state (e.g., not drugged) can cause poorer performance than when training and testing occur in the same internal state or context. Much of this work has revealed that these performance deficits were due to a retrieval failure. Context changes provide one example of the effects of a postconditioning treatment on the CR. This chapter will describe research on the effects of postconditioning manipulations using a CTA procedure.

HISTORICAL ANTECEDENTS: REMINDER EFFECTS AND THE EVENT-MEMORY MODEL

Reminder Effects

Two areas of research conducted in the early 1970s highlight the large impact that treatments administered after conditioning and prior to testing can have on learning. We shall begin by reviewing some findings using procedures other than CTA to illustrate the history of such effects, as well as some of the important concepts that we will be discussing throughout this chapter. First, Miller and Springer (1972, 1973; see also Springer & Miller, 1972) found that rats that received conditioning and then were rendered amnesic through electroconvulsive shock (ECS) could experience a reversal of the amnesia through "reactivation" or "reminder" treatments administered prior to the test. For

instance, subjects could be given one trial of passive avoidance conditioning (i.e., the subjects are placed in a safe compartment of a shuttlebox and receive footshock only if they move to the other side of the shuttlebox). Subjects receiving this treatment typically learn an avoidance response (staying in the safe compartment) to prevent the footshock from occurring. However, if subjects were given ECS 500 ms after performing the avoidance response, then poor performance was found on the subsequent test trial for avoidance, indicating the occurrence of retrograde amnesia caused by the ECS. Of most interest with regard to the present discussion, presentations of a "reminder shock" in a different context after the amnesia-inducing treatment can produce recovery of the avoidance response. In sum, in the absence of ECS during training, subjects perform well on the avoidance test. When the ECS was given, poor avoidance responding resulted for those subjects, but a reminder treatment following ECS for other subjects reversed the effects of the ECS, as evidenced by the recovery of good avoidance responding. Because the subjects were only presented with one component of the target memory (e.g., the footshock US was given in a different context) such a treatment cannot be considered a new pairing of a relevant stimulus with the US. Miller referred to such treatments as "reminder treatments" and suggested that the presentation of the single component from the conditioning episode could reactivate the entire target conditioning memory (see Miller, Kasprow, & Schachtman, 1986). This additional processing induced by the reminder treatment made the target memory more accessible when the subjects were tested. In other words, the retrievability of the conditioning information was enhanced. The effects of US reminder treatments are also sometimes referred to as "US reinstatement" (see next section).

The above-mentioned results are informative for a number of reasons. First, they show that the avoidance memory was "consolidated" in the 500 ms prior to the ECS since the memory was expressed as a result of the reminder. (Note that this is at odds with numerous recent papers in the neuroscience literature that view the consolidation phase as lasting for a much larger interval of time.) Second, it demonstrates that postconditioning treatments can have very dramatic effects on learning, and, specifically, on the retrieval of learned information.

Event-Memory Model and Related Effects

Rescorla's (e.g., Rescorla & Cunningham, 1978; Rescorla & Heth, 1975) research on the event-memory model focused on postconditioning manipulations. This idea was apparently stimulated in part by an early article by Rozeboom (1958), and this focus assessed the "content of learning" that occurred during acquisition of a simple CS–US association. The event-memory model claimed that three memories are acquired when a CS is paired with a US. First, a representation of the CS event is formed in memory. Second, a US representation is also created in memory. Third, an association between the two representations is acquired. When these experiences are acquired and formed in memory, the presentation of the CS (in addition to activating the CS representation) will, via the CS–US association, activate the representation of the US. In addition to describing the potential processes occurring as a result of CS–US pairings, the event-memory model explained extinction, that is, the decrease in CR that occurs when the CS is presented without the US after CS–US pairings. In this model, extinction was viewed as involving two processes: first, presentations of the CS-alone after CS–US pairings had the effect of degrading the US representation in memory and, second, additional CS-alone presentations could weaken the CS–US association.

In accord with the event-memory model, if the US (the same US magnitude used during conditioning) was presented alone following extinction, then the CR was shown to return (Bouton & Bolles, 1985; Rescorla & Heth, 1975; Schachtman, Brown, & Miller, 1985), presumably because the memory of the US representation was reinstated. Rescorla and Heth called this effect "US reinstatement." Therefore, US reinstatement is another procedure (in addition to the work by Miller & Springer mentioned earlier) that occurs between a conditioning phase and a test phase and that can reveal an otherwise unexpressed (but, at least partially, intact) association. According to the event-memory model, if too much extinction occurred, such that the CS–US association had also been greatly weakened, then US presentations may not reinstate the CR. The event-memory model predicted that the CS would not be capable of activating the US through a functional CS–US association.

Spontaneous recovery, although very familiar to conditioning theorists since the time of Pavlov's original work (Pavlov, 1927), is an intriguing phenomenon because it shows that, even after an extinction treatment is successful in reducing the CR, the original CS–US association must remain at least partially intact in memory since the CR returns after a time interval elapses (and, importantly, without additional conditioning). Moreover, it serves as perhaps the simplest treatment that one can administer between the extinction treatment and the test phase to influence the CR. To account for spontaneous recovery, Rescorla (1979) suggested that degrading the US representation after extinction was not necessarily always an enduring change—after a period of time the US representation could revert to its earlier strong status. Randich and Rescorla (1981; see also Rescorla & Cunningham, 1978) found support for the notion that the US representation does spontaneously increase in its effective status with a retention interval following conditioning. Work discussed later in this chapter also examined the effects of a retention interval using an extinguished CS in a CTA procedure.

Rescorla also performed studies involving the modification of the US representation between the conditioning and test phases (Rescorla, 1973, 1974). Much of the work done on this topic since the original experiments by Rescorla has been well described by Delamater and LoLordo (1991), and details of that work will not be repeated here. It is worth noting, however, that Delamater and LoLordo discuss a finding by Mikulka, Leard, and Klein (1977) using a CTA procedure in which US presentations after conditioning produced a decrease in the CR—akin to the habituation-induced US degradation obtained by Rescorla (1973) and also consistent with some theories of conditioning (Miller & Matzel, 1988; Miller & Schachtman, 1985). The findings described in this introduction, albeit using primarily fear conditioning tasks, illustrate the usefulness of administering treatments after conditioning and prior to (or at the time of) testing. Such findings show the richness in theorizing that can result from some treatments, such as postulating the existence of event representations, retrieval processes, and the recovery of otherwise unexpressed associations. Most of the remainder of this chapter will address the use of these tools and hypothetical processes to describe findings obtained with the CTA procedure.

EXTINCTION IN CTA: REINSTATEMENT, RETENTION, REACQUISITION, AND THE RENEWAL EFFECT

Reinstatement

As previously mentioned, the event-memory model predicts that, if a CS is paired with an US and then given CS-alone extinction trials (resulting in a loss of the CR), a subsequent US presentation may "reinstate" the CR to the CS. Schachtman, Brown, and Miller (1985) examined this effect in CTA by giving thirsty rats one pairing of saccharin with LiCl to establish a conditioned aversion to saccharin. In a second phase, this flavor was presented without LiCl once on each of 3 days and the CR was significantly reduced. The rats were then given an injection of LiCl as a "US reinstatement trial" or "reminder trial" that was identical to the US received during conditioning, but it was presented in a different context to minimize the formation of any new appreciable aversion to the conditioning (and test) context. The CR for the rats given the reminder treatment was significantly enhanced (i.e., the extinguished aversion to saccharin was reinstated). This result is consistent with the event-memory model's notion that initial extinction trials will degrade the US representation and that the presentation of the US (reminder trial) can restore this degraded US memory. Moreover, there was no enhancement for groups that had received the CS and US presented unpaired during conditioning, revealing that a CS–US association is needed to obtain the effect. There was also no reinstatement-induced enhancement of the CR for rats that had received more extensive extinction (e.g., six trials rather than three trials). These latter results are also consistent with Rescorla's event-memory model in that, if enough extinction treatment is given, then the CS–US association may be weakened. However, as we will discuss later in this chapter, there are other explanations for such effects, including the role of retrieval processes (Schachtman, Gustavson, Chelonis, & Bourne, 1992) as well as inadvertent context conditioning that may result from the US presentation during reactivation (Bouton & Bolles, 1979). In fact, this recovery of the CR achieved through US reinstatement can be explained in that the presentation of the US after extinction (reinstatement treatment) enhances the accessibility of the conditioning memory (CS–US association) at the expense of the retrievability of the

association formed during extinction of the CR (see Schachtman et al., 1985).

Reacquisition of an Extinguished CTA and Reacquisition Following a Retention Interval

The research just described found that US reinstatement reversed the poor CR elicited by a CS given a moderate amount of extinction, but not the CR elicited by a CS given extensive extinction. Danguir and Nicolaidis (1977) observed that a CS paired with LiCl and then given eight extinction trials resulted in impaired reacquisition of an aversion to the CS relative to a group conditioned with the CS for the first time, an effect referred to as the slow reacquisition effect (Bouton, 1986). Hart, Bourne, and Schachtman (1995) obtained similar results in a study conducted using a CTA preparation. In their study, slow reacquisition was observed following extensive extinction of a previously acquired aversion (but see Revusky & Coombes, 1979). However, following a few extinction trials, Hart et al. observed rapid reacquisition (see also Bouton, 1986, for similar results using a fear conditioning procedure).

Most learning theories are challenged by the observation of slow reacquisition following extinction (cf. Kehoe, 1988; Pearce & Hall, 1980; Rescorla & Wagner, 1972; Wagner, 1981) since such models (including Rescorla's event-memory model) claim that extinction would at most abolish any "advantage" a previously conditioned CS might have in reacquiring excitatory associative strength, rather than producing a "deficit" in relearning. One interpretation of the slow reacquisition effect is that extinction trials produce an inhibitory association between the CS and the US, or a CS–no US association and, with a sufficient amount of extinction training, this association will be more retrievable than the excitatory CS–US association resulting in slow reacquisition. This view posits that the CS can be associated with the US in an excitatory fashion (the intact CS–US association) as well as possess an inhibitory association with the US. For evidence of simultaneous excitatory and inhibitory associations for the same CS see Matzel, Gladstein, and Miller (1988) and Williams and Overmier (1988). Such a view has prompted some researchers to raise the possibility that an extinguished CS could possess net inhibitory properties (Calton, Mitchell, & Schachtman, 1996). For instance, the finding that an extensively extinguished CS results in slow reacquisition demonstrates that such a CS "passes" a retardation test for inhibition.

Miller et al. (1986) viewed the CR recovery after treatments for an extinguished CS as evidence of retrieval processes producing the CR deficit that results from extinction. According to this view, the CS-alone presentations during extinction produce a CS–no US association (or an excitatory association between the CS and a representation of "no US," see Konorski, 1967; Rescorla, 1979). The CS–no US association interferes with retrieval of the CS–US association, resulting in a poor CR. Extinction is therefore viewed as an interference effect in which these two incompatible associations (CS–US and CS–no US) compete for accessibility or retrievabililty. This idea of two "habits" being independently acquired and competing for recall echoes Martin's (1971) description of McGeoch's (1942) verbal learning theory as an "independent dominance hypothesis" such that two associations are acquired that share a common element (i.e., the A–B A–C paired associate paradigm) with one association dominating at the time of recall. McGeoch (1942) was one of the first theorists to raise the notion that poor responding can be the result of impaired retrieval instead of impaired learning (Crowder, 1976, p. 225).

A retention interval is known to produce recovery from extinction, that is, spontaneous recovery (see Rosas & Bouton, 1996, 1998, for demonstrations using CTA), presumably because it hinders inhibitory associations more than excitatory associations (see Hammond & Maser, 1970, for some evidence supportive of this claim). If a retention interval reverses the poor CR that results from extinction (i.e., produces spontaneous recovery), then would it have a similar effect on the slow reacquisition effect? Schachtman, Threlkeld, and Meyer (2000) gave rats a conditioning trial with a flavored solution followed by nine flavor-alone exposures. Rats were then given two additional pairings of the flavored solution with the LiCl injection (reacquisition) prior to testing for the CR to the flavor. Some rats received a 21-day retention interval between the extinction exposures and the reacquisition trials while others did not. Control conditions were also included in which rats received conditioning

on the target flavor for the first time prior to the test (i.e., they were originally conditioned and extinguished with a noncritical, alternative flavor). These rats were also tested immediately or after a retention interval. As expected, the retention interval had no effect on these latter control groups since the interval occurred prior to the initial conditioning of the target flavor. Of most importance, a slow reacquisition effect was found for rats reconditioned on the flavor (without a retention interval following extinction) relative to the control groups that were conditioned to this flavor for the first time, thereby replicating effects seen by Hart et al. (1995) and Danguir and Nicolaidis (1977). However, the interpolation of a retention interval between extinction and the reconditioning phase reversed the slow reacquisition effect. That is, rats conditioned more quickly if they had a retention interval placed between extinction and reconditioning. This effect is not unlike spontaneous recovery, in which the CR returns following a retention interval. One way of interpreting such an effect is that the inhibitory association resulting from the extinction trials is more sensitive to the effects of a retention interval than the excitation acquired during conditioning. Hence, the retention interval renders the CS–no US association less retrievable and the "positive transfer" stemming from the original CS–US association results in more rapid reacquisition. Again, to allude to a topic that we will discuss later about extinction and conditioned inhibition, this finding also shows that a retention interval can attenuate the ability of an extinguished CS to "pass" a retardation test for inhibition. We should also note that Rescorla (2005) has recent evidence using an appetitive conditioning procedure that conditioned excitatory associations are susceptible to spontaneous recovery following a retention interval whereas inhibitory associations are not.

Changing the Context between Training and Testing: The Renewal Effect

Earlier in this chapter we mentioned that the CR can be influenced by a change in context (e.g., Bouton & Bolles, 1979; Bouton & King, 1983). For example, if CSs are conditioned in one context (Context 1) and then extinguished in a second context (Context 2), then a weak CR will occur in

Context 2 (the "extinction context"); but a strong CR will occur outside Context 2. For instance, testing in Context 1 or in a new context (Context 3) will produce a strong CR (e.g., Bouton & Brooks, 1993; Bouton & Ricker, 1994). This effect has been called the "renewal effect" by Bouton (for a review, see Bouton, 1993) and shows that extinction memories are, at least partially, dependent on the context in which they were initially acquired for their subsequent retrieval. Chelonis, Calton, Hart, and Schachtman (1999) obtained a renewal effect in two experiments using a CTA procedure. Rats were given a single conditioning trial with sucrose and LiCl in one context (Context 1). Then, the subjects were given three extinction trials in a second context (Context 2). Other rats received conditioning and extinction in the same context (Context 1). Finally, all rats were tested in Context 1. The rats that received extinction in Context 1 showed a poor CR at test, whereas those that had been extinguished in Context 2 showed a stronger CR. These results parallel those obtained by Bouton and his colleagues using a fear conditioning procedure.

Chelonis et al. (1999) included an additional group that received extinction treatment in multiple contexts. Specifically, after receiving conditioning in Context 1, this group received one extinction trial in each of three contexts (Contexts 2, 3, and 4). The rationale behind this treatment was the notion of "encoding variability"; that is, the idea that learning in several contexts can enhance the retrievability of the target information (or "recall" in the human memory literature; Melton, 1970; Smith, 1982). Although this group received extinction in a context other than Context 1 and were tested in Context 1, the renewal effect was attenuated. Gunther, Denniston, and Miller (1998) observed an effect similar to that obtained by Chelonis et al., but using a fear conditioning procedure (also see Pineño & Miller, 2004, for related results in human predictive learning).

It should be noted that researchers have found that extensive extinction can also reverse the renewal effect (Denniston, Chang, & Miller, 2003; Tamai & Nakajima, 2000). Again, although other interpretations are possible (Denniston et al., 2003; Garcia-Gutierrez, Rosas, & Nelson, 2005), these results are consistent with the notion that extensive extinction produces a CS–no US association that is strong enough (through encoding variability or through extensive extinction) to be retrieved at test regardless of the test context.

THE EFFECTS OF RETENTION INTERVALS, RETRIEVAL PROCESSES, AND OTHER POSTCONDITIONING MANIPULATIONS

The effects of retention intervals on retrieval have been examined using a latent inhibition procedure. The following sections discuss such data using CTA.

Latent Inhibition and Retention

Latent inhibition refers to the poor CR that occurs if a CS is presented a number of times without the US prior to the CS–US pairings (i.e., if the CS is "preexposed"). Kraemer, Randall, and Carbary (1991; see also Aguado, Symonds, & Hall, 1994; Bakner, Strohen, Nordeen, & Riccio, 1991; De la Casa & Lubow, 1995) observed that a poor CR resulting from latent inhibition could be obtained if testing occurred within a day or two of the conditioning phase (see Pineño, De la Casa, Lubow, & Miller, 2006, for review). However, if testing was delayed for 2 or 3 weeks after conditioning, then little latent inhibition was observed; that is, a strong CR occurred. Put differently, if subjects received CS-alone presentations followed by CS–US pairings and then were given a test soon after, then a poor CR occurred, indicative of latent inhibition. By contrast, if the test was delayed, the subjects behaved as though they had not received the CS-alone presentations—a strong CR was observed. Kraemer et al. claimed that the CS–US association must have been formed despite the poor CR that occurred when there was no retention interval, since a CR was found when a retention interval occurred. The intact memory of the conditioning experience was expressed following the retention interval. The retention interval revealed that an excitatory association was acquired and intact but not otherwise expressed.

Latent Inhibition, Extinction, Retention, and Attention

When a retention interval occurs after extinction exposures, the CR returns, that is, spontaneous recovery occurs. Therefore, retention intervals appear to influence latent inhibition and extinction (as just seen in the previous section) in similar ways (Kraemer & Spear, 1992). Other parallels have been investigated. Hall and Pearce (1982) found that if CS-preexposures result in a loss of attention to the CS or, in other words, produce a decrease in the CS associability, a surprising event immediately after the CS preexposure allowed subsequent CS–US pairings to produce strong conditioning (i.e., latent inhibition will not be observed), presumably by restoring the attention/associability to the CS. In a recent study, Dopheide, Bills, Smith, Kichnet, and Schachtman (2005) examined if such an effect occurs for an extinguished CS using a CTA procedure. Although such effects do not involve "postconditioning manipulations" *per se*, a description of these effects is included here because they complement the other findings reported in this chapter. Dopheide et al. gave rats a single pairing of a flavor with LiCl. Then the subjects received eight CS-alone extinction trials. On the ninth and final extinction trial, the rats in the "surprise condition" received an unexpected second flavor immediately after the first target flavor. Then subjects received additional CS–US pairings to assess the degree to which the surprising event might have increased associability or attention and enhanced subsequent conditioning. No effect of this surprising nontarget flavor was seen on conditioning. Groups that received conditioning and extinction of the target flavor conditioned slowly on this flavor and there was no difference between the condition that received the postextinction trial "surprise" and the similarly treated group that did not. (Control groups were conditioned and extinguished with an irrelevant flavor and, hence, were conditioned with the target flavor for the first time when the other groups were receiving "reconditioning." Such groups are needed to document the slow reacquisition effect.) An additional experiment found that a second flavor could influence the habituation of neophobia, thereby showing that rats are sensitive to such treatment. Moreover, other experiments conducted in our laboratory (Walker, Ramsey, Hock, & Schachtman, 2007) administered a very surprising "swim stress" experience immediately after the ninth and final extinction trial and this event also did not influence attention or associability as assessed by the extent to which these rats showed slow reacquisition.

STIMULUS INTERACTION EFFECTS AND POSTCONDITIONING MANIPULATIONS

The experimental manipulation of nontarget events has also been a widely used tool in the study of stimulus interaction phenomena. Stimulus interaction refers to effects in which responding to a target CS is not only determined by the current status of its association with the US, but it is also determined by the associative history of other, nontarget CSs with the US. Although there is evidence of interaction between two CSs trained apart with the same US (i.e., an effect akin to the A–B C–B paired associates paradigm in the verbal learning tradition, e.g., Escobar, Matute, & Miller, 2001; Matute & Pineño, 1998), most stimulus interaction effects involve the training of the target and nontarget CSs (CS X and A, respectively) in either a simultaneous (i.e., AX) or a serial (i.e., A–X or X–A) compound. Stimulus interaction effects can be categorized as either "positive interaction" or "negative interaction" phenomena. In positive interaction phenomena, the response potential of the target CS, X, changes in the same direction as response potential of the nontarget CS, A. Conversely, in negative interaction phenomena, the response potential of CS S X and A change in opposite directions. In the present section, we describe some CTA studies employing manipulations of nontarget events as an attempt to ascertain the processes involved in different stimulus interaction phenomena. Many such manipulations are sensitive to postconditioning effects (e.g., extinction of CS A).

Negative Interaction Phenomena: Blocking and Overshadowing

Perhaps the best-known negative interaction phenomena are blocking and overshadowing. This section discusses evidence related to these compound conditioning phenomena, in which postconditioning manipulation of the nontarget (blocking or overshadowing) CS results in variations in the CR elicited by the target (blocked or overshadowed) CS.

Recovery from Blocking and Overshadowing: Deflation (Extinction) of the Nontarget Stimulus

Kaufman and Bolles (1981; also see Matzel, Schachtman, & Miller, 1985), using a fear conditioning procedure, gave rats a tone and light paired with footshock as an overshadowing treatment in which the control group received the tone paired alone with footshock. The light was found to "overshadow" the tone CS (i.e., a poor CR occurred for the tone on the test trial) for rats trained with a compound CS. Moreover, some subjects receiving the tone and light paired with shock in the conditioning phase also received extinction treatment with the light prior to the test on the tone. For these rats, the overshadowing effect was reversed. That is, the tone produced a strong CR. Once again, such a manipulation reveals how postconditioning manipulations can influence the CR. There are at least two theoretical explanations for such an effect. Matzel et al. (1985) concluded that the results supported the comparator hypothesis (Miller & Matzel, 1988; Miller & Schachtman, 1985). According to this idea, the tone CS (which accompanied the light during training) provided a "background context" for the light (and, conversely, the light provided a "background context" for the tone). On the basis of the comparator hypothesis, the CR to the target CS (the tone) will be directly proportional to the strength of that cue's association with the US (tone–US) and inversely proportional to the strength of two associations: the association between the target CS and its companion CS (i.e., the light, which serves as the "comparator stimulus") and the association between the comparator stimulus and the US (i.e., the light–US association). Hence, in the experiment by Kaufman and Bolles, the light was presumably a comparator cue for the tone and, thus, impaired (overshadowed) the CR to the tone. Extinction treatment with the light prior to testing of the tone presumably weakened both the tone–light and light–US associations, resulting in a recovery of responding to the tone. Since these initial studies were reported, a large number of researchers in the fields of animal learning and human contingency learning have employed this technique of reducing the "validity" of a "competing" cue after initial conditioning/contingency training and prior to final testing on the target cue (e.g., Shanks, 1985; Shanks & Dickinson, 1987; Wasserman, 1990). This effect, has been instrumental in the revision of some traditional models of conditioning (e.g., Dickinson & Burke, 1996; Van Hamme & Wasserman, 1994).

Another explanation of the effect involves retrieval processes. When the tone and light are presented together and paired with the US on a compound conditioning trial, both the tone and the light are associated with the US; however, due to competition for processing, the light–US association could reduce retrievability of the tone–US association, resulting in the overshadowing effect. That is, the two CSs could compete for the processing that is needed for good retrievability of the CS–US association. Thus, assuming that extinction of the light reduces its competitive ability, the tone–US association can be released from interference and is therefore able to be retrieved and expressed.

Schachtman, Kasprow, Meyer, Bourne, and Hart (1992) attempted to demonstrate the findings by Kaufman and Bolles (1981) using a CTA procedure. First, the target flavor, CS X, was presented for 5 min followed by a 40-min interval. Then, a 5-min presentation of the nontarget flavor, CS A, was given immediately followed by an injection of LiCl. The subjects in the "overshadowing control group" received the same treatment except that A was omitted (water was substituted for A). After this single conditioning trial, some of the rats that had been conditioned with A and X were given five exposures (one per day) of A. All rats were then tested on X. Overshadowing was observed for the group conditioned with both flavors compared to the group conditioned with just X; that is, a weaker CR occurred for the group conditioned with A and X. However, no effect of the extinction of A on the CR elicited by X was found. Regardless of whether they received A-alone trials after conditioning or not, the conditions trained with X in the presence of A on the conditioning trial learned relatively poorly about X. A second experiment used a larger number of conditioning and extinction trials and obtained a similar result. An additional experiment used a lengthy 200-min period between the presentation of X and the presentation of A on each of two conditioning trials in order to reduce the opportunity for within-compound (flavor–flavor) associations. No effect of extinction was observed. Two final experiments used a simultaneous compound, one during four conditioning trials prior to the A-alone extinction trials, and the other during two conditioning trials followed by the extinction trials. None of these experiments obtained any evidence of the A-alone trials enhancing the CR to X.

The CTA experiments just described tried to obtain the effect of extinction of the nontarget CS on responding to the target CS found by Kaufman and Bolles (1981) and Matzel et al. (1985; also see Matzel, Shuster, & Miller, 1987). No such effect was observed. It appears as though, in contrast to many successful demonstrations using fear conditioning in rats and a covariation judgment task with human subjects, it is hard to obtain recovery from overshadowing in CTA by extinguishing the overshadowing cue.

These results make the findings of a recent blocking study conducted in one of our laboratories somewhat surprising. This experiment administered an A–LiCl pairing followed by a single X–A–LiCl trial (the presentation of X was followed immediately by the presentation of A, which was immediately followed by the injection of LiCl). This treatment resembled a "blocking condition." One group received three A-alone trials after this compound conditioning trial and prior to testing, and it showed a much stronger CR to X than a group lacking such A-alone trials. This effect is very similar to the "alleviation from competition effect" seen by Kaufman and Bolles (1981) and Matzel et al. (1985). It is not clear why the several experiments conducted by Schachtman et al. (1992) did not obtain a recovery effect while our recent "blocking experiment" did. The latter study involved a blocking procedure rather than an overshadowing procedure as well as different intervals and stimuli. Our laboratory is currently examining the reasons why recovery occurs in some cases but not others. It should also be noted that many recovery effects have been found using a fear conditioning task and a blocking procedure and, therefore, the most recent result from our laboratory is not that surprising.

Attenuation of Blocking by Extinction of the Blocking Stimulus Prior to Compound Conditioning

Given that CS-alone extinction treatment results in an intact but unexpressed CS–US association, one may consider how well an extinguished CS might serve as a competitor for processing in a blocking design. On the one hand, despite the poor CR seen for an extinguished CS, there is retention of the CS–US association, therefore presumably allowing it to compete well with another CS for processing (relative to a CS lacking a CS–US association). On the other hand, it is also reasonable to suspect that an extinguished CS would be poor at competing with another cue: most learning theorists would expect that the learning that occurs during the CS-alone phase would attenuate the competitive potential of a CS.

We tested this idea using a CTA procedure (Bills, Dopheide, Pineño, & Schachtman, 2006). In the first experiment, rats were given a sucrose solution paired with LiCl and then received three CS-alone extinction trials. Then these rats were

given two serial compound conditioning trials on which a target vinegar solution was presented followed by sucrose and then LiCl. A control group received identical treatment except that an alternative control flavor (decaffeinated coffee) was presented during the initial phases of the experiment (initial conditioning and extinction) and, hence, both sucrose and vinegar were novel for this group on the compound conditioning trials. When all rats were tested with the vinegar flavor, the conditioned and extinguished sucrose flavor was a poor competitor compared to the novel sucrose solution in that a stronger aversion to vinegar was found in the former condition. Thus, extinction appeared to reduce the competitive potential of a CS compared to a novel CS. A subsequent experiment used a similar procedure but tested the nontarget (blocking) CS instead of the target (blocked) CS, and found an impaired CR for the CS that had received conditioning and extinction relative to a novel CS. This result shows that an extinguished CS can reveal a "slow reacquisition effect" using this procedure (see Bouton, 1986; Hart et al., 1995), even when it is "reconditioned" in compound with a second CS. Moreover, it also confirms the expected tradeoff in the acquisition of associative strength that many learning models (e.g., Rescorla & Wagner, 1972) postulate should occur during compound conditioning. In the experiment just discussed, the extinguished CS allowed the target CS to acquire a large amount of associative strength on the compound conditioning trials merely because the extinguished CS was itself impaired in acquiring associative strength (i.e., due to slow reacquisition).

Reversal of the Attenuation of Blocking by Extinction of a Blocking Stimulus: Effect of a Retention Interval

Bills et al. (2006) conducted an additional experiment that shed some light on the results of many of the previously described experiments. In this experiment, rats were conditioned and extinguished on one flavor (A) and then received compound conditioning with this flavor and a second (target) flavor, X, (AX trials) paired with LiCl. This treatment reflects that of the experiments just described in the previous section. However, in this experiment, one condition received compound conditioning on the day following the last extinction trial (i.e., as in the previously mentioned experiments), whereas a second group received a

3-week retention interval between the extinction phase and the compound conditioning phase. Similar to the effects that a retention interval has on performance to an extinguished CS (i.e., spontaneous recovery), we examined if a retention interval would enhance the otherwise poor competitive potential that an extinguished CS typically possesses. (The experiment also included groups receiving control solutions during initial conditioning and extinction.) We found that the aversion to the target flavor X was well learned if CS A was conditioned and extinguished just prior to compound conditioning, thereby confirming the results of the previous experiments (see the previous section). However, when CS A received conditioning and extinction treatments 3 weeks prior to compound conditioning, the aversive CR to CS X was impaired ("blocked"). That is, the retention interval reversed the poor competitive ability that is ordinarily found for an extinguished CS—an effect that suggests that retention intervals influence the competitive potential of a CS in the same way that it increases the CR to a CS. As we discussed regarding the poor CR to an extinguished CS, the poor competitive potential of a CS may be due to impaired retrievability of the excitatory CS–US association. A poorly retrieved CS–US association renders the CS a poor competitor (as well as poor at producing a CR), regardless of whether the corresponding CS–US association is still intact (but poorly retrieved).

Enhancement of the Competitive Potential of an Extinguished CS by US Reinstatement

In the previous two sections on Attenuation of Blocking by Extinction of the Blocking Stimulus Prior to Compound Conditioning we discussed how an extinguished CS is a poor competitor when presented along with a novel CS as reinforced compound conditioned stimulus, as well as the competitive potential of the extinguished CS that is reversed by interpolating a retention interval between extinction treatment and compound conditioning (Bills et al., 2006). An earlier study (Schachtman et al., 1992; see also Gustavson, Hart, Calton, & Schachtman, 1992) found that the poor competitive potential of an extinguished CS could also be enhanced by a US-reinstatement treatment. In this study, rats were administered a flavored solution paired with LiCl and then given three extinction trials. These trials were followed by compound conditioning. Importantly,

following extinction treatment, half of the rats received a US exposure (i.e., "US reinstatement") in a separate context (different from the location where other experimental treatments occurred), whereas the other half did not receive such treatment. (Control rats received an alternative flavor during the initial phases of the experiment and, as with the experimental conditions, half of these rats were given reinstatement and the other half of the rats were not—a treatment that had no detectable effect for control subjects.) In sum, some rats were given conditioning and extinction and reinstatement with a flavor that was used as a "competitor" during compound conditioning while other rats were only given conditioning and extinction with the competitor. For the control rats, both CSs were novel at the time of compound conditioning. When the target CS, X, was tested, the pretrained and extinguished flavor was found to be a more effective competitor on the compound conditioning trial if the rats had been given a reinstatement presentation following extinction treatment. In this condition, a weak aversion to X was observed relative to the group given no reinstatement trial. Hence, the reinstatement allowed the extinguished CS to more effectively compete with the acquisition of an aversion to sucrose, a result that parallels that of the experiment of Bills et al. (2006), discussed in the previous section that used a retention interval. It is worth noting at this point that in the 1980s, Miller and colleagues showed that a number of CR deficits in classical conditioning could be reversed by reminder treatments (Miller et al., 1986). Interference and retrieval processes potentially exert an influence on many CR deficits including blocking (Schachtman, Gee, Kasprow, & Miller, 1983), overshadowing (Kasprow, Cacheiro, Balaz, & Miller, 1982), latent inhibition (Kasprow, Catterson, Schachtman, & Miller, 1984), and extinction effects (Calton et al., 1996; Schachtman et al., 2000). Miller and his collaborators (e.g., Kasprow et al., 1982) showed that the poor CR elicited by the overshadowed CS could be recovered by a reminder treatment consisting of presenting the target CS alone prior to test. That is, after compound conditioning, the subjects received a presentation of the target (overshadowed) CS alone, resulting in a strong CR to this CS when presented during testing. Although counterintuitive, this finding is not unique: Gordon and Mowrer (1980) found a related effect. In their study, rats were given extinction treatment; yet, a single CS-alone exposure during a session following the extinction phase produced recovery of the CR at the subsequent test. The reminder treatments (i.e., CS-alone, US-alone, or even exposure to the apparatus cues) presumably reactivate or prime the target CS–US association prior to testing and this "rehearsal" facilitates its subsequent retrieval and expression. It is important to note that similar results have also been found in a blocking procedure (Balaz, Gutsin, Cacheiro, & Miller, 1982). (For reviews of these and related findings, see Miller et al., 1986; Spear & Riccio, 1994.) The success of these reminder treatments reveal that these CR deficits are due, at least in part, to a retrieval deficit.

Given that Balaz et al. (1982) found that the weak CR to a blocked CS was seemingly due to low retrievability of the association between the blocked CS and the US, as well as experiments suggest that poor blocking by the blocking CS occurs due to inadequate retrievability of the association between the blocking CS and the US—blocking seems to result from retrieval competition between the two cues (rather than competition for associative strength).

Other Forms of Recovery from Blocking and Overshadowing: Number of Compound Trials

Blocking and overshadowing may be influenced by other treatments relevant to the present discussion. Bellingham and Gillette (1981), using rats in a classical conditioning procedure with an appetitive US, found that overshadowing was attenuated when an extensive amount of compound conditioning was given (in contrast to fewer compound trials). Similar results were reported by Azorlosa and Cicala (1988) in a blocking procedure. In the latter study, increasing the number of compound conditioning trials resulted in a reduction of blocking. It is possible that additional compound conditioning can improve the retrievability of the otherwise "overshadowed CS" and attenuate the overshadowing deficit (although certain other explanations are possible; see Bellingham & Gillette, 1981, for a discussion of a configuring account). Schachtman et al. (1983), using a fear conditioning procedure, found that blocking was slightly greater with fewer compound conditioning trials (Schachtman et al., 1983, Experiment 2). This finding is consistent with that of Bellingham and Gillette in that additional compound conditioning trials may allow

extra processing of the "blocked association," and reduce the blocking effect since this association can now be expressed due to adequate retrieval. In support of this view, Schachtman et al. (1983) found that US reinstatement given after compound conditioning alleviated the blocking deficit when the rats had received six compound conditioning trials but not when they had received two compound conditioning trials. Presumably, these extra compound trials provided additional processing of the target CS–US association—this extra processing allowed the association to benefit from the US reinstatement presentation (e.g., by bringing the association closer to threshold for retrievability). Schachtman et al. concluded that "after...acquisition to the blocked stimulus is complete, the blocked stimulus continues to be processed during the additional compound stimulus conditioning trials, with a consequent facilitation of retrieval of associations to the blocked stimulus" (p. 154). Reinstatement potentially adds to this retrieval potential. Additional training trials can increase (or decrease) an association's sensitivity to postconditioning manipulations.

Blocking by a Latent Inhibitor and the Effects of a Retention Interval

We mentioned earlier that Kraemer et al. (1991; also see Bakner et al., 1991), using a CTA procedure, observed that a poor CR resulting from latent inhibition (a CS given CS-alone exposure followed by CS–US pairings) could be obtained if testing occurred within a day or two of the conditioning phase, whereas a strong CR occurred when testing was delayed for 2 or 3 weeks. This strong CR reveals that the CS–US association was intact, but poorly expressed, when a weak CR occurred in the absence of the retention interval. Our laboratory examined whether a latent inhibitor could serve as an effective blocking stimulus (since, after all, the CS–US was apparently acquired and retained, but poorly expressed in the absence of a retention interval), and, especially, to examine if such potential could be influenced by a retention interval.

Earlier work used a CTA procedure in which a preexposed CS was conditioned in compound with a novel (target) CS. As expected, such a CS is very poor at competing for expression of associative strength with the added, target CS (e.g., Blaisdell, Bristol, Gunther, & Miller, 1998; Revusky, Parker,

& Coombs, 1977). Indeed, the target CS can be expected to gain more associative strength in such a treatment than in a control condition in which both CSs are novel at the time of the compound conditioning phase. In the latter case, a novel CS is a better "competitor" for processing than a latent inhibitor (Revusky et al., 1977), a procedure usually referred to as "attenuation of overshadowing." However, in the experiments by Bakner et al. (1991) and Kraemer et al. (1991), the nontarget CS was conditioned on its own prior to compound conditioning with the target CS. That is, the nontarget CS was first preexposed, then paired with the US, and then presented in compound with the target CS in additional pairings with the US. Thus, this arrangement of trials constitutes something akin to a blocking procedure in which the blocking CS previously underwent latent inhibition treatment. Experiments by Bills (2000) performed in our laboratory aimed to explore this effect. In one experiment, four different groups of rats were used. The rats in Group LI (i.e., latent inhibition) received presentations of a sucrose solution for each of 6 days prior to compound conditioning with sucrose and a vinegar solution (the target CS) paired with LiCl. Hence, this group received merely CS preexposure prior to compound conditioning (akin to the Revusky et al. [1977] "attenuation of overshadowing" study). Group Block received sucrose paired with LiCl prior to the compound conditioning phase; therefore, this group resembled a conventional blocking condition. Group Control received no prior treatment with sucrose

prior to compound conditioning. Group LI-Block received the six sucrose presentations followed by the sucrose–LiCl pairing (the latter treatment was like that received by Group Block) before compound conditioning. The presentations of sucrose alone followed by sucrose–LiCl trials was akin to Kraemer et al.'s latent inhibition training. (For control purposes, all groups received "control treatments" for any phases not specified above by using a control flavor, 1% decaffeinated coffee. Hence, Group Block received coffee-alone exposures, Group LI received a coffee–LiCl pairing, and Group Control received coffee-alone exposures and a coffee–LiCl pairing.)

All groups were tested on vinegar (the target flavor) using a single-bottle test 48 h after compound conditioning (a relatively short retention interval). The results are depicted in Figure 8.1. As expected, Group LI showed the strongest CR to vinegar since this flavor was presented in compound with a previously preexposed taste (see Revusky et al., 1977). For Groups Block and Control, vinegar conditioned much more poorly, indicating that if the competing CS (sucrose) had not received any CS-alone exposures, then it made a strong competitor (similar to a novel overshadowing cue). Yet, when the CS had been preexposed and conditioned on its own prior to compound conditioning (Group LI-Block), the CR to vinegar was weaker than in Group LI (the pairing made vinegar a better competitor). However, the CR to vinegar for Group LI-Block was stronger than for Groups Control and Block, indicating that

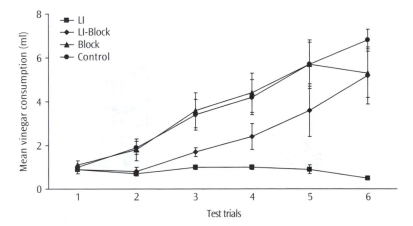

Figure 8.1. Mean vinegar consumption during six test trials for the four groups in Bills (2000). Error bars represent standard error of the means. See text for details regarding group treatments.

that CS-alone exposures made vinegar a poorer competitor. (In addition, there was no apparent blocking in the experiment—Group Block did not differ from Group Control.)

More importantly, in a subsequent experiment conducted in our laboratory, Groups LI-Block-Short and LI-Block-Long received similar treatments to that of Group LI-Block that was just described (the CS is preexposed and then paired with the US), except that compound conditioning occurred either 2 days or 21 days after CS conditioning for Groups LI-Block-Short and Group LI-Block-Long, respectively. You might recall that Kraemer et al. (1991) and Bakner et al. (1991) found that LI was attenuated with a retention interval. If a similar effect is observed with respect to a CS's competitive ability (i.e., just as a "latent inhibitor" shows a weak CR with a short retention interval but a strong CR with a long retention interval), then such a "latent inhibitor" could also be a poor competitor after a short retention interval but a relatively stronger competitor with a long interval. In this case, Group LI-Block-Long should show a weak CR to the target flavor (suggesting good "blocking"). The results from the study confirmed this expectation: Group LI-Block-Long showed a weaker CR to the target CS than Group LI-Block-Short (see Figure 8.2). This finding is consistent with the notion that a retention interval allows the CS–US association formed prior to compound conditioning to be more successfully retrieved and to compete more effectively

with the added CS. The effects just described parallel the findings and conclusions described in previous sections regarding the competitive potential of a conditioned and extinguished CS and the effects of a retention interval and US reinstatement on CR recovery. Although US reinstatement has been found to reverse the poor CR that typically occurs following latent inhibition (Kasprow et al., 1984), it is not yet known if reinstatement would influence a latent inhibitor's competitive ability.

Positive Interaction Phenomena: Second-Order Conditioning and Sensory Preconditioning

Two positive interaction phenomena, second-order conditioning (hereafter, SOC; Pavlov, 1927) and sensory preconditioning (hereafter, SPC; Brodgen, 1939), are examples of the important role that nontarget event manipulations have played in research over the last two decades. In both SOC and SPC, a target CS, X, elicits excitatory responding without being directly paired with the US. Rather, excitatory responding to X is due to the pairings of X with another CS, A, which, in turn, is directly paired with the US. Thus, responding to X is mediated by the associative history of X with A, as well as of A with the US. Procedurally, both SOC and SPC comprise X–A and A–US pairings during treatment and result in excitatory responding to X at test.

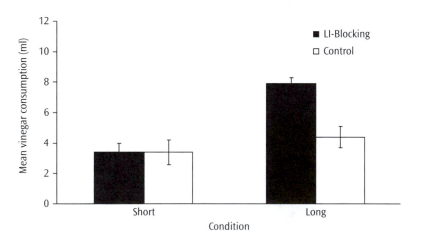

Figure 8.2. Mean vinegar consumption on the test trial for the four groups in an experiment examining stimulus competition with and without a retention interval. Error bars depict the standard error of the means. See text for details regarding group treatments.

The critical difference between these two effects relies in the order in which the X–A and A–US trials are presented during training: in SOC, A–US pairings are given first, followed by X–A pairings. In SPC, X–A pairings are followed by A–US pairings. This difference in the order of presentation of X–A and A–US trials is important because during the AX compound presentations A is either a neutral, to-be-conditioned stimulus (i.e., SPC) or a CS able to elicit a CR (i.e., SOC). Because of this difference in the associative status of A during AX presentations for SPC and SOC treatments, different explanations of each effect can be offered. One theory, the within-compound association view, states that compound AX presentations result in the formation of an association between A and X, which plays a critical role at test of X. Specifically, in this view the presentation of X at test is assumed to retrieve the representation of A (i.e., by means of the previously formed A–X within-compound association), which, in turn, retrieves the representation of the US. The within-compound view does not depend on the order in which the AX and A–US trials are presented in order to explain the observation of a CR to X (i.e., provided that both A–X and A–US associations are functional at the time of testing); and, thus, it can account for both SPC and SOC. The alternative theory proposes the formation of a stimulus–response (S–R) association as a means to explain SOC. Specifically, from this viewpoint, SOC is presumed to be due to X forming an association with the CR elicited by A during presentations of the AX compound. Notably, the S–R association explanation of SOC cannot be applied to SPC because, in this procedure, A is a neutral stimulus (i.e., A does not produce a CR) during the presentations of the AX compound. In sum, only one explanation has been offered for SPC (i.e., the within-compound association view), whereas SOC has been accounted for by two candidate views (i.e., the within-compound association and S–R association theories). Research employing manipulations of nontarget events has therefore been critical in our understanding of the processes involved in SPC and especially in SOC.

Extinction of the Nontarget Stimulus in SOC and SPC
The study by Rizley and Rescorla (1972) is, to our knowledge, the first one employing manipulations of nontarget events as a means to understand SOC and SPC. In their experiments, Rizley and Rescorla evaluated the influence on the CR elicited at test by the target CS, X, on extinguishing the nontarget CS, A, following either SOC (Experiments 1–3) or SPC (Experiment 4). An extinction treatment with CS A given after SOC treatment and prior to test of X was expected to have differential effects upon responding to X according to the within-compound association and the S–R association theories of SOC. From the within-compound association viewpoint, responding to X depends on the X–A and A–US associations being functional at the time of test so that X can retrieve the US memory through the activation of the memory of A. Therefore, presenting A-alone trials prior to test of X should reduce responding to X because of the weakening of the A–US association (as well as possibly a weakening of the X–A association). In contrast, the S–R association account of SOC predicted that A-alone presentations following SOC treatment should be of no effect on the excitatory response elicited by X. From this viewpoint, SOC is due to the formation of a direct association between X and the CR elicited by A during the AX compound presentations and, thus, X could elicit a CR with no need of the mediating role of A (i.e., once the X-response association is established, the associative status of A is no longer important for the CR to X), and the response produced by X was not expected to be affected by changes in the associative status of A performed after the AX trials. The results of Rizley and Rescorla support the S–R association account of SOC, in that the CR elicited by X was not appreciably affected by extinction treatment with CS A (also see Archer & Sjödén, 1982; Holland & Rescorla, 1975a; Nairne & Rescorla, 1981; but see Hittesdorf & Richards, 1982; Rashotte, Griffin, & Sisk, 1977). In contrast to SOC, SPC seems to rely on the formation of a within-compound association, as indicated by the reduction in the CR to X following extinction of CS A that has been reported in different studies (e.g., Archer & Sjödén, 1982, Experiment 3; Rizley & Rescorla, 1972, Experiment 4; for analogous studies in CTA, see Rescorla & Cunningham, 1978; Rescorla & Freberg, 1978).

Outcome Devaluation in SOC and SPC

There are some problems associated with the previously described use of giving an extinction treatment with the nontarget CS, A, which, although not severely so, does undermine one's interpretation of its effect on responding to the target CS, X. One such problem concerns the possibility of extinguishing, during A-alone trials, not only the A–US association but also the A–X within-compound association. This possibility does not pose any problem in attempting to discriminate between the within-compound association and S–R association accounts of SOC (i.e., because extinction of the A–X within-compound association should be of no effect according to the S–R association view but is critical for the other view). However, it is not possible to unequivocally ascertain whether a decrease in the CR elicited by X after A-alone trials is due to a reduction of strength of the A–US association, the A–X association, or both (both processes are possible in the framework of the within-compound theory). An alternative approach, consisting of devaluating the outcome (i.e., the US) associated with CS A, has been successfully employed in the literature and rules out alternative interpretations of the results in terms of the extinction of within-compound associations.

Associative Devaluation in SOC and SPC

Pairing the outcome (i.e., the US; in this case, food serving as the US) with another outcome of opposite motivational valence is one way of devaluing the outcome that is associated with the nontarget CS, A. For example, following the critical phases of SOC treatment, an appetitive outcome, such as food, can be paired with a toxin (e.g., the administration of LiCl). This technique, employed by Colwill and Rescorla (1985) in a study examining instrumental responding, also allows assessment of the role of the US representation in the production of the CR elicited by the target CS. In this manner, one can consider the potential role of the US representation in SOC and SPC. As previously mentioned, according to the within-compound association account, SOC and SPC effects are due to the formation of two essential associations: an A–X within-compound association and a first-order A–US association. The observation of a CR at test of X is thus assumed to take place because of the activation of the US representation through a X–A–US combination of associative linkages. Importantly, if the response elicited by X depends

on such an associative link, pairing the target US with a second US of contrary motivational value should have an important influence on the CR produced by X. Following this rationale, Holland and Rescorla (1975b, Experiment 1) assessed the role of within-compound associations in SOC by pairing the food US with a "devaluing" noxious outcome (i.e., the animal received high-speed rotation after ingesting the food). Although such a treatment dramatically decreased responding to the first-order CS, A, it produced no effect on responding to the second-order CS, X. Thus, Holland and Rescorla's findings are consistent with other studies using extinction of the nontarget CS, A (e.g., Rizley & Rescorla, 1972), in that they indicate that SOC is due to the formation of a direct association between X and the CR that was elicited by A during AX trials.

Manipulation of the Motivational Status in SOC and SPC

Holland and Rescorla (1975b) also provided a second approach to study the role of the activation of the US representation in SOC by changing the animals' motivational status prior to testing. Specifically, animals were tested in either a hunger or a satiation state. The underlying assumption was that, if responding to CS X depended on the anticipation of the occurrence of food based on an active representation of food during testing (i.e., again based on the X–A–food associative link, in which X activates the representation of A and the activation of A causes the activation of the representation of food), then only hungry animals should respond in the presence of X. Sated animals could still expect the occurrence of food following the presentation of X, but they should not produce a CR. As in the case of the associative devaluation treatment, a change in the motivational status (i.e., when animals were satiated prior to test) effectively reduced responding to CS A, but did not affect responding to X, which was similarly strong regardless of whether animals were tested while being hungry or sated.

EXTINCTION IN THE PRESENCE OF A SECOND CS

Following CS–US pairings, CS-alone extinction trials will reduce the CR. However, the rate of CR loss can be influenced by the present of another CS, including those with a past history of conditioning.

Protection from Extinction by a Pavlovian Conditioned Inhibitor

Extensive current research has examined the effects of extinguishing a CS either alone or in the presence of second CS. Traditional associative models such as the Rescorla–Wagner model predict that the addition of a neutral stimulus will slow the rate of extinction to the target CS (i.e., an effect referred to as "overshadowing of extinction," see Taylor & Boakes, 2002, for evidence in CTA). The occurrence of an extinction trial at the time that the US is expected causes a loss of excitatory strength (or a gain in inhibitory strength for a neutral CS), and the presence of a second stimulus will cause a "sharing" of this loss (resulting in less extinction). Recent work by Rescorla (2000) has isolated many of the factors that contribute to this effect (also see section *Compound Extinction of Indepently Trained Excitors*). Protection from extinction has been found using a CTA procedure (Taylor & Boakes, 2002); this report found that the more salient the nontarget CS, the better the "protection."

Moreover, the Rescorla–Wagner model predicts that, when a CS is given extinction in the presence of a conditioned inhibitor, this inhibitor will be especially good at protecting an excitor from extinction (e.g., Lovibond, Davis, & O'Flaherty, 2000; Soltysik, Wolfe, Nicholas, Wilson, & Garcia-Sanchez, 1983). However, Lovibond et al.'s study used humans in a skin conductance procedure, and it should be noted that they found that an excitor protected another excitor from extinction just as an inhibitor protects the CS from extinction. The effects of a concurrently presented excitor on extinction of another excitor will be discussed in the section *Compound Extinction of Indepently Trained Excitors*.

Protection from Extinction by an Extinguished Stimulus and Conditioned Inhibition

As previously mentioned, the fact that an extensively extinguished CS shows slow reacquisition (Bouton, 1986; Hart et al., 1995) implies that such a CS passes a retardation test for conditioned inhibition. It is commonly accepted that—unless a CS can produce a direct measure of inhibition (e.g., a preference for the putative inhibitory flavor relative to a control

flavor in the case of CTA; see Best, 1975)—a CS must pass a retardation and a summation test to be considered a conditioned inhibitor (Rescorla, 1969). Calton et al. (1996) showed that an extensively extinguished CS can pass a summation test for conditioned inhibition (see Blaisdell & Miller, 2001, for a similar finding). This suggests that extensive extinction can produce a net conditioned inhibitor. Such a finding is not particularly surprising in that many researchers (e.g., Bouton, 1993, 1994; Miller et al., 1986; Pearce & Hall, 1980) claim that extinction exposures result in the formation of an inhibitory or a CS–no US association, and the notion of extinction producing net inhibition simply states that this association can be stronger than the original (intact) excitatory association. Some researchers have doubted whether the extensive extinction can produce inhibition. However, these researchers have used dissimilar parameters and procedures from those used by Calton et al. (1996) and Schachtman et al. (2000) in their attempt to demonstrate the effect (Aguado, de Brugada, & Hall, 2001). Brooks, Bowker, Anderson, and Palmatier (2003) found that an extinguished CS passed retardation tests and summation tests in each of their experiments, but they found that their procedure produced summation test results explicable in terms of stimulus generalization decrement in their study. They also obtained evidence (their Experiment 2) that a CS given explicitly unpaired training (as a control condition) in which the CS and US are unpaired passed a summation test, which they interpreted as supporting a stimulus generalization decrement view of extinguished CSs passing such a test. The possibility exists that unpaired presentation(s) of the CS and US can produce conditioned inhibition. If an explicitly unpaired treatment may itself produce conditioned inhibition, then this renders the lack of a difference between the two groups an inappropriate test.

As mentioned earlier, unless a CS can be shown to produce a "direct measure" of conditioned inhibition, the CS must pass a retardation test and a summation test in order to qualify as a conditioned inhibitor. Best (1975; see also Batson & Best, 1981), using CTA, has provided some evidence that a conditioned inhibition training procedure can result in a flavor producing a direct measure of conditioned inhibition (higher consumption of the flavor than in a control condition for which the flavor should be neutral). However, Delamater, Kruse, Marlin, and LoLordo (1986) obtained little evidence for such an effect. In another study, Best and his colleagues (Best, Dunn, Batson, Meachum, & Nash, 1985) used a Pavlovian conditioned inhibition training procedure (often referred to as A+/AX− training) to produce conditioned inhibition for a vinegar flavor. This study is notable for a few reasons. First, Best and colleagues used contextual cues as the excitor (A+). That is, subjects received many pairings of a distinctive context (a chamber besides the animals' home cage) with LiCl (A+ trials in which the context serves as "A"). Then, vinegar was presented in the context in the absence of LiCl (AX− trials). Vinegar was consumed more after such training than it was by a control group that never received LiCl in the context (again, a direct measure of conditioned inhibition). In another experiment, Best et al. found that extinction of the contextual cues after conditioned inhibition training was complete, but prior to testing for inhibition, significantly reduced the inhibition. These authors concluded that inhibition in CTA is a "slave process" in which the inhibition to the CS depends on the excitation to the excitor by which it was trained (see Lysle & Fowler, 1985, for a demonstration of such an effect using a fear conditioning preparation). In a third experiment, Best et al. extinguished the contextual cues and then reconditioned the context cues causing the inhibition to vinegar to return.

A study that used a very different procedure for producing conditioned inhibition and CTA was conducted by Espinet, Iraola, Bennett, and Mackintosh (1995). Thus, there are some demonstrations of conditioned inhibition in the CTA literature, but the status of many issues (such as the potential for a direct measure of inhibition) remain unclear as does the suitability of summation tests given the potential for confounding variables.

Calton et al. (1996, Experiment 4; see also Pineño, 2007), using a CTA procedure, found that if a (target) excitor is extinguished in the presence of a previously extinguished CS, then the latter cue can protect the target excitor from extinction. This finding is consistent with the view that an extensively extinguished CS possesses properties of a conditioned inhibitor. An extinguished nontarget CS permits less extinction when presented along with the target CS during extinction of the latter cue as opposed to when no other CS was presented along with the target CS—or if an excitor was presented along with the target CS (cf. Lovibond et al., 2000, using human subjects, was able to protect

the target CS from extinction, i.e., an effect that could be referred to as "blocking of extinction") presumably because of the nontarget CS being a net inhibitor following extensive extinction treatment. As mentioned earlier, the Rescorla–Wagner model (Rescorla & Wagner, 1972; Wagner & Rescorla, 1972) predicts that the presentation of a conditioned inhibitor in compound (and nonreinforced) with a conditioned excitor will protect the excitor from extinction. The model also predicts that extinction of a conditioned inhibitor in the presence of a neutral stimulus will cause the neutral stimulus to become excitatory (but see Baker, 1974).

Compound Extinction of Independently Trained Excitors

In the previous section we discussed evidence of protection from extinction by presenting the target CS, X, in a nonreinforced compound with another CS, A, previously trained as either a Pavlovian conditioned inhibitor or as an extensively extinguished stimulus. In these two cases, the concurrent presentation of a putative inhibitor, A, presumably slows the rate of extinction. Given that a putative inhibitor can block extinction of the target CS, what outcome should we expect from the nonreinforced presentation of two independently trained excitors? The obvious answer is that presenting a CS, A, previously trained as an excitor should enhance, instead of impair, extinction of a second CS, X (the opposite of the effect produced by an inhibitor). In fact, this is the finding that Rescorla (2000) reported in a series of experiments using two different tasks (i.e., conditioned magazine approach and instrumental discriminative training). This result, however, has not always been observed. Some researchers (e.g., Lovibond et al., 2000; Pearce & Wilson, 1991) observed that the compound extinction of two independently trained CSs resulted in weakened extinction of the target CS. This result was found in different preparations, specifically, a skin conductance response in a fear conditioning preparation with humans (Lovibond et al.) and an autoshaping preparation with pigeons (Pearce & Wilson).

In a recent study that used CTA, we (Pineño, Zilski, & Schachtman, 2007; also see Pineño, 2007) obtained results similar to those of Lovibond et al. (2000) and Pearce and Wilson (1991). In our Experiment 1, the critical group, PP, was first given individual pairings of a target taste (sucrose, CS S) with the US (i.e., a LiCl injection) and a nontarget flavor (vinegar or coffee, CS A) with the US (i.e., separate S–US and A–US pairings), followed by compound presentations of A and S during an extinction treatment (i.e., AS trials). (Note that the group name, PP, stands for "paired–paired": CS A was first paired with the US, and then A was paired with CS S.) The treatment received by group PP resulted in impaired extinction of the conditioned aversion to S (i.e., low consumption of sucrose was found at test) relative to two control groups: PU (i.e., "paired–unpaired": A was paired with the US, but explicitly unpaired with S), and UP (i.e., "unpaired–paired": A was explicitly unpaired with the US, but paired with S). Moreover, group PP consumed S at test in an amount comparable to that of a control group that had received no extinction treatment with S (group NE), a result that indicated that the extinction of aversion to S in group PP, was not only attenuated, but completely prevented. It was hypothesized that this result was indicative of an SOC-like effect (see section *Positive Interaction Phenomena: Second-Order Conditioning and Sensory Preconditioning*) occurring at the time of the compound extinction treatment. That is, compound training of the CSs A and S could result in CS S acquiring further excitatory responding due to its being concurrently presented with another excitor, CS A. This SOC-like effect could produce protection from extinction: the effect of nonreinforcement of S (i.e., extinction of aversive responding) could be counteracted by the SOC-like effect arising from the conjoint presentation of S with A. Congruent with this hypothesis, the results of an additional condition of Experiment 1 (i.e., group PP-E, or "paired-paired-extinction"), in which A-alone presentations were interspersed with AS trials, found a weak aversion at test of S. That is, in this condition, extinguishing A in the same phase in which AS trials were given attenuated the conditioned aversion elicited by A and, in turn, released S from the putative SOC effect, thereby allowing extinction of the aversion to S. These results are depicted in Figure 8.3a.

In Experiment 2 of the same report (Pineño et al., 2007), the effect of extinguishing CS A on the extinction of the aversion to CS S during AS trials was assessed by giving the extinction treatment with A either before or after nonreinforced treatment with the AS compound. This manipulation

was important because, as discussed in section *Positive Interaction Phenomena: Second-Order Conditioning and Sensory Preconditioning*, the within-compound association and S–R association views of SOC make different predictions regarding the impact of performing extinction treatment with A prior to or following AS trials. Specifically, according to the within-compound theory of SOC, A-alone trials should have an equivalent impact on the extinction of S regardless of whether they take place before or after presentations of the AS compound. From this viewpoint, what matters is that, at the time of the test of S, the A–US association (and also perhaps the S–A association) is no longer functional; and, thus, S cannot retrieve the US memory (and, as a consequence, S cannot produce aversive responding). According to the S–R association view, however, A-alone trials could attenuate the SOC-like effect to CS S only if given before AS compound presentations: in this case, because A could not elicit a CR during the AS trials, S would not enter into an association with the CR and, thus, it would extinguish more strongly. In contrast, when AS trials preceded A-alone trials, SOC to S should remain unaffected by the latter treatment according to the S–R association view (see section *Positive Interaction Phenomena: Second-Order Conditioning and Sensory Preconditioning* for further details). The results of this experiment (see Figure 8.3b) replicated the main finding of Pineño et al.'s Experiment 1: the extinction of aversion to S was attenuated in group AS, which received a pairing of CS A with the US, followed by pairings of A and S during the extinction treatment (i.e., a treatment identical to the one received by group PP in Experiment 1). Specifically, the consumption at test of S was comparable in group AS and group NE (i.e., a group given no extinction treatment with S), whereas these two groups consumed less of S than group S (i.e., a group given S-alone presentations during extinction treatment). The critical results of Experiment 2 involved the consumption scores of groups A–AS and AS–A at test of S. These results found a relatively high consumption (i.e., indicative of moderate extinction of aversion to S) when A-alone trials were given prior to AS trials (i.e., group A–AS), but not when they were given after AS trials (i.e., group AS–A). In fact, A-alone trials were completely ineffective when given after AS compound trials, as indicated by the comparable consumption at test of S in group AS–A and group AS, which received no extinction treatment with A

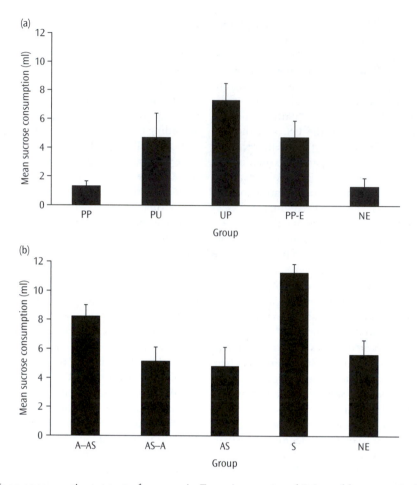

Figure 8.3. Mean consumption at test of sucrose in Experiments 1 and 2 (a and b, respectively) of Pineño et al. (2007). Error bars depict the standard error of the means. See text for details regarding group treatments.

alone. Thus, consistent with the S–R association account, extinction treatment with A following AS compound treatment does not reduce the putative SOC effect. These results strengthened our initial impression that a SOC-like process might be responsible for the protection from extinction that was observed when two individually trained excitors were extinguished in compound.

In sum, the study of Pineño et al. (2007) can be viewed as a demonstration of how a technique that has been used for decades (i.e., manipulating the associative status of the nontarget CS either before or after the treatment with the target CS) can still prove extremely useful in the research of a "new" issue (i.e., protection from extinction by presenting two excitors in a nonreinforced compound). Specifically, in Pineño et al.'s experiments, the

associative status of the nontarget CS was deflated through an extinction treatment, a technique that is common to the study of positive interaction (e.g., Archer & Sjödén, 1982; Holland & Rescorla, 1975a; Nairne & Rescorla, 1981; Rizley & Rescorla, 1972; see section *Extinction of the Nontarget Stimulus in SOC and SPC*) and negative interaction (e.g., Bills et al., 2006; Kaufman & Bolles, 1981; Matzel et al., 1985; Schachtman et al., 1992; see section *Recovery from Blocking and Overshadowing: Deflation [Extinction] of the Nontarget Stimulus*). Interestingly, because this technique was employed by Pineño et al. to study the effect of extinguishing two excitors in compound, the experimental technique involved the very process being studied: extinction was used to study extinction itself.

CONCLUDING COMMENTS

The findings reviewed in this chapter illustrate how the processes of retrieval and interference among associations have a large impact on the CR. These processes exert an influence on extinction as well as compound conditioning phenomena such as blocking, overshadowing, SOC, and SPC. The findings also illustrate the richness of the types of processing and many possible cue interactions that can occur during compound conditioning. The role of retrieval, attention/associability, and within-compound associations can exert a large influence on processing during compound conditioning, including their effects on positive and negative mediation (e.g., Dickinson, Nicholas, & Mackintosh, 1983; Hall, Mackintosh, Goodall, & dal Martello, 1977; Holland, 1982; Robbins, 1990; Rudy, 1982; see also Batsell & Paschall, Chapter 10). It will be valuable to see how future models of conditioning incorporate the potential interrelationships among attention, retrieval, and interference into their views of conditioning.

Acknowledgments The authors would like to thank S. Reilly and an anonymous reviewer for their insightful comments on an early draft of this manuscript. OP received support from the Department of Universities, Research, and Technology of the Andalusian Government (Junta de Andalucía).

References

Aguado, L., de Brugada, I., & Hall, G. (2001). Tests for inhibition after extinction of a conditioned stimulus in the flavour aversion procedure. *Quarterly Journal of Experimental Psychology, 54B*, 201–217.

Aguado, L., Symonds, M., & Hall, G. (1994). Interval between preexposure and test determines the magnitude of latent inhibition: Implications for an interference account. *Animal Learning & Behavior, 22*, 188–194.

Archer, T., & Sjödén, P.-O. (1982). Higher-order conditioning and sensory preconditioning of a taste aversion with an exteroceptive CS1. *Quarterly Journal of Experimental Psychology, 34B*, 1–17.

Archer, T., Sjödén, P.-O., & Nilsson, L.-G. (1985). Contextual control of taste-aversion conditioning and extinction. In P. D. Balsam & A. Tomie (Eds.), *Context and learning* (pp. 225–271). Hillsdale, NJ: Lawrence Erlbaum.

Azorlosa, J. L., & Cicala, G. (1988). Increased conditioning in rats to a blocked CS after the first compound trial. *Bulletin of the Psychonomic Society, 26*, 254–257.

Baker, A. G. (1974). Conditioned inhibition is not the symmetrical opposite of conditioned excitation: A test of the Rescorla–Wagner model. *Learning and Motivation, 5*, 369–379.

Bakner, L., Strohen, K., Nordeen, M., & Riccio, D. C. (1991). Postconditioning recovery from the latent inhibition effect in conditioned taste aversion. *Physiology & Behavior, 50*, 1269–1272.

Balaz, M. A., Gutsin, P., Cacheiro, H., & Miller, R. R. (1982). Blocking as a retrieval failure: Reactivation of associations to a blocked stimulus. *Quarterly Journal of Experimental Psychology, 34B*, 99–113.

Batson, J. D., & Best, M. R. (1981). Single element assessment of conditioned inhibition. *Bulletin of the Psychonomic Society, 18*, 328–330.

Bellingham, W. P., & Gillette, K. (1981). Attenuation of overshadowing as a function of nondifferential compound training trials. *Bulletin of the Psychonomic Society, 18*, 218–220.

Best, M. R. (1975). Conditioned and latent inhibition in taste-aversion learning: Clarifying the role of learned safety. *Journal of Experimental Psychology: Animal Behavior Processes, 1*, 97–113.

Best, M. R., Dunn, D. P., Batson, J. D., Meachum, C. L., & Nash, S. M. (1985). Extinguishing conditioned inhibition in flavour-aversion learning: Effects of repeated testing and extinction of the excitatory element. *Quarterly Journal of Experimental Psychology, 37B*, 359–378.

Bills, C. (2000). *Blocking by a latent inhibitor.* Unpublished masters thesis. University of Missouri, Columbia, MO.

Bills, C. H., Dopheide, M., Pineño, O., & Schachtman, T. R. (2006). Effects of an extinguished CS on competition with another CS. *Behavioural Processes, 72*, 14–22.

Blaisdell, A. P., Bristol, A. S., Gunther, L. M., & Miller, R. R. (1998). Overshadowing and latent inhibition counteract each other: Support for the comparator hypothesis. *Journal of Experimental Psychology: Animal Behavior Processes, 24*, 335–351.

Blaisdell, A. P., & Miller, R. R. (2001). Conditioned inhibition produced by extinction-mediated recovery form the relative validity effect: A test of acquisition and performance models of empirical retrospective revaluation. *Journal of Experimental Psychology: Animal Behavior Processes, 27*, 48–58.

Bouton, M. E. (1986). Slow reacquisition following extinction of conditioned suppression. *Learning and Motivation, 17*, 1–15.

Bouton, M. E. (1993). Context, time, and memory retrieval in the interference paradigms of

Pavlovian learning. *Psychological Bulletin, 114,* 80–99.

Bouton, M. E. (1994). Conditioning, remembering, and forgetting. *Journal of Experimental Psychology: Animal Behavior Processes, 20,* 219–231.

Bouton, M. E., & Bolles, R. C. (1979). Contextual control of the extinction of conditioned fear. *Learning and Motivation, 10,* 445–466.

Bouton, M. E., & Bolles, R. C. (1985). Contexts, event-memories, and extinction. In P. D. Balsam & A. Tomie (Eds.), *Context and learning* (pp. 133–166). Hillsdale, NJ: Lawrence Erlbaum.

Bouton, M. E., & Brooks, D. C. (1993). Time and context effects on performance in a Pavlovian discrimination reversal. *Journal of Experimental Psychology: Animal Behavior Processes, 19,* 165–179.

Bouton, M. E., & King, D. A. (1983). Contextual control of the extinction of conditioned fear: Tests for the associative value of the context. *Journal of Experimental Psychology: Animal Behavior Processes, 9,* 248–265.

Bouton, M. E., & Ricker, S. T. (1994). Renewal of extinguished responding in a second context. *Animal Learning & Behavior, 22,* 317–324.

Brodgen, W. J. (1939). Sensory preconditioning. *Journal of Experimental Psychology, 25,* 323–332.

Brooks, D. C., Bowker, J. L., Anderson, J. E., & Palmatier, M. I. (2003). Impact of brief or extended extinction of a taste aversion on inhibitory associations: Evidence from summation, retardation, and preference tests. *Learning & Behavior, 31,* 69–84.

Calton, J. L., Mitchell, K. G., & Schachtman, T. R. (1996). Conditioned inhibition produced by extinction of a conditioned stimulus. *Learning and Motivation, 27,* 335–361.

Chelonis, J. J., Calton, J. L., Hart, J. A., & Schachtman, T. R. (1999). Attenuation of the renewal effect by extinction in multiple contexts. *Learning and Motivation, 30,* 1–14.

Colwill, R. M., & Rescorla, R. A. (1985). Instrumental responding remains sensitive to reinforcer devaluation after extensive training. *Journal of Experimental Psychology: Animal Behavior Processes, 11,* 520–536.

Crowder, R. G. (1976). *Principles of learning and memory.* Hillsdale, NJ: Erlbaum.

Danguir, J., & Nicolaidis, S. (1977). Lack of reacquisition in learned taste aversions. *Animal Learning & Behavior, 5,* 395–397.

De la Casa, G., & Lubow, R. E. (1995). Latent inhibition in conditioned taste aversion: The roles of stimulus frequency and duration and the amount of fluid ingested during preexposure.

Neurobiology of Learning and Memory, 64, 125–132.

Delamater, A. R., Kruse, J. M., Marlin, S., & LoLordo, V. M. (1986). Conditioned inhibition in taste aversion learning: Testing methodology and empirical status. *Animal Learning & Behavior, 14,* 6–14.

Delamater, A. R., & LoLordo, V. M. (1991). Event revaluation procedures and associative structures in Pavlovian conditioning. In L. Dachowski & C. F. Flaherty (Eds.), *Current topics in animal learning: Brain, emotion, and cognition* (pp. 55–94). Hillsdale, NJ: Lawrence Erlbaum.

Denniston, J. C., Chang, R., & Miller, R. R. (2003). Massive extinction treatment attenuates the renewal effect. *Learning and Motivation, 34,* 68–86.

Deutsch, J. A., & Roll, S. K. (1973). Alcohol and asymmetrical state-dependency: A possible explanation. *Behavioral Biology, 8,* 273–278.

Dickinson, A., & Burke, J. (1996). Within-compound associations mediate the retrospective revaluation of causality judgements. *Quarterly Journal of Experimental Psychology, 49B,* 60–80.

Dickinson, A., Nicholas, D. J., & Mackintosh, N. J. (1983). A reexamination of one-trial blocking in conditioned suppression. *Quarterly Journal of Experimental Psychology, 35B,* 67–79.

Dopheide, M., Bills, C., Smith, S., Kichnet, R., & Schachtman, T. R. (2005). Unexpected post-CS events during extinction and the slow reacquisition effect. *International Journal of Comparative Psychology, 18,* 249–256.

Escobar, M., Matute, H., & Miller, R. R. (2001). Cues trained apart compete for behavioral control in rats: Convergence with the associative interference literature. *Journal of Experimental Psychology: General, 31,* 228–237.

Espinet, A., Iraola, J. A., Bennett, C. H., & Mackintosh, N. J. (1995). Inhibitory association between neutral stimuli in flavor-averion learning. *Animal Learning & Behavior, 23,* 361–368.

Garcia, J., Ervin, & Koelling, R. A. (1966). Learning with a prolonged delay of reinforcement. *Psychonomic Science, 5,* 121–122.

Garcia, J., & Koelling, R. A. (1966). Relation of cue to consequence in avoidance learning. *Psychonomic Science, 4,* 123–124.

Garcia-Gutierrez, A., Rosas, J. M., & Nelson, J. B. (2005). Extensive interference attenuates reinstatement in human predictive judgments. *International Journal of Comparative Psychology, 18,* 240–248.

Gordon, W. C., & Mowrer, R. R. (1980). An extinction trial as a reminder treatment following electroconvulsive shock. *Animal Learning & Behavior, 8,* 363–367.

Gunther, L. M., Denniston, J. C., & Miller, R. R. (1998). Conducting exposure treatment in multiple contexts can prevent relapse. *Behaviour Research and Therapy, 36,* 75–91.

Gustavson, K. K., Hart, J. A., Calton, J. L., & Schachtman, T. R. (1992). Effects of extinction and US reinstatement of a blocking CS–US association. *Bulletin of the Psychonomic Society, 30,* 247–250.

Hall, G., Mackintosh, N. J., Goodall, G., & Dal Martello, M. (1977). Loss of control by a less valid or by a less salient stimulus compounded with a better predictor of reinforcement. *Learning and Motivation, 8,* 145–158.

Hall, G., & Pearce, J. M. (1982). Restoring the associability of a preexposed CS by a surprising event. *Quarterly Journal of Experimental Psychology, 34B,* 127–140.

Hammond, L. J., & Maser, J. (1970). Forgetting and conditioned suppression: Role of a temporal discrimination. *Journal of the Experimental Analysis of Behavior, 13,* 333–338.

Hart, J. A., Bourne, M. J., & Schachtman, T. R. (1995). Slow reacquisition of a conditioned taste aversion. *Animal Learning & Behavior, 23,* 297–303.

Hittesdorf, M., & Richards, R. W. (1982). Aversive second-order conditioning in the pigeon: Elimination of conditioning to CS1 and effects on established second-order conditioning. *Canadian Journal of Psychology, 36,* 462–477.

Holland, P. C. (1982). Interelement associations in classical conditioning. In M. L. Commons, R. J. Herrnstein, & A. R. Wagner (Eds.), *Quantitative analysis of behavior: Acquisition* (Vol. 3, pp. 323–370). Cambridge, MA: Ballinger.

Holland, P. C., & Rescorla, R. A. (1975a). Second-order conditioning with food unconditioned stimulus. *Journal of Comparative & Physiological Psychology, 88,* 459–467.

Holland, P. C., & Rescorla, R. A. (1975b). The effect of two ways of devaluing the unconditioned stimulus after first- and second-order appetitive conditioning. *Journal of Experimental Psychology: Animal Behavior Processes, 1,* 355–363.

Kasprow, W. J., Cacheiro, H., Balaz, M. A., & Miller, R. R. (1982). Reminder-induced recovery of associations to an overshadowed stimulus. *Learning and Motivation, 13,* 155–166.

Kasprow, W. J., Catterson, D. C., Schachtman, T. R., & Miller, R. R. (1984). Attenuation of latent inhibition by postacquisition reminder. *Quarterly Journal of Experimental Psychology, 36B,* 53–63.

Kaufman, M. A., & Bolles, R. C. (1981). A nonassociative aspect of overshadowing. *Bulletin of the Psychonomic Society, 18,* 318–320.

Kehoe, E. J. (1988). A layered-network model of associative learning: Learning to learn and configuration. *Psychological Review, 95,* 411–433.

Konorski, J. (1967). *Integrative activity of the brain.* Chicago, IL: University of Chicago Press.

Kraemer, P. J., Randall, C., & Carbary, T. (1991). Release from latent inhibition with delayed testing. *Animal Learning & Behavior, 19,* 139–145.

Kraemer, P. J., & Spear, N. E. (1992). The effect of nonreinforced stimulus exposure on the strength of a conditioned taste aversion as a function of the retention interval: Do latent inhibition and extinction involve a shared process? *Animal Learning & Behavior, 20,* 1–7.

Lovibond, P. F., Davis, N. R., & O'Flaherty, A. S. (2000). Protection from extinction in human fear conditioning. *Behaviour Research and Therapy, 38,* 967–983.

Lysle, D. T., & Fowler, H. (1985). Inhibition as a "slave process": Deactivation of conditioned inhibition through extinction of conditioned excitation. *Journal of Experimental Psychology: Animal Behavior Processes, 11,* 71–94.

Martin, E. (1971). Verbal learning theory and independent retrieval phenomena. *Psychological Review, 78,* 314–332.

Matute, H., & Pineño, O. (1998). Stimulus competition in the absence of compound conditioning. *Animal Learning & Behavior, 26,* 3–14.

Matzel, L. D., Gladstein, L., & Miller, R. R. (1988). Conditioned excitation and conditioned inhibition are not mutually exclusive. *Learning and Motivation, 19,* 99–121.

Matzel, L. D., Schachtman, T. R., & Miller, R. R. (1985). Recovery of an overshadowed association achieved by extinction of the overshadowing stimulus. *Learning and Motivation, 16,* 398–412.

Matzel, L. D., Shuster, K., & Miller, R. R. (1987). Covariation in conditioned response strength between stimuli trained in compound. *Animal Learning & Behavior, 15,* 439–447.

McGeoch, J. A. (1942). *The psychology of human learning.* New York: Longmans.

Melton, A. W. (1970). The situation with respect to the spacing of repetitions and memory. *Journal of Verbal Learning & Verbal Behavior, 9,* 596–606.

Mikulka, P. J., Leard, B., & Klein, S. B. (1977). Illness-alone exposure as a source of interference with the acquisition and retention of a taste aversion. *Journal of Experimental Psychology: Animal Behavior Processes, 3,* 189–201.

Miller, R. R., Kasprow, W. J., & Schachtman, T. R. (1986). Retrieval variability: Sources and consequences. *American Journal of Psychology, 99,* 145–218.

Miller, R. R., & Matzel, L. D. (1988). The comparator hypothesis: A response rule for the expression of associations. In G. H. Bower (Ed.), *The psychology of learning and motivation* (Vol. 22, pp. 51–92). San Diego, CA: Academic Press.

Miller, R. R., & Schachtman, T. R. (1985). Conditioning context as an associative baseline: Implications for response generation and the nature of conditioned inhibition. In R. R. Miller & N. E. Spear (Eds.), *Information processing in animals: Conditioned inhibition* (pp. 51–88). Hillsdale, NJ: Erlbaum.

Miller, R. R., & Springer, A. D. (1972). Induced recovery of memory in rats after electroconvulsive shock. *Physiology & Behavior, 8,* 645–651.

Miller, R. R., & Springer, A. D. (1973). Amnesia, consolidation, and retrieval. *Psychological Review, 80,* 69–79.

Nairne, J. S., & Rescorla, R. A. (1981). Second-order conditioning with diffuse auditory reinforcers in the pigeon. *Learning and Motivation, 12,* 65–91.

Overton, D. A. (1985). Contextual stimulus effects of drugs and internal states. In P. D. Balsam & A. Tomie (Eds.), *Context and learning* (pp. 357–384). Hillsdale, NJ: Lawrence Erlbaum.

Pavlov, I. P. (1927). *Conditioned reflexes.* London: Clarendon Press.

Pearce, J. M., & Hall, G. (1980). A model for Pavlovian learning: Variations in the effectiveness of conditioned but not of unconditioned stimuli. *Psychological Review, 87,* 532–552.

Pearce, J. M., & Wilson, P. N. (1991). Effects of extinction with a compound conditioned stimulus. *Journal of Experimental Psychology: Animal Behavior Processes, 17,* 151–162.

Pineño, O. (2007). Protection from extinction by concurrent presentation of an excitor or an extensively extinguished CS. *Psicológica, 28,* 151–166.

Pineño, O., De la Casa, L. G., Lubow, R. E., & Miller, R. R. (2006). Some determinants of latent inhibition in human predictive learning. *Learning and Motivation, 37,* 42–65.

Pineño, O., Zilski, J. M., & Schachtman, T. R. (2007). Second-order conditioning during a compound extinction treatment. *Learning and Motivation, 38,* 172–192.

Randich, A., & Rescorla, R. A. (1981). The effects of separate presentations of the US on conditioned suppression. *Animal Learning & Behavior, 9,* 56–64.

Rashotte, M. E., Griffin, R. W., & Sisk, C. L. (1977). Second-order conditioning of the pigeon's keypeck. *Animal Learning & Behavior, 5,* 25–38.

Rescorla, R. A. (1969). Pavlovian conditioned inhibition. *Psychological Bulletin, 72,* 77–94.

Rescorla, R. A. (1971). Variation in the effectiveness of reinforcement and nonreinforcement following prior inhibitory conditioning. *Learning and Motivation, 2,* 113–123.

Rescorla, R. A. (1973). Effect of US habituation following conditioning. *Journal of Comparative and Physiological Psychology, 82,* 137–143.

Rescorla, R. A. (1974). Effect of inflation of the unconditioned stimulus value following conditioning. *Journal of Comparative and Physiological Psychology, 86,* 101–106.

Rescorla, R. A. (1979). Conditioned inhibition and extinction. In A. Dickinson & R. A. Boakes (Eds.), *Mechanisms of learning and motivation: A memorial volume to Jerzy Konorski* (pp. 83–110). Hillsdale, NJ: Erlbaum.

Rescorla, R. A. (2000). Extinction can be enhanced by concurrent excitor. *Journal of Experimental Psychology: Animal Behavior Processes, 26,* 251–260.

Rescorla, R. A. (2005). Spontaneous recovery of excitation but not inhibition. *Journal of Experimental Psychology: Animal Behavior Processes, 31,* 277–288.

Rescorla, R. A., & Cunningham, C. L. (1978). Within-compound flavor associations. *Journal of Experimental Psychology: Animal Behavior Processes, 4,* 267–275.

Rescorla, R. A., & Freberg, L. (1978). The extinction of within-compound flavor associations. *Learning and Motivation, 9,* 411–427.

Rescorla, R. A., & Heth, C. D. (1975). Reinstatement of fear to an extinguished conditioned stimulus. *Journal of Experimental Psychology: Animal Behavior Processes, 1,* 88–96.

Rescorla, R. A., & Wagner, A. R. (1972). A theory of Pavlovian conditioning: Variations in the effectiveness of reinforcement and nonreinforcement. In A. H. Black & W. F. Prokasy (Eds.), *Classical conditioning II: Current research and theory* (pp. 64–99). New York: Appleton-Century-Crofts.

Revusky, S., & Coombes, S. (1979). Reacquisition of learned taste aversions. *Animal Learning & Behavior, 7,* 377–382.

Revusky, S., Parker, L. A., & Coombes, S. (1977). Flavor aversion learning: Extinction of the aversion to an interfering flavor after conditioning does not affect the aversion to the reference flavor. *Behavioral Biology, 19,* 503–508.

Riccio, D. C., Urda, M., & Thomas, D. R. (1966). Stimulus control in pigeons based on proprioceptive stimuli from floor inclination. *Science, 153,* 434–436.

Rizley, R. C., & Rescorla. R. A. (1972). Associations in second-order conditioning and sensory preconditioning. *Journal of Comparative and Physiological Psychology, 81,* 1–11.

Robbins, S. R. (1990). Mechanisms underlying spontaneous recovery in autoshaping. *Journal of Experimental Psychology: Animal Behavior Processes, 16,* 235–249.

Rosas, J. M., & Bouton, M. E. (1996). Spontaneous recovery after extinction of a conditioned taste aversion. *Animal Learning & Behavior, 24,* 341–348.

Rosas, J. M., & Bouton, M. E. (1998). Context change and retention interval can have additive, rather than interactive, effects after taste aversion extinction. *Psychonomic Bulletin & Review, 5,* 79–83.

Rozeboom, W. W. (1958). "What is learned?"—An empirical enigma. *Psychological Review, 65,* 22–33.

Rudy, J. (1982). An appreciation of higher order conditioning and blocking. In M. L. Commons, R. J. Herrnstein, & A. R. Wagner (Eds.), *Quantitative analysis of behavior: Acquisition* (Vol. 3, pp. 371–388). Cambridge, MA: Ballinger.

Schachtman, T. R., Brown, A. M., & Miller, R. R. (1985). Reinstatement-induced recovery of a taste-LiCl association following extinction. *Animal Learning & Behavior, 13,* 223–227.

Schachtman, T. R., Gee, J. L., Kasprow, W. J., & Miller, R. R. (1983). Reminder-induced recovery from blocking as a function of the number of compound trials. *Learning and Motivation, 14,* 154–164.

Schachtman, T. R., Gustavson, K. K., Chelonis, J. J., & Bourne, M. J. (1992). Effects of US reinstatement on the potential of an extinguished CS to attenuate manifest learning about another CS. *Learning and Motivation, 23,* 250–268.

Schachtman, T. R., Kasprow, W. J., Meyer, R. C., Bourne, M. J., & Hart, J. A. (1992). Extinction of the overshadowing CS after overshadowing in conditioned taste aversion. *Animal Learning & Behavior, 20,* 207–218.

Schachtman, T. R., Threlkeld, R., & Meyer, K. (2000). Retention of conditioned inhibition produced by extinction. *Learning and Motivation, 31,* 283–300.

Shanks, D. R. (1985). Forward and backward blocking in human contingency judgment. *Quarterly Journal of Experimental Psychology, 37B,* 1–21.

Shanks, D. R., & Dickinson, A. (1987). Associative accounts of causality judgment. In G. H. Bower (Ed.), *The psychology of learning and motivation* (pp. 229–261). New York: Academic Press.

Smith, S. M. (1982). Enhancement of recall using multiple environmental contexts during learning. *Memory & Cognition, 10,* 405–412.

Smith, S. M., & Vela, E. (2001). Environmental context-dependent memory: A review and meta-analysis. *Psychonomic Bulletin and Review, 8,* 203–220.

Soltysik, S. S., Wolfe, G. E., Nicholas, T., Wilson, W. J., & Garcia-Sanchez, J. L. (1983). Blocking of inhibitory conditioning within a serial conditioned stimulus-conditioned inhibitor compound: Maintenance of acquired behavior without an unconditioned stimulus. *Learning and Motivation, 14,* 1–29.

Spear, N. E., & Riccio, D. C. (1994). *Memory: Phenomena and principles.* Boston, MA: Allyn & Bacon.

Springer, A. D., & Miller, R. R. (1972). Retrieval failure induced by electroconvulsive shock: Reversal with dissimilar training and recovery agents. *Science, 177,* 628–630.

Tamai, N., & Nakajima, S. (2000). Renewal of formerly conditioned fear in rats after extensive extinction training. *International Journal of Comparative Psychology, 13,* 137–146.

Taylor, K. M., & Boakes, R. A. (2002). Extinction of conditioned taste aversions: Effects of concentration and overshadowing. *Quarterly Journal of Experimental Psychology, 55B,* 213–239.

Tulving, E., & Thompson, D. M. (1973). Encoding specificity and retrieval processes in episodic memory. *Psychological Review, 80,* 352–373.

Van Hamme, L. J., & Wasserman, E. A. (1994). Cue competition in causality judgments: The role of nonpresentation of compound stimulus elements. *Learning and Motivation, 25,* 127–151.

Wagner, A. R. (1981). SOP: A model of automatic memory processing in animal behavior. In N. E. Spear & R. R. Miller (Eds.), *Information processing in animals: Memory mechanisms* (pp. 5–47). Hillsdale, NJ: Lawrence Erlbaum.

Wagner, A. R., & Rescorla, R. A. (1972). Inhibition in Pavlovian conditioning: An application of a theory. In R. A. Boakes & M. S. Halliday (Eds.), *Inhibition and learning* (pp. 301–336). London: Academic Press.

Walker, J., Ramsey, A., Hock, R., & Schachtman, T. R. (2008). Effects of swim stress on neophobia and reconditioning using a conditioned taste aversion procedure. Manuscript submitted for publication.

Wasserman, E. A. (1990). Detecting response–outcome relations: Toward an understanding of the causal texture of the environment. In G. H. Bower (Ed.), *The psychology of learning and motivation* (Vol. 26, pp. 27–82). San Diego, CA: Academic Press.

Williams, D. A., & Overmier, J. B. (1988). Some types of conditioned inhibitors carry collateral excitatory associations. *Learning and Motivation, 19,* 345–368.

9

Conditioned Taste Aversions Based on Running or Swimming

ROBERT A. BOAKES AND SADAHIKO NAKAJIMA

Conditioned taste aversions (CTAs) are most commonly established in rats by injecting chemical substances such as lithium chloride (LiCl, e.g., Garcia & Koelling, 1966; Kalat & Rozin, 1970; Nachman & Ashe, 1973), cyclophosphamide (e.g., Dragoin, 1971; Garcia, Ervin, & Koelling, 1967), methyl mercury (e.g., Braun & Snyder, 1973; Levine, 1978), morphine (e.g., Farber, Gorman, & Reid, 1976; Riley, Jacobs, & LoLordo, 1978), apomorphine (e.g., Garcial, Ervin, & Koelling, 1966; Wittlin & Brookshire, 1968), ethanol (e.g., Berman & Cannon, 1974; Eckardt, Skurdal, & Brown, 1974), scopolamine and amphetamine (e.g., Berger, 1972; Braveman, 1975), insulin and formalin (e.g., Domjan & Levy, 1977; Weisinger, Parker, & Skorupski, 1974), among others (see Riley & Freeman, 2004, for database).

However, many nonchemical agents are also effective in inducing CTAs in rats. The pioneering experiments by Garcia and his colleagues (e.g., Garcia, Kimeldorf, & Koelling, 1955) employed gamma radiation. Other ionizing radiations such as X-rays (e.g., Garcia & Koelling, 1966; Revusky, 1968; Smith & Birkle, 1966) and neutron radiation (e.g., Garcia & Kimeldorf, 1960) are also effective (see Rabin & Hunt, 1986, for a review of taste aversion studies using radiation). A taste aversion can also be produced by thiamine deficiency (e.g., Rozin, 1967; Zahorik, 1972), histidine-free amino acid load (e.g., Booth & Simson, 1974;

Simson & Booth, 1974), tumor implantation (e.g., Bernstein & Fenner, 1983; Bernstein & Sigmundi, 1980), exposure to magnetic fields (see Houpt & Smith, Chapter 20, for a review), area postrema cooling (e.g., Wang & Chambers, 2001; Wang, Lavond, & Chambers, 1987), electric shocks (e.g., Braveman, 1977; Krane & Wagner, 1975), motion sickness (e.g., Braun & McIntosh, 1973; Green & Rachlin, 1973, 1976), high ambient room temperature (e.g., Biederman & Davey, 1997; Davey & Biederman, 1997), and exposure to a poisoned conspecific (e.g., Bond, 1984; Coombes, Revusky, & Lett, 1980).

In addition, recent research has found that physical exercise such as running in an activity wheel or swimming in a pool can be effective in establishing in rats an aversion to the taste consumed before the exercise. It is this research that is reviewed in the present chapter. Starting with running-based taste aversion learning, we review the evidence indicating that this displays similar properties to those of more familiar examples of Pavlovian conditioning, discuss the possible relationship between this phenomenon and that of activity-induced self-starvation, examine the apparent paradox that running appears to function both as an aversive and an appetitive US, and finally outline suggestions as to what kind of physiological basis there might be for running-based aversions. Swimming-based taste aversion learning has only recently been investigated so that less is known about its properties or underlying mechanisms. This chapter then reviews the limited number of studies that have directly compared running-based and swimming-based aversions or have compared such aversions to those based on other agents. In the concluding discussion we speculate on possible implications of these activity-based aversions for understanding human food choice and highlight some of the questions that future research might address.

CTAs BASED ON RUNNING

Three kinds of apparatus have been widely used to study the effects of running in rats. The most common is the Wahmann-style activity wheel that has been used for a variety of research purposes over many decades. This consists of a metal drum of about 1.1 m in circumference and a side chamber from which a rat can enter the drum via a closeable door. If the door is left open, the rat is able to move to and fro between chamber and drum throughout a session. We will refer to this as an "open wheel." When a rat is first introduced to such a wheel, it runs very little at first, but typically runs increasingly as sessions are repeated. This increase is accelerated if the rat is food deprived, but running

in general decreases with age (e.g., Boakes, Mills, & Single, 1999; Collier, 1969; Jakubczak, 1973). A simple variant of the open wheel excludes the side chamber so that the rat is unable to escape from within the drum, but whether it runs or not is "voluntary." We will refer to this as a "closed wheel." Relative to the open wheel, this produces higher rates of running in early sessions. The third kind of running wheel imposes "forced" running on the rat in that it is driven at a specified speed by a motor; this will be referred to as a "motorized wheel."

In what appears to be the first experiment to have deliberately used a conditioning procedure in which rats were given a novel taste prior to placement in an activity wheel, Lett and Grant (1996) gave three "wheel days" in which a target taste solution was given prior to a 30-min session in a closed wheel intermixed with three "rest days" in which a control solution was given prior to return to the home cage. The rats came to drink less of the target than of the control solution, as seen in Figure 9.1. Interestingly, one can see with the benefit of hindsight that the first published data showing a running-based taste aversion were reported by Jennings and McCutcheon (1974) but the authors did not identify the effect as such (see also Nikoletseas, 1981).

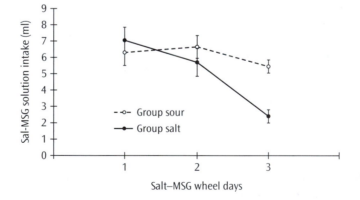

Figure 9.1. Results from the first published study to show taste aversion learning based on wheel running. These intake data for "salt" sessions are replotted from Figure 1 in Lett and Grant (1996). In these three sessions fluid- and food-deprived rats were given 10-min access to a saline + MSG mixture, followed by either 30-min in closed wheels (Group Salt) or return to the home cage (Group Sour). On three other days access to a sour solution was followed by return to home cage (Group Salt) or placement in the wheels (Group Sour); data from these "sour" sessions are not shown here. The error bars indicate standard errors of the mean.

Since the initial discovery, the basic effect has been replicated in a large number of experiments (Aoyama, 2007; Baysari & Boakes, 2004; Eccles, Kim, & O'Hare, 2005; Forristall, Hookey, & Grant, 2007; Hayashi, Nakajima, Urushihara, & Imada, 2002; Heth & Pierce, 2007; Heth, Inglis, Russell, & Pierce, 2001; Hughes & Boakes, 2008; Lett, Grant, & Gaborko, 1998; Lett, Grant, Koh, & Smith, 2001; Masaki & Nakajima, 2006; Nagaishi, Nakanishi, & Nakajima, submitted; Nakajima, 2004, 2008; Nakajima, Hayashi, & Kato, 2000; Nakajima, Urata, & Ogawa, 2006; Salvy, Heth, Pierce, & Russell, 2004; Salvy, Pierce, Heth, & Russell, 2002, 2003, 2004; Satvat & Eikelboom, 2006; Sparkes, Grant, & Lett, 2003). These experiments have used a variety of rat strains (male Sprague-Dawley, albino Wistar, hooded Wistar, JCR:LA-cp rats, and female hooded Wistar rats), rat ages (33–150 days old), deprivation conditions (food-and-water-deprived, food-deprived, water-deprived, and no-deprived conditions), taste substances (sucrose, salt, salt–monosodium glutamate [MSG] mixture, saccharin, citric acid, citric acid–saccharin mixture, ethanol, Kool-Aid, and essence-flavored solutions; flavored pellets and dog biscuits), durations of wheel sessions (usually from 15 min to 2 h, but 21–22.5 h in some studies), wheel types (open, closed, and motorized wheels), amount of training (from one to several daily sessions, with one trial per session), and assessment procedures (a single taste consumption test and a taste choice test). Overall, this research has shown that running-based taste aversion learning in laboratory rats is a robust phenomenon that can be obtained over a wide range of conditions.

Taste aversion learning based on running has been found using both within-subject differential conditioning designs and between-group comparisons involving control groups given either explicitly unpaired wheel versus taste conditions or taste-only conditions without access to a wheel. The dependent variable in all these studies has been fluid or food intake during the conditioning procedure and/or subsequent assessment by single intake or choice intake testing. A single exception is a study by Aoyama (2007) who used wheel running to devalue an instrumental reinforcer. This experiment compared rates of lever-pressing in two kinds of sessions: In one the reinforcers were food pellets containing a distinctive flavor, for example,

banana, and these sessions were followed by 30-min periods in a closed running wheel, while in other lever-pressing sessions the pellets contained a second flavor, for example, chocolate, and these were followed by return to the home cages. As in a previous experiment using LiCl (Aoyama, 2004), response rates were lower for the devalued reinforcer, but the within-session rate of decline of lever-pressing was the same as for the nondevalued reinforcer. Parenthetically, the rats exclusively consumed the nondevalued pellets in the subsequent pellet preference test.

That running, rather than simply confinement in a wheel, is the effective factor for producing a taste aversion was confirmed by both Heth et al. (2001) and Hayashi et al. (2002, Experiment 3), in that confining rats in a locked wheel did not produce an aversion to the paired taste (see also Forristall et al., 2007). Since a correlation between a target taste and running is critical for establishing a taste aversion, running-induced taste aversion learning has been generally treated within the framework of Pavlovian conditioning, whereby the target taste is regarded as the conditioned stimulus (CS), running as the unconditioned stimulus (US), and the acquired taste aversion as the conditioned response (CR).

Properties of Running-Based Taste Aversions

Running-based taste aversion learning has been found to possess many of the properties of Pavlovian conditioning found in traditional experimental preparations and conventional taste aversion studies, as follows.

The Law of US Strength

According to Pavlov (1927, pp. 31–32), the strength of conditioning is, in general, directly related to the intensity of the US within a reasonable range (see e.g., Flaherty, 1985; Hall, 1976; Mackintosh, 1974; Tarpy, 1997, for discussions). This Pavlovian law of US strength is applicable to CTA based on chemical agents (e.g., Andrews & Braveman, 1975; Berger, 1972; Davison & House, 1975; Dragoin, 1971; Elkins, 1973; Garcia et al., 1967; Grote & Brown, 1971; Nachman & Ashe, 1973; Nathan & Vogel, 1975), irradiation (e.g., Garcia et al., 1955; see Rabin & Hunt, 1986, for review), motion sickness (Green & Rachlin, 1973, 1976), and a poisoned conspecific (Bond, 1984).

Conditioned aversion learning based on running is no exception: The acquired aversion can be a positive function of duration of exposure to a wheel, within a reasonable range (Hayashi et al., 2002; Masaki & Nakajima, 2006). For example, Hayashi et al. (2002, Experiment 1B) compared three groups of rats given 10 days of training where on each day drinking saccharin was followed by a period of either 5, 15, or 30 min in a wheel. The weakest aversion to saccharin was found in the 5-min group and the strongest aversion in the 30-min group. In a similar experiment Salvy, Heth, et al. (2004) compared groups given an orange Kool-Aid solution followed by either a 20- or a 60-min period of wheel running. Even though the number of wheel turns was twice as much in the 60-min group than in the 20-min group during the 4 days of training, no difference in acquisition of an aversion to the orange flavor was found, possibly because of a ceiling effect. Because the procedures used in this study differed from those in Hayashi et al. (2002) and Masaki and Nakajima (2006) with regard, for example, to rat strain, wheel type, and taste, its insensitivity to the law of US strength might be ascribed to one or more of these factors.

Sensitivity to Duration of the CS–US Interval

The effective range of interstimulus intervals is much wider in CTA learning than in other Pavlovian conditioning preparations. Nevertheless, the strength of a learned taste aversion based on chemical agents is still sensitive to the length of the CS–US interval (e.g., Andrews & Braveman, 1975; Barker & Smith, 1974; Garcia et al., 1966; McLaurin, 1964; Nachman, 1970), as are those based on irradiation (e.g., Barker & Smith, 1974; McLaurin, 1964; Revusky, 1968; Smith & Roll, 1967), motion sickness (Green & Rachlin, 1976; Haroutunian & Riccio, 1975), and a poisoned conspecific (Coombes et al., 1980).

Hayashi et al. (2002, Experiment 2B) examined the role of the CS–US interval in a simple taste–running conditioning procedure. Placing rats in a closed wheel immediately after they had drunk a saccharin solution was more effective in producing a saccharin aversion than when there was a 30- or 60-min delay between the end of saccharin access and being placed in the wheel. When a differential conditioning procedure was employed a CTA could be detected even with a 60-min delay

(Hayashi et al., 2002, Experiment 2A). In summary, taste aversions based on running are strongest with a minimum CS–US interval but, like CTAs based on other agents, they can be acquired even with CS–US intervals well outside the range required for other forms of Pavlovian conditioning to take place.

CS Preexposure Effect

Attenuation of Pavlovian conditioning when animals are preexposed to a CS in the absence of a US—the so-called latent inhibition effect (Lubow, 1989)—is as robust an effect for CTA learning based on chemicals or irradiation as for any other type of conditioning (see Lubow, Chapter 3). This CS-preexposure effect is also found for running-based taste aversion learning. Experiments from three laboratories using different procedures have found that a conditioned aversion was attenuated if the target taste was familiar (Heth & Pierce, 2007; Satvat & Eikelboom, 2006; Sparkes et al., 2003).

US Preexposure Effect

Previous experience of a US attenuates subsequent acquisition or expression of conditioned responding in traditional Pavlovian conditioning (see Randich & LoLordo, 1979, for a review). This US preexposure effect has also been found in CTA learning based on a variety of US agents, including many chemical substances, irradiation, area postrema cooling, electric shocks, motion sickness, and a poisoned conspecific (see Riley & Simpson, 2000, for a review). As discussed in detail by Hall (in Chapter 4), there are two major accounts of the effect. According to the nonassociative account, repeated exposure to a US habituates its physiological effects and thus reduces its effectiveness as a US during the conditioning phase. On the other hand, the dominant associative account proposes that a context–US association established during the preexposure phase blocks subsequent acquisition or expression of CS–US association.

A US-preexposure effect on running-based taste aversion learning has been reported from three laboratories (Baysari & Boakes, 2004; Hughes & Boakes, 2008, Experiment 3; Nakajima et al., 2006; Salvy et al., 2002). The effect is not attributable to simply the familiarity of wheel but must include an opportunity to run, since confinement in a locked wheel had no effect (Salvy et al., 2002). The effect was found to be a positive function of number of preexposures between 2 and 8, when a 15-min running opportunity was used as the US (Nakajima et al., 2006, Experiment 1). Baysari and Boakes (2004) argued that their effect was unlikely to be due to associative blocking. They gave a group of rats access to one taste solution (saccharin) prior to running on each of four pre-exposure sessions, assuming that this would interfere with context conditioning. However, this had no effect on the US-preexposure effect detected in a subsequent phase when a second solution (almond) was repeatedly followed by running.

Degraded-Contingency Effect

Following Rescorla (1968) it has been commonly accepted that both temporal contiguity between a CS and a US and a positive contingent relationship between them are necessary for excitatory Pavlovian conditioning to occur. A standard procedure for examining the role of contingency is to compare CS–US contingent and noncontingent groups, while keeping the total number of US presentations equated across the groups. Using this design the importance of CS–US contingency has been demonstrated for LiCl-based taste aversion learning by Monroe and Barker (1979). Contingency can also be degraded by presenting extra USs in the intervals between CS–US trials and this procedure also interferes with the acquisition of conditioned responding in Pavlovian conditioning (see Durlach, 1989, for a review).

This second approach was adopted by Nakajima (2008) to test whether running-based taste aversion learning is also sensitive to contingency. Three groups were each given five sessions in which access to saccharin was followed by 30-min confinement in a closed wheel. These were intermixed with five sessions in which Group Unsignaled was placed in a wheel for 30 min, while Group Signaled was given sodium chloride (NaCl) solution before the 30-min running. Group Control had no special treatment. A degraded contingency effect was found in that, although Group Control acquired the expected strong aversion to saccharin in a final 2-bottle test, the saccharin aversion was weak in Group Unsignaled. The results for Group Signaled were intermediate, suggesting that the addition of the cover stimulus, NaCl, had overshadowed context conditioning so that context–running associations provided weaker competition with saccharin–running associations than for Group Unsignaled. These results

correspond to the extra-US effect found in traditional Pavlovian conditioning preparations such as rats' fear conditioning (e.g., Rescorla, 1972, 1984) and approach conditioning (Williams, 1994) and pigeons' autoshaping (e.g., Durlach, 1982, 1983; Goddard & Jenkins, 1987).

Overshadowing

As first noted by Pavlov (1927, pp. 141–144), presentation of another stimulus with a target CS on conditioning trials can reduce conditioned responding to the target CS when this stimulus is subsequently tested by itself. Overshadowing of a target taste by another taste has been reported for taste aversion learning based on chemical agents (e.g., Bond, 1983; Kaye, Gambini, & Mackintosh, 1988; Lindsey & Best, 1973; Nakajima, Ka, & Imada, 1999; Revusky, 1971). Running-based aversion learning is no exception. Nagaishi et al. (submitted) demonstrated an overshadowing effect in each of two experiments in which access to NaCl and saccharin was given prior to wheel sessions. For example, in their Experiment 2, a group of rats was trained on the sequence NaCl → saccharin, followed by placement in a closed wheel. This group was compared with a control group given the sequence, NaCl → water → wheel. Subsequent testing revealed that the conditioned aversion to NaCl was weaker in the first group than in the control group.

Self-Starvation and Running-Based Taste Aversion

Initial interest in running-based taste aversion learning on the part of some researchers, including one of the present authors (RAB), was prompted by its possible relationship to self-starvation in rats. As first clearly documented by Routtenberg and Kuznesof (1967), rats given the combination of unrestricted access to an open wheel plus 1–2-h per day restricted access to food at a fixed time can lose weight progressively to the point when they will die unless removed from these conditions. The effect has been termed "self-starvation" because rats given this *activity-based anorexia* (ABA; Epling & Pierce, 1992) procedure eat less than controls without access to a wheel. Two factors are of prime importance in producing the effect. One is that after running, even for a relatively short period, rats eat less food, whether they are on a restricted food schedule (e.g., Boakes & Dwyer,

1997) or nondeprived (e.g., Looy & Eikelboom, 1989). The second is that, as already mentioned, the more body weight a rat loses, the more it runs in a wheel (e.g., Boakes et al., 1999; Collier, 1969; Jakubczak, 1973). The combination of these two factors can create a vicious cycle whereby weight loss produces more running that keeps food intake suppressed and thus increases weight loss (Boakes, 2007).

Following Lett and Grant's (1996) discovery of running-based taste aversion learning, the question arose as to whether this might shed light on the self-starvation effect and, in particular, on running-based suppression of eating. Two possibilities have been examined. One is that rats acquire a mild conditioned aversion to their food. The other is that whatever internal state serves as the effective US to support taste aversion learning has an unconditioned suppressive effect on food intake. In human terms, after running a long distance or engaging in some other form of vigorous exercise, we are unlikely to find even the most appetizing meal quite as enticing as when we have rested for a while.

The issue was directly addressed first by Sparkes et al. (2003) in experiments that compared food intakes in a group given the standard ABA procedure, with 90-min food access per day and confinement in closed wheels at all other times, and a cage group that was never placed in wheels. They obtained the standard result whereby food intake in the wheel group was much lower than intake in the cage group. What was unusual about the procedure was that, following 5 days of the ABA treatment, 2 days later the rats were given a choice between the food provided during ABA training and a neutral food. In the experiment that used familiar chow on which the rats had been raised there was no indication that the rats had formed an aversion to this food; the wheel and cage groups showed identical preference for the chow. On the other hand, in a second experiment a strong aversion was acquired toward a novel food that had been available during ABA training. Since the self-starvation effect is found when familiar food is available, Sparkes et al. (2003) concluded that taste aversion learning plays little or no role in the effect, presumably because it is prevented by the strong latent inhibition effect produced by familiar chow (Heth & Pierce, 2007).

This conclusion was also reached by Satvat and Eikelboom (2006) on the basis of experiments in which rats had unrestricted access to familiar chow and sometimes to unfamiliar sucrose. By providing, in addition, either continuous access to wheels or alternating between wheel and no-wheel days, they were able to distinguish between unconditioned suppression of intake (that occurred only on wheel days) and conditioned suppression (that occurred on both wheel and no-wheel days), with the latter occurring only to sucrose, as long as no preexposure had been given to this taste. A notable feature of these results was that a conditioned aversion to sucrose developed despite the absence of any explicit pairing between this food and running.

A third study concerned with this question allowed a comparison between rats given familiar chow plus a novel almond flavor prior to running and those given chow alone on how much chow was eaten *following* a wheel session. Despite the potential strong overshadowing of a chow aversion by almond in the first group, postrunning suppression of chow intake was the same in both groups. Thus, it was unlikely that the suppression was due to a conditioned aversion to chow (Baysari & Boakes, 2004, Experiment 1).

In conclusion, although the effect of running is to suppress intake of food presented afterwards, it is unlikely that a conditioned aversion plays a major role in this process, unless a novel food is used. Since the self-starvation effect has routinely been found with highly familiar chow, it is not dependent on any kind of taste aversion learning.

The Bivalent Nature of Running

Running in a wheel can be a highly positive activity for rats. Whereas rats repeatedly placed in a circular alley that contains no rewards will move less and less (e.g., Koh, Lett, & Grant, 2000), rats—and many other species—with access to a wheel will run more and more, suggesting that this activity becomes self-reinforcing (Sherwin, 1998). Furthermore, a wheel-experienced rat will choose this over other forms of activity (Sherwin, 1998), learn to choose the arm of a T-maze that leads to a running wheel (Livesey, Egger, & Meyer, 1972), press a lever at a high rate on a fixed ratio schedule to gain access to a running wheel (Collier & Hirsch, 1971; Iversen, 1993), and persist in running at a high ambient temperature (Gutierrez, Baysari, Carrera, Whitford, & Boakes, 2006). These examples can be seen as ones in which some internal consequence of running functions as an instrumental reinforcer. It can also function as an appetitive US in Pavlovian procedures. Lett, Grant, Byrne, and Koh (2000) used a place preference apparatus whereby on alternating sessions rats were placed in one chamber following 2-h sessions in a closed wheel and in the other chamber following 2-h sessions in a small cage. After giving six of each kind of pairing, rats were given a place preference test. They showed a small, but significant, preference for the chamber paired with the aftereffects of running. A follow-up experiment from the same laboratory used water-deprived rather than food-deprived rats and wheel sessions were reduced to 30 min. In addition, the rats were given distinctive tastes—saccharin or saline—prior to each kind of session. A place preference for the chamber paired with the aftereffects of running was again found, together with an aversion to the taste paired with running (Lett et al., 2001).

As noted by Lett et al. (2001), these results are similar to those found with certain drugs, in that when rats are, for example, given a taste solution in a distinctive chamber after injection with either amphetamine (Reicher & Holman, 1977) or morphine (Sherman, Pickman, Rice, Liebeskind, & Holman, 1980), they acquire a preference for this chamber but an aversion to the taste. This comparison suggests that wheel running, like amphetamine or opiates, has multiple consequences of which the positive are selectively associated with events such as an instrumental response or a place and the negative are selectively associated with tastes.

A simple selective association account of the above kind ignores two factors that have been found to be important in determining the outcome of such experiments. One is the sequence of events. Preference for a chamber associated with running is found when rats are placed in the chamber immediately following wheel sessions, but not if a delay of 30 min is inserted (Lett, Grant, & Koh, 2002). On the other hand, if rats are placed in the target chamber *before* wheel sessions, they acquire an aversion to the chamber (Masaki & Nakajima, in press). Furthermore, if rats are given access to a taste solution *after* a wheel session, they can acquire a preference for the taste (Hughes & Boakes, 2008; Salvy, Pierce, et al., 2004). The second factor is preexposure to the wheel. In the case of morphine, Simpson and Riley (2005) showed that preexposure to morphine weakened conditioned

aversion to a paired taste but strengthened conditioned preference for a paired chamber. As we have already seen, prior exposure to running wheels produces a standard US-preexposure effect in that it weakens subsequent running-based aversion learning. Hughes and Boakes (2008, Experiment 3) found this effect when comparing a preexposed group that had been given eight sessions of wheel training prior to the conditioning phase, with a group for which the wheel was novel at the start of conditioning. The latter acquired an aversion to a flavor given prior to the wheel sessions, but did not acquire a preference for a taste given after these sessions; in contrast, the preexposed group did acquire a preference for the "after" taste.

In attempting to understand this pattern of results indicating the bivalent nature of wheel running, one can assume either that the aversive and appetitive processes are related or that they are independent. One example of the first alternative is to treat the aversive process as primary and the appetitive as a secondary, opponent process (comparable to the b-process in Solomon & Corbit, 1974; see also Schull, 1979; Wagner, 1981). This is consistent with the finding that conditioning of a place or taste preference has been found only with a backward conditioning procedure. Such a procedure can yield inhibitory conditioning (see Hall, 1984; LoLordo & Fairless, 1985, for reviews) and, when used with apomorphine or LiCl agent in repeated drug-taste trials, has yielded conditioned taste preferences rather than aversions (Green & Garcia, 1971; Hasegawa, 1981). The interdependence assumption is also consistent with the idea that repetition weakens the effectiveness of the initial aversive process, but strengthens the secondary, appetitive process.

A second example of a theory that assumes the aversive and appetitive properties to be related makes the opposite claim as to which is primary. According to Grigson and her colleagues, the similar paradox that arises in relation to addictive drugs can be understood in terms of anticipatory contrast: Briefly, animals develop an aversion toward a taste that precedes the effects of a drug such as morphine because "the value of the taste pales in comparison to the powerful drug reward anticipated in the very near future" (Grigson, Twining, Freet, Wheeler, & Geddes, Chapter 5). We have reservations about the generality of such anticipatory contrast effects in view of the many demonstrations of taste *preference* learning that are obtained when a taste CS is repeatedly followed by a highly valued reward (e.g., Higgins & Rescorla, 2004). When applied to wheel running, the anticipatory contrast account would seem unable to account for the US-preexposure effect. As noted earlier, prior experience with wheel running is needed before running acquires appetitive properties and yet such experience weakens its ability to support taste aversion learning.

On the other hand the two processes may be independent. Thus, a number of authors (e.g., Epling & Pierce, 1992) have suggested that the high level of activity produced by repeated access to a running wheel leads to the release of endorphins, as proposed to be responsible for "runners' high." Endorphin release is not believed to be involved in conditioning of aversions to either a taste or a place, but it is believed to provide a basis for the apparent self-reinforcing quality of running and for the acquisition of preferences for tastes or places experienced following a wheel session. In what appears to be the only direct test of this claim Lett, Grant, and Koh (2001) carried out two conditioned place preference experiments in which placement in one chamber of the apparatus followed each of four 2-h wheel sessions. This produced a preference for the wheel-paired chamber in a group given saline injections in between running and placement in the chamber, but not in a group injected with 0.5 mg/kg (Experiment 1) or 0.1 mg/kg of the mu-opioid receptor antagonist, naloxone (Experiment 2).

Further evidence related to the opiate hypothesis comes from the finding that prior wheel running produced cross-tolerance to the rewarding effect of morphine (Lett, Grant, Koh, & Flynn, 2002). Moreover, wheel running, like morphine, can reduce sensitivity to pain (e.g., Shyu, Andersson, & Thoren, 1982). On the other hand there have been failures to confirm predictions from the hypothesis that have led to some skepticism about the role of endorphins in the reinforcing function of running (e.g., Aravich, 1996).

Underlying Mechanisms of Running-Based Taste Aversions

Few studies have directly explored the question as to why wheel running can support taste aversion learning. However, several possible physiological mechanisms have been proposed, as described in the following sections. These hypotheses are not mutually exclusive; combinations of some or all of these factors might contribute to particular instances of running-based taste aversion learning.

Mesolimbic Dopamine System

As noted in the previous section, the similarity between wheel running and drugs such as amphetamine in terms of combining strong rewarding properties with the ability to support taste aversion learning was first noted by Lett and her colleagues, who also pointed out another similarity between wheel running and amphetamine, namely, that in low "doses" both of these agents facilitate feeding in nondeprived rats (Lett et al., 1998; see also Forristall et al., 2007, Experiment 2). Because of these similarities, Lett and her colleagues proposed that the mesolimbic dopamine system, which has played a major role in both rewarding and taste-aversion-inducing effects of amphetamine and morphine (Hunt & Amit, 1987), is also critical in running-based taste aversion learning.

Gastrointestinal Discomfort

Apparently, Garcia ascribed the cause of running-based taste aversion to gastrointestinal discomfort through inhibition of stomach emptying by running (personal communication cited by Lett et al., 1999). This hypothesis seems to have little face validity, because rats running in a wheel display no obvious behavioral symptoms of illness, malaise, or nausea. Given Parker's (2003; Chapter 6) distinction between avoidance of taste and taste disgust and claim that only the latter is based on conditioning of nausea, it would be helpful for assessing the role of nausea in running-based taste aversion to have data from orofacial tests for active rejection of the target taste. Some recent support for Garcia's hypothesis comes from the finding that granisetron, an antiemetic drug, prevented acquisition of a taste aversion based on forced running in a motorized wheel (Eccles et al., 2005). Further research on antiemetics, particularly on their effect on CTA-based voluntary running, would also be valuable.

General Stress

One of the first studies to compare various USs that supported taste aversion learning was carried out by Braveman (1975), employing a cross-tolerance, or cross-familiarization, design to assess the degree to which such agents have common properties. A later experiment, for example, contained a preexposure phase in which one group of rats was given repeated injections of LiCl, a second was given equivalent injections of saline, a third was injected with amphetamine, a fourth was injected with methylscopolamine, and a fifth was rotated on a turntable. In the subsequent conditioning phase all groups were given saccharin followed by rotation, a procedure that was effective in producing a strong saccharin aversion in the saline control group. Preexposure to rotation produced the expected US-preexposure effect, in that no aversion to saccharin was detected in this group. However, there was also no saccharin aversion in the groups preexposed to LiCl, amphetamine, or methylscopolamine (Braveman, 1977). On the basis of such results suggesting complete cross-tolerance between several agents supporting taste aversion learning, Braveman (1977) argued that they must share a common underlying process. He ascribed this to certain stress-induced physiological changes such as the elevation of plasma corticosterone levels (e.g., Ader, 1976; Hennessy, Smotherman, & Levine, 1976).

As reviewed by Riley and Simpson (2000), subsequent research has revealed that US crossover effects are not universal enough to support the hypothesis that all taste-aversion-inducing agents involve the same underlying process, be it general stress or some other factor. Nonetheless, cross-familiarization tests provide a useful tool for assessing whether two agents have anything in common. Thus, Nakajima et al. (2006) examined the effects of preexposure to LiCl on running-based aversion learning and, *vice versa*, of preexposure to running on LiCl-based aversion learning. Preexposure to LiCl interfered with running-based aversion learning, suggesting some commonality between wheel running and LiCl, but there was no detectable effect of preexposure to wheel running on LiCl-based learning. Two experiments by Boakes and Pitts (2005) that used a somewhat different procedure also failed to detect any effect of prior running—in this case, two 22.5-h sessions in an open wheel—on the subsequent acquisition of a LiCl-based saccharin aversion. However, a third experiment failed to find any effect of prior LiCl injections on acquisition of a running-based aversion, even though this pretreatment produced a strong US-preexposure effect on LiCl-based aversion learning.

Despite the failure of Boakes and Pitts (2005) to find any crossover effect, the LiCl-to-running transfer found by Nakajima et al. (2006) suggests that the effects of LiCl and of running have something in common, but whether this is general stress or nausea, as described by Braveman (1977), or something entirely different remains to be determined. It is worth noting that the concept of "general stress" is vague and needs to be better specified.

Motion Sickness

Rats do not run continuously in nonmotorized activity wheels. Alternation of running and stopping produces rocking movements of the wheels. Forristall et al. (2007) suggested that these back-and-forth movements induce motion sickness. To test this hypothesis they compared the effectiveness of voluntary running in a closed wheel with that of forced running in a motorized wheel (that does not allow any back-and-forth movement) in producing a taste aversion, while adjusting the speed of the motorized wheels to match total amount of running in the closed wheels. They found stronger taste aversion learning with voluntary running, as consistent with the hypothesis that rocking is important in producing a taste aversion. On the other hand, since forced running also produced a taste aversion compared with a no-running control group (see Eccles et al., 2005; Masaki & Nakajima, 2006, for other examples of CTA based on forced running), back-and-forth movements of the wheel are clearly not necessary for producing a taste aversion. Furthermore, as acknowledged by Forristall et al. (2007), there were many differences between their free- and motorized-wheel conditions other than the presence or absence of back-and-forth movements. Parenthetically, it is very difficult to use a yoked procedure to exclude these differences, because the behavior of a yoked rat placed in a wheel that unexpectedly stopped and started would be quite different than the running pattern of the master rat.

Energy Expenditure

Although rats run increasingly in wheels, when placed repeatedly in other environments their activity is less vigorous and quickly declines. In an attempt to determine whether activity other than running in a wheel can support taste aversion learning, Lett, Grant, Koh, & Parsons (1999) carried out two experiments in which drinking a taste solution was followed by 30-min placement in a circular alley. They reported that activity in this alley soon declined, but nevertheless placement there induced a small taste aversion. This conclusion needs to be treated with caution, since it is an example of a problem that can arise from the use of two tastes in a differential conditioning design followed by a choice test between the tastes. Briefly, if Taste A is followed by Outcome 1 and Taste B by Outcome 2, then a preference for B over A in a subsequent two-bottle test can indicate either an aversion to A, a preference for B, or both. Such ambiguity does not arise if a decline in intake of A, but not of B or of some control solution, occurs during training. Where no difference in training intakes is detected, the ambiguity can be resolved by testing A and B separately against some neutral solution, but such additional tests are rarely added and finding an appropriate neutral solution is not always straightforward. In the first experiment reported by Lett et al. (1999), Outcome 1 (preceded by Taste A) was placement in a circular alley, as described earlier, and Outcome 2 (preceded by Taste B) was return to the home cage. It is plausible that the latter was a positive outcome that supported a slight preference for B. In a second experiment Outcome 2 was changed to confinement in a small novel chamber and now only a small preference for B over A was obtained. It remains possible that in this context placement in the small chamber was a positive outcome relative to placement in the circular alley. Thus, the safe conclusion to be drawn from these experiments is that placement in an alley that elicits a low and declining level of activity, and thus little energy expenditure, supports little or no taste aversion learning.

When food-deprived rats are given a flavor paired with a calorie-rich nutrient they acquire a preference for the flavor (see Capaldi, 1992, 1996; Fedorchak, 1997; Sclafani, 1990, 1991, for reviews). Nakajima et al. (2000) argued that rats might also learn to *avoid* a flavor or taste that has become associated with calorie expenditure caused by exercise such as running in a wheel. This hypothesis led to the discovery of a new agent for establishing a CTA.

CTAs BASED ON SWIMMING

Forced swimming in a pool involves considerable energy expenditure (e.g., Benthem et al., 1994; Griffiths & Gallagher, 1953). If rats are given a novel taste prior to a swimming session, they acquire an aversion to the taste, as first reported from experiments using both simple and differential conditioning designs (Nakajima & Masaki, 2004). In a representative example of such experiments, three groups of rats were given 15-min access to saccharin in drinking cages and then Group Swim was placed for 20 min in a circular pool, 43–48 cm in diameter, filled to a depth of 36 cm with water. This pairing took place on four successive days, while Group Control was returned to the home cages and Group Shower was given a 20-min water shower instead of being placed in the pool. In a subsequent two-bottle test an aversion to saccharin was found only in Group Swim (Masaki & Nakajima, 2005, Experiment 3).

Properties of Swimming-Based Taste Aversions

The discovery of swimming-based taste aversion learning is relatively new and so its properties have not yet been explored as extensively as those of running-based taste aversion. Nonetheless, some properties are already known. First, the strength of a conditioned aversion is a positive function of duration of water immersion (Masaki & Nakajima, 2005, Experiment 2; Masaki & Nakajima, 2006). Thus, swimming-based taste aversion follows the Pavlovian law of US strength.

It may be noted that, although 30 min of swimming may be needed to obtain a detectable taste aversion after a single taste–swimming pairing (see Figure 9.2), other data suggest that an effect can be obtained with only 5 min of swimming under some settings (e.g., Nakajima & Masaki, 2004, Experiment 1). In one experiment three trials in which saccharin was followed by a 5-min swim period did not produce a detectable saccharin aversion but did facilitate subsequent acquisition of a LiCl-based aversion to saccharin—although this is not the interpretation favored by the authors (Smith, Fieser, Jones, Hock, & Schachtman, in press, Experiment 6). This last study was undertaken in the context of research on stress-based attenuation of taste aversion learning. Thus, 5 min of "swim stress," like other stressors, can interfere with the acquisition of a LiCl-based taste aversion (Bourne, Calton, Gustavson & Schachtman, 1992; Revusky & Reilly, 1989). It may seem paradoxical that swimming can both support and attenuate taste aversion learning. However, we see these

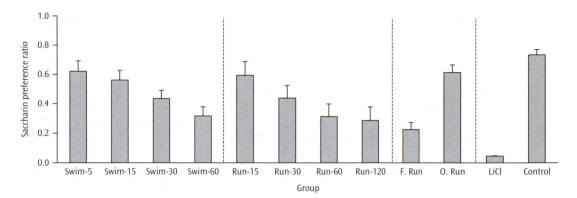

Figure 9.2. Comparison of saccharin aversions based on various USs (from Masaki & Nakajima, 2006). These preferences for 0.2% saccharin over water were obtained from a two-bottle test given to 12 groups of rats (each *n* = 8) following a single conditioning day in which 15-min access to novel saccharin was followed by various treatments, as follows. The four "Swim" groups were placed in a pool for either 5, 10, 30, or 60 min. Likewise, the four "Run" groups were placed in a closed wheel for either 15, 30, 60, or 120 min. The "F. Run" (= forced run) group were placed in a motorized wheel for 60 min and the "O. Run" (= optional run) group were placed in an open wheel for 120 min. The LiCl group was injected with 0.15-M lithium chloride at 20 ml/kg, while the Control group was returned to the home cages after drinking saccharin.

results as indicating that swimming can function both as a general stressor and as a US supporting taste aversion learning; which of these properties will be dominant in a given situation will depend on parameters such as the relative timing of the events.

Swimming-based taste aversion learning can occur with a delay of 30 min between the removal of access to saccharin and the start of a 20-min swimming session (Masaki & Nakajima, 2004b). The delayed group in the latter experiment showed a somewhat weaker aversion than the nondelayed group, but this difference was not statistically significant and both groups were statistically different from the no-water-immersion group. Further research is required to determine the effective range of delays in which swimming-based aversions can be acquired. Finally, as in taste aversion learning based on other US agents, swimming-based aversions show a US-preexposure effect, in that prior experience of swimming attenuates acquisition of such a taste aversion (Masaki & Nakajima, 2004a). A recent study revealed that this effect was unusually strong, in that a single experience of 5-min swimming completely prevented subsequent conditioning of the saccharin aversion that was obtained in a nonpreexposed control following four pairings of saccharin and 20-min swimming (Masaki & Nakajima, submitted).

Underlying Mechanisms of Swimming-Based Taste Aversions

The discovery of swimming-based taste aversion learning is consistent with—and was predicted by—the energy-expenditure hypothesis. However, it could also be explained in terms of activity in the mesolimbic dopamine system, gastrointestinal discomfort, or general stress. Support for the mesolimbic dopamine hypothesis comes from the finding that a conditioned place aversion can be produced by forward pairings of a target chamber with forced swimming (Masaki, submitted), as is the case with voluntary running and rewarding drugs noted earlier. In addition, it is quite possible that lengthy swimming causes gastrointestinal discomfort in rats.

A further factor could be general stress, since being dropped into water is clearly a stressful event. Indeed, forced swimming has been claimed to cause depression in rats and mice and has been widely used as a tool to evaluate antidepressants, following Porsolt, Le Pichon, and Jalefre (1977), though some researchers question its validity (see Borsini & Meli, 1988; Cryan, Markou, & Lucki, 2002; Lucki, 1997 for reviews and discussions). Furthermore, forced swimming causes many stress-related physiological, endocrine, and immune changes in rats, including elevation of plasma corticosterone and alterations of mono-amine levels in a variety of brain regions (Abel, 1993, 1994a, 1994b, 1994c; Connor, Kelly, & Leonard, 1997). Some of these physiological changes might be critical for producing a swim-ming-based taste aversion.

However, there is a further piece of evidence that provides support for the energy-expenditure hypothesis. Masaki and Nakajima (2005, Experiment 4) indirectly manipulated the amount of physical activity of rats by varying water levels in a pool. There was no water at all for the 0-cm group so that these rats could engage in a variety of activities, including resting, walking, exploring, rearing, and jumping in the bottom of the empty pool. For a second group there was always water in the pool to a depth of 12 cm so that rats in this group had to rear on their hind legs to keep their heads above the water; they also jumped up in the water in vain attempts to escape. For a third group the water was 32-cm deep and these rats had to swim, as in the other studies of swimming-based taste aversion. Over four training trials all three of these groups were given saccharin followed by 20-min confinement in the pool, while a control group was returned to the home cages immedi-ately after drinking saccharin. The total amount of energy expenditure was expected to be the least in the control group, followed by the 0-cm group, then the 12-cm group, and greatest in the 32-cm group. Two-bottle tests of saccharin versus water revealed a monotonic relationship between the degree of saccharin aversion and the assumed amount of energy expenditure. Although also consistent with the stress hypothesis, at the very least these results indicate the heuristic value of the energy-expenditure hypothesis for designing new experiments on exercise-based taste aversion.

COMPARISONS BETWEEN RUNNING, SWIMMING, AND OTHER AGENTS

Comparison between Voluntary Running and Forced Swimming

Nakajima (2004) compared taste aversions based on voluntary wheel running, forced swimming, and electric shock. For 6 days of training, drinking a 5% ethanol solution was followed by a 15-min treatment consisting of either running, swimming, or a series of 0.7-ms shocks (0.45 mA) with an intershock interval of 1 min. A subsequent two-bottle test revealed that all three treatments had produced moderate aversions to ethanol relative to an ethanol-alone control group, but no difference between the treatments was detected.

A far more extensive comparison of aversions based on running and swimming was carried out by Masaki and Nakajima (2006), using one-trial conditioning of a 0.2% saccharin solution and varied durations of confinement to a closed wheel or the pool. In addition, they included groups for which saccharin was followed by placement in an open wheel ("optional" running) or a motorized wheel (forced running), as well as a control group (no-US) returned to the home cages after drinking saccharin. As seen in Figure 9.2, the results con-firmed for this one-trial procedure that condition-ing of saccharin aversion follows the Pavlovian law of US strength both for voluntary running and forced swimming. Relative to the no-US con-trol rats, at least 30-min exercise was necessary to endow the rats with taste aversion based on either running or swimming. As seen in the figure, the functions relating strength of saccharin aver-sion to duration of confinement were very simi-lar for these two US agents and not statistically distinguishable.

Despite the surprising degree of similarity of running and swimming in the preceding experi-ments, it is of course always possible that differ-ences would be detected under other conditions. Even if the effectiveness of these USs do prove to be equivalent under a wide range of conditions, it does not follow that their underlying mechanisms are the same. For example, voluntary running and forced swimming appear to differ in sensitivity to the US-preexposure effect. As noted before, sev-eral sessions of prior wheel running are needed to attenuate running-based taste aversion learning (Nakajima et al., 2006), while a single brief preex-posure to swimming in a pool can be sufficient to entirely prevent subsequent acquisition of a swim-ming-based taste aversion (Masaki & Nakajima, submitted). Furthermore, a preliminary study in the laboratory of one of the present authors (SN) failed to yield a cross-familiarization effect between voluntary running and forced swimming. It is worth noting here that Nakajima (2004) and Masaki and Nakajima (2004a) found that, while rats in the wheels showed the usual repeated break-and-run pattern throughout, rats in the pool swam energetically and constantly, at least for the first 5 min before gradually becoming immobile with sporadic swimming during the remaining period.

Comparisons with Other US Agents

As noted in the previous section, in their comparison between running and swimming, Masaki and Nakajima (2006) also included a group of rats placed in motorized wheels for 60 min and a group placed for 2 h in open wheels, where rats could move to and fro between a side cage and the wheel. As seen in Figure 9.2, forced running produced a saccharin aversion that was slightly stronger than, but statistically equivalent to, the effect of 60-min voluntary running in a closed wheel. Unlike in Forristall et al. (2007), the speed of the motorized wheel was not adjusted so as to equate the total number of wheel turns for voluntary and forced running. In fact the speed was such (equivalent to 8 m/min) that these rats ran far more than any rat did in the 60-min voluntary running groups. If this factor had been equated, forced running might have produced a weaker taste aversion than voluntary running, as reported by Forristall et al. (2007).

In contrast, the rats placed in the open wheels—the "optional run" group—ran very little during the 2-h session and failed to acquire a saccharin aversion. Masaki and Nakajima (2006) attributed the failure of the "optional run" rats to the exploratory behaviors evoked by a new situation that prevented wheel running. On the other hand, Boakes and Pitts (2005) successfully demonstrated one-trial taste aversion learning in rats with no prior wheel experience that were given a single 2-h opportunity to run in an open wheel.

The final group to be considered from Masaki and Nakajima (2006) was given an intraperitoneal injection of 0.15-M LiCl at 20 ml/kg (i.e., 127.2 mg/kg). This dosage is at the high end of the range typically employed in LiCl-based taste aversion studies and, as expected, produced a very strong aversion to saccharin (see Figure 9.2). In what appears to be the only other experiment allowing a comparison between aversions based on running and on LiCl, Boakes and Pitts (2005) did not find any difference between an aversion to 0.1% saccharin produced by a single pairing with 0.15-M LiCl at 10 ml/kg and one produced by a single pairing with 2 h in an open running wheel.

CONCLUDING DISCUSSION

One general conclusion to draw from the research reviewed here is that taste aversion learning based on running or swimming is a robust phenomenon, as much so as learning based on any of the various US agents listed at the start of the chapter. One reason for the great interest in Garcia's original studies of taste aversion learning was that it contributed to our understanding of phenomena in naturalistic settings such as bait-shyness and of food choice in general, both in rats and in humans. Arguably, in most people's lives acquisition of a food aversion based on nausea or following ingestion of any of the many agents that can support aversion learning in the laboratory is a rare event. In contrast, most individuals engage in periods of physical activity quite frequently, so that, although the degree of aversion toward a food preceding such a period may be relative mild, activity-based aversion learning may have a very pervasive impact on an individual's choice of foods. Given the obesity epidemic now taking place in many developed countries and consequent public health campaigns to encourage children in particular to take more exercise, one could speculate that any effectiveness of exercise in reducing weight gain might stem as much from reducing liking for otherwise attractive foods as from burning off calories. In this context it is disappointing that to our knowledge there are no published data on activity-based aversion learning in humans; we are aware of only one unpublished experiment that obtained results suggesting that participants exercising in a gym came to dislike a novel taste sampled prior to exercise periods (S.-J. Salvy, personal communication, June 2007).

Returning to the rat laboratory and more theoretical issues, a major question that needs to be resolved is how the positive properties of wheel running are related to its negative properties. As noted earlier, these may reflect either independent internal consequences, the aversive properties might result from anticipatory contrast with its primary positive consequences, or the positive properties may result from an opponent process to a primary aversive state. Two potential experiments that could bear on this last possibility are as follows. One is to test whether an antiemetic such as odansetron or granisetron interferes with acquisition of a preference to a place or taste given after running, as well as interfering with acquisition of an aversion to a place or taste given before running (Eccles et al., 2005).

A result indicating the absence of any effect on acquisition of a preference based on backward conditioning in the context of interference with aversion learning based on forward conditioning would support the independence view, while interference by an antiemetic with both kinds of learning would favor the opponent-process hypothesis. A second experiment would be to carry out a backward conditioning procedure using swimming. Particularly since, unlike running in a wheel, swimming in a pool is not obviously self-reinforcing in rats (and it is unlikely that anyone will succeed in using access to a swimming pool to reinforce an instrumental action such as lever-pressing), a result indicating that rats acquire a preference for a taste given after removal from a pool would provide strong support for the opponent-process view.

This review makes clear major areas of ignorance about the phenomenon. For example, although wheel running appears to be self-reinforcing for a wide variety of species (Sherwin, 1998), there appears to be no research on taste aversion learning based on running in any species other than the rat. Also, very little is known about the physiological basis of this kind of aversion learning. The proposals we have listed in the previous sections on "Mechanisms" have remained little more than general suggestions. Given the simplicity of these procedures and—in the case of swimming-based learning—the need for apparatus no more complex than a bucket of water, such research does not need special facilities or a large grant. We hope that this review will stimulate further study of what until the work of Lett and Grant (1996) seems to have been a completely unsuspected phenomenon.

Acknowledgments The authors would like to thank Virginia Grant, Donald Heth, and David Pierce for their comments on drafts of this chapter, while acknowledging that they might not agree with some of the views expressed here.

References

Abel, E. L. (1993). Physiological correlates of the forced swim test in rats. *Physiology & Behavior, 54*, 309–317.

Abel, E. L. (1994a). Behavioral and physiological effects of different water depths in the forced swim test. *Physiology & Behavior, 56*, 411–414.

Abel, E. L. (1994b). Physical activity does not account for the physiological response to forced swim testing. *Physiology & Behavior, 56*, 677–681.

Abel, E. L. (1994c). A further analysis of physiological changes in rats in the forced swim test. *Physiology & Behavior, 56*, 795–800.

Ader, R. (1976). Conditioned adrenocortical steroid elevations in the rat. *Journal of Comparative and Physiological Psychology, 90*, 1156–1163.

Andrews, E. A., & Braveman, N. S. (1975). The combined effects of dosage level and interstimulus interval on the formation of one-trial poison-based aversions in rats. *Animal Learning & Behavior, 3*, 287–289.

Aoyama, K. (2004). The effect of taste aversion learning on within-session response decrease during a continuous reinforcement (CRF) schedule. *Japanese Journal of Psychonomic Science, 22*, 168–173.

Aoyama, K. (2007). Effects of post-session wheel running on within-session changes in operant responding. *Learning and Motivation, 38*, 284–293.

Aravich, P. F. (1996). Adverse effects of exercise stress and restricted feeding in the rat: Theoretical and neurobiological considerations. In W. F. Epling & W. D. Pierce (Eds.), *Activity anorexia: Theory, research, and treatment* (pp. 81–97). Mahwah, NJ: Lawrence Erlbaum.

Barker, L. M., & Smith, J. C. (1974). A comparison of taste aversions induced by radiation and lithium chloride in CS–US and US–CS paradigms. *Journal of Comparative and Physiological Psychology, 87*, 644–654.

Baysari, M. T., & Boakes, R. A. (2004). Flavour aversion produced by running and attenuated by prior exposure to wheels. *Quarterly Journal of Experimental Psychology, 57B*, 273–286.

Benthem, L., Bolhuis, J. W., Van Der Leest, J., Steffens, A. B., Zock, J. P., & Zijlstra, W. G. (1994). Methods for measurement of energy expenditure and substrate concentrations in swimming rats. *Physiology & Behavior, 56*, 151–159.

Berger, B. D. (1972). Conditioning of food aversions by injection of psychoactive drugs. *Journal of Comparative and Physiological Psychology, 81*, 21–26.

Berman, R. F., & Cannon, D. S. (1974). The effect of prior ethanol experience on ethanol-induced saccharin aversions. *Physiology & Behavior, 12*, 1041–1044.

Bernstein, I. L., & Fenner, D. P. (1983). Learned food aversions: Heterogeneity of animal models of tumor-induced anorexia. *Appetite, 4*, 79–86.

Bernstein, I. L., & Sigmundi, R. A. (1980). Tumor anorexia: A learned food aversion? *Science, 209,* 416–418.

Biederman, G. B., & Davey, V. A. (1997). Taste aversion conditioning with heat as an unconditioned stimulus: The role of taste intensity and preexposure in rats. *Learning and Motivation, 28,* 140–152.

Boakes, R. A. (2007). Self-starvation in the rat: Running versus eating. *Spanish Journal of Psychology, 10,* 251–257.

Boakes, R. A., & Dwyer, D. M. (1997). Weight loss in rats produced by running: Effects of prior experience and individual housing. *Quarterly Journal of Experimental Psychology, 50B,* 129–148.

Boakes, R. A., Mills, K. J., & Single, J. P. (1999). Sex differences in the relationship between activity and weight loss in the rat. *Behavioral Neuroscience, 113,* 1080–1089.

Boakes, R. A., & Pitts, C. (2005, July). *US-preexposure and cross tolerance: Lithium- and activity-based taste avoidance learning.* Paper presented at the joint meeting of the Brain, Behavior, and Cognitive Science Society (Canada) and Experimental Psychology Society (UK), Montreal.

Bond, N. W. (1983). Reciprocal overshadowing in flavour-aversion learning. *Quarterly Journal of Experimental Psychology, 35B,* 265–274.

Bond, N. W. (1984). The poisoned partner effect in rats: Some parametric considerations. *Animal Learning & Behavior, 12,* 89–96.

Booth, D. A., & Simson, P. C. (1974). Taste aversion induced by an histidine-free amino acid load. *Physiological Psychology, 2,* 349–351.

Borsini, F., & Meli, A. (1988). Is the forced swimming test a suitable model for revealing antidepressant activity? *Psychopharmacology, 94,* 147–160.

Bourne, M. J., Calton, J. L., Gustavson, K. K., & Schachtman, T. R. (1992). Effects of acute swim stress on LiCl-induced conditioned taste aversion in rats. *Physiology & Behavior, 51,* 1227–1234.

Braun, J. J., & McIntosh, H., Jr. (1973). Learned taste aversions induced by rotational stimulation. *Physiological Psychology, 1,* 301–304.

Braun, J. J., & Snyder, D. R. (1973). Taste aversions and acute methyl mercury poisoning in rats. *Bulletin of the Psychonomic Society, 1,* 419–420.

Braveman, N. S. (1975). Formation of taste aversions in rats following prior exposure to sickness. *Learning and Motivation, 6,* 512–534.

Braveman, N. S. (1977). What studies on preexposure to pharmacological agents tell us about the nature of the aversion-inducing agent. In L. M. Barker, M. R. Best, & M. Domjan (Eds.), *Learning mechanisms in food selection* (pp. 511–530). Waco, TX: Baylor University Press.

Capaldi, E. D. (1992). Conditioned food preferences. In D. L. Medin (Ed.), *The psychology of learning and motivation* (Vol. 28, pp. 1–33). San Diego, CA: Academic Press.

Capaldi, E. D. (1996). Conditioned food preferences. In E. D. Capaldi (Ed.), *Why we eat, what we eat: The psychology of eating* (pp. 53–80). Washington, DC: American Psychological Association.

Collier, G. (1969). Body weight loss as a measure of motivation in hunger and thirst. *Annals of New York Academy of Science, 157,* 594–609.

Collier, G., & Hirsch, E. (1971). Reinforcing properties of spontaneous activity in the rat. *Journal of Comparative and Physiological Psychology, 77,* 155–160.

Connor, T. J., Kelly, J. P., & Leonard, B. E. (1997). Forced swim test induced neurochemical, endocrine, and immune changes in the rat. *Pharmacology Biochemistry and Behavior, 58,* 961–967.

Coombes, S., Revusky, S., & Lett, B. T. (1980). Long-delay taste aversion learning in an unpoisoned rat: Exposure to a poisoned rat as the unconditioned stimulus. *Learning and Motivation, 11,* 256–266.

Cryan, J. F., Markou, A., & Lucki, I. (2002). Assessing antidepressant activity in rodents: Recent developments and future needs. *Trends in Pharmacological Sciences, 23,* 238–245.

Davey, V. A., & Biederman, G. B. (1997). Heat-induced conditioning of taste aversion and aversion failure in rats: Unconditioned effects, memorial processes, and the attenuation of neophobia. *Learning and Motivation, 28,* 357–367.

Davison, C. S., & House, W. J. (1975). Alcohol as the aversive stimulus in conditioned taste aversion. *Bulletin of the Psychonomic Society, 6,* 49–50.

Domjan, M., & Levy, C. L. (1977). Taste aversions conditioned by the aversiveness of insulin and formalin: Role of CS specificity. *Journal of Experimental Psychology: Animal Behavior Processes, 3,* 119–131.

Dragoin, W. B. (1971). Conditioning and extinction of taste aversion with variations in intensity of the CS and UCS in two strains of rats. *Psychonomic Science, 22,* 303–305.

Durlach, P. (1982). Pavlovian learning and performance when CS and US are uncorrelated. In M. L. Commons, R. J. Herrnstein, & A. R. Wagner (Eds.), *Quantitative analyses of behavior, Vol. III: Acquisition* (pp. 173–193). Cambridge, MA: Ballinger.

Durlach, P. (1983). Effect of signaling intertrial unconditioned stimuli in autoshaping. *Journal of Experimental Psychology: Animal Behavior Processes, 9,* 374–389.

Durlach, P. (1989). Learning and performance in Pavlovian conditioning: Are failures of contiguity failures of learning or performance? In S. B. Klein & R. R. Mowrer (Eds.), *Contemporary learning theories: Pavlovian conditioning and the status of traditional learning theory* (pp. 19–59). Hillsdale, NJ: Lawrence Erlbaum.

Eccles, S., Kim, E.-M., & O'Hare, E. (2005). Granisetron attenuates exercise-induced conditioned taste aversion in the rat. *Appetite, 44,* 325–328.

Eckardt, M. J., Skurdal, A. J., & Brown, J. S. (1974). Conditioned taste aversion produced by low doses of alcohol. *Physiological Psychology, 2,* 89–92.

Elkins, R. L. (1973). Individual differences in bait shyness: Effects of drug dose and measurement technique. *Psychological Record, 23,* 349–358.

Epliing, W. F., & Pierce, W. D. (1992). *Solving the anorexia puzzle: A scientific approach.* Toronto, Canada: Hogrefe & Huber.

Farber, P. D., Gorman, J. E., & Reid, L. D. (1976). Morphine injections in the taste aversion paradigm. *Physiological Psychology, 4,* 365–368.

Fedorchak, P. M. (1997). The nature and strength of caloric conditioning. In M. E. Bouton & M. S. Fanselow (Eds.), *Learning, motivation, and cognition: The functional behaviorism of Robert C. Bolles* (pp. 255–269). Washington, DC: American Psychological Association.

Flaherty, C. F. (1985). *Animal learning and cognition.* New York: Knopf.

Forristall, J. R., Hookey, B. L., & Grant, V. L. (2007). Conditioned taste avoidance induced by forced and voluntary wheel running in rats. *Behavioural Processes, 74,* 326–333.

Garcia, J., Ervin, F. R., & Koelling, R. A. (1966). Learning with prolonged delay of reinforcement. *Psychonomic Science, 5,* 121–122.

Garcia, J., Ervin, F. R., & Koelling, R. A. (1967). Bait-shyness: A test for toxicity with N = 2. *Psychonomic Science, 7,* 245–246.

Garcia, J., & Kimeldorf, D. J. (1960). Conditioned avoidance behaviour induced by low-dose neutron exposure. *Nature, 185,* 261–262.

Garcia, J., Kimeldorf, D. J., & Koelling, R. A. (1955). Conditioned aversion to saccharin resulting from exposure to gamma radiation. *Science, 122,* 157–158.

Garcia, J., & Koelling, R. A. (1966). Relation of cue to consequence in avoidance learning. *Psychonomic Science, 6,* 123–124.

Goddard, M. J., & Jenkins, H. M. (1987). Effect of signaling extra unconditioned stimuli on autoshaping. *Animal Learning & Behavior, 15,* 40–46.

Green, K. F., & Garcia, J. (1971). Recuperation from illness: Flavor enhancement for rats. *Science, 173,* 749–751.

Green, L., & Rachlin, H. (1973). The effect of rotation on the learning of taste aversions. *Bulletin of the Psychonomic Society, 1,* 137–138.

Green, L., & Rachlin, H. (1976). Learned taste aversions in rats as a function of delay, speed, and duration of rotation. *Learning and Motivation, 7,* 283–289.

Griffiths, W. J., & Gallagher, T. J. (1953). Differential dietary choices of albino rats occasioned by swimming. *Science, 118,* 780.

Grote, F. W., Jr., & Brown, R. T. (1971). Conditioned taste aversions: Two-stimulus tests are more sensitive than one-stimulus tests. *Behavior Research Methods, & Instrumentation, 3,* 311–312.

Gutiérrez, E., Baysari, M. T., Carrera, O., Whitford, T. J., & Boakes, R. A. (2006). High ambient temperature reduces rate of body-weight loss produced by wheel running. *Quarterly Journal of Experimental Psychology, 59,* 1196–1211.

Hall, H. F. (1976). *Classical conditioning and instrumental learning: A contemporary approach.* New York: Lippincott.

Hall, J. H. (1984). Backward conditioning in Pavlovian type studies: Reevaluation and present status. *Pavlovian Journal of Biological Science, 19,* 163–168.

Haroutunian, V., & Riccio, D. C. (1975). Acquisition of rotation-induced taste aversion as a function of drinking-treatment delay. *Physiological Psychology, 3,* 273–277.

Hasegawa, Y. (1981). Recuperation from lithium-induced illness: Flavor enhancement for rats. *Behavioral and Neural Biology, 33,* 252–255.

Hayashi, H., Nakajima, S., Urushihara, K., & Imada, H. (2002). Taste avoidance caused by spontaneous wheel running: Effects of duration and delay of wheel confinement. *Learning and Motivation, 33,* 390–409.

Hennessy, J. W., Smotherman, W. P., & Levine, S. (1976). Conditioned taste aversion and the pituitary-adrenal system. *Behavioral Biology, 16,* 413–424.

Heth, C. D., Inglis, P., Russell, J. C., & Pierce, W. D. (2001). Conditioned taste aversion induced by wheel running is not due to novelty of the wheel. *Physiology & Behavior, 74,* 53–56.

Heth, C. D., & Pierce, W. D. (2007). The role of pre-exposure to novel food tastes in activity-based conditioned taste avoidance. *Learning and Motivation, 38,* 35–43.

Higgins, T., & Rescorla, R. A. (2004). Extinction and retraining of simultaneous and successive flavor conditioining. *Learning & Behavior, 32*, 213–219.

Hughes, S. C., & Boakes, R. A. (2008). Flavor preferences produced by backward pairing with wheel running. *Journal of Experimental Psychology: Animal Behavior Processes, 34,* 283–293.

Hunt, T., & Amit, Z. (1987). Conditioned taste aversion by self-administered drugs: Paradox revisited. *Neuroscience and Biobehavioral Reviews, 11,* 107–130.

Iversen, I. H. (1993). Techniques for establishing schedules with wheel running as reinforcement in rats. *Journal of the Experimental Analysis of Behavior, 60,* 219–238.

Jakubczak, L. F. (1973). Frequency, duration, and speed of wheel running of rats as a function of age and starvation. *Animal Learning & Behavior, 1,* 13–16.

Jennings, W. A., & McCutcheon, L. E. (1974). Novel food and novel running wheels: Conditions for inhibition of sucrose intake in rats. *Journal of Comparative and Physiological Psychology, 87,* 100–105.

Kalat, J. W., & Rozin, P. (1970). "Salience": A factor which can override temporal contiguity in taste-aversion learning. *Journal of Comparative and Physiological Psychology, 71,* 192–197.

Kaye, H., Gambini, B., & Mackintosh, N. J. (1988). A dissociation between one-trial overshadowing and the effect of a detractor on habituation. *Quarterly Journal of Experimental Psychology, 40B,* 31–47.

Koh, M. T., Lett, B. T., & Grant, V. L. (2000). Activity in the circular alley does not produce the activity anorexia syndrome in rats. *Appetite, 34,* 153–159.

Krane, R. V., & Wagner, A. R. (1975). Taste aversion learning with a delayed shock US: Implications for the "generality of the laws of learning." *Journal of Comparative and Physiological Psychology, 88,* 882–889.

Lett, B. T., & Grant, V. L. (1996). Wheel running induces conditioned taste aversion in rats trained while hungry and thirsty. *Physiology & Behavior, 59,* 699–702.

Lett, B. T., Grant, V. L., Byrne, M. J., & Koh, M. T. (2000). Pairings of a distinctive chamber with the after effect of wheel running produce conditioned place preference. *Appetite, 34,* 87–94.

Lett, B. T., Grant, V. L., & Gaborko, L. L. (1998). Wheel running simultaneously induces CTA and facilitates feeding in non-deprived rats. *Appetite, 31,* 351–360.

Lett, B. T., Grant, V. L., & Koh, M. T. (2001). Naloxone attenuates the conditioned place preference induced by wheel running in rats. *Physiology & Behavior, 72,* 355–358.

Lett, B. T., Grant, V. L., & Koh, M. T. (2002). Delayed backward conditioning of place preference induced by wheel running in rats. *Learning and Motivation, 33,* 347–357.

Lett, B. T., Grant, V. L., Koh, M. T., & Flynn, G. (2002). Prior experience with wheel running produces cross-tolerance to the rewarding effect of morphine. *Pharmacology, Biochemistry and Behavior, 72,* 101–105.

Lett, B. T., Grant, V. L., Koh, M. T., & Parsons, J. F. (1999). Pairing a flavor with activity in a flat, circular alley induces conditioned taste aversion. *Learning and Motivation, 30,* 241–249.

Lett, B. T., Grant, V. L., Koh, M. T., & Smith, J. F. (2001). Wheel running simultaneously produces conditioned taste aversion and conditioned place preference in rats. *Learning and Motivation, 32,* 129–136.

Levine, T. E. (1978). Conditioned aversion following ingestion of methylmercury in rats and mice. *Behavioral Biology, 22,* 486–496.

Lindsey, G. P., & Best, P. J. (1973). Overshadowing of the less salient of two novel fluids in a taste-aversion paradigm. *Physiological Psychology, 1,* 13–15.

Livesey, P. J., Egger, G. J., & Meyer, P. N. (1972). Wheel running, a rewarding activity for the rat or response to increased drive following deprivation? *Australian Journal of Psychology, 24,* 45–53.

LoLordo, V. M., & Fairless, J. L. (1985). Pavlovian conditioned inhibition: The literature since 1969. In R. R. Miller & N. E. Spear (Eds.), *Information processing in animals: Conditioned inhibition* (pp. 1–49). Hillsdale, NJ: Erlbaum.

Looy, H., & Eikelboom, R. (1989). Wheel running, food intake, and body weight in male rats. *Physiology & Behavior, 45,* 403–405.

Lubow, R. E. (1989). *Latent inhibition and conditioned attention theory.* New York: Cambridge University Press.

Lucki, I. (1997). The forced swimming test as a model for core and component behavioral effects of antidepressant drugs. *Behavioral Pharmacology, 8,* 523–532.

Mackintosh, N. J. (1974). *The psychology of animal learning.* London: Academic Press.

Masaki, T. (submitted). Conditioned place aversion based on forced swimming in rats.

Masaki, T., & Nakajima, S. (2004a). Swimming-induced taste aversion and its prevention by a prior history of swimming. *Learning and Motivation, 35,* 406–418.

Masaki, T., & Nakajima, S. (2004b). Taste aversion learning induced by delayed swimming activity. *Behavioural Processes, 67,* 357–362.

Masaki, T., & Nakajima, S. (2005). Further evidence for conditioned taste aversion induced by forced swimming. *Physiology & Behavior, 84*, 9–15.

Masaki, T., & Nakajima, S. (2006). Taste aversion in rats induced by forced swimming, voluntary running, forced running, and lithium chloride injection treatments. *Physiology & Behavior, 88*, 411–416.

Masaki, T., & Nakajima, S. (in press). Forward conditioning with voluntary wheel running causes place avoidance in rats. *Behavioural Processes*.

Masaki, T., & Nakajima, S. (submitted). Effects of prior- and post-experience with forced swimming on swimming-based taste aversion learning in rats.

McLaurin, W. A. (1964). Postirradiation saccharin avoidance in rats as a function of the interval between ingestion and exposure. *Journal of Comparative and Physiological Psychology, 57*, 316–317.

Monroe, B., & Barker, L. M. (1979). A contingency analysis of taste aversion conditioning. *Animal Learning & Behavior, 7*, 141–143.

Nachman, M. (1970). Learned taste and temperature aversions due to lithium chloride sickness after temporal delays. *Journal of Comparative and Physiological Psychology, 73*, 22–30.

Nachman, M., & Ashe, J. H. (1973). Learned taste aversions in rats as a function of dosage, concentration, and route of administration of LiCl. *Physiology & Behavior, 10*, 73–78.

Nagaishi, T., Nakanishi, M., & Nakajima, S. (submitted). Overshadowing in running-based taste aversion learning.

Nakajima, S. (2004). Conditioned ethanol aversion in rats induced by voluntary wheel running, forced swimming, and electric shock: An implication for aversion therapy of alcoholism. *Integrative Physiological and Behavioral Science, 39*, 95–104.

Nakajima, S. (2008). Effect of extra running on running-based taste aversion learning in rats. *Behavioural Processes, 78*, 470–472.

Nakajima, S., Hayashi, H., & Kato, T. (2000). Taste aversion induced by confinement in a running wheel. *Behavioural Processes, 49*, 35–42.

Nakajima, S., Ka, H., & Imada, H. (1999). Summation of overshadowing and latent inhibition in rats' conditioned taste aversion: Scapegoat technique works for familiar meals. *Appetite, 33*, 299–307.

Nakajima, S., & Masaki, T. (2004). Taste aversion learning induced by forced swimming in rats. *Physiology & Behavior, 80*, 623–628.

Nakajima, S., Urata, T., & Ogawa, Y. (2006). Familiarization and cross-familiarization of wheel running and LiCl in conditioned taste aversion. *Physiology & Behavior, 88*, 1–11.

Nathan, B. A., & Vogel, J. R. (1975). Taste aversions induced by D-amphetamine: Dose–response relationship. *Bulletin of the Psychonomic Society, 6*, 287–288.

Nikoletseas, M. M. (1981). Exercise-induced sucrose suppression in the rat. *Physiology & Behavior, 26*, 145–146.

Parker, L. A. (2003). Taste avoidance and taste aversion: Evidence for two different processes. *Learning & Behavior, 31*, 165–172.

Pavlov, I. P. (1927). *Conditioned reflexes: An investigation of the physiological activity of the cerebral cortex*. Oxford, UK: Oxford University Press.

Porsolt, R. D., Le Pichon, M., & Jalefre, M. (1977). Depression: A new animal model sensitive to antidepressant treatments. *Nature, 266*, 730–732.

Rabin, B. M., & Hunt, W. A. (1986). Mechanisms of radiation-induced conditioned taste aversion learning. *Neuroscience and Biobehavioral Reviews, 10*, 55–65.

Randich, A., & LoLordo, V. M. (1979). Associative and nonassociative theories of the UCS preexposure phenomenon: Implications for Pavlovian conditioning. *Psychological Bulletin, 86*, 523–548.

Reicher, M. A., & Holman, E. W. (1977). Location preference and flavor aversion reinforced by amphetamine in rats. *Animal Learning & Behavior, 5*, 343–346.

Rescorla, R. A. (1968). Probability of shock in the presence and absence of CS in fear conditioning. *Journal of Comparative and Physiological Psychology, 66*, 1–5.

Rescorla, R. A. (1972). Informational variables in Pavlovian conditioning. In G. H. Bower (Ed.), *The psychology of learning and motivation* (Vol. 6, pp. 1–46). New York: Academic Press.

Rescorla, R. A. (1984). Signaling intertribal shocks attenuates their negative effect on conditioned suppression. *Bulletin of the Psychonomic Society, 22*, 225–228.

Revusky, S. (1968). Aversion to sucrose and produced by contingent X-irradiation: Temporal and dosage parameters. *Journal of Comparative and Physiological Psychology, 65*, 17–22.

Revusky, S. (1971). The role of interference in association over a delay. In W. K. Honig & P. H. R. Jones (Eds.), *Animal memory* (pp. 155–213). New York: Academic Press.

Revusky, S., & Reilly, S. (1989). Attenuation of conditioned taste aversion by external stressors. *Pharmacology, Biochemistry & Behavior, 33*, 219–226.

Riley, A. L., & Freeman, K. B. (2004). Conditioned taste aversion: A database. *Pharmacology. Biochemistry and Behavior, 77,* 655–656.

Riley, A. L., Jacobs, W. J., & LoLordo, V. M. (1978). Morphine-induced taste aversions: A consideration of parameters. *Physiological Psychology, 6,* 96–100.

Riley, A. L., & Simpson, G. R. (2000). The attenuating effects of drug preexposure on taste aversion conditioning: Generality, experimental parameters, underlying mechanisms, and implications for drug use and abuse. In R. R. Mowrer, R. R., & S. B. Klein (Eds.), *Handbook of contemporary learning theories* (pp. 505–559). Mahwah, NJ: Erlbaum.

Routtenberg, A., & Kuznesof, A. W. (1967). Self-starvation of rats living in activity wheels on a restricted feeding schedule. *Journal of Comparative and Physiological Psychology, 64,* 414–421.

Rozin, P. (1967). Specific aversions as a component of specific hungers. *Journal of Comparative and Physiological Psychology, 64,* 237–242.

Salvy, S.-J., Heth, D. C., Pierce, W. D., & Russell, J. C. (2004). Conditioned taste aversion induced by wheel running: Further evidence on wheel running duration. *Behavioural Processes, 66,* 101–106.

Salvy, S.-J., Pierce, W. D., Heth, D. C., & Russell, J. C. (2002). Pre-exposure to wheel running disrupts taste aversion conditioning. *Physiology & Behavior, 76,* 51–56.

Salvy, S.-J., Pierce, W. D., Heth, D. C., & Russell, J. C. (2003). Wheel running produces conditioned food aversion. *Physiology & Behavior, 80,* 89–94.

Salvy, S.-J., Pierce, W. D., Heth, D. C., & Russell, J. C. (2004). Taste aversion induced by wheel running: Effects of backward pairings and robustness of conditioned taste aversion. *Physiology & Behavior, 82,* 303–308.

Satvat, E., & Eikelboom, R. (2006). Dissociation of conditioned and unconditioned factors in the running induced feeding suppression. *Physiology & Behavior, 89,* 428–437.

Schull, J. (1979). A conditioned opponent theory of Pavlovian conditioning and habituation. In G. H. Bower (Ed.), *The psychology of learning and motivation* (Vol. 13, pp. 57–90). New York: Academic Press.

Sclafani, A. (1990). Nutritionally based learned flavor preferences in rats. In E. Capaldi & T. L. Powley (Eds.), *Taste, experience, and feeding* (pp. 139–156). Washington, DC: American Psychological Association.

Sclafani, A. (1991). Conditioned food preferences. *Bulletin of the Psychonomic Society, 29,* 256–260.

Sherman, J. E., Pickman, C., Rice, A., Liebeskind, J. C., & Holman, E. W. (1980). Rewarding and aversive effects of morphine: Temporal and pharmacological properties. *Pharmacology, Biochemistry and Behavior, 13,* 501–505.

Sherwin, C. M. (1998). Voluntary wheel running: A review and novel interpretation. *Animal Behaviour, 56,* 11–27.

Shyu, B. C., Andersson, S. A., & Thoren, P. (1982). Endorphin mediated increase in pain threshold induced by long-lasting exercise in rats. *Life Sciences, 30,* 833–840.

Simson, P. C., & Booth, D. A. (1974). Dietary aversion established by a deficient load: Specificity to the amino acid omitted from a balanced mixture. *Pharmacology, Biochemistry and Behavior, 2,* 481–485.

Simpson, G. R., & Riley, A. L. (2005). Morphine preexposure facilitates morphine place preference and attenuates morphine taste aversion. *Pharmacology Biochemistry and Behavior, 80,* 471–479.

Smith, J. C., & Birkle, R. A. (1966). Conditioned aversion to sucrose in rats using X-ray as the unconditioned stimulus. *Psychonomic Science, 5,* 271–272.

Smith, J. C., & Roll, D. L. (1967). Trace conditioning with X-rays as an aversive stimulus. *Psychonomic Science, 9,* 11–12.

Smith, S., Fieser, S., Jones, J., Hock, R., & Schachtman, T. R. (in press). The effects of swim stress on latent inhibition using a conditioned taste aversion procedure. *Physiology & Behavior.*

Solomon, R. L., & Corbit, J. D. (1974). An opponent-process theory of motivation. *Psychological Review, 81,* 119–145.

Sparkes, S., Grant, V. L., & Lett, B. T. (2003). Role of conditioned taste aversion in the development of activity anorexia. *Appetite, 41,* 161–165.

Tarpy, R. M. (1997). *Contemporary learning theory and research.* New York: McGraw-Hill.

Wagner, A. R. (1981). SOP: A model of automatic memory processing in animal behavior. In N. E. Spear & R. R. Miller (Eds.), *Information processing in animals: Memory mechanisms* (pp. 5–47). Hillsdale, NJ: Lawrence Erlbaum.

Wang, Y., & Chambers, K. C. (2001). The role of the dura in conditioned taste avoidance induced by cooling the area postrema of male rats. *Behavioural Brain Research, 122,* 113–129.

Wang, Y., Lavond, D. G., & Chambers, K. C. (1987). Cooling the area postrema induces conditioned taste aversions in male rats and blocks acquisition of LiCl-induced aversions. *Behavioral Neuroscience, 111,* 768–776.

Weisinger, R., Parker, L. F., & Skorupski, J. D. (1974). Conditioned taste aversions and specific need states in the rat. *Journal of Comparative and Physiological Psychology, 87,* 665–660.

Williams, B. A. (1994). Contingency theory and the effect of the duration of signals for noncontingent reinforcement. *Psychonomic Bulletin & Review, 1,* 111–114.

Wittlin, W. A., & Brookshire, K. H. (1968). Apomorphine-induced conditioned aversion to a novel food. *Psychonomic Science, 12,* 217–218.

Zahorik, D. M. (1972). Conditioned physiological changes associated with learned aversions to tastes paired with thiamine deficiency in the rat. *Journal of Comparative and Physiological Psychology, 79,* 189–200.

10

Mechanisms of Overshadowing and Potentiation in Flavor Aversion Conditioning

W. ROBERT BATSELL, JR. AND GAYLA Y. PASCHALL

MECHANISMS OF COMPOUND CONDITIONING IN AVERSION CONDITIONING

Conditioned taste aversions (CTAs) are a form of classical conditioning in which an organism experiences an edible substance (conditioned stimulus or CS) followed by an illness-producing event (unconditioned stimulus or US). As a result of this CS–US pairing, when the organism subsequently reencounters the CS, it will demonstrate a reluctance to consume that food (the conditioned response or CR). One of the enduring questions in associative learning in general is whether CTA operates under the exact rules as other types of classical conditioning such as fear conditioning and conditioned eyeblink (Domjan, 1980; Logue, 1979). This question was originally explored through such manipulations as cue-to-consequence learning (Garcia & Koelling, 1966) and long-delay learning (Garcia, Ervin, & Koelling, 1966), but subsequent research found that these effects could be accommodated in other types of classical conditioning (see Bouton, 2006, for review). Nonetheless, one area in which CTA consistently appears to operate by different mechanisms is in compound conditioning. In other classical conditioning paradigms, the simultaneous conditioning of two or more CSs results in *cue competition* for associative strength, and ultimately, less associative strength to the weaker CS. Although evidence of this cue competition is abundant in the CTA literature,

on many occasions, the simultaneous conditioning of multiple CSs produces the exact opposite of cue competition, *synergistic conditioning*, in which conditioning is actually enhanced to the weaker CS. This chapter will review the research and proposed mechanisms underlying cue competition and synergistic conditioning in aversion conditioning.

EVIDENCE OF CUE COMPETITION

In classical conditioning, the cue competition designs are those in which two or more CSs compete for associative strength with the US. The two cue competition designs that have received the most attention in the CTA literature are the compound conditioning (AX+) and the blocking (A+/AX+) designs. Because relatively little work has explored the mechanisms of blocking with CTA methodology, this work will be reviewed briefly before the more extensive review of compound conditioning. Kamin (1969) used the A+/AX+ design in fear conditioning where rats were given multiple tone–shock pairings in Phase 1, followed by tone–light–shock pairings in Phase 2. Relative to controls that only experienced Phase 2, experimental rats showed high fear to the pretrained tone and no fear to the light. Kamin and others have interpreted this result as the previous learning that the tone signals the shock renders the light redundant during Phase 2. As such, the previous learning to the tone blocks the learning to the light. Kalat and Rozin (1972) reported the results of four A+/AX+ experiments in their attempt to determine if Kamin's blocking effect could be demonstrated in CTA. Although these four experiments differed in a number of procedural variables, in no study did they obtain significant evidence of blocking. Similar studies were conducted by Revusky (1971), but he found evidence for blocking, which was confirmed by other labs (Gillan & Domjan, 1977), but again, the main purpose of these studies was to determine *if* blocking could occur with taste aversion learning, not *how* blocking occurs with taste aversion learning. Since that initial work, the concept of blocking has been explored primarily in relation to the US preexposure effect, and the evidence is that in CTA this effect is due to context blocking (e.g., Batson & Best, 1979; Hall, Chapter 4; Willner, 1978).

Most evidence of cue competition in taste aversion learning comes from compound conditioning (AX+) studies. Procedurally, these AX+ studies have used both simultaneous and sequential conditioning designs. In a simultaneous compound design (AX+), if CS A and CS X are relatively equal along many variables to be described later in this section, and paired with a US, *reciprocal overshadowing* may be observed as conditioning to both A and X is reduced relative to conditioning each cue alone. In a sequential conditioning design (A–X+), A is presented alone, followed by X alone, and then the US. Because X is more proximal to the US, greater associative strength typically accrues to X and A is overshadowed (e.g., Revusky, Parker, & Coombes, 1977). In the sequential design, if the A–X interval was brief (e.g., 0 min), reciprocal overshadowing could be observed as responding to each cue would be reduced (Bond, 1983). Yet, if the A–X interval, the time between CS offset and US onset, was extended to 10 min, overshadowing of X was eliminated (Bond), while overshadowing of A remained intact. In general, increases in the A–X interval produce greater overshadowing of A (e.g., Revusky, 1971). Thus, temporal contiguity has been established as a primary determinant of overshadowing in the sequential design.

Research conducted in the 1960s and 1970s revealed that other variables (novelty, intensity, and salience) could act alone or in conjunction with temporal contiguity to influence the degree of overshadowing. Revusky and Bedarf (1967) conducted the first investigation of two flavors in which one was familiar and the other was novel. Rats received 8 days of pretraining during which they had 1-h access to either milk or grape juice. During conditioning, half of the rats received a presentation order of familiar taste followed by novel taste while the other rats received the presentation order of novel taste followed by familiar taste. Following a 60- to 70-min CS–US interval, illness was induced. During the two-bottle preference test, rats preferred the familiar flavor to the novel flavor. These results indicate that in a sequential procedure, the novelty of the flavor is a better determinant of the target of aversion learning than proximity to the US.

The importance of the intensity of the cues had been evident from the initial compound conditioning work reported by Pavlov (1927, pp. 269–270), who coined the term *overshadowing*. Revusky (1971) reported that conditioning of a saccharin → vinegar → lithium sequence, the strength of the saccharin (SAC) aversion was inversely proportional to the concentration of the vinegar solution (weaker SAC aversions were produced by stronger vinegar solutions). Similarly, Lindsey and Best (1973) reported that at least in some situations, relative intensity can override temporal contiguity in the determination of overshadowing.

In a related experiment, Kalat and Rozin (1970) examined whether the salience of the taste—"the tendency of a solution to be associated with subsequent poisoning" (p. 193)—was more important than temporal contiguity in sequential conditioning. For example, in one study, the aversion to NaCl was also stronger than to vanilla, regardless of whether NaCl was more or less contiguous with poisoning. Thus, in their studies, they were able to demonstrate a relative hierarchy of decreasing salience as follows: casein hydrolysate → sucrose → NaCl → vanilla. Nonetheless, temporal contiguity did play a role as the taste was always avoided more when it was the more contiguous flavor. Another important finding from this work was that salience was different from palatability because although casein was the least palatable and the most salient, sucrose was the most palatable, but second in salience.

Mechanisms of Overshadowing in Taste Aversion Learning

Once the experimental parameters to produce overshadowing were established, ensuing research used this procedure to explore the mechanism of overshadowing. On one hand, some formal theories of associative learning interpret overshadowing as an "acquisition-deficit" phenomenon (e.g., Rescorla & Wagner, 1972) in which the deficits occur at the time of conditioning. In other words, once overshadowing has occurred at conditioning, postconditioning manipulations should be ineffective in reinstating learning to the overshadowed stimulus. On the other hand, a number of studies have suggested that overshadowing is not an acquisition deficit; instead, it is due to expression or retrieval deficits (see R. R. Miller, Barnet & Grahame, 1995, for review), and the deficits occur at the time of testing. The evidence for this expression deficit interpretation are research works that have reported that various postconditioning manipulations such as extinction of the overshadowing stimulus (e.g., Kaufman & Bolles, 1981; Matzel, Schachtman, & Miller, 1985; Matzel, Shuster, & Miller, 1987) or delayed testing (e.g., Batsell & Best, 1992b; J. S. Miller, Jagielo & Spear, 1990; Kraemer, Lariviere, & Spear, 1988) produce recovery from overshadowing.

The first evidence of recovery from overshadowing was demonstrated with the postconditioning extinction paradigm (Kaufman & Bolles, 1981; Matzel et al., 1985, 1987). Matzel et al. (1985) examined lick suppression following pairings of a light–tone compound with footshock. The key group in their studies received extinction of the overshadowing tone following conditioning, and this manipulation produced a recovery in lick suppression to the light relative to controls that did not undergo extinction. Notably, this experiment also demonstrated covariation in the strength of the elements of the compound: As the CR to the overshadowing tone decreased, the CR to the overshadowed light increased. Matzel et al. (1987) established the generality of this recovery effect when they reported similar results following sequential overshadowing; in fact, the recovery from overshadowing was more extensive following sequential conditioning than simultaneous conditioning. R. R. Miller and his colleagues have proposed the comparator hypothesis to account for these results (Matzel et al., 1987). According to the comparator hypothesis, responding to a given CS is determined by the relative associative strengths of the target stimulus and all other elements. In a typical overshadowing experiment, CS X would have greater associative strength, and thus there

would be less responding to CS A. However, if the associative strength of CS X is weakened via extinction, the associative strength (and responding to) CS A increases.

The delayed testing paradigm was first used to examine recovery from overshadowing in taste aversion learning studies by Kraemer et al. (1988). Using groups of adult rats, Kraemer et al. simultaneously paired a chocolate milk solution with banana odor followed by lithium-mediated illness. Controls were given chocolate milk paired with lithium. When chocolate milk testing occurred 1 day after conditioning, a weak aversion was recorded following compound conditioning (e.g., overshadowing was evident). When testing occurred 21 days after conditioning, however, a significantly stronger chocolate milk aversion was present after compound conditioning. Apparently, the overshadowed taste aversion recovered during the retention interval. Moreover, there was no difference in chocolate milk consumption between the two single-element control groups across the retention interval, and the results from nonconditioned controls suggested that the increased aversion in the compound conditioning group was not due to increased neophobia across the retention interval.

In 1990, J. S. Miller et al. replicated the Kraemer et al. findings that an overshadowed taste aversion increases in strength across a 21-day retention interval (see Experiment 1). In Experiment 2, J. S. Miller et al. tested the banana odor component of the compound (the overshadowing cue in Experiment 1), and they found no evidence of overshadowing at the 1-day test (i.e., a strong CR), but a significant overshadowing effect at the 21-day test (i.e., a weak CR). In other words, responding to the overshadowed taste and the overshadowed odor appeared to covary across the retention interval. J. S. Miller et al. concluded that this pattern of results was due to *differential retrievability* of the stimuli across the retention interval. In their retrievability hypothesis, because tastes are more readily associated with illness than are odor cues, the retrievability of the taste increased across the retention interval. This produced a twofold effect. First, retrieval of the taste was enhanced, and an increased taste aversion was recorded at the later test. Second, because the taste was more easily retrieved, this produced greater overshadowing of the odor, and the odor aversion was weaker at the later test.

Curiously, the patterns of recovery from over-shadowing following CTA appear different from those following conditioned suppression (e.g., Matzel et al., 1985). Specifically, all successful demonstrations of recovery from overshadow-ing with delayed testing have occurred with taste testing (e.g., Kraemer et al., 1988), but successful demonstrations of recovery from overshadowing with postconditioning extinction have not been recorded with taste testing. Indeed, multiple stud-ies that have utilized postconditioning extinction to produce recovery from overshadowing with a CTA procedure have failed (Kalat & Rozin, 1972; Revusky et al., 1977; Schachtman, Kasprow, Meyer, Bourne, & Hart, 1992). In a series of experiments that examined both simultaneous overshadowing and sequential overshadowing, Schachtman et al. found no evidence that extinction of the over-shadowing taste had any effect on the aversion to the overshadowed taste. Indeed, following simul-taneous overshadowing, they found that extinc-tion of the overshadowing taste had no effect or appeared to weaken the CR to the overshadowed taste. Thus, although recovery from overshad-owing may have important implications for the-ories of associative learning, and mechanisms of overshadowing, the conditions that reliably produce these effects in different classical condi-tioning preparations are not known at this time. Intriguingly, every demonstration of recovery from overshadowing with delayed testing has occurred after simultaneous conditioning, and the use of the simultaneous conditioning design may be key to explaining this phenomenon because, as described next, the use of this design does not always pro-duce cue competition.

SYNERGISTIC CONDITIONING

In the late 1970s, multiple publications provided evidence of synergistic conditioning following AX+ conditioning (Clarke, Westbrook, & Irwin, 1979; Galef & Osborne, 1978), but Rusiniak, Hankins, Garcia, and Brett (1979) produced the report that has garnered the most attention. Rusiniak et al. presented an SAC taste with an almond (AL) odor in compound, followed by toxi-cosis. During odor testing, the odor aversion in the compound conditioning group was significantly stronger than the odor aversion in the odor-alone group. In other words, instead of the expected outcome of overshadowing, compound condition-ing produced a significantly stronger odor aversion. This phenomenon was termed *taste-potentiated odor aversion* (TPOA). Interestingly, TPOA is an asymmetric phenomenon as the taste aversion was either not affected or it was overshadowed (e.g., Westbrook, Homewood, Horn, & Clarke, 1983). Over the past 25+ years, numerous experiments have demonstrated TPOA, although not without some difficulty in finding the phenomenon (e.g., Bouton & Whiting, 1982). It is worth noting that there have been numerous examinations of the physiological substrates of TPOA (e.g., Ferry, Sandner, & Di Scala, 1995; Hatfield & Gallagher, 1995; Kiefer, Rusiniak, & Garcia, 1982), but a review of the strengths and limitations of this literature is beyond the scope of this chapter.

In addition to TPOA, odor and taste have been used within the "blocking design" (A+/AX+) to produce synergistic conditioning. In our ini-tial studies (Batsell & Batson, 1999; Batson & Batsell, 2000), rats were first given a pairing of AL odor with illness in Phase 1 (A+); next they were given a simultaneous presentation of AL and the bitter taste denatonium (DEN) in Phase 2 (AX+). Subsequent DEN testing revealed a significantly stronger taste aversion compared to a group that only experienced AX+ conditioning. This out-come is noteworthy because most theories of associative learning would predict blocking, not enhancement, of the DEN aversion following A+/AX+ conditioning. Subsequent work confirmed that this phenomenon was symmetrical as pre-training the taste aversion prior to taste + odor compound conditioning produced a significantly stronger odor aversion than that of the TPOA con-trol group (Batsell, Paschall, Gleason, & Batson, 2001). Because this effect is symmetrical, and TPOA is not, we used the term *augmentation* to describe the evidence of synergistic conditioning in the A+/AX+ design.

Besides synergistic conditioning between taste and odor cues, experiments have confirmed that compound conditioning with taste can potentiate other cues as well. For example, taste-potentiated *taste* aversions have been reported by a num-ber of different labs (e.g., Batsell & Best, 1992b; Bouton, Dunlap, & Swartzentruber, 1987; Davis, Best, & Grover, 1988; Davis, Best, Grover, Bailey, Freeman, & Mayleben, 1990; Kucharski & Spear, 1985). Furthermore, taste-mediated potentiation has been reported to cues that cannot be mixed into solution with the taste. Using rat subjects, taste has been reported to potentiate aversions to *auditory* cues (e.g., Ellins, Cramer, & Whitmore, 1985; Ellins & von Kluge, 1987, 1990; Holder, Bermudez-Rattoni, & Garcia, 1988; von Kluge, Perkey, & Peregord, 1996) and *visual* cues (e.g., Galef & Osborne, 1978). It is notable that more reports of taste potentiation of visual cues have occurred with bird subjects than rat subjects (e.g., Jackson & Fritsche, 1989; Lett, 1980; Westbrook, Clarke, & Provost, 1980).

A related area that has stimulated substantial research is taste-potentiated context aversions. The initial evidence for this effect was reported by the late Mike Best and his colleagues (Best, Batson, Meachum, Brown, & Ringer, 1985; Best, Brown, & Sowell, 1984; Best & Meachum, 1986) and subsequently replicated by others (e.g., Boakes, Westbrook, & Barnes, 1992; J. S. Miller, McCoy, Kelly, & Bardo, 1986; Westbrook & Brookes, 1988; Westbrook, Harvey, & Swinbourne, 1988). In these studies, rats would be given multiple pairings of a solution (either water or a novel solution) in a distinctive context prior to illness induction. Later testing in the distinctive context revealed significantly less consumption of a familiar and palatable solution by the compound conditioning group (taste + context). Although the results of this research appeared to provide evidence of taste-potentiated context aversions, work by Geoff Hall and Michelle Symonds has called that conclusion into question. Symonds and Hall initiated their work to eliminate the possibility that evidence of context potentiation was due to generalization from the novel conditioning flavor to the test flavor in the compound conditioning group; to do this, they used an indirect measure in which the strength of the context aversion would be assessed via its ability to block the formation of a new taste–US association. In a series of experiments (Symonds & Hall, 1999), rats consumed a novel taste (HCl) or water in a distinctive context, followed by illness. In a later phase, all groups consumed sucrose in this context, followed by illness. The dependent measure was the strength of the sucrose aversion, which would provide an index of the extent of blocking by the distinctive context, and thus an indirect assessment of the context aversion produced during Phase 1. In these experiments, rats that experienced the novel HCl taste during Phase 1, showed a stronger sucrose aversion, suggesting that the context aversion in this group was

overshadowed, not potentiated. On the basis of these studies, Symonds and Hall concluded that previous demonstrations of taste-potentiated context aversions are artifacts of the testing stimuli and not true evidence of potentiation.

Mechanisms of TPOA

Because TPOA is an outcome that is behaviorally opposite of overshadowing and it has rarely been reported in other types of classical conditioning, it is one of various phenomena that have represented a challenge to modern theories of learning for over 25 years. Indeed, the search for the conditions that will reliably produce the effect and its mechanism has inspired considerable research. Two conditions that appear necessary to produce TPOA include a simultaneous presentation of the cues and the salience of the target cues. In regard to stimulus presentation, CTA experiments that have used a sequential presentation of cues have not yielded potentiation; instead, these studies often produce overshadowing (Batsell et al., 2001; Coburn, Garcia, Kiefer, & Rusiniak, 1984; Holder & Garcia, 1987).

Regarding studies in which the taste can be mixed into solution with the other cue (e.g., odor, taste), the *salience ratio* between the cues determines the degree of potentiation. For example, Bouton, Jones, McPhillips, and Swartzentruber (1986) showed that when the taste and odor were mixed in solution, TPOA occurred only when a 0.1% SAC solution was paired with weaker concentrations of AL odor (0.005% and 0.01% solutions), but not with stronger concentrations of AL odor (2%). The following year, Bouton and his colleagues (Bouton et al., 1987) showed that the salience ratio also applied in taste-potentiated taste aversion as SAC could potentiate a weak salt solution (0.03%), but not stronger salt solutions (0.6% and 1.2%). Finally, a report by Slotnick, Westbrook, and Darling (1997) suggests that the salience ratio may be more important than the sense modality of the CSs in determining the target of potentiation. In their studies, Slotnick et al. varied concentrations of isoamyl acetate (odor CS) and SAC. Compared to single-element controls, rats that experienced higher concentrations of taste paired with weaker concentrations of odor showed TPOA as expected. Interestingly, compared to taste aversions of single-element controls, rats that experienced higher concentrations of odor paired with weaker concentrations of taste showed *odor-potentiated taste aversions*. Thus, their results show that potentiation can occur without taste as the potentiating cue; yet, it is worth noting that this outcome has yet to be replicated by other researchers.

Historically, there have been two primary theoretical explanations of TPOA. One of these has emphasized general principles of associative learning (within-compound association model) whereas the other has focused on mechanisms that would be unique to the feeding system (Garcia's *sensory and gate channeling model*). Durlach and Rescorla (1980) provided the *within-compound association theory*, which describes TPOA through the formation of three associations: a taste–US association, an odor–US association, and a taste–odor association. Following taste + odor compound conditioning, presentation of the odor alone elicits the US representation directly through the odor → US pathway and indirectly through the odor → taste → US pathway. Therefore, the odor aversion produced by compound conditioning is strong because of the contribution of the direct and indirect pathways. In contrast, the control group that received odor-alone conditioning can only activate the direct odor → US pathway. One clear prediction of the within-compound association model is that changes to the indirect taste pathway (taste–US) should change responding to the odor.

In contrast, Garcia and his colleagues offered an explanation of TPOA based on Garcia's extensive research in flavor aversion learning, particularly his demonstrations of selective associations between taste and illness. Thus, the sensory and gate channeling model (Garcia, Lasiter, Bermudez-Rattoni, & Deems, 1985) arose from Garcia's findings that the nervous system uniquely processes information about taste and illness. In the sensory and gate channeling approach, sensory stimulation may be processed via the external defense system or the internal defense system. The external defense system has evolved to protect the organism from threats to the periphery such as shock, and auditory stimuli and visual stimuli would be processed effectively by this system. Gustatory stimuli are incorporated into the body, and they have direct access to the internal or gut defense system. Olfactory stimuli are more difficult to characterize because they could represent external dangers (e.g., smoke) or internal dangers (e.g., spoiled meat). If the odor is experienced in conjunction with a taste, the taste can "gate" the odor into the internal defense system where it will be processed like a taste. Thus, in the sensory and gate channeling model, TPOA arises from the odor being experienced along with the taste at the time of conditioning. One prediction from this approach is that once the odor has been gated into the internal defense system, the strength of the taste can be increased or decreased with no change in responding to the odor.

The key experimental manipulation conducted to compare these accounts of TPOA has been postconditioning extinction of the potentiating taste. As stated earlier, the sensory and gate channeling theory would be supported if taste extinction had no effect on responding to the odor, but if taste extinction decreased responding to the odor this would support the within-compound association theory. The initial use of this procedure was reported by Durlach and Rescorla (1980). In their sixth study, they conducted four taste extinction trials after compound conditioning. During testing, rats drank significantly more of the odored solution that had its taste associate extinguished (a *mediated extinction effect*) than the single-element odored solution or the odored solution that did not have its taste associate extinguished. Thus, they concluded that the integrity of the taste aversion at the time of testing is crucial for TPOA, and their data provided support for their within-compound association model. Many subsequent reports have replicated the finding that postconditioning extinction of the taste eliminated TPOA relative to groups that had received compound conditioning without taste extinction (e.g., Batsell et al., 2001; J. S. Miller et al., 1986; Trost & Batsell, 2004; von Kluge et al., 1996; Westbrook et al., 1983). Yet, the opposite pattern of results also has been reported (Lett, 1984). Lett reported that all compound conditioning groups evinced equally robust TPOA, despite their differential history with taste extinction. To complicate matters further, experimental attempts aimed at resolving the differences between these reports added further to the debate. Droungas and LoLordo (1991) used the same basic procedures in two experiments; they showed no changes (Experiment 1) or a weakening (Experiment 2) in the strength of the odor aversion after postconditioning taste extinction. The inability to obtain clear support for one account of TPOA with the postconditioning taste extinction procedure has been a limitation in this field, but the majority of studies have provided support for the within-compound association account. Moreover, the aforementioned results of odor-potentiated taste aversions (Slotnick et al., 1997) would be contrary to the sensory and gate channeling model's proposal that only taste cues can gate stimuli into the internal defense system. One final deficit of the sensory and gate channeling model is that there are no provisions within the model to account for why the salience of the stimuli is a determinant of TPOA. Taken together, the TPOA evidence accumulated over the past 20 years is inconsistent with the sensory and gate channeling model.

Although more evidence has supported the within-compound association account of TPOA, recent work from our labs has called this explanation into question as well. Over the past decade, in conjunction with John Batson, we have examined synergistic flavor aversion conditioning in variations of the A+/AX+ designs to resolve the long-standing debate of the mechanism of TPOA. In particular, considering that the majority of the data have favored the within-compound association model, we have tested various predictions of the within-compound association model. If the within-compound association model is correct, not only should extinction manipulations be able to influence responding to the elements of the compound, but postconditioning inflation of one of the elements (A+) of the compound AX should also increase responding to the other element (X) of the compound. This prediction was based on the idea that postconditioning taste inflation would strengthen the indirect odor → taste → illness pathway (specifically, the taste–illness component) and, thus, increase TPOA. We conducted a series of four AX+/A+ experiments to test the within-compound association model (Batsell, Trost, Cochran, Blankenship, & Batson, 2003). For example, in Experiment 1, following odor + taste compound conditioning, a subsequent taste + LiCl trial was administered. A group that received compound conditioning followed by taste inflation (AX+/A+) demonstrated a significantly stronger odor aversion than controls that only received taste + odor compound conditioning (AX+), confirming that postconditioning taste inflation increased the significant potentiated odor aversion. Furthermore, the reciprocal effect was shown in Experiments 3 and 4: Odor inflation following taste + odor compound conditioning (AX+/A+ training) produced

a significantly stronger taste aversion relative to the taste aversion of controls that only received taste + odor compound conditioning (AX+) or generalization training (A+/X+). Also, Experiments 2 and 4 confirmed the specificity of this effect because the increase in responding to Stimulus X was only observed when its conditioning associate was inflated (AX+/A+ training), but not when a novel Stimulus B was inflated (AX+/B+ training). Collectively, these results provide strong support for the hypothesis that within-compound associations form during a single taste + odor conditioning trial and that the inflation manipulation is an effective means of demonstrating these associations. Further, these results provide additional evidence that contradicts the prediction of the sensory and gate channeling model that postconditioning manipulations would have no effect on aversion strength.

Interestingly, these results indicate that the within-compound association is bidirectional because taste inflation increased responding to the odor (Experiments 1 and 2) and odor inflation increased responding to the taste (Experiments 3 and 4). If the within-compound association model is correct, a bidirectional taste–odor association should simultaneously increase responding to both odor *and* taste. Yet, this prediction is inconsistent with the results of numerous experiments that have shown that following compound conditioning, responding to the odor is enhanced relative to odor-alone controls, but responding to the taste either is not affected or is overshadowed relative to taste-alone controls (e.g., Bowman, Batsell, & Best, 1992; Westbrook et al., 1983). Therefore, even though the inflation experiment results provide strong evidence for the presence of a within-compound association, the bidirectionality of the association is problematic for the within-compound association model of TPOA.

Although it appears that within-compound associations can form during taste + odor compound conditioning, they may not be sufficient to produce TPOA. To test this hypothesis, a taste inflation experiment and a taste extinction experiment were conducted using a weak concentration of taste and a strong concentration of odor that would *not* produce TPOA (Schnelker & Batsell, 2006). The logic of these studies was that, if within-compound associations can be demonstrated in the absence of TPOA, the within-compound association cannot be the complete explanation. Three groups were the same in each experiment: Group A– was the unpaired odor/illness group; Group A+ was the single-element odor group; Group AX+ was the taste + odor conditioning group. Experiment 1 also included Group AX+/A+, which was the post-conditioning taste inflation group. Experiment 2 also included Group AX+/A–, which received three postconditioning taste extinction trials. In Experiment 1, the postconditioning taste inflation group, Group AX+/A+, drank significantly less than the other groups, and Groups AX+ and A+ did not differ significantly. In Experiment 2, the postconditioning taste extinction group, Group AX+/A–, drank significantly more AL odor solution than Groups A+ and AX+, which did not differ from each other. Collectively, these two experiments point to the same conclusion: Using experimental procedures that in the past have supported the presence of within-compound associations, Schnelker and Batsell found evidence of within-compound associations, but the presence of these within-compound associations (without additional treatment such as A+ trials) was not sufficient to produce TPOA. Schnelker and Batsell proposed that within-compound associations may form during taste + odor compound conditioning; but if only compound conditioning is conducted, these within-compound associations do not influence responding.

Even though the work of Schnelker and Batsell (2006) demonstrated that within-compound associations are not sufficient to produce TPOA, this demonstration occurred with cues that do not produce TPOA. More recently, Batson, Watkins, Doyle, and Batsell (in press) obtained evidence of a within-compound association in the absence of TPOA with cues that reliably produce TPOA. This series of experiments compared the odor aversions produced by A+/AX+ conditioning and AX+/A+ conditioning when A was AL odor and X was DEN in concentrations that have produced TPOA in previous studies (e.g., Batsell et al., 2003). In multiple experiments, AX+/A+ conditioning produced a significantly stronger odor aversion than A+/AX+ conditioning. A subsequent experiment indicated that the stronger AL aversion following AX+/A+ conditioning was due to the absence of TPOA following A+/AX+ conditioning. One explanation for this absence was that prior odor aversion conditioning (A+) prevented the formation of the taste–odor within-compound association during subsequent AX+ conditioning. The key experiment to test this

hypothesis employed both A+/AX+ and AX+/A+ conditioning, followed by extinction of the taste (X). If the within-compound association hypothesis was correct, taste extinction should only have an effect on AX+/A+ conditioning but not following A+/AX+ conditioning. Yet, this was not the case. Taste extinction significantly reduced the strength of the odor aversion relative to nonextinguished controls after both conditioning procedures. Therefore, this study confirmed that the presence of a within-compound association is not sufficient to produce TPOA even with concentrations of taste and odor that have repeatedly produced TPOA.

Taken together, these results indicate limitations in the within-compound association account of TPOA. It is important to note that we have not claimed that within-compound associations do not form during taste + odor compound conditioning—we have shown that they do form—but that these associations are not the sole mechanism of TPOA. Instead, over the past few years, our interpretation of these results has borrowed from previous configural accounts of TPOA. The earliest configural account of TPOA was offered by Rescorla (1981). He proposed this account as an alternative to the within-compound association model offered by himself and Durlach. In 1985, Kucharski and Spear adopted a configural interpretation to account for their taste-potentiated taste aversion results, but as detailed elsewhere (Batsell & Blankenship, 2003), they were unable to support all of the predictions derived from their model. Later, Bouton et al. (1987) evoked a perceptual integration hypothesis, which is similar to a configural account, to accommodate their demonstrations of the importance of relative salience in producing potentiation. We have proposed the *configural–elemental model*, which assumes that both configural and elemental representations are formed during the initial presentation of the taste + odor compound. First, during taste + odor compound conditioning, the organism forms a configural representation of the taste + odor compound. Because this representation contains both taste and odor features, it will be more salient than either stimulus alone. During testing, if one of the elements of the compound is presented, responding to this element will reflect the generalization decrement from the salient compound to this element, similar to the generalization rule for overshadowing described by Pearce (2002) in his configural model. If the test stimulus is relatively weak by itself (e.g., odor), the generalization from the more salient compound will produce a significantly stronger aversion. If, on the other hand, the test stimulus is relatively strong by itself (e.g., taste), the generalization decrement from the compound to this stimulus will be much greater and a significantly weaker or overshadowed aversion will be recorded. Thus, the results of experiments that involve compound conditioning and element testing can be explained in terms of configural representations, and the many previous studies that have demonstrated the importance of the salience ratio are consistent with this interpretation. Second, during the initial odor + taste compound conditioning trial, a within-compound association also forms between the taste and the odor, but because the stimuli have only been experienced in combination, this within-compound association is latent and probably does not influence responding. However, following odor + taste compound conditioning, if extinction or inflation of either element is conducted, this will activate the within-compound association (presumably because the organism is now experiencing the element by itself), and produce mediated extinction or mediated conditioning, respectively. In this case, the activation of the within-compound association will produce an outcome that is consistent with predictions based on the within-compound association model, and the association will appear to be bidirectional (Batsell et al., 2003). One key component of this prediction is that within-compound associations should still be demonstrable with taste and odor stimuli that do *not* combine into a unique configural cue (i.e., do not produce TPOA; cf., Batson et al., in press; Schnelker & Batsell, 2006).

Application of the Configural–Elemental Model to Other Results

Taste + Odor Interactions

Another example of a TPOA data set that is consistent with the configural–elemental model, but inconsistent with the within-compound association model, is our recent work with taste + odor interactions (Trost & Batsell, 2004). Serendipitously, in a follow-up test of our inflation research (Batsell et al., 2003), we observed that following compound conditioning (orange odor [ORG] + DEN conditioning or AL + DEN conditioning), the potentiated ORG odor aversion was significantly stronger than the potentiated

AL odor aversion. This difference was surprising because we had chosen these two odors on the basis of pilot work that had shown that they produced odor aversions of equal strength. Thus, these data suggested that the strength of TPOA might depend on the unique interaction of specific tastes and odors. Moreover, this outcome was of importance because it contradicts a prediction derived from the within-compound association model: If two odors of similar salience are paired with the same taste, this should result in potentiated odor aversions of similar strength. This prediction is based on the premise that the increased responding observed to the potentiated odor is contributed by the indirect taste–illness association. Therefore, two odors with equivalent odor–illness associations and equivalent taste–illness associations should produce equivalent potentiated odor aversions.

Trost and Batsell (2004) conducted three experiments to examine taste + odor interactions in compound aversion conditioning. In Experiment 1, rats received odor-alone conditioning (AL–LiCl or ORG–LiCl) or taste + odor conditioning (DEN+AL–LiCl or DEN + ORG–LiCl). There were no differences in consumption of the odor-alone groups (Groups A+ and O+), but the potentiated ORG odor aversion was significantly stronger than the potentiated AL odor aversion (Group DO+ > Group DA+). This outcome is problematic for the within-compound association model because if the odor–illness pathway is equivalent (equal aversions in Groups O+ and A+), and the taste–illness pathway is equivalent (DEN conditioning), then the potentiated odor aversions should also be equal. Another possible interpretation of these differences to the potentiated ORG and AL odors could be consistent with the within-compound association model. If the taste aversion was stronger following DEN + ORG conditioning, the indirect ORG odor− > DEN− > illness association may have been stronger relative to the indirect AL odor− > DEN− > illness association, and this resulted in the stronger ORG odor aversion. To test for this possibility, we conducted DEN testing after the two odor tests. There was no difference in DEN consumption between the odor-alone groups, but Group AD+ drank significantly less DEN than Group OD+. The fact that the stronger DEN aversion was shown by the compound conditioning group with the weaker TPOA is contradictory to the within-compound association model.

To determine the source of these differences in TPOA, Experiments 2 and 3 were designed to investigate whether taste and odor interact to form a unique perceptual unit. If taste and odor combine to form a unique perceptual unit, extinction of the separate elements or the compound may reveal how the organism perceives the taste + odor compound. Specifically, the following predictions were tested: (1) Elemental extinction will result in stronger responding than compound extinction only for those cues that are perceived to be different from the compound; (2) The patterns of elemental extinction will be different depending on the identity of the odor (ORG vs. AL). Five groups of rats received odor + taste compound conditioning. Next, each group received extinction with a specific stimulus (water, odor, taste, odor + taste, or separate extinction of odor/taste). All groups were tested for their aversion to the odor + taste compound. ORG odor was used in Experiment 2 and AL odor was used in Experiment 3. In Experiment 2, ORG extinction resulted in a weaker compound aversion than taste extinction (Group O− > Group T−), and compound extinction resulted in a weaker compound aversion than taste extinction (Group OT− > Group T−). There was no difference between ORG extinction and compound extinction (Group O− = Group OT−). In Experiment 3, AL extinction and taste extinction resulted in similar aversions to the compound (Group O− = Group T−). In addition, extinction of the elements odor and taste resulted in stronger compound aversions than compound extinction (Group OT− > Group T−; Group OT- > Group O−). It appears that even though ORG odor and AL odor are quite similar when conditioned alone, combining ORG + DEN versus combining AL + DEN creates unique perceptual units that produce different outcomes. Following AL + DEN conditioning and ORG + DEN conditioning, testing of ORG versus AL produces a stronger CR to ORG than the CR to AL because the ORG odor is perceived to comprise a greater part of the ORG + DEN compound than is the AL odor in the AL + DEN compound. The present results and the above interpretation are inconsistent with predictions derived from the within-compound association model; instead, they are most consistent with the configural–elemental account in which the taste and odor are perceived as a unitary stimulus. Presently, too little data are available to make definitive predictions about the strength of the configural

representation and the consequent generalization to its elements.

Recovery with Delayed Testing

In addition to the previously described data, the configural–elemental model can also provide a plausible explanation for the recovery from overshadowing with delayed testing data presented at the beginning of this chapter. In this approach, because the odor + taste compound is processed as a single stimulus, responding to each cue reflects generalization from the salient compound. As described earlier, with the strong taste–weak odor compound, this produces an overshadowed taste aversion and a potentiated odor aversion. Furthermore, because generalization decrements flatten across time (e.g., Thomas et al., 1985), generalization should increase over time, and both the taste aversion and the odor aversion will be stronger at longer retention intervals. The configural–elemental approach allows for two distinct predictions. First, taste + odor combinations that produce potentiation of one element and overshadowing of the other may yield increased responding to both elements with delayed testing. In fact, there is already some evidence to support this prediction because Batsell and Best (1992b) reported that following taste + taste compound conditioning, both the overshadowed taste aversion and the potentiated taste aversion increased in strength across a 21-day interval (it should be noted that these results were confounded with weak aversions in all groups at 1-day testing). Second, because configuration of the cues is a necessary component in this approach, recovery across the retention interval will be observed only following simultaneous conditioning, but not after sequential conditioning.

The following experiments used manipulations of compound conditioning and retention interval to explore the recovery with delayed testing effect; portions of some of these experiments were also included in Paschall's thesis (1998). The initial two studies used DEN and AL odor in simultaneous conditioning, and they were based on the conditioning parameters used by Batsell and Best (1992b), with the exception that the short interval test was conducted 3 days postconditioning to eliminate short-term retention interval effects. Our work has shown that both taste aversions (e.g., Batsell & Best, 1992a, 1994) and odor aversions (Experiment 2, Paschall) are significantly weaker at a 1-day test, but that aversion strength stabilizes by 3 days after conditioning.

Fifty rats were matched to one of four groups, and the groups differed by retention interval (3 days vs. 21 days) and conditioning type (taste [T] vs. taste–odor compound [TO]). Group 3-T received the taste paired with LiCl and was tested 3 days after conditioning. Group 3-TO received the taste + odor compound paired with LiCl and was tested 3 days after conditioning. Group 21-T received taste paired with LiCl and was tested 21 days after conditioning. Group 21-TO received the taste + odor compound paired with LiCl and was tested 21 days after conditioning. During conditioning, each rat received 10-min access to 10 ml of their target fluid. Following a 15-min CS–US interval, these rats were injected with LiCl. Rats were conditioned on different days, but tested on the same day. The primary comparison of interest in this and in subsequent experiments was between the groups that received compound conditioning and were tested at the short (3 days) and long (21 days) retention intervals.

Figure 10.1 displays the mean DEN intake of the four groups at testing. Group 3-TO drank

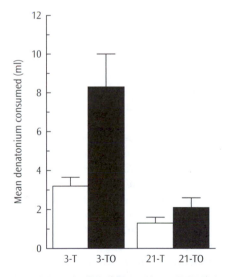

Figure 10.1. Mean (+SE) denatonium (DEN) intake in milliliters of the four groups on Test 1. Groups 3-T and 21-T received a pairing of DEN with LiCl, and Groups 3-TO and 21-TO received a simultaneous presentation of DEN and almond (AL) odor followed by LiCl. Groups 3-T and 3-TO were tested 3 days after conditioning whereas Groups 21-T and 21-TO were tested 21 days after conditioning.

the most DEN, and the comparison with Group 3-T shows a significant overshadowing effect. However, Groups 21-TO and 21-T drank equivalent amounts of DEN, suggesting that overshadowing had diminished across the 21-day retention interval The 2×2 ANOVA yielded a significant retention interval effect, $F(1, 46) = 19.6$, a significant conditioning effect, $F(1, 46) = 10.3$, and a significant retention interval $\times$ conditioning interaction, $F(1, 46) = 5.5$. The planned comparisons confirmed that Group 21-TO drank significantly less than Group 3-TO, $t(23) = 3.5$, but a significant difference was not seen between the two control groups (3-T vs. 21-T).

Because previous explanations of this phenomenon focused on covariation in the taste and odor aversions across time (J. S. Miller et al., 1990), one experimental goal was to assess whether increases in the taste aversion across time were accompanied by loss of the odor aversion at the longer retention interval. Therefore, an AL odor test was given after the single taste test. As expected, Groups 3-T and 21-T, which had never received the odor, drank large amounts, 18.1 ml (SE = 1.9) and 19.2 ml (SE = 1.0), respectively. This outcome confirms that generalization of the DEN aversion to a novel AL odor does not increase across the retention interval. Notably, Group 21-TO ($M = 5.6$ ml; SE = 1.2) drank less AL odor solution than Group 3-TO ($M = 10.5$ ml; SE = 1.7). The 2×2 ANOVA conducted over the AL odor intakes yielded a significant conditioning effect, $F(1, 46) = 41.3$, and a significant retention interval $\times$ conditioning interaction, $F(1, 46) = 4.1$. The planned comparison confirmed that Group 21-TO drank significantly less AL odor solution than Group 3-TO, $t(23) = 2.3$. There was a significant *increase* in the CR to the odor across the 21-day retention interval in the compound group. A subsequent experiment that included odor-alone controls and tested the odor aversion prior to the taste aversion replicated the finding that TPOA produced via simultaneous conditioning is significantly stronger at a 21-day interval ($M = 2.5$; SE = 0.6) than at a 3-day interval ($M = 6.2$; SE = 0.6), $t(35) = 4.5$.

The taste test outcome replicates the finding that an overshadowed taste aversion recovers across a long retention interval (c.f., Batsell & Best, 1992b; J. S. Miller et al., 1990; Kraemer et al., 1988), and the odor test outcome replicates the observation that a potentiated aversion increases across a retention interval (Batsell & Best, 1992b). These results advance this research in two respects. First, the odor test showed that the recovery of the overshadowed taste aversion was not accompanied by any loss in responding to the odor. This outcome contradicts the prediction that the strength of the elements of the compound covaries across the retention interval. Although the odor test may be influenced by the previous taste test, there is no evidence that extinction of a potentiating taste *increases* a potentiated aversion (cf., Davis et al., 1988; Durlach & Rescorla, 1980; Lett, 1984). Second, the evidence from the odor test suggests that an odor aversion can increase across a retention interval. This outcome contradicts the retrievability hypothesis of J. S. Miller et al. that proposed that only taste cues increase in strength across a retention interval.

In two later experiments we investigated recovery from sequential overshadowing after delayed testing. The study that examined an overshadowed taste aversion used 47 naïve rats as subjects matched to four groups. The groups were labeled as in the previous experiment, but a hyphen is used to separate the taste and odor symbols (T-O) to represent sequential conditioning: 3-T, 3-T-O, 21-T, and 21-T-O. During conditioning, all rats received 10-min access to 10 ml of DEN. Once these bottles were removed, the single-element controls (T) were given 10 ml of water for 10 min while the compound groups (O-T) were given 10 ml of AL odor solution for 10 min. All rats received the LiCl injection 5 min after removal of the second bottle. This interval was chosen because the interval between termination of the target CS (DEN) and the US would be the same as in simultaneous experiments (i.e., 15 min).

Figure 10.2 shows the group's mean DEN intake on the initial taste test. Overshadowing occurred at both retention intervals, $F(1, 43) = 12.2$, as the single-element controls drank significantly less than the compound element groups, but there was no recovery from overshadowing across the retention interval or differences in the control groups. Two additional taste tests were conducted to determine if any changes occurred across the retention interval; the only observed change was a significant *weakening* of the taste aversion in Group 21-T-O relative to Group 3-T-O on Test Day 2. Finally, there were no differences between the compound groups on an odor test. These results are intriguing because they show no recovery in responding

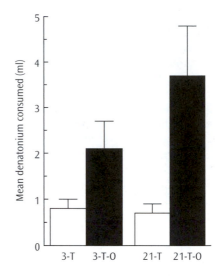

Figure 10.2. Mean (+SE) denatonium (DEN) intake in milliliters of the four groups on Test 1. Groups 3-T and 21-T received a pairing of DEN with LiCl, and Groups 3-T-O and 21-T-O received a sequential presentation of DEN, almond (AL) odor, and then LiCl. Groups 3-T and 3-T-O were tested 3 days after conditioning whereas Groups 21-T and 21-T-O were tested 21 days after conditioning.

across the retention interval to either the overshadowed taste or the overshadowing odor after sequential conditioning. This outcome suggests that the recovery of the overshadowed taste aversion across time is dependent on the simultaneous stimulus presentation during conditioning.

A final experiment was conducted to explore the effects of delayed testing on an overshadowed odor aversion following sequential conditioning. The design of this study mirrored the design just described with the one procedural difference during conditioning being that all groups received 10 ml of AL odor solution for 10 min prior to 10-min access to water (O Groups) or 10-min access to DEN (O-T Groups; i.e., order of the cues was reversed). All rats received two AL odor tests. Figure 10.3 displays the mean AL odor solution consumed by the four groups on Test 1. It can be seen that there was a significant conditioning effect, $F(1, 42) = 9.0$, as overshadowing was seen at both retention intervals, but there was no recovery in overshadowing across the retention interval. The other effects were not statistically significant. These differences remained unchanged on a second odor test.

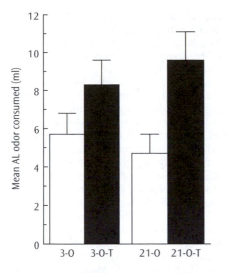

Figure 10.3. Mean (+SE) almond (AL) odor solution intake in milliliters of the four groups on Test 1. Groups 3-O and 21-O received a pairing of denatonium (DEN) with LiCl, and Groups 3-O-T and 21-O-T received a sequential presentation of AL odor solution, DEN, and then LiCl. Groups 3-O and 3-O-T were tested 3 days after conditioning whereas Groups 21-O and 21-O-T were tested 21 days after conditioning.

Collectively, these studies indicate that recovery from overshadowing with delayed testing only occurs within simultaneous conditioning preparations with these stimuli. Therefore, interpretation of this effect should center on learning during the co-presentation of stimuli. Furthermore, these outcomes confirm that increases across the retention interval may not be specific to the overshadowed element or to taste cues. Instead, the results of the preliminary experiments are most consistent with interpretations based on the configural–elemental model. Other unique predictions may be generated from this approach including an exploration of the experiences that may increase or decrease the organism's tendency to configure stimuli.

CONCLUSIONS

One of the enduring theoretical questions of the past 45 years of associative learning research is whether CTA operates by different rules of learning than other types of classical conditioning. One of the areas in which CTA experimentation has produced different results is in regard to compound conditioning. This chapter reviewed some of the results from compound conditioning experiments with a substantial focus on TPOA. In our opinion, the theoretical interpretation that best accommodates the TPOA data is the configural–elemental model, however, the model has yet to be extended to other examples of synergistic conditioning. One obvious next step would be to determine if taste–taste potentiation could be explained with this model; it may be harder to accommodate examples of taste-potentiated auditory aversions and taste-potentiated visual aversions within the configural–elemental framework because it may be more difficult for the organism to configure those combinations of stimuli. Instead, the within-compound association approach may still be the best explanatory framework for these phenomena. Similarly, it is possible that the configural–elemental approach may only be applicable to situations involving tastes and odors or cues that can be rapidly processed as a unitary stimulus. In other words, a few reasons why potentiation-like effects are rarely seen with other classical conditioning preparations include (1) the identity of the cues or their mode of presentation prevents the organism from configuring the cues into a unitary stimulus and (2) the need to conduct multiple training trials allows the organism to discriminate the cues into separate elements. Nonetheless, if experimental preparations can be designed to foster rapid configuration, synergistic conditioning may be observed in other situations as well. Suffice it to say, these directions for future experimentation are numerous and should prove to be quite fruitful.

Regarding the mechanism(s) underlying overshadowing in CTA, the best candidate at this time may be an acquisition-deficit model, perhaps based on the allocation of attentional resources and stimulus characteristics (e.g., intensity, salience, novelty). As detailed earlier, the configural–elemental approach provides a plausible explanation of the recovery from overshadowing with delayed testing phenomenon, and our data suggest that this phenomenon is more an artifact of taste + odor compound conditioning than changes in the strength of the CS–US association across time. As such, there may be no reliable evidence of recovery from overshadowing within the CTA literature from either delayed testing or postconditioning extinction (e.g., Schachtman et al., 1992). The absence of recovery from overshadowing in CTA following postconditioning extinction of the overshadowing stimulus may be another unique aspect of compound conditioning in CTA research, but too little is known at this point to make such a claim. Most of the CTA studies we reviewed here showed that using the AX+/A– design produced a weaker CR to X, commonly termed *mediated extinction*. This outcome is of interest because recent conditioned suppression experiments using the AX+/A– design have reported a stronger CR to X, termed *retrospective revaluation*. Presently, it is clear that both mediated extinction and retrospective revaluation can be obtained with conditioned suppression methodology (Shevill & Hall, 2004), and that the presence of retrospective revaluation may depend on the salience of the A cue (Liljeholm & Balleine, 2006). There has been some work showing that retrospective revaluation and mediated conditioning can occur with CTA methodology (Dwyer, 2003), but much more research is needed to determine if the mechanisms mediating these effects are different across classical conditioning preparations. In conclusion, the results from compound conditioning experiments continue to provide compelling evidence to suggest that different mechanisms may operate in taste aversion learning, and there is every reason to expect this debate to stimulate more research.

References

Batsell, W. R., & Batson, J. D. (1999). Augmentation of taste conditioning by a preconditioned odor. *Journal of Experimental Psychology: Animal Behavior Processes, 25*, 374–388.

Batsell, W. R., Jr., & Best, M. R. (1992a). Investigation of replacement fluids and retention-interval effects in taste-aversion learning. *Bulletin of the Psychonomic Society, 30*, 414–416.

Batsell, W. R., Jr., & Best, M. R. (1992b). Variations in the retention of taste aversions: Evidence for retrieval competition. *Animal Learning & Behavior, 20*, 146–159.

Batsell, W. R., Jr., & Best, M. R. (1994). The role of US novelty in short-term retention-interval effects in taste-aversion learning. *Animal Learning & Behavior, 22*, 332–340.

Batsell, W. R., Jr., & Blankenship, A. G. (2003). Beyond potentiation: Synergistic conditioning in flavor-aversion learning. *Brain & Mind, 3*, 383–408.

Batsell, W. R., Jr., Paschall, G. Y., Gleason, D. I., & Batson, J. D. (2001). Taste preconditioning augments odor-aversion learning. *Journal of Experimental Psychology: Animal Behavior Processes, 27*, 30–47.

Batsell, W. R., Jr., Trost, C. A., Cochran, S., Blankenship, A., & Batson, J. D. (2003). Effects of postconditioning inflation on odor + taste compound conditioning. *Learning & Behavior, 31*, 173–184.

Batson, J. D., & Batsell, W. R., Jr. (2000). Augmentation, not blocking, in an A+/AX+ flavor-conditioning procedure. *Psychonomic Bulletin & Review, 7*, 466–471.

Batson, J. D., & Best, P. J. (1979). Drug-preexposure effects in flavor-aversion learning: Associative interference by conditioned environmental stimuli. *Journal of Experimental Psychology: Animal Behavior Processes, 5*, 273–283.

Batson, J. D., Watkins, J. H., Doyle, K., & Batsell, W. R. Jr. (in press). Differences in taste-potentiated odor aversions with O+/OT+ vs. OT+/O+ conditioning implications for configural associations. *Learning & Behavior.*

Best, M. R., Batson, J. D., Meachum, C. L., Brown, E. R., & Ringer, M. (1985). Characteristics of taste-mediated environmental potentiation in rats. *Learning and Motivation, 16*, 190–209.

Best, M. R., Brown, E. R., & Sowell, M. K. (1984). Taste-mediated potentiation of noningestional stimuli in rats. *Learning and Motivation, 15*, 244–258.

Best, M. R., & Meachum, C. L. (1986). The effect of stimulus preexposure on taste-mediated environmental conditioning: Potentiation of overshadowing. *Animal Learning & Behavior, 14*, 1–5.

Boakes, R. A., Westbrook, R. F., & Barnes, B. W. (1992). Potentiation by a taste of a toxicosis-based context conditioning: Effects of varying the test fluid. *Quarterly Journal of Experimental Psychology, 45B*, 303–325.

Bond, N. W. (1983). Reciprocal overshadowing in flavour-aversion learning. *Quarterly Journal of Experimental Psychology B, 35*, 265–274.

Bouton, M. E. (2006). *Learning and behavior: A contemporary synthesis.* Sunderland, MA: Sinauer Associates, Inc.

Bouton, M. E., Dunlap, C. M., & Swartzentruber, D. (1987). Potentiation of taste by another taste during compound aversion learning. *Animal Learning & Behavior, 15*, 433–438.

Bouton, M. E., Jones, D. L., McPhillips, S. A., & Swartzentruber, D. (1986). Potentiation and overshadowing in odor-aversion learning: Role of method of odor presentation, the distal–proximal cue distinction, and the conditionability of odor. *Learning and Motivation, 17*, 115–138.

Bouton, M. E., & Whiting, M. R. (1982). Simultaneous odor–taste and taste–taste compounds in poison-avoidance learning. *Learning and Motivation, 13*, 472–494.

Bowman, M. T., Batsell, W. R. Jr., & Best, M. R. (1992). Evidence that stimulus generalization does not determine taste-mediated odor potentiation. *Bulletin of the Psychonomic Society, 30,* 241–243.

Clarke, J. C., Westbrook, R. F., & Irwin, J. (1979). Potentiation instead of overshadowing in the pigeon. *Behavioral & Neural Biology, 25,* 18–29.

Coburn, K. L., Garcia, J., Kiefer, S. W., & Rusiniak, K. W. (1984). Taste potentiation of poisoned odor by temporal contiguity. *Behavioral Neuroscience, 98,* 813–819.

Davis, S. F., Best, M. R., & Grover, C. A. (1988). Toxicosis-mediated potentiation in a taste/taste compound: Evidence for within-compound associations. *Learning and Motivation, 19,* 183–205.

Davis, S. F., Best, M. R., Grover, C. A., Bailey, S. A., Freeman, B. L., & Mayleben, M. A. (1990). The effects of taste extinction on ingestional potentiation in weanling rats. *Animal Learning & Behavior, 18,* 444–452.

Domjan, M. (1980). Ingestional aversion learning: Unique and general processes. In J. S. Rosenblatt, R. A. Hinde, C. Beer, & M. C. Busnel (Eds.), *Advances in the study of behaviour* (Vol. 11, pp. 275–336). New York: Academic Press.

Droungas, A., & LoLordo, V. M. (1991). Taste-mediated potentiation of odor aversion induced by lithium chloride: Effects of preconditioning exposure to the conditioned stimulus and postconditioning extinction of the taste aversion. *Learning and Motivation, 22,* 291–310.

Durlach, P. J., & Rescorla, R. A. (1980). Potentiation rather than overshadowing in flavor-aversion learning: An analysis in terms of within-compound associations. *Journal of Experimental Psychology: Animal Behavior Processes, 6,* 175–187.

Dwyer, D. M. (2003). Learning about cues in their absence: Evidence from flavour preferences and aversions. *Quarterly Journal of Experimental Psychology, 56B,* 56–67.

Ellins, S. R., Cramer, R. E., & Whitmore, C. (1985). Taste potentiation of auditory aversions in rats: A case for spatial contiguity. *Journal of Comparative Psychology, 99,* 108–111.

Ellins, S. R., & von Kluge, S. (1987). Preexposure and extinction effects of lithium chloride induced taste-potentiated aversions for spatially contiguous auditory food cues in rats. *Behavioral Neuroscience, 101,* 164–169.

Ellins, S. R., & von Kluge, S. (1990). Auditory food cue conditioning: Effects of spatial contiguity and taste quality. *Quarterly Journal of Experimental Psychology, 42B,* 73–86.

Ferry, B., Sandner, G., & Di Scala, G. (1995). Neuroanatomical and functional specificity of the basolateral amygdaloid nucleus in taste-potentiated odor aversion. *Neurobiology of Learning & Memory, 64,* 169–180.

Galef, B. G., & Osborne, B. (1978). Novel taste facilitation of the association of visual cues with toxicosis in rats. *Journal of Comparative and Physiological Psychology, 92,* 907–916.

Garcia, J., Ervin, F. R., & Koelling, R. A. (1966). Learning with prolonged delay of reinforcement. *Psychonomic Science, 5,* 121–122.

Garcia, J., & Koelling, R. A. (1966). Relation of cue to consequence in avoidance learning. *Psychonomic Science, 4,* 123–124.

Garcia, J., Lasiter, P. S., Bermudez-Rattoni, F., & Deems, D. A. (1985). A general theory of aversion learning. In N. S. Braveman & P. Bronstein (Eds.), *Experimental assessments and clinical applications of conditioned food aversions* (Annals of the New York Academy of Sciences, Vol. 443, pp. 8–21). New York: New York Academy of Sciences.

Gillan, D. J., & Domjan, M. (1977). Taste-aversion conditioning with expected versus unexpected drug treatment. *Journal of Experimental Psychology: Animal Behavior Processes, 3,* 297–309.

Hatfield, T., & Gallagher, M. (1995). Taste-potentiated odor conditioning: Impairment produced by infusion of an N-methyl-D-aspartate antagonist into basolateral amygdala. *Behavioral Neuroscience, 109,* 663–668.

Holder, M. D., Bermudez-Rattoni, F., & Garcia, J. (1988). Taste-potentiated noise–illness associations. *Behavioral Neuroscience, 102,* 363–370.

Holder, M. D., & Garcia, J. (1987). Role of temporal order and odor intensity in taste-potentiated odor aversions. *Behavioral Neuroscience, 101,* 158–163.

Jackson, R. L., & Fritsche, M. B. (1989). Potentiation and overshadowing in pigeons. *Learning and Motivation, 20,* 15–35.

Kalat, J. W., & Rozin, P. (1970). "Salience": A factor which can override temporal contiguity in taste-aversion learning. *Journal of Comparative and Physiological Psychology, 71,* 192–197.

Kalat, J. W., & Rozin, P. (1972). You can lead a rat to poison but you can't make him think. In M. E. P. Seligman & J. Hager (Eds.), *Biological boundaries of learning* (pp. 115–122). New York: Appleton-Century-Crofts.

Kamin, L. J. (1969). Predictability, surprise, attention, and conditioning. In B. A. Campbell & R. M. Church (Eds.), *Punishment and aversive behaviour* (pp. 279–296). New York: Appleton-Century-Crofts.

Kaufman, M. A., & Bolles, R. C. (1981). A nonassociative aspect of overshadowing. *Bulletin of the Psychonomic Society, 18,* 319–320.

Kiefer, S. W., Rusiniak, K. W., & Garcia, J. (1982). Flavor–illness aversions: Gustatory neocortex ablations disrupt taste but not taste-potentiated odor cues. *Journal of Comparative & Physiological Psychology, 96,* 540–548.

Kraemer, P. J., Lariviere, N. A., & Spear, N. E. (1988). Expression of a taste aversion conditioned with an odor–taste compound: Overshadowing is relatively weak in weanlings and decreases over a retention interval in adults. *Animal Learning & Behavior, 16,* 164–168.

Kucharski, D., & Spear, N. E. (1985). Potentiation and overshadowing in preweanling and adult rats. *Journal of Experimental Psychology: Animal Behavior Processes, 11,* 15–34.

Lett, B. T. (1980). Taste potentiates color-sickness associations in pigeons and quail. *Animal Learning & Behavior, 8,* 193–198.

Lett, B. T. (1984). Extinction of taste aversion does not eliminate taste potentiation of an odor aversion in rats or color aversion pigeons. *Animal Learning & Behavior, 12,* 414–420.

Liljeholm, M., & Balleine, B. W. (2006). Stimulus salience and retrospective revaluation. *Journal of Experimental Psychology: Animal Behavior Processes, 32,* 481–487.

Lindsey, G. P., & Best, P. J. (1973). Overshadowing of the less salient of two novel fluids in a taste-aversion paradigm. *Physiological Psychology, 1,* 13–15.

Logue, A. W. (1979). Taste aversion and the generality of the laws of learning. *Psychological Bulletin, 86,* 276–296.

Matzel, L. D., Schachtman, T. R., & Miller, R. R. (1985). Recovery of an overshadowed association achieved by extinction of the overshadowing stimulus. *Learning and Motivation, 16,* 398–412.

Matzel, L. D., Shuster, K., & Miller, R. R. (1987). Covariation in conditioned response strength between stimuli trained in compound. *Animal Learning & Behavior, 15,* 439–447.

Miller, J. S., Jagielo, J. A., & Spear, N. E. (1990). Changes in the retrievability of associations to elements of the compound CS determine the expression of overshadowing. *Animal Learning & Behavior, 18,* 157–161.

Miller, J. S., McCoy, D. F., Kelly, K. S., & Bardo, M. T. (1986). A within-event analysis of taste-potentiated odor and contextual aversions. *Animal Learning & Behavior, 14,* 15–21.

Miller, R. R., Barnet, R. C., & Grahame, N. J. (1995). Assessment of the Rescorla–Wagner model. *Psychological Bulletin, 117,* 363–386.

Paschall, G. Y. (1998). *Retention of single-element and compound-element ingestional aversions.* Unpublished Master's Thesis, Southern Methodist University, Dallas.

Pavlov, I. J. (1927). *Conditioned reflexes.* London: Oxford University Press.

Pearce, J. M. (2002). Evaluation and development of a connectionist theory of configural learning. *Animal Learning & Behavior, 30,* 73–95.

Rescorla, R. A. (1981). Simultaneous associations. In P. Harzem & M. D. Zeiler (Eds.), *Predictability, correlation, and contiguity* (pp. 47–80). New York: Wiley.

Rescorla, R. A., & Wagner, A. R. (1972). A theory of Pavlovian conditioning: Variations in the effectiveness of reinforcement and nonreinforcement. In A. H. Black & W. F. Prokasy (Eds.), *Classical conditioning II: Current research and theories* (pp. 64–99). New York: Appleton-Century-Crofts.

Revusky, S. (1971). The role of interference in association over a delay. In W. K. Honig & P. H. R. James (Eds.), *Animal memory* (pp. 155–213). New York: Academic Press.

Revusky, S. H., & Bedarf, E. W. (1967). Association of illness with prior ingestion of novel foods. *Science, 155,* 219–220.

Revusky, S., Parker, L. A., & Coombes, S. (1977). Flavor aversion learning: Extinction of the aversion to an interfering flavor after conditioning does not affect the aversion to the reference flavor. *Behavioral Biology, 19,* 503–508.

Rusiniak, K. W., Hankins, W. G., Garcia, J., & Brett, L. P. (1979). Flavor–illness aversions: Potentiation of odor by taste in rats. *Behavioral & Neural Biology, 25,* 1–17.

Schachtman, T. R., Kasprow, W. J., Meyer, R. C., Bourne, M. J., & Hart, J. A. (1992). Extinction of the overshadowing CS after overshadowing in conditioned taste aversion. *Animal Learning & Behavior, 20,* 207–218.

Schnelker, J., & Batsell, W. R., Jr. (2006). Within-compound associations are not sufficient to produce taste-mediated odor potentiation. *Behavioural Processes, 73,* 142–148.

Shevill, I., & Hall, G. (2004). Retrospective revaluation effects in the conditioned suppression procedure. *Quarterly Journal of Experimental Psychology: Comparative and Physiological Psychology, 57(B),* 331–347.

Slotnick, B. M., Westbrook, F., & Darling, F. M. C. (1997). What the rat's nose tells the rat's mouth: Long delay aversion conditioning with aqueous odors and potentiation of taste by odors. *Animal Learning & Behavior, 25,* 357–369.

Symonds, M., & Hall, G. (1999). Overshadowing not potentiation of illness-based contextual conditioning by a novel taste. *Animal Learning & Behavior, 27,* 379–390.

Thomas, D. R., Windell, B. T., Bakke, I., Kreye, J., Kimose, E., & Aposhyan, H. (1985). Long-term memory in pigeons: I. The role of discrimination problem difficulty assessed by reacquisition measures II. The role of stimulus modality assessed by generalization slope. *Learning and Motivation, 16,* 464–477.

Trost, C. A., & Batsell, W. R., Jr., (2004). Taste + odor interactions in compound aversion conditioning. *Learning & Behavior, 32,* 440–453.

von Kluge, S., Perkey, T., & Peregord, J. (1996). An ear for quality: Differential associative characteristics of taste-potentiated auditory and odor avoidance. *Physiology & Behavior, 60,* 331–339.

Westbrook, R. F., & Brookes, N. (1988). Potentiation and blocking of conditioned flavor and context aversions. *Quarterly Journal of Experimental Psychology, 1,* 3–30.

Westbrook, R. F., Clarke, J. C., & Provost, S. (1980). Long-delay learning in the pigeon: Flavor, color, and taste-mediated color aversions. *Behavioral and Neural Biology, 28,* 398–407.

Westbrook, R. F., Harvey, A., & Swinbourne, A. (1988). Potentiation by a novel flavour of conditioned place aversions based on both toxicosis and shock. *Quarterly Journal of Experimental Psychology B, 40,* 305–319.

Westbrook, R. F., Homewood, J., Horn, K., & Clarke, J. C. (1983). Flavour–odour compound conditioning: Odour-potentiation and flavour-attenuation. *Quarterly Journal of Experimental Psychology, 35B,* 13–33.

Willner, J. A. (1978). Blocking of a taste aversion by prior pairings of exteroceptive stimuli with illness. *Learning and Motivation, 9,* 125–140.

11

Representation-Mediated Food Aversions

PETER C. HOLLAND AND DANIEL S. WHEELER

In most mammals, pairing a flavored food with gastrointestinal malaise results in the subsequent avoidance and reduction of consumption of that food (e.g., Garcia & Kimeldorf, 1957). Although there is substantial evidence that such flavor aversion learning shares many features with other examples of associative learning, most researchers agree that it reflects a privileged system with impressive capabilities and unique specializations. For example, in rats, flavor aversions may be learned even when the flavor and illness experiences are separated by hours, and illness-induced aversions are much more readily acquired to flavor cues than to auditory, visual, or olfactory stimuli. Nevertheless, research conducted in the late 1970s and early 1980s suggested that these exteroceptive cues may gain access to this privileged system in rats through associative learning. We found that pairing auditory, visual, and olfactory cues with flavored foods endowed those cues with the ability to substitute for their flavor referents not only in the control of action but also in the acquisition of new learning about those flavors. For example, Holland (1981) found that rats would acquire an aversion to a flavored food if they were made ill after presentations of an auditory cue that, days before, had been paired with that food.

In accord with many learning theories of the time, Holland (1981) asserted that as a result of associative learning, conditioned stimuli (CSs) come to activate internal representations of the unconditioned stimuli (USs) with which they are paired. In a series of early

investigations supported by the US National Science Foundation and a more recent series supported by the National Institute of Mental Health, we explored the functions that could be served by such "associatively-activated event representations" (Hall, 1996), and the extent to which those representations shared properties with the events themselves, or more properly, internal representations activated directly by those events. Although most of those experiments exploited the unique properties of flavor aversion learning, they were intended to address basic questions about the features and functions of event representations in associative learning in general.

In this chapter, we first describe some basic *demonstrations* and *properties* of representation-mediated flavor aversion learning. Next, we describe experiments that examined the *contents* of learning that come under the control of exteroceptive cues for flavored foods, and that can later mediate learning of aversions to those foods. Finally, we discuss the studies that addressed the *conditions* under which such mediated learning may occur, as well as limitations on that learning.

DEMONSTRATIONS AND PROPERTIES OF REPRESENTATION-MEDIATED AVERSION LEARNING

As described in more detail in other chapters in this book (e.g., Balleine, Chapter 13), associatively activated representations often play an important role in the expression of learning. For example, at least early in training, a rat's lever pressing for food is apparently mediated by a representation or expectation of that food. If the rat subsequently learns an aversion to the food, its operant behavior will spontaneously decrease, even without further exposure to that food in the context of lever pressing. This outcome suggests that the current motivational value of the food influences conditioned responding. This chapter is primarily concerned with other functions served by associatively activated representations. For example, these representations can allow an animal to learn about absent stimuli, and can modulate learning about other cues in the same way as their directly activated counterparts.

Conditioning

In our first study (Table 11.1a; Holland, 1981), we sought to determine whether a flavor–illness association could be learned when an associatively activated flavor representation was paired with illness. Rats in Group FOR (forward pairings) received 16 pairings of a tone with a flavored food, designed to endow the tone with the ability to activate a representation of that food. Next, the tone was paired with an illness-inducing injection of lithium chloride (LiCl), in the absence of the food, in each of two sessions. Finally, consumption of the food was assessed in the rats' home cages, in the absence of the tone. If the tone-activated representation of the flavor entered into an association with illness, then consumption of the flavored food itself later would be reduced, relative to consumption of various control groups of rats that did not have the opportunity to associate a food representation with illness. Three control groups received tone–food but not tone–LiCl pairings (CTL1), tone–LiCl but not tone–food (CTL2) pairings, or backward food–tone and tone–LiCl pairings (BACK). Indeed, food consumption was significantly lower in Group FOR than in the each of the controls (Figure 11.1a), although not nearly as low as would be anticipated if the food had been directly paired with LiCl twice.

Subsequent experiments (Tables 11.1b and 11.1c; Holland, 1981, 1990) indicated that flavor properties of the associatively activated food representations were involved in these mediated aversions. In these experiments, different auditory or visual CSs were paired with foods that differed in various

Table 11.1a Outline of Procedures of Mediated Learning Experiment Shown in Figure 11.1a.

Group	Phase 1	Phase 2	Consumption Test
FOR	Tone → food	Tone → LiCl	Food
	Light → nothing	Light → nothing	
CTL1	Tone → food	Light → LiCl	Food
	Light → nothing	Tone → nothing	
CTL2	Tone → nothing	Tone → LiCl	Food
	Light → food	Light → nothing	
BACK	Food → tone	Tone → LiCl	Food
	Light → nothing	Light → nothing	

Table 11.1b Outline of Procedures of Mediated Learning Experiment Shown in Figure 11.1b.

Group	Phase 1	Phase 2	Consumption Test
One	Tone → sucrose	Tone → LiCl	Sucrose
	Light → food pellets	Light → nothing	Food pellets

Note: Three additional groups provided complete counterbalancing of the roles of tone and light in Phases 1 and 2.

Table 11.1c Outline of Procedures of Mediated Learning Experiment Shown in Figure 11.1c.

Group	Phase 1	Phase 2	Consumption Test
LiCl	Tone → wintergreen	Tone → LiCl	Wintergreen
	Noise → peppermint	Noise → nothing	Peppermint
Shock	Tone → wintergreen	Tone → shock	Wintergreen
	Noise → peppermint	Noise → nothing	Peppermint

Note: Additional groups provided complete counterbalancing of the roles of tone and noise in Phases 1 and 2. In addition, for half of the rats in each condition received the flavors as sucrose pellets and the other half received them as sucrose solutions.

properties (e.g., sucrose solutions vs. grain pellets or wintergreen vs. peppermint-flavored sucrose solutions). These foods were of equal palatability in most individual rats in the studies, as determined by consumption pretests. One CS was then paired with LiCl injection (in the absence of either food) and the other CS was presented alone. In subsequent consumption tests, consumption of both foods was reduced, but that reduction was significantly greater for the food whose CS partner had been paired with illness (Figure 11.1b and 11.1c).

Relation of Mediated Aversions to Sensory Preconditioning

Our account for these mediated aversions was that associations were formed between the absent flavor and illness when the auditory/visual CSs were paired with LiCl. Thus, we argued that these aversions exemplified *mediated learning*. An alternate account rejects the idea that new associations are acquired to absent events, and instead attributes these aversions to *mediated performance* at the time of the final consumption tests. By this account, the initial tone–food pairings establish backward, food–tone associations, and subsequent tone–LiCl pairings establish tone–illness associations. Presentation of food in the consumption test activates a representation of the tone, which in turn activates a representation of illness, suppressing consumption. Thus, the food aversion is based on a chain of associations, each of which was initially established between physically present events.

This account likens our mediated aversions to sensory preconditioning, in which two neutral stimuli are first paired in the absence of any reinforcer, and then one of those stimuli is directly paired with the reinforcer. In this procedure, the cue that receives direct reinforcement appears to mediate responding to the cue that receives no direct reinforcement (e.g., Rizley & Rescorla, 1972). As such, sensory preconditioning generally results in responding to both of the cues. In contrast, our representation-mediated food aversions did not appear to be mediated by tone–illness associations, but rather were manifested as the establishment of direct flavor–illness associations. Notably, in Holland's (1981) studies, responding to tones paired with LiCl was not reduced compared to responding to tones that were not paired with LiCl. Because the tone itself did not support aversive responding, Holland (1981) concluded that the tone–LiCl pairings allowed the flavor to form a direct association with illness. Furthermore, this sensory preconditioning or associative chaining account depends on the establishment of food–tone associations during initial tone–food pairings. Although some authors have argued that simple conditioning procedures often establish bidirectional associations, it is notable that in Holland's (1981) study, rats in a control group that received explicit food–tone pairings (Group BACK), which should have maximized the food's ability to activate a representation of the tone in testing, failed to show mediated aversion learning (Figure 11.1a).

Selective Association

A hallmark of flavor aversion learning is its substantial reinforcer-selectivity. For example, Garcia and Koelling (1966) observed that animals were more apt to form an aversion to a saccharin solution that was paired with an illness-inducing agent (e.g., LiCl or radiation) than if it was paired with an electric shock. In contrast, water that was distinguishable by a lick-contingent audiovisual stimulus

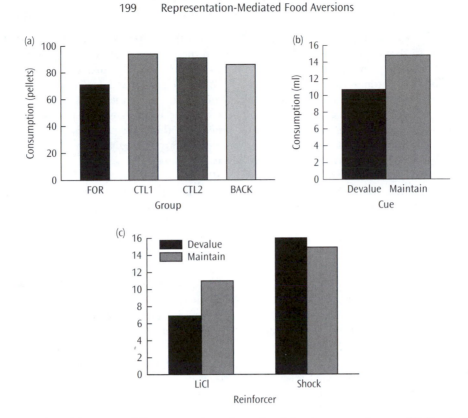

Figure 11.1. Mediated learning of flavor aversions. In each of the three experiments (Holland, 1981), an aversion was established to a flavored food by pairing an auditory cue that had been previously associated with that food, with the illness-inducing toxin, lithium chloride (LiCl). In (a) rats first received either tone → food (Groups FOR and CTL1), light → food (CTL2), or food → tone pairings in an experimental chamber. Then, the rats in Groups FOR, CTL2, and BACK received tone-alone presentations in those chambers, followed 10 min later by LiCl injection; Group CTL1 received light presentations in those sessions. Finally, food pellet consumption was assessed in the home cages in the absence of explicit cues (shown). Group FOR showed significantly less pellet consumption than the rats in each of the other three groups, which did not differ. In (b) each rat first received pairings of two cues (light and tone) with two reinforcers (food pellets and sucrose [counterbalanced]). Then, the rats received LiCl injections after either light-alone or tone-alone presentations. Finally, consumption of food pellets and sucrose was measured in the home cages on two successive days. Consumption of each reinforcer (sucrose consumption only shown) was significantly lower if its partner cue had been paired with LiCl (Devalue) than if it had not been paired (Maintain). In (c) all rats received one cue paired with peppermint food and another cue paired with wintergreen food (in half of the rats the two foods were both liquids and in the other half both were pellets). Then, one of those auditory cues was paired with either LiCl injection or foot shock. Finally, consumption of both foods was measured in the home cages. For rats that received LiCl, every rat showed less consumption of the food whose cue partner had been Devalued with LiCl, but for rats that received cue–shock pairings, food consumption was not affected (only consumption of liquid foods is shown).

was more readily avoided when it was associated with shock rather than LiCl. Garcia and Koelling concluded that animals were prepared to associate certain cues with specific consequences, according to adaptive specializations acquired in the course of evolution. Extensive experimentation later confirmed these observations. Although there is ample

evidence that rats can form flavor–pain and auditory/visual–illness associations (e.g., Delamater & Treit, 1988; Krane & Wagner, 1975), in most cases flavor–illness and auditory/visual–pain associations are formed far more readily.

Holland (1981, Experiment 3) found that an associatively activated representation of a flavor forms the same selective associations as directly activated representations. In that experiment (Table 11.1c), two auditory CSs were each paired with a different flavored food (e.g., tone–wintergreen, noise–peppermint). After this treatment, one of the CSs was reinforced either by LiCl (e.g., tone–LiCl) or by shock (tone–shock) in separate groups. In a subsequent extinction test of responding to the CSs, subjects suppressed food-cup-directed responding considerably more if the tone had been paired with shock than if it had been paired with LiCl. Thus, the tone itself was more readily associated with shock. However, a consumption test with the two different flavors showed the opposite result (Figure 11.1c). Rats suppressed intake of the flavor more if its representation had been paired with LiCl than if its representation had been paired with shock. Thus, the selective associations formed by associatively activated representations were similar to the selective associations observed by Garcia and Koelling (1966).

In contrast to Holland's (1981) study, Ward-Robinson and Hall (1996) conducted a series of experiments that indicated that an associatively activated flavor representation could readily enter into an association with shock. In their Experiment 1, rats received discrimination training in which one auditory stimulus signaled the delivery of flavored food, and another CS signaled nothing (CS1-food, CS2−). After this treatment, half of the subjects received pairings of CS1 with shock, and the other half received pairings of CS2 with shock. After this training, Ward-Robinson and Hall tested the rats' food preference by giving them lever press contingent access to the food, in the absence of either CS. Their latency data indicated that subjects pressed the lever less quickly if CS1 was paired with shock, which suggests that the food had become aversive through representation-mediated learning involving shock. Ward-Robinson and Hall asserted that they detected a flavor–shock association because their operant test of the food's reinforcing power was more sensitive to food–shock associations than Holland's consumption test. If selectivity of associations exists on a continuum, then Holland's observation can stand as evidence that an associatively activated representation maintains the cue-to-consequence properties of the original stimulus, whereas Ward-Robinson and Hall's observation indicates that an association can be formed between an associatively activated representation and shock under the appropriate circumstances.

Recently, we (Holland, in press) directly compared the sensitivity of operant reinforcement and consumption tests to mediated learning procedures. If Ward-Robinson and Hall's (1996) observation of mediated aversion learning with shock reinforcers was due to the greater sensitivity of their test procedure, then that procedure might reveal even more substantial mediated aversions if the tone CS was paired with illness, as in our experiments. We were especially interested in the alternative possibility that the reinforcement value of food might depend on different food attributes than food consumption. Thus, after tone–food pairings, whereas tone–LiCl pairings might especially reduce food consumption, tone–shock pairings might reduce the food's ability to serve as an operant reinforcer. In our first experiment (Table 11.2a), rats first received tone–food pairings, followed by either tone–shock or tone–LiCl pairings, with the other aversive reinforcer presented on intervening days in the absence of the tone. Finally, half of the rats in each of these two conditions received consumption tests and half received chain-pull acquisition tests, in which each chain pull resulted in the delivery of a food pellet. Consistent with Holland's (1981) data, we found that rats that received tone–LiCl pairings consumed fewer pellets than rats that received tone–shock pairings (Figure 11.2a). In contrast, rats that received tone–shock pairings performed fewer chain pulls than rats that received tone–LiCl pairings, confirming Ward-Robinson and Hall's (1996) observation of reduced operant reinforcement power of a food whose representation had been paired with shock. These data suggested that the operant procedure was not simply more sensitive than consumption testing, but rather tapped into different aspects of mediated learning about food.

A subsequent experiment considered a simpler account for these data (and most of Ward-Robinson and Hall's). It is possible that rats that received tone–shock pairings were punished for food-cup entry (because the tone elicited such responses) whereas rats that received tone–LiCl pairings were not. Although those latter rats received shock presentations in the absence of tone on alternate days, those shocks were less likely to occur when rats were in the food cup. During operant testing, rats that received tone–shock pairings may have shown reduced acquisition of chain-pull responding not because of a mediated food–shock association, but because of a reduced tendency to approach the food cup (and hence receive the food reinforcer). Thus, there may be no need to appeal to the notion of mediated conditioning of

Table 11.2a Outline of Procedures of Mediated Learning Experiment Shown in Figure 11.2a.

Group	Phase 1	Phase 2	Test
Consume–shock	Tone → food	Tone → shock LiCl	Food consumption
Consume–LiCl	Tone → food	Tone → LiCl; shock	Food consumption
Reinforce–shock	Tone → food	Tone → shock LiCl	Lever press → food
Reinforce–LiCl	Tone → food	Tone → LiCl; shock	Lever press → food

Note: In Phase 2, one aversive reinforcer was paired with tone and the other was presented alone on alternate days.

Table 11.2b Outline of Procedures of Mediated Learning Experiment Shown in Figure 11.2b.

Group	Phase 1	Phase 2	Test
Consume–shock	Tone → orange Light → grape	Tone → shock Light → nothing; LiCl	Orange consumption (devalue) Grape consumption (maintain)
Consume–LiCl	Tone → orange Light → grape	Tone → LiCl Light → nothing; shock	Orange consumption (devalue) Grape consumption (maintain)
Reinforce–shock	Tone → orange Light → grape	Tone → shock Light → nothing; LiCl	Lever press → orange (devalue) Chain pull → grape (maintain)
Reinforce–LiCl	Tone → orange Light → grape	Tone → LiCl Light → nothing; shock	Lever press → orange (devalue) Chain pull → grape (maintain)

Note: The roles of tone and light stimuli and lever-press and chain-pull responses were completely counterbalanced. In Phase 2, one aversive reinforcer was paired with tone and the other was presented alone on alternate days.

a flavor–shock association to account for reduced operant responding of rats that received tone–shock pairings. Furthermore, because consumption testing in Holland's experiments typically occurred in the home cage, such conditioned responses would be irrelevant to consumption.

To address these issues we conducted another experiment that minimized the impact of potential punishment of food-cup entry by using multiple CSs and foods delivered to a common food cup, as in Holland (1981, Experiment 3). In this experiment (Table 11.2b), rats first received pairings of two auditory/visual CSs with two liquid foods (orange or grape-flavored sucrose). Then, one CS (e.g., tone) was paired with either shock or LiCl and the other (e.g., light) was presented alone, on separate days. As in the earlier experiment, the other aversive reinforcer (LiCl or shock) was presented in the absence of either CS on separate days. Thus, any punishment of food-cup approach should be equivalent in all rats. Finally, consumption of food placed in the food cup was assessed in half of the rats, and for the other rats, the reinforcing power of each food was assessed with operant training of either a chain-pull or a lever-press response.

The left side of Figure 11.2b shows the results of the food-consumption tests. Rats that had received tone–LiCl pairings selectively reduced consumption of the food whose auditory partner had been paired with LiCl (LiCl-Devalue), relative to consumption of the other food (LiCl-Maintain), but rats that had received tone–shock pairings showed no such selectivity. Notably, the latter rats had received shocks after visits to the food cup, whereas rats that received tone–LiCl pairings received shocks in the absence of any CS that would have generated food-cup visits. Thus, the lower food consumption in the rats that received tone–shock pairings than consumption in the LiCl-Maintain condition likely reflected conditioning of fear of the food cup or punishment of food-cup visits. Alternately, tone–shock pairings may have devalued an attribute common to both foods, although the results of Holland's (1981) experiment (Figure 11.1c) in which no such suppression of consumption was observed when food consumption was assessed in the home cage, suggests otherwise.

The right side of Figure 11.2b shows the results of the operant reinforcement tests. In two tests, given in counterbalanced order, each chain pull or lever press was reinforced with the flavored food whose CS partner

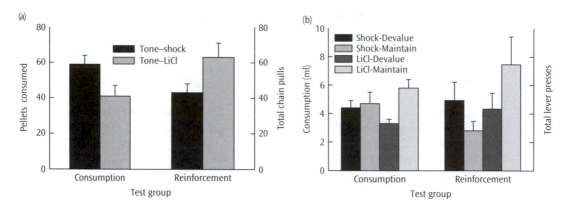

Figure 11.2. Comparison of mediated food aversion learning, measured by food consumption tests or by the ability of the foods to reinforce learning of a new operant response. In (a) all rats first received tone–food pairings. Half of the rats then received tone–shock pairings and the other half received tone–LiCl pairings. Each of those two groups was then subdivided into rats tested for consumption (left side of [a]) or operant reinforcement power (right side of [a]) of the food pellets. Rats that received tone–LiCl pairings consumed fewer pellets than those that received tone–shock pairings, but rats that received tone–shock pairings were less likely to pull a chain to earn those pellets. In (b) all rats received one cue paired with one flavored sucrose (orange or grape) and another cue paired with the other flavor. Then on separate sessions in the experimental chambers, one group of rats received pairings of one cue with shock (Shock-Devalue), nonreinforced presentations of the other cue (Shock-Maintain), and LiCl injections in the absence of any other cue. Another group of rats received pairings of one cue with LiCl (LiCl-Devalue), the other cue alone (LiCl-Maintain) and shocks in the absence of any cue. Finally, half of the rats in each group received consumption tests for each flavor (left side of [b]) and the other half (right side of [b]) received training on each of two operant responses (chain pulls or lever presses). Both food consumption and food reinforcement power were selectively reduced by cue–LiCl pairings but not by cue–shock pairings.

had been paired with shock or LiCl, and the other response was reinforced with the other food. Rats that had received CS1–LiCl pairings showed fewer operant responses when that CS's food partner was used as the reinforcer than when the other food was used as the reinforcer. In contrast, there were no significant differences in responding related to whether the reinforcer's tone partner had been paired with shock or not. Thus, when potentially confounding effects of food-cup response punishment were equated, there was no evidence for selective reduction in reinforcement power of a food whose CS partner had been paired with shock. Hence, operant reinforcement power of a food was selectively responsive to pairings of an associatively activated representation of that food with illness, but not with shock, just as Holland (1981, Experiment 3) found with food consumption. At the same time, as noted earlier for the case of consumption, pairing of an associatively activated food representation with shock might have reduced the reinforcing power of both foods nonselectively, by devaluing a property of the food other than its unique flavor (e.g., Garcia, Kovner, & Green, 1970).

Mediated Extinction of Flavor Aversions

Although taste aversion learning is often exceptionally robust, it can be extinguished through repeated nonreinforced exposure of the CS (e.g., Grote & Brown, 1973). Similarly, repeated nonreinforced exposure of an associatively activated representation of a flavor appears to be sufficient to produce extinction of directly acquired taste aversion learning. Holland and Forbes (1982b; Table 11.3a) paired a tone with a flavor, prior to establishing an aversion to that flavor by direct flavor–LiCl pairings. For some rats, the tone was repeatedly presented in the absence of other stimuli. The mere presentation of the tone caused an alleviation of suppression of flavor consumption in those rats, as measured by savings in extinction when the flavor itself was presented in extinction later (Figure 11.3a). Likewise, in another experiment (Table 11.3b), Holland and Forbes paired two auditory CSs with two flavored foods, then established aversions to both flavors by pairing

Table 11.3a Outline of Procedures of Mediated Extinction Experiment Shown in Figure 11.3a.

Group	Phase 1	Phase 2	Phase 3	Test
EXT	Tone → food Light → nothing	Food → LiCl	Food → nothing	Food consumption
MED	Tone → food Light → nothing	Food → LiCl	Tone → nothing	Food consumption
CTL	Tone → nothing Light → food	Food → LiCl	Tone → nothing	Food consumption

Table 11.3b Outline of Procedures of Mediated Extinction Experiment Shown in Figure 11.3b.

Cue	Phase 1	Phase 2	Phase 3	Test
EXT	Tone → peppermint	Peppermint → LiCl	Tone → nothing	Wintergreen consumption
NON	Noise → wintergreen	Wintergreen → LiCl		Peppermint consumption

Note: The roles of tone and noise in phases 1 and 3 were completely counterbalanced.

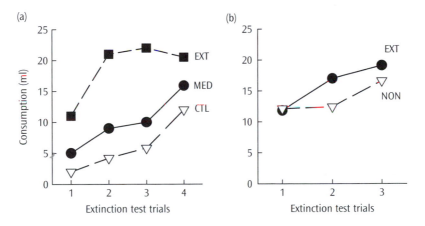

Figure 11.3. Mediated extinction of flavor aversions (Holland and Forbes, 1982b). Nonreinforced presentations of a cue that had previously been paired with food enhanced subsequent extinction of an aversion to that food. In (a) rats in groups EXT and MED first received tone–food pairings. Then all rats received food–LiCl pairings in the home cage to establish an aversion to that food. Next, the rats in Groups MED and CTL received repeated presentations of the tone alone, while the rats in Group EXT received repeated delivery of the food alone, all in the experimental chambers. Finally, extinction of the food aversion was assessed in four test sessions in the home cage. Group MED, which putatively received associatively activated food representations in the absence of illness, consumed significantly more food in test (extinction) than Group CTL, but not as much as Group EXT, which received food itself in second phase. In (b) all rats received pairings of one auditory cue with one flavored sucrose and another auditory cue with another flavored sucrose. All rats then received separate pairings of each flavor with LiCl injection in the home cage. Next, each rat received repeated presentations of one auditory cue in the absence of either flavors or illness. Finally, consumption of both foods was assessed in successive test sessions in the home cage. Each rat consumed more of the food whose partner cue had been presented previously in extinction (EXT) than of the food whose cue partner had not been presented (NON).

each with LiCl, and then presented one CS repeatedly without flavors or illness. Again, extinction of the aversion to the flavor whose partner CS had been extinguished was more rapid (Figure 11.3b). Nonreinforced presentations of a CS appeared to activate a representation of the flavor, partially extinguishing the aversion to that flavor, because that representation was not followed by illness.

Modulation of Learning About Other Cues

The outcome of direct CS–US pairings can be modulated by the presence of other cues. This modulation can be divided into two broad categories, negative and positive. Negative modulation occurs when a cue interferes with the acquisition or expression of another CS–US association, as in overshadowing (e.g., Bouton & Whiting, 1982) and blocking (e.g., Gustavson, Hart, Calton, & Schachtman, 1992) of aversion learning. Positive modulation occurs when a cue facilitates the acquisition or expression of another CS–US association. Examples of positive mediation include potentiation

of odor aversion learning by flavors (Rusiniak, Hankins, Garcia, & Brett, 1979) and augmentation of flavor aversion learning by concomitant odors (e.g., Batsell & Batson, 1999; Batsell & Blankenship, 2003). We have found that both types of modulation may also be produced by associatively activated representations of events.

Negative Modulation

Overshadowing is probably the most broadly known example of negative modulation. Overshadowing refers to the reduced behavioral control exhibited by a CS if it is reinforced in compound with another, often more salient CS, than if it is reinforced by itself (e.g., Mackintosh, 1974). In the taste aversion paradigm, overshadowing can occur when a compound consisting of two flavors is paired with illness, and one of the flavors is later tested alone (e.g., Revusky, Parker, & Coombes, 1977). Holland (1983) conducted two experiments to determine whether an associatively activated flavor representation could overshadow another flavor. In Experiment 1 (Table 11.4a), for rats in a mediated overshadowing group (AT+), a tone was first

Table 11.4a Outline of Procedures of Mediated Overshadowing Experiment Shown in Figure 11.4a.

Group	Phase 1	Phase 2	Consumption Test
A	Tone → saline Light → nothing	Sucrose → LiCl	Sucrose
AX	Tone → saline Light → nothing	Sucrose + saline → LiCl	Sucrose
AT+	Tone → saline Light → nothing	Sucrose + tone → LiCl	Sucrose
AT−	Tone → nothing Light → saline	Sucrose + tone → LiCl	Sucrose

Table 11.4b Outline of Procedures of Mediated Potentiation Experiment Shown in Figure 11.4b.

Group	Phase 1	Phase 2	Consumption Test
A	Tone → sucrose Light → nothing	Almond → LiCl	Almond
AX	Tone → sucrose Light → nothing	Almond + sucrose → LiCl	Almond
AT+	Tone → sucrose Light → nothing	Almond + tone → LiCl	Almond
AT−	Tone → nothing Light → sucrose	Almond + tone → LiCl	Almond

reinforced with a saline solution. Later, that tone was presented in compound with a sucrose solution and followed by an injection of LiCl. Consumption of sucrose was greater in that group than in a group (AT−) that had received a compound of a previously nonreinforced tone as well as sucrose with LiCl (Figure 11.4a, right bars). Holland interpreted this finding as an example of overshadowing by an associatively activated flavor representation. He suggested that the tone activated a saline representation, which effectively overshadowed conditioning of an aversion to sucrose.

That experiment also included a pair of groups that received either sucrose alone (A) paired with LiCl or a saline + sucrose compound (AX) paired with LiCl. The directly presented saline also overshadowed conditioning of the sucrose (Figure 11.4a,

left bars). Notably, the level of overshadowing produced by saline itself (Group AX) was substantially greater than that produced by the associatively activated representation of saline (Group AT+). This finding is consistent with the notion that associatively activated representations are typically of lower salience than directly activated ones, and the frequent observation that less salient stimuli are less effective in overshadowing.

Positive Modulation

Although overshadowing is a common and robust phenomenon, some aversion learning experiments have revealed examples of positive modulation. For example, Durlach and Rescorla (1980) and Rusiniak et al. (1979) observed potentiation of odor aversion learning by flavors. Rats consumed less of an odor

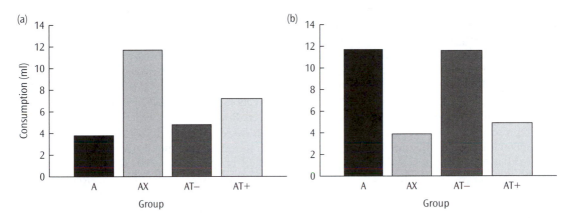

Figure 11.4. Mediated overshadowing (a) and potentiation (b) of an odor aversion (Holland, 1983). Compared to a neutral tone, a tone that had been paired with a flavor overshadowed learning of an aversion to another flavor, but potentiated learning of an aversion to an odor. In the overshadowing experiment (a), water-deprived rats in Group A, AX, and AT first received pairings of a tone with a saline solution, and rats in Group AT− received tone presentations unpaired with saline. The rats in Groups AT+ and AT− then received a single presentation of a sucrose solution in the presence of the tone, rats in group AX received a sucrose + saline solution, and rats in Group A received sucrose alone. All rats received an injection of LiCl immediately after this trial. Test consumption of sucrose alone (shown) was significantly higher in Group AT+ than in Group AT−, suggesting that an associatively activated representation of saline overshadowed conditioning of an aversion to sucrose. That overshadowing was smaller than that obtained when saline itself was combined with sucrose in aversion training (compare Groups AX and A). The potentiation experiment (b) was identical except that sucrose served as the potentiating stimulus and an almond odor served as the added stimulus on the aversion training trial. Water-deprived rats in Group A, AX, and AT first received pairings of a tone with a sucrose solution, and rats in Group AT− received tone presentations unpaired with sucrose. The rats in Groups AT+ and AT− then received a single presentation of an almond solution in the presence of the tone, rats in group AX received a sucrose + almond solution, and rats in Group A received almond alone. All rats received an injection of LiCl immediately after this trial. Both sucrose itself (Group AX) and an associatively activated representation of sucrose (Group AT+) produced comparable potentiation of aversion learning to almond, relative to rats trained in the absence of a flavor or its representation (Groups A and AT−).

solution if it had been paired with LiCl in compound with a flavor than if the odor alone had been paired with LiCl, an outcome diametrically opposed to that of overshadowing. Holland (1983, Experiment 3) sought to determine whether an associatively activated flavor representation would also potentiate learning of an aversion to a directly activated odor. That experiment (Table 11.4b) was similar to the overshadowing experiment just described, except the target solution was an almond odor solution rather than a saline flavor (Figure 11.4b). However, in this case, the tone-activated representation of a sucrose flavor potentiated learning of the odor aversion. Thus, both an associatively activated and a directly activated flavor representation potentiated target learning if the target stimulus was primarily processed as an odor (almond), but overshadowed target learning if the target was primarily processed as a flavor (sucrose).

Although most examples of potentiation involve odor targets and flavor potentiators, there are occasional examples of flavor–flavor and even odor–flavor potentiation as well (Batsell & Blankenship, 2003; Bouton, Jones, McPhillips, & Swartzentruber, 1986; Slotnick, Westbrook, & Darling, 1997). Interestingly, Holland (2006) recently found that in a case of potentiation of a flavor aversion by an odor, an associatively activated representation of that odor also potentiated the aversion learning. Again, the principle observed here was that an associatively activated event representation mimicked the functions of its referent.

CONTENTS OF ASSOCIATIVELY ACTIVATED REPRESENTATIONS

The evidence reviewed in the last section shows that associatively activated flavor representations can participate in new learning and modulate learning about other directly experienced events. In this section, we consider the nature or the contents of such associatively activated stimulus representations. Clearly, there must be some overlap between the features of directly and associatively activated representations, or none of the mediated learning experiments described in the section on Demonstrations and Properties of Representation-Mediated Aversion Learning would have succeeded. In the extreme case, a CS might activate the same representation, in its entirety, as is activated by its referent, such that the real and imaginary events are indistinguishable. Alternatively, directly and associatively activated representations might be largely independent, with only minimal shared features. Or, the features of these representations may overlap substantially, but be activated into different processing states, with distinct functional characteristics (e.g., Wagner, 1981). The studies discussed in this section provide evidence that suggests that directly and associatively activated representations of foods share many properties, including information concerning current gustatory palatability.

Flavor Specificity of Associatively Activated Food Representations

In the previous section we presented several instances in which representation-mediated learning was specific to particular flavors (e.g., Holland, 1981, 1990; Holland & Forbes, 1982b). Clearly, in those experiments, the auditory CSs came to selectively activate sensory properties of food representations sufficiently detailed to distinguish, for example, wintergreen and peppermint flavors of a standard sucrose solution. This detail in associatively activated food representations is also reflected in a variety of other conditioning procedures besides mediated aversion learning, including reinforcer devaluation (Balleine, Chapter 13; Colwill & Rescorla, 1990; Colwill & Motzkin, 1994; Delamater & Holland, 2008; Holland, 1988, 1990), Pavlovian-instrumental transfer (Balleine, Chapter 13; Colwill & Rescorla, 1990; Delamater & Holland, 2008), cue-potentiated feeding (Delamater & Holland, 2008; Galarce, Crombag, & Holland, 2007; Petrovich, Ross, Gallagher, & Holland, 2007), and differential-outcome expectancy (McDannald, Saddoris, Gallagher, & Holland, 2005) procedures. These phenomena have been studied extensively in other laboratories, but the experiments from our laboratory are notable in the present context because they used events and conditioning parameters similar to those used in our mediated flavor aversion learning studies.

Perceptual Nature of Associatively Activated Event Representations

A simple account for the sensory-specificity of associatively activated food representations is that through associative learning, cues acquire the ability to activate the same perceptual processing mechanisms as activated by the foods themselves. Within this perspective, mediated learning occurs because perceptual processing of the represented food occurs even in the absence of that food itself, thereby permitting the association of sensory properties of that food with illness. This view also implies that CSs should activate all downstream markers of perceptual activity related to the represented flavor. That is, if a CS makes a rat "taste" food, then it should act the same way it would act if presented with the food itself in all circumstances, given the appropriate behavioral supports. A series of experiments exploited others' observations of behavioral markers of flavor palatability to explore the extent to which CSs engage processing of their absent referents.

The ingestion of a taste is often accompanied by orofacial and muscular activity that reflects the palatability of the taste (Grill & Norgren, 1978). Delamater, Lolordo, and Berridge (1986) showed that a CS paired with a flavored reinforcer is capable of eliciting the same gustatory responses as the reinforcer itself. In their Experiment 1, one auditory cue was paired with sucrose delivery (CS+) and another cue was presented without reinforcement (CS−). A subsequent test measured the rats' taste reactivity to a water infusion when either the CS+ or CS− was present. Presentation of the CS+ produced more orofacial responses that are typically indicative of a positive gustatory reaction relative to the presentation of the CS− or the delivery of water alone. The authors concluded that the CS+ evoked a representation of the sucrose US that maintained some of the gustatory qualities inherent in the directly activated US representation.

An alternative account of these results is that these motor responses were directly conditioned to the CSs, and thus reflect simple stimulus–response (S–R) learning rather than evidence for perceptual or motivational processes. Holland (1990) and Kerfoot, Agarwal, Lee, and Holland (2007) extended Delamater et al.'s (1986) study by combining the monitoring of orofacial taste-reactivity responses with reinforcer devaluation procedures. In a typical Pavlovian devaluation experiment, a CS is first paired with delivery of a flavored food. After a conditioned response is established, the flavored food is devalued through satiety, illness, or some other means in the absence of the CS. In a

final test of responding to the CS, conducted in the absence of the flavored food itself, responding is found to be reduced, consistent with the new, lowered hedonic value of that food. This phenomenon is important for the present discussion because it helps elucidate the nature of the associatively activated representation. The fact that responding to the CS is affected by a devaluation manipulation that occurs after training is completed indicates that the CS activates a current representation of the flavor. Thus, the associatively activated flavor representation is not merely a static memory of training, but an updated representation of that flavor.

In Kerfoot et al.'s (2007) study (Table 11.5a), rats first received 16 paired (Groups Maintain and Devalue) or unpaired (Group Control) presentations of a 15-s tone and a 5-s intraoral delivery of sucrose solution in a single-conditioning session. For the rats that received paired tone–sucrose presentations, the sucrose accompanied the last 5 s of the tone presentation. In the next session, the rats received infusions of sucrose in the absence of any tones. The rats in Group Devalue and half of the rats in Group Control received an injection of LiCl immediately after the sucrose session, intended to devalue the sucrose. The rats in Group Maintain and the remaining rats in Group Control received that injection delayed by 8 h, intended to expose the rats equally to sucrose and illness but not devalue the sucrose. Two days later, responding to the tone was tested. Each test trial comprised a 15-s presentations of the tone, in which the tone was presented alone for the first 10 s, at which point unflavored water was infused until the time of tone termination, to provide a substrate for orofacial responses. Figure 11.5a shows taste-reactivity responses during no-CS baseline, tone-alone, tone + water, and posttrial periods in the test session. The left side of Figure 11.5a shows positive responses. As in Delamater et al.'s (1986) study, rats that had received tone–sucrose pairings and that had not had sucrose devalued (Group Maintain) showed significantly more appetitive responses during the tone, tone + water, and posttone intervals than rats that had not received tone–sucrose pairings (Group Control). Furthermore, consistent with the results of other reinforcer devaluation studies with more conventional response measures (e.g., Holland & Straub, 1979), rats that had sucrose devalued after tone–sucrose pairings (Group Devalue) showed significantly fewer appetitive responses than the rats in Group Maintain. Indeed, those rats showed no

Table 11.5a Outline of Procedures of Devaluation Experiment Shown in Figure 11.5a.

Group	Phase 1	Phase 2	Test
Devalue	Tone → sucrose	Sucrose → LiCl	Tone → water
Maintain	Tone → sucrose	Sucrose; LiCl	Tone → water
Control	Tone; sucrose	Sucrose → LiCl or sucrose; LiCl	Tone → water

Note: Unflavored water was presented on test trials to provide a substrate for the performance of taste reactivity responses.

Table 11.5b Outline of Procedures of Devaluation Experiment Shown in Figure 11.5b.

Phase 1	Phase 2	Test
Noise → sucrose	Sucrose → nothing	Tone (A1)
Tone → saline	Saline → nothing	Noise (A2)
	Sucrose + saline → LiCl	Tone + noise (A1 + A2)

Note: The roles of noise and tone were completely counterbalanced. Testing was conducted in the presence of unflavored water A. The test notations A1 and A2 refer to the nomenclature in Figure 11.5b.

Table 11.5c Outline of Procedures of Devaluation Experiment Shown in Figure 11.5c.

Phase 1	Phase 2	Test
Noise → sucrose	Sucrose → LiCl	Tone (A1)
Tone → saline	Saline → LiCl	Noise (A2)
	Sucrose + saline → nothing	Tone + noise (A1 + A2)

Note: The roles of noise and tone were completely counterbalanced. Testing was conducted in the presence of unflavored water A. The test notations A1 and A2 refer to the nomenclature in Figure 11.5c.

more appetitive responding than the rats in Group Control, suggesting that the devaluation effect was complete.

More interestingly, the rats in Group Devalue (and only those rats) showed substantial numbers of aversive taste-reactivity responses (right side of Figure 11.5a). These aversive responses ordinarily accompany consumption of unpalatable flavors, such as quinine, or flavors that had been paired with illness. Indeed, assessment of taste-reactivity responses to sucrose infusion alone in a second-test session (administered to a subset of the rats) showed substantial aversive responses in the rats that had received sucrose–LiCl pairings, but few or none in the rats that had received sucrose and illness unpaired.

These data are consistent with the claim that in the test session the tone-activated "tasting" of the sucrose, which now "tasted bad" to the rats in Group Devalue and "tasted good" in the rats in Group Maintain. Notably, none of the rats had exhibited aversive responses in the presence of the tone or sucrose at any time during the initial tone–sucrose or sucrose-alone sessions. Thus, these responses are unlikely to reflect direct S–R learning between the tone and aversive gustatory responses.

Two additional devaluation experiments carried our investigations of the perceptual nature of associatively activated flavor representations a step further, by contrasting the effects of combining CSs and the effects of combining the representations they activated (Tables 11.5b and 11.5c; Holland, 1990, Experiments 2 and 3). In each of these experiments, water-deprived rats first received pairings of a tone with a saline solution and a noise with a sucrose solution. These

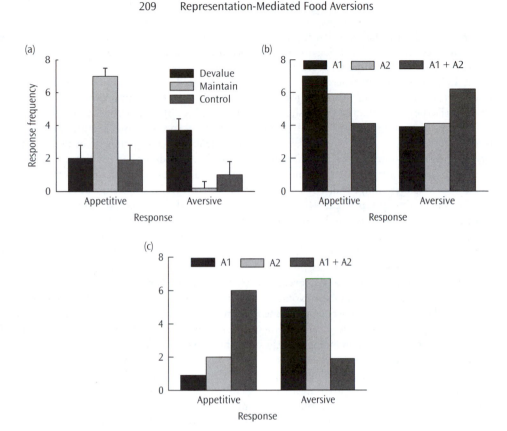

Figure 11.5. Taste-reactivity responses to auditory cues after flavor devaluation. In (a) (Kerfoot, 2007), rats in Groups Devalue and Maintain first received 16 pairings of a tone with intraoral infusion of sucrose, while rats in the control group received those events unpaired. Next, the rats in Group Devalue and half of the rats in the control group received sucrose infusions in the absence of tones, followed by a LiCl injection; rats in Group Maintain and the other half of the Control rats received infusions and LiCl on separate days. Finally, all rats received eight presentations of the tone, each followed by infusions of unflavored water. Occurrences of various appetitive and aversive taste-reactivity measures were scored from slow motion video. Rats in Group Maintain showed appetitive but few aversive responses, whereas rat in Group Devalue showed aversive responses and few appetitive responses. In (b) and (c) (Holland, 1990), rats first received noise and tone cues, one paired with sucrose and one paired with saline delivery. Then the rats were given flavor aversion training, using either positive patterning ([b]: sucrose + saline → LiCl, sucrose alone → nothing, saline alone → nothing) or negative patterning ([c]: sucrose → LiCl, saline → LiCl, sucrose + saline → nothing) procedures. Finally, taste-reactivity responses were recorded in rats while they consumed unflavored water, during presentations of each auditory cue separately (A1 and A2), or during a noise + tone compound (A1 + A2). In all cases, the rats responded to each elemental cue as if its referent were present, and to the noise + tone compound as if the sucrose + saline compound was present.

CSs and reinforcers were chosen to permit additive combinations of each. That is, the identity of each element is maintained within so-called separable (Garner, 1974) stimulus compounds. Thus, a compound of saline and sucrose retains both its sweet and salty properties, and a compound of tone and noise includes recognizable tone and noise components. Next, in their home cages, and in the absence of any auditory cues, half the rats (Table 11.5b) were trained with a positive patterning procedure, to establish an aversion to a sucrose + saline compound but not to saline or sucrose presented separately. Presentations of the compound flavor were followed by LiCl injection whereas presentations of each element separately occurred without consequence. The other half of the rats were trained with the opposite, negative-patterning contingencies (Table 11.5c), in which presentations of sucrose or saline separately were paired with LiCl injection, but sucrose + saline compound presentations were nonreinforced. Previous data (Forbes & Holland, 1980) showed that rats solve these discriminations rapidly, and this was again the case.

Finally, the rats' responses to unflavored water were examined in the presence of the tone, the noise, and a tone + noise compound. For the rats in the positive patterning group (Figure 11.5b), in which the sucrose + saline compound was paired with LiCl, presentations of the tone and noise separately produced substantial appetitive responses and minimal aversive responses, whereas the tone + noise compound produced substantial aversive responses and fewer appetitive responses. Notably, the rats responded to the tone + noise compound the way they would respond to a sucrose + saline compound solution, as if they were combining (for the first time) associatively activated perceptual images of sucrose and saline. In contrast, had the rats simply combined their responding appropriate to the tone and noise elements, the noise + tone compound should have elicited more appetitive responses than either element alone. Likewise, for the rats in the negative-patterning group (Figure 11.5c), in which sucrose and saline each had been paired with LiCl, but the sucrose + saline compound was not associated with illness, presentations of the tone and noise separately each controlled substantial aversive responses and few appetitive responses, whereas presentation of the noise + tone compound evoked mostly appetitive responses, and fewer aversive responses than either element did separately. Thus, in terms of their taste-reactivity responses, which putatively reflect gustatory palatability, both subgroups of rats treated compound auditory stimuli as compounds of the individual elements' associatively activated event representations, rather than as compounds of the peripheral responses elicited by each individual element.

Brain Systems Underlying Associatively Activated Event Representations

At the conclusion of the final test session of the simple devaluation experiment described at the beginning of the previous section (Figure 11.5a), Kerfoot et al. (2007) sacrificed the rats and prepared their

brains for immunochemistry for Fos, the protein product of the activity-dependent immediate-early gene *c-fos*, as a measure of neuronal activation. We evaluated Fos expression in a number of brain regions known to be important in taste processing, the display of appetitive and aversive taste-reactivity responses, and performance in devaluation tasks, as a function of behavioral training condition. As described earlier, rats in Groups Devalue and Maintain first received pairings of a tone with intraoral infusion of sucrose and later either paired (Devalue) or unpaired (Maintain) presentations of sucrose and LiCl, whereas rats in Group Control received tone and sucrose unpaired in the initial phase. The final test session included pairings of tone with plain water infusions.

Our initial predictions were that if tone–sucrose pairings endowed the tone with the ability to activate perceptual processing of sucrose, then the rats in Groups Devalue and Maintain might both show more Fos expression in gustatory sensory brain regions after the tone tests than rats in the Control group. Others in our lab have found learning-dependent activation of neurons in gustatory cortex by odors previously paired with flavors, using both immediate-early gene expression (M. Saddoris, unpublished) and electrophysiological recording (T. Furuyashiki, unpublished) methods. Furthermore, we anticipated differential Fos expression in Groups Devalue and Maintain in two brain regions we have previously shown to be critical to the display of devaluation effects, the basolateral amygdala and orbitofrontal cortex, and in the nucleus accumbens, different subregions of which were found to be involved in the production of both appetitive and aversive taste-reactivity responses (Reynolds & Berridge, 2002). We also examined Fos expression in amygdala central nucleus and the lateral hypothalamus, as likely regions for both activation with the presentation of appetitive CSs (Lee et al., 2005; Petrovich, Holland, & Gallagher, 2005) and convergence of appetitive and aversive information in flavor aversion learning (e.g., Bernstein, Wilkins, & Barot, Chapter 16; Reilly, Chapter 15). Finally, we assessed Fos activation in several control regions in the occipital and parietal cortex that we did not expect to be differentially affected by the behavioral training procedures.

Fos expression did not differ among the three training groups in any of the control regions. Interestingly, Fos expression in gustatory neocortex was significantly greater in each of the groups in which the tone was associated with sucrose (Maintain and Devalue) than in Group Control, in which the tone had not been paired with sucrose, as if in the former groups the tone indeed instigated taste processing. In addition, Fos expression in the basolateral amygdala and orbitofrontal cortex was greater in Group Devalue than in Group Maintain or Group Control, whereas Fos expression in the amygdala central nucleus was similar in both Groups Maintain and Devalue, which in turn was greater than in Group Control. Notably, lesions of either basolateral amygdala or orbitofrontal cortex disrupt performance in devaluation experiments (Hatfield, Han, Conley, Gallagher, & Holland, 1996; Pickens et al., 2003), but lesions of the amygdala central nucleus do not (Hatfield et al., 1996). Finally, and perhaps most interestingly, Fos expression in the shell of the nucleus accumbens showed contrasting gradients over the rostral–caudal extent of that structure. In the rostral shell, rats in Group Maintain showed significantly greater Fos expression than either of the other groups, whereas in the caudal shell, Group Devalue showed reliably greater Fos expression than in the other groups. This observation is consistent with Reynolds and Berridge's (2002) finding that stimulation of rostral shell enhanced appetitive taste-reactivity responses and stimulation of caudal shell enhance the display of aversive taste-reactivity responses. Thus, the pattern of brain Fos activation in Kerfoot et al.'s (2007) study supports the claim that an auditory cue paired with sucrose can initiate activity in brain regions normally associated with processing of taste and palatability information.

CONDITIONS FOR REPRESENTATION-MEDIATED LEARNING

A major component of most learning theories is the specification of the conditions under which learning may occur, such as the role of reinforcement or temporal contiguity (Rescorla & Holland, 1976). Thus, it is important to characterize the conditions under which mediated aversions may be acquired. We considered one of these in the section on Selective Association, the apparently selective nature of flavor aversion learning for illness-inducing USs, or cue-to-consequence specificity (Garcia & Koelling, 1966), as a basic property of mediated flavor aversions. In this section, we describe research, mostly

from our laboratory, which has examined four other conditions that appear important for the occurrence of representation-mediated learning. The first two, the amount of cue–flavor training and the temporal relation of cue and flavor, are straightforward, but the latter two are more subtle. These include the question of whether an associatively activated representation of an illness-inducing US can serve as a reinforcer in flavor aversion learning, and the possibility that by associatively activating a representation of another event, a CS is rendered less able to itself be modulated by associatively activated event representations.

Amount of Training and Mediated Learning

Holland (1998) found that the capacity for a tone to activate a rich representation of a flavor, which is able to participate in flavor aversion learning when paired with illness, is limited by the amount of training that the subject receives with the tone and flavor. Mediated learning was observed only with relatively small amounts of training. In one experiment of that series (Table 11.6a), rats received either 16 or 40 pairings of one auditory stimulus (e.g., a tone) followed by delivery of sucrose, and 16 pairings of another auditory stimulus (e.g., a noise) with flavored food pellets. To equate simple exposure to sucrose, the rats also received 24 interspersed pairings of a visual stimulus with sucrose. After this training, the tone was paired with LiCl for half of the subjects (Devalue groups) whereas the noise was paired with LiCl for the other half (Maintain groups). A subsequent test showed that the sucrose consumption of the rats in Group Devalue depended on the number of tone–sucrose pairings in training (Figure 11.6a). Sucrose consumption was suppressed in the rats that had received 16 tone–sucrose pairings (Devalue-16) but not in the rats that had received 40 tone–sucrose pairings (Devalue-40). Thus, a greater number of tone–sucrose pairings limited the ability of the tone to substitute for sucrose itself in subsequent sucrose aversion learning.

One interpretation for this result is that, early in training, CSs activate a detailed, sensory-based representation of food, but as training proceeds, they come to activate a more impoverished food representation. Indeed, it is frequently asserted that well-practiced behaviors become automatized, such that they are executed without mediation by

Table 11.6a Outline of Procedures of Mediated Learning Experiment Shown in Figure 11.6a.

Group	Phase 1	Phase 2	Test
Devalue-16	16 Tone → sucrose 24 Light → sucrose 16 Noise → pellets	Tone → LiCl	Sucrose consumption
Devalue-40	40 Tone → sucrose 16 Noise → pellets	Tone → LiCl	Sucrose consumption
Maintain-16	16 Tone → sucrose 24 Light → sucrose 16 Noise → pellets	Noise → LiCl	Sucrose consumption
Maintain-40	40 Tone → sucrose 16 Noise → pellets	Noise → LiCl	Sucrose consumption

Note: The numbers refer to the number of tone → sucrose trials in Phase 1. This outline omits some of the groups and experimental procedures used in the original study (Holland, 1998, Experiment 2).

Table 11.6b Outline of Procedures of Devaluation Experiment Shown in Figure 11.6b.

Group	Phase 1	Phase 2	Test
Devalue-16	16 Tone → sucrose 24 Light → sucrose 16 Noise → pellets	Sucrose → LiCl	Tone → nothing
Davalue-40	40 Tone → sucrose 16 Noise → pellets	Sucrose → LiCl	Tone → nothing
Devalue-160	160 Tone → sucrose 16 Noise → pellets	Sucrose → LiCl	Tone → nothing
Maintain-16	16 Tone → sucrose 24 Light → sucrose 16 Noise → pellets	Pellets → LiCl	Tone → nothing
Maintain-40	40 Tone → sucrose 16 Noise → pellets	Pellets → LiCl	Tone → nothing
Maintain-160	160 Tone → sucrose 16 Noise → pellets	Pellets → LiCl	Tone → nothing

Note: The numbers refer to the number of tone → sucrose trials in Phase 1. This outline omits experimental procedures used in the original study (Holland, 1998, Experiment 3).

complex internal outcome representations (Adams & Dickinson, 1981; Allport, 1937; Kimble & Perlmutter, 1970). That is, as Pavlovian training proceeds, conditioned responding may become increasingly S–R in nature, such that the CS does not activate a representation of sensory properties of the reinforcer. However, another experiment in that series (Table 11.6b; Holland, 1998, Experiment 3) showed that rats were still sensitive to a food devaluation treatment after extensive stimulus–food pairings. That experiment was similar to the experiment just described except that after Pavlovian training, either sucrose or food pellets themselves were paired with LiCl. When tested for conditioned responding to the two CSs, all rats spent less time in the food cup in the presence of the CS whose food partner had been paired with LiCl, regardless of the amount of CS–food training (Figure 11.6b). Because in this study, responding to the CSs was sensitive to the contemporary motivational value of the outcome, it is likely that the stimulus still activated a sensorially detailed

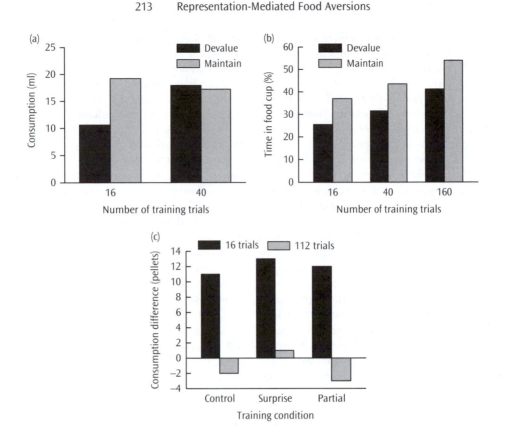

Figure 11.6. Effects of the amount of training on mediated food aversion learning and devaluation. In (a) rats received either 16 or 40 pairings of a tone with sucrose (Holland, 1998). Then, the rats in Group Devalue received tone → LiCl pairings and the rats in Group Maintain received those events unpaired. Mediated aversion learning tone occurred only after 16 and not 40 tone–sucrose pairings. In (b) rats first received either 16, 40, or 160 tone–food pairings (Holland, 1998). Then, rats in Group Devalue received food–LiCl pairings and rats in Group Maintain received those events unpaired. Devaluation was observed regardless of the amount of training. (c) It summarizes the results of two experiments designed to test the effects of associability enhancement on the loss of mediated learning with extended training (Holland, 2005). All rats first received 16 pairings of one cue with food (minimal cue) and 112 pairings of another cue with food (extended cue). Rats in the Partial condition also received 116 nonreinforced presentations of the extended cue, intended to maintain its associability. After a pretest of food consumption in the home cage, half of the rats in each condition then received pairings of the minimally trained cue with LiCl and the other half received pairings of the extensively trained cue with LiCl. Rats in the Surprise condition were also given a session with four nonreinforced cue presentations before the cue–LiCl sessions, also intended to restore the associability of that cue. Food consumption of all rats was then assessed in their home cages. (c) Shows the magnitude of the mediated aversion effect (pretest consumption minus test consumption) in each condition. In all conditions, mediated aversions were established after 16 training trials, but not after 112 training trials. Thus, manipulations known to enhance cue associability in other experimental contexts did not enhance mediated learning after extended training.

representation of the devalued food even after extensive stimulus–food pairings.

Taken together, these two outcomes seem contradictory, with the results of mediated learning procedures suggesting that the more extensively trained CSs did not activate sensorially detailed representations of the foods whereas the results of the devaluation study suggested that they did. To accommodate these outcomes, Holland (1998) suggested that CSs maintain their ability to activate outcome representations, but that the nature of the associatively activated food representation becomes impoverished with extended training. It apparently loses its ability to form a new association with illness, but maintains a representation of the contemporary hedonic value of the food sufficient to mediate previously trained conditioned responding. This view differs from "automatization" accounts because responding to the CS is not driven by an S-R association after extended training, but by an impoverished representation of food that maintains certain characteristics (e.g., flavor properties and motivational value) and loses others (e.g., the ability to enter into new associations).

Recently, we have evaluated different versions of this account (Holland, 2005). One possibility invoked the Pearce and Hall (1980) model of conditioning. Within this model, the ability of a stimulus to enter into new associations (its "associability") is a function of the extent to which a subject was surprised after presentations of that stimulus. Thus, early in Pavlovian training, receipt of the reinforcer is not anticipated on the basis of prior learning, so that reinforcer is surprising. As a result, the associability of the CSs present on that trial is set high, and learning is initially very rapid. However, as learning about the CS proceeds, the reinforcer gradually becomes less surprising, thereby reducing the associability of the CS, and hence reducing the rate of further CS-reinforcer learning. Importantly, within this model, a CS's associability value determines only the rate at which it enters into new associations and not the extent to which it may control previously conditioned behavior. Thus, as conditioning proceeds, CSs become less able to enter into new associations, but are no less able to generate previously trained conditioned responses. This description of the model strikingly resembles our description of the implications of the effects of amount of training on mediated learning and devaluation: A CS-activated food representation becomes less able to enter into new associations (with illness) but maintains its ability to mediate previously trained CRs.

Hall and Pearce (1982) noted that CS associability that was reduced after extended training could be restored by surprise, that is, by violating the outcome expectancies that had led to those reductions. For example, after extended training of a CS with a shock US, they presented one group of rats with a single nonreinforced extinction trial with that CS, before pairing it with a new, larger

shock US. According to the Pearce and Hall (1980) model, the surprising nonreinforcement of the CS should enhance its associability, allowing the rats to learn about the CS-new shock relation more readily than rats that did not receive the intervening an extinction trial. Indeed, this was the case. We applied a similar strategy to consider whether the reduced mediated flavor aversion leaning we observed after extended tone-food training was due to analogous losses in the associability of the food representation, and hence in its ability to be associated with illness. In several experiments, rats received 16 pairings of one CS (CS-16) with a flavored food, intermixed with 112 pairings of another CS (CS-112) with that food. The rats then received pairings of either CS-16 or CS-112 or a control CS with LiCl. As in previous experiments (Holland, 1998), rats that received pairings of CS-16 with LiCl showed food aversions but those that received pairings of CS-112 with LiCl did not. Notably, introducing surprise, either by a few nonreinforced CS presentations or by using partial reinforcement procedures from the onset, had no effect on the amount of mediated learning observed (Figure 11.6c). Thus, these studies did not provide support for an account based on the Pearce and Hall (1980) model.

Another possibility is that the contents of associatively activated event representations change as conditioning proceeds, such that the properties or processing mechanisms needed for new taste aversion learning lose their availability. To account for the taste-reactivity data obtained in devaluation studies, described in the section titled Perceptual Nature of Associatively Activated Event Representations, Holland (1990) suggested that early in training, CSs might control relatively low-level perceptual processing of the absent event, such that a rat may "taste" the absent flavor. A simple prediction from this perspective is that the change in the display of taste-reactivity responses to CSs-alone, observed after reinforcer devaluation, would occur only after small amounts of initial CS-food training. A recent experiment (Table 11.7; Holland, Lasseter, & Agarwal, 2008) confirms this prediction. Each rat received 16 pairings of one CS (CS-16) with intraoral delivery of a sucrose solution and 112 pairings of another CS (CS-112) with intraoral sucrose, intermixed over eight sessions. Half of the rats then received two sucrose-LiCl pairings, while the other half received those events

Table 11.7 Outline of Procedures of the Devaluation Experiment Shown in Figure 11.7.

Group	Phase 1	Phase 2	Test
Devalue	16 Tone → sucrose	Sucrose → LiCl	Tone → water
	112 Noise → sucrose		Noise → water
Maintain	16 Tone → sucrose	Sucrose; LiCl	Tone → water
	112 Noise → sucrose		Noise → water

Note: The roles of tone and noise were counterbalanced. Water was presented in the test to provide a substrate for taste-reactivity responses.

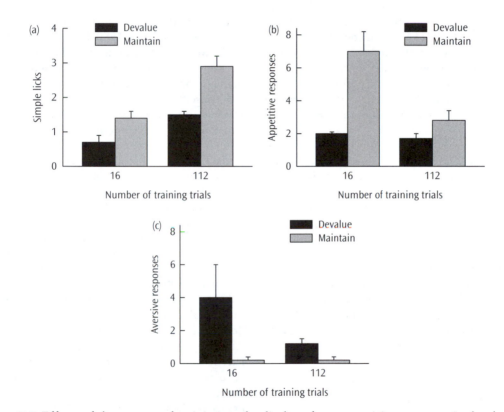

Figure 11.7. Effects of the amount of training on the display of taste-reactivity responses in devaluation procedures. Each rat received 16 pairings of one auditory cue with sucrose and 112 pairings of another auditory cue and sucrose, intermixed. Then the rats in Group Devalue received sucrose–LiCl pairings and the rats in Group Maintain received those events unpaired. All rats were then tested for food-cup entry and taste-reactivity responses in a test session that included pairings of each of the two auditory cues with unflavored water. (a) Shows performance of a simple consummatory (licking) response. (b) and (c) show appetitive and aversive taste-reactivity responses during water presentations after each cue. Although a nonhedonic measure of conditioned responding in devaluation studies (a) showed no sensitivity to the amount of training (as in Figure 11.6b), the display of taste-reactivity responses appropriate to the altered motivational value of the (absent) flavor was observed more obviously with small amounts of training.

individually, separated by 8 h. Finally, the rats were tested in the presence of each CS, paired with the delivery of unflavored water. Figure 11.7 shows the results of this test. Figure 11.7a shows a measure of simple licking/consumption in the presence of each CS. Notably, as with food-cup entry in Holland's (1998) devaluation study, rats that received sucrose–LiCl pairings spent less time performing this learned consummatory during both CSs than the rats that received no such devaluation training. However, Figure 11.7b and 11.7c, which show the taste-reactivity measures, tell a different story. First, in the unpaired rats, there were more appetitive responses (Figure 11.7b) in the presence of CS-16 than CS-112. Second, in the paired (Devalue) rats, although CS-16 controlled significant numbers of aversive responses (Figure 11.7c), CS-112 evoked considerably fewer responses. Thus, in the absence of the flavored reward itself, responses that purportedly reflect palatability judgments (both positive and negative) were more likely to occur in the presence of a minimally trained CS than in the presence of a more extensively trained CS.

Together with Holland's (1998, 2005) findings, these results suggest that the contents of exteroceptive cue–food learning changes quite rapidly over the course of conditioning. Early in training, auditory/ visual CSs activate features of food representations that are responsible for both the display of palatability information (as indicated by taste-reactivity measures) and for the ability to participate in new flavor aversion learning. With extensive training, these features are no longer activated by the CS. At the same time, these features do not seem to be the same ones responsible for the control of simple licking (Figure 11.7a), because those responses maintained their sensitivity to devaluation over extensive training.

Interstimulus Interval and Content of Associatively Activated Event Representations

Temporal contiguity is perhaps the most widely investigated determinant of the ease of associative learning. Typically, the rate, and often the asymptote of learning has been found to be maximal at some small, nonzero optimal forward interval and decreases as that interval is extended (Mackintosh, 1974). Although the range of effective intervals ranges from hundreds of milliseconds for some conditioning preparations, to hundreds of seconds

for others, and hundreds of minutes for flavor aversion learning, comparably shaped CS–US interval functions have been observed across a wide range of conditioning preparations. An interesting property of mediated taste aversion learning in this context is that in our experiments those aversions were readily formed despite intervals of 5–20 min between CS presentations and LiCl injections, more typical of intervals that are optimal for learning about flavors than for learning about auditory or visual stimuli.

More subtle issues relating to variations in interstimulus interval include whether the time of US delivery is coded (typically, it is, e.g., Kirkpatrick & Church, 2000; Miller & Barnett, 1993) and whether variations in CS–US interval produce variations in the content as well as the amount of learning (e.g., Holland, 1980; Silva & Timberlake, 1997). In the context of mediated aversion learning, Konorski's (1967) suggestion that short CS–US intervals encourage the formation of associations with sensory features of the US whereas longer intervals encourage associations with more general affective properties of the US, is especially relevant. If mediated flavor aversion learning depends on the CSs' activating sensory properties of a US representation, then it would seem likely that the ability of CSs paired with flavored foods to participate in mediated aversion learning would be especially constrained by CS–US interval. However, studies of mediated flavor aversion as well as more direct investigations of associatively activated flavor representations have failed to provide evidence that supports Konorski's notion.

Using a variety of tasks to assess the representational content of learning, Delamater and Holland (2008) examined the role of CS–US interval on representation of sensory aspects of USs. They found no support for Konorski's suggestion. Pavlovian-instrumental transfer (see Balleine, Chapter 13) was equally reinforcer-specific across a range of CS–US intervals from 20 to 120 s. That is, the rate of instrumental responding reinforced by a particular food reinforcer was augmented more by a CS that had been paired with that same reinforcer than by a CS that had been paired with a qualitatively different reinforcer. They also found that the use of a 2-s CS–US interval, despite generating more rapid and higher levels of conditioning, provided no evidence for US-specificity in Pavlovian-instrumental transfer, US devaluation, or CS-potentiated feeding procedures, each of which displayed substantial specificity when rats were trained with 20-s CS–US intervals. (CS-potentiated feeding refers to the ability of a CS that had been paired with a food when the rat was food-deprived to enhance food consumption later, when it was food sated.) Thus, contrary to Konorski's suggestion, activation of sensory properties of a US representation was more likely with moderate CS–US intervals (e.g., 20 s) than short (2 s) ones.

Accordingly, an unpublished experiment from our lab showed no evidence for mediated food aversion learning when a 2-s auditory CS was paired first with food and then with illness. Two groups of rats received pairings of a 2-s auditory cue with sucrose and a second 2-s auditory cue with maltodextrin (the same procedures and events used by Delamater and Holland). One group then received pairings of one of the CSs with LiCl, and the other group received unpaired presentations of that CS and LiCl. A subsequent test revealed no differences in consumption across foods or groups. In contrast, paired rats trained and tested in exactly the same manner except with 20-s CS–food intervals showed less consumption of the food whose auditory partner had been paired with LiCl than of the other food, and less consumption of that food than found with either food in the unpaired rats. Thus it seems reasonable to conclude that very short CS–food intervals (2 s) may not permit encoding of food properties needed to establish mediated aversion learning.

Activation Status of CS and US: Learning About Absent USs

The studies we have described so far have all examined situations in which an associatively activated event representation served as a CS, and the US (and in some cases, other CSs) were physically present, that is, their representations were directly activated. Thus, in Holland's (1981) mediated flavor aversion learning studies, the illness-inducing US was physically presented, whereas the flavor CS was physically absent, but its representation was associatively activated by a tone previously paired with that flavor. It seems reasonable to consider whether associatively activated event representations could also serve as USs for physically present CSs, and whether associations between CSs and USs could be formed when both CS and US functions are served by associatively activated

event representations. Much theoretical discussion of these issues has been based on elaborations of Wagner's (1981) SOP theory of learning and memory. Although the power of this model was first brought to bear on these issues in the context of mediated aversion learning (Holland, 1983), most subsequent empirical and theoretical development (e.g., Dickinson & Burke, 1996; Holland & Sherwood, in press; Van Hamme & Wasserman, 1994; Wheeler, Sherwood, & Holland, 2008) in this vein concerned conditioning situations that do not pertain to taste aversion learning. Recapitulation of these theories and issues would require discussion of data from experiments that are outside the scope of this chapter. Thus, we confine our discussion to the empirical issues of whether flavor–US associations can be formed when the CS is physically present and the illness-inducing US is physically absent, but its representation is associatively activated, and whether flavor–US associations can be formed when neither CS nor US is physically present, but representations of both events are associatively activated.

Operationally, simple second-order conditioning procedures provide circumstances under which a flavor aversion might be established by pairing a real CS with an associatively activated US representation. An aversion is first established to one flavor by pairing it with an illness-inducing agent, and then a second flavor is paired with the first flavor, in the absence of the original US (e.g., Bevins, Delzer, & Bardo, 1996; Robertson et al., 1984). On extrapolating from Konorski's (1948) account for second-order conditioning in more traditional settings, because the first flavor activates a representation of the illness-inducing US, the second-order flavor might become directly associated with that US. However, the acquisition of an aversion to the second-order cue is insufficient to claim that such a direct association was formed. Instead, that aversion might be mediated by an association between the two flavors, such that the second-order flavor activates a representation of the now-averted first-order flavor, and thus suppresses consumption indirectly. Alternately, an association might be formed between the second-order flavor and the learned illness response to the first flavor. These three possible structures of learning in second-order conditioning have been explored extensively in more conventional procedures (see Rescorla, 1980, for a review). Although the latter two accounts generally have received the most empirical support, there is evidence for the first, mediated learning, possibility as well (Davey & McKenna, 1983; Ward-Robinson, 2004; Winterbauer & Balleine, 2005). However, there have been few attempts to disentangle these options in flavor aversion learning (e.g., Robertson et al., 1984).

Nevertheless, the question of whether flavor aversions may be formed in the absence of both the flavor CS and the aversion-inducing US has been addressed by Dwyer (1999), who showed that two indirectly activated representations may be associated if they are activated contiguously. In one experiment, rats drank a peppermint solution in one context, and an almond–quinine solution in a second context. After that treatment, some rats drank an almond-only solution in the first context while others drank that solution in the second context. When the rats were tested in a third context, they showed less consumption of the peppermint solution if they had previously consumed the almond solution in the first context than if they had consumed it in the second context. Dwyer concluded that the reduction in consumption was due to an association that was formed between peppermint and the aversive quinine, when the presence of the first context activated a representation of peppermint at the same time that the taste of the almond solution activated a representation of quinine. Dwyer (2001) found a similar outcome when the almond aversion was established by backward pairings with LiCl. Thus, at least under some circumstances, an aversion to a flavor can be formed by pairing an associate of that flavor with an associate of an event that would normally be sufficient to induce aversions. Interestingly, Dwyer, Mackintosh, and Boakes (1998) provided an analogous example of mediated learning of an association between absent events in a taste preference conditioning paradigm.

Redescription of an experiment described in the section titled Mediated Extinction of Flavor Aversions, which concerned mediated extinction of a flavor aversion, provides a somewhat different example of the formation of an association between two absent events (Holland, 1983). Recall that Holland and Forbes (1982b) first paired two auditory cues with two flavored foods, before establishing aversions to both flavors by pairing each of them with LiCl. Then, one auditory cue was presented repeatedly in the absence of either flavors or illness, and finally consumption of the two flavors themselves was assessed in extinction. There was more rapid extinction of the aversion to

the flavor whose auditory partner had been presented alone. Holland and Forbes attributed this outcome to mediated extinction: associative activation of the flavor representation in the absence of illness provided the opportunity for flavor extinction learning. Notably, most theories of extinction attribute it to the acquisition of inhibitory associations between the CS and the US whose representation is aroused by presentation of that CS (see Bouton, 2004; Rescorla, 2004a, for reviews). In support of that assertion, extinction of responding to a CS is often substantially reduced if activation of the US representation is thwarted by, for example, simultaneous presentation of a previously trained conditioned inhibitor (Rescorla, 2003) or reducing the motivational significance of that US by satiation or other methods of US devaluation (Holland & Rescorla, 1975). From that perspective of the nature of extinction learning, Holland and Forbes's demonstration of mediated extinction reflects the acquisition of inhibitory associations between the flavor and the illness-inducing US, neither of which was physically presented in the mediated extinction phase (Holland, 1983). Instead, the flavor was associatively activated by the auditory CS, which in turn activated the representation of the illness US via a chaining or "spreading-activation" (e.g., Collins & Loftus, 1975) process, which has often been used within learning theories to explain phenomena such as sensory preconditioning (e.g., Wagner, 1981).

Dwyer (1999) discussed the discrepancy between his observation of excitatory flavor aversion learning and Holland and Forbes's (1982b) observation of inhibitory learning when associatively activated representations of CS and US were paired, in the context of various theories that include learning about absent events. For example, Dickinson and Burke (1996) asserted that excitatory learning will occur when both CS and US representations are associatively activated and inhibitory associations will be formed when one representation is directly activated and the other associatively activated, whereas Holland (1983) suggested a spreading-activation account for the formation of inhibitory associations between absent events. We have not pursued this issue further in the context of flavor aversion learning in our laboratory. However, based on the results of studies with auditory and visual CSs and flavor USs, we suggest that assumptions that various combinations of actual and associatively activated event representations uniquely produce excitatory or inhibitory associations are misguided. Holland and Sherwood (in press) and Wheeler et al. (2008) found that either excitatory or inhibitory tone–flavor associations could be formed, depending on the temporal relations between associatively activated representations of those events. Simply described, arrangements of associatively activated representations of CS and US produce excitatory or inhibitory CS–US learning depending on the same factors that determine the nature of learning between directly experienced CSs and USs. Again, the guiding principle in this situation seems to be that associatively activated event representations often function in the same manner as their directly activated referents.

Self-Reinforcement and Modulation: Limitations of Mediated Potentiation

Despite our emphasis throughout this chapter on the comparability of associatively activated event representations and their referents, it is clear that they are not indistinguishable. As we have repeatedly noted in this chapter, our mediated aversions are typically an order of magnitude weaker than directly established aversions. A possible exception was observed in the case of mediated potentiation of odor aversion learning (see the section on Modulation of Learning About Other Cues; Holland, 1983, Experiments 3 and 4), in which an auditory cue previously paired with a flavor was as capable of potentiating odor aversion learning as the flavor itself. We capitalized on this large effect size to search for functional differences between directly and associatively activated flavor representations in this context, relatively independent of differences in effect magnitude.

The experiments were based on an observation reported originally by Durlach and Rescorla (1980) and Palmerino, Rusiniak, and Garcia (1980) in their investigations of flavor-potentiated odor aversion learning. It might be recollected that in those studies, pairing a taste + odor compound with LiCl produced more aversion to the odor than pairings of the odor alone with LiCl. In one control condition, rats first received flavor + odor pairings and then odor → illness pairings. Those rats showed no evidence for potentiation of odor aversion learning. From our perspective, however, one might predict that the initial odor + flavor pairings would endow the odor with the ability to activate a representation of the flavor, which could potentiate odor aversion learning, when the odor alone was later paired with LiCl.

Holland (1983) suggested that an event that activates a representation might be immune to associative modification by that representation. Such a limitation might be convenient for avoiding problems of "self-reinforcement" in other contexts, for example, extinction, which might never be observed because each CS presentation would be accompanied by activation of a US representation regardless of the physical presence of the US. Holland (1983, Experiment 4) showed that potentiation does not occur for an odor that activated an association of a flavor, even when that associatively activated flavor representation potentiates the conditioning of an aversion to another odor. In that experiment (Table 11.8), rats were given access to an odor–flavor (sucrose) compound during some sessions, and another odor solution in other sessions (O1F, O2). After this training, rats in a Compound group were injected with LiCl after exposure to a solution consisting of both odors (O1O2 → LiCl). For other rats, in an Elements group, the two odors were paired with LiCl separately in different sessions (O1 → LiCl, O2 → LiCl). In a subsequent consumption test, rats in the Elements group consumed large and roughly equal amounts of both odor solutions (16.0 ml of O1 and 18.0 ml of O2). Thus, consistent with Durlach and Rescorla's (1980) data, there was no evidence for enhancement of aversion learning to an odor that had previously been paired with a flavor. In contrast, the rats in Group Compound consumed 17.6 ml of O1 and 12.4 ml of O2. Although consumption of O1 in Group Compound did not differ from that in Group Elements, consumption of O2 was significantly lower compared to both O2 consumption in Group Elements and O1 consumption in Group Compound. Thus, Holland asserted that the flavor representation activated by O1 apparently potentiated the acquisition of an aversion to O2, but not to O1, suggesting that an associatively activated flavor representation cannot potentiate learning about the cue that activates that representation. O1 appeared to be immune from the effects of the flavor representation that it generated.

More recent studies have confirmed and extended Holland's (1983) arguments. First, it is notable that a plausible alternative account for Holland's (1983, Experiment 4) data, based on the notion of counterconditioning (e.g., Bouton &

Peck, 1992), remained. O1–sucrose pairings may have produced appetitive conditioning of a preference for O1 (e.g., Harris, Shand, Carroll, & Westbrook, 2004), which might then have retarded O1-LiCl learning and perhaps enabled the "superconditioning" (Rescorla, 2004b) of O2–LiCl associations. However, Holland (2006) showed comparable immunity effects even when the flavor used was nonpreferred (relative to water), such that the odor alone was preferred to the odor + flavor compound. In those cases, there would be no reason to expect enhanced preference for the odor and hence resistance to subsequent aversion learning.

Second, although in Holland's (1983, Experiment 4) study an odor cue that activated a flavor representation was immune to potentiation by that flavor, such an odor seems to be normally susceptible to the potentiating effects of a flavor that is physically present. Holland (1990, Experiment 9; 2006; Table 11.8a) preexposed rats to an O1F compound and O2 alone. Rats that then received pairings of a compound of both odors and a real flavor (FO1O2) with LiCl showed potentiation of aversion learning to both O1 and O2 (Figure 11.8a). In contrast, as in Holland's (1983, Experiment 4) study, when the two odors were paired with LiCl in the absence

of the real flavor (O1O2), only the aversion to O2 was potentiated. Thus, although O1's activation of a flavor representation made it immune to potentiation by an associatively activated representation of that flavor, it did not reduce the normal potentiation of O1 aversion learning by the flavor itself.

Finally, Holland (2006) also showed that an odor that has been previously paired with a flavor is immune to potentiation by *any* associatively activated flavor representation, not only by just the one activated by that odor itself. Holland's (1983) original description of the failure of potentiation of O1 learning in his Experiment 4 and in Durlach and Rescorla's (1980) control procedures was that cues could not potentiate themselves. That is, aversion learning about O1 could not be potentiated by a flavor representation activated by O1. Holland (2006) contrasted this "antibootstrapping" account with the possibility that odors that activate flavor representations are generally immune to modulation by other associatively activated flavor representations, regardless of their source. In one experiment (Table 11.8b), rats received preexposure to two flavors and two odors. In Group Two, each of the odors was presented in compound with a flavor (O1F1 and O2F2). In Group One, one odor was presented in compound with a flavor and the other odor and flavor were unpaired (O1F1, O2, F2) and in Group Con, all four stimuli were unpaired. Then, all rats received an O1O2 compound paired with LiCl injection. As in Holland's (1983, Experiment 4) study, relative to the rats in Group Con, the rats in Group One showed potentiated aversion learning to O2 but not O1 (Figure 11.8b). More important, the

Table 11.8 Outline of Procedures of Holland's (1983, Experiment 4) Mediated Potentiation Study.

Group	Phase 1	Phase 2	Test
Compound	O1F, O2	O1O2 → LiCl	O1, O2
Element	O1F, O2	O1 → LiCl	O1, O2
		O2 → LiCl	

Note: O1 and O2 were two olfactory cues, counterbalanced, and F was a sucrose flavor.

Table 11.8a Outline of Mediated Potentiation Experiment Shown in Figure 11.8a.

Group	Phase 1	Phase 2	Test
Real	O1F, O2, or O1, O2, F	FO1O2 → LiCl	O1, O2
Rep	O1F, O2	O1O2 → LiCl	O1, O2
Con	F, O1, O2	O1O2 → LiCl	O1, O2

Note: O1 and O2 were two olfactory cues, counterbalanced, and F was either sucrose or saline.

Table 11.8b Outline of Mediated Potentiation Experiment Shown in Figure 11.8b.

Group	Phase 1	Phase 2	Test
One	O1F1 O2, F2	O1O2 → LiCl	O1, O2
Two	O1F1 O2F2	O1O2 → LiCl	O1, O2
Con	O1, F1 O2, F2	O1O2 → LiCl	O1, O2

Note: O1 and O2 were two olfactory cues, counterbalanced, and F1 and F2 were sucrose and saline flavors, counterbalanced.

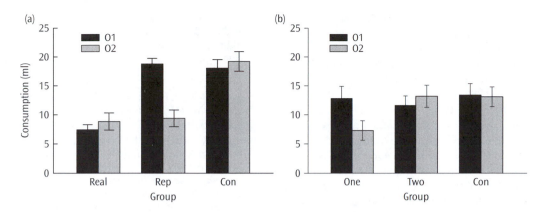

Figure 11.8. Test consumption of odor solutions, showing limitations on mediated potentiation of odor aversion learning (Holland, 2006). (a) In a preexposure phase, rats in Group Rep received presentations of an odor (O1) + flavor compound and of another odor (O2) by itself, and rats in Group Con received those three events separately. Thus, O1 should activate a representation of the flavor in Group Rep but not in Group Con. Half of the rats in Group Real received the former treatment and the other half received the latter. Next, all rats received a compound of the two odors followed by LiCl injection; the odor compound was accompanied by the flavor in Group Real but not in the other two groups. Relative to the performance of rats in Group Con, the presence of the flavor potentiated conditioning of an aversion to both odors in Group Real, but the presence of an associatively activated representation of the flavor in Group Rep potentiated aversion learning only to the odor that did not activate that flavor representation. (b) Rats in Group Two were preexposed to two odor + flavor compounds (O1F1 and O2F2), rats in Group One were preexposed to one odor compound (O1F1) and the other events unpaired, and rats in Group Con received unpaired preexposure to all of the events. All rats then received an O1 + O2 compound paired with LiCl. Relative to Control rats, an odor that activated a representation of a flavor potentiated conditioning of an aversion to another contemporaneous odor if that odor did not itself activate a flavor representation (Group One), but not if the other odor activated such a representation (Group Two).

rats in Group Two showed no evidence for potentiation of aversion learning to either O1 or O2. If the immunity to potentiation shown by an odor previously paired with a flavor is specific to the effects produced by the flavor representation that it activates, then learning of aversions to both odors should have been potentiated: O1 learning would be potentiated by the F2 representation activated by O2, and O2 learning would be potentiated by the F1 representation activated by O1. The fact that neither odor aversion was potentiated shows that the odors that activate flavor representations are immune to potentiation by any associatively activated flavor representation. At the same time, the results of the previous experiment show that odors that activate flavor representations are normally susceptible to potentiation by directly activated (real) flavor representations. Thus, there appear to be at least some processing limitations on associatively activated, relative to directly activated, event representations.

CONCLUSION

The data described in this chapter show that associatively activated flavor representations share many of the features and functions of directly activated representations of those events. Associatively activated flavor representations were found to substitute for their referent flavors in the acquisition of new flavor aversions and the extinction of previously established ones, as well as a variety of modulatory functions including overshadowing, potentiation, and occasion-setting (Holland & Forbes, 1982a). Furthermore, in many cases, associatively activated food representations encoded detailed sensory features of those foods. Indeed, some data, both behavioral and neurobiological, suggested that such activation might include instigation of perceptual processing appropriate to the absent food referents, consistent with the results of many human imaging experiments in which pairing of events from different sensory modalities endows those events with the ability to provoke activity in sensory regions characteristic to the predicted, but absent, event (e.g., Cabeza & Nyberg, 2000; Gottfried et al., 2003; McIntosh, Cabeza, & Lobaugh, 1998).

At the same time, directly and associatively activated event representations are clearly not identical, and the mutual substitution of these representations is constrained in some circumstances. For example, in most of our studies, associatively activated event representations were considerably less salient than directly activated representations. Furthermore, the ability of associatively activated representations to substitute for their referents in some functions was severely constrained by the amount of training or other activity of those representations.

Taken together, the results of our research give further credence to suggestions by other investigators that food aversions mediated by cognitive images, rather than physical illness, may be widespread and may contribute to unusual eating habits and eating disorders (e.g., Batsell & Brown, 1998; Rozin, 1986). Moreover, although we introduced our studies of associatively activated event representations to illustrate how a privileged system of flavor aversion learning may, through associative learning, come under the control of a range of external and internal (imaginary) cues, other research in our laboratory suggest that our results are broadly applicable within a range of conditioning preparations including food- and shock-reinforced learning. Thus, by extrapolation to other associative learning contexts, they provide a substantial empirical basis to the use of imagery procedures in psychotherapy, by which imagined events are meant to substitute, in a potentially controllable fashion, for real-world events that might prove traumatic or damaging in other ways (e.g., Dadds, Bovbjerg, Redd, & Cutmore, 1997). On the other hand, some clinicians (Dadds et al., 1997) have noted that, if of general application, some of our observations of differences in the contents and functions of directly and associatively activated event representations may undermine the utility of these substitution-based therapies. Further exploration of behavioral and neurobiological aspects of associatively activated event representations will help us refine our understanding of associative learning in general, and facilitate the development of more effective learning-based therapies.

References

Adams, C., & Dickinson, A. (1981). Actions and habits: Variations in associative representations during instrumental learning. In N. E. Spear & R. R. Miller (Eds.), *Information processing in animals: Memory mechanisms* (pp. 143–165). Hillsdale, NJ: Lawrence Erlbaum.

Allport, G. W. (1937). *Personality: A psychological interpretation.* New York: Holt.

Batsell, W. R., & Batson, J. D. (1999). Augmentation of taste conditioning by a preconditioned odor. *Journal of Experimental Psychology: Animal Behavior Processes, 25,* 374–388.

Batsell, W. R., & Blankenship, A. A. (2003). Beyond potentiation: Synergistic conditioning in flavor-aversion learning. *Brain and Mind, 3,* 383–408.

Batsell, W. R., & Brown, A. S. (1998). Human flavor-aversion learning: A comparison of traditional aversions and cognitive aversions. *Learning and Motivation, 29,* 383–396.

Bevins, R. A., Delzer, T. A., & Bardo, M. T. (1996). Second-order conditioning detects unexpressed morphine-induced salt aversion. *Animal Learning & Behavior, 24,* 221–229.

Bouton, M. E. (2004). Context and behavioral processes in extinction. *Learning and Memory, 11,* 485–494.

Bouton, M. E., Jones, D. L., McPhillips, S. A., & Swartzentruber, D. (1986). Potentiation and overshadowing in odor-aversion learning: Role of method of odor presentation, the distal-proximal cue distinction, and the conditionability of odor. *Learning and Motivation, 17,* 115–138.

Bouton, M., & Peck, C. (1992). Spontaneous recovery in cross-motivational transfer (counterconditioning). *Animal Learning & Behavior, 20,* 313–321.

Bouton, M. E., & Whiting, M. R. (1982). Simultaneous odor–taste and taste–taste compounds in poison-avoidance learning. *Learning and Motivation, 13,* 472–494.

Cabeza, P. R., & Nyberg, L. (2000). Imaging cognition II: An empirical review of 275 PET and fMRI studies. *Journal of Cognitive Neuroscience, 12,* 1–47.

Collins, A., & Loftus, E. (1975). A spreading-activation theory of semantic processing. *Psychological Review, 82,* 407–428.

Colwill, R. M., & Motzkin, D. K. (1994). Encoding of the unconditioned stimulus in Pavlovian conditioning. *Animal Learning & Behavior, 22,* 384–394.

Colwill, R. M., & Rescorla, R. A. (1990). Effect of reinforcer devaluation on discriminative control of instrumental behavior. *Journal of Experimental Psychology: Animal Behavior Processes, 16,* 40–47.

Dadds, M. R., Bovbjerg, D. H., Redd, W. H., & Cutmore, T. R. H. (1997). Imagery in classical conditioning. *Psychological Bulletin, 122,* 89–103.

Davey, G. C. L., & McKenna, I. (1983). The effects of postconditioning revaluation of CS1 and UCS following Pavlovian second-order electrodermal conditioning in humans. *Quarterly Journal of Experimental Psychology, 35B,* 125–133.

Delamater, A. R., & Holland, P. C. (2008). The influence of CS–US interval on several different indices of learning in appetitive conditioning. *Journal of Experimental Psychology: Animal Behavior Processes, 34,* 202–222.

Delamater, A. R., LoLordo, V. M., & Berridge, K. C. (1986). Control of fluid palatability by exteroceptive Pavlovian signals. *Journal of Experimental Psychology: Animal Behavior Processes, 12,* 143–152.

Delamater, A., & Treit, D. (1988). Chlordiazepoxide attenuates shock-based and enhances LiCl-based fluid aversions. *Learning and Motivation, 19,* 221–238.

Dickinson, A., & Burke, J. (1996). Within-compound associations mediate the retrospective revaluation of causality judgments. *Quarterly Journal of Experimental Psychology, 49B,* 60–80.

Durlach, P. J., & Rescorla, R. A. (1980). Potentiation rather than overshadowing in flavor aversion learning: An analysis in terms of within compound associations. *Journal of Experimental Psychology: Animal Behavior Processes, 6,* 175–187.

Dwyer, D. M. (1999). Retrospective revaluation or mediated conditioning? The effect of different reinforcers. *Quarterly Journal of Experimental Psychology, 52B,* 289–306.

Dwyer, D. M. (2001). Mediated conditioning and retrospective revaluation with LiCl then flavor pairings. *Quarterly Journal of Experimental Psychology, 54B,* 145–165.

Dwyer, D. M., Mackintosh, N. J., & Boakes, R. A. (1998). Simultaneous activation of the representations of absent cues results in the formation of an excitatory association between them. *Journal of Experimental Psychology: Animal Behavior Procsses, 24,* 163–171.

Forbes, D. T., & Holland, P. C. (1980). Positive and negative patterning after CS preexposure in flavor aversion conditioning. *Animal Learning & Behavior, 8,* 595–600.

Galarce, E. M., Crombag, H. S., & Holland, P. C. (2007). Reinforcer-specificity of appetitive and consummatory behavior of rats after Pavlovian conditioning with food reinforcers. *Physiology and Behavior, 91,* 95–105.

Garcia, J., & Kimeldorf, D. J. (1957). Temporal relationships within the conditioning of a saccharine aversion through radiation exposure. *Journal of Comparative and Physiological Psychology, 50,* 180.

Garcia, J., & Koelling, R. A. (1966). Relation of cue to consequence in avoidance learning. *Psychonomic Science, 4,* 123–124.

Garcia, J., Kovner, R., & Green, K. S. (1970). Cue properties versus palatability of flavors in avoidance learning. *Psychonomic Science, 20,* 313–314.

Garner, W. R. (1974). *The processing of information and structure.* Potomac, MD: Lawrence Erlbaum.

Gottfried, J. A., O'Doherty, J., & Dolan, R. J. (2003). Encoding predictive reward value in human amygdala and orbitofrontal cortex. *Science, 301,* 1104–1107.

Grill, H. J., & Norgren, R. (1978). Chronically decerebrate rats demonstrate satiation but not bait shyness. *Science, 201,* 267–270.

Grote, F., & Brown, R. (1973). Deprivation level affects extinction of a conditioned taste aversion. *Learning and Motivation, 4,* 314–319.

Gustavson, K., Hart, J., Calton, J., & Schachtman, T. (1992). Effects of extinction and US reinstatement of a blocking CS–US association. *Bulletin of the Psychonomic Society, 30,* 247–250.

Hall, G. (1996). Learning about associatively-activated stimulus representations: Implications for acquired equivalence and perceptual learning. *Animal Learning & Behavior, 24,* 233–255.

Hall, G., & Pearce, J. M. (1982). Restoring the associability of a pre-exposed CS by a surprising event. *Quarterly Journal of Experimental Psychology, 34B,* 127–140.

Harris, J. A., Shand, F. L., Carroll, L. Q., & Westbrook, R. F. (2004). Persistence of preference for a flavor presented in simultaneous compound with sucrose. *Journal of Experimental Psychology: Animal Behavior Processes, 30,* 177–189.

Hatfield, T., Han, J. S., Conley, M., Gallagher, M., & Holland, P. C. (1996). Neurotoxic lesions of the basolateral, but not central, amygdala interfere with Pavlovian second order conditioning and reinforcer devaluation effects. *Journal of Neuroscience, 16,* 5256–5265.

Holland, P. C. (1980). CS–US interval as a determinant of the form of Pavlovian appetitive conditioned responses. *Journal of Experimental Psychology: Animal Behavior Processes, 6,* 155–174.

Holland, P. C. (1981). Acquisition of representation mediated conditioned food aversions. *Learning and Motivation, 12,* 1–18.

Holland, P. C. (1983). Representation mediated overshadowing and potentiation of conditioned aversions. *Journal of Experimental Psychology: Animal Behavior Processes, 9,* 1–13.

Holland, P. C. (1988). Excitation and inhibition in unblocking. *Journal of Experimental Psychology: Animal Behavior Processes, 14,* 261–279.

Holland, P. C. (1990). Event representation in Pavlovian conditioning: Image and action. *Cognition, 37,* 105–131.

Holland, P. C. (1998). Amount of training affects associatively-activated event representation. *Neuropharmacology, 37,* 461–469.

Holland, P. C. (2006). Limitations on representation-mediated potentiation of flavour or odour aversions. *Quarterly Journal of Experimental Psychology, 59,* 233–250.

Holland, P.C. (in press). A comparison of two methods of assessing representation-mediated food aversions based on shock or illness. *Learning and Motivation.*

Holland, P. C., & Forbes, D. T. (1982a). Control of conditional discrimination performance by CS evoked event representations. *Animal Learning & Behavior, 10,* 249–256.

Holland, P. C., & Forbes, D. T. (1982b). Representation mediated extinction of flavor aversions. *Learning and Motivation, 13,* 454–471.

Holland, P. C., Lasseter, H., & Agarwal, I. (2008). Amount of training and cue-evoked taste-reactivity responding in reinforcer devaluation. *Journal of Experimental Psychology: Animal Behavior Processes, 34,* 119–132.

Holland, P. C., & Rescorla, R. A. (1975). The effect of two ways of devaluing the unconditioned stimulus after first and second order appetitive conditioning. *Journal of Experimental Psychology: Animal Behavior Processes, 1,* 355–363.

Holland, P. C., & Sherwood, A. (in press). Formation of excitatory and inhibitory associations between absent events. *Journal of Experimental Psychology: Animal Behavior Processes.*

Holland, P. C., & Straub, J. J. (1979). Differential effects of two ways of devaluing the unconditioned stimulus after Pavlovian appetitive conditioning. *Journal of Experimental Psychology: Animal Behavior Processes, 5,* 65–78.

Kerfoot, E. C., Agarwal, I., Lee, H. J., & Holland, P. C. (2007). Control of appetitive and aversive taste-reactivity responses by an auditory conditioned stimulus in a devaluation task: A FOS and behavioral analysis. *Learning and Memory, 14,* 581–589.

Kimble, G. A., & Perlmuter, L. C. (1970). The problem of volition. *Psychological Review, 77,* 361–384.

Kirkpatrick, K., & Church, R. M. (2000). Stimulus and temporal cues in classical conditioning. *Journal of Experimental Psychology: Animal Behavior Processes, 26,* 206–209.

Konorski, J. (1948). *Conditioned reflexes and neuron organization.* Cambridge: Cambridge University Press.

Konorski, J. (1967). *Integrative activity of the brain.* Chicago, IL: University of Chicago Press.

Krane, R. V., & Wagner, A. R. (1975). Taste aversion learning with a delayed shock US: implications for the "generality of the laws of learning." *Journal of Comparative Physiology Psychology, 88,* 882–889.

Lee, H. J., Groshek, F., Petrovich, G. D., Cantalini, J. P., Gallagher, M., & Holland, P. C. (2005). Role of amygdalo-nigral circuitry in conditioning of a visual stimulus paired with food. *Journal of Neuroscience, 25,* 3881–3888.

Mackintosh, N. J. (1974). *The psychology of animal learning.* New York: Academic Press.

McDannald, M. A., Saddoris, M. P., Gallagher, M., & Holland, P. C. (2005). Lesions of orbitofrontal cortex impair rats' differential outcome expectancy learning but not CS-potentiated feeding. *Journal of Neuroscience, 25,* 4626–4632.

McIntosh, A. R., Cabeza, R. E., & Lobaugh, N. J. (1998). Analysis of neural interactions explains the activation of occipital cortex by an auditory stimulus. *Journal of Neurophysiology, 80,* 2790–2796.

Miller, R. R., & Barnet, R. C. (1993). The role of time in elementary associations. *Current Directions in Psychological Science, 2,* 106–111.

Palmerino, C. C., Rusiniak, K. W., & Garcia, J. (1980). Flavor illness aversions: The peculiar role of odor and taste in memory for poison. *Science, 208,* 753–755.

Pearce, J. M., & Hall, G. (1980). A model for Pavlovian learning: Variations in the effectiveness of conditioned but not of unconditioned stimuli. *Psychological Review, 106,* 532–552.

Petrovich, G. D., Holland, P. C., & Gallagher, M. (2005). Amygdalar and prefrontal pathways to the lateral hypothalamus are activated by a learned cue that stimulates eating. *Journal of Neuroscience, 25,* 8295–8302.

Petrovich, G. D., Ross, C. A., Gallagher, M., & Holland, P. C. (2007). Learned contextual cue potentiates eating in rats. *Physiology and Behavior.* 90, 362–367.

Pickens, C. L., Saddoris, M. P., Setlow, B., Gallagher, M., Holland, P. C., & Shoenbaum, G. (2003). Different roles for orbitofrontal cortex and basolateral amygdala in a reinforcer devaluation task. *Journal of Neuroscience, 23,* 11078–11084.

Rescorla, R. A. (1980). *Pavlovian second order conditioning: Studies in associative learning.* Hillsdale, NJ: Lawrence Erlbaum.

Rescorla, R. A. (2003). Protection from extinction. *Learning & Behavior, 31*, 124–132.

Rescorla, R. A. (2004a). Spontaneous recovery. *Learning and Memory, 11*, 501–509.

Rescorla, R. A. (2004b). Superconditioning from a reduced reinforcer. *Quarterly Journal of Experimental Psychology, 57B*, 133–152.

Rescorla, R. A., & Holland, P. C. (1976). Some behavioral approaches to the study of learning. In E. Bennett & M. R. Rozensweig (Eds.), *Neural mechanisms of learning and memory* (pp. 165–192). Cambridge, MA: MIT Press.

Revusky, S., Parker, L. A., & Coombes, S. (1977). Flavor aversion learning: Extinction of the aversion to an interfering flavor after conditioning does not affect the aversion to the reference flavor. *Behavioral Biology, 19*, 503–508.

Reynolds, S. M., & Berridge, K. C. (2002). Positive and negative motivation in nucleus accumbens shell: Bivalent rostrocaudal gradients for GABA-elicited eating, taste "liking"/"disliking" reactions, place preference/avoidance, and fear. *Journal of Neuroscience, 22*, 7308–7320.

Rizley, R., & Rescorla, R. A. (1972). Associations in second order conditioning and sensory preconditioning. *Journal of Comparative and Physiological Psychology, 81*, 1–11.

Robertson, D., Krane, R. V., & Garrud, T. (1984). 2nd-order conditioned taste aversion in rats—Shared modality is not sufficient to promote an association between S2 and S1. *Animal Learning & Behavior, 12*, 316–322.

Rozin, P. (1986). One-trial acquired likes and dislikes in humans: Disgust as a US, food predominance, and negative learning predominance. *Learning and Motivation, 17*, 180–189.

Rusiniak, K., Hankins, W., Garcia, J., & Brett, L. (1979). Flavor illness associations: Potentiation of odor by taste in rats. *Behavioral and Neural Biology, 25*, 1–17.

Silva, K. M., & Timberlake, W. (1997). A behavior systems view of conditioned states during long and short CS–US intervals. *Learning and Motivation, 28*, 465–490.

Slotnick, B. M., Westbrook, R. F., & Darling, F. M. C. (1997). What the rat's nose tells the rat's mouth: Long delay aversion conditioning with aqueous odors and potentiation of tastes by odors. *Animal Learning & Behavior, 25*, 357–369.

Van Hamme, L. J., & Wasserman, E. A. (1994). Cue competition in causality judgments: The role of nonpresentation of compound stimulus elements. *Learning and Motivation, 25*, 127–151.

Wagner, A. R. (1981). SOP: A model of automatic memory processing in animal behavior. In N. E. Spear & R. R. Miller (Eds.), *Information processing in animals: Memory mechanisms* (pp. 5–47). Hillsdale, NJ: Erlbaum.

Ward-Robinson, J. (2004). An analysis of second-order autoshaping. *Learning and Motivation, 35*, 1–21.

Ward-Robinson, J., & Hall, G. (1996). Backward sensory preconditioning. *Journal of Experimental Psychology: Animal Behavior Processes, 22*, 395–404.

Wheeler, D. S., Sherwood, A., & Holland, P. C. (2008). Excitatory and inhibitory learning with absent stimuli. *Journal of Experimental Psychology: Animal Behavior Processes, 34*, 247–255.

Winterbauer, N. E., & Balleine, B. W. (2005). Motivational control of second-order conditioning. *Journal of Experimental Psychology: Animal Behavior Processes, 31*, 334–340.

12

Strain Differences in Taste Aversion Learning: Implications for Animal Models of Drug Abuse

ANTHONY L. RILEY, CATHERINE M. DAVIS, AND PETER G. ROMA

THE NATURE OF ANIMAL MODELS

Although the focus on animal models of drug abuse has traditionally been on the reinforcement processes underlying the initiation and escalation of drug intake, recently there has been an increasing interest in the drug's aversive effects (as indexed by the conditioned taste aversion [CTA] procedure) in such models. This chapter describes some of the recent work on the role of aversions (as a protectant factor in drug escalation), focusing primarily on work on inbred strains of mice and rats or rodent models that have been selectively bred for drug reactivity. The chapter closes with an overview of the role of environmental factors in modulating reactivity in such lines and strains, highlighting the importance of gene–environment interactions in the particular phenotype of drug-taking behavior.

The use of animals as models of the human condition has a long and interesting history. Although some of the initial uses in this context were criticized, for example, when the Greek physician Galen (AD 157) used examples of animal organs as illustrations representing human anatomy (see Zimmer, 2004), their use in biomedical settings has provided information on a range of issues related to human development and health such as normal cardiovascular function (Harvey, 1993), the genetics of behavior (Uhl, Hall, & Sora, 2002) and the possibilities for stem-cell transplantation

(Thomson et al., 1995). Interestingly, and despite myriad concerns regarding the use of such models for the complexity of human activity (Dawkins, 1980; Keehn, 1986), a range of human behavioral and psychiatric conditions, including depression, anxiety, schizophrenia, Alzheimer's and Parkinson's diseases, human sexual dysfunction and eating disorders, have analogues in animal research (see Bond, 1984; Davey, 1983; Haug & Whalen, 1999; Keehn, 1979, 1986). Such conditions have all been elucidated by animal models, resulting in insights relevant to the etiology and treatment of the disorders. The popularity and use of such models has recently been highlighted by the NIH Blueprint that provides resources for a variety of animal models (primate, rodent, zebrafish) addressing issues as diverse as mutagenesis, retinal degeneration, aging, and Parkinson's disease (see http://neuroscienceblueprint.nih.gov).

Modeling human behavior in general assumes a number of issues, including an understanding of what is being modeled (i.e., the specific behavior or pathology) as well as how the procedure in question truly models the behavior (i.e., the specific model). In relation to the first issue, one can only model a specific behavior if the phenomenon has been well characterized. By such careful characterization, a model can be crafted to address the properties of the behavior. Further, by knowing the nature of the model, for example, whether the animal model shares a common etiology with the human condition or simply provides a baseline on which manipulations are predictive of changes in that condition, conclusions regarding etiology and treatment may be more confidently made (see Kornetsky, 1977).

One phenomenon receiving extensive interest in terms of the development or creation of animal models is that of drug use and abuse. Although this has been most evident with alcoholism (e.g., see Tabakoff & Hoffman, 2000), such models now address drugs in general as well as their interactions with each other. In these models, animals have been used to examine the initiation, maintenance, and escalation of drug taking, the multifaceted genetic and environmental factors contributing to drug-abuse vulnerability, the physiological, anatomical, and neurochemical mediation of drug-taking behavior and various behavioral and pharmacological treatments for addiction. For each of these issues, a model of drug-taking has to be constructed in such a way that the effects of specific manipulations on these patterns can be detected and controlled. In several recent, comprehensive reviews of investigations into the dynamics and neurobiology of drug-taking behavior, the nature of abuse and addiction has been described, and, in so doing, the characteristics to be modeled by animal work have been noted.

ANIMAL MODELS OF DRUG ABUSE

In their recent analysis of the neurobiology of drug abuse, Koob and LeMoal (2006) provided an overview of the various stages involved in addiction. The model describes the initiation of drug-taking via its acute reinforcing effects that eventually transitions into the escalation of drug intake and compulsive drug use as a consequence of drug-induced neuroplastic changes. These patterns are then followed by dependence and withdrawal that maintain elevated intake. In a related analysis, Meyer and Quenzer (2005) described a similar sequence of drug-taking behavior and provided a number of possible theoretical processes underlying these patterns that develop with chronic use. These possibilities included (1) positive reinforcement (reward), (2) incentive sensitization, (3) physical dependence, and (4) opponent process. Although each theoretical model addresses chronic drug intake, each assumes a different process underlying the maintenance and escalation of drug-taking. For example, in the positive reinforcement model,

there is the creation of a craving to reexperience the initial drug-induced euphoria. In the sensitization model, there is a compulsive desire for the drug as a result of some sensitized incentive value acquired by the drug and drug-related stimuli. In the physical dependence model, the symptoms of withdrawal from the drug are thought to be sufficiently aversive to motivate further drug intake. Finally, in the opponent process model, a lowering of a hedonic "set point" induces further drug intake to overcome the opponent process-induced dysphoria. Independent of the specific model of drug addiction presented, there is an interesting and common element (one also common to the initial pattern described by Koob & LeMoal), specifically, some initial "reinforcement" for drug-taking behavior. That is, although the basis for escalation and compulsive use varies across these theoretical models, for each model proposed there is an underlying assumption that the *initiation* of drug-taking is a function of the acute reinforcing effects of the drug. This could be in the form of some positive reinforcement generated by the drug itself or in the form of negative reinforcement, as drug use may be used to relieve boredom, combat anxiety, or facilitate social interactions. It is interesting that for each of the four models proposed by Meyer and Quenzer, it is some elaboration of this basic reinforcement process (via drug-induced craving, sensitization and wanting, dependence, or opponent process-induced dysphoria) that appears also to motivate continued use and which makes relapse so likely. It is important to note that such analyses do not preclude a host of other factors such as genetic predispositions and environmental stress from operating to impact drug-taking behavior, only that there is a common process that may underlie the motivation for use and abuse (see Shurtleff, Liu, & Sasek, 2004).

ANIMAL MODELS OF THE REINFORCING EFFECTS OF DRUGS

Given the focus on the mechanism of reinforcement as important for the initiation and maintenance of drug-taking, it is no surprise that the majority of recent animal models of drug-taking behavior have focused on this process (whether positive or negative reinforcement). In this context, the animal model that has been used most extensively over the years to assay the reinforcing effects of drugs of abuse is the self-administration preparation (originally introduced by Weeks, 1962). What has generally been found is that drugs that are self-administered by humans are also self-administered by laboratory animals, giving clear face validity to its use as a model of the reinforcing effects of drugs (see Yokel, 1987).

Self-administration is by no means the only model used in assessments of the reinforcing effects of drugs. In one of the most comprehensive summaries of animal models for assessing the reinforcing effects of drugs of abuse, Bozarth (1987) describes a number of laboratory preparations used for just this purpose.[1] These other models include conditioned place preference (CPP) in which specific and distinct sides of a chamber are associated with the drug or vehicle and the animal is then allowed to choose between the drug-associated and vehicle-associated sides in a nondrug state (Bardo & Bevins, 2000; Tzschentke, 1998), drug discrimination learning in which the drug serves as a discriminative stimulus for some other behavior–reinforcer association (Stolerman, 1993) and electrical stimulation of the brain (ESB) in which the effects of a drug on the threshold for brain stimulation are compared to responding for ESB in the absence of the drug (Kornetsky, Esposito, McLean, & Jacobson, 1979). From such preparations, a variety of drugs under a range of conditions in a number of animal species have been shown to have the rewarding and positive effects thought to be important for drug-taking in humans (see Bozarth, 1987). Although these models vary considerably in their face validity for human drug use (compare self-administration vs. drug discrimination learning), these models have been instrumental in identifying abuse potential and in elucidating the neurochemical and anatomical substrates for abuse and addiction.

THE ROLE OF AVERSIONS IN DRUG USE AND ABUSE

Clearly, an understanding of drug reward is critically important for modeling abuse potential; however, it should be noted that the majority of drugs of abuse have multiple stimulus effects, not all of which are positive, reinforcing, or rewarding (Koob & LeMoal, 2006; Lynch & Carroll, 2001; Stolerman, 1992). Although the nature of the aversive effects of drugs has been mentioned with regard

to dependence and withdrawal (or opponent-process-induced dysphoria; see earlier section), these aversive effects are seen primarily with chronic drug use and do not reflect any acutely aversive effects that might impact initial drug intake and escalation. A drug's aversive effects, however, are often noted in the assessments of abuse liability in humans (see Baker & Cannon., 1982; Griffiths, Bigelow, & Ator, 2003; Zacny & Gutierrez, 2003) and have been described in a variety of animal studies addressing the ability of drugs of abuse to induce CTA and condition place aversion (CPA), respectively.

In relation to taste aversions, Garcia, Kimeldorf, and Koelling (1955) reported that in rats the consumption of a sweetened solution prior to exposure to ionizing radiation resulted in the subsequent suppression of consumption of the radiation-paired flavor (tested once the unconditioned effects of radiation had dissipated), suggesting that the aversive effects of radiation conditioned an aversion to the flavor. Although initially demonstrated with radiation, such CTAs have been demonstrated with a wide variety of compounds, including classical emetics (e.g., emetine and lithium chloride [LiCl]) and known toxins (e.g., red squill, sodium monoflourophosphate, barium sulfate; see Riley & Tuck, 1985a; Rzóska, 1954). Interestingly, the majority of drugs of abuse, including morphine, alcohol, cocaine, marijuana, and nicotine, also induce taste aversions (see Cappell & LeBlanc, 1977; Gamzu, Vincent, & Boff, 1985; Hunt & Amit, 1987; Riley & Tuck, 1985b). Such findings have been used to argue that drugs of abuse also have aversive effects and that the relative balance between reward and aversion may be important for the initiation and/or escalation of drug taking (Gaiardi et al., 1991; Riley & Simpson, 2001; Stolerman & D'Mello, 1981).

Although both reward and aversion have been reported with the same drug, such assessments are typically made under very different experimental conditions, such as dose of drug, timing of injection, and route of administration, making it difficult to conclude that the drug under comparable parametric conditions has both effects and that the effects might interact to impact drug taking. However, in preparations that have attempted to control for these potential confounds, others have shown that aversions can be demonstrated with specific drugs of abuse at the same dose and by the same route as those used to demonstrate reward in some of the aforementioned animal models. In one of the first demonstrations of these concurrent effects, White, Sklar, and Amit (1977) trained rats to run down a runway for food located in a specific goalbox. Immediately after eating the food, the animals were injected with morphine sulfate and returned to the goalbox for 50 min. Such conditioning was repeated for four additional trials on subsequent days. Throughout conditioning, the time to reach the goalbox and the amount of food consumed once there were recorded. Over trials, the rats ran faster to get to the goalbox, but they reduced the amount consumed of the morphine-associated food. The increase in running speed was not simply a function of being fed in the chamber because saline-treated animals did not display any changes in running speed (or food consumption). White et al. interpreted these findings as suggestive of the dual effects of morphine: The positive effects of morphine were sufficient to reinforce running, while the aversive effects of morphine conditioned an aversion to the food. Interestingly, LiCl-injected subjects decreased food intake but showed no change in running speed, indicating that the suppression of feeding was not necessarily associated with a change in running speed. Thus, the effects on running speed and food intake appeared to be a function of morphine's ability to produce both positive and aversive effects. In related work, Wise, Yokel, and DeWit (1976) reported similar effects within a self-administration preparation. Specifically, they reported that rats formed aversions to tastes that had been associated with the dopamine agonist apomorphine delivered during self-administration. In this study, rats that drank saccharin immediately before self-administering apomorphine subsequently avoided consumption of the saccharin solution, but maintained the self-administration behavior. As with White et al., Wise et al. interpreted these behaviors as reflecting a rewarding effect that maintained self-administration and an aversive effect that was sufficient to condition a taste aversion. More recently, similar findings have been reported using a combined CTA/CPP preparation in which a novel taste and place were paired with morphine. In this procedure, Simpson and Riley (2005) presented animals with a novel saccharin solution to drink, injected them with morphine (or saline), and then confined them to one side of a place conditioning apparatus (every other day for four conditioning trials). On alternate days, the animals were given water access,

injected with saline, and placed on the other side of the apparatus. Following conditioning, all subjects were permitted free access to the entire apparatus. They were then given access to saccharin in a test of any aversion to the morphine-associated taste. Similar to the early reports described previously assessing the affective properties of morphine and apomorphine, this procedure revealed both positive and aversive effects of the drug. Specifically, animals avoided the morphine-associated taste but preferred the morphine-associated place (see also G. M. Martin, Bechara, & van der Kooy, 1988). Again, given that morphine was administered to the same animals at the same dose and by the same route argues that both effects are produced by morphine. Similar results have been demonstrated with caffeine, alcohol, and amphetamine (see Brockwell, Eikelboom, & Beninger, 1991; Reicher & Holman, 1977; Sherman, Pickman, Rice, Liebeskind, & Holman, 1980; Shram, Funk, Li, & Le, 2006).

CTA AS A MODEL OF DRUG ABUSE VULNERABILITY

As noted above, the fact that drugs of abuse produce both approach and avoidance behaviors may have implications for the development and application of animal models of drug-taking behavior. Traditional analyses of such behaviors have focused on the rewarding effects of drugs, and, as such, the corresponding animal models have focused on these particular characteristics. However, given that drugs have aversive effects as well, it may be more appropriate to argue that both reward and aversion contribute to drug-taking behavior. In fact, some have suggested that it is the balance of these effects that impacts or shapes the vulnerability to initial drug taking and escalation, with the drug's rewarding effects increasing vulnerability to abuse and the aversive effects being in some sense protective (Haertzen, Kocher, & Miyasato, 1983; Neumark et al., 2004). Accordingly, comprehensive models of abuse potential might be expected to incorporate assays of both the drug's rewarding and aversive effects.[2]

Given this possible role of a drug's aversive effects in its abuse vulnerability and the use of the CTA procedure in indexing such effects, an understanding of CTA learning in general and how such learning is impacted by a host of factors, for example, drug history, concurrent drug administration, sex, and strain of subject, may be relevant for modeling vulnerability to drug-taking behavior (initiation, escalation, and relapse; see following text). As described earlier, Garcia et al. (1955) introduced aversion learning in their report on changes in the consumption of a sweetened solution after its pairing with ionizing radiation. Subsequent to this introduction of taste aversion learning (see also Chitty, 1954; Rzóska, 1954; Chapter 2), there were a number of findings that characterized this type of learning as somewhat unique or special. Specifically, it occurred despite long delays between the taste and administration of the aversion-inducing agent (see Garcia, Ervin, & Koelling, 1966; McLaurin & Scarborough, 1963), only with specific CS–US combinations (e.g., taste and illness; Garcia & Koelling, 1966) and was very rapidly acquired, that is, one-trial learning (Garcia et al., 1955; see Bitterman, 1975; Logue, 1979). Although such learning is often rapid and robust, it is nonetheless subject to a wide range of parametric manipulations. Specifically, the rate of acquisition, the overall level of suppression, and the speed of extinction are all influenced by a host of factors, including, but certainly not limited to, sex, route of drug administration, age, body weight, amount of solution consumed, number of conditioning trials, drug history, time of day, degree of deprivation, taste quality (and intensity), aversion-inducing drug (and its intensity), the delay between taste and onset of the drug's effects, need state (e.g., if animals are sodium or calcium deficient), and species (Klosterhalfen & Klosterhalfen, 1983; Riley & Freeman, 2004). What is clear from this is that aversions can be altered significantly by a host of internal and external factors. If a drug's aversive and rewarding effects compete to impact drug-taking behavior and if a drug's ability to induce an aversion (as a measure of its aversive effects) varies by such factors, then understanding how these factors affect aversion learning may yield insights for predicting abuse vulnerability.

GENETIC INFLUENCES IN DRUG-INDUCED CTA

One variable that has received considerable attention throughout the history of taste aversion learning is the influence of genetic factors (e.g., Dragoin, 1971; Rozin, 1968). For drug-induced CTA, the interest in genotype goes beyond simply illustrating yet another parameter relevant to the experimental demonstration of the phenomenon, because this variable addresses the intriguing possibility of predictable genetic variations mediating susceptibility to the aversive effects of drugs which may, in turn, affect vulnerability to drug abuse. To investigate the role of genetic factors in animal models of drug abuse, laboratory researchers utilize a variety of methods. Recent advances in molecular biology have enabled the development of transgenic mouse models with targeted gene deletions or compromised functionality of various central nervous system proteins implicated in the effects of abused drugs (Chen et al., 2006; Hall, Li, Sora, Xu, Caron, Lesch et al., 2002; Hill, Alva, Blednov, & Cunningham, 2003; Risinger, Freeman, Greengard, & Fienberg, 2001; see also Phillips et al., 2002). A more traditional and widely applied method for assessing the effects of genotype on abuse vulnerability is the use of selectively bred lines and inbred strains of rodents (Crabbe, 2002). For this approach, individual animals of the same (often outbred) stock are chosen for reproduction based on a common genotypic feature or similar expression of a phenotype of interest. Selectively bred lines are not inbred, as the constituent members of any given mating pair are not related; however, they still share the common phenotype of interest and presumably the same genetic substrate(s) contributing to that phenotype. In contrast, inbred strains are typically derived through full-sibling matings for at least 20 consecutive generations, thereby maximizing the likelihood of genetic homogeneity (Beck et al., 2000; Billingham & Silvers, 1959). Throughout the last century, hundreds of distinct varieties of mice and rats have been developed (see www.informatics.jax.org/external/festing/search_form.cgi), and regardless of the underlying breeding methodology, this genetic approach has met with considerable success when applied to drug-induced CTA (see Table 12.1).

Selected Lines

Within some selectively bred lines, taste aversion learning in general has been shown to vary by genotype. For example, Elkins (1986) selectively bred multiple generations of Sprague-Dawley rats that showed strong and weak CTAs induced by the emetic cyclophosphamide into the taste

Table 12. 1 Genetic influences in drug-induced CTA and relation to self-administration (SA).

Author(s)/ Date	Species	Selected Lines or Inbred Strains	Drug US and Route	Genotypes	Self-Administration or Origin Background	Major CTA Results
Froehlich et al., 1988	Rat	Lines	Alcohol (IP)	Alcohol Preferring (P); Alcohol Nonpreferring (NP)	P oral consume > NP	NP CTA >P, and longer lasting than P at 1.0 g/kg; Significant saccharin preference during extinction at 0.25 g/kg in P only
Kulkosky et al., 1995	Rat	Lines	Alcohol (IP)	High Alcohol Sensitive (HAS); Control Alcohol Sensitive (CAS); Low Alcohol Sensitive (LAS)	No alcohol SA work. HAS > CAS > LAS sleep time and resting behaviors after alcohol injection	LAS CTA extinction more rapid than CAS or HAS; no differences in LiCl CTA
Gauvin et al., 2000	Rat	Lines	Alcohol (IP)	Alcohol Accepting (AA); Alcohol Nonaccepting (ANA)	AA oral consume > ANA	CTA at 1.5 g/kg retarded in ANA
Quintanilla et al., 2001	Rat	Lines	Alcohol (IP)	University of Chile Low Alcohol Drinking (UChA); University of Chile High Alcohol Drinking (UChB)	UChB oral consume > UChA	CTA to 1.5 g/kg in UchA only; CTA to 2.0 g/kg in both, but UChA > UChB
Elkins et al., 1992	Rat	Lines	Alcohol (IP)	Taste Aversion Prone (TAP); Taste Aversion Resistant (TAR)	No alcohol SA work. TAP CTA to cyclophosphamide > TAR	TAP CTA > TAR at 0.25, 0.75, & 1.25 g/kg
Elkins et al., 2003	Rat	Lines	Cocaine (SC)	Taste Aversion Prone (TAP); Taste Aversion Resistant (TAR)	No cocaine SA work. TAP CTA to cyclophosphamide > TAR	TAP CTA > TAR at 5.0 & 20.0 mg/kg
Martin & Baettig, 1980	Rat	Lines	Apomorphine (IP)	Roman High Avoidance (RHA); Roman Low Avoidance (RLA)	No apomorphine SA work. RHA > RLA active shuttle-box avoidance with light CS and shock US	RHA CTA < RLA at 5.0 mg/kg
Durcan et al., 1988	Rat	Lines	Nicotine (SC)	Roman High Avoidance (RHA); Roman Low Avoidance (RLA)	No nicotine SA work. RHA > RLA active shuttlebox avoidance with light CS and shock US	RHA CTA < RLA at 0.4 mg/kg

(continued)

Table 12.1 *Continued*

Author(s)/ Date	Selected Lines or Inbred Strains	Species	Drug US and Route	Genotypes	Self-Administration or Origin Background	Major CTA Results
Risinger et al., 1994	Lines	Mouse	Alcohol (IP)	FAST; SLOW	No alcohol SA work. FAST > SLOW locomotor response to 2.0 g/kg alcohol	FAST CTA < SLOW at 2.5 g/kg
Chester et al., 1998	Lines	Mouse	Alcohol (IP)	Withdrawal Seizure Prone (WSP); Withdrawal Seizure Resistant (WSR); High Alcohol Withdrawal (HAW); Low Alcohol Withdrawal (LAW)	No alcohol SA work. WSP withdrawal convulsions > LAW after 72 h ethanol vapor inhalation; HAW withdrawal > LAW after single 4.0 g/kg injection	WSP CTA < WSR on Trial 2 only (collapsed 2.5 and 4.0 g/kg doses) HAW = LAW at 2.0 and 4.0 g/kg
Chester et al., 2003	Lines	Mouse	Alcohol (IP)	High Alcohol Preference (HAP); Low Alcohol Preference (LAP)	HAP oral consume > LAP	HAP CTA < LAP at 2.0 and 4.0 g/kg
Phillips et al., 2005	Lines	Mouse	Alcohol (IP)	High Taste Aversion (HTA); Low Taste Aversion (LTA)	LTA oral consume > HTA	LTA CTA < HTA at 4.0 g/kg
Cannon & Carrell, 1987	Strains	Rat	Alcohol (IP)	Wistar Kyoto (WKY); Marshall (M520)	WKY oral consume < M520	WKY acquire CTA at 1.0 and 1.5 g/kg, M520 only at 1.5
Cannon et al., 1994	Strains	Rat	Alcohol (IP)	ACI; Brown Norway (BN); Buffalo (BUF); Fischer (F344); Maudsley Reactive (MR); Marshall (M520); Wistar Kyoto (WKY)	Oral consume: WKY < ACI < F344 < BUF < M520 < MR < BN; WKY < all other strains; BN > all other strains except MR	Dose–response slope (0, 0.5, 1.0, 1.5 g/kg) WKY > M520; Correlation between CTA slope and SA = 0.59 (smaller CTA = greater SA)

Reference	Type	Drug	Species	Strains	Oral consumption	CTA results
Cailhol & Mormède, 2002	Strains	Alcohol (IP)	Rat	Wistar Kyoto (WKY); Spontaneously Hypertensive (SHR); Wistar Kyoto Hyperactive (WHKA)	WKHA oral consume > WKY and SHR	WKHA CTA longer to acquire at 1.0 and 1.5 g/kg, no CTA at 0.5 g/kg
Horowitz & Whitney, 1975	Strains	Alcohol (IP)	Mouse	C57BL/6J (C57); DBA/2J (DBA)	C57 oral consume > DBA	C57 CTA < DBA at 20% concentration; CTAs at 5% and 10% only in DBA
Risinger & Cunningham, 1992	Strains	Alcohol (IP)	Mouse	C57BL/6J (C57); DBA/2J (DBA)	C57 oral consume > DBA	C57 CTA < DBA at 2.0 g/kg
Risinger & Cunningham, 1995	Strains	Alcohol (IP)	Mouse	C57BL/6J (C57); DBA/2J (DBA)	C57 oral consume > DBA	C57 CTA < DBA at 4.0 g/kg
Risinger & Cunningham, 1998	Strains	Alcohol (IP)	Mouse	C57BL/6J (C57); DBA/2J (DBA); Plus 20 BXD Recombinant Inbred Strains	C57 oral consume > DBA	C57 CTA < DBA at 4.0 g/kg
Broadbent et al., 2002	Strains	Alcohol (IP)	Mouse	C58/J, CBA/J, DBA/1J, DBA/2J, NZB/BlNJ, PL/J, SJL/J, SWR/J, 129/J	Oral consumption: C57BL/6J > C57L/J > CBA/J > AKR/J > C3H/HeJ > BALB/cJ > 129/J > PL/J > DBA/2J > SJL/J > A/HeJ > DBA/1J > SWR/J	Significant correlation between the strains' mean CTA and mean oral SA (smaller CTA = greater SA)
Risinger & Brown, 1996	Strains	Nicotine (IP)	Mouse	C57BL/6J (C57); DBA/2J (DBA); BALB/cJ (BALB); C3H/heJ (C3H)	Corrected for total fluid intake: C57 oral consume > DBA; C57 female significant 2-bottle preference at 40 μg/ml	C57 no CTA (0.5, 1.0, 2.0 mg/kg); BALB weak CTA, no dose–response; DBA = C3H CTA all doses

aversion prone (TAP) and taste aversion resistant (TAR) lines, respectively. By definition, the TAP rats exhibit stronger cyclophosphamide CTA than their TAR counterparts, but despite similar general learning ability (Hobbs, Walters, Shealy, & Elkins, 1993; Orr, Walters, & Elkins, 1997), TAP rats are also more prone to CTAs induced by LiCl and emetine hydrochloride (Elkins, Walters, & Orr, 1992). Most relevant to this discussion is the fact that TAP rats also show stronger aversions with drugs that have known reinforcing effects. Specifically, and unlike the TAR line, TAP animals show dose-dependent CTAs induced by intraperitoneal (IP) and subcutaneous (SC) cocaine (see Elkins et al., 2003) and also develop stronger CTAs induced by several doses of IP ethanol (Elkins et al., 1992). Unlike the TAP/TAR line, the Roman high-avoidance (RHA) and Roman low-avoidance (RLA) rat strains were not bred based on CTA performance, but rather differential avoidance responding to stimuli previously paired with shock (Bignami, 1965). Interestingly, when tested in a CTA paradigm the RHA rats are actually less sensitive to the aversive effects of 5.0 mg/kg apomorphine and 0.4 mg/kg nicotine than their RLA counterparts (Durcan, Garcha, & Stolerman, 1988; J. R. Martin & Baettig, 1980).

Aside from the TAP/TAR and RHA/RLA rats described earlier, a number of other rodent lines have been specifically bred based on differential responses to an abused drug, namely alcohol, and subsequently tested for sensitivity to alcohol-induced CTA. Among rats, the lines bred for differential oral consumption of ethanol solutions with published CTA data include the alcohol preferring (P) and alcohol nonpreferring (NP) (Froehlich, Harts, Lumeng, & Li, 1988), the alcohol accepting (AA) and alcohol nonaccepting (ANA) (Gauvin, Baird, & Briscoe, 2000), the University of Chile low-alcohol drinking (UChA) and high-alcohol drinking (UChB) (Quintanilla, Callejas, & Tampier, 2001), and the Sardinian alcohol nonpreferring (sNP) and alcohol preferring (sP) lines (Brunetti et al., 2002). In all cases, the lines with the greater propensity for oral alcohol consumption also show weaker alcohol-induced CTAs. In addition to these lines, the high alcohol sensitive (HAS) and low alcohol sensitive (LAS) lines that differ accordingly in sleep time and resting behaviors following alcohol injection also show differential alcohol CTA, with the LAS rats showing more rapid extinction of ethanol-induced CTA than their more highly sensitive counterparts (Kulkosky, Carr, Flores, LaHeist, & Hopkins, 1995).

Among mice, the high alcohol preference (HAP) and low alcohol preference (LAP) lines bred for differences in oral ethanol consumption also differ in alcohol-induced CTAs, with the HAP animals showing weaker CTAs than their low-preferring counterparts (Chester, Lumeng, Li, & Grahame, 2003). Although we are not aware of any self-administration work in the FAST and SLOW mouse lines that differ in their locomotor responses to ethanol, FAST mice do acquire weaker ethanol CTA (Risinger, Malott, Prather, Niehus, & Cunningham, 1994). In addition, the high alcohol withdrawal (HAW) and low alcohol withdrawal (LAW) lines show equivalent ethanol CTA, but acquisition of ethanol aversions is generally slower in withdrawal seizure-prone (WSP) mice versus withdrawal seizure-resistant (WSR) mice (Chester, Risinger, & Cunningham, 1998). Finally, Phillips et al. (2005) recently engaged in a short-term selective breeding effort with mice specifically showing differential ethanol-induced CTA, and consistent with the literature described above, found that the high taste aversion line (HTA) consumed less ethanol than their low taste aversion (LTA) counterparts.

Inbred Strains

Although there are currently no published reports of rodent strains specifically inbred based on sensitivity to drug-induced CTA, a number of strains of rats and mice have been tested for CTA conditioned by some drugs of abuse. As with the selected lines, much of the genetically oriented CTA work with inbred strains has focused on alcohol, typically involving the Wistar Kyoto (WKY) strain known for its relatively low preference for oral alcohol consumption compared to strains such as the high-consuming Marshall (M520; Li & Lumeng, 1984). Consistent with the selected line work described above, Cannon and Carrell (1987) produced CTAs in the low-preferring WKY animals with 1.0 and 1.5 g/kg IP ethanol, whereas the M520 rats only acquired an aversion at the higher dose. Follow-up work including WKY, M520, and five other inbred strains revealed a steeper CTA dose–response slope in the WKY animals versus M520; in addition, a correlation was revealed between the strains' CTA dose–response slopes and mean oral alcohol self-administration, such that a weaker CTA dose–response function tended to correspond with stronger alcohol consumption (Cannon, Leeka, & Block, 1994). Finally, the Wistar Kyoto hyperactive (WKHA) strain, which consumes alcohol more readily than the WKY or spontaneously hypertensive (SHR) strains, fails to acquire an aversion with 0.5 g/kg IP ethanol and shows weaker CTA at 1.0 g/kg compared to the WKY and SHR rats (Cailhol & Mormède, 2002).

Although a number of strains have been tested, virtually all drug-induced CTA work among inbred mice includes the C57BL/6J (C57) and DBA/2J (DBA) strains. When corrected for total fluid intake, C57 mice orally self-administer more nicotine than DBAs; accordingly, and in contrast to the DBA mice, they also fail to acquire aversions with 0.5, 1.0, or 2.0 mg/kg IP nicotine (Risinger &Brown, 1996). However, the well-known difference in oral self-administration between the alcohol-preferring C57 and alcohol-avoiding DBA mice (McClearn & Rodgers, 1959) has made them a particularly valuable model for exploring genetic influences on sensitivity to the aversive effects of ethanol (see Chapter 19). Over the years, C57 mice have consistently shown reduced or no aversions produced by IP ethanol versus their DBA counterparts. For example, both strains acquire CTA at 20% ethanol, but the C57 aversion is markedly weaker than that of the DBA mice; in addition, the DBAs, but not C57s, acquire aversions at 5% and 10% concentrations of ethanol (Horowitz &Whitney, 1975). Moreover, C57 mice acquire weaker CTAs than DBA mice with 2.0 and 4.0 g/kg alcohol (Risinger & Cunningham, 1992, 1995, 1998). In one of the most comprehensive studies of drug-induced CTA, Broadbent, Muccino, and Cunningham (2002) assessed aversions with 2.0 g/kg ethanol in 15 inbred mice strains (including C57 and DBA) and found a significant correlation between the strains' mean CTA and mean oral ethanol consumption rates, such that smaller CTA corresponded with greater self-administration (see also Rhodes et al., 2006). As with Cannon et al.'s (1994) assessment of CTA and self-administration in inbred rats, these data are consistent with the view that vulnerability to excessive alcohol use is subject to genetic influences on sensitivity to alcohol's aversive motivational effects.

Of course, alcohol and nicotine are not the only drugs of interest to researchers, and the selected lines and inbred strains described above are by no means the only genetically distinct animals suitable for exploring genetic factors in vulnerability to drug abuse. In this spirit, we now redirect our focus on what has become an increasingly popular animal model for the effects of genotype on biobehavioral responses to a variety of drugs of abuse: the Fischer and Lewis inbred rat strains.

THE FISCHER–LEWIS MODEL OF DRUG ABUSE

As is typical with inbred rodent strains, and in contrast to selected lines, Fischer (F344) and Lewis (LEW) rats were bred independently of each other in both place and time. After purchasing the founding stock from a local breeder named Fischer, the F344 strain itself was developed in 1920 by Drs. M. R. Curtis and W. F. Dunning of the Institute for Cancer Research at Columbia University in New York, whereas the LEW strain was bred from Wistar stock beginning in 1945 by Dr. Margaret R. Lewis of the Wistar Institute in Philadelphia (Billingham, Hodge, & Silvers, 1962; Billingham & Silvers, 1959; Tanaka, Segawa, Tamaya, Miyaishi, & Ohno, 2001; see also the Rat Genome Database www.rgd.mcw.edu/strains). Although originally developed as respective stand-alone models for cancer susceptibility and tissue transplantation, many differences between F344 and LEW rats have been identified, leading to direct strain comparisons by investigators interested in exploring genetic contributions to disease-relevant differences in physiology and behavior. Aside from overt disparities in body size, docility, and exploratory behavior (LEW > F344), perhaps the best characterized and widely applied difference between the strains is in regulation of the hypothalamic–pituitary–adrenal (HPA) axis, with the F344 animals being markedly more reactive to physical and psychosocial stressors than the LEW. For example, this phenotypic divergence has been explored in recent years by researchers interested in modeling endogenous differences in stress reactivity in relation to disorders as diverse as inflammatory disease susceptibility, immune function, and pain sensitivity, as well as drug abuse (Dhabhar, McEwen, & Spencer, 1993; Grakalic, Schindler, Baumann, Rice, & Riley, 2006; Kosten & Ambrosio, 2002; Stöhr, Szuran, Welzl, Pliska, Feldon, & Pryce, 2000; Vit et al., 2006; Wei, Listwak, & Sternberg, 2003; Yang & Hou, 2006).

Similar to the models of stress physiology and autoimmune disease mentioned earlier, the relatively recent use of F344 and LEW rats for drug abuse research was not intentional, and the success of the model was quite serendipitous. In the middle to late 1980s, Drs. Frank George, Mary Ritz, Dick Meisch, and colleagues were exploring genetic differences in the reinforcing effects of oral ethanol using the selectively bred AA and ANA rat lines (Ritz, George, deFiebre, & Meisch, 1986). This work was conducted in the United States; however, the rats were shipped from Finland, where they were originally bred in conjunction with Alko, the Finnish national alcoholic beverage retail monopoly. Since the overseas shipping of live animals had become prohibitively expensive, but certain that the influence of genetic factors was worthy of continued study, Meisch asked George if he could name two inbred strains of rats that were (1) commercially and readily available and (2) differed as much as possible in terms of genotype. Being well versed in the rodent line and strain literature, George immediately answered with Fischer and Lewis rats (R. A. Meisch, personal communication, June 18, 2006 and November 30, 2006). The two strains were then successfully used for oral self-administration studies with alcohol and the opioid etonitazene (Ritz, Elmer, Suzuki, Meisch, & George, 1988; Suzuki, George, & Meisch, 1988, 1992). Soon thereafter, other researchers interested in the genetic bases of drug abuse also began directly comparing F344 and LEW rats, and thus was born the Fischer–Lewis model of drug abuse.[3]

Indeed, in addition to the multifaceted differences noted earlier, the F344 and LEW rat strains vary on a wide number of behavioral, physiological, and neurochemical endpoints related to drugs of abuse. As such, the Fischer–Lewis model provides two genetically distinct populations of animals that have enabled researchers to generate insights on the role genotype plays in the physiological and behavioral antecedents and consequences of drug administration, serving as a valuable tool for studying the etiology of drug abuse. One of the main goals of research regarding these strains is the investigation of genetic vulnerabilities or susceptibilities to voluntary drug intake.

Oral Self-Administration

Throughout the drug-abuse literature, research on the F344 and LEW strains has centered on their characterization during self-administration studies and the different patterns of intake each strain exhibits. In the initial investigations into drug self-administration with the two strains, the drug was primarily administered orally (see Table 12.2). In such assessments, LEW rats typically consume more of the drug than F344 rats. For example, in 1988 Suzuki and colleagues (see also Li & Lumeng, 1984) found that although orally-delivered ethanol maintained higher operant response rates than vehicle for both strains, LEW animals exhibited greater responding for and consumption of ethanol compared to the F344 rats, suggesting that ethanol was serving as a stronger reinforcer for the LEW rats (see Taylor, Tio, Bando, Romeo, & Prolo, 2006). In a second report that same year by Suzuki, Otani, Koike, and Misawa (1988), strain differences in preferences for consumption of morphine- or codeine-containing food during daily choice trials were reported. Under these conditions, the LEW strain showed greater preferences than the F344 strain for both types of food, leading the authors to conclude that in addition to alcohol, the reinforcing effects of morphine and codeine also vary by genotype (see also Suzuki et al., 1992). A third oral self-administration study was also published in 1988, by George and Goldberg, in which strain differences in food-induced and nonfood induced home-cage drinking of a 0.57 mg/ml cocaine solution were investigated. In this preparation, food did induce drinking of the cocaine solution in both strains, but to a greater degree in the LEW rats. Nonfood-induced drinking also occurred to a greater extent in the LEW animals; interestingly, for the F344 rats, nonfood-induced intake of the cocaine solution was less than the nonfood induced consumption of the vehicle solution. The results of this study suggested that only the LEW animals found orally administered cocaine rewarding. In addition to these first oral self-administration studies, Suzuki and colleagues (1992) examined operant deliveries of varying concentrations of a solution of etonitazene. Although the ratio of drug intake to body weight was comparable between the strains, LEW rats exhibited a greater number of responses at lower drug concentrations and earned more drug deliveries than F344 rats, indicating a possible strain difference in the reinforcing effects of this potent opioid drug.

Intravenous Self-Administration

Subsequent to this work with oral self-administration, intravenous (IV) preparations were initiated that allowed for an analysis of any possible strain-specific effects with other drugs (and by a route

Table 12.2 Self-administration studies comparing the Fischer (F344) and Lewis (LEW) inbred rat strains.

Author(s)/Year	Drug/Dose	Schedule	Results
Intravenous Opioid			
Ambrosio et al., 1995	Morphine: 1.0 mg/kg	FR1	Acquisition: LEW > F344; Extinction: F344 > response rate than LEW; Reacquisition: LEW > F344
Martín et al., 1999	Food morphine: 1.0 mg/kg	Progressive ratio	Food: No difference in BPs; Morphine: LEW BPs > F344; BPs
Martín et al., 2003	Food morphine: 1.0 mg/kg	Food: VI3, IRT Morphine: PR	Food: LEW shorter IRTs than F344; Morphine: LEW BPs > F344; BPs (most sessions)
Sánchez-Cardoso et al., 2007	Morphine: 1.0 mg/kg	Progressive ratio	LEW BPs > F344
Oral Opioid			
Suzuki et al., 1988b	Morphine or codeine: 0.25, 0.5, 1.0 mg/g in food	Drug-Admixed Food Procedure (DAF)	LEW > preference for 0.5 mg/g morphine or codeine than F344; Mean food intake: F344 < LEW
Suzuki et al., 1992	Etonitazene: 0.625, 1.25, 2.5, 5 µg/ml in water	Operant liquid deliveries (lever press)	LEW > responses at lower concentration than F344; LEW > number of etonitazene deliveries than F344; LEW decrease responding with increasing concentration; Etonitazene intake/body weight: LEW = F344
Intravenous Psychostimulant			
Kosten et al., 1997	Cocaine: 0.25, 0.5, 1.0 mg/kg	FR1	Acquisition: LEW > F344; Maintenance: F344 = LEW; Extinction: F344 = LEW
Haile & Kosten, 2001	Food and Cocaine: Training = 1.0 mg/kg; Testing = 0.25, 0.5, 1.0 mg/kg	FR1 to FR15; FR3	Food: F344 = LEW; F344 > number of cocaine infusions and active lever presses than LEW; F344 = LEW: Cocaine infusions decrease with increasing dose
Haile et al., 2005	Cocaine: 1.0 mg/kg	FR3	F344 >number of cocaine infusions and active lever presses than LEW
Kruzich & Xi, 2006a	Cocaine: 0.5 mg/kg	FR1	Acquisition: F344 intake varied across sessions; LEW intake stable; F344 > LEW on sessions 1, 2, 12, 14. Extinction responding:

(*continued*)

Table 12.2 *Continued*

Author(s)/Year	Drug/Dose	Schedule	Results
			F344 > LEW sessions 1, 3, 6. Reinstatement: LEW = lower doses, F344 = LEW at higher doses
Kruzich & Xi, 2006b	Methamphetamine: 0.6 mg/kg	FR1	LEW > number of infusions than F344. Extinction: No overall strain difference; F344 more responses during first session. Reinstatement: LEW > number of active lever presses than F344
Kosten et al., 2007	Cocaine: Training = 1.0 mg/kg; Testing = 0.0625, 0.125, 0.25, 0.5, 1.0 mg/kg	FR3; progressive ratio for 1.0 mg/kg	F344 > LEW number of infusions at 0.0625 and 0.125 mg/kg and during PR
Xi & Kruzich, 2007	Methamphetamine: 0.06 mg/kg	FR1; progressive ratio for 0.01, 0.03, 0.06 mg/kg	F344 = LEW number of infusions during maintenance and PR; LEW > F344 responses during conditioned reinstatement and methamphetamine-primed reinstatement
Oral Psychostimulant			
George & Goldberg, 1988	Cocaine: 0.57 mg/ml in water	Home-cage drinking	Food-induced cocaine solution intake occurred in both strains; LEW > F344 food- and nonfood-induced intake; F344 nonfood-induced intake of cocaine solution < intake of vehicle solution
Intravenous Nicotine			
Shoaib et al., 1997	0.015, 0.03, 0.06 mg/kg	FR1 to FR5	Neither strain acquired
Brower et al., 2002	0.03 mg/kg	FR1 to FR5	LEW: 88% of subjects acquired FR1; maintained SA at FR1-FR5; F344 did not acquire
Oral Ethanol			
Suzuki et al., 1988a	1.0, 2.0, 3.0, 4.0, 5.7, 8.0, 16.0, 32.0% (v/v) in water	FR1, FR2, FR4, FR8, FR16	LEW > F344 ethanol consumption
Taylor et al., 2006	Liquid diet: 5% w/v	14 days	Males: F344 > LEW (g/kg/ day). Females: F344 = LEW

that better approximates the kinetics of drug self-administration in humans). In such assessments, LEW rats typically acquire self-administration of most abused compounds faster than do the F344 rats (Ambrosio, Goldberg, & Elmer, 1995; Brower, Fu, Matta, & Sharp, 2002; Kosten et al., 1997; Martín et al., 2003; Martín et al., 1999; Suzuki et al., 1988), although the effects reported are a function of the specific drug examined (see below). In one of the first assessments of morphine self-administration with F344 and LEW rats, Ambrosio and colleagues (1995) reported that LEW rats acquired morphine self-administration faster than F344 rats (at a dose of 1.0 mg/kg on an FR1 schedule of reinforcement). Consistent with this report, three other investigations examining morphine self-administration in these strains at 1.0 mg/kg using a progressive-ratio (PR) schedule of reinforcement reported that LEW rats displayed higher breakpoints (BPs) than F344 rats (Martín et al., 1999, 2003; Sánchez-Cardoso et al., 2007). PR schedules of reinforcement require subjects to increase the number of responses for each successive reinforcer. The highest completed schedule, that is, the BP, is generally considered as a measure of the motivation to obtain the reinforcer. Such differences in BPs suggest that the LEW rats were willing to work harder than the F344 rats for the same morphine injection(s). The strains never differed in BPs for food, providing strong evidence that these strains differed in response to drug and not food under this schedule. It is interesting to note that when food-reinforced behavior was examined using a variable interval (VI3) schedule, LEW animals displayed shorter interresponse times (IRT), suggesting that the behavior of this strain was less efficient than the F344 rats (Martín et al., 2003). These shorter IRTs represent hyperresponsive behavior by the LEW animals and correspond to other compulsive behaviors such as wheel running (Werme, Thorén, Olson, & Brené, 1999) and spontaneous locomotor activity (Ambrosio et al., 1995; Camp, Browman, & Robinson, 1994; Paulus, Geyer, & Sternberg, 1998; Rex, Sondern, Voigt, Franck, & Fink, 1996; although see Kosten, Miserendino, Chi, & Nestler, 1994; Simar, Saphier, & Goeders, 1996; Stöhr, Wermeling, Weiner, & Feldon, 1998) often exhibited by this strain.

Cocaine IV self-administration also differs between these strains; however, the results of these studies show that any differences seen are a function of the specific phase in which the animals are tested, that is, acquisition, maintenance, or extinction, preventing any general statement about the relative sensitivity to cocaine between the two strains. For example, Kosten et al. (1997) reported that LEW animals displayed a more rapid acquisition of cocaine (under an FR1 schedule at a dose of 0.5 mg/kg), as indexed by the LEW animals' ability to more quickly display differential selection between the active and inactive levers. However, no strain differences were reported in the maintenance of cocaine self-administration at asymptote or the extinction of responding when cocaine was no longer delivered. Interestingly, during maintenance, F344 animals actually administered more cocaine infusions overall compared to the LEW animals. Subsequent reports by Haile and Kosten (2001), Haile, Zhang, Carroll, and Kosten (2005), and Kosten, Zhang, and Haile (2007) also noted greater numbers of cocaine infusions and active lever presses in the F344 rats during maintenance, with acquisition either not reported or not differing between strains. Haile and Kosten also examined operant food responding between the strains and found no differences on schedules that ranged from FR1 to FR15. In opposition to the Kosten et al. (1997) report, Kruzich and Xi (2006a) did not find consistent strain differences in acquisition (or in extinction) of self-administration for cocaine (a 0.5 mg/kg dose of cocaine on an FR1 schedule). The most notable finding from the Kruzich and Xi report was that the F344 animals varied their intake across sessions, while the LEW animals maintained a rather stable self-administration pattern for the duration of the experiment. Thus, work with cocaine self-administration studies provides a somewhat inconsistent picture of differences in responding by genotype, precluding any general summary of differences between F344 and LEW rats in cocaine self-administration.

Comparisons between the F344 and LEW strains with psychostimulants other than cocaine are rather limited, but are relatively consistent with the patterns seen with morphine. For example, Kruzich and Xi (2006b) reported that LEW rats administered a greater number of infusions of 0.6 mg/kg methamphetamine than F344 rats (FR1 schedule). Although no overall strain differences were found during extinction, the LEW rats displayed a greater number of active lever presses following a priming injection of the drug (i.e., reinstatement; also see Xi & Kruzich, 2007). In an assessment of IV nicotine self-administration,

Shoaib, Schindler, and Goldberg (1997) reported that neither strain acquired self-administration of nicotine. However, Brower et al. (2002) reported that LEW, but not F344, rats did acquire and maintain self-administration of 0.03 mg/kg nicotine under schedules ranging from FR1 to FR5.

In general, self-administration patterns vary between the F344 and LEW strains, with the most consistent findings being that LEW animals more rapidly acquire the self-administration of ethanol, morphine, etonitazene, and nicotine compared to F344 rats. Work with cocaine seems to parallel the findings with these other compounds given that LEW rats display a faster acquisition of self-administration; however, the fact that the F344 animals consistently show a greater number of active lever presses along with a greater number of cocaine infusions compared to the LEW animals does qualify the general conclusion that cocaine is more rewarding in the LEW strain.

These patterns with self-administration suggest a differential reinforcing effect of drugs between the two strains, an effect that is supported in part in other animal models of the rewarding effects of drugs of abuse. For example, behavior of F344 and LEW rats has been examined with a variety of drugs using place-conditioning methodologies (see Table 12.3). In these procedures, LEW animals typically show a greater CPP induced by cocaine (Guitart, Beitner-Johnson, Marby, Kosten, & Nestler, 1992; Kosten et al., 1994), nicotine (Horan, Smith, Gardener, Lepore, & Ashby, Jr., 1997), and morphine (Grakalic et al., 2006; Guitart et al., 1992; although see Davis, Roma, Dominguez, & Riley, 2007). Interestingly, the F344 rats display greater CPPs induced by a 1.0 mg/kg dose of amphetamine (Stöhr et al., 1998) and neither strain shows a preference or an aversion when conditioned with alcohol (Roma, Flint, Higley, & Riley, 2006). It is important to note that several studies reporting CPP in the LEW strain also reported CPA in the F344 strain under the same conditions. For example, LEW animals show a CPP induced by 15.0 and 30.0 mg/kg cocaine, whereas the F344 strain shows no change in time spent on the drug-paired side at 15.0 mg/kg of cocaine but displays a place aversion at 30.0 mg/kg (see Kosten et al., 1994). Horan et al. (1997) reported a similar dissociation with nicotine, with the LEW animals displaying a nicotine-induced CPP after five or ten context-drug pairings and the F344 animals displaying no change after five

pairings but a nicotine-induced place aversion after ten. Similar to the self-administration data discussed above, the place conditioning data also reveal genotype-dependent responses to the rewarding/reinforcing properties of drugs of abuse between the F344 and LEW rat strains.

CTA LEARNING IN THE F344 AND LEW RAT STRAINS

The differences between the F344 and LEW rat strains in drug self-administration and other models of the rewarding properties of abused drugs underscore the importance of genetic contributions to sensitivity to the rewarding effects of drugs. However, given the work with selected lines and inbred strains demonstrating the differential ability of a host of drugs to condition aversions raises the issue of whether these two strains might differ in sensitivity to the aversive effects of drugs, and if so, how such differences might relate to patterns of drug self-administration.

We began our investigations into aversion learning in the F344 and LEW strains with cocaine, a drug with reported differences in self-administration and CPP (see previous section).[4] In this assessment (Glowa, Shaw, & Riley, 1994), water-deprived female rats of both strains were given 20-min access to saccharin that was followed immediately by injection of saline vehicle or one of three doses of cocaine (18.0, 32.0, or 50.0 mg/kg, SC). These doses of cocaine and the route by which they were administered had previously been reported by our laboratory to induce dose-dependent taste aversions in outbred rats (Ferrari, O'Connor, & Riley, 1991). This conditioning procedure was repeated every fourth day for a total of four conditioning trials. On intervening days, all subjects were given access to water during their scheduled fluid-access period.

As depicted in Figure 12.1, although there were no differences between the two strains when saccharin consumption was followed by vehicle, strain differences did emerge on subsequent trials in the cocaine-treated animals. Specifically, LEW subjects drank significantly less saccharin than F344 subjects on Trials 3 and 4 at both the 18.0 and 32.0 mg/kg doses. There were no differences between strains at 50.0 mg/kg, a dose at which both strains displayed robust cocaine-induced aversions. Further, the LEW rats acquired

Table 12.3 Place conditioning studies comparing the Fischer (F344) and Lewis (LEW) inbred rat strains.

Author(s)/Year	Dose/Route	Apparatus/ Drug-Paired Chamber	Conditioning Regimen	Results
Psychostimulants				
Guitart et al., 1992	Cocaine: 15.0 mg/kg (IP)	Unbiased, nonpreferred	Day 1: First chamber vehicle, second chamber drug; 4 cycles; 4 total drug exposures	LEW CPP 2x > F344
Kosten et al., 1994	Cocaine: 7.5, 15.0, 30.0, 60.0 mg/kg (IP)	Unbiased, nonpreferred	Day 1–2: drug; day 3: vehicle; 2 cycles; 4 total drug exposures	LEW: CPP at 15.0, 30.0 mg/kg F344: no CPP; CPA at 30.0 mg/kg
Stöhr et al., 1998	d-Amphetamine: 1.0 mg/kg (IP)	Unspecified, nonpreferred	Day 1: First chamber drug, second chamber vehicle; 3 cycles; 3 total drug exposures	F344 > LEW CPP (both sexes)
(-)-Nicotine				
Horan et al., 1997	0.4 mg/kg (SC)	Unbiased, counterbalanced	5 Drug pairings, 10 drug pairings	LEW: CPP after 5 and 10 pairings; F344: No change after 5, CPA after 10 pairings
Suzuki et al., 1999	Nicotine: 10.0 mg/kg/day, SC infusion for 3 days; Mecamylamine (SC): 0.3, 1.0, 3.0 mg/kg	Unspecified, preferred	Day 1–3: Surgery/recovery; day 4–5: apparatus habituation; day 6: pretest; day 7: conditioning AM = vehicle, PM = drug; day 8: posttest	LEW > F344 CPA
Morphine				
Guitart et al., 1992	4.0 mg/kg (SC)	Unbiased, nonpreferred	Day 1: First chamber = Vehicle, second chamber = drug; 4 cycles; 4 total drug exposures	LEW CPP 2x > F344
Grakalic et al., 2006	1.0, 4.0, 10.0 mg/kg (SC)	Unbiased, counterbalanced	2 Conditioning trials/day; 2 cycles; 2 total drug exposures	No direct strain comparison; LEW mean difference score > F344 at 4.0 mg/kg only
Davis et al., 2007	1.0, 4.0, 10.0 mg/kg (SC)	Biased, nonpreferred	Acquisition: Day 1 = drug, day 2 = vehicle, day 3 = test; 4 cycles; 4 total drug exposures; 4 test days	F344: CPP at 1.0 mg/kg only; LEW: no CPP to any dose

(continued)

Table 12.3 *Continued*

Author(s)/Year	Dose/Route	Apparatus/ Drug-Paired Chamber	Conditioning Regimen	Results
Ethanol				
Roma et al., 2006	1.0, 1.25, 1.5 g/kg (IP)	Biased, counterbalanced	Alternating drug and vehicle days; 4 cycles; 4 total drug exposures	No drug effect

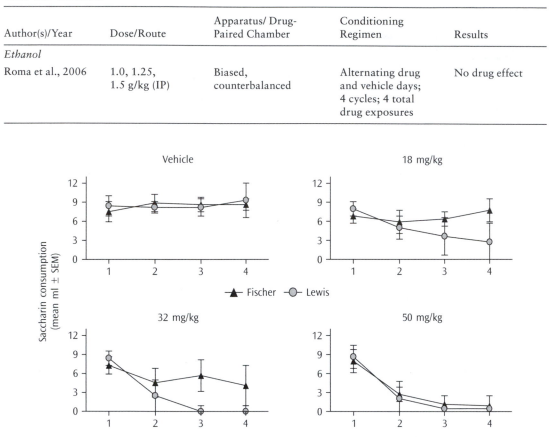

Figure 12.1. Saccharin consumption over repeated conditioning trials in which rats from the F344 and LEW strains were given pairings of saccharin and vehicle or varying doses of cocaine (18.0, 32.0, or 50.0 mg/kg). Redrawn from Glowa et al. (1994).

cocaine-induced aversions significantly faster than the F344 rats at both the 18.0 and 32.0 mg/kg dose (when consumption on each trial was compared to initial baseline consumption of saccharin). Glowa et al. noted that the differential acquisition of taste aversions between the two strains was consistent with other work reporting a greater sensitivity of the LEW strain to cocaine, although the basis for this differential sensitivity to the aversive effects of cocaine was not known or if it reflected a common mechanism to that mediating the differential sensitivity to cocaine's rewarding effects. What was clear was that the two strains differed in yet another behavioral measure of cocaine's effects (Grigson & Freet, 2000; but also see Kosten et al., 1994).

This differential acquisition of cocaine-induced taste aversions could be a function of a number of

differences between F344 and LEW rats such as general learning ability or general insensitivity to the aversive effects of all drugs. The work assessing general learning abilities between the two strains has not shown any consistent differences (e.g., Kearns, Gomez-Serrano, Weiss, & Riley, 2006). However, given that taste aversion learning is acquired under somewhat different conditions than those used with typical learning preparations—for example, learning with one to few trials (Garcia et al., 1955) over long delays (Garcia et al., 1966) and relatively selective to tastes (Garcia & Koelling, 1966; for reviews, see Garcia & Ervin, 1968; Revusky & Garcia, 1970; Rozin & Kalat, 1971)—it was unclear if the differences with cocaine reflected a learning difference within the CTA preparation. To test this and to see if the differential acquisition of taste aversions seen with cocaine generalized to other drugs of abuse, we initiated an assessment of taste aversion learning with morphine (Lancellotti, Bayer, Glowa, Houghtling, & Riley, 2001). Specifically, using the design described above, different groups of water-deprived female F344 and LEW rats were given 20-min access to saccharin followed immediately by a SC injection of vehicle (saline) or various doses of morphine (10.0, 32.0, or 56.0 mg/kg). As with cocaine, these doses of morphine and the route by which they were administered had previously been reported by our laboratory to induce dose-dependent aversions in outbred rats (Hutchinson et al., 2000). Although the conditioning procedure was functionally identical to that described above for cocaine, the results were exactly the opposite. Specifically, F344 rats displayed robust, dose-dependent morphine-induced aversions, while LEW rats displayed no aversions to the morphine-associated solution, drinking at control levels at every dose of morphine, even after repeated conditioning trials (see Figure 12.2). Blood morphine levels at 1, 2, and 4 h postinjection revealed a time-dependent effect but no effect of strain, suggesting that the differential aversions were not simply a function of differential absorption or clearance. Although the basis for the differential aversions was not known, it was clear that morphine had a dramatically different effect than

cocaine in the two strains. Thus, the differential acquisition of taste aversions in the LEW and F344 rats was both drug specific and strain dependent. No obvious general mechanism, for example, general insensitivity to all drugs or differential learning ability, was accounting for the relative sensitivities seen in the two strains, at least with these two drugs.

From the results of our first two assessments of aversion learning in the F344 and LEW strains, it appeared that cocaine and morphine were differentially aversive, with cocaine being more aversive in the LEW rats and morphine being more aversive in the F344 strain. If this were true, then it should be possible to test this in ways other than CTA. Recent work on the neurobiology of taste aversion learning offered such a test. On the basis of a host of findings assessing the effects of lesions in specific brainstem areas on aversion learning, it appeared that the area postrema (AP), nucleus tractus solitarius (NTS), and parabrachial nucleus (PBN) were important for the acquisition of taste aversions induced by a variety of compounds (for a review, see Bermúdez-Rattoni & Yamamoto, 1998). Additional support for the role of these areas in aversion learning was provided by more recent work showing elevated c-Fos levels (indicative of cellular activity) in these areas in response

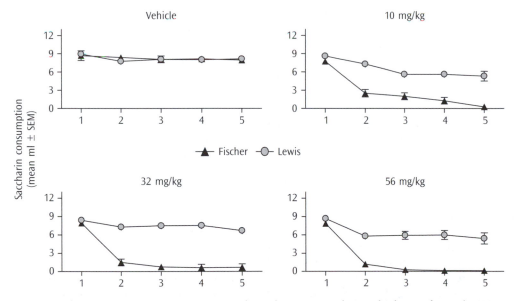

Figure 12.2. Saccharin consumption over repeated conditioning trials in which rats from the F344 and LEW strains were given pairings of saccharin and vehicle or varying doses of morphine (10.0, 32.0, or 56.0 mg/kg). Redrawn from Lancellotti et al. (2001).

to administration of a number of aversion-inducing agents (Bureš, Bermúdez-Rattoni, & Yamamoto, 1998; Swank & Bernstein, 1994; Yamamoto, 1993; see also Bernstein & Koh, 2007). To test whether cocaine and morphine might differentially activate c-Fos in these brainstem areas important for aversion learning, we examined the effects of cocaine and morphine on c-Fos activity in a variety of brainstem nuclei (Grabus, Glowa, & Riley, 2004). Specifically, based on the work of Glowa et al. (1994) and Lancellotti et al. (2001), we administered doses of cocaine and morphine that produced the largest strain differences in CTA and measured c-Fos levels in the AP, intermediate nucleus tractus solitarius (iNTS), central nucleus tractus solitarius (cNTS), PBN, lateral parabrachial nucleus (LPB), caudate nucleus (CN), and nucleus accumbens (NAc), with the last two areas assayed to determine if any differences that were seen in the brainstem areas were specific to those areas or generalized across the brain.

As seen in Figure 12.3, c-Fos levels in the PBN were elevated in both the F344 and LEW subjects following cocaine (relative to that following an injection of saline). This increase was greater for the LEW subjects. Following morphine, c-Fos levels were elevated only for the F344 rats. The same general pattern was evident in LPB following cocaine, although with morphine both strains showed an elevation with no difference between strains. Figure 12.4 shows a similar analysis of c-Fos activation in the AP, iNTS, and cNTS. Interestingly, the same general pattern seen with the PBN was also evident in these structures. For example, in the iNTS, both strains showed c-Fos activation following cocaine and morphine, although the relative increase was strain and drug dependent. Specifically, cocaine induced greater c-Fos activation in the LEW while morphine induced greater c-Fos activation in the F344 subjects (an effect also seen in the cNTS); a similar pattern of differential activation was also seen in the AP. Thus, the drug that produced greater CTAs in LEW rats (cocaine) produced greater c-Fos activation in brainstem nuclei associated with taste aversion learning in outbred subjects. Conversely, the drug that produced greater CTAs in F344 subjects (morphine) produced greater c-Fos activation in the same brainstem nuclei. These differential patterns of activation suggest that the drugs have differential aversive effects in the two strains.

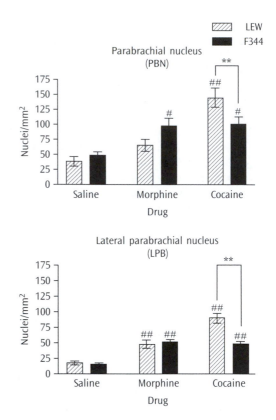

Figure 12.3. c-Fos activation in the PBN and LPN in the F344 and LEW rat strains following injections of saline, morphine, or cocaine. **Significant strain difference; ##significant difference from saline. Reprinted from *Brain Research, 998*, Grabus, Glowa, & Riley, Morphine- and cocaine-induced c-Fos levels in Lewis and Fischer rat strains, 20–28, 2004 with permission from Elsevier.

Importantly, these patterns were specific to the brainstem nuclei associated with aversions. Specifically, in the shell of the NAc (an area associated with the rewarding effects of a range of abused drugs; see Bozarth, 1987; Koob & LeMoal, 2006) both cocaine and morphine produced greater c-Fos levels in LEW rats than F344 rats (an effect consistent with the aforementioned data showing greater sensitivity to the reinforcing effects of cocaine and morphine in the LEW strain). Furthermore, only cocaine induced c-Fos activity in the dopamine-rich CN, and these elevations were similar for the F344 and LEW strains. Thus, the differential effects of cocaine and morphine on c-Fos activity in the F344 and LEW rats appear to parallel the drugs' differential ability to induce taste aversions in these strains.

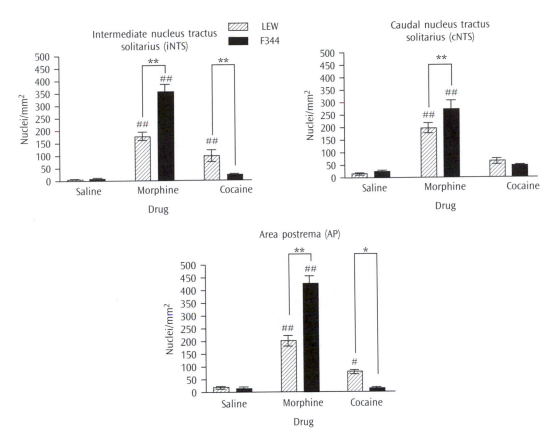

Figure 12.4. c-Fos activation in the iNTS, cNTS, and AP in the F344 and LEW rat strains following injections of saline, morphine, or cocaine. *Significant strain difference; #significant difference from saline. Reprinted from *Brain Research*, *998*, Grabus, Glowa, & Riley, Morphine- and cocaine-induced c-Fos levels in Lewis and Fischer rat strains, 20–28, 2004 with permission from Elsevier.

Subsequent to our initial demonstrations of differential patterns of acquisition of taste aversions induced by cocaine and morphine, we examined two additional drugs for their ability to induce aversions in these two strains, specifically, nicotine and alcohol. The procedures in these assessments were similar, although not identical, to those described above. In the work with nicotine (Pescatore, Glowa, & Riley, 2005), water-deprived male F344 and LEW rats were given 20-min access to saccharin followed by injection of vehicle or varying doses of nicotine (0.1, 0.4, or 0.8 mg/kg, SC) every other day for a total of five conditioning trials (20-min access to water was given on intervening days). Such doses and route of administration have been reported to induce aversions in outbred rats (Kumar, Pratt, & Stolerman, 1983; Parker & Doucet, 1995; Pratt & Stolerman, 1982;

Shram et al., 2006). As depicted in Figure 12.5, although there were no differences between the two strains when injected with vehicle or the two lower doses of nicotine, differences did emerge at 0.8 mg/kg nicotine. Specifically, F344 subjects injected with 0.8 mg/kg nicotine following saccharin consumption displayed a faster acquisition of the aversion and drank significantly less than LEW animals on Trials 4 and 5.

When alcohol at doses previously reported to induce aversions in outbred rats (e.g., Cunningham, 1979) was paired with saccharin consumption under similar conditions to those described for nicotine, male (but not female) F344 rats again displayed significantly greater aversions than the LEW rats (Roma et al., 2006; Roma, Chen, Barr, & Riley, 2007). As illustrated in Figure 12.6, at 1.25 and 1.5 g/kg male F344 rats acquired the

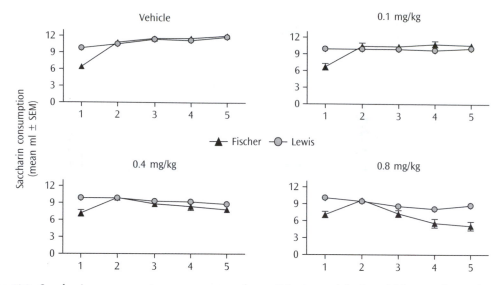

Figure 12.5. Saccharin consumption over repeated conditioning trials in which rats from the F344 and LEW strains were given pairings of saccharin and vehicle or varying doses of nicotine (0.1, 0.4, or 0.8 mg/kg). Redrawn from Pescatore et al. (2005).

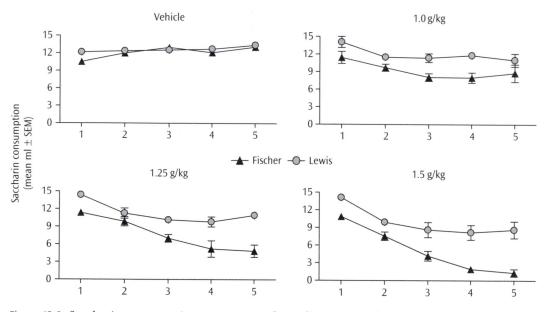

Figure 12.6. Saccharin consumption over repeated conditioning trials in which rats from the F344 and LEW strains were given pairings of saccharin and vehicle or varying doses of alcohol (1.0, 1.25, or 1.5 g/kg). Redrawn from Roma et al. (2006).

alcohol-induced aversions more rapidly than did the LEW rats and drank significantly less of the alcohol-paired solution on Trials 3, 4, and 5. These differential effects with alcohol did not appear to be a function of differences in blood alcohol levels in response to an IP injection of vehicle, 1.0 or 1.5 g/kg alcohol. Specifically, although there were dose and time effects on blood alcohol levels, there was no significant interaction with strain. When one examined peak blood alcohol, the LEW animals did appear to have higher overall levels; however, these differences did not parallel

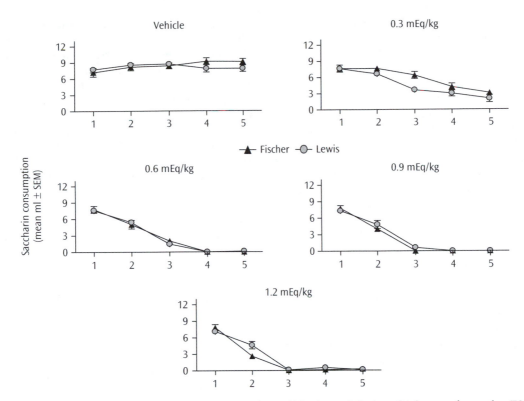

Figure 12.7. Saccharin consumption over repeated conditioning trials in which rats from the F344 and LEW strains were given pairings of saccharin and vehicle or varying doses of LiCl (0.3, 0.6, 0.9, or 1.2 mEq/kg). Redrawn from Foynes and Riley (2004).

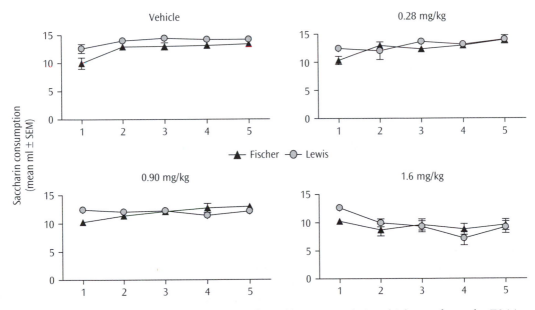

Figure 12.8. Saccharin consumption over repeated conditioning trials in which rats from the F344 and LEW strains were given pairings of saccharin and vehicle or varying doses of (−)–U50,488H (0.28, 0.90, or 1.6 mg/kg). From Davis and Riley (2007b).

the differences seen in alcohol-induced aversions, that is, there was no strain × dose interaction, and the F344 and LEW animals' peak blood alcohol levels did not actually differ from each other at any of the doses tested.

The data thus far indicate that for a variety of drugs with varying physiological effects, F344 and LEW rats differ significantly in their acquisition of CTAs. While cocaine induces stronger aversions in the LEW strain, morphine, nicotine, and alcohol produce greater aversions in F344 rats. It is interesting in this context to note that not all drugs induce different aversions in the two strains. For example, neither the emetic LiCl nor the kappa opioid agonist (−)−U50,488H differentially condition aversions in the F344 and LEW rats. Under conditions similar to those described earlier, animals from both strains were given saccharin followed by varying doses of LiCl (Foynes & Riley, 2004) or (−)−U50,488H (Davis & Riley, 2007b). Although both drugs induced dose-dependent taste aversions, there were no systematic differences between the two strains at any dose tested for either drug (see Figures 12. 7 and 12.8). These data, again, indicate that the differential aversive effects seen in the F344 and LEW strains are drug-dependent and suggest an interesting strain × drug interaction whose basis remains unknown.

BALANCE OF REWARDING/AVERSIVE EFFECTS IN DRUG INTAKE

The premise stated at the outset of the preceding section was that drugs have both rewarding and aversive effects and that the balance of these effects may contribute to overall drug acceptability, and, therefore, their self-administration. Given that F344 and LEW rats differ in their patterns of self-administration of drugs such as morphine, cocaine, alcohol, and nicotine, the question becomes one of whether or not the differential responses to the aversive effects of drugs ultimately impact drug self-administration. Such a question has been recently raised by Broadbent and colleagues (2002) in trying to account for the differential patterns of oral alcohol self-administration in a variety of mouse strains. In their analysis, they reported a significant correlation between the strength of taste aversions induced by ethanol and the preference for a 10% ethanol solution, specifically, the strains of mice showing weaker aversions induced

by ethanol showed an increased preference for the ethanol solution.

Examining self-administration and taste aversion learning in the F344 and LEW rat strains reveals similar correlations. For example, as noted earlier, F344 and LEW rats differ in the self-administration of morphine, with LEW rats displaying a more rapid acquisition of responding than F344 rats, suggesting a greater sensitivity to morphine's rewarding effects in the LEW animals.[5] Consistent with these data is the fact that LEW animals display no morphine-induced taste aversions at any dose tested, even with repeated conditioning trials, whereas the F344 rats display strong taste aversions induced by morphine at low doses and with few conditioning trials, suggesting a greater sensitivity to morphine's aversive effects in the F344 rats relative to their LEW counterparts. That the LEW subjects self-administer morphine is proof that morphine is rewarding in these animals. The fact that morphine has little (if any) aversive effects in these animals increases their vulnerability to its use. That the F344 subjects acquire morphine self-administration at all also provides evidence for its rewarding effects, but the fact that morphine has clear aversive effects may limit their intake of morphine. Although the F344 and LEW strains differ in the rate of acquisition of morphine self-administration, once responding has stabilized and is at asymptote, the two strains do not differ (Ambrosio et al., 1995; Martín et al., 1999, 2003); an effect most likely the result of adaptations in neural systems mediating the effects of morphine in the F344 strain (see Guitart et al., 1992, 1993). It is interesting in this context that morphine history significantly weakens morphine-induced taste aversions in both outbred (Simpson & Riley, 2005) and inbred F344 (Davis & Riley, 2007a) rats, suggesting that animals become tolerant to morphine's aversive effects with exposure, an effect that could be a function of the abovementioned neuroadaptations and one that may contribute to increased drug intake.

Similar inverse relationships between drug self-administration and taste-aversion learning are evident with nicotine and alcohol, although the work on each of these compounds in self-administration and taste aversions is somewhat limited. As described, under conditions in which the LEW animals acquire and maintain self-administration of nicotine, F344 rats do not increase responding above baseline levels (Brower et al., 2002; but see Shoaib et al., 1997). Although nicotine-induced taste aversions are generally weak in outbred subjects (Ossenkopp & Giugno, 1990; Pratt & Stolerman, 1982), F344 rats acquire stronger aversions and do so more rapidly than the LEW strain (Pescatore et al., 2005). Thus, nicotine appears to be mildly aversive in the LEW strain, but it is not sufficiently aversive to prevent its self-administration (although it is difficult to conclude that it had no impact on responding). The fact that F344 subjects fail to self-administer nicotine may be a function of both its weak reinforcing and relatively strong aversive effects. Alcohol is generally difficult to establish as a reinforcer in rat models of self-administration and often is self-administered only after chronic exposure (an effect suggested to be due to the weakening of its aversive effects; see Meisch, 1982). Despite these difficulties, Suzuki and colleagues have reported greater intake of alcohol in male LEW versus F344 rats (Suzuki et al., 1988). As we reported, alcohol-induced aversions were stronger and more rapidly acquired in male F344 rats than in male LEW rats (Roma et al., 2006). Again, we suggest that the differential patterns in self-administration are a function, in part, of the differential sensitivities to alcohol's aversive effects.

It is important to note that this analysis does not suggest that the differential patterns of self-administration of any of these drugs are solely a function of the drug's aversive effects. To establish and maintain self-administration, a drug must have some rewarding effects, and these effects may vary by genotype in concert with known neurochemical and neuroanatomical differences in reward pathways (see Guitart et al., 1992). We are simply suggesting that the drug's other affective properties may also vary by strain and covary with the differences in self-administration. The fact that a number of manipulations that impact the acquisition of taste aversions also impact self-administration suggests that the aversive effects of the drug may serve a protective role against additional or excessive drug intake (see Baker & Cannon, 1982; Gaiardi et al., 1991; Riley & Simpson, 2001; Stolerman & D'Mello, 1981).

Although the relationship between self-administration and taste aversion appears clear for the abovementioned compounds, it is less clear for cocaine. As we reported, LEW animals acquired stronger aversions to cocaine than F344 subjects[6]

(Glowa et al., 1994; Grigson & Freet, 2000; Roma, Davis, & Riley, 2007; although see Kosten et al., 1994), and given the position noted above it might be predicted that LEW subjects would show weaker cocaine self-administration than F344 subjects. However, LEW animals actually have been reported to display a quicker acquisition of a 0.5 mg/kg dose of cocaine during self-administration compared to F344 rats (Kosten et al., 1997). This apparent contradiction is important for several reasons. First, of all the drugs assessed with the F344 and LEW strains in the self-administration preparation, cocaine is the one whose results are least consistent. For example, one study reported quicker acquisition of cocaine self-administration in the LEW animals (Kosten et al., 1997), while another did not show faster acquisition by the LEW subjects, even at the same dose as that for which a difference was reported (Kruzich & Xi, 2006a). In fact, this latter study reported that the F344 animals actually infused more drug on specific sessions compared to LEW rats. Also, F344 animals reportedly emit more active lever presses and obtain a greater number of cocaine infusions than LEW animals (Haile et al., 2005; Haile & Kosten, 2001; Kosten, Zhang, & Haile, 2007). Thus, relating aversions to self-administration is somewhat difficult in the absence of a clearly characterized pattern in the two strains. A second important point raised by the analysis with cocaine, however, is related to interpretation. It is important to dissociate reward from aversion in this analysis and to stress that a greater sensitivity to the aversive effects of any given drug does not necessarily mean a lessened sensitivity to its rewarding effects. What is important in determining a drug's overall acceptability and eventual self-administration behavior is the balance between these two affective properties. Thus, although the LEW subjects may be more sensitive to cocaine's aversive effects (as evidenced in the taste aversion preparation) they may also be more sensitive to its rewarding effects (as evidenced by the CPP data). If sensitivity to cocaine's rewarding effects outweighs sensitivity to its aversive effects, then the balance of the two would still lead to an increased likelihood of self-administration. It is interesting that a related general sensitivity to the aversive and rewarding effects of alcohol has been reported by Broadbent and colleagues (2002) who demonstrated that the inbred DBA mouse strain displays greater alcohol-induced taste aversions *and* place preferences but avoids alcohol self-administration, suggesting that for this strain the relative balance is against over-all acceptability (see Belknap, Belknap, Berg, & Coleman, 1977; Cunningham, Neihus, Malott, & Prather, 1992; Horowitz & Whitney, 1975; Risinger & Cunningham, 1992). For now, at least, it is difficult to understand the relationship between cocaine self-administration and cocaine-induced taste aversions in F344 and LEW rats, precluding any definitive conclusions regarding the possible impact aversion learning might have on patterns of self-administration in these animals. Clearly, more work is needed for this characterization.

The abovementioned discussion on the relation-ship between drug self-administration and taste aversion learning is solely about how the two factors covary and will clearly benefit by systematic analyses of how any one factor would affect the two behav-iors. That is, if the aversive effects of a drug impact its likelihood of self-administration, then manipulations that are known to affect aversion-learning such as lesions, pharmacological antagonism, and drug his-tory should, in turn, affect the likelihood of the drug's self-administration. One such factor has already been noted, that is, drug history. Interestingly, exposure to a drug tends to both weaken aversion-learning (e.g., Riley & Simpson, 2001) and increase drug self-administration (Horger, Shelton, & Schenk, 1990; Valadez & Schenk, 1994; for a review see Schenk & Partridge, 1997). Whether this increase in self-administration reflects only a weakened impact of the drug's aversive effects on self-administration or the net effect of two independent processes—one on reward (unaffected and/or strengthened), the other on aversions (unaffected and/or weakened)—remains to be determined, but such analyses are needed to take the relationship beyond its current correlational state. It will be important in these analyses that the assessments of such manipula-tions on taste-aversion learning and self-admin-istration be done under similar parametric condi-tions to preclude any confounding effects due to doses, routes, and timing of drug injections in the two procedures (see Simpson & Riley, 2005; White et al., 1977; Wise et al., 1976).

CONSIDERATION OF EPIGENETIC INFLUENCES AND GENE–ENVIRONMENT INTERACTION

Regardless of the direction of the effects, the F344 and LEW data presented above (along with the

preceding discussion of other genetically distinct rodents) clearly demonstrate the importance of genotype when modeling initial acceptability of abused drugs. In fact, a number of investigators have unambiguously attributed the neurobiologi-cal and behavioral phenotypic differences between F344 and LEW rats to underlying genomic differ-ences (e.g., Brodkin et al., 1998). Such an inter-pretation is consistent with heritability studies of addiction in humans and recent work implicating specific molecular genetic variations in human drug abuse (see Hurd, 2006; Liu et al, 2006; Oroszi & Goldman, 2004). Although this per-spective certainly seems reasonable given the phe-notypic differences between the strains set against the genetic homogeneity within each strain, some issues both conceptual and empirical present chal-lenges for this traditional view and suggest avenues for expanding the Fischer–Lewis model of drug abuse to more accurately reflect the complexity of the human condition.

While establishing that the contribution of geno-type is critically important for understanding the biological bases of any behavior, the fact is that genes do not exist in a vacuum. Indeed, expres-sion of the otherwise fixed genome within any organism is by nature environmentally influenced (see Ptashne, 2004), and phenotypes can only be expressed within some kind of environmental con-text (Crabbe, 2002). Given the virtually infinite variety of experiences to which one may be sub-jected and the multiple levels that may be affected by such experiences, it should come as no surprise that environmental factors may interact with genetic predisposition(s) to affect vulnerability to drug abuse. Such gene–environment interplay is essentially the default setting for those who study biological and behavioral development (Rutter, Moffitt, & Caspi, 2006; Suomi, 2003), and both the human and primate psychiatric literature, including that on addiction, support the notion that relatedness or genotype alone cannot always account for the emergence of maladaptive pheno-types (Barr et al., 2004; Cloninger, Sigvardsson, Bohman, & von Knorring, 1982; Malone, Taylor, Marmorstein, McGue, & Iacono, 2004; National Institute on Drug Abuse [NIDA], 1996; also see Caspi & Moffitt, 2006). In light of these theoreti-cal considerations and given the many differences between F344 and LEW rats, the questions that naturally follow are (1) whether or not the pre-sumably genetic effects exhibited by these strains could be modulated by environmental input, and (2) if so, are responses to the aversive effects of abused drugs in these strains subject to the kinds of complex gene–environment interaction effects reported by others?

In addition to the conceptual points above, it seems on empirical grounds that some responses to drugs in F344 and LEW rats *must* be shaped to some extent by environmental influences because of the within-strain variability seen in some of our early studies. For example, in Glowa et al.'s (1994) analysis of cocaine-induced aversions in the F344 and LEW strains, LEW rats clearly displayed greater taste aversions than F344 rats (see Figure 12.1). Although the between-strain effect is clear, so too is the within-strain variability: If genotype is directly responsible for phenotype, then how could genetically identical animals respond differently to identical environmental experiences? Since we knew with certainty that all post-weaning housing conditions were uniform across strains and CTA studies in our laboratory, we considered the early maternal environment as a potential source of epigenetic modulation. This approach was justifiable on the premise that with inherited genes usually come inherited environments (West & King, 1987), and even more so given the documented effects of individual differences in rat maternal behavior on developmental trajectories in offspring (Caldji, Diorio, & Meaney, 2000; Champagne, Francis, Mar, & Meaney, 2003).

Perhaps the most straightforward method for assessing gene–environment interaction in laboratory rodents is through reciprocal cross-fostering (Ressler, 1962). For our initial studies (Gomez-Serrano, Sternberg, & Riley, 2002; Gomez-Serrano, Tonelli, Listwak, Sternberg, & Riley, 2001), newborn F344 and LEW pups were fostered to unrelated F344 or LEW dams, yielding the following four groups: F344 pups reared by F344 dams (F/F), F344 pups reared by LEW dams (F/L), LEW pups reared by LEW dams (L/L), and LEW pups reared by F344 dams (L/F). As adults, the rats were tested on a battery of assays known to reveal differences between the strains. The cross-fostering manipulation modulated some of the strain differences typically observed in body weight, corticosterone responses to lipopolysaccharide injection and acoustic startle reactivity, and actually produced differences exclusively between cross-fostered groups in open-field activity.

Encouraged by the fact that some well-established differences between F344 and LEW rats in physiology and behavior are subject to gene–environment interaction effects, we now find ourselves immersed in the task of assessing such effects in responses to the aversive properties of drugs. Although much more work needs to be done, particularly regarding the features of the maternal environment and neurobiological substrates mediating gene–environment interaction effects, our initial efforts look promising. Using the same cross-fostering design as Gomez-Serrano and colleagues (2001, 2002) in conjunction with doses of cocaine and morphine known to generate robust strain differences in CTA (Glowa et al., 1994; Lancellotti et al., 2001), we found significant gene–environment interaction effects among adult female F344 and LEW rats reared by dams of their own strain or the other. Representative data are presented in Figure 12.9 (32.0 mg/kg, SC for both drugs), where it is apparent that the F344 rats that would otherwise acquire a weaker CTA to cocaine compared to LEW rats actually acquired identical CTAs to those of LEW rats if reared in the LEW maternal environment (Roma, Davis, et al., 2007; also see Roma & Riley, 2007). An even more complex effect emerged for morphine, where the F344 animals that generally show strong morphine-induced CTAs were retarded in their acquisition if reared in the LEW maternal environment; conversely, the LEW animals that are virtually immune to morphine CTA acquired a robust CTA if reared in the F344 maternal environment (Gomez-Serrano & Riley, 2006). Clearly, for as genetically different as F344 and LEW rats may be from each other, genotype alone is only part of the answer to the question of why they differ.

CONCLUDING REMARKS

We began the chapter by describing the value of animal models for understanding the nature of many human behaviors and conditions, including drug use and abuse. In so doing, the relative roles of the rewarding and aversive effects of drugs were introduced and their relative balance was noted as being important to overall drug acceptability. The rewarding effects of drugs have traditionally been the focus in animal models of drug abuse, but as more is learned about the aversive effects of drugs and how these effects impact the overall affective

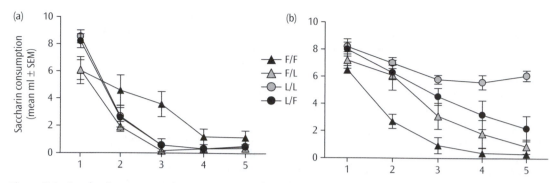

Figure 12.9. Saccharin consumption over repeated conditioning trials in which rats of the F344 and LEW genotypes were given pairings of saccharin and 32.0 mg/kg cocaine (a; from Roma, Davis, et al., 2007) and 32.0 mg/kg morphine (b; from Gomez-Serrano & Riley, 2006). Group F/L refers to F344 pups reared by LEW dams and L/F refers to LEW pups reared by F344 dams. Groups F/F and L/L refer to F344 and LEW pups reared by unrelated dams of their own strain.

response to initial drug exposures, a fuller understanding of both vulnerability and resistance to drug abuse may follow. The present review has focused on these aversive effects of drugs and has described genetic influences on these effects. For most individuals, the concept of genotype naturally conveys a role for genes in the behavior under question. In the present review, we addressed if genetic factors influence taste-aversion learning by examining the ability of a variety of compounds to induce CTAs in the Fischer (F344) and Lewis (LEW) inbred rat strains. The fact that these two genetically distinct strains perform so differently in drug-induced CTA assays argues that genes do play a significant role, and begs the question of what it is exactly that differentiates the strains at the genetic level; but unfortunately, no functional genomics work has been conducted in F344 and LEW rats with respect to CTA (see Lazar, Moreno, Jacob, & Kwitek, 2005; Twigger, Shimoyama, Bromberg, Kwitek, & Jacob, 2007 for the current state of this art). It will be important to characterize the differences between the F344 and LEW strains further to determine their generalization with other drugs and across other parameters such as sex, route, and drug intensity known to impact aversion learning and self-administration and to further determine the neurochemical and molecular bases of these differences. Of course, demonstrating neurochemical and molecular correlates will raise additional questions regarding how they themselves arose, which may eventually lead into assessments of specific genetic mediation (see Crabbe, 2002). It is important in closing to note that the very focus on strain should not limit the analyses to genetic factors (and their mediation). Although the term "strain difference" denotes genetic influences, some of the cross-fostering work from our laboratory presented here indicates a critically important role of the early maternal environment in the pronounced differences between the F344 and LEW rats. Additional work with these strains that isolates the various factors contributing to their behavioral differences may provide additional insight into factors important for the aversive effects of drugs and the role these effects play in animal models of drug use and abuse.

Acknowledgments The work described in the present chapter was supported in part by grants from the MacArthur Foundation and Mellon Foundation to ALR.

Notes

1. Interestingly, although each of these latter procedures is generally classified as an animal model of reinforcement, they may best be seen as assessing some rewarding effect of the drug, an effect that may be important in its ability to serve as a reinforcer in some operant procedure (e.g., self-administration). But given that in none of these latter designs is the drug itself serving as a reinforcer of behavior, it is not truly a reinforcer of behavior in the traditional operant sense. Other preparations that rely on some modification of these basic procedures include secondary reinforcement and reinstatement in which cues associated with the

rewarding effects of the drug are used to establish, maintain, and reinstate drug taking.

2. It is important to note that the above-mentioned analysis of taste aversion learning as reflecting an association between the taste of a solution and the aversive effects of a drug assumes quite a bit, specifically that the drug is aversive. This assumption of the nature of the unconditioned stimulus (US) in taste aversion learning is just that—an assumption. Although sickness (Garcia et al., 1955) and toxicity (Riley & Tuck, 1985a) have been presented as effects sufficient to condition an aversion, others have argued for other bases, for example, stress (Riley, Jacobs, & LoLordo, 1976), disruptions in homeostasis (Gamzu, 1977; Parker, 2003), and even reward itself (Grigson, 1997). This view regarding reward (see Chapter 5) argues that as a result of learning an association between a taste and a drug of abuse such as morphine, when the animal is presented with the taste it pales in comparison to the drug. As a result of this anticipatory contrast, consumption of the taste is reduced. In other words, for drugs of abuse, Grigson argues that the concept of aversion is not needed, and is, in fact, wrong. For the present purposes, we will work with the underlying assumption that there is something aversive about the drug.

3. We use the phrase "Fischer–Lewis Model of Drug Abuse" here in the broadest sense and define it as the direct comparison between the two strains in biological or behavioral responses to a drug of abuse or related compound. The experimental preparation(s) employed for any given study may assay any given aspect of drug taking, with the unifying theme of modeling genetic contributions writ large to individual vulnerability to drug use, abuse, dependence, or relapse.

4. Although a variety of substrains of Fischer and Lewis rats have been developed, and F344 and LEW rats are commercially available worldwide from a number of suppliers, all of the work from our laboratory involving these strains is based on rats purchased from or whose parents were purchased from Harlan Sprague-Dawley (Indianapolis, IN, USA). According to Harlan Sprague-Dawley, the full formal designations for each strain are F344/NHsd (Fischer) and LEW/SsNHsd (Lewis).

5. In this analysis, we are assuming that faster acquisition of self-administration represents a greater sensitivity to the rewarding effects of the drug. However, this is not the only interpretation of this behavior. For example, the fact that these strains differ in the acquisition of a fixed dose of a drug suggests that the LEW strain could actually be *less* sensitive to the rewarding effects of morphine, requiring more infusions during the acquisition phase to maintain self-administration behavior (cf. Davis et al., 2007). This idea is consistent

with findings in outbred rats showing decreases in responding with increasing doses of the drug, suggesting that more drug is needed at lower doses to maintain behavior (Carroll & Lac, 1997).

6. In fact, female LEW animals acquire stronger taste aversions to cocaine than female F344 rats (see Glowa et al., 1994; Roma, Davis, et al., 2007); however, males of these strains acquire comparable taste aversions induced by varying doses of cocaine (Kosten et al., 1994; Roma & Riley, 2007; although see Grigson & Freet, 2000). Given these findings, it is evident that other variables, including sex, play a role in the drug-induced behaviors of these strains and a complete account of the relationship between self-administration and CTA will necessitate an analysis of all these factors.

References

Ambrosio, E., Goldberg, S. R., & Elmer, G. I. (1995). Behavior genetic investigation of the relationship between spontaneous locomotor activity and the acquisition of morphine self-administration behavior. *Behavioral Pharmacology, 6,* 229–237.

Baker, T. B., & Cannon, D. S. (1982). Alcohol and taste-mediated learning. *Addictive Behaviors, 7,* 211–230.

Bardo, M. T., & Bevins, R. A. (2000). Conditioned place preference: What does it add to our preclinical understanding of drug reward? *Psychopharmacology (Berlin), 153,* 31–43.

Barr, C. S., Newman, T. K., Lindell, S., Shannon, C., Champoux, M., Lesch, K. P., et al. (2004). Interaction between serotonin transporter gene variation and rearing condition in alcohol preference and consumption in female primates. *Archives of General Psychiatry, 61,* 1146–1152.

Beck, J. A., Lloyd, S., Hafezparast, M., Lennon-Pierce, M., Eppig, J. T., Festing, M. F. W., et al. (2000). Geneologies of mouse inbred strains. *Nature Genetics, 24,* 23–25.

Belknap, J. K., Belknap, N. D., Berg, J. H., & Coleman, R. (1977). Preabsorptive vs. postabsorptive control of ethanol intake in C57BL/6J and DBA/2J mice. *Behavioral Genetics, 7,* 413–425.

Bermúdez-Rattoni, F., & Yamamoto, T. (1998). Neuroanatomy of conditioned taste aversion. Lesion studies. In J. Bures, F. Bermúdez-Rattoni, & T. Yamamoto (Eds.), *Conditioned taste aversion: Memory of a special kind* (pp. 26–45). Oxford, UK: Oxford University Press.

Bernstein, I. L., & Koh, M. T. (2007). Molecular signaling during taste aversion learning. *Chemical Senses, 32,* 99–103.

Bignami, G. (1965). Selection for high rates and low rates of avoidance conditioning in the rat. *Animal Behaviour, 13*, 221–227.

Billingham, R. E., Hodge, B. A., & Silvers, W. K. (1962). An estimate of the number of histocompatibility loci in the rat. *Proceedings of the National Academy of Sciences of the United States of America, 48*(2), 138–147.

Billingham, R. E., & Silvers, W. K. (1959). Inbred animals and tissue transplantation immunity (with an index of some inbred strains other than mice). *Transplantation Bulletin, 6*(2), 399–406.

Bitterman, M. E. (1975). The comparative analysis of learning. *Science, 188*, 699–709.

Bond, N. W. (1984). *Animal models in psychopathology.* New York: Academic Press.

Bozarth, M. A. (Ed). (1987). *Methods of assessing the reinforcing properties of abused drugs.* New York: Springer-Verlag.

Broadbent, J., Muccino, K. J., & Cunningham, C. L. (2002). Ethanol-induced conditioned taste aversion in 15 inbred mouse strains. *Behavioral Neuroscience, 116*, 138–148.

Brockwell, N. T., Eikelboom, R., & Beninger, R. J. (1991). Caffeine-induced place and taste conditioning: Production of dose-dependent preference and aversion. *Pharmacology, Biochemistry and Behavior, 38*, 513–517.

Brodkin, E. S., Carlezon, W. A. Jr., Haile, C. N., Kosten, T. A., Heninger, G. R., & Nestler, E. J. (1998). Genetic analysis of behavioral, neuroendocrine, and biochemical parameters in inbred rodents: Initial studies in Lewis and Fischer 344 rats and in A/J and C57BL/6J mice. *Brain Research, 805*, 55–68.

Brower, V. G., Fu, Y., Matta, S. G., & Sharp, B. M. (2002). Rat strain differences in nicotine self-administration using an unlimited access paradigm. *Brain Research, 930*, 12–20.

Brunetti, G., Carai, M. A. M., Lobina, C., Melis, S., Serra, S., Vacca, G., et al. (2002). Differences in ethanol-induced conditioned taste aversion in Sardinian alcohol-preferring and Sardinian alcohol-nonpreferring rats. *Alcohol, 26*, 167–172.

Bureš, J., Bermúdez-Rattoni, F., & Yamamoto, T. (Eds.). (1998). *Conditioned taste aversions: Memory of a special kind (Series Volume 31).* Oxford, UK: Oxford University Press.

Cailhol, S., & Mormède, P. (2002). Conditioned taste aversion and alcohol drinking: Strain and gender differences. *Journal of Studies on Alcohol, 63*, 91–99.

Caldji, C., Diorio, J., & Meaney, M. J. (2000). Variations in maternal care in infancy regulate the development of stress reactivity. *Biological Psychiatry, 48*, 1164–1174.

Camp, D. M., Browman, K. E., & Robinson, T. E. (1994). The effects of methamphetamine and cocaine on motor behavior and extracellular dopamine in the ventral striatum of Lewis versus Fischer 344 rats. *Brain Research, 668*, 180–193.

Cannon, D. S., & Carrell, L. E. (1987). Rat strain differences in ethanol self-administration and taste aversion learning. *Pharmacology, Biochemistry & Behavior, 28*, 57–63.

Cannon, D. S., Leeka, J. K., & Block, A. K. (1994). Ethanol self-administration patterns and taste aversion learning across inbred rat strains. *Pharmacology, Biochemistry and Behavior, 47*(4), 795–802.

Cappell, H., & LeBlanc, A. E. (1977). Gustatory avoidance conditioning by drugs of abuse: Relationships to general issues in research on drug dependence. In N. W. Milgram, L. Krames, & T. M. Alloway (Eds.), *Food aversion learning* (pp. 133–167). New York: Plenum Publishing.

Carroll, M. E., & Lac, S. T. (1997). Acquisition of IV amphetamine and cocaine self-administration in rats as a function of dose. *Psychopharmacology (Berlin), 129*, 206–214.

Caspi, A., & Moffitt, T. E. (2006). Gene-environment interactions in psychiatry: Joining forces with neuroscience. *Nature Reviews: Neuroscience, 7*(7), 583–590.

Champagne, F. A., Francis, D. D., Mar, A., & Meaney, M. J. (2003). Variations in maternal care in the rat as a mediating influence for the effects of environment on development. *Physiology & Behavior, 79*, 359–371.

Chen, R., Tilley, M. R., Wei, H., Zhou, F., Zhou, F.-M., Ching, S., et al. (2006). Abolished cocaine reward in mice with a cocaine-insensitive dopamine transporter. *Proceedings of the National Academy of Sciences of the United States of America, 103*(24), 9333–9338.

Chester, J. A., Lumeng, L., Li, T.-K., & Grahame, N. J. (2003). High- and low-alcohol-preferring mice show differences in conditioned taste aversion to alcohol. *Alcoholism: Clinical and Experimental Research, 27*(1), 12–18.

Chester, J. A., Risinger, F. O., & Cunningham, C. L. (1998). Ethanol reward and aversion in mice bred for sensitivity to ethanol withdrawal. *Alcoholism: Clinical and Experimental Research, 22*(2), 468–473.

Chitty, D. (Ed.). (1954). *Control of rats and mice: Vol. 1.* Oxford, England: Clarendon Press.

Cloninger, C. R., Sigvardsson, S., Bohman, M., & von Knorring, A.-L. (1982). Predisposition to petty criminality in Swedish adoptees II: Cross-fostering analysis of gene-environment interaction. *Archives of General Psychiatry, 39*, 1242–1247.

Crabbe, J. C. (2002). Genetic contributions to addiction. *Annual Review of Psychology, 53*, 435–462.

Cunningham, C. L. (1979). Flavor and location aversions produced by ethanol. *Behavioral and Neural Biology, 27*, 362–367.

Cunningham, C. L., Neihus, D. R., Malott, D. H., & Prather, L. K. (1992). Genetic differences in the rewarding and activating effects of morphine and ethanol. *Psychopharmacology (Berlin), 107*, 385–393.

Davey, G. (1983). *Animal models of human behavior: Conceptual, evolutionary and neurobiological perspectives.* Chichester, UK: Wiley.

Davis, C. M., & Riley, A. L. (2007a). The effects of cocaine pre-exposure on cocaine-induced conditioned taste aversion learning in Fischer and Lewis rat strains. *Pharmacology, Biochemistry and Behavior, 87*, 198–202.

Davis, C. M., & Riley, A. L. (2007b). *Lack of strain differences in (−)−U50-488H-induced taste aversions in the Fischer and Lewis rat strains.* Manuscript in preparation.

Davis, C. M., Roma, P. G., Dominguez, J. M., & Riley, A. L. (2007). Morphine-induced place conditioning in Fischer and Lewis rats: Acquisition and dose–response in a fully biased procedure. *Pharmacology, Biochemistry and Behavior, 86*, 516–523.

Dawkins, M. S. (1980). *Animal suffering: The science of animal welfare.* New York: Methuen.

Dhabhar, F. S., McEwen, B. S., & Spencer, R. L. (1993). Stress response, adrenal steroid receptor levels and corticosteroid-binding globulin levels—A comparison between Sprague-Dawley, Fischer 344 and Lewis rats. *Brain Research, 616*, 89–98.

Dragoin, W. B. (1971). Conditioning and extinction of taste aversions with variations in intensity of the CS and UCS in two strains of rats. *Psychonomic Science, 22*, 303–305.

Durcan, M. J., Garcha, H. S., & Stolerman, I. P. (1988). Conditioned taste aversions produced by nicotine in Roman High and Low Avoidance strains of rat. *Psychopharmacology (Berlin), 94*, 532–535.

Elkins, R. L. (1986). Separation of taste-aversion-prone and taste-aversion-resistant rats through selective breeding: Implications for individual differences in conditionability and aversion-therapy alcoholism treatment. *Behavioral Neuroscience, 100*(1), 121–124.

Elkins, R. L., Orr, T. E., Rausch, J. L., Fei, Y. J., Carl, G. F., Hobbs, S. H., et al. (2003). Cocaine-induced expression differences in PSD-95/SAP-90-associated protein 4 and in Ca^{2+}/calmodulin-dependent protein kinase subunits in amygdala of taste aversion-prone and taste aversion-resistant rats. *Annals of the New York Academy of Sciences, 1003*, 386–390.

Elkins, R. L., Walters, P. A., & Orr, T. E. (1992). Continued development and unconditioned stimulus characterization of selectively bred lines of taste aversion prone and resistant rats. *Alcoholism: Clinical and Experimental Research, 16*(5), 928–934.

Ferrari, C. M., O'Connor, D. A., & Riley, A. L. (1991). Cocaine-induced taste aversions: Effect of route of administration. *Pharmacology, Biochemistry and Behavior, 38*, 267–271.

Foynes, M. M., & Riley, A. L. (2004). Lithium-chloride-induced conditioned taste aversions in the Lewis and Fischer 344 rat strains. *Pharmacology, Biochemistry and Behavior, 79*, 303–308.

Froehlich, J. C., Harts, J., Lumeng, L., & Li, T.-K. (1988). Differences in response to the aversive properties of ethanol in rats selectively bred for oral ethanol preference. *Pharmacology, Biochemistry and Behavior, 31*, 215–222.

Gaiardi, M., Bartoletti, M., Bacchia, A., Gubellini, C., Costa, M., & Babbini, A. (1991). Role of repeated exposure to morphine in determining its affective properties: Place and taste conditioning studies in rats. *Psychopharmacology (Berlin), 103*, 183–186.

Gamzu, E. (1977). The multifaceted nature of taste-aversion-inducing agents: Is there a single common factor? In L. M. Barker, M. R. Best, & M. Domjan (Eds.), *Learning mechanisms in food selection* (pp. 477–510). Waco, TX: Baylor University Press.

Gamzu, E., Vincent, G., & Boff, E. (1985). A pharmacological perspective of drugs used in establishing conditioned food aversions. In N. S. Braveman & P. Bronstein (Eds.), *Experimental assessments and clinical applications of conditioned food aversions, Volume 443* (pp. 231–249). New York: The New York Academy of Sciences.

Garcia, J., & Ervin, F. R. (1968). Gustatory-visceral and telereceptor-cutaneous conditioning: Adaptation in internal and external milieus. *Communications in Behavioral Biology, 1*(Part A), 389–415.

Garcia, J., Ervin, F. R., & Koelling, R. A. (1966). Learning with prolonged delay of reinforcement. *Psychonomic Science, 5*, 121–122.

Garcia, J., Kimeldorf, D. J., & Koelling, R. A. (1955). Conditioned aversion to saccharin resulting from exposure to gamma radiation. *Science, 122*, 157–158.

Garcia, J., & Koelling, R. A. (1966). Relation of cue to consequence in avoidance learning. *Psychonomic Science, 4*, 123–124.

Gauvin, D. V., Baird, T. J., & Briscoe, R. J. (2000). Differential development of behavioral tolerance and the subsequent hedonic effects of alcohol in AA and ANA rats. *Psychopharmacology (Berlin), 151*, 335–343.

George, F. R., & Goldberg, S. R. (1988). Genetic differences in responses to cocaine [Monograph]. *NIDA Research Monograph Series, 88,* 239–249.

Glowa, J. R., Shaw, A. E., & Riley, A. L. (1994). Cocaine-induced conditioned taste aversions: Comparisons between effects in LEW/N and F344/N rat strains. *Psychopharmacology (Berlin), 114,* 229–232.

Gomez-Serrano, M. A., & Riley, A. L. (2006). The effects of cross-fostering on morphine-induced conditioned taste aversion in Fischer and Lewis rats. Manuscript in preparation.

Gomez-Serrano, M. A., Sternberg, E. M., & Riley, A. L. (2002). Maternal behavior in F344/N and LEW/N rats: Effects on carrageenan-induced inflammatory reactivity and body weight. *Physiology & Behavior, 75,* 493–505.

Gomez-Serrano, M. A., Tonelli, L., Listwak, S., Sternberg, E., & Riley, A. L. (2001). Effects of cross fostering on open-field behavior, acoustic startle, lipopolysaccharide-induced corticosterone release, and body weight in Lewis and Fischer rats. *Behavior Genetics, 31*(5), 427–436.

Grabus, S. D., Glowa, J. R., & Riley, A. L. (2004). Morphine- and cocaine-induced c-Fos levels in Lewis and Fischer rat strains. *Brain Research, 998,* 20–28.

Grakalic, I., Schindler, C. W., Baumann, M. H., Rice, K. C., & Riley, A. L. (2006). Effects of stress modulation on morphine-induced conditioned place preferences and plasma corticosterone levels in Fischer, Lewis, and Sprague-Dawley rat strains. *Psychopharmacology (Berlin), 189,* 277–286.

Griffiths, R. R., Bigelow, G. E., & Ator, N. A. (2003). Principles of initial experimental drug abuse liability assessment in humans. *Drug and Alcohol Dependence, 70* (Suppl. 3), S41–54.

Grigson, P. S. (1997). Conditioned taste aversions to drugs of abuse: A reinterpretation. *Behavioral Neuroscience, 111,* 129–136.

Grigson, P. S., & Freet, C. S. (2000). The suppressive effects of sucrose and cocaine, but not lithium chloride, are greater in Lewis than in Fischer rats: Evidence for the reward comparison hypothesis. *Behavioral Neuroscience, 114,* 353–363.

Guitart, X., Beitner-Johnson, D., Marby, D. W., Kosten, T. A., & Nestler, E. J. (1992). Fischer and Lewis rat strains differ in basal levels neurofilament proteins and their regulation by chronic morphine in the mesolimbic dopamine system. *Synapse, 12,* 242–253.

Guitart, X., Kogan, J. H., Berhow, M., Terwilliger, R. Z., Aghajanian, G. K., & Nestler, E. J. (1993). Lewis and Fischer rat strains display differences in biochemical, electrophysiological and behavioral parameters: Studies in the nucleus accumbens and locus coeruleus of drug-naïve and morphine-treated animals. *Brain Research, 611,* 7–17.

Haertzen, C. A., Kocher, T. R., & Miyasato, K. (1983). Reinforcements from the first drug experience can predict later drug habits and/or addiction: Results with coffee, cigarettes, alcohol, barbiturates, minor and major tranquilizers, stimulants, marijuana, hallucinogens, heroin, opiates, and cocaine. *Drug and Alcohol Dependence, 11,* 147–165.

Haile, C. N., & Kosten, T. A. (2001). Differential effects of D1- and D2-like compounds on cocaine self-administration in Lewis and Fischer 344 inbred rats. *Journal of Pharmacology and Experimental Therapeutics, 299,* 509–518.

Haile, C. N., Zhang, X. Y., Carroll, F. I., & Kosten, T. A. (2005). Cocaine self-administration and locomotor activity are altered in Lewis and F344 inbred rats by RTI 33, a 3-phenyltropane analog that binds to the dopamine transporter. *Brain Research, 1055,* 186–195.

Hall, F. S., Li, X. F., Sora, I., Xu, F., Caron, M., Lesch, K. P., et al. (2002). Cocaine mechanisms: Enhanced cocaine, fluoxetine and nisoxetine place preferences following monoamine transporter deletions. *Neuroscience, 115*(1), 153–161.

Harvey, W. (1993). *On the motion of the heart and blood in animals* (R. Willis, Trans.). Buffalo, NY: Prometheus Books.

Haug, M., & Whalen, R. E. (1999). *Animal models of human emotion and cognition.* Washington, DC: American Psychological Association.

Hill, K. G., Alva, H., Blednov, Y. A., & Cunningham, C. L. (2003). Reduced ethanol-induced conditioned taste aversion and conditioned place preference in GIRK2 null mutant mice. *Psychopharmacology (Berlin), 169,* 108–114.

Hobbs, S. H., Walters, P. A., Shealy, E. F., & Elkins, R. L. (1993). Radial maze learning by lines of taste-aversion prone and taste-aversion resistant rats. *Bulletin of the Psychonomic Society, 31,* 171–174.

Horan, B., Smith, M., Gardener, E. L., Lepore, M., & Ashby, C. R., Jr. (1997). (−)−Nicotine produces conditioned place preference in Lewis, but not Fischer 344 rats. *Synapse, 26,* 93–94.

Horger, B. A., Shelton, K., & Schenk, S. (1990). Preexposure sensitizes rats to the rewarding effects of cocaine. *Pharmacology, Biochemistry and Behavior, 37,* 707–711.

Horowitz, G. P. & Whitney, G. (1975). Alcohol-induced conditioned aversion: Genotypic specificity in mice (*Mus musculus*). *Journal of Comparative and Physiological Psychology, 89,* 340–346.

Hunt, T., & Amit, Z. (1987). Conditioned taste aversion induced by self-administered drugs: Paradox revisited. *Neuroscience and Biobehavioral Reviews, 11*, 107–130.

Hurd, Y. L. (2006). Perspectives on current directions in the neurobiology of addiction disorders relevant to genetic risk factors. *CNS Spectrums, 11*(11), 855–862.

Hutchinson, A. C., Simpson, G. R., Randall, J. F., Zhang, X., Calderon, S. N., Rice, K. C., et al. (2000). Assessment of SNC 80 and Naltrindole within a conditioned taste aversion design. *Pharmacology, Biochemistry and Behavior, 66*(4), 779–787.

Kearns, D. N., Gomez-Serrano, M. A., Weiss, S. J., & Riley, A. L. (2006). A comparison of Lewis and Fischer rat strains on autoshaping (sign-tracking), discrimination reversal learning and negative automaintenance. *Behavioural Brain Research, 169*, 193–200.

Keehn, J. D. (1979). *Psychopathology in animals: Research and treatment implications.* New York: Academic Press.

Keehn, J. D. (1986). *Animal models for psychiatry.* Boston, MA: Routledge & Kegan Paul.

Klosterhalfen, W., & Klosterhalfen, S. (1983). Conditioned taste aversion and traditional learning. *Psychological Research, 47*, 71–94.

Koob, G. F., & LeMoal, M. (2006). *Neurobiology of addiction.* Boston, MA: Academic Press.

Kornetsky, C. (1977). Animal models: Promises and problems. In I. Hanin & E. Usdin (Eds.), *Animal models in psychiatry and neurology* (pp. 1–9). Oxford, UK: Pergamon Press.

Kornetsky, C., Esposito, R. U., McLean, S., & Jacobson, J. O. (1979). Intracranial self-stimulation thresholds: A model for the hedonic effect of drugs of abuse. *Archives of General Psychiatry, 36*, 321–330.

Kosten, T. A., & Ambrosio, E. (2002). HPA axis function and drug addictive behaviors: Insights from studies with Lewis and Fischer 344 inbred rats. *Psychoneuroendocrinology, 27*, 35–69.

Kosten, T. A., Miserendino, M. J. D., Chi, S., & Nestler, E. J. (1994). Fischer and Lewis rat strains show differential cocaine effects in conditioned place preference and behavioral sensitization but not in locomotor activity or conditioned taster aversion. *Journal of Pharmcology and Experimental Therapeutics, 269*, 137–144.

Kosten, T. A., Miserendino, M. J. D., Haile, C. N., DeCaprio, J. L., Jatlow, P. I., & Nestler, E. J. (1997). Acquisition and maintenance of cocaine self-administration in Lewis and Fischer inbred rat strains. *Brain Research, 778*, 418–429.

Kosten, T. A., Zhang, X. Y., & Haile, C. N. (2007). Strain differences in maintenance of

cocaine self-administration and their relationship to novelty activity responses. *Behavioral Neuroscience, 121*, 380–388.

Kruzich, P. J., & Xi, J. (2006a). Different patterns of pharmacological reinstatement of cocaine-seeking behavior between Fischer 344 and Lewis rats. *Psychopharmacology (Berlin), 187*, 22–29.

Kruzich, P. J., & Xi, J. (2006b). Differences in extinction responding and reinstatement of methamphetamine-seeking behavior between Fischer 344 and Lewis rats. *Pharmacology, Biochemistry and Behavior, 83*, 391–395.

Kulkosky, P. J., Carr, B. A., Flores, R. K., LaHeist, A. F., & Hopkins, L. M. (1995). Conditioned taste aversions induced by alcohol and lithium in rats selectively bred for ethanol neurosensitivity. *Alcoholism: Clinical and Experimental Research, 19*(4), 945–950.

Kumar, R., Pratt, J. A., & Stolerman, I. P. (1983). Characteristics of conditioned taste aversion produced by nicotine in rats. *British Journal of Pharmacology, 79*, 245–253.

Lancellotti, D., Bayer, B. M., Glowa, J. R., Houghtling, R. A., & Riley, A. L. (2001). Morphine-induced conditioned taste aversions in the LEW/N and F344/N rat strains. *Pharmacology, Biochemistry and Behavior, 68*, 603–610.

Lazar, J., Moreno, C., Jacob, H. J., & Kwitek, A. E. (2005). Impact of genomics on research in the rat. *Genome Research, 15*, 1717–1728.

Li, T.-K., & Lumeng, L. (1984). Alcohol preference and voluntary alcohol intakes of inbred rat strains and the National Institutes of Health heterogeneous stock of rats. *Alcohol: Clinical and Experimental Research, 8*, 485–486.

Liu, Q.-R., Drgon, T., Johnson, C., Walther, D., Hess, J., & Uhl, G. R. (2006). Addiction molecular genetics: 639,401 SNP whole genome association identifies many "cell adhesion" genes. *American Journal of Medical Genetics Part B (Neuropsychiatric Genetics), 141B*, 918–925.

Logue, A. W. (1979). Taste aversion and the generality of the laws of learning. *Psychological Bulletin, 86*, 276–296.

Lynch, W. J., & Carroll, M. E. (2001). Regulation of drug intake. *Experimental and Clinical Psychopharmacology (Berlin), 9*, 131–143.

Malone, S. M., Taylor, J., Marmorstein, N. R., McGue, M., & Iacono, W. G. (2004). Genetic and environmental influences on antisocial behavior and alcohol dependence from adolescence to early adulthood. *Development and Psychopathology, 16*, 943–966.

Martin, J. R., & Baettig, K. (1980). Acquisition and extinction of gustatory aversion in two lines of rats selectively bred for

differential shuttlebox avoidance performance. *Behavioural Processes, 5*, 303–310.

Martin, G. M., Bechara, A., & van der Kooy, D.
(1988). Morphine preexposure attenuates the aversive properties of opiates without preexposure to the aversive properties.
*Pharmacology, Biochemistry and Behavior,
30*, 687–692.

Martín, S., Lyupina, Y., Crespo, J. A., González,
B., García-Lecumberri, C., & Ambrosio, E.
(2003). Genetic differences in NMDA and D$_1$
receptor levels, and operant responding for
food and morphine in Lewis and Fischer 344
rats. *Brain Research, 973*, 205–213.

Martín, S., Manzanares, J., Corchero, J., García-
Lecumberri, C., Crespo, J. A., Fuentes, J. A.,
et al. (1999). Differential basal proenkephalin
gene expression in dorsal striatum and nucleus
accumbens, and vulnerability to morphine
self-administration in Fischer 344 and Lewis
rats. *Brain Research, 821*, 350–355.

McClearn, G. E., & Rodgers, D. A. (1959).
Differences in alcohol preference among
inbred strains of mice. *Quarterly Journal of
Studies on Alcohol, 20*, 691–695.

McLaurin, W. A., & Scarborough, B. B. (1963).
Extension of the interstimulus interval in
saccharin avoidance conditioning. *Radiation
Research, 20*, 317–323.

Meisch, R. A. (1982). Animal studies of alcohol
intake. *British Journal of Psychiatry, 141*,
113–120.

Meyer, J. S., & Quenzer, L. F. (2005).
*Psychopharmacology: Drugs, the brain,
and behavior.* Sunderland, MA: Sinauer
Associates, Inc.

National Institute on Drug Abuse. (1996).
*Individual differences in the biobehavioral
etiology of drug abuse* (NIH Publication
No. 96-4034). Washington, DC: Government
Printing Office.

Neumark, Y. D., Friedlander, Y., Durst, R.,
Leitersdorf, E., Jaffe, D., Ramchandani, V. A.,
et al. (2004). Alcohol dehydrogenase polymorphisms influence alcohol-elimination rates in a
male Jewish population. *Alcoholism: Clinical
and Experimental Research, 28*, 10–14.

Oroszi, G., & Goldman, D. (2004). Alcoholism:
Genes and mechanisms. *Pharmacogenomics,
5*(8), 1037–1048.

Orr, T. E., Walters, P. A., & Elkins, R. L. (1997).
Differences in free-choice ethanol acceptance
between taste aversion-prone and taste aversion-resistant rats. *Alcoholism: Clinical and
Experimental Research, 21*(8), 1491–1496.

Ossenkopp, K. P., & Giugno, L. (1990). Nicotine-
induced conditioned taste aversions are
enhanced in rats with lesions of the area
postrema. *Pharmaology, Biochemistry and
Behavior, 36*, 625–630.

Parker, L. A. (2003). Taste avoidance and taste
aversion: Evidence for two different processes.
Learning and Behavior, 31, 165–172.

Parker, L. A., & Doucet, K. (1995). The effects
of nicotine and nicotine withdrawal on taste
reactivity. *Pharmacology, Biochemistry and
Behavior, 52*, 125–129.

Paulus, M. P., Geyer, M. A., & Sternberg, E.
(1998). Differential movement patterns but
not amount of activity in unconditioned motor
behavior of Fischer, Lewis, and Sprague-
Dawley rats. *Physiology and Behavior, 65*,
601–606.

Pescatore, K. A., Glowa, J. R., & Riley, A. L.
(2005). Strain differences in the acquisition of
nicotine-induced conditioned taste aversion.
*Pharmacology, Biochemistry and Behavior,
82*, 751–757.

Phillips, T. J., Belknap, J. K., Hitzemann, R. J.,
Buck, K. J., Cunningham, C. L., & Crabbe,
J. C. (2002). Harnessing the mouse to unravel
the genetics of human disease. *Genes, Brain
and Behavior, 1*, 14–26.

Phillips, T. J., Broadbent, J., Burkhart-Kasch, S.,
Henderson, C., Wenger, C. D., McMullin, C.,
et al. (2005). Genetic correlational analysis of
ethanol reward and aversion phenotypes in
short-term selected mouse lines bred for ethanol drinking or ethanol-induced conditioned
taste aversion. *Behavioral Neuroscience,
119*(4), 892–910.

Pratt, J. A., & Stolerman, I. P. (1982). Conditioned
taste aversions (CTA) produced by nicotine
in rats. *British Journal of Pharmacology
Proceedings Supplement, 77*, 352P.

Ptashne, M. (2004). *A genetic switch: Phage
Lambda revisited* (3rd ed.). Cold Spring
Harbor, NY: Cold Spring Harbor Laboratory
Press.

Quintanilla, M. E., Callejas, O., & Tampier, L.
(2001). Differences in sensitivity to the aversive effects of ethanol in low-alcohol drinking
(UChA) and high-alcohol drinking (UChB)
rats. *Alcohol, 23*, 177–182.

Reicher, M. A., & Holman, E. W. (1977). Location
preference and flavor aversion reinforced by
amphetamine in rats. *Animal Learning &
Behavior, 5*, 343–346.

Ressler, R. H. (1962). Parental handling in two
strains of mice reared by foster parents.
Science, 137(3524), 129–130.

Revusky, S., & Garcia, J. (1970). Learned associations over long delays. In G. Bower & J. Spence
(Eds.), *Psychology of learning and motivation:
Advances in research and theory: Volume 4*
(pp. 1–84). New York: Academic Press.

Rex, A., Sondern, U., Voigt, J. P., Franck, S., &
Fink, H. (1996). Strain differences in fear-
motivated behavior of rats. *Pharmacology,
Biochemistry and Behavior, 87*, 308–312.

Rhodes, J. S., Ford, M. M., Yu, C.-H., Brown, L. L., Finn, D. A., Garland, T., Jr., et al. (2006). Mouse inbred strain differences in ethanol drinking to intoxication. *Genes, Brain and Behavior, 6*, 1–18.

Riley, A. L., & Freeman, K. B. (2004). Conditioned flavor aversions: Assessment of drug-induced suppression of food intake. In J. N. Crawley, C. Gerfen, R. McKay, M. Rogawski, D. R. Sibley, & P. Skolnick (Eds.), *Current protocols in neuroscience* (pp. 8.6E.1–8.6R.12). New York: Wiley.

Riley, A. L., Jacobs, W. J., & LoLordo, V. M. (1976). Drug exposure and the acquisition and retention of a conditioned taste aversion. *Journal of Comparative and Physiological Psychology, 90*, 799–807.

Riley, A. L., & Simpson, G. R. (2001). The attenuating effects of drug preexposure on taste aversion conditioning: Generality, experimental parameters, underlying mechanisms and implications for drug use and abuse. In R. R. Mowrer & S. B. Klein (Eds.), *Contemporary learning theory* (2nd ed., pp. 505–559). Hillsdale, NJ: Lawrence Erlbaum.

Riley, A. L., & Tuck, D. L. (1985a). Conditioned taste aversions: A behavioral index of toxicity. In N. S. Braveman & P. Bronstein (Eds.), *Experimental assessments and clinical applications of conditioned food aversions* (Vol. 443, pp. 272–292). New York: The New York Academy of Sciences.

Riley, A. L., & Tuck, D. L. (1985b). Conditioned food aversions: A bibliography. In N. S. Braveman & P. Bronstein (Eds.), *Experimental assessments and clinical applications of conditioned food aversions* (Vol. 443, pp. 381–437). New York: The New York Academy of Sciences.

Risinger, F. O., & Brown, M. M. (1996). Genetic differences in nicotine-induced conditioned taste aversion. *Life Sciences, 58*(12), 223–229.

Risinger, F. O., & Cunningham, C. L. (1992). Genetic differences in ethanol-induced hyperglycemia and conditioned taste aversion. *Life Sciences, 50*, PL113–PL118.

Risinger, F. O., & Cunningham, C. L. (1995). Genetic differences in ethanol-induced conditioned taste aversion after ethanol preexposure. *Alcohol, 12*(6), 535–539.

Risinger, F. O., & Cunningham, C. L. (1998). Ethanol-induced conditioned taste aversion in BXD recombinant inbred mice. *Alcoholism: Clinical and Experimental Research, 22*(6), 1234–1244.

Risinger, F. O., Freeman, P. A., Greengard, P., & Fienberg, A. A. (2001). Motivational effects of ethanol in DARPP-32 knock-out mice. *The Journal of Neuroscience, 21*(1), 340–348.

Risinger, F. O., Malott, D. H., Prather, L. K., Niehus, D. R., & Cunningham, C. L. (1994). Motivational properties of ethanol in mice selectively bred for ethanol-induced locomotor differences. *Psychopharmacology (Berlin), 116*, 207–216.

Ritz, M. C., Elmer, G. I., Suzuki, T., Meisch, R. A., & George, F. R. (1988). Neither behavioral nor biochemical sensitivity to ethanol is related to self-administration. *Alcohol: Clinical and Experimental Research, 12*, 306.

Ritz, M. C., George, F. R., deFiebre, C. M., & Meisch, R. A. (1986). Genetic differences in the establishment of ethanol as a reinforcer. *Pharmacology, Biochemistry and Behavior, 24*, 1089–1094.

Roma, P. G., Chen, S. A., Barr, C. S., & Riley, A. L. (2007). Dissociation between the aversive and pharmacokinetic effects of ethanol in female Fischer and Lewis rats. *Behavioural Brain Research, 182*, 51–56.

Roma, P. G., Davis, C. M., & Riley, A. L. (2007). Effects of cross-fostering on cocaine-induced conditioned taste aversions in Fischer and Lewis rats. *Developmental Psychobiology, 49*, 172–179.

Roma, P. G., Flint, W. W., Higley, J. D., & Riley, A. L. (2006). Assessment of the aversive and rewarding effects of alcohol in Fischer and Lewis rats. *Psychopharmacology (Berlin), 189*, 187–199.

Roma, P. G., & Riley, A. L. (2007). Cross-fostering and the extinction of cocaine's conditioned aversive effects: Evidence for gene-environment interaction. *Pharmacology, Biochemistry and Behavior, 88*, 1–8.

Rozin, P. (1968). Specific aversions and neophobia resulting from vitamin deficiency or poisoning in half-wild and domestic rats. *Journal of Comparative and Physiological Psychology, 91*, 1326–1336.

Rozin, P., & Kalat, J. W. (1971). Specific hungers and poison avoidance as adaptive specializations of learning. *Psychological Review, 78*, 459–486.

Rutter, M., Moffitt, T. E., & Caspi, A. (2006). Gene-environment interplay and psychopathology: Multiple varieties but real effects. *Journal of Child Psychology and Psychiatry, 47*(3/4), 226–261.

Rzóska, J. (1954). Bait shyness, a study in rat behavior. *British Journal of Animal Behavior, 1*, 128–135.

Sánchez-Cardoso, P., Higuera-Matas, A., Martín, S., del Olmo, N., Miguéns, M., García-Lecumberri, C., et al. (2007). Modulation of the endogenous opioid system after morphine self-administration and during its extinction: A study in Lewis and Fischer 344 rats. *Neuropharmacology, 52*, 931–948.

Schenk, S., & Partridge, B. (1997). Sensitization and tolerance in psychostimulant self-administration. *Pharmacology, Biochemistry and Behavior, 57,* 543–550.

Sherman, J. E., Pickman, C., Rice, A., Liebeskind, J. C., & Holman, E. W. (1980). Rewarding and aversive effects of morphine: Temporal and pharmacological properties. *Pharmacology, Biochemistry & Behavior, 13,* 501–505.

Shoaib, M., Schindler, C. W., & Goldberg, S. R. (1997). Nicotine self-administration in rats: Strain and nicotine pre-exposure effects on acquisition. *Psychopharmacology (Berlin), 129,* 35–43.

Shram, M. J., Funk, D., Li, Z., & Le, A. D. (2006). Periadolescent and adult rats respond differently in tests measuring the rewarding and aversive effects of nicotine. *Psychopharmacology (Berlin), 186,* 201–208.

Shurtleff, D., Liu, R., & Sasek, C. (Eds.). (2004). Frontiers in addiction research: Celebrating the 30th anniversary of the National Institute on Drug Abuse. *Neuropharmacology, 47*(Suppl. 1), 1–367.

Simar, M. R., Saphier, D., & Goeders, N. E. (1996). Differential neuroendocrine and behavioral response to cocaine in Lewis and Fischer rats. *Neuroendocrinology, 63,* 93–100.

Simpson, G. R., & Riley, A. L. (2005). Morphine preexposure facilitates morphine place preferences and attenuates morphine taste aversion. *Pharmacology, Biochemistry and Behavior, 80,* 297–306.

Stöhr, T., Szuran, T., Welzl, H., Pliska, V., Feldon, J., & Pryce, C. R. (2000). Lewis/Fischer rat strain differences in endocrine and behavioural responses to environmental challenge. *Pharmacology, Biochemistry and Behavior, 67,* 809–819.

Stöhr, T., Wermeling, D. S., Weiner, I., & Feldon, J. (1998). Rat strain differences in open-field behavior and the locomotor stimulating and rewarding effects of amphetamine. *Pharmacology, Biochemistry and Behavior, 59,* 813–818.

Stolerman, I. P. (1992). Drugs of abuse: Behavioural principles, methods and terms. *Trends in Pharmacological Sciences, 13,* 170–176.

Stolerman, I. P. (1993). Drug discrimination. In F. Van Harren (Ed.), *Methods in behavioral pharmacology* (pp. 217–243). Amsterdam: Elsevier.

Stolerman, I. P., & D'Mello, G. D. (1981). Oral self-administration and the relevance of conditioned taste aversions. In T. Thompson, P. B. Dews, & W. A. McKim (Eds.), *Advances in behavioral pharmacology* (pp. 169–214). Hillsdale, NJ: Lawrence Erlbaum.

Suomi, S. J. (2003). Gene-environment interactions and the neurobiology of social conflict. *Annals of the New York Academy of Sciences, 1008,* 132–139.

Suzuki, T., Geroge, F. R., & Meisch, R. A. (1988). Differential establishment and maintenance of oral ethanol reinforced behavior in Lewis and Fischer 344 inbred rat strains. *Journal of Pharmacology and Experimental Therapeutics, 245,* 164–170.

Suzuki, T., Geroge, F. R., & Meisch, R. A. (1992). Etonitazene delivered orally serves as a reinforcer for Lewis but not Fischer 344 rats. *Pharmacology, Biochemistry and Behavior, 42,* 579–586.

Suzuki, T., Ise, Y., Maeda, J., & Misawa, M. (1999). Mecamylamine-precipated nicotine-withdrawal aversion in Lewis and Fischer 344 inbred rat strains. *European Journal of Pharmacology, 369,* 159–162.

Suzuki, T., Otani, K., Koike, Y., & Misawa, M. (1988). Genetic differences in preference for morphine and codeine in Lewis and Fischer 344 inbred rat strains. *Japanese Journal of Pharmacology, 47,* 425–431.

Swank, M. W., & Bernstein, I. L. (1994). c-Fos induction in response to a conditioned stimulus after single trial taste aversion learning. *Brain Research, 636,* 202–208.

Tabakoff, B., & Hoffman, P. L. (2000). Animal models (Part 1)—Behavior and physiology. *Alcohol Research and Health, 24,* 77–144.

Tanaka, S., Segawa, T., Tamaya, N., Miyaishi, O., & Ohno, T. (2001). A group of five parameters as a new biological marker on F344/N rats. *Archives of Gerontology and Geriatrics, 32,* 139–150.

Taylor, A. N., Tio, D. L., Bando, J. K., Romeo, H. E., & Prolo, P. (2006). Differential effects of alcohol consumption and withdrawal on circadian temperature and activity rhythms in Sprague-Dawley, Lewis, and Fischer male and female rats. *Alcoholism: Clinical and Experimental Research, 30,* 438–447.

Thomson, J. A., Kalishman, J., Golos, T. G., Durning, M., Harris, C. P., Becker, R. A., et al. (1995). Isolation of a primate embryonic system cell line. *Proceedings of the National Academy of Science, 92,* 7844–7848.

Twigger, S. N., Shimoyama, M., Bromberg, S., Kwitek, A. E., & Jacob, H. J. (2007). The Rat Genome Database, update 2007—Easing the path from disease to data and back again. *Nucleic Acids Research, 35,* D658–662.

Tzschentke, T. M. (1998). Measuring reward with the conditioned place preference paradigm: A comprehensive review of drug effects, recent progress and new issues. *Progress in Neurobiology, 56,* 613–672.

Uhl, G. R., Hall, F. S., & Sora, I. (2002). Cocaine, reward, movement and monoamine transporters. *Molecular Psychiatry, 7*, 21–26.

Valadez, A., & Schenk, S. (1994). Persistence of the ability of amphetamine preexposure to facilitate acquisition of cocaine self-administration. *Pharmacology, Biochemistry and Behavior, 47*, 203–205.

Vit, J.-P., Clauw, D. J., Moallem, T., Boudah, A., Ohara, P. T., & Jasmin, L. (2006). Analgesia and hyperalgesia from CRF receptor modulation in the central nervous system of Fischer and Lewis rats. *Pain, 121*, 241–260.

Weeks, J. R. (1962). Experimental morphine addiction: Method for automatic intravenous injections in unrestrained rats. *Science, 138*, 143–144.

Wei, R., Listwak, S. J., & Sternberg, E. M. (2003). Lewis hypothalamic cells constitutively and upon stimulation express higher levels of mRNA for pro-inflammatory cytokines and related molecules: Comparison with inflammatory resistant Fischer rat hypothalamic cells. *Journal of Neuroimmunology, 135*, 10–28.

Werme, M., Thorén, P., Olson, L., & Brené, S. (1999). Addiction-prone Lewis but not Fischer rats develop compulsive running that coincides with downregulation of nerve growth factor inducible-B and neuron-derived orphan receptor 1. *Journal of Neuroscience, 19*, 6169–6174.

West, M. J., & King, A. P. (1987). Settling nature and nurture into an ontogenetic niche. *Developmental Psychology, 20*, 549–562.

White, W., Sklar, L., & Amit, Z. (1977). The reinforcing action of morphine and its paradoxical side effect. *Psychopharmacologia, 52*, 63–66.

Wise, R. A., Yokel, R. A., & DeWit, H. (1976). Both positive reinforcement and conditioned aversion from amphetamine and from apomorphine in rats. *Science, 191*, 1273–1275.

Xi, J., & Kruzich, P. J. (2007). Black agouti (ACI) rats show greater drug- and cue-induced reinstatement of methamphetamine-seeking behavior than Fischer 344 and Lewis rats. *Pharmacology, Biochemistry and Behavior, 87*, 90–97.

Yamamoto, T. (1993). Neural mechanisms in taste aversion learning. *Neuroscience Research, 16*, 181–185.

Yang, L., & Hou, Y. (2006). Different characters of spleen OX-62 positive dendritic cells between Fischer and Lewis rats. *Cellular & Molecular Immunology, 3*(2), 145–150.

Yokel, R. A. (1987). Intravenous self-administration: Response rates, the effects of pharmacological challenges, and drug preferences. In M. R. Bozarth (Ed), *Methods of assessing the reinforcing properties of abused drugs* (pp. 1–34). New York: Springer-Verlag.

Zacny, J. P., & Gutierrez, S. (2003). Characterizing the subjective, psychomotor, and physiological effects of oral oxycodone in non-drug-abusing volunteers. *Psychopharmacology (Berlin), 170*, 242–254.

Zimmer, C. (2004). *Soul made flesh*. New York: Free Press.

13

Taste, Disgust, and Value: Taste Aversion Learning and Outcome Encoding in Instrumental Conditioning

BERNARD W. BALLEINE

Taste aversion learning, the demonstration that pairing a taste with illness reduces the willingness of animals to consume substances containing that taste, has been shrouded in controversy since its first description about four decades ago. As is well documented elsewhere in this book, reports of robust learning despite long delays between taste and illness, of biological constraints on learning, and of potentiation rather than competition between elements of a compound for association with illness were met with a degree of skepticism when first reported and yet, or perhaps because of this, taste aversion learning has become one of the more thoroughly researched areas of learning in its own right. Just as importantly, the taste aversion paradigm has proven to be a useful tool in the investigation of a variety of other learning processes. This chapter discusses two cases in which taste aversion learning has been used in this way to understand the associative structure of instrumental conditioning; indeed, it was through the use of this procedure that the first and most important evidence that animals can encode the consequences of their actions emerged. Furthermore, using this procedure, it has been established that instrumental performance is not just determined by the association between an action and the outcome but is also a product of the incentive value of the outcome. As such, this chapter begins by reviewing the studies that

have used taste aversion procedures to investigate instrumental conditioning beginning with a description of experiments designed to assess the associative structure of instrumental learning. The second half of the chapter describes studies that have used taste aversion to investigate the motivational processes that control instrumental performance, particularly those processes that determine the reward value of the instrumental outcome.

TASTE AVERSION LEARNING AND THE ASSOCIATIVE STRUCTURE OF INSTRUMENTAL CONDITIONING

Instrumental conditioning allows animals to acquire new behavioral strategies and so exert control over the environment in the service of their basic needs and desires; for example, in the paradigm case, a rat may be trained to press a freely available lever to earn a food reward. Although predictive learning, studied using Pavlovian conditioning procedures, provides animals with the capacity to elicit anticipatory responses as a result of learning about associations between events, the adaptive form of these responses is not acquired and is clearly determined by evolutionary processes rather than by individual learning. As a consequence, because the form of conditioned responses can only adjust through selection, the survival of an animal that can engage only in predictive learning is strongly challenged if the causal consequences of its conditioned responses changes; for example, if a predator develops characteristics that mimic those of an animal's prey. For its responses to remain adaptive in an unstable environment, animals must be capable of rapidly modifying their behavioral repertoire in the face of changing environmental contingencies; that is, they must be capable of exerting control over responses instrumental to gaining access to sources of benefit and avoiding events that can maim or kill.

Despite its adaptive significance, there has long been argument over what animals learn in instrumental conditioning. The answer to this question turns out, however, to be complex; the associative structure of instrumental learning appears to depend on the training conditions. Historically, although various cognitive perspectives were advanced, it was generally accepted that animals acquire new actions using a form of stimulus–response (S–R) learning process. This was partly due to the hegemony of S–R theory at the time, but it was also because it was recognized that this approach provides a more parsimonious account of the way learning results in changes in performance. Cognitive accounts, in contrast, were seen as being unable fully to explain behavior because information that takes the form "action A leads to outcome O" can be used both to perform A and to avoid performing A; knowing which outcome reliably follows an action does not mean that the action will be performed. This criticism of cognitive theories of instrumental conditioning was recognized early in the analyses of animal behavior, the classic critique in that context being Guthrie's (Guthrie, 1935) jibe at the cognitive behaviorism of Tolman (Tolman, 1932), particularly the latter's contention that the performance of a rat learning to traverse a maze to find food was a matter of acquiring a belief about "what (action) leads to what (outcome)." As Guthrie (1935) put it, on this view, "the rat is left buried in thought" (p. 172). Merely believing that, say, "turning left at the choice point is necessary to get food" does not *entail* turning left.

Guthrie himself favored an S–R account of animal action that emphasized the sufficiency of S–R contiguity, a theory that rendered actions homologous to reflexes and that explained performance by confounding action selection and initiation within the function of the stimulus. The most influential

version of this account was later developed by Hull (Hull, 1943) who proposed that S–R associations are strengthened by reinforcement; that is, an association between the situational stimuli (S) and a response (R) is strengthened when R is followed by a reinforcing event (such as food) thereby accounting for the observation that R becomes more probable in S. However, as has been well documented in the past (Adams & Dickinson, 1981; Holman, 1975), one implication of this account is that, in instrumental conditioning, animals do not encode the consequences of their actions; that is, the reinforcer or outcome contingent on the performance of the R does not itself form a part of the associative structure controlling the performance of R. Recognition of this fact produced some of the critical experimental tests of S–R theory notably the *outcome devaluation test* (Holman, 1975), which is where taste aversion learning enters this story.

The outcome devaluation test, conducted after training and so after the formation of any putative S–R connection has been made, has typically involved changing the value of the instrumental outcome by conditioning a taste aversion to it using an injection of lithium chloride (LiCl; Adams & Dickinson, 1981; Colwill & Rescorla, 1986). After the taste aversion phase, the tendency of the rat to press the lever is assessed in extinction, that is, in a test in which no outcomes are delivered. Performance of the devalued action has typically been compared either against that of a nondevalued control group or, in a choice situation, against the performance of another action whose training outcome is not devalued. S–R theories of instrumental performance predict that, because of the S–R association established during training, the presence of the training S guarantees that R will be performed normally during the extinction test irrespective of the change in the value of the training outcome.

Early studies found some evidence to support this prediction. For example, Holman (1975) was able to show that lever-press responses in thirsty rats reinforced on an interval schedule by access to a saccharin solution were maintained in extinction even after the saccharin had been devalued by pairing its consumption with illness. It is important to recognize how maladaptive the lever pressing was in Holman's rats. Although the pairing with illness resulted in the rats no longer consuming or even contacting the previously palatable (but now poisonous) saccharin, their subsequent extinction performance on the lever continued at a rate comparable to that of rats for which the saccharin was not devalued.

Several years later, in a replication of Holman's experiment, Adams and Dickinson (Adams, 1981; Adams & Dickinson, 1981; Dickinson, 1994) found, in contrast, that when lever pressing in hungry rats was reinforced either continuously or on a ratio schedule by sucrose pellets, devaluation of the pellets strongly attenuated subsequent performance on the lever. Although several features of the two studies differed, Dickinson, Nicholas, and Adams (1983) later showed that interval schedules of reinforcement were particularly apt to produce responses that are no longer dependent on the current value of their consequences. When previously reinforced by sucrose on a ratio schedule lever pressing was sensitive to devaluation whereas when reinforced on an interval schedule it was not. These findings using taste aversion learning to change the value of the instrumental outcome ultimately provide evidence that, depending on how different schedules of reinforcement organize the relationship between the rate of instrumental performance and the rate of reward delivery, the performance of instrumental actions can be controlled by either an S–R learning process (i.e., when outcome devaluation does not affect performance) or by the encoded relationship between action and outcome (i.e., when outcome devaluation does affect performance). Thus, when reward delivery is constrained by time within an interval schedule so that changes in the rate of performance have little if any effect on the rate of reward, actions tend to become habitual. When rate of reward is proportional to the rate of performance, as it is on ratio schedules, for example, actions tend to be goal-directed.[1]

Although this conclusion from these studies has generally held up in subsequent years, it should be noted that a successful demonstration of outcome devaluation after training on a single action and outcome does not really demonstrate control by the action–outcome contingency. It is possible, for example, that conditioning a taste aversion to the outcome modifies the ability of sucrose-associated cues, such as the context, to control performance, for example, perhaps devaluing the sucrose reduces performance by removing the excitatory effect of the context–sucrose association. In the first appropriately controlled study along these lines, Adams and Dickinson (1981) assessed this account by

training rats with two types of food pellets, sugar and grain, with only one type being delivered by lever pressing. The other type of pellets was presented independently of any instrumental action. Thus, any particular rat might have to work for sugar pellets by lever pressing, while receiving free deliveries of grain pellets every so often. The issue was whether the animals would reduce lever pressing more after the devaluation of the response-contingent pellets, the sugar pellets in our example, than after devaluation of the free pellets, the grain ones. Such an outcome could only occur if the effect of the devaluation was mediated by the instrumental contingency between lever pressing and the sugar pellets. In this study, the pellets were again devalued using conditioned taste aversion procedures; having trained the rats to lever press, half had a taste aversion conditioned to the sugar and half to the grain pellets. During aversion conditioning the levers were withdrawn and the animals were given a series of sessions in each of which they were allowed to eat one type of pellet. The animals in the devaluation group received a LiCl injection after sessions in which they received the pellets that had been contingent on lever pressing during training but not following sessions with the free pellets. The control group, in contrast, had the aversion conditioned to the free pellets rather than the response contingent ones. Although such food aversions can be established with a single pairing of consumption with illness when the food is novel, the treatment had to be repeated a number of times to suppress consumption in the present study. This is because the pellets were already familiar to the rats, having been presented during instrumental training.

If the motivational property of a reward is mediated by its instrumental relation to an action, then devaluing the response-contingent pellets should have had a greater effect on performance than devaluing the freely delivered pellets. In fact, this is just what Adams and Dickinson found—when subsequently given access to the lever again, the devaluation group pressed significantly less than the control group. Note that this test was conducted in "extinction" during which neither type of pellets were presented because, if the pellets had been presented during testing, the reluctance of the devaluation group to press the lever could be explained simply in terms of the direct suppressive effect of presenting an aversive consequence (i.e., the food pellet paired with LiCl). By testing in extinction, however, different performance in the two groups must have reflected integration of knowledge of the consequences of lever pressing acquired during training with the current reward value of the pellets. This suggestion was confirmed by Colwill and Rescorla (1985a, 1985b) using a choice test similar to that illustrated in Figure 13.1. They trained hungry rats to perform two instrumental actions, lever pressing and chain pulling, with one action earning access to food pellets and the other earning access to a sucrose solution. The rats were then given several trials in which they were allowed to consume one of the outcomes with the levers and chains withdrawn and were then made ill by an injection of LiCl. All animals were then given a choice extinction test on the levers and chains again conducted in extinction, that is, in the absence of either of the outcomes. Colwill and Rescorla found that animals performed fewer of the action the training outcome of which was subsequently paired with LiCl than the other action indicating that the rats had indeed encoded the specific consequences of their actions.

As these demonstrations make clear, taste aversion learning has proven a useful tool in establishing the training conditions conducive to the control of instrumental performance by the S–R association and by the response–outcome association. The importance of these demonstrations of the outcome devaluation effect lies in the fact that, together, they provide strong evidence that animals can indeed encode the specific features of the consequences or outcome of their instrumental actions. Furthermore, these studies show that instrumental performance is not only determined by encoding the action–outcome relation but also by the current reward value of the outcome. It is this second implication of these findings that is the concern of the remainder of this chapter.

HOW DOES TASTE AVERSION MODIFY THE VALUE OF THE INSTRUMENTAL OUTCOME?

Perhaps the simplest account of the way taste aversion learning works to devalue the instrumental outcome can be derived from accounts of aversive conditioning generally. According to most views of aversion conditioning, pairing the instrumental outcome with illness changes the evaluation of the outcome through the formation of a predictive association between the food or fluid and the aversive state induced by illness; that is, as a result of the pairing, the outcome now *signals* forthcoming illness. From this perspective, therefore, the outcome devaluation effect is the product of a practical inference process; that is, the previously encoded action–outcome relation (e.g., "lever pressing leads to sugar") is combined with the learning that the outcome signals an aversive consequence ("sugar leads to illness") to reduce subsequent performance of the action ("therefore stop lever pressing").

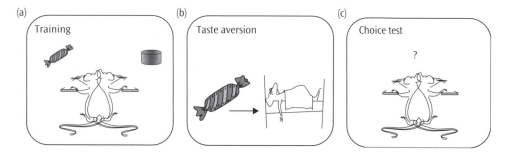

Figure 13.1. Outcome devaluation. Studies assessing changes in the value of the goal on the performance of goal-directed actions have typically used taste aversion learning to devalue the instrumental outcome. In choice studies of this kind rats are trained on two actions each earning a different outcome (a). After this phase, one or other outcome is devalued by taste aversion learning (b). When the outcome is no longer consumed, the tendency of the rats to perform the two actions is tested in the training situation in extinction and, hence, changes in the tendency to perform one or other action must reflect the ability of the rats to integrate information from the training and devaluation phases.

Some time ago, Garcia (1989) introduced a more complex account according to which the change in the evaluation of the outcome induced by taste aversion learning is not due to changing what the outcome predicts but how it tastes. Garcia related the change in taste to negative feedback from a system sensitive to illness that he identified as inducing a disgust or distaste reaction. It is important to see that this view implies that taste aversion learning involves not one learning process but two: (1) an effective pairing of the outcome with illness initially enables a connection between the sensory properties of the outcome and illness (or, more, precisely, a system sensitive to illness); (2) this association is activated when the outcome is subsequently contacted to generate a distaste reaction that then allows the animal to associate the outcome representation with the negative feedback induced by this disgust or distaste reaction. Importantly, this account predicts that it is not sufficient merely to pair the outcome with an injection of LiCl to induce outcome devaluation. Rather, a change in value is not produced until the second process described above is engaged when the outcome is recontacted, a process that we have referred to as *incentive learning* (Dickinson & Balleine, 1994, 2002).

The procedures typically used to induce outcome devaluation do not differentiate between the standard aversive conditioning account and that advanced by Garcia because the conditioning of an aversion to the outcome is usually conducted using multiple pairings of the outcome with illness. Clearly, the pairings themselves would be sufficient to establish a *signaling* relation between the outcome and an aversive consequence, whereas the fact that the animals are typically allowed to contact the outcome on subsequent pairings when it is at least partly devalued provides the opportunity for the animals to associate the outcome representation with distaste. If a substantial aversion to the outcome could be conditioned, using a single pairing of the outcome with illness, however, then these accounts of outcome devaluation make divergent predictions; the *incentive learning account* anticipates that the pairing would not induce devaluation until the outcome had been reexposed after the pairing. In contrast, *the signaling account* predicts that a single effective pairing should induce a devaluation effect without the need for further reexposure.

To test these predictions, Balleine and Dickinson (1991) trained thirsty rats to lever press for access to a sugar solution. Illness was then induced by an injection of LiCl immediately after this session for one group of rats (IMM). A second control group (DEL), was also made ill but after a delay sufficient to prevent any aversion being conditioned to the sugar solution. For reasons not of immediate relevance but that will become apparent, both groups, which we shall refer to as Group IMM-H_2O and Group DEL-H_2O were then allowed to drink water in the test chamber on the next day in the absence of the lever before being tested for their willingness to press the lever on the third day in extinction, that is, in the absence of the sugar. If animals have only to associate sugar with illness to show a devaluation effect, then any effective pairing should be sufficient to generate a change in lever-press performance. If, however, they have to discover that the sugar solution is no longer valuable after the poisoning then giving a single scores–illness pairing without allowing recontact with the sucrose before the test should have no effect on performance. Indeed, this latter effect is exactly what we observed; Group IMM-H_2O, made ill immediately after earning the sugar solution and reexposed to water, pressed just as frequently as Group DEL-H_2O that had experienced the delayed illness. We demonstrated that the sucrose–illness pairing was effective. We found that the rats that received immediate illness had a strong aversion to the sugar solution in a subsequent punishment session in which lever pressing once again delivered the sugar solution. In this session, as soon as these animals started earning and thus making contact with the devalued sugar they stopped pressing, unlike the control rats that showed sustained performance throughout the reacquisition session. This result suggests that, during reacquisition, the animals experienced the nausea or disgust elicited by contact with the sugar and that this experience reduced incentive value to the outcome and, hence, performance of lever pressing.

If contact with the outcome after the devaluation treatment is required to reduce the incentive value of the outcome, as proposed by Garcia (1989), giving this experience prior to the extinction test should induce a devaluation effect and reduce performance in the devalued group relative to the control groups. To test this possibility, a second pair of groups, Group IMM-SUC and Group DEL-SUC, were trained in exactly the same manner as the previous two groups except that they were allowed to contact the sugar solution, rather than water, on the day prior to the extinction test. This experience should have allowed immediately poisoned rats to discover their aversion and, therefore, to refrain from pressing the lever during the test the next day. This is just what happened; Group IMM-SUC pressed significantly less than either of the delay groups, Groups DEL-SUC and DEL-H$_2$O as well as Group IMM-H$_2$O. The significance of this finding is that it allows us to conclude that outcome devaluation induced by taste aversion learning is not a form of signal learning but rather is produced by feedback during consummatory contact with the poisoned outcome. If a change in incentive value were mediated solely by a signaling process, we should expect that pairing the sweet solution with illness would be sufficient to devalue it as a goal of instrumental performance. Indeed, allowing reexposure to it in the absence of illness should serve to weaken, not strengthen, any signaling relation between the outcome and illness acquired in training. The fact that reexposure increased the devaluation effect suggests that the representation of sucrose was only modified as the goal of the rats' instrumental performance when they were allowed to consume it after the pairing with illness.

THE INTERACTION OF EVALUATIVE AND INCENTIVE PROCESSES

The kind of structure that the above discussion suggests underlies the way that taste aversion learning acts to devalue the instrumental outcome is illustrated in Figure 13.2. Pairing the instrumental outcome with illness produces an association between a representation of the sensory properties of the outcome (O) and a structure sensitive to the effects of illness. In line with previous analyses (Dickinson & Balleine, 1994; Rozin & Fallon, 1987), this structure is identified as that reflecting or mediating disgust (D). Thus, it is this association between O and D that is referred to above as underlying the initial conditioning connection following the taste–illness pairing and that, in previous analyses (e.g., Balleine 2001, 2004) has been referred to as *evaluative conditioning*. It is proposed that establishing this association opens a feedback loop that provides the basis for a second-learning process proposed to underlie outcome devaluation, that is, that of *incentive learning*, which is engaged when the outcome is subsequently contacted. This contact activates the representation of the outcome that, through prior evaluative conditioning, then

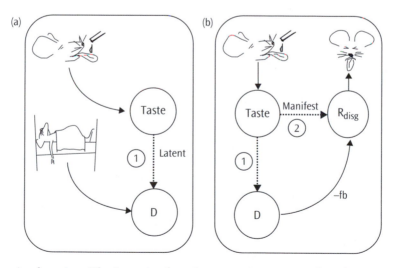

Figure 13.2. Incentive learning. The incentive learning account proposes that the taste–illness pairing establishes (1) a latent connection between the sensory properties of the instrumental outcome and a motivational system sensitive to the effects of LiCl; that is, a disgust system (D—[a]). The taste–disgust association influences outcome value at the time of reexposure to the taste that, through this association, generates a disgust response as negative feedback contiguous with taste exposure allowing a connection between the taste and that response (2—[b]). It is this latter connection that constitutes instrumental incentive learning and that establishes the value of the instrumental outcome.

increases the activity of the disgust system and this latter activity produces negative feedback, Garcia's disgust or distaste reaction, that is contingent on contact with the outcome. It is this feedback that is associated with the representation of the food or fluid itself and that then acts to change the animal's evaluation of the outcome itself.

Of the features of this account, one of the more controversial is the suggestion that the pairing of the outcome with illness establishes a connection between the outcome representation and a disgust system; that is, a system that is activated by the detection of gastric malaise. An alternative, and perhaps more parsimonious suggestion, would be to bring this analysis in line with analyses of aversive conditioning to propose that the outcome representation becomes associated with an aversive system, such as that envisaged by Konorski (1967) or Mowrer (1960) again bringing taste aversion more in line with other forms of aversive conditioning such as that induced by pairing a stimulus with shock. Indeed, there is evidence consistent with this argument; when a flavored solution is paired with an electric shock, the consumption of that solution is reduced to a degree comparable to that induced by pairing the solution with illness (Pelchat, Grill, Rozin, & Jacobs, 1983). There are, however, several reasons for resisting the suggestion that the effects of illness and of shock on consumption are induced by the same associative connection. For example, Berridge, Grill, and Norgren (1981) demonstrated that the ingestive–consummatory response patterns elicited by a palatable commodity, such as sucrose, change after it has been paired with illness to resemble the rejection responses produced by unconditionally noxious substances, such as quinine. The same is not true when sucrose is paired with electric shock; although Pelchat et al. (1983) found that the consumption of a flavor was reduced when it was paired with shock, their animals did not display any rejection reactions when the flavor was subsequently contacted; indeed they continued to display the ingestive reactions produced prior to the pairing. Generally, therefore, pairing a taste with illness both reduces ingestive reactions and increases rejection reactions when the flavor was subsequently contacted after the pairing suggesting that the reduction in consumption produced by illness reflects changes in the palatability of the taste, whereas the reduction produced by shock appears to be based on what the taste predicts (i.e., the shock).

The different effects of shock and illness on taste reactivity responses help to explain a devaluation effect first reported by Rescorla (1992). Rescorla trained rats to lever press and chain pull with one action earning pellets and the other sucrose. He then gave his rats a single pairing of one of the two outcomes with illness before a test in extinction and found that, without reexposure, his rats were able to immediately reduce their performance on the appropriate action. To devalue the outcome, however, Rescorla had used a hypotonic dose of LiCl (0.6 M), something that has been reported to produce immediate somatic discomfort as well as illness (Nachman & Ashe, 1973). Indeed, in a subsequent study we found that, when thirsty rats were given a single injection of 0.6-M lithium (5 ml/kg) following a session in which they were trained to press a single lever for a sucrose solution, they reduced their performance on the lever (relative to delay injected controls) in a subsequent extinction test without reexposure to the sucrose prior to the test (Balleine & Dickinson, 1992). This effect clearly contrasts with that described above when LiCl is injected at a hypotonic concentration (i.e., less than 0.18 M). Perhaps, devaluation produced by somatic feedback is mediated by a different process to that produced by illness.

To assess this interpretation, a second experiment was conducted using six groups of thirsty rats. All of the groups were trained in a single session to press a lever for sucrose solution. After this session, four of the groups were injected with the 0.6-M concentration of lithium except that two of these groups were given the injection while they were anesthetized with halothane. The other two groups served as unpaired controls and were anesthetized immediately following the training session but were given the injection of lithium after a 6-h delay. The day after this treatment, three of the groups, one immediately injected, one immediately injected under anesthesia, and one delay injected, were given brief reexposure to the sucrose in the operant chambers, whereas the other groups were given exposure to water and were then tested on the lever the next day. If the immediate devaluation was produced by pairing the sucrose with the immediate feedback induced by the 0.6-M injection, and the anesthesia acted to mitigate that effect, then an outcome devaluation effect should not be anticipated in that group in the absence of reexposure to the sucrose. This is, in fact, exactly what was found. Irrespective of the reexposure

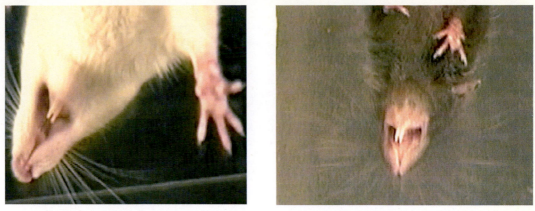

Rat gape   Shrew prevomiting oral response

Figure 6.1. Conditioned gaping in rats reflects nausea "incipient vomiting response." The orofacial characteristics of the rat gape are very similar to those of the shrew retch. Unlike the rat, the shrew vomits in response to emetic stimulation.

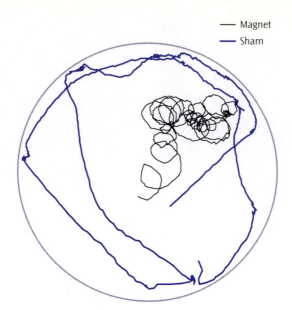

— Magnet
— Sham

Figure 20.2. Traces of individual rats swimming in 2-m diameter pool after 30-min exposure to 14.1 T (thin line) or sham exposure (thick line). The first 50 s of swimming are shown. Exposure to high magnetic fields induces walking in tight circles within an open field; the circling is more apparent when provoked in a swim test. The circling is transient and usually subsides within 2 min.

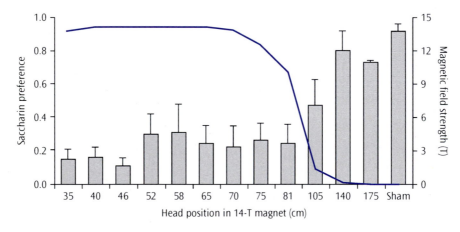

Figure 20.5. Maximal CTA is induced by exposing the head to the maximum uniform field. Rats were "stacked" within the bore of the 14.1-T magnet at different positions, such that their heads (i.e., 65 cm) or their caudal body (i.e., 105 cm) was exposed to the maximum uniform field at the center, or so that they were exposed to the maximum field gradient (i.e., at 105 and 140 cm). The strength of the magnetic field at different positions within the 14.1-T magnet is indicated by the line; magnitude of CTA expressed on the first day of two-bottle testing after exposure at different positions is indicated by the bars. Large CTA was only acquired when the rostral body was exposed to 14.1 T. On the basis of rate of extinction (not shown), the greatest CTA was induced at 65 cm where the entire body was exposed to 14.1 T. Exposure to a large gradient produced little or no CTA, however.

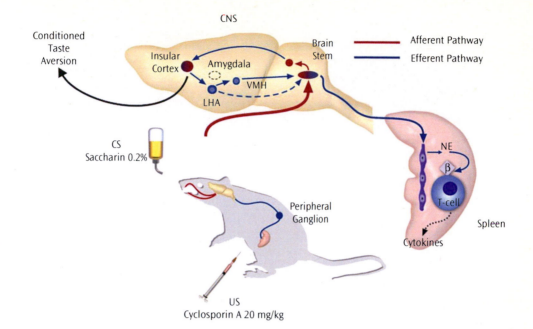

Figure 22.1. Saccharin–cyclosporin association model of TIAL. During the acquisition phase, thirsty animals are motivated to drink saccharin-flavored water (CS). Immediately afterwards these animals receive an intraperitoneal injection of the immunosuppressive drug cyclosporin A (US). At evocation time, the conditioned animals are reexposed to the CS. This gustatory information is centrally processed through brainstem relays (nucleus of the solitary tract and parabracchial nucleus) reaching the insular cortex. This neocortex, together with the amygdala, is indispensable during the acquisition phase, and is also necessary in evoking conditioned ingestive behavior (aversion/avoidance). The ventromedial nucleus of the hypothalamus (VMH) is essential for evoking the immunosuppressive CR in the periphery. The conditioned suppression of cytokine expression and production directly affecting the capacity of splenic lymphocytes to proliferate is not related to hypothalamic–pituitary–adrenal axis activation and is merely mediated by the neural innervation of the spleen, via β-adrenoceptor-dependent mechanisms. LHA, lateral hypothalamic area; NE, noradrenalin.

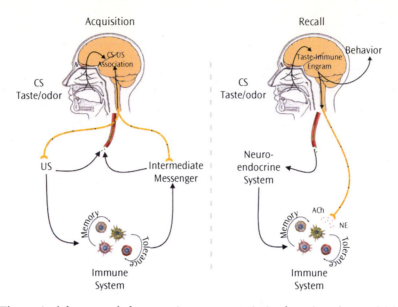

Figure 22.2. Theoretical framework for neuroimmune associative learning. At acquisition time there are two possible USs associated with a CS. The US that is directly detected by the CNS is defined as a "directly perceived US," whereas the one that needs one or more intermediary molecules to be released by another system before it can be detected by the CNS, is called an "indirectly perceived US." For any US, directly or indirectly perceived, there are two possible afferent pathways to the CNS: the neural afferent pathway and the humoral afferent pathway. At recall there are two possible pathways by which the CNS can modulate immune functions: the humoral efferent pathway and the neural efferent pathway. The humoral efferent pathway may imply changes in neurohormones that directly or indirectly modify the immune response. The neural efferent pathway is supported by the direct innervations of primary and secondary lymphoid organs. Regarding the CS, it is important to mention that features such as novelty, intensity, duration and naturalistic relation to the US may explain the feasibility of associating the CS with the US, as well as the stability and strength of such an association. In addition, it is necessary to remember that the immune history (tolerance and memory) of the subject may vary the response to the US, resulting in different associative learning at acquisition time and/or in a different CR at recall. Ach, acetylcholine; NE, noradrenalin. Adapted from: Pacheco-López et al., (2007).

condition, the groups given the hypertonic injection without anesthesia showed an immediate reduction in performance on the lever relative to the delayed injection controls. Of the groups given the injection under anesthesia, however, a devaluation effect was only observed in the group given reexposure to the sucrose. The group exposed to water did not differ from the control groups (cf. Balleine & Dickinson, 1992). This result confirms that devaluation induced by pairing an outcome with somatic feedback and that induced by illness differ and are likely not mediated by the same associative structure and that rather than associating the outcome with disgust, pairing the outcome with somatic feedback might be proposed to condition an association between the outcome representation and a fear system such as that argued to be activated by events such as mild footshock during fear conditioning (Davis, 1998; Fanselow & Gale, 2003; LeDoux, 2000).

If this view is accepted, however, it suggests a further difference between outcome devaluation effects induced by pairing the outcome with illness and with events like shock relating to the lability of the incentive learning process. If pairing the outcome with shock produces an immediate devaluation effect, this account suggests that it does so by (1) conditioning an association between the outcome representation and a fear system and so (2) generating immediate negative feedback that allows the conditioning of the connection between the outcome and an aversive emotional reaction. In contrast, in taste aversion learning, the lengthy delay between exposure to the outcome and the induction of illness, although sufficient for the excitatory association between the outcome representation and the disgust system to form, appears to be too long an interval to associate a new emotional response with the outcome. This suggests that, in instrumental outcome devaluation, the incentive learning process is more sensitive to contiguity than the evaluative process.

VARIATIONS IN OUTCOME ENCODING

The above experiments suggest that reexposure to the outcome is necessary for outcome devaluation by conditioning a taste aversion to influence instrumental performance. There is, however, one published observation that does not accord with this empirical generalization. Rescorla (1994) reported that, in an instrumental choice situation, rats immediately reduced their performance of an action after only a single pairing of its outcome with illness (induced by 0.15-M LiCl) without the need for reexposure. Although Balleine and Dickinson (1991; Balleine, Garner, & Dickinson, 1995) found that, as with overall performance on a single lever, when rats are trained on two actions for different outcomes that are then both paired with illness, choice between instrumental actions is determined by incentive learning; that is, reexposing the rats to one or other outcome biases choice away from the action that, in training, earned that reexposed outcome. If, however, an immediate effect of devaluation can be detected using a sufficiently sensitive within-subjects test, then we need to modify our conclusion: Although incentive learning significantly increases the size of outcome devaluation effects it is not *necessary* to induce outcome devaluation. But, if this is the case then what associative structure mediates outcome devaluation? When does taste aversion learning produce direct effects on instrumental performance and when do these effects depend on incentive learning?

Recent evidence suggests that the answer to this question depends on the *relative contiguity* between an action and outcome delivery. Although incentive learning was required before taste aversion was effective in modifying instrumental performance in the above experiments, it must be conceded that this was not true of *all* the responses performed in the instrumental situation. For example, in these studies we also reported evidence that the rats' tendency to approach the location of food delivery was directly affected by taste aversion learning without the need for animals to recontact the food after its pairing with illness (Balleine & Dickinson, 1991, 1992). Thus, in some groups (most notably the IMM-H_2O group of Balleine and Dickinson's, 1991 study) pairing the sucrose with illness had no effect on lever pressing but directly reduced the tendency to approach the area where the sucrose had been delivered during training. To explain this difference in sensitivity to the effects of devaluation we have at various points argued that this reflects a difference in the *contingency* that controls the performance of these responses, suggesting that instrumental actions, such as lever pressing, are controlled by the action–outcome association whereas anticipatory approach is elicited by Pavlovian stimulus–outcome associations

(Corbit & Balleine, 2003; Dickinson & Balleine, 1993, 1994, 2002). It is possible that outcome devaluation only affects instrumental actions controlled by the action–outcome association after reexposure, whereas outcome devaluation immediately affects responses controlled by Pavlovian stimulus–outcome associations. This would be likely if, given the structure described in Figure 13.2, Pavlovian CR's are controlled directly by motivational components of the taste–disgust association whereas instrumental actions are controlled by incentive learning. Furthermore, this suggestion would help to explain Rescorla's (1994) data if the rats' actions in this study were at least partly controlled by the excitatory influence of Pavlovian stimulus–outcome associations, an influence reduced by outcome devaluation. It remains, however, to establish why the actions in Rescorla's (1994) study and why magazine entry in our experiments should be more open to the influence of stimulus–outcome associations than instrumental lever pressing in the initial studies described earlier.

One potential explanation lies in the relative contiguity of these various responses to outcome delivery. In the free operant situation, lever pressing must precede magazine entry and so has a relatively lower temporal and spatial contiguity to outcome delivery. Indeed, as it is necessary that these two responses be performed as a part of heterogeneous chain if the outcome is to be both earned and retrieved, it is possible that the local contiguity of cues encountered and responses performed around the magazine systematically overshadow the necessarily more distal lever-press action for direct association with the outcome. Furthermore, in our initial experiments it is likely that this overshadowing effect was greater than that induced in Rescorla's study; in our experiment we required rats to push back a transparent panel to enter the recessed magazine area where the food was delivered whereas this panel push response was not required in Rescorla's study. Pavlovian cues may contribute to the performance of responses more proximal to outcome delivery and their rate of performance may be directly affected by outcome devaluation as a consequence. In contrast, more distal responses may be protected from the influence of these cues and hence from the direct effects of outcome devaluation.

In a recent series of experiments designed to assess this issue, we attempted to model the situation where lever pressing is followed by panel pushing/magazine approach by training rats on a heterogeneous chain of actions, and we found that whereas the performance of actions proximal to outcome delivery was directly affected by taste aversion learning, more distal actions were not (Balleine, Paredes-Olay, & Dickinson, 2005). Indeed, the performance of these more distal actions was only affected when the opportunity for incentive learning was given. For example, in one study (Balleine et al., 2005, Experiment 1), thirsty rats were trained to perform two actions (designated R1 and R2) in sequence to gain access to the instrumental outcome, initially water and then, in the critical training session, for a 20% sucrose solution (i.e., R1 → R2 → SUC). Half the rats were required to press a lever then pull a chain, whereas for the other animals this relationship was reversed. Rats had no great difficulty acquiring this relationship and, indeed, during the sucrose training session, the conditional probability of the performance of R2 following R1 was significantly higher than for R1 following R2. After this training, we examined the sensitivity of the performance of R1 and R2 to outcome devaluation by injecting half of the rats with LiCl immediately after the session (Group IMM). The remaining rats were injected after a 6 h-delay (Group DEL). The effects of the devaluation treatment on the performance of R1 and R2 were assessed the next day in extinction where it was found that, although the performance of the distal response, R1, did not differ between groups, the performance of the action proximal to the delivery of the sucrose, R2, was immediately and directly reduced by taste aversion learning in group IMM relative to Group DEL.

In a second study we assessed the role of incentive learning in bringing the performance of the distal action (i.e., R1) under the influence of the taste aversion learning. To achieve this, we trained thirsty rats on the heterogeneous chain for sucrose solution as described above after which all of the animals were given an immediate injection of LiCl. The next day half of the rats were allowed reexposure to the sucrose solution (Group SUC), whereas the remaining rats were given reexposure to water (Group H_2O). Both groups were then given an extinction test on the levers and chains in which we found that, although performance on the proximal action to sucrose, R2, was unaffected by the reexposure and was similar in the two groups, performance on the distal action, R1, was reduced in the reexposed group, Group SUC, relative to Group H$_2$O. As such, the impact of reexposure was most clearly observed in the performance of the action distal to outcome delivery and, in this study, was not observed in the performance of the action proximal to outcome delivery (Balleine et al., 2005, Experiment 2).

The differential effectiveness of taste aversion learning on the performance of actions in an instrumental chain has been used in the past to argue that variations in the encoding of the outcome associated with R1 and R2 might underlie the differences in the sensitivity of these responses to taste aversion learning (Balleine, 2001, 2004). This account is illustrated in Figure 13.3. In essence, as described briefly earlier, this account proposes that variations in outcome encoding arise because the proximal action overshadows the distal action in the formation of an association with the most salient, motivationally relevant features of the instrumental outcome, that is, those sensory features that form a direct association with

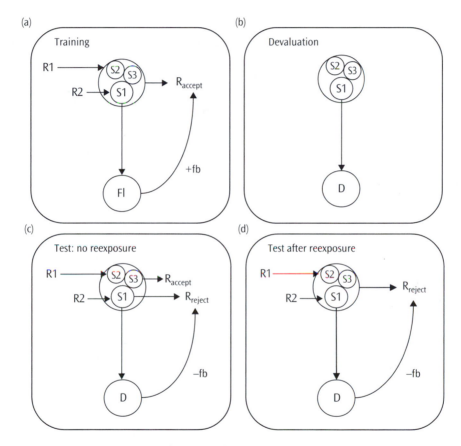

Figure 13.3. Variations in outcome encoding. On this account, the outcome is composed of various sensory elements (S1, S2, S3, etc.) of differing salience. The most salient element becomes associated with the dominant motivational process; for example, S1 becomes associated with fluid system when rats are thirsty (a) and with the disgust system after pairing of the outcome with illness (b). During initial training actions proximal to outcome delivery (R2) become associated with the most salient element of the outcome and overshadow more distal actions for association with that element The latter, therefore, become associated with more diffuse elements of the outcome (e.g., S2, S3 in [a]). After devaluation but without reexposure, the tendency to perform R2 might be reduced because it retrieves S1 and so disgust. In contrast, because R1 is associated with elements that are not linked with motivational processes directly, its performance does not change (refer [c]). After rexposure, not just S1 but also diffuse elements like S2 and S3 are associated with the distaste reaction and, hence, have a reduced value allowing R1 to also reduce (see [d]).

motivation for fluids during initial training when thirsty and with the disgust system during taste aversion learning. As a consequence, the distal action may be predominantly associated with more diffuse, motivationally irrelevant features. As a consequence, the distal (R1) and proximal (R2) actions in the chain may become associated with different features of the outcome representation due to both differences in the salience of specific features of the outcome (here represented as S1, S2, and S3) and the operation of overshadowing. When the value of the sucrose is reduced, the tendency to perform R2 could be immediately reduced by two factors; (1) a reduction in the excitatory influence of specific Pavlovian cues on performance and (2) a direct incentive learning effect driven by the ability of R2 to recall S1 and so activate the disgust system, which, given that sufficient feedback can be generated from this source, might then directly reduce the motivational support for the action.

In contrast, if R1 is associated with motivationally irrelevant features of the outcome, and the incentive value of these features is determined solely by the feed-forward connection established during reexposure, then the tendency to perform R1 cannot directly modify the motivational support for that action through this feedback process. Thus, without the opportunity to revalue these features of the outcome through reexposure, performance after devaluation should not be expected to change and will be maintained by the relatively high value assigned to those elements of the outcome during initial training in the thirsty state. Once reexposure to the sucrose has been given, however, all of the elements of the sucrose having been paired with the distaste response, the performance of both the proximal and distal action should be reduced.

CHANGES IN OUTCOME VALUE AS AN EMOTIONAL PROCESS

The above analysis pins the effects of reexposure to feedback produced by the activation of primary motivational systems, in the form of taste or distaste reactions; that is, ingestive responses, such as licking, chewing, and swallowing in the case of appetitive outcomes and rejections responses in the case of disgust. In the past, however, various accounts of the effect of outcome reexposure after taste aversion learning have proposed that these effects are mediated by the formation of an

association between the outcome representation and the *emotional effects* induced by the arousal of disgust (Balleine, 2001, 2004). Indeed, this kind of suggestion is not new. Neobehaviorist learning theories (e.g., Hull, 1943, 1952; Spence, 1956) argued that conditioned responses could themselves exert a motivational influence on instrumental performance, referred to, in that context, as fractional anticipatory goal responses (i.e., rg-sg). Largely due to the subsequent work of Konorski (1967) and Mowrer (1960) but also due to the description of incentive contrast effects (Flaherty, 1996), however, it is now commonly accepted that these effects reflect the activation of an affective state that can exert a direct modulatory influence over consummatory responses and, through a change in the emotional responses elicited during ingestion, on instrumental performance (Dickinson, 1989; Rescorla & Solomon, 1967). With respect to the effects of outcome reexposure after taste aversion learning, this approach suggests that, during reexposure to the previously poisoned outcome, the reactivation of the outcome representation increases activity in the disgust system to produce an aversive state that is then manifest in feedback in the form of an aversive emotional response, a response that occurs contiguous with contact with the sensory feature of the outcome. This structure is illustrated in Figure 13.4.

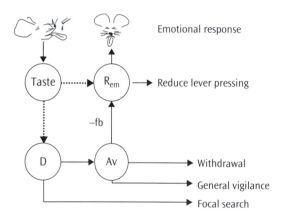

Figure 13.4. Emotional feedback. The role of an aversive affective system in controlling the emotional response and other responses elicited by taste-related activation of the disgust system through the associative link established during taste aversion learning.

On this account, incentive learning depends on two processes: a feedback process and a feed-forward process. Pairing the instrumental outcome with illness conditions an association between the outcome representation and the disgust system (i.e., the evaluative connection) and acts, effectively, to open a feedback loop (fb). When the outcome is reexposed, activation of the outcome representation acts to produce activity in the disgust system to induce activity not only in aversive affective structures (AV) productive of a number of conditioned responses, such as withdrawal and increased general vigilance, but also in the production of an aversive emotional response (R_{em}). On this view, reexposure provides the basis for a feed-forward (ff) association between the outcome representation and this emotional response.

There are several points to make about this account. First, if the effects of reexposure are identified with the conditioning of this feed-forward association it should be clear why devaluation induced by taste aversion should rely on reexposure, whereas devaluation induced by somatic discomfort should not. In the latter case, the aversive response induced by the injection should be relatively contiguous with consumption of the outcome, so allowing a stronger feed-forward association to form at that time; that is, one less likely to be overshadowed by other reactions. In the former case, a comparable degree of contiguity between contact with the outcome and the aversive emotional reaction induced by disgust will only occur during reexposure. Second, it suggests that, in order to establish, and subsequently change, the reward value of the outcome in instrumental conditioning, it is sufficient to elicit an emotional response during contact with the outcome. Although this provides a simple model of the way goal value is established and altered, it makes the very strong claim that this process not only mediates reductions in value induced by taste aversion learning but also changes in value induced by other manipulations too.

In fact, considerable evidence suggests that the reward value of primary incentives, like food or fluid outcomes, is mediated by similar changes in the emotional response associated with these outcomes. For example, specific satiety treatments have been found to be extremely effective in producing selective changes in the incentive value of instrumental outcomes and in the performance of actions that gain access to those outcomes (Balleine & Dickinson, 1998b, 1998c) over and above the effects of satiety on motivation for nutrients generally or even for specific macronutrients. For example, in one study (Balleine & Dickinson, 1998c) hungry rats were trained to press a lever and pull a chain with one action earning sour starch and the other salty starch before they were sated on either the salty or sour starch and given an extinction test on the lever and chain. Although both actions earned equivalent calories in a similar macronutrient structure, the rats still altered their choice performance to favor the action that, in training, delivered the outcome on which they were not sated; that is, they were able to modify their choice based on changes in taste (Balleine & Dickinson, 1998c). In another series we assessed the effects of cell-body lesions of gustatory region of the insular cortex, for some time known to be involved in taste processing, although not taste detection (Braun, Lasiter, & Kiefer, 1982), on specific-satiety induced devaluation and on incentive learning conducted after instrumental training when hungry after a shift to a sated state (Balleine & Dickinson, 2000). Although these lesions had no effect on the ability of rats to detect changes in value when they actually contacted a specific outcome on which they were sated, they were deeply amnesic when forced to choose between two actions based on their memory of satiety-induced changes in value.

These results suggest that the gustatory cortex operates as one component of an incentive system, acting to encode the taste features of the instrumental outcome as an aspect of the representation of the value of that outcome in memory. From this perspective, the gustatory cortex is not involved in detecting changes in incentive value, which would appear to require the integration of taste memory, involving the gustatory cortex, with an affective signal, apparently mediated by a different component of the incentive system (Balleine, 2001). Thus, changes in the value of the taste features of nutritive outcomes appear to be a function of emotional feedback; that is, of the emotional response experienced contiguously with detection of the taste. If the emotional response is pleasant, the value of the outcome is correspondingly increased whereas if it is unpleasant it is reduced. Hence treatments that produce changes in palatability in rats, usually assessed by taste reactivity responses, are also those that which most potently modify the value of the instrumental outcome (Berridge, 2000;

Berridge et al., 1981). For example, Rolls, Rolls, and Rowe (1983) have provided a clear demonstration that, in humans, eating one particular food to satiety strongly reduces the pleasantness rating of that food but not other similar foods. Likewise, in rats, Berridge (1991) has demonstrated that, when sated on milk, ingestive taste reactivity responses were reduced and aversive taste reactivity responses were increased when milk, but not when sugar, was subsequently contacted. These kinds of data suggest that satiety-induced changes in incentive value are not a product of general shifts in motivation but reflect variations in the association of taste features with specific emotional responses.

If incentive learning is determined by an association between sensory and emotional processes, one should suppose neural structures implicated in the formation of associations of this kind to be critically involved in this form of learning. The gustatory cortex maintains strong reciprocal connections with the amygdala (Sripanidkulchai, Sripanidkulchai, & Wyss, 1984; Yamamoto, Azuma, & Kawamura, 1984) and, indeed, this connection has been implicated in taste–affect associations in a variety of paradigms (Gallo, Roldan, & Bures, 1992). The basolateral amygdala (BLA) has itself been heavily implicated in a variety of learning paradigms that have an evaluative component; for example, this structure has long been thought to be critical for fear conditioning and has recently been reported to be involved in a variety of feeding-related effects including sensory specific satiety (Malkova, Gaffan, & Murray, 1997), and in food consumption elicited by stimuli associated with food delivery (Holland, Petrovich, & Gallagher, 2002; Petrovich, Setlow, Holland, & Gallagher, 2002). And, indeed, in two recent series of experiments we have found clear evidence of the involvement of the BLA in incentive learning. In one series we found that lesions of the BLA rendered the instrumental performance of rats insensitive to outcome devaluation, apparently because they were no longer able to associate the sensory features of the instrumental outcome with its emotional or incentive value (Balleine, Killcross, & Dickinson, 2003).

More recently, we have confirmed this suggestion using posttraining infusions of the protein-synthesis inhibitor anisomycin (S. H. Wang, Ostlund, Nader, & Balleine, 2005). It has now been well documented that both the consolidation of the stimulus–affect association that underlies fear conditioning and its reconsolidation

after retrieval depends on the synthesis of new proteins in the BLA (Nader, Schafe, & LeDoux, 2000; Schafe, Nader, Blair, & LeDoux, 2001). In a recent experiment, we first trained hungry rats to press two levers with one earning food pellets and the other a sucrose solution. After this training the rats were sated and given the opportunity for incentive learning, that is, they were allowed to consume either the food pellets or the sucrose solution in the sated state. Immediately after this consumption phase, half of the rats were given an infusion of anisomycin, whereas the remainder were given an infusion of vehicle. In a subsequent choice extinction test that was conducted on the two levers when sated, rats in the vehicle group performed fewer responses on the lever that, in training, delivered the outcome that they were reexposed to when in the sated state prior to the test; that is, the standard incentive learning effect (Balleine, 1992). In contrast, the infusion of anisomycin completely blocked this shift in preference. To assess whether incentive learning is subject to reconsolidation involving the BLA, we gave all of the rats a second reexposure episode to either the pellets or sucrose when sated such that if they had been first given vehicle infusion then they were now given an anisomycin infusion, whereas if they were first given an anisomycin infusion they were now given a vehicle infusion. Although, again, vehicle infused rats showed reliable incentive learning, those given the anisomycin infusion performed indifferently on the two levers despite the fact that these same rats had previously shown clear evidence of incentive learning after the first episode of reexposure (S. H. Wang et al., 2005).

Previous effects of amygdala manipulations on feeding have been found to involve connections between the amygdala and the hypothalamus (Petrovich et al., 2002), and, indeed, it has been well reported that neuronal activity in the hypothalamus is heavily modulated by chemical signals associated with food deprivation and food ingestion, including various macronutrients (Levin, 1999; Seeley et al., 1996; R. Wang et al., 2004; Woods, Schwartz, Baskin, & Seeley, 2000). Conversely, through its connections with visceral brainstem, midline thalamic nuclei, and associated cortical areas, the hypothalamus is itself in a position to modulate motivational and nascent affective inputs into the amygdala. These inputs, when combined with the amygdala's sensory afferents, provide the kind of associative process required to alter incentive value and points both to the associative structure and the larger neural system underlying incentive learning for food and fluid outcomes generally. As described above, this structure is based on a simple feedback circuit within which the goal or reward value of a specific event is set and, indeed, can be reset when subsequently contacted on the basis of the animals' current internal state (see Balleine, 2001, for review).

With regard to taste aversion learning, although the gustatory cortex has been implicated in taste aversion learning, the amygdala, and particularly the BLA, have had a checkered past; some studies have reported effects of BLA manipulations (Simbayi, Boakes, & Burton, 1986) whereas others have not (Dunn & Everitt, 1988). Most studies assessing the role of the BLA on taste aversion learning have, however, used a consumption paradigm. When Pavlovian conditioning procedures have been used, the effects of BLA lesions on taste aversion-induced US devaluation become somewhat more consistent (Hatfield, Han, Conley, Gallagher, & Holland, 1996). The effects of BLA manipulations on devaluation induced by a shift in motivational state suggest that taste aversion induced devaluation may also be affected by BLA lesions. Perhaps the BLA mediates the effects of conditioned taste aversion on outcome value when the outcome is serving as a goal of instrumental actions or as a Pavlovian US but does not mediate its effects on consummatory responding.

SOMATIC AND SYMBOLIC VALUES

One of the main reasons for proposing that pairing the instrumental outcome with illness conditions an association between the outcome representation and the disgust system comes from evidence that antiemetics attenuate both the acquisition and expression of conditioned taste aversions. In one study (Balleine, Garner, et al., 1995, Experiment 1), thirsty rats were given two sessions in one of which they were allowed to drink a sucrose solution, whereas in the other session they were allowed to drink a saline solution. After both sessions all of the rats were given an injection of LiCl (0.15-M, 5 ml/kg) but, 20 min prior to one injection, rats were injected with ondansetron (100 µg/kg), a 5-HT3 receptor antagonist reported to have a strong antiemetic profile in both animals (Higgins, Kilpatrick, Bunce, Jones, & Tyers, 1989)

and humans (Chaffee & Tankanow, 1991). Prior to the other injection of lithium the rats were given a control injection of saline vehicle. The rats were then given a series of two-bottle choice tests in which they were free to consume both the sucrose and saline solutions. Before these tests, half of the rats were injected with ondansetron whereas the remaining were injected with vehicle.

If pairing a taste with illness conditions an association between the taste and disgust, blocking the activity of the disgust system at the time of conditioning using an antiemetic should be predicted to attenuate the formation of that association with the effect that, in the test sessions, rats should prefer the solution poisoned under ondansetron to the other solution. Furthermore, if the expression of a previously conditioned aversion depends on the ability of the taste representation to access the disgust system via an established connection, blocking the activity of the disgust system with ondansetron should be predicted to increase consumption of the solution previously poisoned under vehicle on test. The results of this study largely confirmed both predictions; although initially the consumption of both solutions did not differ, rats injected with vehicle clearly came to prefer the solution poisoned under ondansetron to the other solution over a series of extinction trials. More importantly, this preference was clearly attenuated in rats injected with ondansetron prior to the test and, over the course of extinction, the rats drank more of both solutions.

The finding that ondansetron attenuates the expression of a previously conditioned taste aversion suggests that ondansetron should also attenuate the effect of incentive learning in instrumental outcome devaluation induced by taste aversion learning. Consistent with this suggestion, Limebeer and Parker (2000) reported that the antiemetic ondansetron blocked the expression of the aversive taste reactivity responses induced by a taste previously paired with illness. To assess this prediction directly, we (Balleine, Garner, et al., 1995) trained thirsty rats in a single session to perform two actions, lever pressing and chain pulling, with one action delivering the sucrose solution and the other delivering the saline solution. Immediately after this training session, all the rats were given an injection of LiCl. Over the next 2 days the rats were reexposed to both the sucrose and the saline solutions. Prior to one reexposure session, however, rats were injected with ondansetron whereas prior to the other session they were injected with vehicle. The next day the rats were given a choice extinction test on the lever and chain. If reexposure devalues the instrumental outcome via the ability of the outcome representation to access the disgust system, blocking the activity of that system with ondansetron should be predicted to attenuate the effects of reexposure such that, on test, the action that, in training, delivered the outcome subsequently reexposed under ondansetron should be performed more than the other action. This is, in fact, exactly what we found (cf. Balleine, Garner, et al, 1995, Experiment 2).

Given the role of incentive learning in encoding reward, it is interesting to consider how the value conferred by this process is retrieved to determine choice performance on test. Because the choice tests are often conducted many days after incentive learning and in extinction the rat is forced to rely on its memory of specific action–outcome associations and the current value of the instrumental outcome. *So how is value encoded for retrieval during this test?*

A currently influential theory, the *somatic marker hypothesis* (Damasio, 1994) proposes that value is retrieved through the operation of the same processes through which it was encoded. According to this view, decisions based on the value of specific goals are determined by reexperiencing the emotional effects associated with contact with that goal. With regard to outcome devaluation effects, for example, the theory could not be more explicit.

> When a bad outcome connected with a given response option comes to mind, however fleetingly, you experience an unpleasant gut feeling...that forces attention on the negative outcome to which the given action may lead, and functions as an automated alarm signal which says: Beware of danger ahead if you choose the option that leads to this outcome. The signal may lead you to reject, *immediately*, the negative course of action and thus make you choose between other alternatives.
>
> Damasio, 1994, p. 173

An alternative theory proposes that reward values, once determined through incentive learning, are encoded abstractly (e.g., "X is good" or "Y is bad" etc.) and, as such, from this perspective they are not dependent on the original emotional effects induced by contact with the goal during the encoding of incentive value for their retrieval (see Balleine, 2005; Balleine & Dickinson 1998a, for further discussion).

We have conducted several distinct series of experiments to test these two hypotheses and, in all of these, the data suggest that after incentive learning, incentive values are encoded abstractly and do not involve the original emotional processes that established those values during their retrieval (Balleine, Ball, & Dickinson, 1994; Balleine, Davies, & Dickinson, 1995; Balleine & Dickinson, 1994; Balleine, Garner, et al., 1995). One test of these two accounts was derived from consideration of the role of associations between the outcome representation and the disgust system in outcome devaluation described above. If the impact of outcome devaluation on performance is carried by emotional feedback induced by activation of the disgust system by the outcome representation, then, according to the somatic marker hypothesis, reducing the ability of the outcome representation to activate the disgust system during retrieval of the incentive value on test by administering ondansetron prior to the test should be predicted to attenuate the effects of outcome devaluation on performance. This experiment replicated the procedures used in the experiment described (Balleine, Garner, et al., 1995) except that, prior to the choice extinction test, half of the animals were injected with ondansetron whereas the remainder were injected with vehicle. On the basis of the previous study, it was anticipated that the group given the injection of vehicle prior to the test would perform more of the action that, in training, had delivered the outcome reexposed under ondansetron. More importantly, if activation of the disgust system critically mediates the retrieval of incentive value during the test, as the somatic marker hypothesis suggests, then any difference found in the vehicle group should be attenuated in the group injected with ondansetron on test.

The results of this experiment were very clear; contrary to predictions of the somatic marker hypothesis, the injection of ondansetron on test had no impact whatever on performance in the choice extinction test. Whether injected with vehicle or ondansetron prior to the test, the action that, in training, delivered the outcome reexposed under ondansetron was performed more than the other action and to a similar degree. This finding suggests that, although activity in the disgust system determines the effects of incentive learning, the disgust system does not play a role once incentive learning has occurred; that is, the retrieval of incentive value is not based on the same process

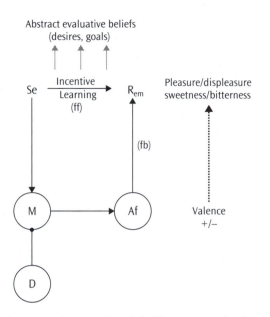

Figure 13.5. A general model of instrumental values. Evidence from studies assessing the effect of drug manipulations during incentive learning and on test suggest that different processes are used to encode and to retrieve incentive value. On this view, incentive value is encoded abstractly as an evaluative belief and so does not require the reengagement of the same emotional state that established the value to be retrieved. This general model of incentive learning emphasizes the relationship between the sensory properties of the outcome (se), motivational (M—modulated by drive, D) and affective (Af) processes in the induction of an emotional response during reexposure for the encoding of incentive value but proposes that, from this experience, an evaluative belief (e.g., X is good; Y is bad) is extracted to guide action selection.

through which it was encoded. In line with the proposal that reward value is encoded abstractly or symbolically and in contradiction to predictions from the somatic marker hypothesis, in this and other similar studies, we have found that the processes that determine the encoding of reward value are not required during the retrieval of that value during free choice tests for animals to select a course of action. This general account of incentive learning is illustrated in Figure 13.5.

SUMMARY AND CONCLUSIONS

As detailed in this chapter, taste aversion learning has been an essential tool in establishing the nature

of the learning and motivational processes that determine instrumental performance. First, taste aversion learning has been critical to the development of the outcome devaluation procedure, which has itself proven to be of critical importance in establishing the conditions under which instrumental performance is goal directed and those under which it is habitual. Second, studies assessing how taste aversion learning affects instrumental performance have contributed to our understanding of the way that basic motivational processes influence changes in incentive value and how these values act to determine instrumental performance. These studies have helped to establish that outcome value is determined by an association between the sensory properties of the instrumental outcome and emotional feedback induced by the activation of affective processes by specific motivational systems. For example, taste aversion learning acts to reduce the value of the instrumental outcome not just by conditioning an association between the outcome representation and the disgust system, sensitive to the induction of illness, but also by the formation of an association between this representation and the aversive emotional feedback produced by disgust's activation of the aversive affective system. Evidence from taste aversion learning also suggests that different aspects of the outcome representation can be associated with different emotional responses and that this variation in outcome evaluation can extend to actions such that, in a heterogeneous chain, even when actions proximal to reward are to be associated with devalued components of the outcome representation, more distal actions are not. As a consequence, paradoxically, distal actions in a chain are often selected and performed even when more proximal actions are not.

Reexposure to the outcome after a shift in motivation, whether this shift is induced by a change in the deprivation conditions or by conditioning procedures, such as those involved in taste aversion learning, provides the opportunity not just to experience the current value of the outcome but to encode that value. Evidence suggests that this encoding is accomplished not by establishing a link with the emotional system but by extracting an abstract value that can be retrieved and deployed without requiring the animal to reexperience the emotion on the basis of which it was encoded. It is clearly through this abstract value that evaluative beliefs are formed and it is in establishing these beliefs that cognitive states—beliefs like what action leads to what outcome—can be integrated with the current motivation and emotional conditions to determine a course of action. It is pleasing to recall that, despite the power and ubiquity of taste aversion learning, our biology found a way to utilize these experiences to direct our actions without requiring us continually to suffer the debilitating effects of conditioned nausea and disgust.

Acknowledgment   The preparation of this chapter was supported by a grant from the National Institute of Mental Health #56446.

Note

1. There are two important qualifications to this account: (1) training two actions concurrently on an interval schedule does not cause actions to become insensitive to the value of their consequences (Colwill & Rescorla, 1985b) whereas (2) overtraining an action on a ratio schedule of reinforcement does (Adams, 1981). These results suggest that it is not the schedules per se but their underlying feedback functions that are critical in determining the relative strength of action-outcome and stimulus–response associations (see Dickinson, 1994, for further discussion)

References

Adams, C. D. (1981). Variations in the sensitivity of instrumental responding to reinforcer devalaution. *Quarterly Journal of Experimental Psychology, 34B*, 77–98.

Adams, C. D., & Dickinson, A. (1981). Instrumental responding following reinforcer devaluation. *Quarterly Journal of Experimental Psychology, 33B*, 109–121.

Balleine, B. W. (1992). Instrumental performance following a shift in primary motivation depends on incentive learning. *Journal of Experimental Psychology: Animal Behavior Processes, 18*(3), 236–250.

Balleine, B. W. (2001). Incentive processes in instrumental conditioning. In R. Mowrer & S. Klein (Eds.), *Handbook of contemporary learning theories* (pp. 307–366). Hillsdale, NJ: Lawrence Erlbaum.

Balleine, B. W. (2004). Incentive behavior. In I. Q. Whishaw & B. Kolb (Eds.), *The behavior of the laboratory rat: A handbook with tests* (pp. 436–446). Oxford: Oxford Univeristy Press.

Balleine, B. W. (2005). Neural bases of food-seeking: Affect, arousal and reward in corticostriatolimbic circuits. *Physiology & Behavior, 86*, 717–730.

Balleine, B. W., Ball, J., & Dickinson, A. (1994). Benzodiazepine-induced outcome revaluation and the motivational control of instrumental action in rats. *Behavioral Neuroscience, 108*(3), 573–589.

Balleine, B. W., Davies, A., & Dickinson, A. (1995). Cholecystokinin attenuates incentive learning in rats. *Behavioral Neuroscience, 109*(2), 312–319.

Balleine, B. W., & Dickinson, A. (1991). Instrumental performance following reinforcer devaluation depends upon incentive learning. *Quarterly Journal of Experimental Psychology, 43B*, 279–296.

Balleine, B. W., & Dickinson, A. (1992). Signalling and incentive processes in instrumental reinforcer devaluation. *Quarterly Journal of Experimental Psychology. B, Comparative and Physiological Psychology, 45*(4), 285–301.

Balleine, B. W., & Dickinson, A. (1994). Role of cholecystokinin in the motivational control of instrumental action in rats. *Behavioral Neuroscience, 108*(3), 590–605.

Balleine, B. W., & Dickinson, A. (1998a). Consciousness: The interface between affect and cognition. In J. Cornwell (Ed.), *Consciousness and human identity* (pp. 57–85). Oxford: Oxford University Press.

Balleine, B. W., & Dickinson, A. (1998b). Goal-directed instrumental action: Contingency and incentive learning and their cortical substrates. *Neuropharmacology, 37*(4–5), 407–419.

Balleine, B. W., & Dickinson, A. (1998c). The role of incentive learning in instrumental outcome revaluation by specific satiety. *Animal Learning & Behavior, 26*, 46–59.

Balleine, B. W., & Dickinson, A. (2000). The effect of lesions of the insular cortex on instrumental conditioning: Evidence for a role in incentive memory. *Journal of Neuroscience, 20*(23), 8954–8964.

Balleine, B. W., Garner, C., & Dickinson, A. (1995). Instrumental outcome devaluation is attenuated by the anti-emetic ondansetron. *Quarterly Journal of Experimental Psychology B, Comparative and Physiological Psychology, 48*(3), 235–251.

Balleine, B. W., Killcross, A. S., & Dickinson, A. (2003). The effect of lesions of the basolateral amygdala on instrumental conditioning. *Journal of Neuroscience, 23*(2), 666–675.

Balleine, B. W., Paredes-Olay, C., & Dickinson, A. (2005). The effect of outcome devaluation on the performance of a heterogeneous instrumental chain. *International Journal of Comparative Psychology, 18*, 257–272.

Berridge, K. C. (1991). Modulation of taste affect by hunger, caloric satiety, and sensory-specific satiety in the rat. *Appetite, 16*(2), 103–120.

Berridge, K. C. (2000). Measuring hedonic impact in animals and infants: Microstructure of affective taste reactivity patterns. *Neuroscience and Biobehavioral Reviews, 24*(2), 173–198.

Berridge, K. C., Grill, H. J., & Norgren, R. (1981). Relation of consummatory responses and preabsorptive insulin release to palatability and learned taste aversions. *Journal of Comparative and Physiological Psychology, 95*(3), 363–382.

Braun, J. J., Lasiter, P. S., & Kiefer, S. W. (1982). The gustatory neocortex of the rat. *Physiological Psychology, 10*, 13–45.

Chaffee, B. J., & Tankanow, R. M. (1991). Ondansetron—The first of a new class of anti-emetic agents. *Clinical Pharmacy, 10*, 430–446.

Colwill, R. M., & Rescorla, R. A. (1985a). Instrumental responding remains sensitive to reinforcer devaluation after extensive training. *Journal of Experimental Psychology: Animal Behavior Processes, 11*, 520–536.

Colwill, R. M., & Rescorla, R. A. (1985b). Postconditioning devaluation of a reinforcer affects instrumental responding. *Journal of Experimental Psychology: Animal Behavior Processes, 11*, 120–132.

Colwill, R. M., & Rescorla, R. A. (1986). Associative structures in instrumental learning. In G. H. Bower (Ed.), *The psychology of learning and motivation* (Vol. 20, pp. 55–104). Orlando, FL: Academic Press.

Corbit, L. H., & Balleine, B. W. (2003). Instrumental and Pavlovian incentive processes have dissociable effects on components of a heterogeneous instrumental chain. *Journal of Experimental Psychology: Animal Behavior Processes, 29*(2), 99–106.

Damasio, A. (1994). *Descartes' error.* New York: G.P. Putnam's Sons.

Davis, M. (1998). Anatomic and physiologic substrates of emotion in an animal model. *Journal of Clinical Neurophysiology, 15*(5), 378–387.

Dickinson, A. (1989). Expectancy theory in animal conditioning. In S. B. Klein & R. R. Mowrer (Eds.), *Contemporary learning theories: Pavlovian conditioning and the status of traditional learning theories* (pp. 279–308). Hillsdale, NJ: Lawrence Erlbaum.

Dickinson, A. (1994). Instrumental conditioning. In N. J. Mackintosh (Ed.), *Animal cognition and learning* (pp. 4–79). London: Academic Press.

Dickinson, A., & Balleine, B. W. (1993). Actions and responses: The dual psychology of behaviour. In N. Eilan, R. McCarthy, & M. W. Brewer (Eds.), *Spatial representation* (pp. 277–293). Oxford: Basil Blackwell Ltd.

Dickinson, A., & Balleine, B. W. (1994). Motivational control of goal-directed action. *Animal Learning & Behavior, 22*, 1–18.

Dickinson, A., & Balleine, B. W. (2002). The role of learning in the operation of motivational systems. In C. R. Gallistel (Ed.), *Learning, motivation & emotion, Volume 3 of Steven's handbook of experimental psychology* (3rd ed., pp. 497–533). New York: John Wiley & Sons.

Dickinson, A., Nicholas, D. J., & Adams, C. D. (1983). The effect of the instrumental training contingency on susceptibility to reinforcer devaluation. *Quarterly Journal of Experimental Psychology, 35B*, 35–51.

Dunn, L. T., & Everitt, B. J. (1988). Double dissociations of the effects of amygdala and insular cortex lesions on conditioned taste aversion, passive avoidance, and neophobia in the rat using the excitotoxin ibotenic acid. *Behavioral Neuroscience, 102*(1), 3–23.

Fanselow, M. S., & Gale, G. D. (2003). The amygdala, fear, and memory. *Annals of the New York Academy of Sciences, 985*, 125–134.

Flaherty, C. F. (1996). *Incentive relativity.* New York, NY: Cambridge University Press.

Gallo, M., Roldan, G., & Bures, J. (1992). Differential involvement of gustatory insular cortex and amygdala in the acquisition and retrieval of conditioned taste aversion in rats. *Behavioural Brain Research, 52*, 91–97.

Garcia, J. (1989). Food for Tolman: Cognition and cathexis in concert. In T. Archer & L.-G. Nilsson (Eds.), *Aversion, avoidance and anxiety* (pp. 45–85). Hillsdale, NJ: Lawrence Erlbaum.

Guthrie, E. R. (1935). *The psychology of learning.* New York: Harpers.

Hatfield, T., Han, J. S., Conley, M., Gallagher, M., & Holland, P. (1996). Neurotoxic lesions of basolateral, but not central, amygdala interfere with Pavlovian second-order conditioning and reinforcer devaluation effects. *Journal of Neuroscience, 16*(16), 5256–5265.

Higgins, G. A., Kilpatrick, G. J., Bunce, K. T., Jones, B. J., & Tyers, M. B. (1989). 5-HT3 receptor antagonists injected into the area postrema inhibit cisplatin-induced emesis in the ferret. *British Journal of Pharmacology, 97*, 247–255.

Holland, P. C., Petrovich, G. D., & Gallagher, M. (2002). The effects of amygdala lesions on conditioned stimulus-potentiated eating in rats. *Physiology & Behavior, 76*(1), 117–129.

Holman, E. W. (1975). Some conditions for the dissociation of consummatory and instrumental behavior in rats. *Learning and Motivation, 6*, 358–366.

Hull, C. L. (1943). *Principles of behavior.* New York: Appleton.

Konorski, J. (1967). *Integrative activity of the brain.* Chicago, IL: University of Chicago Press.

LeDoux, J. E. (2000). Emotion circuits in the brain. *Annual Review of Neuroscience, 23,* 155–184.

Levin, B. E. (1999). Arcuate NPY neurons and energy homeostasis in diet-induced obese and resistant rats. *American Journal of Physiology, 276*(2, Pt. 2), R382–387.

Limebeer, C. L., & Parker, L. A. (2000). The antiemetic drug ondansetron interferes with lithium-induced conditioned rejection reactions, but not lithium-induced taste avoidance in rats. *Journal of Experimental Psychology: Animal Behavior Processes, 26*(4), 371–384.

Malkova, L., Gaffan, D., & Murray, E. (1997). Excitotoxic lesions of the amygdala fail to produce impairment in visual learning for auditory secondary reinforcement but interfere with reinforcer devaluation effects in rheus monkeys. *Journal of Neuroscience, 17,* 6011–6020.

Mowrer, O. H. (1960). *Learning theory and the symbolic processes.* New York: Wiley.

Nachman, M., & Ashe, J. (1973). Learned taste aversions in rats as a function of dosage, concentration and route of administration of LiCl. *Physiology and Behavior, 10,* 73–78.

Nader, K., Schafe, G. E., & LeDoux, J. E. (2000). The labile nature of consolidation theory. *Nature Reviews Neuroscience, 1*(3), 216–219.

Pelchat, M. L., Grill, H. J., Rozin, P., & Jacobs, J. (1983). Quality of acquired responses to tastes by *Rattus norvegicus* depends on type of associated discomfort. *Journal of Comparative Psychology, 97*(2), 140–153.

Petrovich, G. D., Setlow, B., Holland, P. C., & Gallagher, M. (2002). Amygdalo-hypothalamic circuit allows learned cues to override satiety and promote eating. *Journal of Neuroscience, 22*(19), 8748–8753.

Rescorla, R. A. (1992). Depression of an instrumental response by a single devaluation of its outcome. *Quarterly Journal of Experimental Psychology. B, Comparative and Physiological Psychology, 44*(2), 123–136.

Rescorla, R. A. (1994). A note on depression of instrumental responding after one trial of outcome devaluation. *Quarterly Journal of Experimental Psychology. B, Comparative and Physiological Psychology, 47*(1), 27–37.

Rescorla, R. A., & Solomon, R. L. (1967). Two-process learning theory: Relationships between Pavlovian conditioning and instrumental learning. *Psychological Review, 74*(3), 151–182.

Rolls, E. T., Rolls, B. J., & Rowe, E. A. (1983). Sensory-specific and motivation-specific satiety for the sight and taste of food and water in man. *Physiology & Behavior, 30,* 85–92.

Rozin, P., & Fallon, A. E. (1987). A perspective on disgust. *Psychological Review, 94,* 23–41.

Schafe, G. E., Nader, K., Blair, H. T., & LeDoux, J. E. (2001). Memory consolidation of Pavlovian fear conditioning: A cellular and molecular perspective. *Trends in Neurosciences, 24*(9), 540–546.

Seeley, R. J., Matson, C. A., Chavez, M., Woods, S. C., Dallman, M. F., & Schwartz, M. W. (1996). Behavioral, endocrine, and hypothalamic responses to involuntary overfeeding. *American Journal of Physiology, 271*(3, Pt. 2), R819–823.

Simbayi, L. C., Boakes, R. A., & Burton, M. J. (1986). Effects of basolateral amygdala lesions on taste aversions produced by lactose and lithium chloride in the rat. *Behavioral Neuroscience, 100*(4), 455–465.

Spence, K. W. (1956). Behavior theory and conditioning. New Haven, CT: Yale University Press.

Sripanidkulchai, K., Sripanidkulchai, B., & Wyss, J. M. (1984). The cortical projection of the basolateral amygdaloid nucleus in the rat: A retrograde fluorescent dye study. *Journal of Comparative Neurology, 229*(419–431).

Tolman, E. C. (1932). *Purposive behavior in animals.* New York: Century Books.

Wang, R., Liu, X., Hentges, S. T., Dunn-Meynell, A. A., Levin, B. E., Wang, W., et al. (2004). The regulation of glucose-excited neurons in the hypothalamic arcuate nucleus by glucose and feeding-relevant peptides. *Diabetes, 53*(8), 1959–1965.

Wang, S. H., Ostlund, S. B., Nader, K., & Balleine, B. W. (2005). Consolidation and reconsolidation of incentive learning in the amygdala. *Journal of Neuroscience, 25*(4), 830–835.

Woods, S. C., Schwartz, M. W., Baskin, D. G., & Seeley, R. J. (2000). Food intake and the regulation of body weight. *Annual Review of Psychology, 51,* 255–277.

Yamamoto, T., Azuma, S., & Kawamura, Y. (1984). Functional relations between the cortical gustatory area and the amygdala: Electrophysiological and behavioral studies in rats. *Experimental Brain Research, 56,* 23–31.

14

Conditioned Taste Aversion Across the Life Span from Prenascence to Senescence

JAMES R. MISANIN, MATTHEW J. ANDERSON,
AND CHARLES F. HINDERLITER

Although John Garcia published his first paper (Garcia, Kimeldorf, & Koelling, 1955) on conditioned taste aversion (CTA) in the widely read journal, *Science*, it was his seminal paper on the relationship of cue to consequence, which appeared in *Psychonomic Science* over a decade later (Garcia & Koelling, 1966) that triggered an intensive investigation of this unique phenomenon by other investigators. The majority of the investigations over the next decade, parametric studies, were empirical in nature, attempting to delineate a set of functions describing the manner in which different levels of a variable, for example, conditioned stimulus (CS) or unconditioned stimulus (US) amount (Bond & DiGiusto, 1975) or intensity (e.g., Dragoin, 1971a; Kalat, 1974) affect the development of CTA. Other studies focused on the neural structures mediating the association of taste and illness (e.g., Buresova & Bures, 1973, 1974, 1975). During this time there was also much concern and discussion as to whether or not CTA conformed to the general laws of learning (e.g., Kalat, 1977; Kalat & Rozin, 1971; Revusky, 1977; Rozin & Kalat, 1971; Seligman, 1970). There was also much speculation as to whether "stimulus relevance," the focal point of Garcia and Koelling's (1966) paper, was learned or innate (e.g., Mackintosh, 1973; Revusky, 1977). During this decade, however, there was little effort to answer this latter question experimentally. There were very few studies on CTA as a function of age to help answer

this question about the innate status of stimulus relevance. But those that had been conducted led to some very firm beliefs. Revusky (1977), for example, citing Grote and Brown (1971) who reported CTA in 22-day-old rats, said, "it is unreasonable to suppose that young rats could have developed a broad concept of relevance on the basis of experience only with chow, water, and mother's milk" (p. 46). Subsequent studies supported this belief (e.g., Gemberling & Domjan, 1982).

Another early belief was that very young altricial mammals, whose single food source is their mother's milk, would be unlikely to demonstrate CTA because it would be highly improbable that they would ever be poisoned during feeding (Bures & Buresova, 1977). The results of the studies (Bures & Buresova, 1977; Galef & Sherry, 1973; Grote & Brown, 1971) that had investigated CTA in periweanling animals led Bures and Buresova (1977) to conclude that CTA should not occur in preweanling rats. However, it would appear equally improbable that altricial mammals would have to escape or avoid noxious stimuli in their preweaning environment, especially in the early postnatal days. Nevertheless, rats and mice as young as 5 days of age had been shown to learn instrumental escape behaviors (Misanin, Chubb, Quinn, & Schweikert, 1974; Misanin, Haigh, Hinderliter, & Nagy, 1973; Misanin, Nagy, & Weiss, 1970; Misanin, Rose, & Hinderliter, 1971; Nagy, Misanin, & Newman, 1970). Furthermore, rats and mice as young as 10–11 days of age had been shown to retain learned escape behaviors over days of testing (Misanin, Nagy, Keiser, & Bowen, 1971; Nagy, Misanin, Newman, Olsen, & Hinderliter, 1972; Nagy, Misanin, & Olsen, 1972). These studies are significant for a number of reasons:

1. They demonstrated that rats and mice as young as 5 days of age are capable of learning complex defensive behaviors.
2. They made clear that to understand the ontogenesis of an adult behavioral phenotype, researchers have to study behavior at earlier stages of development than they had been doing.
3. They also made it clear that the learning methodologies have to take into consideration the physical capabilities of infant animals.
4. They demonstrated the short-term memory process necessary for learning may appear at an earlier age than memory processes typically associated with long-term memory (cf., Spear, 1978, p. 226).

These four findings were eventually realized in the study of the ontogeny of CTA.

The early studies on CTA in preweanling rats did not make the distinction between learning and retention capabilities. Bures and Buresova (1977), for example, conditioned their young rats at 20, 30, and 50 days of age and tested for acquisition after a 10-day interval. Finding none in the 20-day-old rats and weak aversions in the 30-day-old rats, they reached the conclusion that CTA should appear at the time of weaning. Since periweanling rats show rapid forgetting of other appetitive and defensive behaviors (e.g., Campbell, Jaynes, & Misanin, 1968; Campbell, Misanin, White, & Lytle, 1974), it is possible that Bures and Buresova's 20-day-old rats learned the aversion but did not retain it over the training–test interval. The finding that animals younger than 20 days of age can learn an aversion was subsequently demonstrated by Campbell and Alberts (1979). They conditioned aversions in preweanling animals at 10, 12, 15, and 20 days of age. They then tested the 15- and 20-day-olds after 24 h, and all age groups after 5- and 10-day retention intervals. According to Campbell and Alberts (1979), the 10- and 12-day-old rats showed more rapid forgetting than the 15- and 20-day-old rats. Like Bures and Buresova (1977), however,

Campbell and Alberts (1979) failed to make a distinction between learning and retention capabilities. Before retention comparisons are made, the degree to which subjects are capable of learning a specific response should be determined. Since the 10- and 12-day-olds were not tested immediately at the 24-h retention interval, it is not clear whether their relatively poorer performance at the 5-day retention interval was due to a more rapid age-related forgetting or to an age-related lower level of acquisition. That 10-day-old rats can learn a defensive response and forget it completely over a very short retention interval was subsequently demonstrated with active avoidance learning (Misanin, Lariviere, Turns, Turns, & Hinderliter, 1986). Nevertheless, there was evidence that Campbell and Alberts' 10-day-old rats learned a taste aversion since their aversions were stronger after the 5-day retention interval than after the 10-day interval.

To determine if rats younger than 10 days of age could learn and retain a taste aversion, a procedure was needed that would take into consideration the physical capabilities of the infant rat. Gemberling and her associates provided just that. Using a cannulation procedure developed by Hall and Rosenblatt (1977), Gemberling and her associates succeeded in conditioning aversions in 5-day-old rat pups by following the infusion of a novel taste CS with an intraperitoneal (IP) injection of LiCl. They measured the strength of the aversion 12 h after conditioning by measuring the amount of the infused CS that was swallowed during testing (Gemberling, Domjan, & Amsel, 1980). They went on to demonstrate CTA in 1-day-old rats. In this study the rats were conditioned at 1 day of age and tested at 5 days of age (Gemberling & Domjan, 1982). The strength of the aversion in these 5-day-olds was remarkably similar to that of their previous study (Gemberling et al., 1980), suggesting that there was very little memory loss over the retention interval.

PRENATAL CONDITIONED AVERSIONS

Since CTA had been demonstrated in newborn rats, it seemed reasonable to ask if a taste aversion could also be conditioned prenatally. Investigators who have studied prenatal taste aversion conditioning have done so for various reasons: (1) to see if fetuses can learn an aversion *in utero* from the mother's gustatory experiences (e.g., Gruest, Richer, & Benard, 2004), (2) to see if CTA learned as fetuses carries over into infancy (e.g., Gruest et al., 2004; Stickrod, Kimble, & Smotherman, 1982), and (3) to determine the neural substrates of CTA in prenatal rats (e.g., Mickley, Remmers-Roeber, Dengler, Kenmuir, & Crouse, 2001).

For a fetus to learn an aversion, the neural mechanisms necessary to process chemosensory stimulation must be functioning, and the fetus must be able to discriminate and make associations between stimuli. Moreover, for the investigator to infer learning, the fetus must retain the information past stimulus exposure and demonstrate learning via a behavioral change.

There are three ways in which fetal or prenatal conditioned aversions have been studied and demonstrated. One has been to indirectly manipulate the fetus's experiences by administering both the CS and the US to a pregnant dam and assessing its effect on the fetus after parturition. Another way in which conditioned aversions in prenatal rats have been studied and demonstrated has been to present both the CS and US to the fetus directly and assess the effect postnatally. The third way in which prenatally conditioned aversions have been studied and demonstrated has been to present both the CS and US directly to the fetus and test for conditioning *in utero*. Each of these methods is briefly discussed in the following separate topics.

Indirect Manipulation of the Fetus's Experiences via Stimulation of the Mother

Using the first approach described above, Gruest et al. (2004) subjected pregnant rats to a garlic flavor (CS) followed 45 min later by an IP injection of a LiCl US on embryonic days (E) 15–16 or on E18–19. The offsprings were tested 42 days after the pairings in a free-ingestion "single-choice presentation" (p. 191), that is, pups had access to garlic flavored water via one pipette. Fours groups were included within each embryonic age group, a CS–US group, a CS-only group, an US-only group, and a group whose mothers experienced water followed by a NaCl injection. There were no significant differences among the four E15–16 groups. However, the E18–19 group that experienced the garlic paired with LiCl drank significantly less than the other E18–19 groups. Although the

test involved drinking the solution, it is not clear whether the conditioned aversion was a taste aversion, an odor aversion, or both, since the gustatory and olfactory components of the stimulus reaching the fetuses via the amniotic fluid cannot be separated and both gustatory and olfactory stimuli were present during testing. Also, although the authors suggested that the ability to form an aversion and long-term retention capabilities emerge within the last 3 days of gestation, there is no clear evidence that the E15–16 CS–US group did not form an aversion. Had a shorter retention interval been utilized, evidence for CTA in the E15–16 CS–US group might have been obtained. The authors acknowledged that the lack thereof may have been due to deficits in learning, retention, or performance.

Indirect manipulation of the fetus via stimulation of the mother and assessing the effects of the manipulation postnatally has its drawbacks especially when chemosensory stimulation is used. Not only are learning and retention capabilities confounded, but also the transmission of the stimuli to the fetuses via amniotic fluid cannot be well controlled. The degree of stimulation of the fetus may possibly differ depending on its age (Mickley et al., 2001), size, gender, the surrounding amniotic fluid, position in the uterine horn (cf., Babine & Smotherman, 1984), movements of the mother (cf., Smotherman, Richards, & Robinson, 1984), and so on. And, according to Smotherman and Robinson (1987), every link in the chain of delivery of the stimulus from the mother to the fetus is "unpredictable and lacks the precision necessary to establish causal connections between changes in the intrauterine environment and fetal behavior" (p. 42).

Direct Stimulation of the Fetus and Testing Postnatally

A procedure reported by Strickrod (1981) and Strickrod, Kimble, and Smotherman (1982) allowed for direct stimulation of the fetus. On the twentieth day of gestation, dams were anesthetized, their ventral areas shaved, and their uterine horns exposed through an incision in their abdomens and covered with moist gauze. Amniotic injections of 0.04 ml of either 0.09% NaCl or apple juice were placed adjacent to the nose–mouth areas of the fetuses. Each fetus was then given an IP injection of 0.02 ml of 0.15-M LiCl or 0.09% NaCl. The dams' incisions were then closed and they were allowed to recover and deliver normally. Using this procedure Strickrod et al. (1982) reported a significant taste/odor aversion in rat pups conditioned on day E20 and tested 16 days postnatally. The test consisted of placing an anesthetized dam in the cross arms of a T-maze with her ventral surface facing the runway and six of her nipples coated with apple juice and the other six coated with the saline solution. Each pup was given 10 trials in the maze. A trial consisted of placing each rat individually at the start of the 7 × 15 cm runway and giving it the opportunity to approach and attach to a nipple. A trial ended when the pup had been attached to the nipple for 15 s. The dependent measure was the number of apple coated nipples suckled. Four embryonic groups were run. An apple–LiCl paired group, a saline–LiCl paired group, an apple–NaCl paired group, and a saline–NaCl paired group. Only the apple–LiCl paired group showed a conditioned aversion. When the CS was administered via the amniotic fluid, it is possible that both an odor and a taste aversion were formed. In a subsequent study, employing the same four training groups, animals were allowed to spend time over clean or apple scented shavings that they could smell but not touch or taste. Again, only the apple–LiCl animals showed an aversion for the apple odor. These investigators also demonstrated that the small peptide, Met-enkephalin, enhanced the aversion. These results indicate that early prenatal CTA experiences can have relatively long-term effects. This method of directly stimulating the fetus with both the CS and US, although more refined than the method of injecting the pregnant dam with both the CS and US, still relies on postnatal performance to determine if the conditioning procedure is effective.

Like the method of indirectly stimulating the prenatal organism, this method of directly stimulating the fetus also has its drawbacks. Again, not only must you depend on long-term retention capabilities to assess learning, but the intensity of the fetal taste aversion can be modulated by the anesthesia used on the dam during conditioning (Mickley, Lovelace, Farrell, & Chang, 1995). Mickley and his associates anesthetized dams with sodium pentobarbital, ketamine hydrochloride, and xylazinc or sodium pentobarbital and ketamine hydrochloride. While experiencing these anesthetics, rat fetuses received pairings of saccharin and LiCl or one of a variety of oral and IP control injections.

On postnatal day 15, the animals were given the opportunity to suckle from nipples coated with saccharin or water. The neonates that received the saccharin–LiCl pairing avoided the saccharin coated nipples whereas control subjects preferred those nipples. Rats conditioned while experiencing the ketamine showed significantly stronger aversions than those experiencing the sodium pentobarbital. Thus, although direct stimulation of the fetus allows for better control of the CS and US than the previously described indirect stimulation method, the use of anesthetics may introduce an additional variable that alters the ability of prenatal rats to learn CTA.

Conditioning and Testing *In Utero*

In order to eliminate the effect of the long delay in testing required with the two previously described procedures, some investigators have developed techniques that allow for obtaining measures that can be observed prenatally. Smotherman and Robinson (1985) employed a procedure that permitted direct observation of fetal behaviors. Rat fetuses were exposed to a taste/odor mint solution in the amniotic fluid on day E17 followed by an IP injection of LiCl. Under general anesthesia on the nineteenth day of gestation female rats underwent a chemomyelotomy that involved an injection of 100% ethanol into the mother's spinal cord. This produces irreversible chemical blockade of transmission within the spinal cord posterior to the site of injection. The female rats then had their uteruses exteriorized through a midline laprotomy. The uterus and lower body were immersed in a temperature controlled isotonic saline solution. After the anesthesia wore off and the dam and fetuses became acclimated to the saline bath, observations of the fetuses' behavioral reactions to the CS were recorded. Seven categories of fetal behavior including movements of the head, mouth, foreleg, hindleg, and trunk (twitches, curls, and stretches) were observed. The response to the mint CS on day E19, a suppression of overall behavior, was a reexpression of the unconditioned response to the US on day E17. These results provided clear evidence that prenatal rats as young as day 17 of gestation can learn to associate a taste/odor stimulus with LiCl and retain the association over 2 prenatal days.

Smotherman and Robinson (1991) refined their technique by delivering small amounts of fluid into the fetuses' mouths. This was accomplished by fitting each subject with a dual cannula that consisted of two independent channels with a flanged tip positioned on the fetuses' tongues. The channels were connected to microsyringes containing isotonic saline, sucrose (10% w/v in isotonic saline), or lemon (a 1:3 v/v dilution of pure extract). As was the case for mint in the previous study, isotonic saline and sucrose had little effect on fetal activity. In contrast, the diluted lemon extract, like LiCl in the previous study, had a marked effect on movements of the head, mouth, foreleg, and so on, but the effects were opposite of those produced by LiCl. Lemon increased most activities whereas LiCl decreased them. The fetuses were conditioned and tested on day E20. The sucrose CS–lemon US interval was 2 s and the condition–test interval was 6 min. Controls received a comparable sucrose–saline pairing. Only the experimental fetuses showed an increase in activity to the sucrose CS during testing. In a second experiment, Smotherman and Robinson (1991) included additional controls and a backward conditioning group. In addition to the saline control, there were CS-alone and US-alone control groups. The forward conditioning and the backward conditioning differed significantly from the other three groups and from each other during testing, with the forward conditioning group showing the greatest activity. According to the authors, the backward conditioning groups would have essentially experienced three forward conditioning trials since the intertrial interval was 1 min and the interstimulus interval was 30 s. Thus the weaker conditioning in the backward group may simply reflect fewer forward conditioning trials. Backward conditioning is not easily obtained with most unconditioned stimuli, but it has been repeatedly demonstrated with CTA. However, unlike in the Smotherman and Robinson (1985) study, in which they referred to their conditioning as taste/odor conditioning, Smotherman referred to this conditioning as conditioned activation. If this experiment had been conducted before the 1985 experiments, or, if this experiment had been conducted on fetuses prepared by surgical transaction of the olfactory bulbs in which lemon results in a reduction of responsiveness (Robinson & Brumley, 2005), results would have been interpreted as evidence for CTA. Depending on the organism and the stimulus, aversive stimuli can either increase or decrease behavior. The high concentration of lemon abstract that was used is surely not an appetitive

US. Human infants respond to sour tastes as if they are aversive (Desor, Maller, & Andrews, 1975), and as pointed out by Garcia, Lasiter, Bermudez-Rattoni, and Deems (1985), there are a variety of reactions to a gustatory stimulus paired with a noxious stimulus other than suppression of behavior. As an example of such reactions, they describe the coyote's "disgust" reactions to beef previously paired with poison that include "urinating on the beef and rolling over it as dogs do when they encounter putrid matter" (p. 9). The sour taste of lemon and the accompanying strong taste of alcohol in the lemon extract may have produced the same effect to the fetus as the bitter tasting monarch butterfly does to the eastern bluejay. But since the fetus, unlike the bluejay, cannot avoid the noxious stimulus, the exaggerated movements, in this case, may have represented an aversive reaction. Also, an aversive reaction to a stimulus may decrease or increase activity depending on the age of the organism. Hall and Bryan (1981) found that quinine infusions tend to decrease activity in rats less than 12 days of age and increase it in rats 12 days of age and older. Also, surely the route of administration of both the CS (amniotic fluid vs. intraoral cannulation) and the US (IP injection vs. intraoral cannulation) in the Smotherman and Robinson (1985, 1991) studies, as well as the flavor characteristic of the US (salty vs. sour or illness vs. distasting stimulus), could possibly lead to different unconditioned reactions. Illness, per se, is not a prerequisite for CTA (Gamzu, 1977; Gemberling, 1984). To determine if a CTA had been conditioned in these subjects would require testing them postpartum in a situation in which they could demonstrate the aversion with the more familiar aversive reaction.

This procedure for conditioning and testing *in utero* also has its shortcomings. The movements of the fetus *in utero* can be affected by any number of variables. For example, Smotherman et al. (1984) reported that the method used to sever the spinal cord of the pregnant dam could have differential effects on the pattern of activity as well as the overall activity of the fetus. Also, as pointed out by Hepper and Shahidullah (1994), a factor that must be considered is the comparability of prenatal behavior to their postnatal counterparts. They ask "Are they mediated by the same structures? do they mean the same thing?"(p. 150). Is the suppression of fetal action patterns to the apple taste/odor resulting from being paired with LiCl mediated by the same neural mechanism(s) as the suppression of drinking in postweaning animals?

CONCLUDING REMARKS REGARDING PRENATAL CTA

The studies of prenatal CTA have made it clear that the olfactory/gustatory systems of the rat fetus during the last 4 days of gestation are sufficiently developed for the fetus to sense, perceive, and make distinctions and associations between odor/taste stimuli (Smotherman & Robinson, 1991) and between odor/taste stimuli and an IP injection of LiCl (Smotherman & Robinson, 1985). This does not mean, however, that their sensory systems are fully functional. It has been shown, for example, that, although the gustatory system is functional in perinatal rats, the perinatal rat does not respond to all stimuli in a mature way and that progressive changes in neurophysiological responses occur during a prolonged developmental period (cf., Formaker & Hill, 1990). The studies of prenatal CTA in comparison with studies on the acquisition and retention of instrumental avoidance in infant rats also make it clear that memory is not a singular process, that is, it is not an isolated process that functions independently of the sensory-motor mechanisms used to learn a specific task. For example, rat fetuses exposed to apple juice and LiCl *in utero* on day E20 showed an aversion to the apple juice when tested at 16 days of age (Stickrod et al., 1982), whereas 10-day-old rats trained on an active avoidance response were unable to retain the response over a 30-min retention interval (Misanin, Turns, & Hinderliter, 1985). The ability to learn different tasks may appear at different ages due to differences in sensory-motor capabilities; however, if memory is a singular or isolated process then once it has emerged all *learned* tasks should be remembered equally well.

THE EFFECT OF PRENATAL STIMULATION ON THE ACQUISITION OF POSTNATAL CTA

A variety of substances and other treatments when administered prenatally have been shown to alter normal development, negatively impacting health (Kolberg, 1999) and behavior (e.g., Huizink & Mulder, 2006). Indeed, prenatal exposure to

certain teratogens has proven capable of hindering various aspects of postnatal CTA and its retention (but also see Ferrari & Riley, 1994; Sandner, Silva, Angst, Knobloch, & Danion, 2004). In this section we examine several treatments capable of altering postnatal CTA.

Prenatal Maternal Stress

One form of prenatal stimulation that has been shown to alter certain aspects of CTA experienced after birth is prenatal maternal stress. Maternal stress during pregnancy has been shown to affect offspring in a variety of ways including brain neurochemistry changes (e.g., Takahashi, Turner, & Kalin, 1992) and behavioral disturbances (e.g., Lordi, Patin, Protais, Mellier, & Caston, 2000; Tazumi et al., 2005).

Bethus, Lemaire, Lhomme, and Goodall (2005) have demonstrated that prenatal maternal stress increases latent inhibition to a flavor CS, hindering subsequent conditioning of that flavor in male rat offspring. In this experiment pregnant female Wistar rats were placed in a ventilated transparent tube in the presence of an intense light source three times a day from day E13 until birth. Between 5 and 9 months following birth, some of the male and female offspring were subjected to 3 days of preexposure to a sucrose CS prior to its eventual pairing with a LiCl US. While both prenatally stressed and nonstressed males and all females clearly demonstrated CTA, prenatally stressed male rats exposed to the CS prior to conditioning displayed an increased consumption of sucrose. Bethus and colleagues hypothesized that such prenatal stress-dependent sex differences were due to altered levels of dopamine in the developing animals (Alonso, Navarro, & Rodriguez, 1994; Takahashi et al., 1992). Although the mechanism for such effects is not thoroughly understood, such results indicate that prenatal experiences can have long-term consequences.

Prenatal Ethanol Exposure

Ethanol, unquestionably one of the most widely studied and devastating of all teratogens, is known to have a variety of effects on organ systems (Burd, 1989; Driscoll, Streissguth, & Riley, 1990) and postnatal behaviors (e.g., O'Connor, Kogan, & Findlay, 2002). Prenatal ethanol exposure leads to a later preference for alcohol (e.g., Bond &

DiGiusto, 1976) and has been shown to impair learning in a wide range of tasks (e.g., Becker & Randall, 1989; Blanchard, Riley, & Hannigan, 1987; J. C. Martin, Martin, Sigman, & Radow, 1977; LaFiette, Carlos, & Riley, 1994). Perhaps not surprisingly, CTA is also negatively affected by exposure to ethanol (e.g., Riley, Lochry, & Shapiro, 1979).

Riley et al. (1979) sought to determine whether alcohol exposure *in utero* would affect performance in tasks requiring the withholding of a response given that certain types of hyperactivity have been linked to maternal alcohol consumption during pregnancy (e.g., Bond & DiGiusto, 1976). Having found that prenatal alcohol impaired passive avoidance, Riley et al. sought to determine if it affected CTA also. Pregnant Long-Evans rats consumed 0%, 17%, or 35% of their liquid diets mixed in ethanol. After weaning on the twenty-first day after birth, the progeny were allowed only 6 h of access to liquids on each of the following 11 days. This access was provided in the form of a 1-h period in the morning and a 5-h period each evening. Water was made available during the evening session in order to prevent a growth deficiency due to fluid restriction. During the 1-h morning session, each subject was exposed to either water or a 0.12-M LiCl solution. On days 4, 7, and 10 of the experiment, the subjects were presented with LiCl solution and fluid intake was recorded. In this procedure, LiCl served as both the CS and US (see Hall, Chapter 4, for a similar procedure). As evidenced by greater fluid intake on day 4 than on day 7 or 10, all subjects, regardless of the amount of prenatal alcohol exposure, were capable of developing a taste aversion to the LiCl. The amount of LiCl consumed each day, however, was dependent upon the amount of alcohol that the rat had been exposed to prenatally, with those animals subjected to higher ethanol doses consuming more LiCl. Riley and colleagues concluded that prenatal alcohol exposure leads to a dose-dependent deficit in response inhibition, with ever-higher doses of prenatal exposure increasing the likelihood that animals will consume the illness-inducing substance again in the future. Alternatively, it is possible that alcohol in the amniotic fluid led to olfactory/gustatory imprinting similar to olfactory imprinting often observed in infant rats (cf., Galef & Henderson, 1972; Valliere, Peterson, & Misanin, 1985). Galef and Henderson (1972), for example, found that weanling animals seek and prefer a diet their mother has been eating even though the diet is relatively unpalatable.

Similarly, preweanling rats exposed to ethanol prenatally have been shown to have deficits in CTA. In three experiments, Riley, Barron, Driscoll, and Chen (1984) gave pregnant Long-Evans rats 35% or 0% of their liquid diets in ethanol-derived calories from days 6 through 20 of gestation. Sucrose was again isocalorically substituted for ethanol in the 0% groups. At 5, 10, or 15 days after birth, all subjects received a 0.5% (w/v) solution of sodium saccharin via a cannula inserted into the oral cavity. Following this, pups received either an injection of LiCl or NaCl. When testing was conducted 12-h after conditioning, animals were again infused with saccharin and intake was recorded. One obvious advantage of this infusion procedure is that it allows for a more precise administration of the CS and US than those methods previously employed by Riley et al. (1979). Results demonstrated significant taste aversions for both the 10- and 15-day-olds (marginal support for an aversion at 5-day-olds was also found). At 15 days of age the strength of the aversion was dependent upon the prenatal treatment, with those prenatally exposed to alcohol demonstrating a weaker aversion. In addition, Driscoll, Riley, and Meyer (1985) have demonstrated that if the CS–US interval is lengthened to 2 h, 15-day-old rats whose mothers consumed a 35% ethanol liquid diet display a weaker aversion. Driscoll et al. (1985) claim that "prenatal alcohol exposure causes a deficit in the acquisition of a CTA, and that this deficit is additive, but not synergistic with deficits produced by long-delay conditioning procedures" (p. 279).

Clausing, Ferguson, Holson, Allen, and Paule (1995) sought to examine the effects of prenatal ethanol exposure on retention of CTA. Pregnant female Sprague-Dawley rats consumed 0%, 18%, or 36% of their liquid diets in ethanol-derived calories. On postnatal days 32 to 38, male members of the progeny underwent water restriction. On postnatal day 39, subjects were provided with a 0.15% saccharin solution or tap water for 30 min followed 20 min later by IP injections of either 50 mg cyclophosphamide/kg or saline. Testing occurred on postnatal days 42 and 45 during which animals were once again exposed to the saccharin CS and fluid intake was recorded. Results demonstrated a clear CTA on postnatal day 42 (3 days after conditioning) for all groups, indicating that all subjects were in fact learning. On postnatal day 45 (6 days after conditioning), however, animals prenatally exposed to the higher does of ethanol consumed more saccharin than controls, suggesting that prenatal ethanol exposure is capable of impairing retention of taste aversion conditioning. Results from such studies with rats suggest that prenatal exposure to ethanol is likely to interfere with CTA experiences that occur within the first few weeks of life.

The detrimental effects of prenatal ethanol exposure on later CTA performance could possibly be attributed to a type of US preexposure effect in which the early exposure to alcohol results in illness, thus limiting the ability of illness to enter into associations later in life. This explanation seems unlikely, however, as prenatal ethanol exposure has been shown to lead to a later preference for alcohol (e.g., Bond & DiGiusto, 1976). Indeed, if the prenatal exposure resulted in substantial enough illness to influence CTA later in life, one would expect to observe an avoidance of ethanol at that time, not a preference for it. In light of this, an explanation of the deficit based on a disruption of associative (e.g., Driscoll et al., 1985) or memory (Clausing et al., 1995) processes, or perhaps a decrement in response inhibition (Riley et al., 1979), seems more plausible.

Attenuation of Negative Prenatal Exposure Effects

Given the extreme negative impact of teratogens, it is perhaps not surprising that a great deal of research has been conducted examining the effectiveness of various postnatal treatments at reversing the numerous and devastating deficits resulting from teratogenic exposure. Recognizing that the plasticity of the nervous system and age are negatively correlated, the vast majority of these studies have attempted to modulate the negative effects of prenatal alcohol exposure via certain preweaning experiences (for review see Clausing, Mothes, & Optiz, 2000).

Optiz, Mothes, and Clausing (1997), for example, examined whether postnatal environmental enrichment would attenuate the negative impact of prenatal ethanol exposure in mice. Pregnant females were intubated with an ethanol or sucrose solution twice daily (once in the morning and once in the afternoon) from gestational day 14 to 18. Other pregnant females simply received lab chow and water *ad libitum*. Half of the litters in each condition were reared individually,

the others were group-housed (two dams and litters that received the same prenatal treatment). Moreover, individually housed litters were weaned earlier (postnatal day 21) than those that were group-housed (postnatal day 28). The combination of group-housing and delayed weaning has been shown to be an effective form of environmental enrichment (Mothes, Optiz, Werner, & Clausing, 1996). Beginning on postnatal day 54, male offspring from each group were placed on a restricted water schedule with 10-min access to water in the mornings and evenings. During the morning session on postnatal day 57, a saccharin solution was provided instead of water and 20 min later the subject received an oral intubation of 0.15-M LiCl. Water was again made available during the 10-min sessions until the morning session on postnatal day 59 when the subject was again presented the saccharin and the amount consumed was recorded. For mice prenatally exposed to ethanol and raised in standard, individually housed conditions, CTA was impaired. Mice prenatally exposed to ethanol and raised in the enriched condition, however, were perfectly capable of developing CTA, and performed at a level similar to controls. Thus, preweaning environmental enrichment would appear to be capable of counteracting the negative impact of prenatal ethanol exposure on postnatal CTA.

CONCLUDING REMARKS ON THE EFFECT OF PRENATAL EXPERIENCES ON POSTNATAL CTA

With the numerous and rapid developmental changes occurring prenatally, it should not be surprising that this period is highly sensitive to various forms of stimulation. Prenatal experiences that hinder postnatal CTA impairs an animal's ability to avoid poisonous substances, potentially endangering life itself. Thus, as the already long list of known teratogens continues to grow, the need for additional research into this issue is great.

PREWEANING CTAs

In a number of papers on ingestional aversion learning in preweanling rats, Alberts and his associates describe four feeding stages that altricial mammals pass through from conception to postweaning (Alberts, 1987; Alberts & Gubernick,

1984; Gubernick & Alberts, 1984). The first is the prenatal stage in which the fetus is a passive recipient of nutrients transported via maternal circulation to the placenta and amniotic fluid. The second is a preweanling stage which, in the rat, extends from birth until about 17 days postpartum; during this time, nutrients, initially in the colostrum and then in milk, are provided via the mother's teats to the suckling infant. The third is the weanling stage in which the 18–22-day-old rat obtains nourishment both through the mother's milk and solid foods, and the fourth stage is a postweaning stage during which the animal's nutrient source is physically independent of the mother. The second and third stages are the focus in this section.

Studies on preweaning CTA have been conducted to determine the following: (1) if stimulus relevance is learned or innate (Gemberling & Domjan, 1982), (2) if very young animals can learn and retain stimulus irrelevance or safety (e.g., Kraemer, Hoffman, & Spear, 1988), (3) if infantile amnesia occurs with taste aversion learning (Steinert, Infurna, & Spear, 1980), (4) if animals can form aversions through the mother's milk or during suckling (e.g., Alberts, 1987; Kehoe & Blass 1986), and (5) if substances in the mother's milk or events in the postnatal environment influence the acquisition of taste aversions (e.g., Gabriel & Weinberg, 2001).

Stimulus Relevance in the Newborn Rat

As mentioned earlier, Gemberling and Domjan (1982) demonstrated that a taste aversion can be conditioned in 1-day-old rats. This paper is particularly important because it supports the early belief that "stimulus relevance" is not learned (Revusky, 1977). One-day-old rats learned an aversion to a novel taste paired with lithium-induced illness but not to a taste paired with shock and, conversely, they learned an aversion to a tactile stimulus paired with shock but not to a tactile stimulus paired with illness. The investigators concluded that "selective associations in aversion learning are mediated by innate mechanisms that govern conditioning in the absence of extensive ontogenetic experience" (p. 105). Hoffman and Spear (1988), however, contend that postnatal development of cue-consequence specificity may in part be learned. They gave 5-, 10-, and 15-day-old rats six pairings of 20-s infusions of 15% sucrose and a 1-mA footshock and found significant taste aversions in the 5- and 10-day-olds, but not in the 15-day-olds. They maintain that Gemberling and Domjan's (1982) failure to obtain a taste–shock association was due to their use of ineffective procedures. Might not also the same thing then be said about Garcia and Koelling's (1966) study on the relation of cue to consequence, since Krane and Wagner (1975) were able to arrange conditions so that adult rats would form an aversion to saccharin when followed by electric shock? The answer, of course, is no. Under conditions in which a taste aversion was readily learned using X-rays (e.g., Garcia & Koelling, 1966), a taste aversion could not be conditioned using shock as the US and, if it could be, as in Krane's case, it does not occur as readily. In the terminology of Seligman's (1970) preparedness notion, rats would be "unprepared" to associate taste with footshock rather than "contraprepared" as suggested by Seligman (p. 409). Furthermore, Gemberling and Domjan gave their 1-day-old rats a single flavor–US pairing, the US being a localized shock via electrodes attached to the rat's haunches, whereas Hoffman and Spear's subjects were given six CS–US pairings with a rather diffuse "foot shock" that, according to the authors, may have produced internal effects through the abdomen. In a second experiment, therefore, Hoffman and Spear (1988) put electrical tape around the abdomen of 5-day-olds with the hope of ruling out the possibility that their diffuse shock was producing visceral effects that were easily associated with the sucrose. Their taping procedure, however, would not have localized the effect of "footshock" on the rat's feet. Furthermore, the intensity of the (1.0 mA) "footshock" that they used was 10 times the intensity (0.1 mA) of the shock typically used in studies of escape (Misanin et al., 1973) and avoidance (Misanin, Turns, & Hinderliter, 1985) learning in 5- and 10-day-old rats. It is not unreasonable to assume that more than the animal's feet was shocked and that there still existed the possibility of visceral effects. Animals of these ages cannot effectively support their weight and, more often than not, are straddling the grids when shocked.

Latent Inhibition within the Context of CTA in Preweanling and Weanling Rats

The attenuation of conditioning as a result of CS preexposure has been referred to as *latent inhibition*

(Lubow, 1973) or learned safety (Kalat & Rozin, 1973). This phenomenon has been observed in both preweanling (Kraemer et al., 1988) and weanling (Franchina, Domato, Patsiokas, & Griesemer, 1980; Franchina & Horowitz, 1982) animals within a taste aversion context. Kraemer et al. (1988) examined the effect of flavor preexposure on 6- and 12-day-old rats 20 h or 10 days after conditioning. They found no effect of preexposure in 6-day-old pups and a transitory effect in the 12-day-old pups. Kraemer and Roberts (1984) found that in adult rats the effect of CS preexposure also decreases when a delay is interpolated between conditioning and testing (see also Lubow, Chapter 3; Meehan & Riccio, Chapter 7).

Franchina and Horowitz (1982) gave 19-, and 90-day-old rats, 0, 1, or 3 preexposures to a 12% sucrose solution, conditioned them the day after the last preexposure, and then tested for conditioning on the following day. A two-bottle test yielded a greater effect of preexposure in the 19-day-olds than in the 90-day-olds. This greater effect of flavor preexposure in younger animals than in adults has also been observed in early postweaning (24–25-day-old) rats (Misanin, Guanowsky, & Riccio, 1983). In an earlier study, Franchina et al. (1980) gave 20-day-old rats 0, 1, 2, 4, or 8 half-hour exposures of a 12% sucrose solution or water at the rate of 1 sucrose preexposure or water every 12 h prior to pairing the sucrose with LiCl. The rats were given 9, half-hour, two-bottle tests at the rate of 1 every 12 h beginning 24 h after conditioning. Significant effects of number of preexposures were obtained where groups given more preexposures generally showed a stronger preference for saccharin. The 1-preexposure group had a significantly stronger preference for saccharin than the 0-preexposure group; as expected with latent inhibition, the 1-preexposure group had a significantly weaker preference for saccharin than all other preexposure groups. The 2- and 4-preexposure groups did not differ from each other but both showed a significantly weaker preference for saccharin than the 8-preexposure group. A significant trials effect was also obtained. The sucrose preference increased reliably over the nine test trials most likely due to extinction and/or forgetting of the CTA. These findings are consistent with that found in older animals (e.g., Fenwick, Mikulka, & Klein, 1975). Results from these studies indicate that the ability to acquire and retain latent inhibition (learned safety) emerges prior to weaning age in rats.

Infantile Amnesia for CTA

Infant rats, like adults, can form taste–illness associations with just one pairing of a taste CS with a LiCl US, even when there is a delay between the CS and US (Gemberling et al., 1980). For other types of passive avoidance, immature rats require more trials than mature rats to learn the task. Retention of the passive avoidance response is also poorer in young rats than in adults (Hinderliter & Riccio, 2002; Schulenburg, Riccio, & Stikes, 1971). This greater forgetting in immature animals, "infantile amnesia," has also been observed in rats for active avoidance (Campbell & Campbell, 1962), discriminated escape (Campbell et al., 1974), and for appetitive responses (Campbell et al., 1968). According to Campbell et al. (1974), neurological maturity at the time of training appears to be a major determinant of infantile amnesia. If this is so, then, even though memory may be directly linked with the type of task learned, infantile amnesia for CTA might still be expected. However, CTA conditioned in rats in utero was retained 16 days after birth (Stickrod et al., 1982). Schweitzer and Green (1982) found a gradual forgetting of CTA in 12-day-old rats over three intervals ranging from 13 to 25 days. In contrast, Campbell and Alberts (1979) reported rapid forgetting in 10- and 12-day-olds over a 10-day retention interval; they found, however, that 18-day-olds retain CTA over a 56-day interval as well as adults. Campbell and Coulter (1976) maintain that the onset of adult memory processing is marked by the disappearance of infantile amnesia. In the rat, they set the age at which this occurs for CTA at 15 days of age. However, Steinert et al. (1980) reported forgetting of CTA in 18-day-old weanling rats over a 60-day retention interval, and there are studies that show that even in postweaning rats, infantile amnesia is evident (e.g., Guanowsky, Misanin, & Riccio, 1983). Steinert et al. concluded that relationship between memory and development in rats for CTA parallels that for shock-motivated tasks using audiovisual cues. The same appears to be true for guinea pigs that show no forgetting over long intervals. Kalat (1975), for example, conditioned an aversion to sucrose in infant guinea pigs at 1–2, 3–4, 5–6, 7–8, and 9–11 days of age with interstimulus intervals (ISIs) of 0, 0.5, or 24 h, and tested them after a 30-day retention interval with a two-bottle (sucrose vs. water) preference test. There were no significant differences between the

0- and 30-min ISI groups and both differed from the combined 24-h ISI group and saline controls. Similarly, Campbell et al. found no forgetting of a shock-motivated discrimination task after a 75-day retention interval in young (5 days old) and adult guinea pigs. According to Campbell and Coulter (1976), "the guinea pig's capacity for long-term memory appears to be fully developed at birth whereas the rat's is not" (p. 226). They maintain that "it is not until 20–30 days of age that its [the rat's] central nervous system approximates that of the newborn guinea pig" (p. 226). The differential forgetting of the preweanling rat and guinea pig, according to Campbell and Coulter, provides support for "the importance of neural maturation as a critical substrate for the emergence of long term memory" (p. 226).

There are three ways in which this neural maturation hypothesis of infantile amnesia has been interpreted. One of these views suggests that the neural substrates of long-term memory may not be functioning at the time of the learning event and, consequently, memories are not stored and available at the time of retrieval (Campbell & Spear, 1972). A second interpretation posits that some brain structures continue to develop over the retention interval and make memory inaccessible by inhibiting the structures responsible for the retrieval of memory (Campbell & Spear, 1972). The third interpretation of the neural maturation hypothesis maintains that continued neural growth changes the internal milieu sufficiently to produce massive stimulation generalization decrements which, at the time of recall, are viewed as memory deficits (Gordon, 1979; but see also Anderson & Riccio, 2005). Regardless of the interpretation one wishes to champion, clearly, it would not explain remembering or forgetting of CTA in immature rats. For example, CTAs *in utero* carry over to the postnatal stages and thus these memories survive substantial changes in neural growth and changes in both the internal and external milieu (Gruest et al., 2004). Also, preweanling rats demonstrate encoding, consolidation, storage, and retrieval of CTAs and still show retention deficits (Schweitzer & Green, 1982).

Conditioned Aversions during Suckling

A series of studies by Alberts and his associates (Alberts & Gubernick 1984; Gubernick & Alberts, 1984; L. T. Martin & Alberts, 1979) show that a robust aversion to mother's milk can be conditioned in 10-day-old rats if distinctively flavored milk is experimenter-delivered intraorally and is followed by toxicosis. When the flavored milk is obtained from the mother or foster mother through sucking, an aversion can be conditioned only in weanling-age pups (L. T. Martin & Alberts, 1979). According to these investigators, the failure of preweanling pups to acquire a taste aversion within a sucking context appears to result from an inability to associate taste cues with illness in the nursing situation rather than a failure to detect taste cues obtained from a nipple. Alberts (1987) has referred to this phenomenon as "blockade of toxiphobia" (p. 23). If weaning is delayed, then the age at which pups fail to form an aversion is also delayed (Gubernick & Alberts, 1984). If weaning is hastened by providing earlier access to alternate food sources, however, the age at which pups can form an aversion does not occur earlier (Melcer, Alberts, & Gubernick 1985). The procedure used in this latter study was the cannulation procedure described earlier (Hall & Rosenblatt, 1977). Intraoral injection of almond flavored evaporated milk served as the CS and an IP injection of 0.15-M LiCl served as the US. These stimuli were administered while 16-day-old rats, which had been on solid food and water from 13 days of age up until 4–5 h before conditioning, were attached to a dam's nipple. During a 24-h test, the animal had a choice between consuming either nonflavored or almond-flavored powered rat chow. In these studies (L. T. Martin & Alberts, 1979; Melcer et al., 1985) the flanged end of the cannula was on the posterior of the tongue. There was no evidence of CTA observed in these early weaned rats.

Kehoe and Blass (1986), however, found they could get taste aversion conditioning in 5-day-old pups while sucking if the taste stimulus was placed on the anterior of the tongue, but not if it was placed on the posterior of the tongue. According to Kehoe and Blass, fluid placed at the posterior remains near the site of injection and does not reach taste receptors necessary for taste/odor perception. Thus they conclude that "the infant rat is protected from its own impressive ability to form gustatory associations by...not being able to taste the milk" (Kehoe & Blass, 1986, p. 45). Kehoe and Blass maintain that the posterior receptors necessary for taste/odor are fully available to the rat by 20 days of age. This agrees with research

(L. T. Martin & Alberts, 1979) indicating that nipple position during suckling is the same for rats 10–21 days of age, but only rats 20 days of age and older form an aversion while suckling. However, Alberts (1987) reported that delaying weaning, by preventing young rats access to solid food, had a dramatic effect on the CTA at the "normal" weaning age. Animals past weaning age failed to show an aversion to flavored milk experienced while sucking (on nipple) but showed a strong aversion to the flavored milk if experienced off nipple. They also found that they could lift the blockade by giving the rat experience with solid food either before or after conditioning (Gubernick & Alberts, 1984). Thus, they concluded that the blockade while nursing in weanling-aged pups, but not in younger pups, is related to a failure to express rather than acquire a learned association (Alberts, 1987). If it were the blocking of the expression of CTA in preweaning rats, then preweaning rats subjected to the conditioning treatment should express the aversion after they have been weaned. This does not occur (L. T. Martin & Alberts, 1979).

It should not be surprising that monophageous feeders would fail to develop a CTA because they have no other recourse than returning to the source of the malaise for nutrients. The common vampire bat, which is a monophageous feeder on vertebrate blood, for example, does not learn to associate a novel taste with toxicosis (Ratcliffe, Fenton, & Galef, 2003). Thus, one might expect that the preweaning rat, which is a monophageous feeder on its mother's milk for a limited period in its life, would develop a mechanism that would block the expression of a learned event that would prevent it from ingesting its only source of nutrition during this transitory period. The mechanism that blocks the acquisition of a taste aversion in preweanling rats has yet to be identified. Kehoe and Blass (1986), as mentioned above, suggested that the milk, when injected in the posterior of the tongue, fails to reach the receptors in the anterior of the tongue that allow the preweanling rat to taste it. The finding that early weaned rats who experienced solid food for 3 days prior to conditioning treatment still did not form an aversion while sucking suggests that something like that may be occurring. Alberts (1987) dismissed that explanation since his rat pups did learn the aversion off nipple. It is possible, however, that the position of the teat in the mouth is responsible for the milk or fluid not reaching the anterior portion of the

tongue; but again, this would not explain why delayed weaning should result in the blockade of toxiphobia whereas 20-day-olds readily learn taste aversion while sucking (L. T. Martin & Alberts, 1979). Of course, there may be different mechanisms mediating the blockade of the expression of CTA in weanling rats and the blockade of the acquisition of CTA in preweanling rats.

There is a social mechanism in place that aids the suckling rat in returning to the source of its malaise. In a series of experiments, Gemberling (1984) found that mother rats will develop an aversion to, and stop eating, a novel flavor that is ingested and is followed by the illness of her pups. Gemberling suggested that olfactory characteristics of the pups that signal gastrointestinal distress likely mediate this aversion in the dam. Does the mother's experience likewise influence CTA in her offspring? The next section examines that question.

Environmental Influences during Preweaning on Pre- and Postweaning CTA

Infant rats given an injection of lithium after sampling milk from a female rat eating a diet different than their mother's diet will avoid that female rat's diet during weaning (Galef & Sherry, 1973). Generally, however, weanling rats learn what foods to eat from their mothers rather than what foods to avoid (Galef, 1977). In a number of early studies Galef and his associates showed that a rat dam's milk contains gustatory cues reflecting the flavor of her diet and these cues influence the dietary choice of infant rats (Galef & Clark, 1972; Galef & Henderson, 1972; Galef & Sherry, 1973). These gustatory cues, however, can also influence the development of CTAs.

Alcohol Exposure
Pepino, Lopez, Spear, and Molina (1999), for example, found that on day 15 postpartum, pups that had suckled from alcohol-intoxicated dams showed a stronger taste aversion to alcohol than appropriate control pups. The stronger CTA in the alcohol-experienced pups may have been due to the alcohol-CS itself being aversive. According to Molina, Pepino, Johnson, and Spear (2000), rat pups detect the presence of alcohol, and possibly its affect on their mother, while nursing and can acquire alcohol-related information that constitutes "an aversive hedonic component" (p. 428).

They showed that pups previously exposed to an intoxicated mother not only consumed less alcohol than control pups but also avoided a specific texture that had been associated with the odor of alcohol.

Handling

Gabriel and Weinberg (2001) reported that postnatal handling influences CTA. In order to examine the ability of handling to attenuate prenatal ethanol exposure, mother rats were given either a liquid ethanol diet, a maltose-dextrin liquid diet, or laboratory chow and water during gestation. Offspring were subdivided into postnatal handled and nonhandled groups. The subjects were handled on day 2 through day 15 postpartum and conditioned at 35 days of age. The ethanol-handled offspring showed a weaker CTA than the other two handled groups suggesting that simple postnatal handling is not capable of attenuating the effect of prenatal alcohol exposure, which itself also hinders postnatal CTA (e.g., Riley et al., 1979). Across all prenatal groups in a one-bottle test under deprived conditions, handled rats demonstrated weaker CTA and lower corticosterone levels during reexposure to the saccharin CS than nonhandled rats. Ader (1973), on the other hand, found no effect of handling or electric shock during the preweaning period on the development of a taste aversion at maturity.

Maternal Separation

Maternal separation during the preweaning period also appears to have a disruptive effect on CTA in so much as it enhances the flavor-preexposure effect in adult rats (Lehmann, Logeay, & Feldon, 2000). These investigators separated rat pups from their mothers on postnatal days 4, 9, or 18 for a 24-h period. They then tested the effect of this maternal separation on 8-month-old rats that were preexposed or not preexposed to the 0.1% saccharin CS over three daily 15-min sessions. The day after the last preexposure, the preexposed and nonpreexposed rats were given access to 0.1% saccharin followed immediately by 1.5% body weight IP injection of 0.14-M LiCl. Preexposed and nonpreexposed rats that had not been separated from their mothers during the preweaning period also experienced the conditioning treatment. Beginning the following day, all animals were given five daily 15-min sessions during which they had access to the saccharin CS. The results

indicated that while preexposure reduced CTA in all groups, the preexposed pups separated from their mother at 9 days of age showed an enhanced flavor-preexposure effect (weakened conditioning) in comparison with all other preexposed animals. There was also a tendency for nonpreexposed pups separated from their mother at 9 days of age to show stronger CTA. As mention previously, similar long-term effects of prenatal experiences on latent inhibition and CTA were reported by Bethus et al. (2005). They demonstrated that exposing a pregnant female to an intense light source three times a day from day E13 until the birth of its pups also enhanced the flavor preexposure effect (latent inhibition) in male offspring when examined 5–9 months after birth. The results of the Bethus study and those of Lehmann et al. (2000) described above, demonstrate that prenatal experience can have rather long-term effects.

CONCLUDING REMARKS ON PREWEANING CTAs

Research indicates that CTA (e.g., Gemberling et al., 1982) and latent inhibition (Kraemer et al., 1988) to a novel flavor (e.g., sucrose) can be learned and retained by preweanling animals, but not while sucking on the mother's nipple (e.g., L. T. Martin & Alberts, 1979). Explanations for this effect have focused on not being able to taste the milk as a result of the location of the nipple on the pup's tongue (Kehoe & Blass, 1986) and on a failure to express the aversion rather than an ability to acquire it (L. T. Martin & Alberts, 1979). Variables such as prior experience with alcohol have been shown to produce stronger CTA to alcohol-induced taste aversion (Pepino et al., 1999), whereas handling of pups (Gabriel & Weinberg, 2001) has been shown to result in weaker CTA. Further work examining the effect of preweanling experiences on CTA indicate that maternal separation during preweanling periods enhance latent inhibition training conducted when subjects were 8 months old (Lehmann et al., 2000). In sum, research conducted with preweanling rats indicates that environmental events experienced during this time period can influence behavior for extended periods of time when assessed using CTA procedures.

Although it has been shown that prenatal, preweanling, and weanling animals readily acquire taste aversions, the age at which this behavior becomes adult-like has yet to be determined. This is due, in part, to the number of variables that have been demonstrated to influence CTA as a function of age. In the next topic we will describe some of these variables that researchers have shown to influence acquisition and retention of CTA in postweaning animals.

THE ACQUISITION AND RETENTION OF CTA IN POSTWEANING ANIMALS

Although the weaning process in rat dams may extend to the fourth week of the life of her pups, it has been customary in most laboratories to separate the mother and pups at about 21 days of age. In this section we will consider rats that are 21 days of age and older as being in Alberts' (1987) postweaning stage, during which the pup no longer must depend on the mother's milk to obtain the nutrients necessary for survival. It is in this stage that the capability of acquiring and retaining taste aversion is most important.

Peck (1975) compared 21-day-old and adult (age unspecified) rats on the acquisition and retention of a saccharin aversion. In their first experiment, the rats were given an injection of one of two doses of cyclophosphamide (US) either 0, 0.5, 1. 3, or 6 h after ingesting 1 ml of 0.1% saccharin solution (CS). They were tested 2 days later with a two-bottle (saccharin vs. water) test. The latency to lick each bottle and the number of licks per bottle were recorded. They found that the 21-day-olds and the adults did not differ at the 0-min CS–US interval but at the longer intervals the young animals did not acquire the aversion as well as the adults. In a second experiment he conditioned the young and adult rats with a 0-min CS–US interval and tested them for retention either after 2, 30, or 60 days. While the young animals retained the aversion as well as adults at the 2-day retention interval, they showed a diminished response at the 30-day interval. At the 60-day interval they showed no evidence of conditioning. At all three intervals adults showed evidence of CTA.

The difficulty in determining age differences was demonstrated in a subsequent study. Ader and Peck (1977) found no retention in 21-day-old rats after a 60-day retention interval using a one- or a two-bottle test, but they did find evidence of retention in a competitive situation in which a conditioned and a nonconditioned rat had access to a single bottle during testing. Nonconditioned rats drank more of the CS-flavored water than the conditioned rats. Klein, Domato, Hallstead, Stephens, and Mikulka (1975) showed that the testing procedure also determines, in part, whether or not young animals will display an acquired aversion. They compared 23- and 65-day-old rats on the acquisition of a taste aversion using a sucrose CS and a LiCl US, a 0-min CS–US interval, and either a one-bottle or a two-bottle test. While both age groups showed a strong aversion with the two-bottle test, only the 65-day-olds showed a strong aversion with the one-bottle test. When methyl scopolamine was used as the US, the 23-day-olds failed to express an aversion after six CS–US pairings.

Misanin et al. (1983), using one saccharin–LiCl pairing and a 0-min CS–US interval, conditioned an aversion in 23-, 140-, and 617-day-old rats and tested them for retention after an interval of 1 or 28 days using a two-bottle test. The three age groups did not differ at the 1-day retention interval, but the 23-day-olds showed a significantly weaker aversion than the 140- and 617-day-olds at the 28-day retention interval. The two older groups did not differ on the 28-day retention test. In contrast, Klein, Mikulka, Domato, and Hallstead (1977), after giving their 23- and 65-day-old rats saccharin–LiCl pairings on each of 4 days on which they consumed more than 1 g of saccharin, found no age difference in retention at either the 1- or 28-day intervals. Similarly, Ingram (1979) found no differences in CTA in young (55–78 days), middle age (392–413 days), and old-age (668–692 days) mice during 3 days of testing. Also, after giving subjects saccharin–LiCl pairings until they reached a suppression criterion, he found no differences among age groups in the retention of a CTA across intervals of 7, 14, and 28 days. Martinez and Rigter (1983) gave rats 3–6-months old and 24–27-months old a single 5% glucose–0.15-M LiCl pairing and tested them for retention after intervals of 7, 21, 42, or 84 days. They also found little differences between age groups and both age groups showed good retention of CTA over all intervals. They repeated the experiment using 7-, 42-, and 84-day retention intervals with essentially the same results. Thus, the rate or extent of forgetting CTA was not clearly delineated in this study.

CONCLUDING REMARKS REGARDING CTA IN POSTWEANING SUBJECTS

While the research results on the acquisition and retention of CTA in postweaning animals appears to be a heterogeneous mixture, there are some apparent consistencies that aid in understanding those factors that will determine whether or not equal expression of CTA across ages can be achieved. One of these is the CS–US interval. The shorter the interval, the greater the likelihood that there will be no age differences within a relatively wide range of ages. Another is the number of CS–US pairings: the greater the number of CS–US pairings, the greater the likelihood that CTA will be equal among animals of different ages and over various retention intervals. The type of test procedure employed is also important. Two-bottle tests appear to be more sensitive than one-bottle tests (Dragoin, 1971b; Klein et al., 1975). And although rarely used by other investigators, Ader and Peck's (1977) competitive test (where another rat is in the test cage) appears to be more sensitive than either the typical one- or two-bottle tests. The type of US also appears to be a determining factor, for example, LiCl appears to be more effective than methyl scopolamine in early postweaning rats.

AGE DIFFERENCES IN LONG-TRACE CTA

One of the most striking features of CTA is its apparent violation of the principle of contiguity between a stimulus and its consequence. For CTA, the CS is presented and terminated before the US is presented and thus represents trace conditioning. Smith and Roll (1967), for example, found that rats will form an aversion to saccharin if it precedes X-irradiation by as much as 12 h, and Etscorn and Stephens (1973) found that by using cyclophosphamide as the US an aversion to saccharin could be formed in rats over a 24-h CS–US interval. After reviewing a sizable literature on age effects on learning, Campbell and Coulter (1976) concluded that as a task becomes more complex, by imposing additional requirements such as delays, young animals have greater difficulty learning the task than adults. Although their focus was on instrumental learning, the same appears to be true of classical conditioning. Baker, Baker, and Kesner (1977), for example, compared 23- and 80-day-old rats on their ability to learn taste aversion and found that the 23-day-olds learned aversions only with short CS–US intervals. A 60-min interstimulus interval was sufficient to disrupt taste aversion learning in the 23-day-olds but not in the 80-day-olds. Similarly, G. M. Martin and Timmins (1980) found that 23-day-old rats could form an aversion to a 0.1% saccharin CS with a 3-M LiCl US over 15-, 30-, and 45-min intervals but not over a 60-min interval. However, when G. M. Martin and Timmins increased the intensity of the CS from 0.1% to 1% and also increased the intensity of the LiCl US from 0.3 M to 0.65 M the 23-day-olds formed an aversion over a 2.5-h CS–US interval. They concluded, nonetheless, that the manipulations of stimulus intensity alone were not the only factors that determined the young rat's ability to form a taste–sickness association. They found that whether or not CTA was revealed depended on the length of the one-bottle testing session. Others have similarly reported that the type of test influences the evidence for CTA. For example, Klein et al. (1975) reported that a two-bottle preference test is more sensitive to detect learning in 23-day-old rats than a one-bottle test.

Misanin, Grieder, and Hinderliter (1988), using a two-bottle test, manipulated age (21–24 days, 76–79 days, and 680–825 days) and CS–US interval (0, 0.75, 1.5, and 3 h) during taste aversion conditioning. The CS was a 0.1% saccharin solution and the US was an IP injection of 0.15-M LiCl. They found that increasing the CS–US interval was more disruptive the younger the rat. The various age differences observed were not likely to be due to floor effects or ceiling effects. Neither the weanling and young-adults nor the young-adults and aged groups differed significantly at the 0-CS–US interval even though mean percentages were well above zero for weanlings and young-adults. Also, percent preference never exceeded 90% for the LiCl-treated groups except for weanlings at the 3-h CS–US interval. Thus ceiling effects did not likely contribute to the decrease in aging effects observed with longer CS–US intervals.

Misanin and his associates further discovered that this ability to form associations over extended delays does not occur suddenly in old age but, rather, emerges gradually over the life span of the rat. In one study, for example, when the CS immediately preceded the US, CTA was comparable across a wide variety of ages, from 3 months to

2.5 years. When the CS–US interval was extended to 0.75 h, CTA was weaker in 3-month- and 1-year-olds than in 1.5-year-olds. At a 1.5-h interval, 2-year-olds were superior to 1.5-year-olds and at a 3-h CS–US interval, CTA was stronger in 2.5-year-olds than in 2-year-olds. At the longest interval examined, 6 h, only the 2.5-year-olds demonstrated an aversion (Misanin, Collins, et al., 2002). To determine if the neural representation of the flavor CS is available to aged rats at a time it is no longer available to young-adult rats, Misanin, Goodhart, Anderson, and Hinderliter (2002) systematically varied the intensity of the US and the CS–US interval during long-trace taste aversion conditioning in young-adult and old-age rats. They found that increasing US intensity extends the interval over which trace conditioning is evident in old-age rats but not in young-adults. They concluded that trace decay occurs more rapidly in young-adult rats than in old-age rats.

In a series of experiments, Misanin and his associates ruled out a variety of explanations for this age-related superiority in associative learning. They found that it cannot be attributed to a variety of factors including the following:

1. Physical characteristic such as body weight that might influence US intensity or the absolute or relative (percentage of body weight) amount of the taste CS consumed during conditioning (Misanin & Hinderliter, 1994).
2. An age-related learning deficit such as the aged rat's difficulty in learning safety (Misanin & Hinderliter, 1995b).
3. Age-related differences in environmental experiences such as cage familiarity (Misanin & Hinderliter, 1995a) that could affect context-illness associations (Hinderliter, & Misanin, 1993) or relative CS novelty (Misanin & Hinderliter, 1995b).
4. Debilitating factors that accompany aging, such as renal dysfunction or decreases in sodium or potassium, that could alter US intensity by resulting in greater concentrations of serum LiCl (Misanin, Collins, et al., 2002).

As a possible explanation of age differences in long-trace taste aversion conditioning, Misanin, Wilson, Schwarz, Tuschak, and Hinderliter (1998) hypothesized that aging may slow a metabolic pacemaker, and accordingly, speed up time within an animal's time frame thereby making it more likely to form associations over long-trace intervals. Events that do not appear to be temporally contiguous based on experimenter manipulations may be experienced as contiguous for subjects that have a relatively slow metabolic pacemaker. Metabolic rate per unit of body weight (Kleiber, Smith, & Chernikoff, 1956) or surface area (Davis, 1937) is slower in older rats than in young rats. Misanin, Collins, et al. (2002) suggested that the biochemical organization of the nervous system involved in stimulus association, memory consolidation, and trace decay occurs at a uniform rate (i.e., a fixed number of "ticks") regardless of the animal's time frame. Therefore, if trace decay occurs over 400 ticks of an internal clock in a young rat, then an older rat whose clock has been slowed by a factor of four would experience only 100 ticks over the same temporal interval between two events (as measured by an external clock). Thus, the two events would not only be closer in time for the older rat but also less decay would have occurred for the older rat than for the younger one.

To test this hypothesis, Misanin and his associates slowed metabolic rate in young-adult rats either by lowering their body temperatures (Hinderliter, Goodhart, Anderson, & Misanin, 2002; Hinderliter, Musci, Pollack, Misanin, & Anderson, 2004; Misanin, Anderson, et al., 2002; Misanin et al., 1998) or by anesthetization (Misanin, Christianson, Anderson, Giovanni, & Hinderliter, 2004). Slowing metabolic rate in young-adult rats by either means increased the saccharin–LiCl interval over which conditioning a taste aversion was effective, essentially making the young-adult comparable to the old-age rat in making CS–US associations over long-trace intervals. They also found that the greater the depth of cooling and, hence, the slower the metabolic rate, the more likely young rats were to form an aversion over the longer CS–US intervals. Misanin et al. (1998) went on to show that, with a constant 3-h CS–US interval, delaying cooling for different lengths of time following CS presentation produced a delay of reinforcement gradient that would be expected if reducing body temperature results in time dilation.

In a further test of this metabolic-pacemaker hypothesis, these investigators used tail-pinch stress (Misanin, Kaufold, Paul, Hinderliter, & Anderson, 2006) and chronic water deprivation (Anderson, Hinderliter, & Misanin, 2006) to speedup metabolism in young-adult rats in order to decrease the effective CS–US interval. Using CS–US intervals ranging from 22.5 to 180 min, Misanin et al. (2006) found no evidence of conditioning in stressed rats beyond the 22.5-min interval. The stressed rats, furthermore, showed weaker conditioning at the 22.5-min interval than rats not subjected to the experimentally manipulated stress procedures. Chronic water deprivation, which also increased metabolic rate, had an attenuating effect on CTA across all intervals (Anderson et al., 2006). Thus as predicted, increasing metabolism as a result of stress manipulations decreased the intervals at which CTA was formed in young-adults. On the basis of the notion of an internal pacemaker, stress increased the pacemaker, and as a result, intervals of time measured externally resulted in more "ticks" on the internal clock than that which occurred for subjects whose pacemaker had not been increased.

In contrast to our belief that the memory processes necessary for making associations over long delays occur at a constant rate, and our notion of an age-related time dilation effect, Meehan and Riccio in Chapter 7 suggest that age-related changes in the ability to form associations over long delays between the CS and US in CTA may be due to the memory processes themselves becoming more protracted as animals age. Similarly, they suggest that states such as hypothermia and anesthetization, which also extend the effective CS–US interval, when interpolated between the CS and US, may exert their effects by protracting the gustatory short-term memory of the CS. Currently, both views appear to be plausible explanations for these effects.

Several investigators (Franchina & Horowitz, 1982; Misanin, Blatt, & Hinderliter, 1985; Misanin et al., 1983) found that the function relating latent inhibition or learned safety to age is essentially the inverse of the function relating long-trace CTA to age. That is, very young animals learn safety very rapidly with brief access to the flavor CS whereas old-age animals have difficulty in establishing that a flavor is safe (Misanin et al., 1985). It may be that very young animals have a natural inclination to develop safety. As mentioned previously, young rats learn from their mothers what foods are safe rather than what foods are dangerous (Galef & Sherry, 1973). This, however, does not explain the tendency of old-age rats to resist learning that a stimulus is safe. The difficulty old-age rats have

in establishing learned safety and the ease with which young animals learn it can be explained by age differences in the speed of the proposed metabolic pacemaker (Misanin, Collins, et al., 2002). The faster-running clock of the young animals makes even brief stimuli, as measured by an external clock, very long, making learned safety likely to occur; whereas the slow-running clock of the older rats makes even long-duration stimuli, as measured by an external clock, very brief, making it less likely that they would have the time to learn that the flavor is safe. Ayres, Philbin, Cassidy, Bellino, and Redlinger (1992), using 90-day-old adult rats and a conditioned suppression bar-press task, demonstrated that total CS-preexposure time was the most important parameter of latent inhibition or learned safety.

Evidence suggesting the existence of such a clock can be gleaned from a number of sources. Hoagland (1933), one of the first researchers to test Henri Pieron's (1923) proposal that personal time can be modified by altering the rate of biological processes, showed that an increase in body temperature produced by fever or diathermy increased his human subjects' estimations of temporal intervals. Both Baddeley (1966) and Bell (1975) found that human subjects' estimation of duration was shorter when their body temperatures were lowered. Buresova, Bures, Hassamannova, and Fifkova (1964) showed that forced extinction of a passive avoidance response in rats occurs more slowly, if at all, in rats whose body temperatures have been lowered in comparison to noncooled animals. For the cooled animals, time in the passive avoidance apparatus would be experienced as very brief compared to that of noncooled animals and hence extinction would be less likely to occur for the cooled subjects. Also, it has long been known that forgetting is less pronounced during sleep than during an equal period of waking activity (Jenkins & Dallenbach, 1924). Such findings have been taken as evidence against decay theory and as evidence for interference theory. Gleitman (1991), for example, maintained that "To explain such findings within a decay theory, one would have to assert the processes are slowed down." The research on the effects of hypothermia (Hinderliter et al., 2004; Misanin, Anderson, et al., 2002; Misanin et al., 1998) and anesthetization (Misanin et al., 2004) of long-trace conditioning in rats of different ages suggests just that. Sleep, like cold water immersion and anesthesia, lowers body temperature and slows metabolic rate. French's (1942) work on the effect of low body temperature on retention in goldfish, furthermore, shows that deep body cooling has the same effect as sleep, and his research ruled out interference as a major contributing factor. Metzger and Riccio's (1999) work showing that Ketaset–Rompun anesthesia extends the period over which an amnesic agent is effective disrupting memory is also compatible with the metabolic pacemaker hypothesis.

CONCLUDING REMARKS ON AGE DIFFERENCES ON LONG-TRACE CTA

While long-trace conditioning has to be the most striking feature of CTA, it also has to be one of the most troubling in the sense that the maximum trace interval over which an association can be made differs from laboratory to laboratory, and even from study to study within laboratories. In our laboratory, for example, we have found some LiCl-control young-adult animals to show conditioning only over intervals of 45 min or less (Misanin et al., 2006), whereas others have shown conditioning up to a 3-h interval (Misanin, Collins, et al., 2002). Other researchers have found their animals to form associations over much longer intervals, for example, 9 h (Green & Rachlin, 1976), 12 h (Smith & Roll, 1967), and even 24 h (Etscorn & Stephens, 1973). We believe that the memory processes that are necessary for making associations over long delays between stimuli occur at a constant rate for a given species and that reported differences are due to changes in the proposed metabolic pacemaker. Any manipulation of animals such as handling (Misslin, Herzog, Koch, & Ropartz, 1982), changing cages (Misslin et al., 1982), restraint (Elias & Redgate, 1975), or other experimentally induced stress, for example (Misanin et al., 2006), water deprivation (Anderson et al., 2006), injections (Izumi et al., 1997), anesthetization (Misanin et al., 2004), housing (Hayashi et al., 1998), time of day (Imai-Matsumura, Kaul, & Schmidt, 1995), and so on may alter an animal's metabolism. If the manipulation increases metabolic rate, then two temporally separated events will be experienced as farther apart than they would be for an animal whose metabolic rate has not been altered. If the manipulation decreases metabolic rate, then the animals will experience a shorter interval of time

between events similar to that experienced by aged animals. Evidence to determine whether or not such a metabolic pacemaker exists will require more detailed examination of central nervous system processes and other physiological variables. Regardless of the mechanism, we believe that researchers examining the influence of temporal variables on the formation of CS–US associations must carefully control factors that influence metabolic rate.

FUTURE CONSIDERATIONS

Rats and mice, in comparison with other altricial subjects used for behavioral research, such as cats, dogs, and primates, including man, have a relatively abbreviated life span. This is a reason commonly mentioned for the use of rats and mice in aging research. Feldman (2005), for example, maintains that the shorter life span of rats "allows researchers to learn about the effects of aging in a much smaller time frame than they could by using human participants" (p. 43). The research on the effect of aging on CTA has not taken advantage of this characteristic of rats and mice. The research on CTA in rats and mice as a function of age has been cross-sectional research, comparing rats or mice of different chronological ages at the same point in time. For this type of research, an abbreviated life span is not necessary. To take advantage of the shorter life span of these rodents, longitudinal or sequential research is required. Longitudinal research would assess the change in CTA in a group of rats or mice over time. Sequential research, a combination of cross-sectional and longitudinal procedures, assesses the change in different age groups over time. For example, using a split-litter technique in a sequential study, researchers could begin examining CTA in groups of rats at preweanling, weanling, adolescent, young-adult, middle-age, and old-age stages of development. Each group would be examined at each of the subsequent developmental stages. This technique would allow the investigator to separate the effect of age from other possibly contributing factors, such as prior experience, on the development of long-trace conditioning, long-term retention, and so on. To our knowledge, there have been no longitudinal or sequential studies of CTA in rats or mice.

Animals of the same age group in cross-sectional studies often respond quite differently in a given learning situation. For example, in long-trace CTA, some animals of a particular chronological age group may show strong conditioning at a long CS–US interval whereas others in the same chronological age group may show weaker or no conditioning at all. One possible explanation for this within-group variability is that animals of the same chronological age may be different in biological age and mechanisms that change with biological age may be the important determinants of long-trace CTA. We contend that the speed of a metabolic pacemaker is a biological marker of aging and a determining factor in whether or not a CS–US association will be made over a long interstimulus interval. Measuring an animal's metabolic rate and ability to form associations over long CS–US intervals at various points in its life span would support that contention.

An alternative explanation for the above-mentioned within-group variability is genetically based. Some animals may simply be less capable than others in forming an association over long CS–US intervals as a result of heritable characteristics. If this is so, then we would expect some consistency in their behavior over time. If an animal's behavior is observed at different points in its life span, then the consistency of its behavior can be established and predicted from earlier to later life stages. It should also be possible to selectively breed animals that differ in this capability in the same way that Tryon (1929, 1940) selectively bred maze-bright and maze-dull rats. The study of CTA may also prove useful in examining the role genetics play in associative learning.

The use of CTA to study associative learning as a function of age has many advantages. Stimuli used to form associations, that is, the CS and US, are relatively easy to manipulate in order to control nonassociative processes that are known to change with age, for example, motivational variables, variables related to motor performance, and so on. Thus, the study of CTA in animals, especially when using sequential designs, may prove to be an effective animal model in examining the effects of aging on associative learning, allowing for manipulation of physiological variables that cannot be manipulated with human subjects.

References

Ader, R. (1973). Effects of early experiences on shock- and illness-induced passive avoidance behaviors. *Developmental Psychobiology, 6,* 547–555.

Ader, R., & Peck, J. H. (1977). Early learning and retention of a conditioned taste aversion. *Developmental Psychobiology, 10,* 213–218.

Alberts, J. R. (1987). Early learning and ontogenetic adaptation. In N. A. Krasnegor, E. M. Blass, M. A. Hofer, & W. P. Smotherman (Eds.), *Perinatal development: A psychobiological perspective* (pp. 11–37). Orlando, FL: Academic Press, Inc.

Alberts, J. R., & Gubernick, D. J. (1984). Early learning as ontogenetic adaptation for ingestion by rats. *Learning and Motivation, 15,* 334–359.

Alonso, S. J., Navarro, E., & Rodriguez, M. (1994). Permanent dopaminergic alterations in the n. accumbens after prenatal stress. *Pharmacology Biochemistry and Behavior, 49,* 353–358.

Anderson, M. J., Hinderliter, C. F., & Misanin, J. R. (2006). The effects of chronic water deprivation on metabolic rate and long-trace taste-aversion conditioning in rats. *Neurobiology of Learning and Memory, 85,* 199–205.

Anderson, M. J., & Riccio, D. C. (2005). Ontogenetic forgetting of stimulus attributes. *Learning & Behavior, 33,* 444–453.

Ayres, J. J. B., Philbin, D., Cassidy, S., Bellino, L., & Redlinger, E. (1992). Some parameters of latent inhibition. *Learning and Motivation, 23,* 269–287.

Babine, A. M., & Smotherman, W. P. (1984). Uterine position and conditioned taste aversion. *Behavioral Neuroscience, 98,* 461–466.

Baddeley, A. D. (1966). Time estimation at reduced body temperatures. *American Journal of Psychology, 79,* 475–479.

Baker, L. J., Baker, T. B., & Kesner, R. P. (1977). Taste aversion learning in young and adult rats. *Journal of Comparative and Physiological Psychology, 91,* 1168–1178.

Becker, H. C., & Randall, C. L. (1989). Effects of ethanol exposure in C57BL mice on locomotor activity and passive avoidance behavior. *Psychopharmacology, 97,* 40–44.

Bell, C. R. (1975). Effects of lowered temperature on time estimation. *Quarterly Journal of Experimental Psychology, 27,* 232–234.

Bethus, I., Lemaire, V., Lhomme, M., & Goodall, G. (2005). Does prenatal stress affect latent inhibition? It depends on gender. *Behavioural Brain Research, 158,* 331–338.

Blanchard, B. A., Riley, E. P., & Hannigan, J. H. (1987). Deficits on a spatial navigation task following prenatal exposure to ethanol. *Neurotoxicology and Teratology, 9,* 253–258.

Bond, N. W., & DiGiusto, E. (1975). Amount of solution drunk is a factor in the establishment of taste aversion. *Animal Learning & Behavior, 3*, 81–84.

Bond, N. W., & DiGiusto, E. L. (1976). Effects of prenatal alcohol consumption on open-field behaviour and alcohol preference in rats. *Psychopharmacologia, 46*, 163–168.

Burd, L. (1989). Fetal alcohol syndrome: Diagnosis and syndromal variability. *Physiology & Behavior, 46*, 39–43.

Bures, J., & Buresova, O. (1977). Physiological mechanisms of conditioned food aversion. In N. W. Milgram, L. Krames, & T. M. Alloway (Eds.), *Food aversion learning* (pp. 219–255). New York: Plenum Press.

Buresova, O., & Bures, J. (1973). Cortical and subcortical components of conditioned saccharin aversion in rats. *Acta Neurobiologiae Experimentalis, 33*, 689–698.

Buresova, O., & Bures, J. (1974). Functional decortication in the CS–US interval decreases efficiency of taste aversion learning. *Behavioral Biology, 12*, 357–364.

Buresova, O., & Bures, J. (1975). Functional decortication by cortical spreading depression does not prevent forced extinction of conditioned saccharin aversion in rats. *Journal of Comparative and Physiological Psychology, 88*, 47–52.

Buresova, O., Bures, J., Hassamannova, J., & Fifkova, E. (1964). The effect of decreased body temperature on conditioned reflex activity in the rat. *Physiologia Bohemoslovencia, 13*, 220–226.

Campbell, B. A., & Alberts, J. R. (1979). Ontogeny of long-term memory for learned taste aversions. *Behavioral & Neural Biology, 25*, 139–156.

Campbell, B. A., & Campbell, E. H. (1962). Retention and extinction of learned fear in infant and adult rats. *Journal of Comparative and Physiological Psychology, 55*, 1–8.

Campbell, B. A., & Coulter, X. (1976). The ontogenesis of learning and memory. In M. R. Rosenzweig & E. L. Bennett (Eds.), *Neural mechanisms of learning and memory* (pp. 209–235). Cambridge, MA: The MIT Press.

Campbell, B. A., Jaynes, J., & Misanin, J. R. (1968). Retention of light–dark discrimination in rats of different ages. *Journal of Comparative and Physiological Psychology, 66*, 467–472.

Campbell, B. A., Misanin, J. R., White, B. C., & Lytle, L. D. (1974). Species differences in the ontogeny of memory: Support for neural maturation as a determinant of forgetting. *Journal of Comparative and Physiological Psychology, 87*, 193–202.

Campbell, B. A., & Spear, N. E. (1972). Ontogeny of memory. *Psychological Review, 79*, 215–236.

Clausing, P., Ferguson, S. A., Holson, R. R., Allen, R. R., & Paule, M. G. (1995). Prenatal ethanol exposure in rats: Long-lasting effects on learning. *Neurotoxicology and Teratology, 17*, 545–552.

Clausing, P., Mothes, H. K., & Optiz, B. (2000). Preweanling experience as a modifier of prenatal drug effects in rats and mice—a review. *Neurotoxicology and Teratology, 22*, 113–123.

Davis, J. E. (1937). The effect of advancing age on oxygen consumption of rats. *American Journal of Physiology, 119*, 28–33.

Desor. J. A., Maller, O., & Andrews, K. (1975). Ingestive responses of human newborns to salty, sour, and bitter stimuli. *Journal of Comparative and Physiological Psychology, 89*, 966–970.

Dragoin, W. B. (1971a). Conditioning and extinction of taste aversions with variations in intensity of the CS and UCS in two strains of rats. *Psychonomic Science, 22*, 303–305.

Dragoin, W. B. (1971b). A comparison of two methods of measuring conditioned taste aversions. *Behavior Research Methods & Instrumentation, 3*, 309–310.

Driscoll, C. D., Riley, E. P., & Meyer, L. S. (1985). Delayed taste aversion in prewenaling rats exposed to alcohol prenatally. *Alcohol, 2*, 277–280.

Driscoll, C. D., Streissguth, A. P., & Riley, E. P. (1990). Prenatal ethanol exposure: Comparability of effects in humans and animal models. *Neurotoxicology and Teratology, 12*, 231–237.

Elias, P. K., & Redgate, E. (1975). Effects of immobilization stress on open field behavior and plasma corticosterone levels of aging C57BL/6J mice. *Experimental Aging Research, 1*, 127–135.

Etscorn, F., & Stephens, R. (1973). Establishment of conditioned taste aversions with a 24-hour CS–US interval. *Physiological Psychology, 1*, 251–253.

Feldman, R. S. (2005). *Essentials of understanding psychology* (6th ed.). New York: McGraw Hill.

Fenwick, S., Mikulka, P. J., & Klein, S. B. (1975). The effect of different levels of pre-exposure to sucrose on the acquisition and extinction of a conditioned aversion. *Behavioral Biology, 14*, 231–235.

Ferrari, C. M., & Riley, A. L. (1994). Effect of prenatal cocaine on the acquisition of cocaine-induced taste aversions. *Neurotoxicology and Teratology, 16*, 17–21.

Formaker, B. K., & Hill, D. L. (1990). Alterations of salt taste perception in the developing rat. *Behavioral Neuroscience, 104*, 356–364.

Franchina, J. J., Domato, G. C., Patsiokas, A. T., & Griesemer, H. A. (1980). Effects of number of preexposures on sucrose taste aversions in weanling rats. *Developmental Psychobiology*, 13, 25–31.

Franchina, J. J., & Horowitz, S. W. (1982). Effects of age and flavor preexposure on taste aversion performance. *Bulletin of the Psychonomic Society*, 19, 41–44.

French, J. W. (1942). The effect of temperature on the retention of a maze habit in fish. *Journal of Experimental Psychology*, 31, 79–87.

Gabriel, K. I., & Weinberg, J. (2001). Effects of prenatal ethanol exposure and postnatal handling on conditioned taste aversion. *Neurotoxicology and Teratology*, 23, 167–176.

Galef, B. G. (1977). Mechanisms for the social transmission of acquired food preferences from adult to weanling rats. In L. M. Barker, M. R. Best, & M. Domjan (Eds.), *Learning mechanisms in food selection* (pp. 123–148). Waco, TX: Baylor University Press.

Galef, B. G., & Clark, M. M. (1972). Mother's milk and adult presence: Two factors determining initial dietary selection by weanling rats. *Journal of Comparative and Physiological Psychology*, 78, 220–225.

Galef, B. G., & Henderson, P. W. (1972). Mother's milk: A determinant of the feeding preferences of weaning rat pups. *Journal of Comparative and Physiological Psychology*, 78, 213–219.

Galef, B. G., & Sherry, D. F. (1973). Mother's milk: A medium for the transmission of cues reflecting the flavor of mother's diet. *Journal of Comparative and Physiological Psychology*, 83, 374–378.

Gamzu, E. (1977). The multifaceted nature of taste-aversion-inducing agents: Is there a single common factor? In L. M. Barker, M. R. Best, & M. Domjan (Eds.), *Learning mechanisms in food selection* (pp. 477–509). Waco, TX: Baylor University Press.

Garcia, J., Kimeldorf, D. J., & Koelling, R. A. (1955). Conditioned aversion to saccharin resulting from exposure to gamma radiation. *Science*, 122, 157–158.

Garcia, J., & Koelling, R. A. (1966). Relation to cue to consequence in avoidance learning. *Psychonomic Science*, 4, 123–124.

Garcia, J., Lasiter, P. S., Bermudez-Rattoni, F., & Deems, D. A. (1985). A general theory of avoidance learning. *Annals of the New York Academy of Sciences*, 443, 8–21.

Gemberling, G. A. (1984). Ingestion of a novel flavor before exposure to pups injected with lithium chloride produces a taste aversion in mother rats (*Rattus norvegicus*). *Journal of Comparative Psychology*, 93, 285–301.

Gemberling, G. A., & Domjan, M. (1982). Selective associations in one-day old rats: Taste–toxicosis and texture–shock aversion learning. *Journal of Comparative and Physiological Psychology*, 96, 105–113.

Gemberling, G. A., Domjan, M., & Amsel, A. (1980). Aversion learning in 5-day old rats: Taste–toxicosis and texture–shock associations. *Journal of Comparative and Physiological Psychology*, 94, 734–745.

Gleitman, H. (1991). *Psychology* (3rd ed.). New York: W. W. Norton & Company.

Gordon, W. C. (1979). Age: Is it a constraint on memory content? In N. E. Spear & B. A. Campbell (Eds.), *Ontogeny of learning and memory* (pp. 271–287). New York: Lawrence Erlbaum.

Green, L., & Rachlin, H. (1976). Learned taste aversions in rats as a function of delay, speed, and duration of rotation. *Learning and Motivation*, 7, 283–289.

Grote, F. W., & Brown, R. T. (1971). Rapid learning of passive avoidance by weaning rats: Conditioned taste aversion. *Psychonomic Science*, 25, 163–164.

Gruest, N., Richer, P., & Benard, H. (2004). Emergence of long-term memory for conditioned aversion in the rat fetus. *Developmental Psychobiology*, 43, 189–198.

Guanowsky, V., & Misanin, J. R., & Riccio, D. C. (1983). Retention of conditioned taste aversion in weanling, adult, and old age rats. *Behavioral & Neural Biology*, 37, 173–178.

Gubernick, D. J., & Alberts, J. R. (1984). A specialization of taste aversion learning during suckling and its weaning-associated transformation. *Developmental Psychobiology*, 17, 613–628.

Hall, W. G., & Bryan, T. E. (1981). The ontogeny of feeding in rats IV: Taste development as measured by intake and behavioral responses to oral infusions of sucrose and quinine. *Journal of Comparative and Physiological Psychology*, 95, 240–251.

Hall, W. G., & Rosenblatt, J. S. (1977). Sucking behavior and intake behavior in the developing rat pup. *Journal of Comparative and Physiological Psychology*, 91, 1232–1247.

Hayashi, A., Nagaoka, M., Yamada, K., Ichitani, Y., Miake, Y., & Okado, N. (1998). Maternal stress induces synaptic loss and developmental disabilities of offspring. *International Journal of Developmental Science*, 8, 209–216.

Hepper, P. G., & Shahidullah, S. (1994). The beginnings of mind—evidence from the behaviour of the fetus. *Journal of Reproductive and Infant Psychology*, 12, 143–154.

Hinderliter, C. F., Goodhart, M., Anderson, M. J., & Misanin, J. R. (2002). Extended lowered body temperature increases the effective CS–US interval in conditioned taste aversion for adult rats. *Psychological Reports, 90,* 800–802.

Hinderliter, C. F., & Misanin, J. R. (1993). Context familiarity and delayed conditioned taste aversion in young-adult and old-age rats. *Perceptual and Motor Skills, 77,* 1403–1406.

Hinderliter, C. F., Musci, J. A., Pollack, C. A., Misanin, J. R., & Anderson, M. J. (2004). Hypothermia modifies the effective CS–US interval in conditioned taste aversion in rats. *Neuroscience Letters, 369,* 142–144.

Hinderliter, C. F., & Riccio, D. C. (2002). Intertrial interval manipulations and passive avoidance retention in young Long-Evans hooded rats. *Developmental Psychobiology, 41,* 197–204.

Hoagland, H. (1933). The physiological control of judgments of duration: Evidence for a chemical clock. *Journal of General Psychology, 9,* 267–287.

Hoffmann, H., & Spear, N. E. (1988). Ontogenetic differences in conditioning of an aversion to a gustatory CS with a peripheral US. *Behavioral and Neural Biology, 50,* 16–23.

Huizink, A. C., & Mulder, E. J. H. (2006). Maternal smoking, drinking or cannabis use during pregnancy and neurobehavioral and cognitive functioning in human offspring. *Neuroscience & Biobehavioral Reviews, 30,* 24–41.

Imai-Matsumura, K., Kaul, R., & Schmidt, I. (1995). Juvenile circadian core temperature rhythm in Wistar and lean (Fa/-) Zucker rat pups. *Physiology & Behavior, 57,* 135–139.

Ingram, D. K. (1979). Acquisition, extinction, and retention of a conditioned taste aversion as a function of age in mature male mice. *Dissertation Abstracts International, 39,* 6184–6185.

Izumi, J., Washizuka, M., Hayashi-Kuwabara, Y., Yoshinaga, K., Tanaka, Y., Ikeda, Y., et al. (1997). Evidence for depressive-like state induced by repeated saline injections in Fischer 344 rats. *Pharmacology, Biochemistry, and Behavior, 57,* 883–888.

Jenkins, J. G., & Dallenbach, K. M. (1924). Obliviscence during sleep and waking. *American Journal of Psychology, 35,* 605–612.

Kalat, J. W. (1974). Taste salience depends upon novelty, not concentration, in taste aversion learning in the rat. *Journal of Comparative and Physiological Psychology, 86,* 47–50.

Kalat, J. W. (1975). Taste-aversion learning in infant guinea pigs. *Developmental Psychobiology, 8,* 383–387.

Kalat, J. W. (1977). Status of "learned-safety" or "learned noncorrelation" as a mechanism in taste aversion learning. In L. M. Barker, M. R. Best, & M. Domjan (Eds.), *Learning mechanisms in food selection* (pp. 273–293). Waco, TX: Baylor University Press.

Kalat, J. W., & Rozin, P. (1971). Role of interference in taste aversion learning. *Journal of Comparative and Physiological Psychology, 77,* 53–58.

Kalat, J. W., & Rozin, P. (1973). "Learned safety" as a mechanism in long-delay taste-aversion learning in rats. *Journal of Comparative and Physiological Psychology, 83,* 198–207.

Kehoe, P., & Blass, E. (1986). Conditioned aversions and their memories in 5-day-old rats during suckling. *Journal of Experimental Psychology: Animal Behavior Processes, 12,* 40–47.

Kleiber, M., Smith, A. H., & Chernikoff, T. N. (1956). Metabolic rate of female rats as a function of age and body size. *American Journal of Physiology, 159,* 9–12.

Klein, S. B., Domato, G. C., Hallstead, C., Stephens, I., & Mikulka, P. J. (1975). Acquisition of a conditioned aversion as a function of age and measurement technique. *Physiological Psychology, 3,* 379–384.

Klein, S. B., Mikulka, P. J., Domato, G. C., & Hallstead, C. (1977). Retention of internal experiences in juvenile and adult rats. *Physiological Psychology, 5,* 63–66.

Kolberg, K. J. S. (1999). Environmental influences on prenatal development and health. In T. L. Whitman, T. V. Merluzzi, & R. D. White (Eds.), *Life-span perspectives on health and illness* (pp. 87–103). Mahwah, NJ: Lawrence Erlbaum.

Kraemer, P. J., Hoffman, H., & Spear, N. E. (1988). Attenuation of the CS-preexposure effect after a retention interval in preweanling rats. *Animal Learning & Behavior, 16,* 185–190.

Kraemer, P. J., & Roberts, W. A. (1984). The influence of flavor preexposure and test interval on conditioned taste aversion in the rat. *Learning and Motivation, 15,* 259–278.

Krane, R. V., & Wagner, A. R. (1975). Taste aversion learning with a delayed shock US: Implications for the generality of the laws of learning. *Journal of Comparative and Physiological Psychology, 88,* 882–889.

LaFiette, M. H., Carlos, R., & Riley, E. P. (1994). Effects of prenatal alcohol exposure on serial pattern performance in the rat. *Neurotoxicology and Teratology, 16,* 41–46.

Lehmann, J., Logeay, C., & Feldon, J. (2000). Long-term effects of a single 24-hour maternal separation on three different latent inhibition paradigms. *Psychobiology, 28,* 411–419.

Lordi, B., Patin, V., Protais, P., Mellier, D., & Caston, J. (2000). Chronic stress in pregnant rats: Effects on growth rate, anxiety and memory capabilities of the offspring. *International Journal of Psychopathology, 37,* 195–205.

Lubow, R. E. (1973). Latent inhibition. *Psychological Bulletin, 79,* 398–407.

Mackintosh, N. J. (1973). Stimulus selection: Learning to ignore stimuli that predict no change in reinforcement. In R. A. Hinde & J. Stevenson-Hinde (Eds.), *Constraints on learning: Limitations and predispositions* (pp. 75–100). New York: Academic Press.

Martin, G. M., & Timmins, W. K. (1980). Taste–sickness associations in young rats over varying delays, stimulus, and test conditions. *Animal Learning & Behavior, 8,* 529–233.

Martin, J. C., Martin, D. C., Sigman, G., & Radow, B. (1977). Offspring survival, development, and operant performance following maternal ethanol consumption. *Developmental Psychobiology, 10,* 435–446.

Martin, L. T., & Alberts, J. R. (1979). Taste aversions to mother's milk: The age-related role of nursing in acquisition and expressions of a learned association. *Journal of Comparative and Physiological Psychology, 93,* 430–445.

Martinez, J. L & Rigter, H. (1983). Assessment of retention capacities in old rats. *Behavioral & Neural Biology, 39,* 181–191.

Melcer, T., Alberts, J. R., & Gubernick, D. J. (1985). Early weaning does not accelerate the expression of nursing-related taste aversions. *Developmental Psychobiology, 18,* 375–381.

Metzger, M. M., & Riccio, D. C. (1999). Ketaset–Rompun extends the temporal gradient for hypothermia-induced retrograde amnesia. *Physiology & Behavior, 66,* 737–740.

Mickley, G. A., Lovelace, D., Farrell, S. T., & Chang, K. S. (1995). The intensity of a fetal taste aversion is modulated by the anesthesia during conditioning. *Developmental Brain Research, 85,* 119–127.

Mickley, G. A., Remmers-Roeber, D. R., Dengler, C. M., Kenmuir, C. L., & Crouse, C. (2001). Paradoxical effects of ketamine on the memory of fetuses of different ages. *Developmental Brain Research, 127,* 71–76.

Misanin, J. R., Anderson, M. J., Christianson, J. P., Collins, M. M., Goodhart, M. G. Rushanan, S. G., et al. (2002). Low body temperature, time dilation, and long-trace conditioned flavor aversion in rats. *Neurobiology of Learning and Memory, 78,* 167–177.

Misanin, J. R., Blatt, L. A., & Hinderliter, C. F. (1985). Age dependency in neophobia: Its influence on taste aversion learning and the flavor preexposure effect in the rat. *Animal Learning & Behavior, 13,* 69–76.

Misanin, J. R., Christianson, J. P., Anderson, M. J., Giovanni, L. M., & Hinderliter, C. F. (2004).

Ketaset–Rompun extends the effective interstimulus interval in long-trace taste-aversion conditioning in rats. *Behavioural Processes, 65,* 111–121.

Misanin, J. R., Chubb, L. D., Quinn, S. A., & Schweikert, G. E. (1974). An apparatus and procedure for the effective instrumental training of neonatal and infant rats. *Bulletin of the Psychonomic Society, 4,* 171–173.

Misanin, J. R., Collins, M., Rushanan, S., Anderson, M. J., Goodhart, M., & Hinderliter, C. F. (2002). Aging facilitates long-trace taste-aversion conditioning in rats. *Physiology & Behavior, 75,* 759–764.

Misanin, J. R., Goodhart, M., Anderson, M. J., & Hinderliter, C. F. (2002). The interaction of age and unconditioned stimulus intensity on long-trace conditioned flavor aversion in rats. *Developmental Psychobiology, 40,* 131–137.

Misanin, J. R., Greider, D. L., & Hinderliter, C. F. (1988). Age differences in the outcome of long-delay taste-aversion conditioning in rats. *Bulletin of the Psychonomic Society, 26,* 258–260.

Misanin, J. R., Guanowsky, V., & Riccio, D. C. (1983). The effect of CS-preexpsoure on conditioned taste aversion in young and adult rats. *Physiology & Behavior, 30,* 859–862.

Misanin, J. R., Haigh, J. M., Hinderliter, C. F., & Nagy, Z. M. (1973). Analysis of response competition in discriminated and nondiscriminated escape training of neonatal rats. *Journal of Comparative and Physiological Psychology, 85,* 570–580.

Misanin, J. R., & Hinderliter, C. F. (1994). Efficacy of lithium chloride in the taste aversion conditioning of young-adult and old-age rats. *Psychological Reports, 75,* 267–271.

Misanin, J. R., & Hinderliter, C. F. (1995a). Lack of age differences in context–illness associations in the long-delay taste aversion conditioning of rats. *Perceptual and Motor Skills, 80,* 595–598.

Misanin, J. R., & Hinderliter, C. F. (1995b). Learned irrelevance and age differences in the long-delay taste aversion conditioning of rats. *Psychological Record, 45,* 127–132.

Misanin, J. R., Kaufold, S. E., Paul, R. L., Hinderliter, C. F., & Anderson, M. J. (2006). A time contraction effect of acute tail-pinch stress on the associative learning of rats. *Behavioural Processes, 71,* 16–20.

Misanin, J. R., Lariviere, N. A., Turns, A. E., Turns, L. E., & Hinderliter, C. F. (1986). The effect of home cage stimuli on acquisition and retention of an active avoidance response in previsual rats. *Developmental Psychobiology, 19,* 37–47.

Misanin, J. R., Nagy, Z. M., Keiser, E. F., & Bowen, W. (1971). Emergence of long-term memory in the neonatal rat. *Journal of Comparative and Physiological Psychology, 77*, 188–199.

Misanin, J. R., Nagy, Z. M., & Weiss, E. M. (1970). Escape behavior in neonatal rats. *Psychonomic Science, 18*, 191–192.

Misanin, J. R., Rose, S. J., & Hinderliter, C. F. (1971). Escape behavior in neonatal rats: Methodological and psychometric considerations. *Behavioral Research Methods & Instrumentation, 3*, 253–254.

Misanin, J. R., Turns, L. E., & Hinderliter, C. F. (1985). Acquisition and retention of active avoidance behavior in previsual rats. *American Journal of Psychology, 98*, 485–501.

Misanin, J. R., Wilson, H. A., Schwarz, P. R., Tuschak, J. B., & Hinderliter, C. F. (1998). Low body temperature affects associative processes in long-trace conditioned flavor aversion. *Physiology & Behavior, 65*, 581–590.

Misslin, R., Herzog, F., Koch, B., & Ropartz., P. (1982). Effects of isolation, handling and novelty on the pituitary–adrenal response in the mouse. *Psychoneuroendocrinology, 7*, 217–221.

Molina, J. C., Pepino, M. Y., Johnson, J., & Spear, N. E. (2000). The infant rat learns about alcohol through interaction with an intoxicated mother. *Alcoholism: Clinical and Experimental Research, 24*, 428–437.

Mothes, H. K., Optiz, B., Werner, R., & Clausing, P. (1996). Effects of prenatal ethanol exposure and early experience on home cage and open field activity in mice. *Neurotoxicology and Teratology, 18*, 59–65.

Nagy, Z. M., Misanin, J. R., & Newman, J. A. (1970). Anatomy of escape behavior in neonatal mice. *Journal of Comparative and Physiological Psychology, 72*, 116–124.

Nagy, Z. M., Misanin, J. R., Newman, J. A., Olsen, P. L., & Hinderliter, C. F. (1972). Ontogeny of memory in the neonatal mouse. *Journal of Comparative and Physiological Psychology, 81*, 380–393.

Nagy, Z. M., Misanin, J. R., & Olsen, P. L. (1972). Development of 24-hour retention of escape learning in neonatal C3H mice. *Developmental Psychobiology, 5*, 259–268.

O'Connor, M. J., Kogan, N., & Findlay, R. (2002). Prenatal alcohol exposure and attachment behavior in children. *Alcoholism: Clinical and Experimental Research, 26*, 1592–1602.

Optiz, B., Mothes, H. K., & Clausing, P. (1997). Effects of prenatal ethanol exposure and early experience on radial maze performance and conditioned taste aversion in mice. *Neurotoxicology and Teratology, 19*, 185–190.

Peck, J. H. (1975). Acquisition and retention of an illness-induced taste-aversion as a function of age in the rat. *Dissertation Abstracts International, 36*, 1951.

Pepino, M. Y., Lopez, M. F., Spear, N. E., & Molina, J. C. (1999). Infant rats respond differentially to alcohol after nursing from an alcohol-intoxicated dam. *Alcohol, 18*, 189–201.

Pieron, H. (1923). Les problemes psychophysiologiquesception du temps. *Année Psycholgie, 24*, 1–25.

Ratcliffe, J. M., Fenton, M. B., & Galef, B. G. (2003). An exception to the rule: Common vampire bats do not learn aversions. *Animal Behaviour, 65*, 385–389.

Revusky, S. (1977). The concurrent interference approach to delay learning. In L. M. Barker, M. R. Best, & M. Domjan (Eds.), *Learning mechanisms in food selection* (pp. 319–366). Waco, TX: Baylor University Press.

Riley, E. P., Barron, S., Driscoll, & Chen, J. S. (1984). Taste aversion learning in preweanling rats exposed to ethanol prenatally. *Teratology, 46*, 45–48.

Riley, E. P., Lochry, E. A., & Shapiro, N. R. (1979). Lack of response inhibition in rats prenatally exposed to alcohol. *Psychopharmacology, 62*, 47–52.

Robinson, S. R., & Brumley, M. R. (2005). Prenatal behavior. In I. Q. Whishaw & K. Bryan (Eds.), *The behavior of the laboratory rat: A handbook with tests* (pp. 257–265). New York: Oxford University Press.

Rozin, P., & Kalat, J. W. (1971). Specific hungers and poison avoidance as adaptive specializations of learning. *Psychological Review, 78*, 459–486.

Sandner, G., Silva, R. C. B., Angst, M., Knobloch, J., & Danion, J. (2004). Prenatal exposure of Long-Evans rats to 17á-ethinylestradiol modifies neither latent inhibition nor prepulse inhibition of the startle reflex but elicits minor deficits in exploratory behavior. *Developmental Brain Research, 152*, 177–187.

Schulenburg, C. J., Riccio, D. C., & Stikes, E. R. (1971). Acquisition and retention of a passive-avoidance response as a function of age in rats. *Journal of Comparative and Physiological Psychology, 74*, 75–83.

Schweitzer, L., & Green, L. (1982). Acquisition and extended retention of a conditioned taste aversion in preweanling rats. *Journal of Comparative and Physiological Psychology, 96*, 791–806.

Seligman, M. E. P. (1970). On the generality of the laws of learning. *Psychological Review, 77*, 978–982.

Smith, J. C., & Roll, D. L. (1967). Trace conditioning with X-rays as an aversive stimulus. *Animal Learning & Behavior, 9*, 11–12.

Smotherman, W. P., Richards, L. S., & Robinson, S. R. (1984). Techniques for observing fetal behavior *in utero*: A comparison of chemomyelotomy and spinal transaction. *Developmental Psychobiology, 17*, 661–674.

Smotherman, W. P., & Robinson, S. R. (1985). The rat fetus in its environment: Behavioral adjustments to novel, familiar, aversive, and conditioned stimuli presented *in utero*. *Behavioral Neuroscience, 99*, 521–530.

Smotherman, W. P., & Robinson, S. R. (1987). Psychobiology of fetal experience in the rat. In N. A. Krasnegor, E. M. Blass, M. A. Hofer, & W. P. Smotherman (Eds.), *Perinatal development: A psychobiological perspective* (pp. 39–60). New York: Academic Press, Inc.

Smotherman, W. P., & Robinson, S. R. (1991). Conditioned activation of fetal behavior. *Physiology & Behavior, 50*, 73–77.

Spear, N. E. (1978). *The processing of memories: Forgetting and retention.* Hillsdale, NJ: Lawrence Erlbaum Associates, Inc.

Steinert, P. A., Infurna, R. N., & Spear, N. E. (1980). Long-term retention of a conditioned taste aversion in preweanling and adult rats. *Animal Learning & Behavior, 8*, 375–381.

Stickrod, G. (1981). *In utero* injection in rat fetuses. *Physiology & Behavior, 27*, 3, 557–558.

Stickrod, G., Kimble, D. P., & Smotherman, W. P. (1982). *In utero* taste/odor aversion conditioning in the rat. *Physiological Behavior, 28*, 5–7.

Takahashi, L. K., Turner, J. G., & Kalin, N. H. (1992). Prenatal stress alters brain catecholaminergic activity and potentiates stress-induced behavior in adult rats. *Brain Research, 574*, 131–137.

Tazumi, T., Hori, E., Uwano, T., Umeno, K., Tanebe, K., Tabuchi, E., et al. (2005). Effects of prenatal maternal stress by repeated cold environment on behavioral and emotional development in the rat offspring. *Behavioural Brain Research, 162*, 153–160.

Tyron, R. C. (1929). The genetics of learning ability in rats: Preliminary report. *University of California Publications in Psychology, 4*, 71–89.

Tyron, R. C. (1940). Studies in individual differences in maze ability. VII. The specific components of maze ability, and a general theory of psychological components. *Journal of Comparative Psychology, 30*, 283–335.

Valliere, W. A., Peterson, C. S., & Misanin, J. R. (1985). Age-differences in odor preference following an odor–illness pairing. *Bulletin of the Psychonomic Society, 23*, 427–429.

PART III

NEURAL ANALYSIS AND PHYSIOLOGICAL MECHANISMS

15

Central Gustatory System Lesions and Conditioned Taste Aversion

STEVE REILLY

To eat, or not to eat: that is the question. Faced with a novel food, an animal is confronted with a decision that cannot be taken lightly. While consumption may lead to a nutritious meal, it may, if the food is poisonous, cause death. Unsurprisingly, then, powerful learning effects have evolved to guide ingestive behavior. The present review is concerned with the most important of these phenomena: conditioned taste aversion (CTA; Garcia, Kimeldorf, & Koelling, 1955; Lemere & Voegtlin, 1950; Rzóska, 1954). CTAs not only prevent the repeated ingestion of toxic food but they are also implicated in many other situations relevant to our well-being. Thus, in addition to the intrinsic value of determining the normal functioning of the brain, research into the physiological mechanisms of CTA will surely lead to a better understanding of a wide range of health-related issues, perhaps the most clinically salient of which are the adverse dietary side effects of chemotherapy and the associated anticipatory nausea.

The ultimate goal of research on this subject is to elucidate the neuropharmacological and molecular underpinnings of CTA. However, understanding at these levels is predicated upon knowledge about the basic CTA neurocircuitry and the respective functions of the neural components. There is, then, an obvious sense in which systems-level research informs the selection of neural structures in which the cellular and molecular changes consequent to

the induction of CTA can be most meaningfully investigated. Thus, the present review is focused on the neuroanatomy of first-order CTA. Specifically, we examine which nuclei are essential for a taste (conditioned stimulus, CS) to be associated with visceral malaise (unconditioned stimulus, US).

We view CTA as a process that minimally involves five stages (e.g., Reilly & Bornovalova, 2005). In Stage 1 the taste cue (which will become the CS following pairing with the US) is detected and processed. In Stage 2, the US must be detected and processed. In Stage 3 the neural representations of these two types of stimuli are integrated to form the learned association. Information embodied in the CS–US association is retrieved in Stage 4 and expressed in performance in Stage 5. This model provides the framework within which the empirical data will be assessed. In effect, each stage of the model constitutes a hypothesis about how a brain lesion or other manipulation might disrupt taste aversion learning. We are interested in determining which brain nuclei are essential for CTA acquisition. Historically, this has been achieved by assessing the residual behavioral capacities consequent to the induction of a permanent lesion. To the extent that a lesion of a particular nucleus abolishes CTA acquisition, then we will consider that nucleus to be an obligate structure in the system. This is, of course, just a beginning because an impairment in any of the five stages of CTA leads to the same behavioral deficit (i.e., overconsumption of the taste CS). As such, additional experiments are necessary to accurately identify the nature of the underlying dysfunction.

Despite more than 30 years of research and numerous reviews (including Ashe & Nachman, 1980; Bures, Bermudez-Rattoni, & Yamamoto, 1998; Chambers, 1990; Gallo, Ballesteros, Molero, & Moron, 1999; Gaston, 1978; Kiefer, 1985; Lamprecht & Dudai, 2000; Scalera, 2002), consensus has yet to emerge regarding the basic neuroanatomy of CTA learning in the rat. In part, this reflects the nonsystematic manner in which brain structures have been selected for investigation. Given that CTA is a taste-guided behavior, the present review is organized around the major nuclei of the central gustatory system (described in the next section). In one of the definitive studies in the literature, Grill and Norgren (1978a) determined that decerebrate rats were incapable of acquiring CTAs. We will describe this report, the only study of its type, in some detail prior to the main section of the review that concerns the effects of permanent lesions of central gustatory nuclei on taste aversion learning.

CENTRAL GUSTATORY SYSTEM

A number of excellent reviews are available concerning the organization of the gustatory system within the rat brain (e.g., Finger, 1987; Lundy & Norgren, 2004; Travers, 1993). For present purposes, this system (see Figure 15.1) will be sketched in sufficient detail appropriate for an appreciation of the lesion–CTA review that follows.

Distributed between three cranial nerves (facial, glossopharyngeal, and vagus), taste information from the mouth is believed to project exclusively to the anterior half of the nucleus of the solitary tract (NST) in the brainstem (Contreras, Beckstead, & Norgren, 1982; Hamilton & Norgren, 1984). From this first taste nucleus, axons ascend to the medial region of the parabrachial nucleus (PBN) in the pons (Norgren & Leonard, 1971, 1973). Neurons from the PBN taste area transmit information along two routes to the forebrain. Axons in dorsal pathway first synapse in the gustatory thalamus (GT; the parvicellular division of the ventral posteromedial nucleus; Karimnamazi & Travers, 1998; Voshart & van der Kooy, 1981) before projecting to the gustatory region of the insular cortex (IC) that is located in a narrow band on the dorsal bank of the rhinal sulcus on either side of the middle cerebral artery (Kosar, Grill, & Norgren, 1986; Nakashima et al., 2000). The other route for ascending gustatory information, the ventral pathway, involves projections, mostly reciprocal, from the PBN to a number of forebrain structures including the bed nucleus of the stria terminalis (BNST; Alden, Besson, & Bernard, 1994; Karimnamazi & Travers, 1998), the lateral hypothalamus (LH; Bester, Besson, & Bernard, 1997;

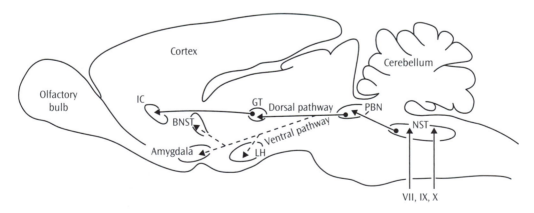

Figure 15.1. Schematic diagram showing the central gustatory system of the rat superimposed onto a sagittal section of the brain. Gustatory information enters the brain along cranial nerves VII (facial), IX (glossopharyngeal), and X (vagus). Abbreviations: BNST, bed nucleus of the stria terminalis; GT, gustatory thalamus (the parvicellular division of the ventral posteromedial nucleus); IC, insular cortex; LH, lateral hypothalamus; NST, nucleus of the solitary tract; PBN, parabrachial nucleus. Modified figure reprinted with permission from Finger (1987).

Halsell, 1992; Norgren, 1976), and the central nucleus of the amygdala (CNA; Bernard, Alden, & Besson, 1993; Karimnamazi & Travers, 1998).

There is also ample opportunity for interactions between the dorsal and ventral pathways. Of relevance to present purposes, connections occur between the GT and the CNA (Halsell, 1992; Nakashima et al., 2000; Ottersen & Ben-Ari, 1979; Turner & Herkenham, 1991; Yasui, Saper, & Cechetto, 1991), the GT and the lateral amygdaloid nucleus (La; Nakashima et al., 2000; Turner & Herkenham, 1991), and the La and basolateral amygdaloid nucleus (Bla; Pitkanen, Savander, & Le Doux, 1997). These latter two subnuclei (La and Bla) are components of a larger anatomical unit termed the basolateral amygdala (BLA), which has been a target for a number of lesion–CTA studies. The IC and the CNA are each recipients of projections from the Bla and La (Krettek & Price, 1977a, 1977b; Pitkanen et al., 1997) and the IC and CNA are interconnected (Norgren, 1976; Ottersen, 1982; Pitkanen et al., 1997; Veening, 1978). Finally, there is a pathway of unknown modality (Lundy & Norgren, 2004) that projects from the vicinity of the PBN to the IC (Lasiter, Glanzman, & Mensah, 1982; Saper, 1982; Shipley & Sanders, 1982) as well as a direct projection from the IC to the PBN (Halsell, 1992; Moga et al., 1990; Saper, 1982). Relevant to interpretation of the effects of lesions of the CNA on CTA, Frey, Morris, and Petrides (1997) demonstrated that these two pathways pass through but do not synapse in the CNA.

The present review will critically evaluate the effects of permanent lesions of the components of the dorsal and ventral gustatory pathways on CTA acquisition. However, before examining the influence of lesions targeted at specific gustatory nuclei, it is first necessary to discuss the influence of decerebration on taste aversion learning.

THE DECEREBRATE RAT AND CTA

The decerebrate preparation, which can involve transection of the neuraxis at one of a number of levels, has long been used to investigate the neural substrates of information processing (e.g., Bell, Horne, & Magee, 1933; Donhoffer & Macleod, 1932; Woods, 1964). In the Grill and Norgren (1978a) CTA study, the rat brain was completely transected in a two-stage procedure at the

mesodiencephalic junction thereby reducing the functional central gustatory system to the two taste nuclei (NST and PBN) located in the brainstem. Because the chronic decerebrate (CD) rat is incapable of spontaneous ingestive behavior, the CD rat is an "intensive care" preparation that must be intubated with nutrients in order to survive. Taste reactivity methodology, which involves monitoring of orofacial responses evoked by the infusion of fluids through an indwelling oral catheter (Grill & Norgren, 1978b; Grill & Kaplan, 1990), is used to assay the behavioral capacities of the CD rat.

CTA was examined in seven subjects (five CD and two surgical control rats) in a procedure that involved four presurgical CS–US pairings and, 19 days later, an additional eight postsurgical trials with the same CS (sodium chloride [NaCl] for four rats and hydrochloric acid [HCl] for the other three animals). During each trial, the CS was infused and immediately followed by an intraperitoneal injection of lithium chloride (LiCl). To investigate whether a lack of endogenous arousal was affecting the performance of the CD rats, some of the postsurgical trials were administered following external stimulation induced either by tail pinch or by injection of amphetamine. The CTA results, unexpectedly, were presented entirely qualitatively; no quantitative assessment was reported. As described, "The decerebrate rats neither retained nor acquired an association of a taste with the LiCl even under conditions of exogenous arousal" (Grill & Norgren, 1978a, p. 268). This experiment provides evidence that the caudal brainstem taste nuclei (NST and PBN) have only minor roles in CTA, which might be viewed as a forebrain-dependent process. The Grill and Norgren CTA experiment with CD rats gave direction to research that clearly would be most profitably directed at determining the identity and functions of forebrain structures that underlie CTA. Indeed, the first studies of the effects on CTA of lesions of the NST and PBN were not to appear until about a decade after the publication of this seminal study by Grill and Norgren. It is to these more recent lesion experiments that we now turn.

EFFECTS OF CENTRAL GUSTATORY SYSTEM LESIONS ON CTA

The challenge of defining the neurocircuitry of CTA has been constrained by the long-standing view that forebrain structures were important for the integrative functions that underlie learning and memory and that "lower" structures were merely "relay stations" for ascending information en route to cortex. The failure of CD rats to acquire CTAs thus fell on fertile ground. Unsurprisingly, then, the first lesion studies examining the role of brainstem taste nuclei in CTA were not published until the late 1980s. However, rather than using a chronological perspective, our exposition, as previously stated, is organized around the components of the central gustatory system beginning first with structures of the dorsal taste pathway (NST, PBN, GT, and IC) before progressing to the forebrain nuclei of the ventral pathway (BNST, LH, and amygdala).

In reading the lesion–CTA, literature a number of interpretational issues become apparent and must be considered when critically assessing the significance and merit of the studies under review. These issues can be separated into two categories: physiological and experimental design. In the first category, the size and accuracy of lesion placement (including bilateral symmetry) undoubtedly influence the quality of the behavioral results. In the following analysis, more weight will be given to the behavioral results obtained from studies that used neurotoxic rather than aspiration or electrolytic lesions; the former method destroys intrinsic neurons while sparing fibers of passage unlike the latter methods that nonselectively destroy all tissue at the target site thereby compromising the attribution of function to structure. In addition, our analysis will exclude studies in which presentation of the histology and/or behavior data are of insufficient detail to allow independent assessment of the results. In the experimental design category, a number of issues undermine accurate assessment of the nature, or even occurrence, of a lesion-induced CTA deficit (e.g., Reilly & Bornovalova, 2005). First, although it is common to use a design with only one conditioning trial, this practice may be insufficient to determine whether the lesion has eliminated or attenuated taste aversion learning. This problem may be avoided by using a design that employs multiple conditioning trials. Second, assessing the strength of an acquired aversion by monitoring CS intake over repeated extinction trials is problematic for the simple reason that extinction does not reflect unlearning of the initial association. Rather, extinction seems to involve the acquisition of a new association about the occurrence of the CS and the absence of the US.

Accordingly, a lesion-induced deficit in extinction cannot unambiguously be attributed to a disruption of original learning processes. Third, two-bottle test trials (e.g., CS vs. water) may be useful for detecting the occurrence of a weak CTA in neurologically intact rat (because, independent of the strength of the aversion, the rat can avoid the CS by drinking the water which, of course, will magnify the apparent strength of the CTA). For the very same reason, the strength of an aversion in a lesioned rat may mistakenly be overestimated or even entirely obscured when a two-bottle test is used. The best way to evaluate the strength, as opposed to the occurrence, of an acquired aversion requires the use of a one-bottle test trial. The final interpretational issue concerns the inadvertent practice of preexposing all subjects to the taste cue that subsequently will be paired with the US. Although this practice is typically undertaken to allow a determination of whether the lesion disrupts taste detection/processing or neophobia, it will also begin to reduce the novelty of the taste stimulus. Because familiar stimuli acquire aversions more slowly than novel stimuli (a phenomenon termed latent inhibition; see Chapter 3), inadvertent preexposure to the taste cue may lead to a misinterpretation of the influence of a lesion on CTA. These interpretational issues guide our evaluations of the studies in the lesion–CTA literature.

Nucleus of the Solitary Tract

Only three studies have examined the effects of bilateral NST lesions on CTA. These studies yield a consistent, if unexpected, outcome: bilateral electrolytic lesions of the NST did not prevent CTA acquisition or retention.

Flynn, Grill, Schulkin, and Norgren (1991), using taste reactivity methodology, reported that NST-lesioned (NSTX) rats, like control subjects, decreased the number of ingestive responses while concomitantly increasing the frequency of aversive responses over the course of three CS–US (alanine–LiCl) pairings. Employing a conventional procedure with voluntary fluid intake as the dependent measure, Grigson, Shimura, and Norgren (1997a) found that NSTX rats developed LiCl-induced taste (alanine) and odor (almond) aversions. To rule out the possibility that the CTA acquired by lesioned animals was mediated by the olfactory component of the taste CS, these researchers further demonstrated that NSTX rats, when rendered anosmic with zinc sulfate, developed a normal CTA to malic acid. Finally, the NSTX rats in the Grigson et al. (1997b) study showed normal retention of a preoperatively acquired CTA to alanine.

Thus, a consistent picture emerges from these studies concerning the influence of NST lesions on CTA. Although this picture is also consistent with the view, derived from the decerebrate rat experiment, that brainstem taste nuclei have little involvement in CTA, such a conclusion may be premature with regard to the NST. Lesions of the NST, the first nucleus of the central gustatory system, if they completely destroy all gustatory neurons, should have a profound influence on CTA and all other taste-guided behaviors because they would block all ascending gustatory information into the brain. That is, such lesions would prevent CTA because of a deficit in Stage 1 (taste detection and processing) of our CTA model. One is left to conclude, then, that the lesions in the three NST studies were incomplete and that the spared gustatory neurons account for the obtained results. An alternative conclusion that gustatory information ascends into the brain via an as yet unidentified route that bypasses the NST seems highly improbable.

Parabrachial Nucleus

Bilateral lesions that damage a large portion of the PBN prevent CTA acquisition (e.g., Bielavska & Bures, 1994; Ivanova & Bures, 1990a, 1990b; Sclafani, Azzara, Touzani, Grigson, & Norgren, 2001; Yamamoto, Fujimoto, Shimura, & Sakai, 1995). Confident interpretation of the nature of this behavioral deficit is difficult, however. The PBN surrounds the brachium conjunctivum in the dorsolateral pons and, although it consists of numerous subnuclei, it is generally divided into two major regions: medial and lateral. The medial PBN, as previously noted, is a component of the central gustatory system whereas the lateral PBN is a component of the central visceral system (Cechetto, 1987; Saper, 2004). To the degree that the lesions in the studies cited above invaded both PBN regions, the attribution of function to structure is compromised. In this context it might be noted that lesions restricted to the lateral PBN prevent taste aversion learning (Cubero, Lopez, Navarro, & Puerto, 2001; López-Grancha et al., 2006; Mungarndee, Lundy, & Norgren, 2006;

Reilly & Trifunovic, 2000, 2001), a deficit that is generally considered to result from a disruption in the transmission of ascending US-related information (see Reilly, 1999, for review).

A number of studies have shown that lesions confined to the medial PBN, a feat that is best achieved by using electrophysiological guidance, also prevent the acquisition of LiCl-induced CTAs (DiLorenzo, 1988; Flynn, Grill, Schulkin, et al., 1991; Scalera, Spector & Norgren, 1995; Spector, 1995b; Spector, Norgren, & Grill, 1992; Spector, Scalera, Grill, & Norgren, 1995). How is this deficit to be interpreted? The failure of medial PBN-lesioned (PBNX) rats to reduce CS intake (or to change from ingestive to aversive orofacial responses when taste reactivity methodology is employed) over repeated conditioning trials could potentially be explained as a disruption in any one of the five stages of the CTA model articulated earlier (i.e., CS detection and processing, US detection and processing, association formation, CS retrieval and the expression of learning in performance).

With regard to a Stage 1 deficit, there is evidence that medial PBN lesions disrupt taste sensibilities (see Spector, 1995a, for review). For instance, Flynn, Grill, Schwartz, and Norgren (1991) reported that medial PBNX rats showed no concentration-dependent changes in ingestive taste reactivity responses when sucrose was infused intraorally, normal performance for NaCl and HCl, and although they were sensitive to changes in quinine hydrochloride (QHCl) concentration they emitted significantly more ingestive and aversive responses at the highest concentration (0.003M) than normal subjects. When the same rats were tested while water deprived using a 15-min single-bottle procedure, their performance was deficient but they nonetheless showed concentration-dependent changes in the consumption of sucrose, NaCl, HCl, and QHCl. Although the medial PBNX rats cannot be considered ageusic, the fact that they drank significantly more of the aversive stimuli than neurologically intact animals indicates an impairment of taste detection. Spector, Grill, and Norgren (1993) reported that electrolytic lesions centered in the gustatory region of the PBN caused a rightward shift in the concentration–response functions for NaCl and sucrose as assessed with a brief-access procedure (comparable results were reported by Spector, 1995b, for QHCl), a pattern of deficits that reflects a blunting of responsivity not a loss of taste detection. Finally, using a taste-cued shock avoidance task, Spector et al. (1995) found that medial PBN lesions that were sufficient to prevent CTA acquisition resulted in detection thresholds for sucrose and NaCl that spanned the entire range from no impairment to profound deficits. These results indicate that medial PBN lesions reduce the perceived intensity of some gustatory stimuli and, given the lack of correspondence between performance in the taste aversion and shock avoidance tasks, a deficit in taste detection is unlikely to account for the absence of CTA in rats with bilateral lesions of the medial PBN.

So, what is the nature of the underlying deficit in medial PBNX rats? In a series of experiments with the same animals, Reilly, Grigson, and Norgren (1993) examined this issue by varying the nature of the CS to be associated with a LiCl-induced US and, conversely, by varying the nature of the US to be associated with a taste CS. In a taste-potentiated odor aversion procedure, rats with electrolytic lesions of the medial PBN developed neither a conditioned odor aversion (COA) nor a CTA. However, the medial PBNX rats subsequently acquired a conditioned flavor preference induced with a calorie-rich US (sucrose) and a conditioned place aversion induced with lithium toxicosis. The pattern of spared and impaired functions was taken as evidence that the absence of CTA in medial PBNX rats could not be explained in terms of deficits of CS or US detection or processing, retrieval of a CS–US association, or expression of that knowledge in performance. By exclusion of these untenable accounts, Reilly et al. concluded that rats with bilateral medial PBN lesions "are unable to form a specific association between gustatory and visceral cues" (p. 1005).

This conclusion was supported in two later reports that replicated and extended the results obtained by Reilly et al. (1993). First, Grigson, Reilly, Scalera, and Norgren (1998) found that rats with ibotenic acid lesions of the medial PBN failed to acquire lithium-based aversions to a taste cue and an olfactory cue (either presented as an airborne odor or consumed in aqueous solution). Importantly, the same lesioned rats were fully able to use an odor cue to avoid consuming an aversive capsaicin solution. This latter result indicates that the absence of COAs in medial PBNX rats cannot be attributed to a failure to detect the odor CS. In the second report, Grigson, Reilly, Shimura, and Norgren (1998) found that ibotenic acid lesions of the medial PBN abolished CTA acquisition but

had no influence on a conditioned flavor preference induced with a calorie-free US (saccharin). Finally, using a CTA procedure with a trigeminal cue substituting for the taste cue, medial PBNX rats suppressed consumption of a weak capsaicin solution that was followed by gastrointestinal malaise induced with LiCl.

Overall, then, the results presented in this section support the conclusion that neurons in the medial, gustatory region of the PBN are critically involved in the association formation mechanism that integrates a taste (or odor) CS with a LiCl-induced US (for a more detailed exposition of this research see Reilly, 1999). The finding that medial PBN lesions prevent CTA acquisition necessitates a revision of our earlier conclusions derived from the decerebrate rat experiment; a brainstem taste nucleus, the medial PBN, clearly is necessary for taste aversion learning. However, the medial PBN although necessary is not sufficient, as demonstrated by the absence of CTA in decerebrate rats. This revision restructures our task into a determination of the forebrain structure or structures that interact with the medial PBN during CTA acquisition.

Gustatory Thalamus

Neurobehavioral studies of the influence of GT lesions on taste-guided behaviors have been ongoing for over 60 years (see Reilly, 1998, for review). Unfortunately, the conclusions derived from much of the early work are compromised by two related problems. First, nonselective lesions were used that caused damage that spread well beyond the boundaries of the GT. Second, in studies using rats, these large lesions had a consequence that could not be appreciated at that time. This latter point turns on the fact that the PBN in the rat was not recognized as a taste nucleus until the early 1970s (Norgren & Leonard, 1971, 1973). Thus, prior to these two publications, the central gustatory system of rats was thought to follow the same route to cortex as that of primates (i.e., serial connections between NST, GT, and IC; for a recent review of the latter system see Pritchard & Norgren, 2004). Of particular relevance, the ventral taste pathway of the rat passes through the medial thalamus near to the GT. Large, nonselective lesions of the GT, then, would likely not only destroy the target nucleus but also damage the medial PBN fibers of passage *en route* to forebrain taste nuclei. Accordingly, the present discussion will focus on research that avoids the aforementioned problems by using discrete, well-placed electrolytic lesions, or lesions induced with a neurotoxin, in studies that also report histology in sufficient detail to allow a meaningful assessment of the obtained results.

From the studies that meet these criteria, the results are clear: GT lesions have little, if any, influence on the acquisition of first-order CTAs. Whether water deprived and tested with a voluntary intake procedure (Mungarndee et al., 2006; Scalera, Grigson, & Norgren, 1997) or water replete and tested using taste reactivity methodology (Flynn, Grill, Schulkin, et al., 1991), GT-lesioned (GTX) rats show normal taste aversion learning. It should also be noted that GTX rats acquire a CTA at the same rate as neurologically intact animals irrespective of whether the CS is novel or familiar (Reilly, Bornovalova, Dengler, & Trifunovic, 2003).

Although GT lesions have little influence on first-order CTA acquisition, a complicated picture emerges when the experimental design moves beyond the single CS procedures of the studies cited above. When multiple CSs (compound stimuli involving either two tastes or a taste cue and an odor cue) are used, GT lesions affect aversion learning in a way that can best be described as confusing. Reilly et al. (2003) reported that ibotenic acid lesions of the GT disrupt blocking. Specifically, irrespective of whether the blocking cue was preconditioned or not, GTX rats showed little or no CTA to the blocked cue. There is no easy explanation for this result; we speculated that, unlike normal animals that do perceive the individual elements of the compound CS, GTX rats treated the taste–taste compound CS as if it were a single, unique taste cue. By this analysis, GT lesions induce a perceptual deficit that is manifest only when multiple CSs are present at the time of conditioning. The finding that GT lesions do not disrupt taste-potentiated odor aversion learning (Lin, Roman, St. Andre, & Reilly, in preparation), would appear to suggest that the perceptual deficit is specific to compound stimuli involving two taste cues. As straightforward as this interpretation may seem, it is inadequate. In another taste–odor compound conditioning experiment, Reilly and Pritchard (1996) found that the taste cue, despite supporting normal CTA acquisition in GTX rats, failed to overshadow the acquisition of a COA in the same animals. Currently, we have no

explanation for the pattern of impaired and spared functions in GTX rats tested with compound CSs. However, whatever the nature of the GT lesion-induced deficits in compound conditioning designs, that dysfunction clearly does not interfere with the acquisition of first-order CTAs.

Insular Cortex

Although some experiments find null effects, the vast majority of studies in the literature report that IC lesions do influence CTA acquisition, a deficit that is best characterized as attenuation. Before examining the nature of the lesion-induced deficit, it is first necessary to discuss some issues that may confuse interpretation of the results.

In a number of studies (e.g., Bermudez-Rattoni & McGaugh, 1991; Dunn & Everitt, 1988; Hankins, Garcia, & Rusiniak, 1974; Kiefer, Cabral, & Garcia, 1984; Lasiter, 1983) all subjects were preexposed to the taste cue that was later paired with the US. Whether inadvertent or intentional, this practice introduces an additional component (latent inhibition) to the learning situation that may confound interpretation of the obtained results. When a more complete experimental design is employed, IC-lesioned (ICX) rats are reported to show normal acquisition when the CS is familiar and attenuated taste aversion learning when the CS is novel (Kiefer & Braun, 1977; see also Roman & Reilly, 2007). As discussed below, these latter findings may be the key that unlocks the role of the IC in CTA acquisition.

A second interpretational issue concerns the nature of the CS. Some studies that found no influence of IC lesions on CTA used CSs that are best described as taste/odor compound stimuli (e.g., Kiefer, Lawrence, & Metzler, 1986; Kiefer, Metzler, & Lawrence, 1985; Kiefer, Morrow, & Metzler, 1988; Mackey, Keller, & van der Kooy, 1986). As most recently demonstrated by Roman, Nebieridze, Sastre, and Reilly (2006), ICX rats that show attenuated CTA acquisition develop COAs at a rate that is indistinguishable from neurologically intact subjects. IC lesions, then, do not disrupt odor aversion learning (see also Kiefer, Leach, & Braun, 1984; Kiefer, Rusiniak, & Garcia, 1982). In some well-designed experiments, Kiefer and colleagues (e.g., Kiefer et al., 1988; see also Kiefer & Orr, 1992) provide evidence that the failure of IC lesions to disrupt CTA when alcohol is the CS occurs because the ICX rats develop an aversion to the olfactory component of the CS. Thus, when taste/odor compound CSs are employed, ICX rats may acquire a COA that masks a disruption of taste aversion learning. This analysis may also explain why the ICX rats in the study by Mackey et al. (1986) showed normal CTA acquisition. Because the unsweetened Kool-Aid solution that served as the CS in the Mackey et al. study has a very noticeable olfactory component, it is difficult to resist the view that the lesioned, and perhaps even the nonlesioned, rats may have acquired a COA rather than a CTA.

The Mackey et al. (1986) study is also relevant to another interpretational issue. These researchers reported that ICX rats demonstrated no evidence of a morphine-induced saccharin aversion while showing normal acquisition of a LiCl-induced aversion to a Kool-Aid CS. This pattern of results would appear to demonstrate that the involvement of the IC in CTA acquisition is dependent upon the nature of the US. However, it is not clear that this conclusion is warranted on the basis of the results reported by Mackey et al. First, as noted above, the normal aversion to Kool-Aid can reasonably be attributed to the acquisition of a COA by ICX rats. Second, while it was commonly accepted in the 1980s that drugs of abuse induce CTAs, more recent research suggests that psychoactive drugs induce saccharin suppression because of their known rewarding properties not their hypothetical aversive properties (Grigson, 1997, 2000). That is, morphine-induced saccharin suppression may be an example of an anticipatory contrast effect rather than a CTA (see Chapter 5). If this analysis is correct, then the Mackey et al. study may be the first demonstration that IC lesions disrupt morphine-induced anticipatory contrast. From this perspective, the original conclusion derived from the results reported by Mackey et al. (i.e., that the role of the IC in CTA learning depends upon the nature of the US) is not valid.

A fourth issue concerns interpretation of the results obtained from experiments in which a single conditioning trial and a single test trial were employed. The use of this design is particularly problematic when the rats with brain lesions display no evidence of CTA on the test trial (e.g., Cubero, Thiele, & Bernstein, 1999; Schafe & Bernstein, 1998). Does such a result represent a lesion-induced elimination of taste aversion learning? Or, alternatively, should the deficit be characterized as an attenuation of CTA in the brain manipulated subjects? There are at least two ways to avoid this interpretational impasse. First, the inclusion in the design of additional control groups (both neurologically intact and brain damaged) that are given the CS but not the US on the conditioning trial. Such groups would permit an accurate assessment of whether the lesion did, in fact, eliminate taste aversion learning (assuming, of course, that the test trial allows proper assessment of the strength of the acquired aversion). Alternatively, by increasing the number of conditioning trials, it is possible to determine whether lesioned rats can or cannot (as is believed to be the case with medial PBNX and decerebrate rats) eventually acquire a CTA.

With the foregoing caveats in mind, the most enduring interpretation of the role of the IC in CTA acquisition was proposed by Braun, Slick, and Lorden (1972) in the first study to investigate the issue. These researchers found that IC lesions disrupted acquisition of a cyclophosphamide-induced aversion to a normally preferred taste cue (saccharin) but had no influence on the development of a conditioned aversion to a normally nonpreferred taste cue (quinine). The selective nature of the deficit was taken as evidence that the lesion induced a reduction in the salience of the saccharin CS. As defined by Kalat and Rozin (1970) salience refers to the ease with which a novel CS can be associated with a US. Salience is a property of the CS. Thus, from the perspective of the CTA model described earlier, the Braun et al. interpretation gives the IC a role in Stage 1 (i.e., taste/CS processing).

In the report that introduced the term to the CTA literature, Kalat and Rozin (1970) state that salience is the name of a phenomenon not an explanation. These researchers went on to differentiate salience from the palatability (Kalat & Rozin, 1970) and the concentration of the taste (Kalat, 1974) of the CS. Most definitively, Kalat (1974) states that salience "depends mainly if not entirely" on the novelty of the taste. Whether termed salience or associative salience (Braun, 1990), the results of a number of IC lesion–CTA acquisition studies have been interpreted in terms of a disruption of this type of CS processing (e.g., Braun et al., 1972; Dunn & Everitt, 1988; Kiefer & Braun, 1977, 1979; Lasiter Deems, Oetting, & Garcia, 1985).

Despite two reviews on the topic (Braun, 1990; Braun, Kiefer, & Ouellet, 1982), associative salience remains an elusive notion. Unsurprisingly, alternative interpretations of the influence of IC lesions on CTA acquisition have emerged. Derived from experiments that found that IC lesions attenuate taste aversion learning when the CS is novel but have little, or no, influence on CTA when the CS is familiar (Kiefer & Braun, 1977), Roman and Reilly (2007) suggested that IC lesions disrupt recognition of taste novelty and, as a secondary consequence, retard CTA acquisition because of a latent inhibition-like effect. The pattern of spared and impaired functions obtained in these experiments provides strong evidence that IC lesions disrupt taste/CS processing but have no influence on taste detection, US detection or processing, association formation, retrieval, or on the expression of knowledge in performance.

If we expand our purview to include the role of the IC in the postoperative retention of a preoperatively acquired CTA, differences begin to emerge between the taste novelty recognition and associative salience accounts. It is unclear whether a lesion-induced disruption in the detection of taste novelty would anticipate an impairment in CTA retention. Yet, just such a deficit has been consistently reported in the literature (Braun, Kiefer, & Ouellet, 1981; Cubero et al., 1999; Kiefer et al., 1986; Kiefer et al., 1984; Kiefer et al., 1985; Yamamoto, Azuma, & Kawamura, 1981; Yamamoto, Matsuo, & Kawamura, 1980). On the other hand, Braun (1990) argued that a loss of associative salience could account for the absence of CTA retention in ICX rats. Indeed, Braun suggested that the somewhat paradoxical finding that ICX rats can relearn a preoperatively acquired CTA (Braun et al., 1981) is also compatible with the associative salience account. Specifically, it was argued that in the absence of taste associative salience other, previously less salient, cues become more effective at guiding the behavior of ICX rats. Such stimuli, it was suggested, include odor cues, postingestive consequences, and perhaps even feedback from orofacial reflex responses.

A loss of associative salience may provide a parsimonious interpretation for the CTA acquisition and retention deficits seen in ICX rats. However, it is not entirely clear how this interpretation can explain the differential effects of IC lesions in the latent inhibition studies noted above (Kiefer & Braun, 1977; Roman & Reilly, 2007). Accordingly, one of the challenges in the IC lesion–CTA literature is to accurately define the nature of the deficits and to determine if the acquisition and retention

data can be explained as the product of a single, or multiple, dysfunctional mechanisms.

Bed Nucleus of the Stria Terminalis

The BNST is a recipient of ascending gustatory input from the medial PBN. Moreover, it has recently been demonstrated that intraperitoneal administration of LiCl induces c-Fos expression in the BNST (St. Andre, Albanos, & Reilly, 2007). This convergence of gustatory and viscerosensory information strongly suggests that the BNST may be implicated in CTA acquisition, perhaps, like the medial PBN, as part of the association formation mechanism. To the best of our knowledge, only one study, that of Roman et al. (2006), has examined the influence of permanent lesions of the BNST on taste aversion learning. To help determine if the BNST has a similar role in aversion learning as the medial PBN, these researchers examined whether lesions of the BNST, like lesions of the medial PBN, also prevent acquisition of a COA. Thus, rats with lesions of the BNST were first tested for CTA and then COA. Using the same rats in both experiments, as opposed to a new group of animals in each procedure, provides greater explanatory power because any differences in behavior that might emerge cannot be explained away as the product of between-experiment differences in the extent or locus of the lesions. The results from this study were clear and unequivocal: electrolytic lesions of the BNST had no influence on the acquisition of CTAs or COAs.

Lateral Hypothalamus

Six studies have investigated the influence of permanent lesions of the LH on taste aversion learning. At the outset, it is important to note that LH-lesioned (LHX) rats are severely hypophagic and hypodipsic, dysfunctions that are more pronounced and longer lasting following electrolytic lesions than neurotoxic lesions (see Bernardis & Bellinger, 1996, for review). These disruptions of ingestive behavior may lead to interpretational problems when assessing the influence of LH lesions on CTA procedures that use voluntary intake as the dependent measure. Somewhat surprisingly, none of the studies discussed below employed taste reactivity methodology.

Using rats that were food and water deprived, Roth, Schwartz, and Teitelbaum (1973) reported that electrolytic lesions of the LH prevented the acquisition of lithium-based aversions to complex flavor (i.e., taste/odor) cues that were added to the liquid maintenance diet. Using the same behavioral and lesion-induction procedures, Schwartz and Teitelbaum (1974) replicated the acquisition deficit in LHX rats that showed normal retention of a preoperatively acquired aversion to the flavor cues. The authors argued that the failure to acquire conditioned flavor aversions could not be explained in terms of a lesion-induced loss of sensitivity to taste or gastrointestinal malaise (the LH is a component of the central visceral system), or to memory, motivation or performance deficits. Rather, it was concluded "that lesions in the LH area prevent the formation of associations between the taste of a diet and the consequences of ingestion" (Schwartz & Teitelbaum, 1974, p. 396).

It is not clear, however, that this conclusion is warranted. In the experiments reported by Teitelbaum and colleagues, all rats were preexposed to the flavor CSs prior to the conditioning trials. In the absence of groups of rats that were not preexposed to the CSs, unambiguous interpretation of the nature of the deficit is compromised. Further challenging the conclusion that the LH is involved in the associative mechanism responsible for flavor aversion learning are studies in which LH neurons were destroyed by neurotoxins which, unlike electrolytic lesions, spare fibers of passage. As discussed below, none of these studies provides any evidence supportive of an associative deficit in LHX rats.

Yamamoto et al. (1995) found that water-deprived rats with ibotenic acid lesions of the LH, although severely hypodipsic, suppressed CS intake following a single saccharin-LiCl conditioning trial. In the Touzani and Sclafani (2001) study, rats with ibotenic acid lesions of the LH were fitted with gastric catheters and food restricted prior to the conduct of a series of experiments that examined conditioned flavor preferences and aversions using saccharin solutions into which various flavors of Kool-Aid were mixed. Using a discrimination procedure in which one flavor (CS+) was paired with intragastric infusions of a US and a second flavor (CS−) was paired with water or saline, LHX rats acquired a conditioned flavor preference when the CS+ was paired with concurrent infusions of Polycose (Experiment 1), failed to acquire a preference when Polycose was infused 15 min after consumption of the CS+ (Experiment 2),

and showed an attenuated preference for a flavor paired with concurrent infusions of corn oil (Experiment 3). Finally, of most relevance to present purposes, the LHX rats acquired conditioned flavor aversions when the LiCl US was intragastrically infused during (Experiment 4A) or 15 min after (Experiment 4B) CS+ intake. The authors argued that the pattern of spared and impaired functions, all obtained in the same set of animals, rule out explanations in terms of lesion-induced disruptions of CS processing, US processing, or association formation. As acknowledged by the authors, the flavors were primarily distinguishable by their distinctive odors (saccharin and the citric acid taste of Kool-Aid were common to all CS+ and CS− solutions) and odors are generally considered less salient than tastes in toxicosis experiments. If the infusions of LiCl induce visceral feedback more rapidly than infusions of Polycose or corn oil, then, as Touzani and Sclafani suggested, the nominal 15-min CS–US delay was effectively longer in the preference procedure than the aversion procedure. By this analysis, LH lesions induce a memory disruption that is revealed in experiments that employ CSs with low salience and a relatively slow-acting, delayed US.

These conclusions received some support from a second study by Touzani and Sclafani (2002) that used the same behavioral procedures, again in rats with ibotenic acid lesions of the LH. As in the earlier study, LHX rats acquired conditioned preferences when the Polycose US was infused concurrently (Experiments 1A and 4) but not when a 15-min CS–US delay was used (Experiment 1B). The same LHX rats also developed conditioned aversions when a lactose US was infused 15 min (Experiment 3), or a LiCl US was infused 30 min (Experiment 2A), after CS+ intake. However, LHX rats failed to acquire an aversion when the flavor–LiCl interval was 120 min (Experiment 2B). As before, Touzani and Sclafani interpret the results of their second study in terms of a lesion-induced impairment of flavor memory, a deficit that is most readily exposed when a less potent appetitive US (Polycose) rather than a more potent aversive US (LiCl or lactose) is employed. This is a plausible explanation of the pattern of results reported in the two papers by Touzani and Sclafani, except that the complex CSs (Kool-Aid dissolved in a saccharin solution) are, as noted in the previous paragraph, discriminable on the basis of their unique odor components not their flavors or tastes. From this perspective, neurotoxic lesions of the LH more readily disrupt odor preferences than odor aversions: nothing definitive can be claimed about taste aversion learning from the Touzani and Sclafani (2001, 2002) studies.

The final study to be considered in this section (Roman et al., 2006) explicitly examined the influence of neurotoxic lesions of the LH on the acquisition of CTAs and, separately, COAs induced with lithium toxicosis. In these experiments, the US (LiCl or saline) was administered 15 min after intake of a taste or aqueous odor CS. The LHX rats suppressed CS consumption in the LiCl condition of each experiment, but showed no intake suppression when the taste or odor cue preceded a delayed injection of saline (the control, no US condition). Although severely hypodipsic, LHX rats nonetheless acquired both CTAs and COAs. While it will clearly be important to determine whether LHX rats can develop CTAs when the CS–US interval is extended beyond the 15-min delay of the Roman et al. study, at the present time there is no compelling evidence that neurons in the LH are critically involved in taste aversion learning.

Amygdala

The CTA–amygdala lesion literature was assessed by Reilly and Bornovalova (2005), and the reader is referred to that source for a more detailed exposition of the topic. The present discussion will focus on the main themes and conclusions of that recent review.

There is no doubt that permanent lesions of the amygdala disrupt taste aversion learning. This has been repeatedly documented in studies that used electrolytic or neurotoxic lesions that caused variable amounts of damage to multiple subnuclei within the amygdala (e.g., Dunn & Everitt, 1988; Nachman & Ashe, 1974). From the current perspective, two questions require answers: which subnuclei are involved in first-order CTA acquisition and what is the nature of that involvement? The first question is approached by using small, discrete lesions that are targeted at a specific subnucleus or region of the amygdala. With regard to the second question, the deficit is typically seen as a retardation of CTA acquisition which, where data are available, is usually accompanied by an elevation of CS intake on the first conditioning trial.

However, before focusing on these two questions, an exception to the latter point concerning

the severity of the CTA deficit in amygdala-lesioned rats merits some discussion. Schafe, Thiele, and Bernstein (1998) reported that large ibotenic acid lesions of the entire amygdala eliminated CTA when the CS was delivered via intraoral infusions. On the other hand, when a conventional, voluntary intake procedure was used, ibotenic acid lesions were considered to have no influence on CTA acquisition. This pattern of results was taken to demonstrate that the involvement of the amygdala is dependent upon the method used to condition the taste aversion. There are, however, reasons to question this interpretation. Taking the results in reverse order, the normal CTA found in rats trained with the voluntary CS intake protocol stands in marked contrast to the attenuation that is typically found following lesions that destroy multiple subnuclei (see earlier text) or are restricted to the BLA (see following text). That is, normal CTA in lesioned rats is not representative of the literature. Neither is a lesion-induced elimination of taste aversion learning as found in the rats that were trained with intraoral CS infusions. Indeed, the severity of this deficit may be more apparent than real. The experimental design, which involved a single conditioning trial and single test trial, does not afford sufficient opportunity to determine whether the lesions caused a genuine abolition or an attenuation of taste aversion learning. One way to evaluate the merits of these alternative views requires an intraoral conditioning experiment employing multiple conditioning trials so that it can be determined whether lesioned rats do, as the literature indicates, eventually acquire CTAs. Until the Schafe et al. results are replicated in such an experiment, claims that different neural substrates underlie aversions conditioned with different procedures are not entirely convincing.

Returning to the question of which subnuclei or regions of the amygdala are involved in first-order CTA acquisition, research has focused on three areas: the medial amygdala, the CNA, and the BLA (which includes the La and Bla). Of the studies that have examined the effects of electrolytic lesions of the medial amygdala on taste aversion learning, only one (Meliza, Leung, & Rogers, 1981) reported a deficit. However, when ibotenic acid lesions were used, virtually complete suppression of CS intake occurred after one conditioning trial (Yamamoto et al., 1995). At the present time, then, there is no evidence that neurons in the medial amygdala have a role in CTA acquisition.

The same conclusion is appropriate for the involvement of CNA neurons in taste aversion learning. While two studies reported attenuations of CTA acquisition consequent to electrolytic lesions of the subnucleus (Aja, Sisouvong, Barrett, & Gietzen, 2000; Lasiter & Glanzman, 1985), three other studies, also using electrolytic lesions, found no impairments (Galaverna et al., 1993; Kemble, Studelska, & Schmidt, 1979; Schoenfeld & Hamilton, 1981). Furthermore, none of the studies that used a neurotoxin reported a deficit of taste aversion learning after lesions of the CNA (Bermudez-Rattoni & McGaugh, 1991; Morris, Frey, Kasambira, & Petrides, 1999; Sakai & Yamamoto, 1999; St. Andre & Reilly, 2007; Touzani, Taghzouti, & Velley, 1997; Yamamoto et al., 1995). As established using tract tracing techniques, electrophysiological recordings, and c-Fos imaging, the CNA is a component of the central gustatory system and the central visceral system. Whatever functions and roles the CNA subserves in these two systems, it clearly is not an obligate component of the system that governs CTA acquisition.

The results obtained from rats with electrolytic lesions of the BLA are highly comparable to those found following large lesions that damaged multiple subnuclei of the amygdala. That is, the typical finding is an attenuation of CTA acquisition that, where data are available, most often co-occurs with an elevation of CS intake on the first conditioning trial (see Table 4, Reilly & Bornovalova, 2005). Nachman and Ashe (1974) interpreted this pattern of results (in their case obtained from rats with large lesions that damaged BLA, CNA, cortical and medial nuclei) as the product of a lesion-induced disruption of taste neophobia. That is, they suggested that lesioned rats treat a genuinely novel taste as if it is familiar, a deficit which accounts for both the elevated CS intake on the first conditioning trial (because a familiar, safe taste is consumed more avidly than a novel taste) and the retardation of CTA acquisition (because of a latent-inhibition-like effect). In support of their account, they also reported that, irrespective of whether the CS was novel or familiar, amygdala-lesioned rats developed a weak CTA of the same strength as the aversion acquired by nonlesioned rats conditioned with a familiar taste. Morris et al. (1999) reported that a similar pattern of latent inhibition results in rats with neurotoxic lesions of the BLA in a study that involved separate experiments for novel and familiar CSs. In explanation of their results, these researchers seemed to suggest an associative deficit

such that "The BLA could therefore constitute a critical node in the integration of the sensory quality of the sucrose solution with the visceral signals of poisoning and its affective consequences" (p. 300).

In the only other study that examined latent inhibition in rats with neurotoxic lesions, St. Andre and Reilly (2007) used a design that prevented lesion-induced intake differences during preexposure from confounding interpretation of the taste aversion data. Furthermore, unlike the previous two studies, St. Andre and Reilly use a procedure that involved multiple conditioning trials thereby allowing an assessment of the rate of taste aversion learning. The results showed that BLA lesions retarded CTA acquisition only when the CS was novel. Normal CTA performance when the CS was familiar suggests that the BLA–lesioned rats were able to detect the CS, detect and process the LiCl-induced US, as well as form, retrieve and behaviorally express the CS–US association. Thus, it was concluded that BLA lesions selectively disrupt processing of the taste cue that becomes the CS following pairings with the US. Like Nachman and Ashe, St. Andre and Reilly favored an account based on a BLA lesion-induced disruption of taste neophobia.

At present research suggests that the BLA is the important amygdala structure for taste aversion acquisition. Moreover, neurons in the BLA appear to be concerned with the perception of CS novelty. Future research clearly will need to clarify the role of the BLA in gustatory neophobia and, given our similar conclusions in the IC section, the nature of the BLA–IC interaction in the perception of taste novelty/familiarity. Finally, it will be recognized that the BLA is not critically involved in taste aversion learning, as is the medial PBN. That is, although lesions of the BLA retard, they do not prevent CTA acquisition; given multiple conditioning trials, BLA-lesioned rats learn to avoid a taste CS.

CONCLUSIONS

In this chapter we reviewed the literature concerning the effects of permanent lesions of central gustatory nuclei on the acquisition of first-order CTAs. Our analysis indicates that the NST, GT, BNST, LH, and CNA are not obligate components in this system. The medial PBN, BLA, and IC, on the other hand, appear to have important roles in taste aversion acquisition. More specifically, the medial PBN seems to be critically involved in the association formation mechanisms by which aversive gastrointestinal feedback is associatively integrated with the taste (and odor) of a previously ingested food. Indicating a role for the BLA in taste/CS processing, lesions of the BLA disrupt CTA acquisition when the taste CS is novel but not when the CS is familiar. We suspect that the BLA plays a critical role in the detection of taste novelty (Roman, Lin, St. Andre, & Reilly, in preparation). In the absence of this mechanism, the BLAX rat may treat a genuinely novel stimulus as if it is familiar and consequently shows retarded CTA acquisition because of a latent-inhibition-like effect. A similar type of deficit (taste/CS processing) seems to occur following lesions of the IC, although whether the dysfunction is novelty detection or associative salience remains to be clarified.

Two fundamental issues emerge from this review. First, given the similarity of behavioral deficits consequent to lesions of the BLA and IC, what is the nature of the interaction between these structures. Clearly, they are not performing identical functions. If this were the case, following the loss of one of these structures, the other would still be available to perform the common function and neophobia would be evident. Presumably, then, the BLA and IC are performing interdependent functions related to novelty detection (or associative salience). But, what are these functions? Furthermore, are the BLA and IC the only components of this system or do they interact with other structures to form a larger novelty detection system? If so, the other components and their respective functions need to be identified (for one approach to this issue see Chapter 16 by Bernstein, Wilkins, & Barot). Is there a separate system involved in the detection of taste familiarity such that a lesion, or other manipulation, would result in a novel taste failing to habituate with repeated presentations? Or, is the detection of taste novelty and familiarity the product of single system (e.g., Figueroa-Guzmán, Kuo, & Reilly, 2006; Figueroa-Guzmán & Reilly, 2008). Either way, answers to these questions will significantly enhance our understanding of the neurocircuitry involved in taste neophobia and habituation (for further discussion see Reilly & Bornovalova, 2005) and the roles of the BLA and IC in this system.

The second issue raised by the present review returns our discussion to the interpretation of the finding that decerebrate rats fail to develop taste aversions. This result (Grill & Norgren, 1978a) seemed to provide compelling evidence that the brainstem has little, if any, involvement in CTA, which appears to be a forebrain-dependent process. However, the subsequent discovery that lesions of the medial PBN prevent CTA acquisition precipitated a revision of this conclusion such that the medial PBN interacts with one or more forebrain structures during CTA acquisition. But, as our analysis has shown, lesions of no central gustatory forebrain structure disrupt taste aversion learning in a manner comparable to the profound deficits found after medial PBN lesions or decerebration. How, then, are the results from medial PBNX and CD rats to be explained?

It is entirely possible that the critical forebrain structure for CTA acquisition has yet to be examined. Our analysis focused on those major components of the central gustatory system that have attracted research attention. There are, of course, other forebrain nuclei that receive taste information and one of these may prove to be critical for taste aversion learning. Or, perhaps, two or more forebrain nuclei interact with the medial PBN during CTA acquisition. Explanations of the latter type have been proposed. Yamamoto (1993), for instance, suggested that interplay between the amygdala and IC underlies taste aversion learning. This study, however, employed a one-trial procedure so it is difficult to determine whether the deficit should be characterized as an attenuation or elimination of CTA. As described in the present review, when the experimental design employs multiple conditioning trials, lesions of the BLA or IC are found to attenuate not eliminate taste aversion learning. Moreover, as detailed above, we propose that lesions of the BLA or IC each disrupt the perception of taste novelty which, in turn, retards CTA acquisition because of a latent-inhibition-like effect. Although combined lesions of the BLA and IC may produce a more pronounced CTA deficit than would lesions of either structure alone, we are not convinced that the deficit would be as profound as that seen following decerebration or medial PBN lesions. Nonetheless, the issue of which forebrain structure(s) is/are interacting with the medial PBN during CTA acquisition remains viable until all possible individual forebrain gustatory nuclei and combinations thereof have been properly examined for their involvement in taste aversion learning. We are, however, becoming increasingly skeptical that a search for the missing structure(s) will prove fruitful.

This doubt encourages speculation about alternative ways to reconcile the CTA data obtained from decerebrate and medial PBNX rats. One of the most readily testable of these accounts proposes that unidentified damage in the brainstem of CD rats underlies that absence of taste aversion learning. As previously noted, Lasiter and Glanzman (1985) reported that electrolytic lesions of the CNA attenuate CTA acquisition, a deficit that does not occur when the lesions are induced with a neurotoxin (e.g., Morris et al., 1999; St. Andre & Reilly, 2007). Mindful that electrolytic lesions damage fibers as well as intrinsic neurons, Lasiter and Glanzman also reported a comprehensive histological analysis of the remote damage induced by CNA lesions. Among a number of areas, the medial PBN sustained significant neuronal degeneration. The medial PBN is monosynaptically and reciprocally connected with the CNA. If electrolytic lesions of a single forebrain nucleus cause damage to the medial PBN we are inclined to suggest that decerebration, which transects all forebrain gustatory pathways to and from the medial PBN, will produce even more damage to the medial PBN. We are suggesting, then, that the absence of CTA in CD rats is not due to disconnection of the medial PBN from one or more as yet unidentified forebrain nuclei. Rather, we hypothesize that PBN damage induced by decerebration results in the failure of CD rats to acquire taste aversions. If this account is supported empirically then only one structure, the medial PBN, will have been found to be critical for the associative mechanism that governs CTA acquisition. This would give important new direction to research concerning the neuropharmacological substrates of, and the molecular changes in, the medial PBN that underlie taste aversion learning.

Acknowledgment Funding from the National Institute of Deafness and Other Communication Disorders supported the author's research reported in, and the preparation of, this chapter.

References

Aja, S., Sisouvong, S., Barrett, J. A., & Gietzen, D. W. (2000). Basolateral and central amygdaloid lesions leave aversion to dietary amino acid imbalance intact. *Physiology and Behavior, 7,* 533–541.

Alden, M., Besson, J. M., & Bernard, J. F. (1994). Organization of the efferent projections from the pontine parabrachial area to the bed nucleus of the stria terminalis and neighboring regions: A PHA-L study in the rat. *Journal of Comparative Neurology, 341,* 289–314.

Ashe, J. H., & Nachman, M. (1980). Neural mechanisms in taste aversion learning. *Progress in Psychobiology and Physiological Psychology, 9,* 233–262.

Bell, D. J., Horne, E. A., & Magee, H. E. (1933). The decerebrate rat. *Journal of Physiology, 78,* 196–207.

Bermudez-Rattoni, F., & McGaugh, J. L. (1991). Insular cortex and amygdala lesions differentially affect acquisition on inhibitory avoidance and conditioned taste aversion. *Brain Research, 549,* 165–170.

Bernard, J. F., Alden, M., & Besson, J. M. (1993). The organization of the efferent projections from the pontine parabrachial area to the amygdaloid complex: A *Phaseolus vulgaris* leucoagglutinin (PHA-L) study in the rat. *Journal of Comparative Neurology, 329,* 201–229.

Bernardis, L. L., & Bellinger, L. L. (1996). The lateral hypothalamic area revisited: Ingestive behavior. *Neuroscience and Biobehavioral Reviews, 20,* 189–287.

Bester, H., Besson, J. M., & Bernard, J. F. (1997). Organization of the efferent projections from the parabrachial area to the hypothalamus: A *Phaseolus vulgaris* leucoagglutinin (PHA-L) study in the rat. *Journal of Comparative Neurology, 383,* 245–281.

Bielavska, E., & Bures, J. (1994). Universality of parabrachial mediation of conditioned taste aversion. *Behavioral Brain Research, 60,* 35–42.

Braun, J. J. (1990). Gustatory cortex: Definition and function. In B. Kolb & R. C. Tees (Eds.), *The cerebral cortex of the rat* (pp. 407–430). Cambridge, MA: MIT Press.

Braun, J. J., Kiefer, S. W., & Ouellet, J. V. (1981). Psychic ageusia in rats lacking gustatory neocortex. *Experimental Neurology, 72,* 711–716.

Braun, J. J., Lasiter, P. S., & Kiefer, S. W. (1982). The gustatory neocortex of the rat. *Physiological Psychology, 10,* 13–45.

Braun, J. J., Slick, T. B., & Lorden, J. F. (1972). Involvement of gustatory neocortex in the learning of taste aversions. *Physiology and Behavior, 9,* 637–641.

Bures, J., Bermudez-Rattoni, F., & Yamamoto, T. (1998). *Conditioned taste aversion: Memory of a special kind.* Oxford, UK: Oxford University Press.

Cechetto, D. F. (1987). Central representation of visceral function. *Federation Proceedings, 46,* 17–23.

Chambers, K. C. (1990). A neural model for conditioned taste aversions. *Annual Review of Neuroscience, 13,* 373–385.

Contreras, R. J., Beckstead, R. M., & Norgren, R. (1982). The central projections of the trigeminal, facial, glossopharyngeal and vagus nerves: An autoradiographic study in the rat. *Journal of the Autonomic Nervous System, 6,* 303–322.

Cubero, I., Lopez, M., Navarro, M., & Puerto, A. (2001). Lateral parabrachial lesions impair taste aversion learning induced by blood-borne visceral stimuli *Pharmacology Biochemistry and Behavior, 69,* 157–163.

Cubero, I., Thiele, T. E., & Bernstein, I. L. (1999). Insular cortex lesions and taste aversion learning: Effects of conditioning method and timing of lesion. *Brain Research, 839,* 323–330.

DiLorenzo, P. M. (1988). Long-delay learning in rats with parabrachial pontine lesions. *Chemical Senses, 13,* 219–229.

Donhoffer, C., & Macleod, J. J. R. (1932). Studies in the nervous control if carbohydrate metabolism. I. The position of the center. *Proceedings of the Royal Society of London, Series B, 110,* 125–141.

Dunn, L. T., & Everitt, B. J. (1988). Double dissociations of the effects of amygdala and insular cortex lesions on conditioned taste aversion, passive avoidance, and neophobia in the rat using the excitotoxin ibotenic acid. *Behavioral Neuroscience, 102,* 3–23.

Figueroa-Guzmán, Y., Kuo, J. S., & Reilly, S. (2006). NMDA-receptor antagonist MK-801 infused into the insular cortex prevents the attenuation of neophobia in rats. *Brain Research, 1114,* 183–186.

Figueroa-Guzmán, Y., & Reilly, S. (2008). NMDA receptors in the basolateral amygdala and gustatory neophobia. *Brain Research, 1210,* 200–203.

Finger, T. E. (1987). Gustatory nuclei and pathways in the central nervous system. In T. E. Finger & W. L. Silver (Eds.), *Neurobiology of taste and smell* (pp. 331–353). New York: Wiley.

Flynn, F. W., Grill, H. J., Schulkin, J., & Norgren, R. (1991). Central gustatory lesions. II. Effects on sodium appetite, taste aversion learning, and feeding behavior. *Behavioral Neuroscience, 105,* 944–954.

Flynn, F. W., Grill, H. J., Schwartz, G. J., & Norgren, R. (1991). Central gustatory lesions: I. Preference and taste reactivity tests. *Behavioral Neuroscience, 105,* 933–943.

Frey, S., Morris, R., & Petrides, M. (1997). A neuroanatomical method to assess the integrity of fibers of passage following ibotenate-induced damage to the central nervous system. *Neuroscience Research, 28,* 285–288.

Galaverna, O. G., Seeley, R. J., Berridge, K. C., Grill, H. J., Epstein, A. N., & Schulkin, J. (1993). Lesions of the central nucleus of the amygdala I: Effects on taste reactivity, taste aversion learning and sodium appetite. *Behavioral Brain Research, 59,* 11–17.

Gallo, M., Ballesteros, M. A., Molero, A., & Moron, I. (1999). Taste aversion learning as a tool for the study of hippocampal and non-hippocampal brain memory circuits regulating diet selection. *Nutritional Neuroscience, 2,* 277–302.

Garcia, J., Kimeldorf, D. J., & Koelling, R. A. (1955). Conditioned aversion to saccharin resulting from exposure to gamma radiation. *Science, 122,* 157–158.

Gaston, K. E. (1978). Brain mechanisms of conditioned taste aversion learning: A review of the literature. *Physiological Psychology, 6,* 340–353.

Grigson, P. S. (1997). Conditioned taste aversions and drugs of abuse: A reinterpretation. *Behavioral Neuroscience, 111,* 129–136.

Grigson, P. S. (2000). Drugs of abuse and reward comparison: A brief review. *Appetite, 35,* 89–91.

Grigson, P. S., Reilly, S., Scalera, G., & Norgren, R. (1998). The parabrachial nucleus is essential for acquisition of a conditioned odor aversion in rats. *Behavioral Neuroscience, 112,* 1104–1113.

Grigson, P. S., Reilly, S., Shimura, T., & Norgren, R. (1998). Ibotenic acid lesions of the parabrachial nucleus and conditioned taste aversion: Further evidence for an associative deficit. *Behavioral Neuroscience, 112,* 160–171.

Grigson, P. S., Shimura, T., & Norgren, R. (1997a). Brainstem lesions and gustatory function: II. The role of the nucleus of the solitary tract in Na+ appetite, conditioned taste aversion, and conditioned odor aversion in rats. *Behavioral Neuroscience, 111,* 169–179.

Grigson, P. S., Shimura, T., & Norgren, R. (1997b). Brainstem lesions and gustatory function: III. The role of the nucleus of the solitary tract and the parabrachial nucleus in retention of a conditioned taste aversion in rats. *Behavioral Neuroscience, 111,* 180–187.

Grill, H. J., & Kaplan, J. M. (1990). Caudal brainstem participates in the distributed neural control of feeding. In E. M. Stricker (Ed.), *Handbook of behavioral neurobiology. Vol 10. Neurobiology of food and fluid intake* (pp. 125–149). New York: Plenum.

Grill, H. J., & Norgren, R. (1978a). Chronically decerebrate rats demonstrate satiation but not bait shyness. *Science, 201*, 267–269.

Grill, H. J., & Norgren, R. (1978b). The taste reactivity test. I. Mimetic responses to gustatory stimuli in neurologically normal rats. *Brain Research, 143*, 263–279.

Halsell, C. B. (1992). Organization of parabrachial nucleus efferents to the thalamus and amygdala in the golden hamster. *Journal of Comparative Neurology, 317*, 57–78.

Hamilton, R. B., & Norgren, R. (1984). Central projections of gustatory nerves in the rat. *Journal of Comparative Neurology, 222*, 560–577.

Hankins, W. C., Garcia, J., & Rusiniak, K. W. (1974). Cortical lesions: Flavour-illness and noise–shock conditioning. *Behavioral Biology, 10*, 173–181.

Ivanova, S. F., & Bures, J. (1990a). Acquisition of conditioned taste aversion in rats is prevented by tetrodotoxin blockade of a small region centered around the parabrachial nucleus. *Physiology and Behavior, 48*, 543–549.

Ivanova, S. F., & Bures, J. (1990b). Conditioned taste aversion is disrupted by prolonged retrograde effects of intracerebral injection of tetrodotoxin in rats. *Behavioral Neuroscience, 104*, 948–954.

Kalat, J. W. (1974). Taste salience depends on novelty, not concentration, in taste-aversion learning in the rat. *Journal of Comparative and Physiological Psychology, 86*, 47–50.

Kalat, J. W., & Rozin, P. (1970). "Salience": A factor which can override temporal contiguity in taste-aversion learning. *Journal of Comparative and Physiological Psychology, 71*, 192–197.

Karimnamazi, H., & Travers, J. B. (1998). Differential projections from gustatory responsive regions of the parabrachial nucleus to the medulla and forebrain. *Brain Research, 813*, 283–302.

Kemble, E. D., Studelska, D. R., & Schmidt, M. K. (1979). Effects of central amygdaloid nucleus lesions on ingestion, taste reactivity, exploration and taste aversion. *Physiology and Behavior, 22*, 789–793.

Kiefer, S. W. (1985). Neural mediation of conditioned food aversions. *Annals of the New York Academy of Sciences, 443*, 100–109.

Kiefer, S. W., & Braun, J. J. (1977). Absence of differential associative responses to novel and familiar taste stimuli in rats lacking gustatory neocortex. *Journal of Comparative and Physiological Psychology, 91*, 498–507.

Kiefer, S. W., & Braun, J. J. (1979). Acquisition of taste avoidance habits absence in rats lacking gustatory neocortex. *Physiological Psychology, 7*, 245–250.

Kiefer, S. W., Cabral, R. J., & Garcia, J. (1984). Neonatal ablations of the gustatory neocortex in the rat: Taste aversion learning and taste reactivity. *Behavioral Neuroscience, 98*, 804–812.

Kiefer, S. W., Lawrence, G. J., & Metzler, C. W. (1986). Learned alcohol aversions in rats: Gustatory and olfactory components. *Alcohol, 3*, 27–31.

Kiefer, S. W., Leach, L. R., & Braun, J. J. (1984). Taste agnosia following gustatory neocortex ablation: Dissociation from odor and generality across taste qualities. *Behavioral Neuroscience, 98*, 590–608.

Kiefer, S. W., Metzler, C. W., & Lawrence, G. J. (1985). Neocortical involvement in the acquisition and retention of learned alcohol aversions in rats. *Alcohol, 2*, 597–601.

Kiefer, S. W., Morrow, N. S., & Metzler, C. W. (1988). Alcohol aversion generalization in rats: Specific disruption of taste and odor cues with gustatory neocortex or olfactory bulb ablations. *Behavioral Neuroscience, 102*, 733–739.

Kiefer, S. W., & Orr, M. R. (1992). Taste avoidance, but not aversion, learning in rats lacking gustatory cortex. *Behavioral Neuroscience, 106*, 140–146.

Kiefer, S. W., Rusiniak, K. W., & Garcia, J. (1982). Flavor–illness aversions: Gustatory neocortex ablations disrupt taste but not taste-potentiated odor cues. *Journal of Comparative and Physiological Psychology, 96*, 540–548.

Kosar, E., Grill, H. J., & Norgren, R. (1986). Gustatory cortex in the rat. II. Thalamocortical projections. *Brain Research, 379*, 342–352.

Krettek, J. E., & Price, J. L. (1977a). The cortical projections of the medio-dorsal nucleus and adjacent thalamic nuclei in the rat. *Journal of Comparative Neurology, 171*, 157–192.

Krettek, J. E., & Price, J. L. (1977b). Projections from the amygdaloid complex to the cerebral cortex and thalamus in the rat and cat. *Journal of Comparative Neurology, 172*, 687–722.

Lamprecht, R., & Dudai, Y. (2000). The amygdala in conditioned taste aversion: It's there, but where. In J. P. Aggleton (Ed.), *The amygdala: A functional analysis* (2nd ed., pp. 331–351). Oxford, UK: Oxford University Press.

Lasiter, P. S. (1983). Gastrointestinal reactivity in rats lacking anterior insular neocortex. *Behavioral and Neural Biology, 39*, 149–154.

Lasiter, P. S., Deems, D. A., Oetting, R. L., & Garcia, J. (1985). Taste discriminations in rats lacking anterior insular gustatory neocortex. *Physiology and Behavior, 35*, 277–285.

Lasiter, P. S., & Glanzman, D. L. (1985). Cortical substrates of taste aversion learning: Involvement of dorsolateral amygdaloid nuclei and temporal neocortex in taste aversion learning. *Behavioral Neuroscience, 99*, 257–276.

Lasiter, P. S., Glanzman, D. L., & Mensah, P. A. (1982). Direct connectivity between pontine taste areas and gustatory neocortex in rat. *Brain Research, 234*, 111–121.

Lemere, F., & Voegtlin, W. L. (1950). An evaluation of the aversion treatment of alcoholism. *Quarterly Journal of Studies on Alcohol, 11*, 199–204.

Lin, J.-Y., Roman, C., St. Andre, J. R., & Reilly, S. (in preparation). Taste-potentiated odor aversion: The roles of the gustatory thalamus, insular cortex, medial and basolateral amygdala.

López-Grancha, M., Sánchez-Amate, C., Navarro, M., Carvajal, F., Sánchez-Santed, F., & Cubero, I. (2006). Lateral parabrachial lesions disrupt paraoxon-induced conditioned flavor avoidance. *Toxicological Sciences, 91*, 210–217.

Lundy, R. F., Jr., & Norgren, R. (2004). Gustatory system. In G. Paxinos (Ed.), *The rat nervous system* (3rd ed., pp. 891–921). San Diego: Academic Press.

Mackey, W. B., Keller, J., & van der Kooy, D. (1986). Visceral cortex lesions block conditioned taste aversions induced by morphine. *Pharmacology, Biochemistry and Behavior, 24*, 71–78.

Meliza, L. L., Leung, P. M. B., & Rogers, Q. R. (1981). Effect of anterior prepyriform and medial amygdaloid lesions on acquisition of taste-avoidance and response to dietary amino acid balance. *Physiology and Behavior, 26*, 1031–1035.

Moga, M. M., Herbert, H., Hurley, K. M., Yasui, Y., Gray, T. S., & Saper, C. B. (1990). Organization of cortical, basal forebrain, and hypothalamic afferent to the parabrachial the rat. *Journal of Comparative Neurology, 295*, 624–661.

Morris, R., Frey, S., Kasambira, T., & Petrides, M. (1999). Ibotenic acid lesions of the basolateral, but not central, amygdala interfere with conditioned taste aversion: Evidence from a combined behavioral and anatomical tract-tracing investigation. *Behavioral Neuroscience, 113*, 291–302.

Mungarndee, S. S., Lundy, R. F., Jr., & Norgren, R. (2006). Central gustatory lesions and learned taste aversions: Unconditioned stimuli. *Physiology and Behavior, 87*, 542–551.

Nachman, M., & Ashe, J. H. (1974). Effects of basolateral amygdala lesions on neophobia, learned taste aversions, and sodium appetite in rats. *Journal of Comparative and Physiological Psychology, 87*, 622–643.

Nakashima, M., Uemura, M., Yasui, K., Ozaki, H. S., Tabata, S., & Taen, A. (2000). An anterograde and retrograde tract-tracing study on the projections from the thalamic gustatory area in the rat: Distribution of neurons projecting to the insular cortex and amygdaloid complex. *Neuroscience Research, 36*, 297–309.

Norgren, R. (1976). Taste pathways to hypothalamus and amygdala. *Journal of Comparative Neurology, 166*, 12–30.

Norgren, R., & Leonard, C. M. (1971). Taste pathways in rat brainstem. *Science, 173*, 1136–1139.

Norgren, R., & Leonard, C. M. (1973). Ascending central gustatory pathways. *Journal of Comparative Neurology, 150*, 217–238.

Ottersen, O. P. (1982). Connections of the amygdala complex of the rat. IV: Corticoamygdaloid and intraamygdaloid connections as studied with axonal transport of horseradish peroxidase. *Journal of Comparative Neurology, 205*, 30–48.

Ottersen, O. P., & Ben-Ari, Y. (1979). Afferent connections to the amygdaloid complex of the rat and cat. *Journal of Comparative Neurology, 187*, 401–424.

Pitkanen, A., Savander, V., & Le Doux, J. E. (1997). Organization of intra-amygdaloid circuitries in the rat: An emerging framework for understanding functions of the amygdala. *Trends in Neuroscience, 20*, 517–523.

Pritchard, T. C., & Norgren, R. (2004). Gustatory system. In G. Paxinos & J. K. Mai (Eds.), *The human nervous system* (2nd ed., pp. 1171–1196). San Diego, CA: Academic Press.

Reilly, S. (1998). The role of the gustatory thalamus in taste-guided behavior. *Neuroscience and Biobehavioral Reviews, 22*, 883–901.

Reilly, S. (1999). The parabrachial nucleus and conditioned taste aversion. *Brain Research Bulletin, 48*, 239–254.

Reilly, S., & Bornovalova, M. (2005). Conditioned taste aversion and amygdala lesions in the rat: A critical review. *Neuroscience and Biobehavioral Reviews, 29*, 1067–1088.

Reilly, S., Bornovalova, M., Dengler, C., & Trifunovic, R. (2003). Effects of excitotoxic lesions of the gustatory thalamus on latent inhibition and blocking of conditioned taste aversion in rats. *Brain Research Bulletin, 62*, 117–128.

Reilly, S., Grigson, P. S., & Norgren, R. (1993). Parabrachial nucleus lesions and conditioned taste aversion: Evidence supporting an associative deficit. *Behavioral Neuroscience, 107*, 1005–1017.

Reilly, S., & Pritchard, T. C. (1996). Gustatory thalamus lesions in the rat: II. Aversive and appetitive taste conditioning. *Behavioral Neuroscience, 110*, 746–759.

Reilly, S., & Trifunovic, R. (2000). Lateral parabrachial nucleus lesions in the rat: Aversive and appetitive gustatory conditioning. *Brain Research Bulletin, 52,* 269–278.

Reilly, S., & Trifunovic, R. (2001). Lateral parabrachial nucleus lesions in the rat: Neophobia and conditioned taste aversion. *Brain Research Bulletin, 55,* 359–366.

Roman, C., Lin, J.-Y., St. Andre, J. R., & Reilly, S. (in preparation). Effects of lesions of the basolateral amygdala, medial amygdala, or insular cortex on neophobia to taste, olfactory, and trigeminal stimuli.

Roman, C., Nebieridze, N., Sastre, A., & Reilly, S. (2006). Effects of lesions of the bed nucleus of the stria terminalis, lateral hypothalamus, or insular cortex on conditioned taste aversion and conditioned odor aversion. *Behavioral Neuroscience, 120,* 1257–1267.

Roman, C., & Reilly, S. (2007). Effects of insular cortex lesions on conditioned taste aversion and latent inhibition in the rat. *European Journal of Neuroscience, 26,* 2627–2632.

Roth, S. R., Schwartz, M., & Teitelbaum, P. (1973). Failure of recovered lateral hypothalamic rats to learn specific food aversions. *Journal of Comparative and Physiological Psychology, 83,* 184–197.

Rzóska, J. (1954). The behavior of white rats towards poison baits. In D. Chitty (Ed.), *Control of rats and mice* (Vol. 2, pp. 374–394). Oxford, England: Clarendon Press.

Sakai, N., & Yamamoto, T. (1999). Possible routes of visceral information in the rat brain in formation of conditioned taste aversion. *Neuroscience Research, 35,* 53–61.

Saper, C. B. (1982). Reciprocal parabrachial–cortical connections in the rat. *Brain Research, 242,* 33–40.

Saper, C. B. (2004). Central autonomic system. In G. Paxinos (Ed.), *The rat nervous system* (3rd ed., pp. 761–796). San Diego: Academic Press.

Scalera, G. (2002). Effects of conditioned food aversions on nutritional behavior in humans. *Nutritional Neuroscience, 5,* 159–188.

Scalera, G., Grigson, P. S., & Norgren, R. (1997). Taste functions, sodium appetite, and conditioned taste aversion after excitotoxic lesions of the thalamic taste nucleus in rats. *Behavioral Neuroscience, 111,* 633–645.

Scalera, G., Spector, A. C., & Norgren, R. (1995). Excitotoxic lesions of the parabrachial nuclei prevent conditioned taste aversions and sodium appetite in rats. *Behavioral Neuroscience, 109,* 997–1008.

Schafe, G. E., & Bernstein, I. L. (1998). Forebrain contribution to the induction of a brainstem correlate of conditioned taste aversion. II. Insular (gustatory) cortex. *Brain Research, 800,* 40–47.

Schafe, G. E., Thiele, T. E., & Bernstein, I. L. (1998). Conditioning method dramatically alters the role of amygdala in taste aversion learning. *Learning and Memory, 5,* 481–492.

Schoenfeld, T. A., & Hamilton, L. W. (1981). Disruption of appetite but not hunger or satiety following small lesions in the amygdala of rats. *Journal of Comparative and Physiological Psychology, 95,* 565–587.

Schwartz, M., & Teitelbaum, P. (1974). Dissociation between learning and remembering in rats with lesions in the lateral hypothalamus. *Journal of Comparative and Physiological Psychology, 87,* 384–398.

Sclafani, A., Azzara, A. V., Touzani, K., Grigson, P. S., & Norgren, R. (2001). Parabrachial nucleus lesions block taste and attenuate flavor preference and aversion conditioning in rats. *Behavioral Neuroscience, 115,* 920–933.

Shipley, M. T., & Sanders, M. S. (1982). Special senses are really special: Evidence for a reciprocal, bilateral pathway between insular cortex and nucleus parabrachialis. *Brain Research Bulletin, 8,* 493–501.

Spector, A. C. (1995a). Gustatory function in the parabrachial nuclei: Implications from lesion studies in rats. *Reviews in Neurosciences, 6,* 143–175.

Spector, A, C. (1995b). Gustatory parabrachial lesions disrupt taste-guided quinine responsiveness in rats. *Behavioral Neuroscience, 109,* 79–90.

Spector, A. C., Grill, H. J., & Norgren, R. (1993). Concentration-dependent licking of sucrose and sodium chloride in rats with parabrachial gustatory lesions. *Physiology and Behavior, 53,* 277–283.

Spector, A. C., Norgren, R., & Grill, H. J. (1992). Parabrachial gustatory lesions impair taste aversion learning in rats. *Behavioral Neuroscience, 106,* 147–161.

Spector, A. C., Scalera, G., Grill, H. J., & Norgren, R. (1995). Gustatory detection thresholds after parabrachial nuclei lesions in rats. *Behavioral Neuroscience, 109,* 939–954.

St. Andre, J., Albanos, K., & Reilly, S. (2007). C-Fos expression in the rat brain following lithium chloride induced-illness. *Brain Research, 1135,* 122–128.

St. Andre, J., & Reilly, S. (2007). Effects of central and basolateral amygdala lesions on conditioned taste aversion and latent inhibition. *Behavioral Neuroscience, 121,* 90–99.

Touzani, K., & Sclafani, A. (2001). Conditioned flavor preference and aversion: Role of the lateral hypothalamus. *Behavioral Neuroscience, 115,* 84–93.

Touzani, K., & Sclafani, A. (2002). Lateral hypothalamic lesions impair flavour-nutrient and flavour-toxin trace learning in rats. *European Journal of Neuroscience, 16*, 2425–2433.

Touzani, K., Taghzouti, K., & Velley, L. (1997). Increase of the aversive value of taste stimuli following ibotenic acid lesion of the central amygdaloid nucleus in the rat. *Behavioral Brain Research, 88*, 133–142.

Travers, S. P. (1993). Orosensory processing in neural systems of the nucleus of the solitary tract. In S. A. Simon & S. D. Roper (Eds.), *Mechanisms of taste transduction* (pp. 339–394). Boca Raton: CRC Press.

Turner, B. H., & Herkenham, M. (1991). Thalamoamygdaloid projections in the rat: A test of the amygdala's role in sensory processing. *Journal of Comparative Neurology, 313*, 295–325.

Veening, J. G. (1978). Subcortical afferents of the amygdaloid complex in the rat: An HRP study. *Neuroscience Letters, 8*, 197–202.

Voshart, K., & van der Kooy, D. (1981). The organization of the efferent projections of the parabrachial nucleus to the forebrain in the rat: A retrograde fluorescent double-labeling study. *Brain Research, 212*, 271–286.

Woods, J. W. (1964). Behavior of chronic decerebrate rats. *Journal of Neurophysiology, 27*, 635–644.

Yamamoto, T. (1993). Neural mechanisms of taste aversion learning. *Neuroscience Research, 16*, 181–185.

Yamamoto, T., Azuma, S., & Kawamura, Y. (1981). Significance of cortical-amygdalar-hypothalamic connections in retention of conditioned taste aversion in rats. *Experiment Neurology, 74*, 758–768.

Yamamoto, T., Fujimoto, Y., Shimura, T., & Sakai, N. (1995). Conditioned taste aversion in the rat with excitotoxic brain lesions. *Neuroscience Research, 22*, 31–49.

Yamamoto, T., Matsuo, R., & Kawamura, K. (1980). Localization of cortical gustatory area in rats and its role in taste discrimination. *Journal of Neurophysiology, 44*, 440–455.

Yasui, Y., Saper, C. B., & Cechetto, D. F. (1991). Calcitonin gene-related peptide (CGRP) immunoreactivity projections from the thalamus to the striatum and amygdala in the rat. *Journal of Comparative Neurology, 308*, 293–310.

16

Mapping Conditioned Taste Aversion Associations through Patterns of c-Fos Expression

ILENE L. BERNSTEIN, EMILY E. WILKINS, AND SABIHA K. BAROT

Conditioned taste aversions (CTAs) constitute a potent learning model that is associative, adaptive/defensive, and amygdala dependent (Bermúdez-Rattoni & Yamamoto, 1998; Bernstein, 1991; Garcia, Hankins, & Rusiniak, 1974; Yasoshima, Yamamoto, & Kobayashi, 2005; see Reilly & Bornovalova, 2005). Moreover, this learning paradigm has a number of features that make it particularly amenable to neurobiological assessment (Bermúdez-Rattoni, 2004). One such feature is rapid acquisition, as CTAs are typically acquired after a single pairing of conditioned stimulus (CS) and unconditioned stimulus (US). One-trial learning provides researchers a clear time window during which the neuronal signaling and molecular mechanisms underlying the learning can be identified. Another distinctive feature of CTA learning is that it can occur despite lengthy delays between exposure to CS taste and US drug (Domjan, 1980; Garcia, Ervin, & Koelling, 1966; Revusky & Garcia, 1970). In other conditioning paradigms, close temporal proximity between presentation of CS and US are critical to effective conditioning. In fact the requirement for temporal contiguity, with an optimal range being 500 ms to 2 s, is so common a feature of associative learning paradigms that it has been used to build models of the cellular signaling processes that might underlie plasticity (Abrams & Kandel, 1988). CTAs, however, are routinely acquired after delays ranging from several minutes to hours between exposure to CS taste and US illness. Given this, CTAs are clearly anomalous in their temporal properties and may require the development of neural learning models that do not depend so strongly on tight temporal contiguity.

In our lab, identifying the critical components of CTA learning has involved assessment of immediate early gene (IEG) expression. Regulatory IEGs, such as c-fos, couple short-term neuronal activity with changes in gene transcription and are potential markers of neurons undergoing modification as a result of experience. This technique has a number of advantages that account for its popularity as a tool for monitoring patterns of neural activity. The technique marks populations of neurons activated in conscious animals by a specific, defined stimulus. Baseline expression is generally low, which provides a relatively high signal to noise ratio. Individual activated neurons can be identified and the method can be combined with other staining procedures (e.g., tract tracers; immunostaining for neurochemicals) to characterize connectivity and other attributes of activated cells (Spray & Bernstein, 2004). Nonetheless, fos immunostaining also has certain limitations that are important to keep in mind when interpreting experimental results. Neurons differ in their capacity to express fos and in their latency to do so. Strong and sustained neural activation is generally required before significant c-Fos expression can be detected. More important, this means that the absence of fos expression in a region does not necessarily mean that no neurons were activated by that specific stimulus. Finally, the nature of the signal allows for only limited temporal resolution and it can be unclear whether a neural response is a direct or indirect consequence of the stimulus.

To date, increases in Fos-like immunoreactivity (FLI) have been reported in brain regions implicated in CTA learning after exposure to the US and CS (Koh, Wilkins, & Bernstein, 2003; Lamprecht & Dudai, 1995; Schafe, Seeley, & Bernstein, 1995; Swank, 1999), and following behavioral expression of a CTA (e.g., Houpt, Philopena, Joh & Smith, 1996; Swank & Bernstein, 1994). Moreover, interference with c-Fos expression by the central administration of *c-fos* antisense mRNA interferes with acquisition, but not expression, of the learning (Lamprecht & Dudai, 1996; Swank, 1996; Yasoshima, Sako, Senba, & Yamamoto, 2006). Thus c-fos represents not only a neuronal marker of activation but also an intriguing candidate for the molecular mediation of CTA learning (Koh et al., 2003). The synthesis and subsequent degradation of a protein product of an IEG transcription factor such as c-fos could function as a biochemical substrate that bridges long CS–US intervals.

In the following studies we have used both behavioral and neuronal assessment tools such as c-fos to identify cellular events involved in taste aversion acquisition. These studies include analysis of the taste information processing that occurs when an animal is exposed for the first time to a new taste and to the taste–illness associations which underlie acquisition of CTAs (Koh & Bernstein, 2005; Koh et al., 2003).

TASTE INFORMATION PROCESSING

Robust and rapid CTA acquisition relies heavily on the novelty of the CS taste (Kalat, 1974; Kalat & Rozin, 1973; Revusky & Bedarf, 1967). In the laboratory, one or two safe exposures to a taste prior to conditioning can dramatically attenuate aversion learning to that taste. Varying taste novelty provides a tool for assessing the molecular mediation of the learning because gene expression and protein synthesis critical to learning should be modulated strongly by the novelty of the taste. Furthermore, the localization of such modulation

should point to regions critically involved in taste memory.

Varying taste novelty provides a potent tool for identifying events preparatory to, and supportive of, learning. Clearly neural responses to novel and familiar tastes differ significantly and this ultimately determines whether the taste becomes the target of an aversion during CTA training. In particular, gene expression and protein synthesis critical to the learning should be modulated strongly by the novelty of the taste; such signals should display anatomical localization allowing convergence with signals generated by the US and should be characterized by a temporal profile allowing overlap with signals generated by the US. Furthermore, the localization of these signals should point to regions critically involved in taste memory.

NOVEL VERSUS FAMILIAR SACCHARIN EXPOSURE

Rats with and without prior experience with 0.5% saccharin solution were compared using immunostaining for the protein product of the IEG, c-Fos, to identify patterns of neuronal activity after exposure to a novel, in contrast to a familiar, taste. Experience consisted of 6 days of preexposure for rats in the familiar group to develop a "safe" taste memory of saccharin. On the test day, familiar and novel groups were given 30 min to consume a maximum of 5 ml of the saccharin solution. They were sacrificed 2 h later and brains were processed for FLI. Regions previously implicated in taste aversion learning were examined; these include the nucleus of the solitary tract (NTS), pontine parabrachial nucleus (PBN), amygdala, and insular (gustatory) cortex (IC).

In brief, exposure to a novel, but not a familiar, saccharin solution was found to induce robust increases in FLI in some, but not all, brain regions previously implicated in taste processing or taste aversion learning. Striking effects of taste novelty on FLI were found in the central amygdala (CNA) and IC, but not the basolateral amygdala (BLA), the medial PBN, or the rostral NTS (Koh et al., 2003).

In addition to taste novelty, the intensity of a taste is important for determining its effectiveness as a CS in aversion learning (Dragoin, 1971). We compared FLI expression in the CNA and IC in response to novel and familiar 0.15% and 0.5% saccharin solutions. In the CNA, only the novel

0.5% solution produced increases in FLI; there was no difference between novel and familiar 0.15% saccharin. In the IC, however, novel saccharin at both concentrations elevated FLI levels above those produced by familiar saccharin. This suggests that the IC, unlike the CNA, responds selectively to the novelty of a tastant, regardless of intensity (Koh et al., 2003).

NOVEL VERSUS FAMILIAR POLYCOSE EXPOSURE: FLI

The previous study used saccharin as the novel/familiar CS taste. Since taste aversions can be conditioned to virtually any novel tastant, it is important to establish that the novelty-based finding obtained with saccharin can generalize to other tastants. In the next studies we examined the generality of these findings to other tastants.

Choices of testable taste qualities other than sweet tastes such as saccharin were constrained by a need for distinct and novel taste qualities with minimal odor cues. Primary tastes are limited to some five or six distinct types: salty, sour, sweet, bitter, and possibly umami (MSG) and polysaccharide (Brand, 2000; Sclafani, 2004). Sour and bitter stimuli, particularly in high concentrations, tend to be innately aversive, thus complicating the investigation of taste aversion learning since animals find the stimulus aversive even before conditioning. Polycose®, a well- studied polysaccharide preparation, was chosen because it is highly palatable to rats in a wide range of concentrations and does not appear to taste sweet, as aversions to Polycose fail to generalize to sweet stimuli (Nissenbaum & Sclafani, 1987; Sako et al., 1994). Animals were exposed to a familiar or novel aqueous solution of Polycose (30% wt/vol). This high, but palatable, concentration was chosen because of the previously mentioned evidence that high taste intensity as well as novelty might be necessary for detecting elevated *fos* gene expression. FLI induced by novel and familiar Polycose were compared in order to determine whether differences in patterns of neuronal activation would be evident with this nonsweet tastant. Procedures for taste familiarization, taste exposure, and FLI assessment were the same as those in the first study with saccharin.

Unexpectedly, behavioral and FLI results with Polycose were quite different from those seen

with saccharin. Across the 6 preexposure days, animals familiarized with Polycose showed no increase in Polycose consumption. This is strikingly different from animals familiarized with saccharin, where mean intakes increased significantly as animals became more familiar with the tastant. Furthermore, animals that were inexperienced with Polycose took no longer to consume the solution on test day than animals that were previously familiarized with Polycose (Figure 16.1). This behavioral lack of neophobia contrasted with previous work in this lab showing large differences in latency to drink familiar and novel saccharin.

Neural correlates of novelty, elevated FLI in central nucleus of the amygdala (CNA), and IC, were also absent in animals exposed to Polycose for the first time. Figure 16.2 displays average FLI expression in IC, CNA, and BLA. Unlike the previous experiment using novel and familiar saccharin, FLI levels were generally very low and no reliable differences were found as a function of taste novelty. In fact, neither group receiving Polycose differed from controls that received only water. These findings imply that a behavioral lack of neophobia to Polycose is associated with a lack of differential FLI in areas previously found to be sensitive to taste novelty (Barot & Bernstein, 2005).

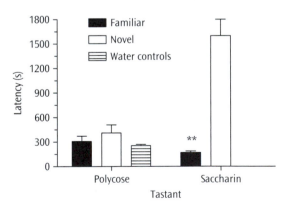

Figure 16.1. Latency (s) to consume 30% Polycose or 0.5% saccharin by novel and familiar animals. Water control animals received only water and were used only in the Polycose experiment. No significant differences were observed between novel Polycose, familiar Polycose, and water control animals. Novel saccharin animals took significantly longer to consume 5 ml of solution than familiar animals. $**p < 0.01$.

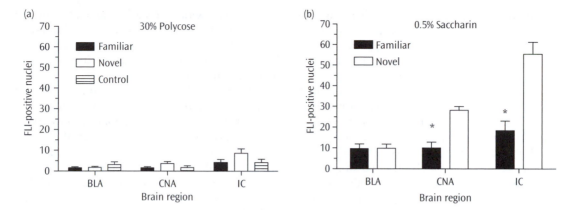

Figure 16.2. Mean number (+ SEM) of FLI-positive nuclei in the basolateral and central nuclei of the amygdala (BLA and CNA, respectively) and insular cortex (IC) following exposure to a familiar 30% Polycose solution, a novel Polycose solution, or water (a) or a familiar or novel 0.5% saccharin solution (b). No differences in FLI as a function of novelty were seen for animals receiving Polycose. Significantly more FLI-positive nuclei were found in the CNA and IC of animals receiving novel than familiar saccharin solution. $*p < 0.05$.

NOVEL VERSUS FAMILIAR
POLYCOSE EXPOSURE: CTA

A more sensitive assessment of a preexposure effect, or latent inhibition, is the marked reduction of CTA learning after preexposure to a taste. To further assess whether rats respond differently to Polycose as a function of taste novelty, we evaluated the effect of Polycose taste preexposure on the strength of CTA learning.

Animals were preexposed to a 30% Polycose solution for 6 days (familiar) or not (novel) as described before. On conditioning day, novel and familiar animals were given access to 5 ml of Polycose and allowed to drink for 30 min, after which they were injected with either 0.15-M LiCl (10 ml/kg) or 0.15-M saline (10 ml/kg). The strength of conditioning was tested 2 days later.

Polycose intake on the test day revealed an effect for conditioning but no difference as a function of taste novelty (Figure 16.3). Both novel and familiar animals that received LiCl on conditioning day drank significantly less than those receiving saline. Thus, animals showed significant CTAs regardless of prior exposure to the taste and did not differ from each other in the amount consumed.

The fact that both familiar and novel conditioned groups showed comparable CTAs again contrasts with studies using saccharin, where familiarized animals showed greatly attenuated, or even no evidence of, learning (Koh & Bernstein, 2005). Thus, differential behavioral and neuronal

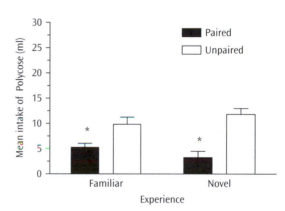

Figure 16.3. Mean intake of Polycose (+ SEM) by novel and familiar animals after pairing with LiCl (paired) or saline (unpaired). Animals learned an aversion regardless of their familiarity with Polycose as is evidenced by the fact that both novel- and familiar-paired animals drank significantly less than unpaired controls. Novel- and familiar-paired animals did not differ from each other. $*p < 0.05$.

responses to novelty were absent with Polycose (Barot & Bernstein, 2005).

NOVEL VERSUS FAMILIAR
NACL EXPOSURE: FLI

The previous experiments indicate that the effects of stimulus novelty commonly ascribed to taste stimuli may not apply to Polycose. Thus, Polycose may be unsuitable as a taste stimulus for assessing the generality of the effects reported by Koh et al. (2003) with saccharin. We next used a third tastant, salt (NaCl), as the novel and familiar taste stimulus. Since solutions with high NaCl concentrations tend to be aversive, and because concentrated NaCl is far less hydrating to thirsty animals, we chose an isotonic (0.9%) concentration of NaCl, a concentration that most strains of rats find to be quite palatable (Midkiff, Fitts, Simpson, & Bernstein, 1985). We examined whether a novel NaCl taste induces a pattern of neuronal activation that is more similar to novel saccharin. Procedures for taste familiarization, taste exposure, and FLI assessment were the same as those in the previous studies with saccharin and Polycose.

As seen with saccharin, animals showed increased intakes of NaCl over the 6-day familiarization period, indicating that animals were hesitant to consume the novel NaCl during their first exposure but that this hesitation decreased as familiarization developed. Table 16.1 provides a comparison for all three tastants in attenuation of neophobia. Evidence for neophobia to novel NaCl was also evident on the test day, when all animals received 5 ml of the NaCl solution. Animals that were unfamiliar with the solution took significantly longer (420 + 14.70 s) to consume 5 ml than those that were familiar with it (144 + 90.32 s).

In line with the behavioral evidence of neophobia, differential FLI induction as a function of taste novelty was evident (Figure 16.4). NaCl taste induced significantly more FLI in IC and CNA

Table 16.1 Intakes of Different Tastants during the First and Last day of Preexposure.

Tastant	Day 1 (ml)	Day 6 (ml)	N	p value
30% Polycose[a]	10.23 + 0.71	11.39 + 0.99	12	0.213
0.5% Saccharin[b]	3.75 ± 0.12	15.84 ± 1.30*	6	<0.01
0.9% NaCl[a]	18.96 + 2.8	24.94 + 2.8*	5	0.021

Note: Mean (+SEM) Intake scores of familiar group animals from three different experiments on the First (Day 1) and Last (Day 6) of their preexposure. Intakes are given in milliliters. Only animals who were familiarized with saccharine and NaCl solutions showed a significantly higher intake of the solution by Day 6. Animals given Polycose did not appear to increase their consumption with increased exposure.

* Indicates significantly higher intake on Day 6 than Day 1 with $p < 0.05$.
[a] Barot and Bernstein (2005).
[b] Koh, Wilkins, and Bernstein (2003).

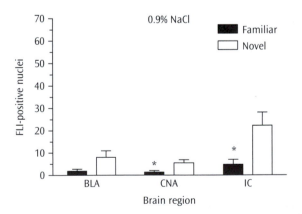

Figure 16.4. Mean number (+ SEM) of FLI-positive nuclei in the basolateral and central nuclei of the amygdala (BLA and CNA, respectively) and insular cortex (IC) following exposure to a familiar or novel 0.9% NaCl solution. As with saccharin, significantly more FLI-positive nuclei were detected in the CNA and IC of novel animals. *$p < 0.05$.

when it was novel than when it was familiar. These data closely replicate the results of aforementioned studies conducted with saccharin, and tend to support the generality of those findings. Moreover, an association was demonstrated between behavioral evidence of neophobia and a difference in FLI as a function of taste novelty. Both saccharin and NaCl show a strong behavioral novelty effect as well as a neural correlate—increased FLI expression in IC and CNA.

NOVEL VERSUS FAMILIAR NACL EXPOSURE: CTA

To confirm the generality of patterns observed with saccharin and taste novelty, we examined patterns of CTA learning as a function of NaCl taste novelty. CTA conditioning was carried out exactly as it was with Polycose, with the only difference being that animals were given a novel or familiar 0.9% NaCl solution to consume.

Intake of NaCl on the test day is shown in Figure 16.5 and depicts CTAs that differed dramatically as a function of taste novelty. No aversions

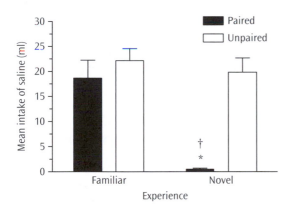

Figure 16.5. Mean intake of a 0.9% NaCl Solution (+ SEM) by novel and familiar animals after pairing the taste with either LiCl (paired) or saline (unpaired). Novel-paired animals drank significantly less than unpaired controls, whereas familiar-paired animals showed no evidence of learning and did not differ from unpaired controls. Novel-paired animals also drank significantly less than familiar-paired animals. $*p < 0.05$ for the difference between paired and unpaired novel animals, $^{†}p < 0.05$ for the difference between paired-novel and paired-familiar animals.

were seen in the familiar animals and aversions were so strong in the novel animals that they consumed virtually none of the solution.

This study confirms, for NaCl, the well-established effect of taste preexposure on CTA learning using an isotonic NaCl taste. Again, results are very similar to those for saccharin (Koh & Bernstein, 2005; Koh et al., 2003) but dissimilar to those seen with Polycose.

WHY IS POLYCOSE ANOMALOUS?

No differences were observed between animals familiarized with Polycose and those for whom it was novel in amount consumed, latency to consume 5 ml, CTA acquisition, or FLI in the CNA and IC. If our findings with novel versus familiar Polycose were limited only to the FLI-dependent measure, we would have questioned the generality of the FLI response as a correlate of taste novelty. However, the consistent absence of preexposure effects across both behavioral and neural outcome measures upholds the existence of an association between FLI expression and taste novelty and raises the question of why Polycose is so unlike other tastants with regard to the novelty–familiarity distinction.

Indeed, it is difficult to ascertain from these studies whether inexperienced and familiarized animals regarded the Polycose taste as novel, familiar, or both. The low FLI response in the brains of animals given novel Polycose, as well as their apparent lack of neophobia, suggests that the taste was perceived somehow as familiar. However, evidence of a significant CTA in familiar animals after a single CS–US pairing indicates that it is processed as somewhat novel.

Although insensitivity to the taste of Polycose might account for some of these findings, such an explanation is not tenable for several reasons. Rats form significant aversions to Polycose, and they prefer it to water even at low concentrations (0.0001 M) (Sclafani & Nissenbaum, 1987). In addition, neural recording indicate that cells in the NTS are responsive to Polycose as well as to other nonsweet tastes (Giza, Scott, Sclafani & Antonucci, 1991). It has been suggested that the taste of polysaccharides such as Polycose may represent a fifth (or sixth) basic taste for rats since its taste quality does not appear similar to sweet, salty, sour, bitter, or umami stimuli (Ackroff, Manza, & Sclafani,

1993; Sclafani, 2004). However, the receptors and distinct coding circuits that underlie this taste are not yet well defined. Whether this "uniqueness" extends to a difference in the role of taste novelty remains to be determined. Although the unusual property of Polycose remains unexplained, the complementary studies with NaCl nonetheless provide important confirmation of the effect of taste novelty on FLI in CNA and IC.

NOVEL TASTE: NEURAL RESPONSES OVER TIME

To understand the spatial and temporal parameters of the FLI response after exposure to a taste CS (saccharin) we analyzed the temporal profiles of FLI activation to a novel taste. Thirsty rats received either 0.5% saccharin solution (familiar condition) or water (novel condition) for 30 min each day during 6 days of preexposure training. On the seventh day, all rats were given saccharin to drink with intake capped at 5 ml in 30 min. Rats were then perfused at one of the following time points: 0.5, 1, 2, 4, or 6 h after taste exposure. Brains were harvested and processed for FLI as previously described (Koh et al., 2003).

Figure 16.6 shows the patterns of FLI in CNA (a) and IC (b) following exposures to either a novel or familiar taste after various delays. For the CNA, main effects of both novelty and time were found to be significant along with an interaction between the two. Direct comparisons between novel and familiar groups at each time point show that a novel taste induced substantially more FLI than a familiar taste after 1 and 2 h delays. Similar patterns of results were observed in the IC (Bernstein & Koh, 2006). Significantly higher FLI expression to novel taste exposure was detected after 1-h delay ($p < 0.01$), but not at other time points. Analyses of FLI expression in other brain regions, including BLA, medial and lateral PBN, rostral and intermediate NTS, failed to show significant effects. Taken together, these results show that novel tastes increased FLI in CNA and IC and that this signal degrades over time, while familiar tastes failed to show any indication of FLI increases within the time course studied.

Manipulations known to reduce the strength of CTA learning (e.g., taste preexposure, reduced CS intensity, and longer CS–US delays) have been shown to be associated with blunting or elimination

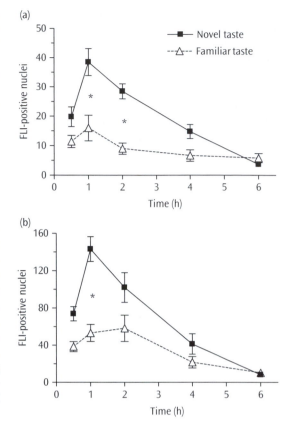

Figure 16.6. Mean number of FLI-positive nuclei in (a) central amygdala and (b) insular cortex 0.5, 1, 2, 4, or 6 h following exposure to either novel or familiar taste. Note the different vertical scales in (a) and (b). *$p < 0.05$ between novel and familiar groups.

of FLI response to a CS. This provides strong support for the idea that FLI marks neural pathways critical to CS processing during CTA acquisition, and further, that key transcriptional events underlying this plasticity may involve *c-fos* expression. A causal link between elevations in Fos protein and CTA acquisition has been indicated by the finding that administration of fos antisense aimed at either the amygdala (Lamprecht & Dudai, 1996) or cerebral ventricle (Swank, 1996) interferes with acquisition of CTA. However, those studies were unable to define whether the critical role of fos was in CS processing, US processing, or the association of the two. The present studies point to a potential role for Fos protein in CS processing. The patterns of results are indicative of involvement of IC and amygdala in taste memory processing. They further suggest that synthesis and subsequent degradation of Fos protein within these cells represents a bio-chemical "trace" of the novel taste which has the potential to bridge some CS–US intervals and play a role in mediating long delay learning. Although only Fos was assessed in the present studies, we readily acknowledge that other molecular events (not necessarily downstream of c-Fos) are likely to be necessary for forming CTAs.

TASTE–ILLNESS ASSOCIATIONS

The next set of studies addressed FLI after stim-ulus exposures known to be sufficient to generate strong CTA learning (i.e., CS–US pairing). Rats were exposed to one of the following conditions, after which their brains were processed for FLI: novel saccharin paired with LiCl, familiar saccha-rin paired with LiCl, or LiCl alone. Familiarization took place as described, with six preexposures prior to the conditioning session. Only the novel CS–US group experienced stimulus exposure known to generate strong CTAs in a single trial. Results indicated strong and widespread induction of FLI only in animals exposed to a highly effective conditioning experience (Koh & Bernstein, 2005). Differential gene expression as a function of CS taste novelty was evident throughout the CTA neu-ral circuit, including brainstem (NTS, PBN) and forebrain (amygdala, IC), but not in areas known to be uninvolved in the learning such as the hippo-campus. The striking behavioral and neural dif-ferences between groups conditioned with novel and familiar tastes provide a remarkable window on the circuitry recruited during the acquisition process.

ROLE OF CONDITIONING METHOD

CTAs can be established using different meth-ods of taste delivery. The most common method involves restricting animals' access to fluids and then allowing them to consume the taste directly from a bottle (Chambers & Bernstein, 1995). More experimenter control over taste exposure can be achieved by infusing the taste solution through an indwelling intraoral (IO) cannula (Schafe et al., 1995; Swank & Bernstein, 1994). Bottle condi-tioning has an active, instrumental component in that the animal must approach the bottle and voluntarily consume the fluid. In IO conditioning,

however, taste exposure does not rely on the animal's behavior. Exposure is under the experi-menter's, not the animal's control, which makes this method closer to "pure" classical conditioning. These two methods can employ different behav-ioral tests for measuring aversions although this is not necessary. Bottle-conditioned aversions are normally measured as decreased voluntary intake of the taste on reexposure (animals passively avoid the CS). With IO delivery animals cannot avoid the infused solution, but aversions can be displayed by active expulsion of the fluid from the mouth.

Most studies aimed at determining the neural circuitry underlying taste aversion learning have employed the bottle method (Chambers, 1990; Dunn & Everitt, 1988). However, there is evidence that CTA learning using the bottle and IO methods may vary in their reliance on specific brain regions, particularly the amygdala (Schafe, Thiele, & Bernstein, 1998; Wang, Fontanini, & Katz, 2006). In these studies excitotoxic lesions of the amygdala were found to eliminate CTA acquisition using the IO method but to have no effect on the learning when animals were bottle conditioned. Results were taken to be indicative of a crucial role for amygdala in IO but not bottle conditioning of CTAs.

This implies that different, but perhaps over-lapping, brain regions are activated during aver-sion conditioning depending on the conditioning method used and raise the question of whether the two methods engage different brain regions during CTA acquisition, that is, when the novel taste was paired with illness. To address this issue we used FLI to assess neuronal activation patterns follow-ing novel or familiar saccharin–LiCl pairing using either bottle or IO delivery.

Half of the rats in this study were implanted with indwelling IO cannulae constructed of poly-ethylene tubing. Both bottle and IO rats received either 0.5% saccharin solution (familiar condi-tion) or water (novel condition) for 30 min each day during 6 days of preexposure training. On the seventh day, all rats were given saccharin to drink with intake capped at 5 ml in 30 min, and then immediately injected with 0.15-M LiCl (5 ml/kg body weight, IP). Ninety minutes after the injec-tion, they were sacrificed and their brains were processed for FLI.

Novel CS–US pairing using bottle condition-ing yielded results similar to Koh and Bernstein (2005). Significant FLI elevations relative to familiar CS–US pairing were observed in a distributed circuit including IC, CNA, BLA, and iNTS. Significant FLI elevations were not observed in PBN, which may have been due to poor staining and low numbers of FLI-positive neurons in all groups. In contrast to bottle conditioning, when the CS was IO-infused, novel CS–US pairing elevations in FLI (relative to familiar CS–US pairing) were restricted to the CNA (Figure 16.7) (Wilkins & Bernstein, 2006).

Thus, patterns of neuronal activation during CTA processing appear to differ considerably based on the method of CS exposure, with a stronger, more widely distributed pattern of activation observed following taste exposure from a bottle. One question that arises from an examination of these different patterns of activation is whether they reflect differences in the strength or effectiveness of conditioning rather than the conditioning method per se. To evaluate this, the strength of conditioning generated by these two methods was assessed. As shown in Figure 16.8, both conditioning methods produced strong aversions using the same CS–US parameters as in the FLI experiment (i.e., 0.5% saccharin and 0.15-M LiCl at 0.5% bodyweight). Further testing using a

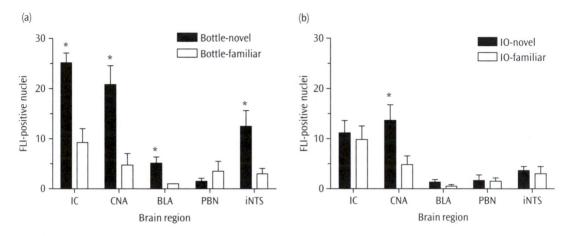

Figure 16.7. Mean (+ SEM) number of FLI-positive nuclei in the insular cortex (IC), central (CNA) and basolateral (BLA) subnuclei of the amygdala, parabrachial nucleus (PBN), and intermediate nucleus of the solitary tract (iNTS) following novel or familiar taste–illness pairing using bottle (a) or IO (b) conditioning methods. *$p < 0.05$ between novel and familiar groups.

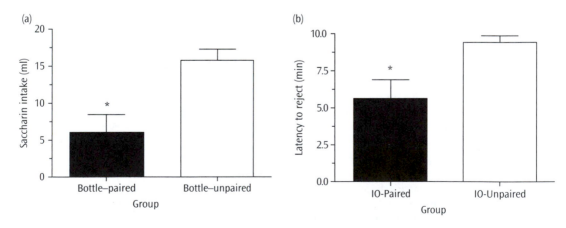

Figure 16.8. (a) Mean (+ SEM) intake of 0.5% saccharin solution by bottle-conditioned animals and controls. (b) Mean (± SEM) latency for IO-conditioned animals and controls to reject infused 0.5% saccharin. *$p < 0.05$ between paired and unpaired groups.

more sensitive two-bottle measure provided no evidence that bottle-conditioned animals developed stronger aversions than IO-conditioned animals. In fact, the trend was in the opposite direction, with bottle groups demonstrating weaker aversions than IO-conditioned animals (Figure 16.9) (Wilkins & Bernstein, 2006).

Overall, patterns of FLI activation suggest a distributed network of involvement in CTA acquisition when animals are conditioned with a bottle, but an activation pattern which is limited to the CNA when animals are conditioned with IO infusions. This difference in distribution of neural activity associated with the two types of conditioning could explain the heavy reliance on amygdala of IO conditioning that was indicated by the lesion data of Schafe et al. (1998). Amygdala-lesioned animals were still able to learn aversions when bottle conditioned, implying redundant processing of the association through activation of a broader neural network, which parallels the FLI results of the present study.

Taken together, the results of this study reveal dramatic differences in the circuitry involved in taste–illness association depending on the method of taste delivery. Koh et al.'s (2003) finding that patterns of FLI elevation to a novel taste do not differ between the two conditioning methods suggests that the patterns seen in the present study occur during associative processing rather than mere taste exposure. Bottle conditioning, which more closely resembles an animal's experience in the wild, engages a broad network of brain areas, implying redundant processing within the circuit. Given the importance of taste aversion learning to an animal's survival, such redundancy ensures that the association will be made and that the animal will be able to benefit from the learning. Though the IO method is closer to classical conditioning, it hardly resembles an animal's natural experience. As previously mentioned, the animal is passively exposed to the taste and this lack of behavioral involvement may somehow relate to the restricted neuronal activation pattern. Of course the choice of model system to study underlying mechanisms is an interesting and important question. There is general agreement that simple systems can often provide advantages in neurobiological assessments. The present findings clearly demonstrate differences in the complexity of the circuits underlying these two ways of conditioning taste aversions. Given the more distributed circuit and greater redundancy in the bottle paradigm, the simpler IO circuit could have advantages in some neurobiological assessments.

Analysis of these two conditioning methods suggests that bottle conditioning has an "instrumental" component while IO conditioning conforms more closely to classical conditioning. The neural mediators of different types of learning have been shown to be dissociable. Interestingly, the amygdala has been shown to be essential for other aversive Pavlovian conditioning tasks (Maren, 2003). Although the role of the amygdala in fear conditioning has been somewhat controversial, much of the controversy can be attributed to differences in conditioning methods. For example, lesions of the BLA have been shown to disrupt Pavlovian fear conditioning, in which CS and US onset are under the control of the experimenter (Muller, Corodimas, Fridel, & LeDoux, 1997). However, when animals are required to press a lever to initiate the conditioning trial or receive footshock following a behavioral response, as in inhibitory avoidance paradigms and "shock-probe" procedures (Lehmann, Treit, & Parent, 2003), BLA lesions have little effect on the learning (Killcross, Robbins, & Everitt, 1997; McNew & Thompson, 1966). Thus, subtle variations in conditioning methods can have dramatic effects on underlying neural circuitry, and this has now been demonstrated in two aversive, adaptive, defensive conditioning paradigms, fear conditioning, and taste aversion learning.

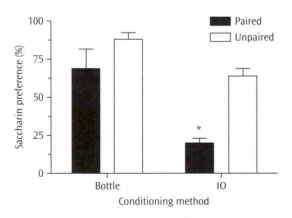

Figure 16.9. Mean (+ SEM) percent saccharin preference during 3-h, two-bottle (water and saccharin) test after previous bottle or IO conditioning. *$p < 0.001$ between IO groups.

Table 16.2 Summary of Effects of CS Taste Novelty and CS–US Pairing on Regional Expression of fos-like Immunoreactivity (FLI).

	IC	BLA	CNA	HPC	lPBN	mPBN	rNTS	iNTS
CS Taste (0.5% saccharin)	↑[a,b]	—[a,c]	↑[a,b]	—[c]	—[c]	—[a,c]	—[a,c]	—[c]
CS–US pairing (bottle)	↑[d]	↑[d]	↑[d]	—[d]	↑[d]	↑[d]	N/A	↑[d]
CS–US pairing (intraoral)	—[e]	—[e]	↑[e]	N/A	—[e,f]	—[e,f]	N/A	—[e]

Notes: IC = insular cortex, BLA = basolateral amygdala, CNA = central amygdala, HPC = hippocampus, lPBN = lateral parabrachial nucleus, mPBN = medial parabrachial nucleus, rNTS = rostral nucleus of the solitary tract, iNTS = intermediate nucleus of the solitary tract, ↑ = significantly higher levels of FLI expression relative to controls, — = no difference, and N/A = not available.

[a] Koh et al. (2003).
[b] See text for details.
[c] Koh and Bernstein (unpublished data).
[d] Koh and Bernstein (2005).
[e] Wilkins and Bernstein (2006).
[f] Lateral and medial subregions were not scored separately.

CONCLUSIONS

Assessment of Fos expression in response to novel tastes implicates IC and amygdala as sites for processing stimuli critical to CTA learning. However, the same stimulus, when paired with LiCl, engages a more distributed circuit that includes multiple brain regions. A summary of the patterns of FLI seen across multiple studies is presented in Table 16.2. The specific roles of these regions in the acquisition process are a topic of investigation in our laboratory. In particular, we are currently examining how the PBN, which has been so strongly implicated in CTA acquisition through lesion studies (e.g., Reilly, Grigson, & Norgren, 1993), fits into this picture. Increased activation in this distributed circuit during acquisition could reflect either the transmission of CS and US information to a site of convergence (e.g., amygdala), the receiving of critical information from the site of convergence to facilitate CS–US association and memory consolidation, or a combination of both. Activation of IC during acquisition, for instance, has been linked to the detection of CS taste novelty and the transfer of that information to the amygdala. Appropriately, lesions of IC were found to reduce FLI expression in the amygdala to novel CS–US pairings, while temporary inactivation of IC during taste familiarization resulted in increased FLI expression in the amygdala to familiar CS–US pairing during CTA acquisition (Koh & Bernstein, 2005). These findings suggest a high degree of interdependence among multiple brain regions for successful acquisition of a CTA.

Our studies have begun to define a distributed circuit in which neural activation is strongly modulated by taste novelty during CS–US pairing. Controls with identical stimulus exposure provide a relatively conservative comparison group. Clearly, the conditions that support CTA learning engage multiple brain sites. By combining FLI with focal and reversible lesions, we get a more nuanced view of how the circuit interacts as it processes CTA associations. Furthermore, it becomes clear that lesions in one site strongly affect activity of other structures in the circuit. By applying these combined approaches at different nodes in the CTA circuit, we expect to better define its functional anatomy.

References

Abrams, T. W., & Kandel, E. R. (1988). Is contiguity detection in classical conditioning a system or a cellular property? Learning in Aplysia suggests a possible molecular site. *Trends in Neurosciences, 11,* 128–135.

Ackroff, K., Manza, L., & Sclafani, A. (1993). The rat's preference for sucrose, Polycose and their mixtures. *Appetite, 21,* 69–80.

Barot, S. K., & Bernstein, I. L. (2005). Polycose taste pre-exposure fails to influence behavioral and neural indices of taste novelty. *Behavioral Neuroscience, 119,* 1640–1647.

Bermúdez-Rattoni, F. (2004). Molecular mechanisms of taste-recognition memory. *Nature Review Neuroscience, 5,* 209–217.

Bermúdez-Rattoni, F., & Yamamoto, T. (1998). Neuroanatomy of conditioned taste aversion: Lesion studies. In J. Bures, F. Bermúdez-Rattoni, & T. Yamamoto (Eds.), *Conditioned taste aversion: Memory of a special kind* (pp. 26–45). Oxford: Oxford University Press.

Bernstein, I. L. (1991). Flavor aversion. In T. V. Getchell, R. L. Doty, L. M. Bartoshuk, & J. B. Snow (Eds.), *Smell and taste in health and disease* (pp. 417–428). New York: Raven Press.

Bernstein, I. L., & Koh, M. T. (2006). Molecular signaling during taste aversion learning. *Chemical Senses, 32,* 99–103.

Brand, J. G. (2000). Receptor and transduction processes for umami taste. *Journal of Nutrition, 130,* 942–945.

Chambers, K. C. (1990). A neural model for conditioned taste aversions. *Annual Review of Neuroscience, 13,* 373–385.

Chambers, K. C., & Bernstein, I. L. (1995). Conditioned flavor aversions. In R. L. Doty (Ed.), *Handbook of medical olfaction and taste* (pp. 745–773). New York: Marcel Dekker.

Domjan, M. (1980). Ingestional aversion learning: Unique and general processes. In J. S. Rosenblatt, R. A. Hinde, C. G. Beer, & M. C. Busnel (Eds.), *Advances in the study of behavior* (Vol. 11, pp. 275–336). New York: Academic Press.

Dragoin, W. B. (1971). Conditioning and extinction of taste aversions with variations in intensity of the CS and the UCS in two strains of rats. *Psychonomic Science, 22,* 303–305.

Dunn, L. T., & Everitt, B. J. (1988). Double dissociations of the effects of amygdala and insular cortex lesions on conditioned taste aversion, passive avoidance, and neophobia in rat using the excitotoxin ibotenic acid. *Behavioral Neuroscience, 102,* 3–23.

Garcia, J., Ervin, F. R., & Koelling, R. A. (1966). Learning with prolonged delay of reinforcement. *Psychonomic Science, 5,* 121–122.

Garcia, J., Hankins, W. G., & Rusiniak, K. W. (1974). Behavioral regulation of the milieu interne in man and rat. *Science, 185,* 824–831.

Giza, B. K., Scott, T. R., Sclafani, A., & Antonucci, R. F. (1991). Polysaccharides as taste stimuli: Their effect in the nucleus tractus solitarius of the rat. *Brain Research, 555,* 1–9.

Houpt, T. A., Philopena, J. M., Joh, T. H., & Smith, G. P. (1996). c-Fos induction in the rat nucleus of the solitary tract correlates with the retention and forgetting of a conditioned taste aversion. *Learning & Memory, 3*(1), 25–30.

Kalat, J. W. (1974). Taste salience depends on novelty, not concentration, in taste-aversion learning in the rat. *Journal of Comparative and Physiological Psychology, 86,* 47–50.

Kalat, J. W., & Rozin, P. (1973). "Learned safety" as a mechanism in long-delay taste-aversion learning in the rat. *Journal of Comparative and Physiolological Psychology, 83,* 198–207.

Killcross, S., Robbins, T. W., & Everitt, B. J. (1997). Different types of fear-conditioned behaviour mediated by separate nuclei within amygdala. *Nature, 388,* 377–380.

Koh, M. T., & Bernstein, I. L. (2005). Mapping conditioned taste aversion associations using c-Fos reveals a dynamic role for insular cortex. *Behavioral Neuroscience, 119*(2), 388–398.

Koh, M. T., Wilkins, E. E., & Bernstein, I. L. (2003). Novel taste elevates c-fos expression in the central amygdala and insular cortex: Implication for taste aversion learning. *Behavioral Neuroscience, 117,* 1416–1422.

Lamprecht, R., & Dudai, Y. (1995). Differential modulation of brain immediate early genes by intraperitoneal LiCl. *Neuroreport, 7,* 289–293.

Lamprecht, R., & Dudai, Y. (1996). Transient expression of c-fos in rat amygdala during training is required for encoding conditioned taste aversion memory. *Learning & Memory, 3,* 31–41.

Lehmann, H., Treit, D., & Parent, M. B. (2003). Spared anterograde memory for shock-probe fear conditioning after inactivation of the amygdala. *Learning & Memory, 10,* 306–308.

Maren, S. (2003). What the amygdala does and doesn't do in aversive learning. *Learning & Memory, 10,* 306–308.

McNew, J. J., & Thompson, R. (1966). Role of the limbic system in active and passive avoidance conditioning in the rat. *Journal of Comparative and Physiological Psychology, 61,* 173–180.

Midkiff, E., Fitts, D. A., Simpson, J. B., & Bernstein, I. L. (1985). Absence of sodium chloride preference in Fischer-344 rats. *American Journal of Physiology, 249,* R438–R442.

Muller, J., Corodimas, K. P., Fridel, Z., & LeDoux, J. E. (1997). Functional inactivation of the lateral and basal nuclei of the amygdala by muscimol infusion prevents fear conditioning to an explicit conditioned stimulus and to contextual stimuli. *Behavioral Neuroscience, 111,* 683–691.

Nissenbaum, J. W., & Sclafani, A. (1987). Qualitative differences in polysaccharide and sugar tastes in the rat: A two carbohydrate taste model. *Neuroscience and Biobehavioral Reviews, 11*, 187–196.

Reilly, S., & Bornovalova, M. A. (2005). Conditioned taste aversion and amygdala lesions in the rat: A critical review. *Neuroscience and Biobehavioral Reviews, 29*, 1067–1088.

Reilly, S., Grigson, P. S., & Norgren, R. (1993). Parabrachial nucleus lesions and conditioned taste aversion: Evidence supporting an associative deficit. *Behavioral Neuroscience, 107*, 1005–1017.

Revusky, S. H., & Bedarf, E. W. (1967). Association of illness with prior ingestion of novel foods. *Science, 155*, 219–220.

Revusky, S. H., & Garcia, J. (1970). Learned association over long delays. In G. H. Bower & J. T. Spence (Eds.), *Psychology of learning and motivation* (Vol. 4, pp. 1–84). New York: Academic Press.

Sako, N., Shimura, T., Komure, M., Mochizuki, R., Matsuko, R., & Yamamoto, T. (1994). Differences in taste responses to Polycose and common sugars in the rat as revealed by behavioral and electrophysiological studies. *Physiology and Behavior, 56*, 741–745.

Schafe, G. E., Seeley, R. J., & Bernstein, I. L. (1995). Forebrain contribution to the induction of a cellular correlate of conditioned taste aversion in the nucleus of the solitary tract. *Journal of Neuroscience, 15*, 6789–6796.

Schafe, G. E., Thiele, T. E., & Bernstein, I. L. (1998). Conditioning method dramatically alters the role of amygdala in taste aversion learning. *Learning & Memory, 5*, 481–492.

Sclafani, A. (2004). The sixth taste? *Appetite, 43*, 1–3.

Sclafani, A., & Nissenbaum, J. W. (1987). Taste preference thresholds for Polycose, maltose and Sucrose in rats. *Neuroscience and Biobehavioral Reviews, 11*, 181–185.

Spray, K. J., & Bernstein, I. L. (2004). Afferent and efferent connections of the parvicellular subdivision of iNTS: Defining a circuit involved in taste aversion learning. *Behavioral Brain Research, 154*, 85–97.

Swank, M. W. (1996). c-Fos antisense blocks acquisition and extinction of conditioned taste aversion in mice. *Neuroreport, 7*, 1866–1870.

Swank, M. W. (1999). Coordinate regulation of Fos and Jun proteins in mouse brain by LiCl. *Neuroreport, 10*, 3685–3689.

Swank, M. W., & Bernstein, I. L. (1994). c-Fos induction in response to a conditioned stimulus after single trial taste aversion learning. *Brain Research, 636*, 202–208.

Wang, Y., Fontanini, A., & Katz, D. B. (2006). Temporary basolateral amygdala lesions disrupt acquisition of socially transmitted food preferences in rats. *Learning & Memory, 13*, 794–800.

Wilkins, E. E., & Bernstein, I. L. (2006). Conditioning method determines patterns of c-fos expression following novel taste–illness pairing. *Behavioural Brain Research, 169*, 93–97.

Yasoshima, Y., Sako, N., Senba, E., & Yamamoto, T. (2006). Acute suppresion, but not chronic genetic deficiency, of c-fos gene expression impairs long-term memory in aversive taste learning. *Proceedings of the National Academy of Sciences, 103*, 7106–7111.

Yasoshima, Y., Yamamoto, T., & Kobayashi, K. (2005). Amygdala-dependent mechanisms underlying memory retrieval of conditioned taste aversion. *Chemical Senses, 30*(Suppl. 1), i158–i159.

17

Molecular Mechanisms of Taste Learning in the Insular Cortex and Amygdala

LIZA BARKI-HARRINGTON, KATYA BELELOVSKY, GUY DORON,
AND KOBI ROSENBLUM

On the assumption that taste learning and conditioned taste aversion (CTA) are not different from any other known forms of learning and memory, and given that the brain loci involved are known, one would look at the cellular (electrophysiological) and molecular/biochemical levels of analysis in order to understand the biological processes underlying taste and CTA learning.

The field of molecular and cellular mechanisms of learning and memory has developed tremendously in the last few years. The current notion in the field presumes that learning has different temporal processes, and it is mediated mainly via modulation of synaptic strength in the relevant brain area/second. Memory formation is expected to be mediated via posttranslational modifications of preexisting proteins, for example, by protein phosphorylation, in a time ranging from milliseconds to minutes. In contrast, the consolidation phase is assumed to be mediated via regulation of cellular translation and modification of gene expression in a time ranging from minutes to hours or days. This proposed concept forms the basis of the work of diverse researchers in the field of biological mechanisms of learning and memory, including those working on taste learning.

In the last few years various researchers have obtained valuable and important data on molecular mechanisms of taste and CTA learning. The behavioral and neuroanatomical aspects (see Figure 17.1 for simplified version of the neuroanatomical circuit underlying taste learning and memory) of taste learning and CTA are not discussed

within this chapter. This chapter aims to cover only few molecular aspects of taste learning occurring in two forebrain areas: the gustatory cortex (GC) and the amygdala. Specifically, the molecular aspects covered in this chapter are the following:

1. The role of the neurotransmitter glutamate and its receptor.
2. The role of mRNA translation regulation in memory consolidation.
3. The role of gene expression, especially c-Fos.

It is not difficult to imagine that the rapid and exciting technological development in life sciences will facilitate our understanding in this highly complex subject of the biological mechanisms underlying learning and memory processes in general, and specifically, those involved in the various forms of taste learning.

ROLES OF GLUTAMATE AND GLUTAMATE RECEPTORS (GluRs) IN THE AMYGDALA AND INSULAR CORTEX DURING TASTE MEMORY FORMATION AND CONSOLIDATION

Glutamatergic Receptors— Introduction

The excitatory amino acid, glutamate is the major transmitter that accounts for most of the fast

Taste pathway

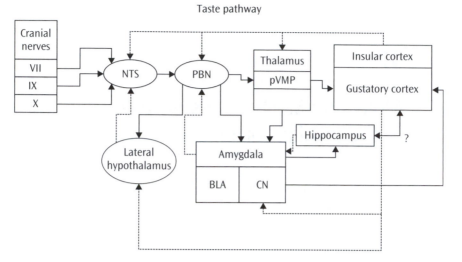

Figure 17.1. The neuroanatomy of the taste system. The processing of gustatory information begins with transduction of chemical stimuli that reach the oral cavity. Taste can be divided among five primary sensations: salty, sour, sweet, bitter, and umami. Typically, taste cells are broadly tuned and respond to several taste stimuli. The sensitivity to taste quality is not uniformly distributed throughout the oral cavity, and the same chemotopic arrangement is preserved to some degree at the gustatory relay.

Taste cells are innervated by cranial nerves, II, V, IX, X, which project to the primary gustatory nucleus in the brainstem (nucleus of solitary tract, NTS). The NTS sends information to three different systems:

1. The reflex system: this comprises medullatory and reticular formation neurons that innervate the cranial motor nuclei (trigeminal, facial, and hypoglossal).
2. The lemniscal system: The gustatory portion of the NTS projects to the secondary nucleus situated in the dorsal pons (parabrachial nucleus, PBN). The PBN sends axons to the ventromedial nucleus of the thalamus (VPMpc), which, in turn, relays gustatory information to the anterior part of the IC (gustatory cortex, GC). The transition from the somatosensory lingual representation to the gustatory representation corresponds to the transition from the granular to the agranular IC. The GC is thus situated dorsally to the intersection of middle cerebral artery and the rhinal sulcus, and can be identified easily using these two markers. Whereas rodents have only a primary taste cortex, humans also have a second one.
3. The visceral-limbic system: The central gustatory pathway involves a collateral network of connections to the hypothalamus and limbic areas in the forebrain. The PBN is connected to the amygdala, the hypothalamus, and the bed nucleus of the stria terminalis. All the limbic gustatory targets are interconnected with each other as well as with the PBN and the GC.

The GC and the thalamocortical system are required for acquisition and retention of taste information. The amygdala is required for learning the negative and possibly positive values of a taste. The prefrontal cortex is involved in CTA extinction. It is not clear what the specific role of the hippocampus is in taste learning, though it is hypothesized that it takes part in novel taste learning.

synaptic transmission in the mammalian nervous system. Glutamate is synthesized in the central nervous system (CNS) and stored in synaptic vesicles, from which it is released in a calcium-dependent manner upon depolarization of the nerve terminal. On release into the synapses, glutamate stimulates several types of receptors to relay several different functions, as discussed later. Its major mode of inactivation is via reuptake by dicarboxylic (glutamate) acid transporters back into presynaptic terminals (reviewed in Dingledine, Borges, Bowie, & Traynelis, 1999).

The actions of glutamate in the CNS are mediated by *metabotropic* and *ionotropic* receptors—two essentially distinct forms of gluta-mate receptors, which vary considerably in their structure and function. *Metabotropic* glutamate receptors (mGluRs) belong to the superfamily of seven membrane-spanning receptors, which relay their signals via binding of ligand to the extra-cellular domain of the receptor, followed by a sequential activation of G proteins and second messenger-generating systems. mGluRs are wide-spread in the CNS, with both pre- and postsyn-aptic functions. Their presynaptic function is as autoreceptors, which modulate neurotransmitter release (Cochilla & Alford, 1998; Koulen, Kuhn, Wassle, & Brandstatter, 1999). Their postsynap-tic functions vary, depending on the G protein to which they couple. Members of the mGluR1 family have been implicated in long-term synap-tic plasticity in many brain areas, including long-term potentiation (LTP) and long-term depression (LTD; Harney, Rowan, & Anwyl, 2006; Nicholls et al., 2006).

The *ionotropic* glutamatergic receptors are ligand-gated ion channels that, when activated, cause neuronal depolarization by generating fast excitatory postsynaptic potentials. These recep-tors belong to the superfamily of P-loop channels, which also includes potassium, sodium, and cal-cium channels. Ionotropic glutamate receptors are thought to be tetrameric, with distinct functional properties for each of their subunits. The amino terminal domain is the site of action for molecules that modulate glutamate receptor function, and it also modulates the assembly of subunits within the receptor complex. The ligand-binding domain consists of two regions; the membrane-associated region consists of three transmembrane-spanning domains and a reentrant loop. An intracellular carboxy terminal domain contains a number of structural motifs that allow the interaction with numerous signal transduction and scaffolding proteins, and it is important for correct regula-tion, trafficking, and localization of the receptor protein, which is reviewed in Chen et al. (2004).

According to their selectivity to nonphysi-ological glutamate agonists, ionotropic gluta-mate receptors are classified into three families: N-methyl-D-aspartate (NMDA) receptors, α-amino 3-hydroxy 5-methylisoxazoleproprionic acid (AMPA) receptors, and kainate receptors (KA). Whereas AMPA receptors are encoded by a single gene family, kinate receptors are encoded by two, and NMDA receptors by three gene families (reviewed in

Dingledine et al., 1999). AMPA receptors can exist as either homomeric or heteromeric assemblies of GluR1–4 receptor subunits, whereas kinate recep-tors are homomeric or heteromeric assemblies of GluR5–7 and KA1 and KA2 subunits. The NMDA receptor (NR) is unique among the glu-tamate receptors in that it requires the binding of both glutamate and the co-agonist glycine to the receptor, to enable the channel to open. Glycine binds to NR1 subunit whereas glutamate binds to NR2A–D subunits. NR can also contain NR3A or NR3B subunits that modulate channel function (Chen et al., 2004).

Expression of Glutamatergic Receptors in the Amygdala and Insular Cortex

Information regarding the distribution of gluta-matergic receptors in the taste cortex and amygdala is of great importance for our understanding of the mechanisms of novel taste and CTA learning. Characterization of receptor distribution makes use of several techniques, including radioactively labeled ligands or immuno-based techniques based on an antibody directed against a specific epitope of the desired receptor. Nonetheless, detailed immunohistochemistry (IHC) and immunocy-tochemistry (ICC) studies of glutamatergic recep-tor distribution in these areas are quite scarce, and sometimes have yielded conflicting results. Thus, these findings alone do not provide a complete picture of which receptors are, in fact, involved in novel taste acquisition, or of their absolute num-bers and relative contributions. Thus, the currently available data have to be integrated with the find-ings of biochemical and electrophysiological stud-ies in order to elucidate the roles of the various molecular participants in taste acquisition.

By using a marked D-serine ligand, which binds to the glycine modulatory site on the ubiquitously expressed NR1, Schell, Molliver, and Snyder (1995) were able to show that in the rat brain the highest levels of NRs are found in the grey mat-ter of the cerebral cortex, hippocampus, olfactory tubercle, and amygdala. A detailed study based on receptor binding and autoradiography techniques also confirmed the existence of high levels of NRs in the insular cortex (IC) of rats and humans (Mugnaini, Meoni, Bunnemann, Corsi, & Bowery, 2001). A closer look at the lateral and basal nuclei of the amygdala revealed the existence of NRs in presynaptic axon terminals. Labeled presynaptic terminals formed asymmetric and symmetric synapses, suggesting presynaptic regulation of both excitatory and inhibitory transmission (Farb, Aoki, & Ledoux, 1995). Examination of the thalamic afferents that lead to the amygdala showed that the majority of the neurons contact dendritic spines that express at least one type of glutamate receptor; this constitutes morphological evidence that thalamic afferents synapse directly onto basolateral amygdala (BLA) neurons that express glutamate receptors (Farb & LeDoux, 1997). At the cellular level, high levels of NR1 were found in pyramidal neurons of the BLA of mouse and monkey brains (McDonald, 1994).

Although probing the NR1 subunit is a useful means of localizing NRs in the brain, it does not distinguish between NR2 or NR3 subunits, which regulate channel properties. Studies in which the distribution of NR2 and NR3 subunits in the amygdala was dissected out are scarce. An electrophysiological study of the interneurons of the BLA revealed a possible involvement of NR2B, which was indicated by sensitivity to the NR2B selective blocker ifenprodil (Szinyei, Stork, & Pape, 2003). A behavioral response to intra-amygdalar infusions of ifenprodil also confirms the presence of functional NR2B in the amygdala (Schroeder, Olive, Koenig, & Hodge, 2003). A study of the various amygdala nuclei showed that synapses in the central nucleus activate NMDA receptors that contain NR1 and NR2B subunits, whereas synapses in the lateral nucleus contain receptors with both NR2A and NR2B subunits (Sah & Lopez De Armentia, 2003). A subsequent study that used real-time PCR and Western blotting found that in adult rats, the ratio of NR2B to NR2A subunit levels was greater in the central amygdala than in the lateral amygdala (Lopez de Armentia & Sah, 2003). Double staining for NR2 subunits in the mouse revealed the expression of both NR2B and NR2C subunits in the cholinergic cells of the basal nucleus (De Souza Silva et al., 2006). Finally, NR3A NMDA mRNA and protein analysis showed high expression throughout much of the adult primate brain including the neocortex and the amygdala (Pende et al., 2004).

Fast excitatory synaptic responses in BLA neurons are mainly mediated by AMPA glutamate receptors. AMPA receptors that contain a GluR2 subunit are calcium impermeable, whereas those that lack this subunit are calcium permeable and are also inwardly rectifying. Therefore, the extent to which synapses in the rat BLA have AMPA receptors with GluR2 subunits is critical to the memory formation mechanisms. Immunoreactivity studies of the localization of the various subunits of the AMPA receptor (GluR1, GluR2/3, and GluR4) in the amygdala revealed an almost constant distribution across neuronal populations, with some variations that may be specific to certain cell types. GluR1 and GluR2/3 were predominantly localized to dendritic shafts and were more widely distributed than GluR4. The distribution of GluR4 was similar to that of NR1, in that it was seen in presynaptic terminals, glia, and dendrites, and was primarily localized to spines (Farb et al., 1995). Conversely, a study by Y. He, Janssen, and Morrison (1999) showed that GluR2 subunits were widely and uniformly distributed in both pyramidal and nonpyramidal cells in the BLA.

Double-label immunohistochemical analyses demonstrated that over 90% of the GABAergic interneurons were labeled for GluR2, and electron microscope analyses further confirmed the presence of GluR2 in the soma and dendrites of GABAergic interneurons as well as in the soma, spines, and dendritic shafts of pyramidal cells in the BLA (Y. He et al., 1999). On the other hand, a two-color immunoperoxidase study found GluR1 subunits only in nonpyramidal neurons, whereas robust GluR2/3 AMPA subunits were seen only in pyramidal cells (McDonald, 1994, 1996). A combined immunocytochemical and electrophysiological recordings from amygdala brain slices revealed that GluR2s were localized to the perikarya and proximal dendrites of BLA neurons. In electron micrographs of the BLA, most of the synapses were asymmetrical, with pronounced postsynaptic densities. Only 11% of morphological synapses in the BLA connected with postsynaptic elements that showed GluR2 immunoreactivity. Synaptic staining in the BLA was exclusively postsynaptic and was particularly heavy over the postsynaptic density (PSD). In whole-cell voltage-clamp recordings, most principal BLA neurons exhibited AMPA receptor-mediated synaptic currents that were elicited by inwardly rectifying external capsule stimulations. Although BLA principal neurons express perikaryal and proximal dendritic GluR2 immunoreactivity, few synapses onto these neurons express GluR2, and a preponderance of principal neurons have inwardly rectifying AMPA-mediated synaptic currents, which suggests that targeting of

GluR2 to synapses is restricted. Many BLA synaptic AMPA receptors are likely to be calcium permeable and could play roles in synaptic plasticity (Gryder, Castaneda, & Rogawski, 2005).

Neurotransmitters Involved in Taste Learning

In the context of taste memory, several neurotransmitters were identified as mediators of this process. As in the case of translation regulation, a glutamatergic activation was widely investigated as a possible candidate for sustaining CTA memory consolidation. A study by H. Gutierrez et al. (1999) found that local injections of the NMDA antagonist, APV, into the IC prior to taste aversion conditioning strongly disrupted the acquisition of this task. Similarly, activation of the NMDA receptor in IC was shown to be necessary for CTA memory formation and consolidation (Berman & Dudai, 2001; Berman, Hazvi, Neduva, & Dudai, 2000; Ferreira, Gutierrez, De La Cruz, & Bermudez-Rattoni, 2002; Rosenblum, Berman, Hazvi, Lamprecht, & Dudai, 1997), and a significant release of glutamate in the IC was observed following lithium chloride (LiCl) injection (Miranda, Ferreira, Ramirez-Lugo, & Bermudez-Rattoni, 2002).

The involvement of NMDA and muscarinic receptors in the nucleus accumbens (NAc) was also confirmed, by showing that pretraining injections of their antagonists, APV and scopolamine, respectively, disrupted taste memory formation (Ramirez-Lugo, Zavala-Vega, & Bermudez-Rattoni, 2006). In a study of the possible interaction between the basolateral nucleus of the amygdala (BLA) and the IC during CTA memory formation, the effects of glutamate and APV injections into these areas prior to the CTA were examined. It was found that glutamate injection into the BLA enhanced the CTA, whereas APV treatment of the IC at the same time as, or 1 h after, the ipsilateral BLA injection reversed the glutamate-induced CTA enhancement (Ferreira, Miranda, De la Cruz, Rodriguez-Ortiz, & Bermudez-Rattoni, 2005).

Another study indicated that alterations in noradrenergic function in the BLA affected the consolidation of both CTA and incidental gustatory memory (Miranda et al., 2002). With regard to the cholinergic activity involved in memory processes, numerous studies have demonstrated that taste aversion memory formation was eliminated when scopolamine or atropine, nonselective antagonists of muscarinic ACh, were injected into the IC several days after CTA acquisition (Berman et al., 2000; Ferreira et al., 2002; Naor & Dudai, 1996; R. Gutierrez, Rodriguez-Ortiz, De La Cruz, Nunez-Jaramillo, & Bermudez-Rattoni, 2003; R. Gutierrez, Tellez, & Bermudez-Rattoni, 2003; Ramirez-Lugo, Miranda, Escobar, Espinosa, & Bermudez-Rattoni, 2003).

Furthermore, it has been demonstrated that injection of scopolamine together with the first presentation of a novel taste blocked latent inhibition (LI; Naor & Dudai, 1996), and, surprisingly, that scopolamine microinjections, either before or after taste presentation, impaired LI in a similar way, which suggests that the cholinergic system is involved in the acquisition and consolidation of taste memory (R. Gutierrez, Rodriguez-Ortiz, et al., 2003; R. Gutierrez, Tellez, et al., 2003). In keeping with these findings, Miranda, Ramirez-Lugo, and Bermudez-Rattoni (2000) showed that presentation of a novel taste led to significant increments of ACh release in the IC.

Effect of Glutamatergic Stimulation in the Amygdala and IC on Taste Memory Formation

The IC plays an important role in the acquisition and storage of various aversion-motivated learning tasks, such as CTA, spatial maze, and inhibitory avoidance. Two major approaches are taken to address the role of glutamatergic stimulation in taste memory formation in the IC: (1) the use of chemical antagonists of the various glutamate receptors and (2) area-specific lesions. Each method is used in conjunction with several different taste behavioral paradigms (e.g., CTA, LI, attenuation of gustatory neophobia), and together they are beginning to elucidate which neurotransmitter/s underlie taste learning in the brain.

Local application of glutamatergic receptor antagonists by microinjection into the IC of rats has proved a useful way to address the role(s) of these receptors in taste memory formation. Neurons containing both NMDA and AMPA receptors are most abundant in the granular area of the IC and application of either the selective NMDA antagonist APV or the non-NMDA antagonist CNQX to this area results in a similar amount of suppression of the taste responses (Otawa, Takagi, & Ogawa, 1995). Several studies addressed the role of NRs in acquisition and consolidation of taste memory. Escobar, Alcocer, and Chao (1998) showed that whereas the administration of the mGluR antagonist MCPG to the IC had no effect, administration of the NR competitive antagonists CPP or APV disrupted the acquisition of CTA, as well as the induction of IC-LTP in vivo. The time point of NR antagonist application was found to be critical to the blocking of taste memory and LTP, as the effect of injection *after* introduction of the taste input was NR independent (Rosenblum et al., 1997). When comparing the roles of NRs in short-term memory (STM) and in long-term memory (LTM), it has been shown that injection of APV during the acquisition state impaired LTM but not STM only if the injection was done prior to presentation of the taste stimulus (Ferreira et al., 2002). On the other hand, the same group found that inhibition of the NRs after the induction of malaise in a CTA paradigm disrupted both STM and LTM, suggesting that perhaps NRs may participate in taste memory consolidation after all.

Whereas the role of NRs in CTA is reasonably well understood, it is more controversial in other behavioral paradigms, such as attenuation of neophobia. Indeed, although microinfusion of the NR antagonist MK-801 into the IC of rats attenuated neophobia in one study (Figueroa-Guzman et al., 2006), injection of APV had no effect, which indicates an NR-independent mechanism (R. Gutierrez, Rodriguez-Ortiz, et al., 2003). One possible explanation for these differences lies in the nature of the antagonism exhibited by the respective compounds: one binding only to activated NRs (MK-801), whereas the other (APV) blocks all NRs.

Another means of determining the role of NRs in taste memory formation is by inducing directed lesions to the IC. Indeed, whereas NR-induced lesions in the amygdala had no effect, lesions to the IC in rats significantly attenuated CTA (Bures, Bermudez-Rattoni, & Yamamoto, 1998). A more detailed study showed that the central but not the anterior or posterior IC was crucial for the acquisition of both the CTA learning and the Morris water maze (Nerad, Ramirez-Amaya, Ormsby, & Bermudez-Rattoni, 1996). These findings support the view that the IC is strongly involved in the acquisition of external as well as visceral aversion-motivated behavior.

Neurons in the amygdala are involved in mediation of hedonic appreciation, emotional expression, and conditioning, particularly as these relate to feeding. The amygdala receives projections from the primary taste cortex, which is thereby offered a route by which it can gain access to the gustatory information required to guide feeding behavior. Tetanic stimulation of the basolateral nucleus of the amygdala was shown to induce LTP in the IC of adult rats via a pathway that requires functional NRs: NR inhibition by CPP and MK-801 disrupted both CTA and IC-LTP induction in vivo (Escobar et al., 1998; Jones, French, Bliss, & Rosenblum, 1999). Further studies that aimed at elucidating the possible interaction between the BLA and the IC during CTA found that a unilateral injection of glutamate to BLA just before lithium administration enhanced CTA. This effect was reversed when APV was injected into the IC at the same time as or 1 h after an ipsilateral injection of BLA, or at the same time as a contralateral IC injection of APV. Injection of APV in IC 3 h after BLA injection did not interfere with the effect of glutamate. These results provide evidence that NR activation in the IC is essential to enable glutamate infusion into the BLA to enhance CTA, and that BLA–IC interactions may regulate the strength of CTA (Ferreira et al., 2005).

Another taste-learning paradigm that requires an intact NR function is that of the taste-potentiated odor aversion (TPOA) paradigm, under which animals acquire a strong aversion to an odor that is followed by delayed intoxication only if a gustatory stimulus is presented together with the odor during conditioning (see also Batsell & Paschall, Chapter 10). Exposure of rats to APV immediately before presentation of the odor–taste conditioned stimulus (CS) or immediately before the test resulted in impaired acquisition of TPOA, with no effect on retrieval. These results suggest that NMDA receptors of the BLA are involved in the formation of potentiation—by taste—of the olfactory memory trace, but not in the maintenance of this process (Ferreira, Ferry, Meurisse, & Levy, 2006).

The role of glutamatergic receptors in the amygdala was examined through the use of reversible and selective blockers of various glutamate receptors (i.e., NMDA, AMPA, and metabotropic receptors) during CTA. Blockade of each of these receptors between the ingestion of the saccharin (CS), and administration of the malaise-inducing LiCl (unconditioned stimulus, US) resulted in impairment of CTA acquisition. However, after acquisition of CTA, only blockade of AMPA receptors was able to impair CTA, indicating that whereas both ionotropic and metabotropic glutamate receptors are necessary for the acquisition of CTA, the expression of acquired CTA is mediated only by AMPA receptors (Yasoshima, Sako, Senba, & Yamamoto, 2006). Interestingly, microinjection of the AMPA antagonist CNQX into the amygdala produced a time-dependent suppression of 30% of the taste neurons in the parabrachial nucleus (PBN), suggesting that AMPA receptors within the amygdala may be involved in the downward modulation in the PBN taste neurons (Kelleher, Govindarajan, Jung, Kang, & Tonegawa, 2004).

Phosphorylation of the NMDA Receptor and Its Role in Taste Learning

NMDA receptors are heteromeric assemblies composed of two NR1 subunits, combined with at least another two types of NR2 (NR2A, NR2D). A third type, NR3 (NR3A, NR3B), does not form functional receptors by itself; it can form them by co-assembly with NR1/NR2 complexes (Cull-Candy, Brickley, & Farrant, 2001; Wisden & Seeburg, 1993). During resting, the NMDA channel is controlled by a voltage-dependent gate of extracellular Mg^{2+} that blocks ion transmission. Upon a change in membrane potential and the simultaneous introduction of both glutamate and glycine, the channel opens briefly, allowing Ca^{2+} and other cations to move into the cell.

The potential importance of NRs in learning processes was initially demonstrated in the induction of LTP in hippocampal slices. The key role of NRs in the induction of a persistent increase in the size of the synaptic component of the elicited response was shown to depend on the occurrence in the channel of the following: (1) removal of the Mg^{2+} in parallel with membrane depolarization; and (2) simultaneous introduction of glutamate, to promote channel opening. Thus, only a strong input, which includes the synchronous activation of enough fibers, can produce sufficient depolarization to enhance the unblocking of NR channels (Collingridge, Herron, & Lester, 1988). Although application of NMDA alone is insufficient to induce LTP, the NR antagonists—including those that bind to the receptor (APV; Collingridge, Kehl, & McLennan, 1983), to the channel itself (MK-801; Coan, Saywood, & Collingridge, 1987), and to the allosteric glycine site (7 chlorokynuric acid; Bashir, Tam, & Collingridge, 1990)—block certain types of LTP (i.e., NMDA-dependent LTP).

Whereas NR1 is fundamental for channel function and is present in all NMDA receptors, NR2 subunits determine the gating of the channel, as well as their pharmacological and functional properties. Therefore, their composition differs in different brain areas and during different developmental stages. For example, an NR1/NR2A channel displays faster inactivation kinetics than NR1/NR2B channels (Cull-Candy et al., 2001). During development and brain maturation, NR2B-containing NRs are thought to be replaced by NR2A-NRs that are incorporated into synapses (Flint, Maisch, Weishaupt, Kriegstein, & Monyer, 1997; Stocca & Vicini, 1998), whereas NR2B-NRs are located predominantly at extrasynaptic sites (Stocca & Vicini, 1998; Tovar & Westbrook, 1999; Y. Huang et al., 2007). Thus, many of the important functional attributes of the native receptors are determined by the expression of the various subunits and isoforms, and the resulting channel combinations.

One of the key mechanisms for regulation of NR function is through phosphorylation of its NR2 subunits. Both NR2A and NR2B were shown to be phosphorylated by both serine/threonine and tyrosine kinases. Phosphorylation of NR1 and NR2 by PKA and PKC (Gardoni, Bellone, Cattabeni, & Di Luca, 2001; Leonard & Hell, 1997) was found to regulate their response to NR agonists (Greengard, Jen, Nairn, & Stevens, 1991; Wang et al., 2001), whereas phosphorylation of NR2B by CaM kinase was found to regulate calcium influx (Omkumar, Kiely, Rosenstein, Min, & Kennedy, 1996; Strack, McNeill, & Colbran, 2000). Both NR2A and NR2B undergo tyrosine phosphorylation under different conditions; however, of the two, NR2B was identified as the major substrate of tyrosine phosphorylation in the PSD (Moon, Apperson, & Kennedy, 1994), with NR2A phosphorylation constituting only about a third of that of NR2B (Moon, 2003). NR2B is phosphorylated by the cytosolic tyrosine kinases Src and Fyn (Asaki, Usuda, Nakazawa, Kametani, & Suzuki, 2003; Lau & Huganir, 1995; Moon et al., 1994) with the main site identified as tyrosine 1472 NR2B.

Several ground-breaking in vitro studies in the mid-1990s used whole-cell currents and intracellular calcium measurements to demonstrate that

NR activity was regulated by the intricate balance between tyrosine kinases and phosphatases (Wang et al., 2001). However, the first clue to the likely pivotal role of tyrosine phosphorylation of the NR in learning and memory processes came from a study that demonstrated that hippocampal LTP was blocked by the application of selective tyrosine kinase inhibitors. Interestingly, these compounds were effective only in attenuating the formation of LTP and had no effect on preexisting LTP (O'Dell, Kandel, & Grant, 1991). Furthermore, LTP induction was found to depend directly on Src activation (Y. M. Lu, Roder, Davidow, & Salter, 1998). These findings were later corroborated in vivo by two independent groups, who showed that the induction of LTP in the dentate gyrus of rats specifically induced an NR-dependent increase in tyrosine phosphorylation of NR2B (Rosenblum, Dudai, & Richter-Levin, 1996; Rostas et al., 1996). Furthermore, deletion of the gene encoding the cytosolic tyrosine kinase Fyn, resulted in impairment of LTP and special learning in transgenic animals (Grant et al., 1992). Similarly, transgenic mice, impaired in their ability to phosphorylate the tyrosine 1472 residue on NR2B, exhibited severe impairment in acquisition of fear-related learning (Asaki et al., 2003).

A potential role for tyrosine phosphorylation in taste learning was demonstrated in a study that examined the phosphorylation profile of proteins in the IC and other brain areas, following CTA. The results revealed specific increases in the extent of tyrosine phosphorylation of several proteins, and the profile was unique to the IC and was not due to the injection of the US (Rosenblum et al., 1995). In those proteins, a marked correlation was observed between sampling of novel taste, whether incidental or in a CTA context, and the increase in tyrosine phosphorylation of NR2B. A subsequent study by the same group showed that application of the NR inhibitor APV during taste learning in LI of CTA impaired taste memory, which suggested that the function of the NR is obligatory for taste learning (Rosenblum et al., 1997), and established a role for the occurrence of posttranslational modifications in a specific brain area, in response to a natural stimulus. This does not role out an additional function for the NR in malaise-inducing memory or an associative learning as expressed in CTA. In addition, although NR function was found necessary for taste learning, its blockade by APV during training did not prevent

tyrosine phosphorylation of NR2B, which suggests that tyrosine phosphorylation of NR2B might be related to the encoding of saliency in the cortex during the first few hours after the introduction of a novel taste, a relationship mediated via an effect on intracellular signaling pathways that interface with the receptor (Rosenblum et al., 1997).

Summary and Further Directions

It is clear that glutamatergic neurotransmission in the GC and amygdala is crucial for taste learning and memory. However, in addition to the glutamatergic neurotransmission, other neurotransmitters are correlated and necessary for taste learning in the amygdala and GC (e.g., Berman et al., 2000). Further studies will examine the molecular, electrophysiological, and circuit aspects of the interactions among the various neurotransmitters in the GC and amygdala that subserve the diverse stages of taste learning; acquisition, consolidation, retrieval, relearning, and reconsolidation. In addition, new phosphoproteomic approaches can elucidate the global posttranslation modifications of many different molecules that occur during learning and consolidation. In any case, it is clear that one major outcome of neurotransmitter and signal transduction activation in the relevant brain area is the regulation of mRNA translation that underlies molecular memory consolidation.

THE ROLE OF mRNA TRANSLATION REGULATION IN TASTE LEARNING AND CTA CONSOLIDATION

Translation in Eukaryotes

Protein synthesis is the last step of gene expression and is a key control point in its regulation. In particular, it enables cells rapidly to manipulate protein production without new synthesis, processing, or export of mRNA (Dever, 2002). Translation proceeds as an ordered process that includes accurate and efficient initiation, peptide chain elongation, and termination. Initiation refers to the assembly of a translation-competent ribosome at the AUG start codon on an mRNA; translation elongation is the codon-dependent assembly of a polypeptide; and termination involves release of the completed protein when the ribosome reaches a termination codon (Klann & Dever, 2004).

The initiation step is facilitated by specific non-ribosomally associated proteins, termed initiation factors (eIFs). The initiation of translation requires three steps. First, the specific initiator methionyl-transfer RNA (Met-tRNA$_i^{met}$) binds to the small (40S) ribosomal subunit to form a 43S preinitiation complex; second, the 43S binds to an mRNA to form a 48S preinitiation complex that scans the AUG start codon; and third, the large (60S) ribosomal subunit joins this complex to form an 80S ribosome. During the initiation phase, multiple initiation factors (eIF1-eIF6) are involved, and the complexity of this biochemical process requires a high level of regulation. Several mechanisms are involved in the regulation of protein synthesis at this level. Among these are posttranslational modification of translation factors, and binding of regulatory proteins to the 5'- or 3'-untranslated regions (UTRs) of specific mRNAs (Klann & Dever, 2004). The process of elongation is also regulated by specific nonribosomal proteins, called elongation factors (eEFs). Elongation of polypeptides occurs in a cyclic manner, such that at the end of one complete round of amino acid addition the A site is empty and ready to accept the incoming aminoacyl-tRNA, as dictated by the next codon of the mRNA (Alberts, 1994).

Translational termination requires specific protein factors, designated as releasing factor (eRF). The signals for termination are termination codons that are present in the mRNA.

Protein Synthesis Inhibitors

Several protein synthesis inhibitors (PSIs) are used in eukaryotic cells. Among these are anisomycin, cycloheximide, and rapamycin. Anisomycin interferes with peptide bond formation and is fairly nontoxic; cycloheximide blocks the translocation reaction on ribosomes, and it inhibits not only translation but also DNA and RNA synthesis (Gale, Cundliffe, Reynolds, Richmond, & Waring, 1981; Stork & Welzl, 1999). Rapamycin, on the other hand, is an immunosuppressant drug and not a general PSI. It inhibits the target of rapamycin (TOR) protein, the activity of which regulates translation in mammalian cells. Rapamycin treatment of mammalian cells specifically inhibits the translation of certain classes of mRNAs, via the regulation of the phosphorylation state of several different translation effector proteins (Raught, Gingras, & Sonenberg, 2001).

In general, PSIs affect LTP or learning consolidation. The various PSIs can prevent different forms of protein-synthesis-dependent synaptic plasticity, such as long-term facilitation in Aplysia and late-phase long-term potentiation (L-LTP) in the hippocampal CA1 region of rodents. However, they do not block short-term forms of synaptic plasticity.

Learning and Protein Synthesis

Inhibitors of protein synthesis have been employed for more than four decades to investigate memory formation in rodents. Data on the subject from the early set of experiments was thoroughly reviewed by Davis and Squire (1984).

Memory is a graded process that can be divided into at least two temporal phases: STM with duration ranging from seconds to hours and LTM that lasts for days, weeks, and even years (Goelet, Castellucci, Schacher, & Kandel, 1986).

A time frame common to the different forms of memory is associated with three stages of memory storage: acquisition—in which sensory information enters STM; consolidation—the conversion of STMs into LTMs; and retrieval—extraction of information from the memory store (Abel & Lattal, 2001).

The consolidation stage is critical for induction of LTMs. During this stage, memory is labile and susceptible to interference (Goelet et al., 1986).

Numerous studies have shown that memory consolidation can be blocked by inhibition of protein synthesis, that is, when blockage of protein synthesis exceeds 90% (Davis & Squire, 1984; Houpt & Berlin, 1999; Rosenblum, Meiri, & Dudai, 1993). This time window for protein synthesis has been identified in both lower vertebrates and mammals, and for learning processes that range in complexity from nonassociative forms such as sensitization to associative forms such as classical and instrumental conditioning (Goelet et al., 1986).

This dependence of consolidation on protein synthesis characterizes the biochemical distinction between STM and LTM. In both vertebrates and invertebrates STM is based on transient modifications of preexisting proteins, most importantly phosphorylation and dephosphorylation of enzymes, receptors, and ion channels. In contrast, the conversion of STM into more stable and self-maintained LTM requires a cellular program of gene expression and regulation of protein synthesis.

Proteins newly synthesized during memory consolidation are likely to contribute to processes of structural changes of existing synapses and, possibly, generation of new neuronal circuits (Stork & Welzl, 1999). Recent studies have shown that individual synapses have the capability to control synaptic strength independently, through the local synthesis of proteins (Steward & Schuman, 2001). A distributed network of translational machinery has been found in dendrites, where polyribosomes and associated membranous elements are positioned beneath synapses (Steward, 1983; Steward & Fass, 1983; Steward & Levy, 1982) and translate a particular population of dendritic mRNAs (Steward, Falk, & Torre, 1996; Steward & Singer, 1997).

Davis and Squire (1984) proposed that cerebral protein synthesis might be involved in memory, in the light of its ubiquitous role in cellular regulatory processes. Thus, synthesis of proteins could be important in changing synaptic efficacy along neuronal pathways. Davis and Squire (1984), on the basis of a review of the literature, suggested that initial acquisition and retention after training are independent of protein synthesis, but that protein synthesis is required for the formation of LTM. This hypothesis applies to many forms of learning, but in the present review we focus on the role of protein synthesis regulation in taste learning.

Houpt and Berlin (1999) demonstrated that short-term expression of a CTA persisted after ICV administration of cycloheximide during the pairing of sucrose and LiCl, whereas long-term expression of a CTA was blocked by cycloheximide administration. Thus, CTA learning appears to be independent of protein synthesis during the first hour after the pairing of sucrose and LiCl, but then requires protein synthesis within at least the first 6 h after the pairing.

Intraventricular injection of cycloheximide prevented the development of aversion against a flavor associated with malaise, as measured 24 h after conditioning (Tucker & Gibbs, 1976). Rosenblum et al. (1993) evaluated the roles of the IC and of protein synthesis within it in the acquisition of taste memory and showed that focal injection of anisomycin into the IC significantly impaired CTA. However, anisomycin did not affect the retrieval of taste memory: animals injected with anisomycin before presentation with a novel taste during the test (96 h post-CTA) displayed normal aversion.

In order to isolate the effect of anisomycin on a memory of novel taste, Rosenblum et al. (1993) used the LI paradigm. They found that whereas prior exposure to a taste attenuated subsequent CTA to the same taste, local application of anisomycin prior to the taste learning significantly impaired this effect. This finding indicates that protein synthesis in the IC is necessary for normal formation of memory of a new taste.

Inhibition of protein synthesis by prior injection of anisomycin into the central nucleus of the amygdala (CeA) blocked the consolidation of long-term CTA memory. Microinfusion into the basolateral amygdalar nucleus (BLA) immediately after retrieval impaired the extinction of CTA (Bahar, Samuel, Hazvi, & Dudai, 2003). These behavioral studies using protein synthesis inhibition determined that translation regulation plays a critical role in taste learning processes.

Neurotransmitters Controlling Translation Regulation

Many recent studies aimed to identify the neurotransmitters that control protein synthesis regulation, in order to understand how neuronal activity is translated to memory consolidation. Most of these studies focused on the role of glutamate and its various receptors in activating the mTOR pathway, and focused mainly on S6K1 phosphorylation. In order to determine the signaling pathways that couple NRs to the translation machinery, hippocampal slices were briefly treated with NMDA (Banko, Hou, & Klann, 2004). Several biochemical markers coupled to translation regulation were examined; they included ERK, eIF4E, and its kinase, mitogen-activated protein kinase-interacting kinase 1 (Mnk1). The brief NMDA activation led to activation of ERK and Mnk1 and increased phosphorylation of eIF4E, indicating that NRs are coupled to protein translation factors in the hippocampus (Banko et al., 2004).

Lenz and Avruch (2005) characterized the differing effects of short and long glutamatergic activation in the mTOR/S6K pathway in cultured mouse neurons, whereas short exposure to glutamatergic activation stimulated S6K1 and increased S6 protein phosphorylation, the opposite effects were observed when the glutamatergic activation was prolonged. These findings emphasize the importance of a short pulse of glutamatergic stimulation for the activation of these pathways, which are known to regulate protein translation.

Similar results were obtained by Y. Huang et al. (2007), who demonstrated that 20 min of NMDA application to cortical neurons (corresponding to the long glutamatergic activation in the study of Lenz & Avruch, 2005) markedly reduced the phosphorylation levels of S6 and 4E-BP, and that these effects were blocked by APV and MK-801. In order to test whether basal, physiological NMDA receptor activation regulated the mTOR pathway, cortical cultures were treated with the NMDA antagonist APV. As a result, pronounced increases in phospho-S6 and phospho-4E-BP were observed.

In a study by Page et al. (2006), stimulation of mGluR subtype 1 in rat striatal and hippocampal synaptoneurosomes resulted in activation of the mTOR signaling pathway, specifically in increased phosphorylation of S6K1. Similarly, activation of group I mGluRs triggered the activation of the phosphoinositide 3-kinase (PI3K)-Akt-mTOR pathway both in total and synaptoneurosomal preparations from hippocampal slices (Hou & Klann, 2004).

In exploring the effect of glutamate treatment of cultured chick cerebellar bergmann glia cells, Gonzalez-Mejia et al. (2006) found a marked decrease in overall protein synthesis after 15 min of exposure to glutamate. Among modifications of proteins regulating the translation was a sustained increase in S6K1 phosphorylation. In order to determine the pharmacological profile of the GluRs involved in phosphorylation of S6K1, the cultures were exposed to both ionotropic (NMDA, AMPA, and KA) and metabotropic (Groups I and III) agonists of glutamate receptors. All of these agonists were shown to increase S6K1 phosphorylation, which was later prevented by the exposure of these cultures to the various antagonists of glutamate receptors (Gonzalez-Mejia et al., 2006).

Taken together, the accumulating data presented above suggest that, according to the duration of its administration, glutamate mainly modulates the initiation phase of translation, by acting on mTOR, S6K1, S6, eIF4E, and 4E-BP phosphorylation and is mediated through ionotropic as well as mGluRs.

The role of NMDA in translation regulation has also been investigated in the context of elongation phase regulation. Belelovsky, Elkobi, Kaphzan, Nairn, and Rosenblum (2005) revealed that NMDA application to hippocampal slices increased eEF2 phosphorylation, whereas the combination of NMDA and APV decreased its levels. These results indicate that activity of a protein that regulates the elongation phase of translation also depends on activation of NMDA receptors.

An additional factor modulating mGluR-dependent protein synthesis is a negative regulator of translation called fragile X mental retardation protein (FMRP); its levels rose in dendrites following activation of group I mGluRs (Huber, Gallagher, Warren, & Bear, 2002).

Translation Regulation during Synaptic Plasticity

Several papers have addressed the effect of induction of LTP or LTD on protein synthesis regulation. A study by Kelleher et al. (2004) stressed the role of MAPK signaling, known to be highly involved in long-term synaptic plasticity and memory, in regulating translational control. Inhibition of ERK, a member of the MAPK family, in hippocampal neurons, blocked neuronal activity-induced translation as well as phosphorylation of the translation factors eIF4E, 4E-BP1, and ribosomal protein S6. All of these proteins have roles in regulation of translation initiation (Mathews, Sonenberg, & Hershey, 2000). Furthermore, mutant mice expressing dominant-negative form of MEK1 (a specific ERK kinase) in the postnatal murine forebrain were generated and hippocampal slices were prepared. The critical role of MAPK signaling in translation control was demonstrated by showing that protein synthesis and translation factor phosphorylation induced in control hippocampal slices by L-LTP-generating tetanization were significantly reduced in mutant slices. With regard to learning and memory, the increase in specific phosphorylation of ERK, S6, and eIF4E that resulted from fear conditioning was smaller in mutant mice than in control mice.

Tsokas et al. (2005) demonstrated that in acute hippocampal slices, the induction of protein-synthesis-dependent LTP increased the expression of 5′ TOP encoded protein elongation factor 1A (eEF1A), a key component of translational machinery. The application of rapamycin blocked this effect, indicating that the increase in eEF1A expression was mediated by the mTOR pathway. Similar results were obtained in a subsequent study, revealing that the mRNA for the eEF1A is present in vivo in the dendrites of neurons that exhibit LTP or LTD (F. Huang, Chotiner, & Steward, 2005).

In an in vivo study of MAPK-dependent translation regulation in LTP, the phosphorylation of eEF2 was found to be modulated following LTP induction: it rose immediately after the stimulation and was down regulated 10 min afterwards Belelovsky, Maroun, and Rosenblum (2007). These results match the findings of Kanhema et al. (2006) regarding increased eEF2 phosphorylation 5 min after the induction of LTP by brain-derived neurotrophic factor (BDNF). In addition, LTP induction resulted in rapid increases in both phosphorylation level and the expression of another key translation factor, eukaryotic initiation factor 4E (eIF4E). Kelleher et al. (2004) obtained similar findings: that inhibition of the MAPK signaling cascade blocked the modulation of translation factor activity.

In summary, the above results show that several different forms of LTP can lead to regulation of both the initiation and the elongation phases of translation, some of which are ERK dependent.

Correlative Changes in Translation Regulation in Learning

Several recent studies have established a role for active protein synthesis regulation following taste learning paradigms. Belelovsky et al. (2005) demonstrated that two kinases—ERK2 and S6K1—known to activate translation factors at the level of initiation, as well as eukaryotic elongation factor 2 (eEF2), a regulator of translation elongation, underwent increased phosphorylation in the IC of rats shortly after novel taste learning. Moreover, in the light of the finding that protein synthesis in the neuron can localize to the synapse to control synaptic strength independently of mRNA synthesis in the cell body (Belelovsky et al., 2005) analyzed the phosphorylation levels of these proteins in the synaptoneurosomal fraction of the IC. The results indicated that eEF2 phosphorylation, but not MAPK activation or S6K1 phosphorylation, was increased in synaptoneurosomal fraction within 20 min after novel taste learning.

In another study, the phosphorylation levels of eukaryotic initiation factor 2alpha (eIF2α) were analyzed following novel taste learning (Costa-Mattioli et al., 2007). Neuronal-activity-dependent modulation of eIF2α phosphorylation is likely to be important for sustained changes in synaptic transmission, because induction of L-LTP in

hippocampal slices, by either tetanic stimulation or treatment with forskolin or BDNF, has been correlated with decreased eIF2α phosphorylation (Costa-Mattioli et al., 2005; Takei, Kawamura, Hara, Yonezawa, & Nawa, 2001). The results obtained by E. Stern et al. (personal communication) show that phosphorylation levels of eIF2α decreased within 5 min of novel taste learning, which implies increased initiation of general protein synthesis.

Necessary Changes in Translation Regulation Subserving Taste Learning

Though several studies indicated that the activity or the expression of various translation factors was modulated following novel taste learning, these correlative studies are not sufficient to confirm the necessity of translation regulation in taste learning. Therefore, many efforts are invested in the preferential inhibition of various translation factors, by genetic modulation, in order to test the effects of such modifications on taste learning and consolidation.

As mentioned above, phosphorylation of eIF2α inhibited general translation, but also selectively stimulated translation of ATF4, a repressor of cAMP response element-binding (CREB)-mediated late-LTP (L-LTP) and LTM (P. D. Lu, Harding, & Ron, 2004; Vattem & Wek, 2004). Costa-Mattioli et al. (2007) used a genetic modification in mice to examine the role of eIF2α phosphorylation in synaptic plasticity and behavioral learning: in eIF2$\alpha^{+/S51A}$ mice, in which eIF2α phosphorylation is reduced, learning of a novel taste under the LI paradigm (see also Lubow, Chapter 3) was significantly enhanced compared with their wild-type littermates. In addition, the decay of the aversion index in eIF2$\alpha^{+/S51A}$ mice was remarkably accelerated over the 5 test days. The authors suggest that the much more rapid extinction of CTA in eIF2$\alpha^{+/S51A}$ mice reflected accelerated learning (reinforcement) of the new taste. These findings highlight the importance of a single phosphorylation site in eIF2α as a key regulator of LTM formation (Costa-Mattioli et al., 2007). In addition, this work opened a new approach to studying the role of transcription regulation (i.e., ATF4 function) by translation regulation (i.e., via phosphorylation levels of eIF2α).

In order to determine how translation initiation is regulated during neuroplasticity, Banko et al.

(2007) utilized mutant C57Bl/6J mice that lack the translation repressor eukaryotic initiation factor 4E-binding protein 2 (4E-BP2). This protein modulates the integrity of the eIF4F cap-binding complex, which is highly important in initiating translation. Specifically, initiation was inhibited by competition between the 4E-BP and eIF4G for binding eIF4E (Pause et al., 1994). The investigators had previously shown that 4E-BP2 plays a critical role in hippocampus-dependent synaptic plasticity and memory. With regard to taste learning, 4E-BP2 knockout mice demonstrated a significantly enhanced memory for CTA: they avoided the saccharin and NaCl CSs to a higher degree than their wild-type counterparts, following a one-trial pairing of saccharin or NaCl with LiCl. These findings emphasized the importance of translation regulatory mechanisms for CTA in mice (Banko et al., 2007).

Another study by Antion et al. (2008) examined whether protein synthesis mediated by S6K1 is critical for the manifestation of learning, memory, and synaptic plasticity. This experimental question was tested by using knockout mice for both the isoforms of S6K that are expressed in the brain, S6K1, and S6K2. In the context of taste memory, mice deficient in S6K1 showed a lower aversion index to novel taste paired with LiCl, under the CTA paradigm. In examination of the strength of the aversive memory, S6K1 knockout mice exhibited more fragile aversive taste memory, as indicated by the extinction curve. In contrast, S6K2 knockout mice displayed normal taste aversion after CTA. However, under the LI paradigm, preexposure to the novel taste did not affect the behavior of the S6K2 knockout mice, indicating that S6K2 is required for LTM of novel taste experience. The results suggest that S6K1 and S6K2 are each uniquely necessary for normal taste learning (Antion et al., 2008).

Recently, we observed that local application of rapamycin to the IC impaired LTM of a novel taste. Under the LI paradigm, the aversion index (i.e., the amount of consumed water divided by the consumption of both water and the novel taste during the test days [see Rosenblum et al., 1993, for further information]) of rapamycin-injected rats was higher than that of vehicle-injected animals. Since rapamycin inhibits subpopulations of mRNA via the regulation of the phosphorylation state of several different translation effector proteins, we conclude that intact activity of translation factors, that

are downstream targets of mTOR, is necessary for long-term taste memory in the rat (Belelovsky & Rosenblum, unpublished results).

Summary and Further Directions

In the last few years, diverse studies have demonstrated that regulation of protein synthesis is a vital step in various forms of molecular consolidation of both learning and synaptic plasticity. Many of these studies specifically examined the role of translation regulation in taste and CTA learning and found that the various phases of translation regulation are involved in taste memory consolidation. The main outcome of such regulation is modification in the amounts of various proteins in several different regions of neurons within the relevant brain circuit that subserves the learning process. It is, therefore, important to identify modulation of mRNA and protein levels, and to understand the contributions of such modifications of gene expression to memory consolidation. Another major research direction is identification of the specific neuronal subtypes that participate in the biochemical process described above.

PROTEIN AND mRNA EXPRESSION IN THE AMYGDALE AND IC CORRELATED WITH TASTE LEARNING AND CTA

Immediate Early Genes as Possible Markers for Neuronal Changes in the CNS

Immediate early genes (IEG) activation can be defined in terms of the capacity to mount a rapid genomic response to stimulation. Hence, IEGs present the first genetic signal in response to cell activation, since their induction is fast and transient and does not depend on *de novo* protein synthesis or on activation of any other preceding genes (Pinaud, 2004). They represent a standing response mechanism that is activated at the transcription level during the first round of responses to stimuli, before any new proteins are synthesized. Thus, IEGs are distinct from "late-response" genes, which can be activated only later, following the synthesis of early-response gene products. IEGs can encode transcription factors (TFs), which are intracellular proteins that control the expression of genes that are responsible for the differentiation, development, functioning, and plasticity of the cell; these include *c-Fos*, *c-Jun*, and *Zif268*. Other IEGs which are not TFs are used to encode membrane and cytoskeletal elements, for example, *Arg3.1*, an IEG that encodes a cytoskeletal-associated protein.

c-Fos Expression in Forebrain Regions Following Taste Learning

Ample experimental data suggest the involvement of cortically dependent c-Fos expression following conditioning under several classical paradigms (see Tischmeyer & Grimm, 1999, for review). CTA is an example in which such a use of c-Fos immunomapping was applied in order to indentify and characterize the neural circuit that mediates taste memory formation. However, careful examination must be applied when using aversion-driven learning paradigms, such as CTA, in order to exclude stress as a possible cause of c-Fos expression (Yokoyama & Sasaki, 1999). Thus, in order to prove an association between a CS, usually in the form of a saccharin solution, and a US in the form of a malaise-inducing agent, for example, LiCl in forebrain areas, it is crucial to examine cortical c-Fos expression levels of different experimental groups such as taste-alone and US-alone in addition to the CS-alone (i.e., a taste previously paired with the US) in the experimental group.

c-Fos Expression in the Amygdala and IC Following Novel Taste Presentation

In order to assess the contribution of sensory stimulation to IEG-dependent expression in the IC, Montag-Sallaz, Welzl, Kuhl, Montag, and Schachner (1999) tested the expression levels of *c-fos* and *arg 3.1* mRNA in several cortical areas, following presentation of either a novel taste (saccharin 0.5%) or a familiar taste (water). The animals were divided into three groups, two of which received either water or saccharin for 8 h on each of 7 consecutive days (controls), while the third group was exposed to water for 6 days and received saccharin only on day 7. The animals were sacrificed at different time points (30 min and 1, 4.5, and 6 h) after they began drinking. Expression of *c-fos* and *arg 3.1* mRNA in the parietal cortex and cingulate cortex 30 min and 4.5 h, respectively, after novel taste presentation were greater than at the same time points after presentation of the familiar taste.

In addition, c-fos mRNA expression was increased in the amygdala 30 min after taste presentation, no such increase was detected in the IC at any time point tested. However, a decrease in c-fos expression between 1 and 4.5 h after the beginning of drinking was found in all three groups. In contrast, Bernstein and Koh (2007) found increased c-Fos protein expression in the IC 1 h after the presentation of a novel taste (see also Bernstein, Wilkins, & Barot, Chapter 16, for review). The authors performed a detailed analysis of the temporal profiles of Fos-like immunoreactivity (FLI) activation, at several time points following exposure to either a novel or a familiar taste, and found a significant difference between the two FLI activation profiles only 1 h after the exposures. A previous study by the same authors (Koh, Wilkins, & Bernstein, 2003) reported an increase in the FLI activation in the IC 2 h after exposure to a novel taste, a result that was not repeated in their more recent report (Bernstein & Koh, 2007). It should be noticed that the elevated c-Fos activation was observed only when a highly neophobic taste saccharin concentration of 0.5% was used, whereas ingestion of 0.15% saccharin did not elicit the same Fos activation in the IC or CeA. Furthermore, a recent study by Doron and Rosenblum (unpublished results), in which the rats received a mild saccharin concentration (0.1%), did not find any difference in c-Fos expression in the dysgranular IC, also referred to as the insular cortex (GC), 2 h following exposure to a novel taste. Thus, although novelty detection remains a crucial component in the gustatory processing of taste memory, its time-dependent presence in the IC, as manifested in the form of IEG expression, remains to be clarified. In contrast, there seems to be little doubt regarding the role of the CeA as a novelty detector in the neural circuit of gustatory processing and taste memory formation. Yamamoto, Sako, Sakai, and Iwafune (1997) and Koh et al. (2003) examined c-Fos expression in the CeA 1.5 and 2 h following exposure of rats to either a familiar or a novel taste, respectively, and reported higher levels of positively stained Fos nuclei after novel taste presentation than after administration of water. In addition, Montag-Sallaz et al. (1999) found elevated expression levels of c-fos mRNA in the amygdala 30 min after novel taste presentation. Moreover, a recent study by Bernstein and Koh (2007), which examined c-Fos kinetics at several time points following novel taste presentation, also found increased FLI activation 1 and 2 h after saccharin presentation.

c-Fos Expression in the Amygdale and IC Following Administration of Malaise-Inducing Agents

Another line of research examined c-fos expression following IP injection of LiCl, normally used as US, to elicit CTA. One hour after LiCl injection, Lamprecht and Dudai (1995) observed increased c-fos mRNA levels in the CeA, as well as in other brainstem nuclei, for example, the nucleus of the solitary tract (NTS) and the PBN. These results were replicated in several studies (Gu, Gonzalez, Chin, & Deutsch, 1993; Koh et al., 2003; Yamamoto et al., 1992, 1997). Spencer and Houpt (2001) examined the c-fos mRNA expression at several time points following LiCl injection and found a peak in the CeA between 20 min and 1 h following injection, with a return to the base level 3 h later. In a recent study, Bernstein and Koh (2007) used the same method to quantify changes in c-Fos protein levels following LiCl injection, and found a significant increase in FLI activation only in the CeA, 1 h following LiCl administration. Other studies (Ferreira et al., 2006; St. Andre, Albanos, & Reilly, 2007) also found elevated c-Fos expression in the CeA and also in the BLA 1.5 and 2 h, respectively, after LiCl injection.

c-Fos Expression in the Amygdala and IC Following CTA Association

A key structure that has been implicated by c-fos expression in the formation of CTA is the CeA. Koh and Bernstein (2005) observed increased FLI activation in the CeA and IC 2 h following novel taste or familiar taste pairing with LiCl; they exposed rats to either novel saccharin (0.5%) paired with LiCl or familiar saccharin paired with LiCl, having used six preexposures prior to the conditioning session in order to familiarize the rats to the saccharin taste. Ferreira et al. (2006) also reported increased Fos expression in the CeA, as well as in the BLA and in the lateral amygdala (LA), 1.5 h after taste presentation, although the last of these was activated only following CTA acquisition, whereas the former two nuclei were also activated in the presence of a familiar taste. Therefore, the authors concluded that the amygdala made a partial contribution to the CS–US association process, via the LA.

Another brain structure that is known to be activated during CS–US association in aversive taste learning is the IC (for reviews see Bermudez-Rattoni, 2004; Bures et al., 1998). However, early studies, which used in situ hybridization techniques to determine mRNA IEG expression, failed to demonstrate its involvement in taste memory association (Lamprecht & Dudai, 1995). Nevertheless, as mentioned above, (Koh & Bernstein, 2005) found elevated FLI expression in the IC 2 h following CS–US association. Similar results were reported by (Ferreira et al., 2006), who found increased Fos activation in the IC 1.5 h after novel taste presentation associated with both low (0.075 M) and high (0.4 M) concentrations of LiCl. In addition, Doron and Rosenblum (unpublished results), using immunofluorescence confocal imaging, found that following CTA, c-Fos elevation was expressed in all cortical layers of the GC. Furthermore, they colabeled c-Fos expression with GABAergic markers and discovered that it was colocalized in contrast to the LiCl-injected animals, which did not exhibit elevated GABAergic activation. This study was the first to yield evidence for the involvement of activation of GABAergic interneurons in aversive memory association in the GC. In a noteworthy study, Chen et al. (2004) examined c-Fos immunomapping in the IC following a conditioned immunoresponse; they used an antigen ovalbumin (OVA, a nonaversive US) as the US after presentation of a novel taste (0.25% saccharin) or a familiar taste (water), in order to investigate the functional activation of the IC after preexposure to the CS. Although the administered US did not contain malaise-inducing information, the CS–US association between the novel taste and the OVA resulted in an elevation of c-Fos expression in the cortical taste area 2 h following taste reexposure. In contrast, Chen et al. (2004) did not observe any c-Fos increase in the IC in response to presentation of the novel taste alone, and they therefore inferred that the CS-induced increase in activation was due not merely to gustatory sensory information but was rather a result of a more elaborate CS–US process of acquisition and storage of associative learning.

Suppression of c-Fos Expression in the Amygdale and IC during Conditioned Taste Memory Formation

An important issue that was raised following the correlative studies described above is that of whether the observed IEG induction that followed behavioral learning procedures was mere correlation or a necessary process in taste memory formation. An early attempt to interpret behavioral learning in mutant mice lacking c-*fos* expression was hampered by the impaired sensory systems and heterogeneous genetic backgrounds of the mice, which made observed behavioral deficits hard to explain or interpret in terms of learning associated behavior (Paylor, Johnson, Papaioannou, Spiegelman, & Wehner, 1994). Thus, an alternative method, involving microinjection of antisense (AS) oligodeoxynucleotides (ODNs) was presented, in order to inhibit the expression of c-fos protein products selectively, locally, and transiently. Blockage of c-*fos* by using AS has been reported to impair several memory-related tasks (Countryman, Kaban, & Colombo, 2005; Grimm et al., 1997; J. He, Yamada, & Nabeshima, 2002; Morrow, Elsworth, Inglis, & Roth, 1999; Tolliver, Sganga, & Sharp, 2000).

The first use of ODNs in a taste–memory-related procedure was by Lamprecht and Dudai (1996), who used local and bilateral microinjection of 5 nmol of c-fos phosphorothioate-modified AS-ODN into the nuclei of the amygdala. This blocked basal and LiCl-induced expression of c-Fos in the CeA, compared with sense ODN or vehicle-treated controls. Furthermore, application of the injection 8 h before CTA training resulted in impairment of aversive memory formation. This did not occur if the AS-ODN was injected 3–5 days before conditioning or into the basal ganglia. Therefore, Lamprecht and Dudai (1996) inferred that there was temporal and localized involvement of c-*fos* induction in the amygdala, and suggested that it filled a critical role in encoding taste aversion memory. Yasoshima et al. (2006) recently elegantly repeated these results by microinjection of 5 nmol of c-fos AS-ODN into the PBN, CeA, and IC, prior to CTA training. Furthermore, they used a control of c-*fos*⁻/⁻ mutant mice in order to assess whether c-fos induction was a sufficient or necessary condition for aversive taste memory acquisition and retention. In order to verify the effectiveness of AS-ODN in disruption of CTA in the PBN, CeA, and IC, the authors examined c-Fos immunoreactivity 1.5 h following saccharin presentation and LiCl injection, and found a marked reduction in Fos positive cells in all these structures compared with the levels in reversed or inverted ODN controls. In addition, after measuring acquisition and retention indices of CTA in all three regions 8 h after AS-ODN application,

Yasoshima et al. (2006) found attenuated acquisition in the PBN only, and an acute reduction in the CeA and IC retention index, a result which implies that the examined regions fill differing roles in aversive memory formation. Interestingly enough, and in contrast to earlier studies, which used chronic c-*fos* gene deficient mutant mice (Paylor et al., 1994), Yasoshima et al. (2006) found unimpaired acquisition of CTA in the c-*fos*⁻/⁻ mutant mice and, moreover, by using a zif268 AS-ODN microinjection, they also found a lack of disruption of CTA in these rats, in contrast to previous findings with zif268⁻/⁻ mutant mice by Jones et al. (2001). In conclusion, although AS-ODN studies shed some light on the role of IEGs in taste memory formation, the question of whether these agents are essential to memory formation and consolidation remains to be clarified.

Expression of Other IEGs in the Amygdala and Insular Cortex during Conditioned Taste Memory Formation

Another protein that is implicated in expression of CTA memory early-response genes is the CREB protein. Lamprecht, Hazvi, and Dudai (1997) used CREB antisense in the amygdala, which resulted in disruption of long-term CTA. In another study, Desmedt et al. (2003) found increased unilateral expression of the phosphorylated form of CREB (pCREB) in the IC 3.5 h following novel taste presentation. However, a recent study by Yefet et al. (2006), which used Western blot analysis to examine the temporal kinetics of pCREB expression in the IC, found no increase in pCREB in the IC at any time point following presentation of a novel taste, that is, 0.1% saccharin. Interestingly, using the same temporal analysis, Merhav et al. (2006) found greater expression of another plasticity related gene, CCAAT/enhancer binding protein (C/EBPβ), 18 h following novel taste presentation than after presentation of a familiar taste.

Summary and Further Directions

The induction of very few proteins in the GC or amygdala was found to be correlated with taste learning or CTA. It is clear that unbiased proteomic research can reveal modulation in the expression of various proteins. An additional issue is the temporal profiling of such screening and

Table 17.1 Time-Dependent c-Fos Expression in IC and Amygdala.

Time (h)	IC				Amygdala			
	0.5	1	1.5	2	0.5	1	1.5	2
Novel taste	$\leftrightarrow$R	$\uparrow$P $\leftrightarrow$R			$\uparrow$R	$\uparrow$P	$\uparrow$P	$\uparrow$P
LiCl injection		$\leftrightarrow$P $\leftrightarrow$R		$\uparrow$P	$\uparrow$R	$\uparrow$R	$\uparrow$P	$\uparrow$P
CTA		$\uparrow$P	$\uparrow$P				$\uparrow$P	$\uparrow$P
AS-ODN		$\downarrow$P				$\downarrow$P		

Notes: R—mRNA expression.

P—Protein product expression.

verification of the results by means of a separate independent measurement. The temporal profile of c-Fos expression has been studied by several groups, and it is clear that the c-Fos expression in the amygdala is correlated both with taste learning and, to a larger degree, with malaise within a wide time window (Table 17.1).

Most of the studies so far used diaminobezidin (DAB) staining for proteins thus did not allow costaining with other markers. In the future the use of fluorescence markers, double or triple staining, together with confocal microscopy should enable elucidation of the details of the local circuit within the amygdalar nuclei or the GC, that is, whether the stained cells are, for example, excitatory or inhibitory neurons. It should enable elucidation of the layers within the cortex that participate in the various phases of the learning process, and better spatial resolution will enable determination of where within the neurons protein induction takes place, for example, in the dendrites or the cell body.

Other routes of research should identify the cellular and molecular processes taking place in the GC and amygdala, from the release of neurotransmitter/s, via translation regulation, and up to the expression of the protein populations of the relevant neurons. The achievement of well-defined understanding of the neuroanatomy and behavior of CTA and taste learning awaits further cutting-edge cellular and molecular analysis.

References

Abel, T., & Lattal, K. M. (2001). Molecular mechanisms of memory acquisition, consolidation and retrieval. *Current Opinion in Neurobiology, 11*, 180–187.

Alberts, B. (1994). *Molecular biology of the cell.* New York: Garland publications.

Antion, M. D., Merhav, M., Hoeffer, C. A., Reis, G., Kozma, S. C., Thomas, G., et al. (2008). Removal of S6K1 and S6K2 leads to divergent alterations in learning, memory, and synaptic plasticity. *Learning & Memory, 15*(1), 29–38.

Asaki, C., Usuda, N., Nakazawa, A., Kametani, K., & Suzuki, T. (2003). Localization of translational components at the ultramicroscopic level at postsynaptic sites of the rat brain. *Brain Research, 972*, 168–176.

Bahar, A., Samuel, A., Hazvi, S., & Dudai, Y. (2003). The amygdalar circuit that acquires taste aversion memory differs from the circuit that extinguishes it. *European Journal of Neuroscience, 7*, 1527–1530.

Banko, J. L., Hou, L., & Klann, E. (2004). NMDA receptor activation results in PKA- and ERK-dependent Mnk1 activation and increased eIF4E phosphorylation in hippocampal area CA1. *Journal of Neurochemistry, 91*, 462–470.

Banko, J. L., Merhav, M., Stern, E., Sonenberg, N., Rosenblum, K., & Klann, E. (2007). Behavioral alterations in mice lacking the translation repressor 4E-BP2. *Neurobiology of Learning and Memory, 87*, 248–256.

Bashir, Z. I., Tam, B., & Collingridge, G. L. (1990). Activation of the glycine site in the NMDA receptor is necessary for the induction of LTP. *Neuroscience Letters, 108*, 261–266.

Belelovsky, K., Elkobi, A., Kaphzan, H., Nairn, A. C., & Rosenblum, K. (2005). A molecular switch for translational control in taste memory consolidation. *European Journal of Neuroscience, 22*, 2560–2568.

Belelovsky, K., Maroun, M., & Rosenblum, K. (2007). MAPK activation in the hippocampus in vivo is correlated with experimental setting. *Neurobiology of Learning and Memory, 88*, 58–64.

Berman, D. E., & Dudai, Y. (2001). Memory extinction, learning anew, and learning the new: Dissociations in the molecular machinery of learning in cortex. *Science, 291*, 2417–2419.

Berman, D. E., Hazvi, S., Neduva, V., & Dudai, Y. (2000). The role of identified neurotransmitter systems in the response of insular cortex to unfamiliar taste: Activation of ERK1–2 and formation of a memory trace. *Journal of Neuroscience, 20*, 7017–7023.

Bermudez-Rattoni, F. (2004). Molecular mechanisms of taste-recognition memory. *Nature Reviews. Neuroscience, 5*, 209–217.

Bernstein, I. L., & Koh, M. T. (2007). Molecular signaling during taste aversion learning. *Chemical Senses, 32*, 99–103.

Bures, J., Bermudez-Rattoni, F., & Yamamoto, T. (1998). *Conditioned taste aversion, memory of a special kind.* Oxford: Oxford University Press.

Chen, J., Lin, W., Wang, W., Shao, F., Yang, J., Wang, B., et al. (2004). Enhancement of antibody production and expression of c-Fos in the insular cortex in response to a conditioned stimulus after a single-trial learning paradigm. *Behavioural Brain Research, 154*, 557–565.

Coan, E. J., Saywood, W., & Collingridge, G. L. (1987). MK-801 blocks NMDA receptor-mediated synaptic transmission and long term potentiation in rat hippocampal slices. *Neuroscience Letters, 80*, 111–114.

Cochilla, A. J., & Alford, S. (1998). Metabotropic glutamate receptor-mediated control of neurotransmitter release. *Neuron, 20*, 1007–1016.

Collingridge, G. L., Herron, C. E., & Lester, R. A. (1988). Synaptic activation of N-methyl-D-aspartate receptors in the Schaffer collateral-commissural pathway of rat hippocampus. *Journal of Physiology, 399*, 283–300.

Collingridge, G. L., Kehl, S. J., & McLennan, H. (1983). Excitatory amino acids in synaptic transmission in the Schaffer collateral-commissural pathway of the rat hippocampus. *Journal of Physiology, 334*, 33–46.

Costa-Mattioli, M., Gobert, D., Harding, H., Herdy, B., Azzi, M., Bruno, M., et al. (2005). Translational control of hippocampal synaptic plasticity and memory by the eIF2alpha kinase GCN2. *Nature, 436*, 1166–1173.

Costa-Mattioli, M., Gobert, D., Stern, E., Gamache, K., Colina, R., Cuello, C., et al. (2007). eIF2alpha phosphorylation bidirectionally regulates the switch from short- to long-term synaptic plasticity and memory. *Cell, 129*, 195–206.

Countryman, R. A., Kaban, N. L., & Colombo, P. J. (2005). Hippocampal c-fos is necessary for long-term memory of a socially transmitted food preference. *Neurobiology of Learning and Memory, 84*, 175–183.

Cull-Candy, S., Brickley, S., & Farrant, M. (2001). NMDA receptor subunits: Diversity, development and disease. *Current Opinion in Neurobiology, 11*, 327–335.

Davis, H. P., & Squire, L. R. (1984). Protein synthesis and memory: A review. *Psychological Bulletin, 96*, 518–559.

De Souza Silva, M. A., Dolga, A., Pieri, I., Marchetti, L., Eisel, U. L., Huston, J. P., et al. (2006). Cholinergic cells in the nucleus basalis of mice express the N-methyl-D-aspartate-receptor subunit NR2C and its replacement by the NR2B subunit enhances frontal and amygdaloid acetylcholine levels. *Genes, Brain, and Behavior, 5*, 552–560.

Desmedt, A., Hazvi, S., & Dudai, Y. (2003). Differential pattern of cAMP response element-binding protein activation in the rat brain after conditioned aversion as a function of the associative process engaged: Taste versus context association. *Journal of Neuroscience, 23*, 6102–6110.

Dever, T. E. (2002). Gene-specific regulation by general translation factors. *Cell, 108*, 545–556.

Dingledine, R., Borges, K., Bowie, D., & Traynelis, S. F. (1999). The glutamate receptor ion channels. *Pharmacological Reviews, 51*, 7–61.

Escobar, M. L., Alcocer, I., & Chao, V. (1998). The NMDA receptor antagonist CPP impairs conditioned taste aversion and insular cortex long-term potentiation in vivo. *Brain Research, 812*, 246–251.

Farb, C. R., Aoki, C., & Ledoux, J. E. (1995). Differential localization of NMDA and AMPA receptor subunits in the lateral and basal nuclei of the amygdala: A light and electron microscopic study. *Journal of Comparative Neurology, 362*, 86–108.

Farb, C. R., & LeDoux, J. E. (1997). NMDA and AMPA receptors in the lateral nucleus of the amygdala are postsynaptic to auditory thalamic afferents. *Synapse, 27*, 106–121.

Ferreira, G., Ferry, B., Meurisse, M., & Levy, F. (2006). Forebrain structures specifically activated by conditioned taste aversion. *Behavioral Neuroscience, 120*, 952–962.

Ferreira, G., Gutierrez, R., De La Cruz, V., & Bermudez-Rattoni, F. (2002). Differential involvement of cortical muscarinic and NMDA receptors in short- and long-term taste aversion memory. *European Journal of Neuroscience, 16*, 1139–1145.

Ferreira, G., Miranda, M. I., De la Cruz, V., Rodriguez-Ortiz, C. J., & Bermudez-Rattoni, F. (2005). Basolateral amygdala glutamatergic activation enhances taste aversion through NMDA receptor activation in the insular cortex. *European Journal of Neuroscience, 22*, 2596–2604.

Figueroa-Guzman, Y., Kuo, J. S., & Reilly, S. (2006). NMDA receptor antagonist MK-801 infused into the insular cortex prevents the attenuation of gustatory neophobia in rats. *Brain Research, 1114*, 183–186.

Flint, A. C., Maisch, U. S., Weishaupt, J. H., Kriegstein, A. R., & Monyer, H. (1997). NR2A subunit expression shortens NMDA receptor synaptic currents in developing neocortex. *Journal of Neuroscience, 17*, 2469–2476.

Gale, E., Cundliffe, E., Reynolds, P., Richmond, M., & Waring, J. (1981). *The molecular basis of antibiotic action*. New York: John Wiley and Sons.

Gardoni, F., Bellone, C., Cattabeni, F., & Di Luca, M. (2001). Protein kinase C activation modulates alpha-calmodulin kinase II binding to NR2A subunit of N-methyl-D-aspartate receptor complex. *Journal of Biological Chemistry, 276*, 7609–7613.

Goelet, P., Castellucci, V. F., Schacher, S., & Kandel, E. R. (1986). The long and the short of long-term memory—A molecular framework. *Nature, 322*, 419–422.

Gonzalez-Mejia, M. E., Morales, M., Hernandez-Kelly, L. C., Zepeda, R. C., Bernabe, A., & Ortega, A. (2006). Glutamate-dependent translational regulation in cultured Bergmann glia cells: Involvement of p70S6K. *Neuroscience, 141*, 1389–1398.

Grant, S. G., O'Dell, T. J., Karl, K. A., Stein, P. L., Soriano, P., & Kandel, E. R. (1992). Impaired long-term potentiation, spatial learning, and hippocampal development in fyn mutant mice. *Science, 258*, 1903–1910.

Greengard, P., Jen, J., Nairn, A. C., & Stevens, C. F. (1991). Enhancement of the glutamate response by cAMP-dependent protein kinase in hippocampal neurons. *Science, 253*, 1135–1138.

Grimm, R., Schicknick, H., Riede, I., Gundelfinger, E. D., Herdegen, T., Zuschratter, W., et al. (1997). Suppression of c-fos induction in rat brain impairs retention of a brightness discrimination reaction. *Learning & Memory, 3*, 402–413.

Gryder, D. S., Castaneda, D. C., & Rogawski, M. A. (2005). Evidence for low GluR2 AMPA receptor subunit expression at synapses in the rat basolateral amygdala. *Journal of Neurochemistry, 94*, 1728–1738.

Gu, Y., Gonzalez, M. F., Chin, D. Y., & Deutsch, J. A. (1993). Expression of c-fos in brain subcortical structures in response to nauseant lithium chloride and osmotic pressure in rats. *Neuroscience Letters, 157*, 49–52.

Gutierrez, H., Gutierrez, R., Ramirez-Trejo, L., Silva-Gandarias, R., Ormsby, C. E., Miranda, M. I., et al. (1999). Redundant basal forebrain modulation in taste aversion memory formation. *Journal of Neuroscience, 19*, 7661–7669.

Gutierrez, R., Rodriguez-Ortiz, C. J., De La Cruz, V., Nunez-Jaramillo, L., & Bermudez-Rattoni, F. (2003). Cholinergic dependence of taste memory formation: Evidence of two distinct processes. *Neurobiology of Learning and Memory, 80*, 323–331.

Gutierrez, R., Tellez, L. A., & Bermudez-Rattoni, F. (2003). Blockade of cortical muscarinic but not NMDA receptors prevents a novel taste from becoming familiar. *European Journal of Neuroscience, 17*, 1556–1562.

Harney, S. C., Rowan, M., & Anwyl, R. (2006). Long-term depression of NMDA receptor-mediated synaptic transmission is dependent on activation of metabotropic glutamate receptors and is altered to long-term potentiation by low intracellular calcium buffering. *Journal of Neuroscience, 26*, 1128–1132.

He, J., Yamada, K., & Nabeshima, T. (2002). A role of Fos expression in the CA3 region of the hippocampus in spatial memory formation in rats. *Neuropsychopharmacology, 26*, 259–268.

He, Y., Janssen, W. G., & Morrison, J. H. (1999). Differential synaptic distribution of the AMPA-GluR2 subunit on GABAergic and non-GABAergic neurons in the basolateral amygdala. *Brain Research, 827*, 51–62.

Hou, L., & Klann, E. (2004). Activation of the phosphoinositide 3-kinase-Akt-mammalian target of rapamycin signaling pathway is required for metabotropic glutamate receptor-dependent long-term depression. *Journal of Neuroscience, 24*, 6352–6361.

Houpt, T. A., & Berlin, R. (1999). Rapid, labile, and protein synthesis-independent short-term memory in conditioned taste aversion. *Learning & Memory, 6*, 37–46.

Huang, F., Chotiner, J. K., & Steward, O., (2005). The mRNA for elongation factor 1alpha is localized in dendrites and translated in response to treatments that induce long-term depression. *Journal of Neuroscience, 25*, 7199–7209.

Huang, Y., Kang, B. N., Tian, J., Liu, Y., Luo, H. R., Hester, L., et al. (2007). The cationic amino acid transporters CAT1 and CAT3 mediate NMDA receptor activation-dependent changes in elaboration of neuronal processes via the mammalian target of rapamycin mTOR pathway. *Journal of Neuroscience, 27*, 449–458.

Huber, K. M., Gallagher, S. M., Warren, S. T., & Bear, M. F. (2002). Altered synaptic plasticity in a mouse model of fragile X mental retardation. *Proceedings of the National Academy of*

Sciences of the United States of America, 99, 7746–7750.

Jones, M. W., Errington, M. L., French, P. J., Fine, A., Bliss, T. V., Garel, S., et al. (2001). A requirement for the immediate early gene *Zif268* in the expression of late LTP and long-term memories. *Nature Neuroscience, 4,* 289–296.

Jones, M. W., French, P. J., Bliss, T. V., & Rosenblum, K. (1999). Molecular mechanisms of long-term potentiation in the insular cortex in vivo. *Journal of Neuroscience, 19,* RC36.

Kanhema, T., Dagestad, G., Panja, D., Tiron, A., Messaoudi, E., Havik, B., et al. (2006). Dual regulation of translation initiation and peptide chain elongation during BDNF-induced LTP in vivo: Evidence for compartment-specific translation control. *Journal of Neurochemistry, 99,* 1328–1337.

Kelleher, R. J., III., Govindarajan, A., Jung, H. Y., Kang, H., & Tonegawa, S. (2004). Translational control by MAPK signaling in long-term synaptic plasticity and memory. *Cell, 116,* 467–479.

Klann, E., & Dever, T. E. (2004). Biochemical mechanisms for translational regulation in synaptic plasticity. *Nature Reviews. Neuroscience, 5,* 931–942.

Koh, M. T., & Bernstein, I. L. (2005). Mapping conditioned taste aversion associations using c-Fos reveals a dynamic role for insular cortex. *Behavioral Neuroscience, 119,* 388–398.

Koh, M. T., Wilkins, E. E., & Bernstein, I. L. (2003). Novel tastes elevate c-fos expression in the central amygdala and insular cortex: Implication for taste aversion learning. *Behavioral Neuroscience, 117,* 1416–1422.

Koulen, P., Kuhn, R., Wassle, H., & Brandstatter, J. H. (1999). Modulation of the intracellular calcium concentration in photoreceptor terminals by a presynaptic metabotropic glutamate receptor. *Proceedings of the National Academy of Sciences of the United States of America, 96,* 9909–9914.

Lamprecht, R., & Dudai, Y. (1995). Differential modulation of brain immediate early genes by intraperitoneal LiCl. *Neuroreport, 7,* 289–293.

Lamprecht, R., & Dudai, Y. (1996). Transient expression of c-Fos in rat amygdala during training is required for encoding conditioned taste aversion memory. *Learning & Memory, 3,* 31–41.

Lamprecht, R., Hazvi, S., & Dudai, Y. (1997). cAMP response element-binding protein in the amygdala is required for long- but not short-term conditioned taste aversion memory. *Journal of Neuroscience, 17,* 8443–8450.

Lau, L. F., & Huganir, R. L. (1995). Differential tyrosine phosphorylation of N-methyl-D-aspartate receptor subunits. *Journal of Biological Chemistry, 270,* 20036–20041.

Lenz, G., & Avruch, J. (2005). Glutamatergic regulation of the p70S6 kinase in primary mouse neurons. *Journal of Biological Chemistry, 280,* 38121–38124.

Leonard, A. S., & Hell, J. W. (1997). Cyclic AMP-dependent protein kinase and protein kinase C phosphorylate N-methyl-D-aspartate receptors at different sites. *Journal of Biological Chemistry, 272,* 12107–12115.

Lopez de Armentia, M., & Sah, P. (2003). Development and subunit composition of synaptic NMDA receptors in the amygdala: NR2B synapses in the adult central amygdala. *Journal of Neuroscience, 23,* 6876–6883.

Lu, P. D., Harding, H. P., & Ron, D. (2004). Translation reinitiation at alternative open reading frames regulates gene expression in an integrated stress response. *Journal of Cell Biology, 167,* 27–33.

Lu, Y. M., Roder, J. C., Davidow, J., & Salter, M. W. (1998). Src activation in the induction of long-term potentiation in CA1 hippocampal neurons. *Science, 279,* 1363–1367.

Mathews, M., Sonenberg, N., & Hershey, J. (2000). Origins and principles of translational control. In N. Sonenberg, J. Hershey, & M. Mathews (Eds.), *Translational control of gene expression* (pp. 1–31). New York: Cold Spring Harbor Laboratory Press.

McDonald, A. J. (1994). Neuronal localization of glutamate receptor subunits in the basolateral amygdala. *Neuroreport, 6,* 13–16.

McDonald, A. J. (1996). Localization of AMPA glutamate receptor subunits in subpopulations of non-pyramidal neurons in the rat basolateral amygdala. *Neuroscience Letters, 208,* 175–178.

Merhav, M., Kuulmann-Vander, S., Elkobi, A., Jacobson-Pick, S., Karni, A., & Rosenblum, K. (2006). Behavioral interference and C/EBPbeta expression in the insular-cortex reveal a prolonged time period for taste memory consolidation. *Learning & Memory, 13,* 571–574.

Miranda, M. I., Ferreira, G., Ramirez-Lugo, L., & Bermudez-Rattoni, F. (2002). Glutamatergic activity in the amygdala signals visceral input during taste memory formation. *Proceedings of the National Academy of Sciences of the United States of America, 99,* 11417–11422.

Miranda, M. I., Ramirez-Lugo, L., & Bermudez-Rattoni, F. (2000). Cortical cholinergic activity is related to the novelty of the stimulus. *Brain Research, 882,* 230–235.

Montag-Sallaz, M., Welzl, H., Kuhl, D., Montag, D., & Schachner, M. (1999). Novelty-induced increased expression of immediate-early genes c-fos and arg 3.1 in the mouse brain. *Journal of Neurobiology, 38*, 234–246.

Moon, I. S. (2003). Relative extent of tyrosine phosphorylation of the NR2A and NR2B subunits in the rat forebrain postsynaptic density fraction. *Molecules and Cells, 16*, 28–33.

Moon, I. S., Apperson, M. L., & Kennedy, M. B. (1994). The major tyrosine-phosphorylated protein in the postsynaptic density fraction is N-methyl-D-aspartate receptor subunit 2B. *Proceedings of the National Academy of Sciences of the United States of America, 91*, 3954–3958.

Morrow, B. A., Elsworth, J. D., Inglis, F. M., & Roth, R. H. (1999). An antisense oligonucleotide reverses the footshock-induced expression of fos in the rat medial prefrontal cortex and the subsequent expression of conditioned fear-induced immobility. *Journal of Neuroscience, 19*, 5666–5673.

Mugnaini, M., Meoni, P., Bunnemann, B., Corsi, M., & Bowery, N. G. (2001). Allosteric modulation of [3H]-CGP39653 binding through the glycine site of the NMDA receptor: Further studies in rat and human brain. *British Journal of Pharmacology, 132*, 1883–1897.

Naor, C., & Dudai, Y. (1996). Transient impairment of cholinergic function in the rat insular cortex disrupts the encoding of taste in conditioned taste aversion. *Behavioural Brain Research, 79*, 61–67.

Nerad, L., Ramirez-Amaya, V., Ormsby, C. E., & Bermudez-Rattoni, F. (1996). Differential effects of anterior and posterior insular cortex lesions on the acquisition of conditioned taste aversion and spatial learning. *Neurobiology of Learning and Memory, 66*, 44–50.

Nicholls, R. E., Zhang, X. L., Bailey, C. P., Conklin, B. R., Kandel, E. R., & Stanton, P. K. (2006). mGluR2 acts through inhibitory Galpha subunits to regulate transmission and long-term plasticity at hippocampal mossy fiber-CA3 synapses. *Proceedings of the National Academy of Sciences of the United States of America, 103*, 6380–6385.

O'Dell, T. J., Kandel, E. R., & Grant, S. G. (1991). Long-term potentiation in the hippocampus is blocked by tyrosine kinase inhibitors. *Nature, 353*, 558–560.

Omkumar, R. V., Kiely, M. J., Rosenstein, A. J., Min, K. T., & Kennedy, M. B. (1996). Identification of a phosphorylation site for calcium/calmodulin dependent protein kinase II in the NR2B subunit of the N-methyl-D-aspartate receptor. *Journal of Biological Chemistry, 271*, 31670–31678.

Otawa, S., Takagi, K., & Ogawa, H. (1995). NMDA and non-NMDA receptors mediate taste afferent inputs to cortical taste neurons in rats. *Experimental Brain Research, 106*, 391–402.

Page, G., Khidir, F. A., Pain, S., Barrier, L., Fauconneau, B., Guillard, O., et al. (2006). Group I metabotropic glutamate receptors activate the p70S6 kinase via both mammalian target of rapamycin (mTOR) and extracellular signal-regulated kinase (ERK 1/2) signaling pathways in rat striatal and hippocampal synaptoneurosomes. *Neurochemistry International, 49*, 413–421.

Pause, A., Belsham, G. J., Gingras, A. C., Donze, O., Lin, T. A., Lawrence, J. C., Jr., et al. (1994). Insulin-dependent stimulation of protein synthesis by phosphorylation of a regulator of 5'-cap function. *Nature, 371*, 762–767.

Paylor, R., Johnson, R. S., Papaioannou, V., Spiegelman, B. M., & Wehner, J. M. (1994). Behavioral assessment of c-fos mutant mice. *Brain Research, 651*, 275–282.

Pende, M., Um, S. H., Mieulet, V., Sticker, M., Goss, V. L., Mestan, J., et al. (2004). S6K1(-/-)/S6K2(-/-) mice exhibit perinatal lethality and rapamycin-sensitive 5'-terminal oligopyrimidine mRNA translation and reveal a mitogen-activated protein kinase-dependent S6 kinase pathway. *Molecular and Cellular Biology, 24*, 3112–3124.

Pinaud, R. (2004). Experience-dependent immediate early gene expression in the adult central nervous system: Evidence from enriched-environment studies. *International Journal of Neuroscience, 114*, 321–333.

Ramirez-Lugo, L., Miranda, M. I., Escobar, M. L., Espinosa, E., & Bermudez-Rattoni, F. (2003). The role of cortical cholinergic pre- and postsynaptic receptors in taste memory formation. *Neurobiology of Learning and Memory, 79*, 184–193.

Ramirez-Lugo, L., Zavala-Vega, S., & Bermudez-Rattoni, F. (2006). NMDA and muscarinic receptors of the nucleus accumbens have differential effects on taste memory formation. *Learning & Memory, 13*, 45–51.

Raught, B., Gingras, A. C., & Sonenberg, N. (2001). The target of rapamycin (TOR) proteins. *Proceedings of the National Academy of Sciences of the United States of America, 98*, 7037–7044.

Rosenblum, K., Berman, D. E., Hazvi, S., Lamprecht, R., & Dudai, Y. (1997). NMDA receptor and the tyrosine phosphorylation of its 2B subunit in taste learning in the rat insular cortex. *Journal of Neuroscience, 17,* 5129–5135.

Rosenblum, K., Dudai, Y., & Richter-Levin, G. (1996). Long-term potentiation increases tyrosine phosphorylation of the N-methyl-D-aspartate receptor subunit 2B in rat dentate gyrus in vivo. *Proceedings of the National Academy of Sciences of the United States of America, 93,* 10457–10460.

Rosenblum, K., Meiri, N., & Dudai, Y. (1993). Taste memory: The role of protein synthesis in gustatory cortex. *Behavioral and Neural Biology, 59,* 49–56.

Rosenblum, K., Schul, R., Meiri, N., Hadari, Y. R., Zick, Y., & Dudai, Y. (1995). Modulation of protein tyrosine phosphorylation in rat insular cortex after conditioned taste aversion training. *Proceedings of the National Academy of Sciences of the United States of America, 92,* 1157–1161.

Rostas, J. A., Brent, V. A., Voss, K., Errington, M. L., Bliss, T. V., & Gurd, J. W. (1996). Enhanced tyrosine phosphorylation of the 2B subunit of the N-methyl-D-aspartate receptor in long-term potentiation. *Proceedings of the National Academy of Sciences of the United States of America, 93,* 10452–10456.

Sah, P., & Lopez De Armentia, M. (2003). Excitatory synaptic transmission in the lateral and central amygdala. *Annals of the New York Academy of Sciences, 985,* 67–77.

Schell, M. J., Molliver, M. E., & Snyder, S. H. (1995). D-serine, an endogenous synaptic modulator: Localization to astrocytes and glutamate-stimulated release. *Proceedings of the National Academy of Sciences of the United States of America, 92,* 3948–3952.

Schroeder, J. P., Olive, F., Koenig, H., & Hodge, C. W. (2003). Intra-amygdala infusion of the NPY Y1 receptor antagonist BIBP 3226 attenuates operant ethanol self-administration. *Alcoholism, Clinical and Experimental Research, 27,* 1884–1891.

Spencer, C. M., & Houpt, T. A. (2001). Dynamics of c-fos and ICER mRNA expression in rat forebrain following lithium chloride injection. *Brain Research. Molecular Brain Research, 93,* 113–126.

St. Andre, J., Albanos, K., & Reilly, S. (2007). C-fos expression in the rat brain following lithium chloride-induced illness. *Brain Research, 1135,* 122–128.

Steward, O. (1983). Polyribosomes at the base of dendritic spines of central nervous system neurons—Their possible role in synapse construction and modification. *Cold Spring Harbor Symposia on Quantitative Biology, 48*(Pt. 2), 745–759.

Steward, O., Falk, P. M., & Torre, E. R. (1996). Ultrastructural basis for gene expression at the synapse: Synapse-associated polyribosome complexes. *Journal of Neurocytology, 25,* 717–734.

Steward, O., & Fass, B. (1983). Polyribosomes associated with dendritic spines in the denervated dentate gyrus: Evidence for local regulation of protein synthesis during reinnervation. *Progress in Brain Research, 58,* 131–136.

Steward, O., & Levy, W. B. (1982). Preferential localization of polyribosomes under the base of dendritic spines in granule cells of the dentate gyrus. *Journal of Neuroscience, 2,* 284–291.

Steward, O., & Schuman, E. M. (2001). Protein synthesis at synaptic sites on dendrites. *Annual Review of Neuroscience, 24,* 299–325.

Steward, O., & Singer, R. (1997). The intracellular mRNA sorting system: Postal zones, zip codes, mail bags and mail boxes. In J. D. M. Hartford (Ed.), *mRNA metabolism and post-transcriptional gene regulation* (pp. 127–146). New York: Wiley-Liss.

Stocca, G., & Vicini, S. (1998). Increased contribution of NR2A subunit to synaptic NMDA receptors in developing rat cortical neurons. *Journal of Physiology, 507*(Pt. 1), 13–24.

Stork, O., & Welzl, H. (1999). Memory formation and the regulation of gene expression. *Cellular and Molecular Life Sciences: CMLS, 55,* 575–592.

Strack, S., McNeill, R. B., & Colbran, R. J. (2000). Mechanism and regulation of calcium/calmodulin-dependent protein kinase II targeting to the NR2B subunit of the N-methyl-D-aspartate receptor. *Journal of Biological Chemistry, 275,* 23798–23806.

Szinyei, C., Stork, O., & Pape, H. C. (2003). Contribution of NR2B subunits to synaptic transmission in amygdaloid interneurons. *Journal of Neuroscience, 23,* 2549–2556.

Takei, N., Kawamura, M., Hara, K., Yonezawa, K., & Nawa, H. (2001). Brain-derived neurotrophic factor enhances neuronal translation by activating multiple initiation processes: Comparison with the effects of insulin. *Journal of Biological Chemistry, 276,* 42818–42825.

Tischmeyer, W., & Grimm, R. (1999). Activation of immediate early genes and memory formation. *Cellular and Molecular Life Sciences: CMLS, 55,* 564–574.

Tolliver, B. K., Sganga, M. W., & Sharp, F. R. (2000). Suppression of c-fos induction in the nucleus accumbens prevents acquisition but not expression of morphine-conditioned place preference. *European Journal of Neuroscience, 12,* 3399–3406.

Tovar, K. R., & Westbrook, G. L. (1999). The incorporation of NMDA receptors with a distinct subunit composition at nascent hippocampal synapses in vitro. *Journal of Neuroscience, 19,* 4180–4188.

Tsokas, P., Grace, E. A., Chan, P., Ma, T., Sealfon, S. C., Iyengar, R., et al. (2005). Local protein synthesis mediates a rapid increase in dendritic elongation factor 1A after induction of late long-term potentiation. *Journal of Neuroscience, 25,* 5833–5843.

Tucker, A., & Gibbs, M. (1976). Cycloheximide-induced amnesia for taste aversion memory in rats. *Pharmacology, Biochemistry, and Behavior, 4,* 181–184.

Vattem, K. M., & Wek, R. C. (2004). Reinitiation involving upstream ORFs regulates ATF4 mRNA translation in mammalian cells. *Proceedings of the National Academy of Sciences of the United States of America, 101,* 11269–11274.

Wang, X., Li, W., Williams, M., Terada, N., Alessi, D. R., & Proud, C. G. (2001). Regulation of elongation factor 2 kinase by p90(RSK1) and p70 S6 kinase. *EMBO Journal, 20,* 4370–4379.

Wisden, W., & Seeburg, P. H. (1993). Mammalian ionotropic glutamate receptors. *Current Opinion in Neurobiology, 3,* 291–298.

Yamamoto, T., Sako, N., Sakai, N., & Iwafune, A. (1997). Gustatory and visceral inputs to the amygdala of the rat: Conditioned taste aversion and induction of c-fos-like immunoreactivity. *Neuroscience Letters, 226,* 127–130.

Yamamoto, T., Shimura, T., Sako, N., Azuma, S., Bai, W. Z., & Wakisaka, S. (1992). c-fos expression in the rat brain after intraperitoneal injection of lithium chloride. *Neuroreport, 3,* 1049–1052.

Yasoshima, Y., Sako, N., Senba, E., & Yamamoto, T. (2006). Acute suppression, but not chronic genetic deficiency, of c-fos gene expression impairs long-term memory in aversive taste learning. *Proceedings of the National Academy of Sciences of the United States of America, 103,* 7106–7111.

Yefet, K., Merhav, M., Kuulmann-Vander, S., Elkobi, A., Belelovsky, K., Jacobson-Pick, S., et al. (2006). Different signal transduction cascades are activated simultaneously in the rat insular cortex and hippocampus following novel taste learning. *European Journal of Neuroscience, 24,* 1434–1442.

Yokoyama, C., & Sasaki, K. (1999). Regional expressions of Fos-like immunoreactivity in rat cerebral cortex after stress: Restraint and intraperitoneal lipopolysaccharide. *Brain Research, 816,* 267–275.

18

Hormonal Modulation of Conditioned Taste Avoidance: The Role of Estradiol

KATHLEEN C. CHAMBERS AND HOURI HINTIRYAN

Hormones are organic compounds that when released into the bloodstream can affect target tissues at long distances from the site of synthesis. They are synthesized and released by secretory cells in the body and brain and those hormones secreted by cells in the body can affect brain function either directly or indirectly through their action on target tissues outside the brain. Although hormones can play an essential role in the display of various behaviors, such as testosterone in male rodent sexual behavior, their role in conditioned taste avoidance (CTA) apparently is modulatory. The study of three different hormones, testosterone, adrenocorticotropin hormone (ACTH), and vasopressin, has revealed that their modulatory influence is both varied and complex. The most striking modulatory effect of these hormones is on the expression of extinction (for reviews see the following: Chambers, 1985; Chambers & Hayes, 2005; Chambers, Yuan, Brownson, & Wang, 1997; Smotherman, 1985). This influence is dependent on whether the hormone is present during the acquisition or extinction processes, on the interaction of the hormone with other hormonal systems, and on whether the circulatory levels of the hormone are high or low.

Both testosterone and ACTH prolong extinction of a CTA induced by lithium chloride (LiCl) and they appear to do so by acting on the extinction process. Their presence during acquisition has no effect on length of extinction while their presence during extinction is required to produce the prolonged effect (Chambers & Sengstake, 1979; Kendler, Hennessy, Smotherman, & Levine, 1976). The modulatory effect of ACTH on extinction is mediated through the testosterone hormonal system. Elevations in ACTH increase circulating testosterone levels and this increased level most likely acts to prolong extinction since ACTH only has an effect on extinction if the testes are intact (Chambers, 1982). Although a number of extinction-based hypotheses have been suggested to account for the modulatory effect of testosterone, an explanation for what testosterone is doing during extinction remains unknown (Chambers & Sengstake, 1979; Clifton & Andrew, 1987; Earley & Leonard, 1979). Evidence does suggest, however, that a delay in passive decay of the memory trace, an increase in the focusing of attention, and an improvement of performance in passive avoidance tasks are unlikely explanations (Chambers et al., 1997; Clifton & Andrew, 1987).

High and low doses of vasopressin have opposite effects on extinction of LiCl-induced CTAs. High doses of vasopressin delay the onset of extinction when they are administered 50 min after pairing a sucrose solution with a high dose of LiCl (1.5 mEq/kg; Hayes & Chambers, 2005a, 2005b). The modulatory effect of these doses of vasopressin is likely due to their aversive properties. They induce CTA when paired with a sucrose solution and strengthen acquisition when administered 50 min after pairing a low dose of LiCl (0.075 mEq/kg) with a sucrose solution (Hayes & Chambers, 2005b). On the other hand, low doses of vasopressin accelerate extinction of a LiCl-induced CTA when they are administered 50 min after LiCl. Existing evidence suggests that they do so by reducing the sensory impact of LiCl during acquisition. Low doses of vasopressin do not induce CTA when paired with a sucrose solution and they can attenuate the unconditioned effects of illness-inducing agents (Dantzer, Bluthe, & Kelley, 1991; Hayes & Chambers, 2002, 2005a). In addition, the completion but not the initiation of extinction of LiCl-induced CTAs is accelerated when the dose of LiCl is lowered from 3.0 to 0.3 mEq/kg, and this is the same kind of attenuated effect that administration of low doses of vasopressin has on extinction of a CTA produced by a 3.0 mEq/kg dose of LiCl (Hayes & Chambers, 2002, 2005a).

Thus, testosterone slows extinction of CTA by acting specifically on the extinction process, ACTH slows extinction by increasing testosterone levels, high levels of vasopressin delay the onset of extinction by acting nonspecifically through the aversive effects it produces, and low levels of vasopressin accelerate extinction by acting specifically on the acquisition process. Recently, we have been investigating the possible reasons for the modulatory effects that the hormone estradiol has on extinction of CTAs induced by LiCl. This hormone is part of a group of steroid sex hormones called estrogens and is present in both males and females. The primary source of estradiol in the circulatory system is the granulosa cells in the ovaries of female rodents and the aromatization of testosterone in the testes of male rodents (De Jong, Hey, & Molen, 1973; Shoham & Schachter, 1996). As such, it is thought of primarily as a gonadal hormone. However, evidence demonstrates that in humans and in rats estrogens are synthesized outside of the gonads as well. For instance, in postmenopausal women and in men, estradiol is produced as a product of androgen aromatization, which occurs locally at various sites like the skin and adipose tissue (Grodin, Siiteri, & MacDonald, 1973; MacDonald, Madden, Brenner, Wilson, & Siiteri, 1979; Nelson & Bulun, 2001). In rats, the presence of aromatase in bone suggests that estradiol is produced at this site as well (Eyre et al., 1998). Because peripheral estradiol freely diffuses

the blood–brain barrier, regardless of its source or whether it is free or plasma protein bound (Pardridge & Mietus, 1979), it can act directly on neural substrates to influence learning processes.

The focus of this chapter is on the modulatory effects of estradiol on CTAs induced by LiCl. In the first section of this chapter, we describe data showing opposite modulatory effects on extinction depending on when estradiol is present during the CTA procedure. Next, we present evidence supporting the hypothesis that these modulatory effects can be explained by the fact that estradiol has unconditioned stimulus (US) properties in a CTA paradigm. Finally, we suggest that there are three different US properties that could induce an apparent CTA and allow estradiol to modulate extinction of LiCl-induced CTAs: aversive, satiating, or positive reinforcing properties. In the second section of this chapter, we review behavioral data relevant to each of these properties and our assessment of these data lead us to the conclusion that the supraphysiological doses of estradiol used to modulate extinction have both aversive and satiating properties. Lastly, in the third section of this chapter, we focus on neural structures implicated in aversion and satiety and our assessment of these data leads us to aversion as the most likely property that accounts for the ability of estradiol to modulate extinction of LiCl-induced CTAs.

MODULATORY EFFECTS OF ESTRADIOL ON EXTINCTION OF CTA

The Data

Elevations in testosterone prolong extinction of CTAs induced by LiCl in gonadectomized female and male rats (Chambers, 1976, 1980). However, the ability of testosterone to prolong extinction is diminished in intact females as well as gonadectomized females and males treated with estradiol (Chambers, 1976, 1980). This reduced effectiveness of testosterone is based on the ability of estradiol to accelerate extinction independent of the presence of testosterone. Elevations in estradiol can accelerate extinction of a LiCl-induced CTA in gonadectomized female and male Sprague-Dawley and gonadectomized female and male Fischer 344 rats in the absence of testosterone treatment (Earley & Leonard, 1979; Yuan & Chambers, 1999a).

In the studies showing the accelerated extinction effects of estradiol on LiCl-induced CTA, nondeprived rats were given access to a 10% sucrose solution for 1 h and then were immediately injected with LiCl. Two days after this acquisition trial, the first extinction trial was given and thereafter, daily extinction trials were given until each rat reached its acquisition consumption level. Estradiol was administered via an implanted Silastic capsule that provided continuous exposure to the hormone starting at least 1 week prior to acquisition and continuing throughout extinction testing. Thus, it was unclear in these studies whether the hormone was required before or during acquisition or before or during extinction to produce its effects. An important first step in understanding what a hormone is doing in learning tasks is to determine the temporal requirements because it potentially allows one to reduce the number of hypotheses that could account for the hormonal effect. Therefore, a series of studies was conducted to determine the temporal requirements for the facilitatory effect of estradiol on extinction (Chambers & Hayes, 2002; Yuan & Chambers, 1999a, 1999b). Exposure to estradiol was given during four different time periods: before acquisition, during acquisition, before extinction, and during extinction (see Table 18.1). When estradiol was given either before acquisition or before extinction of a LiCl-induced CTA, it hastened extinction. On the other hand, when it was given during acquisition, there was a greater suppression of sucrose consumption during the first extinction trial, and when it was given during extinction, it prolonged extinction.

Interpretation of the Data

Substances capable of inducing a conditioned reduction in consumption can be used as both USs and preexposure agents in CTA paradigms. It is a US when it is given after consumption of a novel taste substance and it is a preexposure agent when it is given prior to acquisition in the absence of the taste substance targeted for future conditioning or prior to extinction in the absence of the taste conditioned stimulus (CS). When two agents capable of inducing CTA are both administered after consumption of a novel taste solution, acquisition is stronger and the onset of extinction is slower than when only one of the agents is given (Hayes & Chambers, 2005b). On the other hand, it has been shown for a number of different USs that preexposure attenuates acquisition and accelerates extinction (Cappell, LeBlanc, & Herling, 1975; Colby & Smith, 1977; De Beun, Peeters, & Broekkamp, 1993; Mikulka, Leard, & Klein, 1977; Rabin, Hunt, & Lee, 1989). This is the case if the preexposure agent is the same (intraagent) or different (interagent) than the agent used to induce the CTA (Cannon, Baker, & Berman, 1977). These data suggest that estradiol prolonged extinction when it was given during acquisition and extinction because it was set up experimentally to act as a US. On the other hand, it accelerated extinction when it was administered before acquisition and extinction because it was set up to act as a preexposure agent.

Table 18.1 Effect of the Presence of Estradiol at Different Times during Acquisition and Extinction of CTA induced by LiCl.

Temporal Conditions	Time Periods during which Estradiol was Present	Effect of Estradiol on CTA
Before acquisition[a]	Starting 12 days before acquisition Ending 2 days before acquisition	Extinction hastened
During acquisition[b]	Starting at the time of LiCl injection Ending 18 h later	Acquisition strengthened
Before extinction[a]	Starting 2 days after acquisition Ending 8 days later (1 day before extinction)	Extinction hastened
During extinction[a]	Starting 6 h after the first extinction test Ending after the last extinction test	Extinction prolonged

[a] From Yuan & Chambers (1999b).
[b] From Chambers & Hayes (2002).

Estradiol can act as a US in a CTA paradigm; when paired with a novel taste solution, CTAs can be induced by estradiol in rats and humans (Gustavson, Gustavson, Young, Pumariega, & Nicolaus, 1989; Yuan & Chambers, 1999b). In one of the temporal experiments examining the effects of estradiol on extinction of LiCl-induced CTA, estradiol-filled or empty capsules were implanted after access to sucrose during the first extinction trial (Yuan & Chambers, 1999b). Rats that were given estradiol showed significantly prolonged extinction compared to untreated rats. These results are what one would expect if estradiol acted as a US. Any sampling of the sucrose during the first extinction trial would have been associated with the US properties of estradiol. In effect, then, this would have constituted a second pairing of the sucrose with a US: LiCl in the first pairing and estradiol in the second pairing. Thus, the presence of estradiol during reexposures to the CS would be equivalent to repeated acquisition trials and it is well known that multiple acquisition tests strengthen CTA (Garcia, Kimeldorf, & Hunt, 1956). In another of the temporal experiments, estradiol was administered at the same time as LiCl during acquisition and this combination produced a greater reduction in sucrose consumption during the first extinction trail than LiCl alone (Chambers & Hayes, 2002). These results also are what one would expect if estradiol acted as a US. The combination of estradiol and LiCl would be the equivalent of giving a higher dose of LiCl and it is well established that higher doses of LiCl yield stronger CTAs than lower doses (Chambers & Wang, 2004; Nachman & Ashe, 1973). Finally, in the temporal experiments in which exposure to estradiol was initiated either before acquisition or before extinction of LiCl-induced CTA, extinction was accelerated (Yuan & Chambers, 1999b). Given that estradiol can serve as a US in a CTA paradigm and that preexposure to other USs prior to acquisition or extinction of LiCl-induced CTAs produce attenuation of acquisition and accelerated extinction rates, it seems likely that the presence of estradiol during these time periods served as a preexposure interagent. In addition, studies in another lab have shown that when estradiol is present before acquisition of an estradiol-induced CTA to a glucose solution (4 daily injections starting 5 days before acquisition), avoidance learning is weaker, suggesting that estradiol also can act as a preexposure intraagent (De Beun et al., 1993).

Does this mean that estradiol acts as a US and a preexposure agent because it has aversive properties? Early in the history of the study of CTAs, there was general consensus that if an agent could induce a CTA, then ipso facto, that agent had aversive properties. However, several investigators have challenged this idea. In the 1970s, Booth (1977) suggested that learned reductions in consumption could be a conditioned reaction based on states other than illness and aversive sensations. He conducted several studies showing that pairing a target food with satiation properties can produce subsequent reduction in the consumption of that food. These results led him to suggest that some apparent CTAs are conditioned satiety (Booth, 1985). More recently, it has been suggested that the CTAs induced by reinforcing agents are qualitatively different than those induced by the illness agent LiCl (Hunt & Amit, 1987; Parker, 1988b, 1995). Reinforcing agents, such as amphetamine, are a class of agents that are effective positive reinforcers in a drug self-administration paradigm and that produce conditioned place preferences (Reicher & Holman, 1977; Spyraki, Fibiger, & Phillips, 1982; Wise, Yokel, & DeWitt, 1976). These agents can induce CTAs at the same doses that are rewarding (Wise et al., 1976) but they do not produce aversive responses such as defensive burying and conditioned aversive orofacial and somatic taste reactions such as chin rubbing, mouth gaping, and paw pushing (Parker, 1988a, 1995). One hypothesis that has been suggested to account for this apparent contradiction is based on the results of reward-comparison studies, which have revealed an anticipatory negative contrast effect (Grigson, 1997; also see Grigson, Twining, Freet, Wheeler, & Geddes, Chapter 5). In these studies, animals are given access to a less preferred solution (e.g., 15% sucrose) followed by access to a more preferred solution (e.g., 32% sucrose; Flaherty & Checke, 1982). After such pairings, they learn that the presence of the less preferred solution predicts the future availability of the more preferred solution, and consequently reduce their consumption of the less preferred solution. Accordingly, it has been suggested that when consumption of the CS is followed by an injection of a reinforcing agent, the CS becomes devalued, so that on subsequent exposures animals reduce their consumption in anticipation of receiving the more rewarding stimulus, the reinforcing drug (Grigson, 1997; also see Grigson et al., Chapter 5). Collectively, then, these data raise the possibility that it is satiating or reinforcing properties that allow estradiol to function as a US in a CTA paradigm. In the next section, we discuss existing behavioral evidence that either supports or fails to support the possibility that estradiol is able to modulate extinction because it possesses aversive, satiating, or positive reinforcing stimulus properties.

AN ANALYSIS OF THREE US PROPERTIES THAT MIGHT ACCOUNT FOR THE MODULATORY EFFECTS OF ESTRADIOL

Aversive Properties

Estradiol as an Aversive US
Lithium chloride can serve as both a US and a preexposure intraagent and interagent in a CTA paradigm. When paired with a novel taste solution, LiCl induces CTA (Nachman & Ashe, 1973). In addition, the use of various preexposure regimens has shown that LiCl can attenuate CTAs. For example, three exposures to LiCl that are given 8, 5, and 2 days before pairing LiCl with a novel taste solution and one exposure to LiCl that is given during the interval between acquisition and extinction of a LiCl-induced CTA (on a day that was 2 days after acquisition and 2 days before extinction) produce an attenuation of the learned avoidance (Mikulka et al., 1977; Rabin et al., 1989). Preexposure to LiCl before acquisition also can attenuate CTAs induced by radiation, ethanol, and estradiol (De Beun et al., 1993; Rabin et al., 1989).

Lithium chloride is regarded as a putative aversive US because it produces nausea and vomiting in humans (Schou, 1968) and because a number of different experimental situations reveal it to be a negative stimulus in rats. This agent produces a number of changes after it is paired with a novel taste stimulus that have been interpreted as acquired aversive reactions to the CS. These changes include the following: a greater preference for a more novel taste stimulus when given a choice between that and the CS, despite neophobic reactions of rats to food (Bernstein & Goehler, 1983), a decrease in ingestive and an increase in aversive orofacial and somatic reactions to the CS (Breslin, Spector, & Grill, 1992), redirected gnawing or pica when exposed to the CS (Mitchell, Winter, & Morisaki, 1977), burying the spout of a bottle that

contains the CS (Parker, 1988a), and spilling the CS from its container (Garcia, Hankins, & Rusiniak, 1974). In addition, an animal will avoid a place in which it has experienced the stimulus effects of LiCl (conditioned place avoidance; Cunningham & Niehus, 1993).

Estradiol also can induce nausea and vomiting (Gustavson et al., 1989) and experimental situations reveal that it can function as a negative stimulus as well. After pairing high supraphysiological doses of estradiol with a novel taste stimulus, preferences for the CS are reduced when given a choice between a more novel taste stimulus and the CS and aversive orofacial and somatic reactions are expressed; after pairing a high dose with a place, conditioned place avoidance is exhibited (Bernstein, Courtney, & Braget, 1986; De Beun et al., 1991; Ossenkopp, Rabi, & Eckel, 1996). Additional evidence for the aversive effects of high doses of estradiol has been demonstrated in studies of intracerebroventricular self-administration of estradiol into the lateral ventricles. Male Syrian hamsters do not self-administer high doses of estradiol (0.02 µg/µl; DiMeo & Wood, 2006). Although it is difficult to make comparisons between doses administered neurally and those administered peripherally, the brain uptake index for estradiol is about 85% (Pardridge & Mietus, 1979). Thus, it is not unrealistic to assume that the supraphysiological doses administered peripherally produce supraphysiological levels in the brain as well as in the general circulation.

An Aversive Hypothesis
These similarities in the effects produced by LiCl and estradiol have led researchers to suggest that supraphysiological levels of estradiol induce an illness that parallels that of LiCl (De Beun et al., 1991; Gustavson et al., 1989). Additional support for this hypothesis comes from preexposure studies. Rabin et al. (1989) proposed that the critical stimulus for acquisition of CTA is a stimulus configuration that generates a particular pattern of activity in the neural circuits associated with malaise. In order for a CTA to be attenuated, the neural pattern activated by the preexposure agent would have to be the same or similar to the neural pattern activated by the conditioning agent. This hypothesis is supported by the observation that attenuation of CTA is more easily obtained when the same agent is used as both the preexposure agent and the US. Preexposure studies using

estradiol and LiCl as both preexposure agents and USs have revealed that estradiol and LiCl show symmetrical attenuation. Preexposure to estradiol weakens acquisition and accelerates extinction of CTAs induced by LiCl as well as estradiol (Chambers & Hayes, 2002; De Beun et al., 1993) and preexposure to LiCl attenuates acquisition of both an estradiol-induced and a LiCl-induced CTA (Cannon et al., 1977; De Beun et al., 1993; Rabin et al., 1989). These results are consistent with the hypothesis that the stimulus properties that allow LiCl and supraphysiological levels of estradiol to induce CTAs are similar.

Satiating Properties

Evidence that Estradiol Produces Satiety

There is a substantial amount of evidence establishing the role of estradiol as a satiety hormone. Physiological levels of estradiol have been associated with systemic variations in the amount of food consumed across the reproductive cycle of a number of different mammalian species, including rats (Wade, 1972) and humans (Cohen, Sherwin, & Fleming, 1987). These variations are inversely associated with circulating levels of estradiol such that during the follicular phase, when endogenous estradiol levels are highest, eating is at its lowest, while the opposite is true of the luteal phase, when levels of the hormone are lowest.

Administering estradiol exogenously in ovariectomized female rats has validated that estradiol is responsible for the decrease in eating exhibited across the female reproductive cycle. Ovariectomy induces hyperphagia, accompanied by increased body weight and a 10%–30% increase in body adiposity (Gentry & Wade, 1976; Mystkowski & Schwartz, 2000; Tarttelin & Gorski, 1973). Conversely, estradiol treatment in ovariectomized rats, which mimics physiological levels of the hormone, is sufficient to normalize both eating and body weight (Geary & Asarian, 1999). Estradiol also has specific effects on consumption of sweet substances, producing decreases in consumption of a liquid sweet diet and a glucose solution in rats (Blaustein & Wade, 1976; Hrupka, Smith, & Geary, 1997; Kenney & Redick, 1980). The consistency of the results and the finding that reduction of eating is achieved by decreasing the size of the meals rather than the number of meals (Drewett, 1974), unequivocally establish estradiol as a satiety-inducing agent.

As mentioned in the "Modulatory Effects of Estradiol on Extinction of CTA" section, animals can acquire conditioned satiety (Booth, 1985). Given that estradiol is a satiety hormone, it is possible that the reduction in sucrose consumption after pairing estradiol with a novel sucrose solution is the result of conditioned satiety rather than conditioned avoidance. There is, however, another satiety-based hypothesis that could account for the reduction in consumption. The effects of estradiol on food intake are expressed 24 and 48 h following the increase in circulating estradiol levels (Geary, 2000; Griffin & Ojeda, 1996). It is during this time that most CTA postacquisition tests are conducted. This raises the possibility that a reduction in consumption after pairing estradiol with a sweet taste may actually be an expression of the unconditioned hypophagic effects of estradiol on eating behavior. In all of our temporal studies (summarized in Table 18.1), the females were ovariectomized. Thus, an acute administration of estradiol would be expected to produce a decrease in food intake and withdrawal of estradiol after chronic administration would be expected to produce an increase in food intake. Acceleration of extinction when estradiol is present continuously for at least a week and then is withdrawn 1–2 days before acquisition or extinction of a LiCl-induced CTA could be explained by an unconditioned increase in food intake (including the sucrose solution) after estradiol withdrawal, and prolongation of extinction when estradiol is given during extinction testing could be explained by an unconditioned decrease in food intake (including the sucrose solution) after estradiol administration. This suggests, then, that there are two different satiety hypotheses that could account for the expression of an estradiol-induced CTA, one based on unconditioned satiety and one based on conditioned satiety.

An Unconditioned Satiety Hypothesis: Contribution of Hypophagia to Expression of CTA

Three studies in our lab were conducted to examine whether the unconditioned effects of estradiol on eating are necessary for the development of an estradiol-induced CTA (Hintiryan, Foster, & Chambers, 2008). In the first study, comparisons were made between a group whose extinction tests were begun 2 days following acquisition day (2-Day-Delay), when unconditioned reductions in eating produced by estradiol presumably are evident, and a group whose extinction tests were initiated 8 days after acquisition (8-Day-Delay), when reductions in eating by estradiol presumably are no longer evident. The results indicated that the 8-Day-Delay group exhibited a CTA that was not statistically distinguishable from the CTA acquired by the 2-Day-Delay group even though the 2-Day group exhibited reductions in total caloric intake while the 8-Day group did not (see Figure 18.1). In the second study, we demonstrated that a 1 µg/kg dose of estradiol produced significant reductions in total calorie intake 48 h following its administration without producing a CTA to a sucrose solution (see Figure 18.2). Finally, in the third study, our approach was developed from the proposition that true conditioning demands an effect when pairing is contingent, but not when it is noncontingent. Therefore, we administered a 50 µg/kg dose of estradiol 24 h following the CS sucrose presentation since a 24-h interstimulus interval does not support a CTA (Houpt & Berlin, 1999). Our results showed that there was a reduction in sucrose consumption when pairing was contingent, but not when it was noncontingent (see Figure 18.3). Taken together, these results substantiate the role of estradiol as a US and they

suggest that the unconditioned reductions in eating and the conditioned reductions in sucrose consumption occur via separate mechanisms.

A Conditioned Satiety Hypothesis: Satiety Agents as USs and Aversive Stimuli

Although the possibility that satiety agents can produce preexposure effects remains unexplored a number of different satiety agents have been shown to induce CTA. Peripheral administration of nonphysiological amounts of cholecystokinin (Deutsch & Hardy, 1977) and cerebroventricular infusion of several other satiety agents, such as cocaine-amphetamine regulated transcript, glucagon-like peptide-1, and a melanocortin agonist (Aja, Robinson, Mills, Ladenheim, & Moran, 2002; Thiele et al., 1997, 1998) have been shown to induce CTAs. Administration of high doses of satiety agents also can produce aversive reactions. Cholecystokinin produces abdominal cramps, nausea, and emesis at high doses in humans (Miakiewicz, Stricker, & Verbalis, 1989; Stricker & Verbalis, 1991) and a number of different kinds of aversive responses in rats, including passive aversive orofacial responses, some active aversive responses, and defensive burying when it is paired

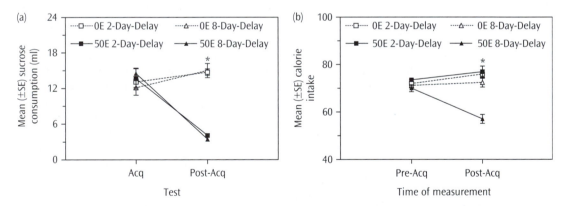

Figure 18.1. (a) Mean (±SE) sucrose consumption of ovariectomized female rats during an acquisition (Acq) test and a postacquisition (Post-Acq) test when there was a 2 day (2-Day-Delay) or 8 day (8-Day-Delay) delay between pairing a 10% sucrose solution with a subcutaneous injection of sesame oil vehicle (0E, $n = 11$ for 2-Day and $n = 10$ for 8-Day) or 50 µg/kg of estradiol (50E, $n = 11$ for 2-Day and for 8-Day) and the Post-Acq test. *Significant difference between the 0E and 50E groups, $F(1,20) = 41.76$, $p < 0.001$ for 2-Day-Delay and $F(1,19) = 97.49$, $p < 0.001$ for 8-Day-Delay, but no difference between the two 0E groups, and the two 50E groups. (b) Mean (+SE) calorie intake of the same ovariectomized female rats during 3 baseline days before acquisition of the CTA (Pre-Acq) and during the 24-h period that started at the beginning of the Post-Acq test. *Significant difference between the 50E 2-Day-Delay group and the other three groups, $F(1,20) = 27.89$, $p < 0.001$ for 0E 2-Day-Delay; $F(1,20) = 19.93$, $p < 0.001$ for 50E 8-Day-Delay; $F(1,19) = 34.51$, $p < 0.001$ for 0E 8-Day-Delay.

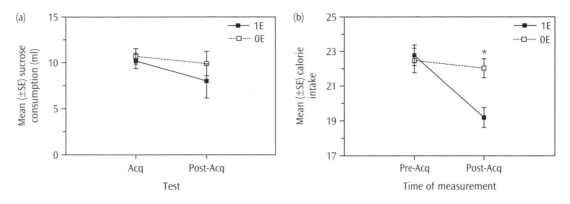

Figure 18.2. (a) Mean (±SE) sucrose consumption of ovariectomized female rats during an acquisition (Acq) test and a postacquisition (Post-Acq) test. A 10% sucrose solution was paired with a subcutaneous injection of sesame oil vehicle (0E, $n = 10$) or 1 μg/kg of estradiol (1E, $n = 10$). No significant differences were found. (b) Mean (+SE) calorie intake of the same ovariectomized female rats during a 24-h period before acquisition of the CTA (Pre-Acq) and during the 24-h period that started at the beginning of the Post-Acq test. *Significant difference between the 0E and 1E groups, $F(2,17) = 4.37$, $p = 0.029$.

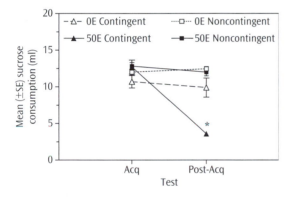

Figure 18.3. Mean (±SE) sucrose consumption of ovariectomized female rats during an acquisition (Acq) test and a postacquisition (Post-Acq) test. A 10% sucrose solution was given either immediately (contingent) or 24 h (noncontingent) before injection of sesame oil vehicle (0E, $n = 11$) or 50 μg/kg of estradiol (50E, $n = 11$) and the Post-Acq test was given 2 days following the oil or estradiol injection. *Significant difference between the E50 contingent group and the other three groups, $F(1,18) = 32.89$, $p < 0.001$ for 0E contingent, $F(1,19) = 57.41$, $p < 0.001$ for 0E noncontingent, and $F(1,19) = 30.72$, $p < 0.001$ for 50E noncontingent.

with a novel taste (Bowers, Herzog, Stone, & Dionne, 1992; Cross-Mellor, Kent, Ossenkopp, & Kavaliers, 1999; Eckel & Ossenkopp, 1995). The physiological basis of these aversive reactions could be similar to that of excess consumption since it is

well known that nimiety produces feelings of nausea. Given that estradiol is a satiety agent, perhaps the illness produced by supraphysiological doses of this steroid is an extreme end of a satiety continuum and the aversiveness of such doses is due to a satiety-based illness rather than a toxin-based illness like that induced by LiCl.

Positive Reinforcing Properties

Positive Reinforcing Agents as USs, Preexposure Agents, and Aversive Stimuli

Reinforcing agents can serve as both USs and preexposure agents in a CTA paradigm. For example, both amphetamine and morphine induce CTAs, and preexposure to amphetamine attenuates a CTA induced by either of these reinforcing agents (Cappell et al., 1975). Because high supraphysiological doses of estradiol function as aversive stimuli (see "Estradiol as an Aversive Unconditioned Stimulus" section) but high doses of reinforcing agents generally do not (Parker, 1995), it would seem unlikely that estradiol modulates extinction of CTA through its reinforcing properties. However, apomorphine is a reinforcing agent that is aversive at high doses. Conditioned place preferences are acquired with low doses (0.1–10.0 mg/kg) while high doses (15.0 or 20.0 mg/kg) elicit aversive orofacial and somatic taste reactions (Parker & Brosseau, 1990; van der Kooy, Swerdlow, & Koob, 1983). In addition, preexposure to apomorphine attenuates an estradiol-induced CTA, which suggests some similarity in the

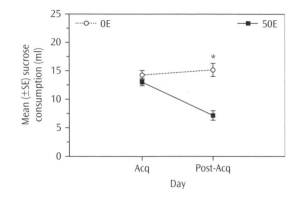

Figure 18.4. Mean (±SE) sucrose consumption of ovariectomized female rats during an acquisition (Acq) test and a postacquisition (Post-Acq) test when there was a 6-h interval between consumption of a 10% sucrose solution and subcutaneous injection of sesame oil vehicle (0E, $n = 12$) or 50 μg/kg of estradiol (50E, $n = 12$). *Significant difference between 0E and 50E, $F(1,22) = 27.76$, $p < 0.001$.

stimulus properties of the two agents (De Beun et al., 1993). Unfortunately, systematic investigation of the possible positive reinforcing properties of low doses of estradiol has yet to be conducted.

The Anticipatory Negative Contrast Hypothesis

Although low supraphysiological doses of estradiol do not appear to be aversive, it is unlikely that the reduction in CS consumption following pairing of a novel taste solution with these doses is due to the anticipatory negative contrast effect (Grigson et al., Chapter 5). As mentioned in an article by Reilly, Bornovalova, and Trifunovic (2004),

> the expression of anticipatory contrast requires that an accurate memory of the future reward [the more preferred substance] be available when the rat consumes the currently available reward [the less preferred substance] so that the relative values of the two solutions can be effectively computed by the comparison mechanism.

This is supported by the findings that anticipatory contrast effects are most evident when the solutions are presented sequentially with no delay, while the effect is eliminated when the interval between the two presentations approaches 30 min (Flaherty & Checke, 1982; Flaherty, Grigson, Checke, & Hnat, 1991). We have demonstrated in our lab that ovariectomized female rats continue to show reliable reductions in CS consumption following a pairing of the CS with a low supraphysiological dose of estradiol (50 μg/kg), which is separated by up to 6 h (see Figure 18.4). This result is consistent with the

suggestion that the decrease in CS consumption is probably not due to the anticipatory contrast effect.

A Discussion of the Behavioral Evidence

There is a dose gradient with respect to the kinds of effects estradiol has when paired with a novel sweet taste. While 50 and 250 μg/kg of estradiol induce CTA after one pairing with a novel saccharin solution, 0.4, 2.0, and 10.0 μg/kg of estradiol fail to do so (De Beun et al., 1991). It is very likely that these lower doses produce physiological blood levels because they represent minimal doses capable of reversing ovariectomy-related changes in pituitary cytology (Davidson, Smith, Rodgers, & Bloch, 1968) and similar doses of estradiol benzoate yield physiological blood levels (ranging from 43.6 to 51.7 pg/ml) after the second consecutive daily injection (Geary & Asarian, 1999).

The ability of estradiol to act as a negative stimulus also is dose dependent. Although both 50 and 250 μg/kg doses induce CTAs in female rats, a conditioned place avoidance is induced with a 250 μg/kg dose but not a 50 μg/kg dose (De Beun et al., 1991). Likewise, although aversive taste reactions are expressed after 2 consecutive days of pairing a taste stimulus with 100 μg/kg of estradiol in male rats (Ossenkopp et al., 1996), similar pairings of lower doses of estradiol benzoate (31–47 μg/kg) with a taste stimulus fail to produce conditioned aversive taste reactions in female rats (Flanagan-Cato, Grigson, & King, 2001). Evidence suggests that all of these doses produce supraphysiological blood levels. One hour after injection of a 40–45 µg/kg dose of estradiol benzoate in ovariectomized female rats, mean blood levels of estradiol are approximately 120 pg/ml and these levels fall to 100 pg/ml at 6 h postinjection and 65 pg/ml at 12 h (Woolley & McEwen, 1993). They reach a similar peak 1 h after a second consecutive daily injection, but maintain that level for at least 12 h before slowly decreasing. On the other hand, physiological levels in cycling female rats range from 1 to 88 pg/ml (Butcher, Collins, & Fugo, 1974; Hawkins, Freedman, Marshall, & Killen, 1975; Overpeck, Colson, Hohmann, Applestine, & Reilly, 1978).

Any hypothesis as to the type of property that estradiol has that allows it to act as a US and pre-exposure agent in a CTA paradigm must include an explanation for the three different dose-dependent effects of estradiol: no CTA or aversive reactions at physiological doses, CTA but no aversive reactions at low supraphysiological doses, and both CTAs and aversive reactions at high supraphysiological doses. We suggested that estradiol has aversive, satiating, or positive reinforcing properties which induce a conditioned reduction in consumption when paired with a novel taste solution. Furthermore, we suggested that it is one of these US properties that allows estradiol to modulate extinction of CTAs induced by LiCl.

With respect to the aversive hypothesis, doses of LiCl ranging from 0.3 to 3.0 mEq/kg can induce CTA after only one pairing (Nachman & Ashe, 1973). However, although the high dose can produce aversive orofacial and somatic taste reactions after only one pairing with a taste solution, it takes multiple pairings before low doses produce aversive taste reactions (Breslin, Spector, & Grill, 1992; Zalaquett & Parker, 1989). In addition, CTAs induced by both low and high doses of LiCl are abolished by lesions of the area postrema (AP) and lateral parabrachial nucleus (lPBN), indicating that the neural mechanisms mediating CTAs induced by different doses are the same (see the section "Neural Substrates for the Effects of Estradiol" that follows; Bernstein, Chavez, Allen, & Taylor, 1992; Chambers & Wang, 2004; Reilly & Trifunovic, 2000; Wang, Lavond, & Chambers, 1997a, 1997b). Taken together with the estradiol dose-dependent effects, these data suggest that aversive properties could be the basis of the ability of estradiol to induce CTA and aversive taste

reactions if two conditions are met. First, doses of estradiol that induce CTA but not aversive taste reactions after one pairing with a taste solution should produce aversive taste reactions after multiple pairings. Second, given that estradiol is an endogenous hormone, aversive reactions and the aversive neural mechanisms mediating them should be activated with supraphysiological doses but not physiological doses.

Estradiol has satiating properties across doses ranging from physiological to supraphysiological. If the CTA induced by estradiol is in fact conditioned satiety, then one would expect that any dose of estradiol that is capable of producing hypophagia would also be capable of inducing conditioned satiety. As discussed above, 1 and 2 µg/kg doses of estradiol fail to induce CTA, yet, similar doses produce hypophagia (De Beun et al., 1991; Geary & Asarian, 1999; Hintiryan et al., 2008, see Figure 18.2). However, in the CTA experiments, only one pairing of estradiol with a sweet solution was given. More than one pairing may be required to produce conditioning when lower doses of estradiol are used. The amount of satiation a particular dose of estradiol produces may determine the ease with which a conditioned satiety can be acquired and the extent of the reduction in consumption that is exhibited. Thus, it must be demonstrated that multiple pairings of low doses of estradiol can induce CTA in order for a conditioned satiety hypothesis to remain viable. In addition, as mentioned above, it must be demonstrated that satiety agents can act as preexposure agents.

A positive reinforcement hypothesis requires demonstration that low doses of estradiol are effective positive reinforcers. As was true for satiation, it also must be demonstrated that low doses can induce conditioned reductions in consumption. Even if future research reveals low doses of estradiol to be reinforcing, higher doses definitely are not. This means that two opposing mechanisms would be needed to account for the effects of estradiol, one based on the positive or rewarding value of estradiol and one based on its negative or aversive characteristics. Given this, it must be determined whether low supraphysiological doses of estradiol are rewarding or whether they produce aversive taste reactions after multiple pairings.

Our assessment of the behavioral data, then, leads us to suggest that there are three viable hypotheses that could account for the ability of estradiol to act as a US and preexposure agent and thus to modulate extinction of CTAs: (1) only supraphysiological doses of estradiol induce a CTA and it is their aversive properties that allow them to do so; (2) both physiological and supraphysiological doses of estradiol induce a CTA and it is their satiating properties that allow them to do so; and (3) both physiological and supraphysiological doses of estradiol induce a conditioned reduction in consumption but it is the rewarding properties of physiological doses and the aversive properties of supraphysiological doses that allow them to do so. Certainly, the behavioral studies suggested above will help determine which of these three hypotheses is more likely. However, there is another approach that can be taken. One would expect the neural pathways mediating aversion, satiation, and reward to be different. Therefore, determination of the neural areas mediating the CTA induced by estradiol should reveal which of these three properties allow this hormone to modulate extinction of LiCl-induced CTAs. Because investigations of estradiol as a US and preexposure agent primarily have involved supraphysiological doses and because we have suggested that these doses are aversive in our positive reinforcement hypothesis, we have directed our attention to the neural basis of satiating and aversive properties. In the next section, we present evidence establishing whether or not the AP, lPBN, and paraventricular nucleus (PVN) of the hypothalamus are involved in satiety and LiCl-induced CTAs. In addition, we discuss evidence for the involvement of these same structures in hypophagia and CTAs induced by estradiol.

NEURAL SUBSTRATES FOR THE EFFECTS OF ESTRADIOL

The Area Postrema

Role of the AP in Satiety and CTA

Satiety. Although animals with lesions of the AP display hypophagia and decreased body weight, which suggests a role for this structure in initiation of eating, the appetite suppressors amylin, calcitonin gene-related peptide, and cholecystokinin are rendered ineffective in animals with lesions of the AP or the AP and surrounding nucleus of the solitary tract (NST; Edwards, Ladenheim, & Ritter, 1986; Lutz et al., 1998; Lutz, Mollet, Rushing, Riediger, & Scharrer, 2001). This suggests that there are neurons in the AP/NST that are necessary for the expression of hypophagia produced by these chemical agents.

CTA. For CTAs induced by LiCl, the prevailing evidence strongly supports the hypothesis that the AP is essential. Temporary cooling lesions made after the CS, such that they overlap with the US duration, prevent acquisition of CTAs induced by LiCl (Wang et al., 1997a, 1997b) and permanent lesions of the AP eliminate both the taste avoidance and aversive taste reactions that occur after pairing LiCl with a sweet solution (Bernstein et al., 1992; Eckel & Ossenkopp, 1996). In addition, the AP contains neurons that respond to LiCl when it is administered directly into the blood or into the fourth ventricle, and electrical stimulation of the AP can serve as a US in a CTA paradigm (Adachi, Kobashi, Miyoshi, & Tsukamoto, 1991; Gallo, Arnedo, Agüero, & Puerto, 1988).

Estradiol. The AP has been implicated in hypophagia and in CTAs that are induced by estradiol. In one study, male rats were given a target diet the night before they were placed under chronic vehicle treatment or estradiol treatment that produced supraphysiological blood levels of estradiol (116.2 or 169.4 pg/ml). The estradiol-treated males showed a decrease in consumption of their target diet across 5 days while the control animals did not. In addition, when the males were offered a choice between their target diet and a new diet, the estradiol-treated males showed a preference for the new diet but the control males preferred the target diet because of their neophobia. This suggests that the estradiol-treated animals developed a CTA to the diet they were exposed to while under estradiol treatment and this contributed to the expressed hypophagia. A subsequent study showed that estradiol-treated males do not express hypophagia or CTA to a target diet following thermal lesions of the AP (Bernstein et al., 1986).

Although these data suggest that the AP mediates hypophagia and CTA induced by estradiol, there are two problems with interpreting the results of AP lesion studies. First, rats with AP lesions develop CTAs to their postlesion diet, as evidenced by preference for a novel food over the postlesion diet even when the novel food is less palatable and daily intake of the postlesion diet has returned to normal levels (Kenney, Tomoyasu, & Burkhart, 1994). Furthermore, they do not appear to recover from their tendency to develop CTAs to postlesion diets as they will develop CTAs to a novel food if kept only on this food for a month. It has been suggested that lesions of the AP provoke some type of unremitting malaise. If the malaise provoked by AP lesioning is similar to that induced by a chemical agent, it could interfere with the ability of rats to acquire a CTA after pairing a novel diet with the chemical agent. The malaise induced by the chemical agent would be interpreted as a continuation or possible worsening of the existing malaise and only the CTA to the postlesion diet would be expressed. A second problem with interpretation is that the body weights of AP- lesioned rats remain 20%–30% lower than those of control rats after their daily intake and rates of weight gain have returned to normal. The evidence strongly suggests that estradiol acts as a long-term satiety agent, that is, it reduces eating as a means of regulating body weight (Tarttelin & Gorski, 1973; Wade, 1972). After ovariectomy, food intake and body weight increase for a time and then intake returns to control intact levels, but body weight remains higher. Similarly, estradiol treatment in ovariectomized females causes only a transient decrease in eating, but a lasting decrease in body weight. However, estradiol fails to induce decreases in food intake in females that do not gain weight after ovariectomy (Wade, 1972). Although the AP lesion study mentioned above allowed for stabilization of body weight before assessing the effects of the lesion (Bernstein et al., 1986), the lower body weight caused by the lesion may have rendered estradiol ineffective in producing reductions in eating.

Despite these interpretive caveats of the AP lesion data, there is some additional evidence that is consistent with the hypothesis that the effects of estradiol are mediated by the AP. Both α and β estrogen receptors have been identified in the AP (Shughrue, Lane, & Merchenthaler, 1997). In addition, estradiol activates c-Fos-like immunoreactivity (c-FLI) expression in the AP (Chambers, Hintiryan, & So, 2008). In a study conducted in our lab, ovariectomized females were injected with sesame oil or 50 μg/kg of estradiol benzoate at the end of the light phase of the light/dark cycle, and 2 h (when neural areas involved in CTA would be activated, see the section "A Discussion of the Neural Evidence" that follows) or 24 h (when neural areas involved in unconditioned hypophagia would be activated, see the section "A Discussion of the Neural Evidence" that follows) later their brains were processed for c-FLI. Estradiol activated c-FLI expression in the AP at both time periods (see Figure 18.5).

Role of the AP in Preexposure Effects

There is evidence to support the hypothesis that the interagent effects of LiCl are mediated by neurons in the AP. Ethanol can induce CTAs and preexposure to LiCl can attenuate ethanol-induced CTA (Rabin et al., 1989). Unlike LiCl, ethanol does not activate the CTA circuitry via the AP. Rather, it is thought to act at a site that is distal to the AP (Hunt, Rabin, & Lee, 1987). When the AP is lesioned, ethanol-induced CTA is not affected, but preexposure to LiCl no longer attenuates the taste avoidance induced by ethanol (Rabin et al., 1989). Recent evidence in our lab suggests that the AP also is implicated in the preexposure effects of estradiol on LiCl-induced CTAs (Chambers, 2008). Ovariectomized females were implanted with empty or estradiol-filled capsules, 10 days later the capsules were removed, and 2 days after capsule removal, LiCl was paired with consumption of a sucrose solution. The brains of the rats were processed for c-FLI 1 h after pairing. Expression of c-FLI was significantly lower in the AP of the females receiving estradiol preexposure than those given no preexposure (see Figure 18.6).

The Lateral Parabrachial Nucleus

Satiety. There is direct evidence that the lPBN mediates the effects of the satiety agents cholecystokinin and D-fenfluramine (a serotonin agonist that releases serotonin and inhibits its reuptake). Excitotoxic lesions of the entire lPBN abolish cholecystokinin-induced hypophagia but medial PBN lesions have no effect (Trifunovic & Reilly, 2001). In addition, injections of cholecystokinin produce c-FLI activation in the lPBN (Inagaki et al., 1984). Unilateral infusions of D-fenfluramine into the lPBN of male rats reduce food intake, while infusions of this satiety agent in surrounding brain regions has no effect (Simansky & Nicklous, 2002). Administering a selective serotonin$_{1B}$ receptor agonist into the lPBN also produces decrements in eating, which is blocked by a selective serotonin$_{1B}$ receptor antagonist, but not by serotonin$_{2C}$ antagonists (Kennett & Curzon, 1988; Simansky & Nicklous, 2002). Immunohistochemical and lesion studies specifically implicate the external subnucleus of the lPBN in serotonergic hypophagia. Administration of D-fenfluramine produces c-FLI activation in the external lPBN and ibotenic acid lesions of the external lPBN block

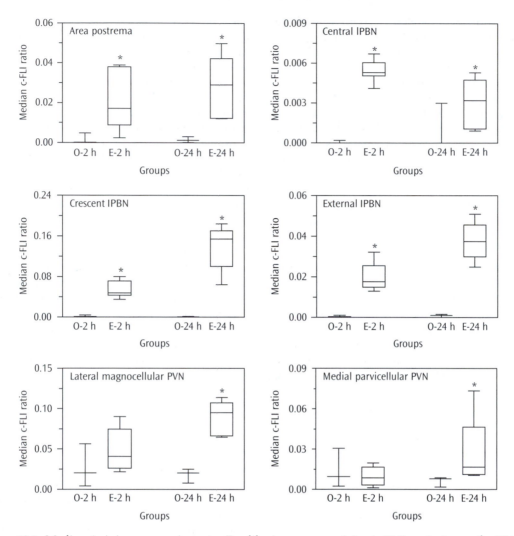

Figure 18.5. Median (minimum–maximum) c-Fos-like-immunoreactivity (c-FLI) ratio (area of c-FLI in neural structure divided by total area of neural structure) for the area postrema, the central, crescent, and external subnuclei of the lPBN and the lateral magnocellular and medial parvicellular PVN of the hypothalamus of ovariectomized females terminated 2 h or 24 h after subcutaneous injections of sesame oil vehicle (O, $n = 4$–5 for O-2 h and $n = 5$ for O-24 h) or 50 µg/kg of estradiol ($n = 7$ for E-2 h and $n = 6$ for E-24 h). *Significant difference between O and E groups at the same hour of termination, Mann-Whitney $U = 0$–3, $p = 0.0062$–0.028.

D-fenfluramine-induced hypophagia (Li, Spector, & Rowland, 1994).

CTA. The lPBN also plays a critical role in CTAs induced by LiCl. Inactivation of the lPBN using various lesioning techniques has yielded congruous results. Confined electrolytic or ibotenic acid lesions and reversible TTX or cooling lesions made after the CS, such that they overlap with the US duration,

block acquisition of a LiCl-induced CTA (Ivanova & Bures, 1990; Reilly & Trifunovic, 2001; Sakai & Yamamoto, 1998; Wang & Chambers, 2002). In addition, administration of LiCl evokes c-FLI in the central, crescent, and external lateral subnuclei of the PBN (Chambers & Wang, 2004; Yamamoto et al., 1992). More importantly, there is strong correlation between the strength of a CTA developed to a sweet solution and c-FLI activation in these

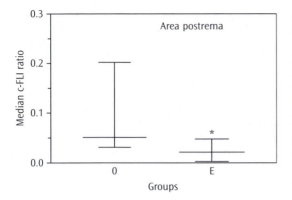

Figure 18.6. Median (minimum–maximum) c-Fos-like-immunoreactivity (c-FLI) ratio (area of c-FLI in neural structure divided by total area of neural structure) in the area postrema of ovariectomized females implanted with empty (0, *n* = 5) or estradiol-filled (E, *n* = 5) capsules before acquisition of a CTA induced by LiCl (10 ml/kg, 0.15 M) and terminated 1 h after pairing the LiCl with a 10% sucrose solution. *Significant difference between 0 and E groups, Mann-Whitney $U = 2$, $p = 0.028$.

three subnuclei of the lPBN following LiCl administration (Chambers & Wang, 2004; Sakai & Yamamoto, 1997). On the other hand, substances that do not induce CTAs, such as electric foot shock, strychnine, and physiological saline, elicit only very modest induction of the protein in the lPBN (Sakai & Yamamoto, 1997).

Estradiol. Although there is no direct evidence that the lPBN plays a role in the hypophagic and conditioned effects of estradiol, two pieces of evidence are suggestive. Both α and β estrogen receptors have been identified in the lPBN (Shughrue et al., 1997) and c-FLI is activated in the central, crescent, and external lPBN both 2 and 24 h after injection of 50 μg/kg of estradiol benzoate (see Figure 18.5; Chambers et al., 2008).

The PVN of the Hypothalamus

Satiety. Lesion and immunohistological studies suggest that the PVN plays a general role in satiety. Lesions of the PVN in the absence of any damage to the ventromedial hypothalamus produce obese rats (Aravich & Scalfani, 1983). In addition, behavioral and immunohistological staining experiments show that the following agents produce hypophagia in animals and are synthesized in neurons residing in the PVN: cholecystonkinin (Kraly, Carty, Resnick, & Smith, 1978; Mezey, Reisine, Skirboll, Beinfeld, & Kiss, 1986), cocaine-amphetamine regulated transcript (Koylu et al., 1997; Kristensen et al., 1998), corticotropin-releasing hormone (Arase, York, Shimazu, Shargill, & Bray, 1998; Sawchenko, Swanson, & Vale, 1984), pro-opiomelanocortin (Koylu et al., 1997; Yaswen, Diehl, Brennan, & Hochgeschwender, 1999), thyrotropin-releasing hormone (Kow & Pffaf, 1991), and vasopressin (Langhans, Grossman, & Geary, 1991; Swanson & Sawchenko, 1980). The inhibitory effect of serotonin infusions in the PVN and the innervation of the PVN by the raphe nucleus, a synthesis site for serotonin, further evince the role of this nucleus in satiety (Larsen, Hay-Schmidt, Vrang, & Mikkelsen, 1996; Smith, York, & Bray, 1999).

CTA. Systematic investigations of the role of the PVN in LiCl-induced CTA have not been conducted. However, evidence suggests that while this hypothalamic nucleus mediates the hypophagic responses of peptides, it is not involved in the expression of CTA produced by these same agents. The inhibitory effect that pro-opiomelanocortin exerts on eating appears to be mediated via melanocortin receptors MC-3/MC-4 (Fan, Boston, Kesterson, Hruby, & Cone, 1997; Poggioli, Vergoni, & Bertolini, 1986). Metallothionein-II, a synthetic agonist for MC3/MC4 receptors, produces both reductions in eating and a CTA when infused into the third ventricle (Thiele et al., 1998). When infused into the PVN directly, however, metallothionein-II produces reductions in eating, but does not induce a CTA, suggesting that the conditioning abilities of this MC3/MC4 agonist are not mediated via the PVN (Wirth, Olszewski, Yu, Levine, & Giraudo, 2001). This same pattern of results has been demonstrated for glucagon-like peptide-1, namely that although infusions of the agent into the third ventricle produce reductions in eating and a CTA (Thiele et al., 1997), discrete infusions into the PVN produce reductions in eating without producing CTAs (McMahon & Wellman, 1998). The assumption has been made that the CTAs induced by these satiety agents are based on aversive properties. However, these CTAs may instead represent conditioned satiety. In either case, the PVN is not involved in conditioning.

Estradiol. The preponderance of evidence supports an involvement of the PVN in estradiol-induced hypophagia. Lesioning the PVN renders estradiol ineffective in producing food decrements in ovariectomized rats (Butera, Willard, & Raymond, 1992) and implanting anisomycin, which inhibits protein synthesis, into the PVN also disrupts the hypophagic effects of estradiol (Butera, Bradway, & Cataldo, 1993). Intracranial application of estradiol into the PVN, but not the ventromedial hypothalamus, posterior hypothalamus, or medial preoptic hypothalamus induces hypophagia in ovariectomized rats (Butera & Beikirch, 1989; Butera, Beikirch, & Willard, 1990). Immunohistological studies also support an association between estradiol and PVN activation. In food-deprived ovariectomized rats, eating increases the expression of c-FLI in the PVN and activation of c-FLI is found within this same neural area when ovariectomized females are given pretreatment with a dose of estradiol that mimics blood levels of estradiol observed during proestrous (Eckel & Geary, 2001). In addition, the magnocellular and parvicellular subdivisions of the PVN contain β estrogen receptors (Shughrue et al., 1997) and c-FLI is activated in the lateral magnocellular and the medial parvicellular PVN 24 h after injection of 50 μg/kg of estradiol benzoate (see Figure 18.5). On the other hand, an involvement of the PVN in estradiol-induced CTAs is not supported by existing data. We have failed to find expression of c-FLI in the lateral magnocellular and medial parvicellular PVN or in any other region of the PVN 2 h after injection of 50 μg/kg of estradiol benzoate (see Figure 18.5; Chambers, et al., 2008).

A Discussion of the Neural Evidence

Anatomical evidence shows that the AP projects the information it receives to the lPBN, but not to the PVN, and the lPBN sends projections to the PVN, some of which have been shown to come specifically from the external subnucleus of the lPBN (Bernard, Peschanski, & Besson, 1989; Saper & Loewy, 1980; Silverman, Hoffman, & Zimmerman, 1981; van der Kooy & Koda, 1983). The lesion and immunohistological evidence suggests that the AP and lPBN are involved in LiCl-induced CTAs and satiety triggered by a number of different agents. On the other hand, the PVN is implicated in satiety but not CTAs induced by satiety agents. Taken together, these data suggest that satiety follows a pathway from the AP to the lPBN and then to the PVN while the pathway for CTAs induced by satiety agents includes the AP and lPBN but not the PVN.

The evidence from our lab suggests that for estradiol, activation of the AP and lPBN does not represent a conditioned satiety pathway. We have found expression of c-FLI in the AP and lPBN both 2 and 24 h after estradiol administration, but activation in the PVN only at the 24-h time period (see Figure 18.5; Chambers et al., 2008). Because hypophagia is expressed a day after elevation of circulating levels of estradiol (Geary, 2000; Griffin & Ojeda, 1996) and because the PVN is implicated in satiety, the 24-h expression of c-FLI in these neural areas most likely represents activation of neurons that mediate satiety. To our knowledge, there are no published reports of reductions in food intake during the first few hours after estradiol administration. However, in a study conducted in our lab, we measured food intake during a 1.5-h and 11.5-h period immediately after injecting ovariectomized females with either 250 μg/kg of estradiol benzoate or sesame oil vehicle. Estradiol benzoate did not produce reductions in food intake during the 1.5-h or 11.5-h periods immediately following the injection. Conversely, the estradiol-treated females consumed less food than the oil-treated females during the 1.5-h and 11.5-h periods that began 24 h after injection (see Figure 18.7). These data, taken together with the fact that c-FLI is expressed in the PVN 24 h but not 2 h after estradiol administration suggest that the hypophagic effects of estradiol are delayed past the time critical for conditioning and therefore satiety is not the stimulus property that allows estradiol to act as a US in a CTA paradigm. Given this is the case, it further suggests that c-FLI expression in the AP and lPBN 2 h after estradiol administration does not represent activation of neurons that mediate CTAs based on satiating properties. In addition, because both LiCl and a low supraphysiological dose of estradiol activate the AP and the same subnuclei of the lPBN during a time that is critical for conditioning, it is likely that the stimulus properties that allow conditioning of taste avoidance are similar for these two agents. The failure of low supraphysiological doses of estradiol to induce aversive reactions to taste and place, then, must be because they provide weaker sensory activation of CTA neural sites.

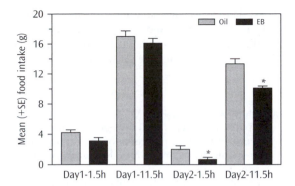

Figure 18.7. Mean (+SE) food intake of ova-riectomized females injected with sesame oil vehicle (Oil, *n* = 9) or 250 µg/kg of estradiol benzoate (EB, *n* = 9) during the 1.5-h or 11.5-h period immediately following injection (Day1) or during the 1.5-h or 11.5-h period that started 24 h after injection (Day2). *Significantly lower food intake than Oil group, $t(16) = 2.42$, $p = 0.028$ for 1.5 h and $t(16) = 4.50$, $p < 0.001$ for 11.5 h).

Unlike estradiol, LiCl activates c-FLI expression in the PVN 2 h after injection (Gu, Gonzalez, Chen, & Deutsch, 1993). If the stimulus properties of estradiol and LiCl are similar, then how do we account for this? The magnocellular and parvicellular areas of the PVN, in particular, have been implicated in satiety. The magnocellular neurosecretory neurons release vasopressin from terminals located in the posterior pituitary gland and the parvicellular neurosecretory neurons, which project to the median eminence release hormones such as corticotropin-releasing hormone and thyrotropin-releasing hormone into the hypothalamo-pituitary portal system (Sawchenko et al., 1984; Segerson et al., 1987; Sherlock, Field, & Raisman, 1975; Swanson & Sawchenko, 1980; Vandesande, Dierickx, & DeMey, 1977). As indicated in the "The PVN of the Hypothalamus" section above, all three of these hormones have been implicated in satiety (Arase et al., 1998; Langhans et al., 1991; Lin, Chu, & Leu, 1983). Expression of c-FLI also is found specifically in the magnocelluar and parvicellular PVN 2 h after LiCl injection (Gu et al., 1993). Given the observation that reductions in eating occur within 45 min of injection for LiCl (Curtis, Sved, Verbalis, & Stricker, 1994), it is likely that at least some of this expression represents activation of neurons that mediate satiety. If this is the case, then the PVN mediates hypophagia induced by estradiol and LiCl. However, unlike estradiol, the AP is not implicated

in LiCl-induced hypophagia since rats with lesions of this structure still exhibit hypophagia after LiCl administration (Curtis, et al., 1994).

CONCLUDING COMMENTS

It has been known for over 30 years that estradiol influences acquisition and extinction of learned behaviors, such as, passive and active shock avoidance learning and nonappetitive and appetitive maze or spatial learning tasks (see Beatty, 1979; van Haaren, van Hest, & Heinsbroek, 1990). The finding that incidences of Alzheimer's disease are lower in elderly women on estrogen replacement therapy than matched controls ignited greater interest in the role of estrogen on learned processes, especially its mnemonic role (Paganini-Hill, Buckwalter, Logan, & Henderson, 1993). However, the results of past investigations using a wide variety of tasks have not produced a uniform or consistent picture (see van Haaren et al., 1990). In addition, the possibility that the influence of estradiol is due to nonspecific effects has been ignored frequently.

Our investigation of the influence of estradiol on extinction of CTAs has led us to conclude that its influence is not due to a direct effect on acquisition or extinction processes. We initially found that extinction is accelerated when estradiol is present during the acquisition and extinction of a CTA. In our attempt to determine whether estradiol acts during acquisition or extinction to produce this effect, we found that when estradiol was present before acquisition or extinction, extinction was accelerated and when it was present during acquisition or extinction, acquisition was strengthened and extinction was prolonged. Because these results are similar to what has been obtained for agents that function as USs in a CTA paradigm and because estradiol can induce CTAs when paired with a novel taste solution, we proposed that it is the US properties of estradiol that allow it to modulate extinction. This means that the effects of estradiol on extinction are not specific to estradiol but rather are a general function of agents that are capable of inducing CTAs.

There is evidence to suggest that there are three different kinds of stimulus properties that can induce a reduction in consumption of a novel taste solution in a CTA paradigm: aversive, satiating, and positive reinforcing properties. Our assessment of behavioral and neural data led us to propose that estradiol has aversive properties paralleling those of LiCl, which allow it to modulate extinction. Like LiCl, estradiol can function as a negative stimulus and it activates c-FLI expression in the AP and lPBN during a time that is critical for conditioning. In addition, it activates c-FLI expression in the PVN (a structure which has been shown to mediate satiety, but not CTAs induced by satiety agents) at a time that is not critical for conditioning but when hypophagia is manifested (a day after administration), and it fails to activate expression in this structure at a time that is critical for conditioning but when hypophagia is not exhibited (hours after administration). Taken together, these data suggest that mediation of estradiol-induced CTAs by the AP and lPBN is not based on satiating properties. To further validate the aversive hypothesis, it must be verified that physiological doses of estradiol do not induce CTA, that low supraphysiological doses of estradiol are aversive and not rewarding, and that beyond the lPBN, estradiol follows the same conditioning neural routes as LiCl.

Our interest in estradiol and CTAs extends beyond determining the mechanism for the modulation of extinction of CTAs by estradiol. It has been suggested that estrogen can be an originating cause of anorexia nervosa in pubertal girls (Chambers & Bernstein, 2003; Gustavson et al., 1989). Specifically, contaminants present during fetal development sensitize the brain to the satiating and aversive properties of estrogen, and consequently, the increased production of estrogen at puberty sets off an exaggerated hypophagic response and a malaise that triggers the development of conditioned food aversions. There is compelling evidence to support this hypothesis. A correspondence between increases in the incidence of anorexia nervosa in 14–20-year-old females and the medical and agricultural usage of diethylstilbestrol, a synthetic nonsteroidal form of estradiol, has been found (Jones, Fox, Babigian, & Hutton, 1980; Willi & Grossmann, 1983) and women who have been exposed to diethylstilbestrol fetally are more likely to exhibit unexplained weight loss and a diagnosis of anorexia nervosa than unexposed women (Gustavson et al., 1989). In addition, female rats exposed to androgens during neural development show persistent reductions in body weight maintenance (Bell & Zucker, 1971) and CTAs that can be induced with lower doses of estradiol than unexposed females (Gustavson et al., 1989).

These data, as well as the ease with which estradiol induces hypophagia and CTA, suggest that rats would make a viable animal model for the study of this serious and intractable eating disorder.

References

Adachi, A., Kobashi, M., Miyoshi, N., & Tsukamoto, G. (1991). Chemosensitive neurons in the area postrema of the rat and their possible functions. *Brain Research Bulletin, 26,* 137–140.

Aja, S., Robinson, B. M., Mills, K. J., Ladenheim, E. E., & Moran, T. H. (2002). Fourth ventricular CART reduces food and water intake and produces a conditioned taste aversion in rats. *Behavioral Neuroscience, 116,* 918–921.

Arase, K., York, D. A., Shimazu, H., Shargill, M., & Bray, G. A. (1998). Effects of corticotrophin releasing factor on food intake and brown adipose tissue thermogenesis. *American Journal of Physiology, 55,* E225–E259.

Aravich, P. F., & Scalfani, A. (1983). Paraventricular hypothalamic lesions and medial hypothalamic knife cuts produce similar hyperphagic syndromes. *Behavioral Neuroscience, 97,* 970–983.

Beatty, W. W. (1979). Gonadal hormones and sex differences in nonreproductive behaviors in rodents: Organizational and activational influences. *Hormones & Behavior, 12,* 112–163.

Bell, D. D., & Zucker, I. (1971). Sex differences in body weight and eating: Organization and activation by gonadal hormones in the rat. *Physiology & Behavior, 7,* 27–34.

Bernard, J. F., Peschanski, M., & Besson, J. M. (1989). A possible spino (trigemino)-ponto-amygdaloid pathway for pain. *Neuroscience Letters, 100,* 83–88.

Bernstein, I. L., Chavez, M., Allen, D., & Taylor, E. M. (1992). Area postrema mediation of physiological and behavioral effects of lithium chloride in the rat. *Brain Research, 575,* 132–137.

Bernstein, I. L., Courtney, L., & Braget, D. J. (1986). Estrogens and the Leydig LTW(m) tumor syndrome: Anorexia and diet aversions attenuated by area postrema lesions. *Physiology & Behavior, 38,* 159–163.

Bernstein, I. L., & Goehler, L. E. (1983). Chronic lithium chloride infusions: Conditioned suppression of food intake and preference. *Behavioral Neuroscience, 97,* 290–298.

Blaustein, J., & Wade, G. (1976). Ovarian influences on the meal pattern of female rats. *Physiology & Behavior, 17,* 201–208.

Booth, D. A. (1977). Satiety and appetite are conditioned reactions. *Psychosomatic Medicine, 39,* 76–81.

Booth, D. A. (1985). Food-conditioned eating preferences and aversion with interoceptive elements: Conditioned appetites and satieties. *Annals of the New York Academy of Sciences, 443*, 22–41.

Bowers, R. L., Herzog, C. D., Stone, E. H., & Dionne, T. J. (1992). Defensive burying following injections of cholecystokinin, bombesin, and LiCl in rats. *Physiology & Behavior, 41*, 969–972.

Breslin, P. A. S., Spector, A. C., & Grill, H. J. (1992). A quantitative comparison of taste reactivity behaviors to sucrose before and after lithium chloride pairings: A unidimensional account of palatability. *Behavioral Neuroscience, 106*, 820–836.

Butcher, R. L., Collins, W. E., & Fugo, N. W. (1974). Plasma concentration of LH, FSH, prolactin, progesterone and estradiol-17 beta throughout the 4-day estrous cycle of the rat. *Endocrinology, 94*, 1704–1708.

Butera, P. C., & Beikirch, R. J. (1989). Central implants of diluted estradiol: Independent effects on ingestive and reproductive behaviors of ovariectomized rats. *Brain Research, 491*, 226–273.

Butera, P. C., Beikirch, R. J., & Willard, D. M. (1990). Changes in ingestive behaviors and body weight following intracranial application of 17α-estradiol. *Physiology & Behavior, 47*, 1291–1293.

Butera, P. C., Bradway, D. M., & Cataldo, N. J. (1993). Modulation of the satiety effect of cholecystokinin by estradiol. *Physiology & Behavior, 53*, 1235–1238.

Butera, P. C., Willard, D. M., & Raymond, S. A. (1992). Effects of PVN lesions on the responsiveness of female rats to estradiol. *Brain Research, 576*, 304–310.

Cannon, D. S., Baker, T. B., & Berman, R. F. (1977). Taste aversion disruption by drug pretreatment: Dissociative and drug-specific effects. *Pharmacology Biochemistry & Behavior, 6*, 93–100.

Cappell, H., LeBlanc, A. E., & Herling, S. (1975). Modification of the punishing effects of psychoactive drugs in rats by previous drug experience. *Journal of Comparative & Physiological Psychology, 89*, 347–356.

Chambers, K. C. (1976). Hormonal influences on sexual dimorphism in the rate of extinction of a conditioned taste aversion in rats. *Journal of Comparative & Physiological Psychology, 90*, 851–856.

Chambers, K. C. (1980). Progesterone, estradiol, testosterone and dihydrotestosterone: Effects on rate of extinction of a conditioned taste aversion in rats. *Physiology & Behavior, 24*, 1061–1065.

Chambers, K. C. (1982). Failure of ACTH to prolong extinction of a conditioned taste aversion in the absence of the testes. *Physiology & Behavior, 29*, 915–919.

Chambers, K. C. (1985). Sexual dimorphisms as an index of hormonal influences on conditioned food aversions. *Annals of the New York Academy of Sciences, 443*, 110–125.

Chambers, K. C. (2007). Estradiol exposure before acquisition of LiCl-induced conditioned taste avoidance reduces expression of c-Fos-like immunoreactivity in the area postrema. Unpublished manuscript.

Chambers, K. C., & Bernstein, I. L. (2003). Conditioned flavor aversions. In R. L. Doty (Ed.), *Handbook of clinical olfaction and gustation* (2nd ed., pp. 905–933). New York: Marcel Dekker.

Chambers, K. C., & Hayes, U. (2002). Exposure to estradiol before but not during acquisition of LiCl-induced conditioned taste avoidance accelerates extinction. *Hormones & Behavior, 41*, 297–305.

Chambers, K. C., & Hayes, U. L. (2005). The role of vasopressin in behaviours associated with aversive stimuli. In T. Steckler, H. Reul, & N. Kalin (Eds.), *Handbook on stress, immunology, and behaviour* (pp. 231–262). Amsterdam: Elsevier Science.

Chambers, K. C., Hintiryan, H., & So, C. (2008). Differential hypophagia and expression of c-Fos-like immunoreactivity two and twenty-four hours after estradiol administration. Unpublished manuscript.

Chambers, K. C., & Sengstake, C. B. (1979). Temporal aspects of the dependency of a dimorphic rate of extinction on testosterone. *Physiology & Behavior, 22*, 53–56.

Chambers, K. C., & Wang, Y. (2004). Role of the lateral parabrachial nucleus in apomorphine-induced conditioned consumption reduction: Cooling lesions and relationship of c-Fos-like-immunoreactivity to strength of conditioning. *Behavioral Neuroscience, 118*, 199–213.

Chambers, K. C., Yuan, D. L., Brownson, A., & Wang, Y. (1997). Sexual dimorphism in conditioned taste aversions: Mechanism and Function. In M. E. Bouton & M. S. Fanselow (Eds.), *Learning, motivation, and cognition: The functional behaviorism of Robert C. Bolles* (pp. 195–224). Washington, DC: American Psychological Association.

Clifton, P. G., & Andrew, R. J. (1987). Gonadal steroids and the extinction of conditioned taste aversions in young domestic fowl. *Physiology & Behavior, 39*, 27–31.

Cohen, I. T., Sherwin, B. B., & Fleming, A. S. (1987). Food cravings, mood, and the menstrual cycle. *Hormones & Behavior, 21*, 457–470.

Colby, J. J., & Smith, N. F. (1977). The effects of three procedures for eliminating a conditioned taste aversion in the rat. *Learning & Motivation, 8,* 404–413.

Cross-Mellor, S. K., Kent, W. D., Ossenkopp, K.-P., & Kavaliers, M. (1999). Differential effects of lipopolysaccharide and cholecystokinin on sucrose intake and palatability. *American Journal of Physiology, 277,* R705–R715.

Cunningham, C. L., & Niehus, J. S. (1993). Drug-induced hypothermia and conditioned place aversion. *Behavioral Neuroscience, 107,* 468–479.

Curtis, K. S., Sved, A. F., Verbalis, J. G., & Stricker, E. M. (1994). Lithium chloride-induced anorexia, but not conditioned taste aversions, in rats with area postrema lesions. *Brain Research, 663,* 30–37.

Dantzer, R., Bluthe, R. M., & Kelly, K. W. (1991). Androgen-dependent vasopressinergic neurotransmission attenuates interleuin-1-induced sickness behavior. *Brain Research, 557,* 115–120.

Davidson, J. M., Smith, E. R., Rodgers, C. H., & Bloch, G. J. (1968). Relative thresholds of behavioral and somatic responses to estrogen. *Physiology & Behavior, 3,* 227–229.

De Beun, R., Jansen, E., Smeets, M. A. M., Niesing, J., Slangen, J. L., & Van De Poll, E. (1991). Estradiol-induced conditioned taste aversion and place aversion in rats: Sex- and dose-dependent effects. *Physiology & Behavior, 50,* 995–1000.

De Beun, R., Peeters, B. W. M. M., & Broekkamp, C. L. E. (1993). Stimulus characterization of estradiol applying a crossfamiliarization taste aversion procedure in female mice. *Physiology & Behavior, 53,* 715–719.

De Jong, F. H., Hey, A. H., & van der Molen, H. J. (1973). Effect of gonadotrophins on the secretion of oestradiol- and testosterone by the rat testis. *Journal of Endocrinology, 57,* 277–284.

Deutsch, J. A., & Hardy, W. T. (1977). Cholecystokinin produces bait shyness in rats. *Nature, 266,* 196.

DiMeo, A. N., & Wood, R. I. (2006). Self administration of estrogen and dihydrotestosterone in male hamsters. *Hormones & Behavior, 49,* 519–526.

Drewett, R. F. (1974). The meal patterns of the oestrous cycle and their motivational significance. *Quarterly Journal of Experimental Psychology, 26,* 489–494.

Earley, C. J., & Leonard, B. E. (1979). Effects of prior exposure on conditioned taste aversion in the rat: Androgen- and estrogen-dependent events. *Journal of Comparative & Physiological Psychology, 93,* 793–805.

Eckel, L. A., & Geary, N. (2001). Estradiol treatment increases feeding-induced c-fos expression in the brains of ovariectomized rats. *American Journal of Physiology, 281,* R738–R746.

Eckel, L. A., & Ossenkopp, K.-P. (1995). Cholecystokinin reduces ingestive taste reactivity responses to water in fluid-replete but not fluid-deprived rats. *Physiology & Behavior, 57,* 599–603.

Eckel, L. A., & Ossenkopp, K.-P. (1996). Area postrema mediates the formation of rapid, conditioned palatability shifts in lithium-treated rats. *Behavioral. Neuroscience, 110,* 202–212.

Edwards, G. L., Ladenheim, E. E., & Ritter, R. C. (1986). Dorsomedial hindbrain participation in cholecystokinin-induced satiety. *American Journal of Physiology, 251,* R971–R977.

Eyre, L. J., Bland, R., Bujalska, I. J., Sheppard, M. C., Stewart, P. M., & Hewison, M. (1998). Characterization of aromatase and 17 beta hydroxysteroid dehydrogenase expression in rat osteoblastic cells. *Journal of Bone & Mineral Research, 13,* 996–1004.

Fan, W., Boston, B. A., Kesterson, R. A., Hruby, V. J., & Cone, R. D. (1997). Role of melano-cortinergic neurons in feeding and the agouti obesity syndrome. *Nature, 385,* 165–168.

Flaherty, C. F., & Checke, S. (1982). Anticipation of incentive gain. *Animal Learning & Behavior, 10,* 177–182.

Flaherty, C. F., Grigson, P. S., Checke, S., & Hnat, K. C. (1991). Deprivation state and temporal horizons in anticipatory contrast. *Journal of Experimental Psychology: Animal Behavior Processes, 17,* 503–518.

Flanagan-Cato, L. M., Grigson, P. S., & King, J. L. (2001). Estrogen-induced suppression of intake is not mediated by taste aversion in female rats. *Physiology & Behavior, 72,* 549–558.

Gallo, M., Arnedo, M., Agüero, A., & Puerto, A. (1988). Electrical intracerebral stimulation of the area postrema on taste aversion learning. *Behavioural Brain Research, 30,* 289–296.

Garcia, J., Hankins, W. G., & Rusiniak, K. W. (1974). Regulation of the milieu interne in man and rat. *Science, 185,* 823–831.

Garcia, J., Kimeldorf, J., & Hunt, E. L. (1956). Conditioned responses to manipulative procedures resulting from exposure to gamma radiation. *Radiation Research, 5,* 79–87.

Geary, N. (2000). Estradiol and appetite. *Appetite, 35,* 273–274.

Geary, N., & Asarian, L. (1999). Cyclic estradiol treatment normalized body weight and test meal size in ovariectomized rats. *Physiology & Behavior, 67*, 141–147.

Gentry, R. T., & Wade, G. N. (1976). Sex differences in sensitivity of food intake, body weight, and running-wheel activity to ovarian steroids in rats. *Journal of Comparative & Physiological Psychology, 90*, 747.

Griffin, J. E., & Ojeda, S. R. (1996). *Textbook of endocrine physiology.* New York: Oxford University Press.

Grigson, P. S. (1997). Conditioned taste aversions and drugs of abuse: A reinterpretation. *Behavioral Neuroscience, 111*, 129–136.

Grodin, J. M., Siiteri, P. K., & MacDonald, P. C. (1973). Source of estrogen production in postmenopausal women. *Journal of Clinical Endocrinology & Metabolism, 36*, 207–214.

Gu, Y., Gonzalez, F., Chen, D. Y., & Deutsch, J. A. (1993). Expression of *c-fos* in brain subcortical structures in response to nauseant lithium chloride and osmotic pressure in rats. *Neuroscience Letters, 157*, 49–52.

Gustavson, C. R., Gustavson, J. C., Young, J. K., Pumariega, A. J., & Nicolaus, L. K. (1989). Estrogen induced malaise. In J. M. Lakoski, J. R. Perez-Polo, & D. K. Rassin (Eds.), *Neural control of reproductive function* (pp. 501–523). New York: Alan R. Liss.

Hawkins, R. A., Freedman, B., Marshall, A., & Killen, E. (1975). Oestradiol-17 beta and prolactin levels in rat peripheral plasma. *British Journal of Cancer, 32*, 179–185.

Hayes, U. L., & Chambers, K. C. (2002). Central infusion of vasopressin in male rats accelerates extinction of conditioned taste avoidance induced by LiCl. *Brain Research Bulletin, 57*, 727–733.

Hayes, U. L., & Chambers, K. C. (2005a). Peripheral vasopressin accelerates extinction of conditioned taste avoidance. *Physiology & Behavior, 84*, 147–156.

Hayes, U. L., & Chambers, K. C. (2005b). High doses of vasopressin delay extinction and accelerate acquisition of LiCl-induced conditioned taste avoidance. *Physiology & Behavior, 84*, 625–633.

Hintiryan, H., Foster, N. N., & Chambers, K. C. (2008). Dissociating the conditioning and anorectic effects of estradiol. Unpublished manuscript.

Houpt, T. A., & Berlin, R. (1999). Rapid, labile, and protein synthesis independent short-term memory in conditioned taste aversion. *Learning & Memory, 6*, 37–46.

Hrupka, B. J., Smith, G. P., & Geary, N. (1997). Ovariectomy and estradiol affect postingestive controls of sucrose licking. *Physiology & Behavior, 61*, 243–247.

Hunt, T., & Amit, Z. (1987). Conditioned taste aversion induced by self-administered drugs: Paradox revisited. *Neuroscience & Biobehavioral Reviews, 1*, 107–130.

Hunt, W. A., Rabin, B. M., & Lee, J. (1987). Ethanol-induced taste aversions: Lack of involvement of acetaldehyde and the area postrema. *Alcohol, 4*, 169–173.

Inagaki, S., Shiotani, Y., Yamano, M., Shiosaka, S., Takagi, H., Tateishi, K., et al. (1984). Distribution, origin, and fine structures of cholecystokinin-8-like immunoreactive terminals in the nucleus ventromedialis hypothalami of the rat. *Journal of Neuroscience, 4*, 1289–1299.

Ivanova, S. F., & Bures, J. (1990). Acquisition of conditioned taste aversion in rats is prevented by tetrodotoxin blockade of small midbrain region centered around the parabrachial nuclei. *Physiology & Behavior, 48*, 543–549.

Jones, D. J., Fox, M. M., Babigian, H. M., & Hutton, H. E. (1980). Epidemiology of anorexia nervosa in Monroe County, New York: 1960–1976. *Psychosomatic Medicine, 42*, 551–558.

Kendler, K., Hennessy, J. W., Smotherman, W. P., & Levine, S. (1976). An ACTH effect on recovery from conditioned taste aversion. *Behavioral Biology, 17*, 225–229.

Kennett, G. A., & Curzon, G. (1988). Evidence that hypophagia induced by *m*CPP and TFMPP requires 5-HT$_{1C}$ and 5-HT$_{1B}$ receptors; hypophagia induced by RU 24969 only requires 5-HT$_{1B}$ receptors. *Psychopharmacology, 96*, 241–250.

Kenney, N. J., & Redick, J. H. (1980). Effects of ovariectomy and subsequent estradiol replacement on intake of sweet solutions. *Physiology & Behavior, 24*, 807–809.

Kenney, N. J., Tomoyasu, N., & Burkhart, M. K. (1994). Food aversion induced by area postrema ablation. *Appetite, 22*, 205–220.

Kow, L., & Pffaf, D. (1991). The effects of the TRH-metabolite cyclo (His-Pro) and its analogs on feeding. *Pharmacology Biochemistry & Behavior, 38*, 359–364.

Koylu, E. O., Couceyro, P. R., Lambert, P. D., Ling, N. C., DeSouza, E. B., & Kuhar, M. J. (1997). Immunohistochemical localization of novel CART peptides in rat hypothalamus, pituitary and adrenal gland. *Journal of Neuroendocrinology, 9*, 823–833.

Kraly, F. S., Carty, W. J., Resnick, S., & Smith, G. P. (1978). Effect of cholecystokinin on meal size and intermeal interval in the sham-feeding rat. *Journal of Comparative & Physiological Psychology, 92*, 697–707.

Kristensen, P., Judge, M. E., Thim, L., Ribel, U., Christjansen, K. N., Wulff, B. S., et al. (1998). Hypothalamic CART is a new anorectic peptide regulated by leptin. *Nature, 393*, 72–76.

Langhans, W., Grossman, F., & Geary, N. (2001). Intrameal hepatic-portal infusion of glucose reduces spontaneous meal size in rats. *Physiology & Behavior, 73*, 499–507.

Larsen, P. J., Hay-Schmidt, A., Vrang, N., & Mikkelsen, J. D. (1996). Origin of projections from the midbrain raphe nuclei to the hypothalamic paraventricular nucleus in the rat: A combined retrograde and anterograde tracing study. *Neuroscience, 70*, 963–988.

Li, B. H., Spector, A. C., & Rowland, N. E. (1994). Reversal of dexfenfluramine-induced anorexia and c-Fos/c-Jun expression by lesion in the lateral parabrachial nucleus. *Brain Research, 640*, 255–267.

Lin, M. T., Chu, P. C., & Leu, S. Y. (1983). Effects of TSH, TRH, LH and LHRH on thermoregulation and food and water intake in the rat. *Neuroendocrinology, 37*, 206–211.

Lutz, T. A., Mollet, A., Rushing, P. A., Riediger, T., & Scharrer, E. (2001). The anorectic effect of a chronic peripheral infusion of amylin is abolished in area postrema/nucleus of the solitary tract (AP/NST) lesioned rats. *International Journal of Obesity, 25*, 1005–1011.

Lutz, T. A., Senn, M., Althaus, J., del Prete, E., Ehrensperger, F., & Scharrer, E. (1998). Lesions of the area postrema/nucleus of the solitary tract (AP/NST) attenuates the anorectic effects of amylin and calcitonin gene-related peptide (CGRP) in rats. *Peptide, 19*, 309–317.

MacDonald, P. C., Madden, J. D., Brenner, P. F., Wilson, J. D., & Siiteri, P. K. (1979). Origin of estrogen in normal men and women with testicular feminization. *Journal of Clinical Endocrinology & Metabolism, 49*, 905–916.

McMahon, L. R., & Wellman, P. J. (1998). PVN infusion of GLP-1-(7–36) amide suppresses feeding but does not induce aversion or later locomotion in rats. *American Journal of Physiology, 274*, R23–R29.

Mezey, E., Reisine, T. D., Skirboll, L., Beinfeld, M., & Kiss, J. Z. (1986). Role of cholecystokinin in corticotrophin release: Coexistence with vasopressin and corticotropin-releasing factor in cells of the rat hypothalamic paraventricular nucleus. *Proceedings of the National Academy of Sciences, 83*, 3510–3512.

Miakiewicz, S. L., Stricker, E. M., & Verbalis, J. G. (1989. Neurohypophyseal secretion in response to cholecystokinin but not meal-induced gastric distention in humans. *Journal of Clinical Endocrinology & Metabolism, 68*, 837–843.

Mikulka, P. J., Leard, B., & Klein, S. B. (1977). Illness-alone exposure as a source of interference with the acquisition and retention of a taste aversion. *Journal of Experimental Psychology: Animal Behavior Processes, 3*, 189–201.

Mitchell, D., Winter, W., & Morisaki, C. M. (1977). Conditioned taste aversions accompanied by geophagia: Evidence for the occurance of "psychological" factors in the etiology of pica. *Psychosomatic Medicine, 39*, 401–412.

Mystkowski, P., & Schwartz, M. W. (2000). Gonadal steroids and energy homeostasis in the leptin era. *Nutrition, 16*, 937–946.

Nachman, M., & Ashe, J. H. (1973). Learned taste aversions in rats as a function of dosage, concentration, and route of administration of LiCl. *Physiology & Behavior, 10*, 73–78.

Nelson, L. R., & Bulun, S. E. (2001). Estrogen production and action. *Journal of the American Academy of Dermatology, 45*, S116–S124.

Ossenkopp, K.-P., Rabi, Y. J., Eckel, L. A. (1996). Oestradiol-induced taste avoidance is the result of a conditioned palatability shift. *NeuroReport, 7*, 2777–2780.

Overpeck, J. G., Colson, S. H., Hohmann, J. R., Applestine, M. S., & Reilly, J. F. (1978). Concentrations of circulating steroids in normal prepubertal and adult male and female humans, chimpanzees, rhesus monkeys, rats, mice, and hamsters: A literature survey. *Journal of Toxicology & Environmental Health, 4*, 785–803.

Paganini-Hill, A., Buckwalter, J. G., Logan, C. G., & Henderson, V. W. (1993). Estrogen replacement therapy and cognitive decline in memory-impaired post-menopausal women. *Biological Psychiatry, 46*, 182–188.

Pardridge, W. M., & Mietus, L. J. (1979). Transport of steroid hormones through the rat blood–brain barrier. *Journal of Clinical Investigation, 64*, 145–154.

Parker, L. A. (1988a). Defensive burying of flavors paired with lithium but not amphetamine. *Psychopharmacology, 96*, 250–252.

Parker, L. A. (1988b). Positively reinforcing drugs may produce a different kind of CTA than drugs which are not positively reinforcing. *Learning & Motivation, 10*, 207–220.

Parker, L. A. (1995). Rewarding drugs produce taste avoidance, but not taste aversion. *Neuroscience & Biobehavioral Reviews, 19*, 143–151.

Parker, L. A., & Brosseau, L. (1990). Apomorphine-induced flavor–drug associations: A dose–response analysis by the taste reactivity test and the conditioned taste avoidance test. *Pharmacology Biochemistry & Behavior, 35*, 583–587.

Poggioli, R., Vergoni, A. V., & Bertolini, A. (1986). ACTH(1–24) and alpha-MSH antagonize feeding behavior stimulated by kappa opiate agonists. *Peptide, 7*, 843–848.

Rabin, B. M., Hunt, W. A., & Lee, J. (1989). Attenuation and cross-attenuation in taste aversion learning in the rat: Studies with ionizing radiation, lithium chloride and ethanol. *Pharmacology Biochemistry & Behavior, 31,* 909–918.

Reicher, M. A., & Holman, E. W. (1977). Location preference and flavor aversion reinforced by amphetamine in rats. *Animal Learning & Behavior, 5,* 343–346.

Reilly, S., Bornovalova, M., & Trifunovic, R. (2004). Excitotoxic lesions of the gustatory thalamus spare simultaneous contrast effects but eliminate anticipatory negative contrast: Evidence against a memory deficit. *Behavioral Neuroscience, 118,* 365–376.

Reilly, S., & Trifunovic, R. (2000). Lateral parabrachial nucleus lesions in the rat: Aversive and appetitive gustatory conditioning. *Brain Research Bulletin, 52,* 269–278.

Reilly, S., & Trifunovic, R. (2001). Lateral parabrachial nucleus lesions in the rat: Neophobia and conditioned taste aversion. *Behavioural Brain Research, 55,* 359–366.

Sakai, N., & Yamamoto, T. (1997). Conditioned taste aversion and c-fos expression in the rat brainstem after administration of various USs. *NeuroReport, 8,* 2215–2220.

Sakai, N., & Yamamoto, T. (1998). Role of the medial and lateral parabrachial nucleus in acquisition and retention of conditioned taste aversion in rats. *Behavioural Brain Research, 93,* 63–70.

Saper, C. B., & Loewy, A. D. (1980). Efferent connections of the parabrachial nucleus in the rat. *Brain Research, 197,* 291–317.

Sawchenko, P. E., Swanson, L. W., & Vale, W. W. (1984). Co-expression of corticotropin-releasing factor and vasopressin immunoreactivities in parvocellular neurosecretory neurons in the hypothalamus of adrenalectomized rats. *Proceedings of the National Academy of Sciences, 81,* 1883–1887.

Schou, M. (1968). Lithium in psychiatry—A review. In D. H. Efron (Ed.), *Pharmacology: A review of progress 1957–1967* (National Institute of Mental Health, Public Health Service Publication No. 1836, Chevy Chase, Maryland, pp. 701–718).

Segerson, T. P., Kauer, J., Wolfe, H. C., Mobtaker, H., Wu, P., Jackson, I. M., et al. (1987). Thyroid hormone regulates TRH biosynthesis in the paraventricular nucleus of the rat hypothalamus. *Science, 238,* 78–80.

Sherlock, D. A., Field, P. M., & Raisman, G. (1975). Retrograde transport of horseradish peroxidase in the magnocellular neurosecretory system of the rat. *Brain Research, 88,* 403–414.

Shoham, Z., & Schachter, M. (1996). Estrogen biosynthesis-regulation, action, remote effects, and value of monitoring in ovarian stimulation cycles. *Fertility & Sterility, 65,* 687–701.

Shughrue, P. J., Lane, M. V., & Merchenthaler, I. (1997). Comparative distribution of estrogen receptor-α and -β mRNA in the rat central nervous system. *Journal of Comparative Neurology, 388,* 507–525.

Silverman, A. J., Hoffman, D. L., & Zimmerman, E. A. (1981). The descending afferent connections of the paraventricular nucleus of the hypothalamus (PVN). *Brain Research Bulletin, 6,* 47–61.

Simansky, K. J., & Nicklous, D. M. (2002). Parabrachial infusion of D-fenfluramine reduces food intake blockade by the $5-HT_{1B}$ antagonist SB-216641. *Pharmacology Biochemistry & Behavior, 71,* 681–690.

Smith, B. K., York, D. A., & Bray, G. A. (1999). Activation of hypothalamic serotonin receptors reduced intake of dietary fat and protein but not carbohydrate. *American Journal of Physiology, 277,* R802–R811.

Smotherman, W. P. (1985). Glucocorticoids and other hormonal substrates of conditioned taste aversions. *Annals of the New York Academy of Sciences, 443,* 126–144.

Spyraki, C., Fibiger, H. C., & Phillips, A. G. (1982). Dopaminergic substrates of amphetamine- induced place preference conditioning. *Brain Research, 253,* 185–193.

Stricker, E. M., & Verbalis, J. G. (1991). Caloric and noncaloric controls of food intake. *Brain Research Bulletin, 27,* 299–303.

Swanson, L. W., & Sawchenko, P. E. (1980). Paraventricular nucleus: A site for integration of neuroendocrine and autonomic mechanism. *Neuroendocrinology, 31,* 410–417.

Tarttelin, M. F., & Gorski, R. A. (1973). The effects of ovarian steroids on food and water intake and body weight in the female rat. *Acta Endocrinologica, 72,* 551–568.

Thiele, T. E., van Dijk, G., Campfield, A., Smith, F. J., Burn, P., Woods, S. C., et al. (1997). Central infusion of GLP-1, but not leptin, produces conditioned taste aversions in rats. *American Journal of Physiology, 272,* R726–R730.

Thiele, T. E., van Dijk, G., Yagaloff, K. A., Fisher, S. L., Schwartz, M., Burn, P., et al. (1998). Central infusion of melanocortin agonist MTII in rats: Assessment of c-fos expression and taste aversion. *American Journal of Physiology, 274,* R248–R254.

Trifunovic, R., & Reilly, S. (2001). Medial versus lateral parabrachial nucleus lesions in the rat: Effects on cholecystokinin- and D-fenfluramine-induced anorexia. *Brain Research, 894,* 288–296.

van der Kooy, D., & Koda, L. Y. (1983). Organization of the projections of a circumventricular organ: The area postrema in the rat. *Journal of Comparative Neurology, 219,* 328–338.

van der Kooy, D., Swerdlow, N. R., & Koob, G. F. (1983). Paradoxical reinforcing properties of apomorphine: Effects of nucleus accumbens and area postrema lesions. *Brain Research, 259,* 111–118.

van Haaren, F., van Hest, A., & Heinsbroek, R. P. W. (1990). Behavioral differences between male and female rats: Effects of gonadal hormones on learning and memory. *Neuroscience & Biobehavioral Reviews, 14,* 23–33.

Vandesande, F., Dierickx, K., & DeMey, J. (1977). The origin of vasopressinergic and oxytocinergic fibers of the external region of the median eminence of the rat hypophysis. *Cell Tissue Research, 180,* 443–452.

Wade, G. N. (1972). Gonadal hormones and behavioral regulation of body weight. *Physiology & Behavior, 8,* 523–534.

Wang, Y., & Chambers, K. C. (2002). Cooling lesions of the lateral parabrachial nucleus during LiCl activation block acquisition of conditioned taste avoidance in male rats. *Brain Research, 934,* 7–22.

Wang, Y., Lavond, D. G., & Chambers, K. C. (1997a). The effects of cooling the area postrema of male rats on conditioned taste aversions induced by LiCl and apomorphine. *Behavioural Brain Research, 82,* 149–158.

Wang, Y., Lavond, D. G., & Chambers, K. C. (1997b). Cooling the area postrema induces conditioned taste aversions in male rats and blocks acquisition of LiCl-induced aversions. *Behavioral Neuroscience, 111,* 768–776.

Willi, J., & Grossmann, S. (1983). Epidemiology of anorexia nervosa in a defined region of Switzerland. *American Journal of Psychiatry, 140,* 564–567.

Wirth, M. M., Olszewski, P. K., Yu, C., Levine, A. S., & Giraudo, S. Q. (2001). Paraventricular hypothalamic alpha-melanocyte-stimulating hormone and MTII reduce feeding without causing aversive effects. *Peptide, 22,* 129–134.

Wise, R. A., Yokel, B., & DeWitt, H. (1976). Both positive reinforcement and conditioned aversion from amphetamine and apomorphine in rats. *Science, 191,* 1273–1275.

Woolley, C. S., & McEwen, B. S. (1993). Roles of estradiol and progesterone in regulation of hippocampal dendritic spine density during the estrous cycle in the rat. *Journal of Comparative Neurology, 336,* 293–306.

Yamamoto, T., Shimura, T., Sako, N., Azuma, S., Bai, W. Z., & Wakisaka, S. (1992). *c-Fos* expression in the rat brain after intraperitoneal injection of lithium chloride. *NeuroReport, 3,* 1049–1052.

Yaswen, L., Diehl, N., Brennan, M. B., & Hochgeschwender, U. (1999). Obesity in the mouse model of pro-opiomelanocortin deficiency responds to peripheral melanocortin. *Nature Medicine, 5,* 1066–1070.

Yuan, D. L., & Chambers, K. C. (1999a). Estradiol accelerates extinction of a conditioned taste aversion in female and male rats. *Hormones & Behavior, 36,* 1–16.

Yuan, D. L., & Chambers, K. C. (1999b). Estradiol accelerates extinction of LiCl-induced conditioned taste aversions through its illness-associated properties. *Hormones & Behavior, 36,* 287–298.

Zalaquett, C. P. & Parker, L. A. (1989). Further evidence that CTAs produced by lithium and amphetamine are qualitatively different. *Learning & Motivation, 20,* 413–427.

19

Genetic Influences on Conditioned Taste Aversion

CHRISTOPHER L. CUNNINGHAM, CHRISTINA M. GREMEL,
AND PETER A. GROBLEWSKI

Individuals differ widely in their willingness to consume certain foods or fluids. Some of these differences can be attributed to innate (unlearned), genetically influenced differences in sensitivity to specific tastes (Drayna, 2005). For example, humans show bimodality in their ability to detect the extremely bitter taste of phenylthiocarbamide (PTC), a phenomenon that can be explained largely by allelic variation in a single gene, *TAS2R38* (Kim et al., 2003). In many cases, however, individual differences in avidity for a food or fluid are more readily traced to the previous consequences, positive or negative, of ingesting those substances. In other words, individuals might differ in their willingness to consume a food or fluid based on previous learning about the postingestive effects of consumption. One common example of this phenomenon is the development of aversion to the taste of a food whose consumption was previously followed by nausea and vomiting, regardless of whether the illness was directly caused by a toxin in the food or was merely coincidental. Individuals who have previously experienced illness after eating a certain food are more likely to avoid that food or to report that it tastes "bad" than individuals who have not (Bernstein, 1999).

Although past experience (i.e., learning) can undoubtedly explain many of the differences among individuals in taste preferences or aversions, individuals who do not differ in their past experience with or innate sensitivity for a substance might still differ as a result of genetic influences on the development of a learned preference or aversion. For example, genotype might affect the basic ability to form an association between a taste and its postingestive consequences. That is, individuals with genotype A might be better able to learn about the relationship between a taste and its outcome than individuals with genotype B. Alternatively, genotype might influence sensitivity to the rewarding or aversive effects of ingestion. For example, in cases where the outcome is aversive, individuals with genotype A might experience a more profound illness than individuals with genotype B, even though both genotypes are exposed to the same dose of toxin.

The broad goal of this chapter is to provide an overview of research that has addressed genetic influences on drug-induced conditioned taste aversion (CTA) over the last 30 years. Because most of this research has been conducted in rats or mice, we focus exclusively on studies involving these two species. Our chapter begins with a review organized according to the major types of genetic animal models that have been used to study CTA: inbred strains, selectively bred lines, and strains with targeted gene mutations (e.g., gene knockouts [KOs]). We also describe recent studies that have used quantitative trait loci (QTLs) mapping techniques to identify genes that influence CTA. Finally, we consider several important issues related to the interpretation of studies that show genetic differences in CTA.

INBRED STRAINS

Comparison across inbred strains is a commonly used technique for demonstrating a genetic influence on behavioral traits. All individuals within an inbred strain are genetically identical, typically as the result of repeated sibling mating for 20 or more generations. Thus, behavioral differences among individuals within a strain can be attributed to nongenetic influences (e.g., environment). However, when two or more inbred strains are studied under the same controlled environmental conditions, differences in strain *means* are presumed to reflect differences in the forms of the genes (i.e., alleles) carried by these strains. That is, the differences between strains can be attributed to genotype not environment.

Tables 19.1 and 19.2 list studies that have compared drug-induced CTA across two or more inbred strains. These studies have been categorized by species (Table 19.1 = mice; Table 19.2 = rats) and by the drug that served as the unconditioned stimulus (US) for taste conditioning. As can be seen, most of these studies have involved two drugs commonly used in the CTA literature: ethanol (EtOH) and lithium chloride (LiCl). To date, only a handful of genetic comparisons have been done using other drugs (e.g., amphetamine, cocaine, morphine, nicotine).

Inbred Mouse Strains

Horowitz and Whitney (1975) were the first to report an inbred strain difference in drug-induced CTA. More specifically, these investigators examined preference for saccharin versus water after a single pairing of saccharin with an intraperitoneal (IP) injection of EtOH in C57BL/6J and DBA/2J mice. These two strains were selected because C57BL/6J mice have consistently shown higher daily EtOH intakes and a greater preference for 10% (v/v) EtOH over water than DBA/2J mice (Crabbe & Phillips, 2004). Horowitz and Whitney found that C57BL/6J mice also developed a weaker EtOH-induced CTA to saccharin than DBA/2J mice, raising the possibility that strain differences in EtOH drinking/preference reflect strain differences in sensitivity to EtOH's ability to induce CTA.

The finding of weaker EtOH-induced CTA in C57BL/6J mice than in DBA/2J mice was later replicated in several studies from other laboratories, making this the most frequently confirmed example of a genetic difference in drug-induced CTA (see Table 19.1). The strain difference was observed not only when saccharin was used as the conditioned stimulus (CS; Risinger & Cunningham, 1998) but also when sodium chloride (NaCl; Broadbent, Linder, & Cunningham, 1996; Broadbent, Muccino, & Cunningham, 2002; Risinger & Cunningham, 1992, 1995) or EtOH itself (Belknap, Coleman, & Foster, 1978) served as the CS. The finding of the same strain difference when acetaldehyde was the US (Dudek & Fuller, 1978) suggests that the strain difference in EtOH-induced CTA might be mediated, in part, by genetic differences in sensitivity to this major metabolite of EtOH.

One question raised by this strain difference in EtOH-induced CTA is whether it reflects a specific difference in sensitivity to EtOH's pharmacological effects, a more general difference in sensitivity to aversive drugs or a difference in the ability to form taste–drug associations. Several later studies addressed this issue by comparing these strains during development of CTAs induced by various other drugs, but the pattern of findings is mixed (Table 19.1). For example, although nicotine (like EtOH) was found to induce a stronger CTA in DBA/2J mice (Risinger & Brown, 1996), two doses of amphetamine produced a similar CTA in both strains (Orsini, Buchini, Piazza, Puglisi-Allegra, & Cabib, 2004). In the case of LiCl, several studies showed stronger CTA in DBA/2J mice (Belknap, Belknap, Berg, & Coleman, 1977; Belknap et al., 1978; Risinger & Cunningham, 2000), whereas others showed no strain difference (Belknap et al., 1977, 1978; Dudek & Fuller, 1978). The discrepancies between the findings reported by Belknap et al. (1977, 1978) can be attributed to the taste used as the CS. When a rich sucrose (15%) served as the CS, the strains developed similar CTAs. However, when the CS was a low concentration (2%–3%) EtOH solution, DBA/2J mice acquired a stronger CTA than C57BL/6J mice. Belknap et al. (1978) hypothesized that the strain difference in CTA to the EtOH CS was due to a strain difference in sensory detection threshold. That is, C57BL/6J mice were relatively impaired at developing CTAs to low concentration EtOH CSs because they were less able to detect EtOH than DBA/2J mice. The finding of equivalent CTAs to the sucrose CS was interpreted to mean that the strains did not differ in their general ability to acquire CTA or in their sensitivity to the aversive effects of LiCl.

The Belknap et al. (1977, 1978) studies underscore an important issue that must be considered whenever one attempts to interpret the outcome of a CTA study that compares multiple genotypes. Although it is tempting to attribute strain differences in CTA to differences in sensitivity to the US properties of the paired drug, one must always consider the possibility that the strains differ in their ability to detect the CS or in their unconditioned response to the CS. Such considerations are especially pertinent when using taste CSs at concentrations near the sensory detection threshold or when using CSs that might differ across strains in terms of their palatability (i.e., unconditioned preference or aversion) or olfactory component.

In fact, several studies of CTA in inbred mouse strains have explicitly used CTA as a tool to study strain differences in gustatory thresholds (Harder, Maggio, & Whitney, 1989; Harder, Whitney, Frye, Smith, & Rashotte, 1984) or to study strain differences in the qualitative similarities and differences among gustatory stimuli (Ninomiya, Higashi, Katsukawa, Mizukoshi, & Funakoshi, 1984; Ninomiya, Nomura, & Katsukawa, 1992). For example, Harder et al. (1984) used the CTA procedure to address whether the lower unconditioned preference of SWR/J mice for the bitter tastant sucrose octaacetate (SOA) was due to a genetic difference in the palatability of SOA (i.e., SWR/J mice find the taste of SOA more aversive) or to a genetic difference in taste detection threshold (i.e., SWR/J mice are able to detect SOA at lower concentrations). After inducing CTA to SOA in 11 different inbred strains using a LiCl US, they estimated detection thresholds by testing across a descending series of SOA concentrations. Although most strains showed a strong CTA of similar magnitude at the training concentration (10^{-3}M), SWR/J mice continued to avoid SOA at concentrations 100-fold weaker than those avoided by any other strain, supporting the suggestion that SWR/J mice were better able to detect SOA, even when CTA was used to match strains for their (conditioned) aversive response to this tastant. A control experiment showed that this outcome could not be explained by greater resistance to extinction in SWR/J mice.

Ninomiya and colleagues (1984, 1992) have used the CTA procedure to ask whether there are strain differences in the pattern of generalization across different tastants. For example, Ninomiya et al. (1992) used LiCl to establish CTAs to the tastes of eight different D-amino acids in separate groups of mice from two inbred strains (BALB/c, C57BL/6). These two strains were chosen because previous research had shown that CTAs to the sweet-tasting amino acid, D-phenylalanine (D-Phe), generalized to sugars and saccharin in C57BL/6 mice, but not in BALB/c mice (Ninomiya et al., 1984). All mice were tested for CTA to their amino acid CS as well as for their response to the other seven amino acids and ten other taste compounds. In both strains, aversions conditioned to five of the amino acids generalized to sucrose. However, CTA to D-Phe generalized to sucrose and saccharin only in C57BL/6 mice. In contrast, CTA to D-Phe generalized to quinine and hydrochloric acid in BALB/c mice. The authors suggested that the *Dpa* (D-phenylalanine) gene mediates this strain difference in the ability of D-Phe to produce a sweet taste.

To date, only two CTA studies have combined a comparison of inbred mouse strains with another manipulation selected to alter development of CTA. In both cases, EtOH-induced CTA was compared in C57BL/6J and DBA/2J mice. One study examined the effect of US preexposure on the later acquisition of CTA (Risinger & Cunningham, 1995) whereas the other study examined the effects of pretreatment with the nonselective opiate antagonist naloxone on conditioning trials (Broadbent et al., 1996). Such studies are of interest because of their potential to shed light on gene–environment interactions (i.e., whether genetic differences are affected by nongenetic variables). However, such studies can be difficult to design and interpret when the strains differ in the ability of the US drug to produce CTA under control conditions. The aforementioned studies attempted to address this issue by giving the more sensitive strain (DBA/2J) a lower dose of EtOH than the less sensitive strain (C57BL/6), thereby producing more similar levels of CTA between strains under control conditions. Interestingly, in both studies, the added manipulation had a greater impact on CTA in the strain that is less sensitive to the taste aversion inducing effect of EtOH. That is, EtOH preexposure produced greater retardation of EtOH-induced CTA (Risinger & Cunningham, 1995) and greater naloxone-induced enhancement of EtOH-induced CTA (Broadbent et al., 1996) in C57BL/6J mice. It should be noted that the strain difference in preexposure was apparent even when

Table 19.1 CTA Studies in Inbred Mouse Strains.

Strains	Reference	CS	US	CTA Outcome
Ethanol (EtOH)				
C57BL/6J, DBA/2J	Horowitz and Whitney, 1975	Saccharin (0.7% w/v)	EtOH (1, 2, 4 g/kg, IP)	DBA > C57
C57BL/6J, DBA/2J	Belknap et al., 1978	EtOH (2%–10% v/v)	EtOH (2%–10% v/v, oral)	DBA > C57 (6%, 7% EtOH)
C57BL/6J, DBA/2J	Risinger and Cunningham, 1992	NaCl (0.2 M)	EtOH (1, 2, 4 g/kg, IP)	DBA > C57 (2 g/kg)
C57BL/6J, DBA/2J, 20 RI strains	Risinger and Cunningham, 1998	Saccharin (0.15% w/v)	EtOH (2, 4 g/kg, IP)	DBA > C57 (4 g/kg); strain differences among RIs (2, 4 g/kg)
BALB/c, C57BL/6, F1	MacPhail and Elsmore, 1980	Saccharin (0.1% w/v)	EtOH (1.5–6 g/kg, IG)	C57 = F1 > BALB
BALB/cBy, C57BL/6By, B6CF1, CB6F1, 7 RI strains, HW23	Crabbe et al., 1982	Glucose (5%)	EtOH (4 g/kg, IP)	Both F1s > BALB (and 5 RIs) > C57 (and 2 RIs, HW23
A/HeJ, AKR/J, BALB/cJ, C3H/HeJ, C57BL/6J, C57L/J, C58/J, CBA/J, DBA/1J, DBA/2J, NZB/B1N/J, PL/J, SJL/J, SWR/J, 129P3/J	Broadbent et al., 2002	NaCl (0.2 M)	EtOH (2, 4 g/kg, IP)	A, C3H, CBA, DBA1, DBA2, SWR, 129 > AKR, NZB, PL, SJL > BALB, C57L > C57BL, C58
EtOH + Other Manipulations				
C57BL/6J, DBA/2J	Risinger and Cunningham, 1995	NaCl (0.2 M)	EtOH (DBA: 2 g/kg, IP; C57: 4 g/kg, IP)	C57 = DBA in nonexposed controls; EtOH preexposure reduced CTA more in C57 than in DBA
C57BL/6J, DBA/2J	Broadbent et al., 1996	NaCl (0.2 M)	EtOH (DBA: 1.5 g/kg, IP; C57: 3 g/kg, IP; Naloxone (1, 3 mg/kg); EtOH + NLX	EtOH: DBA > C57; NLX: no CTA in either strain; EtOH + NLX: C57 showed greater increase in CTA than DBA
Lithium Chloride (LiCl)				
C57BL/6J, DBA/2J	Belknap et al., 1977	EtOH (2% v/v)	LiCl (3 mEq/kg, IP)	DBA > C57 (2% EtOH CS)
C57BL/6J, DBA/2J	Belknap et al., 1978	EtOH (1%–7% v/v)	LiCl (3 mEq/kg, IP)	DBA > C57 (2%, 3% EtOH CS)
C57BL/6J, DBA/2J	Belknap et al., 1977	Sucrose (15% w/v)	LiCl (3 mEq/kg, IP)	C57 = DBA
C57BL/6J, DBA/2J	Belknap et al., 1978	Sucrose (15% w/v)	LiCl (3 mEq/kg, IP)	C57 = DBA
C57BL/6J, DBA/2J	Dudek and Fuller, 1978	Saccharin (0.7% w/v)	LiCl (1.5 mEq/kg, IP)	C57 = DBA

Strains	CS	US	Result	Reference
C57BL/6J, DBA/2J	NaCl (0.2M)	LiCl (0.75, 1.5, 3, 6 mEq/kg)	DBA > C57	Risinger and Cunningham, 2000
C57BL/6JOlaHsd, 129S2/SvHsd	Saccharin (0.5% w/v)	LiCl (2.8 mEq/kg, IP)	C57 > 129	Voikar, Vasar, et al., 2004
C57BL/6J, 129sv, B6x129F2, "wild type" (from unrelated KO study)	Sucrose (5% w/v)	LiCl (2.4 mEq/kg, IP)	No strain differences	De Bruin et al., 2006
A/J, BALB/cByJ, C57BL/6J, C57L/J, DBA/2J, I/LnJ, NZB/B1NJ, RF/J, SWR/J, 129/J	SOA (10^{-8} - 10^{-3} M) in EtOH (4%)	LiCl (12 mEq/kg)	SWR/J > most other strains > C57L	Harder et al., 1984
A/J, BALB/cByJ, BDP/J, C3HeB/FeJ, C57BL/6J, DBA/2J, I/LnJ, NZB/B1NJ, SWR/J, 129/J	Maltose (100 mM)	LiCl (12 mEq/kg)	Most strains > C57 and NZB (based on differences between conditioned and nonconditioned mice)	Harder et al., 1989
C57BL/10Bg, DBA/2J, NZB/B1NJ, P/J, SWR/J	Sodium cyclamate (100nM)	LiCl (12 mEq/kg)	Most strains > DBA (based on differences between conditioned and nonconditioned mice)	Harder et al., 1989
BALB/cCrSlc, C3H/HeSlc, C57BL/6CrSlc	15 different compounds served as CSs	LiCl (5.4 mEq/kg)	Strain differences in pattern of CTA generalization to 15 test compounds	Ninomiya et al., 1984
BALB/cCrSlc, C57BL/6CrSlc	8 D-amino acids served as CSs (+10 other compounds for generalization tests)	LiCl (5.4 mEq/kg)	Strain differences in pattern of CTA generalization to 18 test compounds	Ninomiya et al., 1992
Other Compounds				
C57BL/6J, DBA/2J, B6D2F1/J	Saccharin (0.7% w/v)	Acetaldehyde (200–400 mg/kg, IP)	DBA > F1 > C57	Dudek and Fuller, 1978
C57BL/6J, DBA/2J	Monosodium glutamate (12.5 mM) + NaCl (128 nM) vs. saccharin (0.43 nM + citric acid (1.48 nM)	D-amphetamine (1, 2 mg/kg)	C57 = DBA	Orsini et al., 2004
BALB/cJ, C3H/HeJ, C57BL/6J, DBA/2J	NaCl (0.2M)	Nicotine (0.5, 1, 2 mg/kg, IP)	DBA = C3H > BALB > C57 (2 mg/kg)	Risinger and Brown, 1996

Table 19.2 CTA Studies in Inbred Rat Strains.

Strains	Reference	CS	US	CTA Outcome
Cocaine				
F344, LEW	Glowa et al., 1994	Saccharin (0.1% w/v)	Cocaine (18, 32, 50 mg/kg, sc)	LEW > F344 (18, 32 mg/kg)
F344, LEW	Kosten et al., 1994	Saccharin CS+ (1 mM) vs. HCl CS– (1 mM)	Cocaine (7.5, 15, 30 mg/kg, IP)	F344 = LEW
F344, LEW	Grigson and Freet, 2000	Saccharin (0.15%, w/v)	Cocaine (10 mg/kg, sc)	LEW > F344
Ethanol (EtOH)				
M520, WKY	Cannon and Carrell, 1987	Saccharin (0.1% w/v)	EtOH (0.5, 1.0, 1.5 g/kg, IP)	WKY > M520 (steeper dose–effect curve)
ACI, BN, BUF, F344, M520, MR, WKY	Cannon et al., 1994	Saccharin (0.1% w/v)	EtOH (0.5, 1.0, 1.5 g/kg, IP)	No strain differences
ACI, BN, BUF, F344, M520, MR, WKY	Cannon et al., 1994	EtOH (10% w/v) + cola	EtOH (10% w/v, oral)	WKY and F344 > other strains
F344, LEW	Roma et al., 2006	Saccharin (0.1% w/v)	EtOH (1.0, 1.25, 1.5 g/kg, IP)	F344 > LEW (1.25, 1.5 g/kg)
Lithium Chloride (LiCl)				
M520, WKY	Cannon and Carrell, 1987	Saccharin (0.1%, w/v) or NaCl (0.9% w/v)	LiCl (0.45, 0.9, 1.35, 1.8 mEq/kg, IP)	WKY = M520
ACI, BN, BUF, F344, M520, MR, WKY	Cannon et al., 1994	EtOH (2.5% w/v)	LiCl (0.9 mEq/kg, IP)	No strain differences
F344, LEW	Grigson and Freet, 2000	NaCl (0.15M)	LiCl (0.15M, oral)	F344 = LEW
F344, Wistar	Clarke et al., 2001	NaCl (0.1M)	LiCl (0.5 mEq/kg, IP)	F344 = Wistar
F344, LEW	Foynes and Riley, 2004	Saccharin	LiCl (0.3, 0.6, 0.9, 1.2 mEq/kg, IP)	LEW > F344 (0.3 mEq/kg)
Other Compounds				
F344, LEW	Lancellotti et al., 2001	Saccharin (0.1% w/v)	Morphine (10, 32, 56 mg/kg, sc)	F344 > LEW
F344, LEW	Pescatore et al., 2005	Saccharin (0.1% w/v)	Nicotine (0.1, 0.4, 0.8 mg/kg, sc)	F344 = LEW (two-bottle choice test)
F344, LEW	Pescatore et al., 2005	Saccharin (0.1% w/v)	Nicotine (0.1, 0.4, 0.8 mg/kg, sc)	F344 > LEW (0.8 mg/kg, one-bottle test)
F344, LEW	Grigson and Freet, 2000	Saccharin (0.15% w/v)	Sucrose (1.0M)	LEW > F344

preexposure doses were identical to subsequent conditioning doses, eliminating concerns that the strain difference might be a by-product of using different doses in each phase (Klein, Mikulka, & Lucci, 1986).

Inbred Rat Strains

The most frequent inbred rat strain comparison has been between the Fischer (F344) and Lewis (LEW) strains (Table 19.2). These two strains have drawn interest because they differ in their sensitivity to the reinforcing effects of several abused drugs (e.g., cocaine, morphine, and EtOH), with LEW rats showing greater sensitivity than F344 rats (George & Goldberg, 1988, 1989; Guitart, Beitner-Johnson, Marby, Kosten, & Nestler, 1992; Kosten, 1997; Kosten, Miserendino, Chi, & Nestler, 1994; Suzuki, George, & Meisch, 1988, 1992). However, CTA comparisons between these strains have not shown a consistent strain difference across various US drugs (Table 19.2). For example, although some studies have found stronger CTA in LEW rats when cocaine (Glowa, Shaw, & Riley, 1994; Grigson & Freet, 2000) or LiCl (Foynes & Riley, 2004) is the US, other studies have failed to find a strain difference with these drugs (Grigson & Freet, 2000; Kosten et al., 1994). Moreover, in studies with EtOH (Roma, Flint, Higley, & Riley, 2006), morphine (Lancellotti, Bayer, Glowa, Houghtling, & Riley, 2001), or nicotine (Pescatore, Glowa, & Riley, 2005) as the US, F344 rats have shown stronger CTA than LEW rats. Thus, it does not appear that LEW rats are more sensitive to all effects of these drugs. Rather, for CTA, the direction of the strain difference depends on the type of drug used as the US. Chapter 12 by Riley et al. provides a more comprehensive discussion of comparisons between F344 and LEW rats.

Genetic Correlations Based on Inbred Strains

Inbred strains can be useful for studying pleiotropy, that is, the ability of a particular gene to affect two or more traits (phenotypes). Similarities in the pattern of differences between strains for two different traits might mean that common genes influence those traits, that is, that those traits are genetically correlated. For example, in the comparison of F344 and LEW rats (Table 19.2), the finding that the strain (LEW) that self-administers more cocaine

also shows a stronger cocaine-induced CTA raises the possibility of overlap in the genes that control cocaine-induced CTA and self-administration. Unfortunately, when only two inbred strains are compared, there can be many phenotypic differences between strains that are genetically unrelated to CTA (e.g., body weight, coat color). Thus, the apparent genetic correlation between cocaine-induced CTA and self-administration could simply be a by-product of random fixation of genes in the two strains selected for study (Crabbe, Phillips, Kosobud, & Belknap, 1990).

A more powerful approach for studying genetic correlations with inbred strains is to greatly increase the number of strains tested for each trait. By selecting a relatively large number of strains (e.g., 10–20) that show a wide range of variation for each phenotype, the likelihood that observed correlations reflect chance fixation of genes is greatly reduced. In the case of drug-induced CTA, there are only a few studies thus far that have examined genetic correlations using a large number of inbred strains (Broadbent et al., 2002; D. S. Cannon, Leeka, & Block, 1994; Risinger & Cunningham, 1998). The general strategy used in these studies, all of which involved an EtOH US, was to estimate the genetic correlation between CTA and some other phenotype by calculating Pearson correlation coefficients using the strain means for both phenotypes (Crabbe et al., 1990).

In the first study, D. S. Cannon et al. (1994) examined the genetic correlation between EtOH self-administration and sensitivity to EtOH-induced CTA in seven inbred rat strains (Table 19.2). The Pearson correlation (r) between strain means for daily dose (g/kg/day) in a two-bottle choice drinking task (water vs. 10% w/v EtOH + cola) and strain means for the slope of the dose–effect curve in a study of EtOH-induced CTA to saccharin was 0.59, indicating that strains that showed stronger CTA (i.e., steeper slopes) tended to self-administer less EtOH. This correlation fell short of the criterion for statistical significance ($p = 0.17$), which the authors attributed to the low power offered by only seven pairs of observations. Nevertheless, the outcome encouraged further consideration of the possibility that common genes influence EtOH-induced CTA and EtOH self-administration.

In the next study, Risinger and Cunningham (1998) examined genetic correlations between EtOH-induced CTA (at two doses) and several other EtOH-related phenotypes in 20 of the BXD/ Ty recombinant inbred (RI) strains. Mice in an RI strain are the inbred descendents of the grandchildren (i.e., an F2 cross) of two established inbred strains. The BXD RI strains were derived from crossing the C57BL/6J and DBA/2J strains. Thus, each BXD RI strain carries random combinations of the alleles from these two parental strains at each gene locus. Risinger and Cunningham exposed each RI strain and the two parental strains to a CTA procedure in which saccharin was paired with injection of one of two EtOH doses (Table 19.1). The distribution of strain means for postpairing saccharin intakes at each dose was relatively continuous, suggesting that multiple genes influence EtOH-induced CTA.

Of particular interest, CTA was genetically correlated with several other phenotypes measured in previous studies involving the BXD RI strains. More specifically, there were positive genetic correlations (all r's > 0.45, p < 0.05) between strength of EtOH-induced CTA and sensitivity to onset of ataxia after EtOH (2 g/kg) injection (Gallaher, Jones, Belknap, & Crabbe, 1996), EtOH-induced hypothermia (Crabbe, Belknap, Mitchell, & Crawshaw, 1994), and severity of acute withdrawal (i.e., handling-induced convulsions) during the 12 h after exposure to a high (4 g/kg) EtOH dose (Buck Metten, Belknap, & Crabbe, 1997). In general, strains that showed a greater effect of EtOH on these other phenotypes also showed a stronger EtOH-induced CTA. These genetic correlations support the hypothesis of overlap in the neurobiological mechanisms that underlie EtOH-induced CTA with those that mediate EtOH-induced ataxia, hypothermia, and acute withdrawal. Although the direction of the relationship between CTA and 24-h EtOH (10% v/v) intakes (Phillips, Dickinson, & Burkhart-Kasch, 1994) in the BXD strains was the same as that reported for inbred rat strains (D. S. Cannon et al., 1994), the correlation was not significant, $r(18) = 0.24$, $p = 0.35$.

One limitation in the use of RI strains to study genetic correlations is that genetic variance across strains is necessarily restricted to gene loci where the two parental strains differ. Thus, the ability to generalize across the larger population of laboratory mice is constrained. Broadbent et al. (2002) recently addressed this issue in a study that examined the development of CTA to NaCl at two EtOH doses in 15 inbred strains selected to represent a broad range of mouse genetic diversity (Table 19.1).

As in the study by Risinger and Cunningham (1998), the distribution of strain means for CTA at each dose was continuous, consistent with the hypothesis that multiple genes determine EtOH-induced CTA. Of greater interest, comparison of strain means for CTA with strain means for other EtOH phenotypes previously reported by others revealed significant genetic correlations (both r's ≥ 0.64, p < 0.05) between CTA and 24-h EtOH intake (Belknap, Crabbe, & Young, 1993) and between CTA and severity of withdrawal following 72 h of EtOH vapor exposure (Crabbe, Young, & Kosobud, 1983). Figure 19.1 shows scatter plots of the strain means for both of these genetic correlations. As can be seen, strains that showed stronger EtOH-induced CTA (indexed by a more negative difference between Trial 2 and Trial 1) tended to consume less EtOH (Figure 19.1a) and showed more severe withdrawal after chronic EtOH exposure (Figure 19.1b).

The significant correlation between CTA and EtOH drinking, which is consistent with the trends previously reported by D. S. Cannon et al. (1994) for inbred rats and by Risinger and Cunningham (1998) for BXD RI mice, is of particular interest because it supports the suggestion that genetic differences in sensitivity to EtOH's aversive effects (as indexed by CTA) underlie strain differences in EtOH self-administration (Broadbent et al., 2002; D. S. Cannon & Carrell, 1987). This finding is also of interest because of its implications for theories that attribute CTA induced by abused drugs to the rewarding effects of those drugs (Grigson, 1997; Hunt & Amit, 1987). More specifically, the direction of the correlation is opposite to what would be predicted by such theories. For example, if stronger taste avoidance reflected anticipation of a more highly rewarding drug US (Grigson, 1997; see also Chapter 5), one would expect strains that show stronger CTA to drink *more* EtOH, not less. Thus, an interpretation of EtOH CTA based on EtOH's rewarding effects is not supported (Broadbent et al., 2002).

SELECTIVELY BRED LINES

Selective breeding is another approach for studying genetic influences on CTA and genetic correlations between CTA and other behavioral phenotypes. In a typical selective breeding experiment, individual animals are chosen for breeding based on whether

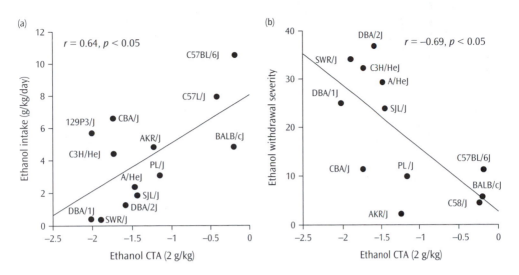

Figure 19.1. Scatterplot of strain means for CTA induced by 2 g/kg EtOH (Broadbent et al., 2002). (a) Strain means for intake of 10% (v/v) EtOH (Belknap et al., 1993) and (b) strain means for severity of withdrawal during the 25 h after exposure to 3 days of EtOH vapor (Crabbe et al., 1983). Taste aversion was indexed as the change in CS taste intake produced by one taste conditioning trial (i.e., Trial 2 minus Trial 1 consumption).

they show extreme high (or low) scores for the selection phenotype. The ability to successfully breed for a specific phenotype indicates that the phenotype is affected by genetic variation within the population. With repeated selection over several generations, alleles of genes that influence the selection phenotype should become fixed in a homozygous state whereas alleles at other genes should vary randomly. Because lines selected to show opposite responses for a selection phenotype are expected to differ only at genes influencing the selection phenotype, a line difference observed in another phenotype implies a genetic correlation between the two phenotypes (i.e., both phenotypes are influenced by common genes). However, due to limitations on the number of breeding pairs that can be maintained in most selection studies, chance fixation of trait-irrelevant genes can also cause selected lines to differ on other phenotypes. The best way to address this potential problem is to test the putative correlated phenotype in a second, independent set of lines (i.e., replicate lines) selectively bred for the same target phenotype (Crabbe et al., 1990).

Tables 19.3 and 19.4 summarize studies that have used selectively bred lines of rats and mice to study genetic influences on CTA. Such lines have

been used to study CTA in two general ways. First, in two selective breeding projects, rats or mice were selected for development of drug-induced CTA (Table 19.3). In one of these projects, Elkins and colleagues selectively bred rats (from a population of Sprague-Dawley rats) that developed strong (taste aversion prone, TAP) or weak (taste aversion resistant, TAR) CTA to saccharin after pairing with injection of an illness-inducing drug, cyclophosphamide (Elkins, 1986; Elkins, Walters, & Orr, 1992). In the other project, conducted in our lab, B6D2F2 mice (derived from crossing the C57BL/6J and DBA/2J inbred strains) were selectively bred for strong (high taste aversion, HTA) or weak (low taste aversion, LTA) CTA to saccharin after pairing with an injection of EtOH (Phillips et al., 2005). In both cases, these lines have been used to study many other behavioral phenotypes, with the goal of identifying traits that are genetically correlated with CTA (Table 19.3). The other major approach has been to examine CTA in lines of rats or mice that were selectively bred for some other phenotype that is hypothesized to be related to CTA (e.g., high or low intake of EtOH). The discovery of line differences in CTA in such lines implies overlap in the genes influencing CTA and those mediating the selection phenotype (Table 19.4).

Table 19.3 Studies in Mouse and Rat Lines Selected for CTA.

Selected Line(s)	Generation	Reference	Selection Phenotype	CS	US	CTA Outcome	Test Phenotype	Test Outcome
Mouse Lines Selected for CTA								
High taste aversion (HTA), low taste aversion (LTA)	1–2	Phillips et al., 2005	CTA	Saccharin (0.15% w/v)	EtOH (4 g/kg, IP)	HTA > LTA	S2: EtOH intake (g/kg) and preference during 24-h choice drinking (3% or 10% v/v EtOH vs. water)	3% intake: HTA = LTA; 3% preference: LTA > HTA; 10% intake and preference: LTA > HTA
HTA, LTA	2	Phillips et al., 2005	CTA	—	—	—	EtOH-induced locomotor stimulation, sensitization, conditioned place preference (2 g/kg, IP)	HTA = LTA
Rat Lines Selected for CTA								
Taste aversion prone (TAP), taste aversion resistant (TAR)	6	Elkins and Harrison, 1983	CTA	—	—	—	CTA: CS = Saccharin (0.1% w/v); US = rotation (6 or 10 min)	TAP > TAR (10-min rotation)
TAP, TAR	6	Hobbs and Elkins, 1983	CTA	Saccharin (0.1% w/v)	Cyclophosphamide (12.5 mg/kg, IP)	TAP > TAR	Bar pressing on CRF, FR6, or DRL-15 s schedules (food pellets)	TAP met initial bar pressing criterion more rapidly, but no line differences on CRF, FR, or DRL
TAP, TAR	1–7	Elkins, 1986	CTA	Saccharin (0.1% w/v)	Cyclophosphamide (12.5–15 mg/kg, IP)	TAP > TAR	Footshock-induced passive avoidance	S1: TAP > TAR; S5–7: TAR > TAP
TAP, TAR	11	Elkins et al., 1989	CTA	—	—	—	Cyclophosphamide-induced suppression of cricket predation (12.5 mg/kg, IP)	TAP > TAR
TAP, TAR	11	Elkins et al., 1989	CTA	—	—	—	Footshock-induced passive avoidance	TAP = TAR

TAP, TAR	n	Reference	Paradigm				Task/Measure	Result
TAP, TAR	14	Elkins et al., 1990	CTA	—	—	—	CTA: CS = Saccharin (0.1% w/v); US = rotation (10, 20, 30, or 40 min)	TAP > TAR (all rotation durations > 10 min)
TAP, TAR	8–22	Elkins et al., 1992	CTA	TAP > TAR	Cyclophosphamide (12.5–15 mg/kg, IP)	Saccharin (0.1% w/v)	S21: EtOH-induced loss of righting reflex and hypothermia (4 g/kg, IP)	TAP = TAR
TAP, TAR	16	Elkins et al., 1992	CTA	—	—	—	CTA: CS = Saccharin (0.1% w/v); US = LiCl (0.15 mEq/kg, IP)	TAP > TAR
TAP, TAR	21	Elkins et al., 1992	CTA	—	—	—	CTA: CS = Saccharin (0.1% w/v); US = emetine hydrochloride (7.5 mg/kg, IP)	TAP > TAR
TAP, TAR	21	Elkins et al., 1992	CTA	—	—	—	CTA: CS = Saccharin (0.1% w/v); US = EtOH (0.25, 0.75, 1.25 g/kg, IP)	TAP > TAR
TAP, TAR	22	Hobbs et al., 1993	CTA	—	—	—	Radial arm maze learning (Fruit Loops cereal)	TAP = TAR
TAP, TAR	22	Orr et al., 1993	CTA	—	—	—	Whole brain amine and amino acid levels	5-HT: TAP > TAR; NE, lysine: TAR > TAP; DA, DOPAC, R-HIAA + 13 amino acids: TAP = TAR
TAP, TAR	23	Orr et al., 1997	CTA	—	—	—	Intake and preference for EtOH (1%–10% v/v vs. water) in 24-h continuous access procedure	EtOH intake/preference: TAR > TAP (2%–10%); total fluid intake: TAP = TAR
TAP, TAR	28	Elkins et al., 2000	CTA	—	—	—	Serotonin uptake in brain synaptosomes	Km: TAR > TAP; Vmax: TAP = TAR
TAP, TAR	32	Elkins et al., 2000	CTA	—	—	—	Paroxetine binding in brain membranes	Kd, Bmax: TAP = TAR

(*continued*)

Table 19.3 *Continued*

Selected Line(s)	Generation	Reference	Selection Phenotype	CS	US	CTA Outcome	Test Phenotype	Test Outcome
TAP, TAR	1–25	Elkins et al., 2003a	CTA	Saccharin (0.1%, w/v)	Cyclophosphamide (12.5–15 mg/kg, IP)	TAP > TAR	Gene expression changes in amygdala 6 h after saline or cocaine injection (25 mg/kg, SC)	Not Specified Greater cocaine-induced expression decreases in TAR than TAP for 11 genes
TAP, TAR	29	Elkins et al., 2003b	CTA	—	—	—	CTA: CS = Saccharin (0.1% w/v); US = Cocaine (5 or 20 mg/kg, SC)	TAP > TAR
TAP, TAR	29	Elkins et al., 2003b	CTA	—	—	—	Gene expression changes in amygdala 6 h after saline or cocaine injection (25 mg/kg, SC)	Greater cocaine-induced expression decreases in TAR than TAP for 6 genes
TAP, TAR	35	Orr et al., 2004	CTA	Saccharin (0.1%, w/v)	Cyclophosphamide (12.5–15 mg/kg, IP)	TAP > TAR	Daily food and water intake; Blood-ethanol concentration (2.5 g/kg, IP)	TAP = TAR
TAP, TAR	35–36	Orr et al., 2004	CTA	—	—	—	Preference for EtOH (10% v/v vs. water) in 2-h limited access and 24-h continuous access procedures	TAR > TAP

Lines Selected for Sensitivity to CTA

TAP rats first showed a significantly greater CTA than TAR rats in the second selected generation (S2), indicating a relatively rapid divergence of trait relevant alleles (Elkins, 1986). After 27 generations of selection (when selective breeding was terminated in favor of random, nonsibling mating within each line), TAP rats showed saccharin preference scores of only 6% compared to 93% for TAR rats (Orr, Whitford-Stoddard, & Elkins, 2004). At various points throughout the selection, Elkins and colleagues examined several other behavioral phenotypes in order to better characterize the line differences. Although studies in early generations suggested the possibility of a line difference in passive avoidance learning induced by footshock (Elkins, 1986), this difference disappeared in later generations (Elkins, Gerardot, & Hobbs, 1989). Moreover, in studies of operant responding (bar pressing) for food pellets (Hobbs & Elkins, 1983) and radial arm maze learning (Hobbs, Walters, Shealy, & Elkins, 1993), both lines performed similarly, providing further support for the conclusion that selection for CTA did not create lines that performed differently in conventional learning procedures. Other studies showed that the line difference in CTA did not depend on the use of saccharin as the CS or cyclophosphamide as the US. For example, TAP rats showed a stronger suppression of cricket predation than TAR rats when ingestion of crickets was followed by cyclophosphamide (Elkins et al., 1989). Also, TAP rats developed stronger CTA to saccharin than TAR rats when saccharin was paired with rotation (Elkins & Harrison, 1983; Elkins, Walters, Harrison, & Albrecht, 1990), cocaine (Elkins et al., 2003b), EtOH, LiCl, or emetine hydrochloride (Elkins et al., 1992). Overall, these data support the authors' general conclusion that selective breeding, in this case, produced lines that differ in taste aversion conditionability that "are subserved by central nervous system differences in CTA associative efficiency" (Elkins et al., 1992). These investigators did not explicitly define "conditionability," but it presumably refers to a heritable trait that determines the rate or asymptote of CTA learning.

Although the selection process did not involve exposure to the taste or pharmacological effects of EtOH, TAR rats consumed more EtOH and showed a stronger preference for EtOH over water than TAP rats in both limited (2-h) and continuous (24-h) access drinking procedures (Orr, Walters, & Elkins, 1997, Orr et al., 2004). This difference was not due to differences in blood EtOH concentration (Orr et al., 2004). Moreover, it was not due to a more general difference in EtOH sensitivity as shown by the lack of line differences in hypothermia or the latency/duration of loss of the righting reflex (Elkins et al., 1992). Finally, it could not be explained as a by-product of line differences in daily food or water intake (Orr et al., 2004). Rather, given the previously observed line difference in EtOH-induced CTA (Elkins et al., 1992), these investigators suggested that the line difference in EtOH drinking was secondary to the line difference in CTA conditionability (Orr et al., 2004). That is, TAP rats drink less EtOH because they are especially sensitive to EtOH's ability to induce CTA whereas TAR rats drink more EtOH because they are less sensitive to this effect.

The genetic relationship between EtOH drinking and sensitivity to EtOH-induced CTA was tested more directly in the recent short-term CTA selection study conducted in our laboratory (Phillips et al., 2005). This study, which continued for only two generations, showed a highly significant response to selection after the first generation, with HTA mice showing a much stronger CTA than LTA mice. Heritability (h^2) across both generations was 0.26 (i.e., 26% of the between line difference in the selection response could be attributed to genetic differences), which was quite similar to the CTA heritability estimates (0.30, 0.29) previously reported for EtOH-induced CTA in 20 BXD RI strains (Risinger & Cunningham, 1998) and 15 inbred strains (Broadbent et al., 2002). Tests conducted in EtOH-naïve S2 mice from both lines showed no line difference in EtOH-induced locomotor stimulation, sensitization, or conditioned place preference, indicating the absence of a genetic correlation between EtOH-induced CTA and each of these other EtOH phenotypes (Table 19.3). However, two-bottle drinking tests showed that LTA mice drank more 10% EtOH and showed a higher preference for EtOH over water than HTA mice (Table 19.3). Thus, the outcome of this study is generally consistent with the inverse genetic correlation between EtOH-induced CTA and EtOH drinking previously reported in inbred strains (Figure 19.1). This outcome is also consistent with the conclusions from the EtOH drinking studies in the TAP and TAR selectively bred rat lines.

Table 19.4 CTA Studies in Mouse and Rat Lines Selected for Other Phenotypes.

Selected Line(s)	Generation	Reference	Selection Phenotype	CS	US	CTA Outcome
Mouse Lines Selected for Other Phenotypes						
Long sleep(LS), short sleep(SS)	23	Dudek, 1982	EtOH-induced loss of righting reflex	Saccharin (0.1% w/v)	EtOH (1.5, 3, 4.5 g/kg, IP); LiCl (1.5 mEq/kg)	LS > SS (only during extinction)
COLD1, COLD2, HOT1, HOT2	12–14	Cunningham et al, 1991	EtOH-induced hypothermia	Saccharin (0.15% w/v)	EtOH (2.25 g/kg, IP)	HOT > COLD (both replicates); saccharin preference: HOT = COLD
FAST1, FAST2, SLOW1, SLOW2	14–17	Risinger et al., 1994	EtOH-induced locomotion stimulation	Saccharin (0.15% w/v)	EtOH (2.5 g/kg, IP)	SLOW > FAST (both replicates); saccharin preference: FAST1 = FAST2, FAST2 > SLOW2
Withdrawal seizure prone (WSP1, WSP2), withdrawal seizure resistant (WSR1, WSR2)	53	Chester et al., 1998	Severity of withdrawal (handling-induced convulsions) after 72-h EtOH vapor exposure	NaCl (0.2 M)	EtOH (2, 4 g/kg, IP)	WSR > WSP (both replicates, Trial 1 only)
High alcohol withdrawal (HAW), low alcohol withdrawal (LAW)	5	Chester et al., 1998	Severity of acute withdrawal (handling-induced convulsions) after a single EtOH injection (4 g/kg, IP)	NaCl (0.2 M)	EtOH (2.5, 4 g/kg, IP)	HAW = LAW
High alcohol preference (HAP1, HAP2), low alcohol preference (LAP1, LAP2)	8	Chester et al., 2003	EtOH intake (g/kg) during 24-h choice drinking (10% v/v EtOH vs. water)	NaCl (0.2 M)	EtOH (2, 4 g/kg, IP)	LAP> HAP (both replicates)
Short-term drinking high (STDRHI), short-term drinking low (STDRLO)	2, 4	Phillips et al., 2005	EtOH intake (g/kg) during 24-h choice drinking (10% v/v EtOH vs. water)	Saccharin (0.15% w/v)	EtOH (4 g/kg, IP)	S2 females: STDRLO > STDRHI; S4: STDRLO = STDRHI
Rat Lines Selected for Other Phenotypes						
Syracuse high avoidance (SHA/Bru), Syracuse low avoidance (SLA/Bru)	21–23	von Kluge and Brush, 1992	Active-avoidance learning	Saccharin (0.1% w/v) + almond extract odor	LiCl (0.24 mEq/kg, ig)	SLA > SHA
Naples high excitability (NHE), Naples low excitability (NLE)	Not Specified	Viggiano et al., 2002	Total activity score (corner crossing, rearing) in Lat maze	Saccharin (0.1% w/v)	LiCl (4 mEq/kg, IP)	NHE > NLE (only during extinction)

Strain/Line	Reference	N	Task	Taste stimulus	Drug (dose)	Results
Spontaneously hypertensive (SHR), Wistar Kyoto hyperactive (WKHA), Wistar Kyoto (WKY)	Cailhol and Mormede, 2002	Not Specified	Hypertension (SHR) and Hyperactivity (WKHA)	Saccharin (0.1% w/v)	EtOH (0.5, 1, 1.5 g/kg, IP)	SHR = WKY > WKHA
Least affected (LA), most affected (MA)	Worsham et al., 1977	5–6	EtOH-induced impairment of motor activity	Saccharin (0.1% w/v)	EtOH (1.5 g/kg, IP)	LA = MA
LA, MA	Worsham et al., 1977	12	EtOH-induced impairment of motor activity	NaCl (1% w/v)	EtOH (1.5 g/kg, IP)	LA = MA
LA, MA	Worsham et al., 1977	5–6	EtOH-induced impairment of motor activity	EtOH (5% w/v)	LiCl (0.75 mEq, IP)	MA > LA
High alcohol sensitive (HAS1, HAS2), low alcohol sensitive (LAS1, LAS2), controls (CAS1, CAS2)	Kulkosky et al., 1995	20, 23	EtOH-induced loss of righting reflex (sleep time)	Saccharin (0.125% w/v)	EtOH (2 g/kg, IP); LiCl (1.8 mEq/kg, IP)	EtOH: HAS = CAS > LAS (both replicates); LiCl: no line differences
Alcohol preferring (P), alcohol nonpreferring (NP)	Froehlich et al., 1988	25	EtOH intake (g/kg) and preference during 24-h choice drinking (10% v/v EtOH vs. water)	Saccharin (0.1% w/v)	EtOH (0.25, 0.5, 1, 1.87 g/kg, IP)	NP > P (at 1 g/kg EtOH dose); at 0.25 g/kg, P rats drank more saccharin than saline P controls; no conditioning at other doses; no line differences in blood EtOH concentration at any dose
Alcohol accepting (AA), alcohol nonaccepting (ANA)	Gauvin et al., 2000	Not Specified	EtOH intake (g/kg) during 24-h choice drinking (10% v/v EtOH vs. water)	Saccharin (0.1% w/v)	EtOH (1.5 g/kg, IP)	EtOH naïve: AA = ANA; prior EtOH intoxicated practice during bar pressing: no CTA in either line; prior EtOH passive exposure: AA > ANA
Low alcohol drinking (UChA), high alcohol drinking (UChB)	Quintanilla et al., 2001	Not Specified	EtOH intake (g/kg) during 24-h choice drinking (10% v/v EtOH vs. water)	Banana-flavored solution (0.015% v/v)	EtOH (0.5, 1, 1.5, 2 g/kg, IP)	UChA > UChB (at 1.5 & 2 g/kg); no CTA at lower doses; no line differences in blood EtOH concentration at any dose
UChA, UChB	Quintanilla et al., 2002	Not Specified	EtOH intake (g/kg) during 24-h choice drinking (10% v/v EtOH vs. water)	Banana-flavored solution (0.015% v/v)	Acetaldehyde (50, 100, 150 mg/kg, IP)	UChA > UChB (UChA rats showed higher cerebral blood acetaldehyde concentrations)
Myers' High-Ethanol-Preferring (mHEP), Sprague-Dawley (SD), Wistar (W)	Lucas and McMillen, 2002	8	EtOH intake (g/kg) and preference during 24-h choice drinking (9%–20% v/v EtOH vs. water)	Saccharin (0.05% w/v) or EtOH (7%, v/v)	LiCl (1 mEq/kg, IP)	Females: SD > mHEP; Males: mHEP = W

One general weakness with both CTA selection projects is that neither selection has yet been replicated. Thus, as noted earlier, one cannot yet eliminate the possibility that the genetic correlations observed in these selected lines reflect the chance fixation of genes that are unrelated to the selection phenotype. However, the finding of a similar genetic correlation between EtOH-induced CTA and EtOH drinking across several different genetic models generally supports the conclusion that this relationship represents the influence of common genes that truly affect both phenotypes.

Lines Selected for Other Phenotypes

Several lines of rats and mice selectively bred for various other phenotypes have been tested in CTA procedures (Table 19.4). The question addressed by such studies is whether there is a genetic correlation between the selection phenotype and CTA, which would indicate that common genes affect these phenotypes. In all but a few cases, the selection phenotype was based on some response to EtOH, for example, loss of the righting reflex, hypothermia, activity changes, withdrawal severity, or EtOH intake/preference. Although some studies tested LiCl, most of these studies also used EtOH as the US for CTA assessment. Interestingly, in most of the studies involving selection for an EtOH phenotype, the line selected for reduced sensitivity to the EtOH effect showed a stronger CTA than the line selected for enhanced sensitivity. For example, the HOT (Cunningham et al., 1991), SLOW (Risinger, Malott, Prather, Niehus, & Cunningham, 1994), WSR (Chester, Risinger, & Cunningham, 1998), and LAP (Chester, Lumeng, Li, & Grahame, 2003) selected lines showed stronger CTA than the COLD, FAST, WSP, and HAP selected lines, respectively (both replicates of all lines). In a few cases, however, lines selected for enhanced sensitivity to the EtOH effect showed a stronger CTA. In two of these cases, lines selected for long sleep times after injection of a large EtOH dose (LS: Dudek, 1982; HAS: Kulkosky, Carr, LaHeist, & Hopkins, 1995) showed stronger EtOH and LiCl-induced CTA (or greater resistance to CTA extinction) than lines selected for short sleep times (SS, LAS). In the third case, a line selected for enhanced EtOH-induced impairment of motor activity (MA) showed stronger LiCl-induced CTA than the line selected for low impairment (LA),

but no CTA difference when EtOH served as the US (Worsham et al., 1977). Because EtOH (5%) served as the CS in the LiCl study, it is quite possible that the line difference in CTA reflected a difference in ability to detect the EtOH CS or in the unlearned motivational response to EtOH's taste.

One of the most consistent outcomes from studies in this category is the finding of an inverse genetic correlation between EtOH intake and EtOH-induced CTA. That is, lines selectively bred for high EtOH intake (HAP: Chester et al., 2003; P: Froehlich, Harts, Lumeng, & Li, 1988; UChB: Quintanilla, Callejas, & Tampier, 2001) showed weaker EtOH-induced CTA than lines selected for low intake (LAP, NP, UChA, respectively). Thus, these studies provide further support for the conclusion that common genes influence sensitivity to EtOH-induced CTA and EtOH drinking/preference.

STRAINS WITH TARGETED GENE MUTATIONS

As in many other fields of genetic research, the ongoing development of mouse strains with targeted gene deletions (KOs), conditional KOs, transgenics, and inducible KOs has allowed researchers to isolate and alter the expression of specific candidate genes and assess the resulting behavioral consequences. In the case of genes related to the classical neurotransmitter pathways, these genetic models can often complement and extend findings derived from conventional pharmacological assessments involving agonists, antagonists, and lesions. However, these models also provide an opportunity to assess the influence of genes in cases where selective pharmacological agents do not yet exist. Thus, these models might provide unique insights into the genetic mechanisms underlying CTA. The studies examining specific gene mutations on CTA are summarized in Table 19.5 and discussed in further detail. Our discussion of these studies is organized according to the target biological system. Although several of these studies involved ethanol-induced CTA, most of them have examined effects of gene mutations on LiCl-induced CTA.

Catecholamines

Pharmacological manipulations have previously implicated several catecholamines in the

Table 19.5 CTA Studies in Strains with Gene Mutations.

System	Reference	Gene Target	CS	US	CTA Outcome
Dopamine	Cannon et al., 2005	D1-receptor (KO)	Sucrose (0.5M)	LiCl (2.95, 6 mEq/kg, IP)	WT > KO
Dopamine	Cannon et al., 2005	D1-receptor (KO)	NaCl (0.2M)	LiCl (.94, 3.54, 6 mEq/kg, IP)	KO = WT
Dopamine	McQuade et al., 2003	D3-receptor (KO)	Sucrose (20%) w/Grape or Cherry Kool-Aid	EtOH (2 g/kg, IP)	KO = WT
Dopamine	Risinger et al., 2001	DARPP-32 (KO)	NaCl (0.2M)	EtOH (2, 4 g/kg, IP)	KO = WT
Norepinephrine	Weinshenker et al., 2000	DA β-hydroxylase (KO)	Saccharin (0.15% w/v)	EtOH (2 g/kg, IP)	KO = Het (but KO > Het during extinction)
Norepinephrine	Weinshenker et al., 2000	DA β-hydroxylase (KO)	Saccharin (0.15% w/v)	LiCl (3 mEq/kg, IP)	KO = Het
Norepinephrine	Kobayashi et al., 2000	TH (heterozygous mutation)	Sucrose (0.5 M)	LiCl (3 mEq/kg, IP)	Het = WT at 24 h (but WT > Het at 48 h)
Serotonin	Risinger et al., 1996	5-HT1b (KO)	NaCl (0.2 M)	EtOH (1, 2, 4 g/kg, IP)	KO = WT
GABA	Blednov et al., 2003	GABA_A receptor (α1 KO)	Saccharin (0.15% w/v)	EtOH (2.5 g/kg, IP)	KO > WT
GABA	Blednov et al., 2003	GABA_A receptor (β2 KO)	Saccharin (0.15% w/v)	EtOH (2.5 g/kg, IP)	KO = WT
GABA	Jacobson et al., 2006	GABA_B(1a)-receptor (KO)	Saccharin (0.5% w/v)	LiCl (3, 6 mEq/kg, IP)	WT > KO
GABA	Jacobson et al., 2006	GABA_B(1b)-receptor (KO)	Saccharin (0.5% w/v)	LiCl (3, 6 mEq/kg, IP)	KO = WT (but KO > WT during extinction)
GABA	Cai et al., 2006	GAT1 (KO)	NaCl (0.2M)	EtOH (2.5 g/kg, IP)	WT > KO
Glutamate	Cui et al., 2005	NR1-receptor (inducible, forebrain-specific KO)	Saccharin (0.1% w/v)	LiCl (3 mEq/kg, IP)	WT > KO when KO induced for 7 d before or for 14 d after conditioning, or for 14 d before test. KO = WT when KO induced for 5 d before test.
Glutamate	Masugi et al., 1999	mGluR7-receptor (KO)	Saccharin (0.1% w/v)	LiCl (3 mEq/kg, IP)	WT > KO
Glutamate	Yee et al., 2006	GlyT1 (KO)	Sucrose (10% w/v)	LiCl (5 mEq/kg, IP)	KO = WT (with and without CS preexposure)

(continued)

Table 19.5 *Continued*

System	Reference	Gene Target	CS	US	CTA Outcome
Protein kinase pathways	Chen et al., 2006	B-raf kinase (forebrain-specific KO)	Saccharin (0.1 M)	LiCl (20 mEq/kg, IP)	KO = WT
Protein kinase pathways	Howe et al., 2002	PKA Cβ (KO)	Saccharin (0.15% w/v)	LiCl (3 mEq/kg, IP)	KO = WT
Protein kinase pathways	Koh et al., 2003	PKA RIIβ (KO)	Saccharin (0.15% w/v)	LiCl (1 mEq/kg, IP)	KO = WT at 3 h; WT > KO at 24 h
Protein kinase pathways	Schafe and Stein, 1996	*fyn* (mutant)	Saccharin (0.15% w/v w/almond extract (1.0%)	LiCl (3 mEq/kg, IP)	Mutant = WT
Gene transcription/expression	Balschun et al., 2003	CREB1 (hippocampal specific KO)	Saccharin (0.5% w/v)	LiCl (2.8 mEq/kg, IP)	WT > KO
Gene transcription/expression	Josselyn et al., 2004	CREB^{αδ} (KO)	Saccharin (0.2% w/v) or Cherry Kool-Aid	LiCl (3 mEq/kg, IP)	WT > KO
Gene transcription/expression	Josselyn et al., 2004	CREB^{IR} (forebrain-specific transgenic)	Saccharin (0.2% w/v) or Cherry Kool-Aid	LiCl (3 mEq/kg, IP)	WT > TG when TG induced 6 h before conditioning
Gene transcription/expression	Banko et al., 2007	4E-BP2 (KO)	Saccharin (0.5% w/v)	LiCl (2.8 mEq/kg, IP)	KO > WT
Gene transcription/expression	Banko et al., 2007	4E-BP2 (KO)	NaCl (0.5% w/v)	LiCl (2.8 mEq/kg, IP)	KO > WT
Gene transcription/expression	Yasoshima et al., 2006	*c-fos* (KO)	Saccharin (0.005M)	LiCl (3 mEq/kg, IP)	KO = WT
Growth factors/immune response	Grota et al., 1987	MRL$^{lpr/lpr}$ (spontaneous mutation)	Chocolate whole milk	Cyclophosphamide (2.5, 50, 100, 200 mg/kg, IP)	KO = WT (25, 50, 200 mg/kg); WT > KO (100 mg/kg)
Growth factors/immune response	Grota et al., 1987	MRL$^{lpr/lpr}$ (spontaneous mutation)	Chocolate whole milk	LiCl (11.8 mEq/kg, IP)	KO = WT
Growth factors/immune response	Blednov et al., 2005	Ccl2 (Chemokine KO)	Saccharin (0.15% w/v)	EtOH (2.5 g/kg, IP)	KO > WT
Growth factors/immune response	Blednov et al., 2005	Ccl3 (Chemokine KO)	Saccharin (0.15% w/v)	EtOH (2.5 g/kg, IP)	KO > WT
Growth factors/immune response	Blednov et al., 2005	Ccr2 (Chemokine receptor KO)	Saccharin (0.15% w/v)	EtOH (2.5 g/kg, IP)	KO > WT
Growth factors/immune response	Blednov et al., 2005	Ccr5 (Chemokine receptor KO)	Saccharin (0.15% w/v)	EtOH (2.5 g/kg, IP)	KO > WT (females only)
Growth factors/immune response	Koponen et al., 2004	BDNF (trkB. TK+ transgenic)	Saccharin (0.5% w/v)	LiCl (2.8 mEq/kg, IP)	TG > WT

Category	Reference	Model	Tastant	US	Result
Growth factors/immune response	Voikar, Rossi, et al., 2004	GDNF (GFRα2 KO)	Saccharin (0.5% w/v)	LiCl (2.8 mEq/kg, IP)	KO = WT at 24 h; WT > KO at 48 h
Obesity and feeding	Lachey et al., 2005	GLP-1R (KO)	Sucrose (20%) w/Grape or Cherry Kool-Aid	LiCl (3 mEq/kg, IP)	KO = WT
Obesity and feeding	Lachey et al., 2005	GLP-1R (KO)	Sucrose (20%) w/Cherry Kool-Aid	GLP-1 (5 µg in 1 µl, icv)	WT > KO
Obesity and feeding	Yamada et al., 1999	BRS-3R (KO)	Saccharin (0.2% w/v)	LiCl (3 mEq/kg, IP)	KO > WT
Obesity and feeding	Yamada et al., 1999	BRS-3R (KO)	NaCl (0.9% w/v)	LiCl (3 mEq/kg, IP)	KO > WT
Obesity and feeding	Ingram, 1981	ob/ob (spontaneous mutation)	Saccharin (0.1% w/v)	LiCl (6 mEq/kg, IP)	KO > WT, KO showed impaired extinction
Stress	Palmer et al., 2004	CRF (heterozygous over-expression transgenic)	NaCl (0.2 M)	EtOH (1.5, 3 g/kg, IP)	TG = WT at 1.5 g/kg; WT > TG at 3 g/kg
Stress	Sharpe et al., 2005	CRF2-R (KO)	NaCl (0.2 M)	EtOH (2, 4 g/kg, IP)	KO = WT
Other	Janus et al., 2004	APP (TgCRND8 transgenic)	Saccharin (0.5% w/v)	LiCl (2.8 mEq/kg, IP)	WT > TG
Other	Pennanen et al., 2004	tau (P301L transgenic)	Saccharin (0.5% w/v)	LiCl (2.8 mEq/kg, IP)	TG = WT at 48 h; WT > TG at 72 h, 1w, 5 w
Other	Shoaib et al., 2002	β2-Nicotinic receptor (KO)	Saccharin (0.9% w/v) and NaCl (0.9% w/v)	Nicotine (0.4, 0.8, 1.2, 2 mg/kg, SC)	WT > KO
Other	Castane et al., 2006	A2A receptor (KO)	Saccharin (0.1% w/v) and NaCl (0.9% w/v)	Nicotine (5 mg/kg, SC)	KO = WT
Other	Hill et al., 2003	GIRK2 (KO)	Saccharin (0.15% w/v)	EtOH (2, 2.5, 3.5 g/kg, IP)	WT > KO at 2, 2.5 g/kg, KO = WT at 3.5 g/kg
Other	D'Adamo et al., 2004	Rab3a (KO)	Saccharin (5% w/v)	LiCl (3 mEq/kg, IP)	KO = WT
Other	Ferguson et al., 2000	Synaptotagmin IV (KO)	Saccharin (0.1% w/v)	LiCl (0.4 mEq/kg, IP)	KO = WT
Other	Stafstrom-Davis et al., 2001	Spinophilin (KO)	Sucrose (5%) or NaCl (0.075M)	LiCl (3, 6 mEq/kg, IP)	WT > KO at 3 mEq/kg; KO = WT at 6 mEq/kg; KO extinguished more quickly after 6mEq/kg.
Other	Stafstrom-Davis et al., 2001	Spinophilin (KO)	Saccharin (0.2% w/v) w/Grape or Cherry Kool-Aid	LiCl (3, 6 mEq/kg, IP)	WT = KO at 3, 6 mEq/kg; WT extinguished more quickly after 3 mEq/kg.
Other	Meiri et al., 1994	aMUPA (transgenic)	Saccharin (0.1% w/v)	LiCl (6 mEq/kg, IP)	WT > TG

development of CTA, especially CTAs induced by abused drugs (e.g., Hunt, Switzman, & Amit, 1985; Lorden, Callahan, & Dawson, 1980; Sklar & Amit, 1977). More recently, several studies using genetically modified mice also have provided evidence that dopamine and norepinephrine might play a role in CTA. For example, C. M. Cannon, Scannell, and Palmiter (2005) eliminated expression of the dopamine D1-receptor gene (*Drd1a*) and assessed its involvement in the development of LiCl-induced CTA to both sweet (sucrose) and salty (NaCl) solutions. When LiCl was paired with NaCl, D1-receptor KO mice showed normal development of CTA, suggesting that a functional D1-receptor is not required for the learning or expression of CTA. In contrast, when sucrose served as the CS, KO mice showed no aversion (relative to vehicle controls) while wild type (WT) littermates developed a strong aversion. Interpretation of this strain difference was complicated, however, by the fact KO mice weighed less and consumed less sucrose than WT mice on the first trial. Moreover, both genotypes showed substantial neophobia (i.e., low sucrose intake on the first conditioning trial) and pairings with LiCl only slowed the loss of neophobia rather than producing a decrease in sucrose intake relative to the first trial. The authors argued against an interpretation based on strain differences in sucrose preference by citing a previous study that showed normal sucrose preference in D1-receptor KO mice (El-Ghundi, O'Dowd, Erclik, & George, 2003). Although they suggested that the difference in KO effects on CTAs to sweet and salty tastes might indicate that D1-receptors only modulate expression of weak CTAs, they could not eliminate alternative interpretations related to procedural differences between the two studies (e.g., food-deprivation in the sucrose study vs. water deprivation in the NaCl study).

The role of the dopamine D3-receptor in CTA learning and expression has also been examined. McQuade, Xu, Woods, Seeley, and Benoit (2003) used a D3-receptor KO mouse to characterize the effects of this receptor on a number of EtOH-related behaviors, including CTA. However, their studies showed no effect of the gene deletion on EtOH-induced CTA or EtOH intake in either continuous or limited access drinking procedures, suggesting that the D3-receptor does not influence either of these behaviors.

Both the dopamine D1- and D3-receptors require a complex cascade of protein phosphorylation for signal transduction. Specifically, dopamine transmission, particularly in the striatum, requires the phosphoprotein, dopamine, and adenosine 3′,5′-monophosphate-regulated phosphoprotein, 32-kDa (DARPP-32; Greengard, Allen, & Nairn, 1999). The recent development of the DARPP-32 KO has provided a way to examine the role of this phosphoprotein in dopamine-related behaviors including CTA. Risinger, Freeman, Greengard, and Fienberg (2001) characterized the motivational effects of EtOH in the DARPP-32 KO mouse using CTA, conditioned place preference, and EtOH self-administration. Although DARPP-32 KO mice showed weaker place preference and lower levels of EtOH self-administration, they developed normal EtOH-induced CTA. Thus, these data suggested a role for DARPP-32 in the rewarding, but not aversive, effects of EtOH.

Other studies have examined the impact of catecholamines on CTA by targeting genes for catecholamine precursor enzymes. For example, Kobayashi et al. (2000) studied mice with a heterozygous (Het) mutation of the tyrosine hydroxylase (TH) gene in several learning and memory tasks including the Morris water maze, active avoidance, fear conditioning, and CTA. Because TH is the first and rate-limiting step in the biosynthesis of catecholamines, TH-mutant mice have reduced levels of catecholamines compared to WT control mice. TH-Het mice displayed impaired learning in the water maze and impaired long-term memory in both the active avoidance and fear conditioning procedures. Also, although TH-Het mice showed normal CTA when tested 24 h after a sucrose–LiCl pairing, they extinguished more rapidly, showing weaker aversion when tested 48 h after conditioning. To test the hypothesis that reduced noradrenergic activity was responsible for the mutation's effect on extinction, another group of TH-Het mice received posttraining treatment with a noradrenaline reuptake inhibitor (desipramine), a manipulation that was expected to increase noradrenaline levels. As predicted, desipramine prevented the more rapid extinction of CTA in TH-Het mice. Overall, these results were viewed as consistent with the broad conclusion that the central noradrenaline system plays an important role in memory formation and long-term memory.

Weinshenker, Rust, Miller, and Palmiter (2000) tested a dopamine β-hydroxylase (DBH) KO mouse in several EtOH-related tasks. They found that mice lacking the gene that controls expression of DBH (and thus unable to synthesize norepinephrine) showed decreased preference for EtOH in a two-bottle choice task and a heightened sensitivity to the physiological effects (sedative and hypothermic) of EtOH. Although DBH-KO mice showed normal acquisition of both EtOH- and LiCl-induced CTA, they were slower to extinguish the EtOH-induced CTA, suggesting that norepinephrine might normally be involved in reducing EtOH's aversive effects or in modulating extinction.

GABA-ergic System

Gamma-aminobutyric acid (GABA) is the primary inhibitory neurotransmitter in the central nervous system and is modulated by both ionotropic ($GABA_A$ and $GABA_C$) and metabotropic ($GABA_B$) receptors. Because GABA receptors are widely dispersed throughout the brain, they have been implicated in the regulation of a wide variety of behaviors, including the acquisition and expression of CTA (Chester & Cunningham, 2002). KO mice lacking specific subunits of both the $GABA_A$ and $GABA_B$ receptor have been characterized using EtOH- and LiCl-induced CTA procedures, respectively. Blednov et al. (2003) evaluated the development of EtOH-induced CTA in two types of $GABA_A$ receptor mutant strains lacking either the α1 or β2 receptor subunit. The α1-KO mice showed stronger CTA than either β2-KO or WT mice, which did not differ. In another study, Jacobson, Kelly, Bettler, Kaupmann, and Cryan (2006) focused on the G-protein coupled $GABA_B$ receptor. Strains carrying targeted mutations in either $GABA_{B(1a)}$ or $GABA_{B(1b)}$ receptor subunits were tested for acquisition and extinction of LiCl-induced CTA. $GABA_{B(1a)}$ mutants mice failed to acquire CTA, whereas $GABA_{B(1b)}$ mutants acquired a CTA similar to WT mice. Interestingly, however, the $GABA_{B(1b)}$ mutants showed no extinction of CTA while WT mice showed substantial extinction. Thus, these data suggest that the two $GABA_B$-receptor isoforms are differentially involved in the acquisition and extinction of CTA.

In another study of the GABA-ergic system's role in CTA, the gene encoding the GABA transporter subtype 1 (*GAT1*) was deleted (Cai et al., 2006). Homozygous GAT1-deficient mice developed significantly weaker EtOH-induced CTA when compared to both the heterozygous GAT1 KOs and WT littermates. GAT1 KOs also showed reduced sensitivity to EtOH's ability to induce conditioned place preference, hyperactivity, and loss of the righting reflex, suggesting that this GABA transporter subtype is broadly involved in modulating behavioral responses to EtOH.

Glutamatergic System

Glutamate, the major excitatory neurotransmitter in the mammalian nervous system, binds to and acts through both ionotropic and metabotropic receptors. Glutamate's fast acting properties are modulated by a group of ionotropic receptors including the AMPA, NMDA, and kainate receptors. In addition, glutamate is able to bind to a variety of metabotropic receptors, all of which have been classified into three groups: Group1 (mGlu1 and 5), Group 2 (mGlu2 and 3), and Group 3 (mGlu 4, 6, 7, and 8). As glutamate and its wide array of receptors are so ubiquitous in the central nervous system, mouse strains with altered glutamate-related genotypes are of great interest.

Because of the well-established role that NMDA-specific glutamatergic signaling plays in different models of learning (including long-term potentiation and depression), several researchers have attempted to create NMDA-specific KO strains. Owing to viability issues with traditional NMDA-related KO strains, a more sophisticated inducible KO mouse was recently created. More specifically, Cui, Lindl, Mei, Zhang, and Tsien (2005) developed an inducible KO model in which the Type 1 NMDA receptor (NR1) can be transiently inactivated in a specific region of forebrain cortex, hippocampus, and striatum. Inducible NR1 KO mice that were treated for a week before conditioning with doxycycline, which knocked-out synaptic NMDA receptor function, showed weaker CTA than controls. Reduced CTA was also observed in KO mice that received doxycycline for 2 weeks immediately after CTA conditioning or for 2 weeks beginning 14 days after conditioning (i.e., during the 14 days before the retention test). However, when induction of the KO was initiated only 5 days prior to the 1-month retention test, NR1 KO mice showed normal levels of CTA. Thus, the NMDA type-1 receptor plays a crucial role in the learning and postlearning consolidation of CTA, but not in the recall of a previously established CTA.

Other studies have examined the role of glutamatergic signaling in CTA by focusing on the metabotropic family of glutamate receptors. More specifically, Masugi et al. (1999) used a type-7 metabotropic glutamate receptor (mGluR7) KO mouse to investigate the role of this receptor in both fear and taste aversion conditioning. The mGluR7 KO mice showed impairments in both conditioned fear and CTA learning when compared to WT mice. Thus, the mGluR7 appears to be importantly involved in both of these forms of aversive learning.

Because NMDA receptors have multiple binding sites that can modulate receptor properties, NMDA current transmission can be regulated not only by glutamate, but also by other coagonists, including glycine. To examine the glycine-specific NMDA signaling pathway, Yee et al. (2006) developed a novel mouse strain that lacks the glycine transporter 1 (GlyT1), thereby eliminating the normally rapid removal of glycine from the extracellular space. Yee et al. predicted that reduction of glycine reuptake would increase available glycine levels and therefore facilitate NMDA transmission. However, GlyT1-KO mice did not differ from WT controls in strength of LiCl-induced CTA, indicating that the GlyT1 does not affect CTA. Although Ye et al. suggested that KO mice showed stronger latent inhibition of CTA than WT mice (induced by preexposure to the taste CS), their overall analysis showed no significant interaction between genotype and preexposure. Nevertheless, GlyT1-KO mice showed enhanced learning and augmentation of latent inhibition in both context fear conditioning and foot shock avoidance conditioning procedures. Thus, Yee et al. concluded that enhancement of extracellular glycine levels caused by mutation of the gene that encodes GlyT1 can improve associative learning.

Protein Kinase Pathway

Second messenger signaling via cyclic-adenosine monophosphate (cAMP) is essential for signal transduction of many membrane impermeable neurotransmitters. The primary role of cAMP in the signaling cascade is the activation of enzymes, such as protein kinases, that can subsequently have a wide variety of downstream effects. Several studies have examined this signaling cascade by using protein phosphorylation inhibitors or by targeting and altering expression of specific genes that code for different proteins within this system. For example, several groups have investigated the behavioral characteristics of different protein kinase KO

strains. Howe, Wiley, and McKnight (2002) used a KO strain of mice that lacked the gene necessary for expression of all catalytic subunits ($C\beta$) of cyclic-AMP protein kinase (PKA). When tested for development and expression of CTA, the $C\beta$-KO and WT controls showed equal decreases in consumption of a saccharin solution after it had been paired with LiCl injection, indicating no effect of the PKA catalytic subunits on CTA. In another examination of the PKA-signaling system, Koh, Clarke, Spray, Thiele, and Bernstein (2003) developed a KO strain lacking the gene required for expression of a specific PKA regulatory subunit, RIIβ. KO mice showed normal CTA when tested 3 h after a saccharin–LiCl pairing, but not when tested 24 h postconditioning. This pattern suggested a role of the regulatory subunit RIIβ in long-term but not short-term memory of the CTA.

Other downstream effectors in the G-protein coupled receptor-signaling pathway, including the mitogen-activated protein kinase (MEK) and extracellular signal regulated kinase (ERK), have also been examined using genetically modified mouse models. For example, Chen et al. (2006) recently found that a forebrain-specific KO of the gene encoding the B-Raf kinase isoform produced no change in LiCl-induced CTA compared to control mice, despite the KO showing other learning deficits.

Gene Transcription, Expression, and Protein Translation

Since acquisition and expression of CTA are thought to depend on long-term memory formation, activation of transcription factors and translation are most likely required for establishing the association (e.g., Baily & Kandel, 1993). Over the past 5 years, experimenters have increasingly used the CTA procedure to characterize transcription and translation processes underlying memory. Although some of these studies have suggested relatively specific effects on CTA memories, other studies have shown (or assumed) a broader involvement of the target gene across multiple types of memory. In most cases, these studies have not provided rigorous assessments of alternative "nonmemory" interpretations of strain difference in CTA (e.g., alterations in US efficacy).

In one recent study, mice lacking the translation repressor 4E-BP2 displayed enhanced LiCl-induced CTAs to two different taste CSs (Banko et al., 2007). Although translation of *de novo* protein seems to be necessary, the exact transcription factors and immediate early genes (IEG) initiating transcription and translation remain unknown. For example, conflicting results exist for the role of the *c-fos* gene. Although studies have shown that pretraining injection of *c-fos* antisense into the amygdala (Lamprecht & Dudai, 1996; Yasoshima, Sako, Senba, & Yamamoto, 2006) impairs retention of CTA, *c-fos* KO mice showed normal acquisition and retention of CTA (Yasoshima et al., 2006). This pattern of findings suggests that FOS-mediated gene transcription may normally be involved in the retention of CTA, but that other signaling pathways may compensate for the chronic *c-fos* deficiency in the KO strain.

A key protein hypothesized to be important in the activation of processes involved in new memory formation is the transcription factor cAMP response element binding protein, CREB. Activation of CREB leads to binding of a regulatory DNA sequence known as CRE (Silva, Kogan, Frankland, & Kida, 1998), activating transcription of many cAMP-responsive genes. Intraamygdala injection of CREB antisense before CTA training, which reduced CREB levels in amygdala, prevented the expression of CTA when tested 3–5 days later (Lamprecht, Hazvi, & Dudai, 1997). However, CREB antisense had no effect on expression of CTA when injected several days before training or when injected 14 h before testing. Of interest, rats that were injected 14 h before training but tested only 2 or 4 h after training displayed similar levels of CTA compared to CREB sense and normal controls. Thus, CREB levels in the amygdala appear to play a critical role in the encoding of long-term, but not short-term CTA memories.

Further support for CREB modulation of CTA comes from a study that showed attenuated CTA in a CREB KO mouse (Balschun et al., 2003). *Creb*[NesCre] mice exhibit a whole brain loss of CREB starting during early development. These mice, which consumed saccharin at levels similar to WT control mice when injected with vehicle, showed weaker CTA when saccharin was paired with LiCl (Balschun et al., 2003). However, *Creb*[NesCre] mice showed no deficits in hippocampal long-term potentiation (LTP), long-term depression (LTD), or contextual fear conditioning suggesting that CREB may play a relatively unique role in mediating CTA memories. Subsequent studies showed that mice with targeted deletions of the two main isoforms of CREB (CREB[αδ-/-]) showed a 90% decrease in CREB protein (Walters & Blendy, 2001) and reduced LiCl-induced CTA compared to WT mice or vehicle treated CREB[αδ-/-] mice (Josselyn, Kida, & Silva, 2004). Furthermore, transgenic mice (CREB[IR]) expressing an inducible and reversible dominant negative form of CREB (αCREB[S133A]) in forebrain regions showed a reduced expression of CTA when the transgene was induced 6 h before conditioning (Josselyn et al., 2004). Thus, CTA was impaired when CREB was disrupted chronically (CREB[αδ-/-]) or acutely (CREB[IR]). Overall, these studies strongly implicate the transcription factor CREB in the memory mechanisms underlying CTA.

Immune Response and Neurotrophic Factors

Researchers investigating the ability of immune system products and growth factors to modulate synaptic transmission have used the CTA procedure to examine their role in learning about aversive stimuli. Early studies took advantage of a spontaneous mutation in a gene (*lpr*, now called *Fas*) that produced lymphoproliferation and a lupus-like disease in mice. More specifically, studies of lupus-prone MRL[lpr/lpr] mice suggested that development of an impaired immune system reduced ability to condition a CTA using the immunosuppressive drug, cyclophosphamide (Ader, Grota, & Cohen, 1987). MRL[lpr/lpr] mice developed weaker CTA compared to MRL[+/+] control mice at an age when the disease had manifested itself in MRL[lpr/lpr] mice but not in MRL[+/+] mice. Since immunosuppressive actions in animals with autoimmune disease increase survival, the authors hypothesized that "the poorer taste aversion performance of lupus-prone mice reflects a recognition of their immunologic dysregulation" (Ader et al., 1987). Subsequent work demonstrated that CTA performance did not differ between MRL[lpr/lpr] and MRL[+/+] strains before disease onset, and that the decreased CTA performance was at least partially specific to cyclophosphamide since no differences were observed when LiCl was used as the US, discounting a general learning deficit in the mutant mice (Grota, Ader, & Cohen, 1987). Overall, these findings implicated the immune system in development of CTA induced by an immunosuppressive drug.

Although chemokines were traditionally viewed as proteins regulating the trafficking of immune cells, recent work has implicated these proteins and their receptors in synaptic transmission underlying EtOH-induced CTA. For example, Blednov and colleagues (2005) proposed that chemokine deficiencies would alter the behavioral actions of EtOH. Null mutant mice for two chemokine genes ($Ccl3^{-/-}$, $Ccl2^{-/-}$) or two chemokine receptor genes ($Ccr2^{-/-}$, $Ccr5^{-/-}$) were created using homologous recombination and subsequently backcrossed to C57BL/6 mice for at least 10 generations. All mutants (except $Ccr5^{-/-}$ males) developed a stronger EtOH-induced CTA than WT control mice. In several cases, reduced EtOH intake and preference was also seen in the mutants that showed enhanced CTA, suggesting that chemokines are important for regulating aversive effects of EtOH that impact drinking.

CTA has also been used to examine genetic manipulations of neurotrophic factors regulating synaptic transmission and plasticity. For example, transgenic mice overexpressing the neurotrophin receptor trkB, which binds brain-derived neurotrophic factor (BDNF), displayed significantly stronger CTA (Koponen et al., 2004). Although no consumption differences were seen during training, trkB overexpressing mice showed greater suppression of saccharin intake after LiCl pairing than WT controls. Transgenic mice also showed better performance in water maze learning and contextual fear conditioning tasks, supporting the general conclusion that overexpression of the trkB receptor significantly enhanced learning and memory.

In a series of studies examining the α-glial cell-line-derived neurotrophic factor receptor (GFRα2), Voikar, Rossi, Rauvala, and Airaksinen (2004) examined LiCl-induced CTA in GRFα2 KO mice. Although KO mice showed a normal CTA 24 h after conditioning, they showed weaker CTA than WT control mice during a second test 48 h after conditioning. When considered in combination with other data, the authors suggested that these findings implicated GRFα2 receptors in memory retention and that CTA differences were not due to the retarded physical growth and development observed in these KO mice. Another possibility might be that extinction was facilitated in mice lacking GRFα2 receptors.

Feeding Related Genes

Genetically modified animals and the CTA procedure have also been used to examine mechanisms that modulate learning about food-related stimuli. In the investigation of obesity and eating disorders, several different mutant strains have been used to examine the role of specific genes in feeding behaviors. The bombesin receptor subtype-3 (BRS-3) is normally expressed in the hypothalamic region that regulates taste perception and feeding behavior (Yamada, Wada, Imaki, Ohki-Hamazaki, & Wada, 1999). When the gene encoding this receptor is deleted, KO mice exhibit the phenotype of hyperphagia and obesity. Yamada et al. (1999) found that BRS-3 deficient mice developed stronger LiCl-induced CTAs to both a saccharin and NaCl CS than WT littermates. These findings are similar to those previously reported in genetically obese *ob/ob* mice carrying a spontaneous mutation in the leptin gene (Ingram, 1981). Overall, these data suggest a possible relationship between obesity and alterations in CTA learning.

Another approach to examining genes underlying CTA learning is to investigate possible central mechanisms mediating the aversive effects of LiCl. In light of pharmacological studies that had previously suggested that glucagon-like peptide-1 (GLP-1) was involved in mediating visceral illness induced by LiCl in rats, Lachey et al. (2005) recently examined the development of CTA in mice carrying a targeted mutation of the GLP-1 receptor gene. Surprisingly, LiCl-induced CTA was similar in mutant and WT control mice, suggesting no effect of GLP-1 on the aversive effects of LiCl. However, GLP-1R KO mice developed a weaker CTA than WT mice when GLP-1 was used as the US to induce CTA. Thus, contrary to the results of the pharmacological studies previously conducted in rats, these studies showed that GLP-1 receptor function is not necessary for the formation of LiCl-induced CTA in mice.

Corticotrophin-Releasing Factor

Candidate gene approaches to investigating the role of corticotrophin-releasing factor (CRF) and its receptors in CTA have thus far revealed limited contributions of the stress system to the development of CTA, specifically EtOH-induced CTA. In one series of studies, mice carrying a transgene that causes overexpression of CRF were tested for EtOH intake/preference and EtOH-induced CTA (Palmer et al., 2004). These investigators hypothesized that the lower

EtOH intake/preference observed in CRF overexpressing transgenic mice might be related to an effect of CRF on the aversive effects of EtOH. However, contrary to this hypothesis, transgenic CRF mice developed a CTA similar to controls at a low EtOH dose (1.5 g/kg) but weaker than controls at a high EtOH dose (3 g/kg). Thus, the lower EtOH intake shown by the transgenic mice could not be attributed to CRF-induced enhancement of EtOH's aversive effects.

A later study examined CTA in mice with a null mutation of the CRF receptor type 2 (CRF2), which was hypothesized to mediate the reduced EtOH drinking observed in CRF overexpressing mice (Sharpe et al., 2005). However, CRF2 KO mice displayed a dose-dependent EtOH-induced CTA similar to that seen in control mice. Thus, these findings suggest that the CRF2 receptor is not involved in mediating EtOH's aversive effects.

Other Candidate Genes

Other candidate genes outside the scope of the aforementioned categories have also been examined for their effects on CTA. Gene targets in these studies include the following:

- Amyloid precursor protein (APP), which leads to generation of plaques commonly observed in Alzheimer's disease (Janus et al., 2004).
- The mutated P301L tau protein that mimics neurofibrillary tangles seen in Alzheimer's disease (Pennanen, Welzl, D'Adamo, Nitsch, & Gotz, 2004).
- The nicotinic receptor beta-2 subunit (Shoaib et al., 2002).
- The adenosine receptor A2A (Castane, Soria, Ledent, Maldonado, & Valverde, 2006).
- The G-protein-coupled inwardly rectifying potassium channel GIRK2 (Hill, Alva, Blednov, & Cunningham, 2003).
- The synaptic vesicle protein Rab3a (D'Adamo et al., 2004).
- Another synaptic vesicle protein synaptotagmin IV (Ferguson, Anagnostaras, Silva, & Herschman, 2000).
- The dendritic protein spinophilin (Stafstrom-Davis et al., 2001).
- The extracellular protease brain murine urokinase-type plasminogen activator (Meiri, Masos, Rosenblum, Miskin, & Dudai, 1994).

Outcomes of these studies are shown in Table 19.5.

QTL MAPPING

During the last 10 years, QTL mapping has been used only a few times in the effort to identify specific genes influencing CTA. Quantitative traits are influenced by multiple genes and, like CTA, they are continuously distributed across individuals within a population. They can be distinguished from single-gene traits, which are either present or absent in individuals. A QTL locus is a region of a chromosome that has been shown on the basis of a statistical mapping procedure to contain one or more genes thought to influence a target phenotype. QTL mapping is done by comparing variations in genetic polymorphisms along the chromosome to variations in the phenotypic responses of individuals or inbred strains. One simple yet powerful approach to QTL mapping involves testing the target phenotype in a relatively large number of RI strains, that is, strains that have been inbred from the F2 cross of two established inbred strains. Because each RI strain possesses only one of two possible alleles at any chromosomal location, a significant correlation between allelic status (genotype) and the phenotypic score can be used to identify a chromosomal region containing one or more genes that influence the phenotype. For example, if most of the RI strains that show strong CTA possess one allele and most of the RI strains that show weak CTA possess the other allele, that gene or a closely linked gene is likely involved in regulating CTA. Additional information about QTL mapping can be found elsewhere (Abiola et al., 2003; Crabbe, Phillips et al., 1999; Phillips et al., 2002).

Risinger and Cunningham (1998) conducted QTL analyses of CTA induced by two different doses of EtOH (2 or 4 g/kg) in 20 of the BXD/Ty RI strains. Point biserial correlation coefficients (r) were calculated by correlating the strain means for CTA at each dose with the strain values for over 1500 genetic markers. At each marker, strains carrying the C57BL/6J allele were coded with the value of 0 whereas strains possessing the DBA/2J allele were coded with the value of 1. These analyses yielded significant QTLs for CTA on nine different mouse chromosomes: 1, 2, 3, 4, 6, 7, 9, 11, and 17. In some cases, both EtOH doses yielded QTLs in similar locations, but in other cases the QTLs appeared to be unique to the low or high EtOH dose. Although many of these CTA QTLs mapped to chromosomal regions containing candidate genes of potential interest (e.g., neurotransmitter receptor genes), it is important to note that this study represents only the first step in the process of identifying specific genes that influence EtOH-induced CTA. The confidence intervals for each of these QTLs are relatively broad, encompassing chromosomal regions that contain dozens (or more) of potential candidate genes. Also, given the relatively liberal criterion used for determining significance ($p < 0.01$), it is possible that some of the QTLs identified in this study were fortuitous. Thus, it will be important in future studies to verify these QTLs in other genetic models and to use models that permit finer mapping of the QTL regions.

Two studies have used the phenotypic data collected by Risinger and Cunningham (1998) to test hypotheses about specific candidate genes located on mouse chromosomes containing CTA QTLs. Encouraged by pharmacological data showing that GABA$_A$ receptors modulate EtOH-induced CTA (Chester & Cunningham, 1999) and several other EtOH effects, Hood and Buck (2000) determined allelic variation across the BXD RI strains for the GABA$_A$ receptor γ2 subunit gene, *Gabrg2*. This gene, which is polymorphic between the C57BL/6J and DBA/2J strains, is located on chromosome 11 proximal to a QTL previously identified for CTA induced by 2 g/kg EtOH. Analysis revealed a significant correlation between allelic status for *Gabrg2* and CTA strain means for mice conditioned with 2 g/kg, supporting the hypothesis that this gene influences EtOH-induced CTA. Groups conditioned at 4 g/kg showed a nonsignificant correlation in the same direction. Interestingly, the direction of the relationship was such that BXD strains with the DBA/2J allele showed *weaker* CTA than strains carrying the C57BL/6J allele. This study also showed that allelic variation in *Gabrg2* was correlated with several other EtOH phenotypes, including acute withdrawal, motor incoordination, and hypothermia.

The other CTA follow-up study examined the role of the syntaxin binding protein 1 gene, *Stxbp1*, which is located on chromosome 2 in the vicinity of a QTL previously identified for CTA produced by 4 g/kg EtOH (Fehr et al., 2005). Allelic status for this gene, which encodes a protein critical for vesicular neurotransmitter release, was significantly correlated with 4 g/kg EtOH CTA strain means. In this case, the genetic relationship was in the same direction as the CTA difference between the two progenitor strains. That is, BXD strains possessing the DBA/2J allele tended to show *stronger* CTA than strains having the C57BL/6J allele. Significant correlations were also found between *Stxbp1* genotype and acute EtOH withdrawal severity, some measures of EtOH consumption and EtOH-induced hypothermia, suggesting that this gene, like *Gabrg2*, influences several different EtOH phenotypes.

In the only study to map CTA QTLs in rats, Bielavská, Kren, Musilova, Zidek, and Pravenec (2002) measured LiCl-induced CTA in RI strains derived from crossing the Brown Norway rat (BN-Lx) and the spontaneously hypertensive rat (SHR). Correlations between strain means for the behavioral data and allelic status at over 700 genetic markers revealed QTLs on rat chromosomes 2 and 4, suggesting that one or more genes in the vicinity of each QTL influence LiCl-induced CTA in rats. The QTL on chromosome 2 was confirmed in a follow-up study that compared CTA between the SHR strain and a congenic strain in which a segment of chromosome 2 from the BN strain was transferred (through selective backcrossing) to the SHR genetic background. The authors noted that rat chromosome 2 is largely homologous to mouse chromosome 3, which had previously been reported to contain EtOH-induced CTA QTLs (Risinger & Cunningham, 1998). Although no specific genes were identified, this observation suggests the possibility of cross-species overlap in the QTLs associated with CTA.

While the studies described in this section have identified several putative QTLs for CTA, much work remains to be done in terms of narrowing the list of candidate genes and providing more compelling evidence in support of the role played by any particular gene. Ultimately, this task will require convergence of information derived from several different approaches, including studies in strains with targeted gene mutations. Fortunately, the techniques and procedures for accomplishing this task continue to improve (Abiola et al., 2003).

INTERPRETATION OF STRAIN DIFFERENCES IN CTA

As illustrated by the studies reviewed in this chapter, there can be many different reasons why strains might differ in CTA, all of which must be considered when attempting to interpret any particular instance of a strain difference in CTA. The major possibilities, which are listed in Figure 19.2, are briefly discussed in this section.

Because the assessment of CTA is generally based on measuring intake (or preference) for the taste CS after a drug pairing, interpretation of strain differences can become complicated when there are strain differences in the initial intake of the taste CS. There are several possible reasons for initial intake differences, including strain differences in body weight, sensitivity to fluid deprivation, or sensitivity to neophobia. In some cases, initial intake differences might also reflect strain differences in the palatability of the CS or in the ability to detect the CS (e.g., Belknap et al., 1977, 1978; Harder et al., 1984). Regardless of the reason, a strain difference in initial intake (or preference) poses a measurement problem because postpairing intakes (or preferences), which are typically used to index CTA, are likely to be genetically correlated with initial intakes. Thus, strain differences in postpairing intake might simply be a by-product of whatever caused the difference in initial intake. Investigators have taken several different approaches to this potential problem, including use of percentage change or ratio scores (Schafe, Stein, Park, & Bernstein, 1996), difference scores (e.g., Broadbent et al., 2002), or residual scores (Risinger & Cunningham, 1998). Although none

of these solutions is ideal, the rationale for such transformations is more compelling when it can be shown that they greatly reduce or eliminate the genetic correlation between initial intake and postpairing intake of the CS (e.g., Broadbent et al., 2002; Risinger & Cunningham, 1998).

A good way to address interpretations based on strain differences in palatability of the CS is to make the same strain comparison multiple times using several CSs that differ in palatability (e.g., sweet, salty, sour, bitter). A strain difference in CTA that persists despite changes in CS palatability is more likely to be explained in terms of differences in learning ability or sensitivity to the US than by differences in the unlearned motivational response to the CS. Similarly, interpretations based on strain differences in ability to detect the CS can be addressed by comparing the strains at several different CS concentrations, including low concentrations near the sensory detection threshold (e.g., Harder et al., 1984). A strain difference in CTA that depends on the use of a threshold level CS concentration, even when different types of drug USs are used, is most likely due to strain differences in the ability to detect the CS.

As indicated by many of the studies reviewed here, much attention has been given to the possibility that strain differences in CTA are representative of more general differences in learning ability, memory consolidation, or the retrieval of those memories. The best examples of this possibility can be found in the recent studies of mice carrying

- Basal fluid intakes, body weight, sensitivity to fluid deprivation

- Ability to detect the taste CS

- Taste neophobia, habituation to neophobia

- Initial preference/aversion for the taste CS

- General learning ability, memory consolidation, retrieval

- Ability to condition taste aversion ("CTA conditionability")

- Sensitivity to extinction

- General sensitivity to aversive events (or aversive drugs)

- Sensitivity to specific US drug

Figure 19.2. Possible reasons for strain differences in CTA.

targeted mutations in genes selected because of their hypothesized involvement in learning and memory (e.g., CREB KOs). Studies that support a learning/ memory interpretation generally do so by finding similar strain differences in other learning and memory tasks (e.g., Kobayashi et al., 2000; Koponen et al., 2004; Masugi et al., 1999). However, in some cases, the strain difference might generalize only to CTAs induced by other aversive USs and not to other types of learning. For example, the TAP and TAR selectively bred rat lines differed in the CTAs induced by several drugs other than the drug used for selective breeding (Elkins et al., 1992), but the lines did not differ in other aversive or appetitive learning procedures (Elkins et al., 1989; Hobbs & Elkins, 1983; Hobbs et al., 1993). Thus, although the strain difference generalized across several different CTA-inducing drugs, it did not reflect a more general strain difference in learning ability.

One conceptual issue that has been inconsistently addressed in this literature is whether an observed strain difference in CTA represents a difference in the acquisition or extinction of the conditioned response. It is quite possible, for example, that two strains might show similar levels of CTA during the first postpairing test, but they may diverge during subsequent extinction tests (e.g., Dudek, 1982; Viggiano, Vallone, Welzl, & Sadile, 2002; Weinshenker et al., 2000). This pattern of findings could mean that the strains do not differ in their ability to learn CTA or in their sensitivity to the drug US, but differ only in their ability to learn a new (presumably inhibitory) association during extinction. The possibility that organismic variables might have differential effects on the acquisition and extinction of CTA is generally supported by previous findings showing sex differences during extinction, but not during acquisition of CTA (Chambers, 1985). However, depending on the parameters used for conditioning, it is also possible that the lack of a strain difference on the initial test is due to a floor effect. That is, intake of the CS may have been maximally suppressed in both strains. In this case, the emergence of strain differences during CTA extinction could reflect differences in learning ability or sensitivity to the US that could not be detected at the end of acquisition.

Another possibility, of course, is that strain differences in CTA are indicative of differences in sensitivity to the aversive effects of the US drug. For example, much of the research on strain differences in EtOH-induced CTA has been guided by an interest in knowing whether strain differences in sensitivity to EtOH's aversive effects can "explain" strain differences in EtOH intake and preference in drinking procedures (e.g., D. S. Cannon & Carrell, 1987; Horowitz & Whitney, 1975; Palmer et al., 2004). There has also been a strong interest in whether sensitivity to EtOH's effects in the CTA procedure is correlated with sensitivity to other unconditioned effects of EtOH exposure, such as hypothermia, ataxia, loss of the righting reflex, and withdrawal (Broadbent et al., 2002; Risinger & Cunningham, 1998). Of course, one approach for addressing the US-specificity of strain differences in CTA is to compare strains for CTAs induced by several different drugs. In some cases (e.g., TAP and TAR selected lines), the strain difference has been found to generalize across many different USs (Elkins et al., 1992). In other cases (e.g., F344 and LEW inbred rats), however, the direction of the strain difference has varied as a function of the US, suggesting that there are drug-specific strain differences in sensitivity to the CTA-inducing effects of these drugs (e.g., Glowa et al., 1994; Grigson & Freet, 2000; Lancellotti et al., 2001; Roma et al., 2006).

Finally, when interpreting strain differences in CTA, one must remain open to the possibility that there could be multiple interacting influences on this behavior and that any given strain difference might be caused by a combination of factors. For example, the difference between two strains might be jointly determined by a strain difference in CS palatability *and* by a strain difference in sensitivity to the drug US. The polygenic nature of CTA is certainly consistent with this possibility. In the case of studies involving targeted gene mutations, one must also recognize that the ability to detect the effect of a mutation may depend critically on background genotype (Phillips, Hen, & Crabbe, 1999) or environment (Crabbe, Wahlsten et al., 1999). Moreover, interpretation may be confounded by unintended differences between the genetic background of the mutant strain and WT control strain (Banbury Conference, 1997; Wolfer, Crusio, & Lipp, 2002). Further discussion of these and other potential problems in the interpretation of studies involving genetically manipulated mice can be found elsewhere (Caine & Ralph-Williams, 2002; Crabbe, Phillips, Harris, Arends, & Koob, 2006; Stephens, Mead, & Ripley, 2002).

CONCLUSIONS

Research conducted over the last 30 years has provided substantial and compelling evidence that CTA is affected by genotype. Much of this research has focused on examining genetic correlations between sensitivity to CTA and sensitivity to various other phenotypes. The pursuit of such correlations has been especially productive in research on EtOH-induced CTA. Thus far, the most frequently confirmed and perhaps the most interesting of these genetic correlations is that between sensitivity to EtOH-induced CTA and EtOH intake/preference (e.g., Broadbent et al., 2002; Chester et al., 2003; Froehlich et al., 1988; Quintanilla et al., 2001). Although this observation shares the interpretive limitations posed by any correlation, it strongly suggests that common, genetically mediated neurobiological processes influence both of these behaviors. The discovery of this and other genetic correlations with CTA will play an important role in guiding future research designed to characterize the neurobiological basis of CTA.

Some of the most exciting advances in the search for CTA-related genes have resulted from the application of QTL mapping procedures and the use of genetically engineered mouse strains (e.g., KOs, transgenics). Both approaches have identified several promising candidate genes that appear to be involved in regulating drug-induced CTA. However, strain differences in CTA, like most quantitative traits, can occur for many different reasons (see Figure 19.2), and we still have much to learn about the specific ways in which these genes influence CTA. Fortunately, this effort will be facilitated by the ongoing development of increasingly sophisticated techniques and tools for the study of gene–behavior relationships.

Acknowledgment Preparation of this chapter was supported by NIH-NIAAA grants AA007468, AA007702, AA013479, AA016041, and AA010760.

References

Abiola, O., Angel, J. M., Avner, P., Bachmanov, A. A., Belknap, J. K., Bennett, B., et al. (2003). The nature and identification of quantitative trait loci: A community's view. *Nature Reviews Genetics, 4*(11), 911–916.

Ader, R., Grota, L. J., & Cohen, N. (1987). Conditioning phenomena and immune function. *Annals of the New York Academy of Sciences, 496*, 532–544.

Bailey, C. H., & Kandel, E. R. (1993). Structural changes accompanying memory storage. *Annual Review of Physiology, 55*, 397–426.

Balschun, D., Wolfer, D. P., Gass, P., Mantamadiotis, T., Welzl, H., Schutz, G., et al. (2003). Does cAMP response element-binding protein have a pivotal role in hippocampal synaptic plasticity and hippocampus-dependent memory? *Journal of Neuroscience, 23*(15), 6304–6314.

Banbury Conference on Genetic Background in Mice. (1997). Mutant mice and neuroscience: Recommendations concerning genetic background. *Neuron, 19*(4), 755–759.

Banko, J. L., Merhav, M., Stern, E., Sonenberg, N., Rosenblum, K., & Klann, E. (2007). Behavioral alterations in mice lacking the translation repressor 4E-BP2. *Neurobiology of Learning and Memory. 87*, 248–256.

Belknap, J. K., Belknap, N. D., Berg, J. H., & Coleman, R. (1977). Preabsorptive vs. postabsorptive control of ethanol intake in C57BL/6J and DBA/2J mice. *Behavior Genetics, 7*(6), 413–425.

Belknap, J. K., Coleman, R. R., & Foster, K. (1978). Alcohol consumption and sensory threshold differences between C57BL/6J and DBA/2J mice. *Physiological Psychology, 6*, 71–74.

Belknap, J. K., Crabbe, J. C., & Young, E. R. (1993). Voluntary consumption of ethanol in 15 inbred mouse strains. *Psychopharmacology (Berl), 112*(4), 503–510.

Bernstein, I. L. (1999). Taste aversion learning: A contemporary perspective. *Nutrition, 15*(3), 229–234.

Bielavská, E., Kren, V., Musilova, A., Zidek, V., & Pravenec, M. (2002). Genome scanning of the HXB/BXH sets of recombinant inbred strains of the rat for quantitative trait loci associated with conditioned taste aversion. *Behavior Genetics, 32*(1), 51–56.

Blednov, Y. A., Bergeson, S. E., Walker, D., Ferreira, V. M., Kuziel, W. A., & Harris, R. A. (2005). Perturbation of chemokine networks by gene deletion alters the reinforcing actions of ethanol. *Behavioural Brain Research, 165*(1), 110–125.

Blednov, Y. A., Walker, D., Alva, H., Creech, K., Findlay, G., & Harris, R. A. (2003). GABAA receptor alpha 1 and beta 2 subunit null mutant mice: Behavioral responses to ethanol.

Journal of Pharmacology and Experimental Therapeutics, 305(3), 854–863.

Broadbent, J., Linder, H. V., & Cunningham, C. L. (1996). Genetic differences in naloxone enhancement of ethanol-induced conditioned taste aversion. *Psychopharmacology (Berl), 126*(2), 147–155.

Broadbent, J., Muccino, K. J., & Cunningham, C. L. (2002). Ethanol-induced conditioned taste aversion in 15 inbred mouse strains. *Behavioral Neuroscience, 116*(1), 138–148.

Buck, K. J., Metten, P., Belknap, J. K., & Crabbe, J. C. (1997). Quantitative trait loci involved in genetic predisposition to acute alcohol withdrawal in mice. *Journal of Neuroscience, 17*(10), 3946–3955.

Cai, Y. Q., Cai, G. Q., Liu, G. X., Cai, Q., Shi, J. H., Shi, J., et al. (2006). Mice with genetically altered GABA transporter subtype I (GAT1) expression show altered behavioral responses to ethanol. *Journal of Neuroscience Research, 84*(2), 255–267.

Cailhol, S., & Mormede, P. (2002). Conditioned taste aversion and alcohol drinking: Strain and gender differences. *Journal of Studies on Alcohol, 63*(1), 91–99.

Caine, S., & Ralph-Williams, R. (2002). Behavioral pharmacologists: Don't just say "no" to knockout mice. Commentary on Stephens et al. "Studying the neurobiology of stimulant and alcohol abuse and dependence in genetically manipulated mice." *Behavioural Pharmacology, 13*(5–6), 349–352.

Cannon, C. M., Scannell, C. A., & Palmiter, R. D. (2005). Mice lacking dopamine D1 receptors express normal lithium chloride-induced conditioned taste aversion for salt but not sucrose. *European Journal of Neuroscience, 21*(9), 2600–2604.

Cannon, D. S., & Carrell, L. E. (1987). Rat strain differences in ethanol self-administration and taste aversion learning. *Pharmacology, Biochemistry, and Behavior, 28*(1), 57–63.

Cannon, D. S., Leeka, J. K., & Block, A. K. (1994, April). Ethanol self-administration patterns and taste aversion learning across inbred rat strains. *Pharmacology, Biochemistry, and Behavior, 47*(4), 795–802.

Castane, A., Soria, G., Ledent, C., Maldonado, R., & Valverde, O. (2006). Attenuation of nicotine-induced rewarding effects in A2A knockout mice. *Neuropharmacology, 51*(3), 631–640.

Chambers, K. C. (1985). Sexual dimorphisms as an index of hormonal influences on conditioned food aversions. *Annals of the New York Academy of Sciences, 443*, 110–125.

Chen, A. P., Ohno, M., Giese, K. P., Kuhn, R., Chen, R. L., & Silva, A. J. (2006). Forebrain-specific knockout of B-raf kinase leads to deficits in hippocampal long-term potentiation, learning, and memory. *Journal of Neuroscience Research, 83*(1), 28–38.

Chester, J. A., & Cunningham, C. L. (1999). GABA(A) receptors modulate ethanol-induced conditioned place preference and taste aversion in mice. *Psychopharmacology (Berl), 144*(4), 363–372.

Chester, J. A., & Cunningham, C. L. (2002). GABA(A) receptor modulation of the rewarding and aversive effects of ethanol. *Alcohol, 26*(3), 131–143.

Chester, J. A., Lumeng, L., Li, T. K., & Grahame, N. J. (2003). High- and low-alcohol-preferring mice show differences in conditioned taste aversion to alcohol. *Alcoholism, Clinical and Experimental Research, 27*(1), 12–18.

Chester, J. A., Risinger, F. O., & Cunningham, C. L. (1998, April). Ethanol reward and aversion in mice bred for sensitivity to ethanol withdrawal. *Alcoholism: Clinical and Experimental Research, 22*(2), 468–473.

Clarke, S. N., Koh, M. T., & Bernstein, I. L. (2001). NaCl detection thresholds: Comparison of Fischer 344 and Wistar rats. *Chemical Senses, 26*(3), 253–257.

Crabbe, J. C., Belknap, J. K., Mitchell, S. R., & Crawshaw, L. I. (1994). Quantitative trait loci mapping of genes that influence the sensitivity and tolerance to ethanol-induced hypothermia in BXD recombinant inbred mice. *Journal of Pharmacology and Experimental Therapeutics, 269*(1), 184–192.

Crabbe, J. C., Jr., Young, E. R., & Kosobud, A. (1983). Genetic correlations with ethanol withdrawal severity. *Pharmacology, Biochemistry, and Behavior, 18*(Suppl. 1), 541–547.

Crabbe, J. C., & Phillips, T. J. (2004). Pharmacogenetic studies of alcohol self-administration and withdrawal. *Psychopharmacology (Berl), 174*(4), 539–560.

Crabbe, J. C., Phillips, T. J., Buck, K. J., Cunningham, C. L., & Belknap, J. K. (1999). Identifying genes for alcohol and drug sensitivity: Recent progress and future directions. *Trends in Neurosciences, 22*(4), 173–179.

Crabbe, J., Phillips, T., Harris, R., Arends, M., & Koob, G. (2006). Alcohol-related genes: Contributions from studies with genetically engineered mice. *Addiction Biology, 11*(3–4), 195–269.

Crabbe, J. C., Phillips, T. J., Kosobud, A., & Belknap, J. K. (1990). Estimation of genetic correlation: Interpretation of experiments using selectively bred and inbred animals. *Alcoholism, Clinical and Experimental Research, 14*(2), 141–151.

Crabbe, J. C., Rigter, H., & Kerbusch, S. (1982). Analysis of behavioural responses to an ACTH analog in CXB/By recombinant inbred mice. *Behavioural Brain Research, 4*(3), 289–314.

Crabbe, J., Wahlsten, D., & Dudek, B. (1999). Genetics of mouse behavior: Interactions with laboratory environment. *Science, 284*(5420), 1670–1672.

Cui, Z., Lindl, K. A., Mei, B., Zhang, S., & Tsien, J. Z. (2005). Requirement of NMDA receptor reactivation for consolidation and storage of nondeclarative taste memory revealed by inducible NR1 knockout. *European Journal of Neuroscience, 22*(3), 755–763.

Cunningham, C. L., Hallett, C. L., Niehus, D. R., Hunter, J. S., Nouth, L., & Risinger, F. O. (1991). Assessment of ethanol's hedonic effects in mice selectively bred for sensitivity to ethanol-induced hypothermia. *Psychopharmacology (Berl), 105*(1), 84–92.

D'Adamo, P., Wolfer, D. P., Kopp, C., Tobler, I., Toniolo, D., & Lipp, H. P. (2004). Mice deficient for the synaptic vesicle protein Rab3a show impaired spatial reversal learning and increased explorative activity but none of the behavioral changes shown by mice deficient for the Rab3a regulator Gdi1. *European Journal of Neuroscience, 19*(7), 1895–1905.

de Bruin, N., Mahieu, M., Patel, T., Willems, R., Lesage, A., & Megens, A. (2006). Performance of F2 B6×129 hybrid mice in the Morris water maze, latent inhibition and prepulse inhibition paradigms: Comparison with C57BL/6J and 129sv inbred mice. *Behavioural Brain Research, 172*(1), 122–134.

Drayna, D. (2005). Human taste genetics. *Annual Review of Genomics and Human Genetics, 6*, 217–235.

Dudek, B. C. (1982, January). Ethanol-induced conditioned taste aversions in mice that differ in neural sensitivity to ethanol. *Journal of Studies on Alcohol, 43*(1), 129–136.

Dudek, B. C., & Fuller, J. L. (1978). Task-dependent genetic influences on behavioral response of mice (*Mus musculus*) to acetaldehyde. *Journal of Comparative and Physiological Psychology, 92*(4), 749–758.

El-Ghundi, M., O'Dowd, B., Erclik, M., & George, S. (2003). Attenuation of sucrose reinforcement in dopamine D1 receptor deficient mice. *European Journal of Neuroscience, 17*(4), 851–862.

Elkins, R. L. (1986, February). Separation of taste-aversion-prone and taste-aversion-resistant rats through selective breeding: Implications for individual differences in conditionability and aversion-therapy alcoholism treatment. *Behavioral Neuroscience, 100*(1), 121–124.

Elkins, R. L., Gerardot, R. J., & Hobbs, S. H. (1989, February). Differences in cyclophosphamide-induced suppression of cricket predation in selectively bred strains of taste-aversion prone and resistant rats. *Behavioral Neuroscience, 103*(1), 112–116.

Elkins, R. L., & Harrison, W. (1983, January). Rotation-induced taste aversions in strains of rats selectively bred for strong or weak acquisition of drug-induced taste aversions. *Bulletin of the Psychonomic Society, 21*(1), 57–60.

Elkins, R. L., Orr, T. E., Li, J. Q., Walters, P. A., Whitford, J. L., Carl, G. F., et al. (2000). Serotonin reuptake is less efficient in taste aversion resistant than in taste aversion-prone rats. *Pharmacology, Biochemistry, and Behavior, 66*(3), 609–614.

Elkins, R. L., Orr, T. E., Rausch, J. L., Fei, Y. J., Carl, G. F., Hobbs, S. H., et al. (2003a). Cocaine-induced expression differences in glutamate receptor subunits and transporters in amygdalae of taste aversion-prone and taste aversion-resistant rats. *Annals of the New York Academy of Sciences, 1003*, 381–385.

Elkins, R. L., Orr, T. E., Rausch, J. L., Fei, Y. J., Carl, G. F., Hobbs, S. H., et al. (2003b). Cocaine-induced expression differences in PSD-95/SAP-90-associated protein 4 and in Ca2+/calmodulin-dependent protein kinase subunits in amygdalae of taste aversion-prone and taste aversion-resistant rats. *Annals of the New York Academy of Sciences, 1003*, 386–390.

Elkins, R. L., Walters, P. A., Harrison, W. R., & Albrecht, W. (1990, May). Congruity of rotational and pharmacological taste aversion (TA) conditioning within strains of selectively bred TA prone and TA resistant rats. *Learning and Motivation 21*(2), 190–198.

Elkins, R. L., Walters, P. A., & Orr, T. (1992, October). Continued development and unconditioned stimulus characterization of selectively bred lines of taste aversion prone and resistant rats. *Alcoholism: Clinical and Experimental Research, 16*(5), 928–934.

Fehr, C., Shirley, R. L., Crabbe, J. C., Belknap, J. K., Buck, K. J., & Phillips, T. J. (2005). The syntaxin binding protein 1 gene (*Stxbp1*) is a candidate for an ethanol preference drinking locus on mouse chromosome 2. *Alcoholism, Clinical and Experimental Research, 29*(5), 708–720.

Ferguson, G. D., Anagnostaras, S. G., Silva, A. J., & Herschman, H. R. (2000). Deficits in memory and motor performance in synaptotagmin IV mutant mice. *Proceedings of the National Academy of Sciences of the United States of America, 97*(10), 5598–5603.

Foynes, M. M., & Riley, A. L. (2004). Lithium-chloride-induced conditioned taste aversions in the Lewis and Fischer 344 rat strains. *Pharmacology, Biochemistry, and Behavior, 79*(2), 303–308.

Froehlich, J. C., Harts, J., Lumeng, L., & Li, T. K. (1988). Differences in response to the aversive properties of ethanol in rats selectively bred for oral ethanol preference. *Pharmacology, Biochemistry, and Behavior, 31*(1), 215–222.

Gallaher, E. J., Jones, G. E., Belknap, J. K., & Crabbe, J. C. (1996). Identification of genetic markers for initial sensitivity and rapid tolerance to ethanol-induced ataxia using quantitative trait locus analysis in BXD recombinant inbred mice. *Journal of Pharmacology and Experimental Therapeutics, 277*(2), 604–612.

Gauvin, D. V., Baird, T. J., & Briscoe, R. J. (2000). Differential development of behavioral tolerance and the subsequent hedonic effects of alcohol in AA and ANA rats. *Psychopharmacology (Berl), 151*(4), 335–343.

George, F. R., & Goldberg, S. R. (1988). Genetic differences in responses to cocaine. In D. Clouet, K. Asghar, & R. Brown (Eds.), *Mechanisms of cocaine abuse and toxicity* (NIDA Research Monograph 88, pp. 239–249). Rockville, MD: National Institute of Drug Abuse.

George, F. R., & Goldberg, S. R. (1989). Genetic approaches to the analysis of addiction processes. *Trends in Pharmacological Sciences, 10*(2), 78–83.

Glowa, J. R., Shaw, A. E., & Riley, A. L. (1994). Cocaine-induced conditioned taste aversions: Comparisons between effects in LEW/N and F344/N rat strains. *Psychopharmacology (Berl), 114*(2), 229–232.

Greengard, P., Allen, P. B., & Nairn, A. C. (1999). Beyond the dopamine receptor: The DARPP-32/protein phosphatase-1 cascade. *Neuron, 23*(3), 435–447.

Grigson, P. S. (1997). Conditioned taste aversions and drugs of abuse: A reinterpretation. *Behavioral Neuroscience, 111*(1), 129–136.

Grigson, P. S., & Freet, C. S. (2000). The suppressive effects of sucrose and cocaine, but not lithium chloride, are greater in Lewis than in Fischer rats: Evidence for the reward comparison hypothesis. *Behavioral Neuroscience, 114*(2), 353–363.

Grota, L. J., Ader, R., & Cohen, N. (1987). Taste aversion learning in autoimmune Mrl-lpr/lpr and Mrl+/+ mice. *Brain, Behavior, and Immunity, 1*(3), 238–250.

Guitart, X., Beitner-Johnson, D., Marby, D. W., Kosten, T. A., & Nestler, E. J. (1992). Fischer and Lewis rat strains differ in basal levels of neurofilament proteins and their regulation by chronic morphine in the mesolimbic dopamine system. *Synapse, 12*(3), 242–253.

Harder, D. B., Maggio, J. C., & Whitney, G. (1989, August). Assessing gustatory detection capabilities using preference procedures. *Chemical Senses, 14*(4), 547–564.

Harder, D. B., Whitney, G., Frye, P., Smith, J. C., & Rashotte, M. E. (1984). Strain differences among mice in taste psychophysics of sucrose octaacetate. *Chemical Senses 9*(4), 311–323.

Hill, K. G., Alva, H., Blednov, Y. A., & Cunningham, C. L. (2003). Reduced ethanol-induced conditioned taste aversion and conditioned place preference in GIRK2 null mutant mice. *Psychopharmacology (Berl), 169*(1), 108–114.

Hobbs, S. H., & Elkins, R. L. (1983, July). Operant performance of rats selectively bred for strong or weak acquisition of conditioned taste aversions. *Bulletin of the Psychonomic Society, 21*(4), 303–306.

Hobbs, S. H., Walters, P. A., Shealy, E. F., & Elkins, R. L. (1993). Radial-maze learning by lines of taste-aversion-prone and taste-aversion-resistant rats. *Bulletin of the Psychonomic Society, 31*(3), 171–174.

Hood, H. M., & Buck, K. J. (2000). Allelic variation in the $GABA_A$ receptor $\gamma2$ subunit is associated with genetic susceptibility to ethanol-induced motor incoordination and hypothermia, conditioned taste aversion, and withdrawal in BXD/Ty recombinant inbred mice. *Alcoholism, Clinical and Experimental Research, 24*(9), 1327–1334.

Horowitz, G. P., & Whitney, G. (1975). Alcohol-induced conditioned aversion: Genotypic specificity in mice (Mus musculus). *Journal of Comparative and Physiological Psychology, 89*(4), 340–346.

Howe, D. G., Wiley, J. C., & McKnight, G. S. (2002). Molecular and behavioral effects of a null mutation in all PKA C beta isoforms. *Molecular and Cellular Neurosciences, 20*(3), 515–524.

Hunt, T., & Amit, Z. (1987). Conditioned taste aversion induced by self-administered drugs: Paradox revisited. *Neuroscience and Biobehavioral Reviews, 11*(1), 107–130.

Hunt, T., Switzman, L., & Amit, Z. (1985). Involvement of dopamine in the aversive stimulus properties of cocaine in rats. *Pharmacology, Biochemistry, and Behavior, 22*(6), 945–948.

Ingram, D. K. (1981). Conditioned taste aversion in genetically obese (*ob/ob*) mice. *Behaviour Analysis Letters, 1*, 199–206.

Jacobson, L. H., Kelly, P. H., Bettler, B., Kaupmann, K., & Cryan, J. F. (2006). GABA(B(1)) receptor isoforms differentially mediate the acquisition and extinction of aversive taste memories. *Journal of Neuroscience, 26*(34), 8800–8803.

Janus, C., Welzl, H., Hanna, A., Lovasic, L., Lane, N., St George-Hyslop, P., et al. (2004).

Impaired conditioned taste aversion learning in APP transgenic mice. *Neurobiology of Aging, 25*(9), 1213–1219.

Josselyn, S. A., Kida, S., & Silva, A. J. (2004). Inducible repression of CREB function disrupts amygdala-dependent memory. *Neurobiology of Learning and Memory, 82*(2), 159–163.

Kim, U. K., Jorgenson, E., Coon, H., Leppert, M., Risch, N., & Drayna, D. (2003). Positional cloning of the human quantitative trait locus underlying taste sensitivity to phenylthiocarbamide. *Science, 299*(5610), 1221–1225.

Klein, S., Mikulka, P., & Lucci, K. (1986). Influence of lithium chloride intensity on unconditioned stimulus-alone interference in a flavor aversion paradigm. *Learning and Motivation, 17,* 76–90.

Kobayashi, K., Noda, Y., Matsushita, N., Nishii, K., Sawada, H., Nagatsu, T., et al. (2000). Modest neuropsychological deficits caused by reduced noradrenaline metabolism in mice heterozygous for a mutated tyrosine hydroxylase gene. *Journal of Neuroscience, 20*(6), 2418–2426.

Koh, M. T., Clarke, S. N., Spray, K. J., Thiele, T. E., & Bernstein, I. L. (2003). Conditioned taste aversion memory and c-Fos induction are disrupted in RIIβ-protein kinase A mutant mice. *Behavioural Brain Research, 143*(1), 57–63.

Koponen, E., Voikar, V., Riekki, R., Saarelainen, T., Rauramaa, T., Rauvala, H., et al. (2004). Transgenic mice overexpressing the full-length neurotrophin receptor trkB exhibit increased activation of the trkB-PLCγ pathway, reduced anxiety, and facilitated learning. *Molecular and Cellular Neurosciences, 26*(1), 166–181.

Kosten, T. A., Miserendino, M. J., Chi, S., & Nestler, E. J. (1994). Fischer and Lewis rat strains show differential cocaine effects in conditioned place preference and behavioral sensitization but not in locomotor activity or conditioned taste aversion. *Journal of Pharmacology and Experimental Therapeutics, 269*(1), 137–144.

Kosten, T. A., Miserendino, M. J., Haile, C. N., DeCaprio, J. L., Jatlow, P. I., & Nestler, E. J. (1997). Acquisition and maintenance of intravenous cocaine self-administration in Lewis and Fischer inbred rat strains. *Brain Research, 778*(2), 418–429.

Kulkosky, P., Carr, B., LaHeist, A., & Hopkins, L. (1995, August). Conditioned taste aversions induced by alcohol and lithium in rats selectively bred for ethanol neurosensitivity. *Alcoholism: Clinical and Experimental Research, 19*(4), 945–950.

Lachey, J. L., D'Alessio, D. A., Rinaman, L., Elmquist, J. K., Drucker, D. J., & Seeley, R. J. (2005). The role of central glucagon-like peptide-1 in mediating the effects of visceral illness: Differential effects in rats and mice. *Endocrinology, 146*(1), 458–462.

Lamprecht, R., & Dudai, Y. (1996). Transient expression of c-Fos in rat amygdala during training is required for encoding conditioned taste aversion memory. *Learning & Memory, 3*(1), 31–41.

Lamprecht, R., Hazvi, S., & Dudai, Y. (1997). cAMP response element-binding protein in the amygdala is required for long- but not short-term conditioned taste aversion memory. *Journal of Neuroscience, 17*(21), 8443–8450.

Lancellotti, D., Bayer, B. M., Glowa, J. R., Houghtling, R. A., & Riley, A. L. (2001, March). Morphine-induced conditioned taste aversions in the LEW/N and F344/N rat strains. *Pharmacology, Biochemistry and Behavior, 68*(3), 603–610.

Lorden, J., Callahan, M., & Dawson, R. (1980). Depletion of central catecholamines alters amphetamine- and flenfluramine-induced taste aversions in the rat. *Journal of Comparative and Physiological Psychology, 94*(1), 99–114.

Lucas, L. A. C., & McMillen, B. A. (2002, September–October). Conditioned taste aversion and the Myer's high-ethanol-preferring rat. *Alcohol and Alcoholism, 37*(5), 427–431.

MacPhail, R. C., & Elsmore, T. F. (1980). Ethanol-induced flavor aversions in mice: A behavior-genetic analysis. *Neurotoxicology, 1,* 625–634.

Masugi, M., Yokoi, M., Shigemoto, R., Muguruma, K., Watanabe, Y., Sansig, G., et al. (1999). Metabotropic glutamate receptor subtype 7 ablation causes deficit in fear response and conditioned taste aversion. *Journal of Neuroscience, 19*(3), 955–963.

McQuade, J. A., Xu, M., Woods, S. C., Seeley, R. J., & Benoit, S. C. (2003). Ethanol consumption in mice with a targeted disruption of the dopamine-3 receptor gene. *Addiction Biology, 8*(3), 295–303.

Meiri, N., Masos, T., Rosenblum, K., Miskin, R., & Dudai, Y. (1994). Overexpression of urokinase-type plasminogen activator in transgenic mice is correlated with impaired learning. *Proceedings of the National Academy of Sciences of the United States of America, 91*(8), 3196–3200.

Ninomiya, Y., Higashi, T., Katsukawa, H., Mizukoshi, T., & Funakoshi, M. (1984). Qualitative discrimination of gustatory stimuli in three different strains of mice. *Brain Research, 322*(1), 83–92.

Ninomiya, Y., Nomura, T., & Katsukawa, H. (1992). Genetically variable taste sensitivity to D-amino acids in mice. *Brain Research, 596*(1–2), 349–352.

Orr, T., Walters, P. A., Carl, G., & Elkins, R. L. (1993, March). Brain levels of amines and amino acids in taste aversion-prone and -resistant rats. *Physiology & Behavior, 53*(3), 495–500.

Orr, T. E., Walters, P. A., & Elkins, R. L. (1997). Differences in free-choice ethanol acceptance between taste aversion-prone and taste aversion-resistant rats. *Alcoholism, Clinical and Experimental Research, 21*(8), 1491–1496.

Orr, T. E., Whitford-Stoddard, J. L., & Elkins, R. L. (2004). Taste-aversion-prone (TAP) rats and taste-aversion-resistant (TAR) rats differ in ethanol self-administration, but not in ethanol clearance or general consumption. *Alcohol, 33*(1), 1–7.

Orsini, C., Buchini, F., Piazza, P. V., Puglisi-Allegra, S., & Cabib, S. (2004, March). Susceptibility to amphetamine-induced place preference is predicted by locomotor response to novelty and amphetamine in the mouse. *Psychopharmacology, 172*(3), 264–270.

Palmer, A. A., Sharpe, A. L., Burkhart-Kasch, S., McKinnon, C. S., Coste, S. C., Stenzel-Poore, M. P., et al. (2004). Corticotropin-releasing factor overexpression decreases ethanol drinking and increases sensitivity to the sedative effects of ethanol. *Psychopharmacology (Berl), 176*(3–4), 386–397.

Pennanen, L., Welzl, H., D'Adamo, P., Nitsch, R. M., & Gotz, J. (2004). Accelerated extinction of conditioned taste aversion in P301L tau transgenic mice. *Neurobiology of Disease, 15*(3), 500–509.

Pescatore, K. A., Glowa, J. R., & Riley, A. L. (2005). Strain differences in the acquisition of nicotine-induced conditioned taste aversion. *Pharmacology, Biochemistry, and Behavior, 82*(4), 751–757.

Phillips, T. J., Belknap, J. K., Hitzemann, R. J., Buck, K. J., Cunningham, C. L., & Crabbe, J. C. (2002). Harnessing the mouse to unravel the genetics of human disease. *Genes, Brain, and Behavior, 1*(1), 14–26.

Phillips, T. J., Broadbent, J., Burkhart-Kasch, S., Henderson, C., Wenger, C. D., McMullin, C., et al. (2005). Genetic correlational analyses of ethanol reward and aversion phenotypes in short-term selected mouse lines bred for ethanol drinking or ethanol-induced conditioned taste aversion. *Behavioral Neuroscience, 119*(4), 892–910.

Phillips, T. J., Dickinson, S., & Burkhart-Kasch, S. (1994). Behavioral sensitization to drug stimulant effects in C57BL/6J and DBA/2J inbred mice. *Behavioral Neuroscience, 108*(4), 789–803.

Phillips, T., Hen, R., & Crabbe, J. (1999). Complications associated with genetic background effects in research using knockout mice. *Psychopharmacology (Berl), 147*(1), 5–7.

Quintanilla, M. E., Callejas, O., & Tampier, L. (2001). Differences in sensitivity to the aversive effects of ethanol in low-alcohol drinking (UChA) and high-alcohol drinking (UChB) rats. *Alcohol, 23*(3), 177–182.

Quintanilla, M. E., Callejas, O., & Tampier, L. (2002). Aversion to acetaldehyde: Differences in low-alcohol-drinking (UChA) and high-alcohol-drinking (UChB) rats. *Alcohol, 26*(2), 69–74.

Risinger, F. O., Bormann, N. M., & Oakes, R. A. (1996). Reduced sensitivity to ethanol reward, but not ethanol aversion, in mice lacking 5-HT1B receptors. *Alcoholism, Clinical and Experimental Research, 20*(8), 1401–1405.

Risinger, F. O., & Brown, M. M. (1996). Genetic differences in nicotine-induced conditioned taste aversion. *Life Science, 58*(12), 223–229.

Risinger, F. O., & Cunningham, C. L. (1992). Genetic differences in ethanol-induced hyperglycemia and conditioned taste aversion. *Life Science, 50*(16), PL113–118.

Risinger, F. O., & Cunningham, C. L. (1995). Genetic differences in ethanol-induced conditioned taste aversion after ethanol preexposure. *Alcohol, 12*(6), 535–539.

Risinger, F. O., & Cunningham, C. L. (1998). Ethanol-induced conditioned taste aversion in BXD recombinant inbred mice. *Alcoholism, Clinical and Experimental Research, 22*(6), 1234–1244.

Risinger, F. O., & Cunningham, C. L. (2000). DBA/2J mice develop stronger lithium chloride-induced conditioned taste and place aversions than C57BL/6J mice. *Pharmacology, Biochemistry, and Behavior, 67*(1), 17–24.

Risinger, F. O., Freeman, P. A., Greengard, P., & Fienberg, A. A. (2001). Motivational effects of ethanol in DARPP-32 knock-out mice. *Journal of Neuroscience, 21*(1), 340–348.

Risinger, F. O., Malott, D. H., Prather, L. K., Niehus, D. R., & Cunningham, C. L. (1994). Motivational properties of ethanol in mice selectively bred for ethanol-induced locomotor differences. *Psychopharmacology (Berl), 116*(2), 207–216.

Roma, P. G., Flint, W. W., Higley, J. D., & Riley, A. L. (2006). Assessment of the aversive and rewarding effects of alcohol in Fischer and Lewis rats. *Psychopharmacology (Berl), 189*(2), 187–199.

Schafe, G. E., Stein, P. L., Park, C. R., & Bernstein, I. L. (1996). Taste aversion learning in *fyn* mutant mice. *Behavioral Neuroscience, 110*(4), 845–848.

Sharpe, A. L., Coste, S. C., Burkhart-Kasch, S., Li, N., Stenzel-Poore, M. P., & Phillips, T. J. (2005). Mice deficient in corticotropin-releasing factor receptor type 2 exhibit normal ethanol-associated behaviors. *Alcoholism, Clinical and Experimental Research, 29*(9), 1601–1609.

Shoaib, M., Gommans, J., Morley, A., Stolerman, I. P., Grailhe, R., & Changeux, J. P. (2002). The role of nicotinic receptor beta-2 subunits in nicotine discrimination and conditioned taste aversion. *Neuropharmacology, 42*(4), 530–539.

Silva, A. J., Kogan, J. H., Frankland, P. W., & Kida, S. (1998). CREB and memory. *Annual Review Neuroscience, 21*, 127–148.

Sklar, L. S., & Amit, Z. (1977). Manipulations of catecholamine systems block the conditioned taste aversion induced by self-administered drugs. *Neuropharmacology, 16*(10), 649–655.

Stafstrom-Davis, C. A., Ouimet, C. C., Feng, J., Allen, P. B., Greengard, P., & Houpt, T. A. (2001). Impaired conditioned taste aversion learning in spinophilin knockout mice. *Learning & Memory, 8*(5), 272–278.

Stephens, D., Mead, A., & Ripley, T. (2002). Studying the neurobiology of stimulant and alcohol abuse and dependence in genetically manipulated mice. *Behavioural Pharmacology, 13*(5–6), 327–345.

Suzuki, T., George, F. R., & Meisch, R. A. (1988). Differential establishment and maintenance of oral ethanol reinforced behavior in Lewis and Fischer 344 inbred rat strains. *Journal of Pharmacology and Experimental Therapeutics, 245*(1), 164–170.

Suzuki, T., George, F. R., & Meisch, R. A. (1992). Etonitazene delivered orally serves as a reinforcer for Lewis but not Fischer 344 rats. *Pharmacology, Biochemistry, and Behavior, 42*(4), 579–586.

Viggiano, D., Vallone, D., Welzl, H., & Sadile, A. G. (2002). The Naples High- and Low-Excitability rats: Selective breeding, behavioral profile, morphometry, and molecular biology of the mesocortical dopamine system. *Behavior Genetics, 32*(5), 315–333.

Voikar, V., Rossi, J., Rauvala, H., & Airaksinen, M. S. (2004). Impaired behavioural flexibility and memory in mice lacking GDNF family receptor α2. *European Journal of Neuroscience, 20*(1), 308–312.

Voikar, V., Vasar, E., & Rauvala, H. (2004). Behavioral alterations induced by repeated testing in C57BL/6J and 129S2/Sv mice:

Implications for phenotyping screens. *Genes, Brain, and Behavior, 3*(1), 27–38.

von Kluge, S., & Brush, F. R. (1992). Conditioned taste and taste-potentiated odor aversions in the Syracuse high- and low-avoidance (SHA/Bru and SLA/Bru) strains of rats (*Rattus norvegicus*). *Journal of Comparative Psychology, 106*(3), 248–253.

Walters, C. L., & Blendy, J. A. (2001). Different requirements for cAMP response element binding protein in positive and negative reinforcing properties of drugs of abuse. *Journal of Neuroscience, 21*(23), 9438–9444.

Weinshenker, D., Rust, N. C., Miller, N. S., & Palmiter, R. D. (2000). Ethanol-associated behaviors of mice lacking norepinephrine. *Journal of Neuroscience, 20*(9), 3157–3164.

Wolfer, D., Crusio, W., & Lipp, H. (2002). Knockout mice: Simple solutions to the problems of genetic background and flanking genes. *Trends in Neurosciences, 25*(7), 336–340.

Worsham, E. D., Riley, E. P., Anandam, N., Lister, P., Freed, E. X., & Lester, D. (1977). Selective breeding of rats for differences in reactivity to alcohol: An approach to an animal model of alcoholism. III. Some physical and behavioral measures. *Advances in Experimental Medicine and Biology, 85A*, 71–81.

Yamada, K., Wada, E., Imaki, J., Ohki-Hamazaki, H., & Wada, K. (1999). Hyperresponsiveness to palatable and aversive taste stimuli in genetically obese (bombesin receptor subtype-3-deficient) mice. *Physiology & Behavior, 66*(5), 863–867.

Yasoshima, Y., Sako, N., Senba, E., & Yamamoto, T. (2006). Acute suppression, but not chronic genetic deficiency, of *c-fos* gene expression impairs long-term memory in aversive taste learning. *Proceedings of the National Academy of Sciences of the United States of America, 103*(18), 7106–7111.

Yee, B. K., Balic, E., Singer, P., Schwerdel, C., Grampp, T., Gabernet, L., et al. (2006). Disruption of glycine transporter 1 restricted to forebrain neurons is associated with a procognitive and antipsychotic phenotypic profile. *Journal of Neuroscience, 26*(12), 3169–3181.

20

Conditioned Taste Aversion Induced by Exposure to High-Strength Static Magnetic Fields

THOMAS A. HOUPT AND JAMES C. SMITH

In the 113 years since the original discovery of X-rays and Roentgen's famous radiogram of the bones of a hand, in vivo imaging of the human body has progressed from the novel to the commonplace. Radiation-based imaging, such as X-rays, computer-assisted tomography, and positron-emission tomography, and more recently magnetic resonance imaging (MRI) are now ubiquitous technologies in many countries. Although there were reports from the very beginning that X-rays were sensible (implying interaction with sensory receptors), X-radiation was initially considered benign and noninvasive. Subsequently, it became clear that X-radiation and other forms of high-energy radiation such as gamma radiation were capable of ionizing atoms within the body, with destructive effect. Similarly, the high-strength magnetic fields used in MRI machines are generally considered benign without significant effects on biological tissue. There are reports, however, of vertigo and nausea in subjects exposed to 4 tesla (T) or higher fields (Kangarlu et al., 1999; Schenck et al., 1992). Furthermore, we found significant interactions of high magnetic fields with the vestibular system in rodents. Although high magnetic fields contain far less energy than clinical X-radiation, the apparent ability of magnetic fields to be detected by humans and rodents implies an action of magnetic fields on sensitive tissues.

In this review we summarize the application of conditioned taste aversion (CTA) learning to determine the sensitivity of animals to high magnetic fields, and to determine the sites of action for their different effects. We also summarize the earlier work of JCS and colleagues on CTA and ionizing radiation, which has served as a model for our analysis of magnetic field effects. In both cases with either radiation or magnetic field exposure used as the unconditioned stimuli (USs), CTA revealed an effect on animals in the absence of other overt behavioral symptoms. CTA experiments also demonstrated that the site of action of ionizing radiation to induce CTA is the histamine-containing mast cells of the abdomen, while magnetic fields interact with the peripheral vestibular apparatus of the inner ear.

IONIZING RADIATION

I (JCS) became interested in taste aversion learning in the late 1950s. My professor, W. N. Kellogg, asked me to review the literature on behavioral effects from exposure to ionizing radiation. W. Roentgen, who has been given credit for the discovery of X-rays in 1895, thought at that time that these rays were not perceptible (Roentgen, 1895). In his third paper in 1897, however, he withdrew this claim and described experiments in which he "saw" the beam as a glow in his eye (Roentgen, 1897). The general belief was that these rays were harmless and it took quite a few years before the deleterious effects on living tissue were fully real-ized. By the middle of the twentieth century, reports were beginning to appear that exposure to X- and gamma-rays had behavioral effects in addition to physiological effects. The seminal paper was pub-lished in *Science* in 1955 by Garcia, Kimeldorf, and Koelling (1955). They showed that one pair-ing of saccharin-flavored water with an exposure to gamma-rays resulted in a subsequent aversion to the sweet solution. CTA had been described earlier by Barnett (i.e., bait-shyness; Barnett, 1963) and others, but most of us date the formal description of CTA from that 1955 paper. I had the good for-tune to spend two summers in 1962–1963 at the Naval Radiological Defense Laboratory working with Donald J. Kimeldorf. With support from the Atomic Energy Commission, and later, the United States Air Force and the National Cancer Institute, we initiated at FSU a long series of studies using X- and gamma-rays as both an US and a condi-tioned stimulus (CS), which are reviewed in greater detail elsewhere (Smith, 1971).

CTA as a result of exposure to ionizing radia-tion provided an interesting challenge since little was known about the unconditioned response to radiation exposure. In the typical design we pre-pared for the conditioning trial by training the rat to drink most of its daily supply of water during a brief 10-min exposure. This insured that the "thirsty" rat would drink a novel 0.1% saccharin solution on conditioning day. The 10-min saccha-rin exposure was followed by, for example, a sin-gle 100 roentgen (R) whole-body exposure of X- or gamma-rays. Control groups were treated in a like manner, but were given either sham exposures to the ionizing radiation or received water (but not saccharin) paired with irradiation on conditioning day. On the first postconditioning day we would initiate a two-bottle preference test between the saccharin solution and water. Saccharin preference was calculated as the ratio of saccharin intake to total fluid intake. The radiation groups showed a profound aversion to the saccharin and the con-trol groups readily showed a strong preference for the sweet solution. Often we continued these daily preference tests until the aversion was extinguished to provide a measure of CTA strength (Spector, Smith, & Hollander, 1981).

Our initial studies focused on the parameters of radiation exposure such as threshold doses, wave length, and rate of irradiation (Smith, Morris, & Hendricks, 1964; Spector et al., 1986).

We showed that novel tastes produced stronger aversions than familiar tastes. We also explored the temporal relations between the initiation of the period of tasting and the onset of the radia-tion exposure (Smith & Roll, 1967), being among the first to demonstrate that CTA learning could tolerate very long time periods between the CS (taste) and the US (irradiation; Carroll & Smith, 1974; Morris & Smith, 1964; Smith & Schaeffer, 1967; Smith, Taylor, Morris, & Hendricks, 1965; Spector et al., 1983).

In her master's thesis, Marilyn Carroll showed that the aversive response to gamma-ray exposure was not immediate, but peaked about 90 min fol-lowing the onset of the exposure period (Carroll & Smith, 1974). She did this by exposing a water-deprived rat to a 100-R dose and then immediately placing the rat in a cage equipped with a lickome-ter, allowing the rat to freely consume saccharin-flavored water. She found that in about 90 min the irradiated rats stopped drinking. Sham-exposed rats, however, kept drinking long after the gamma-ray-exposed rats had stopped. These results raised the question, "was 90 min the period of time that it took the rat to feel the most discomfort from the irradiation, or did it take 90 min to form a conditioned taste aversion?" She answered this by imposing different time delays between the irradi-ation and the initiation of the saccharin drinking period. It became clear that she was measuring the "discomfort," since rats that were given a 90-min delay between irradiation and onset of the drink-ing period failed to drink the saccharin-flavored water at the outset.

It was known that following a 100-R exposure to X-rays there was a build up of histamine in the blood of a rat that peaked 90 min following the exposure (Levy, Carroll, Smith, & Hofer, 1974). There was also evidence that the unconditioned response to a radiation exposure was mediated in the blood (Garcia, Ervin, & Koelling, 1967; Hunt, Carroll, & Kimeldorf, 1965). Using a parabiotic rat procedure in which a pair of male rats were sutured together through the skin, Hunt et al. (1965) showed that if one member of the pair drank saccharin-flavored water and the other member was irradiated, the nonexposed member developed a taste aversion to the saccharin. Furthermore, Garcia et al. demon-strated that plasma from an irradiated rat injected into a thirsty naïve rat, after he drank saccharin-flavored water, developed a taste aversion to the saccharin (Garcia et al., 1967). Our hypothesis was that the "toxic" substance in the blood was hista-mine. We treated rats with an antihistamine, chlor-pheniramine, and found that it blocked acquisition of a CTA in an irradiated rat (Levy et al., 1974). Conversely, injections of histamine into naïve rats paired with saccharin-flavored water induced a CTA to the saccharin solution. Combined with evi-dence that the abdomen was the most sensitive site for radiation-induced CTA (see following section), we concluded that the unconditioned response to the irradiation was the result of tissue damage that resulted in the massive production of histamine, most likely from mast cells in the intestine.

CLINICAL IMPLICATIONS OF RADIATION-INDUCED CTA

In the 1970s the National Cancer Institute put out a request for proposals to study the possible role of taste aversion learning as a contributing factor in the dietary problems experienced by cancer patients undergoing radiation and chemotherapy. The litera-ture on CTA induced by ionizing radiation in rodents typically used procedures that did not match those used in therapy with human patients, however. We focused on three of the obvious differences:

1. Most of the rat studies utilized novel tastes as the CS, whereas the cancer patient would not necessarily be eating novel foods.
2. Most of the rat studies induced CTA in only one trial, whereas the human patient is of-ten given the daily radiation exposure over a several week period.
3. Most of the rat studies involved whole-body exposure, whereas the human patient would typically receive only partial body exposures.

We developed a more suitable rat model for the conditions of human exposure by conditioning rats with familiar taste substances, applying multiple CS–US pairings, and limiting exposure to specific body regions (head, thorax, and abdomen). Rats were individually restrained in Plexiglas tubes. Laminar gamma-rays from a cobalt-60 source were presented through a 2.5-cm slit between two lead plates in order to expose specific parts of the body. We found that we could induce a sig-nificant CTA even with very low radiation doses by administering multiple trials. Furthermore, the

abdominal area was found to be the most sensitive body area (Smith, Hollander, & Spector, 1981). We then spent 3 years in the local hospital demonstrat-ing learned taste aversion in radiotherapy patients (Smith & Blumsack, 1981; Smith, Blumsack, & Bilek, 1985; Smith et al., 1984). Similar studies by Ilene Bernstein also found that chemotherapy could induce CTA in cancer patients (Bernstein, 1978; Bernstein, Webster, & Bernstein, 1982).

If learned taste aversions were to play an impor-tant part in human cancer patients as a result of con-ditioning to radiation or chemotherapy, we needed to quantify the strength of the aversions and how long they lasted. Therefore, in our rat model, we began to add the number of days before extinction of the aversion as a measure of its strength (Spector et al., 1981). This became a standard test for all of our subsequent studies. One thing of interest was the large variation among rats in the time to extinction. Following an aversion conditioned by a 100-R radiation exposure, we found some rats extinguishing in 2 days and others showing no signs of extinction in several weeks (Spector et al., 1981). Presumably, similar variation in sensitivity exists among human patients as well.

RADIATION AS A CS

There was evidence as far back as 1897 that ion-izing radiation could be perceived through the retina if the subject was in a dark-adapted state (Roentgen, 1897). This led us to a series of experi-ments using X-rays as a CS, that is, to determine if our animals (rats, pigeons, and rhesus monkeys) could immediately detect the onset of the X- or gamma-ray beam, as opposed to showing the delayed toxic effects of irradiation. Using a con-ditioned suppression technique, we could measure the threshold for detection of ionizing radiation (Dinc & Smith, 1966; Smith, 1970; Taylor, Smith, Wall, & Chaddock, 1968). The immediate detec-tion of ionizing radiation depended on the rate of the radiation (MR/s) and on head exposure. This was in sharp contrast to irradiation in the CTA experiments, in which the rate of the radiation dose was not important and exposure of the head alone was not an effective US at the lower doses. Subsequent experiments revealed that these animal subjects could immediately "smell" the radiation (i.e., due to the formation of ozone and/or oxides of nitrogen within the olfactory epithelium) and they could "see" the radiation if in a truly dark-adapted state (i.e., due to direct effects on retinal photoreceptors). These forms of detection could be abolished by ablation of the olfactory bulb or optic enucleation, respectively.

HIGH MAGNETIC FIELDS

In 1992, the U.S. National High Magnetic Field Laboratory (NHMFL) was moved from MIT to The Florida State University. At the strong encouragement of my late colleague, Bruce Masterton, we began to make preliminary observations regarding the rat's sensitivity to very high-strength magnets, both in terms of the use of magnets to condition a taste aversion and the immediate detection of the onset of a magnetic field. In the summer of 1994, with the assistance of a NSF high school summer fellow, Ben Kalevitch, we demonstrated that a 9.4-T magnet exposure for 30 min was sufficient to condition a taste aversion that lasted about 2 weeks. Our preliminary studies indicated that the rat needed to be in the core of the magnet for the 30-min period and that passing through the gradient of the magnet for five sweeps was not sufficient to condition the aversion to saccharin-flavored water. In 1996, two neuroscience graduate students, Chris Nolte and David Pittman, quantified the magnet-induced taste aversion and published the first paper on this phenomenon (Nolte, Pittman, Kalevitch, Henderson, & Smith, 1998). Further research on magnet-induced taste aversion lay dormant until the arrival of TAH to The Florida State University in 1998. With the support of a program grant from the University and subsequent funding from the National Institute on Deafness and Other Communication Disorders (NIDCD), we began a series of studies that have continued to this day. Results of these experiments are summarized in the remainder of this chapter.

MAGNETIC FIELDS AND MRI

Advances in MRI are driving the development of more powerful and higher-resolution MRI machines. While MRI machines with static magnetic fields of 1–3 T and resolutions of 2 mm^3 are standard in clinical use, higher resolution requires stronger magnetic fields: 4–8-T MRI machines are becoming available to achieve submillimeter

resolutions. Little is known about the sensory or physiological effects of static magnetic fields of high strength on mammals. (Although there is evidence that lower vertebrates can detect small gradients in weak, earth-strength magnetic fields [~50 µT; Gould, 1998], and the biological effects of oscillatory magnetic fields are well established, Berardelli, 1991, our research is limited to the effects of high-strength, static magnetic fields of 2 T and above.)

MRI signals are generated with a static magnetic field on which radiofrequency (RF) pulses are applied. The RF pulse aligns the spins of protons in the biological sample, and the aligned spins induce a signal voltage in a receiver coil; the strength of this signal and its decay time under different RF pulse protocols allows the differential imaging of tissue components within the samples. The MR signal strength (and hence spatial resolution) is linearly dependent on field strength (Narasimhan & Jacobs, 1996). Thus, there is almost a hundred-fold increase in spatial resolution when the field strength is increased from 0.2 to 12 T. The theoretical limit is 0.5–2 µm resolution (Narasimhan & Jacobs, 1996).

There have been reports of sensory and visceral disturbances in humans exposed to high magnetic fields. Some effects are transient and purely sensory, such as the phenomenon of magnetophosphenes: the perception of flashing light specks long known to be induced by magnetic fields by direct stimulation of retinal cells (Lövsund, Öberg, Nilsson, & Reuter, 1980). More significant are the reports of vertigo and nausea by workers around large magnets. These self-reports were quantified in the safety study of an early 4-T MRI machine (Schenck et al., 1992). Eleven male volunteers each received >100 h of cumulative exposure to 4 T in 90 sessions. Subjects responded to questionnaires on 11 sensory effects experienced during exposure, ranging from vertigo to muscle spasms. Only three effects occurred at a statistically significant level: vertigo, nausea, and metallic taste. Subjects also reported that head movements or rapid advances of the body into the magnetic field increased the sensation of nausea. There has also been a report of vertigo induced within an 8.4-T MRI machine used for human imaging (Kangarlu et al., 1999). The threshold for these side-effects may be close to 4 T, since exposure to lower magnetic fields such as 0.5 T (Winther, Rasmussen, Tvete, Halvorsen, & Haugsdal, 1999) or 1.5 T (Schenck et al., 1992) do not produce them.

Little work has been done in animal models on the effects of high-strength static magnetic fields or MRI protocols. Ossenkopp and colleagues found no acute effects of a standard MRI protocol at 0.15 T on open-field behavior, passive avoidance learning, or spatial memory tasks in rats (Innis, Ossenkopp, Prato, & Sestini, 1986; Ossenkopp, Innis, Prato, & Sestini, 1986). No long-term effect on organ pathology and blood chemistry was found 13–22 months after exposure (Teskey, Ossenkopp, Prato, & Sestini, 1987), although the same group has reported an attenuation of morphine-induced analgesia in mice after MRI exposure at 0.15 T (Ossenkopp et al., 1985). Another group has reported that rats do not form a CTA after exposure to a 1.89-T field (Messmer, Porter, Fatouros, Prasad, & Weisberg, 1987). These experiments, however, were carried out using MRI machines that had weaker fields than are used today in most standard clinical MRI machines (e.g., 3 T) and experimental MRI machines (e.g., 8–11 T).

We have, therefore, been using CTA acquisition and other measures in rodents as an animal model of the behavioral and neural effects of high-strength magnetic fields. We found in rats and mice that exposure to 7-T or greater magnetic fields can induce locomotor circling, CTA, and c-Fos in visceral and vestibular nuclei of the brainstem (Houpt et al., 2005; Houpt, Pittman, Barranco, Brooks, & Smith, 2003; Nolte et al., 1998; Snyder, Jahng, Smith, & Houpt, 2000). Because rotation and motion sickness can induce CTAs (Arwas, Rolnick, & Lubow, 1989; Braun & McIntosh, 1973; Fox, Corcoran, & Brizee, 1990; Green & Rachlin, 1973; Hutchison, 1973) and stimulate similar c-Fos patterns (Kaufman, 1996; Kaufman, Anderson, & Beitz, 1991, 1992, 1993; Marshburn, Kaufman, Purcell, & Perachio, 1997), these results suggest that the rats may be experiencing a vestibular disturbance during magnetic field exposure comparable to the self-reports of humans.

SUPERCONDUCTING AND RESISTIVE MAGNETS

We employed two types of magnets at the NHMFL, superconducting nuclear magnetic resonance (NMR) magnets and a resistive magnet (see Figure 20.1). Both superconducting and resistive magnets are electromagnets. The advantages of the superconducting NMR machines are that they operate on the same principle as MRI machines, they produce extremely homogeneous fields, and

they are available at the NHMFL in a variety of field strengths (from 7 to 20 T). Because they are superconducting, the NMR magnets remain energized for months while drawing little outside current; however, it is very inconvenient to turn the magnetic field off and on again. Thus, we employed a "sham-magnet" for the 0-T controls (e.g., a PVC tube outside the magnetic field); this sham-magnet, of course, lacks many of the potential nonmagnetic characteristics of the NMR machine such as odor, sounds, and so on. Furthermore, the superconducting magnets are designed to be energized only to a set field strength, so that different strengths of magnetic field can only be applied by exposing animals within different superconducting magnets in different physical locations.

In resistive magnets, electric current circles the bore through regular copper wiring (which has some resistance), and not through superconductors (without resistance) as in the NMR magnets. To confirm our observations in the NMR magnets, we employed a resistive magnet at the NHMFL with a vertical bore of 189-mm diameter that can produce fields between 0 T and 20 T (Gao, Bird, Bole, Eyssa, & Schneider-Muntau, 1996) Because the magnetic field generated in a resistive magnet is proportional to the current, the field intensity can be varied by applying up to 40 kA at 500 V (20 MW) through the copper coils. The field strength falls off rapidly with distance, so that when the field is 20 T in the center of the magnet, the field is near 0 T at 2-m distance from the center. The polarity of the field can easily be reversed by reversing the current. The magnetic field also disappears when the current is stopped, so that controls can be run at 0 T within the same magnet. The major limitations on resistive magnets are the availability of electrical power (up to 20 MW for hours at a time) and the capacity to dissipate heat from the copper wiring during operation. While superconducting NMR and MRI magnets are fairly common, large resistive magnets are rare due to their size and cost of operation.

MAGNETIC FIELDS AS THE US FOR CTA LEARNING

Our protocol for determining the behavioral effects of high magnetic fields is very similar to the conditioning protocol described above for radiation treatment. Rats are housed in an animal facility

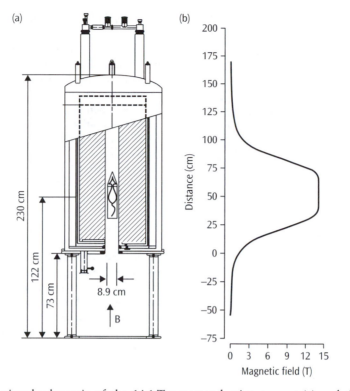

Figure 20.1. Cross-sectional schematic of the 14.1-T superconducting magnet (a) and the corresponding magnetic field (b) relative to the opening of the magnet's bore at 0 cm. Rats were restrained in Plexiglas cylinders and inserted vertically within the bore. Note that while the maximum field is found at the center of the magnet, there are large magnet field gradients (T/m) where the magnetic field strength is rapidly changing. Maximum effects on CTA and other measures were induced, however, when the rats were within the uniform 14.1-T field that extends approximately 15 cm around the center of the magnet's bore.

at the NHMFL. After 10 days on a schedule of water restriction, the rats are given 10-min access to a novel sweet solution of either 3% glucose and 0.125% saccharin (G + S) or 0.125 saccharin alone. Rats are then individually restrained in 6-cm diameter Plexiglas tubes—very similar to the restraint used for exposure to ionizing radiation—and placed inside one of the large magnets at the NHMFL, typically for 30 min of exposure to the magnetic field. (Because of the relatively small bores of most magnets, only one rat can be conditioned at once.) Control rats are restrained but not exposed to a magnetic field.

At the end of exposure, rats are released into a large polycarbonate cage (37 × 47 × 20 cm) with bedding and their locomotor behavior is videotaped for 2 min. When rats are removed from the magnet, they typically display two distinct and abnormal behaviors (Houpt et al., 2003). Compared to sham-exposed rats, magnet-exposed rats show less rearing within the novel chamber (i.e., raising both forepaws from the floor of the cage to stand on their rear legs at the side of the chamber.) Furthermore, magnet-exposed rats tend to walk in tight, counterclockwise circles with a diameter of less than a body length. The tendency to circle is even more evident when rats are exposed within a magnet then placed in a swimming pool to provoke locomotion (see Figure 20.2; see also color Figure 20.2 in the Color insert). These immediate effects of magnet exposure are transient and usually end within 2 min. They are in sharp contrast, however, to ionizing radiation, in which there were no visible signs of a disturbance in behavior following irradiation.

Because magnetic fields are a novel type of US, we have taken pains to establish that the CTA induced by magnetic fields fulfill the basic criteria for CTA learning. Control groups that were given a sweet taste CS and then either exposed within a

— Magnet
— Sham

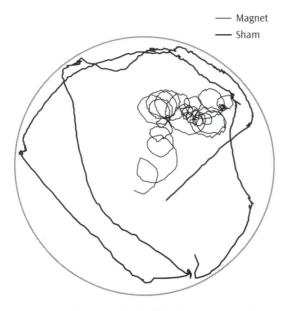

Figure 20.2. Traces of individual rats swimming in 2-m diameter pool after 30-min exposure to 14.1 T (thin line) or sham exposure (thick line). The first 50 s of swimming are shown. Exposure to high magnetic fields induces walking in tight circles within an open field; the circling is more apparent when provoked in a swim test. The circling is transient and usually subsides within 2 min. (See also Color Figure 20.2 in the color insert section.)

"sham-magnet" (a vertical PVC tube placed outside the 5-gauss line of the NMR magnets) or exposed to 0 T within an unenergized resistive magnet do not acquire a CTA. Thus, the association of taste and magnetic field exposure is specific to the presence of a strong magnetic field and not to the exteroceptive stress of restraint or the environs of the magnets' bore.

The acquisition of the CTA is also specific to the taste used at the time of pairing. As a CS, we used 10-min access to sweet solutions of either G + S or 0.125% saccharin. Control rats that received 10-min access to distilled water prior to 10-min exposure to the 14.1 T magnetic field showed a robust preference for novel G + S in subsequent two-bottle preference tests. Thus, decreased preference for G + S or saccharin is not a persistent effect of magnetic field exposure on sweet taste preference, but it requires the contingent association of the novel taste with magnetic field exposure.

LONG INTERSTIMULUS INTERVAL

A cardinal feature of CTA learning is that it can be induced even when there is an exceptionally long interval between exposure to the taste and US treatment. For example, significant CTA has been induced when saccharin consumption was paired with X-radiation after a 12-h delay. Magnetic-field-induced CTAs also tolerate a long delay between taste and magnetic field exposure. A short delay between CS and US has always been obligatory, because the rats usually received their 10-min access to the CS in the NHMFL animal facility some 50 m from the superconducting magnets. Thus there has always been at least a 1–2 min delay after the end of CS access while the rats are placed in the restraint tube, transported to the magnet room, and introduced into the core of the magnet. Even a 2-min interstimulus interval places the phenomenon outside the range of most forms of classical conditioning (reviewed in Kimble, 1961).

More formally, we gave water-restricted rats access to G + S solution for 10 min, paired with 10-min exposure to 14.1-T magnetic field at varying intervals before or after G + S access (T. A. Houpt & J. C. Smith, unpublished data). CTA was accessed with 24-h, two-bottle preference tests. No CTA was observed after backward conditioning (i.e., when magnetic field exposure preceded CS access.) Significant CTA was observed when magnetic field exposure occurred immediately after CS access or 1 h (but not 3 h) after CS access. Thus, magnetic-field-induced CTA also tolerates a long delay.

GRADED EFFECTS OF MAGNETIC FIELD EXPOSURE

An important test of specificity for any treatment is the demonstration of graded effects, along with the determination of the minimal threshold for producing a reliable effect. For magnetic fields, there are three dimensions along which graded effects can be determined: intensity or strength of the magnetic field, duration of exposure to the magnetic field, and number of pairings of the CS with the magnetic field.

We demonstrated a "dose–response" curve for the intensity of high magnetic fields in three ways (see Figure 20.3). First, by exposing different rats to the core of three different superconducting magnets (7, 9.4, and 14.1 T; Houpt et al., 2003); second, by

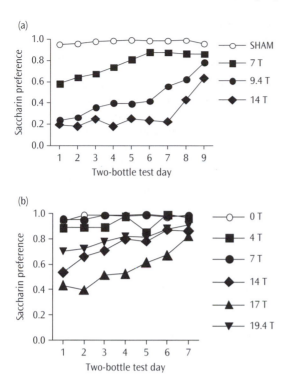

was observed after 19.4 T exposure; in fact, rats looked somewhat stunned and were immobile for several seconds immediately after 19.4-T exposure, and so perhaps nonspecific aversive effects interfered with CTA acquisition.) Importantly, the consistent replication of stimulus thresholds across different experimental preparations and different magnets eliminates the possibility that the observed effects are artifacts of procedure or equipment.

In our experiments, we generally exploited magnetic fields much larger than those used clinically to ensure robust responses. It is relevant, therefore, to determine the minimal field intensity that produces behavioral effects. In the case of CTA, we found that a single pairing of saccharin with 30-min exposure to a magnetic field as low as 0.05 T (within the fringe field of the 14.1-T magnet) was sufficient to produce a small CTA (i.e., a statistically significant decrease in saccharin preference from 0.95 to 0.7). This effect was small and only detected with a large group of rats ($n = 16$), but it suggests that we may be able to extrapolate the effects of high magnetic fields to lower magnetic fields more typical of clinical situations (Houpt, Cassell, Cason, et al., 2007).

Figure 20.3. Magnitude and persistence of CTA is proportional to magnetic field strength, as shown by extinction during consecutive 24-h, two-bottle preference tests. (a) Extinction curves after three pairings of 10-min access of G + S with 30-min exposure within 7 T, 9.4 T, or 14 T superconducting magnets. Repeated pairings with 7 T were sufficient to significantly decrease G + S preference. (b) Extinction curves after one pairing of 10-min access of G + S with 30-min exposure within a 0–19.4-T magnetic field of a resistive magnet. Maximal CTA was observed after 17-T exposure.

exposing different rats in a resistive electromagnet at various current levels (4, 7, 9, 11, 14, 17, and 19.8 T; Houpt et al., 2005); and, third, by exposing different rats at different positions within the magnetic field of a 14.1-T magnet (0.05–14.1 T; Houpt, Cassell, Cason, et al., 2007). The thresholds for behavioral effects are consistent across these three studies: at 3–4 T and above, circling was induced and rearing was suppressed. Acquisition of a maximal CTA (e.g., an average saccharin preference score of 0.1–0.2) required a single pairing with exposure to at least 14 T for at least 30 min, or three pairings with exposure to 7 T for 30 min. (A weaker CTA

DURATION OF MAGNETIC FIELD EXPOSURE

As with ionizing radiation, the duration of magnetic field exposure is also important. In a parametric experiment, rats were given a single pairing of G + S intake with 0–30-min exposure to the 14.1-T magnetic field (Houpt et al., 2003). There was a significant effect of the duration of exposure to the 14.1-T magnetic field on the number of rats circling and rearing. Counterclockwise circling was induced by exposures of 5 min or longer; rearing was significantly reduced after only 1 min of exposure. Two-bottle preference testing showed that rats that received 1-min, or longer, exposure had significantly lower preference for G + S compared to rats that received 0-min exposure. However, longer exposures to 14.1 T produced stronger aversions for G + S that extinguished more slowly.

NUMBER OF PAIRINGS

As with other CS–US paradigms, repeated pairings of CS and magnetic field exposure results in stronger CTA learning. Compared to a single pairing, three pairings of G + S with 30 min of exposure to either 7, 9.4, or 14.1-T magnetic fields produced stronger and more persistent CTAs (Houpt et al., 2003). Rats had only 10-min access to a single bottle of G + S across the three conditioning days, but even so significant decreases in G + S consumption were seen across days. A graded effect was also seen in extinction. For example, a significant CTA after a single pairing of G + S with 14.1 T persisted for 2 days of two-bottle testing, while the CTA after three pairings persisted for 8 days.

ORIENTATION WITHIN THE MAGNETIC FIELD

Magnetic field strength is determined by the density of magnetic flux lines; within the bore of the superconducting and resistive magnets, the flux lines are oriented parallel to the vertical (longitudinal) axis of the bore. We found that the orientation of the rat relative to the field is significant for behavioral effects. Because the superconducting magnets have bores that are only 89 mm in diameter, rats can only be placed with their rostral–caudal body axis parallel to the magnetic field. When placed head-up in the magnet, the rats face +B (equivalent to the magnet's south pole). They can also be placed head-down, facing −B (equivalent to the magnet's north pole). Equivalent CTAs are produced when the CS is paired with 30-min exposure to 14.1 T in either orientation. However, rats placed head-up circled exclusively counterclockwise, while rats placed heads-down circled exclusively clockwise (Houpt et al., 2003).

The source of this asymmetry is unknown. It appears to be a property of the rat's relative orientation and not an effect of heads-down restraint, because the same results were found when rats were restrained in the large resistive magnet in the heads-up position (Houpt et al., 2005). Because the orientation of the field within the resistive magnet can be reversed by reversing the polarity of the applied DC current, rats were exposed heads-up to either +14.1 T or −14.1 T. Again, a comparable CTA was induced, but rats exposed to +14.1 T circled exclusively counterclockwise and rats exposed to −14.1 T circled exclusively clockwise.

The larger 189-mm bore of the resistive magnet also allowed us to orient rats with their rostral–caudal axis perpendicular to a 14.1-T magnetic field (Houpt et al., 2005). Surprisingly, after 30-min exposure in this horizontal orientation, only one of six rats circled. Furthermore, while half the rats showed a decreased preference for G + S, as a group no significant CTA was acquired. Thus it appears that a rostral–caudal orientation parallel with the high magnetic field is required to elicit full behavioral responses. (Note that this is the typical orientation of patients in MRI machines as well.) This may be a significant clue as to the interaction of the magnetic field with possible receptive organs, such as those components of the vestibular apparatus that are oriented approximately orthogonally to the major body axes.

CONSTANT FIELD VERSUS FIELD GRADIENT

Large magnets can not only produce a constant and homogenous magnetic field at their core, but they can also necessarily produce fringe fields with high gradients that drop off rapidly away from the core. Exposure to high gradients or movement of a conductor such as rat tissue through magnetic fields has the potential to generate electric currents that could stimulate the tissue (Halliday & Resnick, 1986). Our data suggests that the behavioral responses to magnet exposure depends on prolonged exposure to the constant high-magnitude magnetic field at the core and not simply on transient passage through the field or exposure to severe magnetic field gradients. Thus, CTA, circling, and suppression increase with time spent (1–30 min) at the center of the 14.1-T magnet while transient passage through the field has no effect (Houpt et al., 2003). Likewise, compared to exposure within the uniform field at the core, exposure to the large gradients (but lower fields) outside the core was not as effective as a US for CTA learning (see below; Figure 20.5; Houpt, Cassell, Cason, et al., 2007). The effects of continuous motion into or within high-strength static magnetic fields have not been evaluated, however.

The dependence on a static uniform field is surprising, however, because translational force (i.e., a pull toward the magnet) is imposed on magnetic objects only when the object is within a field gradient (i.e., outside of the core of the magnet). Within the uniform magnetic field at the core of the magnet, no net translational force will be experienced.

Although translational force would not be experienced within the core, torque would be applied to magnetic substrates within the rat that were not parallel with the uniform magnetic field (Halliday & Resnick, 1986). Alternatively, small motions of the rat's head while restrained within a static field could generate perceptible forces within receptive organs. For example, Schenck has proposed that movement of the inner ear could generate a magnetohydrodynamic force on the charged endolymph of the semicircular canal, thus stimulating the vestibular system and inducing motion sickness (Schenck, 1992).

PARALLELS BETWEEN VESTIBULAR AND MAGNETIC STIMULATION

A link between magnetic fields and the inner ear is suggested by several parallels between the effects of high magnetic fields and the effects of vestibular stimulation or perturbation. The subjective experience of magnetic field exposure may be similar to vestibular perturbation; there are two published reports (and many anecdotes) of vertigo and nausea in humans working around 4-T and 8-T MRI machines (Kangarlu et al., 1999; Schenck et al., 1992). As with magnetic field exposure, pairing a novel flavor with subsequent vestibular stimulation can induce a CTA. The central vestibular system integrates labyrinthine, visual, and proprioceptive inputs to maintain posture and gaze. Aberrant sensation from one input that does not match the other two inputs leads to subjective reports of motion sickness, as well as correlates of malaise in animals such as emesis and pica. Thus, vestibular stimulation can serve as a very effective but nontoxic US for CTA acquisition.

VESTIBULAR INDUCTION OF CTA

CTA can be induced either with constant whole-body rotation (Green & Rachlin, 1973; Haroutunian & Riccio, 1975; Hutchison, 1973), which stimulates mostly the otolith organs of the inner ear by simulating "hypergravity," or with time-varying whole-body rotation (Cordick, Parker, & Ossenkopp, 1999) or compound rotation off-axis (Braun & McIntosh, 1973; Fox, Lauber, Daunton, Phillips, & Diaz, 1984)—both of which strongly stimulate the semicircular canals by constantly altering the

angular velocity. Rotation of the visual field while the subject remains stationary (optokinesis) can also induce CTA in humans (Klosterhalfen et al., 2000; Okifuji & Friedman, 1992).

We examined the magnitude of rotation-induced CTA in our paradigm using constant, off-axis rotation as the US. Water-restricted female rats were given 10-min access to G + S and then restrained on a motor-driven boom at 0, 4, 28, and 49 cm from the center of rotation ($n = 8$/group). The rats were rotated in the horizontal plane (around a dorsal–ventral axis) for 10 min at 60 RPM. The next day, 24-h two-bottle tests were begun to measure CTA expression. The effects of rotation were dependent on the radius of rotation. Constant-speed rotation at or near the center had little or no effect on locomotion and did not induce CTA. At higher radii, rotation induced greater CTA (see Figure 20.4) and suppressed rearing more completely. In addition, rats were also rotated at lower (40 RPM) and higher (120 RPM) speeds, and around the medial–lateral axis or rostral–caudal axis. The same general results were found: regardless of the axis of rotation, greater CTA occurred at greater hypergravity (at higher radii or speed). Similar results were obtained by others for the effects of speed and duration of rotation (Green & Rachlin, 1976).

Vestibular stimulation also has an unconditioned effect on intake. Water-deprived rats show water consumption after whole-body rotation

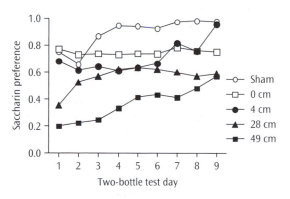

Figure 20.4. CTA extinction after pairing saccharin with sham restraint, or 10-min rotation in the horizontal plane at 60 RPM at 0, 4, 28, or 49 cm radius. Greater radius of rotation causes increased "hypergravity," which stimulates the otolith organs and induced stronger CTA.

(Haroutunian, Riccio, & Gans, 1976; Sutton, Fox, & Daunton, 1988), correlated perhaps with postrotatory postural problems or hypoactivity that would conflict with drinking behavior (Ossenkopp, Rabi, Eckel, & Hargreaves, 1994). Similarly, we found that exposure to 14.1-T magnetic field decreases novel G + S intake by thirsty rats from bottles, largely by increasing the latency to initiate licking (Houpt, Cassell, Riccardi, Kwon, & Smith, 2007). When novel G + S was presented directly into the mouth through intraoral catheters, however, magnetic field exposure had no effect on intake, consistent with a postural effect on ad lib drinking from bottles.

LOCOMOTOR CIRCLING

The circling displayed by rats after magnetic field exposure immediately suggested an asymmetrical effect of the magnetic field on the vestibular system. Destruction (e.g., by unilateral labyrinthectomy [LBX]) of the inner ear leading to asymmetrical labyrinthine inputs also causes pronounced circling behavior in rodents, with turning toward the lesioned ear. Likewise, circling is a common behavioral symptom of rodents with mutations of the inner ear. Although intact rats do not spontaneously walk in circles following whole-body rotation, when provoked by a swim test they display a postrotatory effect by swimming in circles opposite to the direction of rotation (Semenov & Bures, 1989).

There are many other behaviors regulated by the vestibular system that we have not systematically investigated in the context of magnetic field exposure. For example, we have consistently observed "head bobbing" and nystagmus in the rats after magnetic field exposure, but we have not yet quantified these behaviors. Because a critical function of the vestibular system is head and gaze stabilization via the vestibulo-ocular reflex, perturbation of this reflex is another suggestive parallel.

C-FOS IN VESTIBULAR RELAYS

The immediate early gene product c-Fos is commonly used to map neural structures that are activated by the US and CS in CTA paradigms (Houpt, Philopena, Joh, & Smith, 1996a, 1996b; Houpt, Philopena, Wessel, Joh, & Smith, 1994; Swank & Bernstein, 1994; Swank, Ellis, & Chochran, 1996; Swank, Schafe, & Bernstein, 1995). The c-Fos protein is expressed at a very low constitutive levels in many brain structures. Following US or CS stimulation of the animal, however, transynaptic activation of second messenger cascades causes the rapid but transient synthesis of c-Fos protein within 30–180 min. The c-Fos protein is easily visualized by immunohistochemistry and its labeling is discretely localized within cell nuclei. Quantification of the number of c-Fos positive cells provides a measure of response magnitude. Thus, the presence of c-Fos after stimulation in a central relay implies direct or indirect activation of the relay by the stimulus. (An important caveat in the interpretation of c-Fos patterns is that not all neurons express c-Fos after stimulation, and so it is assumed that only a subset of activated neurons are visualized.)

Consistent with high magnetic fields serving as a US in CTA acquisition, 30-min exposure to 9.4-T or 14.1-T magnetic field induced significant c-Fos in visceral relays such as the nucleus of the solitary tract (NTS) and the lateral parabrachial nucleus (lPBN; Snyder et al., 2000). Both the NTS and the lPBN are activated by treatments frequently used in CTA learning, such as systemic LiCl administration. Unlike LiCl, however, high magnetic field exposure also induced significant c-Fos in vestibular relays of the brainstem, such as the medial vestibular nucleus, prepositus nucleus, and supragenualis nucleus. Little or no c-Fos was observed in control rats restrained for 30 min in a "sham-magnet." The c-Fos induction was a consequence of magnetic field exposure and not caused by the magnet-induced locomotor circling, because c-Fos was still expressed in magnet-exposed rats that were prevented from circling by an extra 15 min of restraint.

The pattern of neural activation after magnetic field exposure also parallels the response to vestibular stimulation. These c-Fos results, however, can be interpreted in two additional ways. First, input from specific parts of the labyrinth can be inferred from activation in the projection sites of afferents. Tracing studies have identified specific afferent projection sites (Newlands & Perachio, 2003), for example, the utricle innervates the medial vestibular nucleus but the saccule innervates the superior vestibular nucleus. Second, a considerable database of c-Fos activation by vestibular stimuli has been established by other investigators (simplified and

Table 20.1 Induction of c-Fos in Brainstem Nuclei after Magnetic Field Exposure or Vestibular Treatments.

Brainstem Nuclei	Magnetic Field Exposure	Off-Axis Rotation (Otolith)	Sinusoidal Rotation (Semicircular)	VOR Adaptation (Lateral Canal)	Unilateral LBX (Otolith and Semicircular)
MeV	+	+	−	+	+
Prp	+	−	+	+	+
IOβ	+	−	+	−	+
DMCC	+	+	−	−	+
IOK	+	−	−	+	+

Source: Kaufman (2005).

Notes: Afferent pathways affected are indicated parenthetically. VOR, vestibulo–ocular reflex; MeV, medial vestibular nucleus; Prp, prepositus nucleus; IOβ, inferior olivary complex beta; DMCC, dorsomedial cell column; IOK, inferior olivary complex kappa. +, c-Fos induced by treatment; −, c-Fos not induced.

summarized in Table 20.1). Again, discrete c-Fos patterns are seen to be correlated with stimulation of specific inner ear organs (Kaufman, 2005). In some cases, exclusive c-Fos patterns are induced by different treatments (e.g., off-axis vs. sinusoidal rotation). Conversely, unilateral LBX induces widespread and overlapping c-Fos expression.

Comparison of these patterns with magnetic-field-induced c-Fos in intact rats shows correlations with specific vestibular pathways (Table 20.1). Thus, the magnetic-field-activated brain stem looks similar to the pattern of innervation by both utricular and semicircular afferents, or to c-Fos induction in response to a compound stimulation of both classes of afferents (e.g., unilateral LBX).

SITE OF ACTION FOR MAGNETIC FIELDS

While these parallels suggest an interaction with the vestibular system, the peripheral sites of interaction or detection by magnetic fields are unknown. Typically, the analysis of receptive sites for a stimulus would include the focal stimulation of specific parts of the body. Focused or site-specific application is straightforward for many categories of sensory stimuli and has defined receptive sites in many systems. As described above, during the investigation of the detection of ionizing radiation by mammals, it was possible to limit irradiation of rats or monkeys to either the abdomen or the head using focal X-ray machines or by employing lead shielding to limit exposure. The necessary roles of the abdomen, olfactory system, and retina were subsequently confirmed by pharmacological

blockade of histamine in rats (Levy et al., 1974) and by ablation studies in rats (Dinc & Smith, 1966), monkeys (Chaddock, 1972), and other species (Smith, 1971).

Thus, in the analysis of magnetic field effects it would be helpful to limit exposure to specific somatic regions, for example, the abdomen versus the head. Unfortunately, it is impossible to shield against magnetic fields in the higher range typical of MRI machines. There is no substance that is opaque to these higher magnetic fields as those that exist for electromagnetic radiation (e.g., lead for X-rays), nor are there ways to limit magnetic fields as those that exist for interfering electric fields (e.g., a Faraday cage). The fringe of the high magnetic fields generated by NMR or MRI machines typically falls off across meters, rather than the centimeters needed for localization in rodents. Indeed, it may be this gradient of the magnetic field that imposes a differential field across a region of the rat's body and thereby induces the responses of circling and CTA reported above.

In order to approximate site-specific exposure to the high magnetic field, we placed rats at different positions along the bore of the 14.1-T superconducting magnet (Houpt, Cassell, Cason, et al., 2007). By measuring the current induced in a copper coil pulled through the magnet at a constant speed (see methods below), we mapped the strength of the magnetic field with 1 mm resolution along the center of the magnet's 89-mm bore (see Figure 20.1). It can be seen that the magnet has a uniform central field (B_0) of 14.1 T for a distance of approximately 35 cm in the center of the bore. Along the vertical axis there is a steep field gradient (dB/dz), which reaches a maximum of 56 T/m.

Rats were restrained in Plexiglas restraint tubes and stacked within the bore of the magnet for 30-min exposures. Exposure of the body and head was roughly limited to one or both of the two salient components of the magnetic field: the uniform center of constant 14.1 T or the steep gradient above and below the maximum magnetic field. By varying the vertical position within the bore, rats could be exposed such that (1) both the head and the body would be exposed to the uniform, maximal magnetic field at the center; (2) the head would be exposed in the center to 14.1 T while the body would be in the steep gradient, or vice versa; or (3) both the head and the body would be in the steep gradient above or below the maximal magnetic field at the center.

The results indicated that exposure of the head is necessary for maximal effects of the magnetic field (see Figure 20.5; see also color Figure 20.5 in the Color insert). For example, rats exposed just below the peak magnetic field intensity (at 35 cm, with caudal body at 7 T and head at 14.1 T) showed robust circling and CTA acquisition, while rats exposed just above the peak magnetic field intensity (at 95 cm, with caudal body at 10 T and head at 3 T) showed much weaker responses.

Significantly, the magnetic field effects appeared unrelated to the vertical gradient of the magnetic field experienced by the rats. In the preceding example, both groups of rats positioned at 35 cm and 95 cm within the bore of the magnet experienced large rostral–caudal gradients (20.1 T/m and −30.2 T/m, respectively), yet a much greater response was seen in rats exposed at 35 cm.

EFFECTS OF CHEMICAL LBX

The similarity of responses induced by magnetic exposure or vestibular stimulation and the sensitivity of the rostral body suggest that the vestibular apparatus of the inner ear is acted upon by high magnetic fields. Therefore, we examined the effects of chemical LBX by intratympanic injection of sodium arsanilate. Sodium arsanilate causes a near complete destruction of the vestibular apparatus, although it is nonspecific and destroys both otolith and semicircular organs, as well as the auditory cochlea (Anniko & Wersäll, 1977). The effects of vestibular stimulation on behavioral and neural responses largely depend on an intact inner

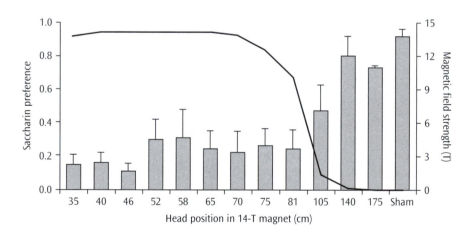

Figure 20.5. Maximal CTA is induced by exposing the head to the maximum uniform field. Rats were "stacked" within the bore of the 14.1-T magnet at different positions, such that their heads (i.e., 65 cm) or their caudal body (i.e., 105 cm) was exposed to the maximum uniform field at the center, or so that they were exposed to the maximum field gradient (i.e., at 105 and 140 cm). The strength of the magnetic field at different positions within the 14.1-T magnet is indicated by the line; magnitude of CTA expressed on the first day of two-bottle testing after exposure at different positions is indicated by the bars. Large CTA was only acquired when the rostral body was exposed to 14.1 T. On the basis of rate of extinction (not shown), the greatest CTA was induced at 65 cm where the entire body was exposed to 14.1 T. Exposure to a large gradient produced little or no CTA, however. (See also Color Figure 20.5 in the color insert section.)

ear. Thus, the effects of whole-body rotation on decreased activity (Ossenkopp et al., 1994), CTA acquisition (Ossenkopp et al., 2003), and c-Fos induction (Kaufman et al., 1992) are abolished by bilateral chemical LBX.

Adult female rats were injected intratympanically with sodium arsanilate (15 mg/50 µl) or saline. LBX was validated by inverting the rats and allowing them to walk upside-down on a Plexiglas sheet apposed to their feet. Two weeks later, the effects of magnetic field exposure (14.1 T for 30 min) on circling, CTA, and c-Fos responses were tested.

After sham exposure, sham-operated rats (*n* = 6) showed little or no circling and some rearing. LBX rats (*n* = 6) showed some circling, but in clockwise and counterclockwise directions. Following magnet exposure, sham-operated rats showed a significant increase in counterclockwise circling, and a significant decrease in rearing. LBX rats, however, did not show an increase in circling nor a decrease in rearing (see Figure 20.6a).

CTA ACQUISITION AFTER LBX

To assess the effects of LBX on CTA acquisition, additional sham-operated and LBX rats were placed on a schedule of water restriction. On conditioning day, rats were given 10-min access to 0.125% saccharin, then restrained and exposed to 14.1-T magnetic field or sham exposed for 30 min (*n* = 6 in each of four groups). On subsequent days, rats received another two pairings of saccharin and exposure. After the last pairing, rats were given 24-h two-bottle preferences tests of saccharin versus water daily until the CTA extinguished. As expected, sham-exposed rats of either surgical group formed no CTA, while sham-operated rats after magnet exposure showed a significant CTA that slowly extinguished. LBX rats showed no CTA at all, however (see Figure 20.6b). These results suggest that the inner ear is a critical site of magnetic field effects capable of inducing CTA.

c-FOS INDUCTION AFTER LBX

Finally, to determine if neural activation by magnetic field exposure depended on the inner ear, sham-operated and LBX rats were exposed to 14.1 T or sham exposed for 30 min, then perfused 1 h after the end of exposure, and their

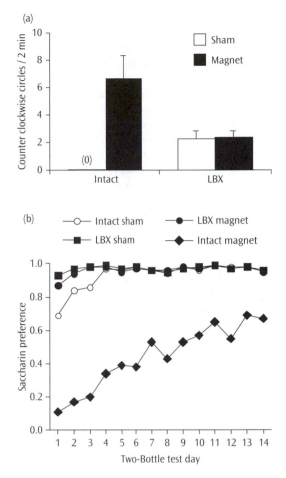

Figure 20.6. (a) Circling in intact and labyrinthectomized (LBX) rats. Intact rats do not spontaneously circle after sham exposure, but walk in tight circles after 14.1 T magnetic field exposure. While LBX rats spontaneously circled after sham exposure, magnetic field exposure did not increase their circling activity. (b) CTA acquisition by intact but not LBX rats. After three pairings of saccharin and 30-min exposure to the 14.1-T magnetic field, intact rats formed a strong CTA that extinguished only gradually. Saccharin preference of LBX rats exposed to the magnetic field was indistinguishable from the preference of sham-exposed rats without a CTA.

brainstems processed for c-Fos immunoreactivity. Quantification of c-Fos positive cells showed that 14.1-T magnetic field exposure (but not sham exposure) induced significantly more c-Fos positive cells compared to sham exposure in brainstem vestibular and visceral nuclei. In LBX rats, however, c-Fos levels were not different from sham-exposed rats. Thus the inner ear is a critical site for magnetic field effects that cause neuronal activation of the brainstem.

Although the inner ear appears critical, other sensory pathways may be necessary or contribute to visceral stimulation mediating CTA acquisition after magnetic field exposure. The other two major pathways contributing to CTA learning are subdiaphragmatic vagal afferents (which detect toxins affecting the gut; Coil, Rogers, Garcia, & Novin, 1978) and the chemoreceptive area postrema (which detects toxin-induced humoral factors or blood-borne toxins; Ritter, McGlone, & Kelley, 1980). These pathways also contribute to rotation-induced CTA (Fox & McKenna, 1988; Gallo, Arnedo, Aguero, & Puerto, 1991; Ossenkopp, 1983). Furthermore, because, the vestibular system integrates sensation from the eyes, inner ear, and proprioceptors, visual and proprioceptive sensation are likely to contribute to magnetic-field-induced CTA.

USE OF INNER EAR MUTANTS

Chemical LBX abolished every effect of high magnetic fields: suppression of rearing, locomotor circling, CTA acquisition, avoidance of high magnetic fields, and vestibular c-Fos induction. Thus, the inner ear is critical to the reception of high magnetic fields by the rat. Chemical LBX, however, destroys all hair cells within the inner ear. Thus it remains unknown if the magnetic field is transduced by the semicircular canals or otolith organs. Unfortunately, ablation of specific vestibular organs (e.g., removal of just otolith organs or plugging of individual semicircular canals) is very difficult in small rodents such as rats; we are unable to use rodents with larger heads and a more accessible inner ear (e.g., chinchilla; Hirvonen, Carey, Liang, & Minor, 2001) because of the small bore size of our large magnets.

To distinguish the contribution of the various parts of the inner ear, therefore, we have begun to screen mutant mouse strains with vestibular disorders. Although many vestibular mutants have nonspecific or gross malformations of the inner ear, it is possible to find some strains with relatively specific deficits in otolith organs (e.g., pallid [*pal*], head-tilt [*het*] mice, and tilted-head

[*tlt*] mice; Jones, Erway, Johnson, Yu, & Jones, 2004) or semicircular canals (e.g., epistatic circler [*ecl*; Cryns et al., 2004] or fidget [*fi*] mice; Cox, Mahaffey, Nystuen, Letts, & Frankel, 2000). Disadvantages of this approach are familiar from the transgenic literature: the mutations exist from conception so that long-term effects or compensation may have occurred; the mutations are irreversible, so that they may modulate both reception during magnetic field exposure and expression of magnetic field effects on subsequent testing; and the mutations may cause unknown deficits in the rest of the body.

Our preliminary findings with *het* mice (indicating a necessary role for otoconia) suggest that this approach will be informative. A swim test was used to phenotype *het* mice and their littermates. Wildtype mice (+/+) swam toward the side of the pool. Homozygous *het* mice (*het/het*) were identified by their inability to swim while keeping their head above water; instead, they swim in circles and "somersault" downward underwater. Heterozygotes (*het/+*) were identified by an intermediate phenotype. Mice were placed on a schedule of water restriction. On three consecutive days, mice were given 10-min access to 0.125% saccharin followed by 30-min restraint within the core of the 14.1-T magnet or by sham exposure, for a total of three pairings. CTA expression was assessed in two-bottle preference tests (see Figure 20.7). While wildtype mice acquired a significant CTA, the saccharin preference of magnet-exposed *het/het* and *het/+* mice was not significantly different from sham-exposed mice. The failure to acquire a magnet-induced CTA was not due to a generalized learning deficit, because all *het* mutant mice were able to acquire a LiCl-induced CTA (data not shown).

CONCLUSION

On the basis of direct observation of postexposure behaviors and the expression of CTA, we have identified graded and specific behavioral responses induced by high static magnetic fields. These effects have been reliably observed with magnetic fields as low as 7 T, which is within the range of MRI machines used for human imaging (Kangarlu et al., 1999). The induction of c-Fos expression in the brain represents neural activity secondary to exposure to magnetic fields, and suggests activation of both visceral and vestibular circuits. Because the

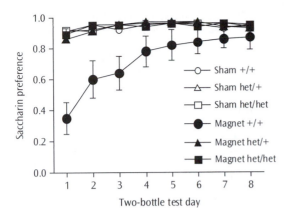

Figure 20.7. CTA in wildtype and head-tilt (*het*) mutant mice. After three pairings of saccharin with exposure to 14.1 T (black symbols), wildtype mice (+/+) acquired a significant CTA. Neither heterozygous (*het/+*) nor homozygous mutants (*het/het*) showed CTA after magnetic field exposure.

magnetic field exposure can serve as a US for CTA acquisition, and because exposure appears to perturb the vestibular system, our results may serve as an animal model for the anecdotal reports of vertigo and nausea around large magnets (Kangarlu et al., 1999; Schenck et al., 1992).

Chemical LBX abolished all the observed effects of magnetic fields, and therefore the vestibular apparatus appears to be the receptive organ. On the basis of our finding that mutant mice lacking otoconia do not respond to magnetic fields, we hypothesize that the magnetic field may interact with the vestibular system via the otolith organs, potentially on the calcium carbonate crystals within the otoconia themselves. Calcium carbonate has a magnetic susceptibility of -38.2×10^{-6} cgs: higher than the susceptibility of calcium hydroxyapatite in bone (0.9×10^{-6} cgs; Hopkins & Wehrli, 1997), but far lower than the susceptibility of ferromagnetic crystals such as Fe_2O_3 (7200×10^{-6} cgs).

Beyond the delayed effect of magnetic fields to induce CTA, there are two additional areas of investigation that we are pursuing. First, as with ionizing radiation, it appears that rats are capable of immediately and consciously detecting the presence of a strong magnetic field. In order to demonstrate immediate detection, we used an operant-type task (Houpt, Cassell, Riccardi, et al., 2007).

Rats were trained to climb up the inside of a 10-m long cylinder made of plastic mesh to reach a food reward at the top. Rats easily learned to climb the "ladder" when it was positioned outside of a magnetic field. When the ladder was inserted through the center of the 14.1-T superconducting magnet, however, rats climbed through the bore of the magnet at most only one time, and on subsequent tests refused to enter the bore of the magnet. Thus they appeared able to detect the presence of the magnetic field, and avoided entry after only one exposure to the center of the magnet. This immediate detection of the magnetic field was also dependent on the vestibular system, because labyrinthectomized rats readily and rapidly climbed the ladder through the 14.1-T magnetic field. As was done with ionizing radiation, we are exploring the immediate detection of magnetic fields using a conditioned suppression apparatus that is adapted for the application of a high magnetic field across the rat's head during an operant task (e.g., licking). Thus, unlike the case of ionizing radiation in which CTA induction and immediate detection were mediated by different receptor systems, CTA and immediate detection both appear to be transduced by the inner ear.

Second, we have consistently observed a diminished response to the magnetic field after repeated exposures. For example, the amount of locomotor circling is highest after the first 30-min exposure to 14.1 T, but decreases after the second and third exposure. Conversely, the amount of rearing increases across exposures (Houpt et al., 2003, 2005). The diminished response could be a form of sensory habituation. We found, however, that the diminished responsivity is very persistent: if rats are preexposed for 30 min to 14.1 T twice, they do not circle in response to a third exposure 30 days later. We are therefore exploring the possibility that repeated exposure to high magnetic fields induces either vestibular habituation, or alternatively delivers a long-lasting perturbation to the vestibular apparatus.

Acknowledgments Supported by the Florida State University Research Foundation and the National Institute of Deafness and other Communication Disorders. We thank Drs. Tim Cross, Zhehong Gan, Riqiang Fu, and Bruce Brandt for assistance and continued access to the magnets of the U.S. National High Magnetic Field Laboratory.

References

Anniko, M., & Wersäll, J. (1977). Experimentally (atoxyl) induced ampullar degeneration and damage to the maculae utriculi. *Acta Oto-Laryngologica, 83,* 429–440.

Arwas, S., Rolnick, A., & Lubow, R. E. (1989). Conditioned taste aversion in humans using motion-induced sickness as the US. *Behaviour Research and Therapy, 27,* 295–301.

Barnett, S. A. (1963). *The rat: A study in behavior.* Chicago, IL: Aldine Press.

Berardelli, A. (1991). Electrical and magnetic spinal and cortical stimulation in man. *Current Opinion in Neurology and Neurosurgery, 4,* 770–776.

Bernstein, I. L. (1978). Learned taste aversions in children receiving chemotherapy. *Science, 200,* 1302–1303.

Bernstein, I. L., Webster, M. M., & Bernstein, I. D. (1982). Food aversions in children receiving chemotherapy for cancer. *Cancer, 50,* 2961–2963.

Braun, J. J., & McIntosh, H. (1973). Learned taste aversions induced by rotational stimulation. *Physiological Psychology, 1,* 301–304.

Carroll, M. E., & Smith, J. C. (1974). Time course of radiation-induced taste aversion conditioning. *Physiology & Behavior, 13,* 809–812.

Chaddock, T. E. (1972). Visual detection of x-ray by the rhesus monkey. *Journal of Comparative and Physiological Psychology, 78,* 190–201.

Coil, J. D., Rogers, R. C., Garcia, J., & Novin, D. (1978). Conditioned taste aversions: Vagal and circulatory mediation of the toxic unconditioned stimulus. *Behavioral Biology, 24,* 509–519.

Cordick, N., Parker, L. A., & Ossenkopp, K. P. (1999). Rotation-induced conditioned rejection in the taste reactivity test. *NeuroReport, 10,* 1557–1559.

Cox, G. A., Mahaffey, C. L., Nystuen, A., Letts, V. A., & Frankel, W. N. (2000). The mouse fidgetin gene defines a new role for AAA family proteins in mammalian development. *Nature Genetics, 26,* 198–202.

Cryns, K., van Alphen, A. M., van Spaendonck, M. P., van de Heyning, P. H., Timmermans, J. P., de Zeeuw, C. I., et al. (2004). Circling behavior in the Ecl mouse is caused by lateral semicircular canal defects. *Journal of Comparative Neurology, 468*(4), 587–595.

Dinc, H. I., & Smith, J. C. (1966). Role of the olfactory bulbs in the detection of ionizing radiation by the rat. *Physiology & Behavior, 1,* 139–144.

Fox, R. A., Corcoran, M., & Brizee, K. R. (1990). Conditioned taste aversion and motion sickness in cats and squirrel monkeys. *Canadian Journal of Physiology and Pharmacology, 68,* 269–278.

Fox, R. A., Lauber, A. H., Daunton, N. G., Phillips, M., & Diaz, L. (1984). Off-vertical rotation produces conditioned taste aversion and suppressed drinking in mice. *Aviation, Space, and Environmental Medicine, 55,* 632–635.

Fox, R. A., & McKenna, S. (1988). Conditioned taste aversion induced by motion is prevented by selective vagotomy in the rat. *Behavioral and Neural Biology, 50,* 275–284.

Gallo, M., Arnedo, M., Aguero, A., & Puerto, A. (1991). Participation of the area postrema in learned aversions induced by body rotation. *Behavioural Brain Research, 42,* 13–23.

Gao, B. J., Bird, M. D., Bole, S., Eyssa, Y. M., & Schneider-Muntau, H.-J. (1996). Design of a 20 T, 200 mm bore resistive magnet. *IEEE Transactions on Magnetics, 32,* 2562–2565.

Garcia, J., Ervin, F. R., & Koelling, R. A. (1967). Toxicity of serum from irradiated donors. *Nature, 213,* 682–683.

Garcia, J., Kimeldorf, D. J., & Koelling, R. A. (1955). Conditioned aversion to saccharin resulting from exposure to gamma radiation. *Science, 122,* 157–158.

Gould, J. L. (1998). Sensory bases of navigation. *Current Biology, 8,* R731–738.

Green, L., & Rachlin, H. (1973). The effect of rotation on the learning of taste aversions. *Bulletin of the Psychonomic Society, 1,* 137–192.

Green, L., & Rachlin, H. (1976). Learned taste aversions in rats as a function of delay, speed, and duration of rotation. *Learning and motivation, 7,* 283–289.

Halliday, D., & Resnick, R. (1986). *Fundamentals of physics* (2nd ed.). New York: John Wiley & Sons.

Haroutunian, V., & Riccio, D. C. (1975). Acqusition of rotation-induced taste aversion as a function of drinking-treatment delay. *Physiological Psychology, 3,* 273–277.

Haroutunian, V., Riccio, D. C., & Gans, D. P. (1976). Suppression of drinking following rotational stimulation as an index of motion sickness in the rat. *Physiological Psychology, 4,* 467–472.

Hirvonen, T. P., Carey, J. P., Liang, C. J., & Minor, L. B. (2001). Superior canal dehiscence: Mechanisms of pressure sensitivity in a chinchilla model. *Archives of Otolaryngology—Head & Neck Surgery, 127,* 1331–1336.

Hopkins, J. A., & Wehrli, F. W. (1997). Magnetic susceptibility measurement of insoluble solids by NMR: Magnetic susceptibility of bone. *Magnetic Resonance in Medicine, 37,* 494–500.

Houpt, T. A., Cassell, J. A., Cason, A. M., Reidell, A., Golden, G. J., Riccardi, C., et al. (2007). Evidence for a cephalic site of action of high magnetic fields on the behavioral responses of rats. *Physiology & Behavior, 92,* 665–674.

Houpt, T. A., Cassell, J. A., Riccardi, C., DenBleyker, M. D., Hood, A., & Smith, J. C. (2007). Rats avoid high magnetic fields: Dependance on an intact vestibular system. *Physiology & Behavior, 92*, 741–747.

Houpt, T. A., Cassell, J. A., Riccardi, C., Kwon, B. S., & Smith, J. C. (2007). Suppression of drinking by exposure to a high-strength static magnetic field. *Physiology & Behavior, 90*, 59–65.

Houpt, T. A., Philopena, J. M., Joh, T. H., & Smith, G. P. (1996a). c-Fos induction in the rat nucleus of the solitary tract by intraoral quinine infusion depends on prior pairing of quinine and lithium chloride. *Physiology & Behavior, 60*, 1535–1541.

Houpt, T. A., Philopena, J. M., Joh, T. H., & Smith, G. P. (1996b). c-Fos induction in the rat nucleus of the solitary tract correlates with the retention and forgetting of a conditioned taste aversion. *Learning & Memory, 3*, 25–30.

Houpt, T. A., Philopena, J. M., Wessel, T. C., Joh, T. H., & Smith, G. P. (1994). Increased c-Fos expression in the rat nucleus of the solitary tract after conditioned taste aversion formation. *Neuroscience Letters, 172*, 1–5.

Houpt, T. A., Pittman, D. M., Barranco, J. M., Brooks, E. H., & Smith, J. C. (2003). Behavioral effects of high strength magnetic fields on rats. *Journal of Neuroscience, 23*, 1498–1505.

Houpt, T. A., Pittman, D. W., Riccardi, C., Cassell, J. A., Lockwood, D. R., Barranco, J. M., et al. (2005). Behavioral effects on rats of high strength magnetic fields generated by a resistive electromagnet. *Physiology & Behavior, 86*, 379–389.

Hunt, E. L., Carroll, H. W., & Kimeldorf, D. J. (1965). Humoral mediation of radiation-induced motivation in parabiont rats. *Science, 150*, 1747–1748.

Hutchison, S. L. (1973). Taste aversion in albino rats using centrifugal spin as an unconditioned stimulus. *Psychological Reports, 33*, 467–470.

Innis, N. K., Ossenkopp, K. P., Prato, F. S., & Sestini, E. (1986). Behavioral effects of exposure to nuclear magnetic resonance imaging: II. Spatial memory tests. *Magnetic Resonance Imaging, 4*, 281–284.

Jones, S. M., Erway, L. C., Johnson, K. R., Yu, H., & Jones, T. A. (2004). Gravity receptor function in mice with graded otoconial deficiencies. *Hearing Research, 191*(1–2), 34–40.

Kangarlu, A., Burgess, R. E., Zhu, H., Nakayama, T., Hamlin, R. L., Abduljalil, A. M., et al. (1999). Cognitive, cardiac, and physiological safety studies in ultra high field magnetic resonance imaging. *Magnetic Resonance Imaging, 17*, 1407–1416.

Kaufman, G. D. (1996). Activation of immediate-early genes by vestibular stimulation. *Annals of the New York Academy of Sciences, 781*, 437–442.

Kaufman, G. D. (2005). Fos expression in the vestibular brainstem: What one marker can tell us about the network. *Brain Research Reviews, 50*, 2200–2211.

Kaufman, G. D., Anderson, J. H., & Beitz, A. (1991). Activation of a specific vestibulo-olivary pathway by centripetal acceleration in rat. *Brain Research, 562*, 311–317.

Kaufman, G. D., Anderson, J. H., & Beitz, A. J. (1992). Fos-defined activity in rat brainstem following centripetal acceleration. *Journal of Neuroscience, 12*, 4489–4500.

Kaufman, G. D., Anderson, J. H., & Beitz, A. J. (1993). Otolith-brain stem connectivity: Evidence for differential neural activation by vestibular hair cells based on quantification of Fos expression in unilateral labyrinthectomized rats. *Journal of Neurophysiology, 70*, 117–127.

Kimble, G. A. (1961). Parameters of reinforcement. In G. A. Kimble (Ed.), *Hilgard and Marquis' conditioning and learning* (pp. 137–166). New York: Appleton-Century-Crofts.

Klosterhalfen, S., Ruttgers, A., Krumrey, E., Otto, B., Stockhorst, U., Riepl, R. L., et al. (2000). Pavlovian conditioing of taste aversion using a motion sickness paradigm. *Psychomatic Medicine, 62*, 671–677.

Levy, C. S., Carroll, M. E., Smith, J. C., & Hofer, K. G. (1974). Antihistamines block radiation induced taste aversions. *Science, 186*, 1044–1046.

Lövsund, P., Öberg, P. Å., Nilsson, S. E., & Reuter, T. (1980). Magnetophosphenes: A quantitative analysis of thresholds. *Medical & Biological Engineering & Computing, 18*, 326–334.

Marshburn, T. H., Kaufman, G. D., Purcell, I. M., & Perachio, A. A. (1997). Saccule contribution to immediate early gene induction in the gerbil brainstem with posterior canal galvanic or hypergravity stimulation. *Brain Research, 761*, 51–58.

Messmer, J. M., Porter, J. H., Fatouros, P., Prasad, U., & Weisberg, M. (1987). Exposure to magnetic resonance imaging does not produce taste aversion in rats. *Physiology & Behavior, 40*, 259–261.

Morris, D. D., & Smith, J. C. (1964). X-ray conditioned saccharin aversion induced during the immediate postexposure period. *Radiation Research, 21*, 513–519.

Narasimhan, P. T., & Jacobs, R. E. (1996). Neuroanatomical micromagnetic resonance imaging. In A. W. Toga & J. C. Mazziotta (Eds.), *Brain mapping: The methods* (pp. 147–167). New York: Academic Press.

Newlands, S. D., & Perachio, A. A. (2003). Central projections of the vestibular nerve: A review and single fiber study in the Mongolian gerbil. *Brain Research Bulletin, 60,* 475–495.

Nolte, C. M., Pittman, D. W., Kalevitch, B., Henderson, R., & Smith, J. C. (1998). Magnetic field conditioned taste aversion in rats. *Physiology & Behavior, 63,* 683–688.

Okifuji, A., & Friedman, A. G. (1992). Experimentally induced taste aversions in humans: Effects of overshadowing on acquisition. *Behaviour Research and Therapy, 30,* 23–32.

Ossenkopp, K. P. (1983). Area postrema lesions in rats enhance the magnitude of body rotation-induced conditioned taste aversions. *Behavioral and Neural Biology, 38,* 82–96.

Ossenkopp, K. P., Innis, N. K., Prato, F. S., & Sestini, E. (1986). Behavioral effects of exposure to nuclear magnetic resonance imaging: I. Open-field behavior and passive avoidance learning in rats. *Magnetic Resonance Imaging, 4,* 275–280.

Ossenkopp, K. P., Kavaliers, M., Prato, F. S., Teskey, G. C., Sestini, E., & Hirst, M. (1985). Exposure to nuclear magnetic resonance imaging procedure attenuates morphine-induced analgesia in mice. *Life Science, 37,* 1507–1514.

Ossenkopp, K. P., Parker, L. A., Limebeer, C. L., Burton, P., Fudge, M. A., & Cross-Mellor, S. K. (2003). Vestibular lesions selectively abolish body rotation-induced, but not lithium-induced, conditioned taste aversions (oral rejection responses) in rats. *Behavioral Neuroscience, 117,* 105–112.

Ossenkopp, K. P., Rabi, Y. J., Eckel, L. A., & Hargreaves, E. L. (1994). Reductions in body temperature and spontaneous activity in rats exposed to horizontal rotation: Abolition following chemical labyrinthectomy. *Physiology & Behavior, 56,* 319–324.

Ritter, S., McGlone, J. J., & Kelley, K. W. (1980). Absence of lithium-induced taste aversion after area postrema lesion. *Brain Research, 201,* 501–506.

Roentgen, W. C. (1895). On a new kind of rays. *Sitzgeber. Physik.-Med.Ges.Wurzburg,* 137.

Roentgen, W. C. (1897). Further observations on the properties of the X-rays. *Math. u. Naturw. Mitt. a.d. Sitzgsber. Preuss. akad. Wiss., Physik-Math.Kl.,* 392.

Schenck, J. F. (1992). Health and physiological effects of human exposure to whole-body four-tesla magnetic fields during MRI. *Annals of the New York Academy of Sciences, 649,* 285–301.

Schenck, J. F., Dumoulin, C. L., Redington, R. W., Kressel, H. Y., Elliot, R. T., & McDougall, I. L. (1992). Human exposure to 4.0-Tesla magnetic fields in a whole body scanner. *Medical Physics, 19,* 1089–1098.

Semenov, L. V., & Bures, J. (1989). Vestibular stimulation disrupts acquisition of place navigation in the Morris water tank task. *Behavioral and Neural Biology, 51,* 346–363.

Smith, J. C. (1970). Conditioned suppression as an animal psychophysical technique. In W. C. Stebbins (Ed.), *Animal psychophysics: The design and conduct of sensory experiments* (pp. 125–159). New York: Appleton-Century-Crofts.

Smith, J. C. (1971). Radiation: Its detection and its effect on taste preferences. In E. Stellar & J. Sprague (Eds.), *Progress in physiological psychology* (Vol. 4, pp. 53–118). New York: Academic Press.

Smith, J. C., & Blumsack, J. T. (1981). Learned taste aversion as a factor in cancer therapy. *Cancer Treatment Reports, 65,* 37–42.

Smith, J. C., Blumsack, J. T., & Bilek, F. S. (1985). Radiation-induced taste aversions in rats and man. In T. G. Burish, S. M. Levy, & B. E. Meyerowitz (Eds.), *Cancer, nutrition and eating behaviors: A biobehavioral perspective* (pp. 77–101). Mahwah, NJ: Lawrence Erlbaum.

Smith, J. C., Blumsack, J. T., Bilek, F. S., Spector, A. C., Hollander, G. R., & Baker, D. L. (1984). Radiation-induced taste aversion as a factor in cancer therapy. *Cancer Treatment Reports, 68,* 1219–1227.

Smith, J. C., Hollander, G. R., & Spector, A. C. (1981). Taste aversions conditioned with partial body radiation exposures. *Physiology & Behavior, 27,* 903–913.

Smith, J. C., Morris, D. D., & Hendricks, J. (1964). Conditioned aversion to saccharin solution with high dose rates of X-rays as the unconditioned stimulus. *Radiation Research, 22,* 507–510.

Smith, J. C., & Roll, D. L. (1967). Trace conditioning with X-rays as an aversive stimulus. *Psychonomic Science, 9,* 11.

Smith, J. C., & Schaeffer, R. W. (1967). Development of water and saccharin preferences after simultaneous exposures to saccharin solution and gamma rays. *Journal of Comparative and Physiological Psychology, 63,* 434–438.

Smith, J. C., Taylor, H. L., Morris, D. D., & Hendricks, J. (1965). Further studies of X-ray conditioned saccharin aversion during the post exposure period. *Radiation Research, 24,* 423–431.

Snyder, D., Jahng, J. W., Smith, J. C., & Houpt, T. A. (2000). c-Fos induction in visceral and vestibular nuclei of the rat brainstem by a 9.4 T magnetic field. *NeuroReport, 11,* 1681–1685.

Spector, A. C., Smith, J. C., & Hollander, G. R. (1981). A comparison of dependent measures used to quantify radiation-induced taste aversion. *Physiology & Behavior, 27,* 887–901.

Spector, A. C., Smith, J. C., & Hollander, G. R. (1983). The effects of postconditioning CS experience on recovery from radiation-induced taste aversion. *Physiology & Behavior, 30,* 647–649.

Spector, A. C., Smith, J. C., & Hollander, G. R. (1986). Radiation-induced taste aversion: Effects of radiation exposure level and the exposure-taste interval. *Radiation Research, 106,* 271–277.

Sutton, R. L., Fox, R. A., & Daunton, N. G. (1988). Role of the area postrema in three putative measures of motion sickness in the rat. *Behavioral and Neural Biology, 50,* 133–152.

Swank, M. W., & Bernstein, I. L. (1994). c-Fos induction in response to a conditioned stimulus after single trial taste aversion learning. *Brain Research, 636,* 202–208.

Swank, M. W., Ellis, A. E., & Chochran, B. N. (1996). c-Fos antisense blocks acquisition and extinction of conditioned taste aversion in mice. *Neuroreport, 7,* 1866–1870.

Swank, M. W., Schafe, G. E., & Bernstein, I. L. (1995). c-Fos induction in response to taste stimuli previously paired with amphetamine or LiCl during taste aversion learning. *Brain Research, 673,* 251–261.

Taylor, H. L., Smith, J. C., Wall, A. H., & Chaddock, B. (1968). Role of the olfactory system in the detection of X-rays by the rhesus monkey. *Phsyiology & Behavior, 3,* 929–933.

Teskey, G. C., Ossenkopp, K. P., Prato, F. S., & Sestini, E. (1987). Survivability and long-term stress reactivity levels following repeated exposure to nuclear magnetic resonance imaging procedures in rats. *Physiological Chemistry and Physics and Medical NMR, 19,* 43–49.

Winther, F. Ø., Rasmussen, K., Tvete, O., Halvorsen, U., & Haugsdal, B. (1999). Static magnetic field and the inner ear: A functional study of hearing and vestibular function in man after exposure. *Scandinavian Audiology, 28,* 57–59.

PART IV

CLINICAL APPLICATION OF RESEARCH AND TARGET POPULATIONS

21

Chemical Aversion Treatment of Alcoholism

SAM REVUSKY

Since the 1970s, it has become solidly established that CTA (conditioned taste aversion) is, by far, the most potent type of learning. CTAs occur when an animal tastes something, becomes sick through some external means (e.g., injection of a toxin), and then avoids substances with that taste. In the chemical aversion treatment (CAT) of alcoholism in the 1930s, a CTA method was used to induce aversions to the flavors of alcoholic beverages in order to facilitate abstinence from alcohol.[1] Because I want to explore the relationship between CAT and subhuman CTA experimentation, the term "CTA" will be used here to refer to subhuman experimental procedures unless otherwise indicated by the context. Also, although CAT is a behavioral intervention, I will not refer to it as such here because I want to contrast it with other types of behavioral interventions to treat alcoholism.

CAT was very successful in terms of treatment outcomes. It was prominent in the medical and psychological literature during the 1940s, 1950s, and 1960s (Rachman & Teasdale, 1969). During those decades and thereafter, it yielded excellent results that are described here. Despite this, interest in CAT rapidly faded away from around 1970. A recent review (W. R. Miller, Wilbourne, & Hettema, 2003) of this literature mentions no clinical studies involving CAT published after 1981 except for reports originating in the Schick-Shadel Hospital, which is apparently the only hospital in North America that regularly offers CAT.

The decline in the use of CAT is astonishing for two major reasons: (1) it was concurrent with the flourishing of a scientific literature on CTA, which gave CAT a solid scientific basis by showing that CTA is the most rapid and long-lasting type of learning and (2) the efficacy of CAT in treating alcoholism was clear by the standards used for evaluating other treatments as shown in reviews by Howard and Jenson (1990) and by Elkins (1991a). There was no equally strong evidence for the efficacy of the behavioral intervention treatments that became more commonly used.

I spent decades conducting CTA experiments, and I am strongly ego-involved with the utilization of the information obtained to justify and improve CAT. Others in my position likely feel the same way. Scientific researchers are substantially motivated by the expectation that if they uncover useful information, it will be utilized. I believe that CTA information has been poorly utilized in alcoholism treatment and that CAT has not been fairly considered by behavior therapists.

Since the lack of viable alternatives justifies the reemergence of CAT, I begin by discussing new material that demonstrates the ineffectiveness of the behavioral intervention treatments that have overshadowed CAT. I then discuss early CAT results and how they reflect a now-rare interplay between alcoholism treatment and basic science. The basic science used was Pavlovian theory, since CAT was developed in the 1930s and 1940s before the development of CTA experimentation in the 1950s and 1960s. However, it is shown in detail that CAT is a type of CTA. Despite this and the known effectiveness of CTA learning, I will claim that there was a strong and unfair bias against CAT. In the 1990s, the CAT treatment at the Schick-Shadel Hospital in Seattle was shown to be more effective than the treatments in extremely well-reputed and otherwise comparable hospitals that treat alcoholism without CAT. CTA work by me and my colleagues in the 1970s was designed to be applied to CAT. In a preliminary clinical investigation (Boland, Mellor, & Revusky, 1978), this application seemed to be successful

BEHAVIORAL TREATMENTS FOR ALCOHOLISM ARE NOT SUPPORTED

The published record indicates that behavioral intervention is useful in the treatment of alcoholism, and this has become the conventional wisdom. However, this record is questionable because publication is biased in favor of positive results. Like newspapers, scientific journals prefer to publish news rather than reports that there is no news. Studies that report negative results are not news and scientific journals are usually unlikely to publish them. Statistical meta-analyses, in which the results of a number of published papers on a particular topic are used to yield a combined statistical significance level, support the existence of a bias against negative results. For instance, the pioneering meta-analysis of psychotherapy indicates that all psychotherapy methods are equally effective (Smith & Glass, 1977), just about at the level required for publication.

Partly because many small studies are likely to be inconclusive, institutional patrons of research began to encourage large multicenter research studies. Presumably, these would not be as fragmented as previous research, and would diminish the role of publication bias. Such large studies were bound to be published and yield definitive data. Project MATCH (Babor & Del Boca, 2003) and Project COMBINE (Anton, O'Malley, et al., 2006; Pettinati, Zweben, & Mattson, 2005), supported by the U.S. National Institute on Alcohol Abuse and Alcoholism (NIAAA) at a total cost

of over $60 million, were two such studies. These were the largest studies of alcoholism treatment to date. Careful reading of them shows that behavioral intervention was not an effective treatment for alcoholism. Remarkably and unfortunately, the investigators in these studies misinterpreted them as evidence for the efficacy of behavioral treatments.

Project MATCH

The designers of MATCH hoped to counter doubts about the effectiveness of treatments for alcoholism by showing that when particular types of patients were matched to particular treatments, the results of the treatments would improve (Allen, Babor, Mattson, & Kadden, 2003, p. 4). The related view of the Institute of Medicine (1990) as cited by these authors was that

> there is no single treatment approach that is effective for all persons with alcohol problems. A number of treatment methods show promise in particular groups. Reason for optimism in the treatment of alcohol problems lies in the range of promising alternatives that are available, each of which may be optimal for different types of individuals.

Despite a minority of participants from other disciplines, psychologists and social workers dominated the 23-member steering committee for MATCH. It was believed that the highly political operation of this committee was an effective way to conduct research (Del Boca, Mattson, Fuller, & Babor, 2003, pp. 27–28). The treatments compared in MATCH were three different behavioral intervention therapies for alcoholism. Each treatment consisted of individual counseling sessions administered in the course of 12 weeks. One treatment was Twelve-Step Facilitation (TSF) related to the Minnesota model of alcoholism treatment (Cook, 1988a, 1988b). It was designed to facilitate membership in Alcoholics Anonymous (AA) and consisted of 12 sessions usually administered by AA graduates. The Cognitive-Behavioral Therapy (CBT) treatment was 12 sessions designed to enhance social and other coping skills. The Motivational Enhancement Therapy (MET) treatment was four sessions more specifically directed to helping the patient understand his alcoholism. Neither nonbehavioral treatments nor control treatments were included in MATCH.

The efficacy of particular treatments did not depend on the characteristics of the patients treated to any important extent. Hence, matching did not counter doubts about the effectiveness of treatments for alcoholism in the way the study's designers hoped it would (Allen et al., 2003, p. 4). Enoch Gordis, then director of NIAAA, stated (NIAAA, 1996):

> The hypothesis that patients who are appropriately matched to treatments will show better outcomes than those who are unmatched or mismatched is well founded in medicine, behavioral science, and alcoholism treatment. These findings challenge the notion that patient matching is necessary in alcoholism treatment.

The reductions in alcohol intake after each MATCH treatment were extremely large with no discernable differences among the three treatments. This led those involved with MATCH to believe that each of these treatments was effective. Gordis claimed (Bower, 1997) that "all three treatments used in MATCH produced excellent overall outcomes." T. F. Babor stated (NIAAA, 1996): "The striking differences in drinking from pretreatment levels to all follow-up points suggest that participation in any of the MATCH treatments would be associated with marked positive change." The COMBINE Study Research Group (2003, p. 1107), with heavy representation from those formerly involved with MATCH, was to refer to "the successful behavioral interventions from Project MATCH." Many other similar statements were made.

However, in an independent statistical analysis of the MATCH data, Cutler and Fishbain (2005) showed that little, if any, of the decline in alcohol intake could be attributed to the treatments. Table 21.1 is a recalculation and radical abridgement of some of their material. Results obtained from patients who chose not to attend any behavioral intervention sessions ($n = 100$) are compared with those from patients who attended all 12 CBT or TSF behavioral intervention treatment sessions ($n = 355$) in terms of mean drinks per day from prior to treatment, the first week of treatment, and 12 months after treatment. Insofar as the decline in drinking is to be attributed to the treatments, it should be absent among the patients who avoided all their scheduled treatments. (MET patients were not included in Table 21.1 since they received only four treatment sessions by design.)

Table 21.1 shows that both cohorts markedly reduced their alcohol consumption during the first week of treatment after at most one behavioral intervention session and this drop was largely retained 12 months after treatment. The decline in drinking after little or no treatment led Cutler and Fishbain (2005) to deny that there was any important effect of the behavioral intervention treatments. An additional consideration was that level of participation in treatment may reasonably be considered a measure of the motivation to abandon excessive drinking, which has been found to be a more important indicator of a positive prognosis for alcoholism than the amount of treatment (W. R. Miller, 1998). If the MATCH results were due to the behavioral intervention treatments, the patients too poorly motivated to attend any behavioral intervention sessions ought not to have shown any important diminution in their drinking. I think the difference between the cohorts in alcohol consumption is smaller than might reasonably be expected with such a difference in motivation and and suspect that the behavioral intervention treatments were detrimental. That the number of treatment sessions attended was correlated to a significant but small extent with the decline in alcohol intake was considered evidence for the efficacy of treatment (Zweben, Del Boca, Mattson, & McRee, 2003), but this may better be attributed to the stronger motivation to relinquish alcoholism among those who select more treatment (W. R. Miller, 1998).

Table 21.1 Recalculation of Some MATCH Data Supplied by Cutler and Fishbain (2005).

Treatment Sessions	Before	Week 1	12 Months
No sessions attended	12.20	0.72	1.96
All 12 sessions attended	10.98	0.12	0.68

Note: Drinking is shown in terms of mean drinks per day before treatment, during the first week of treatment, and 12 months after treatment.

In passing, note that the patients did not seem to think the therapy was very beneficial since, on the average, the CBT and TSF patients missed about a third of the one-on-one therapy sessions (Donovan, Carroll, Kadden, DiClemente, & Rounsaville, 2003, p. 54).

The lack of evidence in MATCH for the efficacy of behavioral intervention was confirmed by W. R. Miller (2005), a leading light in MATCH, in a rebuttal to the critique by Cutler and Fishbain (2005). He denied that any claim was made by those involved in MATCH "suggesting the absolute efficacy of any of the treatments." This is untrue. MATCH investigators clearly suggested that these treatments were effective and did not qualify their claims by referring to "absolute efficacy," whatever that means. W. R. Miller himself stated with Longabaugh (2003, p. 207) that "Three very different treatment methods were associated with similarly positive outcomes."

W. R. Miller (2005) further stated in regard to the material in Table 21.1:

> If one cannot infer from correlations between attendance and outcome that a treatment worked, then surely one cannot infer from nonsignificant correlations (including their comparisons of patients who completed 0, 1, or all 12 sessions) that treatment was ineffective (thus proving a null hypothesis).

This statistical obfuscation implies that treatments cannot be shown by statistical means to be of no substantial value. This and other comments by Miller showed that the criticisms of Cutler and Fishbain (2005) could not be validly answered. The failure of Miller's refutation is very telling due to Miller's eminence as an expert on the behavioral treatment of alcoholism.

I agree with Cutler and Fishbain (2005) that careful selection of patients for participation in MATCH was mainly responsible for the high abstinence rates. The subjects were volunteers and selected so as not to have residential instability, concurrent drug dependencies, problems with the criminal legal system, or serious mental illnesses. Standards for selection were so high that fewer than 1800 of 4481 volunteers were ultimately selected for participation in MATCH (Zweben et al., 2003, p. 65). These criteria differentially eliminated alcoholics with the poorest prognosis for spontaneous remission or successful treatment, leaving drinkers more likely to recover without treatment (Cutler & Fishbain, 2005). R. B. Cutler (personal communication, 2006), who worked on Project COMBINE, in which similar methods were used, believes that the figures reported by Zweben et al. (2003) understate the extent to which patients with good prognoses were selected. He indicated that

> there was a preselection process designed to weed out candidates who are unsuitable. In our drug studies, for every 10 calls from volunteers to the unit, we would typically enroll only one subject in the trial. When we were doing COMBINE, our therapists wanted patients with the best prognoses since, in a way, we were in competition with the other centers.

Project COMBINE

The mandate of Project COMBINE was "to determine if improvements in treatment outcome for alcohol dependence can be achieved by combining pharmacotherapy and behavioral interventions" (COMBINE Study Research Group, 2003, p. 1007). I conjecture that elements within NIAAA wanted investigations of treatments for alcoholism to include more than behavioral interventions. However, this mandate was implemented by many of the same behaviorally oriented activists who had designed MATCH without including anything but behavioral treatments.

Design of COMBINE

Eight groups of patients were each subjected to medical management (MM) for 16 weeks plus different combinations of treatments based on a $2 \times 2 \times 2$ factorial design. The factors were the presence or absence of each of three treatments: (1) CBI (combined behavioral intervention); (2) naltrexone administration; and (3) acamprosate administration. "A ninth group received CBI-only (behavioral intervention without placebos or MM). All patients were encouraged to attend AA. Patients were evaluated for up to 1 year after treatment" (Anton, O'Malley, et al., 2006). Acamprosate and naltrexone were originally believed by the investigators to be effective in the treatment of alcoholism on the basis of meta-analyses of the published record (e.g., Carman, Magro, Munoz, & Maria, 2004) and approved for such use by the U.S. Food and Drug Administration (Project COMBINE Research Group, 2003).

In the following section, we will use materials about COMBINE edited by Pettinati, Zweben, et al. (2005) to supply details of the rationale, design, and methods of COMBINE.

Patient Selection

The 1383 patients in COMBINE were carefully selected after many interviews in the course of 2 years from about 5000 volunteers recently abstinent from alcohol who had been recruited through advertisements. There was a prior telephonic screening before a patient was selected for interviewing and it seems from a previously cited comment by Cutler that the 5000 volunteers did not include patients eliminated in this screening. A major criterion for selection was the potential for cooperation with treatment and follow-ups (Zweben, Barret, Berger, & Murray, 2005, p. 75). This is, of course, also a measure of motivation to relinquish alcoholism.

Combined Behavioral Intervention

CBI was based on the three behavioral intervention treatments used in MATCH. On the presupposition that each of these treatments had been effective, CBI was "expected to produce outcomes equal to or better than prior cognitive behavioral treatment approaches" (Longabaugh, Zweben, LoCastro, & Miller, 2005, p. 181). There was provision in COMBINE to tailor the therapy to the patient's specific desires. That is, patients might match themselves to different combinations of treatments and amounts of treatment. There were from 5 to 20 individual therapy CBI sessions lasting 50 min except that the first session was longer.

One original rationale for the CBI-only treatment was "to study CBI in the context in which it is frequently delivered clinically, that is, in the absence of pharmacotherapy and certainly, in the absence of placebo medication." (Weiss et al., 2005, p. 43). Its effectiveness was to be measured by comparing its results to those obtained with MM-alone, which always included a placebo. A second rationale for CBI-only was to test for the placebo effect in MM through a comparison of CBI plus MM with CBI-only (Weiss et al., 2005, p. 43).

Medical Management

Except for CBI-alone, all other treatments were administered together with MM. Physicians, nurses, and other medical personnel conducted MM sessions. In addition to dealing with medications and taking medical measures, they promoted abstinence and participation in AA. There were up to nine MM sessions. The amount of treatment time spent in MM averaged about 25% of that spent in CBI (Longabaugh et al., 2005; Pettinati, Zweben, et al., 2005).

By the logic of the a priori statistical hypotheses (Weiss et al., 2005), MM was a nontreatment placebo control. In weekly sessions with the MM therapists, COMBINE's supervisors tried to insure that the MM procedure would not deviate from this desideratum. In doing this, they made MM into a control treatment likely to yield results poorer than usually obtained by medical personnel and hence to allow experimental treatments to be considered more effective than they really are. They did this by preventing therapeutic interactions between the MM therapists and patients of the type that might otherwise occur as follows:

> Practitioners who want to deliver MM, as intended, will need to avoid saying or doing anything that is not part of the MM intervention. In nonresearch clinical settings, nonprotocol procedures may or may not be allowable within the overall approach of the MM practitioner, depending on their training and the treatment plan. To this end, the MM practitioner should be clear with the patient about what non-MM elements may or may not occur at MM visits. In research trials, nonprotocol should be strictly avoided.
>
> Pettinati, Weiss, et al., 2005, p. 178

Not only were MM patients likely to be demoralized by being told that otherwise available help was being deleted from the MM therapy, the MM therapists were probably also demoralized: "The most frequent reason in the COMBINE Study for a lower rating in nonprotocol avoidance was the practitioner's use of some form of psychotherapy or counseling beyond the confines of the MM intervention" (Pettinati, Weiss, et al., 2005, p. 178).

The report of the COMBINE results (Anton, O'Malley, et al, 2006) did not indicate that MM was different from the way medical personnel typically treat alcoholism patients.

Overall Results

Given the very large number of patients involved, the COMBINE results should be considered negative since they were not statistically significant a year after treatment. There were very small effects during the treatment period on the preferred measure in COMBINE, the percentage of days during which the patient was abstinent (PDA), and incorrect conclusions were reached on their basis as will be explained in the following text.

Results for Groups that Did Not Receive Active Drugs

Table 21.2 shows the PDA results for Groups CBI-alone, MM-alone, and CBI plus MM during treatment as reported in the abstract of the report by Anton, O'Malley, et al. (2006) together with their original statistical roles as explained by Weiss et al. (2005). The CBI-alone group yielded poorer results ($p < 0.02$, t-test) than Group MM-alone (which, in turn, yielded poorer results than any of the remaining seven groups in COMBINE). The CBI-alone effect was inferior to the CBI plus MM effect (bottom row of Table 21.2) at $p < 0.001$. By the reasoning of Weiss et al. (2005), this indicates that a substantial placebo effect remained in the MM treatment even after MM was reduced in effectiveness by the designers of COMBINE. Finally CBI plus MM produced better results than MM-alone ($p < 0.05$ for rows 2 and 3 of Table 21.2). This small effect is not evidence that CBI was of any net benefit. The benefit may have occurred only due to reinstatement of the normal benefits of the patient–therapist interaction aggressively removed from COMBINE's version of MM. That is, as indicated earlier, MM patients had been told they were missing something in their treatment. The MM patients who received CBI must have believed they were receiving in CBI what was missing in MM. The MM-alone patients remained with the knowledge that something was missing in the only treatment they received.

Results for Groups that Received Active Drugs

There were no significant effects involving acamprosate. Hence Anton, O'Malley, et al. (2006) reduced the original $2 \times 2 \times 2$ factorial design to the 2×2 design shown in Table 21.3: the effects of naltrexone administration and CBI combined factorially when MM was administered throughout. Each cell in Table 21.3 includes data both from patients subjected to acamprosate and those not subjected to it.[2] The main effects were not significant, but the naltrexone by CBI interaction yielded $p < 0.01$. Following the usual procedure for dealing with interactions, I compared PDA during treatment for MM-alone with that when the following treatments were added: CBI, naltrexone, or both CBI and naltrexone. I calculated a separate t-test score for the cases in which acamprosate was not added to the mix and the cases in which it was added. I then combined these two t-scores. Table 21.4 shows that CBI without naltrexone and naltrexone without CBI each yielded a significant increase in PDA over MM-alone. As deduced from the test in Table 21.4 (or any other reasonable test), the combination of CBI and naltrexone was ineffective. The original report of the results from COMBINE claimed that the combination of CBI and naltrexone yielded a higher PDA than MM-alone (Anton, O'Malley, et al., 2006). Representatives of the COMBINE Research Study Group later explicitly stated that "receiving

Table 21.2 A Significant ($p < 0.001$) Difference Among Three Groups in Percent Days Abstinent (PDA) during Treatment in Project COMBINE.

Treatment	Statistical Roles of Treatment from Weiss et al. (2005)	PDA (%)
CBI-alone (without placebo or MM)	To measure effects of behavioral intervention in a nonmedical setting and to serve as a control for placebo effects	66.6
MM-alone (with placebo)	A comparison to test the efficacy of CBI-alone	73.8
CBI plus MM (with placebo)	To serve as a measure of the placebo effect of MM-alone through a comparison with CBI-alone	79.8

Source: Data from Anton, Malley, et al. (2006, p. 2011).

Note: Each mean score is based on over 150 patients. CBI refers to combined behavioral intervention and MM refers to medical management.

Table 21.3 Results in Terms of Mean Percent Days Abstinent of the Factorial Combination of Naltrexone and Combined Behavioral Intervention (CBI).

	Treatment	
	No naltrexone(%)	Naltrexone(%)
No CBI	75.1	80.6
CBI	79.2	77.1

Source: Data from Anton, O'Malley, et al. (2006, p. 2009).

Note: In all cells, MM was administered with a placebo. If naltrexone was not administered, there was a second placebo. Each score is based on over 300 patients. The main effects were not statistically significant: $p = 0.25$ for naltrexone and $p = 0.82$ for CBI. The interaction yielded $p = 0.009$.

Table 21.4 Analysis of Interaction in Table 21.3. The Left-top Cell of Table 21.3 is Treated as a Baseline Value. The Scores in the Remaining Cells of Table 21.3 are Each Compared with It.

CBI without naltrexone as follows	
Without acamprosate	$t(308) = 2.031$
With acamprosate	$t(302) = 0.866$
Combined result: $t(610) = 2.049, p < 0.05$	
Naltrexone without CBI as follows	
Without acamprosate	$t(306) = 2.088$
With acamprosate	$t(299) = 1.635$
Combined result: $t(605) = 2.632, p < 0.01$	
Both naltrexone and CBI as follows	
Without acamprosate	$t(307) = 0.709$
With acamprosate	$t(311) = 0.338$
Combined result: $t(618) = 0.740, p > 0.40$	

Source: Data from Table 5 of Anton, O'Malley, et al. (2006).

Note: This is a comparison of MM-only with groups that have the following three conditions added: CBI, naltrexone, naltrexone plus CBI. For each of these three conditions, a separate $t(df)$ test score was calculated first for groups not receiving acamprosate and then for groups receiving acamprosate. These two t-scores were combined by multiplying their mean by the square root of two.

either the CBI, naltrexone, or both significantly improved outcomes relative to placebo in the context of MM" (Anton, Miller, O'Malley, Zweben, & Hosking, 2006).

The significant result for CBI without naltrexone in Table 21.4 is similar to the significant difference between CBI plus MM and MM-alone in rows 2 and 3 of Table 21.2, and it is similarly explicable by the reinstatement in CBI of the normal benefits of the patient–therapist interaction aggressively removed from COMBINE's version of MM. The MM-only control procedure for naltrexone is also flawed. R. B. Cutler (personal communication, 2006) indicated that it was often obvious to patients and staff whether the naltrexone or a placebo was being used on the basis of discernable drug side effects or their absence. It is not mere pedantry to complain about this defect since the putative naltrexone effect is smaller than 10% of the PDA for any treatment group in COMBINE.

My Conclusions from MATCH and COMBINE

What experts believed to be the most effective behavioral interventions for alcoholism were certainly ineffective in MATCH and COMBINE. I think they were detrimental. That the investigators implied the contrary powerfully contradicts the belief of Del Boca et al. (2003) that committees can perform research effectively, particularly when they have professional involvement with the techniques under investigation and strong preconceptions based on the published clinical research record. In passing, the lack of a detectable effect of acamprosate and the miniscule effect of naltrexone reinforce my suspicion of the published record in this type of research. Alternatively, these failures may be attributable to the careful selection of patients for COMBINE (Jonas & Chabac, 2006; Kiefer & Mann, 2006). This careful selection does not easily account for the ineffectiveness of CBI in MATCH and COMBINE since the patients were selected for amenity to behavioral interventions.

CTA AS A BASIS FOR FURTHER INVESTIGATION

The traditional approach of relying on basic science should be utilized much more in the treatment of alcoholism. In medicine, the preclinical vetting of treatments, usually based on animal research, is the preferred approach. Admittedly, a remarkable amount of medicine is purely empirical in that how the treatment works is unknown but the purely empirical is not the medical desideratum. Physicians are most comfortable with treatments when they know how they work in terms of basic science. In contrast, alcoholism treatment studies often have been disconnected from the strongest basic science and instead have been based on clinical comparisons of various treatments. Addiction treatment studies are very amorphous and hence a preclinical scientific direction is particularly desirable when feasible. Fortunately, there has been a great deal of preclinical work on reward and addiction mechanisms and on cravings for addictive drugs summarized by Wise (2002). I would add preclinical work relevant to CAT to this mix.

Nearly all readers of this book are knowledgeable about CTA, but others who may read this chapter should note that it is the most potent known type of learning. For instance, a single pairing of a sweet solution with a 57-roentgen (R) dose of X-irradiation sickness caused rats to drink much less of the sweet solution than of the unflavored water for over a month of continuous access to both solutions. Before irradiation, over 85% of the fluid intake was the sweet solution (Garcia, Kimeldorf, & Koelling, 1955). The 57-R X-irradiation dose was well below that which produces obvious symptoms in the most susceptible humans (Gerstner, 1960), although rats are more resistant to radiation than humans. Learning after a single pairing of the CS (conditioned stimulus) with the US (unconditioned stimulus) with CS–US delays of many hours (Revusky & Garcia, 1970) occurs in CTA and with no other type of learning. The early CTA work used radiation as the US because it was supported by military funding (Freeman & Riley, Chapter 2) but a variety of toxic states produced by injection were also used from the 1960s (Revusky & Garcia, 1970). Figure 21.2, to be discussed later in detail, shows the long-lasting CTAs produced in rats by emetine and lithium, which, as will be documented, have been used successfully in CAT.

THE FIRST HIGHLY BELIEVABLE CAT TREATMENT RESULTS

While there were sporadic uses of CAT prior to the 1930s, they were not, in retrospect, solid enough to be worth reporting here. Support for the efficacy of CAT comes from papers published in the 1940s and the following two decades by Walter L. Voegtlin, a gasteroenterologist, Frederick Lemere, a biological psychiatrist at the University of Washington, and several of their associates. Voegtlin and Lemere each had distinguished scientific careers in addition to their work with CAT. They based their treatment on Pavlov's work, which they understood much better than the psychologists of their time. The style of their work with its reliance on the basic-science work of Pavlov contrasts starkly with the statistical treatment–comparison approach of Projects MATCH and COMBINE.

Lemere and Voegtlin (1950) reported that from 1935 to 1948, they treated 4468 patients at the Shadel Hospital. They were able in the course of 14 years to obtain accurate follow-up data on 4096 of these patients. They found that 60% remained abstinent for at least 1 year since their first treatment and 23% for at least 10 years. These figures are in line with those obtained later by others who used similar methods (Elkins 1991a; Howard & Jenson, 1990).

These figures are very high and better than those obtained with other therapies, but they are not definitive evidence for the efficacy of CAT. The cost of treatment was mainly covered by private insurance and employers. Therefore the patients were mainly middle class with a good prognosis. Lemere and Voegtlin (1950) were less successful with charity cases. In general, it is hard to determine the efficacy of alcoholism treatment from figures based on reduction in alcohol consumption or abstinence since there is a high rate of spontaneous improvement among the less severely impacted patients (Vaillant, 1995). However, the high abstinence rates obtained by Lemere and Voegtlin (1950) are convincing evidence for the efficacy of CAT when combined with the Pavlovian research they relied on and with the later CTA findings. It will be shown below that the detailed properties of CAT reported by Lemere and Voegtlin were so similar to those later demonstrated for CTA that CAT must depend on the same underlying biological process. The small respects in which there were differences between the Voegtlin–Lemere observations and CTA experiments were diminished by later findings.

The CAT treatment offered at the Shadel Hospital changed slightly over the years, but not in its essentials. I will supply a general picture that may be trivially inaccurate in some details for some of the quarter century over which the treatment was conducted.

A conditioned reflex is established on the basis of the unconditioned nauseant response to the hypodermic administration of emetine. Since it is desired the unconditioned nauseant response be so conditioned as to be evoked by the sight, smell, or taste of alcoholic beverages [these were selected as CSs]...Emetine and liquor were presented just before the onset of the emetine nausea. Following a suitable number of such conditioning experiences, a marked aversion to the sight, smell, and taste of liquor was found to exist.

The sensation of nausea and the act of vomiting [were chosen as unpleasant experiences to build the unconditioned response] for three reasons: (a) There were available at least two drugs, suitable for use as the unconditioned stimulus,

which are easily able to evoke this activity in the average patient. (b) The psychological connection between the ingestion of food and drink, and the resulting nausea and vomiting, is much more potent in creating an aversion to the ingested substances than would be the manifestation of pain, convulsions, syncope, etc. (c) A conditioned vomiting upon attempting to swallow liquor would automatically rid the body of the alcohol before it could be absorbed and exert its narcotic action to a point where the conditioned response would be extinguished.

Voegtlin, Lemere, & Broz, 1940

Here was medical treatment closely and intelligently modeled on experimental findings from the Pavlovian literature. Voegtlin et al.'s point (b) was later supported by Garcia and Koelling's (1966) demonstration with rats that external stimuli (such as sounds and lights) are more readily associated with external threats (such as peripheral pain produced by electrical shock) than tastes, while the converse is true if the US is sickness. Although this result by Garcia and Koelling was a bombshell in Western psychology, the Pavlovian literature had long emphasized the importance in conditioning of modality relationships between the CS and the US. It was on this basis that Voegtlin et al. (1940) expected electrical shock to be an unsuitable agent for producing alcohol aversions. Since then, it has repeatedly been shown that electrical shock does not produce CTAs to alcohol in humans (Elkins 1991a; Howard & Jenson, 1990). In contrast, many psychologists preferred aversion therapy with electrical shock on the basis of the black box approach to conditioning that Pavlov (1932) despised. Nearly two decades after the work of Garcia and Koelling (1966), Nathan (1985, p. 360) commented that the "surprising lack of interest in a treatment as efficacious as chemical aversion with nausea-inducing drugs derived in large part from a much stronger, long-lived interest among behavioral clinicians in electric shock as a stimulus for conditioning aversions to ethanol."

Voegtlin and Lemere not only anticipated the effectiveness of sickness in conditioning CTAs but also anticipated more recent findings about the type of sickness that would be effective. They considered CAT conditioning to be Pavlovian humoral conditioning in which the US is administered through the blood stream.

As it is known that drugs such as pilocarpine and histamine, which act in a purely peripheral manner, are not adequate to allow conditioning to occur, it has been suggested that emetine, by virtue of its peripheral action on the mucous membrane, might fall into this latter category of drugs.

Voegtlin et al., 1940, pp. 501–502

But emetine also has a central action and thus was selected as the US. A similar consideration, expressed in the later terminology of Garcia and Ervin (1968), is that toxins most effective in producing CTAs impinge on the gut defense system; peripherally acting toxins are not as effective. Other investigators not as knowledgeable as Voegtlin et al. tried to produce CAT with, for instance, scoline, a peripherally acting agent that produces muscular paralysis (e. g., Sanderson, Campbell, & Laverty, 1963). This drug specificity was clearly established experimentally in the case of CTA after another decade or so (Ionescu & Buresova, 1977; Lett, 1985). Perhaps the most dramatic demonstration of drug specificity is that a nearly lethal dose of strychnine, which produces muscular paralysis, does not produce appreciable CTAs in rats (Nachman & Hartley, 1975).

The similarities between CAT and CTA are so specific that they clearly indicate that CAT is due to CTA. Table 21.5 contains four of them that will be gradually explained in the course of this paper. That drugs impinging on the gut defense system produce the strongest aversions is the first of these similarities.

Voegtlin et al. (1940, pp. 502–503) did not believe cognitive factors were important for CAT:

A further consideration of the role played by emetine as the unconditioned stimulus gives rise to the most interesting speculation as to whether or not it would be deleterious if the patient knew that the hypodermic injection, at the beginning of the treatment, was in reality the cause of his ensuing nausea and vomiting. It is our opinion that this knowledge would not seriously interfere with the establishment of a satisfactory conditioned reflex.

This opinion was based partly on the frequent observation that when physicians suffer a sickness that they know is due to bacterial infection, they may still develop an aversion to whatever unusual food has recently been consumed. Surely, nearly everybody has a similar story. Seasickness, for instance, frequently results in aversions to food that the victim knows is not responsible for the sickness.

Still, the authors were unwilling to entirely discount the possibility that the patient's knowledge that the sickness was produced by the emetine US might interfere with the efficacy of CAT. Their later discussion of this matter shows how skillful they were:

However, since our opinions on this point are largely speculative, and since evidence to the contrary does exist, it has been our practice to avoid any risk of failure by leading the patient to believe that the hypodermic injection of emetine does not make him ill. The pharmacological characteristics of emetine lend this drug nicely to the technique of deceiving the patient. By a nicety in adjustment of the dosage, it is possible to sensitize the centers of nausea and vomiting in the brainstem to a subnauseant level. In this state, nausea is not apparent unless a simultaneous stimulus of an irritating nature is applied to the mucous membrane of the stomach. This secondary stimulus to the gastric mucosa could be alcohol.

Voegtlin et al., 1940, pp. 503–504

Table 21.5 Extremely Specific Similarities between CAT and CTA.

Effect	Evidence	
	CAT	CTA
Most effective USs related to gut-defense	Voegtlin et al. (1940)	Ionescu and Buresova (1977)
One trial learning with CS–US delay of hours	Logue (1985)	Revusky (1968)
Irrelevance of external stimuli	E. C. Miller et al. (1960)	Garcia and Koelling (1966)
Simultaneous reward and general punishment	Sherman et al. (1988)	Wise et al. (1976) Reicher and Holman (1977)

Voegtlin and his coworkers soon stopped deceiving the patients about what made them ill because it was unnecessary. It probably also was undesirable because a patient's understanding of his medical or behavioral treatment is likely to increase its effectiveness. An administrator at the Shadel Hospital told me in 1968 that their patients were more upbeat in mood than was the case with AA patients. The patients in Shadel Hospital felt the treatment of alcoholism as a disease to be mitigated by CAT denigrated the character of the alcoholic less than AA did. (The section on Later Work at the Schick-Shadel Hospital describes similar recent patient attitudes.) The production of sickness by the emetine meant they were being treated medically rather than moralistically. However, as will be emphasized later, no CAT investigator claimed that CAT alone would cure alcoholism. It does, however, reduce the craving for alcoholic beverages (Howard, 2001).

The authors then discussed adjustment of the emetine dose to the individual patient so that it has little effect until the patient drinks an ounce or two of whisky, thereby potentiating its effect and producing nausea and vomiting. They did not want the sickness to precede exposure to the alcoholic beverage because that would prevent conditioning. Green and Garcia (1971) were later to show that if the sickness preceded exposure of rats to a taste, the taste might actually become more highly preferred due to an association with recuperation from the sickness. The vomiting of the alcoholic beverage was convenient because it substantially reduces the narcotic effect of the alcohol, which the authors expected to interfere with conditioning.

Prior to the Voegtlin–Lemere work, all CAT procedures used the same alcoholic beverage during all conditioning trials. Voegtlin et al. (1940) emphasized the importance of using different alcoholic beverages since the inadvertent omission of one type of liquor sometimes resulted in an early relapse through consumption of the unconditioned liquor. But no more than one alcoholic beverage was to be administered on any single trial. On Pavlovian principles of CS representations competing to become associated with the same US neural center, if more than one beverage was administered during a single session, the aversions to the different beverages would interfere with each other. It might be that a more novel and/or intensely flavored beverage would overshadow

the association of a more familiar and/or milder flavor. It was particularly likely that this would result in only a weak aversion to beer, sometimes an alcoholic's sole alcoholic beverage. Such dangers were removed by using one alcoholic beverage per session. Revusky (1971) later called mutual interference of the conditioning of two CSs presented during the same trial "concurrent interference."

Voegtlin et al. (1940) started with liquor on early trials and usually ended with beer. They believed that a long interval between the last pretreatment drinking of beer and its aversion conditioning made the conditioning more effective. This is also the case in CTA (Mcintosh & Terry, 1977). They also observed that sometimes patients developed aversions to ginger ale and other mixers. They remedied this by freely serving these mixers between conditioning sessions.

I now quote directly from Voegtlin et al. (1940):

Development of Technique. The ability to perform any skilled and delicate operation follows only after long practice. Similarly, in considering the handling of such a delicate operation as a conditioning procedure, the development of a satisfactory technique can follow only after long hours of practice, study, and training. It is felt that we began to develop a suitable technical procedure only after several hundred cases had been treated. Even now occasional changes in procedure are suggested on the basis of continued observation and experience. In developing technicians for this type of work we feel that observation and participation in at least several hundred conditioning séances are prerequisite to the administration of even the earlier and relatively unimportant treatments. The most difficult single technical detail to be mastered is the proper timing of the first administration of alcohol. As was previously mentioned, this first admission of liquor must be just *before* the onset of nausea. Experience alone will enable one to judge the exact moment when the emetine nausea will begin (usually 2 to 8 min.) and consequently the exact moment when the first drink of liquor must be offered. If this timing is not accomplished in the proper manner the results of the entire séance will be unsatisfactory....

A second most important, although less tangible, detail which may be mastered only after considerable experience is the matter of determining the proper number of conditioning experiences which are required in order to reach the optimum conditioned response for each individual patient as well as the interposition of adequate rest periods between séances. An excessive number of treatments will result in the phenomenon of "extinction by adaptation" and the final product of conditioning will be defective.

Voegtlin et al., 1940, pp. 512–513

Not many physicians could train technicians to have the extraordinary skills that Voegtlin et al. demanded. Hence I am glad that CAT is effective without such extraordinary precautions (Elkins, 1991a; Howard & Jenson, 1990). It is almost certain that if the emetine-induced nausea were to begin several minutes after the alcohol ingestion, the delay would not be as deleterious to conditioning as Voegtlin et al. supposed. A quarter century after their work, it was demonstrated that rats can develop an aversion to sugar water after a single pairing in which the CS–US delay is 7 h (Revusky, 1968). Logue (1985) has summarized evidence that humans also can learn CTAs with long CS–US delays. This similarity between animal and human taste aversion is shown in the second row of Table 21.5. There is even a report that a delay of some minutes may produce stronger aversions than very immediate infusion of a poison US (Schafe, Sollars, & Bernstein, 1995). A second more minor elucidating comment about the previous material quoted from Voegtlin et al is that we do not generally find extinction by adaptation in CTA experiments but the clinical situation is different because the dose of the toxic agent used in CAT is much lower than in most animal experiments. With lower doses of toxic agents, such adaptation may occur. In the instrumental conditioning literature, effects similar to extinction by adaptation are the overtraining reversal effects and the overtraining extinction effect (Mackintosh, 1974).

Voegtlin et al. (1940) then supplied details about how the proper number of conditioning sessions should vary for different patients (from 2 to 10). Rest periods between conditioning sessions were used to allow recovery from adaptation. The rest periods must have been at least a day and were probably usually 2 days. (The course of treatment took about 10 days of hospitalization.) Voegtlin and Lemere claimed that excessive rest periods will allow spontaneous extinction of an aversion to previously familiarized alcoholic beverages. This has

only recently been demonstrated with CTA in rats as delay-induced super-latent inhibition (Lubow, Chapter 3). I have not included this in Table 21.5 as a specific similarity between CAT and CTA because it is likely something similar occurs in conditioning involving external stimuli.

Voegtlin et al. (1940) thought it important to use booster CAT sessions some months after the main treatment was completed. It is hard to establish the value of booster sessions as long as the patients select how many booster sessions they receive, since willingness to accept booster treatments is a measure of the patient's motivation. With limited controls for motivation, there is still some evidence to support the efficacy of booster treatments (Voegtlin, Lemere, Broz, & O'Hollaren, 1941). Our knowledge of CTA and common sense indicate that booster sessions are bound to be beneficial. Data regarding boosters will be supplied in a later summary of work by Smith, Frawley, and Polissar (1991).

Pavlov was very careful both to isolate his dogs from extraneous stimuli and to prevent social interaction of his friendly dogs with the investigators. This same method is followed in the sound resistant and light-proof Skinner box. Voegtlin et al. (1940) followed the Pavlovian precedent closely, not even allowing technicians to chat with the patients during CAT sessions. Corresponding precautions are not used in CTA experiments because they are unnecessary, since external stimuli do not readily become associated with sickness and hence do not interfere with CTAs. Such selective association has been called stimulus relevance in the CTA literature (Dietz & Capretta, 1967). Although Voegtlin and Lemere were among the few in North America in 1940 to understand the importance of sensory modality relationships in conditioning, they still underestimated their importance.

That external stimuli do not interfere with CAT was shown by E. C. Miller, Dvorak, and Turner (1960) some years before the Garcia and Koelling (1966) paper that demonstrated this point for CTA. It is shown in Table 21.5 as the third specific similarity between CAT and CTA. E. C. Miller et al. (1960) subjected patients to CAT in squads of four and felt that the interactions between patients improved the treatment. Not only did the sickness of one patient elicit sickness in the other patients but it produced a therapeutic bonding among patients similar in some ways to the bonding among AA patients. Another feature of the E. C. Miller et al. (1960) procedure, based on the elicitation of sickness in patients by observation of sickness in other patients, was to use previously conditioned patients as "scapegoats" to start interactive vomiting. Interestingly, by the way, exposure to a sick rat can also produce a taste aversion in another rat. The effect is small (Coombes, Revusky, & Lett, 1980; Lavin, Freise, & Coombes, 1976), but it may be larger in humans, who typically are more socialized than rats.

It is emphasized that CAT was not used as a stand-alone treatment for alcoholism.

It has always been obvious to us that conditioning alone is not complete therapy by itself. We, at the Schick Shadel Hospitals, therefore have an extensive comprehensive program, with adjunctive individual and family counseling, informational orientation lectures, nutritional advice, and a strong aftercare support system for the patient's recovery. The most important aspect of therapy is to establish a positive attitude toward abstinence. On the other hand, if patients can come out of treatment feeling positive and happy about abstinence, they will be able to enjoy a rewarding life free of alcohol.

Lemere, 1986

ALCOHOL IS SIMULTANEOUSLY REWARDING AND AVERSIVE

A fourth similarity between CAT and CTA in Table 21.5 is that while the effects of recreational drugs are rewarding for motor responses, they can simultaneously produce CTAs (Reicher & Holman, 1977; Wise, Yokel, & DeWit, 1976). This is because these drugs activate reward centers in the brain at the same time as they activate centers related to gut-defense.[3] Thus, a rat that presses a lever for amphetamine injections will develop a CTA to a substance it has consumed prior to the lever-pressing session. The rat develops a CTA because the effects of amphetamine on the gut-defense system are aversive, but it presses a lever for amphetamine injection because it enjoys the amphetamine-induced euphoria.

The difference between the effects of alcohol on reward centers and on gut-defense centers is particularly germane for alcoholism because alcohol is generally taken by mouth. Hence, alcohol itself can cause an aversion to its taste in the alcoholic.

He must overcome this to enjoy the euphoria of inebriation (Logue, 1985). An amusing illustration of this is in Clive Mellor's anecdote (personal communication, circa 1975) of a British regimental Sergeant-Major of his acquaintance. He would retch with his first drink of the day and remark: "That was for the troops. The rest will be for me." I am sure the Shadel investigators were familiar with the frequency of aversions to alcoholic beverages among alcoholics, but I did not notice that they documented it. Other alcoholics do not exhibit or develop an aversion to the alcohol flavor prior to CAT.

It likely is true of both rats and men that all drugs that stimulate reward centers in the brain become more rewarding with additional exposure to them. In nonhuman mammals, the addiction effect with exposure is quite fast with amphetamine and the opiates, and much slower with alcohol (Sherman, Jorenby, & Baker, 1988; Wise, 2002). A similar pattern holds for human addiction. It typically requires many years of alcohol abuse for genetically susceptible humans to become alcoholics (Vaillant, 1995). In these respects, the similarities between humans and rats and other mammals are very close.

Table 21.5 includes only effects characteristic of CTA and CAT and little else. Thus it shows that CTA and CAT are similar in terms of very specific hallmarks. There are, of course, species differences in any general biological process but, in fact, such differences among mammals are remarkably small for CTAs. There is little evolutionary pressure to produce major differences in avoidance of poisoning through learning about tastes (Revusky, 1985b).

A PARADE EXAMPLE OF IDEOLOGICAL BIASES THAT HAVE INTERFERED WITH ACCEPTANCE OF CAT

The bias against the use of basic science to justify CAT treatment of alcoholism is illustrated in a reply by Wilson (1991) to Elkins' (1991a) favorable review of CAT. A related illustration is an earlier critique of CAT (Wilson, 1988). Wilson's (1988) paper was influential in another form as a negative assessment of CAT (Institute of Medicine, 1990, p. 517). Wilson's thinking was badly confused, but, insofar as it was widely accepted, it interfered with wider acceptance and improvement of CAT. Elkins (1991a, 1991b) and Howard and Jenson (1990) pointed out many of the errors and distortions in Wilson's critiques. But they did not mention all of them and did not deal with Wilson's critiques as severely as deserved. Wilson is a pillar of the behavior therapy establishment as the editor of *Behaviour Research and Therapy*, a leading journal in the behavior therapy area. Given the nature of peer review, he would not have reached this position if his views did not reflect those of others. His views need further refutation although I will not duplicate all the points made by Elkins (1991a) and by Howard and Jenson (1990). Wilson (1991, p. 418) commented:

> Elkins recommends the clinical use of chemical aversion conditioning because of a rational theoretical foundation; consistently favorable results from admittedly uncontrolled and methodologically imperfect clinical reports; and the fact that few other alcoholism treatments enjoy the support of controlled experimental evaluations.

For me, the first part of this excerpt is the crux of the matter: Wilson's reference to recommending "the clinical use of chemical aversion conditioning because of a rational theoretical foundation." "Rational theoretical foundation" is a deprecating way to refer to scientific knowledge that fits into a theoretical structure and to Elkins' application of preclinical CTA studies to medical treatment. It may suggest to a reader innocent of knowledge of the CTA literature that Elkins was into abstract philosophy while he, Wilson, was being empirical in his emphasis on treatment comparisons. In the last part of the above-cited comment, Wilson mentioned that "few other alcoholism treatments enjoy the support of controlled experimental evaluations." In fact, no behavioral treatments of alcoholism are supported by strong controlled experimental evaluations. Projects MATCH and COMBINE and smaller studies in the same tradition are certainly what Wilson would have considered "controlled experimental evaluations." As shown in the section on Behavioral Treatments for Alcoholism Are Not Supported, MATCH and COMBINE were to demonstrate the ineffectiveness of the most well-reputed behavioral intervention treatments.

Wilson (1991, p. 41) claimed that "he was not singling out chemical aversion treatment for unduly rigorous evaluation." In fact, however, Wilson consistently set standards for CAT that had never been used for other behavioral treatments of alcoholism. He argued that because CAT is used in conjunction with other methods of helping the patient, no improvement could fairly be attributed to CAT. This argument falsely suggests that other treatments for alcoholism are used in pristine isolation. In fact, treatments for alcoholism almost always include a variety of methods, as was the case in Projects MATCH and COMBINE. AA or involvement with other patient self-support groups is almost universally recommended. According to Elkins (1991b), Bandura (1969), in a book repeatedly cited by Wilson (1991) as highly authoritative, carefully explained why it is not reasonable to try to evaluate CAT in pristine isolation.

Wilson (1991) then worried that CAT was unacceptably intrusive despite the fact that thousands of patients had accepted it (Elkins, 1991b; Howard & Jenson, 1990). Then Wilson (1991) chose to worry about the safety of emetine although thousands of alcoholics had been safely subjected to it (Howard & Jenson, 1990). Earlier, Wilson (1988) chose to worry about the safety of lithium use in CAT when, in fact, it is prescribed to control mania at a daily dose similar to that used intermittently in CAT.

Wilson on Preparedness, Cognitive Learning, and the Bandura Approach

Wilson (1991) had two classes of theoretical considerations with which he buttressed his position. The first class had the heading "Automatic processing and classical conditioning" (p. 415). It is discussed in this section.

Wilson (1988, p. 512) thought that because cognitive processes have been found to be involved in classical aversive conditioning, "the original theoretical justification for the specific use of drug-induced nausea has been undermined." He ignored the clear evidence in the preceding section on how Alcohol is Simultaneously Rewarding and Aversive, (summarized in the bottom row of Table 21.5), that CAT is a type of CTA although this evidence was available at the time he wrote. Instead, he presupposed that there is a single entity called classical aversive conditioning and that one can extrapolate from one instance of this conditioning, presumably eyelid conditioning, to another instance, CTA learning. Hence, if cognitive factors are important for eyelid conditioning, they are bound to be important for CTAs. For Wilson, this theory trumped the clear evidence that cognitive processes are unimportant for CTAs. He amplified this position later:

> Elkins (1991) suggests that chemically conditioned aversions are robust in part because of their "status as Seligman's (1971) type of highly prepared associations." However other instances of what are hypothesized to be prepared associations, such as phobic and obsessional responses, are rapidly eliminated using exposure treatment. Moreover, there is good evidence indicating that prepared fears are no more resistant to extinction than unprepared fears.
>
> Wilson, 1991, p. 416

In reality, Elkins (1991a) claimed that CTAs are robust and resistant to extinction because this has repeatedly been found in many human and animal contexts. For Elkins, the role of theory was to explain this, not to deny it in opposition to the documented facts. As Elkins carefully explained, Garcia (1989) emphasized that different highly prepared associations can have different characteristics because of differences in their neural underpinnings. Elkins briefly mentioned how Seligman's approach was compatible with Garcia's (1989) position and I think that was incorrect. Seligman's (1970) suggestion that there might be general characteristics of prepared associations reflected uncritical acceptance of the general process approach he thought he was opposing. As Revusky (1984) explained, all associations are biologically constrained, or "prepared" in Seligman's terminology.

But neither Seligman nor Elkins intended to use theories to nullify facts in the manner of Wilson. One of the dozens of examples of how readily CTAs are established and how resistant they are to extinction is in Figure 21.2 of the present paper. Logue (1985) has summarized illustrations of this in humans.

Just as he distorted what Elkins wrote, Wilson misquoted Albert Bandura to deny reality: "Modern theoretical analysis, beginning with Bandura's (1969) position, attach no particular advantage to drug-induced nausea" (Wilson, 1988,

p. 513). Bandura's actual opinion was the opposite of Wilson's claim:

> Aversive counterconditioning is thus a simple, brief, economical, and relatively effective method for producing aversion to alcohol for at least a limited period, and for continued total abstinence in approximately 50% of the clients. The aversion form of therapy offers the additional advantages of ready acceptance by clients and wide applicability.
>
> Bandura, 1969, p. 543

In his 1991 paper, Wilson repeatedly cited Bandura (1969) as an authoritative source of opinions Bandura did not hold.

Wilson on Generalization from Rat Studies to Alcoholism in Humans

Wilson's (1991) second theoretical class of objections to CAT was that one cannot generalize from rat studies to the treatment of alcoholics. His main purported evidence was two points made by Sherman et al. (1988): (1) that the rat is especially prone to develop CTAs because it cannot vomit and hence has a stronger evolutionary need for taste aversion learning and (2) that humans are more likely than rats to consume otherwise unpalatable substances due to their tension-reducing effects. I do not fully agree with these points but it would take us too far afield to explain my reasons. It is more important that Wilson (1991) took these points out of context. Sherman et al. (1988, pp. 196–197) clearly stated that CTAs may be useful in the treatment of alcoholism and that "general principles of conditioned food habits derived from study of the rat are applicable across a wide phylogenetic array extending from mollusks to humans" (p. 188).

Even if it were true that the etiology of clinical alcoholism is based on principles unique to humans, this would not invalidate the use of CAT to help treat alcoholism. I find no claim by CAT practitioners that rat and human alcoholism are similar in over half a century of published records. CTA strengthens the case for CAT for a different reason: it is the most potent type of conditioning known and is remarkably similar in all mammalian species.

Wilson (1991) further suggested that CAT of alcoholism makes little sense because alcoholics, presumably unlike rats, can have pretreatment CTAs to alcoholic beverages. As I explained in the preceding section on how Alcohol is Simultaneously

Rewarding and Aversive and summarized in the bottom row of Table 21.5, this is not a difference between rats and humans. If an alcoholic already has a taste aversion to alcohol, CAT can still greatly intensify it. Furthermore, many (possibly most) expert alcoholics do not have strong aversions to the taste of alcohol. They probably have come to drink so slowly that they rarely develop the type of sickness from drinking that produces strong CTAs. Habituation to the alcohol sickness may also be involved (Braveman, 1975).

Wilson on Proper Controls

Early in the study of CTA, some people kept insisting that CTA experiments were not properly controlled because the parametric results that were demonstrated differed from those in widely used experimental paradigms. CTA had been demonstrated with all appropriate controls (Revusky, 1968), but it took a decade for this foolishness to cease. Wilson continued this tradition by demanding proper controls for CAT. But he was luckier than his predecessors in his demand for proper controls because controls for the efficacy of alcoholism treatments are not as straightforward as controls for learning usually are. Recall the absence of good controls in MATCH and COMBINE.

What Wilson (1988, p. 510) considers necessary for proper controls for CAT, that they must be "treated concurrently with the chemical aversion group" (Wilson, 1988, p. 510), is not generally feasible. Nobody can be blind to the presence or absence of therapeutic sickness and the involvement of some placebo effects produced by the sickness itself cannot be excluded. If the two groups are treated at different locations, then there is another violation of statistical assumptions. There is no indication that Wilson understood this problem or that many of those who trumpet "evidenced-based" studies of medical treatments are aware of similar problems. In the "double-blind" studies of clinical psychopharmacology, side effects typically mark the active drug. Then there are such statistical dubiosities as double-blind studies with Antabuse, which I notice in the research literature. Double-blind procedures that are not really blind must be considered suspect.

Methodology should not be allowed to triumph over scientific substance in the manner Wilson advocates. Physicists did not deny the existence of subatomic particles when Werner Heisenberg showed measurement of their individual behaviors to be impossible. Thousands of instances of successful CAT treatment of alcoholism derived from basic scientific information should not be ignored because a double-blind study is impossible. I believe that both this section and the section on Behavioral Treatments for Alcoholism Are Not Supported amply demonstrate how protection of professional turf can trump scientific objectivity.

LATER WORK AT THE SCHICK-SHADEL HOSPITAL

The Schick-Shadel Hospital has continued in the tradition of Voegtlin and Lemere and advertises on a website, www.schick-shadel.com, from which its research papers cited here are available. This website describes the values inherent in the Schick-Shadel treatment for over half a century in a manner that a journal article cannot. It radiates self-confidence, particularly through the boast that its treatment is so beneficial that a consortium of former patients bought the Schick-Shadel Hospital in 2002. Schick-Shadel's description of alcoholism for the potential patient is similar to that of AA. Addiction develops with long-term use of alcohol among the susceptible, but it is a physical problem, not a mental problem. It is maintained through a craving for the rewarding effects of alcohol that becomes connected to external cues. CAT is regarded as a medical method of removing the craving for alcohol, but abstinence from alcohol and changes in lifestyle are still necessary. Although affiliation with alcohol support groups after treatment is recommended, the support group is not usually AA.

A testimonial on the Schick-Shadel website from Glenn Patch, who became a part owner, illustrates some patient attitudes: "I left a 28-day, 12-step program after eight days and entered Schick Shadel. I was impressed that the patients were not beaten down mentally and religion was not pushed down my throat. I completed the 10-day program and haven't had or wanted a drink. This is the only recovery center I know that uses the aversion method. I know it works." As indicated earlier, "12-step" refers to AA. The distaste for AA in Patch's testimonial was frequent among other testimonials on the website. In fact, among the unique advantages of the Schick-Shadel treatment enumerated on the website was "Not a 12-step based program." That the aversion treatment removed the craving for alcohol was another frequent theme in the testimonials.

At the Schick-Shadel Hospital, the patient is detoxified, if necessary, before treatment. The treatment itself is 10 days of hospitalization that includes five occasions at 2-day intervals in which drinking of alcoholic beverages is paired with emetine injection. A minority (about 10%–12%) of patients, not considered healthy enough for the stress of CAT, are administered painful electric shock to the arm instead of emetine. During the course of treatment, the patients receive counseling, family therapy, and other treatments characteristic of good specialized hospitalization for alcoholism. What is unusual is the use of sodium pentathol interviews on days when CAT is not administered. This method was developed in the Voegtlin–Lemere era. The interviews help the therapists identify areas in which the patient needs help. The patients are rehospitalized for booster treatments for 2-day periods on two occasions: about a month and 3 months after the original treatment. During each rehospitalization, the patients receive one CAT treatment, both group and individual counseling, and a sodium pentathol interview.

In general, the Schick-Shadel Hospital personnel detect no difference in treatment effectiveness between emetine and electrical shock (Smith & Frawley, 1993). I do not accept this as definitive because there is plenty of evidence, summarized by Elkins (1991a) and by Howard and Jenson (1990), that electric shock does not produce CTAs. The failure to find inferior results for electrical shock may be due to the selection of less healthy patients for this treatment. Such patients may be more prone to relinquish their alcoholism, particularly if the sickness has recently developed and become paired with alcohol drinking. Bernstein (1995) showed how the growth of some cancers can produce CTAs by causing a coincidence of sickness with eating. The Schick-Shadel Hospital undoubtedly provides excellent alcoholism treatment even without CAT. I do not know whether the electrical shock is helpful to the patients who receive it and respect the Schick-Shadel personnel too highly to dispute their opinion. But, if electrical shock is helpful, it is not through producing an aversion to the alcohol taste.

In passing, I was surprised to notice on the Schick-Shadel website that they use electric shock to treat needle addictions and do not use CAT. Presumably, the Schick-Shadel experience is that shock is better than CAT with needle addictions. Here again, the parallel with animal results is impressive. If rats are sedated through injection and a high dose of lithium is injected afterward, the sedative drug state does not become secondarily aversive. In fact, something like the opposite happens (Revusky, 1985a).

A Comparison of Schick-Shadel CAT Results with Minnesota Model Results

There were a number of good follow-up studies from Schick-Shadel, but the strongest study in methodological terms was by Smith et al. (1991). Its controls contained a condition Wilson (1988, p. 510) considered necessary for CAT, that patients in the control group must be "treated concurrently with the chemical aversion group." However, it avoided the statistical shortcoming in many ostensible double-blind studies when patients and staff know who receives the active drug on the basis of its side effects. It still did not adhere to the strictest statistical canons because the CAT patients and their controls were in different hospitals.

In a study that matched all patients in almost every conceivable way, they used a database from addiction treatment facilities then called "The Chemical Abuse/Addiction Treatment Outcome Registry" (CATOR). Thirty-four treatment facilities, including Schick-Shadel, belonged to CATOR. Shadel was the only CATOR facility in Seattle, while CAT was not available in the other cities where CATOR facilities were located. This reduced the potential contamination of the results by self-selection in which highly motivated patients would select the rigors of CAT more than less motivated patients.

The CATOR facilities (other than Schick-Shadel) had inpatient treatment programs ranging from 3 to 4 weeks, about twice as long as the initial hospitalization at Schick-Shadel. They were designed to prepare patients for a long-term commitment to AA. Such treatment is based on the Minnesota model and related to the TSF treatment in Project MATCH. Vaillant (1995, p. 361), the doyen of life-span students of alcoholism, has conjectured that Minnesota model treatments are very nearly the most effective hospital treatments for alcoholism.

Early in treatment, both Schick-Shadel patients and patients from the other programs were asked to agree to be followed up. From this point on, statistical consultants working for CATOR handled all data and follow-ups. There were 17 variables used to match Schick-Shadel patients with other CATOR patients: gender, age, marital status, education, employment status, performance problem, missed work, lost job, alcohol use pattern, marijuana use, cocaine use, prior treatment for alcoholism, psychiatric hospitalization in past year, medication for psychiatric problems, last alcohol use, ethnicity, and detoxification admittance in past year. Each patient was given a digital score on each variable, 1 or 2 for dichotomous variables such as gender, and up to 6 (in the case of age) for other variables. An exact match for each of 249 Schick-Shadel patients was found among patients at the other CATOR hospitals. The latter were called CATOR-Matches.

Table 21.6 shows that the Schick-Shadel patients reduced their drinking more than the CATOR-Matches both in months 1–6 and in months 7–12 after treatment. The assessment of whether the better Schick-Shadel results were due to CAT must be flawed by the strictest statistical standards because the patients were in different locations. But it is reasonable to suppose that the main factor in the better Schick-Shadel results is CAT. Admittedly, it is logically conceivable that sodium pentathol interviewing, which was only conducted at Schick-Shadel, or something about Seattle itself, had fabulous and previously unnoticed effects on alcoholism.

In all events, any person in need of hospitalization for alcoholism would probably be best off to prefer the shorter Schick-Shadel program to the other programs if he does not wish prolonged involvement with AA. A lead article in *Time Magazine* (Lemonick, 2007) indicates: "evidence is building to support the 90-day rehabilitation model, which was stumbled upon by AA (new members are advised to attend one meeting per day for the first 90 days) and is the duration of a typical stint in a drug-treatment program." This mentions only the first 90 days, where AA typically involves a lifetime commitment. In contrast, the Schick-Shadel program involves 14 days of hospitalization (including booster treatments but not including drying out) in the course of about 100 days after treatment begins.

Table 21.7 shows the beneficial effects of booster treatments. Similar results had previously been reported in Shadel and Schick-Shadel studies (e.g., Voegtlin et al., 1941). The number of booster treatments is self-selected so that, as previously indicated, this comparison is only suggestive.

As might be expected from the difference in ideology between the Schick-Shadel treatment and the AA-oriented treatments in the other CATOR hospitals, the CATOR-Match patients made more use of support groups than did the Schick-Shadel patients. Participation in AA during the first 6 months after treatment was 71% for CATOR-Matches and 22% for Schick-Shadel patients. Among CATOR-Match patients, greater participation in AA was associated with higher abstinence than for the remaining CATOR patients. Not so for the Schick-Shadel patients relative to the other Schick-Shadel patients. For patients who

Table 21.6 Alcohol Relapse in Cohorts of Patients.

	Schick-Shadel (%)	CATOR-Matches (%)
1–6 months after treatment, 249 patients per group: p < 0.01 (chi-square) between groups		
Complete abstinence	85	72
Drinking less than once a month	4	8
Drinking more than once a month	11	20
7–12 months after treatment; 205–207 patients per group after attrition: p < 0.05 (chi-square) between groups		
Complete abstinence	86	74
Drinking less than once a month	3	6
Drinking more than once a month	11	20

Source: From Smith et al. (1991).

Table 21.7 Total Abstinence as a Function of Booster Treatments in the Schick-Shadel Cohort.

	For 6 Months (%)	For 12 Months (%)
No booster	67	47
1 booster	64	60
2 boosters	92	86

Source: From Smith et al. (1991).

Note: In each column, the increase in abstinence with increased booster treatments yielded $p < 0.0001$.

attended AA once a week, the Schick-Shadel and CATOR-Match results were similar. This suggests that patients with personalities and religious convictions amenable to AA do not benefit from CAT as much as patients who dislike AA methods.

A study otherwise modeled on that of Smith et al. (1991) could easily determine which patients are best suited for CAT and which patients may be better suited for the Minnesota model CATOR treatments on the basis of personality tests, religious preferences, ethnic identities, and so on. At the same time, it could be determined in the same study at little additional expense whether the presence of pretreatment alcohol aversions in the patients affects the efficacy of CAT.

The same study might also follow up one of the few successful matches in Project MATCH: that patients high in anger did better with the short MET behavioral intervention than with the other longer psychotherapies. W. R. Miller and Longabaugh (2003, p. 212) found this "consistent with the expectation that the nonconfrontational approach of MET would differentially benefit angry clients by diminishing their resistance." Given that the MATCH treatments were not beneficial at best, it is more likely that MET differentially benefited some patients because it involved fewer sessions (a maximum of four) than the other therapies. Patients high in anger are probably more impatient than other patients and hence differentially benefited by less behavioral intervention. Such patients might be better suited for CAT than for Minnesota model treatment of the type administered in the CATOR-Matches.

POTENTIAL IMPROVEMENTS TO CAT BASED ON CTA RESEARCH AFTER THE WORK OF VOEGTLIN ET AL.

As previously indicated, since the past evidence indicated that CAT was effective and congruent

with basic research, my bottom line was never comparisons of CAT with other alcoholism treatments. If the Schick-Shadel results had not been found to be superior to the CATOR-Matches, it would still remain true that CAT is based on the most potent known type of learning. The proper direction would then be to improve CAT on the basis of CTA data.

To begin the process of improving CAT, Revusky (1973) summarized relevant CTA findings obtained after the work of Voegtlin and Lemere. With one major exception, these findings did not suggest any major changes in the Shadel treatments. Conceivably, they might have prevented practitioners from making countertherapeutic changes in the Shadel procedure on the basis of incorrect beliefs about CTAs. First, Revusky's three minor points that supported the Shadel procedure are the following:

1. The alcohol beverages should be swallowed during CAT, not just tasted because that produces a much stronger taste aversion (Domjan & Wilson, 1972). The amount consumed need not be great.
2. There should be care that the target alcoholic beverage not be consumed after the CAT sickness begins since this might result in association of the alcohol flavor with alleviation of the sickness. The belief that temporal contiguity between the CS and the US was essential for conditioning was so strongly ingrained that counterproductive attempts were made to insure such contiguity in CAT. Such efforts could result in the alcohol taste being experienced while the sickness was at or past its peak and thus become associated with diminution of the sickness. This potential problem had been noted clinically by Hammersley (1957) and was repeatedly confirmed in later CAT work (Elkins, 1991a).
3. To prevent interfering associations that might weaken the clinically important aversion to a particular alcoholic beverage, only one alcoholic substance should be consumed in each CAT session and the session should be temporally separated by many hours from the consumption of other substances.

The major new contribution from later animal research was the suggestion that lithium might be a more effective aversive US than emetine. Voegtlin et al. (1940) selected emetine because it is relatively safe and very effective in producing CTAs. But it has a very long biological half-life, which is a disadvantage when aversive effects are needed for only a few hours to produce near-maximal CTAs. In the CTA literature, lithium had become the preferred toxic agent. In humans, lithium is used for the treatment of mania in almost a mirror image of its short-term use for CAT. During the treatment of mania, the blood level of lithium is gradually increased to a level that controls mania and maintained, sometimes for life. The rise in lithium blood is made gradual to avoid the acute sickness that produces the therapeutic effect in CAT. The lithium is administered frequently and in a slow-release form because its biological life is short. The blood lithium level must be monitored because the gap between the therapeutic blood level for treating mania and a dangerous dose is uncomfortably small, but this danger mainly involves long-term administration. Short lasting rises of blood lithium level, the desiderata for CAT, are not particularly dangerous (Boland et al., 1978). In my laboratory, thousands of healthy rats have been subjected to high doses of lithium every 2 or 3 days without any deaths attributable to the lithium. I have had deaths from apomorphine, a drug once used in CAT, and from emetine although these drugs were used in only two experiments.

Revusky and Gorry (1973) compared the capacity of apomorphine, emetine, and lithium USs to produce CTAs in rats and squirrel monkeys. Equating the doses of these drugs for effectiveness is not as easy as equating apples and oranges for caloric content but these authors did their best. They found the doses of these drugs used in medical practice and expressed them in terms of the number of milligrams per kilogram of body weight. They then determined the magnitudes of CTAs in rats and squirrel monkeys produced by multiples of these doses. These human doses were 0.15 mg/kg of apomorphine hydrochloride, 1.0 mg/kg of emetine hydrochloride, and 31.8 mg/kg of lithium chloride. The lithium dose was based on the daily dose for chronic administration. The emetine dose was based on the package insert; I later discovered that the emetine hydrochloride dose at the Schick-Shadel Hospital was 85 mg (Howard, 2001), about 1.2 mg/kg. Although this was a reasonable way to compare the aversive effectiveness of the three US drugs, it should be noted that with small animals and children, a dose equated to a human adult

dose in terms of mg/kg will produce weaker pharmacological effects (Augsberger, 1962). This is because the site of drug action is likely to be larger relative to total body weight. Hence the US doses used by Revusky and Gorry (1973) in their animal experiments were lower in effectiveness than might be implied by their designations in terms of the human dose.

First I will describe the rat experiment. Water was removed for 2 days and the rats were allowed to drink 0.2% (weight/volume) saccharin solution for 15 min. As they began to drink, the rats were injected intraperitoneally, either with a US drug or with a control injection. After a day, they were allowed 2 days of free access to unflavored water. Then testing began with continuous free access to both unflavored water and the saccharin solution for up to 35 days. Preference for saccharin was defined as the amount of saccharin solution consumed divided by the total fluid intake.

Figure 21.1 shows the saccharin preferences of rats subjected to CTA learning with USs of different multiples of the human dose during hours 5–29 of the saccharin test. Emetine produced stronger aversions than apomorphine, as Voegtlin et al. (1940) had previously noted for CAT, but lithium was still more effective. Because these differences are very large, no reasonable way of equating the US doses for the different drugs should change the direction of these results.

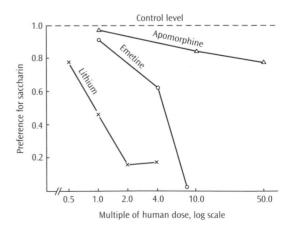

Figure 21.1. Saccharin preferences of rats for 5–29 h of a test trial. On the single acquisition trial, the rats had been injected with different multiples of the human doses of different drugs after drinking saccharin solution. From Revusky and Gorry (1973).

Figure 21.2 shows the results over all test days for both the emetine doses and the lithium doses. Of course, the aversions would not have lasted as long if the rats had not had the choice of drinking unflavored water. Pohl, Revusky, and Mellor (1979) confirmed the superiority of lithium over emetine as an aversive agent when ethanol solution was the CS taste. The rats had been made familiar with the ethanol in a method designed, as much as feasible, to approximate human alcoholism.

The squirrel monkeys were treated differently. For 7 days, they received 20 min of daily access to unflavored water. The next day, they were allowed 20 min of access to 15% (w/v) sugar solution. Thirty minutes later, the bottles were removed; the monkeys were injected intraperitoneally with the human dose of apomorphine, emetine, or lithium. Controls were injected with normal saline. On Days 11 and 12, after 2 days of 20-min access to unflavored water, the monkeys were given 20-min choice tests between the sucrose solution and unflavored water. Table 21.8 shows that the emetine and apomorphine groups did not show significant CTAs, but the lithium group did. Remember that what Revusky and Gorry (1973) designated as the "human dose" was less potent pharmacologically in such small animals as rats and squirrel monkeys than it would be in humans.

When the lithium dose shown in Table 21.8 was doubled to 63.6 mg/kg, Gorry and Ober (1970) found that the mean sucrose preference for the lithium-dosed monkeys was 0.18 compared to 0.66 for the controls. Apomorphine and emetine were not used.

CAT WORK OF BOLAND ET AL. (1978)

The excellent reviews of CAT by Elkins (1991a) and by Howard and Jenson (1990) are better than

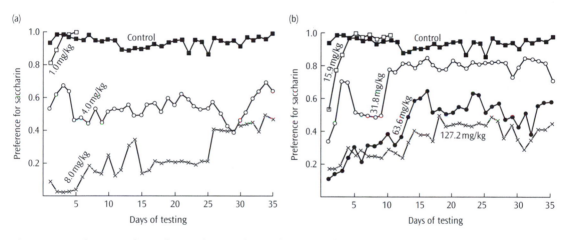

Figure 21.2. Preferences of rats for saccharin solution during 35 days (or less for some groups) of a saccharin preference test as a function of different US doses of (a) emetine hydrochloride or (b) lithium chloride. From Revusky and Gorry (1973).

Table 21.8 Test Preferences for Sucrose Solution in Squirrel Monkeys Following a Single Learning Trial with Various Illness-Inducing Agents.

Toxic Agent and Dosage	Day of Testing	
	1	2
Apomorphine hydrochloride: 0.15 mg/kg	0.66	0.78
Emetine hydrochloride: 1.0 mg/kg	0.71	0.80
Lithium chloride: 31.8 mg/kg	0.51	0.56
Control (no drug)	0.80	0.78

Source: Revusky and Gorry (1973).

I could do unless I plagiarized from them. They mention clinical reports of successful CATs that I will not mention here. Nor will I describe here the work in the Shadel Hospital by Howard (2001) which was superimposed on the Shadel procedures. My main concern is with how CAT has been and can be supported by basic work in CTA, and these points are more easily made in terms of the work at the Shadel Hospital and that of Boland et al. (1978).

The administration of treatments in the latter study was done by Fred Boland, who had once been a problem drinker and was then a master's student in psychology, and Clive Mellor, a practicing biological psychiatrist with a distinguished research history.

The 25 patients treated with CAT came from consecutive admissions to the psychiatric ward of a general hospital in Newfoundland, Canada. Two had refused the treatment. An additional patient died the night before he was due to receive his first lithium treatment. (This frightened Mellor and he later confessed to me, somewhat guiltily, that he was relieved to learn the man had not been subjected to a lithium trial before he died.) No patients were excluded, but none evidenced brain damage, psychosis after detoxification, or other medical contraindications, which might have resulted in exclusion.

The patients were alcoholics with a very poor prognosis for recovery. All of them had "a history of increased tolerance to and craving for alcohol with two or more of the following symptoms; tremors, epileptic fits, or delirium tremens" (Boland et al., 1978). Among them, 64% were admitted as emergency patients (sometimes by the police), 68% were unemployed compared to about 50% in MATCH (Zweben et al., 2003, p. 64), 27% in COMBINE (Anton, O'Malley, et al., 2006, p. 2008), and about 12% (Howard (2001) to 30% (Smith et al., 1991) at Schick-Shadel. Probably due to the close family structure in Newfoundland, 76% lived with a wife or with family. The higher unemployment rate among the Boland et al. patients was probably partly due to the then-poor Newfoundland economy and the generous Canadian welfare system. However, taking all factors into account, these Newfoundland patients had poorer prognoses than those in other studies of alcoholism treatment. Nathan (1985) claimed that CAT studies involved patients with the best prognoses for recovery. He was clearly wrong in the case of the patients treated by Boland et al. (1978), although he referred to their paper.

The control procedure was citrated calcium carbimide treatment, a procedure with a deterrent rationale similar to that of Antabuse. Like Smith et al. (1991), Boland et al. (1978) understood that a valid double-blind control procedure was impossible for CAT. The control procedures did not begin until 6 months after the CAT treatments were completed to allow staff expectations about CAT to dissipate. The control patients were drawn in the same manner and from the same hospital population as the CAT patients and were pretty much statistically identical to them. However, they were hospitalized for a mean of 13.9 days in contrast to 20.0 days for the CAT patients because their treatment was shorter in duration. Although this control procedure was superior to what has been typical in treatment studies, such as COMBINE, its role was not to test the already established value of CAT. It was to aid in assessment of the desirability of lithium as a US for CAT.[4]

The lithium preparation was lithium carbonate. It is pharmacologically equivalent to lithium chloride when the amounts of lithium in both compounds are equated. Lithium carbonate preparations are meant for use to control mania. They are formulated to be slow acting to allow a gradual rise in blood lithium to a therapeutic level for mania without triggering much of the sickness that is the goal of CAT. The desideratum for CAT is a fast-acting preparation. Mellor found a gelatin capsule with relatively fast-acting lithium carbonate in powder form and reformulated it for CAT by putting pinpricks at each end of the capsule so that the drug would dissolve more quickly. The CAT treatments were administered before breakfast to fasting patients to prevent breakfast and mouthwash flavors from becoming associated with the lithium sickness and interfering with the aversion to the alcoholic beverages. The Hammersley (1957) procedure was followed; that is, alcoholic beverages were not tasted at the peak of sickness so that they would not become associated with recovery from sickness. This was probably also the procedure at the Shadel hospital.

Mellor tested blood serum levels of lithium. These never reached a dangerous level and, in fact, remained below the level used to control mania. It may be recalled that the use of lithium for control of mania is continuous, often for a lifetime, in contrast to the intermittent use of lithium in CAT. Mellor also tested for urinary lithium excretion.

There were approximately six conditioning sessions spaced 2 days apart and no booster sessions. In contrast, recall that at Schick-Shadel, five initial sessions were followed by two later booster sessions. The investigators developed a sickness-rating scale to measure the effectiveness of the lithium treatments. The doses used were often too low for maximal aversive effectiveness and sometimes were ineffective at producing emesis. The first 9 patients were started at 1200 mg of lithium carbonate, which did not produce satisfactory sickness reactions, and the remaining 16 patients were started at 1500 mg. These doses were then raised for the patients in the course of later sessions depending on how sick they got. The limit for the first 15 patients was 1800 mg on the basis of work by Trautner, Morris, Noack, and Gershon (1955), who found 1200–1500 mg of lithium carbonate to be near the threshold for sickness. This was very close to the human dose of lithium defined by Revusky and Gorry (1973). For the remaining patients, Mellor felt confident enough to go up to 2100 mg and two patients who were champion lithium excreters were dosed with 2400 mg in late treatment sessions. Blood serum levels of lithium indicated that the administered doses of lithium carbonate were not harmful. No harm produced by lithium was found in any patient during the 6 months after treatment.

The 6-month follow-up was based on personal contact with the patients and at least one informant. Such good follow-up was possible in part because Newfoundland, where the work was conducted, is a small and isolated place compared to the United States. Overall, the percentage of CAT patients abstinent after 6 months was 36% while this percentage for control patients was 12%. This difference was statistically significant at the 0.05 level. The abstinence rate among the CAT patients was not high, but, as the control results show, the patients had far poorer prognoses. Note, by the way, how much larger in actual magnitude this effect is than those reported for Project COMBINE in the section on Behavioral Treatments for Alcoholism Are Not Supported.

If the patients who did not exhibit satisfactory sickness during conditioning were omitted, the abstinence rate increased to 47.4%. Cannon,

Baker, Gino, and Nathan (1986) confirmed the relationship between the intensity of sickness in CAT and the effectiveness of treatment. All in all, these results supported the hypothesis that lithium might be a more effective CAT agent than emetine since the lithium patients had far poorer prognoses than the Schick-Shadel patients.

These results are likely to understate the potential benefits of lithium-based CAT. Boland et al. (1978) began with rather low lithium doses since it was the first use of lithium for CAT. Insofar as these doses were not effective, they ought to have interfered with later conditioning (Braveman, 1975). It also would have been better if there was available a formulation of lithium designed to be fast acting, not slow acting for the treatment of mania. The lack of booster treatments was another defect of the Boland et al. (1978) procedure. Still another probable shortcoming is that it was conducted in the psychiatric ward of a general hospital, not a specialized alcoholism treatment facility such as the Schick-Shadel or other CATOR hospitals.

The work did not continue. Mellor was in the process of switching hospitals after this work and probably did not wish to become an alcoholism specialist.

SUMMARY, CONCLUSIONS, AND RECOMMENDATIONS

The section titled Behavioral Treatments for Alcoholism Are Not Supported showed that the most definitive studies of the use of behavioral interventions to treat alcoholism yielded negative results. The direction of the data suggested that behavioral interventions were countertherapeutic. But this evidence was misinterpreted by investigators professionally involved with behavioral interventions. The earlier publication record in favor of behavioral interventions may be attributed to publication bias. The next section on CTA as a Basis for Further Investigation showed that CTA is an excellent preclinical basis for the development of alcoholism treatments. The following section on The First Highly Believable CAT Treatment Results illustrated the strategy of basing medical treatment for alcoholism (CAT) on the interaction of basic science (Pavlovian conditioning) and clinical work as developed in the 1930s and 1940s. This section and the section titled

Alcohol is Simultaneously Rewarding and Aversive (Table 21.5) showed that, although experimental CTA procedures were not developed until long after the development of CAT on Pavlovian principles, CAT is a form of CTA. The following section (A Parade Example of Ideological Biases that Have Interfered with Acceptance of CAT) illustrated the bias against CAT by some of those committed to behavioral intervention approaches. The section on Later Work at the Schick-Shadel Hospital demonstrated the continuing success of CAT and its superiority to a similar hospital-based AA approach except for patients very amenable to the AA approach. The next section (Potential Improvements to CAT Based on CTA Research after the Work of Voegtlin et al.) described CTA work designed to reinstate the interaction of basic science with the treatment of alcoholism and indicates that lithium may be a better US for CAT than emetine. Finally, the section titled CAT Work of Boland et al. (1978) described preliminary clinical work that supports the possibility that lithium CAT is superior to emetine CAT.

The achievement of behavioral intervention psychologists and social workers in drowning out information about more effective therapies is apparent in a recent *Time Magazine* article (Lemonick, 2007): "AA succeeds about 20% of the time, and other forms of therapy, including behavioral therapy, do no better." In fact, CAT and other therapies not involving much use of behavioral intervention do better (see the section on The First Highly Believable CAT Treatment Results; Table 21.6), even allowing for the likelihood that these patients usually are better candidates for treatment. But what can journalists do other than rely on sources among known experts?

Given bureaucratic inertia and momentum, behavioral intervention psychologists and social workers will continue their harmful influences on recommendations for the treatment of alcoholism as illustrated in the sections Behavioral Treatments for Alcoholism Are Not Supported and A Parade Example of Ideological Biases That Have Interfered with Acceptance of CAT. I wish there was a way to reinstate the type of interplay between basic research and treatment illustrated in the work of Voegtlin and Lemere (see the section on The First Highly Believable CAT Treatment Results) that has been supplanted by treatment–comparison research highlighted by mindless adherence to statistical dogmas (Gigerenzer, 2004).

A study might be conducted at the Schick-Shadel Hospital to help reinstate this earlier interplay through a comparison between the efficacy of emetine and lithium CAT treatments. Unlike nearly all other alcoholism treatment studies, suggestion effects produced by each treatment would be equivalent and hence such a study would be more statistically valid than other alcoholism treatment studies. But I am not optimistic Schick-Shadel will do this because emetine CAT works well and there is risk in medical innovation as illustrated by Mellor's fright when a patient died before he was scheduled for lithium treatment; see the section on CAT Work of Boland et al. (1978). Also, the Schick-Shadel Hospital is run on a business basis and is only peripherally involved with treatment–comparisons.

Acknowledgments   Bow Tong Lett carefully edited this chapter often working harder than I did in the original writing. R. B. Cutler very patiently guided me through the many thickets of clinical research on alcoholism treatment. He also criticized early drafts of this chapter and improved it. I am grateful for the careful and sympathetic editing by Steve Reilly that substantially improved this chapter. A second anonymous review was also helpful. H. K. Taukulis read a very early version of this chapter and sent me a CARE package of research chapters. Graham Skanes and Mike Lavin also read a very early draft of this chapter. The long-distance library facilities of Memorial University were very helpful.

Notes

1. CAT is not to be confused with Antabuse or citrated calcium carbimide treatments, in which there is no attempt to make alcoholic beverages distasteful through systematic conditioning. These are deterrent treatments in which the patient is administered a compound believed to have dangerous effects in synergy with alcohol; the patient is told of these effects and is warned not to indulge.

2. *Ex post facto* manipulation of the data in this way should not have been necessary in a study with as many patients as COMBINE. There was an inconsistency in that the acamprosate data were not used in the comparisons of Table 21.2. If the acamprosate data were included, the results for Group CBI-only relative to the other groups would have appeared even poorer than reported: $p < 0.01$ relative to MM only.

3. As Steve Reilly told me, Grigson, Twining, Freet, Wheeler, and Geddes (Chapter 5) have an alternative explanation for this. The causes of these effects are not critical in the present chapter because the similarity between animals and men remains. There may be reasons to doubt Garcia's terminology (Grant, 1987), but I like its continuity with the Pavlovian tradition.

4. Peter Nathan claimed orally at a conference in 1985 on CTAs that Boland et al. (1978) did not use a proper control procedure. He did not include the objection in the published version of his paper (Nathan, 1985) and cited, without comment, many other papers that did not have any sort of control procedure. Since it seems apparent that both Nathan and G. T. Wilson were unfairly hostile to the work of Boland et al. (1978), I point out that both were associated with the very heavily funded Rutgers Center for Alcoholism Research and produced no improvements in the treatment of alcoholism. Boland et al. were not funded at all but conducted the study as part of Clive Mellor's hospital practice.

References

Allen, J. P., Babor, T. F., Mattson, M. E., & Kadden, M. E. (2003). Matching alcoholism treatment to client heterogeneity: The genesis of Project MATCH. In T. F. Babor & F. K. Del Boca (Eds.), *Treatment matching in alcoholism* (pp. 3–14). Cambridge: Cambridge University Press.

Anton, R. F., Miller, W. R., O'Malley, S. S., Zweben, A., & Hosking, J. D. (2006). Reply to letters about combined pharmacotherapies and behavioral interventions for alcohol dependence. *Journal of the American Medical Association, 296,* 1728–1729.

Anton, R. F., O'Malley, S. S., Ciraulo, D. A., Cisler, R. A., Couper, D., Donovan, D. M., et al. (2006). Combined pharmacotherapies and behavioral interventions for alcohol dependence: The COMBINE study: A randomized controlled trial. *Journal of the American Medical Association, 295,* 2003–2017.

Augsberger, A. (1962). Old and new rules for dosage determination in paediatrics. *Triangle, 5,* 200–207.

Babor, T. F., & Del Boca, F. K. (Eds.). (2003). *Treatment matching in alcoholism.* Cambridge: Cambridge University Press.

Bandura, A. (1969). *Principles of behavior modification.* Boston, MA: Holt.

Bernstein, I. L. (1995). Neural mediation of food aversions and anorexia produced by tumor necrosis factor and tumors. *Neuroscience and Behavioral Reviews, 53,* 177–181.

Boland, F. J. Mellor, C. S., & Revusky, S. (1978). Chemical aversion treatment of alcoholism: Lithium as the aversive agent. *Behavior Research and Therapy, 16,* 401–409.

Bower, B. (1997). Alcoholics synonymous: Heavy drinkers of all stripes may get comparable help from a variety of therapies. *Science News, 151,* 62–63,

Braveman, N. S. (1975). Formation of taste aversions in rats following prior exposure to sickness. *Learning and Motivation, 6,* 512–524.

Cannon, D. S., Baker, T. B., Gino, A., & Nathan, P. E. (1986). Alcohol-aversion therapy: Relationship between strength of aversion and abstinence. *Journal of Consulting and Clinical Psychology, 49,* 360–368.

Carman, B., Magro, A., Munoz, A., & Maria, J. A. (2004). Efficacy and safety of naltrexone and acamprosate in the treatment of alcohol dependence: A systematic review. *Addiction, 99,* 811–828.

COMBINE Study Research Group. (2003). Testing combined pharmacotherapies and behavioral interventions in alcohol dependence: Rationale and methods. *Alcoholism: Clinical and Experimental Research, 27,* 1107–1122.

Cook, C. C. H. (1988a). The Minnesota Model in the management of drug and alcohol dependence: Miracle, method or myth? Part I. The philosophy and the programme *British Journal of Addiction, 83,* 625–634.

Cook, C. C. H. (1988b). The Minnesota Model in the management of drug and alcohol dependence: Miracle, method or myth? Part II. Evidence and conclusions. *British Journal of Addiction, 83,* 735–738.

Coombes, S., Revusky, S., & Lett, B. T. (1980). Long delay taste aversion learning in an unpoisoned rat: Exposure to a poisoned rat as the conditioned stimulus. *Learning and Motivation, 28(11),* 256–266.

Cutler, R. B., & Fishbain, D. (2005). Are alcoholism treatments effective? The Project MATCH data. *BMC Public Health, 5,* 75. Retrieved October 26, 2006, from http://www.biomedcentral.com/4171-2458/5/75

Del Boca, F. K., Mattson, M. E., Fuller, R., & Babor, T. F. (2003). Planning a multisite matching trial: Organizational structure and research design. In T. F. Babor & F. K. Del Boca (Eds.), *Treatment matching in alcoholism* (pp. 15–28). Cambridge: Cambridge University Press.

Dietz, M. N., & Capretta, P. J. (1967). Modification of sugar and sugar–saccharin preference in rats as a function of electrical shock to the Mouth. *Proceedings of the 75th Annual Convention of the American Psychological Association, 12,* 161–162.

Domjan, M., & Wilson, N. E. (1972). Contributions of ingestive behaviors to taste-aversion learning in the rat. *Journal of Comparative and Physiological Psychology, 80,* 403–412.

Donovan, D. M., Carroll, K. M., Kadden, R. M., DiClemente, C. C., & Rounsaville, B. J. (2003). Therapies for matching: Selection, development, implementation, and costs. In T. F. Babor & F. K. Del Boca (Eds.), *Treatment matching in alcoholism* (pp. 42–61). Cambridge: Cambridge University Press.

Elkins, R. L. (1991a). An appraisal of chemical aversion (emetic therapy) approaches to alcoholism treatment. *Behavior Research and Therapy, 29,* 387–413.

Elkins, R. L. (1991b). Chemical aversion (emetic therapy) treatment of alcoholism: Further comments. *Behavior Research and Therapy, 29,* 421–428.

Garcia, J. (1989). Food for Tolman: Cognition and cathexis in concert. In T. Archer & I. Nilsson (Eds.), *Aversion, avoidance, and anxiety: Perspectives on aversively motivated behavior* (pp. 45–85). Hillsdale, NJ: Lawrence Erlbaum.

Garcia, J., & Ervin, F. R. (1968). A neuropsychological approach to the appropriateness of signals and the specificity of reinforcers. *Communications in Behavioral Biology, 1*(Part A), 389–415.

Garcia, J., Kimeldorf, D. J., & Koelling, R. A. (1955). Conditioned aversion to saccharin resulting from exposure to gamma-radiation. *Science, 122,* 157–158.

Garcia, J., & Koelling, R. A. (1966). Relation of cue to consequence in avoidance learning. *Psychonomic Science, 4,* 123–124.

Gerstner, H. B. (1960). Reaction to short-term radiation in man. *Annual Review of Medicine, 11,* 289–302.

Gigerenzer, G. (2004). Mindless statistics. *Journal of Socio-Economics, 33,* 587–606.

Gorry, T., & Ober, S. E. (1970). *Stimulus characteristics of learning over long delays in monkeys.* Paper delivered at the 10th annual meeting of the Psychonomic Society, San Antonio, TX.

Grant, V. L. (1987). Do conditioned taste aversions result from activation of emetic mechanisms? *Psychopharmacology (Berlin), 93,* 405–415.

Green, K. F., & Garcia, J. (1971). Recuperation from illness: Flavor enhancement for rats. *Science, 173,* 749–751.

Hammersley, O. W. (1957). Conditioned reflex therapy. In R. S. Wallerstein (Ed.), *Hospital treatment of alcoholism.* Topeka, KS: Menninger Clinic Monographs.

Howard, M. O. (2001). Pharmacological aversion treatment of alcohol dependence. I. Production and prediction of conditioned taste aversion. *American Journal of Drug and Alcohol Abuse, 27,* 561–585.

Howard, M. O., & Jenson, M. O. (1990). Chemical aversion treatment of alcohol dependence. I. Validity of Current Criticisms. *International Journal of the Addictions, 25,* 1227–1262.

Institute of Medicine (U.S.). (1990). *Broadening the base of treatment for alcohol problems.* Washington, DC: National Academy.

Ionescu, E., & Buresova, O. (1977). Failure to elicit conditioned taste aversion by severe poisoning. *Pharmacology, Biochemistry, and Behavior, 6,* 251–254.

Jonas, J. M., & Chabac, S. (2006). Letter about combined pharmacotherapies and behavioral interventions for alcohol dependence. *Journal of the American Medical Association, 296,* 1727.

Kiefer, F., & Mann, K. (2006). Letter about combined pharmacotherapies and behavioral interventions for alcohol dependence. *Journal of the American Medical Association, 296,* 1727–1728.

Lavin, M., Freise, B., & Coombes, S. (1980). Transferred flavor aversions in adult rats. *Behavioral and Neural Biology, 28,* 15–31.

Lemere, F. (1986). Aversion treatment of alcoholism: Some reminiscences. *British Journal of Addiction, 82,* 257–258.

Lemere, F., & Voegtlin, W. L. (1950). An evaluation of the aversion treatment of alcoholism. *Quarterly Journal of Studies on Alcohol, 11,* 199–204.

Lemonick, M. D. (2007). The science of addiction. *Time Magazine (US edition), 170,* 42–48.

Lett, B. T. (1985). The painlike effect of gallamine and naloxone differs from sickness induced by lithium chloride. *Behavioral Neuroscience, 99,* 146–150.

Logue, A. W. (1985). Conditioned food aversion learning in humans. *Annals of the New York Academy of Sciences, 443,* 316–329.

Longabaugh, R., Zweben, A., LoCastro, J. S., & Miller, W. R. (2005). Origins, issues, and options in the development of the Combined Behavioral Intervention. *Journal of Studies on Alcohol* (Suppl. 15), 179–187.

Mackintosh, N. J. (1974). *The psychology of animal learning.* London: Academic Press.

Mcintosh, H., & Terry, R. M. (1977). Retention of latent inhibition in a taste aversion paradigm. *Bulletin of the Psychonomic Society, 9,* 411–412.

Miller, E. C., Dvorak, B. A., & Turner, D. W. (1960). A method of creating aversion to alcohol by reflex conditioning in a group setting. *Quarterly Journal of Studies on Alcohol, 21,* 424–431.

Miller, W. R. (1998). Why do people change addictive behavior? The 1996 Archibald Lecture. *Addiction, 93*, 163–172.

Miller, W. R. (2005). Are alcoholism treatments effective? The Project MATCH data. *BMC Public Health, 5*, 76. Retrieved October 26, 2006 from http://www.biomedcentral.com/4171-2458/5/76

Miller, W. R., & Longabaugh, R. (2003). Summary and conclusions. In T. F. Babor & F. K. Del Boca (Eds.), *Treatment matching in alcoholism* (pp. 207–221). Cambridge: Cambridge University Press.

Miller, W. R., Wilbourne, P. L., & Hettema, J. E. (2003). What works? A summary of alcohol treatment outcome research. In R. K. Hester & W. R. Miller (Eds.), *Handbook of alcoholism treatment approaches* (pp. 13–63). Boston, MA: Allyn and Bacon.

Nachman, M., & Hartley, P. L. (1975). Role of illness in producing learned taste aversions in rats. A comparison of several rodenticides. *Journal of Comparative and Physiological Psychology, 89*, 1010–1018.

Nathan, P. E. (1985). Aversion therapy in the treatment of alcoholism. *Annals of the New York Academy of Sciences, 443*, 357–364.

National Institute of Alcohol Abuse and Alcoholism (NIAAA). (1996). *News release: NIAAA reports project MATCH main findings.* Retrieved November 2, 2006, from http://www.niaaa.nih.gov/NewsEvents?newsReleases.match.htm

Pavlov, I. P. (1932). The reply of a physiologist to psychologists, *Psychological Review, 39*, 91–127.

Pettinati, H. M., Weiss, R. D., Dundon, W., Miller, W. R., Donovan, D., Ernst, D. B., et al. (2005). A structured approach to medical management: A psychosocial intervention to support pharmacotherapy in the treatment of alcohol dependence. *Journal of Studies on Alcohol* (Suppl. 15), 170–178.

Pettinati, H. M., Zweben, A., & M. E. Mattson (Eds.). (2005). The COMBINE study: Conceptual, methodological and practical issues in a clinical trial that combined medication and behavioral treatments. *Journal of Studies on Alcohol* (Suppl. 15), 1–207.

Pohl, R. W., Revusky, S. H., & Mellor, C. S. (1980). Drugs employed inn the treatment of alcoholism: Rat data suggest they are unnecessarily severe. *Behavior Research and Therapy, 18*, 71–78.

Rachman, S., &Teasdale, J. (1969). *Aversion therapy and the behavior disorders.* Coral Gables, FL: University of Miami Press.

Reicher, M. A., & Holman, E. W. (1977). Location preference and flavor aversion reinforced by amphetamine in rats. *Animal Learning and Behavior, 5*, 343–346.

Revusky, S. (1968). Aversion to sucrose produced by contingent X-irradiation: Temporal and dosage parameters. *Journal of comparative and Physiological Psychology, 65*, 17–22.

Revusky, S. (1971). The role of interference in association over a delay. In H. James & W. Honig (Eds.), *Animal memory* (pp. 155–213). New York: Academic Press.

Revusky, S. (1973). Some laboratory paradigms for the chemical aversion treatment of alcoholism. *Journal of Behavior Therapy and Experimental Psychiatry, 4*, 15–17.

Revusky, S. (1984). Associative predispositions. In P. Marler & H. S. Terrace (Eds.), *The biology of learning* (pp. 447–460). Berlin: Springer.

Revusky, S. (1985a). Drug interactions measured through taste aversion procedures with an emphasis on medical implications. *Annals of the New York Academy of Sciences, 443*, 250–271.

Revusky, S. (1985b). The general process approach to animal learning. In T. D. Johnston & A. T. Pietrewicz (Eds.), *Issues in the ecological study of learning* (pp. 401–432). Hillsdale, NJ: Lawrence Erlbaum.

Revusky, S., & Garcia, J. (1970). Learned associations over long delays. In G. H. Bower (Ed.), *The psychology of learning and motivation* (Vol. 4, pp. 1–82). New York: Academic.

Revusky, S., & Gorry, T. (1973). Flavor aversions produced by contingent drug injection: Relative effectiveness of apomorphine, emetine, and lithium. *Behavior Research and Therapy, 11*, 403–409.

Sanderson, R. E., Campbell, D., & Laverty S. G. (1963). An investigation of a new aversive conditioning treatment for alcoholism. *Quarterly Journal of Studies on Alcohol, 24*, 261–275.

Schafe, G. E., Sollars, S. I., & Bernstein, I. (1995). The CS–US interval and taste aversion learning: A brief look. *Behavioral Neuroscience, 109*, 799–802.

Seligman, M. E. P. (1970). On the generality of the laws of learning. *Psychological Review, 77*, 406–418.

Sherman, J. E., Jorenby, D. E., & Baker, T. B. (1988). Classical conditioning with alcohol: Acquired preferences and aversions, tolerance and urges/craving. In C. D. Chaudron & D. A. Wilkinson (Eds.), *Theories on alcoholism* (pp. 173–237). Toronto: Addiction Research Foundation.

Smith, J. W., & Frawley, P. J. (1993). Treatment outcome of 600 chemically dependent patients in a multimodal inpatient program including aversion therapy and pentothal interviews. *Journal of Substance Abuse and Treatment, 10*, 359–369.

Smith, J. W., Frawley, P. J., & Polissar, L. (1991). Six- and twelve-month abstinence rates in inpatient alcoholics treated with aversion therapy compared with matched patients from a treatment registry. *Alcoholism: Clinical and Experimental Research, 15,* 862–870.

Smith, M. L., & Glass, G. V. (1977). Meta-analysis of psychotherapy outcome studies. *American Psychologist, 32,* 772–777.

Trautner, E. M., Morris, R., Noack, C. H., & Gershon, S. (1955). The excretion and retention of ingested lithium and its effect on the ionic balance of man. *Medical Journal of Australia, 42,* 280–291.

Vaillant, G. E. (1995). *The natural history of alcoholism revisited.* Cambridge, MA: Harvard University Press.

Voegtlin, W. L., Lemere, F., & Broz, W. R. (1940). Conditioned reflex therapy of alcoholic addiction. III. An evaluation of present results in the light of previous experiences with this method. *Quarterly Journal of Studies on Alcohol, 1,* 501–515.

Voegtlin, W. L., Lemere, F., Broz, W. R., & O'Hollaren, R. (1941). Conditioned reflex therapy of alcoholic addiction. IV A preliminary report on the value of reinforcement. *Quarterly Journal of Studies on Alcohol, 2,* 505–511.

Weiss, R. D., Locastro, J. S., Swift, R., Zweben, A., Miller, W. R., Longabaugh, R., et al. (2005). The use of a "psychotherapy" with no pills treatment condition as part of a combined pharmacotherapy–psychotherapy research study of alcohol dependence. *Journal of Studies on Alcohol* (Suppl. 15), 43–49.

Wilson, G. T. (1988). Chemical aversion conditioning as a treatment for alcoholism: A re-analysis. *Behavior Research and Therapy, 25,* 503–516.

Wilson, G. T. (1991). Chemical aversion conditioning in the treatment of alcoholism: Further comments. *Behavior Research and Therapy, 29,* 415–419.

Wise, R. A. (2002). Brain reward circuitry: Insights from unsensed incentives. *Neuron, 36,* 229–240.

Wise, R. A., Yokel, R. A., & DeWitt, H. (1976). Both positive reinforcement and conditioned aversion from amphetamine and from apomorphine in rats. *Science, 191,* 1273–1275.

Zweben, A., Barret, D., Berger, L., & Murray, K. T. (2005). Recruiting and retaining participants in a combined behavioral and pharmacological trial. *Journal of Studies on Alcohol* (Suppl. 15), 72–81.

Zweben, A., Del Boca, F. K., Mattson, M. E., & McRee, B. (2003). Client characteristics and implementation of the research protocol. In T. F. Babor & F. K. Del Boca (Eds.), *Treatment matching in alcoholism* (pp. 62–80). Cambridge: Cambridge University Press.

22

Taste–Immune Associative Learning

GUSTAVO PACHECO-LÓPEZ, HARALD ENGLER, MAJ-BRITT NIEMI,
AND MANFRED SCHEDLOWSKI

AN INTRODUCTION
TO NEUROIMMUNE
ASSOCIATIVE LEARNING

Neuroimmune interactions appear to bring several adaptive advantages to those organisms that acquired and developed them further during phylogeny and ontogeny (Ottaviani, Valensin, & Franceschi, 1998; Schedlowski, 2006; Tada, 1997). This complex repertoire of immune, endocrine, neural, and behavioral responses may be orchestrated to achieve better adaptation of the organism to a constantly challenging environment. In vertebrates, it is well established that there are many intricate interactions between the immune and nervous systems and vice versa (Ottaviani & Franceschi, 1996; Salzet, Vieau, & Day, 2000; Straub & Besedovsky, 2003; Vishwanath, 1996). It was recently shown that invertebrate biology also evolved around acquiring and developing complex neuroimmune communication. For example, interaction between neurons and immune cells has been demonstrated in the mollusk *Aplysia californica* (Clatworthy, 1998). Furthermore, invertebrates also express neuropeptides (e.g., opioids) in the neural and immune tissues and these played a key role as neuroimmune messengers during their evolution (Salzet et al., 2000). Neuroimmune interactions affect the behavior of insects as well, as demonstrated in bees and

humblebees. Noninfected honeybees whose immune systems were challenged by a nonpathogenic immunogenic elicitor (lipopolysaccharide) displayed a reduced ability to associate an odor with sugar reward in a classical conditioning paradigm (Mallon, Brockmann, & Schmid-Hempel, 2003; Riddell & Mallon, 2006).

Ambulatory organisms evolved to face rapidly changing environments (both the internal and external), acquiring the ability to learn. Classical conditioning can be understood as learning about the temporal or causal relationships between external and internal stimuli to allow for the appropriate preparatory set of responses before biologically significant events occur (Rescorla, 1988, 2003). In this regard, the capacity to associate a specific stimulus (e.g., environments or flavors; conditioned stimulus [CS]) with a certain immune response or status (e.g., allergens, toxins, antigens; unconditioned stimulus [US]) seems to be of high adaptive value. Thus, it can be hypothesized that this capacity was acquired during evolution as an adaptive strategy in order to protect the organism and/or prepare it for danger. Furthermore, such associative learning is typically acquired under certain stressful conditions. For example, the exposure to a specific antigen (and its categorization as an allergen) might be associated (*learning*) with a specific environment or food. An adaptive response is then elicited (*memory*), consisting first of behavioral modification, in order to avoid the place or food associated with the antigen (Costa-Pinto, Basso, Britto, Malucelli, & Russo, 2005; Markovic, Dimitrijevic, & Jankovic, 1992). If this is not possible, the organism will try to reduce contact with the allergen, that is, by coughing or sneezing (Pinto, Yanai, Sekizawa, Aikawa, & Sasaki, 1995); at the same time, its immune system may prepare the body for interaction with the antigen by, for instance, mast cell degranulation (Irie, Maeda, & Nagata, 2001; MacQueen, Marshall, Perdue, Siegel, & Bienenstock, 1989; Palermo-Neto & Guimarães, 2000; Russell et al., 1984) or antibody production (Ader, Kelly, Moynihan, Grota, & Cohen, 1993; Alvarez-Borda, Ramírez-Amaya, Pérez-Montfort, & Bermúdez-Rattoni, 1995; Chen et al., 2004; Husband, Lin, Madsen, & King, 1993). Although under experimental conditions such associative learning can be extinguished, it is likely that it will last for a long time, since in natural situations the organism will try to avoid contact with the environmental cues that signal the CS. The influence of behavioral conditioning on immune responses has been reviewed several times before (Ader & Cohen, 1991, 2001; Brittain & Wiener, 1985; Hucklebridge, 2002; Markovic et al., 1993; Pacheco-López, Niemi, Engler, & Schedlowski, 2007). In the present chapter we will focus specifically on those associative learning protocols in which central nervous system (CNS) inputs from chemical senses (gustatory/olfactory) are associated with peripheral immune responses.

TASTE–IMMUNE ASSOCIATIVE LEARNING

Pioneer research on neuroimmune associative learning was based on the association between somatosensory stimulation and peripheral immune challenges (Metalnikov & Chorine, 1926, 1928; Nicolau & Antinescu-Dimitriu, 1929a, 1929b; Ostravskaya, 1930; for a review, see Ader, 1981; Luk'ianenko, 1961; Pacheco-López et al., 2007). However, most of the recent work reporting associative learning affecting immune function has followed a basic protocol pairing taste/olfactory and immune stimuli, originally developed by Ader and Cohen in the mid-1970s (Ader, 1974; Ader & Cohen, 1975). Theoretically, taste–immune associative learning (TIAL) is based on the naturalistic relation of food ingestion with its possible immune

consequences, which may induce behavioral, endocrine, and immune modifications after the engram of this experience is evoked. On the experimental bench, the acquisition step involves contingent pairings of a taste (e.g., saccharin), odor (e.g., camphor), or flavor (e.g., chocolate drink) as a CS with a stimulus that has immune consequences like a US (e.g., immunomodulating drug or antigen). At recall, subjects are normally reexposed to the gustatory/olfactory CS only, but some protocols also employ a vehicle injection as an additional component of the CS. Often, the hedonic value of the CS changes after just a single acquisition trial, modifying ingestive behavior (i.e., conditioned taste/odor avoidance/aversion or reduced palatability). However, the conditioned effects on the immune system may not be evident until several rehearsals are applied (Ader & Cohen, 1975; Ader, Cohen, & Bovbjerg, 1982; Espinosa et al., 2004; Exton, Schult, Donath, et al., 1998; Ghanta, Hiramoto, Solvason, & Spector, 1985). An overview of relevant studies that report immune changes after evoking TIAL is shown in Table 22.1. In addition, it is indicated whether or not these protocols induced conditioned taste/odor aversion/avoidance.

BEHAVIORAL CONSEQUENCES OF TASTE–IMMUNE ASSOCIATIVE LEARNING

The behavioral conditioned response (CR, i.e., conditioned aversion/avoidance/reduced palatability) has been elicited by TIAL using different immunomodulating stimuli as a US, for example,

- T-dependent antigens (e.g., protein antigens; Djuric, Markovic, Lazarevic, & Jankovic, 1987; Husband et al., 1993; Pacheco-López, Espinosa, Zamorano-Rojas, Ramírez-Amaya, & Bermúdez-Rattoni, 2002),
- T-independent antigens (e.g., lipopolysaccharide; Bull, Brown, King, & Husband, 1991; Cross-Mellor et al., 2004; Janz et al., 1996),
- superantigens (e.g., staphylococcal enterotoxin; Kusnecov & Goldfarb, 2005; Pacheco-López et al., 2004),
- immunosuppressive drugs (e.g., cyclophosphamide (CY); Ader & Cohen, 1975; Lambert &

Whitehouse, 2002), and cyclosporine A (CsA) (Exton, von Hörsten, Schult, et al., 1998; S. Klosterhalfen & Klosterhalfen, 1990).

In this regard, the available data document that the magnitude of the behavioral CR seems to be modulated by the intensity of the immune stimulation at acquisition time. For instance, a dose–response relationship between the amount of antigen used (US) and the conditioned ingestive behavior has been demonstrated: the higher the dose of antigen, the more pronounced the conditioned taste avoidance (Djuric et al., 1988; Pacheco-López et al., 2002). Furthermore, following an immune sensitization procedure, a mild dose of antigen is able to induce a strong behaviorally conditioned avoidance response (Markovic, Djuric, Lazarevic, & Jankovic, 1988). Regarding the immunosuppressive drugs used as a US in TIAL protocols, two main substances have been employed: CY and CsA. For both substances, significant modifications of ingestive behavior have been reported. Evoking a *Taste–CY* association consistently induces strong conditioned aversive/avoidance behavior across species (Ader, 1974; Bernstein, 1978; Matsuzawa, Hasegawa, Gotoh, & Wada, 1983; Roudebush & Bryant, 1991). However, after recalling *Taste–CsA* association, experimental subjects displayed different behavioral CRs resulting from TIAL. In mice, this specific taste–immunosuppressant association does not result in conditioned taste avoidance behavior (Niemi et al., 2006), whereas rats display reduced appetitive behavior (Exton, Herklotz, Westermann, & Schedlowski, 2001), and in humans the palatability of the conditioned taste is affected (Goebel et al., 2002). It is important to recognize that these two drugs differ substantially in their immunosuppressive mechanisms, which might be the basis of the differences reported. Briefly, CY is biologically inactive until it undergoes hepatic transformation to the ultimate alkylating agent aldophosphamide commonly called phosphoramide mustard (Moore, 1991). The phosphoramide mustard nonspecifically suppresses the immune response by inhibiting protein synthesis (i.e., antibody), DNA replication, and cell division. In contrast, the immunopharmacologic mechanism of CsA involves its binding to cyclophilins, which leads to inhibition of intracellular phosphatase calcineurin, then selectively reduces the expression of the cytokines interleukin (IL)-2 and interferon (IFN)-γ, which ultimately results in the suppression of T cell specific immune responses (Bukrinsky, 2002).

Additional experimental data deals with conditioned immunomodulation, however using nonimmune US, such as electric shocks (Coussons-Read, Dykstra, & Lysle, 1994; Lysle, Cunnick, Fowler, & Rabin, 1988; Lysle, Cunnick, & Rabin, 1990; Lysle, Luecken, & Maslonek, 1992; Perez & Lysle, 1997; Zalcman, Kerr, & Anisman, 1991; Zalcman, Richter, & Anisman, 1989; for a review, see Lysle & Coussons-Read, 1995), therefore these data are out of the scope from the present chapter, and will not be reviewed in detail.

BEHAVIORAL, ENDOCRINE, AND IMMUNE PARTICULARITIES OF TASTE–IMMUNE ASSOCIATIVE LEARNING

The available literature does not reveal a consistent relationship between the behavioral and immunological consequences of evoking TIAL (Ader & Cohen, 1975; Bovbjerg, Kim, Siskind, & Weksler, 1987; Gorczynski, 1987; Gorczynski, Macrae, & Kennedy, 1984). That is, conditioned taste aversion/avoidance can be expressed without concomitant changes in immune status, and conditioned effects on immune function can be obtained without observable conditioned aversion/avoidance responses.

It is important to mention that compensatory or paradoxical conditioned immune responses have been reported after evocation of some TIAL. For example, Gorczynski and colleagues varied the time of day at which initial acquisition trials began and found that conditioned suppression was acquired by taste cues paired with CY during the light phase of the diurnal cycle (Gorczynski et al., 1984). In contrast, acquisition that began during the dark phase of the diurnal cycle resulted in either no CR or a conditioned immunoenhancement. These investigators also reported that animals exposed to chronic stress were likely to develop conditioned enhancement rather than conditioned suppression of immune responses after *Taste–CY* association was evoked. The authors hypothesized that the background level of neuroendocrine hormones is critical to the direction of the CR to the taste cue paired with CY. However, Siegel and colleagues posited an alternative hypothesis, namely, that the observation that

Table 22.1 Behavioral and Immune Parameters Affected after Recalling Different Taste–Immune Engrams.

CS	US	CTA	Conditioned Immune Response	Relevant References
Saccharin	CY ip	Yes	Antibody production	Ader and Cohen, 1975; Rogers, Reich, Strom, and Carpenter, 1976; Schulze, Benson, Paule, and Roberts, 1988
			Lymphocyte proliferation	Kusnecov et al., 1988; Neveu et al., 1986
			NK-cell activity	O'Reilly and Exon, 1986
			Lupus (murine)	Ader and Cohen, 1982
			Plasmocytoma	Gorczynski, Kennedy, and Ciampi, 1985
			Graft vs. host response	Bovbjerg et al., 1982, 1984
			DTH	Roudebush and Bryant, 1991
			Arthritic inflammation	Klosterhalfen and Klosterhalfen, 1987; Klosterhalfen and Klosterhalfen, 1983
Sucrose	CY ip	Yes	Antibody production	Ader and Cohen, 1981
HCl	CY ip	Yes	Antibody production	Wayner, Flannery, and Singer, 1978
Saccharin/vanilla	CY ip		Total white blood cells	Klosterhalfen and Klosterhalfen, 1987
			Arthritic inflammation	Klosterhalfen and Klosterhalfen, 1983
Saccharin	Methotrexate ip		Antibody production	Ader and Cohen, 1981
Saccharin	Antilymphocyte serum ip	No	Mixed lymphocyte reaction	Kusnecov et al., 1983; Kusnecov, King, and Husband, 1987
Saccharin	CsA ip	Yes	Lymphocyte proliferation	Exton, von Hörsten, Schult, et al., 1998; Goebel et al., 2002
			Allograft rejection	Exton, Schult, Donath, et al., 1998; Grochowicz et al., 1991
Saccharin	CsA ip	No	Lymphocyte proliferation	Niemi et al., 2006
			Arthritic inflammation	Klosterhalfen and Klosterhalfen, 1990

Saccharin	LPS ip	Cytokines	Yes	Janz et al., 1996
Saccharin	LiCl ip	DTH	Yes	Kelley et al., 1984, 1985
Camphor odor	Poly(I:C) ip	NK-cell activity / Neutrophil activity	NR	Ghanta et al., 1985, 1987; Hsueh et al., 2002
		Cytotoxic T-cell activity		Chao, Hsu, Yuan, Jiang, and Hsueh, 2005; Hiramoto, Hsueh, et al. 1993; Demissie et al., 2000
Saccharin	Levamisole s.c.	T-helper/T-suppressor subset ratio	Yes	Husband, King, & Brown, 1987
Chocolate milk	KLH ip	Antibody production	No	Ader et al., 1993
Saccharin	OVA ip	Antibody production	Yes	Chen et al., 2004; Husband et al., 1993
Sacharin	HEL ip	Antibody production	Yes	Alvarez-Borda et al., 1995; Espinosa et al., 2004; Madden et al., 2001
Almond odor	HEL ip	Antibody production	Yes	Ramírez-Amaya and Bermúdez-Rattoni, 1999
Dimethylsulfide/ triethylamine odor	BSA inhaled	Plasma histamine concentrations	NR	Dark et al., 1987; Peeke, Ellman, Dark, Salfi, and Reus, 1987; Russell et al., 1984
Dimethylsulfide odor	BSA inhaled	Plasma histamine concentrations	NR	Irie et al., 2001, 2002, 2004

Notes: BSA, bovine serum albumin; CsA, cyclosporine A; CTA, conditioned taste aversion; CY, cyclophosphamide; HEL, hen egg lysozyme; KLH, keyhole limpet hemocyanin; LiCl, lithium chloride; LPS, lipopolysaccharide; OVA, ovalbumin; Poly(I:C), polyinosinic:polycytidylic acid; SEB, staphylococcal enterotoxin B; NR, not reported.

most conditioning studies of regulatory responses use stimuli other than taste cues suggests that the immunosuppression resulting from evoking a *Taste–CY* association may be unique to the use of taste cues (Siegel, Krank, & Hinson, 1987). Other cues, inadvertently present in the acquisition regimen, may control CRs that are different from those elicited by taste cues. Supporting this view, it has been reported that the CR to environmental or drug state cues that signal CY results in compensatory immunoenhancement (MacQueen & Siegel, 1989). These data suggest that the type of CS used to associate with CY determines the direction of the CR in the immune system. Additional evidence for the existence of compensatory conditioning of host defense reactions can be derived from studies on the role of conditioning in the development of pharmacologic tolerance to repeated injections of polyinosinic:polycytidylic acid (poly [I:C] Dyck, Driedger, Nemeth, Osachuk, & Greenberg, 1987; Dyck, Greenberg, & Osachuk, 1986).

NEUROBIOLOGY OF TASTE–IMMUNE ASSOCIATIVE LEARNING

A discrete neural network involved in taste–visceral associative learning has been documented, including mainly sensory and hedonic neural pathways (Sewards & Sewards, 2002, 2004). Such a neural circuit consistently includes the nucleus of the solitary tract, the parabracchial nucleus, the medial thalamus, the amygdala, and the insular cortex (Yamamoto, Shimura, Sako, Yasoshima, & Sakai, 1994). In particular, the insular cortex is essential for the acquisition and retention of taste–visceral associative learning (Bermudez-Rattoni & McGaugh, 1991; Bernstein, Wilkins, & Barot, Chapter 16; Cubero, Thiele, & Bernstein, 1999), and it has been postulated that the insular cortex may integrate gustatory and visceral stimuli (Sewards & Sewards, 2001). More recently, using the neuronal activity marker c-Fos, it was possible to confirm the preponderant role of the insular cortex in conditioned antibody production (*Taste–Ovalbumin* association) (Chen et al., 2004), which was in agreement with a previous report (Ramírez-Amaya & Bermúdez-Rattoni, 1999). Regarding other forebrain structures, the amygdala seems to play an important role during the formation of aversive ingestive associations (Reilly & Bornovalova, 2005) and is also relevant for limbic–autonomic interaction (Swanson & Petrovich, 1998). A series of reports has indicated that the insular cortex and the amygdala are key structures in conditioned immunosuppression after evoking *Taste–CY* and *Odor–CY* associations (Ramírez-Amaya, Alvarez-Borda, & Bermúdez-Rattoni, 1998; Ramírez-Amaya et al., 1996).

It has also been proposed that the ventromedial hypothalamic nucleus, widely recognized as a satiety center (Vettor, Fabris, Pagano, & Federspil, 2002), is intimately associated with sympathetic facilitation in peripheral tissues (Saito, Minokoshi, & Shimazu, 1989), including modulation of peripheral immune reactivity (Okamoto, Ibaraki, Hayashi, & Saito, 1996). In agreement with previous reports employing a *Taste–CY* engram (Ramírez-Amaya & Bermúdez-Rattoni, 1999; Ramírez-Amaya et al., 1996, 1998), we have identified the neural substrates involved in the immunosuppression resulting from evoking a *Taste–CsA* association in rats (Pacheco-López et al., 2005). The conditioned effect on the immune system, that is, a reduction in splenocyte responsiveness and cytokine production (IL-2 and IFN-γ), was affected by brain excitotoxic lesions; this data shows that the insular cortex is essential for acquiring and evoking this CR. In contrast, the amygdala seems to mediate the input of visceral information necessary at acquisition time, whereas the ventromedial hypothalamic nucleus appears to participate in the output pathway to the immune system, which is needed to evoke the behaviorally conditioned immune response (Figure 22.1; see also Color Figure 22.1 in the color insert).

Using a pharmacologic approach, the neurochemical features of the conditioned effect enhancing NK-cell activity in rodents (*Odor–poly I:C* association) have been reported. Central catecholamines seem to be essential, and glutamate—but not GABA—is also required at recall (Hsueh et al., 1999; Kuo et al., 2001). Furthermore, it has been demonstrated that cholinergic, as well as serotonergic, central systems are required at the acquisition and recall (Hsueh, Chen, Lin, & Chao, 2002).

In addition to classical neurotransmitters, cytokines play an important role within the CNS, modulating neuronal and glial function in nonpathological settings such as learning and memory processes (Balschun et al., 2004; Dantzer, 2004; Tonelli, Postolache, & Sternberg, 2005). Specifically, proinflammatory cytokines, such as IL-1, IL-6, and TNF-α, have been shown to

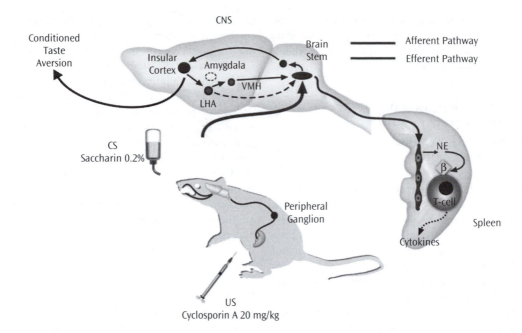

Figure 22.1. Saccharin–cyclosporin association model of TIAL. During the acquisition phase, thirsty animals are motivated to drink saccharin-flavored water (CS). Immediately afterwards these animals receive an intraperitoneal injection of the immunosuppressive drug cyclosporin A (US). At evocation time, the conditioned animals are reexposed to the CS. This gustatory information is centrally processed through brainstem relays (nucleus of the solitary tract and parabracchial nucleus) reaching the insular cortex. This neocortex, together with the amygdala, is indispensable during the acquisition phase, and is also necessary in evoking conditioned ingestive behavior (aversion/avoidance). The ventromedial nucleus of the hypothalamus (VMH) is essential for evoking the immunosuppressive CR in the periphery. The conditioned suppression of cytokine expression and production directly affecting the capacity of splenic lymphocytes to proliferate is not related to hypothalamic–pituitary–adrenal axis activation and is merely mediated by the neural innervation of the spleen, via β-adrenoceptor-dependent mechanisms. LHA, lateral hypothalamic area; NE, noradrenalin. (See also Color Figure 22.1 in the color insert section.)

modulate spatial learning tasks, as well as long-term potentiation phenomena (Banks, Farr, La Scola, & Morley, 2001; Fiore et al., 2000; Gibertini, 1996; Lynch, 2002; Matsumoto, Watanabe, Suh, & Yamamoto, 2002; Matsumoto, Yoshida, Watanabe, & Yamamoto, 2001; Rachal Pugh, Fleshner, Watkins, Maier, & Rudy, 2001; Schneider et al., 1998). In this sense, it is plausible that cytokines are a significant factor in the associative processes occurring during behavioral conditioning of immune functions. Apart from these neuromodulatory properties, proinflammatory cytokines seem to play an important role in the afferent pathway between the immune system and the CNS (Besedovsky & del Rey, 1996; Dantzer, 2004; Turnbull & Rivier, 1999). Therefore, it can be hypothesized that central cytokines act as mediators in the brain during an "immune-sensing"

period in the acquisition phase of TIAL. These hypotheses are supported by the following observations:

1. Receptors for these proinflammatory cytokines are expressed in the CNS (Sredni-Kenigsbuch, 2002; Szelényi, 2001).
2. Peripheral immune changes affect central cytokine production and cytokine receptor expression in the brain (del Rey, Randolf, Pitossi, Rogausch, & Besedovsky, 2000; Pitossi, del Rey, Kabiersch, & Besedovsky, 1997).
3. Cytokines can act as USs to induce conditioned taste aversion/avoidance (Dyck et al., 1990; Hiramoto, Ghanta et al., 1993; Janz, Brown, Zuo, Falk, Greenberg, & Dyck, 1991; Tazi, Dantzer, Crestani, & Le Moal, 1988).

To our knowledge, apart from these reports, there have been no systematic attempts to elucidate the neural substrates underlying immunomodulating effects based on TIAL.

PERIPHERAL MEDIATION OF THE IMMUNE EFFECTS AFTER EVOKING TASTE–IMMUNE ASSOCIATIVE LEARNING

The available data suggest that the effects of conditioning could be mediated mainly by T cells. Conditioned suppression of lymphoproliferative responses in rats and mice, for example, has been observed in response to T-cell mitogens but not (or less reliably) in response to B-cell mitogens (Kusnecov, Husband, & King, 1988; Lysle et al., 1990; Neveu, Dantzer, & Le Moal, 1986). Immune adoptive transfer experiments also suggest that conditioning may be mediated by T cells (Gorczynski, 1987). Splenocytes from conditioned and naïve *donor* animals were transferred to (irradiated) *recipient* naïve and conditioned animals respectively, some of whom were subsequently reexposed to the CS and some not. The reported increases and decreases in the antibody-forming cell response to sheep red blood cells (SRBC) depended on the type of donor cells (T vs. B cells) and the behavioral treatment (conditioning vs. naïve) experienced by the recipient. The separate transfer of enriched T and B cells to naïve and conditioned animals suggested that conditioning effects were mainly attributable to the adoptively transferred T cells and not to B cells (Gorczynski, 1991). However, the specificity of whether the same conditioning can modulate the antibody response to different types of antigen has not been resolved yet.

With respect to adrenocortical influences, it is reasonable to hypothesize that conditioned alterations in immunologic reactivity could be mediated by conditioned neuroendocrine changes; however, relevant experimental data are inconsistent and contradictory. In earlier experiments on humoral immune responses, the recall of a *Taste–LiCl* association did not affect antibody responses to SRBC, in contrast to the immunosuppression that was observed after evoking the *Taste–CY* engram (Ader, Cohen, & Grota, 1979). This finding indicates that an immunosuppressive drug was needed to cause immunosuppression, thus supporting the conditioning interpretation. In the same report but in another experiment, circulation levels of adrenocortical steroids were artificially elevated by exogenous administration of corticosterone at the time of antigen injection, in order to mimic the stress response occurring in animals reexposed to the taste paired with sickness. Elevated glucocorticoid levels did not significantly lower antibody titers. These data would appear, a priori, to exclude the possibility of a stress-mediated phenomenon in the genesis of conditioned immunosuppression. However, experimental data from another research group, in which the delayed-type hypersensitivity (DTH) response was used as an index of T-cell function, support the hypothesis that changes in the immune function of animals subjected to conditioned taste aversion might be better viewed as a secondary consequence of the motivational conflict affecting thirsty animals that are exposed to a taste solution previously associated with sickness (Kelley & Dantzer, 1988). According to this hypothesis, it should be possible to induce immunosuppression in conditioned animals even when no immunosuppressive drug is used (as US). After a *Taste–LiCl* association, conditioned animals showed not only a strong conditioned taste avoidance but also an immunosuppressed status in the T-cell function (Kelley, Dantzer, Mormède, Salmon, & Aynaud, 1984, 1985). Furthermore, additional data indicate that the psychological conflict involved in actively avoiding a sweetened taste solution was sufficient to activate a stress response (Kelley et al., 1985). In contrast, a third research group published a serum corticosterone time-course study performed to examine the possible involvement of glucocorticoids in conditioned immunosuppression of the DTH response (Roudebush & Bryant, 1991). Animals were sacrificed 30, 60, 90, 120 min, and 24 h after evoking a *Taste–CY* engram. No significant differences in serum corticosterone levels were detected between nonconditioned controls and the conditioned groups at any time point. These results are in line with the initial findings, suggesting that conditioned immunosuppression of a cell-mediated immune response is not linked to a rise in glucocorticoid levels. Supporting this line of thinking, several other research groups have consistently reported that the suppression of splenic T-cell proliferation was independent of the stressor-induced increase in adrenocortical activity (Exton, Schult, Donath, et al., 1998; Lysle et al., 1990; Mormede, Dantzer, Michaud, Kelley, & Le Moal, 1988).

Importantly, both conditioned and stressor-induced alterations in immune and nonspecific defense responses have been attributed to the action of central and peripheral catecholamines. For instance, it has been reported that a neuroleptic (chlorpromazine) and an antidepressant (amitriptyline) treatment, both abolish the immunosuppressive status elicited by recalling a *Taste–CY* engram (Gorczynski & Holmes, 1989). Furthermore, it has also been reported that the β-adrenergic antagonist, propanolol, blocked the immunosuppressive effects of a conditioning stress paradigm (Lysle et al., 1992). Supporting the involvement of peripheral catecholamines, nadolol (a β-adrenergic antagonist that does not cross the blood–brain barrier) blocked the electric shock-induced suppression of splenic, but not peripheral, blood lymphocyte proliferation following mitogenic stimulation *ex vivo* (Cunnick, Lysle, Kucinski, & Rabin, 1990). In this regard, we have previously revealed that the immunosuppressed status after evoking a *Taste–CsA* engram is not related to the activation of the hypothalamic–pituitary–adrenal axis and is merely mediated by the neural innervation of the spleen, via noradrenalin- and β-adrenoceptor-dependent mechanisms (Exton et al., 1999, 2002; Xie, Frede, Harnish, Exton, & Schedlowski, 2002); see Figure 22.1. Finally, it has been demonstrated that splenocyte reactivity is modulated, in part, by tonic inhibition from the splenic nerve (Okamoto et al., 1996), and sympathetic splenic innervation seems to be under the central control of the ventromedial hypothalamus (Katafuchi, Ichijo, Take, & Hori, 1993; Katafuchi, Okada, Take, & Hori, 1994). While electrical stimulation of the ventromedial hypothalamus was found to arouse sympathetic activity (Saito et al., 1989), the lateral hypothalamus seemed to do the opposite (Bernardis & Bellinger, 1993). Thus, the lateral hypothalamus may possess immunoenhancing properties (Wrona & Trojniar, 2003) that in part antagonize the ventromedial hypothalamus and thereby reduce sympathetic tone inhibition. Importantly, such hypothalamic regulation of sympathetic activity seems to be modulated by the insular cortex (Allen, Saper, Hurley, & Cechetto, 1991; Butcher & Cechetto, 1998; Cechetto & Chen, 1992; Oppenheimer, Saleh, & Cechetto, 1992). These data provide the peripheral and central neuroanatomical substrates behind the immune effects observed after evoking specific TIAL.

THEORETICAL FRAMEWORK FOR TASTE–IMMUNE ASSOCIATIVE LEARNING

After reviewing the existing data on TIAL, it is possible to summarize guidelines regarding the general mechanisms underlying these neuroimmune phenomena (summary in Figure 22.2; see also Color Figure 22.2 in the color insert). Part of this conceptualization has already been elaborated (Bovbjerg, 2003; Eikelboom & Stewart, 1982; Grossman, Herberman, & Levinat, 1996; Hiramoto et al. 1993; Pacheco-López et al., 2007). According to this theory, in the terminology of behavioral conditioning, both the CS (i.e., changes in the external environment) and the US (i.e., changes in the internal environment) must be inputs to the CNS, which in turn processes and associates this information. Thus, at acquisition time, only a change in the immune system that is sensed by the CNS can serve as a US. Furthermore, both the CR and the unconditioned response (UR) must be outputs of the CNS. This means that only an immune parameter that is detected by the CNS can serve as a US for conditioning, and at recall the CR will resemble that UR.

Acquisition Phase

Two possible kinds of US are employed to induce a given TIAL. The US that is directly detected by the CNS is defined as a *directly perceived US*, whereas the one that needs one or more intermediary molecules to be released by another system before it can be detected by the CNS is called an *indirectly perceived US*. For any US, directly or indirectly perceived, there are two possible afferent pathways to the CNS: (1) *a neural afferent pathway* and (2) a *humoral afferent pathway*. The neural afferent pathway may detect the US and translate this information into neural activity. This sensory process implies the interoceptive capacities, including immunoception, of the CNS (Blalock, 2005; Goehler et al., 2000). Theoretically, this afferent pathway may also be able to codify the stimuli location (local vs. systemic). The humoral afferent

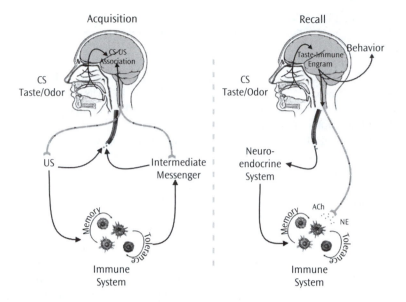

Figure 22.2. Theoretical framework for taste-immune associative learning. At acquisition time there are two possible USs associated with a CS. The US that is directly detected by the CNS is defined as a "directly perceived US," whereas the one that needs one or more intermediary molecules to be released by another system before it can be detected by the CNS is called an "indirectly perceived US." For any US, directly or indirectly perceived, there are two possible afferent pathways to the CNS: the neural afferent pathway and the humoral afferent pathway. At recall there are two possible pathways by which the CNS can modulate immune functions: the humoral efferent pathway and the neural efferent pathway. The humoral efferent pathway may imply changes in neurohormones that directly or indirectly modify the immune response. The neural efferent pathway is supported by the direct innervations of primary and secondary lymphoid organs. Regarding the CS, it is important to mention that features such as novelty, intensity, duration and naturalistic relation to the US may explain the feasibility of associating the CS with the US, as well as the stability and strength of such an association. In addition, it is necessary to remember that the immune history (e.g., tolerance and memory) of the subject may vary the response to the US, resulting in different associative learning at acquisition time and/or in a different CR at recall. Ach, acetylcholine; NE, noradrenalin. Adapted from: Pacheco-López et al. (2007). (See also Color Figure 22.2 in the color insert section.)

pathway is required for any US that is not detected locally or for the molecules induced by a given US (i.e., indirectly perceived US) that reach the CNS via the blood stream. If a given US has effects on several cell types, it is reasonable to assume that several molecules are candidates to be perceived by the CNS (i.e., several directly perceived US). Figure 22.2 indicates that for indirectly perceived US the pathway to the CNS is complex and longer than for the directly perceived US. In this regard, it can be hypothesized that, after administration of a given US, the CNS takes longer to respond to those USs that are indirectly perceived than to those that are directly perceived. This feature can be employed in designing experiments to elucidate the nature of the US. For instance, due

to a long interstimulus interval, backward conditioning should not be possible in the case of a directly perceived US whereas an indirectly perceived US could result in associative learning, since its effects on the CNS may come close to or at the same time of the central perception of the CS.

For an indirectly perceived US that affects immune functions, it has to be remembered that the *immune history* (e.g. tolerance and memory) of the subject may interfere with the response to such a US, resulting in a different immune reaction and thus a different signal intensity to the CNS. For example, the first immune response to a given antigen differs completely from the second, since an immune memory process takes place after the first exposition. Another related example is the immune tolerance phenomenon developed after repeated exposition to the same drug or antigen. Therefore, applying the same conditioning protocol to two subjects with varying immune histories may result in different associative learning processes, which in turn may affect the immune system in diverse ways at recall.

In Pavlovian conditioning, the strength of the association between the CS and the US is affected by the temporal relation between these stimuli, the *interstimulus interval*. Orthodox theory predicts that when the US precedes the presentation of the CS (backward conditioning) learning is poor. In addition, when the CS precedes the US by increasing intervals, the probability of a CR declines (Rescorla, 1988). The specific interstimulus interval that yields the most pronounced CR varies with the species and responses studied. For TIAL, this associative feature could be employed to delineate the nature of the US (directly vs. indirectly perceived) by systematically varying the interstimulus interval between the CS and US, including also backward conditioning protocols.

Regarding the CS, it is important to mention that features such as *novelty*, *intensity*, and *duration* may explain the feasibility of associating the CS with the US, as well as the stability and strength of such an association. In addition, in natural environments, a preexisting relationship between the CS and US, that is, *naturalistic relation*, had facilitated the occurrence of a certain associations. For instance, in contrast to tactile, visual, or auditory stimuli, it is well documented that gustatory and/or olfactory stimuli are strongly and easily associated with visceral USs, since in natural environments consummatory food intake behavior always precedes gastrointestinal consequences (positive or negative; Domjan, 2005). The strength and lastingness of flavor–visceral association is reflected in several features of the CR, such as high magnitude, low forgetting rate, and strong extinction resistance. Finally, the *neutrality* of the CS toward the immune system needs to be assured for each experimental setting.

Recall Phase

The CR is the tacit and unique proof that an associative learning process has occurred at acquisition time. In several TIAL protocols, the experimental subjects display a complex CR, with behavioral and neuroendocrine components in addition to the effects observed in the immune system. Furthermore, it is necessary to consider that the immune system itself displays sensitization and habituation responses to specific stimuli and that, in addition, many immune parameters underlie a circadian rhythm. Thus, the specific time points for acquisition and recall, as well as the immunological history of each experimental subject, may be important variables for the final immunological outcome after recalling a given TIAL. Consequently, some immune parameters modulated at recall might not be the exact reflection of neural activity and may not be explained by established learning and memory rules. For example, the expression of neural activity (e.g., behavior) may follow a normal extinction process during consecutive recall trials, whereas the effects of such neural activity on the peripheral immune response may not display the same extinction slope or may even be enhanced. Such peculiar results could be explained in several ways: It is possible that the interval between the recall trials is not long enough for the specific immune measure to return to baseline, resulting in an additive effect on the conditioned immune response during consecutive, close recall trials (Ader & Cohen, 1975; Hiramoto, Hiramoto, Solvason, & Ghanta, 1987). Another possibility is related to immune processes that may be modulated by neural activity; however, once such a process has started it is basically independent of neural modulation. In addition, it has been demonstrated that a stable and sturdy memory under extinction can, to a considerable extent, be reconsolidated by contingent exposure to the US, even if it is of low intensity (Berman & Dudai, 2001). So it is possible that, after an intensive acquisition phase, the conditioned effect on the immune system work as a putative US, inducing a reconsolidation process of the memory trace at each recall trial and, therefore, maintaining or enhancing the conditioned effects in subsequent recall trials. Finally, it should be indicated that some changes in the immune response after recalling TIAL cannot strictly be described as a CR (Eikelboom & Stewart, 1982). In summary, several physiological responses (including immune responses) can be affected by TIAL, but this does not necessarily imply that such immune responses were behaviorally conditioned (Kelley & Dantzer, 1988).

Regarding the conditioned immune response, there are specific features that may give important clues to its nature, and should be considered in the experimental design in order to differentiate the underlying mechanisms. There are two possible pathways by which the CNS can modulate immune functions: (1) the *humoral efferent pathway* and (2) the *neural efferent pathway*. The humoral efferent pathway may imply changes in neurohormones that directly or indirectly modify the immune response at recall. The peripheral effects evoked after activation of this pathway are diffuse and long lasting like any neuroendocrine response. The neural efferent pathway is supported by the direct innervations of primary and secondary lymphoid organs (Elenkov, Wilder, Chrousos, & Vizi, 2000; Mignini, Streccioni, & Amenta, 2003). There are several immune parameters that are subject to neural modulation, for example, T-cell differentiation (Sanders & Kohm, 2002; Sanders & Straub, 2002), hematopoiesis (Artico et al., 2002; Maestroni, 1998; Miyan, Broome, & Whetton, 1998), T-cell activity, B-cell activity (Downing & Miyan, 2000), natural killer (NK)-cell activity (Hori et al., 1995; Katafuchi, Ichijo, et al., 1993; Katafuchi, Take, & Hori, 1993), and inflammatory response (Czura & Tracey, 2005; Pavlov & Tracey, 2005; Tracey, 2002). We hypothesize that many of these neuroimmune interactions may be affected by TIAL but few have been investigated experimentally so far.

The extinction of the conditioned immune response is another feature that may give some hints about the underlying mechanisms. It has been demonstrated that for behavioral conditioning in which the nervous system directly modulates the CR (e.g., nictitating membrane, gastric secretion, and aversive behavior), an extinction process occurs when the CS is repeatedly presented without the US (active forgetting = extinction). However, if the CR observed is the reflection of neural activity on different types of cells, such as immune cells that exhibit tolerance and memory processes, then CR extinction will not necessarily be elicited in an orthodox Pavlovian manner (see, for instance, Bovbjerg, Ader, & Cohen, 1984). Moreover, if the CR observed reflects neural activity on two or more cellular types, then the picture may be more complicated (e.g., the neuroendocrine efferent pathway may be affecting immune functions). Finally, further consideration is required since the life span of immune cells is short, thus, each recall trial might affect different leukocyte or lymphocyte subsets.

BIOLOGICAL RELEVANCE AND CLINICAL POTENTIALS OF TASTE–IMMUNE ASSOCIATIVE LEARNING

Biological Relevance

Classical conditioning can be understood as learning about the temporal or causal relationships between external and internal stimuli to allow for the appropriate preparatory set of responses before biologically significant events occur (Rescorla, 1988, 2003). In this regard, the capacity to associate a certain immune response or status (e.g., allergens, toxins, antigens) with a specific extereceptive stimulus (e.g., context or flavors) is of high adaptive value. Thus, it can be hypothesized that this capacity was acquired during evolution as an adaptive strategy in order to protect the organism and/or prepare it for danger. For instance, a sensitized individual exposed to a specific antigen (and its categorization as an allergen) might be associated with a specific environment or food. An adaptive response is then elicited, consisting first of behavioral modifications, in order to avoid the place or food associated with the antigen (Costa-Pinto et al., 2005, Costa-Pinto, Basso, De Sá-Rocha, Britto, Russo, & Palermo-Neto, 2006; Markovic et al., 1992). If this is not possible, then the individual will try to reduce the contact with the allergen, that is, by coughing, sneezing (Pinto et al., 1995), or vomiting (Parker, 2006); at the same time its brain may prepare the body for interaction with the antigen by, for instance, mast cell degranulation (Irie et al., 2001; MacQueen et al., 1989; Palermo-Neto & Guimarães, 2000; Russell et al., 1984) or antibody production (Ader et al., 1993; Alvarez-Borda et al., 1995; Chen et al., 2004; Husband et al., 1993). Although under experimental conditions such TIAL could be extinguished, it is likely that it will last for a long time, since in natural circumstances the individual may try to avoid contact with any environmental cues that signal the CS. In humans, we hypothesize that TIAL may significantly affect customer food selection or related place avoidance.

In addition to natural situations, the biological impact of TIAL has been already proved. Based on the power of behavioral conditioning to control the progress of a murine model of systemic lupus erythematosus (Ader & Cohen, 1982), it was documented that mice suffering such autoimmune disease voluntarily drink the taste (CS) that was previously associated with the injections of the immunosuppressive drug; CY (Grota, Ader, & Cohen, 1987; Grota, Schatman, Moynihan, Cohen, & Ader, 1989; Grota, Ader, Moynihan, & Cohen. 1990). The behavioral interpretation indicates that by repeatedly evoking the taste–CY engram, that is, conditioned immunosuppression, autoimmune mice were able to correct homeostatic imbalances within the immune system.

Clinical Potentials

So far, few attempts have been undertaken to specifically investigate conditioned effects that directly modulate peripheral immune functions in human subjects. Since the nineteenth century, anecdotic case studies have reported the occurrence of allergic symptoms in the absence of allergens, provoked simply by different environmental cues (i.e., CS), for example, a picture of a hay field or an artificial rose (MacKenzie, 1886). Several decades later, it was reported that a conditioned dermatitis response was elicited in adolescent male subjects as a result of evoking a specific association (CS: blue solution topically applied/US: 2% raw extract *Rhus venicifera* application; Ikemi & Nakagawa, 1962). In another case report, two asthmatic patients suffering from skin sensitivities to house-dust extract and grass pollen were exposed to these allergens by inhalation (Dekker, Pelser, & Groen, 1957). After a series of conditioning trials, they experienced allergic attacks after inhalation of the neutral solvent used to deliver the allergens. This work showed not only fast conditioning of the asthmatic attack (CR), but also tenacious retention and a lack of extinction. This observation, together with data from animal experiments, resulted in the early hypothesis that asthma could be conceived of as a learned response (Turnbull, 1962). This view was further supported by a TIAL (CS: taste/US: dust mite allergen) in nine patients with allergic rhinitis (Gauci, Husband, Saxarra, & King, 1994). After the acquisition phase, elevated

mast cell tryptase in mucosa was observed when an intranasal saline application was given simultaneously with the CS. Another type of allergic reaction, the DTH response, was tested in seven healthy volunteers who received five monthly tuberculin skin tests (Smith & McDaniel, 1983). In this conditioning protocol both tuberculin (US) and saline were injected; while the latter was taken from a green vial (CS−), tuberculin was drawn from a red vial (CS+). On the test day, the color labeling of the substances was reversed. Although the saline injections did not induce a skin reaction (erythema and induration), the severity of the symptoms was significantly blunted in all the subjects tested when the tuberculin was drawn from the green vial (conditioned effect). However, a similar protocol using various allergens (e.g., mite dust or fur) taken from colored vials did not result in conditioned modulation of skin reactions in the 15 subjects tested (Booth, Petrie, & Brook, 1995).

Associative learning has been consistently reported in the context of cancer treatment, particularly chemotherapy (Bovbjerg, 2003; Scalera & Bavieri, Chapter 24). Chemotherapy agents (e.g., CY) generally have immunosuppressive effects. These agents are typically administered in cycles, with each outpatient treatment infusion followed by a period of recovery prior to the next infusion. From a conditioning perspective, clinic treatment visits can be viewed as "acquisition trials" in which the distinctive salient features of the clinic environment (CS) are contingently paired with the infusion of agents (e.g., CY; US) that have effects on the immune system. For instance, the immune function was assessed in 20 cancer patients in hospital prior to chemotherapy and compared with assessments conducted at home. Proliferative response to T-cell mitogens was lower for cells isolated from blood samples taken in the hospital (i.e., after recall) than for home samples (Bovbjerg et al., 1990). These results were replicated in 22 ovarian patients (Lekander, Fürst, Rotstein, Blomgren, & Fredrikson, 1995) and 19 pediatric patients receiving chemotherapy (Stockhorst et al., 2000). Moreover, chemotherapy patients often develop conditioned nausea (Andrykowski, 1988; Bovbjerg et al., 1990; Matteson, Roscoe, Hickok, & Morrow, 2002; Morrow, Lindke, & Black, 1991), anxiety (DiLorenzo et al., 1995; Jacobsen, Bovbjerg, & Redd, 1993), and fatigue responses (Bovbjerg, Montgomery, & Raptis, 2005) to reminders of chemotherapy. These conditioned nausea and anxiety responses can also be elicited by thoughts and images of chemotherapy (Dadds, Bovbjerg, Redd, & Cutmore, 1997; Redd, Dadds, Futterman, Taylor, & Bovbjerg, 1993), raising the possibility that conditioned effects may affect patients during the course of normal life for years after treatment.

Only a few human studies have so far tried to affect immune parameters on the cellular level by employing behavioral conditioning procedures. On the basis of the knowledge that adrenaline administration leads to the immediate mobilization of leukocytes in the periphery, especially of NK-cell numbers with simultaneous augmentation of their lytic activity (Benschop, Rodriguez-Feuerhahn, & Schedlowski, 1996; Schedlowski et al., 1996), one research group assessed the conditionability of NK-cell numbers and their lytic activity in healthy volunteers following TIAL. Although positive results were reported after evoking a *Taste–Adrenaline* association (Buske-Kirschbaum, Kirschbaum, Stierle, Jabaij, & Hellhammer, 1994; Buske-Kirschbaum, Kirschbaum, Stierle, Lehnert, & Hellhammer, 1992), these effects could not be replicated by other research groups (Kirschbaum et al., 1992). The efficacy of TIAL was also tested in multiple sclerosis patients, for whom 4 monthly CY infusions (US) were contingently paired with the taste of aniseed-flavored syrup (CS; Giang et al., 1996). Long-term treatment with CY decreases blood leukocyte numbers and often leads to leukopenia (UR). Interestingly, 8 out of 10 patients showed reduction in peripheral leukocyte numbers after the mere CS exposure. In addition, by pairing subcutaneous interferon-γ injections (US) with a distinctively flavored drink (CS), it was possible to induce an elevation of neopterin and quinolinic acid serum levels after evoking such an association in healthy volunteers (Longo et al., 1999). However, it has been hypothesized that more than a single associative learning trial pairing a distinctive taste (CS) with interferon-β injections (US) is necessary in order to produce immune conditioned effects (Goebel et al., 2005). This view is supported by experimental data for healthy male volunteers where the immunosuppressive drug cyclosporine A (US) was paired four times with a distinctively flavored/colored solution (CS; Goebel et al., 2002), inducing TIAL. After association, the mere reexposure to the drink (CS)

induced conditioned inhibition of ex vivo cytokine (IL-2 and IFN-γ) mRNA expression and cytokine release, as well as of the proliferative responsiveness of human peripheral blood lymphocytes, similar to the drug effect.

Finally, it should be mentioned that recently both basic and clinical research has focused on elucidating the neurobiology behind the placebo effect. In this regard, experimental data indicate that conscious expectation and unconscious behavioral conditioning processes appear to be the major neurobiological mechanisms capable of releasing endogenous neurotransmitters and/or neurohormones that mimic the expected or conditioned pharmacologic effects. To date, research on placebo responses affecting immune-related diseases is still scarce, but there are consistent indications that skin and mucosal inflammatory diseases, in particular, are strongly modulated by placebo treatments (for a review, see Pacheco-López, Engler, Niemi, & Schedlowski, 2006). As has been reviewed in the present chapter, the brain's capability to modulate peripheral immune reactivity has been impressively demonstrated by paradigms of behavioral conditioning in animal experiments as well as in human studies. Immunomodulatory placebo effects can benefit end organ functioning and the overall health of the individual through positive expectations and behavioral conditioning processes.

SUMMARY AND FUTURE PERSPECTIVE

If we conceptualize Pavlovian conditioning as a mechanism by which an organism anticipates the onset of a biologically important event (the US) and initiates preparatory responses (CR) to allow the organism to deal better with the US effects, this invites the hypothesis that one reason for the neural control of immunity lies in accommodating the adaptive value of classical conditioning (Brittain & Wiener, 1985). In its natural environment, an animal with a cut or a scratch has to build up immunological defense against microorganisms or a sensitized individual may try to avoid food containing the allergen. In the laboratory or a clinical setting, an antigen is reliably preceded by an injection. Therefore, conditioned immune effects may, in fact, be very common. The difficulty for the investigator lies not so much in inducing such responses, but in employing the proper controls, both immunological and behavioral, in order to demonstrate that these responses exist and to explore the underlying mechanism.

Owing to the physiological basis of the conditioned effects, the magnitude of the conditioned immune response should not be expected to override the homeostatic balance of the organism. However, this does not mean that conditioned effects on immune functions are not of biological/clinical significance (Ader, 2003). A very small increase in the potential of the immune system may be of great value in the fight against pathogens when the system reaches an allostatic load (McEwen, 1998; McEwen & Lasley, 2003), but it may increase the occurrence and severity of allergies and autoimmune disorders in other conditions. It is important to emphasize that several immune responses may be affected by TIAL protocols, but this does not necessarily imply that such immune responses were conditioned. Due to the complexity of neuroimmune interaction, such differentiation is not easy to establish. As has been reviewed, the use of a US with immune consequences, such as immunomodulating drugs or antigens, is not the only requirement for *genuinely* conditioning an immune response. A systematic approach should be necessary to clearly differentiate conditioned immune parameters from those immune responses affected after evoking a given association. In addition, each of these responses may be supported by different mechanisms, which might follow different rules. From our own experience and after reviewing the available literature, we conclude that the immune parameter under study to be conditioned should be assessed for several features (e.g., latent inhibition, extinction, CS-specificity, neutrality, CR kinetic vs. US kinetic, CR specificity) to be able to assure that indeed it was subject to be conditioned. However, it is possible that important immune parameters (not truly conditioned) may be affected by evoking specific associations, which indeed have significant impact on the individual's health status, thus it is also of relevance to be understood.

Before TIAL can be implemented as supportive therapy together with standard pharmacologic regimens, it is essential to describe some of its critical features. For example, it is not known how long conditioned immune responses last and how immune specific they are. Since it may be necessary to apply reinforcement at appropriate intervals, the question arises as to whether reconditioning is possible. Since at some time the therapy will stop, what is the forgetting and extinction patterns of conditioned immune responses? How predictable is the conditioned immune response in a human population with different immune and psychological histories? What is the impact of age and gender on immunoconditioning? When using immunomodulating drugs as the US, are some side effects also conditioned?

In summary, we have reviewed and summarized the current data indicating that several immune responses are affected by evoking different kind of TIAL. Conditioning of immune functions is becoming more and more understood and its possible clinical applications seem to be enormous. In future studies it will be essential to analyze the afferent and efferent pathways in brain-to-immune communication before TIAL paradigms can be employed as beneficial tools in a clinical setting, with the aim of maximizing the effects of pharmacologic therapies and reducing undesired side effects (Ader, 1997). Finally, the research on behavioral immunoconditioning has revealed that the organism has important adaptive psychoneuroimmunological strategies, acquired to deal in a better way with a constantly changing and challenging environment.

References

Ader, R. (1974). Behaviorially conditioned immunosuppression. *Psychosomatic Medicine, 36,* 183–184.

Ader, R. (1981). A historical account of conditioned immunobiologic responses. In R. Ader (Ed.), *Psychoneuroimmunology* (pp. 321–352). New York: Academic Press.

Ader, R. (1997). The role of conditioning in pharmacotherapy. In A. Harrington (Ed.), *The placebo effect: An interdisciplinary exploration* (pp. 138–165). Cambridge, MA: Harvard University Press.

Ader, R. (2003). Conditioned immunomodulation: Research needs and directions. *Brain, Behavior, and Immunity, 17*(Suppl. 1), S51–57.

Ader, R., & Cohen, N. (1975). Behaviorially conditioned immunosuppression. *Psychosomatic Medicine, 37,* 333–340.

Ader, R., & Cohen, N. (1981). Conditioned immunopharmacologic responses. In R. Ader (Ed.), *Psychoneuroimmunology* (pp. 185–228). New York: Academic Press.

Ader, R., & Cohen, N. (1982). Behaviorally conditioned immunosuppression and murine systemic lupus erythematosus. *Science, 215,* 1534–1536.

Ader, R., & Cohen, N. (1991). The influence of conditioning on immune responses. In R. Ader, D. Felten, & N. Cohen (Eds.), *Pschoneuroimmunology* (pp. 611–646). New York: Academic Press.

Ader, R., & Cohen, N. (2001). Conditioning and immunity. In R. Ader, D. Felten, & N. Cohen (Eds.), *Psychoneuroimmunology* (Vol. 2, pp. 3–34. New York: Academic Press.

Ader, R., Cohen, N., & Bovbjerg, D. (1982). Conditioned suppression of humoral immunity in the rat. *Journal of Comparative and Physiological Psychology, 96,* 517–521.

Ader, R., Cohen, N., & Grota, L. J. (1979). Adrenal involvement in conditioned immunosuppression. *International Journal of Immunopharmacology, 1,* 141–145.

Ader, R., Kelly, K., Moynihan, J., Grota, L., & Cohen, N. (1993). Conditioned enhancement of antibody production using antigen as the unconditioned stimulus. *Brain, Behavior, and Immunity, 7,* 334–343.

Allen, G. V., Saper, C. B., Hurley, K. M., & Cechetto, D. F. (1991). Organization of visceral and limbic connections in the insular cortex of the rat. *Journal of Comparative Neurology, 311,* 1–16.

Alvarez-Borda, B., Ramírez-Amaya, V., Pérez-Montfort, R., & Bermúdez-Rattoni, F. (1995). Enhancement of antibody production by a learning paradigm. *Neurobiology of Learning and Memory, 64,* 103–105.

Andrykowski, M. A. (1988). Defining anticipatory nausea and vomiting: Differences among cancer chemotherapy patients who report pretreatment nausea. *Journal of Behavioral Medicine, 11,* 59–69.

Artico, M., Bosco, S., Cavallotti, C., Agostinelli, E., Giuliani-Piccari, G., & Sciorio, S., et al. (2002). Noradrenergic and cholinergic innervation of the bone marrow. *International Journal of Molecular Medicine, 10,* 77–80.

Balschun, D., Wetzel, W., del Rey, A., Pitossi, F., Schneider, H., & Zuschratter, W., et al. (2004). Interleukin-6: A cytokine to forget. *FASEB Journal, 18,* 1788–1790.

Banks, W. A., Farr, S. A., La Scola, M. E., & Morley, J. E. (2001). Intravenous human interleukin-1 alpha impairs memory processing in mice: Dependence on blood–brain barrier transport into posterior division of the septum. *Journal of Pharmacology and Experimental Therapeutics, 299,* 536–541.

Benschop, R. J., Rodriguez-Feuerhahn, M., & Schedlowski, M. (1996). Catecholamine-induced leukocytosis: Early observations, current research, and future directions. *Brain, Behavior, and Immunity, 10,* 77–91.

Berman, D., & Dudai, Y. (2001). Memory extinction, learning anew, and learning the new: Dissociations in the molecular machinery of learning in cortex. *Science, 291,* 2417–2419.

Bermudez-Rattoni, F., & McGaugh, J. L. (1991). Insular cortex and amygdala lesions differentially affect acquisition on inhibitory avoidance and conditioned taste aversion. *Brain Research, 549,* 165–170.

Bernardis, L. L., & Bellinger, L. L. (1993). The lateral hypothalamic area revisited: Neuroanatomy, body weight regulation, neuroendocrinology and metabolism. *Neuroscience and Biobehavioral Reviews, 17,* 141–193.

Bernstein, I. L. (1978). Learned taste aversions in children receiving chemotherapy. *Science, 200,* 1302–1303.

Besedovsky, H. O., & del Rey, A. (1996). Immune–neuro-endocrine interactions: Facts and hypotheses. *Endocrine Reviews, 17,* 64–102.

Blalock, J. (2005). The immune system as the sixth sense. *Journal of Internal Medicine, 257,* 126–138.

Booth, R. J., Petrie, K. J., & Brook, R. J. (1995). Conditioning allergic skin responses in humans: A controlled trial. *Psychosomatic Medicine, 57,* 492–495.

Bovbjerg, D. (2003). Conditioning, cancer, and immune regulation. *Brain, Behavior, and Immunity, 17*(Suppl. 1), S58–61.

Bovbjerg, D., Ader, R., & Cohen, N. (1982). Behaviorally conditioned suppression of a graft-versus-host response. *Proceedings of the National Academy of Sciences of the United States of America, 79,* 583–585.

Bovbjerg, D., Ader, R., & Cohen, N. (1984). Acquisition and extinction of conditioned suppression of a graft-vs-host response in the rat. *Journal of Immunology, 132,* 111–113.

Bovbjerg, D., Kim, Y. T., Siskind, G. W., & Weksler, M. E. (1987). Conditioned suppression of plaque-forming cell responses with cyclophosphamide: The role of taste aversion. *Annals of the New York Academy of Sciences, 496,* 588–594.

Bovbjerg, D. H., Montgomery, G. H., & Raptis, G. (2005). Evidence for classically conditioned fatigue responses in patients receiving chemotherapy treatment for breast cancer. *Journal of Behavioral Medicine, 28,* 231–237.

Bovbjerg, D. H., Redd, W. H., Maier, L. A., Holland, J. C., Lesko, L. M., Niedzwiecki, D., et al. (1990). Anticipatory immune suppression and nausea in women receiving cyclic chemotherapy for ovarian cancer. *Journal of Consulting and Clinical Psychology, 58*, 153–157.

Brittain, R., & Wiener, N. (1985). Neural and Pavlovian influences on immunity. *Pavlovian Journal of Biological Science, 20*, 181–194.

Bukrinsky, M. (2002). Cyclophilins: Unexpected messengers in intercellular communications. *Trends in Immunology, 23*, 323–325.

Bull, D. F., Brown, R., King, M. G., & Husband, A. J. (1991). Modulation of body temperature through taste aversion conditioning. *Physiology & Behavior, 49*, 1229–1233.

Buske-Kirschbaum, A., Kirschbaum, C., Stierle, H., Jabaij, L., & Hellhammer, D. (1994). Conditioned manipulation of natural killer (NK) cells in humans using a discriminative learning protocol. *Biological Psychology, 38*, 143–155.

Buske-Kirschbaum, A., Kirschbaum, C., Stierle, H., Lehnert, H., & Hellhammer, D. (1992). Conditioned increase of natural killer cell activity (NKCA) in humans. *Psychosomatic Medicine, 54*, 123–132.

Butcher, K. S., & Cechetto, D. F. (1998). Neurotransmission in the medulla mediating insular cortical and lateral hypothalamic sympathetic responses. *Canadian Journal of Physiology and Pharmacology, 76*, 737–746.

Cechetto, D. F., & Chen, S. J. (1992). Hypothalamic and cortical sympathetic responses relay in the medulla of the rat. *American Journal of Physiology, 263*, R544–552.

Chao, H., Hsu, Y., Yuan, H., Jiang, H., & Hsueh, C. (2005). The conditioned enhancement of neutrophil activity is catecholamine dependent. *Journal of Neuroimmunology, 158*, 159–169.

Chen, J., Lin, W., Wang, W., Shao, F., Yang, J., Wang, B., et al. (2004). Enhancement of antibody production and expression of c-Fos in the insular cortex in response to a conditioned stimulus after a single-trial learning paradigm. *Behavioural Brain Research, 154*, 557–565.

Clatworthy, A. (1998). Neural-immune interactions—an evolutionary perspective. *Neuroimmunomodulation, 5*, 136–142.

Costa-Pinto, F. A., Basso, A. S., Britto, L. R. G., Malucelli, B. E., & Russo, M. (2005). Avoidance behavior and neural correlates of allergen exposure in a murine model of asthma. *Brain, Behavior, and Immunity, 19*, 52–60.

Costa-Pinto, F. A., Basso, A. S., De Sa-Rocha, L. C., Britto, L. R., Russo, M., & Palermo-Neto, J. (2006). Neural correlates of IgE-mediated allergy. *Annals of the New York Academy of Sciences, 1088*, 116–131.

Coussons-Read, M. E., Dykstra, L. A., & Lysle, D. T. (1994). Pavlovian conditioning of morphine-induced alterations of immune status: Evidence for peripheral beta-adrenergic receptor involvement. *Brain, Behavior, and Immunity, 8*, 204–217.

Cross-Mellor, S. K., Kavaliers, M., & Ossenkopp, K. P. (2004). Comparing immune activation (lipopolysaccharide) and toxin (lithium chloride)-induced gustatory conditioning: Lipopolysaccharide produces conditioned taste avoidance but not aversion. *Behavioural Brain Research, 148*, 11–19.

Cubero, I., Thiele, T. E., & Bernstein, I. L. (1999). Insular cortex lesions and taste aversion learning: Effects of conditioning method and timing of lesion. *Brain Research, 839*, 323–330.

Cunnick, J. E., Lysle, D. T., Kucinski, B. J., & Rabin, B. S. (1990). Evidence that shock-induced immune suppression is mediated by adrenal hormones and peripheral beta-adrenergic receptors. *Pharmacology, Biochemistry, and Behavior, 36*, 645–651.

Czura, C., & Tracey, K. (2005). Autonomic neural regulation of immunity. *Journal of Internal Medicine, 257*, 156–166.

Dadds, M. R., Bovbjerg, D. H., Redd, W. H., & Cutmore, T. R. (1997). Imagery in human classical conditioning. *Psychological Bulletin, 122*, 89–103.

Dantzer, R. (2004). Cytokine-induced sickness behaviour: A neuroimmune response to activation of innate immunity. *European Journal of Pharmacology, 500*, 399–411.

Dark, K., Peeke, H., Ellman, G., & Salfi, M. (1987) Behaviorally conditioned histamine release. Prior stress and conditionability and extinction of the response. *Annals of the New York Academy of Sciences, 496*, 578–582.

Dekker, E., Pelser, H., & Groen, J. (1957). Conditioning as a cause of asthmatic attacks: A laboratory study. *Journal of Psychosomatic Research, 2*, 97–108.

del Rey, A., Randolf, A., Pitossi, F., Rogausch, H., & Besedovsky, H. O. (2000). Not all peripheral immune stimuli that activate the HPA axis induce proinflammatory cytokine gene expression in the hypothalamus. *Annals of the New York Academy of Sciences, 917*, 169–174.

Demissie, S., Ghanta, V., Hiramoto, N., & Hiramoto, R. (2000) NK cell and CTL activities can be raised via conditioning of the CNS with unrelated unconditioned stimuli. *International Journal of Neurosciences, 103*, 79–89.

DiLorenzo, T. A., Jacobsen, P. B., Bovbjerg, D. H., Chang, H., Hudis, C. A., Sklarin, N. T., et al. (1995). Sources of anticipatory emotional distress in women receiving chemotherapy for breast cancer. *Annals of Oncology, 6,* 705–711.

Djuric, V., Markovic, B., Lazarevic, M., & Jankovic, B. (1987). Conditioned taste aversion in rats subjected to anaphylactic shock. *Annals of the New York Academy of Sciences, 496,* 561–568.

Djuric, V., Markovic, B., Lazarevic, M., & Jankovic, B. (1988). Anaphylactic shock-induced conditioned taste aversion. II. Correlation between taste aversion and indicators of anaphylactic shock. *Brain, Behavior, and Immunity, 2,* 24–31.

Domjan, M. (2005). Pavlovian conditioning: A functional perspective. *Annual Review of Psychology, 56,* 179–206.

Downing, J., & Miyan, J. (2000). Neural immunoregulation: Emerging roles for nerves in immune homeostasis and disease. *Immunology Today, 21,* 281–289.

Dyck, D. G., Driedger, S., Nemeth, R., Osachuk, T., & Greenberg, A. (1987). Conditioned tolerance to drug-induced (poly I:C) natural killer cell activation: Effects of drug-dosage and context-specificity parameters. *Brain, Behavior, and Immunity, 1,* 251–266.

Dyck, D. G., Greenberg, A., & Osachuk, T. (1986). Tolerance to drug-induced (poly I:C) natural killer cell activation: Congruence with a Pavlovian conditioning model. *Journal of Experimental Psychology: Animal Behavior Processes, 12,* 25–31.

Dyck, D. G., Janz, L., Osachuk, T. A., Falk, J., Labinsky, J., & Greenberg, A. H. (1990). The Pavlovian conditioning of IL-1-induced glucocorticoid secretion. *Brain, Behavior, and Immunity, 4,* 93–104.

Eikelboom, R., & Stewart, J. (1982). Conditioning of drug-induced physiological responses. *Psychological Review, 89,* 507–528.

Elenkov, I., Wilder, R., Chrousos, G., & Vizi, E. (2000). The sympathetic nerve—an integrative interface between two supersystems: The brain and the immune system. *Pharmacological Reviews, 52,* 595–638.

Espinosa, E., Calderas, T., Flores-Muciño, O., Pérez-García, G., Vázquez-Camacho, A., & Bermúdez-Rattoni, F. (2004). Enhancement of antibody response by one-trial conditioning: Contrasting results using different antigens. *Brain, Behavior, and Immunity, 18,* 76–80.

Exton, M. S., Gierse, C., Meier, B., Mosen, M., Xie, Y., Frede, S., et al. (2002). Behaviorally conditioned immunosuppression in the rat is regulated via noradrenaline and beta-adrenoceptors. *Journal of Neuroimmunology, 131,* 21–30.

Exton, M. S., Herklotz, J., Westermann, J., & Schedlowski, M. (2001). Conditioning in the rat: An in vivo model to investigate the molecular mechanisms and clinical implications of brain-immune communication. *Immunological Reviews, 184,* 226–235.

Exton, M. S., Schult, M., Donath, S., Strubel, T., Bode, U., del Rey, A., et al. (1999). Conditioned immunosuppression makes subtherapeutic cyclosporin effective via splenic innervation. *American Journal of Physiology, 276,* R1710–1717.

Exton, M. S., Schult, M., Donath, S., Strubel, T., Nagel, E., Westermann, J., et al. (1998). Behavioral conditioning prolongs heart allograft survival in rats. *Transplant Proceedings, 30,* 2033.

Exton, M. S., von Hörsten, S., Schult, M., Vöge, J., Strubel, T., Donath, S., et al. (1998). Behaviorally conditioned immunosuppression using cyclosporine A: Central nervous system reduces IL-2 production via splenic innervation. *Journal of Neuroimmunology, 88,* 182–191.

Fiore, M., Angelucci, F., Alleva, E., Branchi, I., Probert, L., & Aloe, L. (2000). Learning performances, brain NGF distribution and NPY levels in transgenic mice expressing TNF-alpha. *Behavioural Brain Research, 112,* 165–175.

Gauci, M., Husband, A. J., Saxarra, H., & King, M. G. (1994). Pavlovian conditioning of nasal tryptase release in human subjects with allergic rhinitis. *Physiology & Behavior, 55,* 823–825.

Ghanta, V., Hiramoto, R., Solvason, H., & Spector, N. (1985). Neural and environmental influences on neoplasia and conditioning of NK activity. *Journal of Immunology, 135,* 848s–852s.

Ghanta, V., Hiramoto, R., Solvason, B., & Spector, N. (1987). Influence of conditioned natural immunity on tumor growth. *Annals of the New York Academy of Sciences, 496,* 637–646.

Giang, D. W., Goodman, A. D., Schiffer, R. B., Mattson, D. H., Petrie, M., Cohen, N., et al. (1996). Conditioning of cyclophosphamide-induced leukopenia in humans. *Journal of Neuropsychiatry and Clinical Neurosciences, 8,* 194–201.

Gibertini, M. (1996). IL1 beta impairs relational but not procedural rodent learning in a water maze task. *Advances in Experimental Medicine and Biology, 402,* 207–217.

Goebel, M. U., Hübell, D., Kou, W., Janssen, O., Katsarava, Z., Limmroth, V., et al. (2005).

Behavioral conditioning with interferon beta-1a in humans. *Physiology & Behavior, 84,* 807–814.

Goebel, M. U., Trebst, A. E., Steiner, J., Xie, Y. F., Exton, M. S., Frede, S., et al. (2002). Behavioral conditioning of immunosuppression is possible in humans. *FASEB Journal, 16,* 1869–1873.

Goehler, L., Gaykema, R., Hansen, M., Anderson, K., Maier, S., & Watkins, L. (2000). Vagal immune-to-brain communication: A visceral chemosensory pathway. *Autonomic Neuroscience: Basic & Clinical, 85,* 49–59.

Gorczynski, R. M. (1987). Analysis of lymphocytes in, and host environment of, mice showing conditioned immunosuppression to cyclophosphamide. *Brain, Behavior, and Immunity, 1,* 21–35.

Gorczynski, R. M. (1991). Toward an understanding of the mechanisms of classical conditioning of antibody responses. *Journal of Gerontology, 46,* P152–156.

Gorczynski, R. M., & Holmes, W. (1989). Neuroleptic and anti-depressant drug treatment abolishes conditioned immunosuppression in mice. *Brain, Behavior, and Immunity, 3,* 312–319.

Gorczynski, R. M., Kennedy, M., & Ciampi, A. (1985). Cimetidine reverses tumor growth enhancement of plasmacytoma tumors in mice demonstrating conditioned immunosuppression. *Journal of Immunology, 134,* 4261–4266.

Gorczynski, R. M., Macrae, S., & Kennedy, M. (1984). Factors involved in the classical conditioning of antibody responses in mice. In R. E. Ballieux, J. Cullen, J. F. Fielding, A. L'Abbate, J. Siegrist, & H. M. Wegmann (Eds.), *Breakdown in human adaptation to stress: Towards a multidisciplinary approach* (pp. 704–712). The Hague: Martinus Nijhoff Press.

Grochowicz, P. M., Schedlowski, M., Husband, A. J., King, M. G., Hibberd, A. D., & Bowen, K. M. (1991). Behavioral conditioning prolongs heart allograft survival in rats. *Brain, Behavior, and Immunity, 5,* 349–356.

Grossman, Z., Herberman, R. B., & Livnat, S. (1992). Neural modulation of immunity: Conditioning phenomena and the adaptability of lymphoid cells. *International Journal of Neurosciences, 64,* 275–290.

Grota, L. J., Ader, R., & Cohen, N. (1987) Taste aversion learning in autoimmune Mrl-lpr/lpr and Mrl +/+ mice. *Brain, Behavior, and Immunity, 1,* 238–250.

Grota, L. J., Ader, R., Moynihan, J. A., & Cohen, N. (1990) Voluntary consumption of cyclophosphamide by nondeprived Mrl-lpr/lpr and Mrl +/+ mice. *Pharmacology, Biochemistry, and Behavior, 37,* 527–530.

Grota, L. J., Schachtman, T. R., Moynihan, J. A., Cohen, N., & Ader, R. (1989) Voluntary consumption of cyclophosphamide by Mrl mice. *Brain, Behavior, and Immunity 3,* 263–273.

Hiramoto, R., Ghanta, V., Solvason, B., Lorden, J., Hsueh, C. M., Rogers, C., et al. (1993). Identification of specific pathways of communication between the CNS and NK cell system. *Life Sciences, 53,* 527–540.

Hiramoto, R., Hiramoto, N., Solvason, H., & Ghanta, V. (1987). Regulation of natural immunity (NK activity) by conditioning. *Annals of the New York Academy of Sciences, 496,* 545–552.

Hiramoto, R., Hsueh, C., Rogers, C., Demissie, S., Hiramoto, N., Soong, S., et al. (1993). Conditioning of the allogeneic cytotoxic lymphocyte response. *Pharmacology, Biochemistry, and Behavior, 44,* 275–280.

Hori, T., Katafuchi, T., Take, S., Shimizu, N., & Niijima, A. (1995). The autonomic nervous system as a communication channel between the brain and the immune system. *Neuroimmunomodulation, 2,* 203–215.

Hsueh, C., Chen, S., Lin, R., & Chao, H. (2002). Cholinergic and serotonergic activities are required in triggering conditioned NK cell response. *Journal of Neuroimmunology, 123,* 102–111.

Hsueh, C., Kuo, J., Chen, S., Huang, H., Cheng, F., Chung, L., et al. (1999). Involvement of catecholamines in recall of the conditioned NK cell response. *Journal of Neuroimmunology, 94,* 172–181.

Hucklebridge, F. (2002). Behavioral conditioning of the immune system. *International Review of Neurobiology, 52,* 325–351.

Husband, A. J., King, M. G., & Brown, R. (1987). Behaviourally conditioned modification of T cell subset ratios in rats. *Immunology Letters, 14,* 91–94.

Husband, A. J., Lin, W., Madsen, G., & King, M. G. (1993). A conditioning model for immunostimulation: Enhancement of the antibody responses to ovalbumin by behavioral conditioning in rats. In A. J. Husband (Ed.), *Psychoimmunology* (pp. 139–148). Boca Raton, FL: CRC Press.

Ikemi, Y., & Nakagawa, S. (1962). A psychosomatic study of contagious dermatitis. *Kyushu Journal of Medical Science, 13,* 335–350.

Irie, M., Maeda, M., & Nagata, S. (2001). Can conditioned histamine release occur under urethane anesthesia in guinea pigs? *Physiology & Behavior, 72,* 567–573.

Irie, M., Nagata, S., & Endo, Y. (2002). Fasting stress exacerbates classical conditioned histamine release in guinea pigs. *Life Sciences*, *72*, 689–698.

Irie, M., Nagata, S., & Endo, Y. (2004). Diazepam attenuates conditioned histamine release in guinea pigs. *International Journal of Psychophysiology*, *51*, 231–238.

Jacobsen, P. B., Bovbjerg, D. H., & Redd, W. H. (1993). Anticipatory anxiety in women receiving chemotherapy for breast cancer. *Health Psychology*, *12*, 469–475.

Janz, L. J., Brown, R., Zuo, L., Falk, J., Greenberg, A. H., & Dyck, D. G. (1991). Conditioned taste aversion but not adrenal activity develops to ICV administration of interleukin-1 in rats. *Physiology & Behavior*, *49*, 691–694.

Janz, L. J., Green-Johnson, J., Murray, L., Vriend, C. Y., Nance, D. M., Greenberg, A. H., et al. (1996). Pavlovian conditioning of LPS-induced responses: Effects on corticosterone, splenic NE, and IL-2 production. *Physiology & Behavior*, *59*, 1103–1109.

Katafuchi, T., Ichijo, T., Take, S., & Hori, T. (1993). Hypothalamic modulation of splenic natural killer cell activity in rats. *Journal of Physiology*, *471*, 209–221.

Katafuchi, T., Okada, E., Take, S., & Hori, T. (1994). The biphasic changes in splenic natural killer cell activity following ventromedial hypothalamic lesions in rats. *Brain Research*, *652*, 164–168.

Katafuchi, T., Take, S., & Hori, T. (1993). Roles of sympathetic nervous system in the suppression of cytotoxicity of splenic natural killer cells in the rat. *Journal of Physiology*, *465*, 343–357.

Kelley, K. W., & Dantzer, R. (1988). The importance of conditioning in conditioned immunosuppression. *International Journal of Neuroscience*, *39*, 289–297.

Kelley, K. W., Dantzer, R., Mormède, P., Salmon, H., & Aynaud, J. M. (1984). [Induction of immunosuppression by dietary aversion acquired in the absence of immunosuppressive treatment]. *Comptes rendus de l'Académie des sciences. Série III, Sciences de la vie*, *299*, 123–126.

Kelley, K. W., Dantzer, R., Mormède, P., Salmon, H., & Aynaud, J. M. (1985). Conditioned taste aversion suppresses induction of delayed-type hypersensitivity immune reactions. *Physiology & Behavior*, *34*, 189–193.

Kirschbaum, C., Jabaaij, L., Buske-Kirschbaum, A., Hennig, J., Blom, M., Dorst, K., et al. (1992). Conditioning of drug-induced immunomodulation in human volunteers: A European collaborative study. *British Journal of Clinical Psychology*, *31*(Pt. 4), 459–472.

Klosterhalfen, S., & Klosterhalfen, W. (1987). Classically conditioned effects of cyclophosphamide on white blood cell counts in rats. *Annals of the New York Academy of Sciences*, *496*, 569–577.

Klosterhalfen, S., & Klosterhalfen, W. (1990). Conditioned cyclosporine effects but not conditioned taste aversion in immunized rats. *Behavioral Neuroscience*, *104*, 716–724.

Klosterhalfen, W., & Klosterhalfen, S. (1983). Pavlovian conditioning of immunosuppression modifies adjuvant arthritis in rats. *Behavioral Neuroscience*, *97*, 663–666.

Kuo, J., Chen, S., Huang, H., Yang, C., Tsai, P., & Hsueh, C. (2001). The involvement of glutamate in recall of the conditioned NK cell response. *Journal of Neuroimmunology*, *118*, 245–255.

Kusnecov, A. W., & Goldfarb, Y. (2005). Neural and behavioral responses to systemic immunologic stimuli: A consideration of bacterial T cell superantigens. *Current Pharmaceutical Design*, *11*, 1039–1046.

Kusnecov, A. W., Husband, A. J., & King, M. G. (1988). Behaviorally conditioned suppression of mitogen-induced proliferation and immunoglobulin production: Effect of time span between conditioning and reexposure to the conditioning stimulus. *Brain, Behavior, and Immunity*, *2*, 198–211.

Kusnecov, A. W., King, M. G., & Husband, A. J. (1987). Synergism of a compound unconditioned stimulus in taste aversion conditioning. *Physiology & Behavior*, *39*, 531–533.

Kusnecov, A. W., Sivyer, M., King, M. G., Husband, A. J., Cripps, A. W., & Clancy, R. L. (1983). Behaviorally conditioned suppression of the immune response by antilymphocyte serum. *Journal of Immunology*, *130*, 2117–2120.

Lambert, J. V., & Whitehouse, W. G. (2002). Conditioned inhibition of cyclophosphamide-induced taste aversion. *Journal of General Psychology*, *129*, 68–75.

Lekander, M., Fürst, C. J., Rotstein, S., Blomgren, H., & Fredrikson, M. (1995). Anticipatory immune changes in women treated with chemotherapy for ovarian cancer. *International Journal of Behavioral Medicine*, *2*, 1–12.

Longo, D. L., Duffey, P. L., Kopp, W. C., Heyes, M. P., Alvord, W. G., Sharfman, W. H., et al. (1999). Conditioned Immune Response to Interferon-[gamma] in Humans. *Clinical Immunology*, *90*, 173–181.

Luk'ianenko, V. (1961). The problem of conditioned reflex regulation of immunobiologic reactions. *Uspekhi Sovremennoĭ Biologii*, *51*, 170–187.

Lynch, M. A. (2002). Interleukin-1 beta exerts a myriad of effects in the brain and in particular in the hippocampus: Analysis of some of these actions. *Vitamins and Hormones, 64,* 185–219.

Lysle, D. T., & Coussons-Read, M. E. (1995). Mechanisms of conditioned immuno-modulation. *International Journal of Immunopharmacology, 17,* 641–647.

Lysle, D. T., Cunnick, J. E., Fowler, H., & Rabin, B. S. (1988). Pavlovian conditioning of shock-induced suppression of lymphocyte reactivity: Acquisition, extinction, and preexposure effects. *Life Science, 42,* 2185–2194.

Lysle, D. T., Cunnick, J. E., & Rabin, B. S. (1990). Stressor-induced alteration of lymphocyte proliferation in mice: Evidence for enhancement of mitogenic responsiveness. *Brain, Behavior, and Immunity, 4,* 269–277.

Lysle, D. T., Luecken, L. J., & Maslonek, K. A. (1992). Modulation of immune status by a conditioned aversive stimulus: Evidence for the involvement of endogenous opioids. *Brain, Behavior, and Immunity, 6,* 179–188.

MacKenzie, J. (1886). The production of the so-called rose effect by means of an artificial rose, with remarks and historical notes. *American Journal of the Medical Sciences, 91,* 45–57.

MacQueen, G. M., Marshall, J., Perdue, M., Siegel, S., & Bienenstock, J. (1989). Pavlovian conditioning of rat mucosal mast cells to secrete rat mast cell protease II. *Science, 243,* 83–85.

MacQueen, G. M., & Siegel, S. (1989). Conditional immunomodulation following training with cyclophosphamide. *Behavioral Neuroscience, 103,* 638–647.

Madden, K., Boehm, G., Lee, S., Grota, L., Cohen, N., & Ader, R. (2001). One-trial conditioning of the antibody response to hen egg lysozyme in rats. *Journal of Neuroimmunology, 113,* 236–239.

Maestroni, G. (1998). Catecholaminergic regulation of hematopoiesis in mice. *Blood, 92,* 2971–2973.

Mallon, E., Brockmann, A., & Schmid-Hempel, P. (2003). Immune response inhibits associative learning in insects. *Proceedings: Biological Sciences, 270,* 2471–2473.

Markovic, B., Dimitrijevic, M., & Jankovic, B. (1992). Anaphylactic shock in neuropsychoimmunological research. *International Journal of Neuroscience, 67,* 271–284.

Markovic, B., Dimitrijevic, M., & Jankovic, B. (1993). Immunomodulation by conditioning: Recent developments. *International Journal of Neuroscience, 71,* 231–249.

Markovic, B., Djuric, V., Lazarevic, M., & Jankovic, B. (1988). Anaphylactic shock-induced conditioned taste aversion. I. Demonstration of the phenomenon by means of three modes of CS–US presentation. *Brain, Behavior, and Immunity, 2,* 11–23.

Matsumoto, Y., Watanabe, S., Suh, Y. H., & Yamamoto, T. (2002). Effects of intrahippocampal CT105, a carboxyl terminal fragment of beta-amyloid precursor protein, alone/with inflammatory cytokines on working memory in rats. *Journal of Neurochemistry, 82,* 234–239.

Matsumoto, Y., Yoshida, M., Watanabe, S., & Yamamoto, T. (2001). Involvement of cholinergic and glutamatergic functions in working memory impairment induced by interleukin-1 beta in rats. *European Journal of Pharmacology, 430,* 283–288.

Matsuzawa, T., Hasegawa, Y., Gotoh, S., & Wada, K. (1983). One-trial long-lasting food-aversion learning in wild Japanese monkeys (*Macaca fuscata*). *Behavioral and Neural Biology, 39,* 155–159.

Matteson, S., Roscoe, J., Hickok, J., & Morrow, G. R. (2002). The role of behavioral conditioning in the development of nausea. *American Journal of Obstetrics and Gynecology, 186,* S239–243.

McEwen, B. (1998). Stress, adaptation, and disease. Allostasis and allostatic load. *Annals of the New York Academy of Sciences, 840,* 33–44.

McEwen, B., & Lasley, E. (2003). Allostatic load: When protection gives way to damage. *Advances in Mind-Body Medicine, 19,* 28–33.

Metalnikov, S., & Chorine, V. (1926). Role des réflexes conditionnels dans l'immunité. *Annales de L'Institut Pasteur, 11,* 893–900.

Metalnikov, S., & Chorine, V. (1928). Role des réflexes conditionnels dans la formation des anticorps. *Comptes Rendus des Seances de la Societe de Biologie et Deses Filiales, 99,* 142–144.

Mignini, F., Streccioni, V., & Amenta, F. (2003). Autonomic innervation of immune organs and neuroimmune modulation. *Autonomic & Autacoid Pharmacology, 23,* 1–25.

Miyan, J., Broome, C., & Whetton, A. (1998). Neural regulation of bone marrow. *Blood, 92,* 2971–2973.

Moore, M. J. (1991). Clinical pharmacokinetics of cyclophosphamide. *Clinical Pharmacokinetics, 20,* 194–208.

Mormede, P., Dantzer, R., Michaud, B., Kelley, K. W., & Le Moal, M. (1988). Influence of stressor predictability and behavioral control on lymphocyte reactivity, antibody responses and neuroendocrine activation in rats. *Physiology & Behavior, 43,* 577–583.

Morrow, G. R., Lindke, J., & Black, P. M. (1991). Anticipatory nausea development in cancer patients: Replication and extension of a learning model. *British Journal of Psychology, 82*(Pt. 1), 61–72.

Neveu, P. J., Dantzer, R., & Le Moal, M. (1986). Behaviorally conditioned suppression of mitogen-induced lymphoproliferation and antibody production in mice. *Neuroscience Letters, 65*, 293–298.

Nicolau, I., & Antinescu-Dimitriu, O. (1929a). L'influence des réflexes conditionnels sur l'exsudat peritonéal. *Comptes Rendus des Séances de la Société de Biologie et de ses Filiales, 102*, 144–145.

Nicolau, I., & Antinescu-Dimitriu, O. (1929b). Rôle des réflexes conditionnels dans la formation des anticorps. *Comptes Rendus des Séances de la Société de Biologie et de ses Filiales, 102*, 133–134.

Niemi, M. B., Pacheco-López, G., Kou, W., Härting, M., del Rey, A., & Besedovky, H. O. (2006). Murine taste–immune associative learning. *Brain, Behavior, and Immunity, 20*, 527–531.

Okamoto, S., Ibaraki, K., Hayashi, S., & Saito, M. (1996). Ventromedial hypothalamus suppresses splenic lymphocyte activity through sympathetic innervation. *Brain Research, 739*, 308–313.

Oppenheimer, S. M., Saleh, T., & Cechetto, D. F. (1992). Lateral hypothalamic area neurotransmission and neuromodulation of the specific cardiac effects of insular cortex stimulation. *Brain Research, 581*, 133–142.

O'Reilly, C. A., & Exon, J. H. (1986). Cyclophosphamide-conditioned suppression of the natural killer cell response in rats. *Physiology & Behavior, 37*, 759–764.

Ostravskaya, O. (1930). Le réflex conditionnel et les réactions de l'immunité. *Annales de l'Institut Pasteur (Paris), 44*, 340–345.

Ottaviani, E., & Franceschi, C. (1996). The neuroimmunology of stress from invertebrates to man. *Progress in Neurobiology, 48*, 421–440.

Ottaviani, E., Valensin, S., & Franceschi, C. (1998). The neuro-immunological interface in an evolutionary perspective: The dynamic relationship between effector and recognition systems. *Frontiers in Bioscience, 3*, d431–435.

Pacheco-López, G., Engler, H., Niemi, M. B., & Schedlowski, M. (2006). Expectations and associations that heal: Immunomodulatory placebo effects and its neurobiology. *Brain, Behavior, and Immunity, 20*, 430–446.

Pacheco-López, G., Espinosa, E., Zamorano-Rojas, H., Ramírez-Amaya, V., & Bermúdez-Rattoni, F. (2002). Peripheral protein immunization induces rapid activation of the CNS, as measured by c-Fos expression. *Journal of Neuroimmunology, 131*, 50–59.

Pacheco-López, G., Niemi, M., Engler, H., & Schedlowski, M. (2007). Behaviorally

Conditioned Enhancement of Immune Responses. In R. Ader (Ed.), *Psychoneuroimmunology* (Vol I, pp. 631–660). San Diego, CA: Elsevier Academic Press.

Pacheco-López, G., Niemi, M., Kou, W., Härting, M., del Rey, A., Besedovsky, H., et al. (2004). Behavioural endocrine immune-conditioned response is induced by taste and superantigen pairing. *Neuroscience, 129*, 555–562.

Pacheco-López, G., Niemi, M., Kou, W., Härting, M., Fandrey, J., & Schedlowski, M. (2005). Neural substrates for behaviorally conditioned immunosuppression in the rat. *Journal of Neuroscience, 25*, 2330–2337.

Palermo-Neto, J., & Guimarães, R. (2000). Pavlovian conditioning of lung anaphylactic response in rats. *Life Science, 68*, 611–623.

Parker, L. A. (2006). The role of nausea in taste avoidance learning in rats and shrews. *Autonomic Neuroscience, 125*, 34–41.

Pavlov, V., & Tracey, K. (2005). The cholinergic anti-inflammatory pathway. *Brain, Behavior, and Immunity, 19*, 493–499.

Peeke, H., Ellman, G., Dark, K., Salfi, M., & Reus, V. (1987). Cortisol and behaviorally conditioned histamine release. *Annals of the New York Academy of Sciences, 496*, 583–587.

Perez, L., & Lysle, D. T. (1997). Conditioned immunomodulation: Investigations of the role of endogenous activity at mu, kappa, and delta opioid receptor subtypes. *Journal of Neuroimmunology, 79*, 101–112.

Pinto, A., Yanai, M., Sekizawa, K., Aikawa, T., & Sasaki, H. (1995). Conditioned enhancement of cough response in awake guinea pigs. *International Archives of Allergy and Immunology, 108*, 95–98.

Pitossi, F., del Rey, A., Kabiersch, A., & Besedovsky, H. (1997). Induction of cytokine transcripts in the central nervous system and pituitary following peripheral administration of endotoxin to mice. *Journal of Neuroscience Research, 48*, 287–298.

Rachal Pugh, C., Fleshner, M., Watkins, L. R., Maier, S. F., & Rudy, J. W. (2001). The immune system and memory consolidation: A role for the cytokine IL-1beta. *Neuroscience and Biobehavioral Reviews, 25*, 29–41.

Ramírez-Amaya, V., Alvarez-Borda, B., & Bermúdez-Rattoni, F. (1998). Differential effects of NMDA-induced lesions into the insular cortex and amygdala on the acquisition and evocation of conditioned immunosuppression. *Brain, Behavior, and Immunity, 12*, 149–160.

Ramírez-Amaya, V., Alvarez-Borda, B., Ormsby, C., Martínez, R., Pérez-Montfort, R., & Bermúdez-Rattoni, F. (1996). Insular cortex lesions impair the acquisition of conditioned immunosuppression. *Brain, Behavior, and Immunity, 10*, 103–114.

Ramírez-Amaya, V., & Bermúdez-Rattoni, F. (1999). Conditioned enhancement of antibody production is disrupted by insular cortex and amygdala but not hippocampal lesions. *Brain, Behavior, and Immunity, 13*, 46–60.

Redd, W. H., Dadds, M. R., Futterman, A. D., Taylor, K. L., & Bovbjerg, D. H. (1993). Nausea induced by mental images of chemotherapy. *Cancer, 72*, 629–636.

Reilly, S., & Bornovalova, M. A. (2005). Conditioned taste aversion and amygdala lesions in the rat: A critical review. *Neuroscience and Biobehavioral Reviews, 29*, 1067–1088.

Rescorla, R. (1988). Behavioral studies of Pavlovian conditioning. *Annual Review of Neuroscience, 11*, 329–352.

Rescorla, R. (2003). Contemporary study of Pavlovian conditioning. *Spanish Journal of Psychology, 6*, 185–195.

Riddell, C. E., & Mallon, E. B. (2006). Insect psychoneuroimmunology: Immune response reduces learning in protein starved bumblebees (*Bombus terrestris*). *Brain, Behavior, and Immunity, 20*, 135–138.

Rogers, M. P., Reich, P., Strom, T. B., & Carpenter, C. B. (1976). Behaviorally conditioned immunosuppression: Replication of a recent study. *Psychosomatic Medicine, 38*, 447–451.

Roudebush, R. E., & Bryant, H. U. (1991). Conditioned immunosuppression of a murine delayed type hypersensitivity response: Dissociation from corticosterone elevation. *Brain, Behavior, and Immunity, 5*, 308–317.

Russell, M., Dark, K. A., Cummins, R. W., Ellman, G., Callaway, E., & Peeke, H. V. (1984). Learned histamine release. *Science, 225*, 733–734.

Saito, M., Minokoshi, Y., & Shimazu, T. (1989). Accelerated norepinephrine turnover in peripheral tissues after ventromedial hypothalamic stimulation in rats. *Brain Research, 481*, 298–303.

Salzet, M., Vieau, D., & Day, R. (2000). Crosstalk between nervous and immune systems through the animal kingdom: Focus on opioids. *Trends in Neurosciences, 23*, 550–555.

Sanders, V., & Kohm, A. (2002). Sympathetic nervous system interaction with the immune system. *International Review of Neurobiology, 52*, 17–41.

Sanders, V., & Straub, R. (2002). Norepinephrine, the beta-adrenergic receptor, and immunity. *Brain, Behavior, and Immunity, 16*, 290–332.

Schedlowski, M. (2006). Insecta immune-cognitive interactions. *Brain, Behavior, and Immunity, 20*, 133–134.

Schedlowski, M., Hosch, W., Oberbeck, R., Benschop, R. J., Jacobs, R., Raab, H. R., et al. (1996). Catecholamines modulate human NK cell circulation and function via spleen-independent beta 2-adrenergic mechanisms. *Journal of Immunology, 156*, 93–99.

Schneider, H., Pitossi, F., Balschun, D., Wagner, A., del Rey, A., & Besedovsky, H. O. (1998). A neuromodulatory role of interleukin-1-beta in the hippocampus. *Proceedings of the National Academy of Sciences of the United States of America, 95*, 7778–7783.

Schulze, G. E., Benson, R. W., Paule, M. G., & Roberts, D. W. (1988). Behaviorally conditioned suppression of murine T-cell dependent but not T-cell independent antibody responses. *Pharmacology, Biochemistry, and Behavior, 30*, 859–865.

Sewards, T. V. (2004). Dual separate pathways for sensory and hedonic aspects of taste. *Brain Research Bulletin, 62*, 271–283.

Sewards, T. V., & Sewards, M. A. (2001). Cortical association areas in the gustatory system. *Neuroscience and Biobehavioral Reviews, 25*, 395–407.

Sewards, T. V., & Sewards, M. A. (2002). Separate, parallel sensory and hedonic pathways in the mammalian somatosensory system. *Brain Research Bulletin, 58*, 243–260.

Siegel, S., Krank, M., & Hinson, R. (1987). Anticipation of pharmacological and non-pharmacological events: Classical conditioning and addictive behavior. *Journal of Drug Issues, 17*, 83–110.

Smith, G. R., & McDaniel, S. M. (1983). Psychologically mediated effect on the delayed hypersensitivity reaction to tuberculin in humans. *Psychosomatic Medicine, 45*, 65–70.

Sredni-Kenigsbuch, D. (2002). TH1/TH2 cytokines in the central nervous system. *International Journal of Neuroscience, 112*, 665–703.

Stockhorst, U., Spennes-Saleh, S., Körholz, D., Göbel, U., Schneider, M. E., Steingrüber, H. J., et al. (2000). Anticipatory symptoms and anticipatory immune responses in pediatric-cancer patients receiving chemotherapy: Features of a classically conditioned response? *Brain, Behavior, and Immunity, 14*, 198–218.

Straub, R., & Besedovsky, H. (2003). Integrated evolutionary, immunological, and neuroendocrine framework for the pathogenesis of chronic disabling inflammatory diseases. *FASEB Journal, 17*, 2176–2183.

Swanson, L. W., & Petrovich, G. D. (1998). What is the amygdala? *Trends in Neurosciences, 21,* 323–331.

Szelényi, J. (2001). Cytokines and the central nervous system. *Brain Research Bulletin, 54,* 329–338.

Tada, T. (1997). The immune system as a supersystem. *Annual Review of Immunology, 15,* 1–13.

Tazi, A., Dantzer, R., Crestani, F., & Le Moal, M. (1988). Interleukin-1 induces conditioned taste aversion in rats: A possible explanation for its pituitary–adrenal stimulating activity. *Brain Research, 473,* 369–371.

Tonelli, L. H., Postolache, T. T., & Sternberg, E. M. (2005). Inflammatory genes and neural activity: Involvement of immune genes in synaptic function and behavior. *Frontiers in Bioscience, 10,* 675–680.

Tracey, K. (2002). The inflammatory reflex. *Nature, 420,* 853–859.

Turnbull, A. V., & Rivier, C. L. (1999). Regulation of the hypothalamic–pituitary–adrenal axis by cytokines: Actions and mechanisms of action. *Physiological Reviews, 79,* 1–71.

Turnbull, J. (1962). Asthma conceived as a learned response. *Journal of Psychosomatic Research, 6,* 59–70.

Vettor, R., Fabris, R., Pagano, C., & Federspil, G. (2002). Neuroendocrine regulation of eating behavior. *Journal of Endocrinological Investigation, 25,* 836–854.

Vishwanath, R. (1996). The psychoneuroimmunological system: A recently evolved networking organ system. *Medical Hypotheses, 47,* 265–268.

Wayner, E. A., Flannery, G. R., & Singer, G. (1978). Effects of taste aversion conditioning on the primary antibody response to sheep red blood cells and Brucella abortus in the albino rat. *Physiology & Behavior, 21,* 995–1000.

Wrona, D., & Trojniar, W. (2003). Chronic electrical stimulation of the lateral hypothalamus increases natural killer cell cytotoxicity in rats. *Journal of Neuroimmunology, 141,* 20–29.

Xie, Y., Frede, S., Harnish, M. J., Exton, M. S., & Schedlowski, M. (2002). Beta-adrenoceptor-induced inhibition of rat splenocyte proliferation: Cytokine gene transcription as the target of action. *Immunobiology, 206,* 345–353.

Yamamoto, T., Shimura, T., Sako, N., Yasoshima, Y., & Sakai, N. (1994). Neural substrates for conditioned taste aversion in the rat. *Behavioural Brain Research, 65,* 123–137.

Zalcman, S., Kerr, L., & Anisman, H. (1991). Immunosuppression elicited by stressors and stressor-related odors. *Brain, Behavior, and Immunity, 5,* 262–273.

Zalcman, S., Richter, M., & Anisman, H. (1989). Alterations of immune functioning following exposure to stressor-related cues. *Brain, Behavior, and Immunity, 3,* 99–109.

23

Taste Aversions in Pregnancy

TRACY M. BAYLEY, LOUISE DYE, AND ANDREW J. HILL

Pregnancy is a time that is commonly associated with both food aversions and food cravings.[1] Indeed, there is now substantial research literature characterizing these experiences. The purpose of this chapter is to provide an overview of these findings and to summarize the explanations proposed. Data from three new studies, two of which are prospective in design, looking at the relationship between nausea and food aversions are also presented. Together, this research provides support for learned associations between food exposure, pregnancy nausea and sickness, and food aversions.

THE PHENOMENOLOGY OF FOOD AVERSIONS IN PREGNANCY

Flaxman and Sherman (2000) have summarized the past research on food aversions and cravings during pregnancy in their review of nausea and vomiting of pregnancy (NVP). They collated the results of 20 studies of food aversions during pregnancy that included information from 5432 women, and 21 studies of the food cravings of 6239 women. To be included, studies had to present data on foods that pregnant women craved or found aversive, rather than foods simply listed as "preferences" or "taboos." This ensured the exclusion of dietary habits that were socially desirable reports of food intake or based on the advice of others. Overall,

food aversions and cravings were found to affect 65% and 67% of pregnant women, respectively.

One of the problems with past research has been the lack of standardization regarding the targets of these experiences, that is, the foods themselves. To manage this, Flaxman and Sherman constructed nine food categories broad enough to cater for the variation in nutritional classification in earlier studies. Accordingly, the most common aversions were toward meat, fish, poultry, and eggs (0.28 per woman), nonalcoholic (caffeinated) beverages (0.16 per woman), and vegetables (0.08 per woman). Aversions to alcoholic beverages and ethnic, strong, and spicy foods were only 0.04 per woman, and aversions to dairy and ice cream, and sweets, desserts, and chocolate were even less frequent (0.03 per woman). Aversions to grains and starches, and fruit and fruit juice were very rare (<0.02 per woman). Conversely, the most popular cravings were for fruit and fruit juices (0.20 per woman) and sweets, desserts, and chocolate (0.17 per woman). Cravings were less common (but still notable) for dairy and ice cream (0.12 per woman), meat, fish, poultry, and eggs (0.12 per woman), and grains and starches (0.08 per woman). Pregnant women rarely craved for ethnic, strong, and spicy foods (0.04 per woman), nonalcoholic (caffeinated) beverages (0.03 per woman), or alcoholic beverages (<0.01 per woman). It appears that food items craved were seldom those to which aversions were developed, and vice versa. In addition, there

497

are some categories, such as alcoholic drinks, that are underrepresented in pregnancy-associated aversions compared with those reported in the general population (de Silva & Rachman, 1987). This may reflect either cultural wisdom concerning aversions or adherence to medical advice to avoid alcohol and other substances during pregnancy.

According to Dickens and Trethowan (1971), aversions are most likely to begin in the first trimester and progressively less so in the second and third. Cravings follow a similar pattern but their onset tends to be more evenly distributed across the three trimesters. The approximate duration of cravings and aversions is similar, although there is a tendency for aversions to persist over two or more trimesters as a result of their earlier onset. An examination of the mean week of onset and duration of cravings and aversions by Tierson, Olsen, and Hook (1985) revealed similar findings; aversions tended to start earlier in pregnancy and to last longer than cravings.

Looking at the third trimester and the post-partum period, Worthington-Roberts, Little, Lambert, and Wu (1989) found both aversions and cravings were more frequent before than after delivery. Almost half of the participants (51%) reported some aversion whilst almost all (93%) reported craving some food or drink during the last trimester of pregnancy. Postpartum, aversions markedly decreased but cravings remained common, with over three-quarters of women reporting at least one craving a year after delivery.

EXPLANATIONS FOR FOOD AVERSIONS DURING PREGNANCY

Although food aversions during pregnancy are a well-documented phenomenon, their etiology and functional significance have been hotly debated. The most common categories of explanation are cultural, sensory (taste and olfaction), and maternal and embryo protective.

Cultural

In addition to being a basic requirement of life, food is used as an expression of sociocultural values (Fallon & Rozin, 1983). It has therefore been suggested that food aversions are directed towards the less popular foods (Stewart, Wheeler, & Schofield, 1988). Cravings experienced by pregnant women

from different regional and sociocultural environments are related to the traditional popular foods in that region/culture. Similarly, research that has shown ethnic variation in the experience of food aversions and food cravings has supported these associations. For example, Coronios-Vargas, Toma, Tuveson, and Schutz (1992) compared the food aversions and food cravings during pregnancy of four ethnic groups in the United States (Black, Cambodian, Hispanic, and White). With regard to aversions, Blacks and Whites had significantly more aversions to fermented fish than did Cambodians or Hispanics. Significantly more Cambodians and Hispanics than Blacks and Whites had aversions to peanut butter, and Cambodians reported significantly more aversions to milk, ice cream, and cheese than the rest of the groups. Compared to Blacks and Whites, Cambodians and Hispanics craved significantly more spicy and salty foods. The craving for milk observed in Blacks, Whites, and Hispanics was not observed in Cambodians, and Blacks had more cravings for sweets and fats compared to the other three groups.

So culture can influence food aversions and food cravings during pregnancy, and it is reasonable to associate these changes in liking with the familiarity and regularity of use of foods or flavors within that culture. However, common patterns are also present. For example, cravings for fruit were apparent across all four ethnic groups. Similarly, aversions to meat were apparent in all ethnic groups studied. It has been noted that meat is subject to dietary taboos in many human societies (Fessler & Navarrete, 2003). Meat also has associations with NVP. In an analysis of studies conducted in 21 different countries, Pepper and Roberts (2006) reported a link between NVP rates and intake of all macronutrients. However, NVP rate was better predicted by animal than vegetable produce. It appears that both cultural food familiarity and the constituents of foods themselves influence the reporting of aversions in different countries.

Taste

Taste influences food selection in the nonpregnant population (Clark, 1998). A reduction in taste acuity during pregnancy has been known for some time. It has therefore been suggested that the development of food aversions and food cravings during pregnancy may reflect changes in taste sensitivity (Bowen, 1992).

While responsiveness to sweet, salty, and sour tastes have been associated with food cravings, only bitter taste and fatty foods are associated with food aversions. Pregnant women commonly experience aversions toward nonalcoholic (caffeinated) beverages, and studies specifically cite coffee, a bitter tasting substance, as a target of aversions (Flaxman & Sherman, 2000). Duffy, Bartoshuk, Striegel-Moore, and Rodin (1998) found that intensity ratings of a moderately bitter solution increased from prepregnancy to first trimester and decreased from first to second and second to third trimesters. Since aversions to bitter substances are highest in the first trimester (Rodin & Radke-Sharpe, 1991), aversions to coffee may be the product of this increased sensitivity to bitter tastes.

In a survey of the dietary habits of working-class pregnant women living in Belfast, Knox (1993) found that women tended to become averse to foods containing large amounts of fat. When Knox investigated sensory acuity and fat preference, pregnant women and the nonpregnant controls did not differ in terms of their ability to distinguish between standard and low-fat dairy products. However, preference for low-fat processed cheese over standard processed cheese approached significance among the pregnant women but not the controls. These results suggest that aversions to food containing large amounts of fat during pregnancy may reflect a decreased preference for high-fat-containing foods, but not necessarily a heightened sensory awareness of fat in the diet.

Although there is some indication of changes in taste perception during pregnancy, there is currently little compelling evidence to suggest that aversions are caused by such changes. There is a clear need for more research. For example, in order to determine whether aversions to coffee are the result of increased sensitivity to bitter tastes, studies need to compare the intensity ratings of bitter substances in women who are and are not experiencing aversions to coffee.

Olfaction

The sense of smell is also an important determinant of food choice. Without smell, a potato and an apple are likely to taste very much the same. During pregnancy, pleasant smells are often reported to become obnoxious, and already unpleasant smells become more unpleasant. For example, increased smell sensitivity at an early stage of pregnancy was reported by 67% of pregnant women in Sweden (Nordin, Broman, Olofsson, & Wulff, 2004). Van Lier, Manteuffel, Dilorio, and Stalcup (1993) found the smells least appreciated by pregnant women were onions, perfume, dustbins, nappy (diaper) buckets, vehicle exhaust, and cigarette smoke. Similarly, Hutton (1988) reported that cooking smells, perfume, smoking, anything normally regarded as a "bad smell" and bleach exacerbated pregnancy sickness.

However, research on olfactory acuity during pregnancy has also yielded mixed findings. Early studies indicated that during the first trimester women become hyperosmatic (i.e., developed increased olfactory acuity), but by the third trimester women become hypoosmatic (Doty, 1976). This led to the suggestion that aversions arise in the first trimester of pregnancy in response to a heightened sense of smell (hyperosmaticism), and during the later stages of pregnancy hypoosmaticism counters these early food aversions so that the mother is not deterred from consuming important sources of nutrients during stages of rapid fetal growth (Profet, 1992). In support of this suggestion, aversions are most frequent in early pregnancy and the targets of these experiences (e.g., "nonalcoholic caffeinated beverages," "meat, fish, poultry, and eggs," and "vegetables") can all be regarded as having strong odors (Flaxman & Sherman, 2000). However, more recent experimental studies have failed to find an influence of either the pregnancy state or stage of pregnancy on olfactory acuity (Gilbert & Wysocki, 1991; Laska, Koch, Heid, & Hudson, 1996). Compared to controls, pregnant women in these studies rated many odors as less pleasant. Thus it appears that although olfactory acuity per se may be unchanged during pregnancy there are alterations in the perception of pleasantness (Fessler, 2002).

Maternal and Embryo Protective

It has been suggested that aversions to certain foods and drinks during pregnancy may be due to homeostatic mechanisms, such as NVP, which evolved for fetal protection (Hook, 1978, 1980; Profet, 1988, 1992). Profet (1992, p. 328) argues that, "pregnancy sickness represents a lowering of the usual human threshold of tolerance to toxins in order to compensate for the extreme vulnerability of the embryo to toxins during organogenesis."

According to Hook and Profet, NVP protects the embryo by causing pregnant women to physically expel and subsequently avoid via food aversion learning, foods that contain teratogenic, mutagenic, and abortifacient chemicals (e.g., caffeinated beverages, alcohol, vegetables). Recently, this has been renamed the "maternal and embryo protection hypothesis." This reflects the idea that nausea and vomiting shields both the mother and her embryo from infections by food-borne microorganisms and poisoning from their toxins (such as those found in spoiled meat), in addition to protecting the embryo from teratogens and abortifacients in the mother's diet (Flaxman & Sherman, 2000).

Fessler (2002) has extended the argument, stating that pregnancy sickness and the resulting gestational food aversions protect the mother and her developing organism from infection during the period of immunosuppression necessary during early pregnancy, and that gestational cravings complement this mechanism. Fessler argues that during pregnancy the frequently reported decrease in the appeal of meat is accompanied by an increase in the attraction of alternative protein sources such as dairy products. However, an increase in the presence of calcium is problematic since it inhibits the absorption of dietary iron, which is already lacking due to the decrease in the consumption of meat. Fessler proposes that cravings for fruit resolve this paradox, since vitamin C has the potential to enhance the absorption of iron available in plant foods.

It has also been suggested that pregnancy sickness heightens sensitivity to noxious substances in normally tolerated foods via changes in taste and olfaction (Profet, 1992). This increased sensitivity exacerbates nausea and vomiting, which results in the development of marked aversions to such foods. Thus, the pairing of the taste or smell of a food (conditioned stimulus, CS) with nausea and/or vomiting (unconditioned stimulus, US) results in the former eliciting the illness reaction that was initially produced by the latter. This is a plausible suggestion given the evidence presented above. Furthermore, olfaction is a principal avenue for the remote detection of food properties and plays an important role in the elicitation of nausea (Fernández-Marcos et al., 1996).

Food cravings generally have been attributed to biological need (Hill, 2007). This is also true of those during pregnancy. However, the evidence to support these mechanisms is extremely weak. For example, it is suggested that during pregnancy the increased metabolic energy requirement associated with the developing fetus results in an increased maternal need for calories and calcium (Hook, 1980). If cravings were associated with the developing fetus then there should also be an increased maternal need for protein. However, aversions to high-protein items such as meat, fish, and poultry are common. Pica has been described in some pregnant women who crave nonfood items such as clay (Edwards, McSwain, & Haire, 1954). But if pregnant women crave clay to satisfy caloric and mineral deficiencies, why have studies shown no difference between clay cravers and controls in caloric intake (Edwards et al., 1954), plasma hemoglobin, or incidence of anemia (O'Rourke, Quinn, Nicholson, & Gibson, 1967)? Likewise, Worthington-Roberts et al. (1989) have hypothesized that cravings should be more frequent among lactating women because of the nutritional demands of the lactation process. Yet they found that nonlactators reported a greater number of cravings in the postpartum period and also in the last trimester of pregnancy. This indicates that factors other than the biological attribute associated with nursing or not nursing were responsible for the difference in cravings reported between the two groups.

NAUSEA AND VOMITING OF PREGNANCY

Nature and Frequency

NVP is so pervasive that it is often used in the detection of pregnancy (Jarnfelt-Samsioe, 1987). Research suggests that over 80% of pregnant women experience nausea and over 50% report some degree of vomiting (e.g., Whitehead, Andrews, & Chamberlain, 1992). NVP is frequently termed "morning sickness." However, this term is misleading since very few women who experience NVP report symptoms solely in the morning. Although NVP is typically confined to the early weeks of pregnancy, a small proportion of women suffer from symptoms throughout their pregnancy (Lacroix, Eason, & Melzack, 2000). The symptomatology of NVP can range from mild, occasional nausea to the more serious nausea and vomiting characteristic of hyperemesis gravidarum.

Etiology

A number of explanations for NVP have been proposed. Research into the psychological, social, and demographic correlates of NVP has been copious but generally inconclusive. Some investigators have reported a positive association between symptoms and a particular variable, whereas others have failed to support that association or have even found a negative association (O'Brien & Newton, 1991). For example, some investigators have observed that increased maternal age is associated with decreased nausea and vomiting, whereas others have failed to find such an association. Similarly, the presence of symptoms has been associated with multiparity (having had more than one birth) by some investigators and first pregnancy by others. NVP has also been linked to other variables such as unplanned pregnancy, smoking status, maternal weight, migraine and travel sickness, and infant gender.

Andrews and Whitehead (1990) argue that even if the variables described above influence an individual's experience of pregnancy sickness, each is unlikely to have much influence on the overall incidence in a population. Thus, the major determining factor must be the way in which the body responds to the physiological changes that occur during pregnancy. It is often assumed that nausea and vomiting are due to rising levels of pregnancy-associated hormones. The leading hormonal candidate has been human chorionic gonadotrophin (hCG), since it mirrors the pattern of NVP, rising sharply in early pregnancy, reaching a peak between 8 and 10 weeks of gestation and falling to lower levels between weeks 14 and 18. However, studies have failed to show any consistent relationship between hCG secretions and the incidence and severity of NVP (e.g., Soules et al., 1980). Other endocrine factors investigated in NVP include progesterone and estrogen. In support of a role for estrogens in the development of NVP, Jarnfelt-Samsioe, Samsioe, and Velinder (1983) found that women who did not tolerate oral contraceptives because of side effects (e.g., nausea) had a higher incidence of NVP. However, Masson, Anthony, and Chau (1985) found no difference in estradiol levels between symptomatic and asymptomatic pregnant women. Although progesterone levels peak during the first trimester of pregnancy just when the incidence of nausea and vomiting peaks, some studies have failed to demonstrate a significant difference in serum levels between symptomatic and asymptomatic pregnant women (Soules et al., 1980).

Neural control of nausea and vomiting is coordinated by nuclei in the brainstem, which can be activated by two major pathways, namely, the area postrema ("chemoreceptor trigger zone") and gastrointestinal afferents. Both these pathways appear to be involved in the body's response to ingested toxins. The area postrema also appears to have a role in conditioned taste aversion and the control of food and fluid intake. The lack of correlation between concentrations of reproductive hormones with emesis during pregnancy suggests that hormonal changes function indirectly by activating these neural pathways, rather than being the emetic agents themselves (Walsh, Hasler, Nugent, & Owyang, 1996).

Function

As described above, pregnancy sickness has been suggested to serve a protective function by causing the expulsion and subsequent avoidance of foods that are potentially harmful to the mother and/or her embryo. Central to the arguments of Flaxman and Sherman (2000) are that nausea and vomiting peak at a time when the embryo is most sensitive to developmental disruption by toxins. Women who experience pregnancy sickness are less likely to miscarry than those who do not, and women who vomit suffered fewer miscarriages than those who experience nausea alone (presumably because the latter group do not expel potentially harmful substances). In addition, aversive foods are most likely to contain toxins and their consumption could result in food-borne illness. Most controversially, this has led to the suggestion that alleviating pregnancy sickness through the use of drugs or natural remedies may do more harm than good, since it may interfere with the expulsion of potentially dangerous foods or with learning to avoid them.

However, there are a number of problems with the evolutionary perspective outlined above (see Bayley & Dye, 2002, for a comprehensive discussion of the complexity of these arguments). Ethnographic reviews have revealed that although widely distributed, pregnancy sickness is reportedly absent in some groups. There is also some debate as to whether nausea and vomiting are causes or effects of the reduced probability of miscarriage. Some investigators (e.g., Haig, 1993; Stein &

Susser, 1991) have hypothesized that pregnancy sickness might be a nonfunctional by-product of the physiological changes that accompany pregnancies that do not end in miscarriage. Thus, such investigators view pregnancy sickness as an effect of viable pregnancy rather than a cause. Flaxman (2002) has dismissed the by-product explanation on the grounds that if it were true, pregnancy sickness should occur in every pregnancy that does not end in miscarriage, and in reality many women who do not report nausea and vomiting carry their pregnancies to term. It should be remembered that the hormonal profile of pregnancy exhibits both within- and between-individual variation. Thus, if pregnancy sickness was a mere by-product of hormones it is possible that the absence of nausea and vomiting in the minority of pregnant women may be attributable to varying threshold levels between individuals (Andrews & Whitehead, 1990).

Huxley (2000) provides an alternative adaptationist perspective on NVP. Human and animal studies have shown, counterintuitively, that reduced energy intakes in early pregnancy are associated with increased placental weight (e.g., Godfrey, Robinson, Barker, Osmond, & Cox, 1996). Huxley therefore argues that NVP reduces energy intake, subsequently lowering maternal levels of the anabolic hormones (insulin and insulin growth factor-1 [IGF-1]), which helps to ensure that nutrient delivery to the placenta is sufficient to ensure adequate growth. At this stage in early gestation, embryonic and placental growth is regulated by insulin growth factor-2 (IGF-2), which, unlike insulin and IGF-1, is unaffected by nutrient availability. Thus, embryonic growth is maintained despite lowered energy intake. In mid-gestation and late gestation, the symptoms of nausea and vomiting subside. This coincides with transition to IGF-1, which responds to a reduction in nutrient availability by reducing fetal growth. However, as Fessler (2002) notes, Huxley's hypothesis is inconsistent with the adaptive value of cravings for sweets, fruits, and other high-calorie foods during the same period. Furthermore, animal research indicates that the type of food restriction in combination with the timing of the restriction may be important. Specifically, it appears that although a reduction in energy intake in early pregnancy may be beneficial, restriction of protein intake decreases the availability of essential amino acids required for early placental development (Pond, Maurer, Mersmann, & Cummins, 1992). This is clearly at odds with the high frequency of aversions to meat, an important source of protein, reported in the first trimester.

Other hypotheses concerning the function of nausea and vomiting during early pregnancy have also been proposed. For example, Deutsch (1994) proposes that pregnancy sickness has evolved to reduce the frequency of sexual intercourse during pregnancy. However, counter to this argument is research that indicates that pregnancy sickness does little to inhibit sexual behavior (Robson, Brant, & Kumar, 1981).

In summary, the debate concerning the function of pregnancy sickness, if indeed it serves any function at all, will undoubtedly continue. However, the proposed link between the presence of NVP and the development of food aversions is intuitively sound.

PREGNANCY SICKNESS AND FOOD AVERSIONS—A RELATIONSHIP?

A number of studies have reported that pregnant women often attribute food aversions to pregnancy sickness. Hook (1978) examined changes in consumption during pregnancy for seven beverages, including coffee, beer, wine, and other alcoholic drinks. He reported that approximately half of all women who decreased coffee consumption, and a quarter of those who decreased consumption of alcohol, specifically cited a response to or provocation of nausea as the explanation. Similarly, women in a study by Schwab and Axelson (1984) reported that, "aversions are due to increased sensitivity and queasiness during pregnancy" and that "the taste of [the particular food] causes nausea and vomiting" (p. 150).

Despite the apparent link between pregnancy sickness and food aversions, relatively few studies have explored the exact nature of this relationship. Although Dickens and Trethowan (1971) found no association between the incidence of aversions and NVP, more recent work has indicated that such a link may exist. Rodin and Radke-Sharpe (1991) examined nausea, vomiting, cravings, and aversions in pregnant women followed from baseline (prior to becoming pregnant) up until delivery. They considered whether increased incidence of nausea or vomiting was associated with higher rates of aversions to particular types of foods. Aversions toward poultry, fruits, sugars, and sweets reported during the first trimester appeared to be strongly associated with first trimester vomiting. Vomiting in the second trimester was significantly associated with aversions to red meats, poultry, salty, sour, and spicy foods experienced during the second term of pregnancy. Nausea in the first trimester of pregnancy was significantly related to the incidence of aversions reported to vegetables and sour foods during the first trimester. Second trimester nausea was strongly associated with the number of women reporting aversions to poultry, vegetables, and sour foods in the second term. Aversions to poultry, sour and spicy foods were associated with both nausea and vomiting, whereas aversions toward red meats, fruits, sweet, and salty foods were only related to vomiting. However, as the authors note, since women who experience vomiting also experience nausea it is difficult to discern independent effects.

Since a conditioning explanation of food aversions during pregnancy implies that nausea and/or vomiting precede the development of aversions to specific foods, Rodin and Radke-Sharpe (1991) also examined the relationship between first trimester nausea and vomiting, and second trimester aversions. First trimester vomiting was associated with a higher incidence of aversions reported in the second trimester to red meat, poultry, salty, and spicy foods. First trimester nausea was related only to aversions to spicy food in the second trimester. Thus the strongest associations were between pregnancy sickness and the aversions expressed during the second trimester.

Crystal, Bowen, and Bernstein (1999) compared women with mild ($N = 108$) and severe ($N = 21$) vomiting during pregnancy. They found that women with more severe vomiting reported a greater number of aversions during pregnancy. They also reported more aversions prior to pregnancy suggesting a predisposition to forming aversions when not pregnant. However, there was no significant association between pregnancy nausea severity and the number of reported aversions. Conversely, Baylis, Leeds, and Challacombe (1983) reported that both nausea and food aversions were more common in a group of women with milk allergic children when compared to controls.

Such findings are clearly indicative of a relationship between pregnancy sickness and the development of food aversions during pregnancy. An alternative to the evolutionary perspective is that rather than having an adaptive significance,

food aversions are merely accidental by-products of pregnancy sickness. The literature on food aversion learning reviewed above suggests that proteins, as well as other foods with strong odors, are prime targets for the development of food aversions because of such properties (Mattes, Arnold, & Boraas, 1987; Midkiff & Bernstein, 1985). It is therefore possible that the aversions formed during pregnancy are a result of the flavor properties of the foods or their nutrient composition, rather than their potential to result in food-borne illness or their level of toxicity. However, regardless of whether food aversions serve a protective function or are a mere by-product of pregnancy sickness, the mechanism that links pregnancy sickness to the development of aversions is the same. Clearly, if such a mechanism is responsible for the development of food aversions during pregnancy, then a close relationship between the presence of nausea and/or vomiting and the development of food aversions might be expected.

RECENT INVESTIGATIONS

Retrospective Studies

The outcome of the study by Crystal et al. (1999) provides some evidence of an association between pregnancy nausea and food aversions. Looking at the change in symptoms before and during pregnancy revealed that both nausea and food aversions significantly increased during pregnancy. Moreover, women with the most severe symptoms of vomiting reported significantly more aversions. But as previously noted, there was no correlational association between the severity of nausea during pregnancy and the number of aversions reported. It would appear that women who were more reactive to food before pregnancy, in terms of experiencing both aversions and food cravings, continued to show this heightened response during pregnancy. Critically, the study does not report on the temporal relationships between nausea and food aversions.

To address this we used a similar retrospective methodology to that of Crystal et al. (1999) but targeted participant recruitment at women in the later stages of pregnancy (Bayley, Dye, Jones, DeBono, & Hill, 2002). The intention was to maximize the proportion of women who had already experienced key symptoms and to gather information on their

nature, timing, and persistence. Ninety-nine pregnant women (mean age 30 years), with a median
gestation of 34 weeks, participated in the study.
Four percent were in the first trimester, 29% were
in the second trimester, and 67% were in the third
trimester of pregnancy. Roughly half were recruited
from aqua-natal (exercise) classes and the rest from
antenatal clinics and Primary Care.

Questionnaire responses showed that nausea
and vomiting were reported by 80% and 56% of
women, respectively, and that 61% reported at least
one food aversion. Women who reported one or
more food aversion did not differ from those without a food aversion in terms of age, current week of
pregnancy, or parity. As expected from the existing
literature, the most common aversions were toward
tea and coffee (30%), meat, fish, poultry, eggs, and
fat (16%), and spicy/high flavored foods (12%).
Over the whole study sample, the mean (±SE) number of food aversions reported per participant was
1.3 (±0.2). When the analysis was limited just to
those women who experienced food aversions, the
mean number of aversions increased to 2.2 (±0.2).
All but one of the women who reported food aversions had tasted the item prior to pregnancy and
the mean ratings showed that aversive foods were
at least moderately well liked.

Contingency table analysis showed that
although more women experienced both food
aversions and food cravings than either symptom
alone, reports of food aversions and food cravings
were unrelated. However, there was a significant
association between reports of nausea and of
vomiting. There was also a significant association
between the occurrence of nausea and food aversions. In total, 87% of all women who reported
food aversions also experienced some nausea during their pregnancy. Only 8% of the sample experienced food aversions in the absence of nausea.
There was no relationship between vomiting and
food aversions.

Importantly, there was a significant positive
correlation between the week of first onset of
nausea and the week of first occurrence of food
aversions, indicating that the two symptoms were
temporally related. As can be seen in Figure 23.1,
nausea was the first symptom and appeared in
week six. Food aversions began, on average, less
than 1 week later. The mean onset of vomiting was
2 weeks later than the onset of nausea and a week
later than the onset of food aversions. There was
no significant difference between the week of first

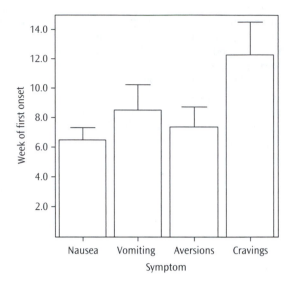

Figure 23.1. Mean (±SE) week of first onset of
nausea, vomiting, food aversions, and food
cravings. From Bayley et al. (2002).

onset of nausea and the week of first occurrence of
food aversions. In 60% of women reporting both
nausea and food aversions, the first occurrence of
nausea and the first food aversion occurred in the
same week of pregnancy (Figure 23.2). A further
4% reported their first occurrence of nausea in the
week preceding their first food aversion.

Looking at symptom persistence, 33 (55%) of
the 60 women reporting food aversions said that
their first food aversion was still present at the
time of completing the questionnaire. There was
no significant difference in the week of pregnancy
when these first food aversion and food craving experiences ended (19.4 ± 1.7 vs. 22.9 ± 2.2
weeks, respectively). In contrast, 60 (76%) of the
79 women who experienced nausea and 41 (75%)
of the 55 who reported vomiting said that their
symptoms had ceased. The average week of cessa-
tion for nausea and vomiting was week 15 and 16,
respectively.

The frequency and nature of these symptoms
are broadly in line with previous research. In the
present context, a key observation was the apparent
temporal association between the week of first onset
of nausea and the week of first occurrence of food
aversions. Interestingly, in women whose nausea
had ceased by the time of data collection, the duration over which bouts of nausea regularly occurred
was approximately 9 weeks. If aversions develop

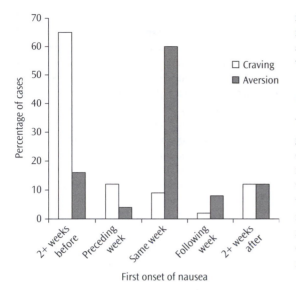

Figure 23.2. Percentage of first reports of food aversions (shaded columns) and food cravings (open columns) in relation to first onset of nausea. From Bayley et al. (2002).

for foods that are paired with nausea it seems surprising that only two aversions were reported. However, the familiarity of dietary items consumed may have limited the acquisition of new aversions. This is consistent with the concept of latent inhibition (see Hall, Chapter 4, for a discussion of this effect). Furthermore, since these participants probably consumed several foods or drinks in the hours preceding the onset of nausea, interference (or overshadowing) may have limited the degree to which any single item became identified as aversive.

Important weaknesses of this approach are the retrospective design and the correlational nature of the data gathered. Although some of these findings are consistent with food aversion learning mechanisms, they do not rule out a third variable explanation. Furthermore, the reliance on recall brings into question the accuracy of responses. For example, women who completed the questionnaire in their third trimester may have provided the least reliable reports since the study required them to recall events that usually occur in the early stages of pregnancy. On this point it should be noted that the 20% of women who reported their first food aversion before the first occurrence of nausea were significantly later in their pregnancy (35.3 ± 1.0 vs. 28.6 ± 1.6 weeks). This may be indicative of such a memory bias. On the positive side, these data do

identify a key time during pregnancy on which to focus if the interest is in the antecedents of food aversion experiences. The problem is how to access women in their early stages of pregnancy.

Prospective Studies

We have recently completed two prospective investigations of the onset, antecedents, and consequences of food aversions and cravings during early pregnancy (Bayley, Dye, & Hill, in preparation). Central to these investigations has been the opportunity to work with women who attend, and staff who organize, assisted conception units (for fertility treatment) in the north of England. The main features of these studies as they relate to food aversions are reported below.

Study 1

One hundred and forty three women, two-thirds of whom were receiving assisted conception services, agreed to take part in the study. They were predominantly Caucasian, with a mean age of 31 years and a mean gestation of 9 weeks. Seventy percent were primiparous and 13% were expecting a multiple birth.

The first part of the study used a questionnaire similar to that of our earlier study (Bayley et al., 2002), providing a retrospective account of their pregnancy so far. Seventy-eight percent of the women had already experienced nausea, 42% had vomited at least once, and 56% reported the onset of at least one food aversion. The targets and frequency of aversions were similar to the previous study. Looking at the relationships between symptoms, the presence of nausea significantly predicted the presence of a food aversion but did not predict the presence of a food craving. Neither aversions nor cravings were predictors of nausea, and the presence of aversions and cravings were not significant predictors of each other. The timings of first onset were more compressed in terms of week of onset but showed the same ordering as described in Figure 23.1, that is, food aversion onset occurring before food craving onset and at a very similar time to the start of nausea. Accordingly, in 41% of women reporting both nausea and food aversions, the first occurrence of nausea and the first food aversion occurred in the same week of pregnancy. A further 27% reported their first occurrence of nausea in the week preceding their first food aversion. By way of contrast, the first occurrence of nausea preceded the development of the first food craving by 2 weeks or more in 48% of cases. Only 21% of food cravings had their first onset during the week of first onset of nausea.

The second part of the study involved a 2-week diary recording of food and drink intake, and experiences of nausea, vomiting, food aversions, and cravings. Two 7-day diaries were provided for participants to record their food and drink consumption, and their experiences of nausea, vomiting, food cravings, and food aversions on a daily basis for two consecutive weeks. Standardized instructions on how to complete the diary were printed on the first two pages and examples were provided. For each day, there were pages dedicated to recording the food and drink consumed and experiences of nausea, vomiting, food cravings, and food aversions. Participants were contacted by phone during the recording period to answer queries and improve compliance. Of the 143 women who provided retrospective data, 103 (72%) completed the 2-week diary phase. A fifth of those who dropped out miscarried in the time before the prospective phase was completed.

Thirty-six percent of women reported experiencing at least one food aversion during the 2-week period, the mean number of aversions in this subgroup of participants being 4.3. Aversions that had not been reported during the retrospective phase and/or at an earlier point during the prospective phase were defined as "new" experiences. Thirty-two percent of these aversion reporters experienced at least one new aversion and amounted to an average of two new aversions over the 2-weeks period.

Contingency table analysis (χ^2) revealed no significant association between the presence of nausea and the type of experience (food aversion or craving). This may reflect the relatively smaller number of participants reporting aversions in this 2-week period compared with the retrospective studies and the associated reduction in statistical power. However, there was a significant association between whether a food aversion was new or old and the presence of nausea on the day of reporting. Eighty-five percent of new aversions were accompanied by nausea on the same day of recording, compared to 67% of aversions that had been reported previously. Unexpectedly, nausea reported prior to old aversion experiences occurred closer in time than nausea reported prior to new aversion experiences (medians = 125 vs. 245 min). But there were no differences in severity of nausea.

The data recorded in the diary were examined to determine whether changes in food aversions and cravings were preceded by eating the target food (either alone or as part of a meal or snack), and/or accompanied by nausea. New experiences were the focus of this analysis. Where the target food had been consumed on several occasions prior to the food craving or food aversion, the eating episode that occurred in closest proximity was the focus of the analysis. Details of nausea occurring in the 24 h prior to and following consumption of the target, but prior to the change in food preference, were noted.

Overall, 45% of new food aversions (vs. 27% of new cravings) were preceded by consumption of the target food or a meal or snack containing the target item. Where consumption of the target food preceded the change in food preference, nausea occurred in the 24 h prior to 93% of food aversions (and 78% of food cravings). Of the new experiences reported, 42% of aversions (and 21% of cravings) were preceded by nausea followed by consumption of the target food. Statistical analysis confirmed that there was a significant association between the type of experience and whether nausea followed by ingestion of the target preceded the change in food preference. It is notable that the duration of nausea prior to ingestion of the target food was significantly longer for food aversions than food cravings (medians = 120 vs. 60 min).

There was also a significant difference between aversions and cravings in the time between the onset of the experience and the next episode of eating. Eating occurred significantly later in cases of aversions compared to cravings (medians = 90 vs. 45 min). Unsurprisingly, nearly three-quarters of all aversions (72%) compared with just over a third of cravings (37%) were followed by consuming an item completely unrelated to the target of the experience.

This study has revealed three important aspects of the antecedents to changes in food preference. First, food aversions were closely associated with both nausea and prior consumption of the target food. Second, there were differences between new and old aversions in the experience of nausea and prior consumption of the target item on the day of recording. Third, a substantial proportion of new aversions was preceded by consumption of the target item and was accompanied by nausea at an earlier time point.

Comparing new and old aversions, nausea was present on a larger proportion of new aversion days and new food aversion experiences were more likely to be preceded by an episode of nausea. A greater proportion of old aversions were preceded by consumption of the target item on the same day of reporting. Thirty-three percent of new food aversions and 17% of new food craving experiences were preceded by food consumption accompanied or followed by an episode of nausea at an earlier point during the prospective recording phase.

Study 2

This study was designed to complement the diary record methodology described above by taking an incident approach to food aversions and cravings. This requires participants to note every occurrence of a food aversion and food craving and to complete a detailed account of the experience once it has passed. The information is noted on a food craving/aversion record, a list of 18 or more questions and ratings of the event listed on a single sheet of paper. Ratings are made on 100-mm visual analogue scales and mood assessed using a mood adjective checklist (see Hill & Heaton-Brown, 1994, for more information). The methodology builds on earlier studies of food cravings in healthy women (Hill & Heaton-Brown, 1994) and in women with bulimia nervosa (Waters, Hill, & Waller, 2001). It differs from a diary study in that participants focus just on the aversion/craving experiences rather that completing successive daily recordings. But the methodology is still most accurately described as quasi-prospective, since while the monitoring for aversions or cravings is prospective, their detailed account is retrospective, only being documented once the experience has passed (Hill, 2007).

Accordingly, 100 women completed a 7-day monitoring period. Again, around two-thirds were attending local assisted conception units. Their mean age was 31 years and their mean gestation 8 weeks, although this ranged from week 5 to 16 of pregnancy. Seventy-three usable food aversion records and 130 food craving records were completed in the week of recording. Thirty-four percent of women reported at least one food aversion and 52% experienced at least one food craving, amounting to just over two episodes of each experience per week (2.1 ± 0.3 and 2.5 ± 0.2, respectively). Looking specifically at new experiences, 27% experienced at least one new aversion and 44% reported at least one new craving.

Aversions and cravings occurred at all times of day, morning, afternoon, and evening. The majority was experienced at home, and only 22% of aversions and 18% of cravings occurred at a location other than home or work. In addition, 76% of aversions and 70% of cravings occurred in the company of others (in contrast to being alone). In 56% of food aversions and 67% of food cravings, participants reported that one form of contact with food preceded the change in food preference. A further 34% of aversions and 23% of cravings were preceded by two forms of contact with food. The most frequent antecedents to food aversions were smelling (53%), seeing (38%), or eating (23%) the target food. Food cravings were most frequently preceded by thinking about (72%) and seeing the target item (18%).

Overall, food aversions were rated stronger and as slower to disappear than food cravings, differences apparent in both new and old experiences (Table 23.1). There was no significant difference in ratings of how difficult the experiences were to resist/overcome. The rating scale values of strength and difficulty in resisting/overcoming were high,

Table 23.1 Mean (±SE) Rated Intensity of Food Craving and Food Aversion Experiences (mm on a 100-mm Visual Analogue Rating Scale).

	Aversions	Cravings
New		
Strength	77.6 (±2.8)	65.8 (±2.4)**
Difficulty in resisting/overcoming	68.1 (±3.4)	60.9 (±3.0)
Speed of disappearance	38.8 (±3.8)	65.0 (±2.7)**
Old		
Strength	86.0 (±2.9)	71.1 (±3.1)**
Difficulty in resisting/overcoming	75.7 (±6.4)	75.3 (±3.8)
Speed of disappearance	27.1 (±6.7)	65.9 (±5.2)**
Overall		
Strength	80.3 (±2.1)	67.2 (±1.9)**
Difficulty in resisting/overcoming	70.8 (±3.0)	64.7 (±2.5)
Speed of disappearance	34.7 (±3.4)	65.3 (±2.4)**

Note: Significant difference between aversions and cravings, **$p < 0.01$.

supporting the contention that these were high intensity experiences. The most common aversions were toward savoury meals (22%), tea and coffee (14%), milk, yoghurt, and cheese (12%), and meat, fish, poultry, and eggs (11%). A quarter of food aversions were for foods or drinks consumed at least once a day and 47% for items consumed infrequently (1–3 times per month or less). The craving/aversion records also showed that 57% of food aversions and 86% of food cravings were followed by eating. In 88% of food cravings followed by eating, the item consumed was either the target of the craving in isolation, or a meal or snack containing the target item. In contrast, in only 5% of food aversion cases followed by eating was the aversion target or a target-containing meal or snack consumed.

Rated nausea and adjective checklist scores of tense arousal (anxiety) were significantly higher prior to the onset of food aversions than cravings (Table 23.2). Postexperience measures showed even greater differences, apparent in nausea and all mood measures. These differences were also reflected in the change scores. Overall,

Table 23.2 Mean (±SE) Pre- and Postaversion and Craving Ratings of Hunger and Nausea (mm on a 100-mm Visual Analogue Rating Scale), and Mood (Adjective Checklist Scores).

	Aversions	Cravings
Hunger		
Pre-	42.1 (±3.9)	45.9 (±2.7)
Post-	28.9 (±3.6)	27.6 (±2.5)
Change	−15.2 (3.4)	−18.9 (±3.2)
Nausea		
Pre-	54.0 (±4.0)	25.8 (±2.4)**
Post-	70.7 (±2.9)	22.6 (±2.3)**
Change	17.3 (±3.6)	−2.8 (±3.0)**
Hedonic tone		
Pre-	7.8 (±0.3)	8.2 (±0.2)
Post-	6.3 (±0.3)	9.3 (±0.2)**
Change	−1.5 (±0.3)	1.2 (±0.2)**
Energetic arousal		
Pre-	4.6 (±0.3)	5.0 (±0.3)
Post-	4.0 (±0.3)	6.1 (±0.2)**
Change	−0.5 (±0.2)	1.0 (±0.3)**
Tense arousal		
Pre-	4.4 (±0.3)	3.4 (±0.2)*
Post-	5.4 (±0.3)	2.7 (±0.2)**
Change	0.9 (±0.2)	−0.7 (±0.2)**

Note: Significant difference between aversions and cravings, *p < 0.05, **p < 0.01.

aversions were associated with a further increase in nausea, a decrease in hedonic tone (happiness), and a increase in tense arousal (anxiety). Food cravings were characterized by an increase in hedonic tone, increase in energy, and decrease in tense arousal: an overall picture of mood improvement. Unsurprisingly, ratings of nausea were significantly and negatively correlated with hedonic tone and positively correlated with tense arousal and energetic arousal, both pre- and postexperience.

There were no significant differences between new and old cravings on any measure. The only significant differences between new and old aversions were that new aversions were associated with higher ratings of hunger both pre- (48.2 ± 4.4 vs. 30.2 ± 7.3) and postexperience (33.1 ± 4.3 vs. 21.2 ± 6.3). It is also of note that hunger decreased significantly across food aversion and craving experiences, regardless of whether food was eaten or not.

This study confirms many of the characteristics of food aversions reported in the diary study above. It confirms the close association with the experience of nausea and has added a change in mildly negative affective state to their description. The contrast with food cravings is also revealing. Cravings were directed at rather different foods, triggered mainly by thinking about those foods (rather than sensory contact), occurred less in the context of nausea and were associated with mild mood improvement. The difference between cravings and aversions in preexperience ratings of nausea and contact with the target food is again consistent with a food aversion learning mechanism.

The most commonly reported trigger or antecedent to an aversion was smelling the food. It has been suggested that in normal circumstances, odor alone is not an effective CS (Bernstein, 1999; Palmerino, Rusiniak, & Garcia, 1980). One possible explanation for this is that food aversions are not reported immediately following the pairing of the target item with nausea. Thus, after an initial pairing of ingestion of the target item with nausea the food aversion is reported following subsequent exposure to the target. Taking account of the phenomenon of taste potentiation of odor (Bernstein, 1999), it is possible that the odor was initially conditioned in conjunction with the taste of the target and became the cue for avoidance. Exposure to the smell of the target item may have elicited nausea, hence the higher ratings of nausea preaversion and the subsequent food aversion report.

Since several components of mood were significantly correlated with nausea, it is difficult to discern independent effects. Both food cravings and food aversions often occurred against some background nausea and both were associated with shifts in mood from pre- to postexperience. In the case of food aversions, nausea was high at the start and increased over the experience. This increase was accompanied by significant decreases in ratings of hedonic and energetic arousal and a significant increase in tense arousal. It is likely that these changes in mood at least partially reflect the change in nausea, and such changes in effect served to further enhance the aversive properties of the target item.

CONCLUSIONS

Nausea and sickness present a potent context for the formation of food aversions, yielding aversions that are different from those generated by other types of symptoms (Pelchat, Grill, Rozin, & Jacobs, 1983; Pelchat & Rozin, 1982). Specifically, nausea appears to be instrumental in the development of hedonic shifts or distaste toward food. Pregnancy therefore is an ideal state to study the acquisitions of food aversions, since NVP is such a common experience. Data from retrospective and prospective investigations outlined in this chapter have provided some evidence supporting conditioning mechanisms in their acquisition. In particular, there was consistency in finding a close temporal association between nausea and food aversions, and of prior physical contact with the food or beverage that became aversive.

Three observations from our prospective studies are pertinent to this argument. First, around one-third of food aversion experiences can be traced back to the pairing of the target food with an episode of nausea occurring during or following food ingestion. These data are consistent with a forward conditioning model (Logue, 1979). Second, participants reported experiencing more nausea on the day that the food aversion was reported and immediately prior to the experience. Third, smelling, seeing, or ingesting the target food characteristically preceded food aversion reports. Collectively these findings indicate that in some food aversions, following an initial pairing of the target item with nausea, the aversion was reported following a subsequent physical exposure to the target. Such an exposure may further increase feelings of nausea.

Past research suggests that food aversion learning may be modified by a number of factors. For example, aversions are more likely if the target food is novel (Revusky & Bedarf, 1967). Our research has provided some support for this in that nearly half of all food aversions in Study 2 were for items consumed infrequently. However, a quarter of aversions were directed at foods or beverages consumed more regularly in the diet. It is also suggested that higher protein foods are overrepresented in lists of aversions (Bernstein, Webster, & Bernstein, 1982; Midkiff & Bernstein, 1985), and this may be due to the flavor properties of such foods (Brot, Braget, & Bernstein, 1987). It is further argued that the presence of an odor in conjunction with a taste may make a food or drink a very potent target for a learned food aversion. Thus, foods with strong smells (e.g., coffee) may frequently become the targets of aversions. In the studies reported above, "tea and coffee" and "meat, fish, poultry, and eggs" were the most frequent targets of aversions. The overrepresentation of protein sources in the aversions of pregnant women is therefore consistent with that of other research where there is evidence of food aversion learning. The high proportion of aversions to caffeinated beverages and high-protein foods indicates that the odors of such items may have rendered them particularly susceptible to aversion formation.

Clearly, ingestion of a target food in the context of feeling nauseous cannot account for the development of all aversions during pregnancy. One possibility is that food consumption might not be necessary for aversion development and in some cases smelling the food in conjunction with nausea may be sufficient to condition an aversion. Although data reported above show smell to be a common antecedent to aversion experiences, this is a long way from showing that smell alone is sufficient to condition the aversion. To investigate this further, food odors or tastes could be incorporated into experimental tests of conditioning mechanisms. An alternative strategy would be to examine the effect of suppressing pregnancy-related nausea on the development of food aversions. However, any such experimental work during pregnancy would be controversial and raise serious ethical issues. For example, authors who have viewed pregnancy sickness as an evolved adaptation have argued that alleviating pregnancy sickness through the use of drugs or natural remedies may be potentially harmful to both mother and embryo, since it interferes with the expulsion of potentially dangerous foods or the opportunity to learn to avoid them (e.g., Flaxman & Sherman, 2000).

What then can be recommended to pregnant women in whom nausea and vomiting occur and in whom food aversions are more like to develop via the conditioning mechanisms described in this chapter? One obvious suggestion would be to avoid foods to which aversions are likely to develop, namely, those with strong odors or tastes, or to avoid contact with these foods during periods of nausea or vomiting. This may be difficult since NVP is not predictable. Alleviating pregnancy sickness via pharmacological intervention will not be advocated by those who support the evolutionary perspective on NVP or, indeed, any view that sees such sickness as valuable for the person or organism.

Finally, how does the evidence presented in this chapter fit with the theories concerning development and function of food aversions during pregnancy outlined earlier? It has been suggested that food aversion experiences, which develop via a food aversion learning mechanism involving pregnancy sickness, represent an evolved adaptation to prevent the consumption of foods that could be harmful to both mother and embryo. These data have provided some support for the only testable component of this theory, namely, the proposed association between prior exposure to the target food, pregnancy sickness, and food aversions. However, we acknowledge that there may be more than one legitimate function for food aversions in pregnancy, just as there are several plausible ways that food aversions can be acquired.

Note
1. The term food aversion dominates the pregnancy literature and in this context is used as synonymous with taste aversion.

References

Andrews, P., & Whitehead, S. (1990). Pregnancy sickness. *News in Physiological Science, 5,* 5–10.

Bayley, T. M., & Dye, L. (2002). Comment on D. M. T. Fessler: Reproductive immunosuppression and diet. *Current Anthropology, 43,* 39–40.

Bayley, T. M., Dye, L., Jones, S., DeBono, M., & Hill, A. J. (2002). Food cravings and aversions during pregnancy: Relationships with nausea and vomiting. *Appetite, 38,* 45–51.

Bayley, T. M., Dye, L. D., & Hill, A. J. Food cravings and aversions in pregnancy: two prospective studies. In preparation.

Baylis, J. M., Leeds, A. R., & Challacombe, D. N. (1983). Persistent nausea and food aversions in pregnancy. *Clinical Allergy, 13,* 263–269.

Bernstein, I. L. (1999). Taste aversion learning: A contemporary perspective. *Nutrition, Immunology, Neuroscience and Behaviour, 15,* 229–234.

Bernstein, I. L., Webster, M. M., & Bernstein, I. L. (1982). Food aversions in children receiving chemotherapy for cancer. *Cancer, 50,* 2960–2963.

Bowen, D. J. (1992). Taste and food preference changes across the course of pregnancy. *Appetite, 19,* 233–242.

Brot, M. D., Braget, D. J., & Bernstein, I. L. (1987). Flavor, not postingestive cues, contribute to the salience of proteins as targets in aversion conditioning. *Behavioral Neuroscience, 101,* 231–249.

Clark, J. (1998). Taste and flavour: Their importance in food choice and acceptance. *Proceedings of the Nutrition Society, 57,* 639–643.

Coronios-Vargas, M., Toma, R. B., Tuveson, R. V., & Schutz, I. M. (1992). Cultural influences on food cravings and aversions during pregnancy. *Ecology of Food and Nutrition, 27,* 43–49.

Crystal, S., Bowen, D. J., & Bernstein, I. L. (1999). Morning sickness and salt intake, food cravings and food aversions. *Physiology and Behavior, 67,* 181–187.

de Silva, P., & Rachman, S. (1987). Human food aversions: Nature and acquisition. *Behavior Research and Therapy, 25,* 457–468.

Deutsch, J. A. (1994). Pregnancy sickness as an adaptation to concealed ovulation. *Biology Forum, 87,* 277–295.

Dickens, G., & Trethowan, W. H. (1971). Cravings and aversions during pregnancy. *Journal of Psychosomatic Research, 15,* 259–268.

Doty, R. L. (1976). Reproductive endocrine influences upon human nasal chemoreception: A review. In R. L. Doty (Ed.), *Mammalian olfaction, reproductive processes, and behaviour* (pp. 295–321). New York: Academic Press.

Duffy, V. B., Bartoshuk, L. M., Striegel-Moore, R., & Rodin, J. (1998). Taste changes across pregnancy. *Annals of the New York Academy of Sciences, 855,* 805–809.

Edwards, C. H., McSwain, H., & Haire, S. (1954). Odd dietary practices of women. *Journal of the American Dietetic Association, 30,* 976–981.

Fallon, A. E., & Rozin, P. (1983). The psychological basis of food rejection by humans. *Ecology of Food and Nutrition, 13,* 15–25.

Fernández-Marcos, A., Martin, M., Sanchez, J. J., Rodriguez-Lescure, A., Casado, A., López Martin, J. A., et al. (1996). Acute and anticipatory emesis in breast cancer patients. *Supportive Care in Cancer, 4,* 370–377.

Fessler, D. M. T. (2002). Reproductive immunosuppression and diet. *Current Anthropology, 43,* 19–39, 48–61.

Fessler, D. M. T., & Navarrete, C. D. (2003) Meat is good to taboo: Dietary proscriptions as a product of the interaction of psychological mechanisms and social processes. *Journal of Cognition and Culture, 3*(1), 1–40.

Flaxman, S. M. (2002). Comment on D. M. T. Fessler: Reproductive immunosuppression and diet. *Current Anthropology, 43,* 41.

Flaxman, S. M., & Sherman, P. W. (2000). Morning sickness: A mechanism for protecting mother and embryo. *Quarterly Review of Biology, 75,* 113–148.

Gilbert, A. N., & Wysocki, C. J. (1991). Quantitative assessment of olfactory experience during pregnancy. *Psychosomatic Medicine, 53,* 693–700.

Godfrey, K., Robinson, S., Barker, D. J., Osmond, C., & Cox, V. (1996). Maternal nutrition in early and late pregnancy in relation to placental and fetal growth. *British Medical Journal, 312,* 410–414.

Haig, D. (1993). Genetic conflicts in human pregnancy. *Quarterly Review of Biology, 68,* 495–532.

Hill, A. J. (2007). The psychology of food craving. *Proceedings of the Nutrition Society, 66,* 277–285.

Hill, A. J., & Heaton-Brown, L. (1994). The experience of food craving: A prospective investigation in healthy women. *Journal of Psychosomatic Research, 38,* 801–814.

Hook, E. B. (1978). Dietary cravings and aversions during pregnancy. *American Journal of Clinical Nutrition, 31,* 1355–1362.

Hook, E. B. (1980). Influence of pregnancy on dietary selection. *International Journal of Obesity, 4,* 338–340.

Hutton, E. (1988). Sickness in pregnancy. *New Generation, 7,* 9–10.

Huxley, R. R. (2000). Nausea and vomiting in early pregnancy: Its role in placental development. *Obstetrics and Gynecology, 95,* 779–782.

Jarnfelt-Samsioe, A. (1987). Nausea and vomiting in pregnancy: A review. *Obstetrical and Gynecological Survey, 42,* 422–427.

Jarnfelt-Samsioe, A., Samsioe, G., & Velinder, G. (1983). Nausea and vomiting in pregnancy: A contribution to its epidemiology. *Gynecologic and Obstetric Investigation, 16,* 221–229.

Knox, B. J. (1993). *Dietary habits, taste acuity and preference for fat during human pregnancy.* PhD thesis, Queen's University, Belfast.

Lacroix, R., Eason, E., & Melzack, R. (2000). Nausea and vomiting during pregnancy: A prospective study of its frequency, intensity, and patterns of change. *American Journal of Obstetrics and Gynecology, 182,* 931–937.

Laska, M., Koch, B., Heid, B., & Hudson, R. (1996). Failure to demonstrate systematic changes in olfactory perception in the course of pregnancy: A longitudinal study. *Chemical Senses, 21,* 567–571.

Logue, A. W. (1979). Taste aversions and the generality of the laws of learning. *Psychological Bulletin, 86,* 276–296.

Masson, G. M., Anthony, F., & Chau, E. (1985). Serum chorionic gonadotrophin (hCG), schwangerschaftsprotein 1 (SP1), progesterone and oestradiol levels in patients with nausea and vomiting in early pregnancy. *British Journal of Obstetrics and Gynaecology, 92,* 211–215.

Mattes, R. D., Arnold, C., & Boraas, M. (1987). Learned food aversions among cancer chemotherapy patients: Incidence, nature and clinical implications. *Cancer, 60,* 2576–2580.

Midkiff, E. E., & Bernstein, I. L. (1985). Targets of learned food aversions in humans. *Physiology and Behavior, 34,* 839–841.

Nordin, S., Broman, D. A., Olofsson, J. K., & Wulff, M. (2004). A longitudinal descriptive study of self-reported abnormal smell and taste perception in pregnant women. *Chemical Senses, 29,* 391–402.

O'Brien, B., & Newton, N. (1991). Psyche versus soma: Historical evolution of beliefs about nausea and vomiting during pregnancy. *Journal of Psychosomatic Obstetrics and Gynecology, 12,* 91–120.

O'Rourke, D. E., Quinn, J. G., Nicholson, J. O., & Gibson, H. H. (1967). Geophagia during pregnancy. *Obstetrics and Gynecology, 29,* 581–584.

Palmerino, C. C., Rusiniak, K. W., & Garcia, J. (1980). Flavor illness aversions: The peculiar role of odor and taste in memory for poison. *Science, 208,* 753–755.

Pelchat, M. L., Grill, H. J., Rozin, P., & Jacobs, J. (1983). Quality of acquired responses to tastes by *Rattus norvegicus* depends on type of associated discomfort. *Journal of Comparative Psychology, 97*, 140–153.

Pelchat, M. L., & Rozin, P. (1982). The special role of nausea in the acquisition of food dislikes by humans. *Appetite, 3*, 341–351.

Pepper, G. V., & Roberts, S. C. (2006). Rates of nausea and vomiting in pregnancy and dietary characteristics across populations. *Proceedings of the Royal Society of Biology, 273*, 2675–2679.

Pond, W. G., Maurer, R. R., Mersmann, H. J., & Cummins, S. (1992). Response of fetal and newborn piglets to maternal protein restriction during early or late pregnancy. *Growth, Development, and Ageing, 56*, 115–127.

Profet, M. (1988). The evolution of pregnancy sickness as protection to the embryo against pleistocene teratogens. *Evolutionary Theory, 8*, 177–190.

Profet, M. (1992). Pregnancy sickness as adaptation: A deterrent to maternal ingestion of teratogens. In J. H. Barkow, L. Cosmides, & J. Tooby (Eds.), *The adapted mind: Evolutionary psychology and the generation of culture* (pp. 327–365). New York: Oxford University Press.

Revusky, S. H., & Bedarf, E. W. (1967). Association of illness with prior ingestion of novel foods. *Science, 155*, 219–220.

Robson, K. M., Brant, H. A., & Kumar, R. (1981). Maternal sexuality during first pregnancy and after childbirth. *British Journal of Obstetrics and Gynaecology, 88*, 882–889.

Rodin, J., & Radke-Sharpe, N. (1991). Changes in appetitive variables as a function of pregnancy. In M. I. Friedman, M. G. Tordoff, & M. R. Kare (Eds.), *Chemical senses: Vol. 4. Appetite and nutrition* (pp. 325–340). New York: Marcel Dekker.

Schwab, E. B., & Axelson, M. L. (1984). Dietary changes of pregnant women: Compulsions and modifications. *Ecology of Food and Nutrition, 14*, 143–153.

Soules, M. R., Hughes, C. L., Garcia, J. A., Livengood, C. H., Prytowsky, M. R., & Alexander, E., III. (1980). Nausea and vomiting of pregnancy: Role of human chorionic gonadotrophin and 17-hydroxyprogesterone. *Obstetrics and Gynecology, 55*, 696–700.

Stein, Z., & Susser, M. (1991). Miscarriage, caffeine, and the epiphenomena of pregnancy: The causal model. *Epidemiology, 2*, 163–167.

Stewart, J., Wheeler, E., & Schofield, C. (1988). Regional differences in British attitudes to diet in pregnancy: Priorities and pragmatism. *Ecology of Food and Nutrition, 20*, 211–229.

Tierson, F. D., Olsen, C. L., & Hook, E. B. (1985). Influence of cravings and aversions on diet in pregnancy. *Ecology of Food and Nutrition, 17*, 117–129.

van Lier, D., Manteuffel, B., Dilorio, C., & Stalcup, M. (1993). Nausea and fatigue during early pregnancy. *Birth, 20*, 193–197.

Walsh, J. W., Hasler, W. L., Nugent, C. E., & Owyang, C. (1996). Progesterone and estrogen are potential mediators of gastric slow-wave dysrhythmias in nausea of pregnancy. *American Journal of Physiology, 270*, G506–G514.

Waters, A., Hill, A. J., & Waller, G. (2001). Internal and external antecedents of binge eating episodes in a group of women with bulimia nervosa. *International Journal of Eating Disorders, 29*, 17–22.

Whitehead, S. A., Andrews, P. L. R., & Chamberlain, G. V. P. (1992). Characterisation of nausea and vomiting in early pregnancy: A survey of 1000 women. *Journal of Obstetrics and Gynaecology, 12*, 364–369.

Worthington-Roberts, B., Little, R. E., Lambert, M. D., & Wu, R. (1989). Dietary cravings and aversions in the postpartum period. *Journal of the American Dietetic Association, 89*, 647–651.

24

Role of Conditioned Taste Aversion on the Side Effects of Chemotherapy in Cancer Patients

GIUSEPPE SCALERA[†] AND MARIO BAVIERI

This chapter will examine problems encountered when trying to assess the role of conditioned taste aversion (CTA) and conditioned food aversion (CFA) in the aversive physical and psychological side effects induced by chemotherapy in cancer patients.

CTA and CFA are widely distributed phenomena in the animal world, from insects to primates including humans, and involves the rejection of fluids or solids whose ingestion had induced the onset of aversive postingestional consequences and/or malaise. CTA has been considered a form of CFA learning, and no substantial differences exist between them. Thus, in this chapter, both CTA and CFA will assume the same meaning, except where noted otherwise.

CTA may be considered a kind of Pavlovian conditioning with some unique properties: (1) strong CTA is established after only one conditioned stimulus–unconditioned stimulus (CS–US) pairing; (2) CTA may also be formed when an interval of several hours (from 30 min to up to 24 h) is allowed between exposure to CS and delivery of US; (3) deep anesthesia does not prevent the CS–US association (Gallo et al., 1999; Revusky & Garcia, 1970; Schafe, LeDoux, Fitts, Thiele, & Bernstein, 2000).

In CFA learning paradigms, taste represents the principal part of the repertoire of elicited responses for CS sensory modality. Other important components include olfactory, thermal, tactile, and visceral stimuli, which may be integrated with taste stimuli in the brain. It must be noted that even if the main CS pathways include the peripheral and central structures of gustatory and olfactory systems, some species use other senses (such as vision) as primary stimulus in CFA learning (Braveman, 1974; Gaston, 1977; Lee-Teng & Sherman, 1966; Wilcoxon, Dragoin, & Kral, 1971). CFA can develop in the course of medical treatments that induce emesis or distress (Bernstein & Webster, 1980; Logue, 1985). Although nausea is a sufficient but not always necessary condition for the development of CFA, it plays a potent role in CFA learning when food becomes distasteful (Pelchat, Grill, Rozin, & Jacobs, 1983; Pelchat & Rozin, 1982).

CTA has been extensively investigated in a wide variety of laboratory and wild animal species but only occasionally in humans. In experimental animals, the most effective drugs and/or treatments producing US are those inducing emetic activity and malaise. The aversive nature of the USs (chemicals, radiation, drugs, etc.) employed

---

[†]Unfortunately, when writing this chapter, doctors diagnosed lung ADK in one of the authors (G. S.). He was treated by chemotherapy and radiotherapy, and he experienced for himself the collateral problems of chemotherapy discussed in this chapter.

in CTA protocols in nonhuman animals has for the most part prevented controlled experiments in human subjects. Nevertheless, interview studies have documented that many people develop CTA as a result of a food–illness pairing (Bernstein & Webster, 1980; Garb & Stunkard, 1974; Logue, 1985). When food consumption is followed by gastrointestinal discomfort (nausea, vomiting, stomachache, etc.), humans may develop a CTA. In humans, as in nonhuman animals, CTAs are more readily learned when the target food is novel rather than familiar, and learning is stronger when the CS precedes the US (Bernstein, 1978; Garb & Stunkard, 1974; Logue, 1985; Midkiff & Bernstein, 1985). Theoretically, any given food or beverage may become aversive when it precedes illness, but the probability is not constant, and unfamiliarity with a food may increase the possibility of forming an aversion.

In rats, taste aversion may be conditioned with radiation exposure when a sweet solution (saccharin) is injected intravascularly (Bradley & Mistretta, 1971). Intravascular injections of a drug (Bradley, 1973; Bures & Buresova, 1989; Coil & Norgren, 1981; Miyagawa, Honma, Sato, & Hasegawa, 1984) or odorant (Maruniak, Mason, & Kostelc, 1983) can increase the blood concentration of that substance (e.g., saccharin, copper sulfide, allyl sulfide, etc.) to a level stimulating the taste buds and/or olfactory receptors in absence of consummatory activity. These results show that the characteristic taste and/or smell of chemotherapeutic drugs injected intravascularly in cancer patients may sometimes produce taste aversion per se.

The cognitive development of humans, which enables them to understand that their discomfort is ascribable to causes unrelated to the foods eaten, does not override the learning mechanisms responsible for CTA (Bernstein & Webster, 1980). Thus, CTAs appear to defy cognition, and strong aversions may arise despite a person's full awareness that the target food was not actually the cause of their illness (Bernstein, 1999). A learned CTA to a particular CS will generalize to other tastes that are qualitatively similar to the CS (Logue et al., 1981).

Usually, in healthy people with a broad range of food preference, CFA plays a relatively minor role in establishing food and fluid intake, but in people disliking many kinds of food, with a fussy appetite or narrow preference ranges, it may assume a relevant aspect because they may experience frequent pairings of specific foods with

symptoms of malaise. Such people may not be able to select alternative nonaversive food choices, and thus they may progressively reduce their food intake (Bernstein, 1991). Most vulnerable to this effect are children, who usually tend to avoid new flavors (Birch, 1998). Some people who are chronically sick or are experiencing unpleasant gastrointestinal distress may more easily develop a CFA against some foods, thus sometimes inducing anorexia (Bernstein & Borson, 1986; MacIntosh, Morley, & Chapman, 2000). The case for learned food aversion as a contributing factor in clinical syndromes of appetite loss is not yet clearly established, but the evidence for involvement of aversion learning in cancer patients anorexia is strong and CFAs might play an etiologic role in appetite and body weight loss (Logue 1979; Logue, Logue & Strauss, 1983).

An interesting matter is the study of factors influencing the tendency of various foods to develop aversive behaviors. Usually, a meal includes many different food items, and thus it is not always easy to identify which food caused the aversion. Taste, smell, flavor, texture, novelty, food preference, and composition are the principal characteristics of foods that increase the associability with illness. Aversions are more likely to be formed to less preferred and less familiar foods, although aversions are acquired to some foods that are also highly preferred. Another interesting aspect of CFA is whether some types of foods are more likely to be targets of aversions than others on account of their nutrients content. The categories of foods that may be considered major protein sources (eggs, red meats, poultry, fish) constitute about 42% of all CFAs (Midkiff & Bernstein, 1985; Mooney & Walbourn, 2001). Categories of foods that infrequently form targets for aversions are sweet (sugar, cakes, pies, etc.) or nonsweet carbohydrates (bread, crackers, flour products, rice, potatoes, etc.; Logue, 1985; Midkiff & Bernstein, 1985). Dairy products (milk, cheese, butter, etc.) are a case apart and controversial data are present in the literature (Logue et al., 1981; Midkiff & Bernstein, 1985).

Nausea and vomiting are among the most intractable and unpleasant experiences of patients undergoing chemotherapy. Despite advances in pharmacological control of chemotherapy-induced nausea and vomiting, up to 80% of cancer patients treated with chemotherapy experience at least mild nausea and about 40% have at least one episode of vomiting (Roscoe, Morrow, Hickok, & Stern, 2000). Patients who have nausea and vomiting after chemotherapy can learn to associate these side effects with their treatments. The taste dysfunction associated with side effects of chemotherapy results in food avoidance with a negative impact on the nutritional status and quality of life of patients.

In addition to physical side effects, cancer patients experience psychological side effects that often compromise patients' quality of life and may lead to the decision to postpone or even reject potentially lifesaving treatments (Carey & Burish, 1988). In particular, the role of CTA and CFA in controlling anticipatory nausea (AN) and anticipatory vomiting (AV), and the nutritional status of cancer patients submitted to chemotherapy will be examined. At last, some pharmacological and cognitive behavioral treatments on reducing aversive side effects of chemotherapy will be discussed.

ETIOLOGY OF PHYSICAL SIDE EFFECTS ASSOCIATED WITH CHEMOTHERAPY

Before the 1950s, no valid therapy against malignant tumors was known. The regional therapies (surgical resection and "curative" radiotherapy) of malignant tumors were the only available tools, but many patients developed recurrent or metastatic cancer. Conceptual constructs and experimental data led to the hypothesis that most primary cancers become systemic in nature by the time the diagnosis is made; consequently, regional therapies cannot provide a realistic probability of cure once micrometastatic deposits have been established (Hortobagyi, 2001). Chemotherapy was introduced as a systemic anticancer therapy in the 1950s and started to be routinely used in the 1970s. Thus, the discovery of cytotoxic chemotherapeutic drugs became the mainstay of cancer drug development in the past decades (Johnson, 2000). From the 1950s, a variety of drugs and regimens have been evaluated for treatments of cancer. Many drugs have been tested for their anticancer activity and new drugs have been constantly developed even now. Some of these drugs have been in use from about 40 years and today clinical oncologists use almost 40 drugs, either alone or in combination (Table 24.1).

Recently, the term "targeted therapy" has been invented to refer to a new generation of cancer drugs designed to interfere with a specific molecular target (typically a protein) that is believed to have a critical role in tumor growth and/or progression. This approach contrasts with the conventional approach used to develop cytotoxic chemotherapeutics (Sawyers, 2004). Even if this new approach offers many exciting targets for treating and/or preventing cancer, classical chemotherapy and radiotherapy approaches remain the mainstay of cancer treatment for tumors that cannot be cured solely by surgical excision. In other words, the conventional cancer therapies (chemotherapy, surgery, radiothearpy) may be combined with "targeted therapy" that disrupts the DNA-repair response; hopefully a more catastrophic cell kill in tumors will result (Sawyers, 2004). But, so far, none has unequivocally proved its superiority and thus no single standard salvage therapy exists yet.

The effectiveness of new cytotoxic chemotherapeutic drugs is more or less the same as that of oldest ones (e.g., cisplatin, carboplatin, etc.), but in some cases, the toxicity is diminished and patients receive a more appropriate individualized dose. Two or more of these drugs are frequently combined in an effort to improve the survival and tumor-related symptoms, even when there is no overt evidence of tumor regression.

The choice and effectiveness of cytotoxic chemotherapeutic drugs depend on many factors, such as the type and characteristic of tumor (origin, localization, extension, etc.), the dosage, age, sex, and general health conditions of the patient.

The concept of "adjuvant" chemotherapy was introduced to define the combination of local/regional and systemic treatments to maximize the probability of cure and long-term survival.

In conclusion, at the present time, cytotoxic chemotherapy is still the treatment of choice for most cancer patients (Jemal et al., 2007; Silverberg & Lubera, 1986), since antineoplastic medications have increased the life expectancy for many patients and, in some cases, have resulted in remission and cure. Unfortunately, such long-term gain in life expectancy can induce considerable short-term cost to the cancer patients in the form of aversive and debilitating side effects. Among the more common antineoplastic-induced side effects are itching, alopecia, stomatitis, immunosuppression, distaste, anorexia, fatigue, insomnia, nausea, vomiting, disrupted gastrointestinal function including dyspepsia and diarrhea, constipation, and retching (Given et al., 2004; Jordan, Kasper, & Schmoll,

Table 24.1 Emetogenic Risk of Intravenously or Orally Administered Chemotherapeutic Agents.

Very High: Emetic Risk > 90% (Without Antiemetic Prophylaxis)

Intravenous Administration		Oral Administration
Actinomycin D	Lomustine >60 mg/m^2	Hexamethylmelamine
Carmustine >250 mg/m^2	Mechlorethamine	Procarbazine
Cisplatin ≥50 mg/m^2	Pentostatin	
Cyclophosphamide >1500 mg/m^2	Streptozotocin	
Dacarbazine (DTIC) ≥500 mg/m^2		

High: Emetic Risk 60%–90% (Without Antiemetic Prophylaxis)

Intravenous Administration		Oral Administration
Carboplatin	Doxorubicin >60 mg/m^2	Cyclophosphamide
Carmustine ≤250 mg/m^2	Lomustine <60mg/ m^2	Temozolamide
Cisplatin <50 mg/m^2	Methotrexate >1000 mg/m^2	Vinorelbine
Cyclophosphamide 750–1500 mg/m^2	Mitoxantrone >15 mg/m^2	Imatinib
Cytarabine ≥1000 mg/m^2	Oxaliplatin	
Dacarbazine <500 mg/m^2	Procarbazine	
Dactinomycin >1.5 mg/m^2		

Moderate: Emetic Risk 30%–60% (Without Antiemetics Prophylaxis)

Intravenous Administration		Oral Administration
Cyclophosphamide <750 mg/m^2	Irinotecan	Capecitabine
Dactinomycin ≤1.5 mg/m^2	Melphalan	Etoposide
Daunorubicin	Methotrexate 250–1000 mg/m^2	Fludarabine
Doxorubicin 20–60 mg/m^2	Mitoxantrone ≤15 mg/m^2	
Epirubicin ≤90 mg/m^2	Temozolamide	
Hexamethylmelamine	Treosulfan	
Idarubicin	Trabectedin	
Ifosfamide		

Low: Emetic Risk 10%–30% (Without Antiemetics Prophylaxis)

Intravenous Administration		Oral Administration
Aldesleukin (IL-2)	Methotrexate 50–250 mg/m^2	Chlorambucil
Asparaginase	Mitomycin	Hydroxyurea
Bortezomib	Mitoxantrone <12 mg/m^2	L-Phenylalanine mustard
Cytarabine <1000 mg/m^2	Paclitaxel	6-Thioguanine
Cetuximab	Pegasparaginase	Methotrexate
Doxorubicin <20 mg/m^2	Pemetrexed	
Docetaxel	Teniposide	
Etoposide	Thiopea	
5-Fluorouracil <1000 mg/m^2	Topotecan	
Gemcitabine	Trastuzumab	

(continued)

Table 24.1 *Continued*

Minimal: Emetic Risk <10% (Without Antiemetics Prophylaxis)

Intravenous Administration		Oral Administration
Bevacizumab	Melphalan	Erlotinib
Bleomycin	Mercaptopurine	Gefitinib
Busulfan	Methotrexate <50 mg/m^2	Melphalan
Capecitabine	Rituximab	
Chlorambucil	Thioguanine	
Cytarabine <100 mg/m^2	Vinblastine	
Fludarabine	Vincristine	
α-, β-, γ-Interferon	Vinorelbine	
Hydroxyurea		

Sources: Data from Roila et al. (2006), Antonarakis and Hain (2004), Jordan, Kasper, and Schmoll, (2005), and Grunberg et al. (2005).

Note: Dosage: mg/m^2 body surface.

2005; Nitenberg & Raynard, 2000; Stockorst et al., 2006). Uncontrolled emesis can have serious consequences and might require delays between treatments, reducing the efficacy of chemotherapy (Miller & Kearney, 2004).

Nausea and vomiting induced by chemotherapy may be (1) acute, when symptoms begin within minutes of drug administration and resolve within 24 h; (2) delayed, when symptoms occur and persist for several hours and days after chemotherapy somministration; (3) anticipatory, when emesis occurs before chemotherapy infusion once an association has been established between contextual cues (taste, odor, sight, thoughts, anxiety, etc.) and nausea and vomiting (Bender et al., 2002).

Nausea and vomiting may be initiated by the activation of 5-hydroxytryptamine (5-HT$_2$, 5-HT$_3$, 5-HT$_4$), dopamine (D$_2$), histamine (H$_1$), and acetylcholine (Ach) receptors that are present in the gut wall, liver, area postrema ("chemoreceptor trigger zone," CTZ), vagus nerve, vomiting center, and so on (Antonarakis & Hain, 2004; Twycross & Back, 1998).

Chemotherapy drugs can cause nausea and vomiting by the damage they cause to cells particularly those in the gastrointestinal tract, and by systemic circulation through their interaction with CTZ and vomiting center. In the first case, the enterochromaffin cells in the intestinal mucosa are rich in 5-hydroxytryptamine (serotonin; 5-HT) and D$_2$ receptors, and the damage to the mucosa due to systemic anticancer drugs (including

cisplatin) may result in a massive release of 5-HT, acting on 5-HT$_3$ receptors, and dopamine, which in turn may start nausea and vomiting (Sanger & Andrews, 2006). In the second case, the area postrema, which is outside the blood–brain barrier but in intimate contact with the blood, is rich in D$_2$ and 5-HT$_3$ receptors that may be directly stimulated by toxic drugs circulating in the blood.

The complex process of vomiting is coordinated by the vomiting center (or "emetic pattern generator"), which may activate the H$_1$, muscarinic ACh, and 5-HT$_2$ receptors inside the blood–brain barrier (Antonarakis & Hain, 2004). The functional connection of vomiting center in the medulla oblongata and the higher cortical structures may be responsible for AN and AV in conditioned patients.

Although the emetogenic potential varies across antineoplastic agents classified as very high (>90%), high (60%–90%), moderate (>30%–60%), low (10%–30%), and minimal (<10%) emetic risk (Table 24.1), in the absence of prophylactic antiemetic therapy, the number of patients experiencing vomiting and nausea after the first treatment would exceed 90% for several widely used chemotherapic agents (e.g., cisplatin; Bovbjerg, 2006).

Typically, patients receive multiple courses of intravenous (i.v.) chemotherapy infusion and antiemetic treatments. A month-long course of repeated cycles of treatment (e.g., infusion followed by 2–3 weeks for recovery) is required for most curative chemotherapy regimens. The interval between two subsequent chemotherapy infusions depends on the recovery time of rapidly dividing normal tissues (e.g., bone marrow, intestines, oral cavity, skin, stem cells, etc.) from the toxicity of chemotherapeutic drugs. Patients receiving chemotherapeutic agents at maximum tolerated doses often require extended treatment-free periods for recovery (Fidler & Ellis, 2000). Usually, in many combined chemotherapy protocols, the recovery interval is 2 weeks and the second cycle may start on the twenty-first day.

With repeated cycles of chemotherapy (usually six cycles), the incidence of emesis and nausea generally becomes higher. Moreover, the percentage of patients reporting emesis increases across subsequent cycles of chemotherapy (Bovbjerg, 2006).

Other risk factors are schedule (morning or afternoon infusions, single or multiple doses), route of drugs administration (i.v. or oral), age (younger patients have more nausea and vomiting than elderly patients), gender (female patients are affected more often than males), alcohol intake, anxiety, experience of emesis, impaired quality of life, and previous experience of chemotherapy; all these are known to increase the risk of nausea and vomiting after chemotherapy (Jordan et al., 2005; Morrow, 1985; Osoba et al., 1997; Roila, Hesketh, & Herrstedt, 2006).

Failure to control side effects such as nausea and vomiting in cancer patients can have serious consequences, since it may require delays between cycles of treatments reducing the effectiveness of chemotherapy; sometimes it may even increase the likelihood that patients will drop out of treatment (Miller & Kearney, 2004). Thus, in the past 20 years, a pharmacological management of emesis have become the standard of care for the control of chemotherapy-induced nausea and vomiting (Jordan et al., 2005).

PHARMACOLOGICAL TREATMENTS OF PHYSICAL SIDE EFFECTS ASSOCIATED WITH CHEMOTHERAPY

Obviously, the principal aim of antiemetic prophylaxis is to reduce or abolish nausea and vomiting induced by chemotherapy. With modern antiemetic therapy, nausea and vomiting can be almost completely prevented in about 70%–80% of patients in accordance with the emetogenic potential of chemotherapeutic agents used (Table 2). In recent years, the development of selective antagonists to the 5-hydroxytryptamine receptors ($5\text{-}HT_2$, $5\text{-}HT_3$, $5\text{-}HT_4$), dopamine receptors (D_2), and neurokinin-1 receptors (NK1 receptors) has changed the treatment of the chemotherapy-induced nausea and emesis (Hesketh & Gandara, 1991; Kris et al., 2005; Perez, Hesketh, & Gandara, 1991). Recently, the Multinational Association of Supportive Care in Cancer (MASCC, 2004), the American Society of Clinical Oncology (ASCO; Kris et al., 2006), and National Comprehensive Cancer Network (NCCN, 2004) published the guidelines for a practical treatment approach for antiemetic prophylaxis in cancer patients.

In accordance with these guidelines, the antagonists of $5\text{-}HT_2$, $5\text{-}HT_3$, and $5\text{-}HT_4$ receptors, in combination with steroids, and aprepitant (NK1 receptor antagonists) have become the standard of care to prevent acute and delayed nausea and vomiting following chemotherapy (Table 24.2). Although the antagonists of the $5\text{-}HT_3$ receptors (ondansetron, granisetron, tropisetron, dolasetron, and palonosetron) differ in receptor specificity, potency, and plasma half-life, each, when given at biologically equivalent doses, has demonstrated equivalent efficacy, interchangeability, and adverse side effects (e.g., headache and constipation being the most commonly reported; Perez, 1995). Steroids are considered to be effective and safe antiemetic and if used in combination with other antiemetics, they significantly raise emetic thresholds. The ASCO update (Kris et al., 2006; Ioannidis, Hesketh, & Lau, 2000) recommends dexamethasone as antiemetic because it is the corticosteroid most extensively studied and widely available, even if its antiemetic efficacy is almost equal to that of other steroids (Jordan et al., 2005). Insomnia and hyperglycemia are the principal side effects of steroids and are dependent on the dosage and duration of somministration of drugs.

NK1-receptor antagonists (aprepitant) represent a new class of antiemetic drugs that increases the antiemetic activity (particularly delayed emesis) of the combination of the $5\text{-}HT_3$- receptor antagonists and dexamethasone in patients treated with cisplatin chemotherapy. The aprepitant treatment versus standard antiemetic therapy reduces the risk of emesis by about 20% (Chawla et al., 2003; Kris et al., 2006; MASCC, 2004; NCCN, 2004).

Table 24.2 Dose and Schedule of Antiemetic Agents to Prevent Acute and Delayed Emesis Induced by Chemotherapy of High, Moderate, and Low Emetic Risk.

Emetic Risk Level Induced by Chemotherapy	Antiemetic	Oral Daily Dose Given before Chemotherapy	Intravenous Daily Dose Given before Chemotherapy
5-HT3 Receptor Antagonists			
High	Ondansetron	24 mg	8 mg or 0.15mg/kg
High	Granisetron	2 mg	1 mg or 0.01mg/kg
High	Dolasetron	100–200 mg	100mg or 1.8 mg/kg
High	Palonosetron	NA	0.25 mg/kg
High	Tropisetron	5 mg	5 mg
Steroids			
High	Dexamethasone	12–20 mg	NA
High	Methylprednisolone	40–125 mg	NA
Neurokinin-1-Receptor-Antagonist			
High	Aprepitant	125 mg day 1, 80 mg days 2 + 3	
5-HT$_3$ Receptor Antagonist			
Moderate	Ondansetron	16 mg	8 mg or 0.15 mg/kg
Moderate	Granisetron	2 mg	1 mg or 0.01mg/kg
Moderate	Dolasetron	100 mg	100 mg or 1.8 mg/kg
Moderate	Palonosetron	NA	0.25 mg/kg
Moderate	Tropisetron	5 mg	5 mg
	Steroids		
Moderate	Dexamethasone	8–12 mg	NA
Moderate	Methylprednisolone	40–125 mg	NA
Neurokinin-1-Receptor-Antagonist			
Moderate	Aprepitant	125 mg,	
D$_2$ Antagonist			
Moderate	Metoclopramide	10–20 mg	0.22–0.46 mg/kg (Pediatric patients)
Moderate	Prochlorperazine	10 mg	
Steroids			
Low	Dexamethasone	8–12 mg	NA
Minimal	None		

Source: Data from Roila et al. (2006); Jordan et al. (2005); Kris et al. (2005); Herrstedt et al. (1998); Herrstedt, Koeller, et al. (2005).

Notes: In some cases, a combination of antiemetics may be used.

Efficacy of the D_2 receptor antagonists as a single antiemetic agent is relatively low; metoclopramide possesses antiemetic activity when given to patients receiving moderately emetogenic chemotherapy (Herrstedt, Aapro, Smyth, & Del Favero, 1998). At high dosage, the main side effects are sedation and orthostatic hypotension.

Antihistamines have not shown any antiemetic effect in the prevention of chemotherapy-induced nausea and vomiting, but they have a role in the treatment of nausea mediated by the vestibular system (Gralla et al., 1999). The main side effects of antihistamines are drowsiness, dry mouth, and blurred vision.

Cannabinoids may be used as antiemetic drugs in the treatment of "refractory" or "breakthrough" emesis, but their employment is limited by the high incident of toxic effects (dizziness, dysphoria, hallucinations; Gralla et al., 1984; Jordan et al., 2005). "Refractory" emesis is generally defined as emesis occurring despite the use of antiemetic prophylaxis during the previous cycle of chemotherapy. "Breakthrough" emesis represents vomiting that occurs on any day of treatment despite the administration of optimal antiemetic prophylaxis. Breakthrough emesis is treated with rescue antiemetics given on the patient's demand (Roila et al., 2006). There is no group of patients for whom metoclopramide, phenothiazines, butyrophenones, and cannabinoids are appropriate as the first-choice antiemetics; these agents should be reserved for patients intolerant or refractory to 5-HT$_3$ receptor antagonists, dexamethasone, and aprepitant. In certain circumstances, benzodiazepines (lorazepam and alprazolam) may be added to the antiemetic therapies since they reduce the anxiety and reduce the risk of AN and AV (Kris, Gralla, Clark, Tyson, & Groshen, 1987), but they are not reccomended as single antiemetic agent.

The progress in the pharmacological treatment of nausea and vomiting has reduced the incidence and/or severity of emesis and nausea in cancer patients. Nevertheless, repeated somministrations of antiemetics may increase adverse symptoms probably because their frequent use may develop CSs (Small, Holdsworth, & Raisch, 2000).

In conclusion, in spite of improvements in controlling nausea and vomiting induced by chemotherapy, the effectiveness of the available antiemetics is still limited; in some cases, the pharmacological prevention of emesis is not complete and that of nausea is still more difficult (Herrstedt, Aapro et al., 1998; Herrstedt, Koeller, et al., 2005; Herrstedt, Muss, et al., 2005; Jordan et al., 2005).

The limited effectiveness of pharmacological antiemetic treatments may depend on the result from psychological processes that occur in the chemotherapy context and that cannot be attributed directly to the antineoplastic medications. For example, patients who have nausea and vomiting after chemotherapy can learn to associate these side effects with their treatments, and they will experience them in response to merely thinking about stimuli connected with treatments. Such symptoms develop in approximately 30% of patients by the fourth treatment cycle and appear to link psychological, neurological, and physiological systems (Burish & Carey, 1986). Once they develop, nausea and vomiting are not well controlled by pharmacologic treatments (Matteson, Roscoe, Hickok, & Morrow, 2002). The ineffectiveness or the practical limitations of pharmacological agents have all prompted researchers to consider the cognitive behavioral treatments (or psychological treatments) as an alternative method of controlling side effects of chemotherapy, and some meta-analysis studies of literature validated the effectiveness of cognitive behavioral therapy treatments for alleviating distress and pain in cancer patients (Carey & Burish, 1998; Mundy, DuHamel, & Montgomery, 2003; Redd, Montgomery & DuHamel, 2001).

ETIOLOGY OF PSYCHOLOGICAL SIDE EFFECTS ASSOCIATED WITH CHEMOTHERAPY

In cancer patients, psychological side effect symptoms are believed to be relatively common, and they can occur before chemotherapy somministration (in which case they are referred to as anticipatory side effects) as well as during and after the actual chemotherapy infusion (Carey & Burish, 1988). Research has focused on such psychological symptoms as nausea, vomiting, dysphoria, CTA and CFA, and conditioned immunosuppression (Ader & Cohen, 1993; Ader, Cohen, & Felten, 1995; Bernstein & Borson, 1986; Smith, Blumsack, & Bilek, 1985). Research has suggested that patients who have a history of motion sickness or of experiencing nausea and vomiting in response to various foods or situations are more likely to report posttreatment and anticipatory nausea and vomiting in response to cancer chemotherapy (Jacobsen et al., 1988; Morrow, 1985). Another major factor that might affect the development of conditioned responses to chemotherapy is a patient's anxiety level. In patients with an increased propensity to be anxious, data suggest that heightened anxiety levels facilitate the development of psychological symptoms, such as AN and AV.

Several suggestions have been offered to explain the development of psychological side effects in cancer patients. One hypothesis suggests that non-pharmacological symptoms represent the negative effect that patients develop toward their chemotherapy treatments. A second hypothesis is that patients may display side effect symptoms in order to gain attention and sympathy with other people. A third hypothesis suggests that the observed symptoms may be produced by local cancer derived factors involving the gastrointestinal tract (Carey & Burish, 1988).

In contrast to these three hypotheses, which are speculative and lack experimental support, a fourth hypothesis, supported by the research and literature, holds that, in cancer patients, psychological side effects develop through an associative process that is strictly similar to the Pavlovian conditioning and closely resembles CTA mechanisms (Bernstein, 1978; Bernstein & Webster, 1980; Bovbjerg, 2006; Carey & Burish, 1988; Garcia y Robertson & Garcia, 1985; Stockhorst, Steingruber, Enck, Klosterhalfen, 2006). According to the most widely accepted conditioning viewpoint, after one or more pairings, an association is established between the pharmacological side effects (the unconditioned response, UR; e.g., nausea and related symptoms) caused by chemotherapy (US; e.g., cytotoxic drugs) and various stimuli associated with the chemotherapy setting (CS; e.g., sights, smells, thoughts, environment, infusion apparatus, room context, color, taste, smell of a soluble capsule containing drugs, etc.). As a result of repeated associations, the CS begin to elicit nausea, vomiting, dysphoria, and other unpleasant effects even in the absence of the US (Bovbjerg, 2006; Carey & Burish, 1988; Stockhorst et al., 2006).

CHEMOTHERAPY TREATMENT AND CTA

About half of cancer patients submitted to chemotherapy have in some degree a temporary taste and smell sensitivity deficit. Modifications in sweet taste recognition occur in about one-third of patients, while bitterness, sourness, and saltiness are less affected (DeWys, 1979). It has been found that measures of taste thresholds assessed by electrogustometry among cancer patients under chemotherapy treatments were significantly higher than that of control subjects (Berteretche et al., 2004; Ovesen, Sorensen, Hannibal, & Allingstrup, 1991). The taste dysfunction associated with side

effects of chemotherapy results in CTA and food avoidance with a negative impact on the nutritional status and quality of life of patients (Bartoshuk, 1990; Berteretche et al., 2004). In about 56% of cancer patients receiving chemotherapy, CTAs were specific and transient, lasting no more than 2 months at the end of therapy, suggesting almost a total recovery of taste sensitivity (Mattes, Arnold, Boraas, 1987a; Mattes, Curran Jr, Alavi, Powlis, & Whittington, 1992).

In healthy subjects, taste receptor cells renew every 5–9 days, and proliferation of taste cells occurs primarily at the base of the epithelium, where cells undergo mitotic division (Beidler & Smallman, 1965). Normally, this very rapid turnover assures new synaptic contacts with taste nerve terminals by a process of mutual recognition, so that taste sensitivity and thresholds always remain constant (Oakley, 1974). Irradiation and chemotherapy are the principal tools used to treat cancer patients since they are most effective with tissue that rapidly turnover and have high metabolic activity.

Since cancerous cells and taste bud cells display these characteristics, it is not unexpected that oral complications are associated with chemotherapy. Usually, the chemotherapy protocols uses chemicals that interfere with mitotic activity and thus destroy proliferating cells. This tends to select cancer cells for elimination in contrast to normal cells of lower mitotic activity. Since taste bud cells possess a short life span, taste cells are also destroyed during chemotherapy. Chemotherapy treatment stops the renewal of cells for the period during which the chemicals remain active and this might disrupt the taste code and decrease taste sensitivity. Moreover, the proportion of taste nerve terminals and cells renewed at the end of chemotherapeutic activity of the drugs might change the normal synaptic connections, which, in turn, might realize an important modification in the neural coding of taste sensitivity. This hypothesis may explain why cancer patients complain that taste is "abnormal, bad, or new" during and for some months after termination of chemotherapy treatments (Berteretche et al., 2004).

Interference between toxic drug administration and taste receptor cell turnover could play a major role in the taste dysfunctions (Beidler & Smith, 1991). These taste aberrations may be crucial factors in the development of CFA and/or CTA through neophobia induced by "abnormal, new" tastes (Rozin, 1968), with decreased nutrient intake, and sometimes with a poor response to chemotherapy (DeWys & Walters, 1975).

Taste function may be modified by the loss of salivary flow experienced by cancer patients submitted to irradiation and/or chemotherapy (Beidler & Smith, 1991). Saliva is a complex fluid mixture containing more than 100 different proteins that play an important role in the health of the oral cavity. Thus, absence of adequate volumes and/or composition of saliva may be very detrimental to the oral cavity, taste function, and food intake and may pose a serious health hazard (Beidler & Smith, 1991). Since a relationship between saliva composition and taste acuity has been discovered (Catalanotto & Leffingwell, 1979; Schmale, Holtgrave-Grez, & Christiansen, 1990; Spielman, 1990), the decline in salivary flow rate may reduce tasting solubilization, decrease lubrication, and change the response of taste receptors.

Accumulating evidences indicate the existence of a relationship between central nervous system and the immune system; in particular, there are reports showing that the limbic structures and the autonomic nervous system receive immune inputs (Abreu, Llorence, Hernàndez, & Gonzalez, 1994; Ader et al., 1995; Haas & Schauenstein, 1997; Jurkowski et al., 2001; Servière, Dubayle, & Menetrey, 2003; Wrona, 2006; YU & Shinnick-Gallagher, 1994). Therefore, it is not surprising that immune responses can be modulated by behavioral conditioning learning procedures (Alvarez-Borda, Ramirez-Amaya, Perez-Montfort, & Bermudez-Rattoni, 1995). Whereas several authors studied conditioned suppression of immune responses (Ader et al., 1995), conditioned enhancement of antibody production has been investigated by Alvarez-Borda et al. (1995) who, in rats, paired a novel taste (saccharin) with injection of a protein antigen and found after reexposure to the conditioned taste a significant increase of antibodies of IgG and IgM classes.

In healthy humans, immune functions can be modified by classical conditioning techniques (Buske-Kirschbaum, Kirschbaum, Stierle, Jabaij, & Hellehammer, 1994; Giang et al., 1996; Goebel et al., 2002; Longo et al., 1999). Nevertheless, the conditionability of immune functions in humans has only seldom been examined despite the clinical relevance for the conditionability of immune function in cancer patients (Bovbjerg et al., 1990; Fredrikson et al., 1993; Lekander, Furst, Rotstein, Blomgren, & Fredrikson, 1995). In cancer patients, natural killer cell activity (NKCA, an immune parameter valid for tumor defense and cytotoxic

competence) has been positively correlated with psychological variables and with a therapeutic group intervention (Fawzy et al., 1990; Levy et al., 1990). Recently, Stockhorst et al. (2000), showed that anticipatory immunomodulation (AIM) is related to conditioning parameters. They showed a higher NKCA and a higher level of IFN-γ (interferon-γ) in the presence of a chemotherapy-related CS (hospital) compared to a lower level in a CS-free (home) environment. A pattern of immunoenhancement had been demonstrated when patients were reexposed to the infusion-related CS situation in hospital environment (Lekander, Furst, Rotstein, Blomgren, & Fredrikson, 1994; Stockhorst et al., 2000).

Consumption of strongly flavored candies before chemotherapy (Broberg & Bernstein, 1987) or specific fruit juice before radiotherapy (Smith et al., 1985) appear to be a simple and effective way to reduce the impact of chemotherapy and/or radiotherapy on preference for normal diets. The basis for this effectiveness is presumed to be the development of aversions to a "scapegoat medium" that then block or interfere with the development of aversions to other foods or tastes (Broberg & Bernstein, 1987). Thus, consumption of a strongly flavored food before chemotherapy may be an effective and simple intervention for preventing or blocking the impact of chemotherapy on the formation of learned aversions.

Cancer patients who experience nausea and vomiting in a clinic after chemotherapy may also develop it in an anticipatory form; that is, they may begin to feel nauseous simply when reexposed to the sight, sound, thought, and smell of the clinic in which treatments are given (Andrykowski & Redd, 1987; Hall & Symonds, 2006). One commonly reported consequence caused by the conditioning effect created by frequent or severe posttreatment nausea (PTN) and vomiting is AN and AV. These symptoms occur before the administration of chemotherapy, namely, in anticipation of it.

ROLE OF CTA IN THE AN AND AV

Anticipatory side effects rarely develop unless posttreatment side effects have occurred, suggesting that the mechanism supporting AN and AV might be classified as a model of classical Pavlovian conditioning learning (Carey & Burish, 1988; Matteson et al., 2002; Stockhorst, Klosterhalfen, Steingruber, 1998). An AN and AV can be a distressing side effect of cancer chemotherapy and still is a serious and relevant clinical problem (Stockhorst, Wiener, et al., 1998).

Pavlovian conditioning is formed in AN and AV in cancer patients (Carey & Burish, 1988) and its etiology may be well explained by classical conditioning paradigms: the infusion of the chemotherapy acts as the US; the stimuli experienced in contingency with the infusion are assumed to be associated with the US, and thus serve as CSs (Figure 24.1). After several pairings of CS and US, which establish a CS–US association, the CS will elicit conditioned nausea even prior to receiving an infusion (Stockhorst, Wiener, et al., 1998). Patients who experience a high frequency of PTN, and thus a high percentage of reinforcement after chemotherapy application, are more likely to develop AN and AV (Tomoyasu, Bovbjerg, & Jacobsen, 1996). Indeed, there is a linear correlation between the frequency of AN and AV and the number of repeated chemotherapy cycles (Aapro, Molassiotis, & Olver, 2005; Morrow & Roscoe, 1997).

The basal autonomic nervous system reactivity (particularly the sympathetic branch) has been related to AN and AV induced by anticancer chemotherapy (Kvale et al., 1991). Patients who experience AN and AV show significantly increased sympathetic reactivity compared with patients who do not experience these aversive symptoms (Kvale et al., 1991; Kvale & Hugdahl, 1994).

Anxiety may also play an important role in AN and AV caused by the chemotherapic treatments (Andrykowski, 1990). Once AN and AV develop, they are difficult to eliminate, do not improve spontaneously, and are not well controlled by pharmacological protocols including the 5-HT$_3$ receptors antagonists (Aapro, Molassiotis, & Olver, 2005; Matteson et al., 2002; Morrow, Arseneau, Asbury, Bennett, & Boros, 1982; Morrow et al., 1998). Paradoxically, the repeated somministration of 5-HT$_3$ receptor antagonists may increase the AN and AV symptoms probably by acting as a CSs itself (Carey & Burish, 1988; Morrow et al., 1982) (Figure 24.1).

Since the chemotherapy regime necessarily implies a "CS–US" pairing, the formation of context–US associations are of special interest since they may have potential clinical interventions

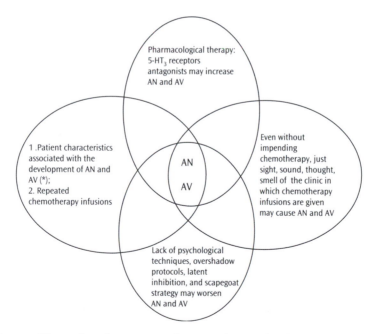

Figure 24.1. *Venn* diagram illustrating the main conditions inducing the development of AN and AV in cancer patients submitted to the chemotherapy. Some interactions between pharmacological and psychological treatments are shown (see text for more details). *Main characteristics associated with the development of AN and AV are age <50 years; nausea and vomiting after last chemotherapy; susceptility to motion sickness; generalized weakness, sweating, feeling warm, or hot after last chemotherapy session; state and trait anxiety; depression; expectation of PTN. Data from Aapro et al. (2005); Bovbjerg (2006); and Matteson et al. (2002).

for the control of AN and AV. In this regard, two interesting classical conditioning paradigms, "overshadowing" and "latent inhibition (LI)," may be successfully applied (Hall & Symonds, 2006) (Figure 24.1).

The phenomenon of "overshadowing" is obtained when the CS is a compound cue (solid and/or liquid) consisting of two separable elements, one more salient than the other. The presence of the more salient element significantly restricts the acquisition of associative strength by the less salient element (Hall & Symonds, 2006). In other words, the overshadowing technique consists of presenting a compound of two stimuli as potential CS that is paired with US. The more salient of the stimuli is assumed to override the effects of the less salient one, and the conditioned response elicited by the less salient compound is weaker than if it alone had been paired with the US (Miller, Jagielo, & Spear, 1990). Thus, a novel salient cue presented during chemotherapy sessions might overshadow the context and thus prevent the development of AN. The cue itself might acquire aversive properties, but this problem will be overcome when as an overshadowing cue a novel-flavored drink that the patient will never encounter again is chosen.

Recently, Stockhorst, Wiener, et al. (1998) used the overshadowing protocol in cancer patients to try to open a new way for therapeutical prevention of conditioned AN and AV established after chemotherapy treatments. They adopted an overshadowing protocol to the chemotherapeutic pre-infusion situation to modify conditioned nausea, and their rationale was that the overshadowing CS will prevent the stimuli typically inherent in the chemotherapy situation (smell, taste, sight of hospital, etc.) from becoming nausea-eliciting CS (Okifuji & Friedman, 1992; Stockhorst, Wiener, et al., 1998). Stockhorst, Wiener, et al. (1998) showed that subjects submitted to overshadowing conditioning technique did not develop AN and AV, whereas in the control group about 23% of subjects complained about AN and AV. Moreover, the overshadowing procedure did not have any adverse effects; rather it seems to attenuate the intensity of postnausea in the test phase. Owing to the clinical relevance of overshadowing technique to prevent AN and AV in cancer patients, it is hoped for further analysis of its effectiveness in a larger sample of subjects.

A taste stimulus that has been repeatedly presented to the animal in the absence of aversive consequences requires more pairing with poisoning to elicit CTA of comparable intensity; this phenomenon has been named "latent inhibition" (LI; Bures, 1998; De La Casa & Lubow, 1995; also see Chapter 3).

In the past, LI has been explained by "interference phenomenon" with the processing of stimuli: LI results in a failure to acquire new association to such stimuli (Bures, 1998; Lubow, 1973). A more recent interpretation of LI asserts that it is due to retrieval failure. In other words, the association of the preexposed CS to the US proceeds normally, but during retrieval the earlier CS–no consequence association competes with the later CS–poisoning association (Bakner, Strohen, Nordeen, & Riccio, 1991; Batsell & Best, 1992; Kraemer, Randall, & Carbary, 1991). Thus, a simple preexposure to the context might provide a useful intervention for the alleviation of AN and AV in cancer patients. Recently, encouraging results have shown that LI may also have potential as a clinical intervention for the alleviation of aversive side effects of chemotherapy treatments (e.g., AN and AV; Hall & Symonds, 2006; Klosterhalfen et al., 2005). But, in this case as well, further analysis of its effectiveness in a larger sample of patients is desired.

CFA AND NUTRITIONAL PROBLEMS CAUSED BY CHEMOTHERAPY IN CANCER PATIENTS

It is important to clarify the influence of CFA on ingestive behavior and nutritional status of cancer patients since the nutritional status of a patient may influence its treatment efficacy (Donaldson et al., 1981; Nitenberg & Raynard, 2000). During the course of cancer and its treatments, patients frequently complain of impaired taste and smell function that may be associated with decreased food intake, anorexia, and body weight loss (DeWys, 1979; DeWys & Walters, 1975; Fearon & Carter, 1988; Kern & Norton, 1988; Shils, 1979). Commonly, malnutrition that occurs in cancer patients during chemotherapy, may adversely affect their quality of life and survival (Holmes, 1993). Malnutrition may be due to a variety of factors, including decreased food intake, side effects of anticancer treatments, and wasteful metabolic processes per se. An analysis of food aversions may provide information to the dietary guidelines and adequate nutrient consumption among cancer patients (McEligot, Rock, Sobo, & Flatt, 2000).

Some antineoplastic drugs (e.g., fluorouracil, adriamycin, methotrexate, cisplatin) induce severe gastrointestinal complications (Mitchel, 1992) such as abdominal cramping and bloating, mucositis, paralytic ileus, constipation, and malabsorption (Nitenberg & Raynard, 2000). Enterocytes are rapidly dividing cells, which make them prone to the cytotoxic effects of chemotherapy that might induce lesions at different levels of the digestive tract (tongue ulceration, mucositis, esophagitis, etc.), acute or subacute enteropathies combining mucosal atrophy, ulcerations, necrosis, leading to the poor nutritional status of patients.

One common nutritional problem in cancer patients is the development of the cancer-anorexia and/or cancer-cachexia syndrome. They remain the most common cause of cancer death as a result of the altered metabolism of fat, carbohydrates, and protein that occurs in cancer patients. The causes of cancer anorexia and cachexia remain poorly understood, but both may come from the disease itself, from other symptoms associated with the illness and from side effects associated with treatments (MacDonald, 2000; MacIntosh et al., 2000; Plata-Salaman, 2000).

Cancer cachexia is the result of multifactorial events that can be grouped into three major categories (Nitenberg & Raynard, 2000):

1. Inadequate food intake and/or appetite loss. In this case, orexigenic agents, such as corticosteroids and pentoxifylline, may be given to increase appetite and ameliorate the anorexia symptoms.
2. Metabolic alterations resulting in a wasting disease. The tumor tissue escapes the normal mechanisms of metabolic control by increasing metabolic demands. It develops whatever the host's nutritional status, and maintains a high level of metabolic activity at the expense of the same host (Lazarus, Kambayashi, Lowry, & Strassmann, 1996). Tumor tissues undergo a high degree of anaerobic glycolysis, a net uptake of amino acids, and produce large amounts of lactate. In cancer patients, the carbohydrate metabolism is characterized by glucose intolerance, with a reduction in the sensitivity of peripheral tissues to insulin (Rofe, Bourgeois, Coyle, Taylor, & Abdi, 1994). Glucose dysregulation depends on two major points: the reduction of hepatic sensitivity to insulin and the decrease in insulin secretion by the Langerhans cells in response to food intake (Nitenberg & Raynard, 2000). In cancer patients, an increase in peripheral fat mobilization and/or an excessive oxidation of fatty acids represent important abnormalities in fat metabolism that may lead to an endogenous lypolysis related with cancer malnutrition. The fat mass reduction could be due to a primary imbalance between lipolysis and lipogenesis. The immunomodulatory effects of essential fatty acids (e.g., omega-3 fatty acids) may alter the rate of eicosanoid's production, which in turn may modulate the immune responses (Alexander, 1998). In fasting healthy subjects, neoglucogenesis may use as precursors some muscle amino acids and/or some visceral proteins. As adaptive mechanism, the protein catabolism decreases slowly and lean body mass is more or less preserved (Nitenberg & Raynard, 2000). On the contrary, in cancer patients, these adaptive mechanisms seem to be completely absent, leading to a remarkable level of protein depletion, and in some patients to an extraordinary muscular atrophy (Smith & Tisdale, 1993). The protein metabolism alterations include the increase in protein turnover, a reduction in muscle protein synthesis, an increase in inflammatory hepatic protein synthesis, a negative nitrogen balance, and various change in plasma protein profile (e.g., hypoalbuminemia) (Nitenberg & Raynard, 2000; Norton, Gorschboth, Wesley, Burt, & Brennan, 1985).
3. Specific humoral and inflammatory circulating factors are suspected in the appetite loss and metabolic disturbances associated with tumor illness, even if the precise role of cytokines and other mediators of appetite regulation and of metabolic loss of homeostasis in cancer patients is poorly documented. The mentioned acute or chronic disorders are associated with one another and with other hormonal disturbances and they may play an important role in the genesis and persistence of metabolic disturbance inducing a catabolic state. It has been shown that cancer anorexia is influenced by sex-related hormones, and probably an interaction exists between cytokines and estradiol (Varma, Chai, Meguid, & Yang, 2001). Many mediators including tumor-derived factors (e.g.,

tumor necrosis factor, interleukin-1, interleukin-6, etc.) and some nutritional problems may be responsible for both cancer-anorexia and cancer-cachexia syndromes (Cohen & Lefor, 2001). The release of cytokines, interleukins, and tumor necrosis factors in cancer patients may produce anorectic effects (Langhans & Hrupka, 1999; MacIntosh et al., 2000; Plata-Salaman, 1998). Cytokine immunotherapy also induces the production of a large array of endogenous cytokines that may act synergistically to cause anorexia, CTA, and other neuropsychiatric manifestations (Plata-Salaman, 2000).

A better knowledge of the mechanisms until now described might lead to new therapeutic strategies against cancer anorexia (Gough, Heys, & Eremin, 1996a, 1996b; Lundholm, Gelin, & Hyltander, 1994; Varma et al., 1999).

Artificial nutrition may be important to correct the metabolic alterations of malnourished cancer patients and might allow a patient to complete a treatment course of chemotherapy (Bozzetti, 1997). It is important to note that artificial nutrition does not limit the treatment-related toxicity and does not improve overall survival (Cohen & Lefor, 2001; Pironi, 1997). Nevertheless, between and during periods of chemotherapy, the health conditions of truly malnourished cancer patients may be improved by artificial nutrition treatment (Bozzetti, 1992). The two main routes of providing nutritional supports are enteral and parenteral (Cohen & Lefor, 2001). Enteral nutrition (EN) and parenteral nutrition (PN) are both effective ways to deliver nutrients directly into the gastrointestinal tract or into the blood stream when patients are unable to ingest food. The role of EN as an adjuvant to anticancer therapy has not been fully evaluated. As an adjuvant to chemotherapy, total PN has not been particularly successful, and the usefulness of this method has not been very encouraging (Cohen & Lefor, 2001; Hill & Daly, 1995; MacIntosh et al., 2000; Nitenberg & Raynard, 2000; Shike, 1996). Artificial nutrition does not appear to significantly modify protein turnover and lead to a reduction in both protein synthesis and catabolism.

Both the EN and PN treatments do not always increase blood levels of nutritional markers of anabolism, such as albumin, transferrin, and cholinesterase, and their effects on humoral and cellular immunity during specific treatments are still controversial (Nitenberg & Raynard, 2000). EN should always be privileged because the PN is more expensive, short-circuits the digestive tract and the entero-insular axis, leads to a reduction in the height of the intestinal villi, and decreases the activity of the brush-border enzymes (Hill & Daly, 1995). Both EN and PN might theoretically develop a CFA that worsens the patient's quality of life (Bernstein, 1986).

CFAs are usually directed to specific foods consumed before cancer chemotherapy (Bernstein, 1978; Bernstein & Webster, 1980; Smith et al., 1984). Frequently consumed and highly preferred items such as chocolate, coffee, and meat (especially red meat) are particularly prone to cause CFA and frequently become targets of learned aversions (Mattes et al., 1992; Scalera, 2002).

To reduce the possibility of CFA, the "interference effect" (Bernstein, Vitiello, & Sigmundi, 1980) was applied to cancer patients. Indeed, Broberg and Bernstein (1987), prompted by these findings, studied the possibility that exposure to novel tastes and/or food may be an effective approach for preventing the formation of CFA to familiar and more nutritious foods. For example, the consumption of an ice cream or strongly flavored candies before chemotherapy (Broberg & Bernstein, 1987) or specific fruit juice before radiotherapy (Smith et al., 1985) appears to be a simple and effective way to reduce the impact of chemotherapy and/or radiotherapy on the aversions that would develop against foods in the normal diet.

The basis for this effectiveness is presumed to be the development of aversions to the novel taste/ food acting as a "scapegoat mean" (e.g., an unusual-tasting ice cream, strongly unusual-flavored candies, specific fruit juice, ethnic foods, etc.), which then "block" or "interfere" with the development of aversions to other foods or tastes (Broberg & Bernstein, 1987). The scapegoat technique is effective in the hospital clinic or ward, and it may be safely employed to reduce conditioned aversions to home-prepared meals that, due to their familiarity, are weaker targets for aversions (Nakajima, Ka, & Imada, 1999). In humans, the scapegoat effect is specific to novel but not familiar foods and what is critical in preventing aversions to familiar foods is that scapegoat food must be consumed any time before the onset of nausea and vomiting (Andresen, Birch, & Johnson, 1990).

In summary, it is recommended that patients with postchemotherapy nausea and vomiting consume a novel food before the onset of nausea since the consumption of an unusual flavored food before chemotherapy may be an effective and simple intervention for preventing or blocking the impact of chemotherapy on the formation of CFA. Chemotherapy in patients who have experienced drug-induced nausea and/or vomiting in the presence of a certain set of contextual cues (such as environment, sight, sound, smell, thought, etc.) report that these cues themselves become capable of evoking nausea and vomiting (AN and AV) (Andrykowski & Redd, 1987; Meachum & Bernstein, 1992). Conditioning occurs not only in conjunction with one single stimulus but also in response to the background within which the stimulus appear, that is, "situation" (Wyrwicka & Chase, 2001). Since the "contextual-conditioning cues," the "complex of environmental stimuli," and the "situation" play a critical role in conditioned behavior and could affect the conditioning process, they might be used as "scapegoat" tools.

Previous attempts to prevent the development of aversions have included diet abstinence before cancer treatments. However, it is not recommended that a patient totally fasts before chemotherapy. In addition, total fasting for the periods of time required to protect foods from aversions is not feasible especially for patients receiving daily treatments. Indeed, aversion conditioning may occur with very long delays (up to 24 h before and after treatment) between the CS (consumption of food) and the US (side effects appearance; Garb & Stunkard, 1974; Logue, 1979; Logue, Ophir, & Strauss, 1981; Mattes, Arnold, & Boraas, 1987b).

A useful recommendation is that patients eat a moderately small meal at least 4 h before cancer therapy and that they avoid categories of foods considered major protein sources (red meats, poultry, fish, eggs, milk, cheese, and some dairy products), since proteins are more salient targets for food aversions than are carbohydrates (Bernstein, Goehler, & Feuer, 1984; Midkiff & Bernstein, 1985). In addition, they should intentionally ingest a novel strongly flavored but not nutritionally important food shortly before treatment ("scapegoat strategy"). Patients should be informed that chemotherapeutic drugs might create food aversions; this knowledge may decrease the possibility to form new adverse conditionings (Beidler & Smith, 1991).

It has been reported (Schiffman, 2000) that breast cancer patients preferred flavor-enhanced to not-flavor-enhanced foods (they did not report aversions to flavor-enhanced foods) and that chemosensory intensification of foods may be helpful in treating anorexia in these patients (Gogos & Kalfarentzos, 1995; MacIntosh et al., 2000).

Recently, ghrelin (an orexigenic peptide produced by the stomach and the hypothalamus) has been shown to increase significantly the energy intake and meal appreciation in cancer patients with impaired appetite (Neary et al., 2004). In rodents, it has been clearly demonstrated that relatively high doses of ghrelin are biologically active to significantly antagonize the side effects induced by cisplatin treatment (e.g., emesis, dyspepsia, impaired appetite, reduced activity, gastric emptying, weight loss; Liu, Malik, Sanger, & Andrews, 2006; Rudd et al., 2006). These results make the activation of ghrelin receptors a potentially valuable target for the treatment of cancer chemotherapy–associated dyspepsia syndrome, widening the potential therapeutic usefulness of ghrelin and its mimetics in the clinic (Liu et al., 2006; Rudd et al., 2006). But further studies are required to investigate the effect of lower dose of ghrelin and the exact sites and spectrum of action in cancer chemotherapy treatments.

COGNITIVE BEHAVIORAL TREATMENTS ON REDUCING SIDE EFFECTS OF CHEMOTHERAPY

Prior to, during, or after chemotherapy administration, at least two factors implicated in a synergistic way may contribute to the development and the expression of psychological side effects, namely, associative learning and psychological stress associated with chemotherapy. In cancer patients, it is interesting to note that, like all clinical symptoms, both anticipatory and postchemotherapy nausea and vomiting do not occur simply as physical phenomena, but they depend on a wider psychological, emotional, and existential context (Antonarakis & Hain, 2004). This multidimensional understanding of symptoms is essential when physicians try to resolve the very unpleasant side effects of chemotherapy.

Pharmacological agents have been used to control the responses to chemotherapy, but even when modern antiemetics provide some relief, they often have side effects of their own. When the antiemetic is given each time the patient becomes nauseated or is vomiting, the drug, as a result, becomes associated with nausea and vomiting and later is able to elicit, on its own, nausea and vomiting (Carey & Burish, 1988; Figure 24.1). Thus, an alternative to or addition to antiemetic pharmacological treatments may be the use of psychological techniques and of complementary and alternative medicine (CAM).

The most promising cognitive behavioral therapy treatments include hypnosis, progressive muscle relaxation training, therapeutic foot massage, guided imagery, acupuncture, acupressure, and acustimulation, systematic desensitization, biofeedback, distraction techniques, and cognitive behavioral strategies. It has been revealed that behavioral interventions are important for reducing emotional distress, AN, and AV, and for relaxation and coping. Massage therapy, muscle relaxation, music therapy, aromatherapy, and exercise conditioning are more effective in pain management; exercise interventions seem effective for fatigue syndrome management (Burish & Jenkins, 1992; Cooley, 2002; Mock, 2002; Morrow, Roscoe, Hickok, Andrews, & Matteson, 2002; Roscoe et al., 2000; Sheard & Maguire, 1999).

A brief description of some effective cognitive behavioral therapy techniques is provided in the following section.

Acupuncture, Acupressure, and Acustimulation

The impact of psychological factors on nausea and vomiting in cancer chemotherapy treatment is widely acknowledged and the efficacy of influencing these psychosomatic aspects has been demonstrated (Mundy et al., 2003). Acupuncture, acupressure, and electroacupuncture are forms of traditional Chinese medicine. Pressure on meridian points of the body can be exerted by insertion of small-gauge needles or a combination of needles and low-frequency electric current (electroacupuncture) or by manual pressure with finger (acupressure) (Menefee & Monti, 2005; Monti & Yang, 2005).

A psychological effect of acupuncture treatment has been hypothesized since acupuncture seems to be effective for depression (influence on the autonomous nervous system), for conditioned learning, and for psychosomatic disorders of the gastrointestinal tract (Schneider et al., 2006). Many randomized and controlled clinical trials showed that acupuncture-point stimulation has some good effect in preventing or attenuating nausea and vomiting in cancer patients treated with chemotherapy (Cohen, Menter, & Hale, 2005; Collins & Thomas, 2004; Ezzo et al., 2005; Streitberger, Ezzo, & Schneider, 2006). In 1977, the National Institute of Health of USA (NIH) convened a panel of experts on acupuncture and chemotherapy, which at the conclusion of their work stated that there exists "clear evidence that needle acupuncture is efficacious for adult postoperative and chemotherapy nausea and vomiting" (NIH Consensus Statement, 1997). It is clear that acupuncture and acupressure are effective in treating chemotherapy-related nausea and vomiting, but their clinical application seems limited as the therapeutic benefit lasted for only 8–12 h.

Although the exact mechanisms by which acupuncture exerts its therapeutic effects are only partially understood; the scientific demonstration of acupuncture's efficacy has eliminated the belief that acupuncture was a placebo (Cohen et al., 2005). Some evidence indicate that acupuncture may release endogenous substances (e.g., oxytocin, steroids, endorphins, etc.) that no single drug treatment could mimic (Filshie & Thompson, 2004). For chemotherapy-induced nausea and vomiting, the effectiveness of acupuncture-point P6 stimulation seems to be modality dependent (Streitberger et al., 2006). For example, acupressure seems to reduce chemotherapy-induced acute nausea on the first day after chemotherapy but not vomiting; on the contrary, only electro-acupuncture is effective for chemotherapy-induced acute vomiting

Acupuncture should be considered a potentially helpful adjunct treatment from the oncologists who are having difficulty controlling nausea and vomiting in patients receiving highly emetogenic chemotherapy (Cohen et al., 2005).

Hypnosis

Hypnosis is probably the first psychological technique used to control the side effects of chemotherapy and probably still is the most widely used procedure with children and adolescent cancer patients.

Hypnosis is a procedure where a person (the patient) is guided by another person (usually the hypnotherapist) to respond to suggestions for changes in subjective experience such as perception, sensation, emotion, thought, or behavioral conditioning and learning (Richardson, Smith,

McCall, & Pilkington, 2006). The hypnotherapist first trains patients to go into a state of deep relaxation and then guides them through relaxation exercises immediately before and during chemotherapy infusions. In almost all patients receiving hypnosis significant reductions are reported in the intensity and severity of both nausea and vomiting, which in some cases may disappear; moreover, the side effects that remain were less bothersome than they were prior to training (Marchioro et al., 2000). Thus, it appears that hypnotic procedures are an effective intervention in the management for reducing both anticipatory and postchemotherapy nausea and vomiting and other negative effects associated with chemotherapy (Marchioro et al., 2000).

Recently, hypnosis has been included as a nonpharmacological intervention for preparing children and adolescents for hospital care management of anticipatory anxiety/distress related to chemotherapy (Prictor, Hill, Mackenzie, Stoelwinder, & Harmsen, 2004). Moreover, a committee of NIH (NIH Technology Statement, 1995) concluded that there was strong supports for the use of hypnosis in alleviating chronic pain associated with cancer. However, the mechanisms by which hypnosis works are not completely understood.

Frequently, hypnotic interventions may include other techniques (e.g., induction, suggestions, progressive muscle relaxation training [PMRT], guided imagery, cognitive behavioral therapy, music therapy, distraction) that usually may produce an increase in therapeutic effect (Kirsch, Montgomery, & Sapirstein, 1995). But similarly dramatic results have been obtained with children by distracting them with video games (Redd et al., 1987).

In conclusion, even if a number of methodological limitations have been identified by reviewing the literature (NIH Technology Statement, 1995; Prictor et al., 2004; Richardson et al., 2006), hypnotic interventions may be used as an adjunct to pharmacological and conditioning treatments to alleviate distress in cancer patients (Liossi & Hatira, 2003).

Progressive Muscle Relaxation Training and Guided Imagery

In several well-controlled investigations, it has been shown that in cancer patients, PMRT is a useful adjuvant technique for reducing anticipatory and postchemotherapy nausea and vomiting

and for increasing food intake during the days following the chemotherapy (Carey & Burish, 1988). The positive effects of PMRT may be potentiated when, at the same time, guided imagery technique (GIT) is applied to the patient. On the contrary, there is no convincing evidence that the application of GIT alone may induce positive effects on physical symptoms such as nausea and vomiting (Roffe, Schmidt, & Ernst, 2005). The positive effects of PMRT potentiated by GIT on postchemotherapy nausea and vomiting are most evident in the initial stage of treatment when patients are unfamiliar with the side effects of chemotherapy, although modest benefits have been also observed in subsequent chemotherapy sessions (Molassiotis, Yung, Yam, Chan, & Mok, 2002; Yoo, Ahn, Kim, Kim, & Han, 2005). In conclusion, combined PMRT and GIT may produce better results in terms of adjuvant in chemotherapy side effects than using one of the two methods alone.

PMRT includes progressive relaxation (tense release) of 11 to 16 groups of muscle (Baider, Uziely, & De-Nour, 1994; Molassiotis et al., 2002). Usually, the PMRT session is followed by GIT, during which the patient is asked to imagine a peaceful scene as a pleasing image from memory. The PMRT and GIT contain both a cognitive distraction and a relaxation component (Redd, Montgomery, & DuHamel, 2001) that may reduce the abnormal muscular contractions in the gastrointestinal tract that accompany postchemotherapy nausea and vomiting (Molassiotis et al., 2002).

Moreover, the immune system may be stimulated since memory retrieval may activate the limbic system that is related to neuroimmunomodulation activity (Felten et al., 1991; Haas & Schauenstein, 1997; Jurkowski et al., 2001; Schiffman, 1997; Servière et al., 2003; Wrona, 2006; see the section titled Conclusion and Perspectives).

Recently, in an empirical study, it has been suggested that physical activity and aerobic exercise programs are means to decrease side effects in cancer patients undergoing chemotherapy (Andersen et al., 2006), but the preliminary results, even if interesting, need to be confirmed.

Other empirical studies describe the use of foot massage and aromatherapy as an intervention technique for achieving the relief from side effect symptoms in patients with cancer, but there is little evidence for its effectiveness (Fellowes, Barnes, & Wilkinson, 2004; Grealish, Lomasney, & Whiteman, 2000). Thus, repeated and larger trials and longer follow-up are needed before validating these methods.

Cognitive Behavioral Strategies

"Cognitive behavioral strategies" were developed to assist patients to reduce the severity of symptoms and their impact on emotional concerns and physical functions, and to assist patients to acquire self-management skills and behaviors to address the problems caused by the symptoms. Four effective classes of cognitive behavioral strategies have been identified from literature: self-care management information, problem solving, communication with provider, and counseling and support (Given et al., 2004; Oliver, Kravitz, Kaplan, & Meyers, 2001). There is little evidence for effectiveness of these strategies, thus repeated trials are needed before they are validated.

CONCLUSIONS AND PERSPECTIVES

Some important reviews clearly and firmly pointed out that psychological symptoms resulting from cancer chemotherapy are the product of both associative learning and the physical stress associated with chemotherapy. Associative learning techniques may become important to solve or reduce drastically the aversive side effects related to chemotherapy that are not prevented or resolved by pharmacological treatments. For example, conditioned scapegoat strategies have significant protective effects and may prevent or decrease aversions toward foods containing important nutrients.

Nausea and vomiting are the most common side effects complained by patients undergoing chemotherapy. Moreover, the first chemotherapy cycle may induce conditioned AN and AV distress. At present, pharmacological treatment (e.g., administration of 5-HT receptor antagonists, NK_1 receptor antagonists, etc.) are used to reduce nausea and vomiting in cancer patients, but prevention of emesis and nausea is not complete and a relevant percentage of patients still suffer from these inconveniences (Herrstedt et al.,1998; Herrstedt, Koeller, et al., 2005; Jordan et al., 2005).

The current point of view is that biomedical and psychological research on nausea and vomiting must be integrative and complementary with the aim to develop the best possible anti–side effect treatment package. For example, a psychological intervention that starts before the beginning of chemotherapy, combined with an effective pharmacological protocol, may be able to prevent or substantially reduce most nausea and vomiting episodes associated with chemotherapy. Most of the psychological research with cancer patients undergoing chemotherapy has focused on AN and AV as the only, or the primary, outcome measures. However, psychological interventions may have positive effects on a number of other side effects related to chemotherapy treatments (e.g., emotional state, anxiety, reduced food intake, pain, immune responses, etc.).

Some interesting results of experimental conditioning on animals have shown that conditioning techniques may have a variety of clinically important applications (Bovbjerg, 1991). For example, animal data show that IL-2 production increases after pairing saccharin with lipopolysaccharide (Janz et al., 1996), and NK concentration is enhanced after pairing an olfactory CS with polyinosinic:polycytidylic acid in tumor-bearing rats (Ghanta, Hiramoto, Solvason, & Spector, 1987).

One interesting and promising field of conditioned response occurring during cancer chemotherapy is the AIM (Stockhorst et al., 2000). Data reveal a higher NKCA and IFN-γ levels in the presence of chemotherapy-related CS (hospital environment) compared to a lower level in the relatively CS-free (home environment). In other words, there is an increase of NKCA and IFN-γ when cancer patients are reexposed to the CS. The immune differences in the two environments (hospital vs. home) could indicate an immunomodulating effect of CS-reexposition to the infusion situation in the hospital (Lekander et al., 1994; Stockhorst et al., 2000). An important question arises from these experimental results: whether the production of interleukins and NKCA might be conditioned in humans as an adjunct immunotherapy in treatment of cancer malignancies (Stockhorst et al., 2000). Moreover, it would be important to implement conditioning-based techniques not only to prevent or reduce the aversive side effects of chemotherapy but also to increase the conditioned responses that induce positive effects on immunomodulatory mechanisms.

Many studies have pointed out a significant role for CTA in several clinical situations in which anorexia and weight loss significantly impair the patient's quality of life (Bernstein & Borson, 1986).

For example, it is evident that cancer patients readily acquire CTA and/or CFA as a consequence of side effects of chemotherapy treatments and that aversions may play an important role in the development of cancer anorexia and/or cachexia.

It is known that 5-HT is involved in normal feeding behavior (Leibowitz & Alexander, 1998; Leibowitz, Weiss, & Shor-Posner, 1988; Meguid, Fetissov, et al., 2000) in the CTA formation (Gietzen, Erecius, & Rogers, 1998) and in cancer anorexia–cachexia syndrome in rats and humans (Edelman et al., 1999; Gietzen, Hammer, Beverly, & Rogers, 1991; Meguid, Fetissov, et al., 2000). Usually, $5-HT_3$ receptor antagonists are used as antiemetics and antinauseatic agents in adjunct to the cancer chemotherapy. Whereas the pharmacological blockade of $5-HT_3$ receptors reduces the side effects of chemotherapy, it does not prevent body weight loss and does not improve significantly the nutritional status of patients (Edelman et al., 1999).

In cancer anorexia, the significant decrease in food intake may depend primarily on reductions in both meal size (MS) and meal number (MN; Meguid, Sato, et al., 2000). Modifications in dopamine and 5-HT levels in the lateral hypothalamus (LH) and ventromedial hypothalamus (VMH) control both MS and MN. Changes in LH dopamine influences MS, whereas in the VMH decreasing dopamine and increasing 5-HT levels influences MN (Varma et al., 1999). In tumor-bearing rats, a significant increase in 5-HT and a decrease in dopamine levels in the VMH has been reported at the onset of anorexia (Varma et al., 1999). Thus, a derangement of the hypothalamic dopamine–serotonin system, secondary to the effects of cancer, might be responsible for the onset of anorexia. The use of pharmacological drugs that are able to "reset" the hypothalamic serotoninergic and dopaminergic system deranged by cancer side effects might be an important therapeutic hypothesis for reducing the onset of cancer anorexia.

In humans, apart from particular dietetic modifications, "social facilitation" might be of importance in cancer patients (mainly children, adolescents, elders) to extinguish the aversions developed by chemotherapy and to prevent the formation of new CFAs. For example, a quiet and relaxed meal atmosphere, a familiar scented (perfumed) environment, and a meal served with the background of a soft, cheerful, uplifting music reminiscent of vacations and/or good times may stimulate a feeling of wellness and reduce fear or intolerance to foods. Healthy people and cancer patients should eat the same food and take note that food is not responsible for malaise and/or disgust. This demonstration might attenuate aversions (CFA and CTA) in patients and persuade them to eat a hypothetical aversive food containing important nutrients (Scalera, 2002).

The flavor of foods arises from the integration of multiple sensory cues including odor, taste, temperature, appearance, and so on. Since olfactory stimuli contribute a significant proportion of the flavors for the majority of foods, they are critical to build up food preferences that are acquired by conditioned learning mechanisms (Small & Prescott, 2005; Yeomans, 2006). The repeated pairing of a novel odor with a hedonically significant taste should result in an enhancement of the flavor. Flavor enhancement of food may improve its acceptability and the absorption of nutrients. Food-related odors impact appetite and reliably stimulate salivation and other cephalic phase responses such as insulin release and gastric and pancreatic secretions. Thus, elevated flavor levels may lead to greater release of digestive enzymes and produce better digestion and absorption of nutrients.

During testing flavor preferences in cancer patients undergoing chemotherapy, almost all patients preferred the flavor-enhanced food to the nonenhanced food, and many patients indicated that the odors stir up the "Proust phenomenon" (Schiffman, 2000). The "Proust phenomenon" is a general phenomenon described in the opening chapter of Marcel Proust's novel "*Swann's way*," and to this day it is the common term for a powerful odor-evoked memory of "pleasant times in the past" (Chu & Downes, 2002; Herz, 2000).

The higher olfactory centers (especially the olfactory tubercle, the amygdala, as well as the hypothalamic, thalamic, hippocampal, and cortical connections) are implicated in limbic functions; therefore, they may communicate and integrate olfactory informations for the control of hormonal, visceral, and emotional state of the subject (Halasz, 1990). Since olfactory processing is directly linked to the limbic system, emotional changes are induced by means of olfactory stimulation as evidenced by neuroimaging studies (Zald & Pardo, 2000).

Thus, odors are capable of altering the emotional state of humans, and an ambient odor of essential oils (orange, citrus, lavander) can decrease the level of anxiety and increase the positive mood and the levels of calmness (Lehrner, Marwinski, Lehr, Johren, & Deecke, 2005). Some essential oils possess pharmacological properties responsible for the emotional effects. For example, the lavander odor acts postsynaptically and may induce sedation modulating the cAMP concentration and lower physiological arousal level by autonomic deactivation without affecting well-being in humans (Lehrner et al., 2005). Since odor signals are processed in the limbic system, which also processes emotions and memories, flavor intensification of ailments might reduce complaints about foods, thereby not only improving sensory qualities but triggering pleasant memories and situations (Schiffman, 1997).

It is important to underline that direct neural–immune connections exist between those parts of the brain that subserve olfaction (mainly the limbic system) and the immune system (Schiffman, 1997). Thus, olfactory stimulation could positively influence immunological functions directly via these connections (Felten et al., 1991) ameliorating mood, reaction to illness and side effects, immunity, functional status, and quality of life. Foods may contain phytochemicals that directly improve immunocompetence due to their biochemical actions. Moreover, flavor enhancement may improve mood and immune response since it reduces circulating cortisol, which in high concentration is known to suppress the immune status (Schiffman, 2000).

Furthermore, repeated taste and smell stimulations increase the salivary flow and salivary IgA concentration (Schiffman & Miletic, 1999). These improvements may have clinical potential for treatment of immune deficiencies and dry mouth that frequently occur in chemotherapy treatments.

In the last few years, CAM has received a tremendous interest and is used in cancer patient undergoing chemo- and radiotherapy. But, while CAM therapies have become popular among patients, their acceptance has lagged within the medical community (Cohen et al., 2005). Now, the time seems right for a major consideration of CAM by the medical community. Although CAM can be effective to resolve the aversive effects of chemotherapy, it should not necessary replace the pharmacological treatments of conventional medicine. On the contrary, CAM should be used, when possible, in conjunction with conventional medicine

protocols to elicit the best possible response in the patients. CAM can also be used as an alternative when conventional therapies do not elicit a desired response for a relatively long time.

Conclusions of many recent and important publications concerning treatments of chemotherapy side effects underline the necessity to combine together the pharmacological and psychological treatments. Sometimes, the pharmacological treatment alone is not enough to eliminate or ameliorate some aversive situations (e.g., AN and AV); in the same manner, in some patients, psychological treatment alone might be ineffective.

Important results of Pavlovian conditioning techniques (scapegoat, overshadowing, LI, etc.) have been shown to be involved in preventing or at least reducing side effects of chemotherapy. The combination of preventive use of scapegoat, overshadowing, LI techniques, and the acupuncture techniques might help oncologists to significantly reduce and/or eliminate the undesired side effects of chemotherapy. Cytoprotection of healthy cells by administration of drug adjuvants before chemotherapy may also reduce the main acute toxicities (Buntzel, Glatzel, Kuttner, Weinaug, & Frohlich, 2002). To improve the patient's feeding behavior after chemotherapy, one recommendation would be to inform them about the aversive side effects of cancer and chemotherapy regarding the "bad taste" perception and lack of appetite.

Since a number of methodological limitations were identified in some reviewed papers, further researches are recommended to confirm and validate the effectiveness and acceptability of CAM therapies. Controlled studies in Cancer Centers should provide CAM therapies and then examining more scientifically, if the integration of behavioral intervention in the standard care of cancer patients has significantly reduced the aversive side effects and improved their quality of life. Further large, high-quality clinical trials are important to identify the clinical value of behavioral therapies, the most practical and effective techniques, and identification of patients who will benefit most (Streitberger et al., 2006).

The application of CAM techniques in cancer clinics probably is limited since they are time consuming, labor intensive, and costly. Costs may be high because traditionally nurses and oncologists are not prepared to deliver behavioral interventions, thus skills of a specialist consultant or psychologist into the cancer care setting must be introduced.

References

Aapro, M. S., Molassiotis, A., & Olver, I. (2005). Anticipatory nausea and vomiting. *Supportive Care in Cancer, 13*, 117–121.

Abreu, P., Llorence, E., Hernàndez, M. M., & Gonzalez, M. C. (1994). Interleukin-1b stimulates tyrosine hydroxylase activity in the median eminence. *NeuroReport, 5*, 1356–1358.

Ader, R., & Cohen, N. (1993). Psychoneuroimmunology: Conditioning and stress. *Annual Reviews of Psychology, 44*, 53–85.

Ader, R., Cohen, N., & Felten, D. (1995). Psychoneuroimmunology: Interactions between the nervous system and immune system. *Lancet, 345*, 99–103.

Alexander, J. W. (1998). Immunonutrition: The role of omega-3 fatty acids. *Nutrition, 14*, 627–633.

Alvarez-Borda, B., Ramirez-Amaya, P., Perez-Montfort, R., & Bermudez-Rattoni, F. (1995). Enhancement of antibody production by a learning paradigm. *Neurobiology of Learning and Memory, 64*, 103–105.

Andersen, C., Adamsen, L., Moeller, T., Midtgard, J., Quist, M., Tveteraas, A., et al. (2006). The effect of a multidimensional exercise program on symptoms and side-effects in cancer patients undergoing chemotherapy—The use of semi-structured diaries. *European Journal of Oncology Nursing, 10*, 247–262.

Andresen, G. V., Birch, L. L., & Johnson, P. A. (1990). The scapegoat effect on food aversions after chemotherapy. *Cancer, 66*, 1649–1653.

Andrykowski, M. A. (1990). The role of anxiety in the development of anticipatory nausea in cancer chemotherapy: A review and synthesis. *Psychosomatic Medicine, 52*, 458–475.

Andrykowski, M. A., & Redd, W. H. (1987). Longitudinal analysis of the development of anticipatory nausea. *Journal of Consulting and Clinical Psycology, 55*, 36–41.

Antonarakis, E. S., & Hain, R. D. W. (2004). Nausea and vomiting associated with cancer chemotherapy: Drug management in theory and in practice. *Archives of Disease in Childhood, 89*, 877–880.

Baider, L., Uziely, B., & De-Nour, A. K. (1994). Progressive muscle relaxation and guided imagery in cancer patients. *General Hospital Psychology, 16*, 340–347.

Bakner, L., Strohen, K., Nordeen, M., & Riccio, D. C. (1991). Postconditioning recovery from the latent inhibition effect in conditioned taste aversion. *Physiology and Behavior, 50*, 1269–1272.

Bartoshuk, L. M. (1990). Chemosensory alterations and cancer therapies. *National Cancer Institute Monographs, 9*, 179–184.

Batsell, W. R., Jr., & Best, M. R. (1992). Variations in the retention of taste aversions: Evidence for retrieval competition. *Animal Learning Behavior, 20*, 146–159.

Beidler, L. M., & Smallman, R. L. (1965). Renewal of cells within taste buds. *Journal of Cell Biology, 27*, 263–272.

Beidler, L. M., & Smith, J. C. (1991). Effects of radiation therapy and drugs on cell turnover and taste. In T. V. Getchell, L. M. Bartoshuk, R. L. Doty, & J. B. Snow, Jr. (Eds.), *Smell and taste in health and disease* (pp. 753–763). New York: Raven Press.

Bender, C. M., McDaniel, R. W., Murphy-Ende, K., Pickett, M., Rittenberg, C. N., Rogers, M. P., et al. (2002). Chemotherapy-induced nausea and vomiting. *Clinical Journal of Oncology Nursing, 6*, 94–102.

Bernstein, I. L. (1978). Learned taste aversions in children receiving chemotherapy. *Science, 200*, 1302–1303.

Bernstein, I. L. (1986). Etiology of anorexia in cancer. *Cancer, 58*, 1881–1886.

Bernstein, I. L. (1991). Flavor aversion. In T. V. Getchell, L. M. Bartoshuk, R. L. Doty, & J. B. Snow, Jr. (Eds.), *Smell and taste in health and disease* (pp. 417–428). New York: Raven press.

Bernstein, I. L. (1999). Taste aversion learning: A contemporary perspective. *Nutrition, 15*, 229–234.

Bernstein, I. L., & Borson, S. (1986). Learned food aversion: A component of anorexia syndromes. *Psychological Reviews, 93*, 462–472.

Bernstein, I. L., & Webster, M. M. (1980). Learned taste aversions in humans. *Physiology and Behavior, 25*, 363–366.

Bernstein, I. L., Goehler, L. E., & Fener, D. P. (1984). Learned aversions to proteins in rats on a dietary self-selection regimen. *Behavioral Neuroscience, 98*, 1065–1072.

Bernstein, I. L., Vitiello, M. V., & Sigmundi, R. A. (1980). Effects of interference stimuli on the acquisition of learned aversions to foods in the rat. *Journal Comparative Physiological Psychology, 94*, 921–931.

Berteretche, M. V., Dalix, A. M., Cesar D'Ornano, A. M., Bellisle, F., Khayat, D., & Faurion, A. (2004). Decreased taste sensitivity in cancer patients under chemotherapy. *Supportive Care in Cancer, 12*, 571–576.

Birch, L. L. (1998). Psychological influences on the childhood diet. *Journal of Nutrition, 128*, 407S–410S.

Bovbjerg, D. H. (1991). Psychoneuroimmunology: Implications for oncology? *Cancer, 67*, 828–832.

Bovbjerg, D. H. (2006). The continuing problem of post chemotherapy nausea and vomiting: Contributions of classical conditioning.

Autonomic Neuroscience: Basic and Clinical,
129, 92–98.

Bovbjerg, D. H., Redd, W. H., Maier, L. A., Holland, J. C., Lesko, L. M., Niedzwiecki, D., et al. (1990). Anticipatory immune suppression and nausea in women receiving cyclic chemotherapy for ovarian cancer. *Journal Consulting Clinical Psychology, 58,* 153–157.

Bozzetti, F. (1992). Nutritional support of the adult cancer patient. *Clinical Nutrition, 11,* 167–179.

Bozzetti, F. (1997). Artificial nutrition in cancer patients: An outlook from Europe. *Nutrition, 13,* 486–489.

Bradley, R. M. (1973). Electrophysiological investigations of intravascular taste using perfused rat tongue. *American Journal of Physiology, 224,* 300–304.

Bradley, R. M., & Mistretta, C. M. (1971). Intravascular taste in rats as demonstrated by conditioned aversion to Na-saccharin. *Journal Comparative Physiological Psychology, 75,* 186–189.

Braveman, N. S. (1974). Poison-based avoidance learning with flavored or colored water in guinea pigs. *Learning & Motivation, 5,* 182–194.

Broberg, D. J., & Bernstein, I. L. (1987). Candy as scapegoat in the prevention of food aversions in children receiving chemotherapy. *Cancer, 60,* 2344–2347.

Buntzel, J., Glatzel, M., Kuttner, K., Weinaug, R., & Frohlich, D. (2002). Amifostine in simultaneous radiochemotherapy of advanced head and neck cancer. *Seminars in Radiation Oncology, 12,* 4–13.

Bures, J. (1998). The CTA paradigm: Terminology, methods, and conventions. In J. Bures, F. Bermudez-Rattoni, & T. Yamamoto (Eds.), *Conditioned taste aversion: Memory of a special kind* (pp. 14–25). Oxford: Oxford University Press.

Bures, J., & Buresova, O. (1989). Conditioned taste aversion to injected flavor: Differential effect of anesthesia on the formation of the gustatory trace and on its association with poisoning in rats. *Neuroscience Letters, 98,* 305–309.

Burish, T. G., & Carey, M. P. (1986). Conditioned aversive responses in cancer chemotherapy patients: Theoretical and developmental analysis. *Journal of Consulting and Clinical Psychology, 54,* 593–600.

Burish, T., & Jenkins, R. (1992). Effectiveness of biofeedback and relaxation training in reducing the side effects of cancer chemotherapy. *Health Psychology, 11,* 17–23.

Buske-Kirschbaum, A., Kirschbaum, C., Stierle, H., Jabaij, L., & Hellehammer, D. (1994). Conditioned manipulation of natural killer (NK) cells in humans using a discriminative learning protocol. *Biological Psychology, 38,* 143–155.

Carey, M. P., & Burish, T. G. (1988). Etiology and treatment of the psychological side effects associated with cancer chemotherapy: A critical review and discussion. *Psychological Bulletin, 104,* 307–325.

Catalanotto, F. A., & Leffingwell, C. (1979). Early effects of desalivation upon fluid consumption and taste acuity in the rat. *Behavioral and Neural Biology, 25,* 190–205.

Chawla, S. P., Grunberg, S. M., Gralla, R. J., Hesketh, P. J., Rittenberg, C., Elmer, M. E., et al. (2003). Establishing the dose of the oral NK1 antagonist aprepitant for the prevention of chemotherapy-induced nausea and vomiting. *Cancer, 97,* 2290–2300.

Chu, S., & Downes, J. J. (2002). Proust nose best: Odors are better cues of autobiographical memory. *Memory and Cognition, 30,* 511–518.

Cohen, J., & Lefor, A. T. (2001). Nutrition support and cancer. *Nutrition, 17,* 698–699.

Cohen, A. J., Menter, A., & Hale, L. (2005). Acupuncture: Role in comprehensive cancer care—A primer for the Oncologist and review of the literature. *Integrative Cancer Therapies, 4,* 131–143.

Coil, J. D., & Norgren, R. (1981). Taste aversions conditioned with intravenous copper sulfate: Attenuation by ablation of the area postrema. *Brain Research, 212,* 425–433.

Collins, K. B., & Thomas, D. J. (2004). Acupuncture and acupressure for the management of chemotherapy-induced nausea and vomiting. *Journal of the American Academy of Nurse Practitioners, 16,* 76–80.

Cooley, M. (2002). Patterns of symptom distress in adults receiving treatment for lung cancer. *Journal Palliative Care, 18,* 150–159.

De La Casa, G., & Lubow, R. E. (1995). Latent inhibition of conditioned taste aversion: The roles of stimulus frequency and duration and the amount of fluid ingested during preexposure. *Neurobiology, Learning and Memory, 64,* 125–132.

DeWys, W. D. (1979). Anorexia as a general effect of cancer. *Cancer, 43,* 2013–2019.

DeWys, W. D., & Walters, K. (1975). Abnormalities of taste sensation in cancer patients. *Cancer, 36,* 1888–1896.

Donaldson, S. S., Wesley, M. N., DeWys, W. D., Suskind, R. M., Jaffe, N., & Van Eys, J. (1981). A study of the nutritional status of pediatric cancer patients. *American Journal of Diseases of Children, 135,* 1107–1112.

Edelman, M. J., Gandara, D. R., Meyers, F. J., Ishii, R., O'Mahony, M., Uhrich, M., et al. (1999). Serotonergic blockade in the treatment of the cancer anorexia-cachexia syndrome. *Cancer, 86,* 684–688.

Ezzo, J., Vickers, A., Richardson, M. A., Allen, C., Dibble, S. L., Issel, B., et al. (2005). Acupuncture-point stimulation for chemotherapy-induced nausea and vomiting. *Journal of Clinical Oncology, 23,* 7188–7198.

Fawzy, F. I., Kemeny, M. E., Fawzy, N. W., Elashoff, R., Morton, D., Cousins, N., et al. (1990). A structured psychiatric intervention for cancer patients. II. Changes over time in immunological measures. *Archives of General Psychiatry, 47,* 729–735.

Fearon, K. C., & Carter, D. C. (1988). Cancer cachexia. *Annals of Surgery, 208,* 1–5.

Fellowes, D., Barnes, K., & Wilkinson, S. (2004). Aromatherapy and massage for symptom relief in patients with cancer. *Cochrane Database of Systematic Reviews Online Update Software, 2,* CD002287.

Felten, D. L., Cohen, N., Ader, R., Felten, S. Y., Carlson, S. L., & Roszman, T. L. (1991). Central neural circuits involved in neural-immune interactions. In R. Ader, D. L. Felten, & D. L. Cohen (Eds.), *Psychoneuroimmunology* (pp. 3–26). San Diego, CA: Academic Press.

Fidler, I. J., & Ellis, L. M. (2000). Chemotherapeutic drugs—More really is not better. *Nature Medicine, 6,* 500–502.

Filshie, J., & Thompson, J. W. (2004). Acupuncture. In D. Doyle, N. C. Hanks, & K. Calman (Eds.), *Oxford textbook of palliative Medicine* (3rd ed., pp. 410–424). New York: Oxford University Press.

Fredrikson, M., Furst, C. J., Lekander, M., Rotstein, S., & Blomgren, H. (1993). Trait anxiety and anticipatory immune reactions in women receiving adjuvant chemotherapy for breast cancer. *Brain, Behavior, and Immunology, 7,* 79–90.

Gallo, M., Ballesteros, M. A., Molero, A., & Moron, I. (1999). Taste aversion learning as a tool for the study of hippocampal and non-hippocampal brain memory circuits regulating diet selection. *Nutritional Neuroscience, 2,* 277–302.

Garb, I. L., & Stunkard, A. J. (1974). Taste aversion in man. *American Journal Psychiatry, 131,* 1204–1207.

Garcia y Robertson, R., & Garcia, J. (1985). X-rays and learned taste aversions: Historical and psychological ramifications. In T. G. Burish, S. M. Levy, & B. E. Meyerowitz (Eds.), *Cancer, nutrition and eating behavior: A biobehavioral perspective* (pp. 11–41). Hillsdale, NJ: Lawrence Erlbaum.

Gaston, K. E. (1977). An illness-induced conditioned aversion in domestic chicks: One-trial learning with a long delay of reinforcement. *Behavioral Biology, 20,* 441–453.

Ghanta, V., Hiramoto, R. N., Solvason, B., & Spector, N. H. (1987). Influence of conditioned natural immunity on tumor growth. *Annals of New York Academy of Sciences, 496,* 637–646.

Giang, D. W., Goodman, A. D., Schiffer, R. B., Mattson, D. H., Petrie, M., Cohen, N., et al. (1996). Conditioning of cyclophosphamide-induced leukopenia in humans. *Journal of Neuropsychiatry Clinical Neurosciences, 8,* 194–201.

Gietzen, D. W., Erecius, L. F., & Rogers, Q. R. (1998). Neurochemical changes after imbalanced diets suggest a brain circuit mediating anorectic responses to amino acid deficiency in rats. *Journal of Nutrition, 128,* 771–781.

Gietzen, D. W., Hammer, V. A., Beverly, J. L., & Rogers, Q. R. (1991). The role of serotonin (5HT) in feeding responses to amino acids. In R. Schwarcz (Ed.), *Kyrunemine and serotonin pathways* (pp. 389–394). New York: Plenum Press.

Given, C., Given, B., Rahbar, M., Jeon, S., McCorkle, R., Cimprich, B., et al. (2004). Effect of a cognitive behavioral intervention on reducing symptom severity during chemotherapy. *Journal of Clinical Oncology, 22,* 507–516.

Goebel, M. U., Trebst, A. E., Steiner, J., Xie, Y. F., Exton, M. S., Frede, S., et al. (2002). Behavioral conditioning of immunosuppression is possible in humans. *FASEB Journal, 16,* 1869–1873.

Gogos, C. A., & Kalfarentzos, F. (1995). Total parenteral nutrition and immune system activity: A review. *Nutrition, 11,* 339–344.

Gough, D. B., Heys, S. D., & Eremin, O. (1996a). Cancer cachexia: Pathophysiological mechanisms. *European Journal of Surgical Oncology, 22,* 192–196.

Gough, D. B., Heys, S. D., & Eremin, O. (1996b). Cancer cachexia II: Treatments strategies. *European Journal of Surgical Oncology, 22,* 286–292.

Gralla, R. J., Osoba, D., Kris, M. G., Kirkbride, P., Hesketh, P. J., Chinnery, L. W., et al. (1999). Recommendations for the use of antiemetics: Evidence-based, clinicalpractice guidelines. *Journal of Clinical Oncology, 17,* 2971–2994.

Gralla, R. J., Tyson, L. B., Bordin, L. A., Clark, R. A., Kelsen, D. P., Kris, M. G., et al. (1984). Antiemetic therapy: A review of recent studies and a report of a random assignment trial comparing metoclopramide with delta-9-tetrahydrocannabinol. *Cancer Treatment Reports, 68,* 163–172.

Grealish, L., Lomasney, A., & Whiteman, B. (2000). Foot massage: A nursing intervention to modify the distressing symptoms of pain and nausea in patients hospitalized with cancer. *Cancer Nursing, 23,* 237–243.

Haas, H. S., & Schauenstein, K. (1997). Neuroimmumodulation via limbic structures—The neuroanatomy of psychoimmunology. *Progress in Neurobiology, 51,* 195–222.

Halasz, N. (1990). *The vertebrate olfactory system.* Budapest: Akademiai Kiado

Hall, G., & Symonds, M. (2006). Overshadowing and latent inhibition of context aversion conditioning in the rat. *Autonomic Neuroscience: Basic and Clinical, 129,* 42–49.

Herrstedt, J., Aapro, M. S., Smyth, J. F., & Del Favero, A. (1998). Corticosteroids, dopamine antagonists and other drugs. *Supportive Care in Cancer, 6,* 204–214.

Herrstedt, J., Koeller, J. M., Roila, F., Hesketh, P. J., Warr, D., Rittenberg, C., et al. (2005). Acute emesis: Moderately emetogenic chemotherapy. *Supportive Care in Cancer, 13,* 97–103.

Herrstedt, J., Muss, H. B., Warr, D. G., Hesketh, P. J., Eisenberg, P. D., Raftopoulos, H., et al. (2005). Efficacy and tolerability of aprepitant for the prevention of chemotherapy-induced nausea and emesis over multiple cycles of moderately emetogenic chemotherapy. *Cancer, 104,* 1548–1555.

Herz, R. S. (2000). Scents of time. *The Sciences (New York Academy of Sciences) 40,* 34–39.

Hesketh, P. J., & Gandara, D. R. (1991). Serotonin antagonists: A new class of antiemetic agents. *Journal of National Cancer Institute, 83,* 613–620.

Hill, A. D., & Daly, J. M. (1995). Current indications for intravenous nutritional support in oncology patients. *Surgery Oncology Clinical North America, 4,* 549–563.

Holmes, S. (1993). Food avoidance in patients undergoing cancer chemotherapy. *Supportive Care in Cancer, 1,* 326–330.

Hortobagyi, G. N. (2001). Progress in systemic chemotherapy of primary breast cancer: An overview. *Journal of the National Cancer Institute Monographs, 30,* 72–79.

Ioannidis, J. P., Hesketh, P. J., & Lau, J. (2000). Contribution of dexamethasone to control of chemotherapy-induced nausea and vomiting: A meta-analysis of randomized evidence. *Journal of Clinical Oncology, 18,* 3409–3422.

Jacobsen, P. B., Andrykowski, M. A., Redd, W. H., Die-Trill, M., Hakes, T. B., Kaufman, R. J., et al. (1988). Nonpharmacological factors in the development of posttreatment nasea with adjuvant for breast cancer. *Cancer, 61,* 379–385.

Janz, L. J., Green-Johson, J., Murray, L., Vriend, C. Y., Nance, D. M., Greenberg, A. H., et al. (1996). Pavlovian conditioning of LPS-induced responses: Effects on corticosterone, splenic NE, and IL-2 production. *Physiology and Behavior, 59,* 1103–1109.

Jemel, A., Siegel, R., Ward, E., Murray, T., Xu, J., & Thun, M. J. (2007). Cancer statistics, 2007. *CA Cancer Journal for Clinicians, 57,* 43–66.

Johnson, D. H. (2000). Evolution of cisplatin-based chemotherapy in non-small cell lung cancer. *Chest, 117,* 133–137.

Jordan, K., Kasper, C., & Schmoll, H. J. (2005). Chemotherapy-induced nausea and vomiting: Current and new standards in the antiemetic prophylaxis and treatment. *European Journal of Cancer, 41,* 199–205.

Jurkowski, M., Trojniar, W., Borman, A., Ciepielewski, Z., Siemion, D., & Tokarski, J. (2001). Peripheral blood natural killer cell cytotoxicity after damage to the limbic system in the rat. *Brain, Behavior, and Immunity, 15,* 93–113.

Kern, K. A., & Norton, J. A. (1988). Cancer cachexia. *Journal Parenteral and Enteral Nutrition, 12,* 286–298.

Kirsch, I., Montgomery, G., & Sapirstein, G. (1995). Hypnosis as an adjunct to cognitive-behavioral psychotherapy; a meta-analysis. *Journal Consulting Clinical Psychology, 63,* 214–220.

Klosterhalfen, S., Kellerman, S., Stockhorst, U., Wolf, J., Kirschbaum, C., Hall, G., et al. (2005). Latent inhibition of rotation-chair-induced nausea in healthy male and female volunteers. *Psychosomatic Medicine, 67,* 335–340.

Kraemer, P. J., Randall, C. K., & Carbary, T. J. (1991). Release from latent inhibition with delayed testing. *Animal Learning Behavior, 19,* 139–145.

Kris, M. G., Gralla, R. J., Clark, R. A., Tyson, L. B., & Groshen, S. (1987). Antiemetic control and prevention of side effects of anti-cancer therapy with lorazepam or diphenhydramine when used in combination with metoclopramide plus dexamethasone: A double-blind, randomized trial. *Cancer, 11,* 2816–2822.

Kris, M. G., Hesketh, P. J., Herrstedt, J., Rittenberg, C., Einhorn, L. H., Grunberg, S., et al. (2005). Consensus proposals for the prevention of acute and delayed vomiting and nausea following high-emetic-risk chemotherapy. *Supportive Care in Cancer, 13,* 85–96.

Kris, M. G., Hesketh, P. J., Somerfield, M. R., Feyer, P., Clark-Snow, R., Koeller, J. M., et al. (2006). American Society of Clinical Oncology Guideline for antiemetics in oncology: Update 2006. *Journal of Clinical Oncology, 24,* 2932–2947.

Kvale, G., & Hugdahl, K. (1994). Cardiovascular conditioning and anticipatory nausea and vomiting in cancer patients. *Behavioral Medicine, 20,* 78–83.

Kvale, G., Hugdahl, K., Asbjornsen, A., Rosengren, B., Lote, K., & Nordby, H. (1991). Anticipatory nausea and vomiting in cancer patients. *Journal Consulting Clinical Psychology, 59,* 894–898.

Langhans, W., & Hrupka, B. (1999). Interleukins and tumor necrosis factors as inhibitors of food intake. *Neuropeptides, 33,* 415–424.

Lazarus, D. D., Kambayashi, T., Lowry, S., & Strassmann, G. (1996). The lack of an effect by insulin or insulin-like growth factor-1 in attenuating colon-2-mediated cancer cachexia. *Cancer Letters, 103,* 71–77.

Lee-Teng, E., & Sherman, S. M. (1966). Memory consolidation of one-trial learning in chicks. *Proceedings National Academy Sciences USA 56,* 926–931.

Lehrner, J., Marwinski, G., Lehr, S., Johren, P., & Deecke, L. (2005). Ambient odors of orange and lavander reduce anxiety and improve mood in a dental office. *Physiology and Behavior, 86,* 92–95.

Leibowitz, S. F., & Alexander, J. T. (1998). Hypothalamic serotonin in control of eating behavior, meal size, and body weight. *Biological Psychiatry, 44,* 851–864.

Leibowitz, S. F., Weiss, G. F., & Shor-Posner, G. (1988). Hypothalamic serotonin: Pharmacological, biochemical and behavioral analyses of its feeding suppressive action. *Clinical Neuropharmacology,* 11(Suppl. 1), S51–S71.

Lekander, M., Furst, C. J., Rotstein, S., Blomgren, H., & Fredrikson, M. (1994). Does informed adjuvant placebo chemotherapy for breast cancer elicit immune changes? *Oncology Reports, 1,* 699–703.

Lekander, M., Furst, C. J., Rotstein, S., Blomgren, H., & Fredrikson, M. (1995). Anticipatory immune changes in women treated with chemotherapy for ovarian cancer. *International Journal Behavioral Medicine, 2,* 1–12.

Levy, S. M., Herberman, R. B., Whiteside, T., Sanzo, K., Lee, J., & Kirkwood, J. (1990). Perceived social support and tumor estrogen/progesterone receptor status as predictors of natural killer cell activity in breast cancer patients. *Psychosomatic Medicine, 52,* 73–85.

Liossi, C., & Hatira, P. (2003). Clinical hypnosis in the alleviation of procedure-related pain in pediatric oncology patients. *International Journal of Clinical Experimental Hypnosis, 51,* 4–28.

Liu, Y. L., Malik, N. M., Sanger, G. J., & Andrews, P. L. R. (2006). Ghrelin alleviates cancer chemotherapy-associated dyspepsia in rodents. *Cancer Chemotherapy and Pharmacology, 58,* 326–333.

Logue, A. W. (1979). Taste aversion and the generality of the laws of learning. *Psychological Bulletin, 86,* 276–296.

Logue, A. W. (1985). Conditioned food aversion learning in humans. *Annals New York Academy of Sciences, 443,* 316–329.

Logue, A. W., Logue, K. R., & Strauss, K. E. (1983). The acquisition of taste aversions in humans with eating and drinking disorders. *Behaviour Research and Therapy, 21,* 275–289.

Logue, A. W., Ophir, I., & Strauss, K. E. (1981). The acquisition of taste aversions in humans. *Behaviour Reserach and Therapy, 19,* 319–333.

Longo, D. L., Duffey, P. L., Kopp, W. C., Heyes, M. P., Alvord, W. G., Sharfman, W. H., et al. (1999). Conditioned immune response to interferon-gamma in humans. *Clinical Immunology, 90,* 173–181.

Lubow, R. E. (1973). Latent inhibition. *Psychological Bulletin, 79,* 398–407.

Lundholm, K., Gelin, J., & Hyltander, A. (1994). Anti-inflammatory treatment may prolong survival in undernourished patients with metastatic solid tumors. *Cancer Research, 54,* 5602–5606.

MacDonald, N. (2000). Cachexia-anorexia workshop: Introduction. *Nutrition, 16,* 1007–1008.

MacIntosh, C., Morley, J. E., & Chapman, I. M. (2000). The anorexia of aging. *Nutrition, 16,* 983–995.

Marchioro, G., Azzarello, G., Viviani, F., Barbato, F., Pavanetto, M., Rosetti, F., et al. (2000). Hypnosis in the treatment of anticipatory nausea and vomiting in patients receiving cancer chemotherapy. *Oncology, 59,* 100–104.

Maruniak, J. A., Mason, J. R., & Kostelc, J. G. (1983). Conditioned aversions to an intravascular odorant. *Physiology and Behavior, 30,* 617–620.

MASCC. (2004). The 2004 Perugia Antiemetic Consensus Guideline process. *Supportive Care in Cancer, 13,* 77–131.

Mattes, R. D., Arnold, C., & Boraas, M. (1987a). Learned food aversions among cancer chemotherapy patients. *Cancer, 60,* 2576–2580.

Mattes, R. D., Arnold, C., & Boraas, M. (1987b). Management of learned food aversions in cancer patients receiving chemotherapy. *Cancer Treatment Reports, 71,* 1071–1078.

Mattes, R. D., Curran, W. J., Jr., Alavi, J., Powlis, W., & Whittington, R. (1992). Clinical implications of learned food aversions in patients with cancer treated with chemotherapy or radiation therapy. *Cancer, 70,* 192–200.

Matteson, S., Roscoe, J., Hickok, J., & Morrow, G. R. (2002). The role of behavioral conditioning in the development of nausea. *American Journal of Obstretic and Gynecology, 186,* S239–S243.

McEligot, A. J., Rock, C. L., Sobo, E. J., & Flatt, S. W. (2000). Food avoidance by women at risk for recurrence of breast cancer. *Journal of Cancer Education, 15,* 151–155.

Meachum, C., & Bernstein, I. L. (1992). Behavioral conditioned responses to contextual and odor stimuli paired with LiCl administration. *Physiology and Behavior, 52,* 895–899.

Meguid, M. M., Fetissov, S. O., Varma, M., Sato, T., Zhang, L., Laviano, A., et al. (2000). Hypothalamic dopamine and serotonin in the regulation of food intake. *Nutrition, 16,* 843–857.

Meguid, M. M., Sato, T., Torelli, G. F., Laviano, A., & Rossi-Fanelli, F. (2000). An analysis of temporal changes in meal number and meal size at onset of anorexia in male tumor-bearing rats. *Nutrition, 16,* 305–305.

Menefee, L. A., & Monti, D. A. (2005). Nonpharmacologic and complementary approaches to cancer pain management. *Journal of the American Osteopathic Association 105*(Suppl. 5), S15–S20.

Midkiff, E. E., & Bernstein, I. L. (1985). Targets of learned food aversions in humans. *Physiology and Behavior, 34,* 839–841.

Miller, M., & Kearney, N. (2004). Chemotherapy-related nausea nd vomiting—Past reflections, present practice and future management. *European Journal of Cancer Care, 13,* 71–81.

Miller, J. S., Jagielo, J. A., & Spear, N. E. (1990). Changes in the retrievability of associations to elements of the compound CS determine the expression of overshadowing. *Animal Learning and Behavior, 18,* 157–161.

Mitchel, E. P. (1992). Gastrointestinal toxicity of chemotherapeutic agents. *Seminars in Oncology, 19,* 566–579.

Miyagawa, M., Honma, T., Sato, M., & Hasegawa, H. (1984). Conditioned taste aversion induced by toluene administration in rats. *Neurobehavioral Toxicology and Teratology, 6,* 33–37.

Mock, V. (2004). Evidence-based treatment for cancer related fatigue. *Journal of the National Cancer Institute Monographies, 32,* 112–118.

Molassiotis, A., Yung, H. P., Yam, B. M. C., Chan, F. Y. S., & Mok, T. S. K. (2002). The effectiveness of progressive muscle relaxation training in managing chemotherapy-induced nausea and vomiting in Chinese breast cancer patients: A randomized controlled trial. *Supportive Care in Cancer, 10,* 237–246.

Monti, D. A., & Yang, J. (2005). Complementary medicine in chronic cancer care. *Seminars in Oncology, 32,* 225–231.

Mooney, K. M., & Walbourn, L. (2001). When college students reject food: Not just a matter of taste. *Appetite, 36,* 41–50.

Morrow, G. R. (1985). The effect of a susceptibility to motion sickness on the side effects of cancer chemotherapy. *Cancer, 55,* 2766–2770.

Morrow, G. R., Arseneau, J. C., Asbury, R. F., Bennett, J. M., & Boros, L. (1982). Anticipatory nausea and vomiting with chemotherapy. *New England Jornal of Medicine, 306,* 431–432.

Morrow, G. R., & Roscoe, J. A. (1997). Anticipatory nausea and vomiting: Models, mechanisms and management. In M. A. Dicoto (Ed.), *Medical management of cancer treatment induced emesis* (pp. 149–166). London: Martin Dunitz.

Morrow, G. R., Roscoe, J., Hickok, J., Andrews, P. R., & Matteson, S. (2002). Nausea and emesis: Evidence for a biobehavioral perspective. *Supportive Care in Cancer, 10,* 96–105.

Morrow, G. R., Roscoe, J. A., Hynes, H. E., Flynn, P. J., Pierce, H. I., & Burish, T. (1998). Progress in reducing anticipatory nausea and vomiting: A study of community practice. *Supportive Care in Cancer, 6,* 46–50.

Mundy, E. A., DuHamel, K. N., & Montgomery, G. H. (2003). The efficacy of behavioral interventions for cancer treatment-related side effects. *Seminars Clinic Neuropsychiatry, 8,* 253–275.

Nakajima, S., Ka, H., & Imada, H. (1999). Summation of overshadowing and latent inhibition in rat's conditioned taste aversion: Scapegoat technique works for familiar meals. *Appetite, 33,* 299–307.

Neary, N. M., Small, C. J., Wren, A. M., Lee, J. L., Druce, M. R., Palmieri, C., et al. (2004). Ghrelin increases energy intake in cancer patients with impaired appetite: Acute, randomized, placebo-controlled trial. *Journal of Clinical Endocrinology and Metabolism, 89,* 2832–2836.

NIH Technology Assesment Conference Statement Online October 16–18, 1–34 (1995). *Integration of behavioral and relaxation approaches into the treatment of chronic pain and insomnia.*

NIH Consensus Statement Online. (1997). *Acupuncture.* November 3–5. 15(5), 1–34.

Nitenberg, G., & Raynard, B. (2000). Nutritional support of the cancer patient: Issues and dilemmas. *Critical Reviews in Oncology/Hematology, 34,* 137–168.

Norton, J. A., Gorschboth, C. M., Wesley, R. A., Burt, M. E., & Brennan, M. F. (1985). Fasting plasma amino acids levels in cancer patients. *Cancer, 56,* 1181–1186.

Oakley, B. (1974). On the specification of taste neurons in the rat tongue. *Brain Research, 75,* 85–96.

Okifuji, A., & Friedman, A. G. (1992). Experimentally induced taste aversions in humans: Effects of overshadowing on acquisition. *Behavioral Research and Therapy, 30,* 23–32.

Oliver, J. W., Kravitz, R. L., Kaplan, S. H., & Meyers, F. J. (2001). Individualized patient education and coaching to improve pain control among cancer outpatients. *Journal of Clinical Oncology, 19,* 2206–2212.

Osoba, D., Zee, B., Pater, J., Warr, D., Latreille, J., & Kaizer, L. (1997). Determinants of postchemotherapy nausea and vomiting in patients with cancer. *Journal of Clinical Oncology, 15,* 116–123.

Ovesen, L., Sorensen, M., Hannibal, J., & Allingstrup, L. (1991). Electrical taste detection thresholds and chemical smell detection thresholds in patients with cancer. *Cancer, 68,* 2260–2265.

Pelchat, M., Grill, H. J., Rozin, P., & Jacobs, J. (1983). Quality of acquired responses to tastes by *Rattus Norvegicus* depends upon type of associated discomfort. *Journal Comparative Physiological Psychology, 97,* 140–153.

Pelchat, M., & Rozin, P. (1982). The special role of nausea in the acquisition of food dislikes by humans. *Appetite, 3,* 341–351.

Perez, E. A. (1995). Review of the preclinical pharmacology and comparative efficacy of, 5-hydroxytryptamine-3 receptor antagonists for chemotherapy-induced emesis. *Journal of Clinical Oncology, 13,* 1036–1043.

Perez, E. A., Hesketh, P. J., & Gandara, D. R. (1991). Serotonin antagonists in the management of cisplatin-induced emesis. *Seminars in Oncology, 18,* 73–80.

Pironi, L. (1997). Nutritional aspects of elderly cancer patients. *Rays, 22*(Suppl.), 42.

Plata-Salaman, C. R. (1998). Cytokines and anorexia: A brief overview. *Seminars in Oncology, 25*(Suppl. 1), 64–72.

Plata-Salaman, C. R. (2000). Central nervous system mechanisms contributing to the cachexia-anorexia syndrome. *Nutrition,* 16, 1009–1012.

Prictor, M. J., Hill, S. J., Mackenzie, A., Stoelwinder, J., & Harmsen, M. (2004). Interventions (non-pharmacological) for preparing children and adolescents for hospital care. *Cochrane Database of Systematic Reviews,* Issue 1, Art. No. CD004564; doi:10.1002/14651858. CD004564.

Redd, W. H., Jacobsen, P. B., Die-Trill, M., Dermatis, H., McEvoy, M., & Holland, J. C. (1987). Cognitive/attentional distraction in the control of conditioned nausea in pediatric cancer patients receiving chemotherapy. *Journal Consulting Clinical Psychology, 55,* 391–395.

Redd, W. H., Montgomery, G. H., & DuHamel, K. N. (2001). Behavioral intervention for cancer treatment side effects. *Journal of the National Cancer Institute, 93,* 810–823.

Revusky, S. H., & Garcia, J. (1970). Learned associations over long delays. In G. Bower, & J. Spence (Eds.), *Psychology of learning and motivation: Advances in research and theory* (Vol. 4, pp. 1–84). New York: Academic Press.

Richardson, J., Smith, J. E., McCall, G., & Pilkington, K. (2006). Hypnosis for procedure-related pain and distress in pediatric cancer patients: A systematic review of effectiveness and methodology related to hypnosis interventions. *Journal of pain and symptom management, 31,* 70–84.

Rofe, A. M., Bourgeois, C. S., Coyle, P., Taylor, A., & Abdi, E. A. (1994). Altered insulin response to glucose in weight-losing cancer patients. *Anticancer Research, 14,* 647–650.

Roffe, L., Schmidt, K., & Ernst, E. (2005). A systematic review of guided imagery as an adjuvant cancer therapy. *Psycho-Oncology, 14,* 607–617.

Roila, F., Hesketh, P. J., & Herrstedt, J. (2006). Prevention of chemotherapy- and radiotherapy-induced emesis: Results of the 2004 Perugia International Antiemetic Consensus Conference. *Annals of Oncology, 17,* 20–28.

Roscoe, J. A., Morrow, G. R., Hickok, J. T., & Stern, R. M. (2000). Nausea and vomiting remain a significant clinical problem: Trends over time in controlling chemotherapy-induced nausea and vomiting in 1413 patients treated in community clinical practices. *Journal of Pain Symptom Management, 20,* 113–121.

Rozin, P. (1968). Specific aversion and neophobia resulting from vitamin deficiencies or poisoning in half wild and domestic rats. *Journal Comparative Physiological Psychology, 68,* 82–88.

Rudd, J. A., Ngan, M. P., Wai, M. K., King, A. G., Witherington, J., Andrews, P. L. R., et al.

(2006). Anti-emetic activity of ghrelin in ferrets exposed to the cytotoxic anti-cancer agent cisplatin. *Neuroscience Letters, 392,* 79–83.

Sanger, G. J., & Andrews, P. L. R. (2006). Treatment of nausea and vomiting: Gaps in our knowledge. *Autonomic Neuroscience: Basic and Clinical, 129,* 3–16.

Sawyers, C. (2004). Targeted cancer therapy. *Nature, 432,* 294–297.

Scalera, G. (2002). Effects of conditioned food aversions on nutritional behavior in humans: A review. *Nutritional Neuroscience, 5,* 159–188.

Schafe, G. E., LeDoux, J. E., Fitts, D. A., Thiele, T. E., & Bernstein, I. L. (2000). The induction of *c*-Fos in the NTS after taste aversion learning is not correlated with measures of conditioned fear. *Behavioral Neuroscience, 114,* 99–106.

Schiffman, S. S. (1997). Taste and smell losses in normal aging and disease. *Journal of the American Medical Association, 278,* 1357–1362.

Schiffman, S. S. (2000). Intensification of sensory properties of food for elderly. *Journal of Nutrition, 130,* 927S–930S.

Schiffman, S. S., & Miletic, I. D. (1999). Effect of taste and smell on secretion rate of salivary IgA in elderly and young persons. *Journal of Nutrition, Health and Aging, 3,* 158–164.

Schmale, H., Holtgrave-Grez, H., & Christiansen, H. (1990). Possible role for salivary gland protein in taste reception indicated by homology to lipophilic-ligand carrier proteins. *Nature, 343,* 366–369.

Schneider, A., Enck, P., Streitberger, K., Weiland, C., Bagheri, S., Witte, S., et al. (2006). Acupuncture treatment in irritable bowel syndrome. *Gut, 55,* 649–654.

Servière, J., Dubayle, D., & Ménétrey, D. (2003). Increase of rat medial habenular mast cell numbers by systemic administration of cyclophosphamide. *Toxicology Letters, 145,* 143–152.

Sheard, T., & Maguire, P. (1999). The effect of psychological interventions on anxiety and depression in cancer patients: Results of two meta-analyses. *British Journal of Cancer, 80,* 1770–1780.

Shike, M. (1996). Nutrition therapy for the cancer patient. *Hematology/Oncology Clinics of North America, 10,* 221–234.

Shils, M. E. (1979). Nutritional problems induced by cancer. *Medical Clinics of North America, 63,* 1009–1025.

Silverberg, E., & Lubera, J. (1986). Cancer statistics, 1986. *CA—A Journal for Clinicians, 36,* 9–25.

Small, D. M., & Prescott, J. (2005). Odor/taste integration and the perception of flavor. *Experimental Brain Research, 166,* 345–357.

Small, B. E., Holdsworth, M. T., & Raisch, D. W. (2000). Survey ranking of emetogenic control in children receiving chemotherapy. *Journal Pediatric Hematology Oncology, 22,* 125–132.

Smith, J. C., Blumsack, J. T., & Bilek, F. S. (1985). Radiation-induced taste aversions in rats and humans. In T. G. Burish, S. M. Levy, & B. E. Meyerowitz (Eds.), *Cancer, nutrition and eating behavior* (pp. 77–102). Hillsdale, NJ: L. Earlbaum Associate.

Smith, J. C., Blumsack, J. T., Bilek, F. S., Spector, A. C., Hollander, G. R., & Baker, D. L. (1984). Radiation-induced taste aversion as a factor in cancer therapy. *Cancer Treatment Reports, 68,* 1219–1227.

Smith, K. L., & Tisdale, M. J. (1993). Mechanism of muscle protein degradation in cancer cachexia. *British Journal of Cancer, 68,* 314–318.

Spielman, A. I. (1990). Interaction of saliva and taste. *Journal Dentistry Research, 69,* 838–843.

Stockhorst, U., Klosterhalfen, S., & Steingruber, H. J. (1998). Conditioned nausea and further side-effects in cancer chemotherapy: A review. *Journal of Psychophysiology, 12*(Suppl. 1), 14–33.

Stockhorst, U., Spennes-Saleh, S., Korholz, D., Gobel, U., Schneider, M. E., Steingruber, H. J., et al. (2000). Anticipatory symptoms and anticipatory immune responses in pediatric cancer patients receiving chemotherapy: Features of a classically conditioned response? *Brain Behavior and Immunity, 14,* 198–218.

Stockhorst, U., Steingruber, H.-J., Enck, P., Klosterhalfen, S. (2006). Pavlovian conditioning of nausea and vomiting. *Autonomic Neuroscience: Basic and Clinical, 129,* 50–57.

Stockhorst, U., Wiener, J. A., Klosterhalfen, S., Klosterhalfen, W., Aul, C., & Steingruber, H. J. (1998a). Effects of overshadowing on conditioned nausea in cancer patients: An experimental study. *Physiology and Behavior, 64,* 743–753.

Streitberger, K., Ezzo, J., & Schneider, A. (2006). Acupuncture for nausea and vomiting: An update of clinical and experimental studies. *Autonomic Neuroscience: Basic and Clinical, 129,* 107–117.

Tomoyasu, N., Bovbjerg, D. H., & Jacobsen, P. B. (1996). Conditioned reactions to cancer chemotherapy: Percent reinforcement predicts anticipatory nausea. *Physiology and Behavior, 59,* 273–276.

Twycross, R., & Back, I. (1998). Nause and vomiting in advanced cancer. *European Journal of Palliative Care, 5*, 39–45.

Varma, M., Chai, J. K., Meguid, M. M., & Yang, Z. J. (2001). Gender differences in tumor-induced anorectic feeding pattern in Fischer-344 rats. *Physiology and Behavior, 74*, 29–35.

Varma, M., Torelli, G. F., Meguid, M. M., Chai, J. K., Blaha, V., Laviano, A., et al. (1999). Potential strategies for ameliorating early cancer anorexia. *Journal of Surgical Research, 81*, 69–76.

Wilcoxon, H. C., Dragoin, W. B., & Kral, P. A. (1971). Illness induced aversions in rat and quail: Relative salience of visual and gustatory cues. *Science, 171*, 826–828.

Wrona, D. (2006). Neural-immune interactions: An integrative view of the bidirectional relationship between the brain and immune system. *Journal of Neuroimmunology, 172*, 38–58.

Wyrwicka, W., & Chase, M. H. (2001). Importance of the environment in conditioned behavior. *Physiology and Behavior, 73*, 493–497.

Yeomans, M. R. (2006). Olfactory influences on appetite and satiety in humans. *Physiology and Behavior, 89*, 10–14.

Yoo, H. J., Ahn, S. H., Kim, S. B., Kim, W. K., & Han, O. S. (2005). Efficacy of progressive muscle relaxation training and guided imagery in reducing chemotherapy side effects in patients with breast cancer and in improving their quality of life. *Supportive Care in Cancer, 13*, 826–833.

Yu, B., & Shinnick-Gallagher, P. (1994). Interleukin-1b inhibits synaptic transmission and induces membrane hyperpolarization in amygdala neurons. *Journal of Pharmacology and Experimental Therapy, 271*, 590–600.

Zald, D. H., & Pardo, J. V. (2000). Functional neuroimaging of the olfactory system in humans. *International Journal of Psychophysiology, 36*, 165–181.

Author Index

Subject Index

Note: Page numbers followed by *f* denote figures, while those followed by *t* denote tables.